The Writings and Speeches of
Oliver Cromwell

With an Introduction, Notes and a Sketch of His Life

by
WILBUR CORTEZ ABBOTT
With the assistance of
CATHERINE D. CRANE

VOLUME I
1599–1649

CLARENDON PRESS · OXFORD

Oxford University Press, Walton Street, Oxford OX2 6DP
Oxford New York Toronto
Delhi Bombay Calcutta Madras Karachi
Petaling Jaya Singapore Hong Kong Tokyo
Nairobi Dar es Salaam Cape Town
Melbourne Auckland
and associated companies in
Berlin Ibadan

Oxford is a trade mark of Oxford University Press

First published 1937
by Harvard University Press,
Cambridge MA, and Oxford
University Press, London
Reissued 1988
by the Clarendon Press
(Oxford University Press), Oxford

ISBN 0-19-821771-4

Printed in Great Britain
at the University Printing House, Oxford
by David Stanford
Printer to the University

TO

"MECCA"

"His pure patriotism, his sacrifice to duty, his public wisdom, and his endeavor for the right course in every difficulty, gave him a transcendent character which, in the history of dangerous epochs, suggests but two men who are worthy to be compared with him as righteous rulers—Washington and Lincoln. Among all the world's rulers he stands high above the rest. . . ."

Church, *Oliver Cromwell.*

"His cruel shuffling ways . . . and the fact that his subjects regarded him as a man in whom there was no truth, who set snares to entrap them shall be published, as far as possible in his own words.

"The Great Rebellion . . . was begun by the craft of a subject directed against his Sovereign. . . . Though wrecked in mind, body, and estate, until his death, the spell cast by that dark Protector brooded not over England only, it stretched across the Channel."

Palgrave, *Oliver Cromwell, the Protector.*

"A complex character, such as that of Cromwell, is incapable of creation, except in times of great civil and religious excitement, and one cannot judge of the man without at the same time considering the contending elements by which he was surrounded. It is possible to take his character to pieces, and, selecting one or other of his qualities as a corner-stone, to build around it a monument which will show him as a patriot or a plotter, a Christian man or a hypocrite, a demon or a demi-god as the sculptor may choose. It should also be possible at this lapse of time to discuss his motives and his career as critically and as dispassionately as we can discuss the dimensions and the architecture of an ancient ruin, or the bones and vestments of a discoffined prelate. But . . . the character of Cromwell is still enveloped in clouds of prejudice and uncertainty, which, like the mists of the Adriatic, magnify the outline while they obscure the detail."

Inderwick, *The Interregnum.*

"The smallest authentic fact, any undoubted date or circumstance regarding Oliver and his affairs, is to be eagerly laid hold of."

Carlyle, *Oliver Cromwell's Letters and Speeches*

TABLE OF CONTENTS

LIST OF ILLUSTRATIONS

MAPS TO ILLUSTRATE CROMWELL'S CAMPAIGNS

PREFACE

It is unfortunate for such a work as a collection of the writings and speeches of Oliver Cromwell that it must inevitably invite comparison with that classic of English biographical writing, Thomas Carlyle's *Letters and Speeches of Oliver Cromwell.* It is especially unfortunate in that Carlyle possessed three enormous advantages over anyone who ventures to follow him in such a task as this. He had an extraordinarily arresting style; he had entire confidence in the infallible righteousness of his subject, his cause and himself; and he had a relatively limited amount of material upon which to base his narrative and his judgments.

In no one of these can anyone nowadays hope to equal him. No one now—least of all an historical scholar—can even pretend to that immanent sense of infallibility which infuses Carlyle's writings with their dogmatic charm. And no one now can possibly confine himself to the comparatively scanty materials on which he based his sweeping and incisive judgments. In consequence it is, and it will be hereafter, impossible for any writer to make such an appeal to such an audience as that which brought reputation and influence to the Sage of Chelsea. It is not probable that his glorification of the great Puritan champion will ever find a rival, or that his portrait of Cromwell will ever be displaced or even greatly modified in popular opinion.

For as earlier two powerful forces worked against the reputation of the Protector, so now two other no less active agencies combine to consolidate his fame. During a great part of the eighteenth century most Tories hated him because he overthrew the monarchy, most Whigs because he overthrew Parliament. Since Carlyle wrote, all Liberals have seen in him their champion and all revolutionists have apotheosized the first great representative of their school; while, on the other side, their opponents have hailed the dictator who put down anarchy. Unless the socialists or the anarchists finally prevail—and perhaps even then—his fame seems as secure as human reputation is likely to be in a changing world.

It is not the purpose of the compiler of these volumes to take sides in the long and acrimonious controversy which from the days of the great Protector to our own has raged about his motives, his aims, his character and his achievements; to traverse either the verdicts of Cromwell's numerous admirers and apologists or those of any of his critics. It is rather the object of this work to set down as fully and as impartially as possible what Cromwell actually wrote and said, with such comment as may make those writings and sayings more intelligible in the light of their time and circumstances, and our own. In such an endeavor to show what kind of man he was, inevitably one must dissent from time to time from the dicta of his greatest champion, inevitably irritate his ardent admirers.

That is inevitable, if for no other reason, because so much has happened in the world of politics, religion and even of historical scholarship since Carlyle wrote. The realms of politics and religion have been revolutionized and the long and patient investigations of a great school of research headed by Ranke and Gardiner and Firth, have unravelled many tangled and knotty threads of seventeenth century affairs. They have cleared away many errors and misconceptions; they have illuminated many dark corners; and—whatever figure of speech may be applied to their labors—they have transformed the chronicle of that century, as was said of Gardiner, from myth into history.

In so doing they have made the task of later workers in that field at once easier and more difficult. They have, indeed, provided an enormous, almost an overwhelming, mass of new materials; they have disposed of many earlier faiths and fallacies. But as no one can ever again be as certain as Carlyle once was of either his own or his subject's infallibility, no one can ever again be as certain as Cromwell was that God was on his side. What we have gained in truth we have, in a sense, lost in certainty. The long development in the field of religious faith—or the lack of it—has not contributed to the dogmatic interpretation of the past and its great characters, nor have more recent political developments provided that implicit confidence in the absolute rightness of all previous steps in the search for "liberty" or even entire satisfaction in some of its later manifestations. For good or ill the Absolute has given way to the Relative in those fields as in others, and few persons nowadays can be as firmly convinced as were Carlyle and Cromwell that what the great Protector stood for is forever Right and all of his opponents and critics forever Wrong.

The appeal to reason has at many times proved its inferiority to the appeal to the emotions and the prejudices of mankind; and it is quite impossible to hope that any reasoned statement of the facts can ever have that powerful influence which Carlyle's great passionate, emotional plea for the Protector achieved. It is the humbler task of the modern scholar to record, as fully, as dispassionately and as accurately as possible, what Oliver Cromwell wrote and said, set down the circumstances of those utterances, and draw from this and from a small infinity of other sources some explanation, however inadequate, of the Protector's actions and his thoughts.

For this purpose it has seemed best to make as nearly as possible a complete collection of Cromwell's utterances, verbal and written. Of these Carlyle accumulated some two hundred and twenty-five letters and eighteen speeches, with other minor notes, for his first edition. To these he added, as they were communicated to him, some seventy-five other documents. At the beginning of the twentieth century the patient industry of Mrs. Lomas added some hundred and eighty-five more items. Unwilling to disturb his own original words, Carlyle, instead of putting his new material in its proper place according to chronology, added it in an Appendix. Mrs. Lomas, still more unwilling to alter the Carlylean system, put her material into a Supplement; with the result that it is necessary to consult three separate collections to unravel the chronological complexities of Cromwell's utterances and activities.

The collection which follows includes the Carlyle-Lomas materials, arranged in the order of their original sequence. It includes, besides, more than seven hundred other items drawn from a great number of sources. Many of them, like most of those in the Lomas-Carlyle collection, have been previously published in more or less—generally less—accessible places; but many, notably a large number from European archives, have not until now been published anywhere. Some letters known to exist, or to have existed, but for one reason or another now inaccessible, are indicated in their proper places and, like the missing speeches, wherever their contents can be surmised from answers to them, or by other means, a brief *precis* has been drawn up as a suggestion of their probable content. Some obvious forgeries, like the dubious letter to Margery Beacham which has furnished Cromwelliana with some of its more sentimental passages, and the so-called Squire Letters, which deceived Carlyle, are omitted, as being of no historical value. A very few, known to exist, for various reasons have not been available, and though they seem to be of little, if any, historical importance, their omission is regrettable, and they are noted in the text. Others, it may be, will turn up in time; and it may be hoped that such a publication as this may draw them from their hiding-places.

Most of what Carlyle included in his original edition had appeared in print before. To those unfortunate scholars, Harris and Noble, especially the latter, on whom the vials of his vituperation were most fluently poured out, he owed the greater part of his material; and his ungenerous denunciation of those "Dryasdust" antiquarians contributes to the spice, though not to the truth, of his account of his hero. He was a master of the adjective, especially in its most virulent form, the epithet, and his description of "Carrion" Heath, and of his "reverend, imbecile friend," Noble, have, no doubt, amused, even while they misled, his army of readers, as his explosive denunciations of the processes of historical scholarship in comparison with his own penetrating and lambent inspiration have delighted many more. Yet it would be less than justice to forget that it is thanks to such persons as those whom he so bitterly denounced that we—and Carlyle among us—have come to a knowledge of the past, and that without such men even such a genius as Carlyle would have found his task infinitely more difficult, if not, indeed, impossible.

It is, then, with profound gratitude to those numerous and painstaking souls who by unearthing this great mass of material which emanated from the mind of Cromwell have made such a collection as this possible, and to them—to Mrs. Lomas in particular—these labors are inscribed. To her careful and accurate scholarship as expressed in her annotations to Carlyle, as well as to the additional materials which she collected; to the great contributions of Professor Firth, Professor Gardiner and their colleagues and followers; to a small army of antiquarians; to the librarians and curators and archivists of many collections of books and manuscripts; to the editors of many periodicals who have published these items, the indebtedness of the present compiler is acknowledged. And not least to Carlyle, whose stimulating rhetoric not merely did so much to make the period of Cromwell and Cromwell himself alive, but drew from their long seclusion such masses of Cromwellian documents, and helped to inspire so much historical interest and investigation in that period. Thus, if one may not accept his dicta unquestioned, extenuating nothing, setting down nothing in malice, it may be hoped that the present compiler may not be reckoned an unworthy follower in the field of Cromwellian historiography, however far he may fall short of the inspired eloquence of the great Protector's greatest advocate.

Scholarship, it has been said bitterly, consists in writing books which no one will ever read out of books which no one has ever read; and to what species of scholarship could that caustic observation be better applied than to such a mass of documents as this? It would seem, on its face, to be merely the product of a "lifetime of horrid industry," for whose completion there was needed only time, patience, paper and pens. Yet to discover the whereabouts of these documents, to copy, or to have them copied, to unravel an infinite number of small but often difficult problems of chronology and authorship, has required not only time and patience, but other qualities. Merely to enumerate the assistants in this task helps to show something of its difficulties. To its completion have been summoned the talents not only of scholars and historians and antiquarians, but those of archivists, librarians, searchers and copyists, photographers, translators, public officials, clergymen and lawyers, men of letters as well as of learning, technicians as well as investigators; and it is to these, rather than to the compiler that the chief credit is due.

It is perhaps proper to say that this collection contains some five hundred and fifty documents previously printed but hitherto uncollected besides the material in Lomas-Carlyle; as well as some hundred and fifty not printed until now. Among them are many of the Cromwellian state papers, of which this collection contains the first even reasonably complete corpus. Of these a considerable number are, of course, derived from the Symmons edition of Milton's State Papers; but many more are taken from the archives where they had lain perhaps unopened since the time they were received. The very list of those archives indicates something of the character of this body of material which, for the first time, provides the opportunity to review Cromwellian foreign policy in so far as it may be derived from his correspondence. Apart from the documents in London and elsewhere in England, the archives of Paris, the Hague, Middleburg, Oldenburg, Basel, Copenhagen, Stockholm, Danzig, Hamburg, Venice, Florence and Turin have each contributed their share.

For the rest, it may be observed that there are included here some speeches hitherto unknown or known only in part; the only Cromwellian major-general's commission as well as the only sheriff's commission yet discovered and the only commission issued to the Generals-at-Sea; and—in an appendix—the lists of letters patent and of privy seal which form a sort of general directory of Cromwellian officials and business. For the sake of completeness and of continuity, as well as because they often throw light on Cromwell's movements and activities, there are included also such lesser documents as warrants, commissions, passes and the like, of no great value in themselves but often contributing details of time or place or circumstance which have a certain measure of importance to the story as a whole.

It will be noted that the Latin letters have been translated. This has been done for two reasons. The first is that the body of Milton letters is chiefly known to us only in translation, and, though all available originals are also included, it seemed best to have all the letters in one form. The second is that there are few, if any, subtleties of thought or of expression in the letters better expressed—or concealed—by the unclassical Latin of the seventeenth century, and where there is doubt, that has been indicated in a note. Whatever their abilities, Cromwell's secretaries were Englishmen as their Latin proves. And it is proper to add that where both Latin original and English translation exist, they have been carefully collated. In some cases where both Latin and English versions are known and errors in translations seemed important, a fresh translation has been made; and in all cases the letters have been carefully scrutinized for omissions or perversions and the whole normalized. As to dates, the Old Style has been retained; that is to say, ten days must be added to the dates of the letters to make them conform to modern chronology, and the old year which began on March 25 has been indicated with the present system when that is necessary. As to spelling, the somewhat individualistic seventeenth century forms have in general been modernized, save in some cases which are left in their original form to show what they were when written.

If it may seem presumptuous to issue another edition of Cromwell's writings, the fact that this collection contains more than twice as many of them as have ever been gathered in one place before may serve to excuse in part such a work as this. For, aside from the arrangement in chronological order which gives a better conspectus of the whole, this is one of the cases in which the whole is somehow greater than the sum of the parts. With no expectation that such a body of material can revolutionize, or perhaps even greatly alter, our opinion of Cromwell, the infinite details, often petty in themselves, the many slight corrections of the time and place of his activities, the more accurate tracing of his movements and his acts, even, in some instances, his thoughts, may provide a truer picture of the man himself.

In one respect, if in no other, the direct contribution is great and obvious. It is in the period of the Protectorate, especially in the field of foreign policy. Here for the first time is assembled the body of letters and despatches to foreign powers, instructions to diplomats and commanders, commissions and orders, from which it is possible to draw a more comprehensive picture of Cromwellian policy than has hitherto been the case. To these the list of Cromwellian officials adds something of another side of the Cromwellian régime, of some importance to an understanding of its character. Those documents have been drawn not only from the archives but from a variety of other sources indicated in the notes. This part of the collection, at least, may be regarded as reasonably complete; and though it may be possible that a document here and there may have escaped the notice of the compiler or the archivists who have been of such service in collecting them, it seems improbable that many of importance have been overlooked.

In conclusion one must put in a plea of confession and avoidance. Completeness is as impossible as faultlessness in such a work as this. It is impossible that such a collection should contain all the writings of Oliver Cromwell. There must have been many orders, notes, letters and commissions which have now disappeared. There are some—though not many—which as has been said before, still exist but which have for one reason or another proved inaccessible. There are doubtless others still which have not come to light, but which will probably appear in time. This collection is, then, only as nearly complete and without errors as time and patience can contrive.

For the rest, one may ask of its critics in the words of the ancient rhyme, "Be to our virtues very kind, and to our faults a little blind"; or, as a more recent rhymester has put it:

> "Our work is done and poorly done, but if we could begin
> And start afresh and take another load,
> The chances are that native, ineradicable sin
> Would meet us and upset us on the road."

With such explanation of the scope and content of this work, it remains only to acknowledge the assistance of those who have contributed so greatly to the collection of this material and to thank them for that contribution: the Marquess of Bath; Sir H. Lincoln Tangye; the Rev. A. C. Moule, Trumpington, Cambridge; H. M. Adams, Esq., Librarian of Trinity College, Cambridge; Professor E. Curtis, Trinity College, Dublin; H. E. Craster, Esq., Librarian of the Bodleian Library, Oxford; Professor J. F. Jameson, Library of Congress; Mrs. Paul Faude; Mr. Godfrey Davies, Huntington Library, San Marino, California; Mr. Victor H. Paltsits, New York Public Library; Professor Willson H. Choate of the University of Rochester; J. V. Kitto, Esq., of the House of Commons Library; H. L. Pink, Esq., of Cambridge University Library; the Cornell University Library; Mr. Harold Russell of the Library of the University of Minnesota; William Le Hardy, Esq.; G. D. Ramsay, Esq.; and the London Museum. To the archivists of the Riksarchivet of Sweden at Stockholm; the Riksarchivet of Denmark at Copenhagen; the Rijksarchief in Zeeland at Middleburg; the Archief of Goes in Zealand; the Algemeen Rijksarchief at the Hague; the Oldenburgisches Landsarchiv; the Archives des Affaires Étrangéres in Paris; the R. Archivio di Stato in Turin; the R. Archivio di Stato di Firenze; the Staatsarchiv der Freien Stadt Danzig; the Staatsarchiv der Freien und Hansestadt Hamburg; the Staatsarchiv des Kantons Basel-Stadt; and to the Clerks of the Peace of co. Essex and co. Wilts; the Town Clerks of Sandwich, Thetford and Reading, in England; and to the Society of Antiquaries of London; the Public Record Office; the British Museum; and the Guildhall of London; and especially to the authorities of the Harvard College Library, to Mr. Walter B. Briggs in particular, and finally to my old friend, R. V. Coleman, who has kindly read the proof and offered many valuable suggestions, grateful acknowledgments are due.

Most of all gratitude is due to the Committee on Research in the Social Sciences in Harvard University for the generous support which it has given at all times to this enterprise, without which the publication of these volumes would have been impossible.

PREFACE TO VOLUME I

Owing to the circumstances of publication, it has seemed necessary to issue the first of these four volumes of the Writings and Speeches of Oliver Cromwell at this time rather than to await the conclusion of the entire work, which, it is hoped, will not be long delayed. This first part covers the period from the birth of Cromwell to the death of Charles I; the second will be devoted to the period of the Commonwealth; the third and fourth to that of the Protectorate. The difference in the scope of these volumes is due, of course, to the increasing amount of documentary material, especially in the last period. There will be included for the first time as nearly complete a collection of Cromwell's speeches, letters, orders, state papers and diplomatic correspondence as it is possible to make, and it is hoped that this will provide the basis for the most complete study of that period and the Protector which has yet been written.

The present volume which covers Cromwell's early life and the Civil War to the death of the King, has, naturally, no such mass of documents as the later period. None the less there are included here not only a considerable number of notes, memoranda, orders, letters and incidental information not brought together in one place before, but the details of his activities in Parliament, which, though known to earlier historians and biographers, have not been used by them in such detail to throw light on his career.

The Writings and Speeches of OLIVER CROMWELL

INTRODUCTION

"They say," wrote Sir William Monson, some three hundred years ago, "that every man is a son to his works, and that what one has by his ancestors can scarcely be called his own; that virtue is the cause of preferment, and honour but the effect." Of all the great figures of history, save Napoleon, this would seem to apply to Oliver Cromwell most of all. That in an age of divine right monarchy an obscure Huntingdonshire gentleman should rise not only to the first place in England, but to almost, if not quite, the first place in the European world, seemed then, and still seems, to argue all but superhuman qualities; and so long as human greatness is measured in terms of power over one's fellow-men, Cromwell must be reckoned as perhaps the greatest of Englishmen.

Yet even the greatest of men must have not merely ability and opportunity but ancestors, and from them derive in no small measure the qualities which make for eminence. While the elaborate genealogies which once introduced biographies have tended to disappear with the faith in heredity which produced them, enough remains of that long enduring faith and of the solid fact which underlies it, to make it necessary to begin the life of any man, not with his own birth and surroundings, but with some account of the human stock from which he was derived. In Cromwell's case that story is not long; for, whatever line of ancestors lay behind him, its first notable figure entered formal history almost precisely sixty years before the birth of Oliver. That entry was spectacular enough.

"On Maie Daie [1540]," wrote Raphaell Holinshed in his *Chronicles of England*, "was a great triumph of justing at Westminster, which justes had been proclaimed in France, Flanders, Scotland and Spaine, for all commers that would against the challengers of England; which were, sir John Dudleie, sir Thomas Seimer, sir Thomas Poinings, sir George Carew, knights, Anthonie Kingston, and Richard Cromwell, esquiers, which said challengers came into the lists that daie richly apparelled, and their horses trapped all in white velvet, with certain knights and gentlemen riding afore them, apparelled all in white velvet and white sarsenet, and all their servants in white dublets, and hozen cut after the Burgonian fashion; and there came to just against them the said daie of defendants fortie six, the earle of Surrie being the formost, lord William Howard, lord Clinton, and lord Cromwell, sonne and heire to Thomas Cromwell, earle of Essex and Chamberleine of England, with other, which were richlie apparelled . . . and after the said justs were doone, the said challengers rode to Durham place, where they kept open houshold, and feasted the king and queene, with hir ladies, and all the court. The second of Maie Anthonie Kingston and Richard Cromwell were made knights at the said place. The third of Maie, the said challengers did turnie on horssebacke with swords, and against them came nine and twenty defendants; sir John Dudleie and the earle of Surrie running first, who in the first course lost both their gantlets, and that daie Sir Richard Cromwell overthrew master Palmer in the field off his horsse, to the great honor of the challengers. On the fift of May, the said challengers fought on foot at the barriers and against them came thirtie defendants, which fought valiantlie; but Sir Richard Cromwell overthrew that daie at the barriers master Culpeper in the field, and the sixt of May the said challengers brake up their houshold."[1]

Thus did the first eminent ancestor of Oliver Cromwell, in a sense, lay the foundations of the fortunes of his family which, in time, came to condition those of his more famous descendant. For, as the worthy Fuller tells us: "This Richard Williams (*alias* Cromwell) came into the place an Esquire, but departed a Knight, dubbed by the King for his valour, clearly carrying away the credit. . . . Hereupon goeth a Tradition in the Familie that King Henry, highly pleased with his prowesse, Formerly, (said He) thou wast My Dick, but hereafter shalt be my Diamond, and thereat let fall His Diamond Ring unto him. In avowance whereof, these Cromwells have ever since given for their Crest a Lyon holding a Diamond Ring in his Fore-paw."[2]

Nor was this Richard Cromwell-Williams's only exploit in arms. "The yere of Christ 1543," wrote the chronicler Cooper, "an Army was sent over by king Henry, of which Sir John Wallop, Captain of Guines, was general, Sir Thomas Seymour, high marshal, Sir Robert Bowes, treasurer, Sir George Carew, Tho. Palmer, John Rainsforthe, John Sainct John, & John Gascoine, knightes, captaines of the footmen, Sir Richard Cromwell, captain of ye horsemen, who departed from Calais the xxii of July, who afterward joyned in the emperours power and besieged Landersey." It was of small avail, for presently "The siege of Landersey was broken up . . . in November ye Englishmen yt were sent thither came home again";[3] and, whether or not as a result of his activities overseas, in less than a twelvemonth Sir Richard Cromwell was dead.

His name, as Fuller notes, was not Cromwell but Williams; his family on the paternal side English only in a transplanted sense. His

[1] Holinshed, *Chronicles* (1808), iii, 815–16. (First ed. 1577). Copied, except for spelling, in Stow, *Annales of England* (1592), pp. 976–7.

[2] Fuller, *Church history of Britain* (1656), p. 370.

[3] T. Lanquet, *Cooper's Chronicle* (1565), pp. 319a, 320a.

father, Morgan Williams, was the son of a certain ap Gwylym of Glamorganshire, who, it is supposed, was one of those Welshmen who followed Henry Tudor's fortunes and accompanied him to England when he became Henry VII. Settled at Putney, steward of the manor of Wimbledon, land agent and accountant, this ap Gwylym, anglicized into Williams, had two sons, Richard and Morgan. Richard entered the church, Morgan inherited the Putney property, had a small place at court, and married Katherine, the daughter of one Walter Cromwell, known also as Smyth, from his trade of a blacksmith to which he appears to have added activities as a fuller, shearman, brewer and innkeeper in Putney. This Walter Cromwell seems to have been a violent as well as a vigorous character; and when, as it is said, he took to drink, his son-in-law succeeded him as owner of the alehouse and brewery.[4]

It was no promising beginning for a great family, especially since, though Morgan Williams seems to have lived in decent and prosperous obscurity, his father-in-law's activities in evading the assize of beer, abusing the privilege of common pasture, erasing the manor records, felonious assault and drunkenness, gave him a permanent if not honorable place in the records of his country. But if the Cromwell-Williams family origins were obscure, Walter Cromwell's son Thomas amply atoned for that obscurity. Trained to business in England, he returned from a varied and stormy career as merchant, soldier and adventurer on the Continent to enter the service of the Marquis of Dorset; then Cardinal Wolsey's, then that of Henry VIII. His character, his experience, his talents and his ambition were suited to his royal master's purposes, and after Wolsey's fall he rose rapidly in favor and position. He improved the royal revenues, he became the active agent in the suppression of the monasteries; and in rapid succession he was created chancellor of the exchequer, king's secretary and master of the rolls, vicar-general and "general visitor to the monasteries," lord privy seal, lord great chamberlain and baron Cromwell. For some five years he was the most powerful man in England, next to the King, and, in effect, chief minister. As such he negotiated the marriage of Henry VIII with Anne of Cleves; and, a few weeks before his nephew Richard Williams distinguished himself in the tournament in celebration of that marriage, he was created Earl of Essex.

His fall was still more rapid than his rise, for within two months, as Holinshed relates, "The ninth of Julie [1540] Thomas lord Cromwell, late made earl of Essex, being in the councell chamber, was suddenlie apprehended and committed to the Tower of London . . . the nineteenth day of the said moneth he was attainted by parlement

[4] Court Rolls of Wimbledon Manor, 15 Edw. IV.

of heresie and high treason . . . and the eight and twentieth of Julie, was brought to the scaffold on the Tower hill."[5] Such was the dramatic end of this extraordinary man, whom in Shakespeare's famous lines Wolsey adjured in vain:

> "Cromwell, I charge thee, fling away ambition,
> By that sin fell the angels . . ."

His sister's son, Richard Williams, was more heedful of such counsel. Though he followed closely in his uncle's steps, he was inclined to take the cash and let the credit go. First in the service of the Dorset family, then in his uncle's, then rising to royal favor, he was a typical figure of the age of Henry VIII. Bold, vigorous, capable, shrewd, acquisitive, ambitious—though rather for wealth than power—perhaps not over-scrupulous, it might have been said of him as it was said of Henry VIII by his apologist, that "he accomplished blessed ends by means which better men might well have thought accursed."

He informed the government of an intended Catholic rising and helped to put it down. He was an active and energetic "visitor" to monastic establishments marked out for destruction.[6] He married the daughter of a lord mayor of London.[7] He took his uncle's name, and dared to wear mourning for his fallen relative before the king who hated black, and he had his reward.

"As he was a good servant to his master," wrote Fuller of the earl of Essex, "so he was a good master to his servants; and foreseeing his own fall (which he might have foretold without the spirit of prophecy some half a year before) he furnished his men, which had no other livelihood to subsist by, with leases, pensions and annuities, whereby after his death they had a comfortable maintenance."[8] Among them his nephew; for when Thomas Cromwell wrote his will, among its provisions were: "Item, I gyue and bequethe to my nephew Richarde Wylliams lxvj^{li} xiij^{s} iiij^{d} sterlinge, my best gowne Dublett and Jaquet. . . . And if it happen him [his own son Gregory] to dye before them [his nephews] then I will all the said partes shall remayn to Rychard Wylliams and Water Williams my nephews."[9]

Nor were these all the benefits he conferred upon his favorite relative. Among a multitude of references to Richard's activities in the destruction of the monastic houses, one finds such notices as his uncle's letter to the Bishop of Coventry and Lichfield: "Forasmoche

[5] Holinshed, *Chronicles*, pp. 816–817.

[6] *Cal. St. Papers, Dom., Henry VIII, passim.*

[7] Francis, daughter of Sir Thomas Murfyn. Noble, *Memoirs of the Protectoral House of Cromwell*, i, 19.

[8] Fuller, *ut supra.*

[9] *Cal. Letters & Papers, Henry VIII*, iv, 5772.

as my nepvoye Richard Cromwell is moche desirous to haue the disposicion and assignment of a prebende in your churche of Lichefeld to preferre a right honest man, and a nere frende of his therevnto. . . . Thiese shalbe to desire and most hertelie praye your Lordshipp to tendre my said napvoyes suet And to send unto him by this bearer the said advouson."[10] Such were the methods of building up fortunes and influence in the days when "the mallet of the monks" was breaking the old establishment into pieces and distributing those pieces among the "new men" of the Tudor régime.

Of them many naturally fell to the share of Richard Cromwell-Williams. Apart from the possessions of St. Helen's nunnery in London,[11] Neath Abbey in Glamorganshire,[12] and lesser properties, the bulk of his gains lay in the eastern counties of England, especially in Huntingdonshire. There Sawtry Abbey,[13] St. Neot's Priory,[14] Hinchinbrook Nunnery,[15] a large part of the holdings of the rich abbey of Ramsey,[16] and the house of St. Mary of the Austin Canons[17] in Huntingdon itself, helped to swell one of the great fortunes which owed their origin to the destruction of the old religious establishment.

Of these vast estates Sir Richard's eldest son, Henry, inherited the greater part, including Ramsey and Hinchinbrook; while Francis, who seems to have been given the Glamorganshire property, lived on his more slender portion as a younger son chiefly at Hemmingford near Huntington.[18] Their pride of family, love of display and liberality were strong. Sir Henry, "the Golden Knight," so-called from these outstanding qualities, besides a summer residence at Ramsey, built on the site and in part out of the nunnery of Hinchinbrook, a splendid mansion whose windows with the quarterings of Glothian, lord of Powis; Mathiaid; Ynyrk of Gwentland, and their successors, at once commemorated and emphasized the Welsh origins of the family.

He was the pattern of a county magnate. Four times sheriff of Cambridge and Huntingdon,[19] a knight of the shire in Parliament, marshal of the county forces in the Armada year, host to Queen

[10] *Ibid.*, xiii, pt. 1, no. 765.

[11] Worth £314 per ann. according to Dugdale, *Monasticon Anglicanum*, (English ed. 1823), iv, 551.

[12] Worth £150 per ann. *Ibid.*, v, 258–60.

[13] Worth £141 per ann. *Ibid.*, v, 522.

[14] Worth £256 per ann. This descended to Francis, younger son of Sir Richard, and thence, in 1597, to his only son Henry. *Ibid.*, iii, 465.

[15] Worth £17 per ann. *Ibid.*, iv, 389–90.

[16] Worth £1716 per ann. *Ibid.*, ii, 546.

[17] *Ibid.*, vi, pt. 1, p. 78.

[18] Sir Richard Williams *alias* Cromwell's will in the Prerog. Office, London, *Allan* 20. Lease of the Glamorganshire property by Francis Williams, *alias* Cromwell, to John ap Henry ap Howell, 1566, in Cardiff Public Library, according to information kindly furnished by the Librarian, Henry Farr, Esq.

[19] Public Record Office, *Lists and Indexes*, vol. ix.

Elizabeth and knighted by her,[20] he was a loyal supporter of church and crown. Like his father, he married the daughter of a Lord Mayor.[21] Of his sons, the eldest, Oliver, inherited the bulk of his father's estate, including Ramsey and Hinchinbrook, where he lived. Like Sir Henry he was knighted by Elizabeth; like him he sat in Parliament for the county and was high sheriff. Like his father, he married twice, first the daughter of a lord chancellor, then the widow of Sir Horatio Pallavicini, collector of Papal revenues in England. Yet, despite rich marriages and an uncle's legacy, Sir Oliver's fortunes gradually declined. Apart from provision for his numerous family, were there wanting evidence of his qualities, the reception which he gave to James I on that monarch's progress from Scotland to the English throne, would help explain how he managed to dissipate his great inheritance.

"His Majestie," wrote Nichols in his *Progresses of James the First*, "passed in state . . . to Maister Oliver Cromwell's house, where his Majestie and all his Followers, with all commers whatsoever, had such entertainment, as the like had not beene scene in any place before, since his first setting forward out of Scotland. There was such plentie and varietie of meates, such diversitie of wines, and those not riffe-ruffe, but ever the best of the kinde, and the cellers open at any man's pleasure. And if it were so common with wine, there is little question but the buttries for beere and ale were more common, yet in neither was there difference; for whoever entred the house, which to no man was denyed, tasted what they had a minde to, and after a taste found fulnesse, no man like a man being denied what he would call for. As this bountie was held backe to none within the house, so for such poore people as would not presse in, there were open beere-houses erected wherein there was no want of bread and beefe, for the comfort of the poorest creatures. Neither was this provision for the little time of his Majestie's stay, but it was made ready fourteen daies, and after his Highnes' departure distributed to as many as had mind to it.

"Also Maister Cromwell presented his Majestie with many rich and respectable gifts, as a very great, and a very faire wrought standing cup of gold, goodly horses, flete and deepe mouthed houndes, divers hawkes of excellent wing, and at the remove gave fifty pounds amongst his Majestie's Officers."[22]

So in time that fortune disappeared. Before his death at ninety-six, Sir Oliver had lost Hinchinbrook to the Montagus, and lived out his days at his summer home of Ramsey. His son and heir Henry, who

[20] Peck, *Desiderata;* Morgan, Sylvanus, *Sphere of Gentry.*

[21] Joan, daughter of Sir Ralph Warren. Noble, i, 23.

[22] Nichols, John, *Progresses* (1828), i, 98–100. The king stayed from April 27th until April 29th, 1603, at Hinchinbrook.

inherited what was left of Sir Oliver's property had a son, Henry, whose son Henry changed his name again to Williams at the Restoration. He had no heir. Thus, within five generations, though the name and family of Cromwell was perpetuated through the younger branches, the direct male line of Sir Richard was extinct.

Thus was the history of the Cromwell family woven in the troubled Tudor and Stuart times—a vigorous, acquisitive ancestor building his fortune on the ruins of the church; descendants of lesser qualities, loyal to the establishment which made them what they were; a fortune dividing and decaying through the years; a family growing in number and alliances, and, with new issues and new interests, dividing against itself, drawing from other strains the strength its own blood lost, merging its qualities into the sources whence it sprang. Such was the stock whence Oliver was derived; and such was, in turn, the history of his own family; for human greatness has no heir, its virtues descend into the people, sometimes, as in Sir Richard's case, to rise once more to eminence, but more often, as in the case of Oliver, never to rise again.

But despite the importance of the physical and material ancestry of Oliver Cromwell, without which he would never have existed at all, if this were all the tale, it would be impossible to explain his character and career—or that of any man. What were the spiritual and intellectual influences which made him what he was and without which he would have played no greater part in history than the rest of his family? As it happened those influences arose in the world just as his ancestor Sir Richard Cromwell-Williams was making his way in that same world, assisted in no small degree but in a very different fashion by the same intellectual, spiritual and even political movements which were to dominate the life of his descendant who was to be their greatest champion.

Those movements owed their origin in large part to the French lawyer-theologian John Calvin, who while Sir Richard Cromwell rose to wealth and power, was busy framing a new theological system destined to exert profound influence on religious thought and on the politics which grew from it. Inspired by the New Learning of the Renaissance, still more by the reforming spirit which had found expression in Luther's defiance of the Papacy, by the work of Erasmus, and by the teachings of the Roman church itself, he framed from them and from the writings of the early Fathers a new system of theology, which, just as Henry VIII broke with the Papacy, he gave to the world in his *Institutes of the Christian Religion*. That volume marked an epoch in religious thought, and when its author moved to Geneva at almost the same moment that Sir Richard Cromwell was distinguishing himself before Henry VIII, he made that city a Calvinistic state on theocratic principles and the center of a communion destined to revolutionize theology and politics alike.

If Calvin's *Institutes* provided a logical system of theology to set against that of Rome and his government of Geneva became a model state, his doctrines and practices combined to inspire an almost fanatical devotion among his followers. It is one of the great mysteries of the human spirit that a faith founded on the assumption that man's fate depends not on his own free will and acts but was predestined from the beginning, should have moved its devotees not to supine inaction but to deeds of heroism and self-sacrifice as vain as they were exalted unless they were "of peculiar grace elect among the rest." Based on the belief that only those "elect" among the infinite masses of mankind were destined to be saved, the "rest" doomed to eternal punishment, it taught the doctrines of "justification" or "salvation" not by works but faith. How that "election" was determined lay beyond the realms of reason to decide. It rested, in the last resort, on one's own innate belief that after "conviction of sin" and "conversion" he was "justified by faith" and in "a state of grace." Nothing that he could do could possibly affect that awful decision of the Almighty made ere time began, "not of will in him but grace in Me," as Milton's God declared. None the less the Calvinist's life was ordered on the straitest lines of an austere, stern and unbending code of rigid morality. He lived according to his faith, expressing in his conduct and his speech his exaltation as one of the "elect." Convinced that God was with him always and always on his side, he was prepared to die for the faith which snatched him from the burning of a literal hell, with "spirit never to submit or yield" or compromise with the Mammon of unrighteousness, least of all with his mortal enemies the followers of Rome.

Clear, logical, systematic, Calvin's stern dogma appealed to many men unmoved by Luther's vaguer teachings, nor was it limited to theology. Against episcopal church government it set the no less ancient system of administration by elders or "presbyters." Against the Roman practice of priestly intervention it joined Lutheranism in teaching man's direct relationship with God. Against the ordered splendor of Catholic liturgy it set extreme simplicity of worship, not in Latin but in the language of the worshippers, not in set forms but with large elements of spontaneity. It glorified the homelier virtues—thrift, honesty, diligence, sobriety—as a means and an expression of man's inner grace. More than this, it lent itself to a sentiment of revolt in resistance to tyranny whether in church or state. "Let us not think," wrote Calvin, "there is given no other commandment but to obey and suffer . . . I affirm that if they wink at kings wilfully raging over and treading down the poor community, their dissembling is not without wicked breach of faith, because they dreadfully betray the people's liberty." His ideal of government was "a mixed aristocracy and democracy"; his practice was theocracy; and each was opposed to unlimited monarchy and episcopacy. Each appealed to the spirit of liberty or self-government, for men determined to administer their consciences or their congregations for themselves tended inevitably to extend that principle into politics, to seek liberty —at least for their own communion—and to oppose authority from above.

It was this spirit which reinforced the general revolt against the Roman church and inspired the fiercest opposition to Papal dominance; which challenged absolutism in civil affairs; which set up at Geneva and presently elsewhere a theocratic state scarcely less autocratic than that of monarchy; which nerved men to resist even to the death all efforts to impose another discipline upon them or limit their individual consciences. It was this spirit which when in power sought to force all others in its mould, and fell little short of Rome in its efforts to impose its will on those who differed from its principles or practices. It was this spirit which moved Calvin to set the ecclesiastical above the civil authorities in his model state and bring his opponent Servetus to the stake. It was this spirit which led men to death defending their determination not to submit to episcopal authority, especially that of the Papacy, and to challenge royal power if it conflicted with their principles.

With all of its rigid convictions, this Calvinistic Presbyterianism was a middle ground, as far from the excesses of those Munster Anabaptists who shocked Europe with their rejection of civil order, church discipline and personal morality as it was from the episcopal authoritarianism of Rome or Canterbury. It influenced, though it did not dominate, the spirit which in Sir Richard Cromwell's time had begun to revolutionize the ancient faith. It conquered the greater part of Scotland in the reign of Elizabeth, and little by little made its way into the English church. It inspired an element in that church; it led to what the rigid Anglicans termed schism and sedition; and as the Cromwell family spread through the eastern counties, this Calvinistic doctrine, "Presbyterian" or as men came to call it, "Puritan," made its chief gains in that same region. In time it came to influence that Cromwell connection in many ways, not least in that it came to dominate the life of its chief representative, who was to become its leading champion.

From these two sources, then, material and spiritual, was derived the life of Oliver Cromwell, the greatest of his name, the hero of the Puritans.

CHAPTER I

CHILDHOOD AND YOUTH

HUNTINGDON, APRIL 25, 1599–APRIL, 1616

Anno domini 1599 Oliverius filius Roberti Cromwell generosi et Elizabethae uxoris ejus Natus vicesimo quinto die Aprilis et Baptisatus vicesimo nono ejusdem mensis[1]—which is to say that in the year of our Lord 1599, on April 25th, there was born to Robert Cromwell, gentleman, and Elizabeth his wife, a son who was baptised "Oliver" on the 29th of the same month. Such was the entry of Oliver Cromwell into recorded history by way of the Register Book of the church of St. John the Baptist in the little town of Huntingdon in eastern England.

The birth of a child in an obscure family in an obscure English town was not a matter of general interest and, save to those most concerned, it seemed at that moment no great or exceptional event. It was by no means unique even in the Cromwell family. Already that register had noted the birth and baptising of Oliver's sister Elizabeth, then six years old; of his brother Henry; and of his two year old sister Catherine. When he was less than two years old was added the name of another sister, Margaret; two years later that of Anna; when he was six, that of Jane; and when he was eight, the record of the birth, baptism and death of a brother, Robert. Nor was this all of his immediate family; for the register of Alconbury-cum-Weston, just outside of Huntingdon, recorded the birth and baptism of his eldest sister, Joan; and to this list was later added the name of his youngest sister, Robina. His brother Henry died, so he became the only son; and, save for the fact that he had seven sisters, a doting mother and two childless uncles, and thus was in a fair way to be completely spoiled, as one of his earliest biographers observed, he "came into the world without any terrible remark."

Nor was there anything more remarkable in his immediate ancestry. He was born into a good if not greatly distinguished family, which, though its fortunes were then somewhat on the wane, had spread and prospered until the Cromwell connection had grown to be one of the most numerous and substantial in the eastern counties, especially in Huntingdon. It was a peculiarly prolific stock. Young Oliver's grandfather, Sir Henry, had ten children who lived to ma-

[1] Noble, *Memoirs of the Protectoral House of Cromwell*, (1787) i, 350–357.

turity,[2] of whom nine married and had children of their own. His uncle Oliver had twelve,[3] and young Oliver's father, Robert, had ten, of whom eight lived.[4] Though none of this numerous connection achieved any great distinction, its members were of importance in Huntingdon affairs. They owned no inconsiderable portion of the county; they served as sheriffs and as lesser officers; they were prominent in all local activities, especially in the great "project" of the draining of the fens which so interested that generation; and in the hundred years between the tournament in which the founder of the family, Sir Richard, distinguished himself before Henry VIII and the Long Parliament of 1640, Huntingdon was seldom unrepresented in Parliament by some member of the Cromwell family. They were intensely loyal to the church and crown which made them what they were and they had their reward. Sir Richard had not only been knighted by Henry VIII but through that monarch's favor he had gained his wide estates; and though his descendants had received no such substantial return for their loyalty, Sir Henry and Sir Oliver had been knighted by Elizabeth, and James I looked upon Sir Oliver's estate of Hinchinbrook, which he often visited, as almost, if not quite, his own.

The Cromwells were, in fact, typical representatives of those county families which in the sixteenth century replaced the clergy as the owners of the soil. England was full of such descendants of the "new men" of the rough Tudor times. Near at hand the Lawrences, deriving from a nephew of the last abbot of Ramsey, held part of the lands of that great foundation which escaped Sir Richard Cromwell's hands. The great rivals of the Cromwells in Huntingdon, the Montagus of near-by Kimbolton, were of like origin. Farther north, the Holles family owed the beginnings of its greatness to a master-baker of early Tudor times who made his fortune in church property. Elsewhere, the Seymours, the Wriothesleys, the Russells, the Audeleys, and many more, had the same history. Successors to the mediaeval baronage as the masters of society, this new nobility and gentry, of which the Cromwell family was a symbol and a type, unlike that older baronage was as yet devoted to the Protestant church and its Defender, the crown, with whose fortunes its own had been so closely bound.

Yet as those fortunes had tended to divide among its members, the Cromwell family, like many others, had tended to divide in interests. Three of young Oliver's uncles lived in Huntingdon; but one of his aunts married a Dunch of Oxfordshire, one a Fleming of Hampshire, one a Whalley of Nottinghamshire, one a Barrington of Essex, one a Hampden of Buckinghamshire, and one of his cousins married Sir

[2] Noble, i, 27–37.
[3] *Ibid.*, 50–60.
[4] *Ibid.*, 88–90.

Richard Ingoldsby—all names of consequence in the years to come and closely bound up with that of Oliver. Besides these, as time went on, he came to number among his relatives by marriage an astonishing list of names of consequence thereafter—St. Johns, Goffes, Trevors, Hammonds, Hobarts, Gerards, Waltons, Pyes, Knightleys and Mashams among others. And it is notable that while, in general, the male Cromwell line remained loyal to church and crown in the ensuing years, the female line with few exceptions inclined to the other side.

This, as it happened, was of profound importance to young Oliver; and—though for very different reasons—his mother's connections were of some consequence to his fortunes. Her family history, if somewhat less distinguished, was not unlike that of her husband. As the Welsh Williams genealogy led back to a shadowy Glothian, lord of Powis, hers traced its beginnings, dubiously, to the Scotch Stuart line.[5] It was, in fact, of Norfolk origin. Her great uncle, Robert Steward, the last Catholic prior of Ely, according to report, had been dealt with so faithfully by Sir Richard Cromwell that he abjured his popery and became the first Protestant dean of the cathedral. Her father, William Steward, farmed cathedral lands; and her only brother, Thomas, much of whose business lay with the cathedral authorities, followed the same course and was a man of substance and of consequence in Ely. Thus as there was a traditional connection between the Cromwell and the Steward families, the fortunes of each were laid on the ruins of the older church.

So far as Robert and Elizabeth Cromwell were concerned, those fortunes, though respectable, were not great. Among the properties which, with the rich spoils of Ramsey and Hinchinbrook, had come into the hands of the Cromwell family was, apparently, property belonging to the Augustine Friars which came in time by way of the portion of a younger son to Robert Cromwell. From the Friary farms and the tithes of the parish of Hartford near by, he drew his livelihood. In a house which had been part of the Hospital of St. John young Oliver was born. With his residence in Huntingdon and a little land about it, a dove-cote and a brew-house and lands outside of Huntingdon, some of which, apparently, like his house, he rented from the church authorities, he had perhaps three hundred pounds a year. His wife seems to have had a jointure from her first husband, a certain William Lynn, of some sixty pounds a year; and with the income from the land, and, later rumor said, from the brewery, the Cromwell family lived, like many of their kind, as lesser gentlefolk in comfort though not in luxury.

Their social position was determined not alone by this but by their

[5] Walter Rye (*Genealogist,* 1885, p. 34) proves that there is no immediate connection between Mrs. Cromwell and the Royal house of Stuart.

membership in the great Cromwell connection, especially by their close relation to its head, Robert's brother, Sir Oliver, who in his splendid mansion of Hinchinbrook just outside of Huntingdon, was the chief figure in the neighborhood. Yet, though overshadowed by his brother, Robert Cromwell was not wholly obscured. Like his father and brother, he had matriculated at Queen's College, Cambridge, though he took no degree; and, like them, he seems to have spent some time at Lincoln's Inn. He became a bailiff[6] and a justice of the peace; a trustee of the Free School of Huntingdon; as a Commissioner of Sewers, a signer of a certificate that the draining of the Fens was feasible;[7] and once represented the town in Parliament.[8] His character, and that of his wife, may be judged not merely from traditional accounts but from their portraits. The contrast between the dark, handsome, aristocratic face of Sir Oliver, with its short, pointed beard, its close cropped hair over its little Elizabethan fluted ruff and dark doublet, and the smooth-shaven, gentler, if not weaker, face of Robert, with long hair falling over a plain "puritanical" white collar is striking enough. But it is not more striking than the contrast between the portrait of Robert and that of his wife, with her capable, determined face, her handsome gown, midway between court costume and that of a country gentlewoman, her head-dress, half cap, half kerchief, covering her hair and tied under her firm chin. A serious, even dreamy, husband, apparently not in the best of health, a shrewd, practical, vigorous, active wife, mother of a large family, good manager and housewife, obviously the stronger character, it is evident whence Oliver derived his more robust qualities. Such was the parentage of Oliver Cromwell and such their worldly circumstance. He came, in short, from that element of society whence most talent comes —good "blood" or family, of not too great fortune, with social standing, background, tradition, education, and necessity to work.

If the circumstances of Oliver Cromwell's family were not unusual, the times which saw his entry in the world were eventful enough. The spacious day of Queen Elizabeth was wearing to a close, but the great sovereign faced no calm and peaceful evening of her reign. Its sky was still shot with the glories of Armada days but it was filled with dark and threatening clouds as shifting conditions of life and thought presaged new and disturbing conflicts everywhere in the European

[6] In 1609. In the church of St. Mary is a panel inscribed "R. CROMWEL. I. TVRPIN. Bailiefs, 1609." Cp. *Victoria County History of Huntingdonshire*, ii, 142. Sanford, *Studies of the Great Rebellion*, says 1599.

[7] Robert, Sir Oliver, and sixteen others subscribed to a certificate to the Privy Council, May 19, 1605, that the work of draining the Great Level was feasible. Dugdale, *History of the Fens* (2nd ed. 1772), p. 379.

[8] In 1593.

world. The revolt of Lutheran and Calvinist from Rome, which had disrupted Germany and France, wrested Great Britain from the Papacy and divided Europe into opposing camps, had, indeed, been calmed for the moment by the great Peace of Augsburg five years before Elizabeth ascended the English throne. But it had brought peace only to the Lutherans; the Calvinists were left naked to their enemies; and it seemed possible that the Geneva communion might fall before its foes. Instead it had become the spear-head of the Protestants. The years of Elizabeth's reign had seen the Calvinistic Netherlands revolt successfully against the Spanish rule; Scotch Presbyterians against Mary, Queen of Scots; French Huguenots against the Catholic monarchy. They had seen the Dutch win their independence; the triumph of the Scotch Presbyterians; and, in the year before Cromwell was born, the Edict of Nantes, by which the Huguenot leader, Henry of Navarre, now king of France, conferred political rights on his Protestant subjects.

Nor was the Calvinistic movement without effect on England itself. The English breach with Rome was partly personal; in part, like Gallicanism in France, due to a spirit of nationalism which resented the intrusion of a foreign power like the Papacy; in part an element of Tudor autocracy. It was due in part to the rise of new doctrines, in part to the rise of new men hungry for the spoils of a monastic system which had outlived its usefulness. It was at all times closely bound up with political ambitions and activities and it was driven to its destiny by forces both within and outside itself. It partook of Calvinistic rather than of Lutheran influence; and following the return of Protestant leaders from the continent after the Catholic reaction under Queen Mary, those who had sought refuge in Germany and who were prepared to support the episcopal system begun under Edward VI found themselves opposed by those who had come under Calvinistic influence in Switzerland.

Every principle of political interest drove the men who framed the Elizabethan settlement of the English church to an episcopal form of church government. Anglicanism bridged the gap between Romanist and Calvinist; it was a compromise suited to the English situation and the English character; and it was peculiarly adapted to the Tudor system of government. That system, like others on the continent, notably in Spain, offered its subjects relief from feudal anarchy in a strong, centralized, autocratic monarchy; and autocracy was as eagerly embraced by men weary of baronial oppression and private wars as was democracy three centuries later. In England as in Spain it was essentially conciliar in form. Through its great Privy Council, its Court of Star Chamber, its lesser courts and councils, like those of the North and the Welsh borders, it controlled affairs of state, with the advice and consent of Parliament, which, in turn, it largely dominated. Now, with the approval of that body, by an Act of Supremacy it assumed the headship of the church as well as of the state. A Prayer Book with Thirty-Nine Articles of church discipline; an Act of Uniformity to compel its subjects to accept the new organization, liturgy and tenets of the Established Church; a Court of High Commission to enforce the law; a Convocation to legislate for the Establishment, completed the ascendancy of the crown in ecclesiastical as in civil affairs; and the government set forth on its programme of organizing and administering the church.

To this Anglican system by no means all men, not even all Protestants, agreed. Calvinists as well as Catholics were equally opposed to this middle way between Rome and Geneva; and though it was accepted by the majority of her subjects, Elizabeth's reign was one long struggle to force the new organization, discipline and liturgy on the rest. The dissenting party had all but succeeded in carrying Convocation with it, and though defeated there as in the Parliament, it had appealed to the nation at large, and at this moment its leaders were striving to organize and inspire a national movement against episcopal government and eliminate the last remnants of what they conceived to be the Roman influence from the English church. And more—the effects of the Protestant Revolt, of Calvinism in particular, went far beyond the confines of theology; they threatened the foundations of the state itself, for men determined to administer their own affairs in matters ecclesiastical were not slow to carry that principle into politics. They had, in theory and to some degree in fact, begun to question royal authority. The doctrines of Calvin, still more those of his disciple John Knox, and most of all those of Knox's follower Buchanan, had pointed the way to an attack on the principles and practices of autocratic power; while in the English Parliament itself there had been heard mutterings of discontent with the activities of Tudor government.

At the moment that Oliver Cromwell was born those problems in church and state were shaping to new issues and new conflicts and England faced questions of profound significance in nearly every field of national life. Those problems touched the Cromwell family close and every circumstance of the boy's life bore witness to the changes which had taken and were taking place in English life and thought. The town in which he lived, his father's property and occupation, the house where he was born, the church where he was christened, the school which he attended, the schoolmaster who directed his education, the university to which he was destined, the Parliament of which he was to become a member, were all typical of the forces then moulding the England in which he was destined to play his part.

That England differed widely from the England of to-day. Just then emerging from its old economy, it was as yet in many parts a rough and ragged land, full of forest and waste and in this eastern region fens. Its roads were poor; the best were still the old Roman highways like that Ermine Street which ran through Huntingdon and which as the Great North Road was to play its part in the boy's later life. Its towns were small; even the capital was scarcely more than the City of London and its neighbor Westminster, connected by the Strand, where great houses had risen among hovels here and there. The town of Huntingdon was typical of its kind. Its twelve or fifteen hundred inhabitants lived for the most part in houses crowded along the main street with fields stretching away from them on every side. With its four churches, the largest, St. Mary's, with a hundred and eighty communicants, the smallest, St. John's, which the Cromwells attended, with eighty-seven, it was the shire and market town, the seat of local government. Its inhabitants were chiefly concerned with the affairs of a farming community, and just then with the great question of extending its fields and pastures by draining of the fens which lay at no great distance.

They and the Cromwells among them, like most of England, were no less concerned with improving what they had. Sheep-grazing which had made that land a great wool-growing country, founding monastic fortunes in the north and those of the merchants of the staple in the west, though still a great if not the greatest source of wealth, was being challenged everywhere, and not least in these eastern counties, by new developments in farming and cattle-raising. Sir Thomas More's complaint in his *Utopia* two generations earlier that 'sheep ate up both towns and men' was being met by these developments; and, farmer, cattle-raiser, petitioner for fen drainage as he was, Robert Cromwell was a characteristic figure of his time.

But the new wealth of England came not wholly from the land. With entry into trade beyond the seas, commerce was rising rapidly into greater consequence. The sea-kings of Elizabeth had done more than capture Spanish galleons and turn back the Armada; they had opened the road for English merchants east and west; they had pointed the way to colonizing lands in North America, claimed but not occupied by Spain. Already plans were being laid to exploit these new sources of wealth and power; already companies had been founded and colonial projects launched. At the moment that Cromwell was born, a group of London merchants was forming an East India Company, from which was to flow presently not merely new adventures and a new empire in the East but companies for the settlement of the West. To this was added another movement which brought still wider issues in its wake. The persecution of the Protestants on the Continent had sent a stream of refugees to England, bringing with them their skill in weaving, not least to the eastern counties where Norwich was rising to eminence in cloth manufacturing. They brought with them, as well, a spirit of religious independence to reinforce the rising revolt against the Anglican establishment especially in this region, and there and elsewhere particularly among merchants and manufacturers, since, as a later observer remarked, "heterodoxy and trade do commonly go hand in hand."

This was the more important in that with new wealth had come new discontents. The huge influx of gold and silver from America, with great increase of trade, had begun to break the bounds of the old economy. Prices were rising rapidly; wages lagged behind; the cost of living and of government had increased and was increasing; wealth and poverty had grown in equal pace with new conditions and new standards of life. Already Parliament men complained openly of the cost, the policy, and even the system of Tudor rule. Already they were framing acts to meet the situation, to free commerce from royal grants of monopoly, to check crown influence upon Parliament, to control the masses of "sturdy beggars" and "deserving poor" thrown up by the developments of the preceding century. Already this active, vigorous society emerging from its older faiths and practices revealed the restlessness which portends a revolution in human affairs. Already the commercial elements made way in politics; and already the new forms of religious faith and discipline were finding their way from theology into political theory; for the great struggles of the Reformation had borne within themselves the seeds of new conflicts now sprouting everywhere.

The very dwellings which housed the Cromwell family typified the changes taking place in the England into which young Oliver was born. Huntingdon had no such memorial of the past as the Earl of Winchester's Basing House or the Earl of Derby's Lathom House, half stronghold and half residence; no castle like that of nearby Ashby-de-la-Zouch or Gainsborough, or more distant Pembroke and Sherborne. It had no walls like those of Chester nor fortress like the London Tower. The great days of those strongholds was past or passing and the stately mansion of Hinchinbrook with a hundred counterparts throughout England testified to the Tudors' gift to their people of domestic peace, revealing the nation's new security as well as its new wealth.

The conflict about to begin, unlike that which had once raged about the old baronial fortresses, tended to center in those other relics of the past, the parish churches and the cathedrals. Like feudalism the monastic age was gone. Abbey and convent, hospital, chantry, priory were wrecked, decayed or turned to other purposes. Their walls were quarries for builders, their lands in private hands, their chapels used as dwellings, sheep-folds or barns, their town-houses occupied by families like the Cromwells, their schools managed by local authorities like those of Huntingdon. But the churches and cathedrals were still there, though, like St. John's in Huntingdon and the cathedral in nearby Ely, they were now the property of the Church of England, in which the government strove to center and confine the nation's religious life. The task was not easy, for the spirit of individual liberty engendered by the Protestant Revolt had made it difficult for many men to be content with faith and forms imposed from above.

For the new Church of England had kept more than the buildings of the older faith. It had retained much of the Roman ritual in English dress; the vestments and the church decorations; the Roman organization and its officers—parish and diocese, bishops, deans, and rectors or vicars in the place of priests. Its bishops raised their mitred fronts in the House of Lords; its clergy met in Convocation to administer church affairs. Church courts clung to their old prerogatives and tithes were levied to support the great Establishment. It was now part of government and since the crown was head of church and state alike, schism and sedition might be considered one.

The way to the assent of the nation to this middle course between Rome and Geneva was long and hard, nor was it lightened by Catholic rebellion and conspiracy nor by the activities of the advanced Protestants determined to force Presbyterianism on the Establishment. It was at once helped and hindered by threats of foreign invasion, by plots against Elizabeth's government and her life, which deepened the hate and fear of Rome and identified the national church with national existence. In time the Roman Catholics were converted, cowed or crushed; the Calvinists—Presbyterians, or as they came to be called "Puritans"—remained. Inside or outside the church, they ranged from moderate men desiring some limits to episcopal authority, to extremists desiring complete religious liberty for congregations or even individuals.

If the bishops were not all or always tolerant or long-suffering, the leaders of that Presbyterian minority were no meek and uncomplaining sufferers for the word. They were active and aggressive controversialists, accomplished agitators, able organizers, gifted in tongues, to whom all times and persons were alike. Apart from all questions of theology, whether Presbyterian, "Disciplinarian," "Brownist" or "Separatist," however divided among themselves, the Puritans were at one in their contention of "Bible, God and conscience" against liturgy and episcopacy; and their opposition to the church establishment took a concrete form. They were not content to have ministers "presented" to them, they wished to choose their own. They were not content with formal services by a ministrant, they desired more share in those services themselves; not music by an organ and a choir, with set readings, responses and sermons, but congregational singing, "lectures," extemporary prayers, even "prophesyings" or "outpourings of the spirit" by individuals. They wanted no rood-screens nor altar-rails; no altar but a communion-table in the middle of the church; no vestments but plain "Geneva" gowns; no Prayer Book but, for the Presbyterians, a Book of Discipline. They objected to "Romish superstitions," to the ring in the marriage ceremony, to the sign of the cross in baptism, to bowing at the name of Jesus, to images, stained glass, saints' days and church festivals, to profanation of the "Lord's day" by games and sports in the afternoons.

Filled with such sentiments, they came to look on themselves as a race apart, a "peculiar," "chosen" people; wore sober clothes, devised a semi-Biblical phraseology, met and interpreted the Scriptures for themselves in "classes" or congregations, set up "lectureships" to supplement or supplant formal church services. They were determined to save their own souls in their own way, for "who can be at rest, or who can enjoy this world with contentment," as Milton wrote, "who hath not liberty to serve God and save his own soul?" Nor were they content to hold such principles themselves and let their opponents be damned in their own way. They were as determined as the Anglicans to compel their countrymen to accept their doctrines and practices; nor did they confine them to the religious sphere, for they soon found their way to Parliament. Thus between the champions of royal and episcopal authority and those of greater popular rights, it was evident in Elizabeth's last years that England faced a struggle between the champions of order and the apostles of liberty.

Such was the great issue which loomed on the political-religious horizon at the moment that Oliver Cromwell came into the world. Yet to most men at that moment there were matters of far more concern than this, for despite their faith and their activity, the Puritans were as yet a small minority. In general men were not then so much concerned with problems of theology or even of church government as with other matters far removed from these. They were then reading Spenser's *Faerie Queene*, whose author died in the year that Oliver was born. They were writing and reading such books as *England's Helicon*, in which were gathered the finest flowers of Elizabethan lyrical and pastoral poetry. It was then that English drama reached a climax in the immortal plays which William Shakespeare of Stratford was writing and presenting on the English stage. Nor were men's interests confined to these; for it was then that the great age of sea-kings neared its end with the deaths of Drake and Hawkins, and another era of overseas adventure opened with the return of Lancaster from harrying Spanish possessions in South America to lead the first voyage of the new East India Company to Asia, as Gosnold explored the coasts of North America seeking location for a colony.

It was at such a period that Oliver was born and amid such influences that he grew to manhood; nor could he have been wholly ignorant of the forces at work in the England of his time. However little touched by the great literary movement of his day—and there seems little evidence that he knew much of either Spenser or Shakespeare—he was in the midst of the struggle then going on in church and state. He saw the king from time to time at Hinchinbrook. His parents and his schoolmaster were concerned with Puritanism in whatever form. His relatives were interested in colonial ventures; and the years of his youth were filled with great events in the world of politics, religion, commerce and colonies. He was born at a great parting of the ways; and in his day and partly at his hands the England which had made his family what it was and had developed the faith that he embraced, was presently transformed into the England in which he was in time to play the leading part.

HUNTINGDON, 1603–1616

The birth of Oliver Cromwell came at a turning-point of English history, his youth fell amid great developments in nearly every field of his country's manifold activity; yet there was little in the circumstances of his early years or in his early promise which gave much evidence of such influences or of the capacity which he showed in later life. There are few men who have played such a great part in affairs who gave less evidence of extraordinary qualities in their youth or of whose early years so little can be told. Despite the efforts of his biographers to find some premonition of greatness, he was a very ordinary youth, and what is there in the ordinary life of ordinary youth to chronicle? The history of his early years is no different from that of a hundred others of his kind. There were some changes in his family. When he was two years old his father's cousin Captain Henry Cromwell, son of Francis Cromwell, died in Robert Cromwell's house, and his uncle, Sir Oliver, whose first wife had died, married the widow of Sir Horatio Pallavicini, sometime collector of Papal revenue in England. That astute Genoese, "robbing the Pope to pay the Queen," had kept the proceeds and loaned them to Elizabeth, who in time repaid them to Sir Oliver; and to further secure the declining fortunes of the Cromwell family, Sir Oliver's younger son Henry presently married Lady Pallavicini's daughter Baptina.

This was of some importance to the Cromwell family since these new resources served, among other things, to contribute to the first great experiences of young Oliver's life. When he was four years old, Elizabeth died and the mourning for her was the earliest national event of which he could well have been conscious. And scarcely had the Hinchinbrook household left off its mourning when it began its

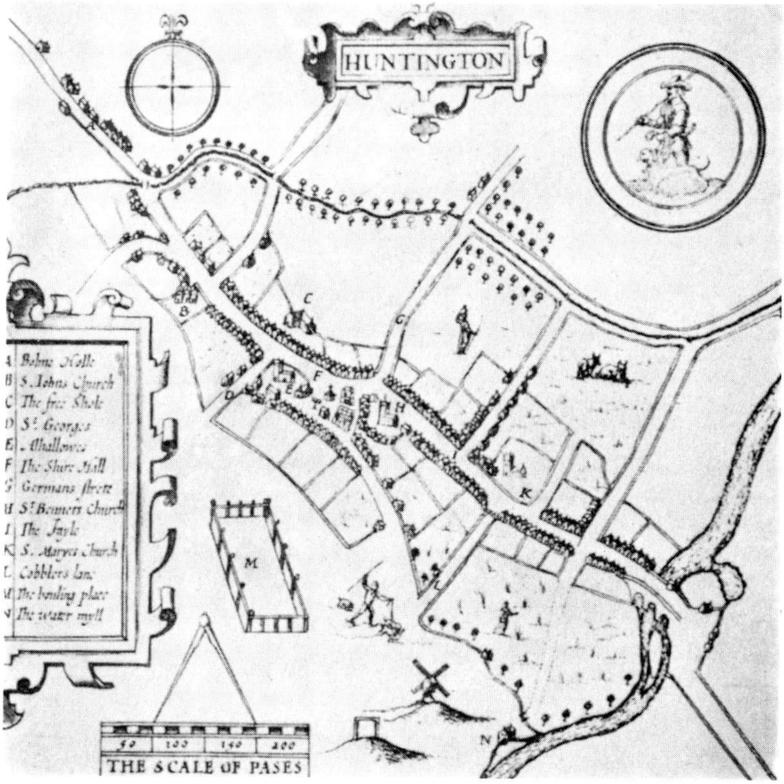

Plan of Huntingdon, from John Speed's Map, 1610.

preparations to welcome the new king, James I, who stopped there on his progress from Scotland to the English throne. There he "had such entertainment as the like had not beene seene in any place before his first setting out of Scotland"; and what with its extravagance and the presents to royalty and its suite, not only did James receive his first impression of the wealth of his new subjects but the Cromwell-Pallavicini fortune was sensibly depleted. There, it seems certain, the boy Oliver must have had his first sight of royalty; and there, later tradition says, he quarrelled and fought with the young prince Charles, then a sickly child of two and a half years.

As he grew older the usual family events marked his advancing years. His grandfather, Sir Henry, died and his magnificent funeral made further inroads on the family fortune. His uncle, Thomas Steward of Ely, was knighted at Whitehall by James. A "visitation" of the diocese held at Huntingdon by Bishop Wickham of Lincoln provided what impression a boy of five might have of episcopacy in action; and the visits of King James to Hinchinbrook again and yet again in the ensuing years gave the community and the Cromwell family in particular a continuing interest in the doings of royalty. The family increased with the births of Oliver's sisters, Margaret, Anna and Jane, and of his short-lived brother, Robert. The bonds between the Cromwell and Pallavicini families were strengthened by the marriage of his cousins, Katherine and Jane to Henry and Tobias Pallavicini. For the rest young Oliver lived the life of a healthy, growing boy. There is a tale of how as a baby he was stolen by a monkey and taken to the roof of Hinchinbrook; but it is a fable told of others, among them Christina of Sweden, and far from credible, nor important if it were. There is another far more probable, of the clergyman who rescued the boy from drowning and lived to repent it publicly. What is of more importance is that he began his education, and, despite the lack of direct evidence, its course is not hard to reconstruct.

In effect its lines had been laid down two generations earlier by Sir Thomas Elyot in his *Boke of the Governour*, whose principles still dominated English schools. It prescribed "first letters" and Latin to the age of seven; from seven to fourteen, removal from all female company, save perhaps that of one "aunciente and sadde matron," and the tutorship of an "aunciente and worshipful man of gentleness mixed with gravity, honest, continent and godly behaviour." And thus, according to custom and such evidence as we have, was Oliver first entrusted to a sort of nurse-governess;[9] then to an elderly clergy-

[9] [Heath], *Flagellum or the Life and Death of Oliver Cromwell, the late Usurper* (1663), p. 5, says Cromwell was under "the slightest governance of a Mistress" before being removed to Beard's care.

man named Long;[10] and finally entered at the Free Schoo of Huntingdon.[11]

That was an event of great if not of determining importance to his life, for he came under the care of a man who was to influence him profoundly. Six months before Bishop Wickham's visitation, there had taken place:

The Institution of Thomas Beard to the Hospital of St. John the Baptist.

On Saturday, to wit the 2nd day of the month, April &c 1604 &c. Thomas Bearde, Clerk, Bachelor in Divinity, presented by the discreet men John Todd and Robert Cooke, of Huntingdon, Gent., the true and undoubted Patrons of the same for this term, by reason of the advowsonship to them by the Burgesses of the Borough of Huntingdon, made and granted to the Hospital of St. John the Baptist, within the Town of Huntingdon aforesaid, &c and the same Thomas Beard, Master or Warden of the same Hospital, with all its rights, members, and appurtenances, canonically and lawfully instituted and invested in the same &c.[12]

It was a notable event for Huntingdon and for the Cromwells, especially for young Oliver. Master and school were typical of the time. Like the house where he was born, the Free School of Huntingdon, of which his father had once been a trustee, had been the property of the Hospital of St. John the Baptist. Its history dated back to the twelfth century, and as early as 1300 it had been in the hands of the town authorities. By this "institution" it was now committed to the care of Thomas Beard, a representative figure of the period and, as it happened, of the party then bent on changes in the Anglican establishment. Some time a member of Jesus College, Cambridge, where he had taken his degree in the Armada year, he had risen presently to M. A.; had been ordained; had become rector of Aythorp in Essex and of Kimbolton, the seat of the rivals of the Cromwell family in Huntingdon, the Montagus; and had written a little book called *The Theatre of God's Judgments*. He was thus an admirable example of the new clergy then rising in the church, especially of the element then coming to be called "Puritan."

He was more than that; he was one of that group of schoolmasters which had arisen to instruct the youth of England in the new learning and the new theology when the monastic and cathedral schools had

10 *Biographia Britannica*. A Sir William Long was vicar of Stranground-cum-Farcet in Yaxley Deanery, Huntingdonshire, in 1584 and also in 1597. Foster, C. W., *State of the Church* (1926), i, 211.

11 *Flagellum*, p. 5.

12 "Institution Book of William Chaderton," Bishop of Lincoln, 1595. Pr. in Gilbert, *Ancient Records Relating to the Borough of Huntingdon* (1827), p. 103. Cp. Dugdale, *Monasticon*, vi, 763.

disappeared. To Beard might have been applied, with some modification, the description of his colleague, John Brinsley of near-by Ashby-de-la-Zouch, who had taken his M. A. at Cambridge when Beard was taking his first degree. "He was," wrote one of Brinsley's pupils, the "astrologer" Lilly, "one in those times of great abilities for instruction of youth in Greek and Latin tongues; he was very severe in his life and conversation; and did breed up many scholars for the universities. In religion he was a strict puritan, not conformable wholly to the ceremonies of the church of England."

Beard was, if not gentler, at least more conformable; and his system of education was almost certainly like that of Brinsley. What that was, appears in Brinsley's book, published at this time. It was called *The Grammar Schoole; shewing how to proceede from the first entrance into learning to the highest perfection required in the Grammar Schooles, with ease, certainty and delight, both to Masters and Schollars; onely according to our common grammar and ordinary Classical Authors.* It covered the years from five to fifteen; and however Beard's instruction may have differed in detail, whatever "ease, certainty and delight" his pupils may have revealed, it was virtually what Oliver Cromwell experienced.

It began with spelling and reading in English, the primer, the Psalms—in metre—the New Testament, notes on sermons, the Bible and its history, the Psalter, the Book of Common Prayer, and the Catechism. In Latin it began with Lily's or the "Eton" grammar, and went on with the *Sententiae Pueriles*, or children's stories, Aesop's *Fables*, Cicero, Ovid and Virgil; then in the upper school, Plautus, Horace, Persius and Juvenal, with themes and verses in Latin. To these were added arithmetic and geometry, some logic and rhetoric, and sometimes Greek.

Nor was the schoolboy's life all work, for Brinsley added what he called "recreations." They took various forms. Sir Thomas Elyot had specified—from the age of fourteen—"throwing the stone or bar, tennis, wrestling, running, swimming, handling weapons, riding, hunting, dancing and shooting with a long bow"; and, if we may believe his earliest biographers, Oliver was more remarkable for these than for the intellectual part of his curriculum.

In another respect Beard's system had a lighter side. He was fond of plays. He wrote brief classical comedies of an improving sort which his boys acted, nor was their acting confined to these; and from this circumstance arises almost, if not quite, the only even tolerably authentic anecdote of Oliver's early years. It had to do, not with his studies, in which, according to gossip, he was so little distinguished that he was often and severely punished, but with the presentation of one of these plays, Anthony Brewer's *Lingua, or the Combat of the Tongue and the Five Senses.* In that, according to the tale, young Oliver took the part of Tactus, or the Sense of Feeling. Coming on the stage, he stumbled over a robe and crown and so began his lines: "High thoughts have slippery feet; I had well nigh fallen." Then, taking up the crown and putting it on his head, he began a long soliloquy ending with:

> "this crown and robe
> My brow and body circles and invests,
> How gallantly it fits me, sure the slave
> Measured my head that wrought this coronet.
> They lie who say complexions cannot change,
> My blood's ennobled, and I am transform'd
> Unto the sacred temper of a KING."[13]

The story sounds too apt to be true, but true or false, such presage of greatness was not to be missed by later writers wise in the event; yet beyond this little is recorded of his years at school. What is of more importance than such tales is the character of his teacher, and that we know about, since Beard rose to prominence in Huntingdon affairs, and played an increasingly important part in those of the Cromwell family, especially in those of young Oliver, nor did that influence cease with his pupil's withdrawal from the school. He was made the rector of St. John's and so became the spiritual as well as the intellectual guide of young Oliver; he became a man of influence in Huntingdon and contributed to the rise of his pupil in politics. It was to him that Oliver's first recorded utterance in Parliament referred; and were these evidences wanting, it requires no great knowledge of Cromwell's career and no stretch of the imagination to perceive that this schoolmaster was one of the great determining influences in his pupil's later life.

We need not speculate as to Beard's character and opinions. They are clearly revealed in his book which ran through at least four editions in some forty years, expanding as it went. In its increasing chapters one somehow perceives the substance of those "lectures," with which, according to the Puritan practice of the times, he edified his parishioners with denunciations of the dissolute habits of his age and of the Papal anti-Christ. These revealed at once his wide reading and the cast of mind of that party in which he was an influential if not an eminent member, for however pluralist and conformist, Beard was essentially a Puritan.

Despite its erudition and its "improving" character, despite the

[13] First edition, 1607. Carrington (*Life of Oliver Cromwell*, p. 3) and Symmonds ("Historical Notes," *Harleian Mss.*, British Museum, 999, p. 22) make the place at which this happened the University of Cambridge. A later edition of the play (Lond. 1657), however, says "First acted at Trinity College Cambridge, after at the Free School at Huntingdon," which may account for their statement.

praise heaped upon it by those who doubtless never read it, Beard's *Theatre of God's Judgments* is not, to modern taste, a pleasant book. It stresses God's immediate concern with all the petty details of men's lives and His presence among them; and divine, angelic and Satanic interference in every-day affairs; but it concerns itself chiefly with the darker side of life. Its God is less the loving Father than a stern avenging Deity much absorbed in the discovery and punishment of sin and in vengeance on the sinners. It stresses the duty of all men, but more especially of rulers, to obey God's laws, "and consequently the Lawes of man and nature." It adduces almost innumerable instances of divine retribution for violation of those laws, from Pharaoh's time to recent Sabbath-breakers, from murder to magic, drawn from an amazing list of sources, sacred and profane, ancient and modern, tales of classical depravity, of wicked continental rulers, of English country-folk. They range from that king of Poland who, like Bishop Hatto, was eaten up by rats to that of the wretch who mistreated his father and whose meat, in consequence, turned to serpents, of which one "leaped in his face and catching hold of his lip, hung there to his dying day, so that he could never feed himself but must feed the serpent withall." It seeks to teach morality by fear; to produce conviction by a cloud of witnesses; it echoes the Old Testament rather than the New. With all its instances of angelic intervention, especially for the poor, it has far more weird tales of Satan and his fiends come among men to deceive them or to hale sinners to eternal punishment; and its erudition is matched only by its credulity.

It was not alone in its appeal to its appreciative audience. The then popular Foxe's *Book of Martyrs* provided earnest Protestants with an account of the sufferings of their fellows for their faith at the hands of the Roman Catholics, just as the Roman Catholic martyrologies of an earlier age had told the stories of Christian persecution by pagan authorities. Like the Lives of the Saints and the books of miracles of the older church, Beard and Foxe supplied that element of the miraculous essential to a faith. To such believers it was not enough to accept the cardinal principles of religion. It must be concrete and imminent; hell and heaven, realities; God's presence, Satan's wiles, a part of human experience; and direct intervention of the Deity visible to all.

It is scarcely conceivable that Oliver Cromwell did not read Beard's book, whose second edition appeared when he was twelve years old; and to its influence was added almost at once the great translation of the Bible which is called the King James Version. That was a notable, even a decisive event in English life. Its simple, splendid style, its noble phraseology, even its exotic, Oriental atmosphere, no less than its content, opened a new world for its generation. Like its English predecessors it offered the very Word of God as an unquestioned and an unquestionable guide to life, a final court of appeal, whose judgments each reader could interpret for himself. It provided something more—figures of speech and arguments, precepts and examples suited to every need and circumstance of life, splendid imagery, threats and judgments, comfort and inspiration, hopes and fears of the hereafter. To Puritans in particular it offered even more than this. It strengthened their concept of themselves as a chosen people like the children of Israel, surrounded by their foes but supported and sustained by a Deity whose chief concern they were, assuring them triumph over their enemies, whether Amalekite or Arminian; and with its coming England and the Puritans in particular became the "land and people of the Book."

It is not difficult to trace the influence of all this on Oliver's later life. His knowledge of some Latin and history and perhaps a little Greek;[14] his remarkable command of the Scriptures and their phraseology; his sense of God's immediate concern with him and his affairs, of His peculiar interest in the success of the "godly"; an enduring hatred of Roman Catholicism and of Spain; all these reflect the training of his youth. They were not all derived from Beard nor from his school. Some were learned at home; some were a part of the air he breathed. He could not help but hear how his grandfather had mustered the forces of the county in the great Armada year; of Catholic conspiracies and of Mary, Queen of Scots. He could not help but know how, when he was six years old, the framers of the dark Gunpowder Plot had planned to blow up the Houses of Parliament, kill the king and restore the ancient faith. He could not help but hear the tales of the sea-kings of Devon of whom only Raleigh remained the last hero of that heroic age. Nor could he have been wholly ignorant of the character of James and his court in their visits to Hinchinbrook as he was growing up, nor of that monarch's quarrels with his Parliaments which made up so much of the politics of the time.

Least of all could he have failed to hear of those rising differences in the church with which his schoolmaster was then much concerned, nor even of the new colonial enterprise then endeavoring to plant a settlement in Virginia. He must have known of them, for all England knew of the struggle between the crown, the bishops and the Puritans, and between the King and Parliament, and some of his own family, his uncle Oliver in particular, had shares in the Virginia Company. He could have known but little of the principles involved in the conflict of "priest" with "presbyter," but he could not well help

[14] Edmund Waller said of him that he was "very well read in the Greek and Roman story" (Waller, *Poems* (1722) pref. p. 30); and Cromwell advised his son Richard to "read a little history, study the Mathematics and cosmography . . . these fit for public services for which a man is born"; and again he recommended Raleigh's *History of the World* as "a good body of history."

feeling something of the spirit which animated Beard. And Beard was more than Oliver's schoolmaster; he was a friend of the Cromwell family, concerned with almost every detail of its life. It was he, apparently, who solemnized the marriage of Joan Cromwell to a certain William Baker[15] when Oliver was twelve; and who prepared him for the next episode in his life, his entrance into Cambridge University, not at his father's college of Queen's but at Sidney Sussex.

CAMBRIDGE UNIVERSITY, APRIL, 1616–JUNE, 1617

Two days before his sixteenth birthday—and, as it happened, on the same day that William Shakespeare died—at the head of the list of students entering that college *A Festo Annunciationis ad Festum Sancti Michaelis Archangeli* was recorded:

Oliverius Cromwell Huntingdoniensis admissum ad commeatum Sociorum Aprilis vicesimo tertio; Tutore Magistro Richardo Howlet.[16]

And with this began another period of Oliver Cromwell's life.

To most men their entry into a university is one of the great experiences of their lives and their stay there one of the determining influences of their later years. For that in Cromwell's case there is no evidence. The college which he entered was a new foundation, closely identified with the Montagu family, which had added to its endowment and one of whose members had lately been its head. Its master, Samuel Ward, had been one of the translators of the new King James Version of the Scriptures, and was presently a delegate to the great Calvinistic Synod of Dort. However timid and perplexed amid the issues of the great theological and ecclesiastical controversy of the time, however devoted to the crown, he was, like Beard, a Puritan, and the college partook of the same character. Its chapel had no stained glass and no images; its services followed the Prayer Book only enough to comply with the law; and it was noted presently by a certain William Laud, sometime archdeacon of Huntingdon, later Archbishop of Canterbury, and, incidentally, a relative by marriage of Cromwell's tutor, Mr. Howlet, that Sidney Sussex was "a hotbed of Puritanism." Otherwise it was in no way remarkable. A new foundation, its tutors were apparently men of little consequence

[15] *Register of St. John's;* Noble, i, 351. Noble says (i, 88) that Robert Cromwell's daughter, Joan was buried at All Saints' in 1601, and (i, 57) that it was Sir Oliver's daughter Joan who married Baker; but he has misread his own records, for in his transcripts of the church records (i, 349) the Joan who died is specifically spoken of as "daughter of Mr. [Sir] Oliver Cromwell." Following Noble, Cromwell's biographers have all supposed that his sister Joan died young.

[16] *Sidney Sussex College Register*, vol. i (1598–1706), p. 151.

and few if any of them rose to distinction. Its students were of like sort. Young Oliver was one of less than a dozen gentlemen-commoners; the rest were ordinary undergraduates and "sizars," who were, in a sense, dependent on charity for their education. To Oliver this was of little consequence, for it nowhere appears that any of his fellow undergraduates ever became very eminent or ever played a part in his later life.

What was of more importance was that in college as in school he was bred in the straitest sect of Puritanism. That for the moment seems to have had as little influence on him as the intellectual stimulus to which he was exposed. From its effects he seems to have been virtually immune. He was an average youth of athletic tendencies and no bent toward books. Making every allowance for its unfriendly spirit, all the evidence we have seems to indicate that young Oliver was a rude, vigorous and unruly youth with little love of learning. His tutor is said to have noted that "neither was he then so much addicted to Speculation as to Action,"[17] and another writer that he was "quickly satiated with study, taking more delight in horse and field exercise."[18]

Heath, enlarging on the same theme without improving it, relates that,

> "During his short residence there . . . he was more famous for his exercises in the Fields than in the Schools (in which he never had the honour of, because no worth and merit to, a degree) being one of the chief match-makers and players at Foot-ball, Cudgels, or any other boysterous sport or game . . ."[19]

If, on the other hand, one prefers another view of the youth of the Protector, written while his son occupied that office, one may find it in the courtly Carrington,[20] who testifies that:

> "Having finished his course of Study at the University, when he had perfectly acquired unto himself the Latine Tongue (which Language, as all men know, he made use of to treat with Strangers) his Parents designed him to Study of the Civill Law . . . he dived not over deep into this study, but rather chose to run a Course in all the rest of the Sciences, and chiefly in the Mathematicks, wherein he excelled, as . . . he yielded to no Gentleman in . . . the rest of the Arts and Sciences!"

Despite Carrington, it seems that Cromwell was, in fact, a fairly common type of undergraduate, then and since. His stay in Cambridge seems to have been limited to one year, but his early departure

[17] *Perfect Politician*, p. 2.
[18] Bate, *Elenchus Motuum Nuperorum* (1663), pp. 273–4.
[19] *Flagellum* (1663), p. 8.
[20] *History of Oliver, Late Lord Protector* (1659), p. 4.

was not due, as one might easily suppose, to any action on the part of the authorities, but to his father's death, which not merely seems to have made an end of his college career but gave rise to an important document, that is to say his father's will. That document is in many ways a significant piece of evidence. In it, as some writers have observed, there is no mention of the name of Oliver; and that has been noted as a surprising circumstance, somehow to his discredit. He is, however, designated as the "heire," which seems to remove whatever reflection on him which the absence of his name implies. It has been further observed that though the will itself does not contain the name Williams, the "Act Book" adds to the name of Cromwell the words "*alias* Williams." Far more important than these trifling circumstances which have engaged the attention of antiquarians, is the spirit and the phraseology of the document. Whether written or dictated by Robert Cromwell, however much it may owe to the spirit of the time or to the person who actually drew it up, it gives one somehow a pleasant impression of the man who thus disposed of his worldly goods, as one of gentle nature, thoughtful character, deep religious feeling and a kindly heart.

Robert Cromwell's Will

In the name of God Amen. The Fiveth day of June in the yeare of our Lord God one Thousand six hundred and seaventeene, I Robert Cromwell of Huntingdon in the County of Hunt, Esquire being taught by longe experyence in others that mans lyfe in his sound and perfect health is like a bubble of water and being at this present sicke in bodie but of sound and perfect remembrance and fyndinge such weaknes in myselfe that by Course of nature I cannott contynewe long in this world, To that end, (being disburthened of all worldly affayres) I may dureing the resydue of that tyme God shall suffer me to breath, the more freely adresse my selfe wholly to the meditacon of Divine and heavenly things, And to that ende I maye leave peace and quietnes to my wyfe and Children together wth that temporall estate God hath endowed me wthdall, Doe make and ordeyne this my last will and testam[t] in manner and forme followeinge, ffirst I doe give and bequeath unto Elizabeth my most loveinge and kynde wyfe Twoe ptes of three pts of all and senguler my Manners lands Tenements and hereditaments whatsoever in the County of Hunt and ellswhere within The Realme of England, To hold to her and her Assignes for and dureinge the terme of one and Twentie yeares next after my decease for and towards the provision of herselfe and mayntenance of all and every of my daughters, Provided allwayes and my will is that none of those lands my said wyfe hath allready assured to her for her joynture shall dureing her lyfe tyme be chargeable wth the mainteynance of any of my said daughters, And my will is allso that my said wife or her Assignes may yf they thinke good at any tyme before the said one and Twentie yeares expired pmitt and suffer my heire to enioy the said two ptes of all and every my mann[rs] lands tenements and hereditaments devysed as aforesaid for the provision of herselfe and mayntenance of my said daughters or so much thereof as my said wyfe or her assignes in their discretions shall thinke meete. Item my will is that the debte due to me by my brother Richard Whaley uppon a statute of sixe hundred poundes shal be equally divided amoungest my daughters for and towards the rayseing of their porcons, And I doe allso will give and bequeath to my said wyfe all and every my Jewells plate household stuffe money goods and chattells whatsoever, And I doe ordeyne and make my said wyfe sole executrix of this my last will and Testament, and my will is that my executrix shall at or shortly after my buriall give and bestowe uppon and amoungest poore people and in deedes of Almes and Charity so much as she in her discretion shall thinke fitt haveinge a Care and respect to the payment of my debtes and funerall charges and the provision of her selfe and my children according to my estate and degree and those meanes I shall leave behynde me, And I doe by these presents revoke and disanull all other wills whatsoever heretofore by me made and have published and declared this my last will the day and yeare first above written in the presence of Robert Cromwell, J. Cromwell, Tho: Bearde, Ry: Cromwell, Paul Kent.[21]

It is not unworthy of remark, as evidencing his continuing interest in the Cromwell family, that the name of Thomas Beard appears among the witnesses. He had meanwhile risen in the world. He issued the second edition of his book a year after he became the rector of St. John's, and whether in recognition of his authorship, his abilities, his conformity, or all three, he became successively a Doctor of Divinity, a prebend of Lincoln, and, besides his rectorship of St. John's, he was presented to the livings of Pertenhall in Bedfordshire and Wiston in Huntingdon. There was still room in the church for a Puritan; and, unlike his colleague Brinsley, he was not only a "pluralist" but he stayed in the church enjoying all its benefits to the last. Meanwhile he continued his connection with the Cromwell family, for the Register of St. John's has a notice in his hand for the year 1617:

Mr. Valentine Walton, and Mrs. Margaret Cromwell marry'd the xxth day of June.[22]

That marriage was of no small significance to Oliver's fortunes, for young Walton, of Great Staughton in Huntingdonshire, a country gentleman like Cromwell himself, was destined to be closely identified with Oliver throughout life.[23] Scarcely had the marriage been per-

[21] From the official copy in the Prerogative Office, London, Welden 78.

[22] Noble, i, 351.

[23] Inheriting from a family who had possessed the Manor of Great Staughton for several generations, Walton was himself lord of the Manor at the time of his marriage. He was presently to sit for Huntingdonshire in Parliament, to be a companion-in-arms of Oliver against the king, whose death-warrant he was to sign; but as a radical republican he refused to support his brother-in-law during the Protectorate and was not included in Cromwell's Upper House.

formed when Oliver's father died, as the Register of All Saints records:

Mr. Robert Cromwell of St. John's parish buryed ye 24 day of June.[24]

Thus were the circumstances of the young "heire" altered in his eighteenth year; and from this arose another incident and another document. The Cromwell property, or part of it, was held by knightly tenure "*in capite*" directly from the king. Was Oliver, then, a royal ward? The case was carried to the Court of Wards and Liveries which duly handed down a decision which, nearly forty years later, Sir James Ley considered important enough to include in his *Reports of divers resolutions in Law arising upon cases in the Court of Wards*, where it has lain all but unnoticed since. It runs as follows:

Cromwels Case

Upon a Diem clausit extremum, after the death of Robert Cromwel, Esquire, it is found by Office That Sir Henry Cromwel, Knight, was seized in fee of a Messuage and certain Lands in Huntingdon, called the Augustin-Friers, holden of the King by Knights service in capite, and suffered a common Recovery thereof, to the use of himself and Dame Joan his wife for their lives, Remainder to the said Robert Cromwel his second Son, and the Heirs males of his body, the Remainder to the right Heirs of Sir Henry Cromwel, as by an Indenture of the limitation of uses appeareth, with a power given in the said Indentures to the said Robert Cromwel to limit the use of the same Lands to his wife for her life for a Joynture: Dame Joan dyeth, Sir Henry Cromwel surrenders his Estate for life to Robert Cromwel who according to the power limiteth the Estate to Elizabeth his wife for her life for her Joynture: Sir Henry Cromwel dyeth, Sir Oliver Cromwel his Son and Heir sueth Livery; Robert Cromwel hath issue a Son, and dyeth seized in fee of other Lands holden in Socage, his Son being within age.

Question. Whether the Son and Heir of Robert shall be in Ward during the life of Elizabeth, who is Tenant for life of all the Capite Lands, and the Remainder thereof is onely descended? Whereupon it was resolved by the Chief Justice and chief Baron, Hubbart and Tanfield, That the said Oliver Cromwel, Son and Heir of the said Robert Cromwel, during the life of the said Elizabeth his Mother, ought not to be in Ward to his Majesty, by reason of the said Office found after the death of the said Robert his Father deceased, nor sue forth Livery for the said Lands in the said Office mentioned, nor any thing therein contained, in regard the said Oliver Cromwel is in by Remainder as aforesaid; and his said Mothers Joynture and Estate for her life in the said Lands was made by vertue of the power given by Sir Henry Cromwel, Father of the said Robert, after whose death the Son and Heir of the said Sir Henry Cromwel sued his Livery; whereupon a Decree was had accordingly.[25]

[24] Noble, i, 350.

[25] Mich. 15 Jacobi Regis 1617. Sir James Ley, *Reports of divers resolutions in Law*, etc. London, 1659, p. 60. The property here in question was granted at the Dissolu-

JUNE, 1617–AUGUST, 1620

His status thus determined, with that of the property, the perennial question soon arose—what was the boy to do? He was still under age; his mother managed the estate; he had revealed no unusual abilities nor aptitudes; he seemed destined, like so many of his kind, to succeed his father as a gentleman farmer—but what was he to do until he came of age? For what he did in those three intervening years we have but little more than presumptive evidence. Whether he returned to Cambridge for a time; whether he stayed at home with his mother and sisters;[26] whether, like so many young men in his position, he went to London to the Inns of Court; or whether, like others, he went abroad to travel or to fight, we have no direct nor wholly trustworthy proof.

The commonest and most generally accepted story is that he went to study law at Lincoln's Inn, though the first of his biographers, Carrington, makes no mention of that circumstance beyond the somewhat indefinite observations that "his Parents designed him to the study of the Civill Law" and that "he dived not over deep into this Study." The author of *The Perfect Politician*, his next biographer, is slightly more specific, declaring that:

"After a good Proficiency in the University, he came to *London*, where he betook himself to the study of the Law in *Lincolns*-Inn; that nothing might be wanting to make him a Compleat Gentleman, and a good Commonwealthsman."[27]

To this may be added the testimony of a third contemporary witness:

tion to one Thomas Ardern and must, therefore, have been purchased by Sir Henry. Cp. Dugdale, *Monasticon Anglicanum*, vi, 1592.

[26] Of Oliver's sisters, four and possibly five were still living at home. Following is a list of them:

1. Joan, at this time 26 years old, had married William Baker in 1611.
2. Elizabeth, 23, never married.
3. Catherine, 20, married Roger Whitstone,—date unknown,—later an officer in the Parliamentary army. She married, much later, Oliver's friend and fellow-regicide, Col. John Jones, of Wales, who was executed at the Restoration.
4. Margaret, 16, married recently to Valentine Walton.
5. Anna, 14, later married John Sewster, of Wistow, Hunts. One of her six children was Robina, who married William Lockhart, ambassador to France during the Protectorate and early Restoration period.
6. Jane, 11, married in 1636 John Desborough, younger son of the lord of Eltisley Manor in Cambridgeshire, later one of Cromwell's Major-Generals.
7. Robina, about 6, married Dr. Peter French, later one of Cromwell's chaplains. Their only child married John Tillotson, archbishop of Canterbury. Robina married in 1656 Dr. John Wilkins, Warden of Wadham College, Oxford.

[27] *Perfect Politician*, p. 2.

"He came to Lincoln's Inn, where he associated himself with those of the best rank and quality, and the most ingenuous persons; for though he were of a nature not adverse to study and contemplation, yet he seemed rather addicted to conversation and the reading of men and their several tempers than to a continual poring upon authors."[28]

Heath, writing for a Restoration audience, is less restrained:

"Weary of the Muses and that strict course of life . . . he returned home. . . . It was concluded to send him to one of the Inns of Court, under pretence of his studying the Laws . . . Lincoln's Inne was the place pitch'd upon . . . where but for a very little while he continued . . . he had a kind of antipathy to his Company and his Converse there . . . and it is some kind of good luck for that honourable Society that he hath left so small and so innocent a memorial of his Membership therein."[29]

In fact he seems to have left no record which has yet been found in Lincoln's Inn nor in any other; and while all his biographers, except the first, Carrington, who presumably had at least as good an opportunity of knowing all the facts, place him at Lincoln's Inn,[30] there is one curious circumstance which may be noted. Though his father, his grandfather and two of his uncles were at Lincoln's, of his other relatives, friends and later associates, only three of much consequence —Oliver St. John, Edmund Waller and John Glyn—seem to have been at Lincoln's Inn, while the records of Gray's Inn during the period when he might have been a member of that society read almost like a list of his relatives, friends and later dignitaries. His uncle, Sir Thomas Steward; his cousins, Henry Cromwell, Robert Barrington, Edmund Dunch, Gilbert Gerard and Robert Waller; his friend John Claypole, whose son married Cromwell's favorite daughter, Elizabeth; Henry Lawrence whose land he rented after he had sold his own to two former members of Gray's Inn; and Colonel John Jones who married Oliver's sister, were all at Gray's, and most of them held office under him in later years.

To these may be added the names of two Cromwellian major-generals—Jephson and Lambert—and those of Admiral Richard Deane and Sir Arthur Haselrig, all men of consequence to his later life. Besides these still, were those of John Bradshaw, who presided over the High Court of Justice which condemned Charles I; Widdrington, the Speaker of the Cromwellian Parliament; three members of Cromwell's Council—Strickland, Mackworth and Pickering; the Presbyterian leader, Denzil Holles; and the Parliamentary general,

[28] *The Portraiture of His Royal Highness Oliver, late Lord Protector* (1659), p. 8.

[29] *Flagellum*, pp. 9–10.

[30] Wood, *Fasti*, ii, c. 88 says "he was taken home and sent to Lincoln's Inn to study the common law but making nothing of it, he was sent for home by his mother."

Sir Thomas Fairfax.[31] Finally no less than twenty-two "regicides" who signed Charles I's death-warrant—more than a third of the entire number—had been at one time or another members of that society.[32]

This is, of course, no proof that Cromwell was ever at Gray's Inn or at the Inns of Court at all. But it argues, at least, that this society contained an unusual number of men opposed to Stuart rule; that sometime and somewhere he came in touch with them—and if he went to Gray's it helps to explain many of his connections in later years.

For the three "lost" years of Oliver Cromwell's life between his departure from Cambridge and his coming of age, trustworthy contemporary evidence is curiously scanty and unsatisfactory. It seems extraordinary that he could have been at the Inns of Court without leaving some record of his residence. Nor does it anywhere appear from what evidence we have that he spent all of this obscure period there, if he went there at all. Carrington gives us no hint of what else he did in those "lost" years. The author of the *Perfect Politician* says:

". . . he returned home again . . . There for some time he spent his life not altogether free from the wildnesses and follies incident to youthful age, to the wasting of some part of that small estate his Father had left him."[33]

Heath, enlarging on that theme, pictures him as returning to Huntingdon, where,

"He fell to his old trade and frequented his old haunts, consumed his money in tipling; in his drink he used to be so quarrelsome as few (unless as mad as himself) durst keep him company; his chief weapon in which he delighted, . . . was a Quarter-staff; in which he was so skilful that seldom did any overmatch him."[34]

Such habits, with the still less attractive custom of accosting, even assaulting, the women whom he met, Heath, "loath to be too large in such particulars," as he assures us, recounts with much detail and more relish. Against these stories may be set two other tales of perhaps no greater validity. The first is that, during some period of his early life, he travelled on the Continent where, in Amsterdam, he met the Jewish leader, Menasseh ben Israel, whose acquaintance he

[31] *Register of Gray's Inn, passim.*

[32] John Carew, John Jones, Simon Mayne, William Purefoy, Thomas Mauleverer, Henry Marten, William Constable, Richard Deane, John Bradshaw, George Fleetwood, William Cawley, John Alured, Gregory Norton, Thomas Scott, H. Edwards, Thomas Waite, John Downes, Richard Ingoldsby, Thomas Harrison, Thomas Grey, John Bourchier, Anthony Stapley.

[33] *Perfect Politician*, p. 2.

[34] *Flagellum*, pp. 10–11.

renewed in later years when that Jewish champion came to England to persuade the Protector to readmit his co-religionists in England.[35] The other story is that during those travels he spent some time in Paris in something of the same fashion that Heath records of his doings in Huntingdon.[36]

It may even be that, like so many young men of his generation, like some of his own relatives in fact, he took service for a time in one of the continental armies. In Holland the Vere regiment had attracted many English volunteers to the Dutch service; and in these lost years of his life recruiting drums were being beaten throughout England for the forces of James I's son-in-law, the Elector Palatine, to whose assistance the Vere regiment was presently despatched as the Thirty Years' War broke out upon the Continent. For this again there is no written evidence. The passport records list no Oliver Cromwell among those who were given permission to leave England; the muster-rolls of the Vere regiment and of the English volunteers are wanting—and in so far the proof is even less than that of his presence at the Inns of Court. Yet if his knowledge of the law in later years be admitted as testimony to his early training in that field, his knowledge of military matters is still more significant; and an assumption that somewhere and somehow in his early life he gained something of his skill in arms by experience on the continent is not beyond the bounds of possibility. Nor is there any reason to assume that he might not have done both—or neither, as the case may be.

But there is still another curious coincidence in these three doubtful years. About the time when he might have been at the Inns of Court, there was entered at Gray's Inn a certain Robert, Lord Rich, with whom he was to have dealings in his later years. Lord Rich's father, the Earl of Warwick, had an estate in Essex near that of Cromwell's cousins the Barringtons, and that of a certain Sir James Bourchier who was distantly related to the Barringtons. At the moment when Oliver might have been entered at the Inns of Court, there were no less than seven Bourchiers at Gray's Inn, besides five more who had been entered since 1610—and on August 22, 1620, the register of the church of St. Giles, Cripplegate, London, records among its list of marriages that of

Oliver Cromwell to Elizabeth Bourcher

Elizabeth was the daughter of Sir James Bourchier; the marriage was arranged, according to gossip, through the Barringtons, and it had various results. It enlarged the circle of Cromwell's connections

[35] Sagredo to Doge, Dec. 21/31, 1655, in *Cal. S. P. Venetian* (1655–56), p. 160.
[36] Leti, *Life of Oliver Cromwell.*

especially in Essex and in London; and it has been suggested, though evidence is lacking, that it increased his resources. His father-in-law was a fur-dealer and leather-dresser, whose father, coming to the City from the west-country, had founded the business and passed it to his son, who in turn flourished. Like many such prosperous men of business of that time and since, he had a town house and a country place—Little Stambridge Hall near Felsted in Essex—and he had been knighted by James I in 1610.

From this marriage arose, among other things, the first document to which Oliver himself seems to have been a party, dated three days after the ceremony:

> " 'Oliv. Cromwell alias Williams, of Huntingdon esq.' enteres into a defeasance of statute staple to Tho. Morley citizen and leather-seller of London in 4000 l. conditioned that he should before the 20th of November following convey and assure to her [his wife, Elizabeth Bourchier] 'for the term of her life for her jointure, all that parsonage house of Hartford with all the glebe lands and tythes' in the county of Huntingdon."[37]

The meaning of this document is obvious enough; the circumstances are not clear. Oliver had come of age four months before, and this agreement—in effect a bond for the performance of an obligation—confirmed to his new wife a part of the inheritance to which he had just succeeded. Worth, it was estimated,[38] some forty pounds a year, the penalty for non-performance seems excessive, unless the figures have been misread for what seems the more reasonable sum of four hundred pounds. The holder of the obligation seems to have been a relative, possibly a business associate of the bride's father. It may be, very possibly, the usual form of securing a marriage settlement for the bride; it may indicate a certain question as to the bridegroom in the minds of his wife's relatives, though that seems less probable. Whatever its significance, it appears that Mrs. Cromwell enjoyed this income for only some twelve years[39] before she surrendered it when her husband disposed of his Huntingdon property, and with the signature of this document ends this first period of his life.

Stripped of the imaginative embroidery of biographers, such is the story and such the evidence for the early years of Oliver Cromwell. It is a commonplace and fragmentary chronicle.[40] It contains noth-

[37] Printed in Noble, i, 124, as he copied it from the original then in the possession of Sir Charles Mackworth. Sir James Bourchier's mother was Elizabeth, the daughter of J. Morley, of London; his father's name was Thomas Bourchier, which indicates that this Tho. Morley was related to the Bourchiers.

[38] By Noble.

[39] It was sold at the time of Cromwell's removal to St. Ives, according to Noble.

[40] Many, on the other hand, have preferred Leti's account (pub. 1692) or some

ing remarkable; there are a thousand like it in English history, Nothing could well be more conventional or more typical of his age and class. The son of a family of the lesser gentry; home-bred; educated in the local grammar-school, with a brief experience in a university—and possibly at the Inns of Court or elsewhere; trained to take his father's place as a small landed proprietor; marrying a London merchant's daughter and so returning home to settle down and make his living as a gentleman-farmer—it is the very type and pattern of such lives. The infinite speculations of biographers, the violence of his partisans and his enemies, have only served to cloud the issue of his early life and character. They give no clue to sources of his strength. Nor could that well be otherwise. Such mysteries lie far beyond our view; they have little to do with the external circumstances of our lives. We can explain the genius of that Stratford boy which flowered into immortal verse in the years when Cromwell grew to manhood as little as we can understand how in the little town of Huntingdon there was developed the great hero of the Puritans.

Yet from the little knowledge that we have we may deduce something of Cromwell's qualities. It is apparent that he had the first requisite of such a life as his. He was strong, active, energetic, fond of rough games and sports, toughened with exercise and full of vigorous life. We know that he was powerfully built; perhaps some five feet nine or ten in height; with a big nose and a wart under the left side of his lower lip; with dark brown hair, one lock of which hung down in unruly fashion on the right side of his forehead. Most painters gave him dark eyes; at least one painted them dark grey or blue, the rest brown or black; but all of them somehow managed to convey an impression of unusually keen, direct and commanding gaze. We know that he seems to have cared less for books than men; that he had as much learning and as much ambition for it as most young men of his station, and no more; that he entered the university at least two years after the usual age of admission in his day; and that he made no mark on it.

Beyond this we know but little of his early life and character. What evidence there is seems to indicate that he was rude and unmannerly, if not worse. Making every allowance for the animus of royalist biographers, it would appear that parts of his early life were not beyond reproach; and all tradition and his own words seem to bear that out. The tales of Cromwell's youth are all of the same

version of it, to the effect that he was a youth of such piety that at five he knew more hymns and prayers than others knew at ten, took such pleasure in sermons that he seemed destined to the church; at ten had "a tincture of mathematics and philosophy"; at twelve went to Cambridge, and at seventeen, after six years of college "possessed perfectly" both subjects. Cp. my *Bibliography of Oliver Cromwell*, Introduction, "The Historic Cromwell."

character; none—save the incredible stories of Leti—paint him as a model of propriety. The most favorable describe him as undisciplined; the most unfavorable as a monster of iniquity. To such charges his partisans have one invariable reply; it is that all these tales are palpably untrue. "The stories about Oliver's wicked youth," says John Morley, voicing the general comment of biographers, "deserve not an instant's notice; and Carlyle's denunciations of "Carrion Heath" are among the classics of vituperation.

It may be that Cromwell's biographers are right; but two things seem to militate against their sweeping exoneration. The first is that, however much or little they owe to each other, the stories of his youth are all alike. Heath, Dugdale, Carrington, Warwick, Baxter, Bate, Cromwell himself, do not differ greatly from each other, save in details and degree. "I have no mind to give an ill character of Cromwell," wrote the moderate Sir Philip Warwick, yet he goes on to say:

> "The first years of his manhood were spent in a dissolute course of life in good fellowship and gaming which afterwards he seemed very sensible of and sorrowful for; and, as if it had bin a good spirit that had guided him therein, he used a good method upon his conversion, for he declared he was ready to make restitution unto any man who would accuse him, or whom he could accuse himself to have wronged; (to his honour I speak this, for I think the publick acknowledgments men make of the publick evills they have done to be the most glorious trophies they can have assigned to them."[41]

The author of the *Perfect Politician*,[42] certainly not a hostile witness, speaks of his "wildnesses and follies" and the wasting of his inheritance. Richard Baxter, who, though a Presbyterian and so not wholly friendly to Cromwell, and, like Warwick, an honest man, testifies that Cromwell was "a prodigal in his youth and afterwards changed to zealous righteousness."[43] Bate, frankly hating Cromwell, asserts that he "wholly run out his estate."[44] We need not accept, yet we can hardly disregard, this testimony, which, whatever its animus, is curiously similar. We need not wholly believe Bate's testimony that Oliver lost his uncle's favor by playing filthy tricks at a Christmas festival and was ducked in a neighboring pond for his misbehavior;[45] yet like stories, of less objectionable character but of greater authenticity, told of his conduct in later life, indicate his love of horse-play and of practical jokes in something less than the best of taste. We need not accept Cromwell's own words as proof of his

[41] Warwick, *Memoirs of the Reign of King Charles I* (1702) pp. 249–50.
[42] *Perfect Politician*, p. 2.
[43] *Reliquiae Baxterianae*, p. 98.
[44] Bate, *The Troubles of England*, p. 77.
[45] *Elenchus Motuum* (1663), p. 273; *Flagellum*, p. 13.

depravity, but we need not, like some of his biographers, brush them aside as irrelevant exaggerations of a too-sensitive conscience.

"You know," he wrote to Mrs. St. John, "what my manner of life hath been. Oh, I lived in darkness and hated light. I was a chief—the chief of sinners. This is true; I hated Godliness, yet God had mercy on me."[46]

It is true, as his champions contend, that men sometimes confess what they have never done or exaggerate their sins—though that seems weak defence of a strong character—but it is also true that such confessions often represent the facts; and to which class Cromwell belongs one must judge for himself. Yet to put all stories of his misdemeanors out of court violates that canon of evidence to the effect that tales not true in all details usually bear some relation to a man's character. Amusing anecdotes are not commonly fathered on men with no sense of humor, nor deeds of heroism attributed to notorious cowards; pious men are seldom charged with atheism, nor generous men with penuriousness. It seems more reasonable to accept, with whatever reservations one may choose, the natural inference from the evidence we have, in default of any other, that young Oliver Cromwell was not so unlike many of his kind in habits or in character as his defenders urge. For Oliver Cromwell was a great man. His strength was not so small as to require unqualified defence: his weakness not so great as to demand unqualified praise. There seems no reason to depict him as either stately, statuesque or saintly from his earliest youth; it seems far better, in his own famous words, to "paint him wart and all."

To this conclusion another circumstance seems to give some weight. It is that, even in the most flattering accounts of the most favorable of his eulogists, it is admitted, even strongly urged, that somewhere in the next period of his life that life was greatly changed by what is called "conversion." For that there is no better evidence than the best—Cromwell's own words, confirmed by every piece of testimony that we have from other hands.

From all of this two things seem evident. The first is that he was a strong man, vigorous, turbulent, uncontrolled, passionate, tending to that melancholy which is often associated with the "Celtic temperament," whose times and training were Puritanical, with what mystical elements were common to Celt and Puritan; and that such natures till tempered by age and experience tend to extremes. The second is that there was little or no premonition of greatness in his youth. There seemed few men of his age and station in England from whom as much might not have been expected. He had developed

[46] Cromwell's letter, 13 Oct., 1638.

slowly and there seemed no reason to believe when he came back to Huntingdon with his bride, nor for long thereafter, that he would not live out his life like his father in comparative obscurity.

It is easy to read into a great man's youth the qualities he revealed in later years. But when he came of age and married, Oliver Cromwell seemed destined to the oblivion which has since enfolded his fellows in school and college; to sink into the mass of country gentlemen with no more trace of his existence than their common lot of useful lives reveals, active in their communities, rising, perhaps, to Parliament, and leaving behind them only their estates and families as part of the common heritage of their race. Of the young men in England at that time there were hundreds from whom as much might have been hoped; scores who seemed to have more promise of greatness and a few who seemed certain to play a greater part in history. As his great admirer, Marvell, wrote of these early years:

> "For neither didst thou from the first apply
> Thy sober spirit unto things too High
> But in thine own fields exercisedst long
> An healthful Mind within a Body strong;
> Till at the Seventh time thou in the Skyes
> As a small cloud, like a Man's hand didst rise."[47]

[47] Marvell, "First Anniversary of the Government under Oliver Cromwell," *Works*, pp. 229–234.

CHAPTER II

EARLY MANHOOD

HUNTINGDON, 1620–1631

With his coming of age and his marriage in the summer of 1620, Oliver Cromwell entered the world of practical affairs. In the three years since he left the university that world had seen a succession of dramatic events full of momentous consequence to Europe, to Protestantism, to Calvinism in particular, to England, and to his own fortunes. At the moment that he left the university there had begun that quarrel between the Protestants and the Catholics in Bohemia which was to lead to the greatest of Europe's religious wars. In May of the following year that quarrel had flamed into open conflict and there began thirty years of religious and political conflict, as each side poured troops into Bohemia: and even while the forces of the Protestant princes overran that land debatable, the theologians of the faith that they professed met in the Dutch town of Dort to determine, if possible, the foundations on which that faith rested.

The greatest assembly of Calvinistic or "Reformed" ministers ever held met in November, 1618, and through a hundred and forty-four sittings debated the theological bases of their communion for which their followers were fighting farther south. It was a difficult task. For two generations the Calvinistic theologians had been busy with the problems set by its founder and dissensions had arisen among them. To some, known from their leader as "Arminians," the dogmas of Calvin had come to seem too unyielding, his logic too severe, his conclusions too terrible to be borne by weak human nature. Was it necessary to assume the grim premise that it was essential for man to fall from grace that God might exercise his omnipotence to pardon the "elect" and condemn all others to eternal punishment? Did He decree, permit, or only foresee that fall from grace? Was "election" purely arbitrary on His part, and unconditional, or did it depend somewhat on man's own acts or faith? Was there such a thing as "total depravity" which could deprive its possessor of all hope of salvation? Was "grace" "irresistible or enduring," or was it possible, as Cromwell was to inquire in almost his last words, for one who had once been in a "state of grace" to decline from that high estate? Would the "saints" who were "elect" to salvation inevitably "persevere" or triumph over their worldly enemies despite everything?

These problems seem now the echo of far-off forgotten things. They were then the breath of life to multitudes, the motive force not only of theology but of politics; and when the Remonstrants who pleaded for a less rigid faith, for a more merciful interpretation of the intentions of the Almighty, were finally defeated, it was an event of profound importance to the affairs of nations, not least to Englishmen. For "Arminian" became a term of contempt to those sterner souls who refused to yield to softer emotions, to look with tolerance on human imperfections and infirmities. To that sterner school Cromwell came in time to belong, counting himself numbered among the "saints" of the "elect," through "conviction of sin," "conversion" and—certain of divine approval of his cause, his party and his acts—convinced of his "sanctification" and his ultimate "salvation" through faith not works.

From the beginning this religious issue was intimately associated with politics. The Amsterdam republicans inclined to Arminianism; the Orange party, with Maurice of Nassau at its head, overpowered its rivals, imprisoned the republican John van Oldenbarneveldt and the great jurist Hugo Grotius, and girded up its loins to renew that long conflict with Spain which had been checked by the Twelve Years' Truce.

From these events flowed great results. When at this moment James I's Calvinistic son-in-law, Frederick, Elector Palatine, accepted the crown of Bohemia and stood forth as the Protestant champion, the European conflict took a wider range. Its earliest phase was disastrous to the Protestants. Just as Cromwell married and moved to Huntingdon, the forces of the Catholic League, Spain and the Empire gathered against Frederick. On November 8, 1620, he was defeated at the Battle of the White Hill near Prague. His followers were dispersed, their faith proscribed throughout Bohemia, and Frederick sought refuge in Holland. James chose that moment to open negotiations with the Spanish court, and for the time being it seemed that Protestantism, and Calvinism in particular, was destined to eclipse.

Yet at the same time, by a curious coincidence, it found expression in another field. At the very moment that Frederick's followers fled from White Hill, a little group of Puritans who, when Oliver was nine years old, had left their Yorkshire home to seek religious liberty in Holland, were sailing for the coast of what was known as "New England." Even as these "Pilgrim Fathers" landed, the Virginia colony founded some thirteen years before and in which young Oliver's uncle was a stockholder, received an accession to its numbers which, with the New England settlement, secured the future of England in America. Nor was this all, for that Virginia colony had held its first Assembly; and the New England settlers had signed a "Compact" on their ship, the *Mayflower*, which looked to a system of self-government. Were this not enough of coincidence, it was at this juncture that James I was driven to summon a new Parliament, in which, as it happened, the various threads of this religious-political situation were to be combined, and with the choice of whose members Oliver Cromwell made his entrance into politics.

The coincidence of Frederick's overthrow and the meeting of the Parliament was unfortunate for the English king. The defeat of the Elector Palatine was a heavy blow to Protestants everywhere, not least to Englishmen. It hurt the pride of a people which still thrilled to the memory of the brave days of great Elizabeth, which looked with disfavor and distrust on a royal policy which endeavored to make peace with the old enemy and sought to still the tempest on the continent not with a threat of force but with smooth words and dubious diplomacy. It increased James's unpopularity and it brought the national temper to the breaking-point.

England had learned much in eighteen years of that son of Mary, Queen of Scots, whom Oliver had first seen on his progress to the throne, and often in later years at Hinchinbrook, where, as it chanced, he was at this moment a visitor, and closer acquaintance had inspired little confidence in its king. Of unroyal bearing, timid, even pusillanimous, his qualities were in striking contrast to the courage, tact and dignity which had made the Tudor despotism, with all its arrogance, endurable. Of all its qualities the only one which he exemplified was a belief in autocracy. With a vivid sense of the divine right of monarchy, with "more learning than became a king," with all the obstinacy of a weak character, disputatious, vain, he was a theorist in a realistic world, a pacifist in a warlike period, an absolutist in a country tending toward parliamentary government. He dreamed of erecting into a system that which in Tudor hands had been an understanding; of determining by reason what was at bottom a religious emotion or national ambition; of substituting phrases for force and logic for passion.

His political creed was simple. "It is atheism and blasphemy," he wrote, "to dispute what God can do; it is presumption and high contempt to dispute what a king can do; or to say that a king cannot do this or that."[1] Against that theory of royal dominance, Sir Thomas Smith in Elizabeth's reign, had pictured a Parliament which "abrogateth old laws and maketh new . . . establisheth forms of religion . . . giveth forms of succession to the crown . . . appointeth subsidies, taxes and impositions."[2] Between these views, conflict was inevitable. From the moment that James told his first Parliament that it "derived all matters of privilege from him and by his

[1] Cp. his *True Law of Free Monarchies* for his theory of government.
[2] *De Republica Anglorum* (after 1589, *The Common Welth of England*).

grant," and was answered that its privileges were "a due right and inheritance no less than our lands and goods," the history of his reign was a long commentary on the struggle between royal prerogative and parliamentary privilege.

It took three forms—religion, revenue and foreign policy. Elizabeth's prestige, her "gift of governance" and Parliament's expressed "cause to tender her in regard to her age and sex"—a reason which appealed but slightly to the Virgin Queen—had prevented the situation from growing acute while she was still alive, but with James's accession this was quickly changed. The Presbyterians had been first to seize their opportunity and from the time when on his progress from Hinchinbrook to London the King had been handed their "Millenary Petition" to the time when Cromwell joined his fellow-countrymen in choosing members to this Parliament, the agitation grew. That petition—not only not signed by a thousand ministers as its name implied, but not signed at all—embodied the Presbyterian programme of church reform. From the use of the ring in the marriage ceremony to Sabbath observance, from church rites to the Book of Common Prayer, from vestments to limitations on church courts and authorities, it protested against the Anglican system. Denounced by church authorities, condemned by Oxford and Cambridge, it was reinforced by a multitude of other petitions, "moving for more or less alteration as the promoters of them stood affected," "not for the paring, pruning and purging but for the extirpating and abolishing of bishops and conforming church government to foreign presbytery," as the church historian wrote.[3]

The King had called the conference they desired within a twelvemonth at Hampton Court, presiding over it himself. The Presbyterians were heard and some concessions granted them, some changes made in the Prayer Book. But their Book of Discipline was rejected, the chief Anglican ceremonies kept; and when discussion turned from theology to politics the King had put an end to it. For "presbyter" had an ugly sound to James. He recalled the long humiliations he and his mother had endured from the Scotch ministers, the democratic teachings of his tutor Buchanan. "When I mean to live under a presbytery," he observed, "I will goe into Scotland againe"; and when the Presbyterian leader, Reynolds, had pressed his case, James ended the conference with his fateful words, "if you aim at a Scotch Presbytery, it agreeth as well with a monarchy as God and the Devil," "No bishop, no king." "If this be all they have to say," he concluded, "I shall make them conform, or I will harrie them out of the land, or else do worse."[4]

His words went far beyond his acts. Reynolds had received pre-

[3] Fuller, *Church History of Britain* (ed. Brewer) v, 305–13.

[4] Cp. Gardiner, *History of England 1603-1642*, vol. ii, *passim.*

ferment in the church, he had been entrusted with direction of the new version of the Scriptures; and the ensuing visitation of the church, whose representatives Oliver had seen in Huntingdon, had demanded only the legal minimum of conformity—the recognition of royal supremacy, of the Thirty-Nine Articles, and of canonical ordination of church authorities. Most of the clergy had "conformed" at once, some after "admonition," and only a handful had been "deprived" of their livings or "silenced" for contumacy. But the harm was done. To the issue of prerogative against privilege had been added that of religious order against religious liberty, and as Oliver grew to manhood the breach between the crown and its Puritan subjects had widened from year to year.

It had reinforced the quarrel over the Commons' demands for freedom of elections and freedom from arrest which began in the first Parliament, and the conflict over customs duties or "impositions" levied by prerogative in which a London merchant, Bate, became a national figure and his cargo of currants a national issue. That quarrel had led to protests against the Court of High Commission and royal proclamations with the force of law. It had defeated the proposed union of England and Scotland and wrecked a "Great Contract" by which James would have exchanged some of his feudal rights for regular revenue. It had been embittered by popular dislike of young, handsome, incompetent favorites like George Villiers, presently created Duke of Buckingham, who ill supplied the loss of the Elizabethan statesman and added an element of scandal to the case. James's second Parliament had been dissolved without the passage of a single act; four of its members had been sent to the Tower; and thereafter for seven years no Parliament had been called, while James raised revenue by prerogative, legally indeed, but in defiance of popular sentiment. It was under such conditions that Oliver Cromwell was brought up and he was profoundly influenced by them.

To the issues of religion and revenue was added foreign policy. James had set himself to play the part of peacemaker to Europe, signed a peace with Spain, married his daughter to Frederick, begun to negotiate a marriage between his son and the Spanish Infanta, sent Raleigh to the scaffold as a sop to Spain, agreed to tolerate the Roman Catholics, and endeavored to mediate between the Catholics and Protestants in Germany. But his plans were as ineffective as they were unpopular. He only managed to infuriate his own subjects; he failed to conciliate their ancient enemy; and he united Anglican and Puritan in opposition to a policy which, whatever its noble spirit and purposes, was destined to futility.

Such was the political-religious atmosphere in which young Oliver had grown to manhood; such the situation which confronted him as he took his place as a burgess of Huntingdon; and, as it happened, five days after the battle of White Hill, and two days after the Pilgrim Fathers signed the Mayflower compact of government, writs[5] for a new Parliament were prepared which gave rise to Oliver Cromwell's first act in politics:

Parliamentary Indenture

This Indenture, made between Thomas Maples, Esquire, Sheriff of the County of Huntingdon of the one part, and Robert Arkensall and George Lambe, Bailiffs of the Town of Huntingdon, and Oliver Cromwell [and fourteen other names], and others, Burgesses of the said Town and Borough of the other part, Witnesseth, that the aforesaid Bailiffs and Burgesses of the Borough aforesaid have caused to be elected by the Burgesses abovesaid, and others, being the maj[or part] of the Burgesses of the said Borough and residing within the said Borough, who were present at such election, two Burgesses of the most sufficient and discreet of the said Borough, according to the form of the statute thereupon enacted, and provided and according to the effect of the Mandate aforesaid to be for the Borough aforesaid, at the Parliament in the said Mandate specified, to wit, Henry Saint John, Knight, and Miles Sandes, Knight and Baronet, which said two Burgesses have full and sufficient power for themselves and the Commonalty of the Borough of Huntingdon aforesaid, &c. In Witness whereof, as well the aforesaid Sheriff, as the Electors aforesaid, have alternately set their Seals to these Indentures, this instant 9th day of January, 1620.

H. Cromwell, Tho. Bearde, R. Coke, John Turpin, Gilbert Wiseman, T. Cromwell, John Peacocke, Willyam Pateryck, John Rygges, Francis Ringsted, John Cooper, William Powes, Robert Arkens . . . , George Lambe, O. Cromwell.[6]

As in all events of his life hitherto, there is nothing remarkable in this save the surrounding circumstance—in this case the character of these representatives. They were, indeed, men of no great consequence then or thereafter but they bore names which were to resound throughout the conflict between crown and Parliament, and they brought Cromwell into touch with the great men and the great affairs of his later life. Sir Miles Sandys[7] was a brother of Sir Edwin Sandys, son of an archbishop of York, a leader of the "popular" party both in church and state, eminent in colonial enterprise, still more eminent in Parliament as an opponent of the crown. And more—for it was from the Sandys estate of Scrooby in Yorkshire that the Pilgrim Fathers had moved to Holland and now to New England. He was a

[5] Dated November 13, 1620.

[6] Printed in Griffith, *Ancient Records relating to the Borough of Huntingdon*, pp. 104–5.

[7] His son Miles was a member of the Committee for Cambridge, in the Eastern Counties Association, with Cromwell.

member of the East India Company, of the Council of the Virginia Company, and of the Council for New England, and it was through his influence that the Puritan pioneers had received their patent to colonize in America. Sir Henry St. John was a relative of Cromwell's cousin, that Oliver St. John who was in time to argue the ship-money case in which a mutual connection of Cromwell and St. John, John Hampden, was the leading character. That these men were chosen for Huntingdon was doubtless due in part to the circumstance that St. John's brother was lord-lieutenant of the county; in part to their friendship with the Montagus; in part to their Puritan tendencies which made them acceptable to the Huntingdon burgesses.

They were, in fact, typical of the men and issues of the new Parliament. Those issues centered about the three great problems which had filled James's reign. The first was that of foreign policy. The nation was eager to help Frederick and the continental Protestants. James, counting on his diplomatic skill, had at first refused; then, when diplomacy broke down, consented; then with the return of the Spanish ambassador, Gondomar, to amuse him with the revival of the project of a Spanish marriage, he had drawn back again. Frederick's defeat again unsettled him; and he met Parliament with a demand for money that he might 'treat for peace, sword in hand.' Balked of war, the Commons fell on the second issue, corruption in government; attacked monopolies, compelled the punishment of the chief offenders, impeached and drove from office the Lord Chancellor Bacon; and defended Sir Edwin Sandys against the Spanish ambassador's charge of infringing on the preserves of Spain in North America and the suspicions of the government that, with the new Virginia constitution and the New England settlement he projected a 'Puritan and republican' state overseas. Finally on the question of their right to debate general public policy, not merely such matters as were laid before them by the crown, they entered on their journals a great "Protestation."[8]

That momentous document declared their liberties and privileges "the undoubted birthright of the subjects of England; the State, the defence of the realm, the Church, the laws and grievances, proper subjects for debate; members entitled to freedom of speech and from imprisonment for speaking on any matters touching the business of Parliament." The king, infuriated by this defiance of what he conceived his unquestionable right to conduct the nation's affairs, tore the offending Protestation from the Commons journals with his own hands; dissolved the Houses; sent the chief offenders like Sir Edwin Sandys, John Pym, Sir Edward Coke and John Selden to the Tower,

[8] *Proceedings and Debates*, ii, 359. Quoted in Gardiner, as above, iv, 262. For detailed account of 1621 Parliament see Notestain, Relf and Simpson, *Diaries* (1935).

to other prisons, to Ireland or the Palatinate; and reaffirmed his royal right to rule.[9]

Such tyranny might once have been endured, but times had changed and it proved a fatal blunder for a Stuart king. It convinced the country that it had nothing to hope from James; it increased the power of the reigning favorite, Buckingham; it encouraged Gondomar; and though James pursued his vacillating course, raised money to send aid to the Palatinate by "benevolences" or "voluntary" gifts, while despatching agents to Madrid to seek peace and a Spanish marriage, he was no longer able to control events. His son Charles hurried to Spain with Buckingham on a romantic and foolhardy enterprise of bringing the Spanish marriage to a successful conclusion—and hurried back again, disappointed and disillusioned. James met his last Parliament in 1624 with virtual confession of his failure; yet only under strong pressure from the Houses did he consent to dissolve the Spanish treaties. In all other respects this Parliament was but a continuation of the former session, so disastrous to the cause of English monarchy.

With this final defeat James virtually ceased to rule. Authority fell to Charles and the imperious and incapable Buckingham; and, infuriated by the blow to his vanity, that minister joined Parliament in urging war with Spain. A marriage treaty was arranged with France; monopolies were declared illegal; the Treasurer, Middlesex, impeached; and with this last expression of its independence, Parliament was dissolved. In March, 1625, James died; his son Charles succeeded him; Buckingham was despatched to France to bring back Charles's bride, Henrietta Maria, daughter of Henry IV and sister of the French king, Louis XIII; and with this began a new chapter of English history.

And what of Oliver Cromwell in these years of violent dispute between the king and Parliament, of foreign war and oversea adventure? Again the answer is simple—only that of any Englishman of his age and class. He was absorbed in details of domestic life; of farm and fireside; in birth, death and marriage; in sowing, reaping and disposing of his crops; in the small but exacting duties of a country life. The Register of the church of St. John's reveals its chief events:

Robert, the son of Oliver Cromwell, Esquire, bapt. the xiij of October [1621].

[9] *Old Parliamentary History* says: "To the Tower, Sir Edward Coke and Sir Robert Phillips." Mr. Selden, Mr. Pym and Mr. Mallory to "other prisons and confinements." Sir Nathaniel Rich and Sir James Perrot to Ireland. Sir Peter Hayman "of Kent" to the Palatinate. *D. N. B.* says: Sandys and Selden to the Tower, Pym "confined to his house in London," Coke to the Tower, Perrot to Ireland.

Oliver, the son of Oliver Cromwell, gent. bapt. the vjth of February [1622–3].
Bridget, the daughter of Oliver Cromwell, Esquire, bapt. the v of August [1624].[10]

There is in these nothing of history or of fame; yet beyond these there is little to chronicle in Cromwell's life during this period. While the nation pressed on to new conflict between crown and Parliament, he went about his every-day affairs as yet little touched by the struggle at Westminster. He, no doubt, took his share in the election to the Parliaments of 1624, 1625 and 1626; though no record seems to remain of its result in Huntingdon save the names of two new members who replaced St. John and Sandys, men of different stamp, though of the same party.

HUNTINGDON, 1625–1628

To Oliver Cromwell as to his fellow-Englishmen—and in greater measure as the years were to prove—the accession of Charles I to the English throne was a momentous event. Braver, more dignified, no wiser than his father, if as wise, Charles was no less strongly convinced of the divine right of monarchy. He had, like his father, all the obstinacy of a weak character, all his dependence upon favorites, and, supported by the influence of his wife, true daughter of French absolutist monarchy, and of his favorite, the arrogant and incompetent Buckingham, he began where his father had left off. His entry into power was unfortunate, for when he met his first Parliament England was seething with discontent over the failure of James's last effort to send help to the Palatinate, the loss of three-fourths of the expedition by the government's neglect to furnish supplies and clothing; over the favor shown to Catholics, as exemplified in the king's marriage and the tenderness towards Romanists; and over the favorite's insolence and incapacity.

The old quarrels were revived as Charles's first Parliament demanded stronger measures against the Catholics and refused adequate supply unless and until the king chose counsellors whom it could trust. Hoping to regain his ascendancy by a triumphant foreign policy, Charles launched an expedition against Cadiz and sought to pawn the crown jewels on the continent to finance the Danes in an attempt to relieve the hard-pressed German Protestants. Like all of Buckingham's enterprises, both failed ingloriously and in 1626 Charles was forced to resort again to Parliament. Again the Houses fell on Buckingham, and under the lead of Sir John Eliot and Sir Edwin

[10] Register of St. John's quoted in Noble, i, 351–2. Carlyle says Bridget was baptised the 4th of August and that Noble is in error.

Sandys sought to impeach that minister. Charles refused to give up his favorite, dissolved the Parliament, demanded a "free gift" from the counties, and that denied, turned to forced loans. Meanwhile the foreign situation went from bad to worse. The Danes were defeated at Lutter; and the feeling between England and France was strained to the breaking-point. The Huguenots rebelled against the determination of Richelieu to make them submit like the rest of France to royal authority; and to the relief of their stronghold of Rochelle the Duke of Buckingham led an army and a fleet. Once more that minister proved incompetent and returned from his unfortunate expedition to the Isle of Rhé to find himself the most hated man in the nation. "Since England was England," wrote Denzil Holles to his brother-in-law, Sir Thomas Wentworth, "it received not so dishonourable a blow"; and in that temper there came together a new Parliament.

It was at this dramatic moment that Oliver Cromwell made his first entry into national politics, not by helping to elect representatives but in person. Whatever his interest in the country's affairs, the years between 1625 and 1628 had given him no opportunity to make his influence felt. If Marvell's poetic license seems a little strained, if Cromwell did not precisely confine himself to

"his private Gardens, where
He liv'd reservéd and austere,
As if his highest plot
To plant the Bergamot,"

at least there remains no record yet discovered of those activities beyond the usual family chronicle. The Register of St. John's continued its record of births:

Richard, the son of Mr. Oliver Cromwell, was borne the fourth day of October, and baptized the 19th day of October [1626].

And from this flows the first letter of Oliver Cromwell which has come down to us. On Richard's birth he wrote in connection with the christening:

To my approved good friend, Mr. Henry Downhall,[11] *at his chambers in St. John's College: These*

Loving Sir,

Make me so much your servant by being Godfather unto my child. I would myself have come over to have made a more formal invi-

[11] Of Northamptonshire, Fellow of St. John's College, Cambridge, Apr. 12, 1614, Vicar of St. Ives, 1631–43. Archdeacon of Huntingdon, 1667. Died at Cottingham, 1669. *Alumni Cantab.*

tation, but my occasions would not permit me; and therefore hold me in that excused. The day of your trouble is Thursday next. Let me entreat your company on Wednesday.

By this time it appears, I am more apt to encroach upon you for new favours than to show my thankfulness for the love I have already found. But I know your patience and your goodness cannot be exhausted by

Your friend and servant,
OLIVER CROMWELL.[12]

Huntingdon,
Oct. 14, 1626.

Such seems to be the only recorded connection between Cromwell and any of his former associates at Cambridge, for Downhall—who was a fellow of St. John's College when Oliver was an undergraduate—had apparently been of some service to him then or thereafter. This was not the end of the connection; for when, nearly ten years later, Cromwell moved from Huntingdon to St. Ives he found Downhall there as vicar.

Nor was this the end of the chronicle of the Cromwell family in the Register of St. John's. It goes on to note at almost the same moment that Oliver was making his entry into politics:

Henry, the son of Oliver Cromwell, Esquire, was born the xxth day of January [1627–8], bapt. the xxix of the same month.[13]

To this may be added an entry in the register of the neighboring parish of Upwood, of importance to Cromwell's fortunes:

Oct. 29 [1628]. Richarde Cromwell, gentelman, was buried.[14]

For this was Oliver's uncle, who, dying without issue, left his property to his nephew and so contributed to that nephew's worldly state.[15]

Beyond these scanty and humble records of these years there are two notices, both in the Register of St. John's, both scandalous, and both denounced as "forgeries"—which they are not—or "later entries in another hand"—which it would seem they were, for the writing, though apparently seventeenth century, is certainly not that of the

[12] Hearne, *Liber Niger Scaccarii* (Lond. 1771), i, 261n. Carlyle, App. 1. Sanford, *Studies and Illustrations of the Great Rebellion*, p. 227, prints the letter and says the original used to be in the Ashmole Museum in Oxford until it was stolen, possibly by Hearne, whose character was not immaculate in that respect.

[13] Noble, i, 352.

[14] *Ibid.*, 356.

[15] The only evidence available for this is the fact that when Oliver sold his Huntingdon property a few years later, some which had formerly belonged to his uncle Richard was included in the sale.

rest of the register. Both echo the tone of the Royalist biographers; and, undated save for the years, they run as follows:

Oliverius Cromwell filius Robt[i] reprehensus est coram tota ecclesia pro factis. J. T. [1621]

Oliverius Cromwell fecit paenitentias coram tota ecclesia. J. T. [1628][16]

Whether these entries reflect old scandalous local traditions or whether they are merely later interpolations of some one intent on smirching Cromwell's character, they have been disregarded by historians and biographers, or mentioned merely to refute their probability. Certainly the next authentic document in his life would seem to make them more improbable; for in the first months of 1627–8 the borough records of Huntingdon include the return of Oliver Cromwell and James Montagu, third son of the Earl of Manchester, to Parliament:

Indenture

This Indenture[17]****
Between Robert Hugar, Esquire, Sheriff of the County of Huntingdon aforesaid of the one part, and Lionel **** of the King's Town or Borough aforesaid, for the time being, Thomas Beard, Professor of Sacred Divinity **** William Walden, Thomas Phillips, William Patrick, William Powes, Robert Farley, **** Bludwicke, Thomas Gynne, and John Turpin, Gentlemen, and many other persons, Burgesses &c. **** who as the major part of the whole Borough aforesaid, then there **** have chosen James Montague and Oliver Cromwell **** for the Borough aforesaid, Burgesses dwelling within the Borough aforesaid of the more discreet and sufficient Men of the same Borough, giving to [the said] Burgesses full and sufficient power for themselves and the whole Community of the Borough aforesaid &c. [Witness] whereof **** of this Indenture remaining with the said Lord the King, the parties abovesaid have put their seals, and to the other part of the same indenture **** hath put ****

Given on the day and year and at the place abovesaid, Lionel Walden, William Lilburne, Thomas Beard, Robert Bernard, Robert Arkenstall, William Walden, T. Phillips, William Patryke, William Pow, R. Farley, John Abbot, John Bowton, William Blodwicke, Thomas Gynne, ****

Sealed and delivered in the presence of Adam Hill, Edward Spaderowe, Henry Maton.[18]

[16] *Register of St. John the Baptist.*

[17] Asterisks indicate where the original is decayed.

[18] Original in the borough records of Huntingdon. Printed in Edward Griffith, *Collection of ancient records relating to the Borough of Huntingdon* (1827), p. 106. The indenture reproduced in Smith, *History of the English Parliament*, facing vol. i, 416, and there said to be for the borough of Huntingdon, for this Parliament, and bearing Cromwell's signature, is in reality the indenture for the county, and the signature is Sir Oliver's.

THE PARLIAMENT OF 1628

If the Williams-Cromwell connection was the physical, and Calvinism the spiritual, ancestry of Oliver Cromwell, this was his political background. Born into a family of Puritan leanings, brought up under the influence of a leader in that faith, his youth was spent in a period of political and ecclesiastical conflict. He was bred in a school opposed at nearly every point to the claims of royal and episcopal supremacy. He was connected by marriage with many of the most eminent of the opponents of the existing system, and his education brought him into contact with the great movement which they championed. Like many of them, he was most bitterly opposed to the church of Rome, which, rallying from the blows of Luther and Calvin, reforming its own system and setting forth on a new crusade to recover as much of its lost provinces and pre-eminence as possible, revealed a strength and an activity which inspired its communicants with fresh courage and its opponents with fresh fears. He came into politics at the moment when these various elements gathered to new conflict, when Europe endured the outbreak of a religious war beside which even the struggles of the preceding century seemed almost insignificant, and when in England the forces of monarchy and episcopacy were challenged as never before in English history. With such a background and such a training as his, it was inevitable—if not foreordained—that episcopacy in whatever form should find in him an unrelenting enemy, and that even monarchy, if it stood forth as the champion of episcopal church government, should feel scarcely less the weight of his animosity. It was, then, a portent of dire consequence to Stuart monarchy that at this critical moment in its history there was added to the forces of its opponents a man of such character and abilities as Cromwell was to show, inspired by such principles as these.

The return of Oliver Cromwell to the Parliament of 1628 was a notable event not only in his own history and that of England but in the affairs of Huntingdon and of the Cromwell family. It promised to restore something of the position of that family which had of late declined. The extravagance and bad management of Sir Oliver had brought him into difficulties from which, apparently, only the king's favor had for a time preserved him. More and more James stayed at Hinchinbrook and more and more came to regard it as his autumn residence. He had been there in October of the fateful years of 1619 and 1620; and in October, 1622 it was reported that "the King continues . . . at Hinchinbrook that was Sir Oliver Cromwell's."[19] Thus early it seems to have passed from his possession, and though

[19] Nichols, *Progresses of King James I*, iv, 780.

he lived on in the great house for five years more, it seems to have been rather as a tenant than as its owner. That did not long endure the death of James; and whether as a means of raising money or for some other reason, whatever claim the crown had on Hinchinbrook was extinguished with its purchase for £3000 by the Earl of Manchester who transferred it to his brother,[20] Sir Sidney Montagu, in June, 1627.

That purchase was reflected in the political situation in Huntingdonshire and its representation in Parliament. To that body the county had sent as its knights of the shire in 1621, Sir Robert Bevill and a friend of the Montagus, Sir Robert Payne. In the Parliaments of 1623–4 and 1625 the county was represented by Edward Montagu and Sir Oliver Cromwell; in that of 1625–6 by Payne and Montagu; and now in 1627–8 by Payne and another friend of the Montagus, Sir Capell Bedell, Edward Montagu having taken his place as Baron in the House of Lords. While the Cromwell influence was being thus replaced by that of the Montagus in the county, the borough representation had undergone like changes. In 1623–4 and 1625 Sir Henry St. John had retained his seat, but Sir Miles Sandys had been replaced by a certain Sir Arthur Manwaring. He, in turn, kept his place in 1625–6 but St. John was replaced by one John Goldsborough. Finally, in this new Parliament of 1627–8, the old Cromwell-Montagu rivalry was revived, as Huntingdon borough divided its representation between James Montagu and Oliver Cromwell.[21]

Nor were these all of the local and family concerns which surrounded and conditioned the election of Oliver to this Parliament. Of his relatives by marriage then or thereafter, no less than six had been imprisoned for refusal to subscribe to the forced loan of 1627;[22] and when he took his seat in the House of Commons, he found there six of that connection as members—Oliver St. John, John Hampden, Edmund Dunch, Sir Francis Barrington and his sons Thomas and Robert; with three others—Richard Knightley, Sir Miles Hobart and Sir Robert Pye—who were to join it later. He was, then, neither a total stranger nor wholly without friends and relatives in a House of Commons which contained, besides these, a considerable number of men who had been at Cambridge in his time, as well as a large contingent of members of the various Inns of Court. One thing seems certain; it is that this group, as in others like and allied to it, formed the nucleus of a party opposed to royal policy, and in this company Cromwell took his place.

[20] See Earl of Manchester's letter, *Hist. MSS. Comm. Rept.* (1899), i, p. 266; and Carruthers, *Hist. of Huntingdon*, p. 311.

[21] *Returns of Members of Parliament.*

[22] Sir Francis Barrington, Sir William Masham, John Hampden, Sir Edmund Hampden, and by later marriage, Richard Knightley and Sir John Trevor.

They were no less opposed to royal principles, which, in this fateful year of 1627, had hardened into a dogma, reinforced by ecclesiastical pronouncements, repugnant to Parliamentarians and still more to Puritans. "A king," Laud had declared in a sermon before Charles when he opened his first Parliament, "is God's immediate lieutenant upon earth; and therefore one and the same action is God's by ordinance and the king's by execution."[23] In this summer of 1627, two churchmen pushed this doctrine still further. It was the duty of the prince, said a Northampton vicar, Sibthorpe, in an assize sermon urging compliance with the forced loan, to "direct and make laws," of the subjects to obey them, and not resist even when 'obedience was impossible or contrary to the laws of God or nature.'[24] Parliaments, declared one of the royal chaplains, Manwaring, preaching before the king at this same time," though the highest and greatest assemblies . . . most sacred and honourable . . . and necessary . . . yet were not ordained . . . to contribute any right to kings, whereby to challenge tributary aids and subsidiary helps"—in this case the forced loan—nor could any man "that should not satisfy such demands defend his conscience from that heavy prejudice of resisting the ordinance of God, and receiving to himself damnation."[25]

Such was the extension of James I's doctrine of the divine right of kings; such the arguments advanced in favor of forced loans; and such the utterances which Charles, defying the archbishop Abbot, and differing even with Laud himself, ordered to be printed in defence of his attempt at unparliamentary taxation. From his prison in the Gatehouse, Sir John Eliot protested against such language and upheld the rights of Parliament; and his petition became the rallying-point of opposition to such extension of the prerogative. From their confinement five knights, then prisoners for refusing the forced loan, Cromwell's relative Sir Edmund Hampden among them, appealed to King's bench for a writ of *habeas corpus;* and four days after Buckingham returned from his failure at Rhé, on November 15th, 1627, they were brought to the bar. A week later their trial began; and in another week the judges determined the case in favor of the crown. Meanwhile money was raised by the prerogative, by forced loans, by excise, by writs of the privy seal; and meanwhile, too, the situation of the government grew more desperate as the country all but openly rebelled against the royal policy. It resented especially the billeting of soldiers on the populace and the proposed levy of ship-money to fit out a fleet against the threat of France, while the imprisonment of a London merchant, Chambers, added fuel to the flame of the City's discontent.

[23] Laud, *Works*, i, 93.
[24] Sibthorpe, *Apostolike Obedience* (1627).
[25] Manwaring, *Sermons* (1627).

In this temper the elections were held and the Houses met on March 17, 1628.[26] Five peers who had felt the displeasure of the crown for their resistance to its policy, were presently restored to their place in the Lords, but the storm broke in the Commons over the imprisonment of those who had resisted the forced loan. The question was acute. Could the king imprison at his will; could he levy taxes without consent of Parliament; could he defy the "ancient laws and liberties" of England? In the ensuing debate Eliot, now at liberty by virtue of his privilege while Parliament was in session, led the way, denouncing firmly the royal attack on those liberties, not least on that of religion. But to Eliot's eloquence was added a greater voice, that of Sir Thomas Wentworth, member for Yorkshire who, ignoring the religious issue, attacked those "projectors," who "have extended the prerogative of the King beyond its just symmetry." To these, in turn, was added the weight of opinion of the greatest of English jurists, Sir Edward Coke. It was in vain that spokesmen of the Court pleaded the ancient and legal authority of the crown; that the king urged the necessity of supply if French Huguenots were not to be destroyed. It was in vain that Wentworth sought a compromise, and the Lords sought to mediate. Between a king who held the doctrines of the divine right to rule, with sole responsibility to God, and a Commons determined to become not merely the advisers but the partners of that rule, a compromise was all but impossible.

The issue thus raised at the moment of Cromwell's entry into public affairs went to the root of the whole problem of the English constitution. What was the relation between crown and Parliament; what were the rights and duties of the king; what was the function of the Houses in the government? The royal position was simple; it was that England should be ruled for its own good by the wisdom and skill of its monarch and his chosen counsellors, financed and advised, but not impeded, much less controlled, by Parliament. Against this was set the doctrine urged by such men as Eliot: that Parliament was not merely an advisory body, but equal in wisdom, skill and authority with the crown, and, by virtue of its ancient right to vote taxation, even superior. Between these contending theories the party represented by Wentworth took its stand for compromise, holding that the final authority lay neither in king nor Parliament, but in the laws of England, its ancient "rights and liberties," to be violated by exercise of the prerogative only in cases of extreme "necessity" or "emergency."

The difficulty was two-fold. The Parliament had no confidence in the wisdom and capacity of the royal counsellors, especially Buckingham; and it feared the definition of "emergency" and "necessity"

[26] Cp. *Commons Journals*, 1628, *passim* and Gardiner, *History*.

might be extended to fit any action that the crown might take, for those two words have been at all times the defence of dictatorship. More practically and more immediately, it resented that exercise of the prerogative which had raised money by unparliamentary means, quartered soldiers on the people, imprisoned men for refusing to loan money to the government and even sent members of Parliament to prison for venturing to oppose the royal—or ministerial—policy. To these were joined two other elements—the distrust and dislike of Charles's foreign policy, as of the minister who advised it, and the favor shown to Roman Catholics.

The first issue Charles and Buckingham had tried to meet with their attempts to aid the Huguenots and to support the Danish king, but questions of foreign policy were now overshadowed by more pressing issues at home, especially those of religion and of revenue. The question of religious liberty did not greatly disturb Wentworth, who was no Puritan, and even Eliot, who was inclined to that party, subordinated that issue to those of Buckingham's incapacity and the crown's policy of arbitrary taxation and imprisonment. But religion had played a larger and larger part in Parliamentary discussion; it had absorbed much of the session of 1621; and it had found a champion in the member for Tavistock, John Pym.[27] If Eliot was the orator and Wentworth the statesman of the movement, Pym was the organizer and exponent of the opposition to Charles, the link between the City and the country; and, as chairman of the committee on religion, the mouthpiece of the Puritans. He was, in fact, the typical leader of a revolutionary movement, deeply convinced of the righteousness of his crusade against Catholics and Anglicans, able, discontented with a system of government and society in which he had been unsuccessful and, his enemies hinted, not uniformly honest, a past master of political management, he had found in this situation an opportunity denied to his talents in other fields. More and more in the successive Parliaments he had come to be the center of the party opposed to the government, gathering about him a group of likeminded men, among them Cromwell's relatives, John Hampden and Oliver St. John, and now Cromwell himself.

It was under such conditions and such auspices that Oliver Cromwell took his place in Parliament in 1628, to hear the fervid eloquence of Eliot, the statesmanlike appeals of Wentworth, the legal arguments of Selden and of Coke, to take part in the divisions which accompanied the struggle between the champions of crown and Commons, and, finally, to join with his colleagues in the great protest which, in June 1628, brought the long struggle to a dramatic climax in the passage of one of the great landmarks of constitutional history.

[27] For Pym see article in *D. N. B.* and Wade, *Pym* (1912).

On June 5th, the so-called "Petition of Right" passed the Commons; two days later it received the King's assent and took its place among the statutes of the realm. Thereafter, it decreed, no man should "be compelled to make or yield any gift, loan, benevolence, tax, or such like charge, without common consent by Act of Parliament . . . to make answer, or take such oath, or to give attendance, or be confined, or otherwise molested or disquieted concerning the same, or refusal thereof." It decreed, also, that billeting be given up, with martial law; and that none "of your Majesty's subjects be destroyed or put to death, contrary to the laws and franchise of the land."[28] Such was the affirmation of the rights of Englishmen and of their Parliament which reinforced the doctrines of Magna Charta; and to it was added within a fortnight a Remonstrance against levying without consent of Parliament those customs duties which made up a third of royal revenue, and presently a protest against misgovernment denouncing Buckingham by name.

This was the crowning blow to the prerogative. The next day the King prorogued the Houses, refusing his assent to the Remonstrance. "I must avow," he said, "that I owe the account of my actions to God alone." He was unwilling, he declared, to receive any more remonstrances, least of all that which proposed "to take away . . . one of the chiefest maintenances of my crown . . . for none of the Houses of Parliament, either joint or separate (what new doctrine soever may be raised) have any power to make or declare a law without my consent."[29] With that pronouncement he not merely defined his own position, he challenged the whole contention of the party then rising to power in the Parliament.

Nor did the king confine himself to words. Parliament was prorogued on June 26th. Five days later, William Laud was promoted to the bishopric of London; and within three weeks Sir Thomas Wentworth was created Baron Wentworth by the king as a mark of that royal favor which was soon to take more substantial form. These appointments were startling enough, but they were overshadowed by a tragic incident. On August 23rd, the Duke of Buckingham, while on a visit of inspection at Portsmouth, was assassinated by a certain John Felton, sometime an officer in the Rhé expedition, driven to desperation by failure to receive promotion and his pay.

The rejoicings over the death of the man whom the public regarded as its chief enemy had no effect on royal policy, but Buckingham's death had one important consequence, for Charles became in fact as in name the head of the government. He presided over the Council, he was his own chief minister, and only in one respect was there any

[28] *Statutes*, v. 23.

[29] *Lords Journals*, iii, 879. *Parl. Hist.*, ii, 434. Gardiner, *History of England*, vi, 324-5.

change in the direction of affairs. Though preparations for a new attempt to relieve Rochelle went on, though it was still proposed to send aid to German Protestants, those preparations and those proposals came to little; for on October 18th, the Rochellois, abandoning their hope of help from England, surrendered; and in the following spring the Danish king made peace with the Emperor. Meanwhile the Dutch prince Frederick Henry began his victorious career against the Spaniards in the Low Countries; and a Dutch commander, Piet Hein, captured the Spanish Plate fleet. On behalf of France, Richelieu was prepared to treat for peace. Spain was no longer able to keep up the war; the hopes and fears of a Spanish marriage had been long since destroyed; and as the war fever in England waned, king and people found their hands free for their domestic differences.

Those differences had by now become clearly defined; but if there remained any question as to the King's attitude it was soon dispelled. In November he issued his Declaration on Religion prefixed to the Book of Common Prayer, defining categorically the position of the crown. "Being by God's ordinance, according to our just title, Defender of the Faith, and Supreme Governour of the Church, within these our dominions," it began, "we hold it most agreeable to this our kingly office, and our own religious zeal, to conserve and maintain in the Church committed to our charge, in the unity of true religion and in the bond of peace; and not to suffer unnecessary disputations, altercations, or questions to be raised, which may nourish factions both in the Church and Commonwealth." He therefore required all his subjects "to continue in the uniform profession" of the articles of the Church of England, "allowed and authorized heretofore, and which our clergy generally have subscribed unto," "prohibiting the least difference from the said articles." To that end, "if any difference arise about the external policy . . . the injunctions, canons and other constitutions," they should be determined by Convocation; and he further commanded "churchmen do the work which is proper unto them," according to the doctrine and discipline of the Church of England, "from which we will not endure any varying or departing in the least degree." Admitting that, "for the present, some differences have been ill raised," he ordered "that all further curious search be laid aside," and that no one, especially any officer of the universities, should print or teach "any new sense to any article" save "in the literal and grammatical sense," else "he shall be liable to our displeasure, and the Church's censure . . . and we will see that there shall be due execution upon them."

It was the voice of Charles but the language of Laud. That champion of order in a church now threatened with chaos by the Puritan movement, had risen rapidly in favor and in office. In the spirit which had led him to seek royal intervention in the case of Montagu three years earlier, that the Church of England "could not be able to preserve any unity among Christians if men were forced to subscribe to curious particulars disputed in the schools," he had prepared the King's speeches in defence of Buckingham. He had, as his reward, been promoted to the see of Bath and Wells; then to the deanship of the royal chapel; then to a place in the privy council; now to the bishopric of London; and was marked for succession to the conciliatory Archbishop Abbot of Canterbury, just now in disgrace for his efforts to compose the quarrel between the high church Anglicans and the Puritans.

To that pronouncement the reply of the committee on religion of the House of Commons when it reassembled in February, 1629, was prompt and firm. It had condemned Manwaring and compelled Charles to withdraw his sermon. Now it went further. Noting what it declared were "innovations" in religion,—that is to say the efforts of the Laudians to introduce more order into church services and affairs,—it protested vigorously against the "unfaithfulness and carelessness" of Charles's ministers; against the "combined counsels, forces, attempts and practices" of the Roman Catholics, the weak resistance made to them, the "stirs and insolences" of that party in Scotland, its spread in Ireland, its successes on the continent, and "the extraordinary growth of Popery" even in England. These it adduced by numerous instances; it offered remedies, as pointed as they were specific; it named names, like those of Barrow and Barret at Cambridge and Bridges at Oxford; it did not hesitate to denounce the Earl of Manchester's brother, Walter Montagu, a recent convert to Rome, and the lately established college of the Jesuits. It pointed, not obliquely, at the Queen's influence in encouraging the rising tide of Catholic influence, and summoned the nation to oppose this threat.[30]

The protest was, in effect, the work of Pym as chairman of the committee on religion. It was followed almost at once by the protestation of the House of Commons, which, joining religion to revenue, declared that anyone who "should bring in innovation of religion, or by favour or countenance seem to extend Popery or Arminianism," "counsel or advise the taking and levying of the subsidies of Tonnage and Poundage, not being granted by Parliament," or even "voluntarily yield or pay the said subsidies," "shall be reputed a capital enemy of this Kingdom and Commonwealth."[31]

The royal answer was immediate and complete. A week after this protestation Charles dissolved the Parliament and issued a Declaration defending his course. Again he began, "Princes are not bound

[30] Cobbett, *Parl. Hist.*, ii, col. 483. Gardiner, *Const. Documents*, p. 11.
[31] Rushworth, *Historical Collections* (1692), i, 660; *Const. Doc'ts* as above, p. 16.

to give account of their actions but to God alone." Again he defended his policy; again he affirmed his good intentions and his patience with the discussion on "many of our high prerogatives . . . which in the best times of our predecessors had never been questioned without punishment or sharp reproof." And, having stated the case for monarchy and for his policy, he denounced "those provocations of evil men" who had ventured to question the wisdom of the crown and ministers, and even the prerogative; promising to maintain "the true religion" and order in the church, to defend his ministers, to cherish his merchants and not to "burthen them beyond what is fitting, but the duty of five in the hundred for guarding of the seas and defence of the realm." From his subjects he demanded obedience; adding significantly, "if any factious merchant will affront us in a thing so reasonable," "we shall find honourable and just means to support our estate, vindicate our sovereignty, and preserve the authority which God hath put in our hands."[32]

Thus were the lines of the ensuing conflict drawn; and with this Oliver Cromwell took his part in the great debate. With the constitutional issue he was as much concerned as his countrymen in general. In the matter of foreign policy, in that of billeting and of levying money by prerogative, which grew, in a sense, out of foreign policy, he had the same interest as any man with house and property; in the question of impositions he had no more immediate concern than the son-in-law of a London merchant might be supposed to have. In none of these great issues does it appear from what evidence we have that he raised his voice in Parliament. But the question of religion was different. Here he had an active interest, as it chanced one personal to him, and through it he entered on the fray.

During the course of an inquiry as to how pardons had been obtained for certain persons accused of preaching "popery," including that champion of divine right, Manwaring, who had been previously censured by Parliament, it appeared that they had been solicited by Dr. Neale, Bishop of Winchester. The matter roused a storm of protest, to which Cromwell contributed. On February 11, 1629, he rose to address the chairman of the committee on religion to make his contribution to the long debate. His speech was brief and personal; his contribution neither insignificant nor ineffectual:

Speech in the House of Commons, Feb. 11, 1628–9

"Manwaring," he declared, "who by censure of the last Parliament for his sermons was disabled from holding any ecclesiastical dignity in the church, and confessed the justice of that censure, was, nevertheless, by this same bishop's means, preferred to a rich living. If these be the steps to pre-

[32] Rushworth, i, App. 1; *Const. Doc'ts*, p. 17 ff.

ferment," he inquired, "what may we not expect? Dr. Beard told me some time ago," he continued, "that one Dr. Alablaster, in a sermon at Paul's Cross, had preached flat popery. Dr. Beard was to rehearse [refute?] Alablaster's sermon at the Spittle, but Dr. Neale, Bishop of Winchester, sent for him and charged him as his diocesan to preach nothing contrary to Dr. Alablaster's sermon. He went to Dr. Felton, Bishop of Ely, who charged him as a minister to oppose it, which Dr. Beard did; but he was then sent for by Dr. Neale, and was exceedingly rated for what he had done."[33]

Such seems to be the first recorded utterance of Cromwell in Parliament; from which appears his great concern for his old master and that master's teachings. Nor did the thing end there. The House resolved on the same day to send for Dr. Marshall and Dr. Beard for further questioning. As a result, Neale and Laud were "named to be those near about the King who are suspected to be Arminians and . . . unsound in their opinions that way," and so reprehended.

To this was added a more violent means of opposition. On March 2, Cromwell, with Holles and others, refused to adjourn at the King's command until the resolution of Sir John Eliot against popery and subsidies not granted by Parliament was passed. Their opposition was successful—but only by the aid of force. Fearful of being anticipated by the King, the Speaker of the House was held in his place by Holles and Valentine, while Eliot read his resolutions amid the tumult of the members. The resolutions were recited by Holles while the Speaker was held in his seat just as Charles came down to prorogue the Houses; and in this turbulent fashion came to an end the last Parliament which was to be held in England for eleven years, with Oliver Cromwell playing his part in the scenes of violence which accompanied its end.

HUNTINGDON, 1628–1629

England was now divided into two camps. On the one side stood the champions of the crown with men like Laud and Wentworth at their head; on the other the champions of Parliament led by men like Eliot and Pym. It is easy for those bred in the democratic tradition of the nineteenth century to denounce the tyranny of the one and to uphold the virtues of the other; and liberty is always a more popular cause than order. At that moment, indeed, it seems probable that the

[33] First part in Sanford, *Studies*, p. 229, from "The Book of Speeches." Three slightly different reports of the speech, of which the above is a composite, are in Notestein and Relf, *Commons Debates for 1629*, pp. 59, 139, 192–3. Bishop Neale (or Neile) was bishop of Rochester 1608–1610 and appointed Laud as his chaplain. He was bishop of Lichfield 1610–14; of Lincoln, 1614–17; of Durham, 1617–27; of Winchester, 1627 to his death in 1640. He was a member of the Privy Council and courts of Star Chamber and High Commission, a Laudian high-churchman and a divine right monarchist.

majority of Englishmen were opposed to the pretensions of the King, and the apparent "apostacy" of Wentworth seemed the more hateful to them in consequence; nor did the character of Charles command their confidence.

Yet there was much to be said for the royal contention. With all the grave defects of their personal qualities, James and Charles would have been more or less than human had they not believed that they were set apart by their office from the common lot of men. They had not merely been crowned but anointed; there was a divinity which hedged about a king. To the hereditary principle, as yet unchallenged even by political philosophers, was added the authority of a Parliament which had recognized the crown as head of both church and state. From time immemorial the direction of foreign affairs had lain in the king's hands and mismanagement had immemorially been attributed to evil counsellors. Even in the most recent protests of this Parliament that form had been observed. Moreover autocracy had been the accepted principle of Tudor government; it was the system of the continent; it was supported by the church; it was all but unquestioned by the people themselves. It was no wonder that Charles and James clung to the old traditions of the monarchy; that they constantly adduced the practices of their predecessors to support their case; that they constantly appealed to ancient law and custom of the constitution as to their divine appointment and responsibility; that they constantly denounced the "innovations" of their enemies. And had they not fallen on such evil times for monarchy, had their policies been as successful as those of Elizabeth, had they been possessed of Tudor qualities, they might well have weathered even this threatening attack.

On the other hand, their opponents appealed no less to law and constitution, to ancient customs and practices; and, so various had been the course of English history, if the crown could cite instances of unquestioned use of the royal power, the Commons could adduce as many instances of its authority. If the King clung stubbornly to his prerogative, the Commons pressed the extension of its privilege. The lawyers divided in opinion according to their sympathies or interests. The courts in general decided the cases sent before them in favor of the crown, for it was their business not to make but to declare the law by statute and precedent and those in general were favorable to the crown.

To men like Pym there was but one solution—the surrender of the crown to popular opinion as expressed in Parliament. To men like Wentworth this was unthinkable, for to him sovereignty resided in the monarchy. The problem seemed insoluble. As this obscure member of Parliament, Cromwell, observed when confronted by the same issue in later years, "When two men ride a horse, one must ride behind." It is easy to say that Charles and James were "wrong," as the event proved, or that had they been of different character, the problem might have been settled amicably; but there are no "ifs" in history, and compromise is impossible when each side is certain it is "right" and neither side will yield.

Yet government must go on, and as yet authority resided in the crown. As soon as dissolution deprived Parliament men of their privilege, Charles hastened to punish those who had opposed him; sent Eliot with others to the Tower, and summoned such talents as he could then command to rule by sheer prerogative: the shrewd, capable, if subservient and unscrupulous, Weston as Treasurer and the adroit Noy as attorney-general; and these, with Coventry, Wentworth and Laud, became, in effect, the government. Laud set himself to reorganize the church; Wentworth to direct administration; Weston to find money; Noy to explore the legal technicalities by which it could be raised; Coventry, who, like Wentworth, had earlier taken the side of Parliament, lent his advice and assistance in matters of policy; and thus equipped, Charles set forth on his attempt at personal government.

What, then, of Oliver Cromwell in these years; how had he developed since his coming of age and his marriage; what effect had the events of these intervening years had on his opinions and his character; what sort of man was he at the beginning of this fateful period? The answer is not easy; there is little evidence, and none of it direct, as to the changes time had wrought in him. Yet there is some; and from it we may draw some notion of what the years had done to him. He had obviously become not merely a Puritan in a religious sense, but, as his single recorded utterance proves, an active and aggressive member of that sect. Whatever the time and cause, he had apparently gone through that searching religious experience known as conversion; and for various reasons it would appear that it had been caused, or accompanied by, or had resulted in, profound disturbances, emotional and perhaps physical. For this, apart from the words of Cromwell's earliest biographers, there are two pieces of apparently indubitable evidence. The first is the case-book of a certain Dr. Theodore Mayerne, sometime physician to James I,[34] who, in the course of his practice, which seems to have been in part at least what is now called "psychiatry," set down under date of September 15, 1628, that, consulted by "Mons. Cromwell," he had found him "*valde melancholicus*,"[35] that is to say, extremely melancholy. That is not, perhaps,

[34] Consulted by Baxter after the siege of Worcester. Cp. *Reliq. Baxterianae.*

[35] Mayerne, *Ephemerides* (Journal of his cases, 1603–1649), quoted from the Sloane Mss., British Museum, 2069, f. 92–6, in Ellis, *Original Letters illustrative of English History*, second series, iii, 248.

surprising for there were many melancholy men in England at that time; but adding some weight to it is a second bit of testimony, written some years later by Sir Philip Warwick:

"After the rendition of Oxford, I living some time with the Lady Beadle (my wife's sister) near Huntingdon, had occasion to converse with Mr. Cromwell's physician, Dr. Simcott, who assured me that for many years his patient was a most splenetic man, and had fancies about the cross in that town, and that he had been called up to him at midnight, and such unseasonable hours, very many times, upon a strong fancy, which made him believe he was then dying; and there went a story of him, that in the day-time, lying melancholy in his bed, he believed that a spirit appeared to him and told him that he should be the greatest man (not mentioning the word King) in this kingdom. Which his uncle, Sir Thomas Steward, who left him all the little estate Cromwell had, told him it was traitorous to relate."[36]

To which Sir Philip adds, after some account of Cromwell's earlier years and his "conversion:" "When he was thus civilized, he joined himself to men of his own temper, who pretended unto transports and revelations." To this again, though in a very different and far more hostile vein the royalist author of the *Flagellum* adds his testimony:

"By this time," Heath asserts, without satisfying our curiosity as to when the change occurred, "and by these ways, Oliver had run himself out of that little patrimony he had, and brought his Mother to the same near Ruin; when taking a sad prospect from the brink of this destruction, of his present desperate condition, a giddy inspiration seized him, and all of a sudden so seemed to change and invert him, that he now became the wonder, who just before was the hissing and scorn of all people. And that this Conversion might seem true and real, he manifested it with the Publican first in the Temple (the Church) which he devoutly and constantly frequented, affecting the Companies and Discourses of Orthodox Divines, no way given to that Schisme of *Nonconformity;* into which *Oliver* soon after fell, not out of *Seduction* and Ignorance, but *Sedition* and Malice, and treasonable design."[37]

Similar to Heath, but without his animus, is another account:

"Growing to years of greater discretion and solidity, he became as remarkable for his sobriety and religiousness, as before for his vanity. . . . And though at his first leaving off of his extravagancies he adhered to the Church of England, frequenting with great devotion the publick assemblies, yet in a short time he began to associate himself with the Puritans, and to entertain their preachers at his house. And he became not only thus zealous in Religion, but as just in his dealings with men, even to scrupulosity."

Finally, one of Cromwell's friends in later years records the same event in somewhat different form and spirit:

[36] Warwick, *Memoirs*, p. 249.
[37] *Flagellum* (1663), pp. 13–14.

"This great man is risen from a very low and afflicted condition; one that hath suffered very great troubles of soul, lying a long time under sore terrors and temptations, and at the same time in a very low condition for outward things; in this school of afflictions he was kept, till he had learned the lesson of the Cross, till his will was broken into submission to the will of God." Religion, he adds, was "laid into his soul with the hammer and the fire"; it did not "come in only by light into his understanding."[38]

With all of the suspicious similarity between the stories of Heath and Carrington, they agree with Warwick, with hints from other witnesses, with the words of Cromwell's friend, of Cromwell himself and with the medical evidence. Whatever remorse he may have experienced for his youthful course of life, however innocent that life may have been; whatever his financial difficulties; whatever effect his health may have had on his spiritual processes, it seems apparent that his moody, undisciplined nature underwent some profound alteration, accompanied by such physical and spiritual disturbances as are common to such experiences.

As to when that change occurred, opinions have differed widely. On the ground that Sir James Bourchier would not have allowed his only daughter to marry a rake, it has been urged that his conversion took place before his marriage. It has been argued that his marriage produced the change. The medical evidence seems to indicate that it was some time between his marriage and his election to Parliament, and not much before; that it was, in cause or effect, still going on while he was a member. The testimony seems to indicate that it was connected with the decline of his fortunes, which would place it either about the time he left Huntingdon or extending into the period of his residence in St. Ives; and this seems not improbable. Somewhere between his twenty-eighth and his thirty-second year seems a not unlikely date for this period of conversion.

HUNTINGDON, 1629–1631

Such was the Oliver Cromwell who now entered on the third great period of his life. As to the events and character of that life, the evidence is disjointed and scanty, aside from tales of gambling and extravagances—though they are not incredible—yet something may be made of it. One senses somehow that his estate had diminished, that, like all his family since Sir Richard's time, he had not been a good man of business. On the other hand he had become a public character, a leader of one of the groups into which Huntingdon was divided, and so far as we can judge, he belonged to the "popular" or "Puritan" element. He had defeated Robert Bernard's party in the election of

[38] Quoted in Firth, *Cromwell*, p. 39.

1627 with the aid, apparently, of his old master, friend and ally, Dr. Beard, in whose behalf he had made his first appearance in the House.

It is not easy at this distance and in default of more evidence to unravel the details of Huntingdon politics in these years; but that Cromwell took a leading part in them and that it had some effect upon his later life, there is no cause to doubt. Its chief event was a change in the form of borough government. On February 9, 1630, the bailiffs and burgesses petitioned for a new charter, changing the administration from a corporation governed by two bailiffs and a common council of twenty-four, freely elected year by year, to twelve aldermen and a recorder chosen for life, and a mayor chosen annually from and by the aldermen. In addition to naming the first mayor, Lionel Walden, and the first aldermen, the charter, granted July 15, 1630, contained the following provision:

"Thomas Beard, doctor of divinity, Robert Bernard, Esqre, and Oliver Cromwell, Esqre, burgesses of the borough aforesaid, are appointed during their several lives, and the longer liver of them, justices to preserve and keep the peace of us, our heirs and successors, within the borough of Huntingdon."[39]

Despite his part in the new government of Huntingdon, Cromwell expressed the dissatisfaction of the disfranchised inhabitants a few months later, in a manner more vigorous than seemly. He had been appointed to preserve the peace, but the mayor and aldermen soon found it necessary to appeal to a higher authority to quiet Cromwell himself, as the *Privy Council Register* relates:

26 Novr. 1630

This day Oliver Crumwell, Esqr and Willyam Kilborne, gent. having bene formerly sent for by warrant from the board, tendered their appearances accordingly, wch for their indempnities is entered in the register of Counsell causes. But they are to remain in the custody of the messenger untill they shalbe dismissed by their Lpps.[40]

Perhaps out of consideration for the mayor and aldermen who were apparently in London to prosecute their case, an early date was set for the formal hearing, with the chief of the King's advisers[41] on hand

[39] *Additional Mss.*, British Museum, 15,665, fols. 131–135. Part of the new charter is printed in Griffith, *Ancient Records of Huntingdon*, pp. 109–115. The section here quoted is also in Sanford, *Studies*, pp. 232–3.

[40] Extract taken from the *Privy Council Register* by John Bruce, in *The Athenaeum*, Oct. 13, 1855, p. 1187.

[41] Present were: Lo. Keeper (Sir Thomas Coventry), Lo. Trea^{r} (Lord Weston), Lo. President, Lo. Privie Seale, Ea. Marshall (Earl of Arundel), E. of Danby, E. of Kelley, Lo. Visc. Wimbledon, Lo. Visc. Falkland, Lo. Bp. of London (Laud), Lo.

to decide not only the merits of the complaint against the disturbers of the peace, but of the charter itself. The Register continues:

1st Dec[r]. 1630

Whereas a peticon was presented to the Board by the Major and Aldermen of the towne of Huntingdon, complayning against Mr. Crumwell and William Kilborne, whereupon the parties complayned of were sent for by warrant from the board, And both sides having this day had a long hearing, there appeared much contrariety and difference in the allegacons on each side, Whereupon their lpps. thought fitt and ordered, that the examinacon of the whole businesse should bee referred to the Lord Privie Seale, as well touching the charter of the said towne, as alsoe that his ldpp. should, in particular, consider what satisfaction were fitt to be given to the said Mayor and Mr. Bernard for the disgracefull and unseemly speeches used unto them, and should settle and end the differences amongst them, if it may bee, or otherwise to make report to the board how the state of these differences stands, together with his opinion touching the same, that such further course may be taken as shall bee fitt. And whereas there was a paticon read with divers complaints therein made against the said Kilburne and Brookes his man for much oppression to the country, and many great abuses to particular persons, It was likewise ordered that the Lord Privie Seale shall take examinacon thereof and make reporte to the board what he finds touching the same.[42]

The Lord Privy Seal who, as it happened, was Henry Montagu, the Earl of Manchester, set to work to collect his evidence, of which the following seems to have been provided by the plaintiffs, for it was despite this agreement that Cromwell and Kilborne abused their opponents:

Certificate of Thomas Beard, D.D.

"That Oliver Cromwell, Esquire and Willm. Kilborne, gent., with a free assent and consent did agree to the renewing" of the charter of Huntingdon, and to the substitution of the word "Mayor" for that of "Bailiffs" in that document.[43]

Basing his decision on this and other evidence, the Earl made the following report to the Council on December 6:

Henry Earl of Manchester, Lord Privy Seal, to the Council

Whereas it pleased your Lordships to refer unto me the differences in the town of Huntingdon, about the renovation of their charter, and some wrongs done to Mr. Mayor of Huntingdon, and Mr. Barnard, a counsellor-at-law,

Newburgh, Mr. Trea[r] (Sir Thomas Edmonds), Mr. Vice Chamberlain (Sir Henry May), Mr. Sec. Coke. *Ibid.*

[42] *Ibid.*

[43] *Hist. MSS. Comm. Rept.* 8, App. II, p. 50 (*Manchester Mss.*).

by disgraceful and unseemly speeches, used of them by Mr. Cromwell, of Huntingdon, as also the considerations of divers abuses and oppressions complained of against one Kilborne, post-master of Huntingdon, and Brookes, his man; I have heard the said differences, and do find those supposed fears of prejudice that might be to the said town, by their late altered charter, from bailiffs and burgesses to mayor and aldermen, are causeless and ill-grounded, and the endeavour used to gain many of the burgesses against this new corporation was very indirect and unfit, and such as I could not but much blame them that stirred in it. For Mr. Barnard's carriage of the business in advising and obtaining the said charter, it was fair and orderly done, being authorized by common consent of the town to do the same, and the thing effected by him tends much to the good and grace of the town.

Then, evidently to appease Cromwell and his friends, the Earl directed three "constitutions" or local regulations on special points to be made, and continued:

For the words spoken of Mr. Mayor and Mr. Barnard by Mr. Cromwell, as they were ill, so they are acknowledged to be spoken in heat and passion, and desired to be forgotten; and I found Mr. Cromwell very willing to hold friendship with Mr. Barnard, who, with a good will, remitting the unkind passages past, entertained the same. So I left all parties reconciled, and wished them to join hereafter in things that may be for the common good and peace of the town.[44]

So Cromwell returned to Huntingdon silenced but not appeased. The new charter was upheld and the town sank rapidly into the "spiritless condition of a rotten borough" in which it remained until the passing of the Reform Act. There seemed small likelihood of his sitting in Parliament again for his native town, nor was there further opportunity, for a few months later he sold his lands and moved out of its jurisdiction.

Before he left Huntingdon, however, an incident occurred which throws light on another side of Oliver's character. He was, it appears, fond of the ancient sport of hawking, then still popular in England. One of his humbler friends in Huntingdon had lost a hawk identified by the small rings or "varvells" attached to it as belonging to Cromwell. It had been taken in by a Warwickshire gentleman, a Mr.

[44] *St. P. Dom. Charles I*, clxxxvi, 34. Printed in *Calendar* (1629–31), pp. x–xi.

For a somewhat different view of Cromwell's career in Cambridge, see S. H. Church, *Oliver Cromwell*, p. 13. "It can be well understood how this pastoral life, unfolding its beautiful domestic incidents, and strengthening from day to day the ties of family love, would gradually develop the divinity that slept in the soul of Oliver Cromwell," *etc.* and Milton's account, quoted there, (p. 14) "Noted for nothing so much as the culture of pure religion and an integrity of life, he was grown rich at home; and enlarging his hopes with reliance in God for any the most exalted times, he nursed his great soul in silence."

Newdigate, whose nephew, Richard, was then in Gray's Inn with Cromwell's cousin, Henry, the son of Sir Philip. To him Cromwell, advised of its whereabouts, wrote a letter which runs as follows, spelling and all:

To John Newdigate

SIR,

I must with all thankfulnesse acknowledge the curtesye you have intended me in keeping this hawk soe long, to your noe small trouble, and although I have noe interest in hir, yet if ever it fall in my way, I shalbe ready to doe your service in the like of any other kinds. I doe confesse I have neglected you in that I have received two letters from you without sending you any answer, but I trust you will pass by it and accept my true and reasonable excuse. This poore man, the owner of the hawke, who, living in the same towne with me, made use of my varvells, I did daly expect to have sooner returned from his journey than he did, which was the cause whie I protracted time, and deferred to send unto you, until I might make him the messinger, whoe was best able to give an account, as also fittest to fetch hir, I myself being utterly destitute of a falconer att the present, and not having any man whom I durst venture to carrie a hawke of that kinde soe farre. This is all I can apologise. I beseech you, command me, and I shall rest, your servant,

Huntingdon, OLIVER CROMWELL.
April 1, 1631.

[P.S.] My cousin Cromwell of Gray's Inn was the first that told me of hir.[45]

It is not surprising that Cromwell was remiss in answering Mr. Newdigate's courteous inquiries; for he was at that moment involved in another controversy with authority, of somewhat less consequence but of wider interest than the quarrel over the charter of Huntingdon. It arose from the "lawful but extraordinary" means by which Charles's government, in default of Parliament, was raising revenue. Among its devices was the enforcement of an old statute by which anyone possessed of freehold land worth forty pounds a year was compelled by law to attend the ceremony of the coronation of a new sovereign and have thrust on him the honor or "distraint" of knighthood, or pay a fine or "composition" for his absence. The statute had in recent years not been generally enforced, and many men, seeking escape from the additional taxation which knighthood involved, had failed to comply with its provisions. It was a promising source of revenue, and

[45] Printed by Lady Newdigate-Newdegate, *Cavalier and Puritan*, p. 5, from the Newdigate Mss at Arbury, co. Warwick; Lomas-Carlyle, Suppl. 1. This letter has been left in its original form as a specimen of the spelling to be found in Cromwell's letters.

commissioners were appointed in each county to enforce it. Among them in Huntingdon were Sir Oliver Cromwell, Sir Sidney Montagu, and the Earl of Manchester; and before the Earl again appeared the name of Oliver Cromwell. For though Oliver's uncle Henry, of Upwood, promptly made his composition, took the tally of his payment into the Exchequer and showed it to the commissioners, Oliver, disregarding the order of that body, paid no attention to it.

With other citizens of Huntingdon he was promptly returned as a defaulter. The sheriff of the county was provided with their names and writs summoning them before the Court of the Exchequer for delinquency, though the commissioners were authorized to give them one more opportunity to escape the penalty for contumacy. In consequence the name of Oliver Cromwell again found a place in his country's official records, as follows:

The names of such persons who were summoned to appeare in his ma^{ts} Court of Exchequer xv^{ne} Pasche to fine for theire contempt in not receivinge the order of K^{t}hoode, and have compounded wth vs 20 April and 28 Apr. 1631.

Oliver Cromwell, of Huntingdon, Esq. . . . . x^{li}
Beniamin Smyth, of Stibbington-cum-Sibson, gent. . . . . x^{li}
Thomas Torkington, of Steukeley magna, gent. . . . . x^{li}
Richarde Wynde, of St. Ives, gent. . . . . x^{li}
Thomas Henson sen^{r}, de Ellington, yeoman . . . . x^{li}
William Curtis, of Stilton, yeoman. . . . . x^{li}
Robert Haylocke, of Abbotsley, yeoman. . . . . x^{li}[46]

His name heads the list, yet it is apparent from the manuscript that it was added after the list was made. Whether Cromwell recanted at the last moment or whether his composition was paid by someone else, he none the less escaped the penalty for his refusal to obey the law. In any event, this is the last, or almost the last of his connection with Huntingdon—and with Beard—for ten days later, on May 7, 1631, he joined with his wife, his mother and his uncle, Sir Oliver, to convey his property there to Richard Oakeley of Westminster and Richard Owen of Middlesex for £1800, as appears by the deed which enumerates those possessions, of which the following is an extract:

"All the capital messuage called the Augustine Fryers, alias Augustine Friers, within the borough or town of Huntingdon, and the messuages &c belonging to it, and one close, called the dove-house close, and all those three cottages or tenements, with a malt-house, and a little close, by estima-

[46] This, with lists of those who had previously compounded, those who failed to respond to the summons, and those who claimed an insufficient freehold estate, were inclosed in a letter from Sir Oliver Cromwell, Sir Sydney Montagu, Robert Bevill and Robert Osbern, the Commissioners, to the Privy Council. *St. P. Dom. Charles I*, clxxxix, 46. *Calendar*, 1631–33, p. 23. Documents printed in the *Proceedings of the Society of Antiquaries*, i, 294–7 (1861).

tion one acre, lying together in Huntingdon aforesaid, theretofore of Edm. Goodwyns, and also all those seven leas of pasture, containing by estimation two acres, called Toothill Leas, lying in Huntingdon; and also all those two acres and three roods of meadow, lying and being in Brampton, in the said county of Huntingdon, in a meadow there called Portholme; and also all those two acres of meadow, in Godmanchester, in the said county of Huntingdon; all the above premises are called either late, or now or late in the possession of the said Eliz. Cromwell, widow; and all other the lands and tenements of the said Eliz. Cromwell, widow, Oliv. Cromwell., esq. or either of them in Huntingdon, Godmanchester, or Brampton aforesaid, or any of them. And also all the rectory and parsonage of Hartford, in the said county, and the tythes both great and small of the same, with all and singular the rights, members, and appurtenances thereof, to the late dissolved priory or monastry of the blessed Virgin Mary, in Huntingdon aforesaid, heretofore belonging, or appertaining, and being sometime parcel of the possessions thereof.[47]

It is a document not without some interest and importance in Oliver Cromwell's life; not merely because it reveals the nature and extent of the possessions of his family, but in some measure his circumstances at the time. It was not all he owned; for it appears from other evidence that he retained possession of some nineteen acres of land in Stucklefield, in the parish of St. Bennet in Huntingdon, which, with the dove-cote, seems to have come to him from his uncle Richard who had died four years before. And it appears as well, that not only did he and his family dispose of their holdings in Huntingdon proper, but that his mother and his wife joined in the transfer to add their jointures to the other property which thus changed hands. Nor is this all the interest of this land transfer; for some twenty years later this property was conveyed by Mr. Oakeley to two members of the Cromwell-Williams family, one John Williams of Brampton and a Henry Williams described as of Lincoln's Inn; that thereafter it was transferred to Sir Sidney Montagu; and that as late as the end of the eighteenth century there was a small parcel of land in Godmanchester known as "Cromwell's Swath" and two acres in Portholme called "Cromwell's Acres."[48]

Such trifles remain to us, with the fact that his mother seems to have stayed on in Huntingdon for some years; but as to the far more important question of just why he made the change there is no direct evidence. It has been plausibly suggested that the circumstances of his last days in Huntingdon, his summons before the Privy Council, his quarrel with Bernard, his contest with the Exchequer, made his position uncomfortable. It has been further suggested that his cir-

[47] Printed in Noble, i, 103–104, from the original in the possession of the Earl of Sandwich.

[48] Noble, i, 104n.

cumstances were now strained, that the sale of his property, if not actually forced upon him, served to relieve him from financial embarrassment, and that it seemed on the whole desirable to move and begin life again under more favorable conditions.

Finally, and not improbably, it has been suggested that the disposal of his property may have been connected with a design of going to America. The tale of his proposed emigration to New England with Hampden, Haselrig, and others having been stopped by a Council order of May 1, 1638, as told by various authors and widely copied and believed, has been disproved.[49] But, as it has been pointed out, Lords Saye and Brooke, Pym and Hampden were interested in the movement which resulted in the foundation of Saybrook—named for Saye and Brooke—in Connecticut, and there is still a tradition there that Cromwell was not merely concerned in that project but went so far as to have foundations laid for a house to which he proposed to remove his family.[50]

If he had that project in mind, it was abandoned at least for the time, for with his wife and children he moved to St. Ives, rented land and entered on the life of a farmer and grazier. Nor is it without interest to note that this land was owned by a Henry Lawrence,[51] some time of Gray's Inn, two years his junior, who lived five miles down the river, and who some twenty years later when his new tenant had come to the headship of the state, came to be President of the Protector's Council and a member of his Upper House.

Such was the little drama played on the narrow stage of an obscure English country town by men as yet unknown beyond their neighborhood. It was set against a background of great movements and events which though they had as yet touched its characters lightly, were to become the dominating influence in their lives. For while Oliver had been absorbed in quarrels with his neighbors and the government, the world outside his circle had been profoundly changed. At the moment that Charles had dissolved his Parliament, the Emperor and the Danish king had come to an agreement by which the latter regained his lands at the price of his withdrawal from Germany and the abandonment of his Protestant allies. By an Edict of Restitution, all the ecclesiastical estates in the Empire which had changed hands during the struggle of the preceding years were restored. The Lutherans who adhered to the Augsburg Confession were allowed to exercise their religion in peace; but all other "sects" were left to the tender mercies of the Emperor's victorious general, Wallenstein, and the armies of

[49] Forster, *Life of Pym*, pp. 81–83.
[50] I am indebted to William B. Goodwin, Esq. of Hartford, Conn. for this story.
[51] *Victoria History of the County of Huntingdon*, ii, 218–219.

the Catholic League. For the time the Calvinists seemed lost and despite the antagonism between the League and Wallenstein, their cause and perhaps ultimately that of Protestantism in general, appeared all but desperate.

But at this moment that cause received new impetus. In July, 1630, the same month that Cromwell was made justice of the peace in Huntingdon,—and no two circumstances could well seem to have been more remote from each other nor more dissimilar in importance, —Gustavus II, Adolphus, "King of Sweden, of the Goths and Vandals, grand prince of Finland, and duke of Esthonia," led his Swedish legions to the rescue of the German Protestants, of his dispossessed kinsman, the Duke of Mecklenburg, and of his own position on the Baltic shores threatened by the Imperialist victories. For the next two years his warlike successes were the wonder of the world until his death at Lützen at the moment of victory over the Imperialists extinguished for the time being the hopes of the Protestants.

Nor was the heroic career of "the Star of the North" the only event of importance to the world of Protestantism, in which the English Puritans, and Cromwell among them, were becoming an increasingly powerful element. Their position was now reinforced by a new movement. In the very days that Charles dissolved his Parliament, on March 4, 1629, was confirmed a charter to the Governor and Company of Massachusetts Bay. Under its provisions the elements of a powerful combination for the settlement of the New World were brought together under the direction of a Puritan leader, John White of Dorchester. In August of that year twelve gentlemen met in Cambridge to pledge themselves to emigrate with their families if the charter and its administration could be transferred to the new settlement. That was arranged by the influence and the adroitness of their allies in the government, notably the Earl of Warwick and Sir Edwin Sandys, and in the summer of 1630 there began the greatest emigration which had as yet left English shores. It was a chosen company, not of adventurers, nor of religious fanatics. Its membership included many men of property and social position; among whom were, it was estimated, more than seventy graduates of the university of Cambridge. It soon outnumbered all other New England settlements, though these had grown remarkably in the few years just past. It formed not merely a colony but a commonwealth; it carried its charter with it; and so far was not merely outside the jurisdiction of the bishop of London but in a sense beyond even that of the crown itself. It spread its boundaries rapidly and widely in the ensuing years and secured once and for all the future of Puritan New England.

It was not alone. Following the granting of the Massachusetts Bay charter, another was issued to a group of "Adventurers" known as the Providence Company to colonize the "Islands of Providence,

Henrietta and the adjacent Islands" of the Bahama group. Among its members were not only the leaders of the Puritan party but many men closely connected with Cromwell. At its head was the Earl of Warwick and among its Adventurers were John Pym, John Hampden, Oliver St. John, Sir Gilbert Gerard, Sir Richard Knightley and Sir Nathaniel Rich, all relatives or colleagues of Cromwell, with others like Henry, Earl of Holland; William, Lord Saye and Sele; Robert, Lord Brooke, and Sir Benjamin Rudyerd, all Puritans and all at one time or another opposed to the crown and among them many interested in the foundation of Connecticut. Deriving their rights from the Council for New England, formed a dozen years before, under the lead of Warwick who more and more opposed the financial and ecclesiastical policy of the crown, the Puritan element found in this colonial enterprise not merely an outlet for the dissatisfaction with that policy in settling the New World with members of their party, but a means of organization in England itself. The biographer of Pym has not hesitated to place in the Providence Company the beginnings of that close-knit group at the center of the opposition to the crown in the ensuing Parliaments, in fact the nucleus of the revolutionary organization bent on the overthrow of Charles.[52] Whether or not we accept the doctrine that no revolution can take place without a more or less organized minority ready to make or seize an opportunity to oppose or overthrow a government, one thing seems evident. It is that there was in this group of men a nucleus about which opposition could crystallize and, under its leadership, offer an organized resistance to church and monarchy.

Whatever truth lies in his charge, two things seem certain. The one is that the members of this group were, in fact, the same men who were presently to lead the attack on personal government and the laws which made it possible and that Oliver Cromwell was in the midst of them. The second is that it is inconceivable that Cromwell did not know of this movement among the men with whom he was more and more closely associated. Nor is it improbable that, despite the lack of direct documentary evidence, he joined, or planned to join, in these activities which coincided so closely with his disposal of his Huntingdon property. That he considered moving to America we know; and no time seems more probable than this.

To such a resolution men like him were driven by the development of Charles's personal government and the activities of Laud. After the dissolution of the Parliament in 1629, Charles had become, in effect, his own chief minister. He was assisted not only by Weston, Noy and Coventry but by Archbishop Laud, who strove with all his

[52] Wade, *John Pym*. See my Chapter I of the *History of Massachusetts* (ed. A. B. Hart), and A. P. Newton, *Colonizing Activities of the English Puritans* (1914).

might to reduce the Church to order "being still of the opinion that unity cannot long continue in the church where uniformity is shut out at the church door." Finally and most of all he was advised by Wentworth, who on the death of Buckingham had become the right hand of the crown. Equally opposed to the rule of the rich and powerful and to government by waves of unregulated and undirected public opinion or emotion, that minister believed in a benevolent autocracy, and in that spirit exercised his great authority and talents in behalf of the peace and the prosperity of the people. Whatever may be thought of the principles which its rulers held, England seems to have been not ill governed in those early days of Charles's personal rule. Laws were enforced; distress relieved; "sturdy beggars" and vagabonds repressed; commerce encouraged and peace maintained with continental powers.

Whatever the grievances of men rich enough to feel the impositions of the crown; whatever the complaints of the unconstitutional actions of the government—and there had been no threat of doing away with Parliament—whatever the feelings of the Puritan minority, the first five years of Charles's personal government seem to have been in general neither unsuccessful nor unpopular. It was not only like contemporary administration on the continent but in most respects like that of the Tudors in the preceding century. It ruled by Tudor machinery to which the nation had long been accustomed. Headed by the great Privy Council, its Courts of Star Chamber, Exchequer, High Commission, its Councils, like the Council of the North where Wentworth held sway, were in fact and theory the conciliar form of government devised and administered in the preceding century. Nor was there anything extraordinary in the failure to summon Parliament. Many such periods of five years or more had seen no meeting of the two Houses, for there was as yet neither law nor custom which prescribed such meetings at regular intervals. If times had changed, if there was discontent, in default of Parliament there was at first but little general expression of the nation's grievances. So long as England was at peace, so long as the resources of the crown were not strained by unusual demands, there seemed no reason why this system should not endure for many years.

Only—and in this lay the great difference between Tudor and Stuart autocracy—the world had changed. The cause of Protestantism, of Puritanism in particular, had advanced with the years. Religion had been added to the "liberties of Englishmen," and the Puritans had increased in numbers, resources and audacity in proportion to the efforts of the Establishment to suppress them. Against their plea for religious liberty, that Establishment had set its principle of unity through uniformity. To this was added the hardening of the doctrine of royal supremacy into a dogma as Parliament had challenged royal authority more and more; till the opposing forces, no longer kept apart by Tudor tact and gift for compromise, stood face to face prepared to fight it out.

ST. IVES, 1631–1636

It was at this moment when English affairs hung in the balance that Oliver Cromwell entered on a new chapter of his life. The circumstances under which he moved to St. Ives were as commonplace as the existence which he led there for the next five years. Of that life there is but scanty and insignificant record, nor is that surprising. The daily existence of a cattle-grazier, however exacting and however important to himself, is of but little consequence to the world at large, nor does it find expression in many written documents. So he lived for some five years, a man almost without a history. This is more natural in that he was no longer the figure he had been in Huntingdon. He was no longer a freeholder, burgess and justice of the peace. He was the tenant of a rented farm; and if he had not precisely fallen in the social scale, if he was still entitled to be called "esquire" or "gentleman," he played no such part and occupied no such position as in the years just past.

The documents belonging to this period of Cromwell's life bear out this view of his altered status in the world. They are as insignificant as they are few. That he still retained his interest in Huntingdon, the Register of St. John's indicates with its brief and tragic entries of 1631–2.

> James, ye son of Oliver Cromwell, Esq., bapt. January viijth.
> James, the son of Oliver Cromwell, Esq. buryed January ye ixth.[53]

That he took his part in the petty affairs of local administration such as the election of keepers, supervisors or custodians of the "streete" and "greene" is evidenced by the parish records—but it is a far cry from them to the events in which he had played a part in Huntingdon and Westminster, and their character indicates his altered status in the world.

The xxijth day of Aprill, an^{o} Dom. 1633.

Memorand^{u} that (the day and year above-written) we the inhabitants of the towne of St. Ives cum Slepa, in the country of Huntingdon (together wth mr. Bell curate thereof) whose names are here underwritten, doe nominate and appoint and elect mr. Thomas Filby and John Ibbit for the streete, and Thomas Larke for the greene.

[53] Noble, i, 352.

Moreover we nominate and elect Robert Pitts, and Richard Perret, and Thomas Simnell, overseers of the high waies for the street of the towne aforesaid, and John Beale, for the sleap.

EDWARD BELL, curate as ibidem.
FRANCIS WOOD.
THOMAS CARTER.
JOHN PARNELL.
ROBERT INGRAM.
THOMAS TIMBS.
ROBERT R. PITTES.
WILLIAM MARRITT.
FRANCIS DORINGTON.
"Oliver Cromwell writes his name here, but it was cut out, supposedly by John Bentley, in 1732, the then church warden."
JOHN BINKMAN.
JAMES BAYLEY.
BENET MESEN.
HENRY PERRY.
ROBERT CORDELL.[54]

It is, perhaps, significant that Cromwell's name has moved up to first place in a similar record the following year:

The 7th of Aprill, anno Dom. 1634

Memorando, the daye and yeare above righten, we the inhabbin of St. Ives, cum Sleape, in the county of Huntingdon, together wth Mr. Downett,[55] vicare theire, whose names are herein under righten, doe nominate and appoint and elect Seackinge Boyden for the greene, William Merrett, & William Parnel for the streete.

Moreover, we nominat and electe John Johnson, William Chadbourne, for the street, & Thomas Field & Danell Golde, overseers for the heighwayes for the towne of St. Ives cume Sleape.

OLIVER CROMWELL.
HENRY PERRY.
THOMAS CARTERS.
JOHN ABBOT.
ROBERT INGRAM.
WILL^M^ SCARLE.
ROBERT CORDELLS.
JOHN FILBEY.
THOMAS COOLSTON.
FRANCIS WOOD.[56]

The birth and death of another son, a share in the election of petty local officers, seem a great contrast to a struggle over a borough charter, a seat in Parliament, and a conflict with royal authority and royal officials, but beyond these insignificant documents there is little evidence of his mode of life in St. Ives. Yet that evidence is of importance to an understanding of his character. It is told by Heath with his usual animosity:

"His estate still decaying," says the author of the *Flagellum*, "he betook himself to a Farm, being parcel of the Royalty of *St. Ives*, where he intended to Husband it, and try what could be done by endevour, since nothing (as

[54] Noble, i, 260, from a book kept at St. Ives for registering parish officers, etc. Facsimile in Clifford, *List of Books*, St. Ives, 1925. Noble's suggestion that Cromwell's name was written in and later cut out seems based only on oral tradition but not improbable.

[55] This is Downhall, to whom Cromwell wrote a letter in 1626.

[56] Noble, i, 261.

yet) succeeded by design; and accordingly took servants, and bought him all Utensils and Materials, as Ploughs, Carts &c, and the better to prosper his own and his Mens Labour, every morning before they stirred out, the Family was called together to prayers, at which Exercise very often, they continued so long, that it was nine of the Clock in the morning before they began their work; which aukward beginning of their Labour sorted with a very sorry Issue; for the effects of those prayers was, that the Hinds and Plowmen seeing this zeal of their Master, which dispensed with the profitable and most commodious part of the Day for their labour, thought they might borrow the other part for their pleasure; and therefore they commonly went to the plough with a pack of Cards in their Pockets, and having turned up two or three Furrows, set themselves down to game till dinner time; when they returned to the second part of their Devotion, and measured out a good part of the afternoon with Dinner and a repetition of some Market Lecture that had been preached the day before. And that little work that was done, was done so negligently and by halves that scarce half a Crop ever reared itself upon his Grounds; so that he was (after five years time) glad to abandon it, and get a friend of his to be the Tenant for the remainder of his time."[57]

It was at this time, Heath goes on to say, that:

"During his continuance here, he was grown (that is he pretended to be) so just, and of so scrupulous a Conscience, that having some years before won thirty pounds of one Mr. *Calton* at play, meeting him accidentally, he desired him to come home with him and to receive his money, telling him that he had got it by indirect and unlawful means, and that it would be a sin in him to detain it any longer; and did really pay the gentleman the said thirty pounds back again.

"Now was he therefore thinking of transporting himself and his family into *New England*, a receptacle of the *Puritan*, who flocked there amain, for Liberty of Conscience. But he indeed, for that his purse and credit were so exhausted that he could no longer stay there."[58]

So Heath, following the story of Carrington as to Mr. Calton, almost word for word, is echoed if not confirmed by the story of Sir Philip Warwick to the same effect[59] adding that: "When he was thus civilized, he joyned himselfe to men of his own temper, who pretended unto transports and revelations."

It seems fairly certain, at least, that Cromwell was deeply concerned with religious questions at this time. The only letter which has been preserved to us from the period of his residence in St. Ives relates to this side of his character; and it reveals not merely Cromwell's interest in what may be called missionary enterprise but that of the Puritans in general and the means taken by their increasingly

[57] *Flagellum* (1663), pp. 16–17. Heath neglects to mention here the real reason for Cromwell's removal from St. Ives, his inheritance in Ely.

[58] *Ibid.*, p. 17.

[59] Warwick, Sir Philip, *Memoirs of the reign of King Charles I* (1702), pp. 249–250. Cp. above, p. 38.

powerful organization to promote their cause. By means of collections in their congregations, by contributions from their wealthier members, particularly the most prosperous London merchants of Puritan leanings, there had been set up in many towns throughout England such "lectureships" as those of which Heath speaks so disparagingly. Whether in church or chapel or in public places, these "lecturers" or preachers or missionaries carried on their work in a fashion not unlike that of the Methodists a century later. They were a scandal to the orthodox then as thereafter; but then as thereafter they were a powerful agency among the people at large but little touched by more formal services. They were endured, even encouraged, by the Puritan clergy still within the church; they were supported vigorously by such men as Cromwell; and they contributed perhaps more than any other force to the movement then making head against the Establishment. It was on behalf of one of these that Cromwell wrote:

To my very loving Friend Mr. Storie, at the Sign of the Dog in the Royal Exchange, London: Deliver these.

MR. STORIE,

Among the catalogue of those good works which your fellow-citizens and our countrymen have done, this will not be reckoned for the least, that they have provided for the feeding of souls. Building of hospitals provides for men's bodies; to build material temples is judged a work of piety; but they that procure spiritual food, they that build up spiritual temples, they are the men truly charitable, truly pious. Such a work as this was your erecting the lecture in our country; in the which you placed Dr. Welles, a man for goodness and industry, and ability to do good every way, not short of any I know in England; and I am persuaded that, sithence his coming, the Lord hath by him wrought much good amongst us.

It only remains now that He who first moved you to this, put you forward to the continuance thereof: it was the Lord; and therefore to Him lift we up our hearts that He would perfect it. And surely, Mr. Storie, it were a piteous thing to see a lecture fall, in the hands of so many able and godly men as I am persuaded the founders of this are, in these times, wherein we see they are suppressed, with too much haste and violence by the enemies of God his truth. Far be it that so much guilt should stick to your hands, who live in a city so renowned for the clear shining light of the gospel. You know, Mr. Storie, to withdraw the pay is to let fall the lecture; for who goeth to warfare at his own cost? I beseech you therefore in the bowels of Christ Jesus put it forward, and let the good man have his pay. The souls of God his children will bless you for it; and so shall I; and ever rest,

Your loving Friend in the Lord,

OLIVER CROMWELL.

St. Ives,
January 11th, 1635.

[P.S.] Commend my hearty love to Mr. Busse, Mr. Bradly, and my other good friends. I would have written to Mr. Busse; but I was loath to trouble him with a long letter, and I feared I should not receive an answer from him. From you I expect one so soon as conveniently you may. *Vale.*[60]

Yet, however puritanical he may have been, all the evidence we have seems to prove that Cromwell was still within the circle of the Establishment. Apart from the continuance of the records of his family in St. John's, among the lesser traditions of that time which endured into the eighteenth century is Noble's story of the clerk of St. Ives, "a very intelligent old man," who said that he had heard from old people who had known Cromwell when he lived there, that he "usually frequented divine service at church, and that he generally wore a piece of red flannel round his neck, as he was subject to an inflammation of the throat,"[61] a not uncommon complaint in that watery region. This then, was the Cromwell of St. Ives.

The gossip and the documents tell the same story—that of a man "afflicted in mind, body and estate," as the Prayer Book says; somewhat depressed in worldly circumstance;[62] troubled about his health; still more troubled, as men are apt to be in such a situation, about his spiritual welfare; and in general ill at ease as to his own condition, the cause he had at heart, and that of the nation in general. It is small wonder that his thoughts turned to things of the spirit, still less that he looked back upon a past which, however spent, gave him small comfort, and sought consolation in religion.

It is, moreover, to this period there belongs a story whose details are obscure and known to us only from the accounts of his enemies. The case seems simple enough, yet there resides in it a mystery. Writing many years later, Sir William Dugdale relates it:

"By his exorbitances at last he so wasted his patrimony that, having attempted his uncle Steward for a supply of his wants, and finding that on a smooth way of application to him he could not prevail, he endeavoured by

[60] Sloane Mss, 2035b, fol. 5. Printed in Harris, *Life of Cromwell,* (1762), p. 12; Sanford, *Studies*, p. 244; Carlyle, Letter I. Dr. Samuel Wells became chaplain to the Earl of Essex's regiment of horse. On July 20, 1644, Essex wrote to the Treasurer of War asking him to pay Wells £10 on account; and again to the same effect in January, 1645, "he being at present in much want and necessity." (*Comm. Excheq. Papers, P. R. O.*) He received and receipted for the money; and Cromwell wrote in his favor. *See* January 17, 1644–5. This seems to be the only surviving letter with the seal described by Henfrey (*Numismata Cromwelliana*, p. 179) as Cromwell's "private seal no. I."

[61] Noble, i, 105n.

[62] Sir James Bourchier's will, drawn on Mar. 15 and probated Apr. 30, 1635, left his property of Little Stambridge Hall and in Much Stambridge to his four sons, Richard, James, William and Oliver, the two latter being minors. His daughter Elizabeth is not mentioned.

colour of law to lay hold of his estate, representing him as a person not able to govern it; but therein he failed."[63]

To this story Bishop Hacket in his *Memorial of the Life of Arch-Bishop Williams of York*, a distant relative of Oliver's, added, still later, that the archbishop warned Charles in 1645 against Cromwell as the most dangerous man in the kingdom, continuing:

"Your Majesty did him but justice in refusing his petition against Sir Thomas Steward of the Isle of Ely; but he takes them all for his enemies that would not let him undo his best friend."[64]

There was, it would seem, some dispute; but later biographers have made light of it, and have pointed out that, whatever the disagreement, the parties were reconciled and that Sir Thomas Steward actually left his property to his only nephew. That reconciliation Heath attributes to the Puritan clergy, relating it, after his scandalous fashion, to Cromwell's conversion:

"This appearance of such a Reformation," Heath goes on to say, "did effectually conduce to his present purpose; for these Reverend Divines, glad of the return of this Prodigal, made it their business to have him received and welcomed with the fatned Calf . . . and therefore severally and joyntly they dealt with Sir John [sic] Steward, his Uncle, . . . to take him into his favour; & did at last prevail so upon him that he declared him his Heir, and dying soon after, left him an Estate of Four or five hundred pounds a year. . . ."[65]

Whatever the circumstances, this much is true. Oliver's only maternal uncle, Sir Thomas Steward, who had married a certain Bridget Poole in 1592, had no children, and after his wife's death in January, 1636, executed a will on the twenty-ninth of that month by which he left the bulk of his estate to his nephew.

To summarize the will,[66] prolix as all such documents are, it appears that to his executor, Humphrey Steward, Sir Thomas left the manor of Vernes [Barnes?] and lands in Elm and Emneth, out of which were to be paid his debts and a few legacies. To his sister Elizabeth, Oliver's mother, he left an annuity of £30 a year; to his brother-in-law, Rowland Poole, an annuity of £10 a year. To his cousin Robert Orwell, to Orwell's wife, and to Oliver Cromwell's "eldest son" he gave £5 apiece; and to Humphrey Steward he gave £100. His cousin Arthur Needham, Austin Brograve, and the Ely workhouse were each to receive £20. The rest of the estate, chiefly

[63] Dugdale, *Short View* (1681), p. 459.

[64] Hacket, Bishop John, *Scrinia Reserata: A Memorial of the Life of John Williams, Archbishop of York* (Lond. 1693) ii, 212.

[65] *Flagellum* (1663), p. 14.

[66] In Probate Court Registry, Somerset House, London, 9 Pile.

leases from the Deans and Chapter of Ely, was left to Oliver. Its extent was considerable, both in amount and distribution. It included certain properties there specified as Chapman's Close and Tilekylne Close in Wichford, just west of the town field of Ely;[67] seven acres in Outwell in Norfolk;[68] Paradise Close on Newenham Street, Ely; the Rectory of the Holy Trinity,[69] the Chapel at Chestisham, the Sextry Barn and other houses and barns belonging to it and a pasture called the Mill Close, all in Ely; ninety acres of glebeland in the common fields of Ely; eight acres of pasture called Bishops or Pinfolds, in the Manor of Upwell in the Isle of Ely; and Barton in Ely with its houses, barns and lands.[70] It was, in all, a handsome, if somewhat complicated inheritance; for the transfer of which two documents remain. One is a parchment much worn and in places illegible, with the date gone.[71] Were it possible to decipher its dim and incomplete writing, some of the details of the property transfer might be made clear, for it has to do with a suit in chancery between Oliver Cromwell and Humphrey Steward, as executor of Sir Thomas. Those lands spoken of in the will as Elm and Emneth, the parcel out of which all special legacies and expenses were to be paid, is the property with which the suit was concerned, so it seems fairly certain that the suit was a result of the execution of the will.

The original of the other document, which may or may not have been a result of the chancery suit, has long since disappeared, but we have Noble's transcript:

Acquittance

For ten pounds given by the attorney-general Noy, and received of the executors of Sir Thomas Steward. June 7, 1636. [Signed by]

OLIVER CROMWELL.[72]

This, then, seems to have been the end of Cromwell's connection with St. Ives. What happened to his lease from Lawrence we do not know. It was either commuted for by Cromwell or more probably

[67] Cp. the renewal of this lease, (Oct. 29, 1638) on p. 100.

[68] A renewal of this lease includes other lands as well, see p. 97.

[69] Cp. the renewal of this lease (Oct. 20, 1638), on p. 99.

[70] Cromwell paid rent regularly until 1641, at least, on Ely Barton, Ely Fair, Ely Toll and Upwell. In 1641, "Mr. Cromwell pd to ye Archdeacon at Christmas quarter" according to a folio paper volume called "A Rentall of the Rents due to the Bpp of Ely," quoted in Gibbons, *Ely Episcopal Records* (1891), pp. 98–100n.

[71] Chancery Proceedings, 1626–1639, Bundle 399, Public Record Office. The document speaks of the "late" Sir Thomas Steward.

[72] Noble, i, 106–7. Carlyle, misquoting Noble because of the proximity of the figures "10 l," dates this June 10, and Sanford follows Carlyle.

taken over by some other tenant, as Heath suggests; for it nowhere appears from what small remnants of evidence we have that he continued with his grazing activities in St. Ives. Still less does it appear what happened to his investment there. It seems most probable that he gradually worked out of his commitments, sold or moved his stock and equipment and withdrew from that not too successful venture on the best terms he could. In any event the early months of 1636 saw the end of it and his entry into another field of residence and activity.

ELY, 1636–1639

With his removal to Ely in the spring or early summer of 1636 there began a period of comparative peace and greater prosperity in Cromwell's life. His fortunes restored by his uncle's generous legacy, he lost no time in establishing himself in his new home. By this reversal of fortune he was now again a man of property and position, the owner of a considerable estate, and evidently his uncle's successor as farmer of the tithes and lessee of cathedral properties. His house, according to later accounts, was that which his uncle had occupied, close to St. Mary's churchyard at the corner of the "Sextry Barn,"—a great square of offices and storehouses in which were gathered the payments in kind from the cathedral properties and which formed, the Ely people fondly believed, "the biggest barn in England but one." There, it seems, his sisters Elizabeth and Robina and his mother joined him later in this house where, as it happened, she had been born and in which the family was to live for some ten years.[73]

Almost at once there were some changes in that family. From the records of the parish church in Eltisley in Cambridge it appears that

Johes Disbrowe et Jane Cromwell connubio juncti fuerunt vicessimo tertio die Junij [*1636*].[74]

Nor is that entry unimportant in Cromwell's later life or even in English history. Younger son of the lord of the manor of Eltisley and with a law practice worth perhaps some seventy pounds a year, this John Disbrowe or Desborough was destined to follow his new brother-in-law's fortunes throughout life, to rise to be a major-general and a member of the Protectoral council in ensuing years.

Cromwell's improved position was reflected in another circumstance, for it was at this time, apparently, that he began to send his

[73] Noble, i, 106–7.
[74] *Ibid.*, 358.

boys to school. Influenced perhaps by the nearness of the Bourchier estate to Felsted in Essex, perhaps by the Barringtons, he sent his sons one by one to the Felsted Grammar School which, under the direction of a new master, Holbeach, was then rising to eminence. It had perhaps a hundred boys from every part of England; and under the patronage of the Rich family of the neighborhood drew its clientele chiefly from the Puritan element. With this Cromwell was increasingly identified and his connection with the group of which the Earl of Warwick and his son, Lord Rich, were members grew still closer.[75]

Thus in the shadow of the Establishment and partly in its service, he lived in such state as his means permitted and began to play an active part in the affairs of the community. Among them was one with which he became connected almost immediately, taking, it may be, his uncle's place. This was a philanthropic foundation known as Parsons' Charity, chartered some three years before his arrival in Ely. The board of governors, trustees or "feoffees" consisted of three members chosen from the cathedral authorities and nine citizens of Ely who formed a permanent and self-perpetuating group. To this body Cromwell was chosen on August 30, 1636,[76] and so was brought into close touch with the bishop, Francis White; the Dean, Dr. William Fuller; John Goodricke, Anthony Page, William Austin and others, with whom he presently had other relations. A few weeks later he signed a renewal of the lease for the house in which he lived, the barn, and other property:

Ely Rectorie to Oliver Cromwell Esqr for one & Twentie yeares.

This Indenture made the * and Twentieth day of October in the Twelfth yeare of the Raigne of our Sovereigne Lord Charles by the grace of God of England Scotland ffraunce & Ireland Defender of the faith etc. *Betweene* William ffuller Doctour of Divinitie Deane of the Cathedrall Church of the holie & undevided Trinitie of Ely, & the Chapter of the same place of the one partie. And Oliver Cromwell of Ely w^th^in the Isle of Ely & Countie of Cambridge Esqr of the other partie *Witnesseth* that the said Deane & Chapter with one assent & consent, Have demised graunted & to ferme letten & by these presents doe demise graunte & to ferme lett unto the said Oliver Cromwell *All* that the Rectorie of the holie Trinitie & the blessed Mary the Virgin of Ely within the Towne of Ely. And also the Chappell of Chetesham with all their rights & appertenaunces whatsoever within the said Isle of Ely in the said Countie of Cambridge. And one Barne Called the Sextrey Barne, & all houses, barnes, stables, & other edifices there built perteyning or belonging to the Grange called the Sextrey barne in thc same

[75] *Annals of Felsted School.*
[76] Noble, i, 107.
* Blank in MS.

towne of Ely. And one Close of land or pasture called the Mill Close wth the appertenaunces cont' by estimacion two acres, & fower score & Tenn acres of Gleabe land lyinge devidedly in the Common feild called Breewoodes, & in the other feilds of Ely aforesaid And all & all manner of Tythes of Corne & Haye, And all other Tythes oblacions profittes Commodities & emoluments whatsoever to the said Rectorie & Chappell or to eyther of them in anie wise belonging or apperteyning All & singuler wch premisses are scituate lying & being in Ely & Chetesham w^th^in the Isle aforesaid in the said Countie of Cambridge (except & alwayes reserved out of this present demise to the said Deane & Chapter & their successors) All & all manner of Tythes profitts & Commodities whatsoever belonging or apperteyning to the Chappell of Stuntney in the Countie aforesaid the Church yards belonging to both the Churches videlicet Trinitie & St. Maryes in Ely aforesaid And all Duties for Marriages Churchinges & burialls within the said parishes of Trinitie & St. Maryes in Ely aforesaid *To Have* & to hold the said Rectorie & Chapell & all & singuler the premisses before mencioned wth all their appurtenaunces (except before excepted) unto the said Oliver Cromwell his Executours administrators & assignes from the day of the date herof, during & untill the full end & terme of One & twentie yeares then next ensuing & from thenceforth to be fullie compleate & ended Yeilding & paying therfore yearly during the said terme to the said Deane & Chapter & their Successors or their certaine Atturney ffortie & eight pounds of good & lawfull monie of England And the Summe of Twentie pounds of like lawfull English monie at fower feasts in the yeare, that is to say, At the feast of the Nativitie of our Lord Jesus Christ, The annunciacion of the blessed Virgin Mary, The Nativitie of St John Baptist & St Michaell the Archangell by equall & even porcions. And also five quarters of the best wheate well & sufficientlie dressed & dight to be delivered at the feasts of the Nativitie of our Lord & of the annunciacion of the blessed Virgin Mary by equall & even porcions *And* if it happen the said Rent of fortie eight pounds, & the said summe of Twentie pounds, or the said five quarters of wheate to be behynd & not paid, & undelivered in part or in all in anie yeare during the said terme by the space of Thirtie dayes after anie of the said feasts at wch it ought to be paid and delivered Then the said Oliver Cromwell for hymselfe his executours administrators & assignes doth Covenaunte & agree to & with the said Deane & Chapter & their Successors by these presents to pay unto the said Deane & Chapter & their Successors (for everie such defaulte of payment) Twentie shillings sterlinge in the name of a payne or penaltie And that then it shalbe lawfull for the said Deane & Chapter & their Successors into the said Rectorie & Chappell with all & singuler their appertenaunces & everie parcell therof to enter & distreyne & the distresses soe taken to lease drive & carrie away & in their handes to retaine & keepe untill they be fullie satisfied & paid as well of the said rent of ffortie & eight pounds, & of the said summe of Twentie pounds & of the said five quarters of wheate together with the arreragies (if any shall be) as also of the said Twentie shillinges to them graunted in the name of a payne or penaltie, as is before mencioned. And if it happen the said rent or ferme of ffortie eight pounds, & the said Somme of Twentie pounds or the said five quarters of wheate or anie part thereof to be behynd in parte or in all & not paid by the space of three monthes after anie of the feasts aforesaid in wch it ought to be paid (being lawfullie demaunded) that then & from thence forth & at all tymes after it shalbe lawfull to the said Deane & Chapter, their successors or assignes into the said Rectorie & other the premisses with their appertenaunces to reenter, & the same to have againe & repossesse to them & their Successors as in their former estate. And the said Oliver Cromwell his executors administrators & assignes thereout wholie to expell & amove this Indenture or anie thinge therein conteyned to the contrarie therof in anie wise notwithstanding *And* the said Oliver Cromwell for hym selfe his executors administrators and assignes doth Covenaunte & graunte to & wth the said Deane & Chapter & their Successors by these presents that he the said Oliver Cromwell his executors administrators & assignes shall from tyme to time during the continuance of this presente lease or demise discharge and acquite the said Deane & Chapter & their Successors of & from all burthens as well ordinarie as extraordinarie (that is to witt) of & from all pencions porcions & other summes of monie whatsoever, yssuing or to be paid out of the said Rectorie and Chappell & other the premisses above by these presents demised or out of anie parte thereof. And shall from tyme to tyme during the continuance of this presente demise discharge & pay the yearlie Sallaries & Stipends of two Chaplains to be appointed by the Deane of the said Cathedrall Church for the time being during all the said terme wch doe or shall celebrate divine service & attend the Cure in the parochiall Churches of the holie Trinitie & blessed Mary the Virgin within the towne of Ely aforesaid And the said Oliver Cromwell for hymselfe his executors administrators & assigns doth covenaunt & graunte by these presents to & with the said Deane & Chapter & their Successors, that he the said Oliver Cromwell his executors administrators & assignes shall at his & their owne proper costs & charges during the continuance of this presente demise mainteyne susteine & reedifie the Chauncell of the Church of blessed Mary the Virgin in Ely, & all other edifices, walls & hedges & other reparacions to the said Rectorie belonging, as ofte as upon the veiw, & surveighe of the said Deane & Chapter & their Successors or of their Receivor for the time being, that shalbe by them thought expedient, & all the premisses soe sufficientlie repayred reedified & mainteyned shall leave & yield upp, at the expiracion of this presente demise. *And* that the said Oliver Cromwell his executors administrators or assignes yearlie at the feast of St. Luke the Evangelist during the said terme shall deliver unto the said Deane & Chapter & their Successors one good Bore or fortie shillings of lawfull English monie in liew of the said Bore at the eleccion of the said Deane & Chapter & their Successors. *And* also the said Oliver Cromwell his executors administrators & assignes shall make or cause to be made, One true Terrar of all the arrable lands pastures & meadowes to the said Rectorie & other the demised premisses perteyning within three yeares next after the beginning of this presente demise & the same faire written in parchment shall deliver to the said Deane & Chapter & their Successors or to their Receiver for the tyme being, And the said Oliver Cromwell his executors administrators & assignes the like Terrar within twelve yeares then next following during the said terme shall renew, & the same soe renewed to the aforesaid Deane & Chapter or to their Surveior for the time being or their Successors shall deliver as is aforesaid (if they shalbe therunto required by the said Deane & Chapter & their Successors or their Surveyor generall for the tyme being. *And* Further it is Covenaunted betweene the parties aforesaid by these presents That it shall not be lawfull for the said Oliver Cromwell his Executors administrators or assignes at anie tyme during the terme aforesaid to aliene or sell all their right or interest in the aforesaid Rectorie with all & singuler the appertenaunces to anie person or persons, except to such person or persons as shalbe sufficient honest & able to performe all & singuler the Covenaunts Condicions & payments in this Indenture specified & expressed. And that the foresaid Oliver Cromwell his executors administrators & assignes shall procure the same person or persons to whom such alienacion or sale of the premisses shalbe made to require & demaund of the said Deane & Chapter or their Successors that this Indenture of all & singuler the premisses may be for soe many of the said yeares as then shalbe unexpired at the time of such alienacion renewed & sealed in their owne names wch shall soe have & possesse the said Rectorie with all and singuler the appertenaunces *And* the said Deane & Chapter doth Covenaunte & graunte for them & their Successors by these presents to renewe & seale againe A new Indenture of demise of all & singuler the premisses with their appertenaunces (under such Condicions Covenaunts & payments as in this presente Indenture are specified & expressed for the terme of soe manie of the said yeares as shall then be unexpired to the use of the foresaid person or persons being sufficient honest & able as is aforesaid, So that the said person or persons doe then pay to the said Deane & Chapter & their Successors & Officers such ordinarie fees as others doe use to pay for writing ingrossing Sealing & Registring of the like *And* it is further Covenaunted betweene the parties aforesaid by these presents That the said Oliver Cromwell his executors administrators or assignes shall yearlie deliver unto the said Deane and Chapter of Ely and their Successors during the terme of this presente demise, Five Carte Loads of wheate straw, & five Carte Loads of Barley strawe, Att the feast dayes of All Sts, the Nativitie of our Lord & the Purificacion of the Virgin Mary by equall porcions to be delivered at the stables of the said Deane & Prebendaries within the precincte of the Colledge of Ely aforesaid being by them or their severall assignes lawfullie demaunded *In witnes* wherof to the one parte of these Indentures with the said Oliver Cromwell remayning the said Deane and Chapter have putte their Common Seale, & to the other parte therof with the said Deane and Chapter remayning the said Oliver Cromwell hath put to his Seale Dated at Ely in the Chapter house of the said Deane & Chapter the day & yeare first above written. Anno Domini 1636.[77]

This seems to be the first legal document connected with Cromwell's residence in Ely; but it was followed by others which, like it, reveal something of his life there. He still retained an interest and a connection in Huntingdon where, it would appear, his mother and sisters had continued to reside during his stay in St. Ives and for

[77] From the "Leiger Book" of the Dean and Chapter of Ely, No. 2 (1615 to 1639) ff. 94b–96a.

some months after his removal to Ely, for it was there another child was taken for christening, as the Register of St. John's records:

> Mary, the daughter of Oliver Cromwell, gent. bapt. the ix of February [1636–7].[78]

If he was present at the christening, he hurried back to Ely, as the minutes of the Feoffees of Parsons' Charity bear witness:

	l.	s.	d.[79]
Given to divers Poore People at ye Workhouse in the presence of Mr. Archdeacon of Ely, Mr. Oliver Cromwell, Mr. John Goodricke and other, 10th February, 1636[–7] as appeareth	16	14	0

Established with his mother, his two sisters, his wife and now seven children, busy with the affairs of his property and his office, with enough to absorb his energy, again it seemed that he was destined to live out a useful life in the comparative obscurity of a farmer and factor. His affairs tended to increase rather than to diminish. There are various entries relating to his activities in connection with Parsons' Charity; and on October 27, 1637 he was party to a lease which apparently had some relation to that foundation:

Lease

This Indenture made the Seaven & twentieth daie of October in the Thirteenth Yeare of the Reigne of our Soveraigne Lord Charles by the grace of God of England Scotland ffrance & Ireland King Defender of the faith etc. *Betweene* the Right wor^{pll} William ffuller D^{r} of Divinitie Deane of the Cathedrall Church of the holie & undivided Trinitie of Elie & the Chapter of the same place on the the one parte And the Right Reverend father in God ffrancis Lord Bi^{p} of Elie And William March of Ely in the Isle of Ely & Countie of Cambridge Esqr John Gooddericke Oliver Cromwell & Anthony Page of Elie aforesaid Esqrs Henry Gooddericke William Aunger John Hand William Crauford William Austen of Ely aforesaid gent on the other parte *Witnesseth* that the said Deane & Chapter with one assent & consent for them & their Successors Have demised granted & to farme letten & by these presentes doe demise grant & to farme lett unto the said ffrancis Lord Bi^{p} of Elie William March John Gooderick Oliver Cromwell Anthonie Page Henry Gooddericke William Aunger John Hand William Crauford & William Austen to & for such intents & purposes as are mencioned in one ffeoffement made to them bearing date the Sixt of January in the nynthe yeare of King Charles 1633 as by the same more at large appeareth All that their holte called Denvers Holte lying neere Stuntney the east head thereof abutteth upon A holte sometimes Sr John Dunham Chaplayne now Stephen Newcome

[78] Noble, i, 352.

[79] From *The Accompts of Mr. John Hand and Mr. Wm. Crauford*, in Ely; printed in Carlyle, App. 2. The old books are badly mutilated with many leaves cut out, says Carlyle, possibly for Oliver's autograph.

Clerke, the west head thereof abutteth toward the holte called Spiggot Holte, And abutteth toward the North upon the middle fenne Common & toward the South upon the Common of Stuntney To Have & to holde the said Holte with thappertinances unto the said ffrancis Lord Bi^{p} of Elie, William March, John Goodderické, Oliver Cromwell, Anthonie Page, Henry Goodericke, William Aunger, John Hand, William Crauford, & William Austen to the use aforesaid from the making hereof for and during the full end & terme of one and Twenty yeares thence next ensueing fully to be compleat & ended Yeelding & paying therefore yearely during all the said Terme to the said Deane & Chapter & their successors their certain Atturney or Receivir generall of the said Church for the time being At the Common hall of the said Deane & Chapter Called the Colledge Hall in Ely aforesaid the full & iust summe of Eleven shillings of lawfull English money At the feast of thannunciacion of our blessed Lady St Mary the virgin & St Michaell tharchangell by equall & even porcions *And* if it shall happen the said yearely Rent of Eleven shillings or any parte thereof to be behinde unpaid in parte or in all after eyther of the said feasts or daies of payment in which it ought to be paid by the space of Twentie daies (being lawfully demaunded) that then & from thence forth it shall & may be lawfull to the said Deane & Chapter or their Successors or certaine Atturney into the aforesaid Holte to reenter & the same to have againe & repossesse as in their former estate anything in these present Indentures conteyned to the contrary in any waies not withstanding *And* furthermore the said Lord Bp William March John Goodderické Oliver Cromwell Anthonie Page Henry Goodericke William Aunger John Hand William Crauford & William Austen doe Covenant & grant to & with the said Deane & Chapter & their successors by these presentes, that they shall from time to time during all their said terme sufficiently maintaine & keepe the said Holte with thappertinances inclosed with ditches, & plant the same with willowes, & the said Holte in the end of the terme aforesaid well & sufficientlie ditched & planted with willowes as aforesaid in as good state or better then the said Holte in the begining of their said terme is, at the end of the same shall leave the same And also the said Holte with the plantes willowes Oyziers & sallowes so often as need is shall ditch plant & scowre & so deliver the same up at the end of their said terme & all other things belonging to the said Holte as well for ditching as otherwise shall performe mainetaine & keepe during all the said terme *In witness* whereof as well the said Deane & Chapter their Common seale as the other said parties their seales to these Indentures interchangeably have sett: the day & yeare above written Aunnoque Domini 1637.[80]

ELY, 1638–1639

It was under these circumstances that Cromwell's life was passed during the first eight years of Charles's personal government. Unlike his residence in Huntingdon, his activities in St. Ives and Ely bore

[80] From the "Leiger Book" of the Dean and Chapter of Ely, No. 2 (1615 to 1639) f. 97.

but small relation or none to national affairs, but those affairs had moved fast and far in that period. With the death of Archbishop Abbot in 1633, Laud had been advanced to the headship of the English church, and at almost the same time Wentworth had landed in Ireland as Lord Deputy. Their appointments marked a turning-point in the great controversy then brewing in church and state. Laud's elevation, in particular, infuriated the Puritans. As part of their hatred of Catholicism, intensified by the long conflict with Spain, they had opposed with increasing violence all forms and practices of the Establishment which seemed to reflect Roman influence. Laud's activities, they believed, concealed a design to reintroduce Catholicism into England.

There was no ground for that belief; but the first acts of the administration served to further alienate the Puritans. Laud's efforts to suppress the lectureships and Charles's Declaration of Sports which, in opposition to "Puritans and precise people," "took order that . . . unlawful carriage should not be used by any of them hereafter in the prohibiting and unlawful punishing of our good people for using their lawful recreations and honest exercises upon Sundays and other Holy-days after the afternoon sermon or service,"[81] struck at the very heart of the Puritan sabbatarian convictions. When to these were added the act of the Privy Council against the placing of the communion-table according to ' the discretion of the parish, much less to the particular fancy of any humorous person," ordering it placed according to "the judgment of the ordinary" or church official, the worst suspicions of the Puritans were confirmed. Were these not enough, the activities of the Queen and of her favorite, Walter Montagu, the second son of the Earl of Manchester, who had embraced Catholicism and was an active agent of that faith, provided convincing evidence of the great design.

On his side, the new archbishop,[82] for the most part ignoring the theological dispute and rejecting the advances of Rome, directed all the force of his strong, orderly, legalistic mind to the rebuilding of the Church of England, its buildings, its services and its authority, especially the uniformity of its services according to the Book of Common Prayer. He believed that the firm, steady enforcement of uniformity would in time bring the Establishment into an ordered, "seemly" unity. Industrious, conscientious, determined, uncompromising, he was no "precisian," much less a "Puritan." He shared in that spirit of broader religious thought then current in the church and wholly compatible in the minds of its champions with strict ceremonialism. No less than ritualism, that Renaissance spirit was ana-

[81] Printed 1633. Text in *Sel. Docts.*, pp. 31 ff.

[82] For an account of Laud see his *Works*, his *Life* by W. H. Hutton, and the *Essays* of Canon Mozeley for the High Church position.

thema to the Calvinists. Though some among them loved the graces and amenities of life, though among them were many of the new rising school of "scientists," the greater number resented the "worldly" spirit of the Anglicans. They resented the "laxity" of Sabbath observance, dancing, plays, amusement in general, but especially the gayety which the young Queen had brought into the English court. And at almost the very moment that Laud and Wentworth entered on their new offices, a Presbyterian lawyer, William Prynne, devoted a thousand pages of vituperative adjectives culled from every tongue, ancient and modern, to the denunciation of those amateur theatricals with which the Queen and her followers amused themselves.

With this another element was injected into the argument. Prynne's *Histriomastix* was scarcely less a sign of the times than the appointments of Wentworth and of Laud. While Wentworth organized Irish administration and Laud the English church, the Puritan attack took form in a burst of pamphleteering which echoed the bitterness of the Martin Marprelate tracts of sixty years before. Like them it spurred the government to retaliate. Prynne's works were judged not merely a reflection on the Queen's character—which they were—but a reflection on that of a monarch who permitted what most men regarded as harmless little plays but Prynne interpreted as dissolute performances. He was haled before the Star Chamber, imprisoned, expelled from Lincoln's Inn, deprived of his Oxford degree, fined £5000 and sentenced to lose his ears in the pillory. The sentence was as severe as the language which inspired it and it was destined to have great consequence, for he took a terrible revenge on Laud whom he regarded as his chief enemy. At the moment that Cromwell moved to Ely, Prynne renewed his attacks.[83] He was joined by others, notably a Dr. John Bastwick and a clergyman, Burton, and on them, with Prynne, the vengeance of the outraged authorities was once more visited.

This incident hurt Charles's government even more perhaps than its exactions. Men recalled how Charles had refused Sir John Eliot's petition to be allowed liberty to go home to die, and even that of his family to bury him in his own churchyard. They remembered the King's cruel judgment, "Let Sir John Eliot be buried in the church of that parish where he died." They recalled the heavy penalties lately inflicted on Dr. Leighton for his attacks on prelacy. They adduced instances of the exercise of arbitrary power by the courts of Star Chamber, of High Commission, of the Marshal, of the councils of the North and of Wales and the Welsh border; and the stories lost nothing in their telling of the insults and injustices of their sentences, for the High Commission, at least, had been notably mild.[84] That

[83] *D. N. B.*; E. Williams, *William Prynne.*
[84] Cp. Gardiner, *History of England,* vol. x, App.

agitation strengthened the irritation of the nobility over the revival of old royal forest rights; of the gentry over the distraint of knighthood, which Cromwell had opposed; of the merchants over the revival of royal monopolies; of the City over the confiscation of their Ulster settlement and their fine for its mismanagement. It intensified their dislike of Laud's visitation of the church in 1635, and increased their fear of Wentworth's activities in Ireland which sought to extend royal authority there.

As yet they had no outlet for their discontent, and had it not been for another circumstance, despite its growing unpopularity, Charles's personal government might have found no effective opposition. That circumstance arose from those activities which since the peace with Spain had been largely in abeyance—foreign affairs. Under Richelieu France had in these years developed a powerful, centralized autocracy. The nobles and the Huguenots had been crushed, and France aspired to play a part in continental politics. For that the German war afforded an opportunity, and the Cardinal turned to the Swedes who after Gustavus's death and the assassination of the Emperor's great general Wallenstein, had dominated the central European stage. His purposes were less religious than political, and concerned England but little. But when he turned to colonial and commercial enterprise, and when Holland, having conquered her Spanish enemies, rose to the position of a first-rate naval power, Charles's government, confronted by this two-fold threat, felt itself driven to increase its strength on the sea.

For this money was needed, and, in default of Parliament, Noy drew on ancient precedent for ship-money levied on port towns to rebuild the English fleet. As part of their customary obligations, it roused but little protest there, but when at the same time that Laud conducted his visitation of the church it was extended to the inland towns and counties, it met resistance everywhere. Appealed to for construction of the law, the judges decided, rightly enough as the law stood, that "when the good and safety of the kingdom in general is concerned, and the kingdom in danger," the crown might exercise its powers to levy the new tax, and further that it "is the sole judge both of the danger and when and how the same is to be prevented and avoided." To this there was violent dissent, and just as Cromwell entered on the lease of Stuntney, there began the trial of his cousin, John Hampden,[85] for refusing to pay his assessment of twenty shillings ship-money levied on his property in Buckinghamshire.

With that trial, among its other results, Oliver Cromwell was

[85] H. R. Williamson *Life of Hampden*, (1933). Nugent's *Hampden* is now out of date. Goldwin Smith's *Essay* is an uncritical apology. The best accounts are the brief sketches by Firth in the *D. N. B.*, and by Gardiner in the *Encyc. Brit.* and in his *History*.

brought one step nearer to an active part in national affairs. For the time being that was far from evident, but he, like all men of his condition, was touched close by the great arguments which as the trial went on found their way throughout England. For Hampden there appeared Cromwell's other cousin, Oliver St. John, and his plea voiced the contention of Charles's opponents. Admitting that the king was "*Pater familiae*," whose "vigilance and watchfulness discovers who are our friends and foes and . . . he only hath power to make war and peace"; that the subject had no power to do anything without royal commission, that the King was the fountain of bounty, justice, in a sense of law and government, St. John argued none the less that these powers were exercised through and subject to the law. In effect he contended that "without assistance in Parliament, His Majesty cannot in many cases communicate either his justice or power unto his subjects"; and he concluded that even in this case of emergency the crown could not, "without consent in Parliament, alter the property of the subject's goods even for the defence of the realm."[86]

Against this Sir Robert Berkeley argued for the crown. Admitting in his turn that the King derived his power from the laws, that his subjects had an inalienable right to their property, and that laws could not be altered without consent of Parliament, he contended none the less, amid a mass of legal subtlety, that the law contemplated no "king-yoking policy." "I never heard," he said, that "*lex* was *Rex*, but it is common and most true that *Rex* is *lex*." "There are two maxims of the law of England," he went on, "the first is 'That the King is a person to be trusted with the state of the commonwealth.' The second is 'That the King cannot do wrong' . . . the King of mere right ought to have and the people of mere duty are bound to yield . . . supply for the defence of the kingdom . . . Parliament is the greatest, the most honourable and supreme court in the kingdom . . . yet it is but a *concilium*, the King may call it, prorogue it, dissolve it at his pleasure."[87]

These were the great fundamental arguments which made their way through England in 1638 as Cromwell was absorbed in the immediate concerns of his business and office; and however much he was concerned with the judgment passed against his kinsman, we lack much evidence that he took more interest in it than any other Englishman of his time. Whatever his feelings in regard to the activities of the government, he was absorbed in the management of his property, in his relations with the cathedral authorities, in the details of his family life. For the time being there is no hint of such concern for religion as he had showed in the years just past; there is no record

[86] Rushworth, ii, 481. Extract in Gardiner, *Const. Docts.*, 41–6.
[87] *State Trials*, iii, col. 1090. Extract in Gardiner, *Const. Docts.*, 46–54.

of ill health. The period of storm and stress seems to have passed; he was now secure and comfortable; and there is no proof that he suffered any longer that profound discouragement which had afflicted him. Whether it was due to his connection with the cathedral authorities; whether it was mere chance, or the improvement of his worldly circumstances, or his better health; whether his daily round of business absorbed his energies; or whether in the language of his sect he "had found peace"; there is no record of those spiritual strivings which had so greatly disturbed him earlier, though there is evidence that he was as active in Puritan concerns as ever.

Such testimony as we have seems to indicate that apart from the conduct of his business he concerned himself more and more in a cause which had not hitherto been conspicuous in his life, that is to say with what is called in general "the poor." It was expressed in his connection with Parsons' Charity, or "Ely Feoffees' Fund," as it was then called, by such undated entries in its accounts as:

Item to Jones, by Mr. Cromwell's consent . . . . £1–0–0[88]

It found further expression in a letter:

[*To Mr. Hand at Ely*]

MR. HAND,

I doubt not but I shall be as good as my word for your money. I desire you to deliver forty shillings of the Town money to this bearer to pay for the physic for Benson's cure. If the gentlemen will not allow it at the time of account, keep this note, and I will pay it out of my own purse. So I rest,

Your loving friend,

September 13th, 1638. OLIVER CROMWELL.[89]

It is apparent that he still took interest in national affairs and that his connection with the Puritan party grew closer. With his usual malicious exaggeration which has done so much to discredit his account, Heath describes Cromwell after his conversion:

"He was grown so cunning as to comply with those silent modes of Kindnesses and private conveyance of Friendships, which imported him a great deal more than he exported, for he was very much in the esteem of the best of the Faction.

"Nor did he omit any other duty or civility or Office of love to any, especially to those of the Household, as they then termed the people of the

[88] "The Disbursements of Mr. Crauford, 1636–1641" in the old Ely book quoted in Carlyle App. 2.

[89] Oliver Cromwell, (a descendant of the Protector), *Memoirs of the Protector*. Carlyle, App. 2, says this note is no longer among the Feoffees' papers at Ely, from which Cromwell's descendant printed it.

Separation; insomuch that he had scrued himself into the affections of many well-meaning people, whose assistance he obtained against his use for it in his election to the long Parliament. . . ."[90]

Besides which, Heath goes on to say, after Cromwell's remove to Ely,

"he more frequently and publickly owned himself a Teacher, and did preach in other mens as well as in his own house, according as the brotherhood agreed and appointed.[91]

Making every allowance for its animus, this seems in general what happened. Apart from its malice, there is nothing incredible in Heath's account, and it is not merely supported by such documents as this letter to Mr. Hand, but by another bit of testimony. His kinsman, Bishop Williams of Lincoln, then lived at the episcopal residence of Buckden near Huntingdon, and, according to his biographer Hacket, told Charles I in later years that Oliver was "a common spokesman for the sectaries and maintained their part with great stubbornness."[92] Were further evidence wanting, Cromwell himself supplied it with a letter to his cousin, Mrs. Oliver St. John:[93]

To my beloved Cousin Mrs. St. Johns, at Sir William Masham his House called Oates, in Essex: Present these

DEAR COUSIN,

I thankfully acknowledge your love in your kind remembrance of me upon this opportunity. Alas, you do too highly prize my lines, and my company. I may be ashamed to own your expressions, considering how unprofitable I am, and the mean improvement of my talent.

Yet to honour my God by declaring what He hath done for my soul, in this I am confident, and I will be so. Truly, then, this I find: That He giveth springs in a dry and barren wilderness where no water is. I live (you know where) in Mesheck, which they say signifies *Prolonging;* in Kedar, which signifieth *Blackness:* yet the Lord forsaketh me not. Though He do prolong, yet He will (I trust) bring me to His tabernacle, to His resting-

[90] *Flagellum*, (1672 ed. only), p. 23. The last paragraph is also in the earlier edition.

[91] *Ibid.*, (1672), p. 23–24.

[92] Hacket, *op. cit.*, ii, 212.

[93] We are forced to speculate as to which of his cousins this Mrs. St. John is because Oliver St. John married two of them. The date of the second marriage is uncertain but, although the first one was Joanna Altham, daughter of Cromwell's cousin, Lady Masham, by her first husband, and would therefore at first glance seem to be the one, the letter sends regards to the recipient's sister and, as far as we know, Joanna had no sister. The second Mrs. St. John was a daughter of Cromwell's uncle, Henry Cromwell, who died leaving his two daughters, aged 12 and 14, orphans. It is very likely that Lady Masham took in the two girls, who were also her cousins, and that it was at her house that Oliver St. John became acquainted with his second wife. Cromwell says "Salute all my good friends in that family whereof you are yet a member," which seems to indicate that her membership is not taken for granted.

place. My soul is with the congregation of the firstborn, my body rests in hope, and if here I may honour my God either by doing or by suffering, I shall be most glad.

Truly no poor creature hath more cause to put forth himself in the cause of his God than I. I have had plentiful wages beforehand, and I am sure I shall never earn the least mite. The Lord accept me in His Son, and give me to walk in the light, and give us to walk in the light, as He is the light. He it is that enlighteneth our blackness, our darkness. I dare not say, He hideth His face from me. He giveth me to see light in His light. One beam in a dark place hath exceeding much refreshment in it. Blessed be His name for shining upon so dark a heart as mine! You know what my manner of life hath been. Oh, I lived in and loved darkness, and hated the light. I was a chief, the chief of sinners. This is true; I hated godliness, yet God had mercy on me. O the riches of His mercy! Praise Him for me, pray for me, that He who hath begun a good work would perfect it to the day of Christ.

Salute all my good friends in that family whereof you are yet a member. I am much bound unto them for their love. I bless the Lord for them; and that my son, by their procurement, is so well. Let him have your prayers, your counsel; let me have them.

Salute your husband and sister from me. He is not a man of his word! He promised to write about Mr. Wrath of Epping; but as yet I received no letters. Put him in mind to do what with conveniency may be done for the poor cousin I did solicit him about.

Once more farewell. The Lord be with you; so prayeth

Your truly loving cousin,

Ely, OLIVER CROMWELL.
October 13th, 1638.

[P.S.] My wife's service and love presented to all her friends.[94]

That these activities and sentiments did not interfere with his worldly concerns, nor with his relation to the cathedral authorities, seems evident by two documents, executed a fortnight later, confirming to him the "farm" or lease of various cathedral properties:

Well Mullicourt cum aliis to Oliver Cromwell Esqr for xxi yeers.

This Indenture made the Nyne & Twentieth day of October in the yeare of the Reigne of our Soveraigne Lord Charles by the grace of God of England Scotland ffrance and Ireland King Defender of the faith etc. the foureteenth *Betweene* the right wor[pll] William ffuller Doctor of Divinitie Deane of the Cathedrall Church of the holy & undivided Trinitie of Ely and the Chapter of the same Church on the one partie And Oliver Cromwell of Ely

[94] Thurloe, *State Papers* (1742), i, 1. In the Birch Collection, 4292, f. 112, as calendared in Ayscough, *Cat.*, p. 808. A copy was in Mrs. Prescott's collection, no. 33, and is calendared in *Hist. MSS. Comm. Rept.* II, App. Carlyle, Letter II. Cp. Sanford's remarks in his *Studies*, pp. 221, 257.

within the Isle of Elie in the Countie of Cambridge Esqr on the other partie *Witnesseth* That the said Deane and Chapter for Diverse good causes & consideracions them thereunto moving Doe by these presentes for them & their Successors with one assent & consent Demise grant & to ffarme Let unto the said Oliver Cromwell and his assignes All that their Mannor in Outwell called Mullicourte house with the landes therunto belonging And the landes called Boxted alias Mullicourte Landes And also the Landes Tenementes & hereditamentes of the said Deane & Chapter, scituate Lying and being in Lynne, Downham Market Wisbich Leverington Newton Walsoken Emneth Elme Upwell Outwell March Doddington Wimblington Boughton & Wigenhall St Maries within the Isle & Countie aforesaid & in the Countie of Norffolk heretofore Demised or mencioned to be Demised by the then Deane and Chapter to Edward ffincham Esqr (except to the said Deane & Chapter & their Successors) All the parsonage & Pencion with thappertinances in Wisbich, their Mannor of Leverington with all such Landes thereunto belonging as sometime were in the tenure of Thomas Bendish Esqr And also their Rentes in Terrington, their Mannor in Murrowe and their Mannor and Parsonage in Fodeston, withall the ffreehold & Coppiholde belonging to all the aforesaid excepted Mannors & Parsonages with their appertinances And also except to the said Deane & Chapter & their Successors Thirtie six Acres which formerlie had beene surrendered by Robert Fincham gent. unto the said Deane & Chapter & their Successors And the Mannor of Tilney Fenne house formerlie granted by the then Deane & Chapter to Robert Russell gent, and Denvers holte in Stuntney. *To have* & to holde the said Mannor & all other the landes Tenements & hereditaments aforemencioned to be Demised with all & singular their appertinances (except before excepted) unto the said Oliver Cromwell his executors administrators & assignes for & during the tyme and terme of one and twentie yeares from the making hereof then next following fully to be compleat & ended *Yeelding* & paying therefore yearely during all the said terme to the said Deane & Chapter & their Successors or unto the Receivor generall of the said Church of Elie in or at the Common Hall of the said Deane & Chapter called the Colledge Hall in Elie above said At or upon the feast day of St Michaell Angell onlie Twentie poundes five shillings Eleaven pence of lawfull money of England *And* if it shall happen the said yearely Rent of Twentie poundes five shillings eleven pence to be behinde unpaid in all or in parte in any yeare after the feast in which it ought to be paid by the space of six weekes being lawfullie demaunded in the same Colledge Hall, then it shalbe lawfull for the said Deane & Chapter & their Successors or certaine Atturney into the premisses with the appertinances & every parte & parcell thereof to reenter & the same to reposses enioye & have againe as in their former estate right & interest And the said Oliver Cromwell & his assignes, clearely to expell or put out of the said Demised premisses anything in these present Indentures conteyned to the contrary not with standing *And* it is Covenanted granted & agreed betweene the said parties that the said Oliver Cromwell his executors administrators & assignes from time to time during all the said terme at his & their proper costs & charges shall repaire sustaine & maintaine or cause to be maintained & sustained the said demised premisses with the appertinances as well freeholde as Coppiholde as also all & singular fences to the same belonging with all other reparacions unto the same needfull & convenient And in the end of their terme soe sufficientlie repayred fenced and maintained shall leave & yeeld upp the same *And* also the said Oliver Cromwell for himselfe his executors administrators & assignes Covenanteth & granted to & with the said Deane & Chapter & their Successors to discharge the said Deane & Chapter & their Successors of all charges in the Countrie & other charges arising & growing by reason of the said Landes *And* further the said Deane & Chapter for them & their Successors doe Covenant & grant by these presentes to & with the said Oliver Cromwell his executors administrators & assignes That it shalbe lawfull for the said Oliver Cromwell his executors administrators & assignes to sue & implead all manner of persons which shall withholde anie of the rentes due unto the said Deane & Chapter & their Successors for any of the premisses *And* also the said Deane & Chapter for them & their Successors doe ordaine & assigne appoint & authorise that the same Oliver Cromwell his executors administrators & assignes shall & may lawfully at any time hereafter during all the continuance of this present demise sue implead & prosecute any manner of accion in Lawe to execute any Lawfull entrie recoverie or seisure in the name of the said Deane & Chapter to the only use & behoofe of him the said Oliver Cromwell & his assignes against any of the tenauntes ffarmers occupiers & possessors of the said Landes & Tenementes or any parte or parcell thereof against the executors administrators or assignes of them or any of them, for the breach or not performing or not payment of any Covenantes grantes Articles rentes paymentes condicions or agreementes which of any of the parties of the said Tenauntes farmers & occupiers or possessors are or ought to be observed performed fulfilled paid done or accomplished by vertue of any writing made betweene the said Deane & Chapter & the said Tenauntes farmers occupiers or possessors, and after any such lawfull entrie recoverie or seisure of & in any of the said landes & tenementes to be had & made by the said Oliver Cromwell his executors administrators & assignes to have & enioye the same to the said Oliver Cromwell his executors administrators & assignes during all the terme hereby demised & then next ensueing & unexpired yeelding doeing paying & performing to the said Deane & Chapter & their Successors all & every such the same rentes Covenants grants articles & agreements onlie as be heretofore rehearsed expressed & declared & none other. *And* the same Oliver Cromwell & his assignes shall make or cause to be made a true & perfect Terrar of all the houses landes tenementes & hereditamentes belonging to the said Mannor with the true buttalls of all the Landes before mencioned within three yeares next after the comencement of this present Lease. And shall deliver or cause to be delivered the same ingrossed in parchment to the Deane or Receivor generall of the said Church for the time being. *Provided* alwaies that the said Oliver Cromwell his executors nor assignes shall not sell nor alienate this Indenture of Lease with his interest of & in the premisses with out the leave & lysence of the said Deane & Chapter first had & obteyned *In witness* whereof as well the said Deane & Chapter as the said Oliver Cromwell have interchangeablie set their seales the day & yeare first above written Annoque Domini 1638.[95]

[95] From the "Leiger Book" of the Dean and Chapter of Ely, No. 2, (1615 to 1639) ff. 100b–101a.

Beele Closes to Oliver Cromwell, Esqr for one & Twentie yeares.

This Indenture made the Nyne & twentieth day of October in the fowertenth yeare of the Raigne of our Sovereigne Lord Charles by the grace of God of England Scotland ffrance & Ireland King Defender of the faith etc. Betweene the Right worp[ll] William ffuller Dr in Divinitie Deane of the Cathedrall Church of the holie & undevided Trinitie of Ely and the Chapter of the same on the one partie, And Oliver Cromwell of Ely within the Isle of Ely in the Countie of Cambridge Esq[r] on the other partie *Witnesseth* that the said Deane & Chapter have demised graunted & to ferme letten & by these presents for them & their successors doe demise graunte & to fferme lett unto the said Oliver Cromwell, Their two closes lying within the bounds of Witchford, The one called Chapmans Close, & the other called Tyle Kilnes Close, betweene Beele on the Weste parte, & the towne feild of Ely called Debden feild on the east parte, as they be inclosed with hedges & ditches their (except & alwaies reserved unto the said Deane & Chapter and their Successors All Ashes, Oakes & Elmes growing in or about anie of the said Closes) *To have* and to hold the said Two closes with thappertenaunces (except before excepted) to the said Oliver Cromwell his Executors administrators & assignes from the day of the date hereof during & untill the full end & terme of One & twentie yeares then next ensuing & from thenceforth to be Compleate & ended. *Yielding & Payinge* therfore Yearlie during the said terme unto the said Deane & Chapter & their Successors to their generall Receivor for the tyme being or to their certeine Attorney, Att the Cathedrall Church of Ely aforesaid, ffyftie shillings & eight pence of lawfull money of England Att the feasts of thannunciacion of the blessed Virgin Mary & Ste Michael tharchangell by even porcions *And* if it shall happen the said yearlie Rent or anie parte thereof to be behynd unpaid to the said Deane & Chapter or their Successors or to the Receivor generall for the tyme being by the space of Thirtie dayes next and ymmediatelie following anie of the dayes & termes aforesaid during the said terme when it ought to be paid, then the said Oliver Cromwell for hym his executors and assignes Covenaunteth & graunteth to & With the said Deane & Chapter and their Successors by these presentes to Content & paye unto them for everie such defaulte Twentie shillings of lawfull monie of England (*Nomine pene*) over & above the said yearlie rent & ferme above reserved, & that for defaulte of payment of the said yearlie rent of Twentie shillings of lawfull monie of England graunted (Nomine pene) it shalbe lawfull to the said Deane & Chapter & to their Successors or to their certeine Atturney to enter into everie & singular the said demised Closes, & there to distreyne, & the distresse there founde from thence to chase leade drive & carrie away, & it to deteine untill they be fullie satisfied & paid as well of the said rent & arreragies thereof, as of the said penaltie of twentie shillings. *And* if it happen the said yearlie rent to be behynde & unpaid to the said Deane & Chapter & to their Successors by the space of three score dayes next & ymmediatelie following anie of the dayes & termes aforesaid during the said terme (being lawfullie required) that then or at any tyme after, it shalbe lawfull to the said Deane & Chapter & to their Successors to reenter into the said demised Closes & the same to have, hold, repossesse & retaine as in their former estate anie thinge in these presente Indentures to the contrarie notwithstanding. *Also* the said Oliver Cromwell for hym his executors & assignes doth Covenaunte & graunte to & with the said Deane & Chapter & their Successors to pay and deliver to them & their Successors or to their Receivor generall for the tyme being or to their certaine Attorney, One fatt Calfe or Six shillings eight pence of lawfull monie of England everie yeare at the feast of Easter during all the said terme at the eleccion of the said Deane & Chapter & their Successors And the said Oliver Cromwell his executors & assignes shall make & skower all manner of Hedges & Ditches about the said Closes & everie of them at his and their owne proper costs & charges during all the said terme & in the end of the same well & sufficientlie hedged ditched & skowred to the said Deane & Chapter & their Successors shall leave & yield upp the same. *Furthermore* it is Covenaunted betweene the said parties, That the said Oliver Cromwell his executors & assignes may cutt lopp & shredd in seasonable tymes All manner of willowes thornes & maple growing within and about the said two Closes at all times during the said terme with out anie lett or interruption of the said Deane & Chapter or their Successors or anie other in their names, & that to be bestowed onelie upon the fencing & hedging of the said Closes. *Provided* alwaies that the said Oliver Cromwell his Executors administrators or assignes shall not sell or alienate this Indenture of Lease with his interest of & in the premisses without the expresse consent of the said Deane & Chapter for the tyme being *In witnes* whereof to the one parte of these Indentures with the Deane & Chapter remayninge, The said Oliver Cromwell hath putte his Seale, And to the other parte therof with the said Oliver Cromwell remayning. The said Deane & Chapter have putte their Common Seale. Dated at Ely in the Chapter house of the said Deane & Chapter the day & yeare first above written. Annoque Domini 1638.[96]

Such was the last of the legal arrangements by which Cromwell replaced his uncle as lessee of the Cathedral properties and settled himself and his family in his uncle's place; and to complete the family record it may be noted that some five or six weeks after these transactions, the parish register of the church of St. Mary's in Ely notes among its list of baptizings:

Frances ye daught. of Oliver Cromwell & Elizabeth his wife, december 6 [1638].[97]

With the birth of this, his last child, the Cromwell family was complete. There were now four sons; Robert, seventeen; Oliver, fifteen; Richard, twelve; and Henry, ten; and four daughters—Bridget, aged fourteen; Elizabeth, nine; Mary, a year and a half; and now Frances; the boys now being sent to Felsted school, the girls remaining at home.

[96] From the "Leiger Book" of the Dean and Chapter of Ely, no. 2 (1615–1639), ff. 103a–104b.

[97] Noble, i, 359.

THE FEN DISPUTE, 1638–1639

Amid the activities arising from cathedral business, his own personal concerns, his increasing interest in the Puritans and the poor, it was at this moment that Cromwell entered on another conflict with authority, of some importance to his later life. This was the project of the draining of the fens which was a leading interest of his time and neighborhood. It was a long-standing problem of the eastern counties, especially of the Isle of Ely. From Roman times the low-lying lands of that region had been annually overflowed by its slow-moving rivers. This was a source of much concern, especially to those who saw in the prospect of drainage and dykes the possibilities of greatly increasing the area of arable and pasture lands and incidentally their own fortunes. In 1601 the government had taken the matter in hand; and despite the opposition of the fen-dwellers and others who, like the people of Cambridge, felt their interests threatened by this system of flood control, the work was pushed forward in the reign of James.

The Cromwell family was interested in this great enterprise and in general favored it.[98] But among its opponents Sir Thomas Steward had been conspicuous in his championship not only of those whose lands were adversely affected by the scheme, but of the fen-dwellers and "poor commoners" who wrung a scanty livelihood from the waste and swamps. The failure of the plan of the Dutch engineer, Vermuyden, who had been brought over to superintend the work had strengthened the opposition to the whole design which fell for a time in disrepute. But with Charles's accession it was revived by "Adventurers" among whom the Earl of Bedford who had extensive possessions in the Fens, and Sir Miles Sandys, were conspicuous, reinforced in time by various stockholders of whom Oliver St. John was one. Of the 360,000 acres to be drained, 95,000 were to be awarded to the Adventurers on completion of the drainage, and they in turn were to convey 12,000 acres to the King and set aside 40,000 as security for upkeep. The work went on for three years until, in 1637, it was adjudged completed and it remained only to parcel it out among the shareholders and Adventurers.

With that disputes began among the new proprietors; the neighboring landholders, many of whom claimed their land was seldom inundated and therefore had objected to the arrangement in the first place; the fen-dwellers now threatened with dispossession; and even

[98] Cromwell's father and his uncle Oliver were Commissioners of Sewers with the eighty-eight appointed in 1604. *C. S. P. Dom.* (Addenda 1580–1625), p. 445; Dugdale, *History of the Fens*, (2nd ed. 1772) p. 379.

among the Adventurers themselves. By the summer of 1638 the crisis was acute. In June mobs began to gather to break down the enclosures and peace was preserved with difficulty.[99] An undated statement preserved in the Record Office mentions crowds of men and women armed with scythes and pitchforks and goes on to say that it was

"commonly reported by the commoners in Ely Fens adjoining that Mr. Cromwell of Ely had undertaken, they paying him a groat for every cow they had upon common, to hold the drainers in suit for five years and in the meantime they should enjoy every foot of their common."[100]

Cromwell had apparently taken up the cause of the fen-dwellers where his uncle Sir Thomas Steward left off. Sir Thomas had been complained of to the Privy Council twenty years before because of his activity against the drainage which was then being done,[101] and what was then his interest became his nephew's. Whether that interest was selfish, because possibly their land would not benefit by drainage or whether they were unselfishly championing the poor commoners, Sir Thomas Steward and Oliver Cromwell led the opposition in Ely to the great project. The Earl of Bedford succeeded in pleasing no one. The Adventurers felt that they had been treated unfairly; the local landowners objected to contributing to a scheme which increased the value of their property little if at all, if it had not actually injured them; Vermuyden was offended because he had not been employed by the Adventurers, although until it became evident that public opinion was opposed to him, the Earl of Bedford had intended to use his services.

Finally the King, having heard all these complaints and being persuaded by Vermuyden that it would be profitable to him to take the whole project into his own hands, undertook it in behalf of the crown in return for an additional 57,000 acres and chose Vermuyden[102] as his engineer, despite his previous failures and adverse expert opinion. To this Cromwell was as much opposed as he had been previously

[99] *Cal. S. P. Dom.* (1637), 447, 503; (1638–9), p. 301.

[100] *Ibid.*, (1631–3), p. 501.

[101] He had apparently gone before a meeting of the Commissioners of Sewers and had been instrumental in reducing the proportion of land to be given to the drainers from 1/2 to 1/40. Sir Miles Sandys complained that he had infused fears into the people and courted popularity and that bonfires had been lit for joy at his return. Sir Henry Montagu, Lord Chief Justice, sent an opinion to the Council favorable to Sir Thomas. *Cal. S. P. Dom.* (1619–1623), p. 96.

[102] Vermuyden had been hired in 1622 but within a year complaints had begun to come in to the effect that the land was in worse condition than before. The Commissioners of Sewers had agreed that the loss of landowners was great and the drainage was generally considered to be a dismal failure. Smiles, *Lives of Engineers*, i, 56, observes that "one of the principal labours of modern engineers has been to rectify the errors of Vermuyden and his followers."

to the projects of the Adventurers, and, in the words of Sir William Dugdale, he

"was especially made choice of by those who ever endeavored the undermining of Regal authority, to be their Orator at Huntingdon, unto the . . . King's Commissioners of Sewers there, in opposition to His Majesty's most commendable design."[103]

Whatever his motives and whatever his connection with the opposition to the royal plans, with this incident Cromwell re-entered public affairs. As the champion of the local landowners and the poor commoners, he seems to have gained a following which led his opponents in later years to dub him contemptuously "The Lord of the Fens."

THE FIRST BISHOPS' WAR, 1638

In the midst of this dispute while he was busy with lesser concerns of his own neighborhood, affairs in the world outside had come to another crisis. The war in Germany, indeed, after the heroic episode of Gustavus's invasion and death, and the romantic tragedy of the rise and fall of his great antagonist Wallenstein, had lost much of its dramatic interest. France under Richelieu and Sweden under Oxenstierna had pursued their national ambitions as religious elements gave way to politics. But what the continental struggle lost, the British Isles soon gained as a center of strife. The three years of Cromwell's residence in Ely saw the quarrel between Charles and his subjects grow more and more acute, and at the moment that the fen dispute came to a head, it was overshadowed by a greater struggle.

The causes and the circumstances of that quarrel are among the best known episodes of English history. The raising of money by unparliamentary taxation and the efforts to enforce uniformity in the church combined to rouse the animosity of both Puritans and men of property. The coincidence of Laud's visitation of the church, of Hampden's ship-money case and the punishment of Prynne, Bastwick and Burton, the suspension and imprisonment of Bishop Williams for favoring moderation toward the Puritans, the discontent of the City of London with royal policies and exactions, the favor shown to Roman Catholics, and the activities of Wentworth in Ireland magnified by distance and rumor, united to produce what later ages called a "revolutionary atmosphere."

Whether or not that would have caused an explosion in England without some impulse from outside, it was at this moment that Charles lit the spark which set his realm in flame. It came from the

[103] Dugdale, *Short View*, p. 460.

effort to impose not only bishops but the Prayer Book on Scotland. In June 1637 Prynne, Bastwick and Burton had been pilloried; in November Hampden's ship-money case had been brought to trial, and five months later judgment was given against him; and while all England was filled with protest, Scotland had acted. In July 1637, a riot broke out on the attempt of the Dean of Edinburgh cathedral to read the service from the new Scottish Prayer Book. As if it were a signal, all Presbyterian Scotland hastened to sign a Covenant. "We believe with our hearts, confess with our mouths, subscribe with our hands and constantly affirm," so it began, "that this is the only true Christian faith and religion pleasing to God and bringing salvation to man . . . received, believed and defended by many and sundry notable kirks and realms but chiefly by the Kirk of Scotland . . . as God's eternal truth and only ground of our salvation." And it concluded, "we promise and swear by the great name of the Lord our God to continue in the profession and obedience of the aforesaid religion, that we shall defend the same and resist all contrary errors and corruptions according to our vocation and to the utmost of that power that God hath put into our hands all the days of our life."[104]

Such was the fierce, proud answer of the Scotch Presbyterians to Laud's attempt to extend episcopacy to that kingdom. In that spirit nobles, clergy and commoners hastened to sign the Covenant; while four committees, or "Tables," virtually assumed control of government; and began to arm. It was in vain that Charles endeavored to calm the storm by revoking the Prayer Book, offering to limit episcopal authority and abandon the Laudian policy.

The King's position in July, 1638 was extremely difficult. It was imperative to fortify Berwick, Carlisle and other northern towns, and raise a navy which could blockade Scotland, if his northern kingdom was to be forced to surrender. He had only £200 in his exchequer and the amount which he could borrow would fall far short of equipping an army and a navy. It was, moreover, extremely doubtful whether the English people, irritated by the Ship-money case and the Laudian visitations, would rally to his aid rather than to that of the Scots.

There is no direct documentary evidence of Cromwell's position at this time, but there is one curious information laid before the government which involves the Cromwell name. It appears that in August, 1638, one Captain Napier, a Scottish gentleman who had been in London some months, called at the lodging of a Mrs. Cromwell on behalf of his sick wife and disclosed to Dr. Edward May a plot for 40,000 English to bring in 300,000 Scotch, all well armed. He made dark allusions to Laud and the joining of English and Scotch to have

[104] Rushworth, ii, 734. Quoted in Gardiner *Const. Docts.*, 54–64.

a parliament, about which business he was supposed to be engaged. To the statement,[105] endorsed by Laud "Concerning the plot between English and Scottish in this business," Dr. May, a Mrs. Cromwell, a neighbor, Mrs. Southcott, and also "Mr. Cromwell" sign themselves as witnesses to the treasonable speeches. It is interesting to note that Mrs. Cromwell, in the words of the information, "lies at one Mr. Stewart's house in Drury Lane;" and it may be recalled that Oliver's mother was a Steward and that he lodged his family in Drury Lane in 1647, their first year in London. It further appears that Captain Napier was well acquainted with Bishop Williams of Lincoln,[106] whom Cromwell claimed as a kinsman.

This curious story, whether or not it relates to any of Cromwell's family, is characteristic of the situation of affairs at this moment in the two kingdoms. The Scots had all but declared their independence by the end of 1638, since the Glasgow Assembly of clergy and nobility, refusing to disband, became in effect a national government, deposing the bishops and establishing Presbyterianism as the national form of faith. Its leaders gathered forces and summoned Alexander Leslie, sometime high in the service of Gustavus Adolphus, to the command of the Covenanting army. To his standard flocked his old companions now returned or returning from the German wars and he soon found himself at the head of more than twenty thousand men, for the most part well-equipped, well-disciplined and with experience in war.

It was a challenge which Charles could not ignore. He called on the lord-lieutenants for levies of men and money; he demanded a "voluntary" loan from men of property; and in the spring of 1639 he led his ill-equipped and ill-disciplined troops to meet the Scots in the first "Bishops' War." It was a hopeless enterprise from the first. He had opposed to him not only Leslie's army but influential English elements which looked on the Scots as their saviors. Merchants, Puritans, nobles, gentry, men of property, even the common people, united against the government. Nor was the hatred of the Courts of Star Chamber and of High Commission the only ground of their reluctance to support the monarchy. They were afraid of the activities of Wentworth in Ireland. That able administrator, besides reducing the island to peace, and giving it a certain amount of prosperity, had overawed nobles and Parliament alike, and had begun to gather an army to support royal authority, men feared, not only in Ireland itself but in England as well. He advised Charles not to attack the Scots and suffer certain defeat. He even offered presently to bring troops from Ireland to "subdue this Kingdom"—a fatal phrase which,

105 *St. P. Dom.* cccxcvii, 26, 27; *Calendar* (1637–38), pp. 591–2.
106 *Ibid.*, ccclxxii, 78; *Calendar*, p. 21.

betrayed by his enemies the Vanes, was interpreted to mean not Scotland but England, and was to prove his undoing.[107]

The mere suggestion of sending help from Ireland revealed the weakness of the royal cause, and Charles bowed to the inevitable. The Treaty of Berwick which he signed with the Scots authorized an assembly to administer church affairs and a parliament for affairs political. The first lost no time in abolishing episcopacy; the second proposed constitutional changes which would have weakened or destroyed royal authority in Scotland. At the same moment Charles's foreign policy broke down and it appeared that nothing could stop the French advance in Germany. He turned to a project of a Spanish alliance; he summoned Wentworth from Ireland; but nothing availed to evade the demand for a Parliament. Wentworth urged it; the other councillors agreed; and Charles was presently driven to issue writs for an election in the early months of 1640.

In all of this Cromwell had, naturally, no share. He was concerned with another matter of sad consequence. At the moment that the English forces gathered against the Scots, among the entries for the year 1639, the parish register of Felsted church records:

"*Robertus Cromwell, filius honorandi viri Mri Oliveris Cromwell et Elizabethe uxoris ejus sepultus fuit 31mo die Maii: iste Robertus fuit eximie spei juvenis deumque timens supra multos.*"[108]

It was the first breach in the Cromwell household as it was constituted at this time; and it was perhaps fortunate that the father was absorbed in the grave dangers which menaced the country. Those dangers had increased; and only in this new Parliament could men see any hope of betterment.

THE SHORT PARLIAMENT, APRIL 13–MAY 5, 1640

With the election to the new Parliament Cromwell re-entered national politics, nor was there any question which side he would take. However biassed, there is evidence that he, like his party, looked to Scotland for relief, to which Heath offers his testimony:

"He was a great stickler likewise against Ship-money, in which danger his great friend and Patron Mr. *Hampden* was so far embarqued; nor was he

107 For a full account of Strafford, see Lady Burghclere, *Strafford,* especially ii, 233 ff. For Vane see Willcock, *Sir Henry Vane, the Younger.*

108 Due to an earlier misreading of "Mtis" (Militis) for "Mri" (Magistri) until Mrs. Lomas discovered the error, attempts were made to prove that this was Sir Oliver's son. But his sons by his first wife Elizabeth were grown men at this time and there is no Robert among them. Lomas-Carlyle, i, 42n.

better affected to the *Scotch* War, then growing on, as he to his hazard discovered himself to some chief Commanders of the *English* Army, who in their march against the Scots quartered at his house; which Discourses drawing suspicion upon him, made him the more popular in those parts which were generally infected with Puritanisme."[109]

It is evident that by this time Cromwell was not merely a member of the "popular" party, but was in touch with its leaders, Hampden, St. John, Pym, the Rich's, and many more besides, and as such he made his next appearance in public affairs as a candidate for Parliament for the city of Cambridge. The grounds of his immediate connection with that constituency are somewhat obscure, but there probably lurks some truth in Heath's account, however deficient it is in details and in sympathy:

"Whilst he continued here [in Ely] there were discourses of new Writs issuing out for the Parliament in 1640, and about the same time or a little before, it was the hap of one Richard Tyms, since Alderman of Cambridge, and a man generally known throughout all the late times, having sate in all the *Juncto's* thereof to be at a Conventicle (as he usually every Sunday rode to the Isle of *Ely* to that purpose, having a brother who entertained them in his course) where he heard this *Oliver*, with such admiration, that he thought there was not such a precious man in the Nation; and took such a liking to him, that from that time he did nothing but ruminate and meditate on the man and his Gifts. . . . *Richard Tyms* before the writs were issued out (in which time he had opportunity of hearing once and again) began to hammer in his head a project of getting him chosen a Burgess for Cambridge, himself being then but one of the 24, and with this device he presently repaired to one Mr. Wildbore a Draper, a Kinsman of *Cromwels* and a Nonconformist likewise; and after some commendatory language of *Oliver*, propounded to him the choosing of him Burgess; to which Wildbore answered that it was impossible because he was no Freeman of the Town."[110]

Whereupon Heath, with minute detail—most of which is palpably untrue—explains how Cromwell was first made a burgess, then chosen as member of Parliament. Yet the main facts are clear enough. Cromwell was well known as a leading Puritan and opponent of the royal policy; he doubtless attended conventicles and prayed and exhorted there; he may well have come to the attention of someone like Tyms, if not Tyms himself; and there is other testimony to his connection with Cambridge. He was a cousin of John Hampden, reputed the richest commoner in England, of much importance in these eastern counties and now a national figure through his resistance to ship-money; and the mayor of Cambridge, Thomas French, was probably

[109] *Flagellum*, (1672), p. 23.

[110] *Ibid.*, 24. Mr. Tyms or Timbs was not one of the "24" at this time but he was an alderman and M. P. for Cambridge in the 1653 Parliament. The story does not appear in the 1663 edition of Heath.

related to a certain Dr. Peter French who later married Cromwell's sister. Nor is it conceivable that one of the best known men in that little area bounded by Ely, Huntingdon, St. Ives and Cambridge had not many connections in the latter place, or that he should not have acquaintances and admirers among the close-knit Puritan congregations there. To this again may be added the story of Sir William Dugdale that Cromwell occupied "mean lodgings" in Cambridge[111] to qualify for election as burgess, which would, of course, have been essential, and the local tradition which assigns his residence to the yard of the White Bull Inn in Bridge Street.[112]

The fact of his election first as a burgess then as member of Parliament, at any rate, is indisputable. The Corporation Book of Cambridge records:

On Tuesday, the 7th of January 1639[-40], Oliver Cromwell of Huntingdon, in the county of Huntingdon, Esq., on the presentation of the mayor of the town, according to the ancient custom recognized in the said town, hath the freedom of the said town gratis, on payment of 1d. to the poor; and is sworn in.[113]

He thus became eligible for Parliament and the contest began. It was apparently strenuous and was accompanied by the usual circumstances of such events. The Lord Keeper Finch sent a letter urging the choice of Mr. Meautys, Clerk of the Privy Council;[114] and it appears from the corporation records that Mr. Meautys donated venison and five pounds for a corporation feast.[115] For the first time in twelve years, note of an election to Parliament was written into the Corporation records:

25 March, 1640, Thomas French, gen., Maior. This day the greatest part of the burgesses of this town being present at the Guildhall, have chosen for burgesses, for the ensuing Parliament, for this town, Thomas Meautys, Esqr, and Oliver Cromwell, Esqr.[116]

The Cambridge election, like many then taking place in an England which was aroused in opposition to the royal policy, was hard fought and bitter; nor can one doubt that this bitterness was due in no small part to the rise of the Puritan party to political importance. Still less can it be doubted that Cromwell was an ideal candidate. He was now forty years old, at the height of his vigor and capacity, hardened by active outdoor life, a man of substance and position, well known

[111] Dugdale, *Short View*, p. 460.
[112] *Cambridge Portfolio.*
[113] *Corporation Common Day book*; printed in Sanford *Studies*, p. 267.
[114] *Ibid.*, printed in Cooper, *Annals of Cambridge*, iii, 296.
[115] *Ibid.*
[116] *Ibid.*, printed in Sanford, *Studies*, p. 262.

in the community, with wide relationships through his family, business and church associates. He had much experience as a landowner and grazier, as a burgess of Huntingdon and a member of Parliament, as a lessee of cathedral lands, and in the fen dispute. He had developed his talents as a speaker; and somewhere and somehow, as his letters amply prove, he had become a master of Puritan phraseology, of vigorous and moving expression, a rude eloquence, filled with Biblical references and infused with emotion. To this he joined a sense of leadership, deep sympathy with those who seemed to him oppressed, and confidence in his cause and in himself. So far from being the unknown and obscure figure he has sometimes been painted on his entrance into Parliament, he was a well-known and rising man, closely connected with powerful interests and strongly supported by one of the most closely-knit and influential groups in England.

With such support, he took his seat in the Parliament which met on April 13, 1640 in an atmosphere of revolt against Charles's policy. Its members were as determined to put a check upon the King as he was determined to pursue his course. To the speech from the throne demanding their support, under Pym's leadership the Commons retorted with a demand for the investigation of existing evils and redress of grievances. Whether Anglican or Puritan, the greater part of the country and its representatives were weary of incompetence and exactions. They had lost confidence in the wisdom of the crown. They distrusted its purposes and its promises; they feared its chief supporter, Strafford. They were opposed to Laudian policies and to the arbitrary exercise of royal authority under guise of ancient and outworn statutes. They resented the continuation of Tudor conciliar government as expressed in courts of Star Chamber and High Commission. They were irritated at the long intermission of Parliament, and still more at the oppressive and often petty exactions of the crown without the sanction of that Parliament; and it was to this spirit that John Pym appealed in words that were as conciliatory as their spirit was revolutionary.

He protested against "the new ceremonies and observances which had put upon the churches a shape and face of Popery" and an ecclesiastical policy which seemed to admit that "any other vice almost may be better endured in a minister than inconformity." To these he added the grievances of eleven years of unparliamentary government —collection of tonnage and poundage without Parliamentary grant, increase of customs, monopolies, distraint of knighthood, ship-money, afforestation, revival of obsolete statutes to raise revenue, and now a new grievance arising from the war, "coat and conduct money" exacted from the very men on whom the duty of military service fell most heavily. Thus far he went with the old principles and his speech differed little from his utterances eleven years before; but when he added to these a statement of his constitutional theory, he broke new ground. Conservative as it seemed in its language, his doctrine was the essence of revolution; for in words portentous of coming change he declared, "The powers of Parliament are to the body politic as the rational faculties of the soul to a man." In that sentence he challenged the whole traditional theory of sovereignty residing in the crown.

It was in vain that Charles offered to abandon ship-money for a grant of subsidies; that every effort was made to shake the opposition; that Strafford hurried back from Ireland with a vote of men and money from his subservient Parliament; that a letter from Scotland addressed apparently to the King of France was adduced to show the effort of the Scots to gain foreign aid. The Commons stood its ground. Its programme as voiced by Pym—though it was not as yet so clearly evident as it was to become presently—involved not merely correction of immediate grievances but a new system of government. It went to the heart of the great issue—were the English people, through their representatives, to rule, or was authority to remain in royal hands?

That issue was not met. Hopeless of gaining what he sought, Charles dissolved Parliament on May 5 and went on with his efforts to subdue the Scots in what was called the Second Bishops' War. In that dispute, so far as we know now, Cromwell took no part, nor was he in a position then to make his influence felt. Like his fellow-members of Parliament, he seems to have returned to his own concerns or those of his neighborhood, and as it happens there is evidence of this. Among his various activities he seems to have been a commissioner of arbitration in a dispute between father and son, in which capacity, some nine days after the dissolution, he drew up a certificate that a settlement had been achieved:

Certificate

Being desired by William Kirbye, of Upton, in the county of Huntingdon, gent., to certify my knowledge of what passed at the speeding of a commission between Thomas Kirbye, the father, and Thos. Kirbye, the son, sat upon at Oundle, co. Northampton, about Michaelmas last past. I being one amongst and with others authorized to execute the same, I do hereby testify and affirm that by and with the consent of both the said parties, and upon a full and final agreement then had and made between the father and son, of the matters then in difference to the searching out the truth of which the said commission tended. It was then and there agreed and consented unto by both the parties that further execution of the commission and return of depositions should cease, and that the same should be suppressed, which accordingly was done, and that this was so and is true I do by these presents testify under my hand.

May 14, 1640. OLIVER CROMWELL.[117]

The dissolution of Parliament was unpopular. "There could not a greater damp have seized upon the spirits of the whole nation," wrote Clarendon in later years, than it produced; but as Oliver St. John observed to him, "It must be worse before it is better"; and in that spirit the leaders of the opposition appealed to the nation for support. As Charles summoned to his side his greatest adviser, Strafford, and strained every nerve to gather forces against the Scots, men like Pym and Hampden drew together the threads of organization to oppose the king.

This was no mere question of popular sentiment nor abstract political philosophy. No movement such as theirs can long depend on general discontent or spontaneous opposition to a government; if it is to be successful it must have an organization superior to that government. The English people faced not reform but revolution. The first stage—that of the development of a "revolutionary atmosphere"—had been passed in the eleven years of unparliamentary government. The second stage—that of evolving an organization—was well under way. The opposition which had long since begun under the lead of men like Eliot and Sandys had gradually developed under the leadership of Hampden and of Pym into a powerful company. It had centered about those Puritan elements which formed a solid core of opposition to the Laudian policy. It had recruited nobles and country gentlemen who, whatever their religious opinions, had been alienated by infringement of their privileges and levies on their property. It had found powerful support from the City whose merchants were at odds with the crown on questions of duties and their Irish colony. It attracted lawyers who were convinced Parliamentarians.

To weld these diverse elements into a coherent group was the work of Pym and Hampden in particular. The one was the orator and the agitator of the movement, the other the organizer; and they found support from others of like sympathies and gifts. Peers like Essex and Manchester, Warwick, Saye and Sele, Russell, Bedford and Brooke; commoners like Strode, Holles, St. John, Erle, Fiennes and Cromwell rallied to the cause. Nor did they lack the elements of organization. In the colonizing companies which had poured thousands of emigrants into New England, they had first found opportunity for united action, and the list of the directors of those companies—Providence, Connecticut, and the rest—read like a list of the Puritan leaders of later years. They were backed by hundreds of

[117] *St. P. Dom. Charles I*, ccccliii, 49; *Calendar* (1640), p. 164.

ministers and as many congregations which provided colonists, then support in elections, and presently fighting-men. What the mother society of the Jacobins was to the French Revolution, what the committees of correspondence and the Sons of Liberty were to the American Revolution, this Puritan group was to the English Revolution. What the provincial Jacobin clubs and the Freemasons were to France, what caucusses, fire-companies and congregations were to America, the Puritan gentry and congregations were to this movement; and what Mirabeau and Sieyès were to the one, what Adams, Henry, Franklin and Jefferson were to the other, Pym, Hampden and St. John, Holles and Cromwell were to this uprising against royal authority in England in these years.

THE SECOND BISHOPS' WAR AND THE ELECTION TO THE LONG PARLIAMENT, 1640

The situation developed rapidly and tragically for Charles. He was bent on a war that was hopeless from the start; for the Scots were not merely superior in resources, men and leadership, but a great part of England looked on them as their saviors from the King. "Never," said Strafford, summoned to bring order out of chaos, "came a man to so lost a business." The army was a mob which defied discipline, killed officers suspected of Popery, broke down altar-rails, moved communion-tables to the middle of the churches, and in every way expressed its opposition to authority. Behind it lay the passive resistance of the country at large. It took the form of refusal to supply money for the war. Strafford vainly sought a loan from Spain, the Queen from Rome; and though Convocation voted subsidies, the City refused to pay ship-money or to lend to Charles. His seizure of a cargo of pepper from the East India Company, its sale for less than the market price, and the borrowing of money at double the usual rate on its security, revealed the desperate straits of monarchy, and served to further irritate financial interests. Save for a few men like Strafford who feared the effect of successful Scottish resistance upon Charles's authority, the greater part of the nation was opposed to the war. Nor was the least disturbing aspect of the situation to the King's counsellors, the fact that behind this opposition to the war lay widespread opposition to the government itself.

Meanwhile the King set out for York, the Scots crossed the Tweed, and in the one brief skirmish at Newburn they drove back the royal troops. The royal strongholds in Scotland were taken one by one; Newcastle was occupied by the Scotch army which advanced as far as the river Tees. Meanwhile, too, the opposition leaders, Saye and

Sele, Essex, Warwick, Bedford and his son Lord Russell, Pym, Hampden, and others held meetings in London and it was an open secret that the Scots had friends and supporters there. The City petitioned Charles for a Parliament and disturbances broke out, including a mob attack on the Court of High Commission and riots in St. Paul's and elsewhere. Whichever way he looked, Charles found no support and he was driven to come to terms with the Scots. By the treaty of Ripon they agreed to accept £850 a day for two months for the support of their army, the first month's payment to be secured by personal bonds of the leading gentry of the counties they occupied, while Charles agreed to summon a Parliament on which they relied for payment for the second month's subsidy. The City promised the King a loan if he would call a Parliament. Under Bristol's lead the great council added its weight to the general demand and Charles, dissolving the council, was driven to issue writs for a general election.

Under such circumstances was the election held. The Corporation records in Cambridge record the re-election of Cromwell[118] and the defeat of the government candidate, Meautys by a representative of the Puritan element:

> October 27th, 1640—Magister Robson, Maior. This day the greatest part of the burgesses of this town being present in the hall, have chosen for burgesses of the next ensuing Parliament for this town Oliver Cromwell, Esq., and John Lawry, of the common council of 24.[119]

Who John Lawry or Lowry was we do not know beyond the fact that he is said to have been a chandler and, as the record states, a member of the town council, and that in later years he became a Parliamentary colonel and was named for the High Court of Justice at the King's trial, though he never served.[120]

The Cambridge election was a typical contest of the time and Cromwell and Lowry characteristic figures in the Puritan host mustering against the crown. With this election ended the first great period of Cromwell's life. To this time, with the exception of his brief appearance in the Parliament of 1628–9, he had been, as it were, a local figure; and though he was to retain that character in some measure for some years, with his entry into the Long Parliament he took his place upon the wider stage of national affairs which he was not to leave until his death. Even now, though he was well known to a few of the leaders of his party who had great confidence in him, he was not yet, nor could he well have been, regarded as more

[118] The poet Cleveland who was then a tutor in St. John's College and was opposed to Cromwell bemoans the fact that Cromwell by a single vote was elected and so "ruined both church and kingdom." Cleveland's Life prefixed to his *Works* (1687).

[119] *Corporation Common Day Book*, quoted in Sanford, p. 264.

[120] Cooper, *Annals of Cambridge*, iii, 304.

than an aggressive Puritan, influential in his immediate neighborhood and potentially a danger to Charles's government, with which he had come into conflict more than once. Yet, apart from his connection with the leaders of the opposition, he seemed no more dangerous than many other men who, like him, were not of the first rank in the Parliamentary opposition. He was to play a great part in politics, but, aside from his activities as a private member which were numerous and important, it was not on the floor of the House of Commons that this part was played, then or thereafter.

CHAPTER III

THE LONG PARLIAMENT.

NOVEMBER, 1640–FEBRUARY, 1641

The Parliament which met on November 3, 1640 was destined to the longest and most eventful life of any English Parliament. It met in an atmosphere of crisis and deep emotion. A Scottish army was encamped on English soil; the remnants of the English royal forces were quartered in the north; and Strafford's troops were ready in Ireland. The air was full of rumors of plots and conspiracies; of suspicions of the Queen whose plan to visit the Continent was construed as an attempt to gain assistance from her brother; of the coming of William of Orange to marry the Princess Mary as a move to get help from Holland; of negotiations with Rome for aid against the Parliament; of English troops and Irish levies to support the monarchy. The language and activities of Strafford in particular were regarded as evidence of his intention to make Charles absolute. For Strafford, though he had earlier supported the movement which resulted in the Petition of Right, was now convinced that the crown must be supreme. "The king," he declared, "is loose and absolved from all rules of government." "In an extreme necessity," he told Charles, "you may do all your power admits. Parliament refusing, you are acquitted towards God and man."

For all of this the Parliamentary leaders were ready, and more than ready, they were eager for the fray. "There was observed," wrote Clarendon,[1] "a marvellous elated countenance in most of the members of Parliament before they met together in the house; the same men who six months before were observed to be of very moderate tempers, and to wish that gentle remedies might be applied without opening the wound too wide and exposing it to the air, and rather to cure what was amiss than too strictly to make inquisition into the causes and original of the malady, now talked in another dialect both of things and persons." The Parliamentary leaders had reason for encouragement. Their organization was now complete. They had a great majority of the Commons on their side; the country, London in particular, supported them; they had friends who betrayed the most secret deliberations of the Privy Council to them; and they had at

[1] *History of the Rebellion*, ed. Macray (1888), iii, 3.

their command not only the machinery of publicity but the City mob. Nor were their purposes less clear. "They must now be of another temper than they were the last Parliament," said their leader, Pym, of the members as the session began. "They must not only sweep the house clean below, but must pull down all the cobwebs which hung in the top and corners, that they might not breed dust and so make a foul house thereafter; that they had now an opportunity to make their country happy, by removing all grievances and pulling up the causes of them by the roots."[2]

It was in that spirit that Pym entered the struggle. Sometime a lawyer, sometime a man of business, and, apparently, not over successful in either, he had developed from a master of Parliamentary procedure, a skilled debater, an unrivalled agitator, into an ideal revolutionary leader. He had long been connected with the Puritan party in many capacities, as a sharer in colonial enterprise, as a leader in the House, as an associate and champion of the London merchants and the Puritan clergy. His colleague Hampden, "a man of much greater cunning . . . of the most discerning spirit and of the greatest address . . . to bring anything to pass which he desired, of any man of that time and who laid the design deepest," as Clarendon described him, was supported, in turn, by St. John, a reserved man "of a dark and clouded countenance, very proud and conversing with very few," who "never forgave the Court" for being summoned before the Star Chamber for "a design of sedition." These, with the Earl of Bedford, long an opponent of the court and now doubly irritated by the fen dispute; Viscount Saye and Sele and his son, Nathaniel Fiennes; the Earl of Warwick and his son, Lord Rich; the two Vanes; Denzil Holles, the brother of the Earl of Clare and brother-in-law of Strafford; Sir Gilbert Gerard; William Strode, sometime admonished by the Star Chamber and bitter against Strafford; and Strode's friend, Sir Walter Erle—such were some of the leaders of the new House of Commons, all having suffered at one time or another from the government and all opposed to it.

Under such conditions and such leadership the Parliament began its work by an attack upon the government and its advisers. Finch and Windebank sought refuge on the Continent, but greater men remained, Strafford by the king's express command. Against him Pym began the session with a fierce attack, denouncing those things "done and contrived maliciously, and upon deliberation, to change the whole frame and to deprive the nation of all liberty and property . . . and subjected to the arbitrary power of the Privy Council which governed the kingdom according to their will and pleasure." He charged the authorities of church and state with "innovations" designed to sub-

[2] Clarendon, *op. cit.*

vert the ancient liberties, directing his bitterest invective against the man whom he perceived to be the ablest of the crown advisers and his most dangerous enemy, that "grand apostate of the commonwealth," "the greatest enemy to the liberties of his country and the greatest promoter of tyranny that any age hath produced"—the Earl of Strafford.

It was a shrewd if obvious maneuvre. The country had a multitude of grievances, it needed that prime requisite of all such situations, an individual to personify its hatreds, a scapegoat on whose head its sins could now be laid. For that part Strafford was now cast; and the attack on him was not pushed by the slow legal process of investigation and trial. It was transferred from law to politics, to an impeachment for high treason which required only a majority of the House. Betrayed by the Vanes, hated by many men for his activities in Ireland, and by many more for his avowed convictions as to monarchy, denied an opportunity to defend himself, Strafford's case was hopeless from the start. He was condemned on charges which had hitherto not been recognized as valid in either law or politics. He was abandoned by a king who had pledged his word to protect his faithful servant, in a vain attempt to preserve his own position. Of all his many errors none was more damaging to Charles than his betrayal of Strafford. It spurred the opposition to fiercer assault; it disheartened the King's followers; it revealed the fundamental weakness, instability and selfishness of Charles, whose vacillation cost Strafford his life, for the Commons could not trust him to banish his minister. There was no way but death, since, as Strafford's enemy, the Earl of Essex, said, "Stone-dead hath no fellow."

The trial dragged through a great part of the first session of the Parliament and it was not until May, 1641 that the great minister was finally condemned. It was a fierce struggle and in what spirit it was conducted St. John's argument before the Lords revealed. "We give law to hares and deer," he said in arguing for the death penalty, but "it was never accounted either cruelty or foul play to knock foxes and wolves on the head." It was accompanied by desperate efforts on both sides—by plans to rescue Strafford by force from the Tower, by levying men for that purpose under pretence of service for the king of Portugal, by appeals to the London mob against these court maneuvers, by endeavors to set the Lords against the Commons, by repeated invasions of Whitehall by armed Londoners to overawe the court and Parliament. Every portent of revolution marked the trial. On it hung not merely Strafford's life but that of his enemies and of their cause. They knew Charles for a vengeful man; they had gone too far to draw back; and they never doubted but that it was a case of "my head or thy head" from the first. Nor were they content with him, for Laud soon followed Strafford to the Tower on his way to the scaffold; and with the removal of these pillars of the throne, the real work of the Parliament went on unchecked.

Its progress, once begun, was rapid and complete. In eleven months the Tudor system of government was wrecked. One by one its institutions fell before the reforming zeal of the Parliament. Star Chamber, Court of High Commission, Marshal's Court, the levying of money by prerogative, whether by ship-money, customs, forced loans or voluntary gifts, distraint of knighthood, reafforestation, all disappeared. A Root and Branch Petition sought the destruction of the "government of archbishops, lord bishops, deans, archdeacons, with all its roots and branches . . . and government according to God's word be rightly placed amongst us." A Triennial Act compelled the meeting of Parliament every three years, with or without royal summons. Another act prevented the dissolution of this Parliament without its own consent. And infusing all of this activity was that fiercest of spirits continually invoked by Pym to force his programme through—the spirit of fear which infuses all revolutionary periods. In this case it was the threat of Popish and Jesuit designs and plots, of efforts on the part of church and crown to "subvert the fundamental laws of England and Ireland," of Popish armies levied in Ireland for that purpose, of "endeavors . . . to bring the English army into a misunderstanding of this Parliament, thereby to incline that army . . . to pass these wicked counsels" of the royal government. His pleas were effective, and under the combined influence of reform, revenge and fear, the Parliament pressed forward on its revolutionary course.

And what of Oliver Cromwell in this feverish time; what part did he play in this great revolt? Was he, as has too often been assumed, one of a silent majority which supported Pym, unknown, unnoticed and insignificant? Nothing could be much farther from the fact than to assume that this period between the meeting of Parliament and the outbreak of war was unimportant in his life or that he was an obscure figure in the House. Of his relatives, there were eighteen in the Commons in 1640, among them Hampden and St. John, and before the Parliament ended there were many more, besides others who later married into the family.[3] As he sat on Speaker Lenthall's right,

[3] Of his close relatives who sat in Parliament there were: Oliver St. John, Sir Thomas Barrington, Sir William Masham, Sir Gilbert Gerard, Francis Gerard, John Hampden, Sir Richard Knightley, Sir Robert Pye, Sir John Trevor, Edmund Dunch, Valentine Walton; more distant were Edmund Waller and his relatives Sir William Waller and Sir Hardress Waller, Thomas Trevor, Sir Oliver Luke and Sir Samuel Luke. His relatives who were later elected to sit in the Long Parliament were: Sir Richard Ingoldsby, John Barrington, William Masham, Sir John Bourchier, Col. John Jones, Henry Ireton and, distantly, Richard Salwey, Thomas and John Hutchinson. Charles Fleetwood, Francis Russell and several others later married into the

near him were Vane, Strode, Mildmay, Rudyerd and Evelyn, opposite them the younger Vane, St. John, Holles, Marten, Sir Thomas Barrington and Sir John Hotham, all in opposition to the government.

But this was not all his close connection with that party. Its headquarters were in a house of Sir Richard Manly just behind Westminster Hall where Pym and Hampden with others kept a common table, and though there is no documentary evidence that Cromwell was of that number it seems probable that he was in its counsels.[4] For this there is some proof. Despite the part they occupy in history, the orators are not always the most important figures of such assemblies, for there remain those men who find small notice from historians but play a great rôle in practical affairs, the committeemen who carry on much of the real business of Parliament. It was in committee work that Cromwell came to be eminent. The very enumeration of those of which he was a member sheds light on the work of the Long Parliament, on the dominant party and on Oliver Cromwell, hard to overestimate. That he was so chosen indicates not merely his own qualities but his close relationship with Hampden and with Pym, and were other evidence lacking, Hampden's own words presently revealed his intimate acquaintance with his cousin Cromwell and his confidence in Cromwell's qualities. Nor, as time went on, was Oliver slow to take a more vocal and aggressive part in the proceedings of the House.

From the beginning of the Long Parliament he was active in many phases of its concerns, and though the record of his activities may seem a dull and uninspiring chronicle, it reveals at once the character of the business which pressed upon the House and Cromwell's place in it. Within a week after Parliament assembled he presented a petition on behalf of a man whose case brought him in touch with one of the great issues of the time, and it is one of the small ironies of history that his first appearance in the Long Parliament should have been to defend one who was to play such an irritating part in his later life. This was a certain John Lilburne, who, apprenticed to a London cloth merchant, had spent his leisure devouring Foxe's *Book of Martyrs* and the works of Puritan divines. He had come into touch with Bastwick and, apparently, with Prynne, and had been arrested in 1637 for printing and distributing unlicensed pamphlets, among them Prynne's famous libel *News from Ipswich.* He had challenged the court's procedure; had been fined, whipped, pilloried and imprisoned; but from his cell had managed to have printed further attacks upon the government, including an account of his sufferings entitled *The Work of the Beast.* Released on the meeting of Parliament, his

Cromwell connection. For more details and for doubtful relationships, see Weyman, "Oliver Cromwell's Kinsfolk," *English Historical Review*, vi, 48–60 (1891).

[4] See Firth, *Cromwell*, pp. 48–50.

petition for redress was now presented and referred to the committee appointed to consider the case of that Dr. Leighton, so severely punished ten years earlier and still a prisoner in the Fleet.

On that committee sat the leaders of the opposition, Pym, Hampden, Holles and St. John, and to that committee Cromwell was now named and thus early took his place among "those who managed."[5] It was a tribute not only to his close connection with Hampden, but to the spirit and ability he showed on this first appearance in this Parliament; and as it happens there is evidence of this.

On that day, apparently, by a fortunate chance Sir Philip Warwick was present, heard the speech, and later recorded his impressions both of the speech and the speaker in a well-known passage of his *Memoirs:*

> "I came into the House well clad and perceived a gentleman speaking (whom I knew not) very ordinary apparrelled, for it was a plain cloth-sute, which seemed to have bin made by an ill country taylor; his linen was plain, and not very clean; and I remember a speck or two of blood upon his little band, which was not much larger than his collar; his hatt was without a hatband, his stature was of a good size, his sword stuck close to his side, his countenance swoln and reddich, his voice sharp and untunable, and his eloquence full of fervor; for the subject matter could not bear much of reason; it being in behalfe of a servant of Mr. Prynn's[6] who had disperst libells against the Queen for her dancing and such like innocent and courtly sports; and he aggravated the imprisonment of this man by the Council Table unto the height, that one would have believed the very Government itselfe had been in great danger by it. I sincerely professe it lessened much my reverence unto that great councill; for he was very much harkened unto."[7]

It was probably on this same occasion that Sir Richard Bulstrode observed Lord Digby, going down the steps after Cromwell, turn to Hampden and ask who that man was. "For I see," he said with some reference to Cromwell's appearance, "he is of our side, by his speaking so warmly this day." "That slovenly fellow which you see before us," replied Hampden, "who hath no ornament in his speech; I say that sloven, if we should ever come to have a breach with the King (which God forbid) in such case will be one of the greatest men of England."[8]

In such fashion did Oliver Cromwell make his entrance into the work of the Long Parliament. In this work he continued. He was first named to a committee of thirty-two to deal with claims arising from the fen dispute. Among them was that of a certain Dr. Tomson who begged for satisfaction for the tithes of 3500 acres of marshland

[5] *Commons Journals*, ii, 24; D'Ewes' *Diary*, ed. Notestein, pp. 18–19.
[6] Lilburne was Prynne's clerk.
[7] Warwick, *Memoirs* (1701), pp. 247–8. Cp. *C. J.*, ii, 24.
[8] Bulstrode, *Memoirs* (1721), pp. 192–3.

due Sutton parish in Lincolnshire, and another from a Mrs. Margaret Kirby who claimed fen lands due to her husband as one of the Adventurers, and whose name somehow echoes the family dispute which Cromwell had been lately called upon to arbitrate. The next day the petition of Lady Dymock and all others of like nature were referred to the same committee.[9]

It was a field peculiarly suited to his talents and experience; but he was almost immediately engaged in another cause, for on that same day he was put on a great committee of sixty to consider the petitions of Prynne, Burton and others for release from prison and to look into the jurisdiction and abuses of the courts of Star Chamber and High Commission. A fortnight later he became a member of a like committee to consider the case of Dr. Bastwick; and with this he came in touch with greater things. The importance of these committees and the increasing connection of Cromwell with the leaders of the opposition is indicated by the fact that on the first sat Pym, Hampden, Fiennes, Holles, St. John, and others like Sir Arthur Haselrig; and on the second the first three, with others like Sir Philip Stapleton.[10] Finally, on December 19, he was named to a subcommittee of the grand committee on religion, once more with Pym, Hampden, Haselrig, Sir Oliver Luke and Valentine Walton[11]—all men with whom he was to be closely associated thereafter, both in war and peace.

On the work of these committees was based the legislation which led to the extinction of the great engines of Tudor autocracy; and his activities in the House thenceforth—with one striking exception, the impeachment of Strafford—are almost an epitome of the history of the Parliament itself. He was especially concerned with questions of "religion," that is to say of the Establishment, the attacks upon it, the punishment of its detractors, and, in particular, the grievances of the Puritans. Nothing illustrates this better than the fact that the committee to which he was now named was directed to receive petitions bearing on the shortage of "preaching" ministers, their maintenance, and the methods of removing "scandalous" incumbents. The matter touched him the more closely in that on December 22 he was named as a member of a special committee to consider petitions and complaints against the man from whom indirectly, in a certain sense, he derived part of his livelihood, Matthew Wren, Bishop of Ely.[12]

[9] *C. J.*, ii, 44; *St. P. Dom., Charles I*, cccc, 70; ccccxxviii, 36; ccccli, 65.

[10] *C. J.*, ii, 44, 52. On February 25, the House resolved to give Bastwick reparation for damages sustained by the sentence. On March 2, Laud and the Star Chamber were ordered to give him satisfaction.

[11] *C. J.*, ii, 54. During the next few months many petitions were referred to this committee. On March 20, they were ordered to draw up a bill against scandalous ministers.

[12] *C. J.*, ii, 56.

Wren represented all of the grievances of which the Puritans complained. He was a strong and convinced Laudian and had helped Laud prepare the Scottish Prayer Book. He was a favorite of both James and Charles, able, active, aggressive; as capable a master of Peterhouse College, Cambridge, as he was vigorous in his efforts to stamp out Puritanism, in his capacity first as Bishop of Norwich then as Bishop of Ely. He had, it was complained, "passionately and furiously" proceeded against the foreign congregations of the eastern counties, and, under Laud's direct supervision, roused the Puritans of that region to "rebellious fury." He was thus a shining mark for Puritan attack, and the day after Laud's impeachment, Hampden had moved against him in the Commons and carried his complaint before the House of Lords. In consequence the committee of which Cromwell was a member brought in nine articles of impeachment against Wren, and on July 5, 1641, the Commons voted that he was unfit to hold office in either church or commonwealth.

With all his committee work, it does not appear that Cromwell took any special share in the more direct activities of the House until almost the last day of 1640, when, on December 30 he moved the second reading of the bill for the "Yearly Holding of Parliaments," which had been introduced by Strode some six days earlier. It was referred to a committee on which Cromwell sat, as usual, with Pym, Hampden, St. John, Strode and Holles, together with those eminent lawyers, Selden and Whitelocke, and some forty others.[13] It seems probable that he addressed the House before this time; but—apart from his appearance on behalf of Lilburne—his first recorded speech seems to have been on February 9, 1641, when he rose to rebut the arguments of Sir John Strangways. Speaking on the subject of petitions from Gloucester and Hertford against episcopacy, Strangways had declared "if we make a parity in the church we must come to a parity in the Commonwealth; since the bishops are one of the three estates of the kingdom and have a voice in Parliament."

Against this argument which raised the whole issue of government and society, Cromwell protested violently. "He knew," he said, "no reason of those suppositions and inferences which the gentleman had made." His manner, if not his words, served to irritate his opponents; he was interrupted, reproved for his unparliamentary language, and it was proposed to call him to the bar of the House to apologize. At once Pym and Holles sprang to his defence. 'If the gentleman had said anything which might offend,' they argued, 'he might explain himself in his place and not be called before the bar.' Their plea prevailed, and Cromwell rose presently to explain his words. His explanation was, if possible, worse than his original offence:

[13] *C. J.*, ii, 60; D'Ewes Diary, *Harleian Mss.*, British Museum, clxii, f. 101.

"He did not understand why the gentleman that last spoke should make an inference of parity from the church to the Commonwealth; nor that there was any necessity of the great revenues of Bishops. He was more convinced touching the irregularity of Bishops than ever before, because, like the Roman Hierarchy, they would not endure to have their condition come to a trial."[14]

Such is D'Ewes account of his explanation, which, however parliamentary, served to aggravate his first utterance and give still deeper offence to the episcopal party. It apparently seemed better to them to let the matter drop than to risk another outburst from this firebrand. It was a brief episode, yet it revealed two things with great clearness. The first was Cromwell's animosity against the bishops; the second was that lack of restraint in his language which had hitherto marked all his controversies.

PARLIAMENT, FEBRUARY–MAY, 1641

The month of February, 1641, saw the House absorbed in a multitude of minor grievances, and Cromwell appointed to four more committees. On February 10 he was named to a sub-committee of the great committee on grievances to consider complaints against the inland posts. Three days later he was appointed to a committee of sixty-eight to consider "An Act for the Abolishing of Superstitition and Idolatry and for the Better Advancing of the True Worship and Service of God"—in effect a measure against the Anglican system; and on these as on many of Cromwell's committees sat his relatives, Barrington, Gerard, Pye, Masham and Walton.[15] On February 17, he was named to another body of like size to consider the question of lands in the fen district which had been granted to the Queen by Charles and sold by her to Lord Mandeville. A week later he was put on a committee of twenty-four, including Hampden, Strode and Haselrig, to consider the breach of privileges of the Parliament of 1628.[16]

It is apparent from the barest record of these appointments that while there were many men in Parliament who served on many committees, and few escaped such service, there were few who at this moment were so closely identified with the leaders and issues of the time as Oliver Cromwell. Nor was this due entirely to his connection with Hampden. He approved himself to his colleagues as a man peculiarly suited to their purposes, able, active, aggressive to a fault, courageous,

[14] Notestein, Wallace, ed., *Journal of Sir Simonds D'Ewes*, p. 340.

[15] *C. J.*, ii, 81–2, 84.

[16] *C. J.*, ii, 87, 91. The first committee remained active for several months.

and all but fanatically opposed to episcopacy, a speaker who, whatever his defects of manner or manners, whatever his disregard or contempt for the amenities of debate, commanded the attention of his hearers and was a man to be feared by any antagonist.

It is, therefore, the more surprising that his name seems nowhere to appear in the proceedings against Strafford which absorbed the House for the next three months. It may be that he had a certain sympathy and respect for one who, however differing in principles, was in some ways not unlike Cromwell himself. It may be, as often appears in his actions, that he had no great interest in constitutional concerns. It may be that he was too absorbed in the religious issue; and only in regard to that is there any evidence of his activities in these feverish months. In that he showed deep interest. The debates on religion which went on in the early part of 1641 centered, among other things, in the proposals of the Scottish commissioners, looking toward a settlement of the dispute between their countrymen and Charles. They had drawn up their "Demands towards a Treaty" as a basis for negotiation. The first seven articles were concerned with "secularities," that is to say the payment of damages, the recalling of Charles's proclamation against them, and like questions arising from the war. But the eighth article, besides a demand for the dismantling of the strongholds of Berwick and Carlisle, included a provision for "uniformity in religion," that is to say the Presbyterian system, before "a solid peace between the Nations" could be achieved. These demands raised thorny questions in the House. They were considered exorbitant. The English merchants were opposed to freedom of trade which the Scotch required; the episcopal party was infuriated by the suggestion of the extension of the presbyterian system to England. Inevitably Cromwell was profoundly interested in such proposals; and so wrote presently to a certain George Willingham, a London merchant, apparently in touch with Scottish affairs, to find out what he could. In the midst of his committee work he made the inquiry:

To my loving friend Mr. Willingham, at his House in Swithin's Lane

SIR,

I desire you to send me the reasons of the Scots to enforce their desire of Uniformity in Religion, expressed in their 8th Article; I mean that which I had before of you. I would peruse it against we fall upon that debate, which will be speedily.

Yours,

[London, Feb. 1640–1.] OL. CROMWELL.[17]

[17] *Sloane, Mss*, 2035b, fol. 5. Printed in Harris, *Life of Cromwell*, p. 538. Carlyle, Letter III. This was George Willingham, a prominent London merchant and later

What share, if any, he took in that debate we have now no means of knowing; nor is there any record remaining, apparently, of his course in that period of intrigue and agitation, mobs and conspiracy which ended in Strafford's execution. Only at the end of that long struggle is there any mention of his name and that is connected with religion. On May 3, nine days before Strafford went to the scaffold, Sir Simonds D'Ewes notes in his *Diary* that "Mr. Cromwell moved that we might take some course to turn the Papists out of Dublin." It was seconded; but after some debate this effort to depopulate the Irish capital seems to have been laid aside.[18]

Cromwell's motion was but an incident in the great debate on religion which, once Strafford's fate was determined, absorbed the attention of the House. On that same day was passed the great Protestation of the Commons, agreed to by the Lords on the day following, which summed up in brief the whole contention of the party led by Pym. Its preamble defined the case against the King; its "protestation" was, in effect, not unlike the Scottish Covenant in English dress; and its passage marked another step in the great movement to revolutionize the government and the church.

A Preamble, with the Protestation made by the whole House of Commons, the 3d of May 1641, and assented unto by the Lords of the Upper House, the 4th of May.

We, the Knights, Citizens and Burgesses of the Commons House, in Parliament, finding, to the grief of our hearts, That the designs of the Priests and Jesuits, and other Adherents to the See of Rome, have [been] of late more boldly and frequently put in practice than formerly, to the undermining, and danger of ruin, of the True Reformed Religion in his Majesty's Dominions established: And finding also that there hath been, and having caused to suspect there still are even during the sitting in Parliament, endeavours to subvert the Fundamental Laws of England and Ireland, and to introduce the exercise of an Arbitrary and Tyrannical Government, by most pernicious and wicked counsels, plots and conspiracies: And that the long intermission, and unhappier breach, of Parliaments hath occasioned many illegal Taxations, whereupon the Subjects have been prosecuted and grieved: And that divers Innovations and Superstitions have been brought into the Church; multitudes driven out of his Majesty's dominions; jealousies raised and fomented between the King and People; a Popish Army levied in

a member of the London Sequestration Committee. The letter is conjecturally dated "Feb." because it was the 28th of Feb. when Baillie expected the question to come up "this very day," and Mar. 3 when the two houses had a conference on it. *C. J.*, ii, 96–7. Parliament finally voted approval of the Eighth Article on May 17, 1641.

[18] D'Ewes Diary, quoted in Sanford, *Studies*, p. 370–71. That autumn a conspiracy was discovered which might have resulted in the Papists massacring all the Protestants in Dublin. D'Ewes, who spoke against Cromwell's motion, thanked fortune then that the plot did not succeed.

Ireland, and Two Armies brought into the bowels of this Kingdom, to the hazard of his Majesty's royal Person, the consumption of the revenue of the Crown, and the treasure of this Realm: And lastly, finding great causes of jealousy that endeavours have been and are used to bring the English Army into misunderstanding of this Parliament, thereby to incline that Army by force to bring to pass those wicked counsels,—

Have therefore thought good to join ourselves in a declaration of our united affections and resolutions; and to make this ensuing

PROTESTATION

I, A. B., do in the Presence of Almighty God promise, vow and protest, To maintain and defend as far as Lawfully I may, with my life, power and estate, the True Reformed Protestant Religion, expressed in the Doctrine of the Church of England, against all Popery and Popish Innovations, and according to the duty of my allegiance to his Majesty's royal Person, Honour and Estate: as also the Power and Privileges of Parliament, the Lawful Rights and Liberties of the Subject; and every Person that maketh this Protestation in whatsoever he shall do in the lawful pursuance of the same. And to my power, as far as lawfully I may, I will oppose, and by good ways and means endeavour to bring to condign punishment, all such as shall, by force, practice, counsel, plots, conspiracies or otherwise, do anything to the contrary in this present Protestation contained.

And further I shall, in all just and honourable ways, endeavour to preserve the union and peace betwixt the Three Kingdoms of England, Scotland and Ireland; and neither for hope, fear nor other respect, shall relinquish this Promise, Vow and Protestation.[19]

That Cromwell, like most of his fellow-members, signed it there can be no doubt; and it so happens that there is evidence that he not only supported it but urged an organization to make it more effective; for the note-book of these proceedings kept by a certain John More, member for Liverpool, records "Mr. Cromwell for an Oath of Association,"[20] which in effect, echoes and emphasizes the Protestation. It further appears from his letter to his Cambridge constituents that he was deeply concerned with this question of association or what he calls "combination," which Pym strongly favored:

To the right worshipful the Mayor and Aldermen of Cambridge, with the rest of that Body: Present these

Gentlemen,

We heartily salute you; and herewith (according to the directions of the House of Commons in this present Parliament assembled), send unto you a Protestation by them lately made, the contents whereof will best appear

[19] *C. J.*, ii, 132.

[20] *Harl. Mss. loc. cit.*, 477, f. 485. This must have been a speech.

in the thing itself. The preamble therewith printed doth declare the weighty reasons inducing them, in their own persons, to begin.

We shall only let you know that, with alacrity and willingness, the members of that body entered thereinto. It was in them a right honourable and necessary act; not unworthy your imitation. You shall hereby as the body represented avow the practice of the representative. The conformity is in itself praiseworthy; and will be by them approved. The result may (through the Almighty's blessing) become stability and security to the whole kingdom. Combination carries strength with it. It's dreadful to adversaries; especially when it's in order to the duty we owe to God, to the loyalty we owe to our King and Sovereign, and to the affection due to our country and liberties, the main ends of this Protestation now herewith sent you.

We say no more, but commit you to the protection of Him, who is able to save you; desiring your prayers for the good success of our present affairs and endeavours, which indeed are not ours but the Lord's and yours, whom we desire to serve in integrity; and bidding you heartily farewell, rest,

Your loving friends to be commanded,

[London, May 8th, 1641.]

OLIVER CROMWELL.
JOHN LOWRY.[21]

That Cromwell's chief concern was religion further appears in his next move in Parliament. On May 21, within a fortnight after Strafford's death, "A Bill for the utter abolishing and taking away all Archbishops, Bishops, their Chancellors and Commissaries, Deans, Deans and Chapters, Archdeacons, etc.," was introduced into the Commons by Sir Edward Dering.[22] This was the measure which was to become famous as the "Root and Branch Bill," proposing as it did to destroy episcopal government in all its 'roots and branches.' It was not Dering's work. It was handed to Sir Arthur Haselrig by Oliver Cromwell and Sir Henry Vane the younger just before it was introduced,[23] and it is reasonable to suppose that, if it was not wholly their handiwork, they had been instrumental in preparing it. It was a drastic measure in accord with all of Cromwell's expressed opinions and activities, and there is little doubt but that it represented his sentiments if it did not actually owe its phraseology to him. It was the outcome of what was known as the Root and Branch Petition

[21] *Cambridge Corporation Common Day Book*, printed in Cooper, *Annals of Cambridge*, iii, 311. Printed also in O. Cromwell, *Memoirs of the Protector*, i, 406; and Carlyle, App. 3. The letter is undated but as Lowry was absent and only signed the Protestation on Friday, May 7, and the letter was read in the Cambridge Common Council on Tues. May 11, it was probably written on Saturday.

[22] *C. J.*, ii, 159; *Old Parl. Hist.*, ix, 331.

[23] Moore's Diary, *Harl. Mss.*, vol. 477, f. 106. In his *Collection of Speeches*, p. 62, Dering says "Upon Thursday, *May* 21, I subjected myselfe to the obloquy I suffer. The Bill for *Abolition* of our present Episcopacy was pressed into my hand by S[ir] A[rthur] H[aselrig] (being then brought unto him by S[ir] H[enry] V[ane] and O[liver] C[romwell]). Cp. D'Ewes, Diary, *Harl. Mss.*, 162, f. 366b for identity of "O. C."

which had been introduced in Parliament on December 11, from "many of His Majesty's subjects in and about the City of London, and several Counties of the Kingdom." That petition recited that "the government of archbishops, lord bishops, deans and archdeacons &c" had "proved prejudicial and very dangerous both to the Church and Commonwealth" and prayed that "the said government, with all its dependencies, roots and branches be abolished," for some twenty-eight reasons which it then adduced. It laid especial stress on "the suppressing of that godly design set on foot by certain saints and sugared with many great gifts by sundry well-affected persons" of lectureships like that which had earlier engaged Cromwell's interest. It emphasized the publishing of "lascivious, idle and unprofitable books," the spread of "Popish" and "Arminian" tenets, and denounced in particular "bishops' rochets and lawn sleeves" with other ecclesiastical millinery, and the position of the communion-table, all in the best Calvinistic manner.[24]

It was a cause dear to Cromwell's heart, and the bill now brought before the House, though it omitted many of the non-essential details of this bill, embodied the fundamentals of the petition. It was of more consequence to him in that most of the problems with which he was concerned had been or were being settled, though not precisely in the form which had been first proposed. Prynne, Burton, Bastwick, Leighton and Lilburne were at liberty. The Triennial Act had been passed, with that preventing the dissolution of this Parliament without its own consent. The Tonnage and Poundage Act was well under way, and the five great measures for the abolition of the courts of Star Chamber and High Commission, ship-money, afforestation, and knighthood fines were being framed as rapidly as possible. Strafford had gone to the block the day after Cromwell's letter was read to the Cambridge Corporation, and had been blessed on his way by Laud from the window of his cell in the Tower.

The way for the attack on the Establishment was thus cleared; and the new bill not merely expressed Cromwell's opinions but provided him and his party with a new issue. It was sponsored in the Lords by his relative, Bishop Williams of Lincoln, and it gave an opportunity to review the whole problem of the church. It was not destined to be passed in its original form, nor in any form, but as a measure not for the abolition but for the "better regulating" or reformation of the church, the investigation of its revenues and its courts, it offered the Puritans a means of attacking or undermining the whole fabric of the great Establishment. Nor was Cromwell's activity confined to this. Though his committee work went on, there seems to be no record of it left, but there were many issues to absorb

[24] Rushworth, *Historical Collections*, iv, 93.

his energies in this spring and summer of 1641, and of at least one of them—the fen dispute—we have some evidence.

PARLIAMENT, MAY–SEPTEMBER, 1641

Among the various issues which confronted the Long Parliament was that perplexing and perennial problem of the fens in which Cromwell had interested himself so much as the champion of the "poor commoners" in Ely and Huntingdon, and in which he now appeared as their advocate in Parliament. The case was simple enough. When, in 1638, Charles had taken over the project from the Adventurers, he had given a considerable area to the Queen as part of her jointure. She had in turn sold it to Edward Montagu, Lord Mandeville, the son of the Earl of Manchester, who, with other proprietors, had begun to enclose their new properties. On May 22, 1641, Denzil Holles presented to the House a petition from Mandeville and Sir Thomas Hatton to the effect that rioters had beaten down their fences while the matter was still under consideration in Parliament by virtue of the petition of these commoners which had not yet been passed upon. That former petition recited that the lands had been enclosed in violation of the agreement that they were to remain common lands until the drainage project was complete. The new petition urged that the enclosures should remain until the first petition should be determined.

At once Cromwell sprang to the defense of the "poor commoners." This question, he declared, concerned the privilege of the House; for, while the first petition had been under consideration, the Lords had made an order against the commoners,

"settling the possession, which made the people to commit this outrage, which he did not approve nor desire to justify; and that since they had made another order to settle possession again by the sheriff and by force of arms with the trained bands."[25]

Behind Mandeville's petition and Cromwell's speech lay, it is evident, a long story of violence and disorder. Into that the Commons, despite Cromwell's insistence, for the moment declined to go, because of the breach on the Lords' part. This was not the end of the matter, but before it went further, various other things claimed his attention. The first was his appointment, on May 29, to a committee formed on May 11, to confer with such persons as they thought might be induced to lend money to pay the army. There he found among his colleagues Holles and Sir Thomas Barrington, with others like Henry

[25] D'Ewes Diary, quoted in Sanford, p. 368–9. Cp. *C. J.*, ii, 155.

Marten and Sir Robert Pye, and in its activities he was, apparently, brought into touch with those City interests which were presently to be of such great importance to him and his party.[26]

Two days later, on June 1, he moved that a certain Sir James Thynne[27] appear before the House on the ensuing Friday to show cause why Sir James had used his position as a member of Parliament to secure copies of documents in connection with a dispute between him and his younger brother over some family property in a case which had long been pending in the Court of Wards.[28] To that abuse of privilege Cromwell objected and the House agreed with him. Three days later, on June 4, he was appointed to a committee of sixteen which included Sir Gilbert Gerard and Bulstrode Whitelocke—both of whom were to play no inconsiderable part in his later life—to consider a petition from his own constituency, the town of Cambridge. On that same day, according to D'Ewes, as part of the general cleaning up of the abuses of the royal administration, on Cromwell's motion:

"It was ordered that the consideration of the office of the Clerk of the Burcels in the Exchequer should be referred to the same committee that was appointed to consider of the fines given for the original writs in Chancery, and . . . to consider what benefit accrues by it to the King, and what loss and danger to the subject. Divers spoke to the matter, as well as Mr. Cromwell, before it was referred, and showed that the office had formerly been questioned in Parliament, and the execution of it suspended for the time, and that it was a grievance to the subject."[29]

Meanwhile, however, the old question of the fen dispute had been under consideration, and on June 9 it came again to the attention of the House, with Cromwell as the motive force. On that day he moved:

"That the Earl of Manchester hath sent forth sixty writs against the poor inhabitants in Huntingdonshire for putting down enclosures and desired that the Committee for the Queen's jointure be renewed and that the petition be considered by it."[30]

It was therefore ordered that this committee consider the petition of the inhabitants of Somersham in Huntingdonshire, and in consequence, some three weeks later, about June 29, the committee on the Queen's jointure was revived, and Mr. Edward Hyde, later the Earl of Clarendon, was made chairman, and when he wrote his *Life* he

[26] *C. J.*, ii, 143, 160, 161.
[27] Elder brother of the ancestor of the Marquess of Bath.
[28] D'Ewes *Diary*, quoted in Sanford, p. 371n; *C. J.*, ii, 162.
[29] Quoted in Sanford, p. 371 n; See also *C. J.*, ii, 166.
[30] D'Ewes, *Diary*, quoted in Sanford, p. 369. Cp. *C. J.*, ii, 172.

described what he could remember of the scene. The enclosed lands, he explained, had been sold to the Earl of Manchester, who, with his son, Lord Mandeville, 'was most concerned to maintain the enclosure.' Against that procedure, Hyde wrote:

"As well the inhabitants of other manors, who claimed Common in those wastes, as the Queen's tenants of the same, made loud complaints, as a great oppression, carried upon them with a very high hand, and supported by power. . . . The Committee sat in the Queen's Court; and Oliver Cromwell being one of them, appeared much concerned to countenance the Petitioners, who were numerous together with their Witnesses; the Lord Mandevil being likewise present as a party, and by the direction of the Committee sitting covered. Cromwell, who had never before been heard to speak in the House of Commons, ordered the Witnesses and Petitioners in the method of the proceeding; and seconded, and enlarged upon what they said, with great passion; and the Witnesses and persons concerned, who were a very rude kind of people, interrupted the Counsel and Witnesses on the other side, with great clamour, when they said anything that did not please them; so that M. Hyde (whose office it was to oblige men of all sorts to keep order) was compelled to use some sharp reproofs, and some threats, to reduce them to such a temper that the business might be quietly heard. Cromwell, in great fury, reproached the Chairman for being partial, and that he discountenanced the Witnesses by threatening them: the other appealed to the Committee; which justified him, and declared that he behaved himself as he ought to do; which more inflamed him, who was already too much angry. When upon any mention of matter-of-fact, or of the proceeding before and at the Enclosure, the Lord Mandevil desired to be heard, and with great modesty related what had been done, or explained what had been said, Mr. Cromwell did answer, and reply upon him with so much indecency and rudeness, and in language so contrary and offensive, that every man would have thought, that as their natures and their manners were as opposite as it is possible, so their interest could never have been the same. In the end, his whole carriage was so tempestuous, and his behaviour so insolent, that the Chairman found himself obliged to reprehend him; and to tell him, That if he proceeded in the same manner, he would presently adjourn the Committee, and the next morning complain to the House of him."[31]

It is evident from Clarendon's account that Cromwell had not changed. As in his career in Huntingdon, in his activities in the Parliament of 1628, and his earlier appearances in this Long Parliament, he revealed the same qualities of unrestrained passion which continually brought him under censure. As Hampden, who sat on this committee, observed, "he was a man to sit well to the mark."[32] There is, besides, another characteristic which marks his utterances.

[31] Clarendon's *Life* (Oxford, 1761), i, 78. This was written from memory, and at least one statement—that Cromwell had never been heard to speak in the House before—is incorrect. Cromwell's violence was perhaps magnified by Clarendon, for D'Ewes, who was on the same committee does not mention such conduct.

[32] Sanford, *Studies*, pp. 371–2.

It is the personal animus against his opponents which impressed itself on those who recorded his speeches. He was not content to regard those who opposed him as merely wrong in principle; he seems to have denounced them personally, and his vituperation served to get him into trouble with the authorities. It was at once his weakness and his strength. His energy and conviction, his gift of strong, if provocative, language, his persistence, his audacity, his courage, his disregard of persons and procedure, marked him out as a man to be feared in any controversy with which he was concerned.

It was perhaps those qualities which made him so useful to men like Hampden and Pym as evidenced by the assignments given him. On July 3 he was appointed to a committee of thirty-one charged with the curious task of considering an "Act for better Enabling Members of Parliament to discharge their Consciences in the Proceedings of Parliament."[33] On the 28th he was put on a committee of twenty-seven, including Hampden, Fiennes, Barrington, Sir Robert Pye and Masham, to "consider an act explanatory of an act to raise money speedily."[34] On August 6 he was on a committee to consider the question of disafforesting the lands of that Sir James Thynne against whom he had earlier appeared.[35]

It was the first of many Parliamentary activities in that busy month of August 1641 when Charles set out for Scotland. That journey was bitterly opposed by Pym and his party, filled with anxiety lest the King escape their grasp and find support against them either in the English forces in the north or from the Scots themselves. Against the journey Cromwell, with others, protested and in a great debate on August 9 concerning the dangers of the kingdom in the King's absence, he voiced his objections forcibly. What, he inquired, was the necessity for Charles going, and what was his "own particular occasion?" Answering his own queries he continued:

> "If we can give the Scots satisfaccion, we disengage from the tye of publick faith which may be done by an ample commission for passing there acts; if we can propose consideracions equivalent, if [they do] not satisfy, yet will acquitt us. [There is] danger to his person going through the Armyes; factions stand up in Scotland; [and there is] danger in this kingdome if he go instante."[36]

Moreover what of the Prince of Wales and his governor, the Marquis of Hertford? He, scarcely less than the King himself, was

[33] *C. J.*, ii, 198.
[34] *Ibid.*, 228.
[35] *Ibid.*, 239.
[36] *Harleian Mss*, 5047, f. 60a, quoted in Barber, Helen B., ed., *D'Ewes Diary*, (July 5–Sept. 9, 1641), p. 344 (Thesis deposited in Cornell University Library, 1927).

the concern of the Commons; and Cromwell moved that two leaders of his own party, the Earl of Bedford and Lord Saye and Sele, be added to Hertford, but his motion was not seconded.[37] There was some reason for the Commons' fear. In March there had been discovered the "first army plot," by which certain courtiers, Suckling, Goring, Percy and Jermyn had planned to bring the army from the north to overawe the Parliament. Charles had refused to countenance that design but the fear remained and the Houses were still pursuing its authors. Returning, on August 12, to debate on the conspiracy of Henry Percy and Henry Jermyn, some would have gone to the question, but at this point, it is noted in a Parliamentary diary, "Mr. Cromwell" moved "to remove the Bishops of the Lords house before we proceed in this," in which the House again refused to follow him.[38]

In that he merely anticipated later action; but meanwhile the matter of Charles's visit to Scotland had been arranged in a way wholly favorable to the Commons and, as it happened, of inestimable advantage to Pym and his followers. On August 14 a "committee of defence" was appointed, which two days later brought in a recommendation that "authority shall be given to some person during the King's absence to putt the kingdome in a present posture of defence."[39] From that committee which, headed by Pym, was to play such a great part in the ensuing revolution, its chairman reported on the same day a recommendation to consider what authority should be given the commissioners who were to accompany Charles to Scotland. There was doubt, he said, whether it could be given without commission under the broad seal and whether the House had any power to command the Lord Keeper to set the Seal to such a commission. "Divers having spoaken, some that wee might cause a Commission to be sealed, others that wee could not, and others that wee might authorize Commissioners by the order of the two howses,"[40] presently, as an anonymous diarist records, "Mr. Cromwell" rose to say that "the putting of the seale wilbe as necessary for a commission to put the Kingdome to a posture as in this" matter of the commissioners to accompany the King, "desiring a committee of long robe may consider it."[41]

Meanwhile Charles had started for Scotland on August 10. There was, in effect, no government in England save the Committee of De-

[37] *Harleian Mss*, 5047, f. 61; D'Ewes Diary, *Harleian Mss*, 164, f. 13b. *Loc. cit.*, pp. 346, 350.

[38] *Harleian Mss*, 5047, f. 63a. Cp. D'Ewes Diary, *Harleian Mss*, 164, f. 22b. *Loc. cit.*, pp. 383, 397.

[39] D'Ewes Diary, *Harl. Mss*, 164, f. 32b.

[40] *Ibid.*

[41] *Harl. Mss*, 5047, f. 74b.

fence which was charged with consideration of the Tower, the forts, the militia and magazines of arms. In the absence of a secretary of state, the Lord Keeper was asked to authorize the appointment of the commissioners to accompany Charles. He had refused and at the suggestion of D'Ewes, the Commons sent to the Lords an "ordinance" to legalize the status of the commissioners. Thus was born the second great engine of government—the Parliamentary ordinance—which, with the Committee of Defence, began to replace royal with parliamentary authority. Another device in whose formation Cromwell played a part grew out of the desire to despatch funds to York to supply the army and the King. There was no authority to levy it but Parliament assumed that power also. On August 24 it was resolved to have the sheriffs of certain counties including Cambridge and Huntingdon send money to York under convoy and it was decided that knights of those shires should write to the sheriffs to that effect. Mr. Walton, Cromwell's brother-in-law, "undertooke that hee would give timely notice to the sheriffe of Huntingdonshire, being one of the knights of that countie." Other knights of shires did likewise, as, apparently, did "Mr. Cromwell one of the burgesses of the towne of Cambridge," as it seems that both of the knights of the shire were at that moment absent.[42]

Such were some of the effects of the King's visit to Scotland, as during his absence the Houses seized the opportunity to get into their hands a part at least of the executive authority through a Committee of Defence which was, in fact, scarcely less than a regency. Reinforced with the new device of ordinances and the levying of money on the counties, it was but one step to the control of the armed forces which they now proposed; and it was evident from their words as from their acts that at least some among them aspired to substitute the House of Commons for the crown.

In all of these activities Cromwell had taken part in some capacity, and on August 24 he was entrusted with another duty which often fell to him as the months went on. When the ordinance was brought in for despatching funds to York, the debate was resumed and Cromwell moved to send a message to the Lords to suggest "a conference by a committee of both Houses touching the speedy sending of money to [York] for the disbanding of the Armies." Himself appointed to go with the message, he brought back the Lords' assent.[43] Four days later, on August 28, Cromwell delivered to the House two petitions, one from the prisoners in the Fleet, the other from the prisoners in the King's Bench, both pointing out that formerly in times of pestilence they had been permitted to go into the country upon good bail,

[42] D'Ewes Diary, *Harl. Mss*, 154, f. 55b.
[43] D'Ewes Diary, *Harl. Mss*, 164, f. 57b; *C. J.*, ii, 270.

and asking the same favor. As a result he was named as one of thirteen to consider the petitions and find some way to release the prisoners on security.[44] On August 30, with Vane, Barrington, Masham and Pye, he was put on a committee of twenty-seven to consider a petition from some freeholders of Hertfordshire.[45] Finally, on September 1, he was named to a committee of twenty-five to consider the petitions of a certain Sir Frederick Hambleton, a Mr. Cope, and "Widow Linche," and to advise what Irish causes were to be recommended from the English to the Irish Parliament.[46] Thus, little by little, he was drawn into connection with those affairs which were to be of such importance to his later life, Scotland, the City and now Ireland.

Before Parliament adjourned in September, he is noted as having some share in two other matters of importance. In the debate on the "Ordinance against Innovations in the Worship of God," which passed the Commons on September 1, he spoke against the Common Prayer Book "shewing that there were many passages in it which divers learned and wise Divines could not submit unto and practice."[47] With the debate on this measure, the lines were finally drawn between the Anglicans and the Nonconformists. It was, in the words of its greatest historian, "the commencement of civil war." Though the Root and Branch bill seems to have been tacitly laid aside, the House agreed to move communion tables from the east end of the churches, to take down communion rails, remove all crucifixes and "scandalous pictures" of the Trinity and the Virgin Mary, with "tapers, candlesticks and basins" on communion tables, to dispense with "all corporal bowing at the name of Jesus or towards the east end of the church," to forbid all dancing and sports on the Lord's day, and permit sermons in the afternoon. Save for the abolition of episcopacy and the Prayer Book, the Puritans had won. With the attack upon that citadel of Anglicanism, the last phase of the long struggle to rid England of the "rags of Rome" began.

In it Cromwell had played a leading part, and on September 8, upon his motion, it was ordered that "sermons should be in the afternoon in all parishes of England at the charge of the inhabitants of those parishes where there were no sermons in the afternoon." The order was afterwards printed and the "liberty of Lecture" to be set up on week days was added to it.[48] On the same day, the day before the Parliament adjourned, Cromwell, with Henry Marten, Edmund Waller, Serjeant Wilde and a Mr. Wheeler, was added to a committee

[44] D'Ewes Diary, *Harl. Mss*, 164, f. 71a; *C. J.*, ii, 274.
[45] *C. J.*, ii, 276.
[46] *Ibid.*, 280.
[47] D'Ewes, Diary, *Harl. Mss*, 164, f. 84a. Cp. *C. J.*, ii, 279–81.
[48] D'Ewes, *op. cit.*, f. 101a.

to consider levies then being made, in the words of the resolution, "for the King of Spain and the French King's service";[49] and with this final assignment, he returned to his home and his constituents.

Such was the career of Oliver Cromwell in this first session of this momentous Parliament. It has attracted little notice from historians or biographers, yet it was an important, if not a determining period of his life. He had been brought into close contact with the great issues and great leaders of the time; he had gained wide acquaintance with many forms of public business; he had touched nearly every side of public affairs in his committee work; and he had called attention to himself by his uncompromising hostility to the church, by his ill-regulated and undisciplined but dangerous qualities as an antagonist. Apart from Strafford's trial, his career is almost an epitome of the activities of this session of the Long Parliament, and he emerged from it a notable if not a leading figure of the Puritan party. That party was now in the ascendant. Its path was strewed with the wreck of the old system of government; it had begun its last great assault on the old order, that upon the church; and at this moment it appeared that it might succeed in even that and remake England in ecclesiastical as in civil government.

THE RECESS, SEPTEMBER 9–OCTOBER 20, 1641

What of the King during this critical period when his power was being filched from him; what of his advisers, of the bishops, of the Scotch and English forces in the north; what of Ireland? How was this revolt to be checked or crushed or conciliated? Stripped of his ablest counsellors, Charles was left to his own uncertain temper and judgment, the advice of his devoted but inexperienced and injudicious wife and his incompetent courtiers, faced with a situation as unfamiliar as it was threatening. That little group was no match for the leaders of the Parliament. It had entered on conspiracy to defeat what it regarded as conspiracy. It had approved fantastic designs to rescue Strafford, to seize the Tower, to bring the army from the north. It had appealed to foreign powers, to the house of Orange, to the Pope, and now to the Scots. It strove to sow dissension among its opponents; and the King had even tried to call some opposition Lords to the Privy Council.

It was all in vain. The steps which might have saved the King he refused to take. He would not abdicate his right to choose his own ministers; he would not give up the Established church; he would not

49 *C. J.*, ii, 284.

accept a new view of monarchy; he would not turn from a constitutional to a mere parliamentary king. He agreed to join Parliament in abolishing the Laudian "innovations" in the church; he assented to the Triennial bill; in the face of threats from the London mob, he abandoned Laud and Strafford to their fate. By accepting the Tonnage and Poundage act he gave up one of his prerogatives; by agreeing that this Parliament would not be dissolved without its own consent, he gave up another. The abolition of the Tudor courts and councils had reduced his powers and by the end of August, 1641, he was left but a shadow of that great authority which he and his predecessors had wielded. The great question which confronted his opponents was whether he would submit to this or whether he would try to regain his old position in the state.

There still remained some hope and in that hope he had set out for Scotland to seek her support. The dream of re-establishing episcopal supremacy in that kingdom was already doomed; the hope of securing Scotland in his interest was more promising despite the adherence of the Scotch Presbyterians to the cause of the Parliament. Though Charles did much to conciliate the Scots, a wild design of some of his adherents to seize the opposition leaders, Argyll, Lanark and Hamilton, undid much of his work and this "Incident," though he had no part in it, did much harm to his cause. In other ways he was wiser and more fortunate. He declared his purpose to restore the church of Elizabeth on his return to England, and won wide support. Had it not been for the distrust of his advisers and of his own sincerity, and the exaggerations of his enemies, it might have given him the ascendancy in his conflict with Parliament. But at this moment another circumstance brought all his plans to naught and introduced another and a fatal element into the already all too difficult situation of affairs.

This was the Irish Massacre.[50] In October 1641, while Charles was still in Scotland, the native Irish attempted to seize Dublin, and, foiled in that design, fell on the English and Scottish colonists, especially in Ulster. According to the wild rumors which reached England, growing as they went, some thirty thousand of these colonists were put to death under circumstances of the greatest cruelty. Whatever the truth or falsehood of the tales which reached Westminster, nothing could have been worse for Charles or better for his opponents than the news of the Irish massacres. Whatever his connection with the Irish leaders—and there seems no reason to believe that it was such as to produce this rebellion, or that he was in any way responsible for it—the suspicion of his purposes put a deadly weapon into the

[50] For the Irish massacre and its results see Gardiner, *History;* Bagwell, *Ireland under the Stuarts;* and Dunlop, *Ireland under the Commonwealth*, Introd.

hands of Pym. None realized this more than Charles himself. It was the crowning blow to all his plans; and his absence had given his enemies an opportunity to undermine his power.

With no royal officials left in England, the Parliamentary leaders had not merely appointed a Committee of Defence, passed "ordinances" with virtually the force of law and levied taxes without the King's consent, but they had taken steps to secure the militia and the fortresses, ordering Holland to occupy Hull and Newport to take charge of the Tower. They had named commissioners not only to watch his movements in Scotland but to keep in touch with the Scottish leaders. But their assumption of great powers with the burden of taxation which made the royal requests seem moderate in comparison, had turned many against them. Moreover, government had begun to disintegrate. Riots had broken out in many places, especially in London; disbanded soldiers had turned highwaymen; the posts were stopped and robbed; and fanatics made their appearance here and there after the fashion of the Munster Anabaptists. Men desired peace and ordered government, such as they had enjoyed under monarchy. The English army was disbanding; the Scots returning home; and had it not been for this Irish rising and the Scotch "Incident," it is not improbable that Charles might have returned in triumph from the north.

THE GRAND REMONSTRANCE
OCTOBER 20–NOVEMBER 25, 1641

It was a critical moment for Pym and his party, for men began to fear the rising of "the blatant beast" of the masses, and this was not lessened by the conflict of authority. When Parliament assembled on October 20, it was met with demands for consideration of a Popish plot, news of the Irish rising and the Scotch "Incident." At that moment Charles sent his declaration of royal policy—monarchy and the church of Elizabeth. It rallied to him the forces of discontent which had been gathering against Pym and his followers, who found that power brought responsibilities and dissatisfaction in its train. Not even the appointment of new bishops by the king served to check his rising popularity. Discontent with "King Pym" increased greatly. This Parliamentary leaders tried in vain to check by the discovery of a new "army plot"; but it was evident that sterner measures were essential and November 1 was set apart for a great assault upon the monarchy. It took the form of a Grand Remonstrance against royal policy, to bring to a head the whole sum of Parliamentary grievances against the crown.

Whether by accident or design—and if it was a mere coincidence, it was one of the most remarkable in history—it was on that very day that the news of the Irish rebellion reached Westminster, and the reading of the despatches of the Irish justices on its outrages accompanied the presentation of the Remonstrance. Never was a political sensation better timed. Whatever their other differences, the Houses were at one in their passionate desire to maintain English supremacy in Ireland and to punish the rebels. Laying all other matters to one side, they voted fifty thousand pounds for suppression of the rebellion, ordered Leicester to proceed to Dublin, authorized an army of eight thousand men, and asked for volunteers. At almost the same moment Charles appealed in person to the Scottish Parliament for aid, transmitted their assent to Westminster, and both nations prepared to put rebellion down.

It was at this moment that Pym launched another attack upon the King, in the form of "Additional Instructions" to the Parliamentary commissioners in Scotland, to the effect that unless the King would remove his 'evil counsellors' and 'take such as might be approved by Parliament,' the Houses would refuse him aid against Ireland. Though bitterly opposed, Pym pressed his proposal and it was carried in the House. It was the essence of revolution, a declaration of war against the monarchy; and as the Root and Branch Petition had divided men into Episcopalians and Puritans, this resolution divided them into Royalists and Parliamentarians. Meanwhile the Grand Remonstrance, read in the Commons in this same session, became the rallying-point of Pym's party in the oncoming struggle between crown and Parliament, into which the quarrel between church and Puritan was thenceforth to be merged.[51]

For some reason now unknown to us, Cromwell seems not to have played the part in the events of August and September, 1641, which one might naturally expect. He was not conspicuous enough to be put on the Committee of Defence, much less to accompany Hampden to Scotland, and his committee assignments in comparison with those of the earlier months of the Long Parliament seem of no great consequence. He was as yet, apparently, known only as an aggressive controversialist, not as an administrator, and certainly not as a diplomat.

With the opening of the second session he became more prominent. He began, as usual, with opposition to the church. The first day of the session, October 20, saw the introduction of a bill to disable "all persons in Holy Orders to exercise any temporal jurisdiction or au-

[51] *C. J.* and *L. J. passim; Parliamentary History;* and Parry, *Parliaments and Councils;* Gardiner, *History.*

thority," and so exclude the bishops from the House of Lords. To this Cromwell naturally gave his support, and the bill was passed on the 23rd, though, as Falkland drily pointed out, it was certain to be rejected by the Lords as it was not the province of the Commons, nor within its powers, to determine the membership of the Upper House. None the less, Pym pressed his attack, and on October 26, as D'Ewes relates, he moved to ask the Lords to sequester the votes of the thirteen bishops in the vote on the bishops' 'crimes.' Vane suggested that this might be done by alleging that they had taken the oath of the new canons binding themselves never to consent to the bill previously sent up taking away their votes permanently. Whereupon,

"Mr. Cromwell gave this reason for it, because we did but suspend their voices for a time only till this bill was passed."[52]

After an interlude in which, on October 27, Cromwell "moved about the late election of a knight of the shire in Hertfordshire"[53]— Sir Thomas Dacres *vice* Arthur Capel called to the Lords as Baron Capel—he returned to the attack, as D'Ewes notes:

"Mr. Cromwell renewed againe the motion which had been first moved by myselfe yesterday and was this day renewed by Sir Walter Earle, touching a conference with the Lords for the staying of the investiture of the five new Bishopps that were to bee made and did speak somewhat bitterly against doctor Howlsworth, others opposed it and Sir John Hotham saied we might runn into a *premunire* by endeavouring to stay the creation of any Bishopps after the King had sent the *Conge de lier*."[54]

The case of Dr. Holdsworth, master of Emmanuel College, Cambridge, vice-chancellor of the University, staunch churchman, strong royalist and royal chaplain but moderate Puritan, "a most learned man . . . most ready to further a reformation of the church," as D'Ewes notes, had been referred to a Parliamentary committee in the preceding July. Now, after long debate, the motion for a conference with the Lords was carried by 71 to 53 and another committee named, "of which," D'Ewes says, "Mr. Cromwell was nominated first and myselfe the second."[55]

To this quarrel with the crown and church and disagreement with the Lords over Charles's appointment of new bishops and their right to vote in the Upper House was added another issue, that of the

[52] D'Ewes Diary, *Harl. Mss*, 162, f. 41b. (Coates, W. H., *Journal of Sir Simonds D'Ewes*, Oct. 20, 1641–Jan. 10, 1641/2, a thesis deposited in the Cornell University Library in 1926.) But, as D'Ewes points out, if it were passed the Bishops would forever lose their vote. Cromwell meant that the Bishops should not be allowed to bring about the rejection of the bill if, without their vote, the bill would be passed.

[53] *Ibid.*, 162, f. 43b.

[54] *Ibid.*, 162, f. 53b, 54b; *C. J.* ii, 298.

[55] *Ibid.*, 162, f. 52b.

education of the Prince of Wales. In that Pym's party took an active interest. On October 30 the Lords consented to a conference concerning an order to the Marquis of Hertford to take Prince Charles into his charge, and there ensued one of those petty squabbles not unknown to such assemblies. Sir John Hotham moved that the members in the Painted Chamber, apparently in conference with a committee of the Lords, might be sent for; Mr. Pearde that some one should take their names instead; and Pearde, Hotham and Cromwell were named for that service. Hotham begged to be excused; Sir Symonds observed acidly that 'only in schools did monitors take names.' The serjeant-at-arms was sent with his mace to bring the members back, and it was ordered presently that Hertford should take the Prince and permit only "safe" people to be near him.[56]

What part Cromwell played in the feverish events of November 1 we do not know, but in the acrimonious discussion of the "army plot," three days later, D'Ewes records that:

> "Mr. Cromwell shewed that Mr. Ashburnham who had been accused heere of the late designe had visited Sir John Barklay in the Tower being ther a prisoner for the same; and therefore hee desired that the saied Mr. Ashburnham, Mr. Wilmot and Mr. Pollard should noe longer goe upon baile but be remannded to prison."[57]

Two days later it appears from the same source that:

> "Another head of the conference [with the upper House on the safety of the kingdom] was added upon Mr. Cromwells motion that wee should desire the Lords that an ordinance of Parliament might passe to give the Earle of Essex power to assemble at all times the trained bands of the kingdome on this side Trent for the defence thereof till further order were taken by Parliament."[58]

This was part of the conflict of authority between King and Parliament. Charles had named Essex to command the trained bands during his own absence in Scotland; this measure continued the appointment during the pleasure of the Houses, and so pushed forward another step the controversy over the respective powers of crown and Commons in this all-important question of control of the militia.

Three days later the Grand Remonstrance was read for the first time, and it was moved that a consideration of the particulars should be assigned to various men according to their knowledge, interests and capacities, to find out and specify these grievances, high and low, particular and general in this grand indictment of the Stuart monarchy. Among a multitude of complaints of misgovernment and mis-

[56] D'Ewes, Diary, *Harl. Mss.* 162, f. 58b.
[57] *Ibid.*, f. 86b.
[58] *Ibid.*, 162, f. 106b; *C. J.*, ii, 305.

management the fen dispute found place, and Cromwell was named to 'farther explain the Commission of Sewers,' that is to say the drainage of the fens.[59]

It was proposed to bring the results of this long and painstaking scrutiny of Charles's government before the House on November 20; but its opponents asked for time to consider the charges, which was secured against the opposition of Pym's party, among them Oliver Cromwell. He, like others of that group, was irked by the delay. Certain of victory, they wished to push the matter to a swift conclusion. Of his impatience and his confidence in the outcome, Clarendon has left some record in his *History* of a conversation on that day.

"Cromwell (who at that time was little taken notice of)," he says, "asked the Lord Falkland 'why he would put it off, for that day would quickly have determined it.' He answered 'There would not have been time enough, for it would take some debate.' Cromwell replied, 'A very sorry one,' supposing few would oppose it."[60]

In that, at least, he was mistaken. On November 22 the debate began on the great indictment of the monarchy, and so far from being short it lasted from noon till two o'clock[61] the next morning; so far from being 'sorry,' it was the most bitterly fought and most momentous argument in the history of the English Parliament. The Grand Remonstrance itself was an extraordinary document. In every line it betrayed the bitter animus of its authors against the system of English government both in church and state which had prevailed until that time. In one long undigested mass of articles it enumerated all the grievances which the combined ingenuity of Pym and his followers could collect to discredit Charles's administration. It included everything from government by bishops to the vexations of "saltpetre men," from evil counsellors to conversion of arable into pasture land, from Roman Catholics to the sale of timber in the Forest of Dean to Papists, from the Court of Star Chamber to the taking of "common and several grounds . . . from the subject by colour of the Statute of Improvement, and by abuse of the Commission of Sewers, without their consent and against it." Thus did the old fen dispute find its way into a great constitutional document, and thus did Oliver Cromwell make his contribution to the Grand Remonstrance.

That document, in which Thomas Jefferson was to find the inspiration for the American Declaration of Independence a hundred and

[59] *C. J.*, ii, 309.

[60] Clarendon, *History* (1826), ii, 42.

[61] D'Ewes says midnight and that they wrangled two more hours over whether or not it should be printed. Gardiner makes a curious slip in placing the end of the session at four o'clock; Sir Philip Warwick says it lasted until three; Whitelocke places it at ten [two?] the next morning.

thirty-five years later, was, like that Declaration, not merely a "battle-cry of liberty," and a statement of the case against the English monarchy; it was an appeal to the people to resist that monarchy. It was, in effect, a call to arms. It was a desperate attempt of Pym and his followers to maintain that ascendancy which they felt was slipping from them. The alteration in worship pushed forward in September, 1641, without consent of the king or assent of the Lords had alienated the Episcopalians; the demand that Charles must choose only such "counsellors and ministers as should receive parliamentary approval," however much it appealed to later generations, was far in advance of its time, and had turned Episcopalians into Royalists. The Irish rising brought matters to a head. An army must be raised and money provided for suppression of the rebellion; but was that army and that money to be put at the disposal of a king who might well use them to suppress not the Irish but the Parliament? It was essential to make that impossible; and to accomplish this it was necessary to discredit Charles's administration once and for all.

In consequence the protest which had been begun in the first session but allowed to lapse was now revived, augmented and presented to the House. The first part, that against the church, prepared earlier, it has been suggested, by Fiennes and Vane, was reinforced by a second instalment relating to political affairs and specific grievances prepared by Pym and his followers, Strode, Culpepper, Cromwell, and Hampden, with others.[62] The Irish rising provided an extraordinary opportunity to rouse again the fears of the country; nor were the usual circumstances of agitation wanting to spur the matter on. The old Gunpowder Plot was revived in another form, this time by a tailor who appeared before the House with a fantastic tale of having miraculously overheard a design to kill a hundred and eight of its members and extend the activities of the Catholic Union to England. Another army plot was called in to further incriminate the King; the Irish rising stressed; the King's complicity more than hinted at; and in an atmosphere charged with fear and suspicion, with many members absent, the Remonstrance was carried by eleven votes (159–148).

But its passage through the Commons was not enough. "It appeared," wrote Clarendon of these proceedings, "that they did not intend to send it up to the House of Peers for their concurrence" but to appeal to the people; and though it was against precedent, Hampden moved that it might be printed. That roused a storm of protest. It came near precipitating bloodshed in the House; but "after scarce any quiet and regular debate," at about two o'clock in the morning, the weary House, after the manner of such assemblies worn out with long conflict, passed Hampden's motion and adjourned. So

[62] Schoolcraft, *Genesis of the Grand Remonstrance;* Forster, *The Grand Remonstrance.* The Remonstrance is printed in *Old. Parl. Hist.* x, 60–88.

as Clarendon later moralized, "a handful of men, much inferior in the beginning in number and interest, came to give laws to the major part."

Among those men Cromwell was numbered; and some record remains of his deep feeling in the matter, for Clarendon observes:

"As they went out of the House the Lord Falkland asked Oliver Cromwell [in obvious continuation of their former conversation] 'Whether there had been a debate?' to which he answered, 'that he would take his word another time,' and whispered him in the ear, with some asseveration, 'that if the Remonstrance had been rejected he would have sold all he had the next morning, and never have seen England more; and he knew there were many other honest men of the same resolution.' "[63]

"So near," wrote Clarendon, "was the poor kingdom at that time to its deliverance." Yet, as he records also, Pym's party was deeply disturbed, for "they discerned well enough that the House had not at that time half its members, though they had provided that not a man of their party was absent, and that they had even then carried it by the hour of night, which drove away a greater number of old and infirm opposers that would have made those of the negative superior in number." They were, as their leaders realized, in a minority. Their only hope was to win support in the nation.

THE ATTEMPT ON THE FIVE MEMBERS, NOVEMBER 25, 1641–JANUARY, 1642

To gain support in the nation was no easy task for Pym's party. Charles returned from Scotland on November 25, 1641, more popular than when he went away. He replied indirectly by a proclamation on religion and by a direct answer to the Remonstrance—which he noted was "already abroad in print," contrary to previous practice—reasserting his intention to meet his people's wishes "in a parliamentary way," both as to reforms in the church and as to the presence of the bishops in the House of Lords. He refused to give up "that natural liberty all free men have" in choosing his own ministers. He thanked the Houses for their aid in suppressing the Irish rebellion, but he noted with strong disapproval the remarks on "malignity" and "malignant advisers," and "endeavors to sow among the people false scandals and imputations against the government." In this he was supported by a considerable body of public opinion even in London itself, which in turn irritated the opponents of Charles in the Com-

[63] Clarendon, *op. cit.*, ii, 43–44.

mons. Two days after the King's return, on November 27, Cromwell called this to the attention of the House.

"Mr. Cromwell," D'Ewes notes in his Diary, "brought in a testimonial of one James Best dwelling in Pater Noster Row [at the sign of the Death's Head in the Old Bailey][64] by which he witnessed that one (whome hee named not least hee should withdraw himselfe) had saied: That this howse was offended that the cittie of London gave the King such great entertainment and that the said howse did send to the saied cittie not to intertaine him. It was thereupon ordered after the clarke had read it: that the said Best should be sent for to the howse to witness the same."[65]

Meanwhile excitement grew and as during Strafford's trial and like crises earlier, that familiar phenomenon of revolution, mob violence, was invoked against the bishops. What Boston was to be to the American and Paris to the French Revolution in the succeeding century, what the mobs of those cities were to be to those movements, the London mob was to this revolt. As it had earlier gathered to demand Strafford's head, it now began to flock to Westminster again to shout "No bishops! No bishops!" and to threaten the palace itself. It attacked the bishops on their way to the House of Lords, and, pushed on by the party of Hampden and Pym, used every means to intimidate the champions of church and crown in this movement to drive the bishops from the Upper House. That attack was extended to the supporters of monarchy, and in this latter activity, at least, Cromwell took his part. On December 6 he moved that:

"The Earl of Arundel had written a letter to the borough of Arundel, in Sussex, for the election of a new burgess there, and desired that the Speaker would write a letter to make a free election."[66]

To this it was objected that it had been an immemorial custom, if not a right of peers to write such "recommendatory letters."[67] None the less a committee was appointed to consider the matter, on which sat Pym and Cromwell, Strode and Lisle, with Royalists like Hyde and Falkland;[68] and on December 10, Cromwell reported for the committee and "brought an order to prevent that election and all others of the same kind."[69] Ten days later he was named to a com-

[64] *C. J.*, II, 325.

[65] D'Ewes, Diary, *Harl. Mss*, 162, f. 191b.

[66] D'Ewes Diary, *Harl. Mss*, 162, f. 213b.

[67] It was also pointed out that a member had been refused a seat for giving money to be elected and that a judge might be corrupted by a great man's letter as well as by a bribe. *Ibid.*

[68] *C. J.*, ii, 333.

[69] D'Ewes, *op. cit.*, f. 226b. The election objected to was of Mr. Harman, the Earl's secretary.

mittee of thirty-five to consider "An Act for the present disarming of Romish Recusants."[70]

Feeling was running higher from day to day and when on December 22 Charles appointed his unpopular follower, Lunsford, to the charge of the Tower, as "a man he could trust," he was protested as 'an outlaw, a ruined and desperate character and a non-attender at church'—besides a rumor that he was a child-eating cannibal. The Lords refused to request his removal but the Commons, supported by the City authorities, forced Charles to replace him with Sir John Byron on December 26. The growing fear of the Roman Catholics, especially of the Irish, and of the possibility of Charles's appeal to force, was increasing in Pym's party. In that Cromwell joined wholeheartedly. On December 28, in the course of a debate in connection with a request to the Lords to join in an address to Charles to remove the Earl of Bristol from his Council, Cromwell voiced the reasons for that request. In the words of D'Ewes:

"Mr. Cromwell moved that hee conceived it fitt for this howse to desire the Lords to joine with them in moveing his Majestie that the said Earl of Bristow might be removed from his Counsell who had thus perswaded his Majestie, and the rather because when the late designe was of bringing upp the armie, hee had perswaded his Majestie to putt the said Armie into a posture, which could have no ordinarie meaning in it, because the saied [army] was then in its due posture of standing still."[71] Mr. Strode and others seconded him.

To this fear was added that of Ireland, in which Cromwell more and more interested himself. On December 29, D'Ewes records that:

"Mr. Cromwel shewed that the Lord Leiftenant of Ireland had not yet bestowed upon Owen Occonelle a captaines place over a companie of Dragoones. His petition was read wherein hee desired againe to have some place of preferment in Ireland in the Province of Munster to serve in the warrs against the Rebels. We had formerly voted that he should have some place of preferment in the armie. Soe the said Mr. Cromwell and Mr. Hotham weere appointed to goe to the Lord Leiftenant to desire in the name of this howse that the saied Occonelle might be preferred."[72]

In consequence Cromwell and Hotham approached the Lord Lieutenant of Ireland, the Earl of Leicester, in behalf of this O'Connell

[70] *C. J.*, ii, 349–50.

[71] D'Ewes, *op. cit.*, f. 287b. Cp. Sanford, p. 453. Gardiner (*History* x, 119) says there is little doubt that Cromwell was mistaken, but the Commons were in no mood to interpret Bristol's conduct favorably.

[72] *Ibid.*, 162, f. 290b. Owen O'Connell was the servant of Strafford's enemy, Sir John Clotworthy, of co. Antrim in Ireland.

who had frustrated the surprise of Dublin by his information to the government of the intended rising. To this they were further instructed to add a request to Leicester to reserve the command of one of the two regiments to be sent into Munster for the President of that province, and that a certain "Mr. Jepson," member for Stockbridge, then in Ireland where he had raised a troop of horse, be serjeant-major of the regiment. And when, two days later, on December 31, Hotham reported that their message had been delivered but no answer had been received, he and Cromwell were ordered to go again and "desire a speedy answer."[73]

But at this moment even the Irish crisis gave way to events nearer home. Charles's none too great patience had been exhausted. He knew the plots against him and his royal authority. He believed that opposition leaders like Kimbolton in the Lords, Pym, Hampden, Holles, Strode and Haselrig in the Commons planned the overthrow of the old system of monarchy. He knew that even while they had denounced him for his attempts to gain aid for his cause, they had negotiated with the Scots before Leslie had crossed the Tweed, and he believed that they had actually invited the invasion. He knew that even while they accused him of "sowing false scandals," they had published attacks on him. He more than suspected that, if they had not actually instigated the mob violence which at critical moments threatened Whitehall, they had at least been cognizant of it; that they had been in touch with City elements, and if they had not planned they had done little or nothing to punish the mob and its leaders. In consequence, on January 3, 1642, he instructed the Attorney-general to impeach them of treason. Immediately their party in the Commons rose in their defence, and it seemed evident that they would resist an effort to bring these men to the same jeopardy in which they had placed Strafford nine months before.

Advised of what he naturally believed an attempt to obstruct justice, Charles took a fatal resolution. The next day, on January 4, accompanied by some five hundred armed followers, he went down the street to the Commons to arrest these men himself. He left his followers outside, entered the House and demanded the five members. Warned of his approach they had sought refuge in the City, and the Speaker, Lenthall, asked for them, made his historic answer: "I have neither eyes to see nor tongue to speak in this place, but as this House is pleased to direct me"; so, followed by shouts of "Privilege! Privilege!" Charles made his way back to Whitehall, and within the week he left that palace not to return till he came back to die.

[73] *Ibid.*, f. 298b; *C. J.*, ii, 360, 361, 365.

CHAPTER IV

THE EVE OF CIVIL WAR

JANUARY, 1642

It was only too evident that with the attack on the five members, barring some miracle of statesmanship, England was faced with the threat of civil war. The Commons' Committee of Defence sought the protection of the City authorities and met in Grocers' Hall. The London trained bands under Skippon were called out to protect them. The City authorities ignored the King's demand for the surrender of the five members; the seamen offered their assistance; the apprentices joined in; and some thousands of Hampden's constituents were reported on their way to support the cause. On January 10 Charles reached Hampton Court; the next morning the Committee of Defence and the five members returned to Westminster in triumph; and each side began to prepare for possible conflict.

Their first concern was the control of strongholds, ports and magazines. As Hampden's constituents arrived, Lunsford's Cavaliers gathered at Kingston to secure its store of arms. Charles ordered Pennington to seize Portsmouth and Newcastle to be governor of Hull, but his plans as usual were betrayed to the Commons who appointed Sir John Hotham to secure the northern port. Charles moved to Windsor and each side turned its attention to the trained bands or militia. Under guise of danger from the "Papists," on January 14 Pym moved that the House go into committee on the state of the kingdom and Cromwell asked for a committee "to consider of means to put the kingdom in a posture of defence," which was accordingly ordered.[1]

Slight as his share was in this first move toward war, it is significant that thus early Cromwell foresaw, if he did not welcome, the arbitrament of arms and joined Pym in this step to prepare for it. They did not waste much time. On that same day the Houses issued a general order to the sheriffs to secure all stores of arms and to suppress all unlawful assemblies—among them, one suspects, of Royalists. At the same time they ordered the Marquis of Hertford to resume his post as governor or tutor of the Prince of Wales and not to let the heir to the throne be taken from the kingdom. Three days later the Houses

[1] D'Ewes Diary, *Harl. Mss*, 162, f. 328b.

issued a declaration concerning a "late breach of privilege." It noted not only the attempt on the five members by "soldiers, Papists and others," but the publication of a charge of high treason against these men, which, they declared was "a high breach of the privilege of Parliament, a great scandal to His Majesty and his government, a seditious act manifestly tending to the subversion of the peace of the kingdom."

It was a deliberate challenge to a king who, whatever his misdeeds, could hardly as the head of the government be charged with sedition against himself. It was, in effect, a notice that the Commons, not the crown, was now the sovereign power. That power it proceeded to exercise in the same manner as the old Star Chamber, and in this again Cromwell played some part. On January 17, he and his brother-in-law Walton "informed the House of dangerous words spoken by a Huntingdonshire gentleman," otherwise unidentified, and a warrant was promptly issued for his arrest and a summons for the informer to appear.

Three days later the individual had apparently been identified, arrested and examined, for, as D'Ewes records:

"A little after 4 of the clocke in the afternoon, Mr. Cromwell moved that Mr. Ravenscroft, a Justice of the Peace in Huntingdonshire, might be bailed, who was sent for upp and kept in the serjeant's custodie, but not as a delinquent. It had been witnessed against him under a minister's hand that hee had said that if the King and Parliament should differ, the most of the gentrie would be for the King, and that he had 1,000 readie to assist him. Divers spake against it for the present but upon my seconding it this afternoon againe as followeth afterwards, it was ordered accordinglie."

This was not quite the end of the matter, for on January 26, D'Ewes notes:

"Upon Mr. Cromwell's motion it was ordered that the two witnesses which were come about the information put in against Mr. Ravenscroft . . . touching words by him spoaken, should be referred to the Committee for Intelligence to examine."[2]

It is apparent from this little incident that, like all revolutionary bodies, the Parliament had felt itself impelled to create a committee to keep itself informed of its opponents' doings and actions. If it was not precisely like the French Committee of Surveillance, as the Committee of Defence was not precisely like the Committee of General Security of the French Revolution, each was, in some measure, intended for the same purpose, and each, as appears from this incident, was supported by its adherents throughout the nation. From this, as

[2] *C. J.*, ii, 386; Nalson, John, *Impartial Collection of Great Affairs of State*, (1682), ii, 888. D'Ewes, Diary, *Harl. Mss.*, 162, f 337b; see also f. 338b, and f. 354.

from other circumstances, it appears that a new authority was rising in the state, prepared to enforce its policies and defend its newly-won position.

Meanwhile excitement grew, with all the usual phenomena of the breakdown of authority in such times of revolution. The continued threat of mobs in Westminster produced orders from the Commons for their dispersal and a request for London trained bands as a guard for Parliament, and the Commons had a new lock put on its doors. The Lords concurred with the Commons in a bill to enable the Houses to "adjourn themselves respectively to any place"; and a design to kill five of their members was reported to the Lords. The Lieutenant of the Tower, Sir John Byron, refused to obey the command of the Peers to appear before them without a warrant from the King, and, voting this contempt of "the Authority and Privileges of Parliament," they ordered his removal from his post. The Lords refused permission for Lord Holland and the Lord Chamberlain to join the King at Windsor as he commanded them. The Attorney General asked for time to prove that the charge of treason which he had drawn against the five members was legal, but the Commons resolved that the impeachment was "a high crime" and Lord Kimbolton demanded an immediate trial.

Meanwhile, too, the Commons sent another resolution to the Lords against the King's "evil counsellors" and an order for a declaration concerning "the defence of the King, the Parliament and the kingdom" and "the treaty with the Scots." To this was added another on the breach of privilege in the case of the five members, the Grand Remonstrance, and other documents, in an appeal to the people against the King—or at least in behalf of Parliament. More and more events shaped toward conflict. The Houses had adjourned after the attempt on the five members, the Commons appointing a committee to sit at Grocers' Hall to maintain their privilege; and when they met again the controversy entered on another stage.

The English revolution was, unlike the French, unmarked by an attack upon the Tower but it fell only short of that. The King sent a conciliatory message for which the Lords returned their thanks, but the Commons refused until Charles put "the Tower, all other forts and the militia into such hands as the Parliament can confide in." That proposal the Lords rejected over the protests of thirty-two of their members, and it became evident that the next move would be to secure control of the only armed force of the kingdom, the trained bands of the counties. A week later Pym again addressed the House and through it the nation on reformation in church and state in what was virtually an arraignment of the monarchy which was at once printed and distributed. At the same time the Duke of Richmond was reprimanded by the Lords for his proposal to adjourn the Houses for six months, and condemned by the Commons for endeavoring to influence elections and "make a party in the House."

It is perhaps not unnatural that those who clung to the crown and church should be infuriated by what seemed to them the "hypocrisy" and dishonesty of Pym's followers whose tactics seemed to them to accuse the king of the very measures in which they themselves indulged—in publishing "scandals," in stirring up the populace, in endeavoring to secure the magazines of arms, and now by a crowning piece of irony, of "making a party in the House." Party feeling rose to such a height and personal encounters increased to such extent that the Commons felt impelled to instruct the Speaker to issue warrants for such of its members as should "send, receive or entertain challenges" to duels; for it was charged that hot-headed Royalists would find in such measures a way to check the activities of even men like Pym by the arbitrament of the sword according to the code then prevalent. In such fashion during the first months of 1642 an appeal to force on either side took form; though each side was reluctant to take up arms and still more reluctant to appear as the aggressor.

But force was not the only argument. While the long struggle between the church and its opponents had gone on, while Laud had striven to enforce uniformity in the establishment, if only by lip-service and outward conformity, many men of many minds had been busy not only with attacks upon each other but with proposals for a settlement of the church problem. But three solutions were possible. The first was unity in uniformity; the second, complete religious liberty; the third, some form of toleration or "comprehension" in a state church broad enough to include within itself all reasonable men, or generous—or indifferent—enough to tolerate nonconformity. Upon these various alternatives—uniformity, comprehension or toleration—discussion had long raged; and there were now three parties in the state, Episcopalians, Presbyterians and "Separatists" of some sort.

By the beginning of the Long Parliament, the conflict took another turn as these parties became more and more clearly defined and their various principles found spokesmen. Among these spokesmen four were conspicuous, and, as it happened, in the twelvemonth which saw the struggle between crown and Commons come to a head, each issued a programme of his policy. The first was Archbishop Ussher of Armagh who left Ireland at this moment to advise the King. A friend of Laud, an advocate of divine right, his plan was none the less liberal. It was, in effect, a limited episcopacy not unacceptable to moderate Presbyterians, admitting certain elements of lay control into church government.[3] The second was that of the Presbyterian

[3] *A Body of Divinity*, and earlier writings.

Edward Calamy, who, in reply to the *Humble Remonstrance* by Bishop Hall, the author of *Episcopacie by Divine Right Asserted*, which embodied the Laudian thesis, denied the apostolic origin of bishops and liturgies and was prepared to accept episcopacy "if reduced to primitive simplicity" and a liturgy "reformed by a consultation of divines."[4]

This was, in a measure, the principle of Sir Edward Dering in moving the first reading of the Root and Branch Petition in the House. To these was added the proposal of Robert, Lord Brooke, a Puritan colleague of Pym and his party, who pleaded for complete religious liberty of the individual, prepared to admit even "vulgar and ignorant" persons to teach and preach, believing in a spiritual equality sufficient to extinguish all differences of education and ability.[5] Finally that Henry Burton who had been pilloried with Prynne and Bastwick for describing the bishops as "(cater)pillars of the church" and "anti-Christian mushrumps" produced a plan for a tolerant national church "surrounded by 'voluntary' churches" which was, in time, to solve the great problem.[6] To these may be added the "latitudinarian" school within the church itself, of which Lord Falkland was a great representative. In the Root and Branch debate he attacked divine right episcopacy—urging that bishops be retained but controlled by civil magistrates and deprived of power to impose ceremonies. Fearing sectarian dominance even more than episcopacy, and seeing intellectual liberty threatened no less in Geneva than in Rome, he championed the Establishment as "the nurse of high thought and high morality," striking a loftier note than most of his antagonists.[7]

These did not exhaust the list of those who at this moment pleaded for a new heaven and a new earth. In the midst of the political activities of January, 1642, Henry Archer published his vision of *The Personal Reign of Christ upon Earth*, which set forth the doctrines of that school of millennialists which, founding themselves on the more visionary passages of Scripture, especially on the Book of Revelation, looked forward to a Fifth Monarchy of King Jesus which they, His Saints, should rule. Again at this moment that little group of so-called Baptists, basing their peculiar faith on their interpretation of the doctrine of baptism held by other Christian communions, divided against itself into two schools, so-called General and Particular Baptists one led by Henry Jessey, the other by that Praisegod Barebone, who has achieved such prominence in history for his peculiarly Puritanical first name. Denying bitterly their connection with the fanati-

[4] Calamy and others, *An Answer to a Booke entitled An Humble Remonstrance*, 1641.
[5] *A Discourse opening the nature of . . . Episcopacy*, 1641.
[6] *The Protestation protested . . .* 1641.
[7] *D. N. B.* and Marriott, *Falkland.* See also Clarendon, *History*, *passim.*

cal Munster sect of Anabaptists whose doctrines of complete liberty verged on anarchy in civil as in ecclesiastical affairs, these English Baptists, none the less were the most advanced of these communions in what came to be called "democracy."

It was evident by such phenomena in the religious world that, apart from the concurrent developments in Parliament, the old ecclesiastical dispute had merged into a political struggle of the first magnitude. Religious differences at once expressed and concealed political differences. From the strict "authoritarianism" of the high church Laudians to the extreme "libertarianism" of the newer, "wilder," or more fanatical sects, they ran the whole gamut of political thought from divine right monarchy and episcopacy through limitations of each in greater or in less degree by synod or Parliament, to Parliamentary supremacy and congregationalism and so to extreme individualism or what might be called in later phraseology, "philosophical anarchy" in church and state alike. Each was in some measure connected with and defined in terms of theological and ecclesiastical divergences and each found followers both in church and state.

In no direction was this more evident than in the development of the press during the preceding months and increasingly as the struggle between conflicting principles deepened into armed conflict. With the decline of authority went that of the censorship which had been enforced by the Privy Council, the Star Chamber and Court of High Commission; and a multitude of men of every conceivable shade of opinion rushed into print their plans for settlement, their attacks and defences of this cause or that, and their often fantastic visions of this world or the next. Inevitably this tended to the advantage of Pym's party. Attack is always superior to defence in such a case as this, and, as has been aptly said, if ever a monument is erected to the inventor of printing, it should be by revolutionists, whose greatest weapon the press has always been.

That was never truer than at this time, as the list of the collection now begun by that far-sighted bookseller of St. Paul's, George Thomason, testifies. In 1640 when he began that collection for which all students of the period must be eternally grateful, he brought together some 22 pamphlets—though it is obvious that he did not get them all. In 1641 he secured 717 and with them four specimens of a new phenomenon, the newspaper, and one may trace the developments of later years in his collection as it went along. In 1642 he found nearly two thousand tracts and 167 newspapers; in 1643, when the war had begun, more than a thousand pamphlets and more than four hundred newspapers. In 1644, as arms more and more replaced argument, he found just under seven hundred tracts and nearly as many newspapers; and the next year the latter outnumbered the former by 722 to 694. It was, in fact, a golden age for the printers and news writers who then gained a position they have never lost; and among the many results of the civil war, as among its incidents—and its weapons—this tremendous burst of pamphleteering is not the least notable.[8]

The publications were of every sort conceivable, and some all but inconceivable. They ranged from newsletters of events on the various fighting fronts, the speeches, declarations of both King and Parliament, petitions, sermons and official notices of all sorts, to satires in both prose and verse, visions and prophecies. The posture to be used in taking the sacrament, "The Organ's funeral," "Strange news from Turkey," of a miracle there, "A Divine Balsam, to cure the wounds of this bleeding time," "The personall Reign of Christ upon Earth," which proclaimed the faith of the Fifth Monarchists, "The Butcher's Blessing, or the bloody intentions of Romish Cavaliers against the city of London," "Jehovah-Jireh," "The Humerous Tricks and Conceite of Prince Roberts Malignant She-Monkey," revealed the wide range of the new literature laid before the English people and the appeal to every element by every party in the state and church, but most especially against monarchy and episcopacy in this orgy of publication which was presently to play its part in Cromwell's life.

Even in such matters as these Cromwell was concerned, as soon appeared by a curious and interesting episode. Toward the end of 1641, Sir Edward Dering, the antiquarian-politician, who had been chairman of the committee on religion and had moved the first reading of the Root and Branch Bill, had published "A Collection of Speeches . . . in the Matter of Religion." There, as in the committee, he had argued for "primitive" or modified episcopacy, limited by the voice of the clergy, and so roused the animosity of those opposed to episcopal government of any sort. In the debate on the bill to exclude bishops from the Lords, he had urged the calling of a national synod. In the debates on the Grand Remonstrance he urged the retention of the bishops and finally voted against it and joined the Royalist-episcopalian party. In consequence he became anathema to the anti-episcopalians and the appearance of his book which defended his position so infuriated them that, as D'Ewes records on February 2, 1642:

> "Upon Mr. Cromwels motion Sir Edward Dering's booke was ordered to be burnt on Friday next by the sheriffs of London and Middlesex."

That was the usual, formal motion of disapproval; but as Dering's book had now been published for some months and it was obviously impossible to call in all the copies which had been distributed, so that

[8] *Catalogue of the Pamphlets . . . collected by George Thomason.*

the harm was done, Cromwell sought an antidote. Five days later, on February 7, as D'Ewes says:

"Mr. Cromwel moved that Sir Edward Dering's booke latelie sett out by him had many dangerous and scandalous passages in it by which many might be deceived and hadd into an ill opinion concerning the proceedings of this house and therefore desired that some able member of the house might bee appointed to make a short confutation of the same and then he nominated mee, which made mee presently stand up and answer that I conceived the gentleman who had last spoke did not dreame that it was now neare 7 of the clocke at night or else that hee would not at this time have made such a motion as hee did for if I could but gaine some spare time from the publicke service of the house I have other things to print of more publicke use and benefit than the confutation of Sir Edward Dering's speech could bee and therefore I desired that the gentleman himself who made the motion might be desired to undertake the work."[9]

In the interval, Dering was imprisoned in the Tower for the week of February 4–11; but this was not the end of this curious episode nor of the implications which seem to lie in it. It may be—it very possibly was—purely a matter of principle which lay behind Cromwell's attack on Dering and his book, but there is one interesting circumstance in connection with it worth notice. It is that though St. John has sometimes been credited with drafting the Root and Branch Bill, whoever wrote the bill, Dering noted in an aside in his book that it was handed to him by "S. A. H. and O. C."—obviously, and more or less provably, Sir Arthur Haselrig and Oliver Cromwell; and Cromwell's protest against a volume which might lead people into "an ill opinion concerning the proceedings of this house," might possibly not be unconnected with that revelation of the origin of the bill.

In any event the episode throws into relief the fact that Cromwell was not merely opposed to episcopacy in whatever form but that he had taken a more active share in the events of the preceding twelvemonth than has been generally recognized, and that his habit of attacking individuals had not lessened with experience in Parliament. He had had a definite part in framing the Grand Remonstrance and in the introduction, if not the composition, of the Root and Branch Bill. He had been personally concerned with the Triennial Act as one of the committee which drafted it. He had been instrumental in releasing Prynne, Bastwick, Burton and Leighton from confinement; and in other matters of scarcely less importance there are hints of his activity. Obscured by abler and more frequent speakers who fill a larger place in history, as yet not entrusted with the conduct of affairs in any leading capacity, he was none the less an active and

[9] D'Ewes, Diary, *Harl. Mss.*, 162 f. 373.

influential figure in the party's counsels, and, as it were, a leader of the second line in the attack on monarchy and almost, if not quite, a leader of the attack on episcopacy.

PREPARATION FOR WAR, FEBRUARY–MARCH, 1642

The situation developed rapidly in the early months of 1642. Despite the advantage which his efforts to seize the five members had put into the hands of his opponents, the King had gained support. He had been hissed in the City, but even there he had been cheered, and his departure from Whitehall had been a blow to his enemies. His messages had been marked by studious moderation and his expressed intention to rule through and with Parliament both in church and state had rallied many moderates to his side. The country at large knew as little of court as of Parliamentary intrigues. It sensed but dimly the "army plots" to rescue Strafford. It knew nothing of the Queen's efforts to get help from the House of Orange and the Pope. It could not know that she first advised, then unconsciously betrayed, the attempt on the five members. It knew, indeed, that she was a Roman Catholic and that she had great influence with the King, but only the Parliamentary leaders realized her great importance in affairs. She played a part, in fact, curiously like that of the queen of Louis XVI a century and a half later; but her husband differed from that unfortunate French king in that he was prepared to fight for his principles and his inheritance. To the daughter of Henry IV and Marie de Medici there was nothing appalling in the thought of civil war or help from abroad. Her father had come to the throne of France after a long period of civil strife. She had seen the efforts of the nobility and of the Huguenots to weaken or overthrow her royal brother's power suppressed by Richelieu. She had seen the Huguenots call on England for support, and the Puritans welcome or even invite the aid of the Scots. It was only natural that she should urge Charles to resist and that she should look abroad for help to save the monarchy. In consequence it became increasingly evident that if they were to win, Pym and his followers must appeal to arms, and it was natural that they looked on the Queen as their most dangerous enemy.

But King and Commons were equally reluctant to begin civil war. Each was still more reluctant to incur the odium of initiating such a conflict; and each lacked money, men and munitions for hostilities. Each, in consequence, strove to evade responsibility for war and at the same time to provide against such an eventuality. For such a purpose the Irish situation offered the Parliamentary leaders an opportunity to secure both men and money to suppress rebellion there, and, if occasion rose, to put down "Popish conspiracy" in England itself. There was no standing army to support the monarchy or be seduced from its allegiance by the Parliament; but there remained the militia, the strongholds and their stores of warlike materials. The month of February, therefore, saw the beginnings of preparation for the possible eventuality of war. It began on February 1 with the King's refusal to give up control of the militia, the Tower and the forts, and the Lords' retort that "whoever advised this Answer is of the Malignant Party and an Enemy to the Publick Peace and Safety." It continued with an "Act for the better raising and levying of soldiers for the present defence of the kingdoms of England and Ireland," whose title revealed a double purpose. It was marked by a struggle for the command of the Tower which compelled Charles to replace his devoted adherent, Sir John Byron by a man more satisfactory to the Houses, Sir John Conyers. It involved Charles's agreement to place the forts and the militia in the hands of men "such as both Houses approve or command, unless where there are great and unquestionable exceptions"; to which the Houses retorted that this was a "Denial of dangerous consequence" and that the King's proposed removal to York would be "a great hazard to the Kingdom and Prejudice to the Proceedings of Parliament."[10]

They had reason to be alarmed. Five days before this vote, on February 23, the Queen had sailed from Dover with the crown jewels to pawn them in Holland, to buy munitions and to secure support, if possible, from continental powers. She had advised the King to put himself at the head of the forces raised for Ireland, to seize Hull, and so secure an army and supplies. On its part the Parliamentary party had begun to raise loans from its own members and from the City, to impress soldiers and sailors, to draw up a list of lord-lieutenants and take steps to secure command of the militia. To these measures it added further attacks on the crown and church. On the first day of February it had passed an act to "disenable all persons in holy orders to exercise any temporal jurisdiction or authority"—and to this, after some delay, the King agreed. But when the Commons resolved that all privy councillors and great officers of state save hereditary officials be removed, drew a bill to forfeit the property of the twelve bishops on trial as enemies of Parliament, and to imprison them for life, opened Lord Digby's letters to the Queen, and impeached him and the Attorney General of treason, the King drew back.

If there wanted evidence that the quarrel was deepening in intensity, a new Remonstrance presented to the King removed the last

[10] For the following cp. *C. J.*, Feb.–Mar. 1642, *passim;* and *Old Parl. Hist.*

doubt in the minds of the Royalists that Pym's party looked not merely to reform but to a constitutional revolution, peaceful or warlike as the case might be. It put the blame on the Queen, her "priests and Jesuits," and her "admission . . . to intermeddle with the great affairs of state." It demanded "due reformation" in the church, a "preaching ministry," the disfranchisement of the Popish Lords, and complained of breaches of privilege. It virtually commanded the King to replace his councillors with nominees of Parliament; to raise to the Upper House only those approved by the Commons; to provide that House with the names of his advisers and correspondents in the Commons; to refuse his wife's advice and compel her to take an oath not to offer it. To give up his council, his control of the armed forces, his right to create peers, even his wife's advice, seemed to deliver him bound hand and foot to his enemies. He could lose little more even by unsuccessful war; yet he, like Pym and his followers, shrank from precipitating armed conflict. He called his son Charles to his side; and as he had earlier appointed Falkland to be secretary of state, he now appointed Hyde his secret, unofficial adviser and correspondent in Westminster, and set out for the north. He hoped to rally the loyal northern gentry and nobility, secure the strongholds, Hull in particular, and gain control of the militia. The Parliamentary leaders, pushing through a resolution to put the kingdom in "a posture of defence," appointed lord-lieutenants and ordered them to suppress "all rebellions, insurrections and invasions." As the result of an interview between their representatives and Charles as he pushed north, they published another declaration reiterating their charges of a Popish Plot, on which they blamed all the disturbances of the preceding months, including the Scotch war, expressing regret that the king's "presence and confidence had been withdrawn from Parliament" in this critical period.

On March 16 the issue came to a head in the reply to the King's letter dated from Huntingdon in which he declared that no act or ordinance which had not his consent could have the force of law. To that Pym's party answered by a resolution that "When the Lords and Commons . . . declare what the law of the land is, to have this not only questioned and controverted but contradicted . . . is a high breach of privilege." It was a bold defiance—too bold, in fact. Most men were not prepared to change the constitution. They stayed away or voted against it, and by the Speaker's casting vote in a House with scarcely more than a hundred members present, it was voted down. The King's reply, drafted perhaps by Hyde, was a shrewd answer to Pym's party. 'Are bills for triennial parliaments, relinquishing impositions, abolition of courts, of forest rights, of bishops in the Lords, for the continuation of this present Parliament, and complete political amnesty—are these but empty words?,' he asked.

'What more can you desire?' The followers of Pym desired much more, but by a vote of 43 to 36 they were defeated on a motion to declare this was another breach of privilege.

From all of this two things were evident. The first was that there was a party even in Parliament unwilling to go farther on the road to revolution now that the royal power had been curbed. The second was that Parliament itself was breaking up. Already many of the peers had left and the Commons were going or had gone. Hyde was gathering a party favorable to a King who had renounced the Strafford-Laudian policy. Already before the end of March the Commons had received petitions, especially one from Kent, praying for restoration of the bishops, liturgy and Book of Common Prayer. The Kentish petition, unlike the petitions against the Establishment, they voted seditious and against privilege and peace and imprisoned its signers, among them Sir Edward Dering and the antiquarian Twysden. Already they had named a committee to "consider the fittest course for keeping the members together." The third step in revolution had been reached. From the "creation of a revolutionary atmosphere" through the period of the formation of an opposition party and the reform of abuses, to the stage where men divided into moderates and conservatives on the one side and extremists on the other, the turning-point had come. It was apparent that men would have to choose between a King and constitution which, whatever their defects, were definite and understandable, and an uncertain and undefined supremacy of Parliament.

The share of Oliver Cromwell in this activity was increasingly important. He was at all times in the thick of it. On February 1—the day when Charles first refused to yield control of the militia and the fortresses—Lord Capel, Sir Gilbert Gerard, Henry Marten and Sir John Francklyn offered to continue the loans they had made to the "Commonwealth," and Oliver Cromwell offered to lend £300 "for the succour of Dublyn."[11] On the 16th, as D'Ewes notes:

"Mr. Cromwell moved that Sir John Clotworthie had done great service for setling these propositions at the Committee and soe desired that some time might be allowed him to stay still and not yet goe into Ireland for the furtherance of this particular business. Sir Walter Earle said that the said gentleman had indeed done great service at the Committee. I moved [to send Clotworthy, notwithstanding Cromwell's motion, and it was ordered that he must go to Ireland.]"[12]

[11] *C. J.*, ii, 408. Carlyle's statement that this took place on Feb. 7, was not corrected by Mrs. Lomas. Sanford, p. 488, apparently following Carlyle, makes the same error in date. On the 17th of Feb. the City of London offered £60,000 toward suppressing the rebellion in Ireland.

[12] D'Ewes, Diary, *Harl. Mss.*, 162 f. 388b. For Clotworthy see *D. N. B.*

Whatever those propositions were, this apparently insignificant notice is of more interest than might appear. Sir John Clotworthy, M. P. for Maldon, was a great landowner in County Antrim in Ireland, a bitter enemy of Strafford in whose prosecution he took an active part, and, according to Carte, "an agent between the English and Irish malcontents." He was an Adventurer in Irish lands, an enemy of Laud, and later a member of the Committee of Both Kingdoms. He was extremely active in the efforts to put down the Irish rebellion, and it was his servant, Owen O'Connell, in whose behalf Cromwell had already bestirred himself, who had been approached by the conspirators who planned to seize Dublin and had given information of the plot. He, like his wife, was a Presbyterian, and was presently employed, unsuccessfully, to help to pacify the English army, charged by them with embezzlement, deprived of his seat in the House and compelled to flee to France.

It was a sample of the work in which Cromwell was engaged from day to day; and, besides membership on a committee to consider a petition from the barristers and students of Gray's Inn, appointed on February 18, he went on to other employments connected with the great issues which confronted Parliament.

On February 24, Pym reported from the committee for Irish affairs the names of members agreed upon to be Commissioners "for the Speeding and Dispatching of the Businesses for Ireland." Among its fourteen names were those of Pym himself, Holles, the younger Vane, Marten, and Oliver Cromwell; and it was noted that Hampden was nominated but was excused on account of his duties with the commission for the Scots.[13] In such fashion did the country enter on preparations for war and Oliver Cromwell become one of the small body entrusted with this great enterprise. It is not necessary, perhaps, to accept Clarendon's dictum that "they fell to raising of moneys under pretence of the relief of Ireland," but it can hardly be doubted that the possibility of armed conflict in England was not absent from their minds, nor that this Irish situation provided them with an opportunity to prepare for a greater conflict if occasion arose.

In any event the month of March saw Cromwell active in many matters, small and great, in the Commons. On March 1, with Pym, Hampden, Marten, Fiennes and Sir Philip Stapleton, he was added to a committee to consider the King's reply to Pym's speech about royal passes which had been issued to Irish rebels.[14] The next day he was sent to the Lords with a request to appoint a committee to meet at once to consider the case of William Murray, a groom of the bedchamber, who had, with others, joined the King and were now ordered to "absent themselves from the King's person." Cromwell

[13] *C. J.*, ii, 440, 453, 456.
[14] *C. J.*, ii, 463.

reported that the Lords acquiesced, and the committee was ordered to examine "Mr. Murray and others."[15] On that same day he, with six others, was added to the Committee for Innovations in the church. On March 5, he was added, with seventeen others, to the committee for the bill disenabling the bishops;[16] and named to the committee to consider an act for "the speedy and effectual reducing" of the Irish rebels. On that same day, too, he informed the House that "dangerous words had been spoken by a colonel latelie and that the witnesses were at the doore who could testifie." Accordingly Mr. Grant and Mr. Parker gave evidence that the colonel was a certain Francis Edmunds, an Irishman, who expressed the wish that the King would 'raise his standard and maintain his prerogative by force of arms, and that if he knew where Pym, Hampden and Strode were, he would ease the King of further trouble from them;' whereupon the valiant colonel was ordered sent for as a delinquent.[17] On the 7th, when the nine leaders were in a committee and matters of a minor character were considered in the House, Cromwell was a teller for the Yeas who lost their plea to recommend a lecturer at the neighboring church of St. Giles-in-the-Fields.[18] A week later, on March 41, the Lords approved of the Commission "for the Speeding and Despatching of the Businesses of Ireland" which was to be composed of seven peers and fourteen commoners, of whom Cromwell was one.[19] On March 16, he introduced some gentlemen from Cambridge with a petition asking for a lecturer and protesting allegiance to Parliament.[20] The next day, besides being a teller for the Noes on a question of doubling the duties on sugar save that imported from English or Portuguese plantations,[21] he, with Pym, Hampden, Holles, Marten, Vane, Whitelocke and thirteen others, was named to an important committee to meet with a like body from the Lords to "examine where his Majesty's last message was framed and who were the advisers thereof."[22] On March 28, he, with sixteen others was added to a committee to consider the list of grievances presented by the committee of the Common Council of London, including a peti-

[15] *Ibid.*, 465; *L. J.*, iv, 622. Murray, the man suspected by Clarendon of having betrayed the King's intention to arrest the five members, was created Earl of Dysart in 1643.

[16] *C. J.*, ii, 465, 467.

[17] *Ibid.*, 468; D'Ewes, Diary, *Harl. Mss.*, 163, ff 23b, 24.

[18] *C. J.*, ii, 470.

[19] *L. J.*, iv, 644. Passed by the Commons on Feb. 24.

[20] *C. J.*, ii, 480. D'Ewes Diary, *Harl. Mss.*, 163, f. 35, quoted in Sanford, p. 485, who dates it Mar. 15. Printed in *L. J.*, and in Kingston, *East Anglia*, p. 41. The King was in Cambridge two days before.

[21] *C. J.*, ii, 482. The Noes won by the Speaker's vote.

[22] *Ibid.*, 484. The letter, dated March 15th and sent from Huntingdon, on the King's progress northward, urged the expediting of the Irish business and reminded Parliament of his Jan. 20th message concerning the militia, the church and the revenue.

tion of a certain Leonard Tillot, prisoner in the Compter in Wood-street. It was on that day, also, that there arose a debate on the printing of scandalous papers of various sorts, in an account of which Sir Symonds D'Ewes reveals the source of Cromwell's animus against Sir Edward Dering. In discussing the matter of a paper by one William Newton, he observes that,

". . . Newton did in particular lay an aspersion upon this house that we had sent out especially to watch the Queen of which he describes three by six great or capital letters as a member of the House (Sir Edward Dering) lately did in a booke hee printed setting down O. C. (*viz.* Mr. Oliver Cromwell) and others and we can already see what effects one omission of this hath produced for there is another wicked false letter pretended to bee sent from the Queenes Ma[tie] to the King here being merely abstracted out of these two false letters. . . ."

Finally, on March 29, as D'Ewes records in his Diary:

"Mr. Cromwell then delivered in a certificate from Mr. Symonds and three other ministers of Monmouthshire directed to Sir Arthur Haselrigg, himselfe and Mr. Pym, bearing date Mar. 23, 1641, by which they shewed that the strength of Papists was soe great about the towne of Monmouth as they feared if some speedie course were not taken it would be in as great danger shortlie as Ireland."[23]

To that Mr. Pym answered that he had received a letter from the Mayor of Monmouth assuring him that the magazine was safer there than in Newport. None the less, the letter was referred to the Committee of Information, the magazine ordered removed and the Mayor ordered to appear before the House. In such fashion did the party opposed to Charles's government function—accusation by local members, very often ministers, reference to the Committee of Information, and a summons for the accused to appear before the House—phenomena common to all such revolutionary movements and parties, and borrowed by them from the governments they opposed.

The mere enumeration of his activities in this month of March, 1642, reveals that Cromwell was rising rapidly to a position of greater importance in the party of Pym and Hampden. It reveals no less the lines of that activity. The relations of the King to the Irish rebellion, his controversy with the Parliamentary leaders, the gathering of a party about him recruited even from the members of the two Houses, the continuing attack on the bishops, the pledges of support from constituencies like Cambridge, the grievances of London, and, above all, the preparations for the Irish war, all these went to the heart of the great issue then confronting the country, and in all of

[23] *Ibid.*, 500; D'Ewes Diary, *Harl. Mss.*, 163, f. 51b, 54.

them, with Pym and Hampden, Holles, Vane, Strode and Marten, Cromwell was involved.

Nor was his last appearance in the affairs of the Commons in this month of less significance. While the King at York gathered about him a group of devoted followers and, under Hyde's guidance, strove to manoeuver the party of Pym into an unfavorable position before the nation, as they meanwhile used every art to discredit him; while the Scots pushed forward preparations to avenge their countrymen in Ireland and while the troops poured across the Irish Sea were being disposed, the remaining members of the two Houses of Parliament strained every nerve to strengthen their position at home and prepare for war abroad. In effect the orderly processes of government broke down in the face of this double emergency. Parliament had found it as difficult to collect the heavy assessments it had laid on the country as Charles had found it difficult to collect ship-money, and the protests against the one were scarcely less violent than against the other. In the disturbed situation of affairs it was hopeless to attempt to collect taxes for the Irish war, and had it not been, there was no time.

Immediate supplies were necessary and as the lord-lieutenants and the justices embarked on the enterprise of collecting men by impressment, the Houses appealed to their members for contributions to pay them and provide supplies and ships. Subscription lists were opened at the beginning of March[24] and one by one men came forward to subscribe to a loan for that purpose. It was scarcely to be expected that the Royalists would join in an enterprise which they believed was directed, or might be directed, against the King, and few of their names appear on the subscription lists. Those lists, indeed read like a roster of the party of Pym and Hampden. The commonest subscription was six hundred pounds, and in that category are found the names of Pym, St. John, Fiennes, Sir William Masham, Sir Walter Erle, John Lisle and Bulstrode Whitelocke. But Sir Gilbert Gerard subscribed two thousand pounds; William, Lord Monson, twenty-four hundred; Sir Arthur Haselrig, Henry Marten, Sir Thomas Barrington and a few others, twelve hundred pounds apiece; John Hampden, Sir Samuel Rolls, Sir William Brereton and some others, a thousand. A few like Miles Corbet gave less. But one thing in this

[24] The list for the Parliament was started March 8. Thirteen had signed by Mar. 25; thirty-seven, including Cromwell, signed on Mar. 26; twenty-five had signed by the time the list went to the printers on Apr. 9. *The Names of such members of the Commons House of Parliament as have already subscribed in pursuance of the Act of Parliament for the speedy reducing of the Rebels and the future peace and safety of this Kingdome.* Pr. for John Francks, Apr. 9, 1642. Partially repr. in Rushworth, iv, 564; and in Husbands.

long list is notable. It is that it contained most of Cromwell's relatives then in Parliament; that many of its signers rose to eminence in the civil wars on the side of Parliament, many held office under Cromwell in later years, and of the men who signed the death-warrant of Charles I seven years later, nearly all then in Parliament signed this subscription list.

Its signers were inspired not only by patriotism and piety. As early as February 11 certain "worthy and well-disposed" citizens of London had pointed out that two and a half million acres of Irish land were subject to confiscation by the rebellion and that a million pounds might be raised on that security. The Commons leaders were quick to take the hint. A bill was pushed through both Houses on February 24, and assented to by Charles March 19, by which subscriptions were taken on terms which explain the curious amounts set against the names. A thousand acres in Leinster was to be had for six hundred pounds, in Munster for four hundred and fifty, in Connaught for three hundred, and in Ulster for two hundred pounds. Each subscriber was to pay down a twentieth of the whole amount to a committee of four London aldermen, and possession was guaranteed on the suppression of the rebellion for a trifling quit-claim rent of from one to three pence an acre. Under such conditions "Master Oliver Cromwell," with a subscription of £500, became the prospective owner of nearly a thousand acres in the most favored district of Ireland, the province of Leinster, as what was to be known as an "Adventurer" in Irish lands.[25]

Despite the fact that some sixty thousand pounds was subscribed by the members of the Commons, the extension of the time, the rebate offered for prompt payment, even the inclusion of Dutch Protestants in the scheme, the total fell far short of the promised million. But it had one great consequence—it provided the Commons with the sinews of war—for on July 30 they required the treasurers of the fund to hand over a hundred thousand pounds, which was never repaid.[26] It was, then, not without reason that Charles refused to compel the Adventurers to pay their subscriptions until security was given that it should not be used against him,[27] and that his followers declared this was only a device to raise money to fight the King.

[25] Eleven years later, when lands were being assigned these Adventurers, Alderman Andrewes certified that, in April 1642, Cromwell had subscribed £300 for adventure in Ireland and paid in the whole sum, that he subscribed in the same month £300 for the Additional Adventure by Sea, which was paid in. The receipts therefor had been lost, but when lots were drawn to assign the property, Cromwell was given lands in Kings county in West Leinster. *Cal. St. P. Ireland*, (Adventurers, 1642–59), p. 319.

[26] *C. J.*, ii, 698.

[27] *L. J.* and *C. J. passim*, Feb.–July 1642. See also Dunlop, *Ireland under the Commonwealth*, i, cxxiii–cxxv.

THE TWO PARTIES, APRIL, 1642

The controversy which had raged since the beginning of the Long Parliament was not confined to its sessions. It had spread to every part of England. The four thousand supporters of Hampden who had ridden to London, the London mobs, the mutinous soldiers, the riotous congregations characterized the disturbed spirit which had filled England since ship-money times. The country folk who thronged into London to see Strafford die and rode back in triumph, shouting "His head is off! His head is off!"[28] were typical of the hatred engendered by the struggle between the parties into which England was dividing. Nowhere was that spirit more evident than in the eastern counties and nowhere there more than in the places which Oliver Cromwell represented in Parliament. The Puritans who refused to attend services in Ely Cathedral unless there was also a sermon or lecture; the refusal of Huntingdon men to pay ship-money; the rioting of the levies for the Scotch war in Cambridge; all these revealed the bitterness of the East Anglians against the church and monarchy. But even they were far from unanimous. The Protestation sent or carried to Cambridge by Cromwell and Lowry was signed by "nine of the corporation and most of the commonalty," but that very fact reveals that the majority of the corporation was opposed to it. The colleges in particular were strongly royalist and the summoning of Dr. Holdsworth, the vice-chancellor, before Parliament for reflecting on the action of the Houses and approving the refusal of the vicar of St. Ives, Cromwell's old friend Downhall, to give communion to those who would not come forward to the communion rails, showed that even his own constituents and friends were divided in their sympathies.[29]

As the struggle deepened in intensity, the district which he represented in Parliament became typical of the whole resistance to the crown. When the order went forth to put the counties in a state of defence, the Lord Lieutenant of Cambridgeshire was appealed to by some of its inhabitants as representatives of the assize meeting as early as February, 1642, to muster men, supply them with arms and drill them as the neighboring counties were then doing;[30] and to spend certain sums in the possession of the county authorities for arms. As the King moved north through Cambridge and Huntingdon, he was acclaimed by his supporters everywhere, and not least by the

[28] Warwick, *Memoirs*, p. 164.
[29] Kingston, *East Anglia, and the great Civil War* (1897), p. 28.
[30] *L. J.*, iv, 25 Feb. 1641–2.

University. Yet within a fortnight a group of knights, gentlemen and freeholders of Cambridge, Huntingdon and Ely petitioned in favor of Parliament, especially in defence of Lord Kimbolton "of our shire," then threatened with impeachment with the five members.

If Cambridge was divided between town and gown, and the townsmen divided among themselves, the old companions and neighbors of Cromwell were no less at odds. Of the county members for Cambridge, North was for the Parliament, Chicheley for the King. The old Earl of Manchester supported Star Chamber, ship-money and Bishops' War; his son, the future Earl, was all for Parliament and presently became its general; and of the Cromwell family, old Sir Oliver was for the King, young Oliver, his son Oliver and Sir Philip's son Oliver took the other side. Thus England divided against itself, district against district, neighbor against neighbor, son against father, as county by county it took up the mustering and training of a militia whose part in the conflict was as yet undetermined, and began to raise men and money for the Irish war, and, it might well be, for conflict nearer home.

It was, then, in these early months of 1642, as lord-lieutenants and justices began impressment and the militia was called out for "drill and exercise," that men considered which side they would take; and King and Commons bid for their support. The Royalists entered the contest with heavy hearts, the King not least. "My father," wrote the young prince Charles from Royston on the journey to the north, "is very disconsolate and troubled, partly from my Royal mother's absence, and partly for the disturbance of the kingdom. I could wish and daily pray that there might be a conjunct and perfect uniting between my father's Majesty and his Parliament."[31] It was the wish of the greater part of England. "O that the swete parliment would come with the olive branch in its mouth, it would refrech and glad all our harte . . . Wee are soe many frighted people," wrote Mrs. Eure to her relative Ralph Verney in Parliament; and to this Lady Sussex added her supplication, "I pray god there may bee agreement between the kainge and his pepell." However spelled, it was the hope of most Englishmen in this spring of 1642, but it was not the only hope. "Peace and our liberties are the only things wee aime at; till wee have peace I am sure wee can enjoy no liberties, and without our liberties I shall not heartily desire peace," wrote Ralph Verney,[32] and in those words summed up the position of the followers of Pym.

To Charles the situation was incomprehensible. He could not understand why his concessions had not conciliated his opponents. He

[31] Quoted in Kingston, *East Anglia*, pp. 35–6.

[32] Verney, *Memoirs of the Verney family during the Civil War and Commonwealth* (1892–99), i, 252–4.

could not see that the eleven years of unparliamentary government had sown the wind and that he was now reaping the whirlwind. He could not grasp the fact that while he distrusted Pym and his followers, they distrusted him so much that it seemed that no concession he could make, short of abdicating all pretensions to sovereignty, would meet their increasingly vigorous demands. On the other hand, to many men there was much to be distrusted in the activities of this remnant of a Parliament now virtually controlled by Pym and Hampden and their followers. In the name of liberty they had gone far on the road to arbitrary power. They had claimed for the diminished Parliament an authority as high as Charles had ever asserted for the monarchy. They had treated the petitions favoring episcopacy as severely as Laud had treated the Puritan demands. They had exercised powers as great as those of Star Chamber or High Commission. It was well for John Milton to declare—ironically—in these very days that if "the bishops be put down, a deluge of innumerable sects will follow; we shall all be Brownists, Familists, Anabaptists"; but that was precisely what many people felt as the bonds of authority were loosened in church and state. Nor were they comforted by his assertion that "Jurisdictive power in the church, there ought to be none at all."

There was strength in his argument that "when the Church without temporal support is able to do her great works upon the unforced obedience of men it argues a divinity about her; but when she thinks to . . . better her spiritual efficacy . . . by strutting in the false vizard of worldly authority, it is evident that God is not there." But it was also true that all human institutions, whatever their spiritual origin, must have some form of organization and authority, whether episcopal or presbyterian. What that should be, was, as the Puritans would have said, "according to conscience," and the conscience of England was still in general on the side of episcopacy, however modified. It was still on the side of monarchy. It was not ready to exchange King Charles for King Pym—and his party realized that, whatever the righteousness of their cause, they were a minority; that if a general election had been held, the principles of Hyde would almost certainly have won.

Those principles were simplicity itself. While Pym spoke of liberty, Hyde appealed to law. He favored what Hobbes called a "mixed monarchy" and was not averse to a modified episcopacy; and time brought these to pass. It is easy to say that Pym was only in advance of his generation; it is still easier to say that the ensuing war was due to Charles's efforts to undo the work of the first twelve months of the Long Parliament. But two things seem to weaken that argument. The first is that the fight was already won; the second is that, when all was said and done, in the ensuing years Hyde's principles prevailed. Pym and his followers disliked the King; they hated episcopacy; and they had now gone too far to draw back. They were determined to secure the complete supremacy of Parliament over crown, church and the judiciary. They feared the vengeance of their enemies; and, apart from their convictions of the righteousness of their cause, despite the disclaimers of their later champions, despite the accusations of the Royalists, they were for the most part men with personal grievances and not without personal ambitions. Without these they would have been more or less than human; and at this very moment those qualities were evidenced. For Charles, urged on by the Queen, dismissed Essex and Holland from their household offices and threw them into the arms of his enemies.

It is better to face the facts. As Chatham is reported to have said, "There was ambition, there was sedition, there was violence; but no man shall persuade me that it was not the cause of liberty on one side and of tyranny on the other." That the end justifies the means is no new doctrine, nor was it in their time, nor used openly by them. They had, indeed, the worst of the debate for it was difficult, it was, in fact, impossible to meet Hyde's arguments. They could not well deny his contention that their acts were unconstitutional. They fell back on agitation and on force, but most of all on fear. They revived the old stories of the Popish plots, they terrified the Houses with rumors, petitions and mob violence, they appealed to the nation to support them against the efforts of the Queen and her co-religionists to re-establish the old faith. What, then—now that the limitation of monarchy and episcopacy had been achieved—was their object? Was it to preserve the fruits of victory; was it to save themselves; was it to overthrow both monarchy and church; was it to establish the supremacy of Parliament and nonconformity; was it to make themselves the masters of the state; or was it a deep passion for liberty? The answer is not clear, for men are seldom moved by single and simple motives, and in all such companies those motives are extremely various. "The Commons," Pym had said to the Lords, "will be glad to have your concurrence and help in saving the kingdom; but if they fail of it, it shall not discourage them in doing their duty."

What did he mean by that? From what was England to be saved—from a tyrannical monarchy, from arrogant episcopacy, from insidious Popery? If it meant anything beyond the usual platitudes of the demagogue, it was that the House of Commons should be supreme in church and state alike. To that, in the mid-seventeenth century, there could be but one answer—it was unconstitutional. The grievances had now been redressed; the courts of High Commission, Star Chamber, and the rest had gone, with the crown's claims to unparliamentary taxation, the bishops had been driven from the House of Lords and deprived of their temporal authority. There remained now legally only the monarchy and the Established church. Were they to be suppressed or dominated by the Commons? This was the great issue on which the Civil War was fought. Put in a thousand ways by a thousand pens, at the root of the great argument which had raged with increasing violence for the past two years, this was the fundamental problem as men went on to fight.

PARLIAMENT, APRIL–MAY, 1642

The activities of the Houses in these critical months of April and May, 1642 were naturally concerned chiefly with the quarrel with the King. They were disturbed at the continual withdrawal of members and every effort was made to keep men in their places.[35] They were no less disturbed by the petitions which began to pour in favoring monarchy and episcopacy and took vigorous steps to discourage them and their promoters, especially the supporters of the men of Kent. They reviewed the London militia; they entered into the business of Hull in great detail; they continued a company of guards under Serjeant-Major Skippon, who was summoned to York, unavailingly, by the King. They busied themselves greatly with the problem of the divided authority of Parliament at Westminster and the King at York. The Lords "finding the Business of the Kingdom to lie upon a very Few" desired a committee of both Houses to keep men at their posts. A conference between the Houses on May 20, reported its resolves "That, seduced by wicked counsels, the King, as it appears, intends to make war against the Parliament"; that this was a breach of trust, and those assisting him were traitors. They tried to stop the Lord Keeper from taking the Great Seal to Charles; they demanded the arrears of taxes of all sorts; and above all day after day they sought means to prevent the officers of state, their own members and all others from joining Charles in this great exodus.[36]

In all of this Cromwell played his part, with increasing frequency and importance as the weeks went on. On April 4 as part of the effort to raise money, he acted as teller on a motion to postpone action by the collectors of the subsidies voted by Parliament against the "Merchant Strangers of the Intercourse"—that is to say aliens doing business in England—until their petition had been heard.[37] That was the day when the House leaders named a committee for

[35] A roll-call on June 16 revealed 45 members absent without leave. *C. J.*, ii, 626.

[36] *C. J.; L. J., passim.*

[37] *C. J.*, ii, 509. The Yeas, for whom Cromwell and Moore were tellers, won. Haselrig and Sir Hugh Cholmley told for Noe.

ecclesiastical policy and ordered Warwick installed as vice-admiral in defiance of the King. In that Cromwell took no recorded share, but on the next day, April 5, he, with Strode, Haselrig, the younger Vane and twenty-six others, was appointed a committee to consider information from the King's Counsel concerning that disturbing phenomenon of petitions in favor of church and crown, "seditious pamphlets and tumults" against the activities of Parliament.[38] Four days later he was named with St. John, Gerard, Strode and Haselrig to a committee of twenty-five to investigate the petition of one Lieutenant Robert Davies as to mismanagement of Charterhouse and the Savoy.[39]

More and more he came into prominence as the quarrel between King and Commons moved to war. On April 16 he was named to a committee to look into the number and quality of those persons who had refused to sign the Protestation.[40] Five days later, on April 21, Pym brought in a commission in the King's name appointing twenty-one men, resident in England, to administer the defence of Ireland, and among them Cromwell was numbered.[41] On April 28 he was sent to the Lords with important news. Its first item was to the effect that "a great meeting was to be held next day on Blackheath to back the rejected Kentish petition" in favor of episcopacy.[42] The second was a request to the Lords to remain in session until the Commons could bring something of importance before them relating to the town of Hull. When the Lords replied that they would reconvene again at two o'clock he was sent to repeat the original request, to which the Lords finally agreed.[43]

The matter, as the Commons indicated, was urgent, if not vital to their plans. John Hotham, whose father, Sir John, described by Clarendon as a 'rough and rude man of great covetousness, great pride and great ambition,' under orders from the Parliament, had anticipated the King's agents in securing Hull. He had refused Charles admission to the town on April 23 and had been declared a traitor by the King. The news had now reached Parliament which promptly declared this a "high breach of privilege," and despatched six members to prevent any effort to seize Hull by force, and possibly to keep an eye on Hotham. To this the Commons added an order for the payment of £2,000 to the garrison, which Cromwell carried to the

38 *C. J.*, ii, 512.

39 *Ibid.*, 519.

40 *Ibid.*, 530.

41 This was the commission whose members were first proposed on Feb. 24, and approved by the Lords Mar. 14. The commission, amended somewhat, was passed by the Lords on Apr. 25. *C. J.*, ii, 536; *L. J.*, v, 15.

42 *Old Parl. Hist.*, x, 463. *C. J.*, says Vane carried this first message but very likely Cromwell was sent in his place.

43 *C. J.*, ii, 545; *L. J.*, v, 25.

Lords. It received their approval and for the moment it seemed that Hull was safe.[44]

Three days after this matter of Hull, on a request from the Lords a committee of twenty-nine, including Cromwell and all the leaders of the House, was named to confer upon a letter from the Marquis of Hertford, governor of Prince Charles, refusing the demand of the Parliament that the heir-apparent should not be conveyed out of the kingdom.[45] Meanwhile the question of Ireland and the Adventurers had come up again. Matters went ill and a new "Act for the advancement of an effectual and speedy reduction of the rebels in Ireland" was referred to a committee appointed earlier to consider a bill relating to the Adventurers. To this committee Cromwell was added with his cousins and co-subscribers to the Irish fund, Sir Thomas Barrington, Sir Gilbert Gerard and Sir William Masham, with nine others.[46] Two days later he with nineteen others was ordered to consider the proposals of certain merchants to supply the Irish forces with provisions;[47] and that a great part of his energy was absorbed in the difficult task of dispatching ten thousand men to Irish soil, there is no reason to doubt. That he was recognized as an important figure seems to be indicated by a memorandum on a petition from Monmouth complaining of its dangerous proximity to the Irish war, that the document be "sent to Mr. Cromwell."[48]

Meanwhile the struggle for the militia enlisted his support. On May 23, an important committee of fourteen including Pym, Strode, Holles, Marten, Haselrig, the younger Vane, Lisle, Ludlow and Sir Thomas Barrington, with Oliver Cromwell, was ordered to prepare an answer to the committee at York in regard to publishing the orders of Parliament in Yorkshire to suppress all forces in that county and to require obedience to the Parliament.[49] At the same time, he seems to have carried out instructions given him two days earlier to ask concurrence of the Lords in the appointment of Sir Walter Pye as deputy lieutenant of Buckinghamshire, to which they agreed.[50] The next day the committee appointed on May 23 to publish orders in York was ordered to supervise the publication of Parliamentary orders and declarations in the several counties and prepare instructions for those members to be sent into Lincolnshire.[51]

Amid this feverish activity of the Parliamentary remnant going

[44] *C. J.*, ii, 555; *L. J.*, v, 40.
[45] *C. J.*, ii, 562.
[46] *Ibid.*, 569.
[47] *Ibid.*, 571.
[48] *Hist. Mss. Comm. Rept.* 13, App. (Welbeck Abbey), i, 39; *C. J.*, ii, 575.
[49] *C. J.*, ii, 583.
[50] *Ibid.*, 582–3; *L. J.*, v, 79.
[51] *Ibid.*, 585.

forth to war, the figure of Cromwell looms larger day by day; and that war was increasingly inevitable was apparent from the Commons declaration of May 20 that the King was preparing to attack the Parliament. Nor was this the only concern of Pym and his party. The Irish question, in which Cromwell was now deeply involved, shared honors with their preparations for hostilities at home. That was apparent in Cromwell's activities. On May 26 he carried two messages to the House of Lords. The one requested them to expedite the ordinance for raising men for Irish service, the ships now being ready to carry them. The second was to recommend Sir Richard Samuel as deputy lieutenant of Northamptonshire; and to both the Lords agreed.[52] Two days later his importance in these warlike councils became still more apparent. On that day he carried two more messages to the Lords; the one to hasten instructions for Hull and Lincolnshire and add a clause putting the militia ordinance in effect; the other asking approval of his relative Mr. Ingoldsby, as deputy lieutenant of Buckinghamshire and of Sir John Bamfield for Devon.[53] On information that quantities of saddles and other warlike materials were being bought and carried out of London, he put through a motion in the House that the wardens of the Company of Armourers should inquire what store of saddles, arms and muskets were being made and to whom they were sold, and to report weekly to the House.[54] On that day, too, he was brought in touch with another aspect of the oncoming war, for he was named to a committee to consider misdemeanors committed in Anglesey by a certain Captain Baker and his troop and one Lieutenant Mason of Mr. Sydney's troop.[55]

On May 30 he carried up to the Lords an order for the beating of recruiting drums for additional volunteers for Ireland[56] and on the same day was appointed to a committee of ten to consider the Bill of Subscriptions for the support of the forces then being raised.[57] The next day he was named to a committee of seven to consider the reports of the preparation of a navy in Norway and Denmark to assist the King.[58] The following day, June 1, Cromwell reported from that Committee and moved that two ships be posted to guard Tynemouth and Newcastle to prevent the landing of arms from Denmark and the Low Countries[59] and Holles was instructed to move

[52] *C. J.*, ii, 588; *L. J.*, v, 85.
[53] *C. J.*, ii, 591–2; *L. J.*, v, 90.
[54] *C. J.*, ii, 592; D'Ewes *Diary*, quoted in Sanford, p. 490–1.
[55] *C. J.*, ii, 591.
[56] *Ibid.*, 594; Approved by Lords, *L. J.*, v, 92.
[57] *C. J.*, ii, 595.
[58] *Ibid.*, 596.
[59] *C. J.*, ii, 598; D'Ewes *Diary*, quoted in Sanford, p. 491.

the Lord Admiral, Warwick, in the matter. He seconded a motion of a Mr. Toll that all 'mayors, customers and searchers' of the northern ports 'stay ships bringing arms out of Denmark or the Low Countries.'[60] He presented the petition of a Colonel William Stewart and others in behalf of some 3,500 Scots who had maintained themselves against the Irish rebels, without English aid, and made an appeal to the House for them.

"Mr. Cromwell," wrote D'Ewes, "showed that they had all this time but a thousand arms amongst them and that there were certain merchants that did now offer to furnish the House with victuals and arms to relieve the said Scots and to give six months time for the payment of the same."[61]

The petition was referred to the Committee on Irish Affairs; and the next day, June 2, an Ordinance of both Houses to raise new forces by land and sea was committed to the care of Cromwell, Holles, St. John, Selden, Prideaux and three others;[62] and on June 2 propositions for a settlement were sent to the King.[63]

Recorded day by day in the formal and uninspired minutes of the House, these motions, messages and committees in which Cromwell was more and more involved, seem dull enough; yet there resides in them the very essence of the great issue now coming to a head. Behind these formal entries in the journals of the Houses loomed the great cloud of war growing from day to day in darkness and intensity. In these entries we perceive the feverish preparation for that conflict —the raising of money, men and arms, the fear of foreign intervention and of supplies from abroad. We perceive the Queen and her followers striving to supply her husband with war materials bought with the proceeds of the crown jewels and seeking the aid of foreign powers and Parliament's efforts to prevent the entry of these war supplies. We see the frantic efforts of Pym and his party to organize the militia under their appointees, to suppress protests against their actions and their policy, their appeals for loans, their seizure of the magazines, their attempts to send succor to Ireland and the forces there, their declarations, proclamations and ordinances, designed to win the country to their side, but above all their preparations for war against the King. We see how, as that war approached, Cromwell

[60] *C. J.*, ii, 598; D'Ewes, *Diary*, quoted in Sanford, p. 491.

[61] D'Ewes *Diary*, quoted in Sanford, pp. 488–89.

[62] *C. J.*, ii, 599. On June 4 it was again recommended to the same committee, *ibid.*, 607.

[63] *Ibid.*, ii, 600.

was rising to greater influence. While the Queen poured supplies into the northern ports; while members of both Houses flocked to York, while the militia drilled and men rode out from London and from York to win it for the King or Parliament; while the recruiting drums were beating throughout England and ships made ready to sail for Ireland; while the handful of Parliament under Pym strove day and night to legislate, administer and prepare to fight, appealing to liberty as the King's followers appealed to loyalty; while in every town and county in England earnest men on each side gathered in opposing camps, Cromwell at the very heart of these activities and concerned with most of them, was being trained for his part in the great conflict.

It was apparent by this time that he was no orator like Pym or Eliot; no political manager like Hampden, no lawyer like Whitelocke or Selden, no man of subtlety like Vane, no republican like Marten or Haselrig, no Presbyterian like Rous or Holles. He was not even a fierce and resentful martyr like Prynne and Valentine and Strode seeking revenge for long sufferings. He was essentially a man of practical qualities absorbed in practical affairs, a willing, able and industrious lieutenant of his leader Pym, a useful agent in the great work of organizing the resistance to the King. What he, or even his great leader, Pym, conceived would be the end of all this striving no one now can tell. Whether they had a great vision of a dominant Parliament and a subservient monarchy, a church free from episcopal authority, or many churches independent of each other and the state; whether, as their opponents claimed, they merely sought to replace the existing order with their own authority; whether it was an unselfish passion for liberty or whether there were personal motives in each case, it is now hard to disentangle and interpret the infinite complexities of the reasons which led them to this pass. Those reasons doubtless differed in each case; but whether moved by personal grievances or the loftiest motives of pure devotion to an abstract ideal of liberty, or by both, they were at one in their opposition to Charles Stuart. They were determined to put an end to those pretensions of divine right monarchy which they believed he still cherished; and they were no less determined to put an end to episcopacy. Whether Presbyterian like Holles or republican like Haselrig, they were at one in this; and in this company and very near its heart Cromwell was numbered as an enemy of monarchy and especially of the episcopal establishment. Whatever goal Pym sought, whatever dream of a new order of society his followers may have cherished, whatever vision of a future state they had, for the moment their immediate purpose was simple enough. It was to crush Stuart "tyranny" both in church and state and to this great purpose they bent all their energies.

THE NINETEEN PROPOSITIONS

As the end of May, 1642, approached, it was increasingly evident that hostilities could not be long delayed and while the presses poured forth arguments to a degree unparalleled hitherto in history, King and Commons strove for a position of advantage. From the moment that the Kentish petitioners for episcopacy were sent to prison and their petition voted seditious, it seemed the die was cast. The greater part of the nobility and gentry and virtually all the clergy rallied to the King as the champions of order against what they conceived to be little less than anarchy. On the other side the Puritan ministers and congregations, some peers and country gentlemen, the more influential part of the City and many townspeople, especially in the manufacturing districts, supported the remnant of Parliament in its crusade for liberty. April and May were filled with their activities and among these three circumstances in particular absorbed the attention of both sides.

The first of these was the control of Hull which Sir John Hotham held for the Parliament. It was essential to the King to have a port where he could land supplies sent by the Queen from the Continent; it was no less important to Pym's party to prevent that aid and to secure the magazines of war material stored there. The Commons had been successful in securing that great port and Charles's efforts to persuade or compel Hotham to yield up the place had failed. The second was a quarrel between Charles and the Houses over the command of the fleet, the King preferring Sir John Pennington, Parliament the Earl of Warwick who, in time, succeeded to that post. The third question was the control of the only armed force in England, the county militia, then being drilled and armed under the direction of the local authorities. There too, as at Hull, Pym's party had anticipated Charles and by virtue of its Militia Ordinance on March 5, and its prompt naming of lords and especially deputy lieutenants had begun to lay its hands on this important force. Against this the King began to issue "commissions of array" after the old custom; and on May 27 a royal proclamation finally forbade his subjects "belonging to the trained bands or militia . . . to rise, march, muster or exercise by virtue of any order or ordinance . . . of Parliament," without his royal consent.

The answer to this proclamation was prompt and decisive. On June 2 the remaining members of the two Houses sent to the King at York their Nineteen Propositions for a peaceful settlement. In them was nothing new. They demanded the dismissal of the privy councillors and great officers of state, "either at home or beyond the sea," save those approved by Parliament, and their replacement by men acceptable to the Houses and under such oaths as those Houses should devise. They demanded further that "the great affairs of the kingdom" "be debated, resolved and transacted only in Parliament"; that members of either House dismissed from place or office—like Essex and Holland, though their names were not mentioned—be restored; that judges and "all the officers placed by the approbation of both Houses of Parliament" hold their places during good behavior, under an oath to be framed by Parliament. They demanded that the education of the royal children be in the hands of those approved by Parliament, that "such servants as are now about them against whom both Houses shall have any just exceptions" be removed, and that no royal marriages be treated for or concluded without the consent of the Houses. They demanded that the laws against Catholics be strictly enforced, that the votes of the Popish peers be taken away and that a bill be drawn for educating the children of Papists by Protestants in the Protestant religion. As to religion they proposed that "such a reformation be made of the Church government and liturgy as both Houses of Parliament shall advise," after "consultations with divines"; that maintenance be provided for "preaching ministers" and laws be drawn for the "taking away of innovations and superstition . . . pluralities, and against scandalous ministers." They demanded a general pardon "with such exceptions as shall be advised by both Houses of Parliament"; that the forts and castles be put in the hands of men approved by Parliament; that the Militia Ordinance be approved and the royal declarations against it withdrawn; and that the "extraordinary guards and military forces" then around the King be disbanded and no such guards or forces raised in the future "but according to law in case of actual rebellion or invasion." They demanded an alliance with the United Provinces and other Protestant states "against all designs of the Pope and his adherents" and the recovery of the Palatinate. They demanded the recall by act of Parliament of the proceedings against Lord Kimbolton and the five members; and, finally, that no peers be created in the future without consent of both Houses.[33]

Such was the answer of Pym and his party to the doctrines of the supremacy of the crown held by the Stuart monarchy, the retort to the eleven years of unparliamentary government, the declaration of the entire ascendancy of Parliament. If the motive which inspired this document was, as its framers asserted, the peaceful settlement of the differences between King and Parliament, never was a proposal less likely to achieve its end. There are only three explanations pos-

[33] *L. J.*, v, 97.

sible—it was designed to make the quarrel irreconcilable and to put an end to monarchy as even a co-ordinate branch of government, to extinguish episcopacy and to make crown, church administration and judiciary subject to Parliament; it was an extreme claim put forward for trading purposes; or it was merely a programme on which to appeal to the country for support. In return for a surrender of sovereignty its framers offered to provide Charles with a revenue "beyond the proportion of any former grants of the subjects of this kingdom to your royal Majesty's predecessors"; to give up Hull; and to "deliver a just account of all the magazines"—whatever that may have meant.

To Charles the proposal seemed scarcely less than an insult. It seemed to him like betraying his birthright for a mess of pottage. It required him to abdicate his constitutional position. There was not a sovereign in the world who would have considered it for an instant; there was hardly a king of England even in the next two centuries who would have entertained all of its provisions. To the Royalists, knowing Pym as an able man, it appeared deliberately provocative; and the King's answer was prompt and decisive. Its proposers, he replied, not only assumed autocratic power, seized his forts, magazines and militia, "awed his subjects" with their "pursuivants," censures, imprisonments and charges of sedition, restrained his servants and cut off his supplies, but they had "totally suppressed the known law of the land." The only answer that he could make to this remnant of Parliament—according to Clarendon a fifth of the Lords and scarcely more than half of the Commons, including the opposition to Pym's party—was *Nolumus leges Angliae mutari*, "We are unwilling to have the laws of England changed."

The issue thus drawn was fought out in the press by proclamations, declarations, tracts and broadsides by both sides seeking to gain the support of the country. It increased in virulence in these early months of 1642; but, as Clarendon observed, "These paper skirmishes left neither side better inclined to the other; but by sharpening each other drew the matter nearer to an issue." The Nineteen Propositions defined the position and brought the matter one step nearer armed conflict. They were not merely the programme of Pym and his followers; they were, in effect, scarcely less than a declaration of war against the monarchy and were so interpreted by both sides. If the struggle between Pym and Strafford had resolved itself into a question of "My head or thy head," these proposals carried that principle one step higher, and each side strained every nerve to prepare for a conflict now seen to be inevitable.[34]

[34] Clarendon, *History*, v, 325 ff.

JUNE–JULY, 1642

It was a task sufficient to absorb their energies. Though they waited for the King's answer to the Nineteen Propositions, no one, least of all such a man as Pym, could doubt what that answer would contain, and he and his party strove in every way to secure themselves. They forbade the royal Lord Admiral, Northumberland, and the Earl of Pembroke to obey the King's order to join him at York. They denounced the Earl of Lindsey as a "delinquent" and declared him a public enemy for opposing the Militia Ordinance. They descended to lesser men; to punish clergymen for asserting that their votes had no authority without the royal sanction, even to "certain fiddlers" for making songs about them. They attacked the printers for publishing the royal proclamations; ordered the Lord Mayor of London not to divulge the King's appeal for money or for plate, and when the King's reply to their Propositions came, they forbade him to publish it at his peril. Finally, on July 12, they voted to raise an army "for the safety of the King's person and the defence of both kingdoms." They named the Earl of Essex as its general, put the fleet under the Earl of Warwick and ignored the protests of men like Whitelocke and Rudyerd against civil war. They ordered their agents to suppress the levies against Parliament and instructed Essex to hasten his preparations.

Nor were these all of their activities. They found time amid these various distractions to appoint a committee to consider "taking down the glass windows in the churches." They voted the petitions from Yorkshire and Lincoln high and insolent invasions of their privilege. They disabled man after man from sitting in the House, among them Edward Hyde who had left to join the King as his chief secretary. They ordered new elections to fill their depleted ranks; and, like the "deputies on mission" of the French Convention a century and a half later, they sent their members here and there throughout England to organize resistance to the King. They impeached of treason all who should aid the monarchy, including the Marquis of Hertford, the Earl of Northampton and Henry Hastings, the second son of the Earl of Huntingdon. They had, in short, now assumed or usurped supreme authority; and what royal prerogative had been, parliamentary privilege became.[64]

Meanwhile the King at York gathered about him a court and guards. From Hyde's pen poured declarations and proclamations against the activities of Parliament. To Charles's side hastened great

[64] *C. J.* and *L. J., passim.* See also Cobbett, *Parliamentary History;* Parry, *Parliaments and Councils of England;* and Gardiner, *History.*

nobles of the realm, with many members of Parliament, country gentlemen, Charles's nephews, the princes Rupert and Maurice, sons of the Elector Palatine, until York was transformed into an armed court and camp. Whatever his shortcomings hitherto, whatever the evils of his eleven years of unparliamentary government, now that the choice had come, the greater part of England sympathized with him, especially since the remnant of Parliament had assumed such powers. In answer to his plea for plate and money, the Marquis of Worcester's son brought him a hundred thousand pounds and with it and lesser contributions from like sources Charles began to equip his troops, as meanwhile the Parliament levied new excises, borrowed from the City and laid hands on the money of the Irish Adventurers for military purposes.

Again in all this movement Cromwell played a part largely neglected by historians and biographers. At best it has been described as an obscure career to which he was not suited; at worst it has been ignored. Yet it was not insignificant in itself and it served as preparation for much greater things. The catalogue of his activities in these months throws light not merely on him but on the great events of these important days. On June 4 he and Prideaux were selected to manage a conference with the Lords on the matter of additional forces for Ireland.[65] It was a delicate question which went to the heart of the problem then pressing on the House. The King demanded security that the forces thus raised should be used against the Irish rebels, not against the crown; and before he would consent to the commission drawn up by the Commons on February 24 and sent to him in April for raising these forces, he insisted on seeing the names of the officers; a plea which seems not to have been granted finally.

On that same day Cromwell carried to the Upper House letters from Hull requesting money for the garrison and a Commons order for supplying it. With this he took a list of the commanders for the fleet then being prepared for Ireland,[66] which he had earlier that day delivered to the Commons and had approved by them. What was even more significant his name appears on a new subscription list. In a "Book of the Members of the House of Commons that Advance Horse, Money and Plate for Defence of Parliament" is an entry, "Die Veneris, June v°, 1642. Mr. Cromwell will bring in five hundred pounds. Mr. Lowry will find a horse ready furnished."[67] This, it seems, was in addition to his subscription to the Irish fund which

[65] *C. J.*, ii, 607.

[66] *C. J.*, ii, 607; *L. J.*, v, 103; D'Ewes *Diary*, quoted in Sanford, p. 491.

[67] *Tanner Mss*, lxiii, f. 57, in the Bodleian Library, and noted by Sanford, p. 491. June 5 fell on Sunday in 1642.

presently was joined to this new source of supply for the equipment of the forces raised against the King, so that in all it seems that Oliver contributed something more than a thousand pounds to the cause.

By this time the pretence of raising men and money entirely for the Irish enterprise was growing thin, if pretence there was, for it was becoming impossible to keep the issues separate. On June 6, Cromwell was named to a committee of thirty-four including all the House leaders save St. John, to consider information which had come from York;[68] and on that day he was commissioned to perfect an order enabling certain captains to recruit their companies for the Irish war.[69] On the next day he, with Gerard and Lord Dungarvon, was sent to the Committee of the Adventurers to ask for a loan of a hundred thousand pounds for the relief of Munster to be repaid from a like sum which had been promised by the City.[70] The request was in time granted, and in time his two subscriptions joined to finance the war against the King.

His next appearance was as teller with Holles for the Yeas on the question as to whether the nine Lords who had left the House contrary to its orders to join the King at York should be suspected of promoting war against the Parliament; and that being carried by a vote of 109 to 51, Cromwell was sent to the Upper House to request its members to "sit awhile" and confer upon a method to convey this message to their impeached fellow peers.[71] Those peers who had been summoned to Westminster on May 30 had replied on June 7 that they had gone to York by Charles's command and stayed there by the same authority. In such fashion there came to a head a new conflict of allegiance, whether to crown or Parliament.

The manifold problems and duties of the Parliamentary party at this time are revealed with great clearness in the activities of Oliver Cromwell.[72] On June 9 he and Hampden were appointed members of a committee of six men to see that despatches were sent from the House to committees appointed by that House;[73] and two days thereafter he carried a message to the Lords asking concurrence in an order enjoining the justices of peace of Yorkshire to keep all Papists' arms in custody, to which the Lords agreed.[74] On the next day he took up to the Lords another order in regard to the setting forth of

[68] *C. J.*, ii, 609. They met that day and again June 14 and 15.

[69] *Ibid.*

[70] *Ibid.*, 610.

[71] *Ibid.*, 620. They were the Earls of Northampton, Devonshire, Monmouth, and Dover, and Lords Rich, Grey de Ruthyn, Coventry, Capel and Howard of Charlton.

[72] *C. J.*, ii, 619 ff.

[73] *Ibid.*, 622.

[74] *Ibid.*, ii, 625; *L. J.*, v, 136.

ships provided by the Adventurers for additional forces to be used by sea against the Irish rebels.[75]

Thus hand in hand the two great issues went as England turned to war. On June 13 the King ordered Commissions of Array sent out for organizing the militia in his name to be executed on June 16. On the 17th Cromwell carried to the Lords four messages. The first had to do with hastening the ordinance for the ships for additional forces for Ireland. The second was to ask if an answer had come from the King concerning the bills for calling an assembly of divines to consider church reform; the third "for enlarging the time of subscriptions and the Adventurers for Ireland"; the fourth to ask agreement to the appointment of another "deputy on mission," Timothy Middleton as deputy lieutenant of Essex and to set July 1 for putting into execution the formation of the militia in Devonshire.[76] On that same day he was named to a committee of sixteen, including Pym, Holles, St. John, Fiennes, Gerard, Barrington and Sir William Waller to get information of warlike provisions being sent to York, to stop them if possible and report daily to the House; and later that same day he brought to the Commons a message from the Lords agreeing to the melting and coining of plate brought in by virtue of the appeals of the Parliament to its supporters for the sinews of war.[77]

It is natural to assume that in such critical times as these the actors in such a great tragedy are conscious of the parts they play; that as history romanticizes them, they dramatize themselves. That is no doubt true in some cases. There are men who, like Sir Symonds D'Ewes, record events from day to day; there are others like Thomason who collect the fugitive literature of their time; there are leaders like Napoleon who heroize themselves. But in the main, even at such times as these, however conscious they may be of the great issues at stake, most men do their work from day to day with little effort to picture themselves as heroes or as protagonists in a great drama. Few men are conscious of themselves as historic characters, at least until their work is done and they sit down to write out their memoirs and *apologiae*. They are too absorbed in the business of the moment; and apart from some such compelling circumstance as the Grand Remonstrance or Strafford's trial, most of that business is of the character which Cromwell's activity typifies. In the sum it is important and imposing; but its details are often apparently insignificant. Yet that must not blind us to the fact that it was on precisely such apparently trifling pieces of business as those which employed the time of men like Cromwell there was raised the edifice of revolution. And, except for the fact that like all those of his faith, he con-

[75] *C. J.*, ii, 627.
[76] *Ibid.*, 629; *L. J.*, v, 142.
[77] *C. J.*, ii, 630; *L. J.*, v, 142.

ceived himself a confidant and an agent of the Almighty, he did not dramatize himself or his activities. It is, indeed, difficult to dramatize such a multiplicity of business as that on which he was engaged.

On June 18 he was appointed as one of a committee to go to the City to a conference in regard to a letter to the Lord Mayor from the King concerning the stopping of subscriptions for raising of horse for the royal service,[78] and he was added to a committee to consider the petitions of a Mr. Chichester and a Mr. Hill.[79] On that same day Philip, Lord Wharton, was appointed Colonel-General of the forces raised by the Adventurers, and in a "List of Field Officers chosen and appointed for the Irish Expedition"[80] appears the name of "Oliver Cromwell, Ensign," probably Cromwell's cousin, Sir Philip Cromwell's son.

Meanwhile preparations for war had gone on apace. Money and plate had poured into York and Westminster and as rapidly as possible had been transmuted into war materials. King and Parliament had strained and were straining every nerve to secure control of the militia and the strongholds. Though Hull remained in the hands of the Parliament, Goring had seized Portsmouth for the King; and on June 17 the Earl of Newcastle took possession of Newcastle. It was a matter of importance to both sides. Charles now had what he had long needed, a northern port as entry for supplies. It was a new threat to Parliament and on June 20 a committee of nineteen including Cromwell, Strode and Vane was ordered to report on information in regard to its capture, and a week later a committee of nine, including this time, Hampden, Barrington, Stapleton and Cromwell was instructed to investigate the whole business of Newcastle.[81] At the same time he carried three messages to the Lords—recommendations for the appointment of two deputy lieutenants for Warwickshire, instructions for that county, and a request to send for the Earl of Northampton as a "delinquent" since it was reported that he was being sent to Warwick by the King to oppose the militia ordinance and execute the Commission of Array.[82]

The month of July saw the activities of each side redoubled and Cromwell brought more and more into affairs. It is almost possible to trace the development of events from his activities. On July 1 he was sent to request the Lords to agree that the counties of Norfolk, Suffolk, Cambridge, Hertford, Dorset and Derby should put the Militia Ordinance into execution; to recommend deputy lieutenants for Cambridge, Surrey and Leicester, and to hasten the declaration

[78] *C. J.*, ii, 632.
[79] *Ibid.*, 631.
[80] Pr. for Edward Paxton, Lond., June 1642. Cp. *C. J.*, ii, 631.
[81] *C. J.*, ii, 634, 642.
[82] *Ibid.*, 641; *L. J.*, v, 163.

against the Commission of Array.[83] Four days later he and Gerard were appointed to draft a letter to be sent to Sir William Brereton, Mr. Booth and others, congratulating them on the cheerful obedience of the county of Chester to the Militia Ordinance. Read in the House and signed by the Speaker on July 7, it produced a reply from Brereton to Cromwell on July 27, which, among other matters, complained of the severity of the Commissioners of Array against the agents of the Parliament.[84]

The struggle for the advantage of position grew from day to day. There was some question even of the Tower, for it was felt that the Royalists might surprise and seize that threat to the City and on July 5, the same day that he was instructed to write to Brereton, Cromwell was appointed with Gerard, Glyn, Pye and three others to confer with the Lieutenant of the Tower, Sir John Conyers, to consider measures for its safety.[85] Again, three days later, Cromwell and Gerard, with Barrington and Mildmay, were added to the Committee for Subscriptions to consider what counties should first be urged to bring in money, plate and horse.[86] On July 11 Cromwell and Sir William Lewis were ordered to bring in instructions for the committee appointed to go into Wiltshire, especially since there, as in Cornwall and the western counties, measures had to be taken to prevent horses being sent to York for the King's forces.[87] To this was added another matter of some importance. On that same day Cromwell, Rous, Constantine and Alderman Pennington were appointed to manage and report a conference requested by the Lords on two curiously unrelated pieces of business.

The first was the answer of the French ambassador to a letter from Sir Thomas Roe, ambassador to the Diet of Ratisbon, denying the charge that he had offered English support to Austria against France. It was a far cry from that remote and unreal realm of foreign politics to the other matter which the conference considered. This was the question of the Lord Mayor of London, that devoted royalist, Sir Richard Gurney.[88] That question touched the Commons close. Chosen Lord Mayor a year earlier over the bitter opposition of the Puritan element, opposing the City petitions favoring Pym's policy, suppressing disorder and imprisoning the most notorious offenders against the peace, Gurney had none the less successfully protested Lunsford's appointment as Lieutenant of the Tower and declined to proclaim the five members traitors. Despite this the Commons re-

[83] *C. J.*, ii, 647–8; *L. J.*, v, 172.

[84] *C. J.*, ii, 653, 657; *Hist. Mss. Comm. Rept.* 13, App. pt. I (Welbeck Abbey), i, 44–45. Cp. Brereton's letter to Lenthall, 30 July, *Ibid.*, p. 47.

[85] *C. J.*, ii, 654.

[86] *Ibid.*, 660.

[87] *Ibid.*, 665.

[88] *Ibid.*; *Perfect Diurnall*, July 8.

fused to entrust him with the militia; and when he had permitted the King's proclamation against the Militia Ordinance to be read and refused to store the war material from Hull in the City, he was impeached and on the very day of this conference, doubtless as one of its results, he was sent to the Tower by the Parliament.

This was the last act before the formal declaration of the existence of a state of war. Having, as it were, secured their rear, on the next day the Commons issued that declaration, named Essex commander and resolved to live and die with him "for the safety of the King's person and the defence of both kingdoms."[89] Two days later, Cromwell was put on a committee of ten to treat with representatives from Ireland as to the steps to be taken for the good of Munster and the general situation of the island, and was instructed to inform the officers then being sent to Munster of the plans of Parliament.[90]

Meanwhile, though the business of Ireland ran through the affairs of Parliament like a crimson thread and absorbed much of Cromwell's energy, it became subordinate to the more pressing problems nearer home. The first of these was the universities. Oxford and Cambridge had been prompt to express their loyalty to Charles by sending him money, the one ten thousand pounds, the other six. It was now proposed to reinforce those gifts with contributions from their great stores of college plate, and on the day that Essex was appointed general, Oxford was commanded not to send such contributions and a guard was ordered thrown about the town. Cambridge came next, and in it Cromwell had an immediate interest. On July 15 he moved that the town be authorized to raise and officer two companies of volunteers. Already, it appeared, he had taken the liberty to send down arms to his constituents for their defence and Sir Dudley North had been ordered to pay Cromwell a hundred pounds of money received from the late sheriff of Cambridge, a certain Mr. Crane, to reimburse him for his outlay in the affair. Though there was opposition, it was finally decided that Cromwell should move the Lord Lieutenant to permit the men of Cambridge to train and exercise in arms;[91] and on the day following the Commons ordered the serjeant-at-arms to stop a shipment of arms said to be destined for the University.[92]

Throughout the next month his activities were divided between the two great issues of Ireland and the oncoming English civil war. On the same day that the serjeant-at-arms was ordered to stop the arms destined for Cambridge University, Cromwell seems to have

[89] *C. J.*, ii, 668.
[90] *Ibid.*, 672–3. Reynolds reported from the committee on July 16.
[91] D'Ewes, *Diary*, quoted in Sanford, p. 513; *C. J.*, ii, 674.
[92] *C. J.*, ii, 675.

carried a message to the Lords recommending the despatch of forces from Ulster and Leinster to Munster which was then the danger point of Irish rebellion.[93] On that same day, he, with Hampden, Strode, Barrington, Rous, Pickering, Erle and Heyman, was added to a committee for distributing various orders and declarations of the House, to stop a troop of horse raised by Captain John Digby for the King and to secure the magazine of arms at Dorchester.[94]

Four days after the House ordered Sir Dudley North to reimburse Cromwell the money seems to have been paid over to him:

Memorandum

Receipt for £100 from Sir Dudley North in satisfaction of arms sent to Mr. Blackly of Cambridge, a high constable for the county, to be disposed of by Lord North, Lord Lieutenant of the said county. July 19, 1642.

OLIVER CROMWELL.[95]

The same day Cromwell carried three messages to the Lords; the first an order to a Mr. Loftus for £10,000 to indemnify the volunteers of Shrewsbury and Hertfordshire; the second to permit Sir John Clotworthy to apply £1,000 of his loan "toward adventuring in Ireland"; the third was a request for "speedy resolution" on the Commons vote to draw forces from Ulster and Leinster to the siege of Limerick in Munster then held by the Irish rebels.[96] That question was acute. On July 20 Cromwell and Strode were ordered to prepare a letter to the Lord Justices of Ireland requiring them to send a regiment of a thousand foot from the Leinster forces to relieve Lord Esmond then hard pressed in Duncannon fort;[97] which, the next day, was read, approved, and sent to the Lords by Cromwell's hands.[98] On August 1 the Commissioners for Irish affairs resolved that four of their number, with Cromwell's assistance, prepare a plan for the speedy despatch of volunteers to Ireland to be presented to the Commons on the next day.[99]

This was the last appearance of Cromwell in the House before an

[93] *C. J.*, ii, 675; *L. J.*, v, 214. Sir Henry Mildmay was originally ordered to carry the message.

[94] *C. J.*, ii, 676.

[95] *St. P. Dom. Charles I*, ccccxci, f. 71I; *Calendar*, 1642, p. 354. The account of Sir Dudley North for £100 received of Wm. Crane by the appointment of John Crane of Cambridge, with a notation that the whole sum was paid to Oliver Cromwell, is filed with the latter's receipt in the Record Office.

[96] *C. J.*, ii, 680; *L. J.*, v, 218.

[97] *C. J.*, ii, 683.

[98] *Ibid.*, 684–5; *L. J.*, v, 229. The next day Cromwell brought a message that the Lords would send their answer by their own messenger. Later they amended the letter slightly and returned it.

[99] *St. P. Ireland*, cclxii, 9, p. 28; *Calendar*, 1633–47, p. 485.

exploit which raised him from the relative obscurity of an active, hard-working member of the Commons to a national, even a romantic, position in the eyes of his party. Since the beginning of the Parliament he had been deeply, if unobtrusively, concerned with nearly every phase of its business; with the attack on the old system, with the measures taken to prepare for armed conflict, with the problem of the Irish war. That problem was vexatious and to the last degree complex. In it was involved not merely the question of suppressing rebellion but the more delicate problem of relations with the King. It had, in the minds of the Royalists, been used as a stalking-horse for warlike preparations nearer home, as earlier the activities of Strafford had been regarded as preparations for intervention in the King's behalf; nor was it easy to separate the two issues, had it been desired.

THE OUTBREAK OF WAR, AUGUST, 1642

Even the Irish question had now begun to yield to matters nearer home; and August finally saw the outbreak of hostilities. At the same moment that he was entrusted with framing the plan to send more troops to Ireland, Cromwell, with Sir John Cutts, Mr. Castle, Mr. Bendish and Mr. Thomas Duckett, were noted in the Commons Journals as having "the general order for advancing the propositions for bringing in money, plate and horses."[100] It was a curious note, the more so in that of these men only Cromwell was a member of the House, though all were from Cambridge. Cutts had been a member for the county in the Short Parliament and he and Castle were soon to be appointed deputy lieutenants, and Castle was member for Cambridge in a later Parliament. They were all devoted to the cause of Parliament and the reason for their notification was soon evident. News had come to Westminster that the University authorities were preparing to follow the example of Oxford and send college plate to York, in response to the King's plea which he had sent the Universities on July 24.

The colleges hastened to pack up their plate, whose value may be guessed from the fact that the contribution of St. John's College, Cambridge was worth two thousand pounds. To guard it a company of volunteers was formed, chiefly, it would appear, from members of the colleges. The sheriff of Huntingdon, Sir Richard Stone, lent his active assistance, the sheriff of Cambridge, Sir John Cotton, his passive consent. Mr. John Barwick, then Fellow of St. John's and later Dean of Westminster, with others, formed a party of horse as an

100 *C. J.*, ii, 698.

escort.[101] Mr. Barnabas Oley, President of Clare Hall, "acquainted with all the bye-ways" about Cambridge acted as a guide, and a considerable part of the treasure was thus spirited away. Meanwhile Cromwell with his brother-in-law Valentine Walton and his friend Francis Russell had hastened from Westminster, gathered forces from the western part of Cambridgeshire as they went to prevent the removal of the plate. They arrived too late, and though the main roads were guarded, the first convoy got through to the King at Nottingham, despite the efforts of the agents of Parliament to catch the convoy at Lowler Hedges between Cambridge and Huntingdon.[102]

Thus balked, Cromwell and his colleagues did not hesitate, but marched straight to Cambridge, to King's College. There Captain James Docwra of the Cambridge trained bands, with Lewis Phillips the undersheriff of Cambridge, Sir John Cotton, Sir Capel Bedell and others, with their followers, with flags flying and drums beating were prepared to send off more plate and it even appeared for the moment that the first blood of the war might be shed. Forces were summoned from every side. Walton had sent out warrants for two hundred men. Sir Oliver Cromwell's son Henry with fifty men came to take the plate. Crowds gathered in Cambridge and along the road to Huntingdon to see the fight or take part in it. Cromwell had placed musketeers, hidden in the fields, along the road, and the sons of Sir John Bramston, the old Ship-money judge, riding along the great North Road were stopped by them to be searched and ordered to "goe before Mr. Cromwell and give account from whence wee came and whither we were going." Mr. Cromwell, they said, was some four miles off; and, the Bramstons protesting and giving the man twelve pence, they were allowed to proceed.[103]

The details of the ensuing events are somewhat obscure, but one thing about the incident is beyond dispute, the plate was not sent.

Mr. Cromwell was, in fact, then engaged in an enterprise which was briefly but comprehensively reported to Parliament on August 15. "Mr. Cromwell, in Cambridgeshire, has seized the magazine in the Castle at Cambridge, and hath hindered the carrying of the plate from that University; which, as some report, was to the value of £20,000 or thereabouts."[104] Two days later, on August 17, the

[101] Cp. *C. J.*, ii, 726; and *Cal. Comm. for Comp.*, pp. 881, 895.

[102] Barwick, *Querela Cantabrigiensis;* Peter Barwick, *Life of John Barwick* (1903), pp. 12–14.

[103] Kingston, *East Anglia*, pp. 55–61. Kingston derives his account from *St. P. Interr. G.*, lxxxviii, pp. 649–655; *Duke of Manchester's Papers*, p. 503; *Autobiography of Sir John Bramston* (Camden Society), pp. 85–6.

[104] *C. J.*, ii, 720; Edwards, *Sidney Sussex*, p. 107, says the value was greatly exaggerated. Valentine Walton reported on Aug. 12 that several persons had tried to prevent the Parliamentary order, to stop the plate, from being executed, whereupon three men were ordered to be brought as delinquents. *C. J.*, ii, 717.

Houses instructed Cromwell, Thomas Sherwood, Mayor of Cambridge, and three aldermen to "care for the peace and safety of the town, exercise the trained bands and volunteers and disarm recusants,"[105] and the next day the Commons voted a committee to prepare an order for the indemnity of Cromwell, Walton, and "those that have or shall assist them in stopping of the plate that was going to York," mentioning incidentally Francis Russell, newly appointed deputy lieutenant of Cambridge.[106] On the next day, so important had the matter become, the Houses ordered Cromwell, Sir John Potts and others

> "to set strong watches, sufficiently armed day and night, upon the several bridges of Germanes, Maudlyn, Soame, Stow, Downham, and all other bridges and ferries between the town of Cambridge and King's Lynn, for the apprehending of all horses of service for the wars, arms, ammunition, or plate sent to His Majesty, and also to prevent persons coming from the North into these counties for the purpose of executing the King's Commission of Array."[107]

Though some undergraduates like Cromwell's son Oliver were on the side of Parliament—and one senses that there was little studying done in Cambridge at this time—most of the members of the colleges were on the royal side. The undergraduates armed and drilled for the King; the heads of the colleges protested against the measures of the Parliament, and Cambridge which had been a center of Puritanism seemed only less loyal than Oxford which had been so strongly Anglican. It was, then, natural, that Cromwell as member for the city should be detailed to prevent the sending of aid to the King and the execution of the commissions of array; and it appears from various pieces of evidence that he was there or in the neighborhood for some little time after his exploit of intercepting the plate and seizing the magazine of arms.

The last week of August 1642 was a decisive period of English history. On August 22 Charles I raised the royal standard at Nottingham; on August 29 Oliver Cromwell began to raise a troop of horse at Huntingdon, and with these two events the Civil War may be said to have begun in form. At the moment, indeed, it would have seemed absurd to compare two such events so different in character and circumstance. The contrast between a sovereign surrounded by his court and an army growing rapidly in numbers and enthusiasm for his cause, and a relatively obscure member of Parliament haranguing prospective volunteers in the market-place of a small English

[105] *L. J.*, v, 299.
[106] *C. J.*, ii, 726, 729; *L. J.*, v, 307.
[107] *L. J.*, v, 306; *C. J.*, ii, 728.

town was as striking as that between the men who were, in time, to be the chief protagonists of the ensuing civil war.

For, despite his close connection with the heads of the revolt, despite his numerous activities in Parliament, Cromwell was not as yet one of the leaders of the party to which he had devoted his life and his estate. He had, indeed, been one of its most energetic members, he had been engaged in most of its numerous activities, he had approved himself a vigorous and capable agent. He may have been—he doubtless was—deep in the counsels of Hampden and of Pym. But if he had served on many committees, there were men in the House who had served on more. If he had been entrusted with much business, there were others who had been given positions of far more importance. He was but one of many who carried messages to the House of Lords. He was no speaker and his voice was seldom heard in the debates. Though a man of business competent to treat with the City, he was no diplomat and was not entrusted with the more delicate and important negotiations which Pym and his party had carried on. He was not recognized as a great administrator, still less as an agitator, least of all as a statesman. He was a man of every-day affairs, able, active, competent, almost fanatically devoted to the destruction of the church establishment, aggressive to a fault, and increasingly competent in the conduct of the business of raising men and money, ships and supplies for the Irish war.

With the seizure of the Cambridge plate and magazine of arms, he found at last his true sphere in life. He was a man of action, prompt, decisive, brave, and unhampered, like so many of his side, like even the new General, Essex, himself, by any doubts of the justice of the cause in which they were embarked. Over them, as over his enemies, he had the enormous advantage of absolute conviction of the utter righteousness of that cause and of himself, the utter wrongness of those on the other side. He had no scruples as to his course or its consequences, such as disturbed the more thoughtful of each side. He was prepared to follow it to its last conclusion; and after he came back to Parliament to receive its thanks and transmit them to his colleagues in the Cambridge exploit, he hastened back to Huntingdon to raise his troop of horse; and in the scanty and inconclusive evidence we have of his utterances there we may perceive the whole of his simple purpose and philosophy.

For those utterances there are only two pieces of evidence. The first is that of Clarendon who, writing in later years from hearsay, testifies that Cromwell assured his men:

"That he would not deceive or cozen them by the perplexed and involved expression in his commission to fight for 'King and Parliament', and therefore that if the King chanced to be in the body of the enemy that he was to charge, he would discharge his pistol upon him as at any other private person, and if their conscience would not permit them to do the like, he advised them not to list themselves in his troop or under his command."[108]

However distant Clarendon was in time and place from the event he thus records, however prejudiced he may have been in the light of Cromwell's later activities, his story had a certain ring of truth. It is in keeping with Cromwell's character and utterances; it is full of that direct and appealing call to action which characterizes so many of his speeches on such occasions. It sounds like Cromwell and it certainly expresses his purpose. It was his business and that of his men to beat the King; all else mattered but little until this was done; and there was nothing else to do till this was done. What the result would be might well be left to a later time. It was not his nature to anticipate the future more than he could help. He met his problems as they came along. Throughout his whole career it was his principle, in the words of a later hymn:

"I do not ask to see the distant path,
One step enough for me."

What was his general purpose another piece of evidence reveals. It is the testimony of a witness who was or who professed to have been there, "Theauro John" as he called himself, who ten years later gave an account of it.

"Hear, my Lord Cromwell," he begins, "I claim protection from you by virtue of the oath you have sworn unto the people, and confirmed by many iterations, vows and protestations, as that protest at Huntingdon in the Market House, myself being there present, and those words I challenge you to make good which you declared, the words are these: You sought not ours but us and our welfare, and to stand with us for the liberty of the gospel and the laws of the land."[109]

In whatever words expressed and in which cause, such a scene as that of Cromwell appealing for volunteers in the Market House of Huntingdon was typical of all England in that summer of 1642 as King and Commons sent out their summons and their messengers to raise men and money for the armies then being formed.

The task was difficult. Except for a handful of royal guards there was no armed force in England; there was no body of trained soldiers on either side; there were only the untrained or half-trained militia and a group of men who had gained some experience of war upon the continent. With such materials King and Commons set out to improvise armies of volunteers. In that enterprise the King had an advantage in the most important arm, the cavalry. He could call upon

[108] Clarendon, *History*, x, 170.

[109] *Theauro John his disruptive Challenge to the Universities of Oxford and Cambridge* (Mar. 1651–2).

the nobles and the country gentlemen and their followers, grooms, game-keepers, and the like, men accustomed to horses and to arms. The Commons on the other hand, with its command of the capital had the advantage in foot-soldiers and supplies, though it did not lack some cavalry, however deficient in comparison with the dashing horsemen of Rupert's regiments.

If the armies on each side were composed for the most part of men who had never seen a shot fired in anger, the high commands were not without men of experience in war. For that the events on the continent during the preceding quarter of a century had afforded an unrivalled opportunity. The struggle between the Dutch and the Spaniards in the Low Countries had long attracted young Englishmen desirous of a military career, and the Vere regiment in particular had drawn many of them to its ranks. In it had served at one time or another the Royalist general Goring and a long list of Parliamentary leaders including the Fairfaxes, father and son, Essex, and Skippon. The service of the Princes of Nassau had attracted others like the Earl of Lindsey, the two Hothams and Sir Edward Massey, as well as the two Palatine princes, Rupert and Maurice, and Sir Jacob Astley, the commander of the royal foot during a great part of the ensuing war.

To these were added the men who had fought under the Elector Palatine, Mansfeld or Gustavus in the Thirty Years' War. In general the Scots like the two Leslies, Monro and Ruthven, had served under Gustavus Adolphus. Some like Sir Ralph Hopton and his antagonist and friend Sir William Waller, had been in the Palatinate; others like Sir Richard Grenville, Sir William Balfour and George Monk had even been at Cadiz and Rochelle; and among the curious circumstances of the time, of the commanders in the English civil war at least five—Rupert, Maurice, Goring, Skippon and Monk—had been at the famous surrender of Breda.

There were, on the other hand, men of no previous experience in war. Of these some men of high rank like Manchester and Newcastle held command rather by wealth and station than by talents or experience. Others rose, as it were, from the ranks. Browne the "woodmonger," Okey the brewer's assistant, Rainsborough the sailor, with Blake, Haselrig, Harrison and others, had neither rank nor wealth nor experience. To which class Cromwell belonged it is impossible to say on the basis of direct evidence, though the assumption has been that he was wholly ignorant of military matters at the outset of the war. If so, there is nothing more remarkable in this than that Blake with no previous experience became one of the greatest of English admirals, though either circumstance is astonishing enough.

Nor was there any very definite plan of campaign, nor was that possible in the confused situation of the time. In general the King's support came largely from the north and west, that of the Commons from the south and east. But England was dotted with towns and castles which held out for one side or the other with small regard to their locality. In the main the towns were for the Parliament and from Plymouth and Exeter to Hull and Newcastle nearly all the ports were held for Parliament. The manufacturing towns from Norwich to Manchester, Bradford, Sheffield, and many in the west, were Puritan as well. On the other hand the castles from Sherborne on the south to Pontefract on the north were held for the most part by the King's followers. Yet even this division was confused. Whole areas like the West Riding of Yorkshire were dominated by the Puritan element, while the King had staunch supporters in all the southern counties as in those of the east, and on the efforts of each side to control or overawe their opponents in every district of England the first feverish months of the struggle were absorbed.

But guerrilla war was not enough, and though it continued throughout the whole struggle, ultimate victory came by other means. The nature of the conflict determined in some measure the disposition of the forces and the plans of the antagonists. The main armies under Essex and the King confronted each other in that great triangle between York, Worcester and London. In the north the King commissioned the Duke of Newcastle to oppose the Hothams and the Fairfaxes, father and son. To the west he sent the Marquis of Hertford with Sir Ralph Hopton to command the horse and secure the six western counties with South Wales against the Parliamentary commanders, Stamford and Sir William Waller. Sir Charles Cavendish was to operate in that land debatable along the edge of the eastern counties, chiefly in Lincoln and Nottingham. Those eastern counties, which with London formed the chief stronghold of the Puritan party, though not abandoned to the Parliament, had no such unified command as the north and west, and it was on them as his great objective Charles designed to move, believing rightly that the capture of London would bring the Parliament's resistance to an end. None realized this better than Pym and his followers and their military dispositions were made accordingly.

While members of Parliament had been riding to and fro, acting as deputy lieutenants or as emissaries to enforce the Militia Ordinance or prevent the execution of the royal commissions of array, and securing strongholds and magazines of arms, the Committee of Safety and the Houses had been busy raising money and commissioning officers for Essex's army, among them many of their own number. In such fashion Hampden, Fiennes, St. John, Stapleton and many more were made colonels; and among eighty others Cromwell was commissioned to raise a troop of horse. Like each of them he was voted a sum of £1,104 "mounting money" to equip his men; and summoning to his aid his brother-in-law, John Desborough, as quartermaster, and two officers, Lieutenant Cuthbert Baildon and Cornet Joseph Waterhouse, he soon enlisted sixty men in Cambridge and Huntingdon.

His relatives were no less active. His son Oliver, apparently leaving St. Catherine's College, became a cornet in Lord St. John's troop.[110] His brother-in-law, Valentine Walton, became the captain of another troop of horse in which his son Valentine was an officer; while in these eastern counties, as in all England, men gathered to be armed and drilled, to harass their opponents, to rabble "Papists" and search for arms and money for the "cause," whether Royalist or Parliamentarian.

That last week of August, 1642, was a busy and tumultous period in English history and nowhere more than in the region where Cromwell was raising his troop of horse. Nothing more clearly illustrates the feeling of the times and the general spirit of unrest and destruction, especially in these eastern counties, than the events of the day that troop was mustered in. That day Sir Dudley North and Sir John Cutts were sent from Westminster to put the Militia Ordinance into effect and Mr. Russell of Shingay appeared in Cambridge with the King's commission of array, while his brother, the Earl of Bedford, was leading a troop from London against the Cavaliers at Ware and thence to search the house of Lord Capel for arms destined to serve the King. Twelve trunks from Holland were seized in Skegney creek with their guard of royalists; and a troop of horse met at Cherryhinton to "search Papists' houses" for more arms. Finding none, they marched to Bishop Wren's palace at Downham, but "the bird had flown" to Cambridge, and as the "Joyful News from Ely" informed the Londoners they seized a thousand pounds' worth of money and of plate with a great piece of ordnance.

What share Cromwell had in these events, if any, we have no evidence save the story of Dr. Barwick to the effect that while Mr. Russell was endeavoring to proclaim the commission of array in Cambridge, assisted by the heads of some colleges,

"Down he comes again in a terrible manner, with what force he could draw together, and surrounds divers colleges, while we were at our devotions in our several chapels; taking away prisoners several doctors of divinity, heads of colleges, viz., Dr. Beale, Master of St. John's College, Dr. Martin, Master of Queen's College, and Dr. Sterne, Master of Jesus College, and these he carries with him to London in triumph . . . they were led captive through Bartholomew Fair and so far as Temple Bar, and back through the

[110] *List of the Army raised under the command of his Excellency Robert Earle of Essex*, Lond. 1642, which lists "C[aptain] Oli. Cromwell" as captain of Troop 67, and "C[ornet] Oliver Cromwell" as cornet in St. John's troop—no. 8.

City to prison in the Tower, on purpose that they might be houted at or stoned by the rabble rout."[111]

To these names has been added that of Cromwell's own college head, Dr. Samuel Ward, but whether or not he was subjected to this indignity, this much seems certain, that he died a year later a prisoner in St. John's College. Whether Cromwell actually accompanied his prisoners on their penitential pilgrimage through London or not, it seems at least possible that he returned to London about this time. In such fashion were the eastern counties, like all England, stirred as on every hand mobs rose, troops were enlisted and equipped and drilled and Essex prepared to march against the King.

Meanwhile each side endeavored to strengthen and consolidate its position. In this Pym's party had a great advantage from the first. It held, as it were, the inner lines, including the capital and the wealthiest and most populous part of England, the south and east. It controlled what remained of the machinery of government; it was supported by the chief sources of ready money in the kingdom; it was experienced in administration as in agitation; and in all these ways superior to a King who had not merely to organize an army but an administration and who was himself both inexperienced and incapable in such affairs. He was, moreover, hampered by his courtiers and his relatives. He had, indeed, his nephews Maurice and Rupert at his side and Rupert in particular was a great cavalry leader capable of inspiring his men with courage and devotion. He had in the Earl of Lindsey, whom he named commander-in-chief, an experienced soldier; but he made Rupert independent of Lindsey and so broke the first rule of success in war.

In this, as in so many other instances, as has so often been pointed out, his inexperience, his vacillation, his instability and his incapacity to deal with men and situations in such a crisis as this, made him an ineffective leader. It is easy to say this; it is easy to point out the defects of his character and policy; it is easy to say that had he done this or that at any given moment, or had he been of different character, the situation might have been cleared up without a war, that he might have kept his head and throne. It is easy but it is not necessarily true. It has been said of many rulers at many times. The same was said of Louis XVI and the French Revolution; and of President Buchanan and the American civil war. It has been said of every leader who failed to prevent or to suppress such a movement as the Puritan Revolution. Yet it has been remarked that no one who has observed the progress of great waves of emotion which from time to time sweep over nations but must feel that no character, no

[111] Barwick, *Querela Cantabrigiensis.*

policy, no leadership of those in authority can prevail against them for the time. They seem to run their course like a fever, and, like a fever, the best that one can do is to assist nature, not attempt to reverse her processes, and so await return to health. This, it has been said, is pure fatalism—and possibly not true. But if one thing seems more certain than another in such times as these it is the old maxim that when things go right nothing one does can go wrong; and that when things go wrong, nothing he does goes right; and in some measure at least, this might well be applied to Charles I and his various policies and activities. Like other rulers in such a situation, he confronted the whirlwind and faced the storm, and whether or not another man might have succeeded where Charles failed, he, at least, was no man to ride the one or direct the other.

He had but a small force and he did not want to fight. Three days after his standard was raised, he asked Parliament to appoint commissioners to treat for peace. It refused to act until he took his standard down and recalled his proclamation of treason against its members. Its leaders were bent on war, and among their preparations they passed an ordinance against stage-plays as inconsistent with "a season of humiliation." Once more the King appealed to them. On September 5 he sent Falkland and Spencer with an offer to take down his standard and withdraw his charges of treason, if the Houses would do the same, agreeing privately to consent to a "thorough reform of religion." To this the Houses under Pym's lead replied that they would never lay down their arms until Charles had ceased to protect persons who had been or might be thereafter voted "delinquents" and that all who had advanced money to the Commonwealth should be repaid "out of the estates of the said delinquents and of the malignant and disaffected party." The proposition was impossible, as he felt it was meant to be. From the beginning to the end the King clung to the three things which he declared he would never forsake—the crown, the church and his friends. The party of Pym had now demanded the surrender of all three and with this final requirement there seemed nothing left but war.

For that Charles was ill prepared. His forces were small and minor skirmishes had revealed no great disposition on his part or theirs to fight. A clash at Manchester between Lord Strange's followers, another at Coventry, a demand by Rupert on Leicester for two thousand pounds, immediately disavowed by Charles, with such occurrences as those in the eastern counties, had comprised the whole of the struggle so far. But the proscription of his supporters by the Parliament with threat of confiscation of their property brought him an army almost overnight. Within a week he found himself at the head of some ten thousand men prepared to contest the sentence pronounced against them by the remnant of Parliament, to defend the crown, the church, the constitution and their lives and estates.

Against them Pym and his party, having secured the greater part of the south, endeavored to bring the King between two fires and on the same day that the payment to Cromwell's troop was authorized, September 7, a letter was drawn up to be sent to the Scots, assuring them that episcopacy was to be destroyed and hinting at an alliance between them and the Parliament. Thus supported by the capital, a great part of England, an army of some twenty thousand men and by possible assistance of the Scots, it seemed that the party of Pym must be able to impose what terms it liked on Charles. In that faith it entered on the war, little doubting, apparently, that it would be short and successful. As D'Ewes wrote, Charles was a "distressed sovereign, being now reduced to the greatest calamity of any person living . . . nothing but the name and shadow of majesty," his followers "everywhere pursued, taken and made captives, and like to be utterly ruined in their fortunes" by the votes of confiscation passed in Parliament. Without men, money or arms, it seemed that Charles must submit at once and that this great army which Essex led north on September 9 was scarcely more than a military promenade. Yet the very words of their votes, their commissions and their proclamations revealed their realization of the position which they occupied. They knew that only a relatively few of even their supporters would follow them in a war openly declared against the King. They knew that even their own general was not disposed to push matters to extremities.

CHAPTER V

THE OUTBREAK OF CIVIL WAR

SEPTEMBER, 1642

It is small wonder in the face of the declarations and votes of the Houses and the proclamations of the King that there was confusion in the popular mind as to the real causes of the conflict about to begin. The position of a party which had passed a Militia Ordinance to secure armed forces "for the safety of His Majesty's person, the Parliament and the kingdom" against the "bloody counsels of the Papists and other ill affected persons" who had raised rebellion in Ireland and might proceed to stir up rebellion in England, was dubious at best. That possibility must have seemed remote even to the authors of the ordinance and the situation was not clarified by Essex's commission as Lord General of the army of "the King and Parliament," or the Commons' vote to live and die with him "for the safety of the King's person and the defence of both Houses of Parliament." The next words "and of those who have obeyed their orders and commands and for the preservation of the true religion, laws, liberties and peace of the kingdom," at once clarified and clouded the issue.

Even the great modern historian of the period found those words "incongruous," though he observes with apparently some slight hesitation that "they were doubtless a true expression of the feelings of those who uttered them." What those feelings were, may be a matter of dispute; but to Royalists they seemed the height of ironical hypocrisy. To set on foot a powerful army under a commander but lately high in the royal service under guise of protecting Charles's person against rebellion seemed preposterous and the King lost no time in proclaiming Essex a traitor. The Parliamentary general himself received his commission in a melancholy mood and, denied the title of High Constable and the permission to treat with the King which he desired, set forth sadly enough. Marching north through Hertfordshire with his forces converging on Northampton, "his features grave and melancholy," his coffin, shroud and family escutcheon in his baggage as earnest of his sincerity of purpose, not all the enthusiasm of the City which speeded his parting, the cheering crowds which met him on the march, the Parliamentary colors with their motto, "God with us," the brightly uniformed regiments of the London trained bands, nor the companies which joined him as he went

Boroughbridge
Ripley
FOREST OF GALTRES
Knaresborough
Marston Moor 1644
YORK
Wetherby
Pocklington
Market Weighton
Sherburn in-Elmet
Selby
Leeds
CLOTH (Broadcloth)
Howden
Ouse
Pontefract
Wakefield
Snaith
Kilham
Driffield
Beverley
HULL
Hedon
1643
Barton
Burton
HATFIELD CHASE (drained by Vermuiden)
Barnsley
Doncaster
Brigg
Grimsby
Spurn Hd
MOUTH OF THE HUMBER
Caistor
Kirton
Rotherham
Bawtry
Gainsborough 1643
Market Rasen
Saltfleet
Louth
Blyth
Littleborough
Retford
Worksop
Alford
LINCOLN 1644
Horncastle
Winceby 1643
Spilsby
Bolingbroke
SHERWOOD FOREST
Mansfield
Alfreton
Newark 1644
Beckingham
East Fen Deeps
Wainfleet
Tattershall
Southwell
COAL
Sleaford
BOSTON
The Wash
Brancaster Roads
Blakeney
Wells
Burnham Market
Holt
Cromer
IRON
Derby (Silk)
NOTTINGHAM (Silk)
Belvoir Cas.
1643
Grantham
Folkingham
Donington
Snettisham
Walsingham
Fakenham
North Walsham
Aylsham
Worstead
Holbeach
Whaplode
Spalding
Bourne
KING'S LYNN
Reepham
Cawston
Hickling
Norfolk
Waltham on the Wolds
Loughborough
Melton
Burton-upon-Trent

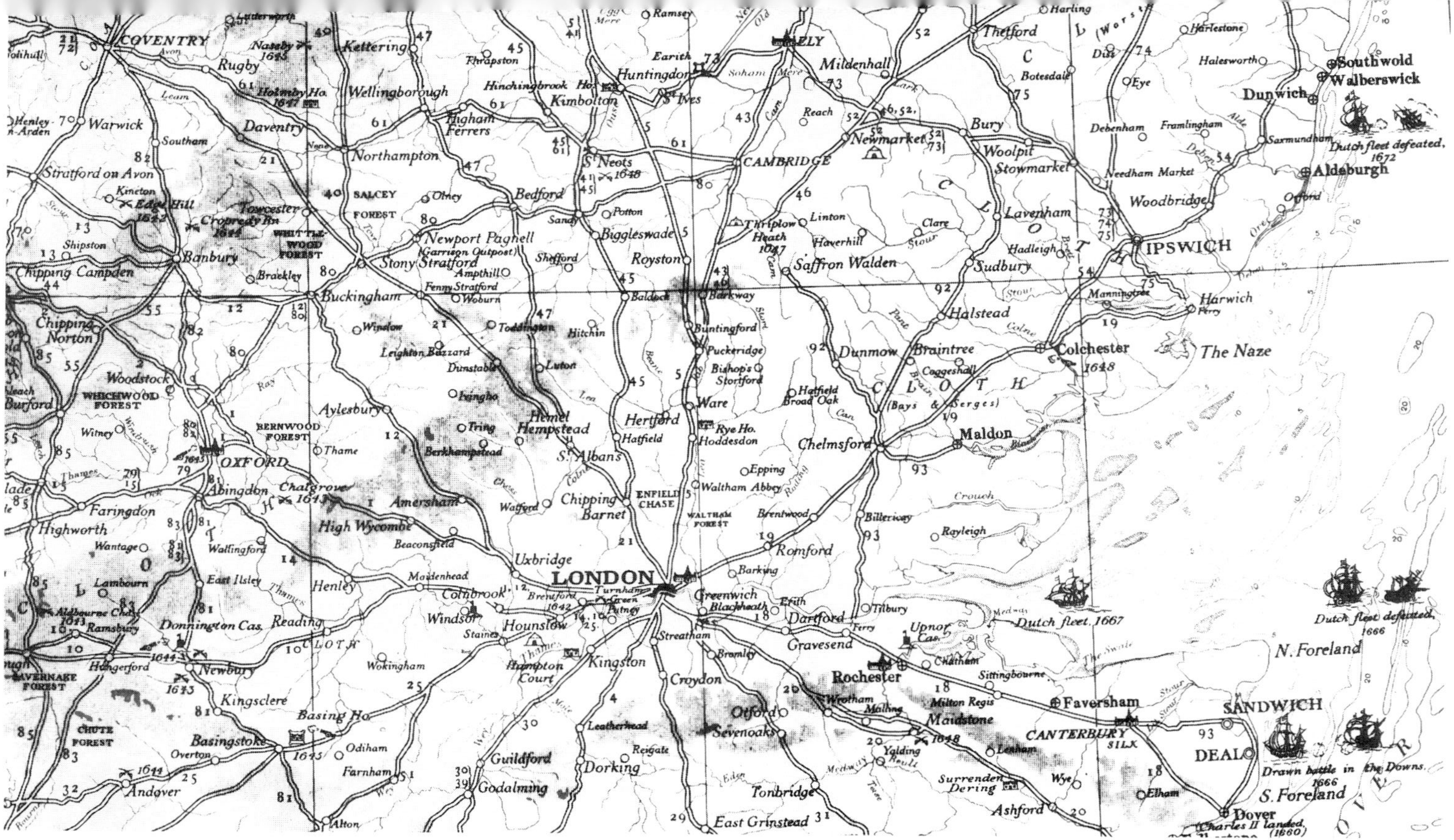

COVENTRY
Rugby
Naseby 1645
Holmby Ho. 1647
Kettering
Wellingborough
Daventry
Northampton
Warwick
Stratford on Avon
Edge Hill 1642
Cropredy Br. 1644
Banbury
Chipping Campden
Chipping Norton
Woodstock
WHICHWOOD FOREST
Burford
Witney
OXFORD
Abingdon
Chalgrove 1643
Faringdon
Highworth
Wantage
Wallingford
Lambourn
Aldbourne Chase 1643
Ramsbury
Hungerford
Newbury
Donnington Cas.
Kingsclere
Basingstoke
Basing Ho. 1645
Andover
CHUTE FOREST
SAVERNAKE FOREST
Towcester
WHITTLEWOOD FOREST
SALCEY FOREST
Brackley
Buckingham
Stony Stratford
Newport Pagnell (Garrison Outpost)
Olney
Bedford
Higham Ferrers
Thrapston
Hinchingbrook Ho.
Kimbolton
St. Neots 1648
Huntingdon
St. Ives
Earith
Ramsey
ELY
Mildenhall
Newmarket
Reach
CAMBRIDGE
Thriplow Heath 1647
Linton
Haverhill
Saffron Walden
Royston
Biggleswade
Potton
Sandy
Shefford
Ampthill
Woburn
Fenny Stratford
Winslow
Leighton Buzzard
Dunstable
Toddington
Luton
Hitchin
Baldock
Barkway
Buntingford
Puckeridge
Bishop's Stortford
Ware
Hertford
Hatfield
Rye Ho.
Hoddesdon
St. Albans
Hemel Hempstead
Tring
Ivinghoe
Berkhampstead
Aylesbury
BERNWOOD FOREST
Thame
Amersham
High Wycombe
Beaconsfield
Uxbridge
Watford
Chipping Barnet
ENFIELD CHASE
WALTHAM FOREST
Waltham Abbey
Epping
LONDON
Turnham Green
Brentford 1642
Putney
Colnbrook
Maidenhead
Henley
Reading
Windsor
Staines
Hounslow
Hampton Court
Kingston
Wokingham
Odiham
Farnham
Alton
Guildford
Godalming
Dorking
Reigate
Leatherhead
Croydon
Streatham
Greenwich
Blackheath
Bromley
Barking
Romford
Brentwood
Erith
Dartford
Gravesend
Tilbury
Otford
Sevenoaks
Tonbridge
East Grinstead
Wrotham
Malling
Yalding
Maidstone 1648
Rochester
Chatham
Upnor Cas.
Dutch fleet, 1667
Sittingbourne
Milton Regis
Faversham
CANTERBURY
SILK
Lenham
Wye
Surrenden Dering
Ashford
Elham
Dover
Charles II landed (1660)
DEAL
SANDWICH
Drawn battle in the Downs, 1666
S. Foreland
N. Foreland
Dutch fleet defeated, 1666
Chelmsford
Billericay
Rayleigh
Maldon
Hatfield Broad Oak
Dunmow
Braintree
Coggeshall
(Bays & Serges)
CLOTH
Halstead
Colchester 1648
The Naze
Harwich
Manningtree
Sudbury
Hadleigh
Lavenham
Clare
Bury
Woolpit
Stowmarket
Needham Market
IPSWICH
Woodbridge
Orford
Aldeburgh
Dutch fleet defeated, 1672
Saxmundham
Framlingham
Debenham
Eye
Diss
Botesdale
Thetford
Harling
Harleston
Halesworth
Dunwich
Southwold
Walberswick

prepared "to make short work of the King and his supporters," could blind him to the real nature of his enterprise. Like Charles, he did not want to fight.

At Northampton Essex found himself at the head of an army reported, doubtless with exaggeration, as numbering some twenty thousand men "assembled for the defence of His Majesty and the maintenance of the true Protestant religion"; and, avoiding more definite statement of his purposes, he contented himself with a promise to live and die with them. Against this, the King marching down from York with a far smaller force though it grew day by day, was more specific. "You shall meet no enemy but traitors," he told his men, "and most of them Brownists, Anabaptists and atheists, such as desire to destroy both Church and State." He, too, promised to live and die with his supporters, as the forces designed to suppress Papist rebellion advanced toward those determined to put down Brownists and atheists.

No thoughtful man on either side believed this in his heart. At the most, one thought that the ancient edifice of the system of government was in danger, the other that liberty of the subject was threatened both in church and state. If the watchword of one was loyalty, that of the other was liberty. If one looked back to the stately and ordered development of law and custom broadening down from precedent to precedent, moulding almost imperceptibly the fabric of English life, the other looked forward to a new order in which popular will should no longer be hampered by the bonds of the past and the voice of the people should be the voice of God. If the one viewed the church as the expression of the nation's soul, within whose noble ceremonies might be expressed its varying religious experiences, the other looked on it as imprisoning the spirit of mankind, limiting the liberty of the individual to seek God in his own way, a clog on his religious development, an enemy to truth. If the one saw in the crown the outward and visible expression of national unity, the symbol of law and justice, honor and security, the other saw in it a power to be curbed or replaced by popular representatives in Parliament. If one recognized the lightness and the grace of life and its amenities, and noble birth as part of nature's law, the other tended to despise these vanities and to turn unconsciously to democracy. If the one was in some measure the child of the Renaissance, the other was almost wholly the offspring of the Reformation; and, with all the contempt of the one for the "vulgar" and of the other for the "vanities" of life, there was enough of nobility of purpose on each side to produce heroes and martyrs, and enough bitterness of antagonism between these two ideals of human life and organized society to turn neighbor against neighbor and brother against brother in a fratricidal strife.

The month of September, 1642, was spent in preparing for impending war. Parliament began with a unanimous vote of the remnant of the Commons to abolish "the government of the church by archbishops, bishops" and lesser officers. It continued with the rejection of proposals from the King until he withdrew his protection from delinquents, and the impeachment of Lord Strange, the Earl of Lindsey, Lord Willoughby and his son, with many lesser men; the summoning of various individuals to account for their actions, and the disabling of many more from sitting in the Parliament. In August some twenty-four members were expelled, in September twenty-five, and only two new writs were issued. The result of these measures combined with the absence of so many men on mission was to reduce the Commons to a handful. The two divisions in June revealed no more than eighty-five members present; in July the largest number present on division was a hundred and seventy, the smallest eighty-three; by August those numbers had sunk to ninety-five and fifty-nine. Two divisions in September showed respectively sixty-nine and eighty-nine members present; and October had no divisions at all; nor were the Lords in any better case.[1]

The interest had shifted to the field, where the commanders feverishly prepared their armies for the fight and each side plundered the other seeking arms, ammunition, money, plate, horses and equipment. In this the royal forces gained steadily. The declaration of the Houses against the King's proposals for a treaty, the vote of September 1 abolishing episcopacy, the denunciation of "delinquents" and "malignants," the proscription of the Royalists and the threat of confiscating their property, rallied thousands to Charles's cause. On the other hand, Pym and his followers had gone too far to retreat. They distrusted the King with reason, for they knew that no promises he made could possibly prevent a charge of treason against them; and none knew better than John Pym that he would be the first to follow Strafford to the scaffold if his cause went down. Thus, like his colleagues and his opponents, he prepared to push the issue to the arbitrament of war. There was an infinity of business which pressed upon them. There were consultations and negotiations, committee meetings, speech-making, and the framing of documents of all sorts. There was much hard riding to and fro, securing of arms, munitions, money and strongholds; and the few brief notices we have of this member for Cambridge transformed into a captain of horse are typical of many of his kind at this moment. There are only three such notices of Cromwell, but each reveals a problem of its own such as confront men like him in times like these.

Returning from his recruiting, he was at Westminster again on

[1] *C. J.; L. J.; Parl. Hist.;* Parry's *Parliaments, passim.*

September 6, where, with a committee of eight, he was instructed to meet with a delegation from the Upper House and the Common Council of London to consider subscriptions of money and plate.[2] That very day, however, the two Houses instructed him to go with Sir Dudley North, son of the Lord Lieutenant of Cambridge, to the Isle of Ely.[3] The next day John Desborough, his brother-in-law and quartermaster, received a month's pay for his troop of sixty mounted men mustered August 29,[4] from which it appears that Cromwell's first command was well on its way to completion. In such fashion many men in England and especially in Parliament were busy in this month of September fashioning new and unfamiliar instruments of war and providing means to lead them into action when occasion came.

EDGEHILL, OCTOBER, 1642

By mid-September, 1642, the two armies were in motion. On the 13th the King left Nottingham and on that day the *Perfect Diurnall* reported that

> "The committee appointed to settle the affairs of the kingdom ordered that Captain Cromwell, Captain Austin and Captain Draper should forthwith muster their troops of horse and make themselves ready to go to his Excellency the Earl of Essex."

That commander meanwhile reviewed his troops, sent to London for more money, with which, "and God's blessing" he believed that he would "bring these unhappy distractions to an end suddenly," and despatched Lord Saye to drive Sir John Byron from Oxford and secure that place for the Parliament. Byron in turn seized Worcester and while Charles moved west toward Shrewsbury, Essex marched parallel to the royal army in the same direction, sending Fiennes forward with some horse to drive Byron out. On September 23 Prince Rupert who had been sent to cover Byron's force met Fiennes cavalry at Powick Bridge and in this first engagement of the war the Royalists were victorious. None the less Worcester was occupied by Essex, and in a series of lesser movements the Parliamentary forces finally took Hereford and some smaller places in the west while Charles was held at Shrewsbury for want of supplies.

By October 12 he finally began his march upon the capital. He had refused Essex's petition for an armistice and a treaty; and on October 20, when he had reached Coventry, London had been put in some posture of defence and Pym had pushed through the Houses

[2] *C. J.*, ii, 754.
[3] *L. J.*, v, 342; see also, *ibid.*, 329–31.
[4] Desborough's receipt is in the Commonwealth Exchequer Papers, Public Record Office, according to Mrs. Lomas, Lomas-Carlyle, i, 113n.

an "Association" like the Scottish Covenant. Meanwhile the King came on. Passing Warwick and Coventry, by October 23 he had reached Edgehill while Essex on his track arrived at Kineton some seven miles away. There the two armies met and there throughout that Sunday there was fought that promiscuous engagement known as the battle of Edgehill. The forces were fairly equal, with between ten and fourteen thousand each. The Royalist center was commanded by Lindsey who on the eve of the battle had been superseded by the Earl of Forth as commander-in-chief; the right wing by Rupert with the bulk of the cavalry; the left by Lord Wilmot. Opposite Rupert was the main body of Essex's horse; in the center his foot; on his right wing, opposite Wilmot, the Lord General's own regiment of horse under Sir Philip Stapleton, with the regiments of Sir William Balfour and Lord Feilding. The battle which began about three in the afternoon was bloody and confused. The Royalists charged on their whole front; the left wing of Essex's army fled almost without a blow; Rupert drove them before him as far as Kineton where his men stopped to plunder Essex's baggage-train till Hampden's brigade, coming up too late for the main battle, drove them back. Meanwhile the remaining regiments fought it out. Stapleton's cavalry broke through the line of pikes and charged the Royalist Red Regiment, while Balfour took the King's cannon. But there was little order and less generalship. At one time each side believed that it was beaten; and Essex and the King each proposed to head his army and die on the field. How confused the situation was, two stories of the battle evidence. The first is that Stapleton's horsemen found themselves among the royal cavalry guarding the standard and each side was so confused that before they discovered their mistake they were shaking hands with their friends in the other ranks. The second is that the royal standard, captured by the Parliamentarians, was regained by Royalists who put on the Parliamentary insignia of orange scarfs and went and asked for it. Each side ran out of ammunition, each was exhausted, it grew dark and, as if by mutual consent, the inconclusive engagement came to an end. Essex withdrew to Warwick and Charles, taking Banbury as he went, marched to Oxford on his way to the capital without hindrance; and each side claimed victory.

The part that Cromwell played at Edgehill is a matter of dispute. Since it appears that Captain Austin's troops arrived at Worcester just too late to take part in the skirmish with Rupert but in time to help compel the Royalists to retreat,[5] it is a not unreasonable supposition that Cromwell was present at that time. Thence, it would seem, he went on to join Essex's main army. As to his presence at

[5] *Perfect Diurnall.*

Edgehill there are various—and varying—bits of evidence. In Fiennes's account of the battle there is a note to the effect that "These persons underwritten were all of the right wing and never stirred from their troops, but they and their troops fought till the last minute," and among those names is that of "Captain Oliver Cromwell." But there are corollaries to that statement even in Fiennes's account; for in a letter accompanying his despatch it is noted that "Captain Cromwell" was among the fugitives driven from the field by the Royalist attack.[6] That, it has been suggested, was young Oliver, a cornet in Lord St. John's regiment; but it has also been suggested that it is highly improbable that one cornet out of the whole army should have been singled out for such mention.

Several years later Denzil Holles, who commanded a regiment of the reserve, brought against Cromwell a charge of cowardice—which does not appear in the account of the battle which he wrote at the time. It accuses Cromwell with

> "base keeping out of the field at Keinton Battle; where he with his troop of horse came not in, impudently and ridiculously affirming, the day after, that he had been all that day seeking the army and place of fight, though his quarters were but at a village near hand, whence he could not find his way, nor be directed by his ear, when the ordnance was heard, as I have been credibly informed, 20 or 30 miles off."[7]

To this Sir William Dugdale adds a fantastic touch of libel to the effect that Cromwell was not merely not at the battle:

> "but got up into a steeple within view of the battel; and there discerning by a perspective-glass the two wings of their horse to be utterly routed, made such hast to be gone, that instead of descending the stairs by which he came up, he swing'd down by a Bell-rope and ran away with his troop."[8]

It is not necessary to refute the charge of personal cowardice, for, whatever Cromwell was, he was not a coward, as those who met him in the field testified. Yet that there may be something of truth lurking in these libellous accounts even Fiennes's letter seems to suggest. Describing the actions of his brother John who arrived at Kineton just in time to meet the fugitives flying from the field, and endeavoring to check the rout, Fiennes relates that his brother

> "gathered a pretty body upon a hill together and with them (there being Captain Keightlye's and Captain Cromwell's troops at length come to them also) he marched towards the town"[9]—joining Hampden's brigade on the way to the battle.

[6] Fiennes, *True Relation of . . . Edgehill* [and] *Worcester*, 1642. Cp. Vicars, *God in the Mount*, p. 198.

[7] Holles, *Memoirs* (1647), p. 17.

[8] Dugdale, *Short View*, p. 110.

[9] Fiennes, *True Relation*, as above.

The fact seems to be that the various parts of the Parliament's forces were widely distributed and, like Hampden's command, came into the engagement at different times. It seems quite possible that Cromwell's troop was driven back on the charge of the Royalists and reformed at Kineton, or that it was quartered in a near-by village and came up, like Hampden's command, after the battle actually began. It seems probable also that it took part in the engagement at the end and contributed to the Parliamentary counter-attack. Nor is it inconceivable that there is truth even in Dugdale's account that Cromwell was in a church steeple looking for the battle, if we assume that he slid down the bell-rope in his haste to get into the battle not away from it.

Despite his slight share in the battle of Edgehill, it was a great event in Oliver Cromwell's life. He learned much from it, especially it would appear, from the flight of the left wing of Essex's army. Years later he referred to it:

"I was a person, who, from my first employment, was suddenly preferred and lifted up from lesser trusts to greater; from my first being a captain of a troop of horse; and I did labour as well as I could to discharge my trust; and God blessed me as it pleased Him. And I did truly and plainly —and then in a way of foolish simplicity, as it was judged by very great and wise men and good men too—desired to make my instruments help me in that work. . . . I had a very worthy friend then; and he was a very noble person and I know that his memory is very grateful to you all—Mr. John Hampden. At my first going into this engagement, I saw our men were beaten at every hand. I did, indeed, and I desired him that he would make some additions to my Lord Essex's army, of some new regiments; and I told him I would be serviceable to him in bringing such men in as I thought had a spirit that would do something in the work. . . . 'Your troopers,' said I, 'are most of them old decayed servingmen and tapsters and such kind of fellows; and,' said I, 'their troopers are gentlemen's sons, younger sons and persons of quality; do you think that the spirits of such base and mean fellows will be ever able to encounter gentlemen that have honor and courage and resolution in them? . . . You must get men of a spirit; and take it not ill what I say—I know you will not—of a spirit that is likely to go on as far as gentlemen will go, or else I am sure you will be beaten still. . . . He was a wise and worthy person, and he did think that I talked a good notion but an impracticable one."[10]

Whether or not that conversation came immediately after Edgehill, it can hardly be doubted but that his experience there is somehow reflected in this speech. It was not that alone. As Baxter wrote in later years:

"At his first entrance into the wars, being but a captain of horse, he had special care to get religious men into his troop. These men were of greater

[10] Speech, April 13, 1657.

understanding than common soldiers and therefore more apprehensive of the importance and consequence of war and making not money but that which they took for the public felicity to be their end, they were the more engaged to be valiant. . . . These things it's probable Cromwell understood, and that none would be such engaged valiant men as the religious. But yet I conjecture that at his first choosing such men into his troop, it was the very esteem and love of religious men that principally moved him; and the avoiding of those disorders, mutinies, plunderings and grievances of the country which deboist men in armies are commonly guilty of. By this means he indeed sped better than he expected. Aires, Desborough, Berry, Evanson and the rest of that troop did prove so valiant that as far as I could learn they never once ran away before an enemy."[11]

LONDON, NOVEMBER–DECEMBER, 1642

There is little or no real evidence as to Cromwell's movements after Edgehill. He probably accompanied Essex as that general made his way, first to Warwick, then to London, where he arrived on November 8 to receive the thanks of the Houses and the offer of a gift of £5,000 from the Commons. There, it appears, the Parliamentary forces were quartered in the City and the surrounding villages, while Charles recruited and reorganized his forces at Oxford; and that Cromwell remained in or about London, like some of his companions in arms, in his dual capacity as captain of horse and member of Parliament, though unlike some of them there seems to be no record of his activities in the House.

Meanwhile that House had revealed divisions in its membership. The spread of plundering, the successes of Newcastle in the north and of Hopton in the west, with that lingering suspicion of the rights and wrongs of the quarrel which haunted many minds, and the disruption of men's lives and business, combined to form a peace party in the City and the Parliament. A week after Edgehill it found voice in both Houses so powerful that what D'Ewes called "Pym's party," though it was still for war and had appealed to Scotland for support, was forced to heed its plea. The demand that Charles must lower his standard as the first step in negotiations was tacitly abandoned and commissioners were sent to the King who had advanced to Reading. He was in no mood to treat; and another set of commissioners appealed to him on November 9 with no more success. He was bent on the capture of London and the quick suppression of the rebellion and in this spirit Rupert was ordered to clear the way to the capital.

On November 12 that leader fell on Holles's regiment at Brentford, which, despite the aid that Hampden brought, was lost to Parliament. But that night the City trained bands and Essex's forces poured out

[11] *Reliquae Baxterianae* (1696), p. 98.

against this threat, and on the morning of November 13 Charles found himself confronted at Turnham Green by a force reckoned at more than twenty thousand men. To attack such numbers, however ill-disciplined, with the far smaller body at his command was hopeless, and he withdrew to Kingston while Essex threw a bridge across the Thames from Putney to Fulham to connect his scattered forces and protect the capital.

Again there was a stalemate and again the Parliament under the influence of the peace party offered to negotiate. Each side accused the other of bad faith and there arose dissensions in Parliament itself. It was evident that, for the moment, despite his reverse at Turnham Green, the balance inclined somewhat to the King. Pym's party held the capital, with the south and east. It commanded a majority in the reduced Parliament, but there was grave dissatisfaction with its policy even there. Holles broke with Pym and though a compromise was reached and Charles was requested to return and settle liberty of religion in accord with Parliament, he was also asked to abandon "delinquents" to the justice of the Houses, which he naturally refused. He retired to Oxford which thenceforth became his capital. Essex set up his headquarters at Windsor; and the Houses took the last step toward sovereignty. Spurred on by revelations of aid from Denmark and the continent for the King, they voted a new tax on the whole nation to carry on the war, and the City agreed to this final expression of the supremacy of Parliament.

More and more the Commons took on greater powers. At Lenthall's own request it named him to the post of Master of the Rolls. It authorized the tax collectors to administer an oath. Yet more and more the peace party grew, especially in the City where as crowds had earlier gathered to bring pressure on the King, they now assembled to force the City authorities and the Parliament to peace. Meanwhile Charles and his advisers framed a plan to crush their enemies. In the north the Marquis of Newcastle had crossed the Tees on December 1, beaten the younger Hotham, disarmed the levies of the Parliament and seized York. At the same time, Sir Ralph Hopton had cleared Cornwall of his enemies, and though his Cornishmen refused to follow him across the Tamar "into England," he had raised fresh troops, taken Tavistock and occupied north Devon, even threatening Plymouth and Exeter which held out for Parliament. Thus Pym's party was cut off from their allies in the West Riding and their potential allies in Scotland. If Charles could hold back Essex, bring Newcastle from the north and Hopton from the west, the capital thus surrounded might well be driven to submit and Parliament, deprived of its chief stronghold, be completely crushed.

The Houses were alarmed; blamed Essex for his inactivity; pushed forward measures to raise more money for the war. But it was imperative to find other means of checking the rising tide of royalism, and while the main forces rested on their arms, a new engine of defence was contrived to bolster up the cause of Parliament. This was found in the principle of "Association." On December 15 an ordinance was passed to accomplish this. "Whereas His Majesty," it began, "by the instigation and advice of divers about His Royall person hath raised forces against the Parliament for the most part consisting of Papists, notorious Delinquents and other malignant persons, and that hereby the well affected of the Kingdome are ruinated in their estates," the House resolved that there be organized an association of the midland counties—Leicester, Derby, Nottingham, Northampton, Buckingham, Bedford, Rutland and Huntingdon, to defend the cause of the Parliament.[12] Five days later, on December 20, another ordinance established a like Association for the eastern counties, including Essex, Suffolk, Norfolk, Cambridge and Hertford.[13] To the headship of the first was named Lord Grey of Groby, son of the Earl of Stamford, with the rank of major-general under Essex; to that of the second, Lord Grey of Wark; and thus equipped the Houses entered on another phase of the civil war.

This was accompanied by fresh proposals of peace to the King. On December 20, as the Eastern Counties Association was being authorized, the Lords sent down their propositions for settlement. They differed little from their numerous predecessors. Charles was asked to agree to pass such bills for chuch reform as Parliament should frame with the assent of an assembly of divines; to secure and vindicate the privileges of Parliament; to agree to bills for payment of its debts; to agree that all votes of the Privy Council be signed by those who had advised them; to bring Digby and all others impeached before January 1, 1642 to trial before Parliament; and to exclude Bristol, Wilmot, Hertford, Herbert, Percy and Jermyn from office and the court; to reinstate Northumberland as Lord High Admiral; and to assent to a new Militia Bill. It was passed through both Houses; the nation clamored for peace; but peace on such terms was inconceivable; and it was equally inconceivable to Charles's followers that such terms were not put forward merely to be denied. If, as Pym claimed, the King had no thought of peace save on terms which meant the abandonment of the whole Puritan contention, it seemed no less evident to Charles that nothing but the abdication of his sovereignty would satisfy the revolutionary element.

In consequence, despite the fervid appeals from every quarter, each side pushed on to war, with Cromwell among those who followed Pym against the peace party of Holles; and at the moment that

[12] *L. J.*, v, 443.
[13] *C. J.*, ii, 897; *L. J.*, v, 505.

the Association ordinances were making their way through Parliament, another document testifies to his activities.

Warrant

Theis are to will and require you forthwith, out of the Treasure remayning in yor hands, to paie unto Captaine Oliver Cromwell, Captaine of a troope of Eightie Harquebuziers, for one halfe monthes paie of the said Troope, comencing from the tenth daie of this instant December inclusive, the some of Two hundred and four pounds and thirteene shillings, and for soe doeing this shalbe yor warrant, dated this xvijth daie of December, 1642.

ESSEX.

To Sir Gilbert Gerrard,
Baron^{t}, Trea'r of the
Army, or his deputie.

Capt. Vernon, I desire you to pay this bearer, George Barton, my Servant, the monie accordinge to this warrant from his Excellencye due to mee and my Troupe, and I shall rest

Your lovinge friend,

Decr 17, 1642
To Captn Vernon
present theise.

OLIVER CROMWELL.

Rec^{d} the 19 of December 1642, by virtue of this warrant, two hundreth and four pounds xiij £204 13 0

George Bartons + marke
P^{d} by order of Captn Cromwell.[14]

CAMBRIDGE, JANUARY–FEBRUARY, 1643

The month of January saw the peace movement rise to new heights. The London apprentices who a year before had rioted against the bishops now presented a peace petition to the Houses in which Essex, Bedford and Hertfordshire joined. The Commons refused to follow Pym into an association with Scotland. But when Charles's answer came to the Common Hall of the City, denouncing the assumption of arbitrary power by Pym's party and calling on his subjects to throw off the yoke of Parliament, Pym convinced the City that Charles had no thought of peace, and the Houses pushed on their preparations for continuing the war. While Hopton and Grenville routed the forces of the Parliament in the west, while Gloucester was brought

[14] Original in the Library of Congress at Washington, D. C. Pr. in *Proceedings of the London Society of Antiquaries*, i, 286 (1861). Cromwell's order (holograph throughout) is pr. in the *Third Report of the Hist. MSS. Comm.*, Appendix, p. 420 (Webster Mss.) and in Lomas-Carlyle, Suppl. 2. Mrs. Lomas notes the contents of Essex's warrant in *ibid.*, i, 113n, but quotes the sum as £404 instead of £204. Cromwell's order is also pr. in Waylen, *House of Cromwell* (1891), p. 273 with "John Barton" by mistake.

under the King's authority, Newcastle had been driven from his attempt on Bradford by a new commander, Sir Thomas Fairfax, and Sir William Brereton had defeated the Royalists in Cheshire.

It was at this moment that Cromwell once more entered on the scene. As the first result of the formation of the Associations of the midland and the eastern counties, he was named a member of the committees for both Cambridge and Huntingdon, and so became an active spirit in both Associations. It was, on the face of it, no great office, for the committee of the Midland Association numbered a hundred and thirty-three men, among them Cromwell's old opponent in Huntingdon, Robert Bernard. But to this new enterprise Cromwell applied himself with such vigor that he became presently one of the chief agents of Parliament in his neighborhood. He was in the House on January 6, when he acted with Long as a teller for the Noes against Hampden and Fiennes as tellers for the Yeas on a motion as to whether the Act of Oblivion should be voted on. In that his side was successful and the King's supporters were deprived of any prospect of indemnity.[15] The Commons had sunk to less than a hundred members on divisions, the Lords to a mere handful; but the diminished Houses had not hesitated to pass the bill against episcopal government, summon men for delinquency, punish others for publishing the royal proclamations, deny petitions for peace which poured in on them from every side, and vote taxes on the whole nation. Meanwhile no small number of their members, like Cromwell, were busy on missions connected with the war; and with this he, in particular, found the true field for the exercise of his talents.

On January 12 the Commons voted that the money contributed for Ireland in Cambridge and the Isle of Ely which was in the hands of Sir John Cotton, the sheriff of Cambridge, and other collectors, should be turned over to Dr. Eden, member for Cambridge University. With that the last pretense of separating the Irish and the English war broke down. Six days later, on January 18, it was voted that "Captain Cromwell" should take Dr. Eden's place.[16] He was, it would appear, already in Cambridge with his troop, sent down by Parliament to secure the town and county and to raise more men. His journey had not been without significant incident. Passing through St. Albans, six of his troopers saw a proclamation posted in the market-place by Sir Thomas Coningsbye, high sheriff of Hertfordshire, proclaiming Essex and his adherents traitors. They pulled it down and took the sheriff prisoner. He was promptly rescued by "a great multitude," went to the market-place and was proclaimed 'lawful high sheriff'; whereupon twenty of Cromwell's troopers

[15] *C. J.*, ii, 917.
[16] *Ibid.*, 924, 932.

charged the crowd, seized him again and he was sent to London to prison;[17] and with this Cromwell proceeded on his way to Cambridge, to carry out his commission to deal with disaffected persons.

From some point on this journey, apparently, Cromwell wrote a letter to his old antagonist, Bernard, now on the committee for Huntingdon of the Midland Counties Association. Moved possibly by his old dislike, more probably by some information brought him by his neighbors, it appears that he sent men to investigate Bernard's activities; and it would further seem that Bernard resented and protested this in his capacity as a member of the committee. To him in consequence, Cromwell wrote with some question of Bernard's good faith:

To my assured friend Robert Bernard, Esquire: Present these

MR. BARNARD,

It's most true, my Lieutenant with some other soldiers of my troop were at your house. I dealt freely to inquire after you; the reason was, I heard you reported active against the proceedings of Parliament, and for those also that disturbe the peace of this county and this kingdom—with those of this county who have had meetings not a few, to intent and purpose too, full of suspect.

It's true, Sir, I know you have been wary in your carriages: be not too confident thereof. Subtlety may deceive you; integrity never will. With my heart I shall desire that your judgment may alter, and your practice. I come only to hinder men from increasing the rent,—from doing hurt; but not to hurt any man; nor shall I you. I hope you will give no cause. If you do, I must be pardoned what my relation to the public calls for.

If your good parts be disposed that way, know me for

Your servant,

January 23, 1642[-3]. OLIVER CROMWELL.

Be assured fair words from me shall neither deceive you of your houses nor of your liberty.[18]

With such stern admonition and veiled threats he proceeded on his way to carry out his main purpose in Cambridge, where he was on January 26. Somehow in the meantime he had risen in rank; for where he was designated by the Commons on the 18th as "Captain Cromwell," he was now noted in the proceedings of the Norfolk Committee of the Eastern Counties Association as "Colonel Cromwell,"[19]

[17] *Perfect Diurnall*, Jan. 16–23; Vicars, *God in the Mount*, p. 246. On January 16th, the Commons ordered him imprisoned in London House. *C. J.*, ii, 930.

[18] Printed in the catalogue of the collection of C. J. Toovey, sold by Sotheby, April 25, 1912; repr. in *New York Times*, April 21, 1912. Carlyle, Letter IV, derived his text from copies, made by friends, of the original then in the possession of a descendant of Bernard.

[19] *Tanner Mss*, xiv, 125.

and a fortnight later, on February 6, Lord Grey, the major-general of the Eastern Counties Association so designates him.[20] The change in title indicates his increasing importance. As a member of both the Eastern and the Midland Counties Associations, commander of a troop of horse on its way to becoming a regiment, member of Parliament for Cambridge, and now in this triple capacity a "deputy on mission" in his constituency, he had already, within five months, risen to equality with those who, like Stapleton and Hampden, had begun the war with superior rank. In his capacity as a member of the Cambridge Committee of the Eastern Association, he signed a letter which illustrates at once the situation of affairs, and the preparations to meet the threatened Royalist threat:

To our noble Friends, Sir John Hobert, Sir Thomas Richardson, Sir John Potts, Sir John Palgrave, John Spelman, Knights and Baronets, and the rest of the Deputy-Lieutenants for the County of Norfolk: Present these.

GENTLEMEN,

The Parliament and the Lord General have taken into their care the peace and protection of these Eastern parts of the kingdom; and to that end have sent down hither some part of their forces,—as likewise a Commission, with certain Instructions to us and others directed; all which do highly concern the peace and safety of your county. Therefore, we intreat that some of you would give us a meeting at Millnall[21] in Suffolk, on Tuesday the 31st of this instant January. And in the mean time that you would make all possible speed to have in a readiness, against any notice shall be given, a considerable force of Horse and Foot to join with us, to keep any enemy's force from breaking in upon your yet peaceable country. For we have certain intelligence that some of Prince Rupert's forces are come as far as Wellingborough in Northamptonshire, and that the Papists in Norfolk are solicited to rise presently upon you.

Thus presenting all our neighbourly and loving respects, we rest,

Your respective friends to serve you,

TERRELL JOCELYN. MILES SANDYS.
WILLM. MARCHE. FRANC. RUSSELL.
EDW. CLENCHE. OLIVER CROMWELL.
JAMES THOMSON. THOMAS SYMONS.
ROBERT CLERKE.[22]

[Cambridge,
January 26th, 1642 [-3].]

The same day Cromwell received a letter from his former superior officer, Sir Philip Stapleton,[23] suggesting the apprehension of two

[20] *Ibid.*, 157.

[21] *I.e.*, Mildenhall.

[22] Original in *Tanner Mss*, lxiv, 116, with corrections in Cromwell's hand. Carlyle, App. 4.

[23] Stapleton's letter to Cromwell, Jan. 25, 1642–3, is printed in *Norfolk Archaeological Society Papers*, ii, 45–46 (1848).

Norfolk Royalists, Framlingham Gaudy, M.P. for Thetford, and Sir Henry Bedingfield of Oxburgh. This and the possibility of Charles moving his headquarters to Norfolk inspired a second letter to the same Deputy-Lieutenants:

To our worthy Friends, Sir John Hobert, Sir Thomas Richardson, Sir John Potts, Sir John Palgrave, Sir John Spelman, Knights and Baronets: Present these

GENTLEMEN,

The grounds of your jealousies are real. They concur with our intelligences from Windsor; the sum whereof we give unto you:

From a prisoner taken by Sir Samuel Luke[24] (one Mr. Gaudy, a Captain of dragooners) this confession was drawn, that the Papists by direction from Oxford should rise in Norfolk. Whereupon it was desired from thence that Sir Henry Benningfield and Mr. Gaudy their persons should be seized, and that we should do our endeavour to make stay of the person and letter which contained this encouragement to them,—he being described by his horse and clothes. But we believe [he] was past us before we had notice, for our Scouts could not light on him.

As for the other consideration of his Majesty's forces being invited into these parts, we have confirmation thereof from all hands; and there is this reason to doubt it will be so, because his Majesty is weary of Oxford, there being little in those parts left to sustain his army. And surely the fulness of these parts and fitness of them for horse are too, too good arguments to invite him thither. Thus we agree in the grounds of our doubt and fear.

The next thought is of remedy. And in this we account it our happiness to consult with you of common safety, to be had either by the Association you speak of, or by any other consideration by communication of assistance, according to necessity. Wherein I hope you shall find all readiness and cheerfulness in us, to assist you to break any strength that shall be gathered; or to prevent it, if desired,—having timely notice given from you thereof. The way will be best settled, if you give us a meeting, according to our desire by a letter particularly prepared before we received yours, and now sent unto you for that purpose together with these.

This is all we can say for the present, but that we are,

Your friends and servants,

THOM. MARTYN. MILES SANDYS.
OLIVER CROMWELL. FRANC. RUSSELL.
WILLM. MARCHE. THOS. SYMONS.
ED. CLENCHE. ROBERT CLERKE.
JAMES THOMSON.
TERRELL JOCELYN.

Cambridge,
January 27th, 1642.

[P.S.] We sent to Sir William Spring to offer him our assistance for the apprehension of Sir H. Benningfield, &c. We have not yet received any

[24] Sir Samuel Luke, Scout-master General, (said to be the original of Hudibras) was M. P. for Bedford, governor of Newport Pagnell and colonel of horse.

answer. We knew not how to address ourselves to you. It's our desire to assist you in that or any other public service.[25]

The next letter, written about this time, was in behalf of the captain of a Cambridge trained band who under the orders of the sheriff, Sir John Cotton, had played a part in the little drama of the Cambridge plate in the preceding August. For that he had, apparently, been arrested by the Cambridge Committee, deprived of his horses and sent as prisoner to London. Somehow he had managed to make his peace and Cromwell now wrote in his behalf:[26]

To William Lenthall, Speaker of the House of Commons

From "Captain Cromwell and others of the Committee of the County of Cambridge," asking that Captain James Dockwray, sent up by that Committee, be discharged, and his horses be delivered to him. [January c.31, 1642][27]

Nothing is more characteristic of the situation in which England found itself in these first months of 1642 than Cromwell's letters and his activities. It was entirely typical of a civil war in which counties and parishes, neighborhoods and families were divided against each other. The seizure of the sheriff of Hertfordshire, his rescue by his supporters, and his re-arrest; the warning to Bernard; the rumors and alarms; the suspicion; the anxiety; the fears of risings and of treachery; the perpetual hope or fear that the King might overpower his enemies or come to some accommodation with them; the dread of Rupert and his plundering Cavaliers; all these are reflected in Cromwell's words and acts. Meanwhile he was diverted from his purpose of securing his old neighborhood for the Parliament by none of them, but pushed forward steadily and whole-heartedly on that enterprise, ferreting out "delinquents," raising men, fortifying the castle, and recruiting his troop into a regiment.

On its part Parliament was not idle. The immediate and pressing need was for money to carry on the war and at the beginning of February the Commons voted to assess such of its own members as had not contributed in proportion to their estates and followed this by disabling such as had resorted to the King. It began to sequester the profits of livings held by Royalist clergy and those of imprisoned supporters of the King, and thus not merely carried out its earlier threat of making its opponents pay for the war but inaugurated a policy of sequestration, confiscation and "compounding for delinquency" which was to play a great part in its future activities. To that end it appointed a committee on February 3 and proceeded to

[25] Original in Cromwell's hand in *Tanner Mss*, lxiv, 129; Carlyle, App. 4.

[26] *Cal. Comm. for Comp.*, p. 895.

[27] Read and acted upon in Parliament, 2 Feb., 1642–3. *C. J.*, ii, 952.

disable, imprison and sequester the estates of its Royalist members with increasing frequency.[28]

But its great problem was accommodation with the King. On February 6 it was resolved to print the King's reply to the propositions of the Houses which had been presented to him at Oxford on February 1. Those propositions began with a request that the King disband his forces, as Parliament would theirs, and return to Westminster; leave delinquents to trial by the Houses; disarm Papists; assent to the bill for abolishing episcopal government of the church; agree to more stringent laws against Popish recusants; remove the Earl of Bristol and Lord Herbert from the court; settle the militia in accordance with the wishes of the Houses; restore their members to their old employments; issue a general pardon—except to Irish rebels, Lord Digby and the Earl of Newcastle; appoint a long list of men, headed by Bramston and Lenthall to various offices; restore all justices of the peace and such local officers as had been put out of their commissions since the preceding April; drop the proceedings against the five members and Lord Kimbolton; make an alliance with the United Provinces; and assent to a bill of costs and damages for the war.[29]

The propositions had been read to Charles by the Earl of Northumberland. "They that principally contrived and penned them," the King observed, "had no thoughts of peace in their hearts, but to make things worse and worse." His answer was in kind. He agreed to "propagate and promote" the true Protestant religion and to govern according to law and to uphold the privileges of Parliament. But he demanded that the Houses recall their declarations in contravention of his power; disclaim the right to tax and imprison his subjects; give back his revenue, forts and ships; and prepare a bill to 'preserve the Book of Common Prayer from the scorn and violence of Brownists, Anabaptists and other sectaries.' The Houses had proposed disbandment; he proposed an armistice. The Commons would consent to this only after Charles agreed to disbandment, and though they agreed to a treaty before disbanding, they ended the month by voting on February 28 that the four commissioners who had treated at Oxford be not despatched again. So, at the end, the peace party of Holles, Waller and Rudyerd was overborne by Pym and the war went on.[30]

Four days earlier, on February 24, the Commons had given their real answer to the King by an ordinance "for the speedy raising . . . of money for the army . . . by a weekly assessment upon . . . every county and city of the Kingdom." It was, in effect, the old ship-money policy, which became the cardinal principle of Parliamentary

[28] *C. J. passim*, Feb. 1642–3.
[29] Rushworth, v, 165.
[30] Gardiner, *Civil War*, i, 89 ff.

finance. Committees for putting the ordinance in effect were appointed, with Cromwell as a member of the Cambridge and Huntingdon groups. The amounts to be paid were drawn up, based, it would appear, on the ship-money lists adapted to the political complexion of the various districts;[31] and three days later the Commons instructed Essex to omit no advantage of war as the House did "not find so quick and speedy a despatch of the treaty and cessation as they expected and desired."[32]

CAMBRIDGE, MARCH–APRIL, 1643

By the first of March, 1643, it was apparent that the peace negotiations had broken down and each side turned again to war. In this the Cambridge Committee, with Cromwell as its leading spirit, had not awaited the orders sent to the Lord General. The King had not invaded the Eastern counties, but "upon a hot and true report and intelligence that the Lord Capel with some of his troops of horse intended to march for Cambridge," to take it for His Majesty, Vicars observes that "noble and active Colonell Cromwell happily prevented him" by summoning volunteers to protect the town.[33] Parliament, aware of his activities, relieved him of his receivership of the money for the Irish expedition, reappointing Dr. Eden and freeing Cromwell's hands for the more important business of recruiting his regiment.[34] By March 2 it was reported, doubtless with exaggeration, that 12,000 men had flocked into Cambridge from Norfolk, Suffolk and Essex to join him, and had been sent back with orders to be ready for action.[35] Ordnance and ammunition was arriving and Cambridge was being fortified and garrisoned; so if Capel had ever intended to seize the place, it was now securely held for Parliament. The *Perfect Diurnall* continued its report of the situation in Cambridge:

> "Colonel Cromwell having possessed himself of Cambridge for the King and Parliament and having in the town about 800 horse and foot which were raised in the associated counties, the Parliament have ordered that four pieces of ordnance and some other ammunition be sent thither."[36]

Under such conditions Cromwell began to transform his troop into a regiment, that famous body known later as the "Ironsides." His principle of selecting his "instruments" he had already outlined to

31 Firth and Rait, *Acts and Ordinances*, i, 85.
32 *C. J.*, ii, 982.
33 Vicars, *God in the Mount* (1644), p. 273.
34 *C. J.*, ii, 982.
35 *Perfect Diurnall*, Mar. 2.
36 *Perfect Diurnall*, Mar. 6.

Hampden. In later years Whitelocke enlarged on it. The men of the new regiment, he wrote, were

> "most of them freeholders and freeholders' sons, and who upon a matter of conscience engaged in this quarrel, and under Cromwel. And thus being well armed within, by the satisfaction of their consciences, and without by good iron arms, they would as one man stand firmly and charge desperately."[37]

To this the Earl of Manchester added his testimony three years later:

> "Col. Cromwell raysing of his regiment makes choyce of his officers not such as weare souldiers or men of estate, but such as were common men, pore and of mean parentage, onely he would given them the title of godly, pretious men . . . I have heard him oftentimes say that it must not be souldiers nor Scots that must doe this worke, but it must be the godly to this purpos. . . . If you looke upon his owne regiment of horse, see what a swarme ther is of thos that call themselves the godly; some of them profess they have sene vissions and had revellations."[38]

Such was the character of the men he sought, believing that there was only one element which could be pitted against the Royalist cavalry with a chance of success. To birth and honor he opposed religious faith verging often on fanaticism, and such men he sought and found. By March he had five troops of perhaps four hundred men; by September he had ten; and in the end he had, as Baxter testifies, "a double regiment of fourteen full troops, [of eighty men each] and all these as full of religious men as he could get," all, or nearly all, recruited from the eastern counties.[39]

For officers he relied on the same element. The officers of his first troop, except Desborough, disappeared from history; but Desborough became the captain of the third troop of the new regiment. The command of the first or "colonel's" troop or company was given to James Berry who rose in time to be a major-general; the second to Cromwell's cousin, Edward Whalley, who rose to a like rank. Young Oliver Cromwell was captain of the fourth, coming to the regiment from his post as cornet in Lord St. John's troop of horse. The fifth was headed by young Valentine Walton, Cromwell's nephew; and these, it would appear, raised as early as March, 1643, were the original nucleus of the "Ironsides."[40]

The conditions under which civil wars are begun are always the

[37] Whitelocke, *Memorials* (1702), p. 72.

[38] Bruce, J., and Masson, D., *Documents relating to the Quarrel between the Earl of Manchester and Oliver Cromwell.* Camden Soc. Misc. 8 (1875), p. 72.

[39] *Reliquiae Baxterianae*, p. 98.

[40] Firth, "Raising of the Ironsides," *Trans. Royal Hist. Soc.* xiii, (1899), pp. 16 ff.

same—hurried improvising of measures for raising men and money; recruiting, arming, drilling inexperienced levies; endeavors of each party to hamper and harass its opponents; excursions and alarms; hard riding to and fro by earnest and harried men; and infinite confusion everywhere. Such was the situation in every part of England at this time; and such were Oliver Cromwell's circumstances and activities. It was a part suited to his temper and abilities; and the nervous notes and letters which he wrote indicate a man keyed to a high point, enthusiastic in the performance of his duties, direct and simple in act and thought, with no plans beyond those of the moment, and, despite the infinite worries and difficulties of his position, on the whole enjoying it.

The work of raising men in Cambridge was progressing satisfactorily, but Cromwell and the rest of the county Committee were faced with the additional necessity of getting money for fortifications. To this task they addressed themselves, sending to each parish church in the vicinity of Cambridge a request for contributions to the cause, of which one specimen remains to us:

To all and every the Inhabitants of Fen Drayton in the Hundred of Papworth

COM. CANT.

WHEREAS, we have been enforced, by apparent grounds of approaching danger, to begin to fortify the town of Cambridge, for preventing the enemy's inroad, and the better to maintain the peace of this country:

Having in part seen your good affection to the cause, and now standing in need of your further assistance to the perfecting of the said fortifications, which will cost at the least two-thousand pounds. We are encouraged as well as necessitated to desire a freewill offering of a liberal contribution from you, for the better enabling of us to attain our desired ends, viz. the preservation of our county; knowing that every honest and well-affected man, considering the vast expenses we have already been at, and our willingness to do according to our ability, will be ready and willing to contribute his best assistance to a work of so high concernment and so good an end.

We do therefore desire that what shall be by you freely given and collected may with all convenient speed be sent to the Commissioners at Cambridge, to be employed to the use aforesaid. And so you shall further engage us to be

Yours ready to serve,
OLIVER CROMWELL.

Cambridge, this 8th
of March, 1642.

and twenty-four others.

[P.S.] What shall be by you gathered, deliver it to Tho. Noris this bearer.[41]

[41] Cooper, *Annals of Cambridge* (1845), iii, 340, from *Bowtell Mss.* ii, 123. Carlyle (Lomas edition), i, 119. The letter was delivered to the churchwardens by Constable Norris on March 12th.

As this appeal brought in exactly 1 l. 19s. 2d. from fifteen contributors,[42] the sum extracted from the Cambridge parishes was probably not great and, with the need for additional sums to support the new forces, Cromwell turned to other means of collecting money. On March 9, the day the Commons ordered him to take into custody six prisoners from Norwich and do with them as he saw fit,[43] the House received word that the King's army was in motion and approved of the Lord General's resolution to march. The next day, as a meeting was being held with the London Council to arrange a loan,[44] Cromwell appealed to Suffolk for the support of a troop:

To my honoured Friends the Deputy Lieutenants for the County of Suffolk

GENTLEMEN,

I am sorry I should so often trouble you about the business of money: it's no pleasant subject to be too frequent upon. But such is Captain Nelson's occasion, for want thereof, that he hath not wherewith to satisfy for the billet of his soldiers. And so this business for Norfolk, so hopeful to set all right there, may fail. Truly he hath borrowed from me, else he could not have paid to discharge this town at his departure.

It's pity a gentleman of his affections should be discouraged! Wherefore I earnestly beseech you to consider him and the cause. It's honourable that you do so. What you can help him to, be pleased to send into Norfolk; he hath not wherewith to pay a troop one day, as he tells me. Let your return be speedy, to Norwich,

Gentlemen, command

Your servant,

Cambridge,
March 10th, 1642. OLIVER CROMWELL.

[P.S.] I hope to serve you in my return. With your conjunction we shall quickly put an end to these businesses, the Lord assisting.[45]

The expedition hinted at in his letter to Suffolk was not long delayed. By Sunday, the 12th, Cromwell was marching toward Norwich with a thousand horse, intending to go on from there to Lowestoft, a port of great consequence, said to be a hot-bed of Royalists. Parliament had become aware of the gathering of Cavaliers in Norfolk and Suffolk and sent orders to Cromwell on March 14 to go there at once,[46] but on that day, having heard that Sir John Wentworth

[42] *Ibid.*
[43] *C. J.*, ii, 995.
[44] *Ibid.*
[45] Carlyle, Letter V, from the original autograph then in the possession of C. Meadows, Esq., Great Bealing, Woodbridge, Suffolk. Captain Nelson was later the Lieutenant-colonel John Nelson who undertook the sending of the Irish soldiers to Spain.
[46] *Mercurius Aulicus*, Mar. 18.

and Captain Allen coming from Lowestoft to "change dollars" had been captured and that Lowestoft was being fortified, he had already left Norwich with his own regiment and eighty Norwich volunteers and, having picked up additional recruits at Yarmouth, had surprised and defeated the Royalists gathered in Lowestoft. The story of that exploit is told in a letter from his colleague, John Cory:

"The town had blocked themselves up, all except where they had placed their ordnance, which were three pieces; before which a chain was drawn to keep off the horse. The Colonel summoned the town and demanded if they would deliver up their strangers, the Town and their Army?—promising them then favour if so; if not, none. They yielded to deliver up their strangers, but not to the rest. Whereupon our Norwich dragoons crept under the chain before mentioned; and came upon their cannoneer, who fled; so they gained the two pieces of ordnance and broke the chain; and they and the horse entered the Town without more resistance. Where presently eighteen strangers yielded themselves . . . Mr. Brooke, the sometime minister of Yarmouth and some others escaped over the river. There was good store of pistols and other arms; I hear above fifty cases of pistols. The Colonel stayed there Tuesday and Wednesday night."[47]

On Friday, the 17th, Cromwell reached Norwich; on Saturday he despatched the prisoners to Cambridge,[48] and the same day notified the authorities of King's Lynn of his intended arrival there:

To the Mayor of King's Lynn

Regarding the putting down of the Royalists and advising them to expect him presently. March 18, 1642/3.[49]

The next day, Sunday, March 19th, the Mayor invited him and his "equipage to come at the Town's charge." After church service in Norwich, Cromwell set out for King's Lynn,[50] and by riding hard all night he and his troopers entered the town the following morning, disarmed the "malignants," secured the town and "seized upon a small barque with arms coming from Dunkirk."[51] It was perhaps there that he wrote another letter, of which the following is a summary:

To the Chief Constables of the Hundred of Holt [*co. Norfolk*]

"Ordering them to give warning to all such in their Hundred as found

[47] Letter from John Cory to Sir John Potts, March 17, *D'Ewes Mss.* f. 1139, printed in Carlyle (Lomas ed.), i, 122.

[48] *Ibid.*

[49] The Mayor's reply to Cromwell's note is mentioned in an order, March 20, for "Free entertainment of Cromwell and gentlemen accompanying him." In *Hist. Mss. Comm. Rept.* 11, App. iii, p. 181 (*King's Lynn Mss.*).

[50] *Certain Informations.*

[51] *Perfect Diurnall*, Mar. 27.

cuirassiers under the command of Sir William Paston, Bart., to appear at Thetford on Monday the 27th inst., completed, to march away under command of Capt. Robert Rich, for the defence of Norfolk." March 20, 1642/3.[52]

Three days later, "having since Sunday week ridden from Cambridge to Norwich, from Norwich to Yarmouth and Lowestoft, from Lowestoft back to Norwich, and thence to King's Lynn,"[53] Cromwell, on his way back to Cambridge, stopped for a night in Thetford where the Guildhall records contain a memorandum of his desecration of St. Mary's church by billeting his men and horses there.[54] Meanwhile the Lord General had written in great haste at three in the morning to Hampden and Stapleton of the arrival of Prince Rupert with a great force before Aylesbury,[55] and had sent orders to Cromwell to send immediate assistance from the Eastern Association. At Thetford, therefore, Cromwell signed another request for troops:

To the Deputy Lieutenants of Norwich

For the raising, arming and sending 100 men towards Cambridge. Written by command of the Earl of Essex. Thetford, March 23, 1642/3.[56]

Later that same day Cromwell reached Cambridge to find that some of the Essex men from Colchester were ready to disband and go home for want of pay. With the Lord General's recent orders in mind, he at once despatched a letter to the Mayor of Colchester pointing out to him the urgency of meeting their demand.

To the Mayor of Colchester and Captain John Langley

GENTLEMEN,

Upon the coming down of your townsmen to Cambridge Captain Langley, not knowing how to dispose of them, desired me to nominate a fit Captain, which I did—an honest, religious, valiant gentleman, Captain Dodsworth, the bearer hereof.

[52] Original in the Mss. of the Earl of Leicester; calendared in *Hist. Mss. Comm. Rept.* 9, App. II, p. 367.

[53] The House of Commons voted on March 21st "that Colonel Cromwell shall have power to dispose of the prisoners he hath taken in the Isle of Lothingland, in the county of Suffolk or Yarmouth or places thereabouts, to such places of safe custody as he, in his discretion, shall think fit. And that thanks be returned unto him for his great service. *C.J.*, iii, 11.

[54] Letter from the Town Clerk to the author.

[55] *C. J.*, iii, 10.

[56] Original, signed by Cromwell in the Upcott Collection, a large part of which was originally collected by Sir John Evelyn, in the possession of Monsieur A. Donnadieu until it was sold at auction in July 1851 by Puttick and Simpson. Puttick and Simpson, *Catalogue*, (1851).

He hath diligently attended the service, and much improved his men in their exercise; but hath been unhappy beyond others in not receiving any pay for himself, and what he had for his soldiers is out long ago. He hath, by his prudence, what with fair and winning carriage, what with money borrowed, kept them together. He is able to do so no longer. They will presently disband if a course be not taken.

It's pity it should be so. For I believe they are brought into as good order as most companies in the army. Besides, at this instant there is great need to use them. I having received a special command from my Lord General to advance with what force we can, to put an end (if it may be) to this work, God so assisting, from whom all help cometh.

I beseech you, therefore, consider this gentleman, and the soldiers; and if it be possible make up his company a hundred and twenty, and send them away with what expedition is possible. It may (through God's blessing) prove very happy. One month's pay may prove all your trouble. I speak to wise men. God direct you. I rest,

Yours to serve you,

[Cambridge?]
March 23rd 1642. OLIVER CROMWELL.[57]

It was on the 23rd also, according to the Royalist newspaper, *Mercurius Aulicus*, and Dr. Barwick's account,[58] that Cromwell and Lord Grey imprisoned some of the University authorities, including the vice-chancellor, in their own quarters for refusing to loan £6,000 "for the public use." They would, Cromwell was reported to have said, "have been content with a thousand pounds or even less, not that so little money would have done much good, but they wanted the people to think that one of the universities was on the side of Parliament."[59] To this Barwick adds a tale that Puritan spirit ran so high that the Book of Common Prayer in St. Mary's was torn to pieces in Cromwell's presence and he ordered the wood carvings in the same chapel to be broken up. Nor is this piece of gossip without interest. It is, apparently, the first of those innumerable tales of the destruction of images, glass, rood-screens and church decorations "by Cromwell," which have helped to blacken his name and bring discredit on the Puritans through the activities of their iconoclastic element.

Despite Cromwell's remark that a thousand pounds would have done little good, no amount of money was too small to be accepted, as the receipt signed by Cromwell and another member of the Cambridge Committee bears witness:

[57] Printed in Morant, *History of Colchester* (1748), i, 55; repr. in Thomas Cromwell, *History of Colchester* (1825), p. 94n. Carlyle, Letter VI. Cf. Kingston, *East Anglia*, p. 95.

[58] Barwick, *Querela Cantabrigiensis*, p. 188.

[59] *Mercurius Aulicus*, Apr. 22.

Receipt to John Annis

	l.	s.	d.
Recd of John Annis of Landbeach in the county of Cambridge for the use of the King and parliament the sum of Five pounds to be repaid according to the propositions of parliament.	5	00	00

OLIVER CROMWELL.
28 March 1643. THO. MARTYN.[60]

Yet with all of this activity, Cromwell had not come into the main theatre of war nor had the main armies moved. For this there were two reasons. The first was the difficulty of conducting military operations on a large scale during the winter and early spring when roads softened by snow, rain and frost made movement of large bodies of troops and especially of munitions and supplies extremely difficult. The second was the plan of campaign, if movements more or less unconnected may be called a plan. The activities of Cromwell in these and succeeding months were accompanied by those of other commanders in other fields. In the west Hopton drove the Parliamentary commander, Ruthven, from Cornwall by his victory at Bradock Down in January; while the Parliamentary general Waller took Malmesbury, drove the Welsh from their siege of Gloucester and the Royalists under Maurice from their control of south Wales. In the north Newcastle dominated the Yorkshire district despite the efforts of the Fairfaxes to gain control. On February 23 the Queen had landed at Bridlington Quay, bringing money and munitions. Thence she was conducted to York by Newcastle, whom she provided with an experienced military adviser, General King, created Earl of Ruthin, and there a new campaign was planned.

Throughout February the Royalists gained ground in the Midlands till they held a line of posts from Newark in the east to Stafford and Stratford in the west, designing a junction of the forces of Newcastle with Charles's main army. A dash by Rupert against Bristol failed and Brereton won some successes for the Parliament in Cheshire; but against these Parliamentary successes the Royalists set the fact that Cholmley, the governor of Scarborough, was won over by the Queen, and the allegiance of the Hothams was shaken. On March 19, in an endeavor to retake Lichfield, Northampton was killed in the battle of Hopton Heath near Stafford with the forces of Gell and Brereton, and Charles's first attempt to open the way for Newcastle's advance was checked. But Rupert seized and sacked Birmingham and retook Lichfield—where Lord Brooke was killed—on April 21, and it seemed possible that a junction might be effected between the two armies. Apart from a few successes like those of Waller and Cromwell, the

60 *Additional Mss*, 4182, f. 3, in the British Museum. Calendared in Ayscough's *Catalogue*, i, 234.

Parliamentary cause had been weakened and the danger of an attack on the Eastern counties and London by the Royalists increased.

Pym's party was fully conscious of its precarious position and the months of February and March were filled with measures to combat this threat. From the Ordinance of the Weekly Assessment in February to the Ordinance for Sequestering Delinquents' Estates at the end of March,[61] every effort was made to raise money for the new campaign. This was accompanied by other ordinances to strengthen resistance against Royalist attack; for trained bands to defend Taunton against Hopton and "the bloody counsels of the Papists"; for the fortification of London; and with the beginning of April as the Royalist plans developed, like measures to preserve the Isle of Wight, the cities and counties of Warwick, Coventry, Lichfield and the neighboring districts; the increase of the London militia; the supplying of Plymouth; the fortification of Yarmouth; and aid for Waller and Haselrig in the west.

Among the places where measures had been taken for defence was Cambridge, in its strategic position as center of the Eastern Association; and warlike activities there as elsewhere interfered with normal life in both town and University. For students or professors who enjoyed an occasional stroll, the gates of Cambridge were not easy to pass unchallenged at that time, but the librarian of the university, who was also professor of Arabic,[62] solved the difficulty by getting signatures of members of the Cambridge committee and an inscription in Cromwell's hand written on the fly-leaf of an Arabic volume which he was apparently accustomed to carry in his pocket:

Pass for Mr. Abraham Whelocke

Suffer the bearer hereof, Mr. Abraham Whelocke, to pass your guards so often as he shall have occasion, into and out of Cambridge, towards Little Shelford or any other place; and this shall be your warrant.

	THO. COOKE.	OLIVER CROMWELL.
April 4th, 1643.	EDW. CLENCHE.	JAMES THOMPSON.[63]

With the defences of the eastern counties being extended to include the bridges over the Ouse at Huntingdon, St. Ives, and elsewhere, another circular letter like that of March 8th, to Fen Drayton, was sent out to be read throughout the parishes on April 9th. Because

[61] Firth & Rait, *Acts and Ordinances*, i, 111, 113.

[62] Carlyle describes Whelocke as a student in the University who later became "the celebrated Professor of Arabic at Oxford." He had, as a matter of fact, been professor at Cambridge since 1630 and he died in 1653.

[63] Written in an Arabic version of one of Bellarmin's books, pr. in Rome, 1627, and showed to Carlyle by a Dr. Lee, Hartwell, Bucks. Carlyle, App. 3. The next year the Earl of Manchester signed a renewal of the pass in the same book.

Cambridge was "of great concernment for a place of retreat and rendezvous in any pressing danger," a further contribution was solicited. The members of the Association committee, including Cromwell, ordered the constables in addition "to return unto us the names of all them that are rated to the poor that refuse or do not give towards so good a work,"[64] so that this "voluntary" contribution was not without a threat. Nor was the alarm which prompted it without foundation. With Royalist successes in the West and North, with Newcastle preparing an advance from Yorkshire, and Charles, Rupert, and lesser commanders threatening the Eastern counties from the West, their defence became one of the chief concerns of Parliament and Cromwell increasingly important to its cause.

HUNTINGDON, PETERBOROUGH AND CROYLAND, APRIL, 1643

Meanwhile men were pouring into Cambridge in response to orders inspired by alarming reports of Royalist advances toward the Eastern counties. The *Perfect Diurnall* announced on April 7th that Cromwell had summoned 12,000 men from Cambridge, Norfolk, and Suffolk. Three days later some of them had arrived and Lord Grey of Wark had marched with 5,500 men to join the Earl of Essex before Reading and help secure that place from Charles's attack. By that time Cromwell was in Huntingdon seeking help from Bedford to cope with the "Camdeners," followers of Noel, Viscount Camden, who were driving cattle and stealing horses and provisions in south Lincolnshire. To combat this new menace Cromwell appealed for aid to Sir John Burgoyne, some time sheriff of Bedfordshire and now member of Parliament for Warwick:

To my honoured Friend Sir John Burgoyne, Baronet: These

SIR,

These plunderers draw near. I think it will do well if you can afford us any assistance of dragooners, to help in this great exigence. We have here about six or seven troops of horse; such, I hope, as will fight. It's happy to resist such beginnings betimes.

If you can contribute to our aid, let us speedily participate thereof. In the meantime, and ever, command

Your humble servant,
OLIVER CROMWELL.[65]

[Huntingdon?]
April 10th, 1643.

Though forces were assembling rapidly Cromwell's own regiment was still far from complete. That the third troop, Desborough's, was

[64] *Stowe Mss*, 807, ff. 204–5.

[65] Facs. in Burgoyne, M., *Letter to church wardens of the Diocese of Lincoln* (1831). Printed from an old copy, in Carlyle, who says it was sent from Huntingdon. Letter VII.

still in the process of formation in April is evidenced by a warrant for pay of a trooper, Lewis Browne of Cambridge, said to have enlisted on April 12th,[66] and by the following commission:

Commission to Cox Tooke

Appointing Cox Tooke quartermaster "to that troop of horse whereof John Disbrowe is captain, in my own regiment raised for the defence of the king, parliament and the kingdom."

OLIVER CROMWELL.[67]

April 12, 1643.

While, then, the eastern counties were being thus secured for Parliament against the threat of Newcastle, the Newark Royalists and presently Rupert at Lichfield, the main armies had begun to move. On April 13 Essex advanced to Reading on his way to Oxford, and, alarmed by a Parliamentary raid which seized Caversham Bridge, Charles summoned Rupert from Lichfield and set out with him to relieve Reading. The air was full of rumors. The day Essex began his march, a London news sheet reported that Cromwell's Cambridge men were advancing toward Oxford[68]—though the commander was, in fact, Lord Grey. Another declared that Cromwell was advancing with five or six thousand men into Lincolnshire.[69] Again this was not quite true. Though he had received orders from Essex to march northward to meet the Royalist threat from that quarter, Cromwell seems to have been still in Huntingdon preparing for this move, and incidentally still plaguing his old antagonist, Robert Bernard. Omitted from the Weekly Assessment committee and from the Sequestration committee for Huntingdon, Bernard seems to have somehow made himself liable for punishment as a "delinquent," and, escaping to London, had appealed to the Earl of Manchester. Each had written to Cromwell, who replied sternly:

To Robert Bernard, Esquire

SIR,

I have received two letters, the one from my Lord Manchester, the other from yourself, much to the same effect. I hope, therefore, one answer will serve both, which is in short this: that we know you are disaffected to the Parliament; and truly if the Lords, or any friends, may take you off from a reasonable contribution, for my part I should be glad to be

[66] Firth, "Raising of the Ironsides," *op. cit.*, p. 27.

[67] Listed in various sales catalogues of private collections: that of Walter V. Daniell, in 1912 (with the date of 22 Apr. 1643); that of J. B. Thacher, in 1920, for sale by the Anderson Galleries; and twice again, in 1925 and 1929.

[68] *Continuation of Special and Remarkable Passages*, Apr. 13.

[69] *Perfect Diurnall*, Apr. 18.

commanded to any other employment. Sir, you may, if you will, come freely into the country about your occasions. For my part, I have protected you in your absence; and shall do so to you.

This is all, but that I am ready to serve you, and rest,

Your loving friend,

[Huntingdon]
April 17, 1643. OLIVER CROMWELL.[70]

About the same time another news sheet noted his activities:

"Colonell Cromwell is for present at Huntingdon with some five troops to which are added some countrymen of Hunts and other counties; the enemy fled as is conceived to Newarke, upon the noyse of him. The Colonell exercises strict discipline; for when two troopers would have escaped he sent them back, caused them to be whipt at the market place in Huntingdon."[71]

The *Perfect Diurnall* for April 20 confirms his presence there, observing that he had marched through Huntingdon, disarmed the malignants and increased his force to 2,000 foot and ten troops of horse and dragoons. With such a constantly growing force, he was on his way toward Lincolnshire where the Newark Royalists had succeeded in dominating the county. He established his headquarters in Peterborough on April 22, and there at the hands of his troops occurred more iconoclasm. It was typical of the movement which on April 24 was formally approved by the Commons, under whose direction the stained glass windows and the images in Westminster Abbey and St. Margaret's church were destroyed, while the City, not to be outdone, tore down the Cheapside cross.

At Peterborough Cromwell's men amused themselves by burning books in the cathedral. From that holocaust chance saved one volume, on whose title-page an inscription reveals the means by which it was preserved:

"Pray let this scripture book alone, for he hath paid me for it, and therefore I would desire you to let it alone, by me, Henry Topclyffe soldier under Captain Cromwell, Colonel Cromwell's son . . . April 22, 1643."[72]

While so engaged the Commons authorized Cromwell and captains Charles Fleetwood, Whalley and Desborough, to seize the persons, arms, horses, money, plate and chattels of delinquents.[73] On that same day, Tuesday, April 25, with his own forces and the regiments of Sir Miles Hobart and Sir Anthony Irby, he began the siege of Croyland, where his cousin, another captain Cromwell, with some

[70] *Gentleman's Magazine* (1791), lxi, 44. Carlyle, Letter VIII.

[71] *Speciall Passages and Certain Informations.*

[72] Gunton, *History of Peterborough.*

[73] *C. J.*, iii, 60. It did not pass the House of Lords until May 2. Printed in *L. J.*, v, 26.

eighty or ninety other Royalists had fortified themselves and held prisoner some Parliamentary sympathizers, including the Puritan minister of nearby Spalding.

The siege of Croyland was Cromwell's first experience of that kind. It was neither great nor glorious. Heavy rains and water made military operations difficult and it was not until Thursday afternoon that the besiegers assaulted the place from its one accessible side. Against such overwhelming force the garrison realized that defence was hopeless and began to steal away. By daylight Friday morning the few that remained proposed terms of surrender, and when terms were refused, allowed the besiegers to enter without opposition. Their fate is unrecorded, but the Parliamentary losses were five dead and 18 or 20 wounded;[74] and with this success Cromwell continued his activities from his headquarters at Peterborough.

There, according to a contemporary account, his men continued to enjoy 'eating up the fat clergy of Peterborough' and damaging their cathedral, burning books, demolishing the woodwork and shattering the great west window, encouraged by their commander who told the protesting spectators, "that they did God good service in that action";[75] and there remains a curious tradition of Cromwell's presence there:

"A finger of divine vengeance touched Cromwell. . . . For being at that time quartered in the house of Mr. Cervington, commonly called the Vineyard, at the east end of the Cathedral, out of the court of which dwelling there was a passage into the churchyard, ascending by three or four stone steps, Cromwell, as others did, riding up those steps, his horse fell under him, and rising suddenly under the lintels of the door, dashed his head against the lintels, so that he fell to the ground as dead, was so carried into the house, and it was about a fortnight ere he could be recovered; those who were eye-witnesses affirmed that the blow raised splinters in his scalp near a finger's length."[76]

Whatever the truth or falsehood of these stories, it appears that he spent nearly three weeks drilling his forces and recruiting, there and in Huntingdonshire. On one of his excursions he seems to have paid a visit to his old uncle, Sir Oliver Cromwell who, after the loss of Hinchinbrook, had retired to Ramsey. Sir Philip Warwick who visited there later, was told indignantly of how Colonel Cromwell came with a strong party of horse to ask the old man's blessing, and though he refused to keep his hat on in Sir Oliver's presence, on his departure he "not only disarmed" the old knight, "but plundered him, for he took away all his plate."[77]

[74] *Divers Remarkable Passages.*
[75] Ryves, *Mercurius Rusticus* (ed. 1685), p. 213.
[76] Gunton, *Peterborough*, p. 92.
[77] Warwick, *Memoirs*, pp. 251–252.

GRANTHAM, MAY, 1643

It had now been some eight months since Cromwell had first raised his troop. He had contributed greatly to the cause of the Parliament in the Eastern counties, taken part in the battle of Edgehill, been commissioned colonel, and raised and drilled a regiment. He had become the leading figure of the cause throughout East Anglia and was so recognized by Parliament and the press. But apart from Edgehill and the siege of Croyland he had thus far had small experience of real war, for that war had as yet scarcely touched the Eastern counties. But it was coming fast, for though Essex had taken Reading on April 26 and with the main army was moving toward Oxford, though Waller had occupied Hereford and had repulsed Hopton, the Royalists were gathering in force about Newark preparing to move against the Eastern counties. The cause of Parliament seemed, on the whole, promising, but on May 2, the House ordered eight men to help Cromwell secure Lincolnshire against the Royalist threat,[78] and the next day Cromwell wrote to the Lincoln committee to explain why he had not obeyed Essex's order to join with Lord Grey of Groby at Stamford:

To the Right Honourable the Lords and others the Committees of Lincoln: These

My Lords and Gentlemen,

I must needs be hardly thought on because I am still the messenger of unhappy tidings and delays concerning you, though I know my heart is to assist you with all expedition.

My Lord Grey hath now again failed me of the rendezvous at Stamford, notwithstanding that both he and I received letters from his Excellency commanding us both to meet and, together with Sir John Gell and the Nottingham forces, to join with you. My Lord Grey sent Sir Edward Hartop to me, to let me know he could not meet me at Stamford according to our agreement; fearing the exposing of Leicester to the forces of Mr. Hastings and some other troops drawing that way.

Believe it, it were better, in my poor opinion, Leicester were not than that there should not be an immediate taking of the field by your forces to accomplish the common end, wherein I shall deal as freely with him when I meet him as you can desire. I perceive Ashby-de-la-Zouch sticks much with him. I have offered him now another place of meeting, to come to which I suppose he will not deny me; and that to be tomorrow. If you shall therefore think fit to send one over unto us to be with at night, you do not know how far we may prevail with him to draw speedily to a head with Sir John Gell and the other forces, where we may all meet at a general rendezvous, to the end you know of, and then you shall receive full satisfaction concerning

[78] *C. J.*, iii, 67. The eight men were Sir Sam Ofeild, Sir Anthony Irby, Sir John Brownloe, Sir William Brownloe, Sir Tho. Trollopp, Captain Hatcher, Captain Lister, and Mr. Wm. Ellis.

my integrity; and if no man shall help you, yet will not I be wanting to do my duty, God assisting me.

If we could unite those forces and with them speedily make Grantham the general rendezvous, both of yours and ours, I think it would do well. I shall bend my endeavours that way. Your concurrence by some able instrument to solicit this, might probably exceedingly hasten it, especially having so good a foundation to work upon as my Lord General's commands. Our Norfolk forces, which will not prove as many as you may imagine by six or seven hundred men, will lie conveniently at Spalden; and, I am confident, be ready to meet at Grantham at the general rendezvous.

I have no more to trouble you, but begging of God to take away the impediments that hinder our conjunction, and to prosper our designs, take leave.

Your faithful servant,

May 3d, 1643. OLIVER CROMWELL.[79]

This letter was sent at once to the House of Commons by Captain John Hotham, Sir Edward Ayscough, and Sir Christopher Wray, of the Lincolnshire Committee, as a defence against the charge of a lack of diligence which they had heard was brought against them.[80] Whether or not that committee was innocent of the charge, hardly a day passed at this time without Captain Hotham writing to the Royalist Earl of Newcastle. Though the Parliamentary party was naturally not aware of his intended treachery, he and his father had planned to follow the example of their cousin, Sir Hugh Cholmley, and the younger Hotham's letter[81] agreeing to turn traitor to Parliament and hinder Cromwell's marching to Lincolnshire was, in fact, written three days before Cromwell's explanation to the Lincolnshire authorities. The reading of Cromwell's letter on May 8 brought immediate action in Parliament which resolved that the order for the eight men to join him was to be served on them at once and that a letter should be prepared requiring Lord Grey to join Cromwell without delay.[82]

By May 9 the forces under Cromwell, Lord Willoughby of Parham, and Sir John Hotham had assembled at Sleaford, on the road from Peterborough to Lincoln, for an attack on the Royalist stronghold of Newark.[83] On the 11th, they marched across to Grantham where they spent the next day resting, and two days later, on May 13, there took place a skirmish at Belton near Grantham on whose results, it has been said, perhaps with some exaggeration, 'rested the whole fortune of the Civil War.' The best description of the engagement is

[79] Carlyle, Letter IX, from the *Tanner Mss* (Oxford), lxii, 94.

[80] *C. J.*, iii, 75. At the same time a letter of May 2 was read, from Ayscough and Wray, complaining that Cromwell had been retarded and the place was in danger. In *Hist. Mss. Comm. Rept.* 13 App. I (*Welbeck Abbey*) i, 706.

[81] In *Tanner Mss*, lxii, pt. i, pp. 90–1.

[82] *C. J.*, iii, 75.

[83] *Perfect Diurnall*, May 12; *Special Passages*, May 9–16.

that of Cromwell himself in his letter to the commander of a Norfolk regiment, written at Syston Park, a mile and a half from the scene of the fight:

To Sir Miles Hobart[84]

NOBLE SIR,

God hath given us, this evening, a glorious victory over our enemies. They were, as we are informed, one-and-twenty colours of horse troops, and three or four of dragoons.

It was late in the evening when we drew out. They came and faced us within two miles of the town. So soon as we had the alarm, we drew out our forces, consisting of about twelve troops, whereof some of them so poor and broken, that you shall seldom see worse. With this handful it pleased God to cast the scale. For after we had stood a little above musket-shot the one body from the other and the dragooners having fired on both sides for the space of half an hour or more, they not advancing towards us, we agreed to charge them, and, advancing the body after many shots on both sides, came on with our troops a pretty round trot, they standing firm to receive us; and our men charging fiercely upon them, by God's providence they were immediately routed, and ran all away, and we had the execution of them two or three miles.

The true number of men slain we are not certain of, but by a credible report and estimate of our soldiers, and by what I myself saw, there were very little less than a hundred slain and mortally wounded, and we lost but two men at the most on our side. We took 45 prisoners, besides divers of their horses and arms, and rescued many prisoners whom they had lately taken of ours, and we took 4 or 5 colours, and so marched away to Lincoln.

Shaston, [OLIVER CROMWELL.][85]
May 13th, 1643.

Neither in the numbers engaged, the losses on each side, nor in immediate results does the skirmish at Grantham seem to rank among the important battles of the Civil War. But it was none the less of great consequence. It disrupted the plans of the Royalists; it proved that Cromwell's men could meet their enemies on more than equal terms; and it revealed him as a leader of power and resource so greatly needed at this moment on the side of Parliament. Despite his dis-

[84] Sir Miles Hobart, bart., had a son John who married John Hampden's fourth daughter, Mary, and thus became one of the great Cromwell connection. Hampden's other sons-in-law, Sir Richard Knightley, Sir Robert Pye, and Sir John Trevor, were all members of the Long Parliament, all Parliamentarians.

[85] There are three versions of this letter, differing considerably from each other: The *Perfect Diurnall*, May 22–29; Vicars, *God in the Mount*, p. 336; *A true relation of a great victory*. The present text is from the Perfect Diurnall, except for the last paragraph, which is from Vicars. Pr. also in Carlyle, Letter X (from *Perfect Diurnall*) who has "Thasten" instead of "Shaston"; in Street, *Notes on Grantham* (1857), pp. 97–98 (from Vicars). Cf. *Lincolnshire Notes & Queries*, xiii, 38–47, for the circumstances of the letter and a discussion of the fight, by Lieutenant-colonel A. C. E. Welby.

paragement of the numbers and the quality of his men, *Special Passages* sang their praises and his:

"As for Cromwell, he hath 2,000 brave men, well disciplined: no man swears but he pays his twelve pence; if he be drunk he is set in the stocks, or worse, if one calls the other 'Roundhead' he is cashiered; insomuch that the countries where they come leap for joy of them, and come in and join with them. How happy were it if all the forces were thus disciplined."[86]

From Grantham these forces circled around Newark and took up their headquarters at Nottingham to await additional troops and money. The two Fairfaxes were in Yorkshire in desperate straits and were asking for aid from the Eastern Association, to which Huntingdonshire was added on May 26.[87] Essex, meanwhile, was held impotent for lack of money to pay his troops; the Queen's convoy of arms reached the King; and on May 16 the Earl of Stamford's forces were beaten at Stratton in Devon by less than half their numbers under Hopton, Grenville and Berkeley with great loss of supplies and prisoners. Stamford's second in command, Chudleigh, went over to the King after the battle and for the moment the west seemed lost to Parliament.

The shifting of Huntingdonshire to the Eastern Association may have been due in part to the fact that Cromwell's regiment comprised men from that county as well as from Cambridge, in part perhaps to the fact that the Eastern counties were now almost the last hope of Parliament in that region and Cromwell their chief reliance there. This change terminated his relations with the Midland Counties Association; in the future he was to deal only with the Eastern counties, where Parliament had recently ordered additional collections.[88] The situation in the north was not promising, despite the success of Lord Fairfax at Wakefield on May 21. The Parliamentary officers in Nottingham had not only found it hard to raise the additional forces necessary, but they had great difficulty in securing money to support those they had; and, faced with the danger from Newcastle, Cromwell appealed again to Colchester:

To the Mayor &c. of Colchester

GENTLEMEN,

I thought it my duty once more to write unto you for more strength to be speedily sent unto us, for this great service.

I suppose you hear of the great defeat given by my Lord Fairfax to the Newcastle forces at Wakefield. It was a great mercy of God to us, and had it not been bestowed upon us at this very present, my Lord Fairfax had not

[86] *Special Passages*, May 9–16.
[87] *C. J.*, iii, 102, 104; *L. J.*, vi, 63.
[88] *C. J.*, iii, 91.

known how to have subsisted. We assure you, should the force we have miscarry, expect nothing but a speedy march of the enemy up unto you.

Why you should not strengthen us to make us subsist! Judge you the danger of the neglect, and how inconvenient this improvidence, or unthrifty, may be to you! I shall never write but according to my judgment. I tell you again, it concerns you exceedingly to be persuaded by me. My Lord Newcastle is near 6000 foot, and about 60 troops of horse; my Lord Fairfax is about 3000 foot, and nine troops of horse; and we have about 24 troops of horse and dragooners. The enemy draws more to the Lord Fairfax. Our motion and yours must be exceedingly speedy, or else it will do you no good at all.

If you send, let your men come to Boston. I beseech you, hasten the supply to us; forget not money. I press not hard, though I do so need that, I assure you, the foot and dragooners are ready to mutiny. Lay not too much upon the back of a poor gentleman, who desires, without much noise, to lay down his life, and bleed the last drop to serve the Cause and you. I ask not your money for myself; if that were my end and hope (viz. the pay of my place), I would not open my mouth at this time. I desire to deny myself; but others will not be satisfied. I beseech you hasten supplies. Forget not your prayers.

Gentlemen, I am yours,

Nottingham
May 28th, 1643. OL. CROMWELL.[89]

Even such an urgent appeal did not bring immediate response, if we may judge from a later letter to the Deputy Lieutenants of Essex which mentions his having borrowed £100 from the Mayor of Nottingham for his Essex men.[90] Nevertheless, Lord Grey and Sir John Gell finally joined forces with Cromwell,[91] and six thousand men, the newspapers said, under those three commanders, Lord Willoughby of Parham and the younger Hotham, were gathered in Nottingham early in June to march into Yorkshire to rescue the Fairfaxes from Newcastle's army.

NOTTINGHAM AND NEWARK, JUNE, 1643

The situation at the end of May, 1643, was unfavorable to Pym's party in and out of Parliament. While Cromwell had been busy in the eastern counties, a quarrel between Northumberland and Henry Marten in April though composed had smoldered on and the Commons had fallen out with the Lords on a question of privilege growing out of

[89] Morant, *History of Colchester*, i, 56; Cromwell, Thomas, *History of Colchester* (1825), p. 95n; Carlyle, Letter XI.

[90] Cromwell's letter, Aug. 1. On July 15th, according to the records of Nottingham, £115 was loaned to Cromwell. Bailey, *Annals of Nottingham*, ii, 682.

[91] During Cromwell's absence to meet these two commanders, "200 of his musqueteers and a troop of horse were surprised by 20 troops of Cavaliers. Only 20 or 30 escaped," according to the *Perfect Diurnall*, May 29–June 5.

orders of sequestration. Differences between the Houses had arisen over the title of the Clerk of Parliament, others over the disposition of the case of the Earl of Chesterfield, now a prisoner. Difficulties had been multiplied by the absence of the Great Seal of England, which had been taken to the King, and by a vote of 86 to 74 it was resolved to make another for the use of Parliament as its assumption of sovereignty advanced another step. A whole group of individuals, including the Queen, were declared traitors; and it appearing that the Lords had sunk to "a miserable state," steps were taken to remedy that situation if possible. The business of Ireland arose to complicate affairs and the desertion of Essex's soldiers alarmed the Houses. Almost day by day measures were taken to raise money, by loans and levies, especially by the ordinance of May 7 to tax all who had not contributed hitherto "according to their estates or their abilities," and from the list of the Cambridge commissioners the name of Cromwell is significantly absent for the first time. With all these causes of uneasiness, the great concern of the Houses was money and still more money for the war, for horses and supplies, but most of all for men.

That was the more important in that Pym and his followers were threatened from another quarter, the so-called "Waller Plot," by which a group of men—Holland, Northumberland, Bedford, Clare, Conway and Portland in the Lords and Edmund Waller, Sir Nicholas Crisp and others in and outside the Commons—planned to seize the City for the King. The plot was discovered; two City merchants involved in it were hanged in front of their own houses; Waller, saved by his confession and, it was rumored, by Cromwell's intervention, was merely fined; and the charges against the peers were summarily dismissed. The cause of Parliament was too weak to make more enemies, and in an endeavor to strengthen it the Houses voted a "covenant" to test the loyalty of its remaining members, passed an ordinance for censorship of the press and authorized an assembly of divines to reform the church.

There were reasons outside of the purely military situation which at this moment inspired the policy of Pym and his party in the conduct of affairs. While the armies maneuvred, and men and money were being raised for the cause of the Parliament, the religious question demanded attention if support was to be obtained from the only source whence it could be expected in their attack on monarchy and episcopacy—the Presbyterians and the "sects." In consequence, on June 6, taking advantage of the revelation of Waller's plot and of Charles's negotiations with the Irish rebels, Pym secured from the Commons an agreement to take the "vow" or "covenant" to support the forces raised against the King "so long as the Papists now in open war against the Parliament shall by the force of arms be protected from the justice thereof." Under the same stimulus the Lords accepted an ordinance for the calling of an Assembly of Divines to consider the ecclesiastical situation. To it the Scottish ministers were requested to send delegates; some Episcopalians were invited but refused or were expelled; and on July 1 the Assembly met in the chapel of Henry VII in Westminster Abbey. Summoned at first nominally to revise the Thirty-Nine Articles, before it met, the religious situation had gone beyond that mandate; and it had begun almost at once to debate the question of an ecclesiastical system to replace that episcopacy which it presently condemned and, as a preliminary, Archbishop Laud, though not yet brought to trial, was enjoined from exercising his authority.

Of its hundred and fifty members, thirty were chosen from the Houses, but their attendance was perfunctory and the problem of church establishment was left in the hands of the Puritan divines, supervised and regulated by the authority of Parliament. From the beginning, the problem of the Covenant was difficult, nor did the Assembly, much less the Parliament, adopt it whole heartedly and without reservation; and in each there came that division which was to become more and more important as the war went on—the irreconcileable breach between the rigid Presbyterians and the more tolerant "Dissenters" or "Independents" of which Cromwell was becoming more and more the champion.

Meanwhile the Parliament's forces remained at Nottingham. They did not move for reasons which soon became too evident. Against Cromwell's protests Hotham was able to prevent an advance against the Royalists on the ground that they dared not leave Lincoln undefended; and on June 2 the commanders sent a letter, penned by Hotham, to Fairfax to explain their inaction:

For the Right Honourable Ferdinando Lord Fairfax, General of the Northern Forces: These present at Leeds

MAY IT PLEASE YOUR LORDSHIP,

We were even ready to march with all the forces here to attend you, when we had certain intelligence of the state of my Lord Newcastle's army, so weak and in such a distraction, that we conceive it far unfit to force your Lordship in your quarters. We had certain notice likewise that a good strength of horse and foot were marched from him to Newark, to face and attend the moving of the forces of horse and dragooners appeared in a body some four miles from this place; and we hear behind them stood their foot. We drew out to fight them, but they had chosen such a ground as we could not come to them without great disadvantage. At night they drew away and are still within six or seven miles hovering up and down the country. Until we see what these people intend, or which way my Lord Newcastle will move, we think it best to stay here, and not to draw down into Yorkshire, to eat up that small remainder of provisions that is left, and by that means do your lordship more prejudice than the enemy can do. This we thought fit to offer to your consideration; and if, notwithstanding all this, you shall think it fit for us to move towards you, it shall be readily done by your lordship's humble servants,

JOHN GELL JOHN HOTHAM
Nottingham, OLI. CROMWELL. MI. HOOBERT.
June 2nd, 1643, THO. GREY.[92]

Two days later, according to Dugdale, "Ye Rebells under ye comand of ye E. of Stamford and Cromwell, plundered Botsford, Com. Leic."[93] The latter was striving to make his position more secure, riding here and there to suppress Royalist activities. On June 10, while Essex marched to Thame on his way to Oxford, threatening Islip without success, and without money to pay his troops, Cromwell left Boston for Donnington, and thence went to Newark to drive out the Cavaliers, only to find that they had already gone.[94] Meanwhile, he was becoming increasingly disturbed by excuses and delays which prevented more active efforts against the Royalists, and finally wrote demanding the regiment of Sir John Palgrave, deputy lieutenant of Norfolk, with or without its commander.[95]

To my honoured friends, the Commissioners for the Association: Present these at Cambridge

GENTLEMEN,

Because I understood Sir John Palgrave was resolved to come to you, and knowing he is very much mistaken in my Lord General's meaning concerning the coming of his regiment to the Army; and finding too, too many delays therein, excuses sometimes put upon the lieutenant-colonel, sometimes upon captains, sometimes upon want of money, upon Lieutenant Hotham and myself, upon misunderstanding his Excellency,—by all which the service is neglected and delayed and the kingdom endangered,—least you upon his coming should be led also into mistakes upon pretences, I make this short address to you, desiring you to believe me it exceedingly imports the kingdom, the Association, and you all, that he hasten to us.

Let no words whatsoever lead your resolutions any other way. I maintain and affirm to you, as I would deal faithfully with you, and love the Associa-

[92] Bell, *Memorials of the Civil War*, (1849), i, 46.

[93] Hamper, W. ed., *Diary of Sir William Dugdale* (1827), p. 51. It would be easier to understand this statement if we could assume that Dugdale put his diary in shape some years after this occurrence, after Thomas, Lord Grey, had inherited his father's title of Earl of Stamford. The Earl of Stamford does not seem to have been with Cromwell at this time.

[94] *Perfect Diurnall*, June 12–19.

[95] Palgrave was with Cromwell on July 24th at Burleigh House. *Hist. Mss. Comm. Rept.* 7, App. (*Lowndes Mss.*), pp. 555–556.

tion, two or three hundred men in those parts are enough. Holland is fronteer to it. Horsea Bridge[96] over the river out of Huntingdonshire being made a draw bridge makes the advance thither altogether fearless. If the enemy's horse advance to Stamford, what can they do? Nothing at all as to that place. If we be strong in the field, you are very well secured, and be assured if the enemy advance towards you we shall follow him in the heels. For Sir Miles Hobart and myself doubt not we shall not be so unfaithful to you to give the enemy leave to march into the Association and tarry behind. My Lord General's express command is that we all advance if he draw towards the south with his army. His care is for you; so we trust shall our faithfulness.

Let no words therefore from Sir John Palgrave prevail but command him to march up with all the volunteers, both the two companies which you send, and all the rest of the volunteers. If he cannot be spared let Sir Edward Ashlye bring them. Let him not keep a volunteer at Wisbeach—I beseech you, do not. He hath a mind to this company and the other company to please himself in composing his regiment. This is not a time to pick and choose for pleasure. Service must be done. Command, you, and be obeyed! The Queen is marching with 1200 horse, and 3000 foot. We are much under that number. We trust to endeavour our duties with these we have, but it will not be good to lose the use of any force God gives us, by negligence. The Lord give you, and us, zeal.

I take leave and rest,

Your faithful servant,

[Newark?
June 13th, 1643.] OLIVER CROMWELL.

[P.S.] I beseech you, inform yourselves fully of the numbers of your men at Wisbeach, and send what you think may well be spared. You need few when we are in the field, whereof doubt not when his comes up to us.[97]

The immediate result of this letter was an appeal from the Committee at Cambridge to the Deputy Lieutenants of Essex for three foot companies and money.[98] There was reason for alarm. Not merely was there danger from the Queen's threatened advance but there was dissension among the Parliamentarians. It had become apparent to Cromwell and the rest of the officers that young Hotham, who had "carried himself marvellous scornfully toward Colonell Cromwell and used Lord Grey of Grobie with like disrespect,"[99] was not to be trusted. In a dispute with Grey's men over some oats he had turned a cannon on Cromwell, whereupon Grey, Colonel John Hutchinson and Cromwell laid information against him before the

[96] *I.e.*, Horsey Bridge, on the northern boundary of Hunts.

[97] Photostat facsimile in National Library of Wales, and printed in Calendar of Wynn Papers (1926), no. 1722A. Printed also in *Athenaeum*, Feb. 4, 1905, p. 145, from the original in the possession of a Mrs. Alan Gough, of Gelliwig, Carnarvonshire, who got it from the family seat of the Hollands.

[98] Letter, June 15th, *Hist. Mss. Comm. Rept.* 7, App. pp. 551–2 (*Lowndes Mss*).

[99] Vicars, *God in the Mount*, p. 366.

Committee of Safety.[100] It was sent to Essex who ordered Hotham's arrest and despatched Sir John Meldrum to take command in Nottingham. Hotham was taken into custody on June 18 by Meldrum and imprisoned in Nottingham Castle, whence he escaped to Lincoln, where he wrote to Speaker Lenthall explaining that though he was still faithful to the House,

'Colonel Cromwell had employed an anabaptist against him, and that one Captain White had been employed against him, who was lately but a yeoman. The valour of these men had only yet appeared in their defacing of churches.'[101]

But Hotham's days of liberty were short. He fled to Hull where he and his father were seized by the Mayor and sent as prisoners to London. Hull was saved; but on June 30 Newcastle routed Fairfax at Adwalton Moor. Bradford and the other towns were lost; the Fairfaxes took refuge in Hull; and though the Royalist effort to seize Lincoln failed, the Queen set out for Oxford on July 3 with every hope of bringing the war to a speedy end.

The King's party was the more certain of this in that the Parliamentarians had suffered a great loss. While Essex threatened Oxford, Rupert, endeavoring to cut off his supply of money from London, though he missed his prize, met the Parliamentary forces at Chalgrove Field on the same day that Hotham was arrested in Nottingham. There, in trifling skirmish John Hampden was mortally wounded and six days later died. It was a blow to Pym's party which they could ill afford, especially at such a time as this. A week later Rupert's cavalry swept around Essex, defeated Stapleton and plundered Wycombe. The City was alarmed. Pym wrote sharply to Essex who offered to resign; and the King, encouraged by these successes, replied to the new covenant with a proclamation denouncing Parliament's assumption of sovereignty and offering indemnity to all of his opponents save five lords and thirteen commoners, if they would recognize his authority.

BURGHLEY HOUSE AND GAINSBOROUGH, JULY, 1643

The month of July was a critical period in the fortunes of Pym and his party. Newcastle began his long threatened advance toward the eastern counties, the Queen joined Charles at Edgehill on July 13; Essex had failed in his offensive and withdrew first to Aylesbury,

[100] *Parliament Scout.* Pym reported from the Committee of Safety, on June 21st, that Hotham was in custody on the word of Lord Grey and Cromwell that he had been plundering and quarreling with Cromwell and Lord Grey, and had turned guns against Cromwell. *C. J.*, iii, 138.

[101] D'Ewes, Diary. *Harl. Mss*, 164, f. 234. Letter, June 24th, read in the House, June 27th. *C. J.*, iii, 146.

then to Brickhill near Bedford to keep his communication open with the eastern counties and the capital. Hopton meanwhile was joined by Prince Maurice, took Taunton and Bridgewater, and at the moment that the Fairfaxes rode into Hull on July 5, defeated Waller at Lansdown, drove him back to Bath, and on July 13 destroyed his army at Roundway Down. Nor was the month to end without further disaster for on July 26 Fiennes surrendered Bristol to Rupert. Confronted by such a series of reverses Pym and his followers took prompt steps to repair the loss. On July 19 they passed an ordinance for commissioners to go to Scotland to appeal for aid. Three days later they passed another for an increase of excise to support the armed forces. On the 25th, to meet the threat of Newcastle's advance, they appointed the Earl of Manchester commander-in-chief of a new body of horse from the fifteen counties which still remained to them, with Oliver Cromwell as his second in command in the counties of Cambridge and Huntingdon, with full powers in Manchester's absence.[102]

While the forces of the Parliament had been driven back on every front, Cromwell and Meldrum for a time remained at Dunsmore Heath near Nottingham where, on July 3, they were waiting for the Queen's expected march.[103] To support them Parliament had ordered that most of the money raised by sequestrations in Huntingdon should be paid to Cromwell for his troops.[104] When the news that the Queen had joined her husband reached Essex, he summoned to his assistance all forces within sixty miles, and on July 17 it was reported that Meldrum with Cromwell and Lord Grey, at the head of forty troops of horse and six regiments of foot were marching to his aid.[105] "My Lord General is now at Stony Stratford," wrote Sir William Masham to Sir Thomas Barrington on that day, "and we hope now that Colonel Cromwell with his forces is joined with him."[106]

That hope was without foundation. Cromwell was, in fact, chiefly concerned with Newcastle's advance from the north and the precarious position of Lord Willoughby of Parham who had just seized Gainsborough. It was on his behalf that Cromwell wrote, about July 22:

[102] Firth and Rait, *Acts and Ordinances*, i, 215–219.

[103] *Perfect Diurnall*, July 3–10.

[104] June 20th. *C. J.*, iii, 136. Two days earlier the House noted the fact that two brass sacres had been sent to Norwich to replace two field pieces loaned to Cromwell. *Ibid.*, 134.

[105] *Perfect Diurnall*, July 17–24.

[106] Letter July 17th, in *Hist. Mss. Comm. Rept.* 7, App. p. 554.

To the Committee at Cambridge

The enemy is approaching. Two troops are needed at once and further reinforcements as soon as possible, to help Fairfax and Lord Willoughby, who has taken Gainsborough but is holding it with great difficulty.[107]

Hard upon that piece of news, the Huntingdon Committee sent out an account of the taking of Burghley House near Stamford where a party of Cavaliers, fleeing from Cromwell, had taken refuge:

"Our scout, now returned from Stamford, tells us that this morning early noble Col. Cromwell, Col. Hobert, with Col. Palgrave sat down before Burleigh House by Stamford (wherein was 2 colonels, six captains, with about 200 horse and 300 foot). At the first sitting down Cromwell sent a trumpet to summon the cavaliers, with offer of free quarter to leave only the place and their arms; thereto the cavaliers returned they would neither give nor take quarter, but fight it out to the last man. Whereupon the col. caused the ordnance to play upon the house, but after a few hours proved no good would be done that way. Whereupon our colonels caused their musketeers in 3 squadrons to draw up to the house; that in a little time the cavaliers sounded a parley. Whereupon the colonel sent to the * * * * * * not to kill a man more upon pain of death (notwithstanding their first peremptory refusal). In this manner the house, all the commanders and soldiers were taken, with all arms and whatever else, and not above 6 men slain on both sides. And while this was doing the colonel sent out Captain Dodson, Wauton, and Disborow to meet with 400 of the enemy and had notice [they?] were coming to assist the cavaliers. Capt. Dodson being first in with them was wounded and beaten from his horse, but rescued by Capt. Wauton, and then together falling upon that rabble slew about 50 of them and wholly dispersed and routed the rest. Our scout tells us Col. Cromwell gave great commendation of Col. Palgrave's men. Col. Cromwell took it extremely ill that Capt. Paes was not sent unto him, seeing he so earnestly desired it."[108]

Among those innumerable traditions of Cromwell which linger here and there in England there are two connected with his presence at Burghley House. The one is that he stayed with a relative of his, a Miss Wingfield who persuaded him not to destroy the place; the other that his "usual gallantry to Royalist ladies" led him to present the Countess of Exeter with a portrait of himself by Walker which is still preserved at Burghley.[109] What is more certain is that he sent some

[107] The letter itself has not survived, but it was enclosed with one from the Committee to the Deputy Lieutenants of Essex which mentions its receipt on July 23rd. A copy was sent by Sir Edw. Ayscough to the House of Commons and read there July 24th. *C. J.*, iii, 180. The troops required by Cromwell had been sent and the garrison at Cambridge was left "destitute." *Hist. Mss. Comm. Rept.* 7, App. p. 555 (*Lowndes Mss*).

[108] *Hist. Mss. Comm. Rept.* 7, App. p. 555b. Letter dated July 24th.

[109] *Fenland Notes and Queries*, quoted in Kingston, *East Anglia*, p. 118.

200 Cavalier prisoners to Cambridge, and that the Committee there, agreeing that the town was "malignant" enough already, hastened to despatch them to London. It was probably on his march north after taking Burghley House that he wrote a letter:

To the Deputy Lieutenants of the county of Suffolk

Earnestly pressing for the assembling of the Committee out of all the Associated counties at Cambridge. [c. July 25, 1643.][110]

The letter of the Suffolk Committee, dated July 27, to the Committee for Essex, which mentions the receipt of this communication from Cromwell, notes also the receipt of the ordinance for the raising of a new force of horse and the appointment of Manchester to its command. The forces thus authorized were to consist of 6,400 men of whom 2,200 were to come from the Eastern Association. Places of rendezvous were named and five commanders were ordered to receive the recruits. The men from Norfolk and Suffolk were to report to Sir Miles Hobart, those from Cambridge and Huntingdon to Cromwell, both commanders to receive them at Cambridge.[111]

Continuing northward after the siege of Burghley House, Cromwell and his forces marched toward Gainsborough where Lord Willoughby of Parham was hard pressed by Newcastle's younger brother, Charles, Lord Cavendish. Three letters tell the story of the rendezvous on July 27th, of the relief of the town with powder and provisions the next day, before Newcastle's army appeared, and of the ensuing encounter, as well as the Parliamentary forces' "masterly retreat before overwhelming numbers." The first, though obviously not written by Cromwell, was signed by him and two Lincolnshire committeemen:

For the Honourable William Lenthall, Esquire, Speaker of the Commons House of Parliament: These

NOBLE SIR,

We, having solicited a conjunction of forces towards the raising of the siege of Gainsborough, did appoint a general rendezvous at North Scarle to be upon Thursday the 27th of July. To the which place Sir John Meldrum with about three-hundred horse and dragoons, and Colonel Cromwell with about six or seven troops of horse and about one-hundred dragoons, came. With these they marched towards Gainsborough; and meeting with a good party of the enemy about a mile from the town, beat them back; but not with any commendations to our dragooners. We advanced still towards the enemy, all along under the Cony-Warren, which is upon a high hill above Gainsborough. The Lincoln troops had the van, two North-

[110] Mentioned in Suffolk Committee to Essex Committee, July 27, in *Hist. Mss. Comm. Rept.* 7, App. p. 556. (Barrington Mss).

[111] Firth and Rait, *Acts and Ordinances*, i, 215–219.

ampton, and three small troops of Nottingham the battle, and Colonel Cromwell the rear; the enemy in the mean time with his body keeping the top of the hill.

Some of the Lincoln troops began to advance up the hill; which were opposed by a force of the enemy; but our men repelled them, until all our whole body was got up the hill. The enemy kept his ground; which he chose for his best advantage, with a body of horse of about three regiments of horse, and a reserve behind them consisting of General Cavendish his regiment, which was a very full regiment. We presently put our horse in order; which we could hardly do by reason of the cony-holes and the difficult ascent up the hill, the enemy being within musket-shot of us, and advancing towards us before we could get ourselves into any good order. But with those troops we could get up, we charged the greater body of the enemy, came up to the sword's point, and disputed it so a little with them, that our men pressing heavily upon them, they could not bear it, but all their body ran away, some on the one side of their reserve, others on the other. Divers of our troops pursuing had the chase about six miles.

General Cavendish with his regiment standing firm all the while, and facing some of our troops that did not follow the chase, Colonel Cromwell with his Major Whalley and one or two troops more, were following the chase, and were in the rear of that regiment. When they saw the body stand unbroken [they] endeavoured, with much ado, to get into a body those three or four troops which were divided, which when they had done,—perceiving the enemy to charge two or three of the Lincoln scattered troops, and making them retire by reason of their being many more than they in number, and the rest being elsewhere engaged and following the chase,—Colonel Cromwell with his three troops followed them in the rear, brake this regiment, and forced their general, with divers of their men, into a quagmire in the bottom of the hill, where one of Colonel Cromwell's men cut him[112] on the head, by reason whereof he fell off his horse; and his[113] Captain-Lieutenant thrust him into the side, whereof within two hours he died, the rest chasing the regiment quite out of the field, having execution of them, so that the field was left wholly unto us, not a man appearing. Upon this, divers of our men went into the town, carrying in to my Lord Willoughby some of the ammunition we brought for him, believing our work was all at an end saving to take care how to bring further provisions into the town to enable it to stand a siege in case my Lord Newcastle should draw up with his army to attempt it.

Whilst we were considering of these things, word was brought us that there was a small remainder of the enemy's force not yet meddled with beyond Gainsborough, with some foot and two pieces of ordnance. We having no foot, desired to have some out of the town, which my Lord Willoughby granted, and sent us about six-hundred foot. With these we advanced towards the enemy. When we came thither to the top of the hill, we beat divers troops of the enemy's horse back, but at the bottom we saw a regiment of foot; after that another (my Lord Newcastle's own regiment consisting of nineteen colours) appearing also and many horse, which indeed was his army. Seeing these there so unexpectedly we advised what to do.

[112] General Cavendish.

[113] That is Cromwell's captain-lieutenant, James Berry, later the Major-General Berry of the Protectorate.

Colonel Cromwell was sent to command the foot to retire, and to draw off the horse. By the time he came to them, the enemy was marching up the hill. The foot did retire disorderly into the town which was not much above a quarter of a mile from them, upon whom the enemy's horse did some small execution. The horse also did retire in some disorder about half a mile, until they came to the end of a field where a passage was, where, by the endeavour of Colonel Cromwell, Major Whalley, and Captain Ayscoghe, a body was drawn up. With these we faced[114] the enemy, stayed their pursuit, and opposed them with about four troops of Colonel Cromwell's and four Lincoln troops, the enemy's body in the mean time increasing very much from the army. But such was the goodness of God, giving courage and valour to our men and officers, that whilst Major Whalley and Captain Ayscoghe, sometimes the one with four troops faced the enemy, sometimes the other, to the exceeding glory of God be it spoken, and the great honour of those two gentlemen, they with this handful forced the enemy so and dared them to their teeth in at least eight or nine several removes, the enemy following at their heels; and they, though their horses were exceedingly tired, retreated in this order, near carbine-shot of the enemy, who thus followed them, firing upon them; Colonel Cromwell gathering up the main body and facing them behind those two lesser bodies, that, in despite of the enemy we brought off our horse in this order without the loss of two men.

Thus have you a true relation of this notable service, wherein God is to have all the glory. And care must be taken speedily to relieve this noble Lord from his and the state's enemies by a speedy force sent unto us, and that without delay, or else he will be lost, and that important town, and all those parts, and way made for this army instantly to advance into the south. Thus resting upon your care in speeding present succours hither, we humbly take our leaves, and remain,

Your humble servants,
Edw. Ayscoghe.
Oliver Cromwell.
Jo. Broxholme.[115]

Lincoln,
July 29th, 1643,
(six o'clock at night).

Gainsborough temporarily relieved, Cromwell made what haste he could back to Huntingdon, and the second letter concerning their activities after leaving Burghley House is Cromwell's own, written on his march thither. The surname of "Sir John" to whom the letter is addressed was effectively crossed out, but Carlyle suggests that it was Sir John Wray. A member for Lincolnshire and on the Committee for that county, his home, Glentworth House, says Carlyle, "is almost within sight and sound of these transactions." His "noble kinsman" was probably the second Earl of Manchester, first cousin to Sir John,[116] and ten days later, commander of the armies of the Eastern Association.[117]

[114] "Forced" in Ms.
[115] *Tanner Mss*, lxii, 194; and *Baker Mss*, xxviii, 434; printed in Carlyle, App. 5.
[116] Burke's *Peerage*, and G. E. C., *Complete Baronetage*.
[117] *C. J.*, iii, 199; *L. J.*, vi, 174.

To my noble Friend Sir John [Wray,] Knight and Baronet: Present these

SIR,

The particular respects I have received at your hands do much oblige me, but the great affection you bear to the public much more. For that cause I am bold to acquaint you with some late passages wherein it hath pleased God to favour us, which, I am assured, will be welcome to you.

After Burlye House was taken, we went towards Gainsbrowe to a general rendezvous, where met us Lincolnshire troops; so that we were nineteen or twenty troops, when we were together, of horse and about three or four troops of dragooners. We marched with this force to Gainsbrowe. Upon Friday morning, being the 28th day of July, we met with a forlorn-hope of the enemy, and with our men brake it in. We marched on to the town's end. The enemy being upon the top of a very steep hill over our heads, some of our men attempted to march up that hill; the enemy opposed; our men drove them up and forced their passage. By that time we came up, we saw the enemy well set in two bodies, the foremost a large fair body, the other a reserve consisting of six or seven brave troops. Before we could get our force into order, the great body of the enemy advanced; they were within musket-shot of us when we came to the pitch of the hill. We advanced likewise towards them; and both charged, each upon the other. Thus advancing, we came to pistol and sword's point, both in that close order that it was disputed very strongly who should break the other; but our men pressing a little heavily upon them, they began to give back, which our men perceiving, instantly forced them; brake that whole body, some of them flying on this side, some on the other side, of the reserve. Our men, pursuing them in great disorder, had the execution about four, or some say six miles, with much ado. This done, and all their force being gone, not one man standing but all beaten out of the field, we drew up our body together and kept the field, the half of our men being well worn in the chase of the enemy.

Upon this we endeavoured the business we came for, which was the relief of the town with ammunition. We sent in some powder, which was the great want of that town; which done, word was brought us that the enemy had about six troops of horse, and three-hundred foot, a little on the other side of the town. Upon this we drew some musketeers out of the town and with our body of horse marched towards them. We saw two troops towards the mill, which my men drove down into a little village at the bottom of the hill. When we came with our horse to the top of that hill we saw in the bottom a whole regiment of foot, after that another and another, and, as some counted, about fifty colours of foot, with a great body of horse, which indeed was my Lord Newcastle's army, with which he now besieges Gainsbrowe.

My Lord Willoughby commanded me to bring off the foot and horse, which I endeavoured; but the foot (the enemy pressing on with the army) retreated in some disorder into the town, being of that garrison. Our horse also, being wearied, and unexpectedly pressed by this new force so great, gave off, not being able to brave the charge. But with some difficulty we got our horse into a body, and with them faced the enemy and retreated in such order that though the enemy followed hard, yet they were not able to disorder us, but we got them off safe to Lincoln from this fresh force, and lost not one man. The honour of this retreat, equal to any of late times, is due to Major Whalley and Captain Ascough, next under God.

This relation I offer you for the honour of God, to whom be all the praise, as also to let you know you have some servants faithful to you to incite to action. I beseech you let this good success quicken your continuing to this engagement; it's great evidence of God's favour; let not your business be starved. I know, if all be of your mind, we shall have an honourable return; it's your own business. A reasonable strength now raised speedily may do that which much more will not do after some time. Undoubtedly, if they succeed here, you will see them in the bowels of your Association. For the time, you will have it from your noble kinsman and Colonel Palgrave. If we be not able in ten days to relieve Gainsbrowe a noble Lord will be lost, many good foot, and a considerable pass over Trent into these parts. The Lord prosper your endeavours and ours. I beseech you present my humble service to the high honourable lady. Sir, I am

Your faithful servant,

[Stamford?]
July 30th, 1643. OLIVER CROMWELL.

[P.S.] I stayed two of my own troops, and my Major stayed his—in all three. There were in front of the enemy's reserve three or four of the Lincoln troops yet unbroken. The enemy charged those troops, utterly broke and chased them, so that none of the troops on our part stood but my three. Whilst the enemy was following our flying troops I charged him on the rear with my three troops, drove him down the hill, brake him all to pieces, forced Lieutenant-General Cavendish into a bog, who fought in this reserve. One officer cut him on the head and, as he lay, my Captain-Lieutenant Berry thrust him into the short ribs, of which he died, about two hours after, in Gainsbrowe.[118]

The third letter describing Gainsborough is addressed to the Deputy Lieutenants of Suffolk:[119]

To my noble Friends, Sir Edmon Bacon, Knight and Baronet, Sir William Springe, Knight and Baronet, Sir Thomas Bernardiston, Knight, Maurice Barrowe, Esquire: Present these

GENTLEMEN,

No man desires more to present you with encouragements than myself, because of the forwardness I find in you (to your honour be it spoken) to promote this great cause. And truly God follows you with encouragements, who is the God of blessings. And I beseech you let Him not lose His blessings upon us. They come in season, and with all the advan-

[118] Pr. in *Norfolk Arch. Soc. Papers*, ii, 45–50 (1848), from the original then in the possession of Dawson Turner, Esq., of Great Yarmouth. Carlyle, App. 5.

[119] A letter, identical with this except for the omission of the first paragraph and most of the last, is printed in Rushworth, Vicars, a pamphlet, and in contemporary newspapers, and said to be to the Committee at Cambridge. It may be that a similar letter (omitting the passages specially meant for the Suffolk Committee) was sent to Cambridge.

tages of heartening. As if God should say, "Up and be doing, and I will help you and stand by you," there is nothing to be feared but our own sin and sloth.

It hath pleased the Lord to give your servant and soldiers a notable victory now at Gainsborough. I marched after the taking of Burlye House upon Wednesday to Grantham, where met me about 300 horse and dragoons of Nottingham. With these, by agreement with the Lincolners we met at North Scarle, which is about ten miles from Gainsbrowe, upon Thursday in the evening, where we tarried until two of the clock in the morning, and then with our whole body advanced towards Gainsbrowe.

About a mile and a half from the town, we met a forlorn-hope of the enemy of near 100 horse. Our dragoons laboured to beat them back; but not alighting off their horses, the enemy charged them, and beat some four or five of them off their horses. Our horse charged them, and made them retire unto their main body. We advanced, and came to the bottom of a steep hill, upon which the enemy stood; we could not well get up but by some tracts, which our men assaying to do, a body of the enemy endeavoured to hinder; wherein we prevailed, and got the top of the hill. This was done by the Lincolners, who had the vantguard.

When we all recovered the top of the hill, we saw a great body of the enemy's horse facing of us, at about musket-shot or less distance, and a good reserve of a full regiment of horse behind it. We endeavoured to put our men into as good order as we could, the enemy in the mean time advancing towards us, to take us at disadvantage; but in such order as we were, we charged their great body, I having the right wing. We came up horse to horse, where we disputed it with our swords and pistols a pretty time, all keeping close order, so that one could not break the other. At last, they a little shrinking, our men perceiving it, pressed in upon them, and immediately routed this whole body, some flying on one side, others on the other of the enemy's reserve; and our men, pursuing them, had chase and execution about five or six miles.

I, perceiving this body which was the reserve standing still unbroken, kept back my major, Whaley, from the chase, and with my own troop and one other of my regiment, in all being three troops, we got into a body. In this reserve stood General Cavendish, who one while faced me, another while faced four of the Lincoln troops, which were all of ours that stood upon the place, the rest being engaged in the chase. At last the General charged the Lincolners, and routed them. I immediately fell on his rear with my three troops, which did so astonish him, that he gave over the chase, and would fain have delivered himself from me, but I pressing on forced them down a hill, having good execution of them, and below the hill, drove the General with some of his soldiers into a quagmire, where my captain-lieutenant slew him with a thrust under his short ribs. The rest of the body was wholly routed, not one man staying upon the place.

We then, after this defeat which was so total, relieved the town with such powder and provisions as we brought, which done, we had notice that there were six troops of horse and 300 foot on the other side of the town, about a mile off us. We desired some foot of my Lord Willoughby, about 400; and, with our horse and these foot, marched towards them. When we came towards the place where their horse stood, we beat back with my troops about two or three troops of the enemy, who retired into a small village at the bottom of the hill. When we recovered the hill, we saw in the bottom, about a quarter of a mile from us, a regiment of foot; after that another; after that Newcastle's own regiment, consisting in all of about 50 foot colours, and a great body of horse, which indeed was Newcastle's army, which, coming so unexpectedly, put us to new consultations. My Lord Willoughby and I, being in the town, agreed to call off our foot. I went to bring them off, but before I returned, divers of the foot were engaged. The enemy advancing with his whole body, our foot retreated in some disorder, and with some loss got the town; where now they are. Our horse also came off with some trouble, being wearied with this long fight, and their horses tired; yet faced the enemy's fresh horses, and by several removes got off without the loss of one man, the enemy following in the rear with a great body. The honour of this retreat is due to God, as also all the rest. Major Whaley did in this carry himself with all gallantry becoming a gentleman and a Christian.

Thus have you this true relation, as short as I could. What you are to do upon it, is next to be considered. If I could speak words to pierce your hearts with the sense of our and your condition, I would. If you will raise 2,000 foot at the present to encounter this army of Newcastle's, to raise the siege, and to enable us to fight him, we doubt not, by the grace of God, but that we shall be able to relieve the town, and beat the enemy on the other side Trent;—whereas if somewhat be not done in this, you will see Newcastle's army march up into your bowels; being now, as it is, on this side Trent. I know it will be difficult to raise thus many in so short time; but let me assure you, it's necessary, and therefore to be done. At least do what you may, with all possible expedition. I would I had the happiness to speak with one of you. Truly I cannot come over, but must attend my charge; our enemy is vigilant. The Lord direct you what to do.

Gentlemen, I am
Huntingdon, Your faithful servant,
July 31st, 1643. OLIVER CROMWELL.

[P.S.] Give this gentleman credence; he is worthy to be trusted. He knows the urgency of our affairs better than myself. If he give you intelligence, in point of time, of haste to be made, believe him; he will advise for your good.[120]

HUNTINGDON, PETERBOROUGH AND CAMBRIDGE, AUGUST, 1643

Extraordinary as was the exploit of Cromwell, Whalley and Ayscough and brave as were Cromwell's words, the fact was that he was back in Huntingdon and by the time his letters were received Gainsborough had fallen before Newcastle's conquering advance.

[120] *Norfolk Arch. Soc. Papers*, ii, 51–54, from the original, then in the possession of Dawson Turner, Esq., Great Yarmouth, and later in the collection of Alfred Morrison. It was sold in 1917 and a year later offered for sale, with facs. of the beginning and end of the letter, for 350 l., in Maggs Catalogue, no. 365, p. 66 (1918). Carlyle XII Cp. Rushworth, v, 278; Vicars, *God's Ark*, pp. 8–10; *The copy of a letter written by Colonel Cromwell to the Committee at Cambridge* (1643).

Save for outlying posts the whole country as far south as Lincoln and beyond, like the north and west, seemed all but lost to Parliament. There remained only Essex and Cromwell to oppose the King and Newcastle who were closing in on the Eastern Association and the capital; and there was profound dissatisfaction with Essex which it took all Pym's authority to repress. Already that leader had taken steps to remedy the situation and by the time Cromwell arrived in Huntingdon he was no doubt aware of the new post assigned to him. On July 24 the Houses had asked the committee for "the six associated counties" of the Eastern Association to consider placing a governor over the Isle of Ely. It was in itself a counsel of despair, for with its single approach by land, it could conceivably, if worst came to worst, be used as it had often been before, as an impregnable retreat from an overwhelming enemy. After four days of deliberation the Commons voted to ask Essex to commission Cromwell as governor of the Isle of Ely.[121]

To this they added two other measures of defence. The day Cromwell reached Huntingdon the Parliament had news of Gainsborough and promptly despatched fresh forces to reinforce Willoughby, meanwhile appointing three members to attend to sending Cromwell a shipment of arms for 1,000 foot and 500 horse which had been seized in an attempt to smuggle them into England from Denmark for the royal troops.[122] At the same time the Eastern Association was ordered to consider raising money for Cromwell's men; and that the need was urgent is revealed in his letter to the Deputy Lieutenants of Essex. They had ignored his letter to them two months earlier and as the Mayor of Nottingham who had supplied the necessary funds at that time was apparently pressing for repayment, Cromwell again appealed for men and money for the cause:

For my Loving Friends the Deputy Lieutenants of the County of Essex

GENTLEMEN,

The time I was absent from Nottingham, this bearer was forced to borrow of the Mayor of Nottingham 100 l. for the payment of the three companies belonging to your counties, besides shoes, stockings, shirts and billet-money, which I promised should be repaid. I receiving no money out of your counties wherewithal to do it, I can but refer it to your considerations, for I think it is not expected that I should pay your soldiers out of my own purse. This is the sum of his desire who rests,

Your truly loving friend,

Huntingdon,
Aug. 1st, 1643.

OLIVER CROMWELL.

121 *C. J.*, iii, 180, 186.
122 *Ibid.*, 188.

[P.S.] I desire you would recruit your two companies and send them up with as much haste as may be, that they may help on in the public service.[123]

There was more enthusiasm elsewhere. The day after Cromwell reproached the Essex men for their lukewarmness, he wrote a letter—to whom we can not say for the address is gone from the original—accepting the generous offer of some "bachelors and maids" to raise and at least partially equip a company. This is obviously the "Maiden Troop" noted by a Royalist newspaper,[124] presently incorporated into Cromwell's regiment as the eleventh company, under the command of Captain Robert Swallow.[125] Within three weeks that "brave company of about 80 men" was in action.[126]

To ....

Sir,

I understand by these gentlemen the good affections of your men and maids, for which God is to be praised.

I approve of the business; only I desire to advise you that your foot company may be turned into a troop of horse; which indeed will (by God's blessing) far more advantage the cause than two or three foot companies; especially if your men be honest godly men, which by all means I desire. I thank God for stirring up the youth to cast in their mite, which I desire maybe employed to the best advantage; therefore my advice is, that you would employ your twelve-score horses; for 400 l. more will not raise a troop of horse. As for the muskets that are bought, I think the country will take them of you. Pray raise honest godly men, and I will have them of my regiment. As for officers, I leave it as God shall or hath directed to choose, and rest,

Your loving friend,

[Huntingdon,]
August 2nd, 1643.

Oliver Cromwell.[127]

His regiment was now nearly complete. To its original five companies had been added a sixth commanded by Captain Ayres; a seventh first under Captain Patterson then under Captain Horsman; an eighth under Captain Grove; a ninth under Captain Samuel Porter; a tenth under Captain Adam Lawrence; now an eleventh under Captain Swallow. To these were added presently a twelfth composed chiefly of Anabaptists and Levellers under Captain Christopher Bethell; while the thirteenth, raised by its captain Ralph

[123] Barrington Papers, *Egerton Mss*, 2643, p. 11. Calendared in *Hist. Mss. Comm. Rept.* 7, App. p. 557 (*Lowndes Mss*). Pr. in Lomas-Carlyle, Supp. 4. Signed only, by Cromwell. Cf. his letter of May 28th.

[124] *Mercurius Aulicus*, Aug. 3, 1643.

[125] Firth, "Raising of the Ironsides," *Royal Hist. Soc. Trans.*, xiii, 32.

[126] *Certain Informations*, Aug. 29. Quoted in Mason, *History of Norfolk*.

[127] Printed in *Fairfax Correspondence* (1849), iii, 56; thence Carlyle, Letter XIII. Original, formerly in the Upcott Collection, sold at auction in 1851. Partly printed in Puttick & Simpson's Catalogue, July 1851, which says it is signed only, by Cromwell.

Margery in Suffolk, was gladly taken over by Cromwell when the committee of that county expressed a desire to get rid of them; and the fourteenth, originally raised by Henry Ireton in Nottingham for Sir Francis Thornhaugh's regiment, became part of the garrison of Ely soon after Cromwell was made governor of that place[128] and Ireton himself was appointed deputy commander of Ely.

Cromwell's regiment was thus gradually enlarged with dependable fighting men, but money was needed as well as men. He had sent many letters to the various counties in the Association, begging, pleading, even demanding support, with no result; so he finally resolved to appeal to Parliament. The House of Commons, in consequence, ordered on August 4, not only that the £3,000 already levied in the Associated counties for him be sent for the pay of his forces, but they gave an order for 2,000 additional men to be raised, with a month's pay for each.[129] On the same day the Speaker sent him a letter:

> "The House hath taken into consideration your letter; they have commanded me to send you these enclosed orders, and to lett you know that nothing is more repugnant to the opinion and sence of this house, and dangerous to the kingdome, then the unwillingnesse of their forces to march out of their severall countys; they hope now the miserys of other places will be a warning to the Association. . . . For your selfe, as they doe exceedingly approve of your faythfull endevours for god and the kingdome, soe they have commanded mee to assure you that noe power they have shall be wanting to improve the good affections of these Associated countys."[130]

Nor was this the only relief that was sent to the threatened districts and its commander at this crisis. It was generally recognized that if the eastern counties were lost, the cause of Parliament was certain to go down, and Pym's party bestirred itself to save the situation, urging local authorities to give what aid they could.

The Deputy Lieutenants of Essex sent a sum of money to Cambridge, possibly in response to Cromwell's letter of August 1, more probably as a result of one from William Lenthall, Speaker of the Commons,[131] informing them of an order for £6,000 and 2,000 soldiers to be raised in the Eastern Association for the forces with Cromwell, and advising them that their proportion was 480 men and £720. The Committee at Cambridge wrote to them on August 1,[132] reminding them of the Parliament's order, with a postscript by Sir Anthony Irby and Miles Corbett, who had been sent to Cambridge by Parliament

[128] Firth, "Raising of the Ironsides," *loc. cit.*, pp. 29–35.
[129] *C. J.*, iii, 193.
[130] Letter pr. in Firth, "Raising of the Ironsides," *loc. cit.*, App. III, from *Tanner Mss*, lxii, 224.
[131] Printed in *Hist. Mss. Comm. Rept.* 7, App. p. 556 (*Lowndes Mss*). Cp. *C. J.*, iii, 179.
[132] *Hist. Mss. Comm. Rept.* 7, App. p. 557.

on July 31 to see that forces were rushed to Gainsborough.[133] It would appear from the following letter that a disagreement had arisen as to the purpose for which the money was sent and Cromwell, sure that it was intended for him, wished to have the doubt removed:

To my Honoured Friends the Deputy Lieutenants of the County of Essex:

GENTLEMEN,

I being at Cambridge, and meeting there with some moneys which came from you, some doubt was made whether that money was intended to be your proportion of the 3000 l. assigned me by the House of Commons towards the payment of my troops. If it be in pursuance of their order, I beseech you send word. Your letters make it clear to me, but yet because doubt is made thereof, none being able to resolve it better than you, I should be very glad to have it from yourselves; and rest,

Your humble servant,

August 4th, 1643. OLIVER CROMWELL.[134]

He had need of all the help that could be given him. He had sent reinforcements back to Gainsborough, but, learning that Lord Willoughby had surrendered the town to Newcastle, they retired with Sir John Meldrum to Lincoln,[135] and Cromwell presently received from Willoughby, now in Boston, a letter so alarming that he had copies made and enclosed them in letters to the Commissioners at Cambridge, and to the Deputy Lieutenants of Suffolk, Norfolk, and Essex. Willoughby's letter and Cromwell's appeal to Cambridge and Essex for reinforcements, without which he believed the enemy could not be checked and the road would soon be clear to London, clearly reveal the fear of a Royalist advance and the consequent collapse of the Association unless help were forthcoming at once:

"*To Colonel Cromwell*

"NOBLE SIR,

"Since the business of Gainsborough, the hearts of our menn have been so deaded, as we have lost most of them by running away, so as we are forced to leave Lincoln on a sudden, and if I had not done it, then I should have been left alone in it. So as now I am at Boston, where we are but very poor in strength, so as without some speedy supply I fear we shall not hold this long neither.

133 *C. J.*, iii, 188.

134 Calendared in *Hist. Mss. Comm. Rept.* 7, App., p. 558. Now in Barrington Papers, *Egerton Mss.* (British Museum), 2643, p. 15. Printed in Lomas-Carlyle, Supp. 4. Underwritten are letters from Captain William Harlackenden and Miles Corbett, both members of the Cambridge committee, urging them to send money and recruits and to return all runaways.

135 Cf. Willoughby to House of Lords, Aug. 1, in Firth, "Raising of the Ironsides," *loc. cit.*, pp. 69–71.

"My Lord General I perceive hath writ to you to draw all your forces together. I should be glad to see it; for if that will not be, there can be no good expected. If you will stop my Lord Newcastle, you must presently draw them to him and fight um; for without we be master of the field we shall all be pulled out by the ears one after another.

"The foot, if they come up, may march very securely to Boston, which, to me, will be very considerable to your association, for if they get that town, which is now very weak for defence for want of men, I believe they will not be long out of Norfolk and Suffolk.

"I can say no more but desire you to hasten, and rest,

"Boston, Aug. 5th, 1643. "FRANCIS WILLOWBY."[136]

To the Commissioners at Cambridge

GENTLEMEN,

You see by this enclosed how sadly your affairs stand. It's no longer disputing, but out instantly all you can. Raise all your bands; send them to Huntingdon; get up what volunteers you can; hasten your horses.

Send these letters to Suffolk, Norfolk and Essex, without delay. I beseech you spare not, but be expeditious and industrious. Almost all our foot have quitted Stamford; there is nothing to interrupt an enemy, but our horse, that is considerable. You must act lively; do it without distraction. Neglect no means. I am

Your faithful servant,

Huntingdon, ye 6th of
August, 1643. OLIVER CROMWELL.[137]

To the Deputy Lieutenants of Essex: These, haste, haste, posthaste

GENTLEMEN,

You see by this enclosed, the necessity of going out of our old pace. You sent indeed your part of the 2,000 foot, but when they came, they as soon returned. Is this the way to save a kingdom? Where is the doctrine of some of your county concerning the trained bands and other forces not going out the Association?

I wish your forces may be ready to meet with the enemy when he is in the Association. Haste what you can; not your part only of 2,000 foot, but I hope 2,000 foot at least. Lord Newcastle will advance into your bowels. Better join when others will join and can join with you, than stay till all be lost; hasten to our help. The enemy in all probability will be in our bowels else in ten days; his army is powerful. See your men come, and some of your gentlemen and ministers come along with them, that so they may be de-

[136] The original was apparently enclosed with the letter to Essex and is now, with Cromwell's letter, in the Barrington Mss, *Egerton*, 2647, f. 120. Printed in *Hist. Mss. Comm. Rept.* 7, App. p. 558. Copies are in *Baker Mss.* in Cambridge University Library, and *Tanner Mss,* the latter apparently the one sent to the Commissioners at Cambridge. Carlyle, before Letter XIV. "um" in *H. M. C. Rept.* = "him" or "them."

[137] *Tanner Mss*, lxii, 229 (copy); printed in Cooper, *Annals of Cambridge,* iii, 355; from *Baker Mss*, xxxiv, 429; thence Carlyle, Letter XIV.

livered over to those shall command them; otherwise they will return at pleasure. If we have them at our army we can keep them.

From your faithful servant,

August 6th, eleven of
the clock, 1643. OLIVER CROMWELL.[138]

With no one else to assume the responsibility of organizing the poorly equipped, inadequate number of troops to meet the threatened Royalist invasion of the eastern counties, the next two days were busy ones for Cromwell. He had a reply to his last letter to the Committee at Cambridge,—not a very encouraging one, judging from his next appeal to the same Committee, written from Peterborough:

To my honoured Friends the Commissioners at Cambridge: These present

GENTLEMEN,

Finding our foot much lessened at Stamford, and having a great train and many carriages, I held it not safe to continue there, but presently after my return from you, I ordered the foot to quit that place and march into Holland; which they did on Monday last.[139] I was rather induced so to do because of the letter I received from my Lord Willowby, a copy whereof I sent you.

I am now at Peterborough, whither I came this afternoon. I was no sooner come but Lieutenant Colonel Wood sent me word from Spalding that the enemy was marching, with twelve flying colours of horse and foot, within a mile of Swinstead; so that I hope it was a good providence of God that our foot were at Spalding.

It much concerns your Association and the Kingdom that so strong a place as Holland is be not possessed by them. If you have any foot ready to march, send them away to us with all speed. I fear lest the enemy should press in upon our foot, he being thus far advanced towards you. I hold it very fit that you should hasten your horse at Huntingdon, and what you can speedily raise at Cambridge, unto me. I dare not go into Holland with my horse lest the enemy should advance with his whole body of horse this way into your Association; but am ready, endeavouring my Lord Grey's and the Northamptonshire horse to me, that so, if we be able, we may fight the enemy or retreat unto you with our whole strength. I beseech you hasten your levies what you can, especially those of foot. Quicken all our friends with new letters upon this occasion, which I believe you will find to be a true alarm. The particulars I hope to be able to inform you speedily of more punctually, having sent in all haste to Colonel Wood for that purpose.

The money I brought with me is so poor a pittance when it comes to be

[138] Barrington Papers, *Egerton Mss*, 2643, p. 17; calendared *Hist. Mss. Comm. Rept.* 7, App. p. 558. Lomas-Carlyle, Supp. 4.

[139] "Yesterday," in other words. On Aug. 8, Parliament voted to send Cromwell an order to send men from his regiment (to be replaced by others) for the defence of Boston. They voted also to send about 500 muskets from the Danish ship, and the next day ordered 100 pikes, 60 clubs and 30 barrels of powder sent to Cromwell in Ely. *C. J.*, iii, 198, 199.

distributed amongst all my troops that, considering their necessity, it will not half clothe them, they were so far behind. If we have not more money speedily they will be exceedingly discouraged. I am sorry you put me to it to write thus often. It makes it seem a needless importunity in me; whereas, in truth, it is a constant neglect of those that should provide for us. Gentlemen, make them able to live and subsist that are willing to spend their blood for you. I say no more, but rest,

Your faithful servant,

August 8th, 1643.

OLIVER CROMWELL.[140]

THE COVENANT AND NEWBURY, SEPTEMBER, 1643

There was every reason for Cromwell's anxiety and his activity. The Parliament's situation was all but desperate and Cromwell was one of the few commanders on whom it could rely. Save for a few places like Hull, Plymouth and Gloucester, the west and north were virtually lost. Pym's party was reduced nominally to the fifteen counties for which they legislated and actually to scarcely more than the six of the Eastern Association, to which were added the capital and presently Lincoln. There was grave dissatisfaction in Kent which soon broke into open mutiny. Of the handful of peers remaining, seven left their places in that House on the refusal of the Commons to concur with the Lords in new peace proposals. On August 9 five thousand women appeared in Westminster with a petition for peace and were not dispersed without bloodshed. The Houses quarrelled over their respective rights, and the attendance in them sank so low that sequestration of their estates was invoked against members "wilfully" absent from the City or Westminster. Every step was taken to save the situation. Weekly assessments were laid upon the counties still within the power of Parliament, with the duty of impressment of men for the armies. Cromwell was named to the committee to enforce the ordinance, of which seven members or more were ordered to meet at Cambridge "or any other frontier town of the Association."[141] Dragoons were ordered to be raised in Essex; and on August 16 as rebellion broke out in Kent, it was voted to raise twenty thousand men in the Associated counties, Norwich and Ely. The next day a covenant was ordained for London and "the lines of communication," with an oath abjuring papal supremacy and avowing that "salvation cannot be merited by works."

The forces of the Eastern Association were almost the only troops to be depended upon. Essex was at Aylesbury with scarcely more

[140] *Fairfax Correspondence*, iii, 58; thence Carlyle, Letter XV. Original, signed by Cromwell, was in the Upcott Collection until it was sold at auction. Partly printed in Puttick & Simpson's catalogue, July 1851.

[141] Firth & Rait, *Acts and Ordinances*, i, 223.

than 3,000 foot and 2,500 horse fit for service. Yet propositions of the peace party in the House of Lords had been rejected by the Commons on August 7, and on August 10 the ordinance organizing the Eastern Counties Association was passed with Manchester as "Serjeant Major of the Associated Counties" and Cromwell as one of his four colonels of horse and a member of the Cambridge and Huntingdon committees.[142]

In this desperate situation of affairs Pym's party sought aid elsewhere. On August 7 commissioners from the Houses arrived in Edinburgh to seek assistance from the Scots. The two lords appointed had refused to serve; and four commoners, headed by the younger Vane, with two ministers—the Presbyterian Stephen Marshall and his son-in-law, Philip Nye, an "Independent"—presently agreed on a Solemn League and Covenant between the two nations. Ratified on August 17, the day that Charles returned from Oxford to the siege of Gloucester, which he had summoned on the 10th, it agreed to the preservation of the Church of Scotland and the reformation of the Church of England, the abolition of episcopacy, the independence of the two parliaments and the bringing to justice of "incendiaries and malignants." To this was added a treaty by which the Scots agreed to furnish an army to their new allies in return for a monthly payment of £30,000 with a down payment of £100,000. It was a desperate remedy for a desperate disease. To those who opposed the introduction of a foreign force and an alien church, and pointed out that this had been one of the main charges against Charles, Pym had his answer ready. The church, he said, was like a sick man who saw a murderer approaching and must either 'cast away his medicine and betake himself to the sword, or take his medicine and suffer himself to be killed.'

The Solemn League and Covenant reached Westminster on August 26 and was immediately forwarded to the Assembly of Divines. Meanwhile the army had begun to move to relieve Colonel Massey in Gloucester, aided by an ordinance passed three days earlier for the assistance of Essex, and accompanied by another authorizing the destruction of "monuments of superstition and idolatry." Two thousand recruits and six regiments of London trained bands were authorized for the enterprise and a compulsory loan levied on the capital to support this force. The citizens of London were exhorted to strain every nerve in this great crisis; the shops were closed, the churches opened. On August 22 Essex reviewed his army on Hounslow Heath; within a week he found himself at the head of 15,000

[142] Firth & Rait, *Acts and Ordinances*, i, 242.

men and by the first of September he had swept round Oxford and by the 8th he had forced the Royalist army to raise the siege.

To his aid had been summoned every man available. On August 28 Cromwell, then at Cambridge, had received an order from Essex by way of Huntingdon to advance with his horse and dragoons to join the main army at Brackley in Northamptonshire on the 29th.[143] Presumably he sent a considerable force to the rendezvous, but he himself remained in Cambridge, absorbed in the defence of the eastern counties,[144] for on that day he signed two letters demanding more troops and supplies:

To Sir Thomas Barrington and the rest of the Deputy Lieutenants of Essex

Divers of your companies arriving here at Cambridge made demand of us of arms, and as they inform us by your directions, which we believe to be a mistake . . . We beseech you therefore to give us some speedy and certain order for the supply of this want that so they may be fit for action.

	W. Rowe.	William Harlakenden.
	Oliver Cromwell.	T. Winche.
	Tho. Martyn.	Tho. Duckett.
	Ralph Freman.	Henry Meautys.
Aug. 29, 1643.		Edm. Harvey.[145]

To my noble Friends the Deputy Lieutenants of the County of Essex: Present these

Gentlemen,

I thought it my duty to send unto you this order from my Lord of Manchester; you will see what it purports, and I beseech you to cause all your horse and dragoons immediately to repair to me to Huntingdon; this order of his Lordships bears date since any he sent you, and therefore supersedes them. Not doubting of your favour herein I take leave and rest,

Your most humble servant,

[Cambridge,]
August 29th, 1643. Oliver Cromwell.[146]

[143] William Harlakenden to Sir T. Barrington, Aug. 27, calendared, with the Barrington Papers, in *Hist. Mss. Comm. Rept.*, 7 App. p. 561.

[144] He was not alone in his fear for the Eastern Association. Sir W. Rowe, of the Committee at Cambridge wrote on Aug. 26, "For the dragooners under Major Moore, my Lord General having sent for some of Col Crumwell's company to go march with him to Glocester, 'tis conceived fit that they, as likewise all other so returned should rather be remitted for that service, as concurring with the same and safety of the whole association." *Hist. Mss Comm. Rept.* 7, App. p. 560.

[145] This is signed by the Committee at Cambridge. Calendared with the Barrington Papers, *loc. cit.*, p. 561. Printed as calendared.

[146] *Ibid.*

About the same time, probably the same day,[147] Cromwell wrote to the Suffolk Committee, telling them of the need for troops and for "godly honest" officers. Mr. Ralph Margery, the bearer of the letter, recruited his troop for the Suffolk Committee and later, upon that Committee's complaint of his not being a gentleman, was taken by Cromwell with his men as the thirteenth troop of the Ironsides.

To my noble Friends, Sir William Springe, Knight and Baronet, and Maurice Barrowe, Esquire, etc., Present these

GENTLEMEN,

I have been now two days at Cambridge, in expectation to hear the fruit of your endeavours in Suffolk towards the public assistance. Believe it, you will hear of a storm in few days. You have no infantry at all considerable; hasten your horses;—a few hours may undo you, neglected. I beseech you be careful what captains of horse you choose, what men be mounted; a few honest men are better than numbers. Some time they must have for exercise. If you choose godly honest men to be captains of horse, honest men will follow them, and they will be careful to mount such.

The King is exceeding strong in the West. If you be able to foil a force at the first coming of it, you will have reputation; and that is of great advantage in our affairs. God hath given it to our handful; let us endeavour to keep it. I had rather have a plain russet-coated captain that knows what he fights for, and loves what he knows, than that which you call a gentleman and is nothing else. I honour a gentleman that is so indeed.

I understand Mr. Margery hath honest men will follow him: if so, be pleased to make use of him. It much concerns your good to have conscientious men. I understand that there is an order for me to have 3,000*l.* out of the Association; and Essex hath sent their part, or near it. I assure you we need exceedingly. I hope to find your favour and respect. I protest, if it were for myself, I would not move you. This is all, from

[Cambridge, Your faithful servant,
August 29th, 1643.] OLIVER CROMWELL.

[P.S.] If you send such men as Essex hath sent, it will be to little purpose. Be pleased to take care of their march; and that such may come along with them as will be able to bring them to the main body; and then I doubt not but we shall keep them, and make good use of them. I beseech you, give countenance to Mr. Margery. Help him in raising this troop; let him not want your favour in whatsoever is needful for promoting this work; and command your servant. If he can raise the horses from malignants, let him have your warrant; it will be of special service.[148]

[147] His remark about the poor troops from Essex suggests that the letter was written at the same time as the two foregoing letters. On the 31st the Committee at Cambridge wrote that the Essex men were "in so naked a posture that to employ them were to murder them." Cromwell's signature does not appear on this letter, from which it may be inferred that he had left Cambridge. *Ibid.*, p. 561.

[148] *Norfolk Archaeol. Soc. Papers*, January 1848, pp. 59–60, from the original then in the possession of Dawson Turner. Carlyle, Letter XVI.

The relief of Gloucester after the gallant defence of Massey for the moment raised the spirits of Pym's party, and with the adoption of the Solemn League and Covenant and the promise of a Scotch army to offset the successes of Newcastle, their cause took on new strength. But the Royalists were scarcely less encouraged. Charles had raised the siege only to seek more favorable ground to fight Essex. Barnstaple and Bideford had been taken; the Parliamentary admiral Warwick had been beaten off in his attempt to relieve Exeter by sea; and though Plymouth, Lyme and Dartmouth still held out for Parliament, Bristol and Exeter had been lost, and it remained only to block Essex's way back to London to bring the cause of Parliament to the ground before Scotch aid arrived. In consequence Charles hastened to throw himself between Essex and the capital and by September 18 he reached Newbury where Essex endeavored to break through. There in a desperate day's fighting, with heavy losses on each side, including the heroic Falkland, Essex's army fought its way through, and four days later entered Reading.

LINCOLNSHIRE, SEPTEMBER, 1643

Indecisive in its results, the battle of Newbury not only saved London but it proved that with such equal forces Charles could not take the capital nor could Parliament conquer him. It proved scarcely less that neither side had as yet developed a great general nor a competent military organization. Yet each was in the making as Parliament was coming more and more to realize. For the moment it relied on Manchester and the Eastern Counties Association. There while the main army was busy in the west the chief concern was to hold back Newcastle. The center of operations for the time was Lincoln, and to that district it appears that on September 4 William Harlakenden of the committee at Cambridge "was with Colonel Cromwell at Ely for dinner to let him know by word of mouth Lord Manchester's pleasure that Essex forces should come, horse and dragoons, to Lincolnshire."[149]

To that Cromwell replied that he had sent away all his troops toward Lincoln and would himself start the next day, "for his scouts brought word of 8,000 of the Earl of Newcastle's forces appeared."[150] Newcastle's orders, "which I have seen, "wrote Fairfax, "were to go into Essex and block up London on that side,"[151] as Manchester's orders were to prevent this movement. But Newcastle was hampered

[149] Harlakendon to Barrington, Sept. 5, *Egerton Mss*, 2647, f. 229; *Hist. Mss Comm. Rept.* 7, App. p. 562.

[150] *Ibid.*

[151] Fairfax, "Short Memorial," in Maseres, *Tracts*, p. 431. Clarendon, *History*, vii, 177.

by the reluctance of his Yorkshiremen to leave their own county and the fear of leaving Hull in the rear. For six weeks, therefore, he had laid siege to Hull, while Manchester's first efforts were directed to the capture of Lynn. Lord Willoughby of Parham remained in Boston and to his aid Cromwell set out on September 5. Four days later news reached London that Lord Fairfax had sent sixteen troops of horse to join Cromwell at Boston,[152] and the next day Manchester was calling for more Essex men to help reduce Lynn, most of his horse and dragoons having been sent Cromwell to stop Newcastle.[153] Manchester's horse—a poor lot, wrote Cromwell, in comparison with his own "lovely company"—reached Boston, but more money was urgently needed, and in desperation he appealed for help to his cousin, "Mr. Solicitor":

To my honoured Friend Oliver St. John, Esquire, at Lincoln's Inn: These Present

SIR,

Of all men I should not trouble you with money matter, did not the heavy necessities my troops are in, press me beyond measure. I am neglected exceedingly!

I am now ready for my march towards the enemy; who hath entrenched himself over against Hull, my Lord Newcastle having besieged the town. Many of my Lord Manchester's troops are come to me: very bad and mutinous, not to be confided in; they paid to a week almost; mine no ways provided for to support them, except by the poor Sequestrations of the County of Hunt. My troops increase. I have a lovely company; you would respect them, did you know them. They are no Anabaptists, they are honest, sober Christians: they expect to be used as men.

If [I] took pleasure to write to the House in bitterness, I have occasion. [Of] the 3,000 l. allotted me, I cannot get the part of Norfolk nor Hertfordshire: it was gone before I had it.[154] I have minded your service to forgetfulness of my own and soldiers' necessities. I desire not to seek myself; I have little money of my own to help my soldiers. My estate is little. I tell you, the business of Ireland and England hath had of me, in money, between

[152] *Perfect Diurnall*, Sept. 8.

[153] Manchester to Deputy Lieuts. of Essex, Sept. 9, *Egerton Mss*, 2647, f. 241. *Hist. Mss. Comm. Rept.* 7, App. p. 563.

[154] In November 1643 the Norfolk Committee drew up a statement of money paid by them to the Association, to which the following account was appended:

Colonel Cromwell had of Sir Richard Berney, March 19..........	48 l.
Colonel Cromwell had of Mr. Heyward, March 25...............	20 l.
Wee paid Colonell Cromwell at Boston........................	500 l.
Colonel Cromwell received of Mr. Roger Castle, March 19.......	50 l.
Paid more to Col. Cromwell by Coll. Pagrave....................	50 l.
1643, May 22, to Col. Cromwell wch was sent by Major Sherwood..	400 l.

Tanner MSS. lxii, 348. In another account (*Tanner MSS.* lxvi, 1) the Committee mention a further payment made to Cromwell later, making a total of 1,068 l., although the items above total just that amount. Firth, *Raising of the Ironsides*, p. 48.

eleven and twelve hundred pounds; therefore my private can do little to help the public. You have had my money: I hope in God I desire to venture my skin. So do mine. Lay weight upon their patience; but break it not. Think of that which may be a real help. I believe [5,000 l. is due.][155]

If you lay aside the thought of me and my letter, I expect no help. Pray for

Your true friend and servant,

[Boston?]
Sept. 11th, [1643.] OLIVER CROMWELL.

[P.S.] There is no care taken how to maintain that force of horse and foot raised and a-raising by my Lord Manchester. He hath not one able to put on [that business.] The force will fall if some help not. Weak counsels and weak actings undo all. [Send at once or come][156] or all will be lost, if God help not. Remember who tells you.[157]

Money or no money, within a week, at the head of 5,000 horse and foot Cromwell marched north out of Boston to the relief of the Fairfaxes in Hull. Some of his troops, sent on ahead, appeared at Barton, on September 18, on the Lincolnshire side of the Humber, to meet twenty-one troops of horse from Hull, which crossed at every tide as fast as they could in the available boats.[158] Before Cromwell with the rest of his troops could reach them, however, Newcastle seems to have discovered his intention, for, some time between the 19th and the 23rd, Manchester, to whom Lynn was surrendered on September 16, received a letter from Cromwell and at once sent to him all the horse and foot he could spare:

To the Earl of Manchester

Sir Thomas Fairfax is landed in Lincolnshire, between Grimsby and Barton, and the enemy's forces are interposed between his and those of Fairfax. [Lincolnshire, c. Sept. 18, 1643.][159]

Cromwell's letter of September 28, to the Suffolk Committee, intimates that it was not long before he was able to join the Hull troops, but the enemy was on their heels, and his letter of the same date

[155] Erased. Precisely this amount was mentioned when Parliament talked about borrowing money for Manchester and Cromwell, on Sept. 1st. Cf. *Perfect Diurnall.*

[156] A portion of the margin has been torn away and what remains seems to be ". . . once or come, *etc.*"

[157] *Additional* (*Ayscough*) *Mss*, 5015, f. 6; copy in *Stowe Mss*, 154, f. 11. Pr. in *Annual Register*, xxxv, 358; Carlyle, Letter XVII. A facs. of this letter was published by Theodore Roosevelt, in his "Oliver Cromwell" in *Scribner's*, May, 1900, facing p. 541. It is said to be "to Sir E. Hartopp, . . . from the original manuscript hitherto unpublished, by permission of Sir Charles Hartopp, Bart." The facsimile was rightly omitted from Roosevelt's *Life of Cromwell*, when published in book form.

[158] Letter from Thos. May, Sept. 19, *True relation from Hull* (1643).

[159] Mentioned in Manchester's letter to the House of Lords, Sept. 23, House of Lords Mss, cal. in *Hist. Mss Comm. Rept.* 5, App. p. 107.

to the Committee at Cambridge tells of the narrow escape they had from being annihilated by Newcastle due to carelessness on the part of Lord Willoughby of Parham. By September 22, Cromwell was in Hull with a store of muskets and powder,[160] in time to take part in a day of fasting and humiliation. Lord Willoughby arrived the next day but their stay was short; on the 26th Sir Thomas Fairfax met them in Boston.[161]

Although this marked the beginning of the long and pleasant association of Cromwell with the man who was later to become Lord General, their first meeting was not cheerful. Cromwell's troops needed clothing and were behind in their pay, and Manchester's Essex men, mutinous from having been pressed against their will from the harvest fields, were not made more docile by the lack of their wages. Cromwell confidently expected to find that the Eastern counties had responded to the various pleas and orders from Parliament and the Committee at Cambridge. "He wept," wrote Harlakenden to Barrington, "when he came to Boston and found no moneys for him from Essex and other counties"; and "he says he regards money as little as any man, but for his troops if they have not money speedily they are in an undone condition. He says he wonders how I will be able to see the troops of horse and dragoons and have no money for them."[162] Moreover Cromwell complained bitterly of the conduct of Lord Willoughby's men in his letter quoted by Harlakenden:

To the Committee at Cambridge

Safely returned to Boston, he desires them to give God the praise of such a mercy; "for divers troops of Lord Willowby of Parham had an alarum from the enemy, Lord Newcastle's forces, that were and are returned into Lincolnshire. And all those troops did run away and gave no alarum to any of the rest of his forces." Urgently asks more aid from Cambridgeshire. Boston, Sept. 28, 1643.[163]

His next letter, to two members of the Suffolk Committee, is in the same strain:

[160] *Certain Informations.*

[161] Rushworth, *Historical Collections*, v, 280.

[162] Harlakenden to Barrington, Oct. 2, 1643. *Egerton Mss*, 2647, f. 296; *Hist. Mss. Comm. Rept.* 7, App. p. 565.

[163] Harlakenden to Barrington, Sept. 30, 1643, *loc. cit.*, p. 564. Harlakenden adds that there was a suspicion of treachery amongst Willoughby's regiment and a court martial is to be held. Cromwell later charged him with dereliction of duty in abandoning Gainsborough and Lincoln. D'Ewes *Diary*, quoted in S. R. Gardiner, *Civil War*, i, 304.

To my honoured Friends, Sir William Springe and Mr. Barrow: These present

GENTLEMEN,

It hath pleased God to bring off Sir Thomas Fairfax his horse over the river from Hull, being about one-and-twenty troops of horse and dragoons. The Lincolnshire horse laboured to hinder this work, being about thirty-four colours of horse and dragoons. We marched up to their landing-place, and the Lincolnshire horse retreated.

After they were come over, we all marched towards Holland; and when we came to our last quarter upon the edge of Holland, the enemy quartered within four miles of us and kept the field all night with his whole body. His intendment, as we conceive, was to fight us, or hoping to interpose betwixt us and our retreat, having received, to his thirty-four colours of horse, twenty fresh troops, ten companies of [dragoons;][164] and about a thousand foot, being General King's own regiment. With these he attempted our guards and our quarters, and, if God had not been merciful, had ruined us before we had known of it, the five troops we set to keep the watch failing much of their duty. But we got to horse, and retreated in good order, with the safety of all our Horse of the Association, not losing four of them that I hear of; and we got five of theirs. And for this we are exceedingly bound to the goodness of God, who brought our troops off with so little loss.

I write unto you to acquaint you with this the rather that God may be acknowledged, and that you may help forward, in sending such force away unto us as lie unprofitably in your country, and especially that troop of Captain Margery's, which surely would not be wanting, now we so much need it. The enemy may teach us that wisdom who is not wanting to himself in making up his best strength for the accomplishment of his designs.

I hear there hath been much exception taken to Captain Margery and his officers, for taking of horses. I am sorry you should discountenance those who (not to make benefit to themselves, but to serve their country) are willing to venture their lives, and to purchase to themselves the displeasure of bad men, that they may do a public benefit. I undertake not to justify all Captain Margery's actions, but his own conscience knows whether he hath taken the horses of any but malignants, and it were somewhat too hard to put it upon the consciences of your fellow deputy lieutenants, whether they have not freed the horses of known malignants, a fault not less, considering the sad estate of this Kingdom, than to take a horse from a known honest man, the offence being against the public, which is a considerable aggravation. I know not the measure that every one takes of malignants. I think it is not fit Captain Margery should be the judge; but if he, in this taking of horses, hath observed the parliament character of a malignant, and cannot be charged for one horse otherwise taken, it had been better that some of the bitterness wherewith he and his have been followed had been spared. The horses that his Cornet Boallry took, he will put himself upon that issue for them all.

If these men be accounted troublesome to the country, I shall be glad you

[164] Manuscript defective.

would send them all to me. I'll bid them welcome. And when they have fought for you, and endured some other difficulties of war which your honester men will hardly bear, I pray you then let them go for honest men. I profess unto you, many of those men which are of your country's choosing, under Captain Johnson, are so far from serving you, that, were it not that I have honest troops to master them, although they be well paid, yet they are so mutinous that I may justly fear they would cut my throat. Gentlemen, it may be it provokes some spirits to see such plain men made captains of horse. It had been well that men of honour and birth had entered into these employments, but why do they not appear? Who would have hindered them? But seeing it was necessary the work must go on, better plain men than none, but best to have men patient of wants, faithful and conscientious in the employment, and such, I hope, these will approve themselves to be. Let them therefore, if I be thought worthy of any favour, leave your country with your good wishes and a blessing. I am confident they will be well bestowed, and I believe before it be long, you will be in their debt; and then it will not be hard to quit scores.

What arms you can furnish them withal, I beseech you do it. I have ever hitherto found your kindness great to me: I know not what I have done to lose it; I love it so well, and price it so high, that I would do my best to gain more. You have the assured affection of

Your most humble and faithful servant,
OLIVER CROMWELL.

[Boston,]
September 28th, 1643.

P.S.—I understand there were some exceptions taken at a horse that was sent to me, which was seized out of the hands of one Mr. Goldsmith of Wilby. If he be not by you judged a malignant, and that you do not approve of my having of the horse, I shall as willingly return him again as you shall desire, and therefore, I pray you, signify your pleasure to me herein under your hands. Not that I would, for ten thousand horses, have the horse to my own private benefit, saving to make use of him for the Public, for I will most gladly return the value of him to the State. If the gentleman stand clear in your judgments, I beg it as a special favour that, if the gentleman be freely willing to let me have him for my money, let him set his own price: I shall very justly return him the money. Or if he be unwilling to part with him, but keeps him for his pleasure, be pleased to send me an answer thereof: I shall instantly return him his horse; and do it with a great deal more satisfaction to myself than keep him. Therefore I beg it of you to satisfy my desire in this last request; it shall exceedingly oblige me to you. If you do it not, I shall rest very unsatisfied, and the horse will be a burden to me so long as I shall keep him.[165]

On September 20 Lincolnshire had been added to the Eastern Counties Association[166] and five days later the Commons had signed

[165] The original, once in the possession of Dawson Turner and pr. in *Norfolk Arch. Soc. Papers*, ii, 55–58 (1849), is now in the Tangye Collection in the London Museum. Carlyle, Letter XVIII.

[166] Husbands, *Ordinances*, ii, 331. The ordinance states that at this time Cromwell's regiment consisted of ten troops. Each troop averaged about eighty men.

the Solemn League and Covenant.[167] As Pym's party thus reformed and strengthened their lines, the second day of October found Cromwell in King's Lynn conferring with Manchester and two members of the Eastern Association Committee—Harlakenden and that Colonel Francis Russell who had helped Cromwell in the incident of the Cambridge plate—and they agreed to move on the following day to Boston with the main body of infantry which was no longer needed at Lynn.[168] It would appear that on his way back to Boston he visited his family in Ely for among the various papers of the Ely Committee is a warrant, written, apparently, by his deputy, Ireton, and signed by Cromwell. Since his transfer from Sir Francis Thornhaugh's regiment of horse in Nottinghamshire and his part in raising the siege of Gainsborough by Meldrum, which had attracted Cromwell's attention, Ireton had acted as deputy governor of Ely[169] and it was there apparently that romance began which was to end presently in his marriage with Cromwell's nineteen-year-old daughter Bridget. Meanwhile his troop which was to be incorporated into the Ironsides was, it would seem, part of the garrison of Ely as this order indicates:

To Robert Brown, Deputy Treasurer of Ely

These are to require you forthwith out of the treasure in your hands to pay to Sarj. Maj. Henry Ireton the sum of seventy pounds upon account towards the pay of his troop and officers, and also the sum of thirty pounds to be by him paid over to Capt. Gervase Lomax upon account towards the pay of his foot company and officers. Hereof fail not at your peril, and this shall be your warrant.

Given under my hand this 3rd day of October 1643,

OLIVER CROMWELL.[170]

This, then, was the Cromwell of the summer of 1643, riding, recruiting, raiding, begging and threatening every one for men, money and arms, but most of all for money for "the cause." However much he and his fellow officers were prepared to sacrifice, however "godly" his common soldiers were, they had to be paid, or else they would not fight. Looking neither to the right nor to the left, not at all behind him, and not very much ahead, he sought with furious and feverish energy but one thing—to beat off the enemy. Yet even in the midst

[167] *C. J.*, iii, 389. There were 112 signatures of the House of Commons set to it the first day. Yonge's *Diary*, *Add. MSS.* 18,778, f. 56, quoted in Gardiner, *Civil War*, i, 235. Rushworth's list, v, 475, is much longer and includes Cromwell's name, which, of course is impossible, and dates the signing Sept. 22nd.

[168] Harlakenden to Barrington, Oct. 2, *Hist. MSS. Comm. Rept.* 7, App. p. 565.

[169] Cf. Firth, *Raising of the Ironsides*, p. 35.

[170] *Ibid.*, p. 35n. The warrant is endorsed with a receipt showing that the money was paid on October 6.

of this amazing display of intense activity, one thing stands out. It is his insistence on what later generations were to call "democracy" or "equality." It was not only his conviction, it was his only hope of ultimate success, and if that desire for success inspired conviction, he was neither the first nor last who confused the two. If the gentry had not come forward to support "the cause", so much the worse for them. He would and did appeal to other elements, and if he identified these with the "godly" and "honest" party, he had at least two good reasons—they were on his side and they were not Episcopalians. In such a state of mind he went forth conquering and to conquer after the manner of the Old Testament, secure in his belief that God was on his side, and, unlike many men of his time and even of his own party, untroubled with either doubts or fears of the future.

For the moment he left Ely to Ireton while he was active in the field. While Charles and Essex recruited their shattered forces after Newbury, the one in Oxford, the other in London and then Windsor; while Waller was empowered to raise another army in the west under Essex; while the Scots prepared an army to cross the Tweed, and Parliament, still further reduced in numbers, enforced the covenant and sought means to pay their allies, Cromwell came nearer the center of the stage. He was bent on driving the Royalists from Lincoln, and he was still seeking money for his troops. He had appealed to the Deputy Lieutenants of Essex of whom his cousin, Sir Thomas Barrington, was chief. To him Harlakenden had also appealed, but apparently with small result or none, and at this point Cromwell wrote again not only to ask money but to deny aspersions on his regiment:

To Sir Thomas Barrington

Sir,

It is against my will to be too troublesome to my friends. I had rather suffer under some extremities, were it my particular; but that which I have to offer concerns those honest men under my command, who have been, who are in straits if want of clothes, boots, money to fix their arms, to shoe their horses be considerable, such are theirs not in an easy degree, truly above what is fit for the state to suffer. Sir, many may complain they are many weeks behind of pay, many who can plunder and pillage; they suffer no want. But truly mine (though some have stigmatised them with the name of Anabaptists), are honest men, such as fear God, I am confident the freest from unjust practices of any in England, seek the soldiers where you can. Such imputations are poor requitals to those who have ventured their blood for you. I hear there are such mists cast to darken their services. Take no care for me, I ask your good acceptance, let me have your prayers, I will thank you. Truly I count not myself worthy to be employed by God; but for my poor men, help them what you can, for they are faithful. The last ordinance hath provided for me, but paper pays not, if not executed. I beg your furtherance herein.

Sir, know you have none will more readily be commanded by you, than your cousin and humble servant,

OLIVER CROMWELL.[171]

Boston, October 6th, 1643.

WINCEBY, OCTOBER, 1643

The war was now definitely shifting to the east and for the moment in favor of the Parliament. Having successfully accomplished the junction of their armies, with their rear secured by Manchester's foot in Boston and in Lynn, with other forces elsewhere, Cromwell and Fairfax advanced northward in Lincolnshire, through territory under Royalist domination, as far as Louth. On October 9 Manchester, hearing that they had retreated because their lack of foot made risky a possible meeting with Sir John Henderson, the governor of Newark, who had appeared with a great force in the vicinity, drew all his forces toward Bolingbroke Castle. The next afternoon he met Cromwell and Willoughby at Kirby, a mile from the Castle, and learned that Fairfax was five miles away at Horn Castle.[172] When it became known that evening that Henderson was advancing from the west to the relief of Bolingbroke, the entire night was spent in drawing the horse to a rendezvous to meet him.

Though Cromwell was much disturbed by the weariness of his horse from two or three days of hard duty,[173] an engagement could not safely be avoided. The Royalists had nearly twice as many colours as Manchester but the latter's troops were fuller and extraordinarily well armed,[174] so the two forces were fairly equal in strength. Meeting near the little hamlet of Winceby, the Parliamentary dragoons led the charge, closely followed by Cromwell with his own and Manchester's regiments of horse.[175] Of the fight which ensued, Vicars gives us a vivid picture:

"Our men went on in several bodies singing Psalms . . . Colonel Cromwell fell with brave resolution upon the Enemy, immediately after Dragooners had given him the first volley, yet they were so nimble as that within half pistol shot they gave him another. His horse was killed under him at the first charge and fell down upon him; and, as he rose up, he was knocked down again . . . but afterwards he recovered a poor horse in a soldier's hands, and bravely mounted himself again. Truly, this first charge was so

[171] Holograph original was in the Morrison Collection until it was sold, according to *Autograph Prices Current*, in 1918. Lomas-Carlyle, Supp. 5.

[172] Vicars, *God's Ark*, p. 44–6; Rushworth, v, 280.

[173] Vicars, *op. cit.*, p. 44. See Firth's remarks on this as an example of Cromwell's solicitude for his horses in *Macmillans's Magazine*, lxx, 301.

[174] Vicars, *op. cit.*, p. 45; Rushworth, ii, 281–2.

[175] *L. J.*, vi, 256.

home-given and performed with so much admirable courage and resolution by our troops that the Enemy stood not another."[176]

The second charge led by Fairfax put the entire enemy force to flight after only a half hour's fighting, and after a short pursuit they were scattered; about six hundred were killed, more were taken prisoners, many were drowned in the waters of the fens, and the remainder took refuge in Newark.[177]

Though, like Gainsborough, Winceby was not to be compared with Edgehill or Newbury, it had an importance beyond even its losses. At the moment that Henderson's men were driven from the field, a sally of the Hull garrison compelled Newcastle to raise the siege of that fortress. The freeing of a great part of Lincolnshire from Royalist control by Winceby fight, and the threat of Newcastle's army for a time removed, the wedge between him and the King's forces was driven deeper. With Manchester taking Lincoln and minor garrisons, it might seem that the position of the eastern counties was secure.

But meanwhile in this land debatable the Cavaliers had captured and begun to fortify Newport Pagnell just west of Bedford and taken Bedford itself. The Cambridge Royalists were getting the better of the supporters of Parliament and it seemed that Rupert might well have taken the capital of the Association. But, relieved of pressure from the north, Manchester was able to send Cromwell with a considerable part of his army toward Huntingdon to interrupt the "Oxford Cormorants" in their activities about Cambridge,[178] while Essex, moving from Windsor to St. Albans, recaptured Bedford and Newport Pagnell.[179] Meanwhile Waller gathered forces in the south, and with the situation now in hand, Essex ordered Cromwell to return to service in the north.[180] On November 2 he had joined Fairfax in besieging Newark and a few days later that Royalist stronghold which held, it was reported, 4,000 Royalist horse, had capitulated.[181] Within a month Waller had beaten the Cavaliers at Alton in Hampshire, taking a thousand prisoners and southern England was safe for Parliament.

When Manchester came back from Lincoln to Cambridge, he dismissed some 6,000 of the trained bands of the Association who had flocked in to defend their capital, leaving five or six hundred as a garrison. Part of his foot was about Gainsborough, part in Newport

[176] Vicars, *God's Ark Overtopping the World's Waves*, p. 45.

[177] *Ibid.*, p. 46; *Scottish Dove*, Oct. 13–20; Manchester's Letter, in *L. J.*, vi, 256. Other accounts of Winceby are to be found in *Parliament Scout*, Oct. 13–20; Ludlow (Firth's ed.), i, 58; *True relation of the victories . . . in the North; True relation of the fight . . . near Horn Castle.*

[178] Vicars, *God's Ark*, p. 55.

[179] *True Informer.*

[180] Vicars, *op. cit.*, p. 56.

[181] *Perfect Diurnall*, Oct. 30 to Nov. 6; Vicars, p. 67.

Pagnell, and the rest around Huntingdon and Cambridge, and he himself remained in Cambridge, while Essex took up winter quarters at St. Albans. Meanwhile the Scots poured across the Tweed, the districts under the control of Parliament were busy taking the Covenant; and though the King held court and parliament in Oxford, for the moment the revolutionary cause was saved.

Relief came just in time. Pym had long been ill and his tremendous efforts in the preceding months had greatly weakened him. The Scotch alliance was his last great achievement and when on September 25 he was the first to sign the Solemn League and Covenant, it was evident that his strength was failing. On December 8 he died and a week later was given a great public funeral. His loss seemed for the moment irreparable. Since his first entry into Parliament, almost precisely thirty years before, he had been the unswerving foe of Stuart monarchy and episcopacy. From the preparation of a petition against "papists" in 1621 to his last public utterance, he exhibited an almost fanatical hatred of Roman Catholicism. He had helped to manage the impeachment of Buckingham; he had pushed forward the Petition of Right; he had sent Strafford to the scaffold; he had framed the Grand Remonstrance; and had become the head and front of that party which led the Parliament to war. From first to last he had been the champion of Parliament against the crown, of Puritanism against Anglicanism, of liberty even against law, of popular will, even popular tumults, against authority. He had refused to check the mobs that rioted against the bishops. "God forbid," he said, "that the House of Commons should proceed in any way to dishearten people to obtain their just desires in such a way."[182] He was, in fact, the ideal revolutionary leader, the heart and soul of opposition to the monarchy and the church and the Royalists rejoiced at the passing of what they conceived to be their most dangerous enemy.

They rejoiced too soon. Pym's death was not the great catastrophe it seemed, and his passing made place for still more dangerous antagonists. In effect Sir Henry Vane the younger, who, with Oliver St. John, headed the war party and had made the covenant with the Scots, succeeded Pym as the chief figure in the party opposed to Charles. "He was that within the House which Cromwell was without," wrote Baxter, and though the Committee of Safety continued to function as the guiding force of the Parliamentary party, it had apparently been as early as the mission to Scotland that Vane conceived the plan of a new body to direct the policies of the two nations now in alliance against English monarchy and episcopacy. If Pym was a capable agitator, Vane was a still more subtle diplomat. "There

[182] Dover's notes, *Clarendon Mss*, 1, f. 603, quoted in *D. N. B.*, "Pym."

need no more be said of him," wrote Clarendon with reluctant admiration, "than that he was chosen to cozen and deceive a whole nation which excelled in craft and dissembling"; and his insertion of the seemingly harmless words in the covenant to reform religion "according to the word of God," left the door open to introduce that form of faith which was to count Cromwell as its greatest champion, so-called "Independency," to oppose not merely episcopacy but presbyterianism.

ELY AND LONDON, DECEMBER, 1643–JANUARY, 1644

Though Vane and Cromwell were to play a great part in each other's lives, for the time being Cromwell had little to do directly with Pym's successor. On November 2 he was appointed with seventeen others as a Commissioner for Plantations, with the Earl of Warwick as Governor.[183] At the beginning of December he was still in Lincolnshire with Manchester about Sleaford;[184] but he seems to have spent much of his time during the winter at home in Ely, of which he was still governor. In this capacity he put his seal to the commission of a friend, a certain Francis Underwood, of the neighboring town of Whittlesea, who, after some two years as captain,[185] became a colonel, and whose son, according to Noble, married Anne Russell, a sister of the wife of Cromwell's son Henry.[186]

To Francis Underwood, Esq.

A commission as captain of foot in a company consisting of 150 men for duty in the Isle of Ely. Dec. 12, 1643.[187]

To this may be added another document connected with his duties as governor. Almost entirely surrounded by water as it was, the garrison of Ely obviously needed a boat and Cromwell accordingly applied to the Ely committee to pay for it:

To my very noble Friends the Committees of the Isle of Ely: Present these

GENTLEMEN,

There is a boat framing for the defence of these parts; I believe it's of consequence. I therefore desire you to let the officer that

[183] *L. J.*, vi, 291–2.
[184] *Mercurius Britannicus*, Nov. 30 to Dec. 7.
[185] *See* Letter, June 6, 1645.
[186] Noble, ii, 411n.
[187] Noble, ii, 411n.

directs the framing of it to have twenty marks for the perfecting of it, and I shall rest,

Your true servant,

[Ely]
Jan. 10th, 1643. OLIVER CROMWELL.[188]

[With note that Lieut. Thomas Selby was accordingly paid £13.]

While Cromwell was thus engaged in Ely and the neighborhood, events in the world outside had taken a new turn. The signing of the Solemn League and Covenant, however necessary it may have seemed to Pym, met with strong opposition from two very different quarters. On the one hand the Royalists and Episcopalians naturally denounced it as a betrayal of England; on the other the various "sects," the Anabaptists, the Separatists, and now the Independents among whom Cromwell was numbered, were scarcely less opposed to presbyterianism than to episcopacy, for, as Milton wrote, "new presbyter is but old priest writ large." The Assembly of Divines contained five men who, like Philip Nye, sought this middle way of Independency between the "wilder" sects and rigid presbyterianism, and, scarcely less than the Royalists, they looked with suspicion on the calling in of the Scots and the commitment of England to their form of faith. As the Assembly of Divines revealed its leanings toward strict presbyterianism, Royalists and sectarians joined in a new appeal to Charles, proposing the deprivation of the existing bishops but the retention of episcopacy, the abolition of obnoxious ceremonies, trial of delinquents by "known law" or in full Parliament and the indemnity of those who had suffered in past times. Thus amid plot and counter-plot among the Royalists and the Parliamentarians, while the main armies lay in winter quarters, Charles, though he refused the proferred terms, proposed to summon a Parliament at Oxford of such members as would come to him and agree to some measure of liberty of conscience. Meanwhile he negotiated with the party favorable to him in London, with France, and with Ireland, planning to bring about a "cessation" of hostilities there and land an Irish army in England to counterbalance the Scots gathering on the Tweed.

Thus at the beginning of 1644 the situation seemed to preclude any thought of peace and each side girded itself again for the renewal of the war. As the Irish began to land in Wales and the Scots crossed the Tweed, the minor engagements which took place here and there during the winter, as this castle and that town fell to one party or the other, shrunk in importance before the new alignment of forces

[188] Printed in Firth, "Raising of the Ironsides," *loc. cit.*, p. 66. from the "Commonwealth Exchequer Papers" in the Public Record Office. Lomas-Carlyle, Supp. 6. Firth suggests that Lieut. Selby was probably the Capt. Selby of Fleetwood's regiment, who was killed at Naseby in 1645.

and the new direction of affairs in the hands of a reorganized Committee of Safety on its way to becoming a Committee of Both Kingdoms.

Though he was shortly to play a great part in the new order of affairs, for the moment Cromwell was concerned with one of those minor matters which were characteristic of another side of Puritanism. Amid its warlike activities Parliament had found time to issue ordinances against stage-plays, bear-baiting and other amusements, authorizing the destruction of "images" and other evidences of "superstition and idolatry," forbidding the wearing of vestments, choir-singing and the use of the Prayer Book; and, in the absence or the abstention of church officers, the interruption of such services and the suppression of such "stage property" by military men. The situation in Ely was acute, for one of the canons of the cathedral, a certain Mr. Hitch, persisted in fulfilling his ecclesiastical functions in the old fashion. Such a defiance naturally came to Cromwell's attention, and rather than let his soldiers interfere, he sent a note to the offender:

[*To the Reverend Mr. Hitch, at Ely*]

MR. HICH,

Lest the soldiers should in any tumultuary or disorderly way attempt the reformation of your Cathedral Church, I require you to forbear altogether your choir-service, so unedifying and offensive; and this as you will answer it, if any disorder should arise thereupon.

I advise you to catechise, and read and expound the Scriptures to the people, not doubting but the Parliament, with the advice of the Assembly of Divines, will in due time direct you farther. I desire the sermons may be where usually they have been, but more frequent.

Your loving friend,

Ely, January
10, 1643.

OLIVER CROMWELL.[189]

Mr. Hitch ignored the warning and the result is told by a contemporary:

"Cromwell, with a party of soldiers attended by the rabble, came into the church in time of divine service, with his hat on; and directing himself to Mr. Hitch, said 'I am a man under authority and am commanded to dismiss this assembly.' Upon which Mr. Hitch made a pause; but Cromwell and the rabble passing up towards the communion table, Mr. Hitch proceeded with the service; at which Cromwell returned; and laying his hand on his sword in a passion, bid Mr. Hitch leave off his fooling and come down; and so drove out the whole congregation."[190]

[189] Facsimile of holograph original in *Isographie des hommes celebres;* thence Lomas-Carlyle, Letter XIX. There are several contemporary MS. copies, from one of which the letter is pr. in *Gentleman's Magazine*, lviii, 225 (1788).

[190] Walker, *Sufferings of the Clergy*, pt. ii, p. 23.

Three days later, it appears, Cromwell was in Cambridge, his regiment of horse at Bedford;[191] but military operations were for a time at a stand and, in the absence of more pressing concerns, Cromwell, Manchester and others of the officers went up to London once more to discharge their duties as members of Parliament. There the business was not so much the organization of any army as the discussion of intercepted letters, Royalist plots for foreign aid, and counterplots. On January 18, the Sheriffs and Aldermen of London entertained the Scots Commissioners, the Assembly of Divines and the two Houses at a banquet, as evidence that the Parliamentary suspicions of them were unfounded and that they were resolved to cooperate with the bodies who were their guests. To this banquet it seems likely that Cromwell went, for on the next day he was in London when he signed an authorization to the Treasurer of Wisbeach, one of the Fen towns north of Ely:

To Mr. [William][192] *Edwards, Treasurer for Wisbeach, etc.*

MR. EDWARDS,

You being Treasurer for Wisbich and Northwichford hundred of such moneys as are raised within the same by authority of Parliament for such soldiers as are for the defence of the Isle of Ely, these are to authorize and require you to pay unto Major Dodson the sum of six hundred pounds with all possible speed you can, which he is to have in part of his arrears until his account can be taken and the remainder paid him that so he may have wherewith to satisfy the poor people, which quarter with his soldiers and so march away to his charge under Colonel Pickering.

OLIVER CROMWELL.
MILES SANDYS.[193]

London, this 19th
of January, 1643.

On Monday, January 22, Cromwell was being heard in the House of Commons. He had something to say about the case of Sir John Hotham, which was being investigated by a committee,[194] and, with the conduct of Lord Willoughby on the occasion of Newcastle's pursuit of the forces under Fairfax and himself[195] in mind, Cromwell made a speech which, although D'Ewes was not present, is noted in his *Diary:*

[191] *Certain Informations*, quoted in Cooper, *Annals of Cambridge*, iii, 368.

[192] *Cf.* James Edwards, son and heir of William Edwards of Wisbeach. *Alumni Cantabrig.*

[193] Original in *St. P. Dom.*, Charles I, dxxxix, no. 175; *Calendar* (1625–1649), p. 657. John Pickering commanded one of Manchester's foot regiments.

[194] *C. J.*, iii, 373.

[195] *See* Cromwell's letter, Sept. 28, 1643.

Speech in the House of Commons, January 22, 1643

During my absence, Cromwell stood up, and desired that the Lord Willoughby of Parham, who had commanded in Lincolnshire as serjeant-major-general of the forces there, might be ordered to stay here, and to go no more thither; and that the Earl of Manchester might be made serjeant-major-general of that county, as well as of the other associated counties. That the Lord Willoughby quitted Gainsborough, when he [Cromwell] was not far off, with forces to relieve him. That he quitted the city of Lincoln, etc., and left powder, match, and arms there, and seven great pieces, mounted, with all the carriages, which the enemy made use of against the Parliament's forces. That he had very loose and profane commanders[196] under him, of the conduct of one of whom he gave instance.[197]

"Sir Christopher Wray," continued D'Ewes, had "much ado to have patience to hear this out to the end. To cast dirt" on one "who had so well deserved!" The debate continued for some time, Sir Arthur Haselrig and Sir Harry Vane entering into it, until the House decided to grant a commission to the Earl of Manchester to be major-general of the county of Lincoln as well as the other six associated counties;[198] and ordered that the case of Lord Willoughby, who had previously been removed from his command, be considered by a special committee.[199]

It was on the same day, apparently, that Cromwell was made lieutenant-general. When he was advanced to the rank of major-general is not known, but the question of the date of his appointment to the higher office is settled by an account of pay due him at the end of 1644 which states that there was owing to him:

From the 22th of January to the 23th of December, 1644, being 48 weekes half pay att 50s. per diem as Lieutenant Generall of horse and foot.......................... £840 0s
For the same tyme as Colonell and Captain of horse, with allowance for 6 horses at 42s. half pay per diem........ £705 12s[200]

Cromwell had now reached the third great stage of his career. The years of youth and early manhood were behind him, with his service in Parliament and the beginnings of his military life. He was now a

[196] The three Wrays—William, Christopher and Theophilus—are the commanders to whom Cromwell refers. Cf. *C. J.*, iii, 387.

[197] D'Ewes, *Journal*, quoted in Sanford, p. 580.

[198] *C. J.*, iii, 373; D'Ewes, *op. cit.*, p. 580–1.

[199] The Horse *formerly* under his command was to be left in Lincolnshire. *C. J.*, iii, 373. On Feb. 16th, he was declared a delinquent by Parliament. *Ibid.*, 401.

[200] Firth, "Raising of the Ironsides," *loc. cit.*, p. 53, from the "Commonwealth Exchequer Papers." The same account includes the item: "From January 1, 1643[–4] to the 22nd of the same, being three weeks' half-pay at 1 l. 15s. per diem as major-general of horse & foot, 36 l. 15s." *Ibid.* The higher officers had agreed to take half pay until the end of the war when the remainder would fall due. *Ibid.*, p. 52.

man of experience in war, at the head of a considerable force which he had himself in large measure raised and trained. He had approved himself a brave, competent and resourceful commander, to be relied on in emergency. He had found his true vocation. The spirit of combativeness which had marked his course hitherto was no longer a hindrance but a help. The deep religious emotion which he had revealed since his conversion added to his strength as a leader of men of like spirit and he had used it as a weapon against his enemies. He was now more than ever convinced that God was on his side, that his was the "honest" as well as the "godly" party, and his the righteous cause.

He was essentially a man of action, a man of single purpose, determined to succeed in the immediate design of overthrowing his opponents at whatever cost. Beyond that he thus far revealed no definite or far-reaching plan. He was an uncompromising foe of the Establishment, above all a fighting-man, as dashing as Rupert but far more cautious; an able organizer and administrator as he had proved within the limits hitherto set to his activity; and the most uniformly successful of the Parliamentary commanders to this time. He was therefore becoming, or had even become, not only the hero of his party but their rising hope, and with his appointment as Lieutenant-general on the way to the headship of its more advanced revolutionary elements.

CHAPTER VI

CROMWELL AS LIEUTENANT-GENERAL

JANUARY, 1644–JANUARY, 1645

With the death of John Pym and the signing of the Solemn League and Covenant, the Civil Wars entered on another stage. Many of the original protagonists had gone. Brooke had died at Lichfield, Hampden at Chalgrove Field, Falkland at Newbury, and especially on the side of Parliament the conduct of affairs was coming to new men. The first stages of revolution were long past, all efforts at compromise had broken down, and it was evident that the war was about to change its spirit and its form. The coming of the Scots had altered the whole situation, the charges of incompetence brought by Cromwell against Lord Willoughby were earnest of future quarrels, and though plundering went on, though raids and the taking of castles and towns continued, though men were still reluctant to fight beyond their own districts, the elevation of Cromwell to the rank of lieutenant-general was a symptom of changes in the field as the ascendancy of Vane was indicative of a change in Parliament.

Cromwell, like some of his fellow officers during this winter season, was again in Parliament where some time between January 22 and February 1 he seems to have received his new commission at the moment of his charges against Lord Willoughby. At the same time he was called on to take part in an affair which did not immediately concern him but was none the less important to his cause. Through Lord Lovelace, Charles had sent to Vane an offer of liberty of conscience; but Vane had kept the letter secret because, not believing Charles had any thought of making good his offer, he hoped by a pretense of giving it serious thought, to unravel the King's plans. Essex, discovering what he considered a slight to himself if not a piece of treachery, had brought the matter before the Lords and precipitated a quarrel between the Houses.[1] The matter was delicate as well as dangerous, and on January 24, Cromwell, with St. John, Holles and eighteen others, was appointed to consider the examinations taken by the Advocate of the Army in the business.[2] Meanwhile the King with 44 Lords and 118 commoners of the Oxford

[1] Robert Baillie, *Letters and Journals*, ii, 135; see also S. R. Gardiner, *Civil War*, i, 274.

[2] *C. J.*, iii, 376.

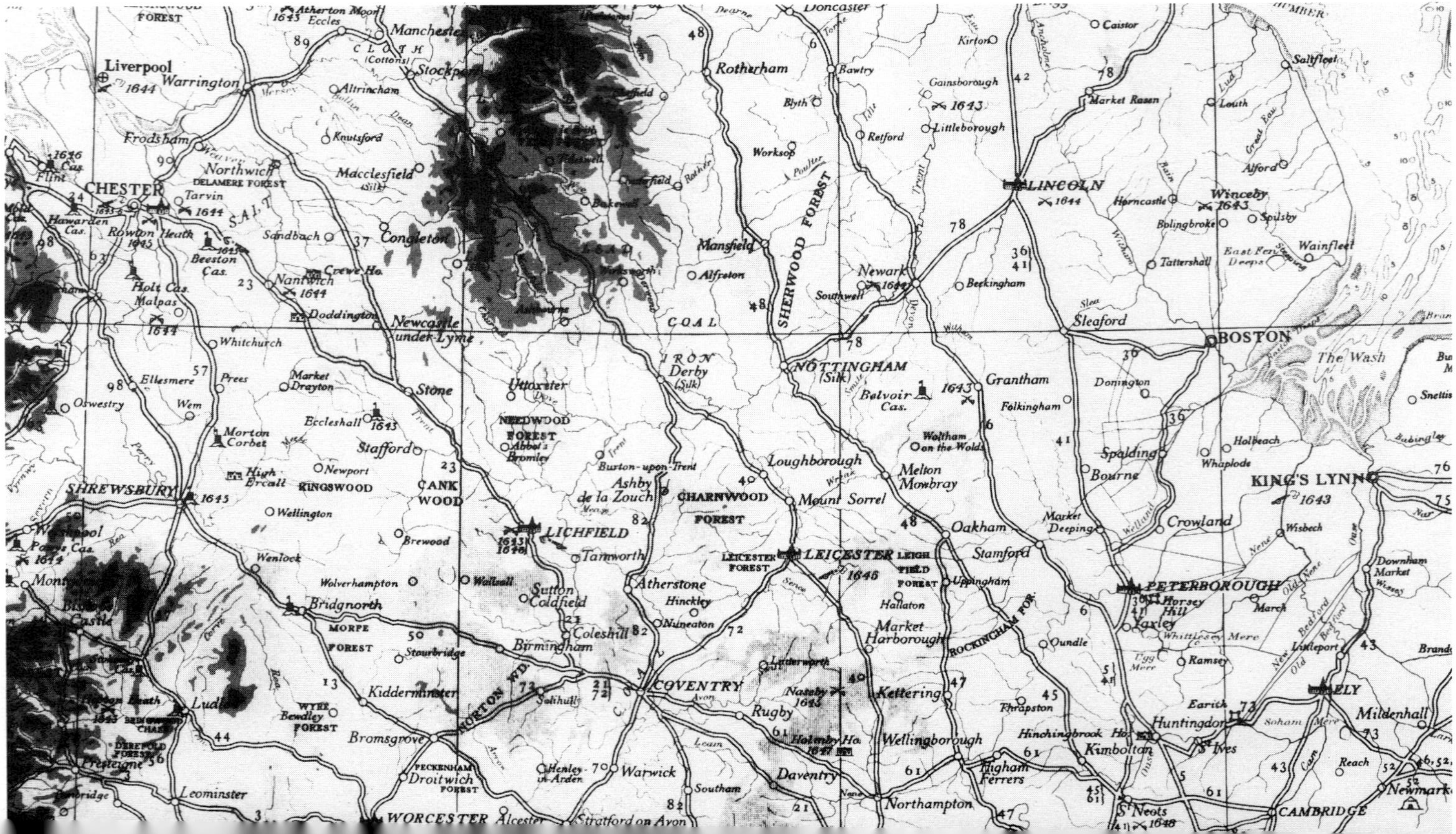

Liverpool
1644
Warrington
Frodsham
Northwich
DELAMERE FOREST
CHESTER
Flint
Tarvin
1644
Hawarden Cas.
Rowton Heath
1645
Beeston Cas.
Holt Cas.
Malpas
1644
SALT
Sandbach
Nantwich
1644
Crewe Ho.
Doddington
Atherton Moor
1643
Eccles
Manchester
CLOTH
(Cottons)
Stockport
Altrincham
Knutsford
Macclesfield
(Silk)
Congleton
Newcastle under-Lyme
Whitchurch
Ellesmere
Oswestry
Prees
Wem
Market Drayton
Stone
Eccleshall
1643
Stafford
Morton Corbet
High Ercall
Newport
KINGSWOOD
Wellington
CANK WOOD
SHREWSBURY
1645
Wenlock
Bridgnorth
MORFE FOREST
Wolverhampton
Walsall
Brewood
Stourbridge
Kidderminster
WYRE FOREST
Bewdley
Bromsgrove
Droitwich
FECKENHAM FOREST
WORCESTER
Alcester
Leominster
Presteigne
Ludlow
Uttoxeter
NEEDWOOD FOREST
Abbot's Bromley
LICHFIELD
Tamworth
Sutton Coldfield
Coleshill
Birmingham
NORTON WD.
Solihull
Henley in Arden
Warwick
Stratford on Avon
Southam
Rotherham
Doncaster
Bawtry
Blyth
Worksop
Retford
Mansfield
Alfreton
COAL
IRON
Derby
(Silk)
SHERWOOD FOREST
NOTTINGHAM
(Silk)
Southwell
Newark
1646
Burton-upon-Trent
Ashby de la Zouch
CHARNWOOD FOREST
Loughborough
Mount Sorrel
Atherstone
Hinckley
Nuneaton
LEICESTER FOREST
LEICESTER
1645
LEIGH FIELD FOREST
COVENTRY
Rugby
Lutterworth
Naseby
1645
Holmby Ho.
1647
Daventry
Northampton
Market Harborough
Hallaton
Kettering
Wellingborough
Higham Ferrers
Gainsborough
1643
Littleborough
Kirton
LINCOLN
1644
Beckingham
Grantham
1643
Belvoir Cas.
Woltham on the Wolds
Melton Mowbray
Oakham
Uppingham
Stamford
ROCKINGHAM FOR.
Oundle
Thrapston
Hinchingbrook Ho.
Kimbolton
St Neots
1648
Caistor
Market Rasen
Louth
Saltfleet
Alford
Horncastle
Winceby
1643
Bolingbroke
Spilsby
Tattershall
East Fen Deeps
Wainfleet
Sleaford
Folkingham
Donington
BOSTON
The Wash
Spalding
Bourne
Market Deeping
Crowland
Holbeach
Whaplode
KING'S LYNN
1643
Wisbech
PETERBOROUGH
Horsey Hill
Yaxley
Whittlesey Mere
Ramsey
March
Downham Market
Littleport
ELY
Huntingdon
St Ives
Earith
Mildenhall
Reach
CAMBRIDGE
Newmarket
Snettisham

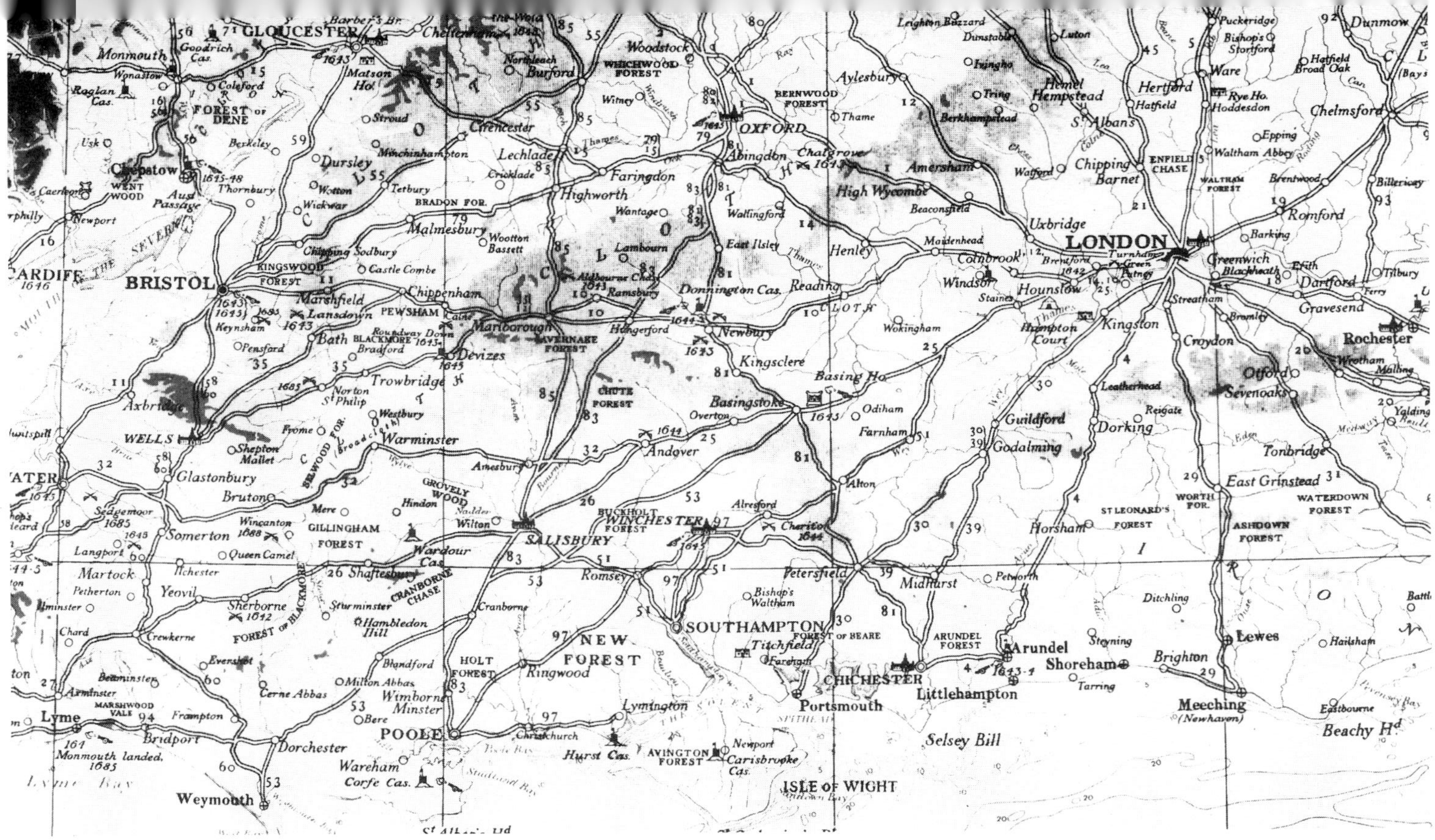

GLOUCESTER
Monmouth
Goodrich Cas.
Raglan Cas.
Coleford
FOREST OF DENE
Chepstow
Newport
CARDIFF
BRISTOL
Cheltenham
Matson Ho
Stroud
Dursley
Berkeley
Thornbury
Aust Passage
Tetbury
Malmesbury
Chipping Sodbury
KINGSWOOD FOREST
Marshfield
Lansdown
Keynsham
Pensford
Bath
Chippenham
Castle Combe
Wootton Bassett
Cirencester
Minchinhampton
Lechlade
Cricklade
Highworth
Faringdon
Burford
Northleach
Woodstock
WHICHWOOD FOREST
Witney
OXFORD
Abingdon
Wantage
Wallingford
Lambourn
Marlborough
SAVERNAKE FOREST
Devizes
Roundway Down
Hungerford
Ramsbury
Newbury
Donnington Cas.
East Ilsley
Trowbridge
Bradford
Norton St Philip
Westbury
Frome
Warminster
SELWOOD FOR.
Shepton Mallet
WELLS
Axbridge
Glastonbury
Bruton
Sedgemoor 1685
Somerton
Langport
Martock
Ilchester
Queen Camel
Wincanton
GILLINGHAM FOREST
Mere
Hindon
GROVELY WOOD
Wilton
Amesbury
SALISBURY
Andover
CHUTE FOREST
Wardour Cas.
Shaftesbury
CRANBORNE CHASE
Yeovil
Sherborne
Crewkerne
Chard
Ilminster
Petherton
Evershot
FOREST OF BLACKMORE
Sturminster
Hambledon Hill
Blandford
Milton Abbas
Cerne Abbas
Dorchester
Weymouth
Bridport
Frampton
Lyme
Monmouth landed, 1685
Axminster
Beaminster
MARSHWOOD VALE
Bere
Wimborne Minster
POOLE
Wareham
Corfe Cas.
HOLT FOREST
Cranborne
Ringwood
NEW FOREST
Christchurch
Lymington
Hurst Cas.
Romsey
SOUTHAMPTON
WINCHESTER
BUCKHOLT FOREST
Alresford
Cheriton
Basingstoke
Overton
Kingsclere
Basing Ho
Odiham
Farnham
Alton
Bishop's Waltham
Titchfield
Fareham
Portsmouth
CHICHESTER
Petersfield
Midhurst
Petworth
Arundel
ARUNDEL FOREST
Littlehampton
Selsey Bill
ISLE OF WIGHT
Newport
Carisbrooke Cas.
Reading
Henley
Thame
Chalgrove
BERNWOOD FOREST
Aylesbury
Wokingham
High Wycombe
Amersham
Beaconsfield
Maidenhead
Windsor
Colnbrook
Staines
Hounslow
Hampton Court
Uxbridge
Watford
Berkhampstead
Tring
Hemel Hempstead
St Albans
Luton
Dunstable
Leighton Buzzard
Chipping Barnet
ENFIELD CHASE
Hertford
Hatfield
Ware
Hoddesdon
Rye Ho.
Bishop's Stortford
Puckeridge
Waltham Abbey
WALTHAM FOREST
Epping
LONDON
Brentford
Turnham Green
Putney
Kingston
Greenwich
Blackheath
Streatham
Croydon
Bromley
Romford
Barking
Brentwood
Billericay
Chelmsford
Hatfield Broad Oak
Dunmow
Dartford
Gravesend
Tilbury
Rochester
Wrotham
Malling
Otford
Sevenoaks
Tonbridge
Reigate
Dorking
Leatherhead
Guildford
Godalming
Horsham
ST LEONARD'S FOREST
WORTH FOR.
East Grinstead
ASHDOWN FOREST
WATERDOWN FOREST
Lewes
Ditchling
Steyning
Shoreham
Tarring
Brighton
Meeching (Newhaven)
Hailsham
Eastbourne
Beachy Hd

Parliament appealed to Essex to bring about a peace. This appeal Essex declined to present to the Westminster Parliament and sent in return a copy of the Covenant and a declaration offering pardon to all who would sign it. At the same time, on February 5, the Westminster Parliament issued an ordinance commanding all Englishmen over the age of eighteen to take the Covenant, and on that day Cromwell with four others signed that document, though he was certainly not in sympathy with it and probably signed it only because his position made it compulsory.[3]

Two days later, on February 7, with fourteen other members of the lower House he was nominated by the Lords to meet with seven peers and the Scotch commissioners to consider the formation of a new engine of government, the Committee of Both Kingdoms. With the formation of that committee the whole balance of affairs was changed. Of the old Committee of Safety, seven sat on the new body, among whose twenty-one members the Independents were a majority, and among those now appointed to "advise, consult, order and direct concerning the carrying on and managing of the war" for a period of three months, the name of Oliver Cromwell was conspicuous.[4] It was a war measure but it was more than that. Thenceforth the Parliamentary commanders received frequent and definite instructions and, far more than Pym's Committee of Safety, it became, in a sense, not only a device of government but a general staff not unlike that Committee of Public Safety which a century and a half later directed the fortunes of the French in their revolution, and though Vane was no Robespierre he occupied a position not unlike that of the great exponent of the Terror in that later time.

BEDFORD, OXFORD, AND CAMBRIDGE, MARCH–APRIL, 1644

The Committee of Both Kingdoms found itself in a strong position. The Scots had crossed the Tweed; the Fairfaxes had recovered the greater part of Yorkshire; and Newcastle, so far from bringing aid to Charles, was calling on the King for assistance. The landing of the Irish had alienated many of Charles's followers; the Parliamentary cause was rising in the west and Parliament seemed to have the upper hand. The Royalists were conscious of their altered and altering position. With the beginning of hostilities in March, Rupert, having

[3] *Ibid.*, p. 389.

[4] *C. J.*, iii, 391–2, 400–1; *L. J.*, vi, 418–30, 440. The members of this Committee were: Wm. Pierrepont, Sir Philip Stapleton, Sir Wm. Waller, Sir Gilbert Gerard, Sir Wm. Armyn, Sir Arthur Haselrig, John Crew, Robert Wallopp, Oliver St. John, Sam. Browne, Recorder John Glyn, Cromwell and the two Vanes; the Earls of Northumberland, Essex, Warwick and Manchester, Viscount Saye and Sele, Lord Wharton, and Lord Roberts. The Scotch members were Loudon, Maitland, Johnston of Warriston, and Barclay.

recruited forces in Wales and the west, set out to relieve Newark, then besieged by Meldrum and Willoughby. Meanwhile, Cromwell had been active. Early in March he was reported to have given alarm at Oxford, 'falling into their quarters and taking sixty horse besides arms and good pillage';[5] or, as Burgoyne wrote to Verney, "Colonel Cromwell faced Oxford last week with 1500 men, and drove all the cattell from the very wall to his quarters."[6] In this disputed land between Charles's capital of Oxford and the Eastern Association's capital of Cambridge, he was as active as Rupert, especially about Newport Pagnell, with orders to keep in touch with Warwick to ensure the safe arrival there of an ammunition train destined for Gloucester.[7] From Padbury, midway between Newport Pagnell and Oxford, he sent out a party on March 3 toward Hillesden House, an advanced post of the Royalists and before six o'clock on the following morning he appeared there with Major-General Crawford and their forces. Their offer of quarter refused, the place was stormed and within fifteen minutes was in possession of Parliament; and, leaving Major Bradbury there with two hundred foot to hold the post, he returned to his quarters near Padbury.[8]

He had only anticipated the plans of the Committee of Both Kingdoms who sent him orders that day to stay about Hillesden House and annoy the enemy until further orders, keep Hopton from joining Charles and maintain intelligence with Warwick for the Gloucester convoy.[9] This evidently he did; and his next letter,[10] to Sir Samuel Luke, then in command of Newport, intimates that his forces were still there with Crawford at Buckingham some five miles from Padbury:

To Sir Samuel Luke[11]

Noble Sir,

I beseech you cause three hundred foot, under a captain, to march to Buckingham upon Monday morning, there to quarter with four hundred foot of Northampton, which Mr. Crew[12] sends thither upon Mon-

[5] *Perfect Occurrences of certain passages in Parliament*, No. 11 (Mar. 1–9, 1643, quoted in *Cal. S. P. Dom* (1642), p. 562.

[6] Sir R. Burgoyne to Sir R. Verney, Mar. 7, *Hist. Mss Comm. Rept.* 7, App. (*Lowndes Mss*), p. 446.

[7] *Scottish Dove; cp.* orders to Manchester and Cromwell from the Committee of Both Kingdoms, Mar. 4, *Cal. S. P. Dom.* (1644), p. 34.

[8] Sir S. Luke to Essex, Mar. 4, *Tanner Mss*, lxii, 591–2, quoted in Sanford, *Studies*, App. B.

[9] *Cal. S. P. Dom.* (1644), pp. 33, 34.

[10] Written at Padbury or on his way to Cambridge. Newport Pagnell is just off the direct route to Bedford where he was to call at the *Swan* for news.

[11] The son of Sir Oliver Luke, M. P. for Bedfordshire, Sir Samuel Luke was himself member for Bedford Borough. Through Cromwell's aunt, Elizabeth Hampden, the Lukes and Cromwells were distantly related.

day next. There will be the Major-General to command them. I am going for a thousand foot more at least to be sent from Cambridge and out of the Association. If any man be come to you from Cambridge, I beseech you send him to me to Bedford with all speed; let him stay for me at the Swan.

Sir, I am your humble servant,

March 8th, 1643. OLIVER CROMWELL.

P.S. Present my humble service to Colonel Aylife and tell him he promised me his coat of mail.[13]

Major-General Crawford, whom Cromwell left in charge at Padbury, was a capable military commander, but Cromwell was not without annoyance and trouble in his association with him. Crawford was a Puritan, but of the strictest sect of Scotch Presbyterianism and had no use for Cromwell's tolerant policy which permitted men of any belief to enter the army as long as they came under the broad heading of Puritans. Cromwell was satisfied with a man who was godly, well-behaved, and faithful to "the cause," and in his troops the sectaries were strong. When the army was at Bedford that spring Crawford arrested one Lieutenant William Packer, a notorious Anabaptist, for an offence probably of a religious rather than a military nature; and upon Packer's complaint to Cromwell, Lieutenant-Colonel Rich was sent to remonstrate with Crawford for "checking such a man . . . he being a godly man."[14] Another case reveals Cromwell's position even more clearly. Crawford sent his own Lieutenant-Colonel, Henry Warner, to Manchester, who was busy at Cambridge University carrying out orders to turn out any who refused to sign the Covenant,[15]—too busy, thought Cromwell, to bother with Crawford's complaints. The charge against Warner seems to have been his Anabaptist convictions which would not permit him to sign the Covenant; a charge which, as Cromwell gives the Major-General to understand in the following letter, was not sufficient grounds for sending away a godly man from an army which needed him.[16]

To Major-General Crawford

SIR,

The complaints you preferred to my Lord against your Lieutenant-Colonel, both by Mr. Lee and your own letters, have occasioned

[12] John Crew, M. P. for Brackley, Northants, was a member of the Committee of Both Kingdoms.

[13] Luke's Letter Book, in *Egerton Mss*, Printed in Ellis, *Original Letters*, 3rd series, iv, 225; Carlyle, app. 6.

[14] "Manchester's Quarrel with Cromwell," *Camden Society Misc.* VIII, p. 59.

[15] Cooper, *Annals of Cambridge*, iii, 371.

[16] Carlyle and Gardiner both assume that this letter refers to Packer but, as Firth points out in his "Raising of the Ironsides," p. 57, Packer was never a lieutenant-colonel and Crawford's lieutenant-colonel was, according to army accounts, Henry Warner. Lee was a Presbyterian chaplain.

his stay here, my Lord being [so] employed, in regard of many occasions which are upon him, that he hath not been at leisure to hear him make his defence, which, in pure justice, ought to be granted him or any man before a judgment be passed upon him.

During his abode here and absence from you, he hath acquainted me what a grief it is to him to be absent from his charge, especially now the regiment is called forth to action: and therefore, asking of me my opinion, I advised him speedily to repair unto you, and thought good by him thus to write unto you. Surely you are not well advised thus to turn off one so faithful to the Cause, and so able to serve you as this man is. Give me leave to tell you, I cannot be of your judgment; that if a man notorious for wickedness, for oaths, for drinking, hath as great a share in your affection as one that fears an oath, that fears to sin, that this doth commend your election of men to serve as fit instruments in this work.

Ay, but the man is an Anabaptist. Are you sure of that? Admit he be, shall that render him incapable to serve the public. He is indiscreet. It may be so, in some things, we have all human infirmities. I tell you, if you had none but such indiscreet men about you, and would be pleased to use them kindly, you would find as good a fence to you as any you have yet chosen.

Sir, the State, in choosing men to serve them, takes no notice of their opinions, if they be willing faithfully to serve them, that satisfies. I advised you formerly to bear with men of different minds from yourself; if you had done it when I advised you to it, I think you would not have had so many stumblingblocks in your way. It may be you judge otherwise, but I tell you my mind. I desire you would receive this man into your favour and good opinion. I believe, if he follow my counsel, he will deserve no other but respect from you. Take heed of being sharp, or too easily sharpened by others, against those to whom you can object little but that they square not with you in every opinion concerning matters of religion. If there be any other offence to be charged upon him, that must in a judicial [way] receive a determination. I know you will not think it fit my Lord should discharge an officer of the Field but in a regulate way. I question whether either you or I have any precedent for that.

I have not further to trouble you, but rest,

Cambridge, Your humble servant,
March 10th. OLIVER CROMWELL.[17]

Cromwell's position, as in the case of the 'russet-coated captain who knew what he was fighting for' was clear. It had little to do with those abstract principles of toleration and democracy urged by political theorists. It was pre-eminently practical. There was a war to be won; a king to be defeated; a bench of bishops to be overthrown; and any instrument which would assist in the accomplishment of this great task was to be seized upon and used. That this involved toleration and democracy—if it did—was incidental to the immediate design. In comparison with men like Essex and Manchester, Cromwell

[17] Carlyle, Letter XX, from a copy then in the possession of the Duke of Manchester; but now, says Mrs. Lomas, in the Public Record Office.

seemed democratic in his tendencies; in comparison with men like Holles and Crawford he seemed tolerant; but had he been democratic and tolerant in a modern sense he could never have accomplished what he did, for his was not a democratic or tolerant age.

It would appear from Cromwell's letter that Manchester was more occupied with the reformation of the University than was his lieutenant-general, but it is Cromwell of whom Barwick complains bitterly in his *Querela Cantabrigiensis*, that he encouraged soldiers to tear up the Book of Common Prayer before the faces of the University church divines; that he openly rebuked the University clerk who ventured to protest; and that he ordered the demolishing of a beautiful carved structure which had "not one jot of imagery about it."[18] Perhaps Cromwell was more thorough than Manchester; almost certainly he was more picturesque and far less restrained in what he did; but such measures were taken in accordance with the orders of Parliament and involved more than mere wantonness. They were part of a settled policy to destroy the influence of these things upon the people's minds, to turn their thoughts away from the old church, to break whatever hold it still maintained through its music and art, its noble services, its splendid vestments and the subtle appeal it made to the senses. Iconoclasm had long been practiced by the continental Protestants in their struggle against the Roman Catholics and it now took its place in the effort to destroy the English church. Of that movement Cromwell was now a leading representative, already challenging the position of his superior officer, as the Scotchman Baillie observed:

> "Manchester himself, a sweet, meek man, permitted his Lieutenant-general, Cromwell, to guide all the army at his pleasure. The man is a very wise and active head, universally beloved, as religious and stout. Being a known Independent, the most of the soldiers who loved new ways put themselves under his command."[19]

Such was the Cromwell of 1644, devoted to the task of overthrowing prelacy and, if monarchy stood in the way of his attack on the bishops, prepared to overthrow the King himself. Unlike some of his co-revolutionists, he was none the less a deeply religious man and in the midst of these activities he had need of his religion, for while he was occupied with the work of reformation and of recruiting new forces, he had an interruption. His son, Captain Oliver Cromwell, "a civil young gentleman and the joy of his father," lay dead of smallpox at Newport Pagnell.[20] Exactly when the boy died, or whether Crom-

[18] Barwick, *Querela Cantabrigiensis* (1646), pp. 11, 17.

[19] Baillie's letter to David Dickson, quoted in Sanford, p. 583; and in Masson, *Milton*, iii, 85.

[20] *Parliament Scout*, Mar. 15–22. A considerable amount of controversy has arisen

well journeyed back to the garrison near which his army was quartered to be present when his son was buried, is not known, nor even the place of burial. There is nothing definite to indicate where Cromwell was between when he wrote the letter to Crawford and March 25th, when he and Manchester were quartered at Huntingdon on their march to Newark which Rupert had relieved three days before. In any event the next document is connected with the death of young Oliver, for on March 28, Cromwell and Manchester signed an order to the Cambridge Committee regarding the troop of Captain Browne, who replaced Oliver as captain of the fourth troop of the Ironsides:

To the Committee at Cambridge

Deliver to Mr. Alexander Akehurst for Captain Browne's troop these twenty-six horses lately come to Cambridge. Hereof fail not. xxviiith of March 1644.

MANCHESTER.
OLIVER CROMWELL.[21]

While Cromwell was thus concerned with his iconoclasm and his private griefs, the war had come nearer. On March 13 Rupert had started for Newark, on the 21st he defeated Meldrum's forces which surrendered to him the next day, and had it not been for the difficulty of keeping his own troops together and the troubles in the south, he might have been able to join Newcastle in holding off the Fairfaxes and the Scots and perhaps even have invaded the eastern counties. But while he was engaged in capturing Meldrum's troops, Waller defeated Forth and Hopton at Cheriton in Hampshire and put to an end the projected invasion of Sussex and Kent and the envelopment of London which had long played a part in Royalist strategy. None the less, under the influence of the Dutch ambassadors who had meanwhile come to England to consider the marriage of Prince Charles to the daughter of Frederick Henry, new negotiations for peace began, with not much sincerity on either side. The situation was further complicated by the necessity of seeking a refuge for the Queen; so that at the beginning of April, with Royalist disaster in the west and Newcastle caught between the Scots and the Fairfaxes, with the Oxford Parliament prorogued until autumn, Charles reviewed his army near Newbury, sent the Queen to Exeter on her way to France, and prepared to meet his enemies. At the same time the

as to the fate of Oliver Jr., due to the account in the forged "Squire Papers" of his being killed in a skirmish near Knaresborough. Cp. *Fraser's Mag.* Dec. 1847; Gardiner, *Civil War*, i, 314; Lomas-Carlyle, i, 176–177n. His death by small-pox is corroborated by Richard Cromwell's Memoirs.

[21] Original in *St. P. Dom. Charles I*, dxxxix, no. 186; *Cal. St. P. Dom.* (1625–1649), p. 658.

forces of Essex and Manchester were ordered to rendezvous at Aylesbury and thus the campaign of 1644 which had begun with the defeat of the Royalists saw the further decline of their fortunes.

Its next phase was as disastrous in the north as Cheriton had been in the west. On April 11 the Fairfaxes stormed Selby, taking 3,000 prisoners, and Newcastle, confronting the Scots at Durham and finding his position with the Fairfaxes in his rear untenable, retired with his 5,000 horse and 6,000 foot within the walls of York as the armies of Leslie and the Fairfaxes advanced to besiege this last stronghold of the Royalists in the north. For the moment Cromwell played but little part in this new disposition of the forces. On March 30, he had left Northampton for Rugby with 1,500 horse and two regiments of foot, intending to go to Coventry;[22] but on the day the Fairfaxes stormed Selby he was back in Cambridge issuing an order to provide for the company stationed at the Hermitage in the Isle of Ely. The order was countersigned by one William Marche and Miles Sandys, the son of Sir Miles, both members of the Committee at Cambridge:

To Mr. Robert Browne, Deputy Treasurer for the Isle of Ely

April 11, 1644.

MR. BROWNE,

What monies you have in hands of the last three months' tax I desire you to pay to Lieut. Bolton, to Captain West's uses for the payment of his company, which I now order him to receive upon account. If you have not so much, yet let him have what is in your hands. And for so doing this shall be your warrant. Given under my hand the day and year above written.

OLIVER CROMWELL.[23]

Two days later he issued another order, evidently authorizing payment to his wife out of money due to himself. It also is countersigned by Marche and Sandys, indicating that it was regular enough, but it was used against him a few months later in his quarrel with Manchester. "I saw at Ely," that commander wrote, "upon the file of letters to that Committee, a letter from Col. Cromwell to them that they should pay his wife 5 l. per week towards her extraordinaries, which hath been duly paid her a great while. I am sure there is no ordinance of Parliament for that."[24]

22 *Perfect Occurrences*, Mar. 28–Apr. 4; pr. in *Cromwelliana* under date 1645.

23 Pr. in Firth, "Raising of the Ironsides," *loc. cit.*, p. 67, from '*Exchequer Mss*' in the Public Record Office. Lieutenant Roger Bolton and Captain Nicholas West are the officers to whom the order refers.

24 Statement printed at the end of "The Quarrel of the Earl of Manchester and Cromwell," *Camden Society Misc.* VIII.

To Dr. Richard Stane, at Ely[25]

DR. STANE,

I do hereby require you to pay my wife 5 l. a week to bear the extraordinary charges. This shall be your warrant. Take her hand in your notes.

April 13, 1644. OLIVER CROMWELL.

Countersigned by Marche and Sandys.[26]

Five days before that order was written Essex had protested to the Lords against the delay in furnishing him with troops. "Newark is not taken, Lincolnshire is lost, Gloucester is unsupplied and the last week there was but a step between us and death, and—what is worse —slavery." That situation had been largely remedied by the victory at Cheriton and the capture of Selby almost before Essex's letter had reached its destination; but his further complaint revealed his real grievance. "You have been pleased to reduce my army to 7,000 foot and 3,000 horse," he told the Committee, "when my Lord of Manchester is allowed an army of 14,000 and receives 34,000 l. a month for the pay of it."[27] His appeal to the City was more successful, and its officials, all but equal to the Committee of Both Kingdoms in resources and authority, met his request with a grant of money to be drawn from the estates of papists and delinquents, and three regiments of trained bands, with three more in reserve.

But Essex's letter revealed the weakness of the Parliamentary situation. The difficulties of carrying on a war by local levies who were inclined to object to serving outside their immediate neighborhood or go home after an engagement, had been felt severely by both sides. Both sides, too, had experienced dissensions among rival commanders; and Parliament, despite its successes in the field, faced controversies between Essex and Waller, between Essex and Manchester, between Cromwell and Willoughby, and presently a growing coolness between Cromwell and Manchester. At the end of April, drawing all their forces from around Bedford and Newport Pagnell, Cromwell and Manchester were near Belvoir Castle in Lincolnshire, prepared to meet Rupert, if he should return, or to retake the various garrisons in the county.[28] On May 6, while Cromwell and his horse held Goring's relieving force in check, Manchester's foot stormed Lincoln.[29] Thence,

[25] Dr. Stane was a Sidney Sussex man a few years after Cromwell and was licensed to practice medicine in 1637. The brother of Wm. Stane to whom Cromwell wrote on Jan. 6, 1644–5, it was his house in which Cromwell's sister Elizabeth lived in 1651.

[26] Firth, "Raising of the Ironsides," *loc. cit.*, p. 67, from the original in the Public Record Office.

[27] *L. J.*, vi, 505.

[28] *Mercurius Civicus*, Apr. 25–May 2.

[29] Vicars, *God's Ark*, pp. 218–220.

with Gainsborough and the rest of the county presenting no difficulties, Cromwell and his cavalry continued northward, joining Fairfax and the Scots before York within a few days, and raising the strength of the besieging forces to "a brave body of horse, 8,000 complete."[30]

YORK AND MARSTON MOOR, JUNE, 1644

With the main strength of the Parliamentary forces in the north under Manchester, Cromwell and the Fairfaxes, Essex and Waller were left to guard the capital against Charles. London and the Eastern Association would have seemed a tempting prize, but the King, unable to decide upon a definite plan of action, divided his forces. To recruit his depleted strength, he ordered the fortifications of Reading destroyed and its garrison incorporated into his army. Instead of throwing it against the capital and the eastern counties, Rupert was despatched to relieve York; Hopton sent to secure Bristol; and Maurice went on with the siege of Lyme. Charles himself marched here and there across Buckinghamshire and Bedfordshire, in search of supplies for his troops, alarming his enemies only by the uncertainty of his movements. Meanwhile a new ordinance continued the Committee of Both Kingdoms,[31] among whose twenty-one members Cromwell was numbered, and thôse of the Committee left in London wrote constantly to vulnerable places, warning them to look to their defences and encouraging them with assurances that Waller would follow the movements of the King.

Meanwhile, too, on June 3, the day that Manchester arrived at York with the remainder of his forces, the younger Vane was sent to urge the army before York to oppose Rupert's advance. That commander had turned aside to relieve Lathom House where the Countess of Derby had long resisted the Parliamentary besiegers, and to plunder the country to support his troops. The commanders at York refused to abandon their siege; nor were they more favorable to the other, and perhaps the real, reason for Vane's mission. He had a proposal to make which Parliament had refused but which he hoped would appeal to the army men: the deposition of the King. Neither Leven, Fairfax, nor Manchester would listen to Vane but Cromwell's position is not so clear. It has been suggested that he saw even then the futility of attempting a settlement with Charles which would secure Puritanism and that his quarrel with Manchester and the Scots started with his inclination to accept Vane's proposal to crown the Prince of Wales.[32]

[30] *Mercurius Britannicus*, May 13.

[31] *C. J.*, iii, 503–4; *L. J.*, vi, 564–6.

[32] Agostini to Doge, June 7/17; June 21/July 1. *Venetian Transcripts*, Record

The attention of the commanders centered on the siege. On June 17 Crawford, now beginning to supplant Cromwell in Manchester's favor, exploded a mine which had been in progress for several days, without warning any but Manchester's troops who endeavored to storm the place. The attempt of so small a body to enter the breach was promptly repulsed, and, with insufficient time to prepare another before Rupert's expected arrival, the disappointed commanders could only turn their attention to his coming. After a fortnight they learned that their wait was at an end when intelligence came that Rupert with 15,000 men had advanced by Skipton to Knaresborough, but twelve miles from York. Fearing to be caught between Rupert and Newcastle, the Parliament's forces hastily withdrew while Rupert, advancing toward York by way of Boroughbridge, sent word to Newcastle to join him. The following letter, written at Cromwell's command by the Scoutmaster General, whose narrative of the battle remains as one of the best accounts,[33] indicates the close intelligence kept between the several parts of the Parliamentary army, from the strategic positions they had taken in the hope of drawing Rupert into battle before he could relieve York:

"*To the Right Honourable the Earl of Manchester, These humbly present*

"My Lord,

"Our intelligence from divers places agreeing that the enemy's horse and foot did advance this day towards Otley, and quarter there and the towns thereabouts this night, hath occasioned us to draw all our horse of both nations into a body upon the moor close by Long Marston, within five miles of York, where now we are, expecting what further orders we shall receive from your Lordship and the other generals.

"My Lord, I humbly offer this, that exact orders might be sent to my Lord Fairfax's troops that are in general parts of this country to march up either to us or you, that they may not by their absence be made useless. The Lieutenant-General commanded me to send this express to your Lordship, being in expectation to hear your Lordship's further resolutions. My Lord, I am

"Your Lordship's most humble servant,

Long Marston, this 30th of June, 1644
Between one and two o'clock in the morning. "Leon. Watson.

P.S. "The enemy's whole body is about 15,000."[34]

With the junction of Rupert and Newcastle it was evident that York was saved, and to bar Rupert's way to the Eastern Association, the Parliamentary commanders decided to fall back in the direction

Office; Sabran to Mazarin, Aug. 29/Sept. 8. *Archives des Affaires Etrangeres*, li, f. 106, both quoted in S. R. Gardiner, *Civil War*, i, 368n.

[33] Watson, *A more exact Relation of the late Battle* (1644).

[34] Printed in Bell, *Memorials of the Civil War*, i, 111.

of Tadcaster. Newcastle was loath to follow them, but Rupert, as usual, was eager for the fray and was strengthened in his resolution by his interpretation of the King's ambiguous orders. Crossing the bridge of boats at Poppleton during the night, by the morning of July 2 his advance guard of horse was at Long Marston Moor in sight of the rearguard of the Parliament cavalry under Cromwell, Fairfax and David Leslie covering the retreat of the foot under Leven which was near Tadcaster. It was evident that the Royalists would attack and Fairfax sent hasty orders to Leven to turn back. By two o'clock in the afternoon they had arrived and Rupert's and Newcastle's men were in position on the moor, which was to be the scene of the battle.

Perhaps a mile and a half in length, Marston Moor was bounded on the east by the village of Long Marston, on the west by the hamlet of Tockwith. Its western end was chiefly furze and broom; on its southern edge was a ditch and hedge from which fields of rye and wheat sloped up to a little hill. At the end of the ditch toward Tockwith was a marsh and a rabbit warren, and at the Long Marston end rough ground and furze. It was on such a field of battle that the armies were drawn up, the Royalists on the moor north of the ditch, the Parliamentarians on the south, so close to the ditch and to each other, as Oliver's scoutmaster said, "their foot were close to our noses." As usual, the foot formed the centre of each army. On the Royalist side the first line was formed of Byron's men on the right centre and Rupert's Bluecoats on the left, with Newcastle's White-coats behind them and in the rear Rupert's life-guards. Opposite them the Parliament foot under the general command of Fairfax was composed chiefly of the Scotch regiments, with Manchester on the left, opposite Byron; Baillie on the right opposite Rupert's Bluecoats, and Crawford, some Scots regiments and Lumsden in the second line.

Thanks to their superiority in numbers of some three to two, the Parliamentary forces overlapped the Royalists. On the right a body of Scotch horse opposed the Royalist left composed of Goring's cavalry. On the left wing of Fairfax's army was Cromwell with his horse, opposed to Rupert's command made up of Byron's three regiments of horse, supported by three regiments under Molineux and his own regiment in the rear. In such formation the armies lay all afternoon until six o'clock, till, tired of inaction and hungry, Rupert went to his supper and Newcastle retired to his coach to smoke a pipe. It was the moment for which the Parliament's forces had waited and about seven o'clcock Cromwell's cavalry charged, fell on Byron's horse whose extreme right had advanced beyond the slough and was broken up by Frizel's dragoons, who cleared the ditch of Royalist musketeers and opened the way for the charge of the main body of Cromwell's Ironsides. They fell on Byron's first line and with pistol and sword-point soon drove it before them "like a little dust." It seemed that they were on the point of victory, but even while they were disorganized by success, there burst on them the charge of the regiments of Rupert and of Molineux, and Cromwell's first and second lines were stopped. A pistol bullet grazed his neck, the flash of the shot blinded him, and for the moment he was near defeat. But at that moment the Royalist attack was stayed by the attack of Leslie with his 800 Scots upon their flank, and in the confusion which it brought, Cromwell was able to reform his men, head them in another and successful charge against the Royalists now fighting on two fronts, and after a brief, bloody hand-to-hand conflict, drive them before him and send Leslie and his Scots to pursue the fugitives, while he himself turned to attack the Royalist centre on the flank.

It was high time, for while Cromwell had broken Rupert's cavalry, the battle elsewhere had gone ill for Parliament. Its left centre under Manchester had passed the ditch and, helped by the rout of Byron's horse, had driven back his foot and Rupert's Bluecoats. But on their right Newcastle's Whitecoats had checked then routed Fairfax's infantry, with their reserves of Scots. Still beyond them on the farther right centre, Baillie's flank was thus left open to the Royalist attack, and though some of the Scots stood off the Royalist advance, they were in evil plight, for Goring had fallen on the Parliamentary right wing with his horse, driven Fairfax's raw levies before him, and while some of his cavalry pursued the fleeing Parliament men as far as Tadcaster and began to plunder the baggage-train, the rest had turned against the exposed centre. Even the Parliamentary commanders began to abandon the field. Lord Fairfax fled toward Hull, Leven toward Leeds. Sir Thomas Fairfax slipped through Lucas's horse and managed to join Manchester, and the day seemed lost. The right wing was gone except for the handful of the Scottish regiments fighting for their lives. The centre was broken and though Crawford had been successful on the left, the Parliamentary army was disorganized and ready to follow its leaders in their flight. There were left only the remnants of the five Scotch regiments on the farther right and the command of Crawford with Cromwell's Ironsides on the left.

That, as it happened, was enough to turn the tide. Ordering a wheel to the right against Newcastle's Whitecoats, supported by Leslie's horse now returned from pursuing Rupert's men, Cromwell led a charge against Goring's cavalry and drove them before him. Then with Crawford's infantry and Baillie's Scots he fell on Newcastle's Whitecoats and, fighting to the last, driven foot by foot to a cattle-fold in the midst of the moor, at White Syke Close, like the Redcoats at Edgehill the Whitecoats died where they stood. Seldom in history has there been a more dramatic reversal of fortune on the field than that accomplished by Cromwell at Marston Moor, and from it he emerged the hero of the army and his cause.

The royal army was not merely beaten, it was destroyed. Newcastle, with Eythin and a crowd of Royalist officers, hastened to Scarborough and thence sailed to the Continent. Rupert, collecting some 6,000 horse in York, retreated toward Wales. York surrendered and it was evident that, with his army gone and his principal supporters on their way to the Continent, Charles's cause was lost in the north. It was no less evident that the battle of Marston Moor had strengthened the position of the Independents and of Cromwell. When he appeared in the House two months later, he was thanked publicly for his "fidelity in the cause in hand, and in particular for the faithful service performed in the late battle near York where God made him a special instrument in obtaining that great victory." The only record he himself left of the engagement occurs in a letter of condolence to his brother-in-law, Valentine Walton, whose eldest son, Valentine, was killed; and such account of the battle as he wrote is only designed to assure the bereaved father that his son had not died in vain:[35]

To Colonel Valentine Walton

DEAR SIR,

It's our duty to sympathise in all mercies; that we may praise the Lord together in chastisements or trials, that so we may sorrow together.

Truly England and the Church of God hath had a great favour from the Lord, in this great victory given unto us, such as the like never was since this war began. It had all the evidences of an absolute victory obtained by the Lord's blessing upon the godly party principally. We never charged but we routed the enemy. The left wing, which I commanded, being our own horse, saving a few Scots in our rear, beat all the Prince's horse. God made them as stubble to our swords, we charged their regiments of foot with our horse, routed all we charged. The particulars I cannot relate now, but I believe, of twenty-thousand the Prince hath not four-thousand left. Give glory, all the glory, to God.

Sir, God hath taken away your eldest son by a cannon-shot. It brake his leg. We were necessitated to have it cut off, whereof he died.

Sir, you know my trials this way; but the Lord supported me with this: that the Lord took him into the happiness we all pant after and live for.

[35] Historians have censured Cromwell severely for his failure to give the Scots their due in this letter, accusing him of direct falsehood. But, as Firth has observed, the facts stated in the letter are rigidly accurate. The left wing, under Cromwell's command, did beat all the royalist horse, and it did consist of the cavalry of the Eastern Association, with a few Scots as its reserve. Cromwell was hailed by his contemporaries as the great agent in that victory. *C. J.*, iii, 62. Cp. Firth, "Marston Moor," in *Trans. of the Royal Historical Society*, (1899), p. 61.

There is your precious child full of glory, to know sin nor sorrow any more. He was a gallant young man, exceeding gracious. God give you His comfort. Before his death he was so full of comfort that to Frank Russel and myself he could not express it, it was so great above his pain. This he said to us. Indeed it was admirable. A little after, he said one thing lay upon his spirit. I asked him what it was. He told me that it was, that God had not suffered him to be no more the executioner of His enemies. At his fall, his horse being killed with the bullet, and as I am informed three horses more, I am told he bid them open to the right and left, that he might see the rogues run. Truly he was exceedingly beloved in the Army, of all that knew him. But few knew him, for he was a precious young man, fit for God. You have cause to bless the Lord. He is a glorious saint in Heaven, wherein you ought exceedingly to rejoice. Let this drink up your sorrow; seeing these are not feigned words to comfort you, but the thing is so real and undoubted a truth. You may do all things by the strength of Christ. Seek that, and you shall easily bear your trial. Let this public mercy to the Church of God make you to forget your private sorrow. The Lord be your strength; so prays

Your truly faithful and loving brother,

July 5th, 1644. OLIVER CROMWELL.

[P.S.] My love to your daughter, and to my Cousin Percevall, Sister Desbrowe and all friends with you.[36]

With more than 4,000 Royalists killed and 100 of their colours, "enough to make surplices for all the Cathedrals in England" taken, from this catastrophe Prince Rupert and his surviving forces managed to escape to Lancashire, then to Wales. Cromwell with 5,000 horse was ordered to disperse the remainder of the Royalist army, but gave up the pursuit after a few days and returned to the leaguer before York. The city was surrendered by Sir Thomas Glemham on July 16,[37] and the victorious commanders turned their attention to another matter, which presently all but superseded the conduct of the war.

This was, in form at least, the settlement of the church; but behind that lay the question of the relations of the Parliamentary leaders to each other, to the Committee of Both Kingdoms, to the Scots, and, finally, to the issue of peace and the King. It had begun with the struggle between Essex and Vane, as a result of which the astute Parliamentarian had first succeeded in making his committee superior to the Lord General, and after Marston Moor had put control of military operations and negotiations with the King into the hands of the Committee dominated by himself, St. John and the Independents, under oath of secrecy. The Lords, now reduced to some seven-

[36] Pr. in Seward's *Anecdotes* (1796), iv, 371; Ellis, *Original Letters*, (First series, 1824), iii, 299. Pr. in Lomas-Carlyle, Letter XXI, from the holograph original, in the Morrison Collection until it was sold in 1917.

[37] Earl of Denbigh to Committee of Both Kingdoms, July 11, *Cal. S. P. Dom.* (1644), p. 339; *Parliament Scout*, July 19; Rushworth, iv, 640.

teen members of whom not more than thirteen or fourteen were ever present, were overpowered by a House of Commons of which scarcely more than a hundred and fifty took part in divisions. In effect the government was vested in the Committee of Both Kingdoms, and, thanks to the absence of some of its members who, like Cromwell, were on military service, the little coterie about Vane and St. John found themselves for the time the masters of the situation.

They were in the main Independents, like Cromwell himself, and like him committed to the overthrow of Charles. But Manchester and Leven, like Essex, were Presbyterians, and Fairfax, though more acceptable to the Independents, was described as belonging to that group whose chief concern was not so much the destruction of the King as the "reformation" of the church, that is to say the establishment of presbyterianism, with peace and parliamentary government. For that the victory of Marston Moor seemed to offer an opportunity and within a fortnight Manchester, Leven and Fairfax addressed a letter to the Committee to that effect. To this Cromwell and his immediate followers like Ireton and Pickering were opposed, and with this came the beginning of an open breach among the commanders. Councils of war were given up and the efforts of Cromwell and his party to follow up the victory and advance on Royalist Newark were opposed.[38] None the less Cromwell had gained new prestige from the victory and how great his reputation had become is evidenced by the fact that Leslie had refused to command the cavalry at Marston Moor, preferring to serve under him. "Europe," he said of Manchester's army, "hath no better soldiers"; and it was apparently at this time that Rupert gave Cromwell the name of "Ironside."

THE EASTERN COUNTIES, JULY–AUGUST, 1644

After Marston Moor the victorious armies divided; Leven to besiege Newcastle; the Fairfaxes to reduce Scarborough, Pontefract and Helmsley; Manchester and Cromwell to defend the eastern counties. On the way from York to Lincoln, Crawford was detached to secure Sheffield while Manchester seized Newcastle's mansion of Welbeck. But he was unwilling to embark on a more vigorous policy and when Lieutenant-colonel Lilburne in defiance of his orders took Tickhill Castle, Manchester threatened to hang him. To prevent this Cromwell, who had directed Lilburne to quarter in the place, rode over with Crawford, ostensibly to see that the articles of surrender were duly performed.[39] It was apparent that the breach between the two commanders was widening. Though Cromwell continually urged a more aggressive policy, Manchester refused to secure Belvoir Castle

[38] Exam. of Col. J. Pickering, 12 Dec. *Cal. S. P. Dom.* (1644–5), p. 151.
[39] *Ibid.*, p. 152; Lilburne's testimony, Nov. 30, *Ibid.*, 148–9.

or attempt Newark,[40] much less to march against Rupert at Chester, or even to help Brereton against him.

Meanwhile Cromwell weeded out of his regiments all opposed to liberty of the "sects" or who hoped to end the war by negotiation rather than by arms. "I will not deny," he was later accused of saying, "but that I desire to have none in my army but such as are of the Independent judgment"; and, asked by Manchester for his reasons, said boldly, "that in case there should be propositions for peace, or any other conclusion of a peace, such as might not stand with the ends that honest men should aim at, this army might prevent such a mischief." Men with whom distinctions of birth counted, Manchester told his fellow-peers, felt instinctively that Cromwell was their bitterest enemy. Cromwell hoped, Manchester added, to 'live to see never a nobleman in England' and spoke of loving some persons better than others 'because they did not love lords,' and that 'it would not be well until Manchester was but Mr. Montague.'[41] Nor did he love the Scots much more. 'In the way they now carry themselves,' he was reported to have said to Manchester, 'pressing for their discipline, I could as soon draw my sword against them as against any in the King's army.'[42] It was no wonder that Presbyterians, English and Scotch alike, as well as Royalists, were antagonized; that they spoke of the Isle of Ely as "a mere Amsterdam," "that nest of unclean birds" as it was described by other pens in later years.

With such dissension among its commanders, the activity of the Parliamentary armies was all but paralysed and the Royalists seized their advantage. While Rupert secured Chester, Waller, whose forces were now reduced to some four thousand men, threw himself into Abingdon but Charles had no mind to be shut up in Oxford and, eluding his enemies by a masterly night march, escaped from Oxford to Evesham. Essex, despite his orders from the Parliament, advanced to the west to the relief of Lyme with Charles in hot pursuit. Outmarched, outnumbered and outmaneuvered by the King and seeking help in vain from Parliament, on September 1, Essex was cooped up at Lostwithiel, and while his cavalry escaped and he himself fled by sea to Plymouth, Skippon was compelled to lay down his arms, though he and his men went free. The decision of Marston Moor was not, indeed, reversed; but with Rupert holding Chester and North Wales; with scattered Royalist forces still unsubdued in the north; with Charles's success at Cropredy Bridge over Waller and at Lostwithiel over Essex; with Waller's force disorganized and Essex's army disarmed; and with dissensions among the Parliamentary commanders, the King had some hope of ultimate success.

[40] Vicars, *God's Ark*, p. 294.

[41] Manchester to House of Lords, *Camden Miscellany*, VIII; Holles, *Memoirs*, p. 14.

[42] *Ibid.*

Meanwhile, after weeks of inactivity save for a gradual movement to the south, on September 1 Cromwell was with Manchester in Lincoln, where he wrote in regard to the reorganization of the government of the Isle of Ely with whose administration he was dissatisfied:

For my noble Friends the Committee for the Isle of Ely: Present these

GENTLEMEN,

I understand that you have lately released some persons committed by Captain Castle, all upon clear and necessary grounds as they are represented unto me; rendering them as very enemies as any we have, and as much requiring to have them continued secured.

I have given order to Captain Husbands to see them recommitted to the hands of my Marshal, Richard White. And I much desire you (for future) not to entrench upon me so much as to release them, or any committed in the like case by myself, or my Deputy and Commanders in the Garrison, until myself or some superior authority be satisfied in the cause, and do give order in allowance for their enlargement, for I profess I will be no Governor, nor engage any other under me to undertake such a charge, upon such weak terms.

I am so sensible of the need we have to improve the present opportunity of our being master in the field and having no enemy near the Isle, to spare what charge may be towards the making of those fortifications which may make it more defensible hereafter if we shall have more need, as I shall desire you, for that end, to ease the Isle and Treasury from the superfluous charge of two several Committees for the several parts of the Isle; and that one Committee, settled at March, may serve for the whole Isle.

Wherefore I wish that one of your number may, in your courses, intend and appear at the Committee to manage and uphold it the better for all parts of the Isle.

Resting upon your care herein, I remain,

Your friend to serve you,

Lincoln,
This 1st Sept., 1644. OLIVER CROMWELL.[43]

The disagreement between Cromwell and Manchester had deepened almost from day to day; but the first open expression of complaint from Cromwell of Manchester's inactivity and justification of his own troops seems to occur in his letter to his brother-in-law, Walton, who had apparently urged him to go to the assistance of Essex. He had reached Sleaford just south of Lincoln with his troops on September 3,[44] whence he wrote with veiled but bitter reflections on his superior officer:

[43] Copy in the Tangye Collection in the London Museum. Printed in the *Athenaeum*, Dec. 13, 1845, from which Carlyle printed it with some alterations, Letter XXII.

[44] Pickering's examination, Dec. 12, *Cal. S. P. Dom.* (1644–5), p. 152.

For Colonel Walton: These in London

Sir,

We do with grief of heart resent the sad condition of our Army in the West, and of affairs there. That business hath our hearts with it, and truly had we wings, we would fly thither. So soon as ever my Lord and the foot set me loose, there shall be no want in me to hasten what I can to that service, for indeed all other considerations are to be laid aside, and to give place to it, as being of far more importance. I hope the Kingdom shall see that, in the midst of our necessities, we shall serve them without disputes. We hope to forget our wants, which are exceeding great, and ill-cared for; and desire to refer the many slanders heaped upon us by false tongues to God, who will, in due time, make it appear to the world that we study the glory of God, the honour and liberty of the Parliament, for which we unanimously fight, without seeking our own interests.

Indeed we find our men never so cheerful as when there is work to do. I trust you will always hear so of them. The Lord is our strength, and in Him is all our hope. Pray for us. Present my love to my friends: I beg their prayers. The Lord still bless you.

We have some amongst us much slow in action: if we could all intend our own ends less, and our ease too, our business in this Army would go on wheels for expedition. Because some of us are enemies to rapine, and other wickednesses, we are said to be factious, to seek to maintain our opinions in religion by force, which we detest and abhor. I profess I could never satisfy myself of the justness of this War, but from the authority of the Parliament to maintain itself in its rights; and in this Cause I hope to approve myself an honest man and single-hearted.

Pardon me that I am thus troublesome. I write but seldom; it gives me a little ease to pour my mind, in the midst of calumnies, into the bosom of a friend.

Sir, no man more truly loves you than

Your brother and servant,

Sleeford,
Sept. 5th. Oliver Cromwell.[45]

In Peterborough the next day, September 6, and in Huntingdon the day, following Cromwell tried again without success to persuade Manchester that their presence in the west was imperative and that the orders of Parliament should be obeyed, but even the news of the surrender of Essex brought only a threat from the Earl that he

[45] Carlyle, Letter XXIII, from Seward, *Anecdotes*, iv, 369, which is professed to have been taken from the original in the Bodleian, dated "6th or 5th Sept." Cromwell would not have dated a letter that way, and, since Seward's claim to have taken his copy of the July 5th letter from the "Original at the Bodleian" is certainly erroneous, it is more than likely that this letter, too, was from some copy, probably the one which was once amongst "Mrs. Prescott's Mss," cal. in *Hist. Mss. Comm. Rept.*, 2 App., p. 98, and was dated thus because of the inability of the copyist to read the date with certainty. The *Athenaeum*, 19 June 1869, prints the letter and dates it Sept. 5th, which is probably correct, since on Sept. 6th Cromwell is known to have been in Peterborough, some thirty miles from Sleaford. Cp. Pickering's exam. *Op. cit.*

would hang anyone who attempted further to advise him.[46] His obvious duty was to throw his army between Charles and the capital, but he was the less inclined to move because the dissensions in his forces were so deep that, as he testified, some of his Independents were as joyful over the defeat of the Presbyterian Essex as if they themselves and not the King had gained a victory.[47]

Believing Crawford to be the author of all the trouble, Cromwell assured Manchester that his colonels would resign in a body if a new major-general were not appointed. By September 11, as Baillie says, unable to settle their dispute, "at last Manchester, Cromwell and Crawford come up themselves. Our labour to reconcile them was vain: Cromwell was peremptor; notwithstanding the kingdom's evident hazard, and the evident displeasure of our nation, yet, if Crawford were not cashiered, his Colonels would lay down their commissions." Moreover, as he goes on to say:

> "While Cromwell is here the House of Commons, without the least advertisement to any of us [the Scottish Commissioners in London], or of the Assembly, passes an order that the Grand Committee of both Houses, Assembly, and us, shall consider of the means to unite us [the Presbyterians] and the Independents; or, if that be found impossible, to see how they may be tolerate. This has much affected us."

The matter having been laid before the Committee of Both Kingdoms, the result was that Cromwell withdrew his demand for Crawford's dismissal in return for Manchester's promise to go at once to the aid of the Parliamentary army in the west.[48]

But this was not the only business which occupied Cromwell's attention during his presence at Westminster in the interval between campaigns. The difference of opinion between Cromwell and Manchester ran deeper than mere personal incompatibility or even than the question of the conduct of the war. It was founded on ecclesiastical antagonism, now increasing to the breaking-point. In June, 1643, a Parliamentary ordinance had authorized the calling of an Assembly of Divines to which a delegation of Scotch ministers had been invited. It had met on July 1 and its hundred and fifty delegates, of whom four-fifths were ministers, had begun by agreeing that church government by bishops and archbishops should be abolished. As to what should take its place, opinion had divided, though inclining toward Presbyterianism. Vane's adroitness, however, had left the way open for another system if Parliament should direct, and from that time until now the arguments had raged over the precise nature

46 Pickering's examination, *loc. cit.*, p. 152. Depositions of Cromwell and Hammond, *ibid.*, pp. 150, 154.

47 Bruce, *Quarrel of Manchester and Cromwell*, p. 76.

48 *Perfect Diurnall*; Manchester to Lords, *Camden Miscellany*, VIII; Baillie, ii, 230.

of a new establishment. Little by little, under the guidance of Vane in the House and of Cromwell in the army, the Independent party had grown in numbers and determination and with Cromwell's rise to greater importance, it was preparing to challenge the Presbyterians.

The battle of Marston Moor and Essex's defeat at Lostwithiel strengthened the position of the new party immeasurably, and on September 13 in a debate concerning the form of ordination for the ministers of the proposed church, Cromwell, in the House again after an absence of seven months, seized the opportunity to intercede for the "sectaries." He suggested to St. John the wording of a motion which resulted in an order that

"the Committee of Lords and Commons appointed to treat with the Commissioners of Scotland and the Committee of the Assembly do take into consideration the differences in opinion of the members of the Assembly in point of church-government, and to endeavour a union, if it be possible; and, in case that cannot be done, to endeavour the finding out some way, how far tender consciences, who cannot in all things submit to the common rule which shall be established, may be borne with according to the Word, and as may stand with the public peace, that so the proceedings of the Assembly may not be so much retarded."[49]

It was the voice of St. John but the spirit of Cromwell; and with it there began a struggle between the rigid Presbyterian system and the looser bond of Independency. Each was equally opposed to episcopacy, but it was evident that their mutual hatred of that system which had held them together in opposition to the King was threatened with this division of opinion as to the character of the new church establishment. Already Cromwell had indicated his leanings toward greater religious liberty than his Presbyterian superiors, Essex and Manchester, desired. But he had accepted Manchester's promises of activity in the field, while by his defeat at Lostwithiel Essex was practically eliminated from consideration either by Cromwell or Vane.

Taking the oath of secrecy as a member of the Committee of Both Kingdoms on September 14, Cromwell was sent three days later with 2,000 horse to Banbury, to meet Rupert who, however, had disappeared when he reached there.[50] Still at Banbury on the 26th, he passed on intelligence of the enemy's movements to Westminster:

To the Committee of Both Kingdoms

"Sir Thomas Glemham with 21 colours of horse and dragoons is marched

[49] D'Ewes Diary, *Harl. Mss*, 166, f. 113b. Quoted in Gardiner, *Civil War*, ii, 30· Cp. also, Baillie, ii, 230; Masson, *Milton*, v, 168–170.

[50] *Cal. S. P. Dom.*, (1644), pp. 500–501.

from Newark by Ashby-de-la-Zouch, it is believed, with intention to raise the siege of Banbury or join with Rupert." Banbury, Sept. 26, 1644.[51]

This elicited a reply telling of reinforcements ordered to him and at about the same time Cromwell sent another letter of intelligence with similar news:

To Sir Samuel Luke, Governor of Newport Pagnell

The King is back at Oxford with great strength. [Banbury, c. Sept. 26, 1644.][52]

That information, at least, was incorrect. After his success at Lostwithiel, the King had given his opponents every opportunity to reorganize. Whether from disinclination or inability he did not follow up his victory, but leaving Grenvile to besiege Plymouth, and detachments to block up Lyme and Taunton, he had turned back and reached Chard on September 23, while Manchester was pushing beyond Watford and the Committee was preparing to send some City regiments to his aid. To prevent Charles's return from the west, on October 1 the Commons resolved to join the forces of Essex to those of Waller and Manchester. The eastern counties demanded their army for their own protection, but without avail, for a week after sending the letters asking for reinforcements, Cromwell was still at Banbury with orders to make haste southward toward Reading. There Manchester awaited him, impatient to follow the Association's bidding, but feeling obliged to obey the order from the Committee of Both Kingdoms to join Waller to prevent Charles from coming out of the southwest.[53] Less reluctant than Manchester to fall in with the plan of the Committee, and with fresh equipment ordered by Parliament for his soldiers,[54] Cromwell set out toward Reading, stopping on his way to arrange for the quartering of some soldiers who had fallen ill:

To ....

SIR,

I would desire you to let these sick soldiers have convenient quarter in your town until they be recovered of their sickness.

Octob: 5th, 1644. OLIVER CROMWELLE.[55]

[51] Cromwell's letter has not been preserved but the reply, dated Sept. 28, is in *Cal. S. P. Dom.* (1644), pp. 541–2.

[52] Luke's request to Sir W. Botteler, Sept. 28th, for additional forces is our only information concerning this letter of Cromwell's. *Hist. Mss Comm. Rept.* 8, App. I, p. 3a (Marlborough).

[53] Manchester to Committee of Both Kingdoms, *Camden Society*, N. S., xii, 35–7.

[54] *C. J.*, iii, 652.

[55] *S. P. Dom. Charles I*, dxxxix, f. 227. Underwritten is a note: "Pd Eliz. Cley and others for quartering these souldiers, 1–12–0."

Before he was able to reach Reading, Cromwell wrote again to Luke to give directions made necessary by the receipt of fresh orders —presumably from Manchester who, it seems, was purposely delaying action—to return to Banbury:

To Sir Samuel Luke

NOBLE SIR,

I thank you for your letters. I have sent them both to the Earl of Manchester. I met here with a command to send me back again to intend this business at Banbury. I march that way this evening. We must still desire the continuance of your assistance in this business. I hope, Sir, if you hear of the King's advancing near to these parts or to Oxford, we shall have timely notice from you. It will behove us to be vigilant, because the King horseth his foot.

Sir, no man is more yours than,

Your humble servant,

October 6. OLIVER CROMWELL.

[P.S.] Sir, I expect two of my troops, Capt. Horsman's and Capt. Porter's, to come up to me. If you hear of them, I pray you send them up towards Banbury. I fear lest they should march towards Aylesbury.[56]

Two days later Cromwell was in the vicinity of Banbury again, at Syresham in Northamptonshire, with plans for a rendezvous a few miles away, at Sulgrave, the next morning, as we learn from another letter:

To Sir Samuel Luke

SIR,

I believe you are assured I take no pleasure in keeping your troop here. Its only for that end to which it was commanded hither at the first by the Committee of Both Kingdoms. I was very loath to detain it, and leave it wholly to yourself either to continue or dismiss it; only Col. Fiennes sent me word early this morning that about a thousand of the enemy's horse were gathering together about Evesham, and endeavouring to mount as many musketeers as they could; upon which, and to draw nearer to the rest of our horse, I have a rendezvous this morning at Sougrave.

Sir, not having more to trouble you, I rest,

Your humble servant,

Siseham,
October 8, 1644. OLIVER CROMWELL.

[P.S.] I doubt the drawing away of your troop may occasion the Aylesbury troops to long to be going also.[57]

[56] Copy in Sir Samuel Luke's letter book. *Stowe Mss*, cxc, f. 42b. Lomas-Carlyle, Suppl. 8. Samuel Porter and Robert Housman were captains of Cromwell's seventh and ninth troops.

[57] Luke's letter book. *Stowe Mss*, cxc, f. 57. Lomas-Carlyle, Suppl. 8.

THE SECOND BATTLE OF NEWBURY, OCTOBER 14–NOVEMBER 15, 1644

It was not until October 14, the day the Lords passed an ordinance for raising money to arm Cromwell's troops,[58] that Cromwell finally joined Manchester at Reading. The same day the Committee of Both Kingdoms agreed to put the command of the Parliamentary army in a commission under a Council of War including Essex, Manchester and Waller, thus avoiding the necessity of appointing one commander of the armies which were about to join forces.[59] The next day the King entered Salisbury and, with Manchester planning to meet Essex at Basingstoke, Waller knew that his only course was to retreat and join forces with the other two commanders. Manchester, with Cromwell, reached Basing on October 17; Waller two days later; and on the 21st Essex was with them, making an army which, with five regiments from London, numbered about 19,000 men.[60]

Meanwhile Charles reached Whitchurch, scarcely fifteen miles away, with an army of 10,000, determined to relieve Basing House. For the moment, however, that task seemed impossible and he withdrew to Newbury, where on October 26 he was confronted by the Parliamentary army.

The Royalist position was strong, with its right wing at Newbury, the left on the Lambourne River with a strongly fortified manor, Shaw House, protecting the crossing, and the rear in command of Prince Maurice at Speen Hill. In the open ground in the centre were the infantry with cavalry supports, and still farther back the stronghold of Donnington Castle. It was apparent that the position was impregnable from the front and flanks, and it was resolved to send Balfour, Skippon, Waller and Cromwell on a wide encircling march around Donnington Castle and attack the rear under Prince Maurice at Speen, while Manchester diverted attention from their march by an attack on Shaw House. The night of the 26th the troops for the encircling movement bivouacked at North Heath, four miles north of Newbury, out of range of the guns of Donnington Castle. At daybreak they were on the move, ordered to attack while Manchester launched a diversion against the Royalist left centre.

But the Royalists were fully aware of the whole plan. Maurice was ordered to face west and prepare to receive the attack of the encircling force and when they reached their objective about three o'clock in the afternoon, with Balfour on the right, Cromwell on the left with their cavalry, and Skippon and Waller in the centre with the infantry, Maurice was ready to receive them. Through lanes and

[58] Manchester to Committee of Both Kingdoms, *Camden Society*, N. S. xii, 44–5; *L. J.*, vii, 24; *C. J.*, iii, 662.

[59] *Cal. S. P. Dom.* (1644–5).

[60] Manchester to Comm. of Both Kingdoms, *Camden Society*, N. S. xii, p. 47.

hedges and across a long strip of open ground commanded by Maurice's five cannon, they forced their way, and, despite Maurice's preparations, stormed his breastworks and captured his guns. The main body of Royalists hastened to send supports. Had Manchester then attacked Charles's weakened lines, the battle might well have been won. But he delayed too long; and though the flanking force had all but cut its way through to a position where it could attack the Royalist cavalry, at the last hedge Balfour was beaten back by a Royalist counter-charge and Cromwell found himself unable to advance. Not until near night did Manchester yield to the solicitations of his officers, and then it was too late. His attack stalled on the defenses of Shaw House; and under cover of the dark Charles's army marched toward Wallingford and so to Oxford undisturbed.[61]

After the escape of the King was discovered, Waller and Cromwell dashed off in pursuit, but left their forces at Blewbury and hurried back to urge Manchester and the rest of the officers to follow, in the hope of routing the King's army before a junction with Rupert could be effected. But Manchester, perhaps wisely, considered the season, the exhausted condition of his men and the failure to receive fresh supplies as good and sufficient reason for delaying his pursuit. His real reason, however, was manifest. He had rejected Vane's proposal to depose the King; he did not want Charles killed or captured, but weakened; and, as a Presbyterian, more and more he feared the rising power of what a later Presbyterian called the "intolerable sects" of Anabaptists and Independents who filled Cromwell's ranks.

While the Parliamentary commanders, despite the efforts of Cromwell and Waller, spent their time in fruitless and acrimonious discussions, Charles found refuge in Oxford where he was joined by Rupert to whom he gave command of his army. By November 1 Manchester, following the advice of Cromwell and Waller too late, was at Compton and the next day advanced the foot to Blewbury, taking two days to go eleven miles. At Harwell on November 3, another council of war was held and Cromwell agreed to keep the army together in retirement on Newbury, though, as he said, all were against drawing back save Manchester. On Tuesday, the 5th, Manchester appointed a rendezvous for the next morning on Compton Downs, four or five miles back toward Newbury. Cromwell spent Tuesday night on Chilton plain and went to Compton on the 6th, where, on the ground of weakness of the soldiers and lack of provisions, Manchester, dispensing with the formalities of a council of war, commanded the army to retire to Newbury. The same day came orders to that effect from the Committee of Both Kingdoms. Once at Newbury further dissensions

[61] The various contemporary reports of the battle are admirably summed up in Gardiner, *Civil War*, ii, 44 ff. and his account has in general been closely followed by later writers.

immediately arose. Donnington Castle, though besieged, was still in the hands of the Royalists and Rupert determined to relieve its defenders. Ordered on November 7 to return and check him, Cromwell virtually rebelled against Manchester. "My Lord," he was reported as saying, "your horse are so spent, so harassed out by hard duty, that they will fall down under their riders if you thus command them; you may have their skins but you can have no service." [62]

The Parliamentary army was around Newbury again on November 8. No resistance was made to the Royalist relief of Donnington Castle the next day, and, although the King drew up his army and offered battle, the Parliamentary officers remained inactive. Cromwell, with most of the horse, which had scattered in search of forage, was on the south side of the Kennet River, and a great body of what was apparently his command was seen by the Royalists "almost at a stand whether to come down or retire." [63] He awaited the order of the commanders to engage but none came, and, fearing to leave Newbury unprotected and hoping to engage the King the next day under more favorable circumstances, it was decided not to fight, and with this feeble conclusion of a great matter each side withdrew.

In the face of such divided counsels and indecision among Manchester's officers, the Royalists relieved Donnington and on November 10 the Parliamentary commanders held another council of war in a cottage near Shaw Field. All realized that their army was in no shape to fight, but Cromwell's voice was still for war. He spoke a quarter of an hour, acknowledging the difficulties of the situation but pointing out that if the King were left undefeated the French would aid him in the following spring.[64] But Manchester, apparently having just learned that French aid was no longer to be feared, again opposed further action; and with this the argument came to a head at last. "If we beat the King 99 times, yet he is King still," said Manchester, "but if the King beat us once we shall all be hanged." "My Lord," Cromwell retorted, "if this be so, why did we take up arms at first? This is against fighting ever hereafter. If so, let us make peace, be it never so base." [65]

When, however, the officers received a letter from the Committee intimating that they understood that the commanders were not abiding by the decisions of the Council of War,[66] even Cromwell came to the defense of Manchester, who had taken the rebuke very much to

[62] Ashe, *True Relation* (1644), p. 6. The facts for the operations around Newbury have been taken mostly from Money, *First and Second Battles of Newbvry* (1881).

[63] Sir Edward Walker, *Historical Discourses* (1705), p. 118.

[64] Money, *op. cit.*, p. 191; Crawford, in Bruce, "Quarrel of Manchester and Cromwell," *Camden Society*, p. 69.

[65] Examination of Haselrig, Dec. 6, *Cal. S. P. Dom.* (1644–5), p. 151. Cromwell's examination, Dec. 10 (*Ibid.*) verifies all the details of what transpired at this meeting.

[66] Nov. 12, *Ibid.*, p. 117.

heart. Impatient as Cromwell was with his general, after twice reading the letter he said, according to Crawford, "I hold him for a villain and a knave that do any man ill offices, but there was nothing done but what was justifiable and by the joint consent of the Council of War, and there was nothing done but what was answerable." [67] Whether or not Crawford afterward twisted his words in Manchester's favor, he continues:

"In my Lord of Manchester's lodging in Newbury, in the presence of my Lord of Manchester, Sir William Belfore, Sir William Waller, Major-General Skippon, Coll. Barklet, and Major-General-Crauford [and Cromwell] there was presently thought fitt that there should bee a letter drawne and sent to the Committee of Both Kingdoms . . . which was referred to bee done by Leif.-Generall Cromwell, which accordingly was done, wherein hee gave a full relation of the weakness of the army."[68]

In consequence Cromwell drew up a reply, signed, in the absence of Essex, by Manchester, Waller, Balfour, and Skippon, which was at once a statement of the position of the army, a defence of its actions, and, with all deference to its authority, was not without a hint of reproof to the Committee itself:

To the Committee of Both Kingdoms

"According to your commands we shall endeavour to keep the forces together, and with them to seize every advantage against the enemy, and endeavour to prevent the relief of Basing House. We hold it our duty to represent the state of the army, and also the nature of the service you require.

"The horse are so tired out with hard duty in such extremity of weather as hath seldom been seen, that if much more service be required of them you will quickly see your cavalry ruined without fighting. The foot are not in better case, besides the lessening of their numbers through cold and hard duty; sickness also is much on the increase, which we dare not conceal from you, daily regarding their extreme sufferings with not a little sorrow. The places we are in do not afford firing, food, or covering for them, nor is the condition of the people less to be pitied, who both within our horse and foot quarters are so exhausted that we may justly fear a famine will fall upon them.

"Having represented these things to you, we are notwithstanding ready to obey what you shall command us, and to undertake to prevent the enemy's relieving of Basing House. We find but two ways to accomplish this object; the one is by guards with half of our horse upon that duty night and day, which will undoubtedly destroy our body of horse, so weakened as before [stated]; the other by marching our whole army thither, which must lie from under covert, there being no place of shelter, until the house be reduced by famine, whose provisions we doubt not will last longer than is imagined.

[67] Crawford's narrative, *loc. cit.*, p. 69.
[68] Crawford's narrative, *loc. cit.*

How certainly this would break our army and cause all the foot to leave us we humbly submit to your judgment.

"If any inconvenience should come to the State by not keeping such castles and houses from relief, we conceive the error lies in the first undertaking such sieges and the loose prosecution of them; we hope nothing of that can be laid to our charge. Having represented to you what the waiting on this place is like to cost you at this season, we will obey your commands, if you please to let us know them.

"For the present to that force already there, we send this day one of the City regiments of foot and three of the Earl of Manchester's to quarter in Basingstoke. We have also appointed all the horse to several rendezvous this day, that so we may quarter them conveniently near Basing and be ready with them to prevent relief. But we desire you to remember what we before stated, that we can lie so but a very little time for want of provisions both for horse and man.

"If what we have here represented does not give your Lordships satisfaction, but that you would have anything more done either in relation to that place or the enemy, upon the signification of your pleasure it shall be obeyed." [Nov. 15, 1644.][69]

CROMWELL'S QUARREL WITH MANCHESTER

It was only too evident that matters had come to the breaking-point and with the permission of the Committee of Both Kingdoms to go into winter quarters,[70] the army left Newbury on November 17 for Reading where it began to arrive on the day following. With this its commanders were free to take their places in Parliament and transfer their differences to Westminster. There, on November 22, Cromwell and Waller as members of the Committee of Both Kingdoms were asked to give an account to the House of "what was done at the late relief of Donnington Castle by the King, what was done at Basing House, and the present posture of the armies."[71] On Saturday, November 23, they went into the House and were ordered to prepare 'a statement of the proceedings of the armies since their conjunction.'[72] In consequence, on Monday, Cromwell presented to the House a statement of the case, setting forth all his grievances against Manchester, attributing every mistake made by the army to Manchester's disinclination to fight. No one in London seemed to understand the business; in most instances Manchester was the one accused of refusing to go into action; in others Manchester accused Cromwell of the same offense; but Cromwell attempted to prove that Manchester's delays were intentional and that his own were for strategical reasons. The narrative which follows is probably what Cromwell set down on

[69] *Cal. S. P. Dom.* (1644–5), p. 125.
[70] Committee of Both Kingdoms, Nov. 16, *Ibid.*, p. 128.
[71] *Ibid.*, pp. 138–9.
[72] *C. J.*, iii, 703.

paper soon after his speech in the House, possibly with the aid of some of his friends.[73]

CROMWELL'S NARRATIVE

An accompt of the effect and substance of my narrative made to this House for so much thereof as concerned the Earl of Manchester.

Being commanded by the House to give an account concerning the many opportunities lost and advantages given to the enemy since the late conjunction of our armies which seemed to be by some miscarriage or neglect in the conduct of the armies, and especially of our not prosecuting the victory at Newbury in time to prevent the King's rallying, of our suffering him (after he had recollected and got to an head again) to relieve Dennington Castle and fetch off his ordnance (with all he had left there) in the face of our armies, and to go off without fighting; of our quitting of Newbury afterwards, and withdrawing the siege from Basing. I did in my narrative of the story freely declare that I thought the Earl of Manchester was most in fault for most of those miscarriages and the ill consequences of them. And because I had a great deal of reason to think that his Lordship's miscarriage in these particulars was neither through accidents (which could not be helped) nor through his improvidence only, but through his backwardness to all action, and had some reason to conceive that that backwardness was not (merely) from dullness or indisposedness to engagement,[74] but (withal) from some principle of[75] unwillingness in his Lordship to have this war prosecuted unto a full victory, and a design or[76] desire to have it ended by accommodation (and that) on some such terms to which it might be disadvantageous to bring the King too low. To the end therefore that (if it were so) the state might not be further deceived in their expectations from their[77] Army, I did (in the faithful discharge of my duty to the Parliament and kingdom) freely discover those my apprehensions, and what grounds I had for them, and, to that purpose,

1. I did not only in the account of the particulars in question (since the conjunction of the armies), but also in many precedent[78] carriages upon former opportunities since our coming from York (whereof I had been a witness), declare his Lordship's continued backwardness to all action, his averseness to engagement or what tends thereto, his neglecting of opportunities and declining to take or pursue advantages upon the enemy, and this (in many particulars) contrary to advice given him, contrary to com-

[73] Bruce, in editing the "Narrative," suggests Waller, Haselrig, and Vane had a hand in drawing it up; Masson thinks Cromwell wrote it himself with suggestions from Waller and Haselrig. The footnotes are quoted from Bruce. Cp. the summary of Cromwell's speech in Parliament, in Carlyle, from Rushworth, v, 732; and *C. J.*, iii, 703, 705.

[74] Originally written "fighting," but altered by another hand into "engagement."

[75] A word struck out here—perhaps "great."

[76] "a" has been struck out here.

[77] Altered from "the."

[78] Altered from, perhaps, "pretenced."

mands received, and when there had been no impediment or other employment for his army.

2. I did likewise declare how his Lordship had (both in words and actions) expressed much contempt and scorn of commands from the Parliament,[79] or the Committee of Both Kingdoms, which have required his advancing westwards, and his desires and endeavor to have his army drawn back into his Association to lie idle there, while the business of the kingdom hath needed it, and the aforesaid commands required it to be employed elsewhere.

3. I did also declare in divers circumstances of the said omissions and miscarriages what shuffling pretences and evasions his Lordship had used, sometimes to delay and put off (till 'twas too late), sometimes to deny and avoid things propounded to him, tending to action or engagement, when the advantage and security of the same hath been clearly urged upon him, in which he had seemed studiously to decline the gaining of such advantages upon the enemy, and sometimes to design the drawing of the army off from the advantages it hath had, into a posture of less advantage.

4. I did also declare some such speeches and expressions offered by his Lordship concurrent with the said series of his actions and carriages, whereby he hath declared his dislike to the present war, or the prosecution thereof, and his unwillingness to have it prosecuted unto a victory or ended by the sword, and desire to make up the same with some such a peace as himself best fancied.

Of these heads the particulars of the first and third which I either touched upon or related more at large in my narrative are briefly these:

That at our coming from York (which was about the middle of July last) his Lordship having many advantages represented to him and time enough to have taken or blocked up Newark before he was commanded into the south, and having then no other employment or impediment to hinder his army from the attempt thereof, did lie first, with his whole army, eight or ten days about Doncaster, and afterwards with the greatest part of it about Lincoln for a month or more, without attempting anything either to reduce Newark or secure the country against it.

That lying at Doncaster, and Tickhill Castle being hard by, and Welbeck House with Sheffield and Bolsover Castle not far off, he was very unwilling to the summoning of Tickhill Castle, and expressed much anger and threats against him that (being sent to quarter in the town) did summon it, though upon the bare summons it was surrendered. And whereas, while he lay thereabouts, he might in that time have taken in those other garrisons also, so as to have had his army entire to march with him in good time against Newark, he would not be persuaded to send any party against any of them till he marched from Doncaster, and then sending a party against Sheffield, and afterwards (with much difficulty) giving way for the same party in their return to attempt Bolsover and Wingfield Manor, he made that serve for an excuse for that greater part of his army which went with him into Lincolnshire to lie idle there, till the return of the other, without attempting of anything against Newark, Belvoyr,[80] Wereton, or Shelford.

[79] This and many other similar passages look like an attempt to excite a prejudice against the accused.

[80] Originally written "Bolsover."

That in his way to Lincoln he was very backward and hardly persuaded to march near Welbeck, to induce the surrender of that house.

That at Lincoln his Lordship being much pressed by some of his officers to certain propositions for the taking or blocking-up of Newark, although the forces he had there with him all the while were sufficient for the service propounded, yet his Lordship first put off the consideration thereof till the return of that party from Sheffield, pretending that then he would advise upon it.

But, when that party was returned, he further deferred the consideration of it, till, at last (through importunity), a council being called, his Lordship, laboring with various objections to avoid the service, made the time left by those delays a main argument against it. And when (notwithstanding all) the council did conclude and his Lordship thereupon seemed to agree to draw down to quarter about Newark, and do what we would while we had time, yet his Lordship after this put it off again with other pretences, and at last did nothing at all.

That during the suspense of those propositions his Lordship, having letters from the Committee soon after his coming to Lincoln to march into Cheshire, was very angry and much displeased thereat, sent up reasons against it, pretending a necessity of doing something against Newark to secure those parts before he would march so far thence, and in the answer thereto, being left to follow the service of those parts with his army, and required only to send some horse into Cheshire, he was utterly against that also, and (notwithstanding many letters out of Cheshire pressing him thereto, and signifying the great need and danger of those parts) yet he would not, nor ever offered to send any till after that resolution taken against Newark as before, and then, though by later letters thence he was advertised that their danger was past, and their need less than before, yet he pretended that he must needs send horse thither, and thereupon broke off the resolution against Newark (that being so put off there went none).

That he caused his army (while it lay about Lincoln) to quarter upon our friends in the more secured parts of the country, leaving the other parts free for[81] the enemy to range on, rather than he would allow a sufficient part thereof to draw down towards Newark to quarter upon the enemy and to straighten and keep them in.

That though his Lordship while he thus lay idle about Lincoln (to avoid the considerations against Newark) did sometimes pretend he would attempt the lesser garrisons about it (Belvoir, Wereton, and Shelford), and was much desired thereto in case he would not meddle against Newark, yet having put off the one, he did nothing against the other, not so much as to secure the country against any of them.

That by the said neglects thereof, while he had time, he was occasioned for securing of the country (when he was called southward) to leave much the more force behind out of his field army, besides the force of the country, which otherwise [by themselves [82]] might have served to secure it, and the country so cleared (as it might have been in that time) might have raised

[81] "from" originally written.

[82] "by themselves" is an insertion. Words in brackets throughout the remainder of the narrative are insertions in the original made shortly after it was first written.

and maintained a great accession [of force] to our field armies; at which (with much more of the advantages of that service and disadvantage by the neglect) was timely and often foretold and urged to his Lordship by his officers while he lay idle as before, but his Lordship, from the time he came from York (which was about July the fifteenth) till his coming from Lincoln (which was about September the third), did not vouchsafe to call his Council of War to advise on any action or employment for his army, saving that one Council before mentioned upon the propositions against Newark, when, indeed, the best opportunity and advantages for that service were lost by the former delays.

That though when (before any real danger in the South appeared) these things were propounded for the clearing and securing of his Association, and that expressly to them his army might be the more free to leave those parts for the southern service (if there should be need), his Lordship then (to avoid these services) would sometimes pretend the keeping of his army free and ready to advance into the west if he should be required, yet when he saw a real danger and need of him in the West, being called up and commanded thitherwards, he was then much displeased thereat, and averse thereunto, pretending that he must provide for the security of his Association, that that was his proper business, and accordingly his Lordship hath showed himself both extremely backward to be drawn from his Association toward the West, and (being with much reluctance drawn but a little that way) he was averse to all good service thereabouts, and desiring and endeavoring to be drawn back to his Association again, as may appear by what follows.

The first letters for his advance from Lincoln coming about the end of August, he made it September 13th ere his army got to St. Albans, lying by the way about Peterborough and Huntingdon four nights or more, though he was in that time quickened by fresh letters and desired to hasten by his chief officers, whom he threatened to hang for such advice.

At St. Albans he caused the army to lie still 8 or 9 days, and then marching slowly to Reading he stayed there till about October 16th, and then advanced not westwards [directly] to Sir William Waller, but southwards to Basingstoke, notwithstanding a desire from this House, an Ordinance of both Houses, and many letters from the Committee of Both Kingdoms, all requiring his speedy advance westward to Sir William Waller, and Sir William Waller's earnest desires in frequent letters to that purpose; there being this while nothing justly to hinder but that his army must have advanced directly to Sir William Waller, and the Lord General's and the City foot might so have marched securely after them to have had the conjunction about Salisbury.

This might have been securely done, the Earl of Manchester's foot with his own and Sir William Waller's dragoons, being then above 6,000 (without the Lord General's and the City regiments), and the King's not so many, and their horse with the Lord General's much superior to the King's. And, if his Lordship had advanced [thither] accordingly, the King would not (in probability) have passed Salisbury river, or the plains, for this winter; and so the sieges of Dennington, Basing, and Banbury Castles had been secured and those places ours ere now, and the King by this time not had a foot on this side Salisbury, except Oxford, [Winchester Castle,] and Wallingford, and those distressed by our quarters.

That by neglect hereof Sir William Waller being forced to give back to Andover and from thence to his Lordship, and the King coming on, his Lordship being then at Basingstoke, the City regiments then with him and the Lord-General's within seven miles, and the King not come much nearer than Andover, his Lordship drew out his army in all haste to retreat to Odiam [leaving Basing and the besiegers exposed to the enemy] had not Sir William Waller and Sir Arthur Haslerig, coming in the nicke, disuaded him from the dishonour of it.

That after this conjunction, we being at Basing, near 11,000 foot and about 8,000 horse and dragoons, and the King (with not above 10,000 horse and foot) marching by Kingscleare to Newberry, on Tuesday, October the 21st, it being agreed (as we thought) to march towards him or to interpose betwixt him and Reading about Aldermaston Heath, and our horse marching before to the Heath, our foot struck down to Swallowfield, and thence next day to Reading, as if we had declined to fight; and thus making four days' march from Basingstoke to Newberry (which might have been little more than one the other way), we gave the King opportunity to have got clear to Oxford (if he would) without fighting, and staying there he had [thereby] time to fortify himself against our approaches to Newberry, and by our coming that way we gave him the advantage of Dennington river interposed betwixt him and us, the passes whereof he so commanded by the Castle and Dolman's house as put us to the hazard of dividing and the difficulty of marching about by Boxford to come upon him by Speene, which took two days more, whereas by a direct march from Basing, on the other side of Newberry river, we had had no such interposition betwixt us and Newberry, but the town open and[83] naked to us, and neither the Castle nor the horse to annoy us (as they did) in our falling on; and our horse being thus for [these] six days, and two before, kept together out of quarter waiting for that service (which [the other way] might have been dispatched in two [days]) were both lessened and disabled for the service when they came to it, and from pursuing the victory when we had it.

That on Saturday, [October 26,] when we came up to Redhill Field within shot of Shaw, and found the passes of the river[84] so possessed against us, it was agreed that the Lord General's and the City foot with the greatest part of the horse should march about by Boxford and attempt to break in upon the enemy on that side by Speene, and that his Lordship with his own foot and about 1,500 horse should stay behind at Shaw side and fall on there at the same instant that he should perceive the other part to fall on at Speene (which was already in his view), yet that other part falling on upon Speene side about two o'clock next day, though he had notice of our engagement by the first fireing of cannon on both parts, and saw the enemy retreating from hedge to hedge in disorder, and was much importuned to fall on by divers about him (and his men likewise all the while within shot of Shaw), yet his Lordship would not suffer the men to fall on, but commanded the contrary,

[83] A deep river, the Kennet, however, flows through the town of Newbury, so that if some of the King's forces had possessed it the capture of the town would not have been easy.

[84] The Lamborne.

till almost half an hour after sunset,[85] about which time we on the other side (having gained most of the hedges towards Newberry Field) did cease and draw our men together to avoid confusion in the dark by that scattered way of fighting; and his Lordship going on so late, his men presently fell foul one upon another, and were put to assault Dolman's house on that only side where it was inaccessible (whereas it was open on the other), by which means he lost two pieces of ordnance and many gallant men; whereas had he fallen on by daylight and according to agreement he might, on the open side, have taken that house with the men and ordnance in it, and, if so, we had betwixt our two bodies in probability ruined the enemy, who had then had no free pass over that river [to get away,] nor ground to stand on betwixt it and Newberry, nor commanded by us.

That the enemy flying away in the night, his Lordship's body lying close by Dolman's house on that side of the river to which they fled, suffered them to pass over the river and go by [him] without prosecution; yea, suffered those in Dolman's house, which was on the same side of the river so near him, to go clear away with their own and his ordnance.

The next morning, being Monday, October 28th, all the horse on Speen side marching after the enemy, His Lordship with all the foot stayed at Newbury, and the horse coming to Blewberry late that night, the enemy being got clear over the river at Wallingford many hours before, and we having no pass to follow them nearer than Abingdon, and our horse being tired out with eight or nine days continued hard duty without any quarters (as before), it was thought fit to let them go to quarters that night, but something close together, and upon consultation it was judged both hazardous and useless to pursue further with the horse alone and entangle them amongst rivers and woodlands without foot; whereupon Sir William Waller, Sir Arthur Haselrig, and myself (meeting by the way a letter from the Earl of Manchester to desire our return to Newbury) did go back thither to get some foot to enable the horse for further pursuit. There we pressed earnestly first to have the whole army march speedily into the quarters beyond Oxford (about Witney, Burford and Woodstock), where the enemy began to rally, and that being denied to have two or three thousand foot sent with the horse, but neither would be granted, his Lordship expressing extreme unwillingness [thereto,] making excuses and delays, speaking for his return into his Association, and much for peace; neither would he be persuaded to stir till the Saturday following, [November 2,] and then marching but to Harwell (eleven miles towards Abingdon) in two days (which at his return he dispatched in one) he stopped there and would advance no farther at all, some excuses being found, but especially unpassableness of the ways to Abingdon and beyond (though they were indeed good enough and proved both before and since to be passable for the enemy but not for us; and at this time, ere we went away, his Lordship allowed them passable to Abingdon for the heavy carriage of his victuals, all which he sent thither); and the Lord Warreston and Mr. Crewe going from Harwell to London, possessed with that and other suggestions against advancing further and for our drawing back, his Lordship engaged himself by promise to them not to stir thence

[85] This is probably correct in spite of other accounts to the contrary. See S. R. Gardiner, *Civil War*, ii, 49n.

till he received from them the directions of Both Kingdoms, and made that promise[86] serve while he stayed at Harwell to stop their mouths that moved for advancing further.

And whereas (as it was timely represented to his Lordship) our timely marching into those quarters about Oxford and so forward would have forced the enemy westward, prevented his re-collecting, occasioned his broken forces in frequent and hasty motions to drop [off] and dissipate still more, had hindred the conjunction with Rupert's and Gerard's forces, and kept the King from re-enforcing his army to appear any more in the field for this year. By our neglect thereof the King gathers the head again with Rupert's and Gerard's forces and others out of garrisons, gets all to Oxford, and thence reinforces his train and (the old being left at Donnington) resolves to fetch it thence and relieve that place; and in order thereto ere we came from Harwell he drew through Oxford, had a rendezvous or two at Bullington Green, yet drew in again, not daring to come on that way till we, drawing back to Newbury, gave him the way clear by Dorchester and Wallingford, [as follows.]

We being thus brought to the defensive part again, while we lay [at] Harwell, some of us thought our present posture or some other thereabouts very good for lying in the King's way to fight ere he got over those plains, and others propounded to cross the rivers to Dorchester, to possess that town and pass, and to quarter on this side the rivers, for more secure quarter and nearer interposition in the King's way to Dennington, and to prevent all other hazards of his impressions towards London or other parts on this side Thames. All were against drawing back to Newbury that I know or heard save his Lordship only. The inconveniencies of that, and the great advantages of the other postures, were represented to his Lordship. But those that were for any advance beyond Harwell his Lordship silenced with pretence of his promise not to remove till the directions came, yet the day before they came he did [on Tuesday, November 5,] appoint a rendezvous for next morning at Compton, 4 or 5 miles back towards Newbury, without any council that I or those that were for the other postures know of, but (to stop our mouths) he pretended he would have a council [at the rendezvous] before he would resolve whether to dispose the army from thence, yet his Lordship going early to the rendezvous when we came thither we found the army ordered before to Newbury, in such haste as (I believe) the van was by noon at or[87] near Newbury, and this before any council met; his Lordship (when they were [come] together) alleging for what was done that he had there received the letters from the Committee of Both Kingdoms commanding his return to Newbury.

From this rendezvous all the victuals (which were come up by water for the army) were sent by his Lordship to Abingdon to excuse his not going beyond the river nor staying thereabouts to secure it. And that sending away of our victuals served afterwards for an occasion to necessitate the army to draw homewards the sooner.

That our drawing back to Newbury was the chief or only cause of our loss of the business of Donnington, giving the King a clear advantage to

[86] Originally written "made this serve."

[87] "by noone at or" inserted in place of "then."

relieve it, and putting us almost out of possibility to hinder him for having thus left the King the way clear by Dorchester to[88] Wallingford, and a large secure quarter in that corner on the north side of Thames close by his post at Wallingford (beyond which we could not come to disturb or discover him, and by which he could come to annoy or discover us even to our quarters, and beat in small guards at pleasure). In that case if we at Newbury (upon every party appearing to draw over at Wallingford and beat in our scouts) should have drawn our horse together, the King might lie quiet with his body beyond the river till we had been forced to dismiss them back to quarters weary and faint, and then might he have taken the opportunity to draw speedily over, and be at the Castle before we could recall them, so as there was no end of our drawing our horse together till certain notice that the King's [main] body was drawn over at Wallingford, and staying for that (since the notice would not come to us till three hours after or more) he might, in that time, be got over the plains, and consequently (before we could possibly after that draw our horse together or[89] get our foot out to interpose) he might be at the Castle and have done his business.

And this being foretold and demonstrated before his Lordship upon the first intelligence of a party drawn out from Wallingford the day after we came to Newbury (which after drew in again), and it being therefore moved to remove thence with our whole army to some better posture of interposition, his Lordship was content indeed to have had our horse drawn together if we would (which the King would soon have made us weary of as before), but would not hearken to draw the foot thence till the King should come on, alleging that he might not quit Newbury; neither would he as yet seem to acknowledge but that (lying still till the King came on[90]) we might well enough prevent the relief of the Castle.

On the Friday after, [November 8,] the King drawing over in earnest, about two o'clock advanced forward, and about five [certain] word was brought us by a fugitive (sooner than we could otherwise expect). We sent orders immediately for our horse to meet at Redhill field, but a council being called it was then found infeasible to draw out time enough to interpose, and concluded that we must give the Castle for relieved, and should only stand upon our guard till the enemy retreated, but then to fall on. And upon this the rendezvous for the horse was altered to Newbury wash on the south side of the town and river, the Castle and the enemy being on the north side. The next morning (our horse being come together before day, and the King, contrary to expectation, staying all night at Ilsley, six miles short of the Castle) it was then urged by divers that we might draw out, but the debate being held long till we could not do it time enough to interpose, the former resolution stood, his Lordship in these debates being most ready to find the danger or infeasibility of drawing out to interpose, most earnest against it, and (in that last dispute) to protract time.

The enemy came on, relieved the Castle, drew down into Newbury field, braved us at our works, and (that while drawing their ordnance and carriages out of the Castle) in the evening they retreated up to the Castle and the

88 "to" instead of "and."
89 "Or" inserted instead of "and."
90 "there" as first written altered to "till the King came on."

heath beyond it. Upon intelligence that they continued their retreat in the night it was concluded that our horse should be drawn over into Shaw Field by three in the morning to pursue the enemy and endeavor to put them to a stand till our foot could come up, which were to follow by break of day. By light day we discovered the enemy not gone but drawn up on Winterbourne Heath, and whereas before (while we thought they would be gone) we seemed forward to fight and regain our lost honor, being now pressed to hasten out the foot, there appeared much backwardness thereto, especially in his Lordship (the foot with much importunity being [not got out] till about eleven o'clock), and the enemy being not yet gone, so as we might fight if we would and have the advantage (before pretended to be looked for) of a retreating enemy. His Lordship having now no further evasion left to shift it off under another name, plainly declared himself against fighting, and having spent much time in viewing the enemy while they drew off, and preparatory discourses, a council being called, he made it the question whether it were prudent to fight. With all earnestness and solicitousness he urged all discouragements against it, opposed all that was said for it, and, amongst other things, it being urged that if now we let the King go off with such honor it would give him reputation both at home and abroad to draw assistance to him, especially from France, where (we heard) endeavors were to get aid for him. But, if we beat him now, it would lose him everywhere, and therefore it concerned us now to attempt it before such aid came. His Lordship replying told the council he would assure them there was no such thing, adding (with vehemence) this principle against fighting: that if we beat the King 99 times he would be King still, and his posterity, and we subjects still; but if he beat us but once we should be hanged, and our posterity be undone. Thus it was concluded not to fight, the King suffered to march off unsought (being within a mile of us), and we retreated into Newbury.

The King (thus encouraged) retires not back towards Oxford, but goes to Marleborough, hovers there for an opportunity to relieve Basing also. The Earl of Manchester[(the while)] hangs homewards to be gone into his Association his agents, and savor (some) to procure command for it, (others) to stir up the soldiers minds to it, for both extremities are needlessly put upon the soldiers, and pretended to be great where they are not; his Lordship's treasurer telling the soldiers (when they complained of their wants) that they should have neither money nor clothes till they came into the Association, but then they should have both.

And whereas (for our coming back to Newbury [from Harwell]) it was sometimes pretended by his Lordship that Newbury must be fortified for a winter quarter, yet when we came there no order was taken for it, and though the importance of that place (especially in reference to the siege of Basing) was by the former council judged to be great, and it was readily apprehended by his Lordship as a reason to avoid our marching out to fight the King, least he should wheel about into Newbury and so relieve Basing, yet afterwards (the King staying at Marlebrough for an opportunity to relieve Basing) the Earl of Manchester was very forward to quit Newbury, and at last, upon intelligence of a great party drawn out from Marleborowe to go to Basing another way, we did draw out from Newbury; but then it was pretended to the council that we should go to Kingscleare for a more direct interposition in the King's way to Basing, and that there we might fight with him upon the downs, if he came that way, and lie ready (if he should bend towards Newbury) to repossess it before him; and on those grounds only and to that end was our remove agreed to in a full council. But being thus got out, and upon our way to Kingscleare, having intelligence that the King was coming [on] by Hungerford towards Newbury, his Lordship would then neither go on to Kingscleare nor return into Newbury, but upon new pretences (without the council of war) turned his course to Aldermarston (which was five miles homewards from Newbury, and seven miles nearer home than Kingscleare). And, though Kingscleare was the known direct road to Basing, yet he pretended to turn to Aldermarston with intent to go directly to Basing, and that he would fight the King there which way soever he should come if he attempted to relieve it. This gave some satisfaction for present, but from Aldermarston his Lordship would not be got to Basing (making excuses);[91] but with much ado being got out next day to Mortimer Heath, he would not be persuaded to go on any further, alleging that many of his soldiers were run to Reading, and more would go thither (being got so near it); that (when he pretended for Basing) drawing the army to Aldermarston (which was clear out of the way) he brought the soldiers so near Reading that they would be running thither, and then made their running thither an occasion to avoid going to Basing at all, and at last to draw all to Reading.[92]

Indorsed "Lieutenant-General Cromwell's Narrative."[93]

Such was the long, involved and circumstantial charge brought against his commanding officer by Cromwell and supported by the Independent officers and members of Parliament. The past two hundred years have seen many such accusations, but this is the first of the kind which was brought into public by such means as these. Those familiar with such documents will recognize all the characteristics of this species of attack in this momentous document—the

91 "excuses" an alteration; originally written "promises."

92 The words "and withdrew the siege from Basing," with which the paper concluded, have been struck out.

93 This narrative may or may not correspond exactly with the charge of Cromwell in the House. Probably it differs in many particulars. It is quite unlike the usual style of Cromwell. This document is compiled with great care and skill, and is remarkable for terseness and perspicuity; and is also notable for the absence of scriptural language and allusions common to most of Cromwell's speeches and letters. It may be the work of several hands. Probably Waller and Haselrig had something to do with it. A question might arise as to whether Vane, who was no doubt very active in the "Independent Plot," may not have had a chief hand in its compilation. It does not appear by any means certain that the Earl of Manchester was ever permitted to see this particular document. It is worthy of note that no allusion is made to the failure of the attempt to take Donnington Castle by assault as described by Clarendon in his *History*, viii, 161. Narrative and footnotes from Bruce, "Quarrel between the Earl of Manchester and Oliver Cromwell," *Camden Soc.* N. S. xii, pp. 78–95.

minute, detailed and circumstantial charges of errors both of omission and commission, the interpretation of every act in a sense hurtful to the accused, the implicit assumption that the authors of the charge knew and could have carried out the precise policy which would have led to success, had they been permitted to follow their own plans. It is the species of attack most difficult to meet and it reveals at once the fact that, whatever Manchester's unwillingness to proceed to extremities and whatever his limitations as a commanding officer, he had in Cromwell an antagonist of extraordinary resource and ingenuity, skilled in controversy and political maneuvering.

Manchester and his friends had not been idle while Cromwell appealed to the Commons. To one of his acquaintances he is reported to have said that Cromwell had once remarked to him, "My Lord, if you will stick firm to honest men, you shall find yourself at the head of an army that shall give the law to king and Parliament," which, as Clarendon, who tells the story, notes, "startled those who had always an aversion to Cromwell and had observed the fierceness of his nature, and the language he commonly used when there was any mention of peace." [94] To the Lords on November 28 Manchester made "a large narrative of the carriage of the affairs of the army at Newbury and of some speeches spoken by Lieutenant-colonel (*sic*) Cromwell which concerns much the Honour of this House and the Peers of England and the good and interest between . . . England and Scotland," which Essex, Warwick, Northumberland, Salisbury, Pembroke and North were named to consider.[95] As a result the Lords sent a statement of the case to the Commons with the suggestion of a joint committee.

The dispute between the commanders thus resolved itself into a disagreement between the two Houses, each of which appointed its own committee to look into the matter. There is no form of controversy more acrimonious and more unsatisfactory than a military quarrel thrown into politics, and the parties to the dispute were not slow to find allies. On December 2 Manchester presented a written narrative[96] which attacked his "factious and somewhat inert officer," not omitting to bring in his opinion of the Assembly of Divines. The next day, Essex, jealous of Cromwell's popularity, invited the lawyers, Maynard and Whitelocke, to confer with the Scots' commissioners as to the possibility of charging Cromwell with being an "Incendiary." But the lawyers decided that it would be difficult to prove such an accusation to the satisfaction of Parliament, and since it appeared

[94] Clarendon, *History*, viii, 184, 185.

[95] *L. J.*, vii, 76.

[96] *Camden Miscellany*, VIII, from *Tanner MSS; C. J.*, iii, 713; Rushworth, v, 733; Baillie, ii, 245.

that Cromwell was in great favor not only in the Commons but with some of the peers as well, that plan was abandoned.[97]

The plan to impeach him soon reached Cromwell's ears, and on December 4, the day Manchester's narrative was read in the House of Commons, he made another speech, denying accusations against him and making a fresh attack on Manchester.[98] On that same day, called for the first time as a witness by the special committee, he told of Manchester's threat in September to hang anyone who advised him to leave the eastern counties for the west in response to orders.[99] Manchester's letters to the Committee of Both Kingdoms were brought in evidence. Crawford, aided by Balfour, added his "Narrative of the Earl of Manchester's campaign" which in general, though it reflected on Cromwell, was unfavorable to the Earl's contentions, accusing him directly and indirectly of strong indisposition to fight. Before the committee this was strengthened by the evidence of various officers. Besides Cromwell's own testimony, Colonels Norton, Jones, Hooper, Sir Arthur Haselrig, and, apparently, Harrison, Rich, and Walton, with others, all testified that Manchester's "backwordnesse to action, and unwillingnesse to ingage with the enimys, hath lost many faire advantages and opportunityes, and hath neclected the commands of Parlement, and booth Kingdomes in matters of importance." [100]

In effect, military opinion was all but unanimous in supporting Cromwell's charges of Manchester's dilatory procedure; and had it not been, the result spoke for itself. The King had not been beaten; he was still prepared to fight; and in this universal condemnation of Manchester for not having brought about a decisive victory, the failures of Essex and the ineffectiveness of other commanders was forgotten. Parliament, the army, and the Independents, had what they desired most, a scapegoat for the failure of the war. Against this the defence of Manchester that he had been hampered by the failure of supplies, the weather, the exhaustion of his men, the lack of co-operation of his officers, bore but little weight. His further charges against Cromwell, that he was mutinous and defiant, that he plotted the overthrow of crown and aristocracy, that he favored the wilder and more dangerous of the sects, that his language was fierce and unrestrained, if not actually dangerous to the state, while it was in keeping with Cromwell's character, and no doubt was true in part or altogether, was of no avail. Cromwell had become a hero of the party by his con-

[97] Rushworth, vi, 2–3; Whitelocke, p. 116.

[98] *C. J.*, iii, 713; D'Ewes Diary, *Harl. Mss*, 483, f. 120; *Mercurius Britannicus*, Dec. 2–9; *Perfect Occurrences*, Dec. 9; *Perfect Diurnall*, Dec. 4; *Parliament Scout*, Dec. 4.

[99] *Cal. S. P. Dom.* (1644–5), p. 150.

[100] "Manchester's Quarrel with Cromwell," *Camden Society*, xii, 96–99.

duct at Marston Moor; he was the only commander thus far all but uniformly successful in the field; he was supported in Parliament by the Independents under Vane; he was worshipped by his men. And his speeches in the House on December 9 revealed him in a new capacity.

THE SELF-DENYING ORDINANCE

His enemies had made an effort to oust him; he now took the offensive against them; but he knew that he must not antagonize the Lords. The situation required tact as well as firmness; and, sure of the support of most of the members, he arose on December 9, after Mr. Zouch Tate had reported to a crowded House from the committee on the quarrel that the "chief causes of division are pride and covetousness," [101] to pave the way for a resolution to be made later in the morning which would effectively dispense with the troublesome Essex and Manchester.

Speech to the House of Commons, on Monday, December 9th.

It is now a time to speak, or forever hold the tongue. The important occasion now is no less than to save a Nation out of a bleeding, nay almost dying, condition, which the long continuance of this War hath already brought it into; so that without a more speedy, vigorous and effectual prosecution of the War,—casting off all lingering proceedings like [those of] soldiers-of-fortune beyond sea, to spin out a war,—we shall make the kingdom weary of us, and hate the name of a Parliament.

For what do the enemy say? Nay, what do many say that were friends at the beginning of the Parliament? Even this, that the Members of both Houses have got great places and commands, and the sword into their hands; and, what by interest in the Parliament, what by power in the Army, will perpetually continue themselves in grandeur, and not permit the War speedily to end, lest their own power should determine with it. This [that] I speak here to our own faces, is but what others do utter abroad behind our backs. I am far from reflecting on any. I know the worth of those Commanders, Members of both Houses, who are yet in power: but if I may speak my conscience without reflection upon any, I do conceive if the Army be not put into another method, and the War more vigorously prosecuted, the People can bear the War no longer, and will enforce you to a dishonourable Peace.

But this I would recommend to your prudence, Not to insist upon any complaint or oversight of any Commander-in-chief upon any occasion whatsoever; for as I must acknowledge myself guilty of oversights, so I know they can rarely be avoided in military matters. Therefore waving a strict inquiry into the cause of these things, let us apply ourselves to the remedy; which is most necessary. And I hope we have such true English hearts, and zealous affections towards the general weal of our Mother Country, as no

[101] *Perfect Occurrences;* Whitacre's *Diary*, quoted in Gardiner.

Members of either House will scruple to deny themselves, and their own private interests, for the public good; nor account it to be a dishonour done to them, whatever the Parliament shall resolve upon in this weighty matter.[102]

For the first time Cromwell spoke in Parliament as a statesman. That he had a definite purpose behind his words was clear to his listeners, but in order not to startle them with the radical suggestion to be made later by another, he carefully prepared them by mentioning the ill, remaining guarded, indirect, allusive, as to the remedy. Immediately afterward Tate moved, "That during the time of the war no member of either House shall have or execute any office or command, military or civil, granted or conferred by both or either of the Houses."[103] The motion was seconded by Vane in a speech during which he offered to lay down his commission as co-treasurer of the navy. In the course of a short debate Cromwell, it seems, spoke twice again. His next speech is to be found only as a summary, in Clarendon's *History:*

Speech in the House of Commons, December 9, 1644.

"When the ice was thus broke, Oliver Cromwell, who had not yet arrived at the faculty of speaking with decency and temper, commended the preachers for having dealt plainly and impartially, and told them of their faults, which they had been so unwilling to hear of: that there were many things upon which he had never reflected before, yet, upon revolving what had been said, he could not but confess that all was very true, and till there were a perfect reformation in those particulars which had been recommended to them, nothing would prosper that they took in hand: that the Parliament had done very wisely in the entrance into this war to engage many members of their own in the most dangerous parts of it, that the nation might see that they did not intend to embark them in perils of war whilst themselves sat securely at home out of gunshot, but would march with them where the danger most threatened; and those honourable persons who had exposed themselves this way had merited so much of their country that their memories should be held in perpetual veneration, and whatsoever should be well done after them should be always imputed to their example; but that God had so blessed their armies, that there had grown up with it and under it very many excellent officers, who were fit for much greater charges than they were now possessed of; and desired them not to be terrified with an imagination that if the highest offices were vacant they would not be able to put as fit men into them; for, besides that it was not good to put so much trust in any arm of flesh as to think such a cause as theirs depended upon any one man, he did take upon him to assure them, that they had officers in their armies who were fit to be generals in any interprise in Christendom.

[102] Rushworth, vi, 4; *Old Parliamentary History*, xiii, 376–7; Carlyle (Lomas ed.) i, 186.

[103] *C. J.*, iii, 718; Whitelock, p. 118.

"He said, he thought nothing so necessary as to purge and vindicate the Parliament from the partiality towards their own members; and made a proffer to lay down his commission of command in the army; and desired that an ordinance might be prepared, by which it might be made unlawful for any member of either House of Parliament to hold any office or command in the army, or any place or employment of profit in the State; and so concluded, with an enlargement upon the vices and corruptions which were gotten into the army, the profaneness and impiety and absence of all religion, the drinking and gaming, and all manner of license and laziness; and said plainly that, till the whole army were new modelled and governed under a stricter discipline, they must not expect any notable success in anything they were about."[104]

Cromwell's third speech on that day was an answer to objections, an assurance that the substitution of other commanders for those who were members of Parliament would not affect the fidelity of the army.

Speech in the House of Commons, December 9, 1644

MR. SPEAKER,

I am not of the mind that the calling of the Members to sit in Parliament will break, or scatter our armies. I can speak this for my own soldiers, that they look not upon me, but upon you; and for you they will fight and live and die in your cause; and if others be of that mind that they are of, you need not fear them. They do not idolize me, but look upon the cause they fight for. You may lay upon them what commands you please, they will obey your commands in that cause they fight for.[105]

With little or no opposition an ordinance was directed to be drawn up—the measure which was later given a name suggested by a phrase of Cromwell's first speech of the morning, the Self-Denying Ordinance. In more ways than one the quarrel of Manchester and Cromwell, the latter's speeches on December 9, and the passage of the Self-Denying Ordinance in the Commons mark a decisive turning-point in the struggle between Charles and the Parliamentary party, and they were accompanied by other events which emphasized that change. On November 24, the day after Cromwell took his seat in Parliament, there was presented to Charles at Oxford at his own request a new set of propositions from the revolutionary party. They differed from the

[104] Clarendon, *History of the Rebellion*, Bk. VIII (1826), vol. v, p. 23. Repr. in *Old Parl. Hist.*, xiii, 381–2. No date is given but it seems clear from the text of the summary that it followed Tate's resolution.

[105] *Perfect Occurrences of Parliament*, Dec. 6–13, 1644; Carlyle (Lomas ed.) i, 187. Either Cromwell did not realize the extent of his soldiers' loyalty to himself personally or he made these assurances because he knew that the resolution could not be passed otherwise. Early in January news reached London that his regiment, hearing that they were to be put under another colonel, a Scotchman, threatened mutiny. Luke's Letter Book, *Stowe Mss*, 190, f. 104b.

earlier proposals only in the changes which the preceding years had brought. They demanded the revocation of all oaths, declarations and proclamations against the Parliament, the King's assent to the Solemn League and Covenant, to the bill abolishing episcopal government, the reformation of the church according to the Covenant, and the former measures against Roman Catholics both in Scotland and England. To these was added a demand that the King give his assent to various acts of Parliament, for "due observation of the Lord's day," abolishing pluralities, reforming the universities, suppressing stage plays forever, abolishing all feudal dues and obligations, and meeting the expenses of the war, including pensions for incapacitated soldiers, their widows and orphans. Charles was further required to agree to all the treaties made between the Scots and Parliament, to "void" the "cessation" in Ireland and give over the conduct of Irish affairs to the Houses, to put the control of all armed forces of both kingdoms and their commanders in the hands of Parliament and the Scottish Estates respectively, consent to whatever treaty those bodies should agree upon, turn the Tower of London over to the City, and grant new liberties to its citizens including the control of the militia.

They insisted that no peers created since Lyttleton had taken the Great Seal to the King in May, 1642 should be allowed to sit in Parliament; that the government of Ireland and the education of the King's children be put in the hands of Parliamentary appointees; that foreign affairs be turned over, in effect, to Parliament; that material indemnity be given to any member of either House deprived of office, and that the armies be disbanded at the pleasure of the Parliaments of both Kingdoms. Finally they exempted from pardon a long list of Charles's followers, beginning with Rupert and Maurice and including all his principal advisers and commanders then or theretofore, among them Mr. Edward Hyde, Archbishop Laud, then under penalty of high treason, and all the chief Scottish Royalists, and ending with a comprehensive and threatening phrase of "all such others, as being processed by the Estates for treason, shall be condemned before the Act of Oblivion be passed."

It was inconceivable that any monarch should assent to such sweeping destruction of his prerogative and to this demand Charles gave his old answer that he could not and would not abandon his church, his crown and his friends. He once more appealed to Whitelocke and Maynard who were members of the commission and known advocates of peace, and who, like many others, including Essex and Holles, hoped for some compromise. That hope was vain and the peace party found itself still outnumbered and the demands of the war party multiplied at the moment that the dissensions among the Parliamentary commanders reached their height. Nor were its demands confined to words. Nine months earlier the trial of Laud for high treason had begun, but not until October had his counsel been heard on points of law. Their pleas had been countered by a petition from many Londoners for his execution and the Commons had, as in Strafford's case, turned from impeachment to attainder. Urged on by Prynne, an ordinance to that effect passed the House and was sent to the Lords who, on December 17, a week after Cromwell's speech, gave way on points of fact, accepted the ordinance on January 2 and eight days later Laud went to the scaffold.

Such were the circumstances which accompanied the introduction and discussion of the Self-Denying Ordinance proposed in the Commons by Tate and seconded by Vane on December 9, on the lines laid down in Cromwell's speech. Whether or not it was the result of collusion between these men must remain a matter of dispute; but, supported by those who saw in it a means of getting rid of Cromwell as well as those who sought to displace Manchester, it passed the Commons on December 19, and a committee was appointed with Cromwell as one of its members to consider the allowances for those thrown out of office and salaries for those to be newly appointed.[106] Thus was ended the dissension which a month before had threatened to split the Parliamentary party in twain. As Baillie wrote of the passage of the Self-Denying Ordinance:

> "The House of Commons in one hour has ended all the quarrels which was betwixt Manchester and Cromwell, all the obloquies against the General, the grumblings against the proceedings of many members of both Houses. This done on a sudden, in one session, with great unanimity is still more and more admired by some as a most wise, necessary and heroic action; by others as the most rash, hazardous and unjust action that ever Parliament did. Much may be said on both hands, but as yet it seems a dream and the bottom of it is not understood."[107]

It went up to the Lords on the next day where it remained, while the quarrel between the Houses over Laud went on, without action. Whether it was a measure of profound statesmanship or a shrewd political device, or both, it was eminently fitted to compose the military situation where agreement among the commanders seemed impossible.

It was a critical period in Cromwell's career. The idol of his soldiers and the populace, the favorite of the Commons, he was none the less opposed by powerful interests; by the Lords, startled at his democratic tendencies; by the Scots and the English Presbyterians, infuriated by his Independent sympathies; and by some of his fellow-officers, alarmed or envious at his popularity and not in sympathy with his religious and political utterances. While, then, the business

[106] *C. J.*, iii, 728–9.
[107] Baillie, ii, 247.

of Laud and the Self-Denying Ordinance took up the time of the Houses during December, Cromwell, now on the defensive, now taking the offensive against his opponents, was too busy to attend more than seven of the twenty-one meetings of the Committee of Both Kingdoms, though Manchester, no less concerned with his own defence and his attack on Cromwell but involved in no subtle plans for the future, found time to attend twice that number.[108] On December 10, Cromwell appeared once more before Tate's committee on the quarrel which seems to have been in session almost daily.[109] On December 16, with other members of both Houses he was appointed to meet with the Duke of Richmond and the Earl of Southampton who brought the King's reply to the Oxford Propositions; and three days later he was a teller on the question of the answer to be sent to the King, which was to the effect that Charles's reply was unsatisfactory.[110]

From these activities Cromwell was summoned to help settle an old issue, that of the Hothams, father and son, now prisoners in the Tower whither they had been sent after Cromwell's charges against the younger Hotham had been more than justified by evidence secured at Marston Moor in Newcastle's papers. Cromwell was still interested in the case and favored no leniency, acting as teller when the question of a reprieve for Sir John came up and again when the Lords wanted to spare his life.[111] They were both executed in January, a few days before Laud went to the scaffold.

Finally, in the last week in December, he was appointed to two important committees, one by the Commons to help draw up a letter to Scotland suggesting friendly relations between the Parliaments;[112] the other by the Committee of Both Kingdoms to make decisions in regard to garrisons and the number of forces necessary in the army in a contemplated reorganization;[113] and with this he turned to face another crisis of his career and of the Civil Wars.

It was in this spirit and situation that Cromwell directed his attack on Manchester; but it is obvious that this was more than an effort to displace an unsatisfactory commander. It was an attempt to reform the whole spirit and conduct of the war. It was, in fact, even more than that; it was a bid for power on the part of the Independents who felt that they and they alone were able to bring the conflict to a successful conclusion, a conclusion which would ensure that religious liberty for which they stood against Anglican and

108 *Cal. S. P. Dom.* (1644–45), *passim.*
109 *Ibid.*, p. 151.
110 *C. J.*, iii, 725, 729.
111 *Perfect Diurnall*, Dec. 9–16; *C. J.*, iii, 734; iv, 4; *Old Parl. Hist.* xiii, 358, 360.
112 *C. J.*, iv, 3.
113 *Cal. S. P. Dom.* (1644–45), p. 205.

Presbyterian alike. Yet it was not possible to put their claims and conclusions so baldly. They were not strong enough to demand the resignation of Manchester and his Presbyterian colleagues in high command. There must be devised some plan by which, without too obvious wounding of Presbyterian sensibilities or those of the Lords, the change in the army's high command could be accomplished in general terms, with no immediate personal implications, and at the same time the army could be reorganized under new commanders and in accordance with the principles of the Independents. In consequence two plans not unconnected with each other were devised; the one centering in the Self-Denying Ordinance, the other in a design for a New Model army; and to these the Independents now addressed themselves.

CHAPTER VII

THE NEW MODEL ARMY

JANUARY-MARCH, 1645

The year 1645 opened on a House of Commons which had just passed the Self-Denying Ordinance and was avoiding with all of Vane's subtlety any serious discussion of peace with the King. While he and his colleagues strove to keep on good terms with the House of Lords and strengthen the bonds with the Scottish Estates, send Laud and the Hothams to the scaffold and lull the suspicions of the Presbyterians, they were engaged as well in forging a new instrument of war. That seemed essential to their purposes. If the two years of conflict had proved one thing more than another it was that under existing conditions no decision over their Royalist opponents was possible. The raids and counter-raids, the seizure and the loss now of this town or castle and now that, with an occasional engagement of the principal forces, while it had ravaged the countryside, destroyed much property and many lives, and little by little had weakened the royal cause, had not been crowned with definite victory. Nor, as events had proved, was such decision desired by the principal commanders on their side. Neither Essex nor Manchester had shown any wish to crush Charles once for all, and they were supported in that view by many of their Presbyterian followers. To them, as to the Scots, the chief purpose was the establishment of their system of church government and the weakening of the power of the crown.

To men like Vane and Cromwell this was not enough. Like Pym they distrusted Charles; feared his return to power; above all, perhaps, they were bent on the total destruction of episcopal government in the church of which Charles was the defender. In this they had enlisted the aid of a new force. As Charles was supported by the Anglicans and the Catholics, and men like Essex, Manchester and Holles by the Presbyterians, as time went on Cromwell and Vane had gathered under them a new politico-religious party. From the beginning of the struggle in the church there had been groups like the so-called Brownists or Separatists who refused equally the discipline of the Anglicans and that of the Presbyterians. To them had been added that still more democratic communion known scornfully as Anabaptist by its enemies, no less determined than its allies not to submit to any church authority but its own. The breakdown of all authority had set free other bodies, each with its own peculiar tenets and observances. New prophets rose to found new sects in this crisis. From and among the Anabaptists grew a sect of millennialists, the Fifth Monarchists, believing in a second coming of Christ upon the earth. The Baptists themselves divided into factions; and presently there arose, among these minor sects, another group to be known in time as "Quakers" or the Society of Friends.

With this development of groups and congregations under the lead of those who sought complete religious freedom went the progress of new doctrines of society, like those of the so-called "Levellers" and "Diggers," chiefly communistic in their principles; until on every hand were to be found individuals and groups determined on salvation, material or spiritual, on their own system—preachers, prophets and exhorters, agitators and social theorists. However differing among themselves, they formed a force which, properly organized, might be set even against the Anglicans and the Presbyterians, and, fiercely convinced of the justice and righteousness of their causes, formed no small part of the best fighting-men of the Parliamentary forces, especially Cromwell's troops. Divided in all else, they were at one in their desire for religious liberty and opposed to discipline of either bishop or of presbyter. They had allies and champions, and in the very months of the campaign of Newbury, they enlisted the greatest pen in England on their side as John Milton published his *Areopagitica*, or a plea for liberty of the press, and soon followed that with other and like appeals to freedom in other fields extending to that of divorce to those who, like himself, had found their marriages unfortunate.

Little by little these groups coalesced into a larger force known in general as Independents, at the head of which stood men like Vane and Cromwell, finding here at once a principle and a party with which to oppose both Anglican and Presbyterian monarchists. They were indeed a relatively small minority; but at the beginning of 1645 it seemed that their opportunity had come. Despite the aid from Scotland, the King was still unconquered; the Anglicans and Presbyterians had reached a deadlock; the Presbyterian generals had been unable or unwilling to push the issue home; and the dissensions among the commanders made a decision seem remote. It was, then, time for a new alignment of forces and a new engine of war.

For these the rise of Cromwell to new eminence provided at once a leader and an opportunity. As early as June, 1644, Waller had told Parliament that no army formed as most armies were on either side, of local levies "would do their business," and, seconded by Cromwell and Massey, steps had been taken to reorganize the forces of Essex, but with small result. Each side had impressed men to its service; each had relied on volunteers from threatened regions as their forces moved here and there more or less aimlessly about the land. The London bands, like the Cornishmen and the men of other counties, took part in campaigns and battles or left the army as the spirit or occasion moved, and though the men under arms reckoned as high as sixty or seventy thousand for the Parliament, what with towns and castles to be held or beseiged, neither side had ever mustered twenty thousand men in any pitched battle. There was as little provision for regular recruiting as there was for regular supply, and men deserted constantly. To this the lack of regular pay contributed, and the dissipation of the forces was in large part due to the necessities of providing food and maintenance in a hundred neighborhoods.

All this came to a head with the quarrel between Cromwell and Manchester and the roots of that quarrel lay partly at least in the wretched condition of the Parliamentary forces after the second battle of Newbury. The letter of their commanders brought action and Parliament lost no time in ordering the Committee of Both Kingdoms to look into the matter. On November 23, the day Cromwell resumed his seat in the House, it urged the Committee to consider "a frame or model of the whole militia and present it to the House";[1] and when Cromwell made his speech on December 9 he declared it was more necessary to "put the army in a new method" than to investigate its generals. By January 7 the Lords, delaying consideration of the Self-Denying Ordinance, gave as part of their reasons a desire to have "a new model" army first.[2] The scheme was all but complete, and it is scarcely beyond the evidence to say that it was in greater or less degree due to Cromwell.

That he was recognized by this time, even among his enemies, as one of their deadliest foes, two circumstances prove. The first was that he was of enough importance to have a number—"88"—in the cipher used by Lord Digby in his letters to the King.[3] The second was the warning of Archbishop Williams to Charles at Oxford:

"That Cromwell, taken into the Rebels Army by his Cousin Hampden, was the most dangerous Enemy that his Majesty had. For tho' he were at that time of mean Rank and Use among them, yet he would climb higher. I knew him at Bugden, but never knew his Religion. He was a Common Spokesman for Sectaries, and maintain'd their Part with stubbornness. He never discours'd as if he were pleas'd with your Majesty, and your great Officers; and indeed he loves none, that are more than his Equals. Your Majesty did him but justice in repulsing a Petition put up by him against Sir Thomas Steward, of the Isle of Ely; but he takes them all for his Enemies, that would not let him undo his best Friend; and above all that live, I think he is the most mindful of an Injury. He talks openly that it is fit some

[1] *C. J.*, iii, 703.
[2] *L. J.*, vii, 129.
[3] Rushworth, v, 812.

should act more vigorously against your Forces, and bring your Person into the Power of the Parliament. He cannot give a good Word of his General the Earl of Essex, because he says the Earl is but half an Enemy to your Majesty, and hath done you more Favour than Harm. His Fortunes are broken, that it is impossible for him to subsist, much less to be what he aspires to, but by your Majesty's Bounty, or by the Ruin of us all, and a common Confusion. In short, every Beast hath some evil Properties; but Cromwel hath the Properties of all evil Beasts. My humble Motion is, that either you would win him to you by Promises of fair Treatment, or catch him by some Strategem, and cut him short."[4]

If he had not the properties of all evil beasts, and if the words attributed to Williams may be somewhat exaggerated, in the beginning of 1645 his was certainly a name greatly dreaded in Royalist circles. Meanwhile, however, though he was engaged in important matters, his letters during the first months of that year are few and insignificant. Only three have been preserved which he wrote during that three month period when he was not with his regiment, all of them requests for payment of army men whose pay was in arrears and whose need was urgent.

The first is to the clerk, or as he was sometimes called, the auditor, of the Eastern Association Committee at Cambridge, Dr. Stane, M.D., a Fellow of the University, who was afterwards a Commissary-General of the army and one of Fairfax's Committee of Officers in 1647. It was his older brother Richard whom Cromwell asked to pay his wife £5 the previous April and in whose house his sister Elizabeth afterwards lived. The signature, "Your loving father," is curious and impossible to explain. Cromwell was a boy of about twelve years when Dr. Stane was born[5] so he could not have been Stane's godfather, but he may have been his adviser, and must have been a close friend. The Captain Coleman mentioned may have been Captain Henry Coleman in Holborne's foot regiment or Captain William Coleman, later in Fleetwood's regiment of horse in the New Model Army.

For Dr. William Staines at Cambridge: These

Dr. Staines,

I desire you to do me the favour to let this bearer have five pounds of my money for his captain, Capt. Coleman. His want is great, and I should be loath he should be sent away to him empty. You must not fail me herein.

I rest, your very loving father,
Oliver Cromwell.[6]

Jan. 6 1644.

[4] Hacket, *Life of Archbishop Williams* (1693), ii, 212; Philips, Ambr., *Life of John Williams*, (1700), pp. 290–291.

[5] *Alumni Cantabrigiensis.*

[6] *Commonwealth Exchequer Papers*, Public Record Office. Printed in Firth, *Raising*

In the next letter Cromwell requests payment to two needy army chaplains, Dr. Samuel Welles—in whose behalf Cromwell wrote to Mr. Storie in 1635[7] and who in 1644 was considerably in arrear of his pay as chaplain to the Earl of Essex's regiment of foot[8]—and Sedgwick who may have been chaplain to Cromwell as Governor of Ely at this time.[9]

To the Sequestrators of the Isle of Ely

GENTLEMEN,

If I have found any respect or favour from you, or may any ways seem to deserve any, I entreat you most earnestly and as for myself that you will pay to Dr. Wells and to Mr. William Sedgwick the money which the Earl of Manchester hath given them a warrant to receive. I am informed that moneys are not very plentiful with you; howbeit I entreat you to do this for my sake and for their sakes that should have it; for let me speak freely, whatsoever the world may judge, they do fully deserve what I desire for them. I have not been often troublesome to you. I have studied to deserve the good opinion of honest men, amongst which number as I have cause to account you, so I hope I have the like esteem with you, which I desire you to testify by fulfilling this my request; giving you the assurance of his unfeigned friendship who is,

Your very loving friend,

London,
Jan. 17th, 1644. OLIVER CROMWELL.[10]

A letter of like character is in behalf of one of Cromwell's own soldiers whose illness had, doubtless, compelled him to leave his troop and take quarter in some private dwelling where he had been unable to pay for his keep.

[*To the Committee at Cambridge?*]

GENTLEMEN,

This soldier of mine (Mr. Frayne) is a man who on my knowledge hath very faithfully served you, his arrears are great, his sickness much and long, by occasion whereof he is brought to great lowness, and is

of the Ironsides, p. 66; Lomas-Carlyle, Suppl. 6. Underwritten is a request from W. Stane to Commissary-General Harlackenden for payment of the above, and order for payment, signed by the Earl of Manchester, Nath. Bacon, and Bra. Gurdon, and dated January 1644. Later Quartermaster-general, with whom Sir John Berkeley negotiated in 1647. Cp. Clarendon, *History*, x, 135.

[7] See Letter, Jan. 11, 1635.

[8] Essex to Treasurer-at-War, July 20, 1644, *Comm. Exch. Papers*. Cp. Lomas-Carlyle, i, 81n.

[9] Cp. Firth, "Raising of the Ironsides," *Royal Hist. Soc. N. S.* xiii, p. 56. Mrs. Lomas says he was later intimately connected with William Dell, who was Cromwell's chaplain in 1644.

[10] *St. P. Dom. Charles I*, dxxxix, no. 256. Printed in Firth, *op. cit.*, p. 56; Lomas-Carlyle, Suppl. 9.

much indebted. If now upon my recommendation of his person and condition unto you, you will please to help him with some competent sum of money to discharge his debt and relieve himself, I shall take it for a great favour and be ready to repay such a respect with a thankful [acknow]ledgment, and ever [be]

Your real and faithful,

Jan. 21, 1644
London.

OLIVER CROMWELL.[11]

Besides these letters there is a note recommending the consideration of a petition to himself from John Desborough, husband of Cromwell's sister Jane, and major of his regiment:

"*To the Right Honourable Lieutenant-General Cromwell the Petition of John Disbrowe, showeth*

"That whereas he was commanded by my Lord of Manchester to conduct a company of pressed men out of the Isle of Ely into Lincoln with the promise of satisfaction for the said service which he never could obtain, he hath since repaired to the Committee of the Isle of Ely for pay for the said service. But they informed him they could pay nothing without express order from your Honour. May it therefore please you to order the said Committee herein, and your petitioner shall upon all occasions be ready to serve you."

To the Committee for the Isle of Ely

GENTLEMEN,

I desire you to take this petition into consideration, and to do therein as to your judgments shall seem meet, and what you please to do herein shall content me.

Your servant,

Jan. 30th, 1644.

OLIVER CROMWELL.[12]

As often happens in certain periods of his life, Cromwell's activities during the month of January, 1645, are revealed not in his letters, which are insignificant, but in other ways. The minutes of the Committee of Both Kingdoms show that he was present for the three days preceding the presentation to the Commons by that committee, on January 9, of the plan for a New Model Army, in whose preparation there can be no doubt he took a leading part.[13] Two days later, having been approved by the Commons, it was sent to the Lords.[14] That

[11] *Commonwealth Exchequer Papers*. Printed in Firth, *op. cit.*, p. 54; Lomas-Carlyle' Suppl. 6. Underwritten is a warrant dated January 24, for the payment of the money to "George Frane, trooper in Lieut.-General Cromwell's own troop," the £5 to be charged "upon the Lieut.-General's account." Noted as paid January 25.

[12] *Commonwealth Exchequer Papers;* printed in Firth, *op. cit.*, App. I, p. 67.

[13] *Cal. S. P. Dom.* (1644–5).

[14] *C. J.*, iv, 15, 16.

body, under the influence of Essex and Manchester, was not prepared to accept the Self-Denying Ordinance which was involved in the plan for the reorganization of the armed forces, and which, it was evident, was directed against them. None the less it was apparent that something must be done, for on January 10 Cromwell had informed the House that forty of Manchester's officers had signed a petition to Parliament to continue the General in his command, and that a colonel at Henley had refused to obey an order to move his quarters until he heard the reply to the petition.[15]

The dissension in the army which had been expressed in Cromwell's quarrel with Manchester threatened to resolve itself into a division not only between Presbyterian and Independent, but between Lords and Commons. On January 13 the Lords, with only four dissentients, voted down the Self-Denying Ordinance; and on the 15th the Commons retorted by ordering the committees on the charges against Manchester to make their reports.[16] These were considered at great length on the 20th with the result that the Lords were voted guilty of a breach of privilege in naming a committee on December 2 to inquire into Cromwell's conduct without permission of the House of which he was a member.[17] During that long session of the Commons, the Committee of Both Kingdoms met with only the peers present and—probably as a jest at Cromwell's expense—ordered a discussion for the day following on the views of some of Cromwell's regiment against fighting in any cause whatsoever,[18] a discussion which it is perhaps needless to say never took place.

On the next day, January 21, the officers of the New Model were chosen. With Cromwell's assurance that Sir Thomas Fairfax, one of the few officers who were not members of Parliament, "was very equal" to the post as commander-in-chief of the army, he was chosen as the new general by a vote of 101 to 69, Cromwell and Vane being tellers for the Yeas.[19] Skippon was named as major-general and the post of lieutenant-general was significantly left vacant. A week later, on January 27, a committee including Cromwell and Waller was appointed to consider instructions for the new army and the next day the ordinance creating it was sent up to the Lords.[20] The New Model Army thus constituted was composed of ten regiments of horse of 600 men each; twelve foot regiments of 1,200 men; and a regiment of 1,000 dragoons; to which a week later was added another regiment of horse; making 21,400 men in all. It was to be supported by an assessment of £56,000 a month on the districts under control of Parliament.

15 Whitacre's Diary, *Add. Mss.*, 31, 116, f. 185b.

16 *C. J.*, iv, 21.

17 *Perfect Diurnall*, Jan. 20–27; *Cal. S. P. Dom.* (1644–5), p. 263; *C. J.*, iv, 25.

18 *Cal. S. P. Dom.* (1644–5), p. 264.

19 *C. J.*, iv, 26; Clarendon, viii, 201; *Old Parl. Hist.* xiii, 402.

20 *C. J.*, iv, 31.

The whole plan from the beginning of the movement for a Self-Denying Ordinance to the election of Fairfax reflects the influence and opinions of Cromwell, and evidences at once the adroitness by which the quarrels of the commanders were composed and the Presbyterian influence supplanted by that of the Independents. From its inception, Cromwell had been active in the great design, of which his speeches on December 9 had been the opening move, and from the beginning the end was clearly seen by him. On the election of Fairfax as general, Whitelocke wrote that "Cromwell was to have the power, Sir Thomas Fairfax only the name, of general, he to be the figure, the other the cypher." [21]

For a month after the New Model Ordinance had been sent to the Upper House the Committee of Both Kingdoms devoted much of its time to ordering the disposition of the troops[22] and making plans for the new army establishment. In both of these measures Cromwell was apparently much concerned, for he missed only two meetings of the Committee from January 29th until he left London a month later.[23] More than once he acted as spokesman for the Committee before the House, on January 30th requesting it to consider favorably the paper regarding the projected advance of the Scots army toward the south, on the 31st asking for £500 for the defence of Newport Pagnell.[24] The next day, no less occupied with the business of the Commons and no less faithful in attendance, he was appointed to the committee to consider a petition from the committee for Kent.[25]

These last activities were characteristic of the situation which, while the Houses were busy with the problem of the new army, had developed outside their walls. The New Model was not their whole concern, nor, indeed, the whole of the forces under the control of Parliament. In the north was an army of Scots reckoned at more than twenty thousand, under Leven, which it was conceived were the forces of Presbyterianism and perhaps of the House of Lords.[26] In and about Nottingham were ten thousand under Major-General Poyntz; as many more in the west under Massey; perhaps five thousand horse and foot in the eastern counties, the local levies of the Midlands under Major-General Browne and scattered forces in Wales; in

[21] Whitelocke, *Memorials* (1732), p. 34.

[22] On January 29 the Committee had ordered seven of Cromwell's troops to march to Sir William Waller—who was to go immediately to Farnham, southwest of London—as soon as they had convoyed an ammunition train to Abingdon. Two of his troops were at Henley. *Cal. S. P. Dom.* (1644–5), p. 278.

[23] *Ibid., passim.*

[24] *C. J.*, iv, 37; *Perfect Diurnall*, Jan. 27–Feb. 3.

[25] *C. J.*, iv, 38.

[26] On February 20, the Lords assented to the ordinance suggested by Cromwell, speaking for the Committee of Both Kingdoms three weeks before, for raising £20,000 monthly to maintain this army. *L. J.* vii, 224–30; *C. J.*, iv, 51.

all some sixty or seventy thousand men, besides the Scots, in the pay of Parliament.

Against these there were perhaps scarcely more than half that number in the ranks of Charles, though, as events had proved, his forces had fluctuated even more widely than those of Parliament and a false move on its part might bring new thousands to his aid almost over night. Nor was Parliament unanimous as to what it should do. There was still a peace party in each House; there were divisions between Independents and Presbyterians; there was still the possibility that if Charles could make terms with the Scots and the Presbyterians, the Independent war party might be crushed. It was necessary to walk warily; and on January 29, the day after the New Model Ordinance was sent to the Lords, commissioners from the Parliament arrived at Uxbridge to negotiate with the King's representatives. They demanded that the King take the Covenant, agree to abolish episcopacy and the Prayer Book and to establish Presbyterianism and the Presbyterian Directory; put the army and navy under officers named by the Scotch and English Parliaments; and leave Irish affairs to the English Parliament. They were, in fact, the same provisions Charles had already rejected, and rejected now, thus leaving matters in the hands of the war party in Parliament. His counter proposals of reformation in the church were refused; and the news of the probable breakdown of negotiations moved the Lords to accept the New Model Ordinance, on February 4, with certain provisos.

These were to the effect that all officers above the rank of lieutenant be nominated by both Houses and that both officers and soldiers should not only take the Covenant but submit "to the form of church government voted by both Houses." With this Cromwell, as one of the chief framers of the plan for the New Model and a leading Independent, again came to the fore. On February 5 he was named to the committee to consider these propositions[27] and two days later opposed the Lords' proviso, arguing for appointment of the officers by the commander-in-chief. By a vote of 82 to 63, a compromise measure was adopted by which the General was to appoint with the approval of the Houses, Cromwell appearing as a teller in the negative.[28]

To the second proviso, that all should take the Covenant, the Commons assented but rejected the attempt to impose a form of church government which had not yet been determined, declaring that the taking of the Covenant made this provision unnecessary. When a few days later the Lords proposed that the Covenant be taken in the presence of the commander-in-chief or a major-general, that a return be sent to Parliament for each soldier and those who refused to take it be dis-

[27] *C. J.*, iv, 42.
[28] *Ibid.*, 43.

placed, Cromwell again opposed it as a teller for the Noes who were this time in the majority.[29] It was during this discussion, says Whitelocke, that it was declared, doubtless as an argument against such rigid regulations, that "no men appeared so full and well armed and civil as Colonel Cromwell's horse."[30]

All revolutionary movements are a series of crises, and this was no exception to the rule. With the formation of the New Model, the appointment of Fairfax, Skippon, and presently Cromwell, to its command, the crisis of the struggle between the Independents and the Presbyterians, the quarrel between Cromwell and Manchester, and the peaceful replacement of Essex and Manchester by the new generals, had been successfully met without open breach. While the fruitless negotiations with the King went on at Uxbridge, Parliament faced another of these crises. There was dissension among the authorities themselves; there was a lack of money for carrying on the war. Sir William Waller's cavalry had mutinied; Essex's men refused to fight under Waller; the Eastern Association demanded the return of its troops quartered in Hampshire and Surrey; Buckinghamshire complained of the burden of free quarter; and news came that Weymouth and Melcombe Regis, almost the only Parliamentary garrison in the west, was in danger of capture.

Moved by this news and by the unfavorable reports from Uxbridge, the Lords finally passed the New Model Ordinance on February 15, naming Fairfax as commander-in-chief with Skippon as Major-general, settling the monthly charge on the counties for its support, and appointing commissioners to collect it, among them Cromwell for Cambridge and Huntingdon.[31] Meanwhile he had been designated by the House to consider the matter of intercepted letters from the Navy commissioners to the Speaker, and a request for supplies from Colonel Browne at Abingdon.[32] He was now commissioned to meet this new crisis. His troops, declared *Perfect Passages*, "in what posture so ever they were, that were it at midnight, they were always ready to obey . . . Parliament, and there was none of them known to do the least wrong by plunder or any abuse to any country people, but were ready to advance with Sir William Waller". A letter from the Commons to the Lords confirmed this good report, and on such grounds, he was appointed on February 18 to consider the mutiny in Waller's regiment and report the next day.[33] To this was added another commission of a different character. In the previous session he, with his brother-in-law Walton and twenty-eight others, had been

[29] *L. J.*, vii, 174, 191; *C. J.*, iv, 44, 48.
[30] Whitelocke, p. 131.
[31] Printed in *L. J.*, vii, 204–209.
[32] *C. J.*, iv, 43.
[33] *C. J.*, iv, 52, *Perfect Diurnall*, Feb. 14.

named to a permanent committee to take charge of recruiting for the army.[34] To supply their needs, the House voted to ask an advance of £80,000 from the City on security of the assessments for the New Model, and Cromwell with fourteen others was now directed to "endeavour to their utmost" to persuade the City to lend them this sum.[35]

The need for men, money and, above all, a firm hand, was pressing. The soldiers in winter-quarters, with no outlet for their energies, unpaid, ill-fed and ill-supplied, found time to air their grievances and from this even Cromwell's men were not entirely free. The Committee of the Eastern Association, ordered to give his regiment ten days' pay, had refused because the troops were not engaged in defending the Association, and the soldiers had refused to march until they were supplied with money, pistols and recruits. The order was repeated; new levies were ordered, new supplies prepared, and the armies were equipped as rapidly as possible for the spring campaign.[36]

That campaign was already under way. The Uxbridge negotiations had not only broken down, as they were perhaps meant to do, but, as the contrivers of the petition to the King possibly foresaw, Charles had antagonized the Scots by his refusal to agree to Presbyterian government. The proposal urged by some of his counsellors to settle the militia in the hands of Essex, Manchester, Warwick, Northumberland, Fairfax and Cromwell, had been dropped;[37] and there seemed nothing left but war. War had, in fact, begun, and with it came the end of Cromwell's activities in Parliament for the time. When, on February 27, news came that Melcombe was surrounded by Royalists, he was ordered to join Waller with all speed, taking with him his quartermaster Ireton, and picking up three troops at Henley, while the Eastern Association was ordered to give him £1,000 for his forces.[38] Delaying only to make a report from the Committee of Both Kingdoms to the House and to attend a meeting of the Committee that afternoon, he hastened to put himself under Waller's orders and march to the west, and so began the spring campaign.[39]

The report which he made to the House of Commons on the day of

[34] *Ibid.*, p. 51.

[35] *Ibid.*, p. 52.

[36] *Ibid.*, 52, 56; Whitacre's *Diary*, *Add. MSS.* 31, 116, f.195. Cambridgeshire money assigned for Cromwell's regiment had already been paid to Mr. Watson, gunsmith. *C. J.*, iv, 35.

[37] Clarendon, viii, 250

[38] *C. J.*, iv, 63. There is an order by the Committee of Both Kingdoms for this money to be paid by the Committee of the West, to be repaid by the Eastern Association (*Cal. S. P. Dom.* 1644–5, p. 323) and another order for the money to be paid on March 4 (*C. J.*, iv, 67). All the letters written by the Committee of Both Kingdoms speak of Cromwell's *two* troops at Henley.

[39] *C. J.*, iv, 63; *Cal. S. P. Dom.* (1644–5), p. 331.

his departure was concerned with another and increasingly important side of the activities of Parliament. Its result was a vote that £30,000 be provided for the Scotch army by the Committee at Goldsmiths' Hall.[40] This raised the whole question of Parliamentary finance in a form which was to be of growing significance in the war and in the period which followed. It was the climax of a long development. As early as September, 1642, the policy of confiscation of the property of the crown, the church, and the opponents of Parliament had been initiated, and with the passage of the Ordinance of Sequestration on March 27, 1643, it was organized as part of the means of supplying the armies of the Parliament. With the tax of five per cent; the monthly contributions which were transformed into "assessments" of increasing severity; the loans from the City on the strength of these confiscations and assessments; and lesser amounts like the money secured from the Irish Adventurers and the plunder of the war, the Parliamentary finances, however precarious, had been somehow recruited.

Now something more was done. In the preceding September the Houses had appealed to the City authorities for a joint committee to get money for the Scots and there were established two bodies, which were in time united—one to pay the Scots, the other, known from its place of meeting as the Committee at Goldsmiths' Hall, to collect the funds for that purpose, first by loans from the City, then from "delinquents" in payment of their obligations to the committee on sequestrations. Such delinquents were at the outset, apparently, prisoners taken in battle or raid; then those pronounced delinquent by Parliament; and, by March, 1645, any who would surrender on "composition", or fines for opposing Parliament. Within six months this arrangement had been transformed into a system of "compounding for delinquency" on a fixed scale of payments. By October, 1645, the Committee at Goldsmiths' Hall, authorized to receive such funds, took its place as part of the machinery of government, and, with the Committee on Sequestrations, provided not merely a source of revenue but a means of weakening their enemies.

THE FIRST CAMPAIGN IN THE WEST

With such arrangements for supply, and with Manchester's scoutmaster-general, Lionel Watson, ordered to join Cromwell,[41] all was prepared, but Waller apparently refused to move, since the Melcombe Regis situation did not seem to him desperate. The Commons, however, ordered him on March 4, "all excuses set aside," to go with

[40] *C. J.*, iv, 63.
[41] *C. J.*, iv, 64.

Cromwell to the west, and on the next day, with Colonel Fiennes and some 5,000 horse and dragoons, they finally set out.[42]

The reasons for this move lay in the activity of the two parties in regions distant from London. While the main armies had lain inactive and mutinous, Meldrum had taken Scarborough and Colonel Mitton, Shrewsbury, for the Parliament, and though Weymouth was surprised by the Royalists, the Parliamentary garrison of the adjoining town of Melcombe Regis had driven them out a week before Cromwell and Waller set out for its relief. The chief danger was from Goring who had been sent into Hampshire in December with the rank of lieutenant-general, and after quartering for the winter in Salisbury had allowed the recapture of Weymouth and the relief of Taunton, but remained a threat to the Parliamentary position in the west. To check that threat, to crush the other Royalist forces there and to threaten or, if possible, capture Bath and Bristol, and secure that region for the Parliament was their chief design.

Their first exploit was at once romantic and amusing. At Andover, half way to Weymouth, on March 9, they captured a small party of Royalists under Henry, Lord Percy, [43] and Waller, being indisposed, desired his second in command to entertain his prisoner "with civility." As Waller recalled later, in this little group of some thirty prisoners Cromwell discovered "a youth of so fair a countenance that he doubted of his condition; and, to confirm himself, willed him to sing, which he did with such a daintiness, that Cromwell scrupled not to say to Lord Piercy that, being a warrior, he did wisely to be accompanied by Amazons. On which that lord, in some confusion, did acknowledge that she was a damsel." [44]

Giving Percy and his followers passes to go into France—subject to the approval of Parliament—Waller, with Cromwell and Sir Hardress Waller, advanced the next day to Amesbury, where the troops were allowed to rest for a few hours while the scouts located a Royalist regiment under a Colonel Long. That accomplished, about midnight the Parliamentary forces were divided into three parts to surround the Royalists. Cromwell's command was detached to cut off their retreat to Devizes, Sir Hardress Waller's to block the way to Trowbridge, and together they forced Long's regiment back on Sir William Waller's force. In the skirmish which followed near Lavington in Somerset, not more than thirty of their enemies escaped. Three hundred,

[42] *J. C.*, iv, 67; *Perfect Diurnall*, Mar. 5.

[43] Letters from Waller, Mar. 9, read Mar. 11. *C. J.*, iv, 76. Whitelocke, p. 136, notes that "Letters from Waller and Cromwell certified the taking of the Lord Percy . . ." and were received Mar. 11. He mentioned Cromwell's name probably because the two were together and at the time Whitelocke wrote Cromwell was the one in whom the readers were interested.

[44] Waller, *Recollections*, p. 124; quoted in Seward, *Anecdotes*, (1798), pp. 357–8.

including Long and most of his officers, were taken prisoner and with this the three commanders pursued their progress through Dorset.[45]

It was in connection with this engagement that Waller, who had seen Cromwell in action at Newbury but had not, apparently, been particularly impressed, set down his revised opinion:

"Here I cannot but mention the wonder which I have oft times had to see this eagle in his eirey; he at this time had never shewn extraordinary parts; nor do I think that he did himself believe that he had them; for, although he was blunt, he did not bear himself with pride or disdain. As an officer he was obedient, and did never dispute my orders, nor argue upon them. He did indeed seem to have great cunning; and whilst he was cautious of his own words (not putting forth too many, lest they should betray his thoughts) he made others talk, until he had, as it were sifted them, and known their most intimate designs."[46]

But Waller and Cromwell had not come merely to beat up the quarters of scattered regiments, nor did their scanty supplies permit them to waste time. On the 13th they set out to meet Colonel Holborne who had joined Blake at Taunton in December, but who was now dismissed for lack of provisions, and escaped through Goring's lines.[47] Meanwhile Cromwell's command drew up a petition to Parliament which he enclosed in a letter which reached London on March 19:

[*To William Lenthall, Speaker of the House of Commons*]

Informing him that, "since his coming to his Regiment, their carriage had been obedient, respective [sic] and valiant; a good testimony whereof they gave in the late defeat of Long's regiment, that they were sorry for their former mutinous carriage, and desired him to send their most humble petition to both Houses." [c. Mar. 17, 1644–5.][48]

While Waller threatened Bath and Bristol with no result, Cromwell advanced to Cerne, six miles from Dorchester, where he arranged to meet Colonels Holborne and Popham; and an encounter with the Royalists, who had come within three miles of them undiscovered, was only averted by the Royalist retreat. Thence they marched to Ringwood in the New Forest, where they were joined by Colonels Norton

45 Waller's letter, Mar. 13, printed in Sanford, *Studies*, p. 617, from the *Weekly Account*. Cp. Vicars, *Burning Bush*, pp. 124–5; Clarendon, ix; *Mercurius Britannicus*, Mar. 17–24.

46 Waller, *Recollections*, p. 124, quoted in Seward, *Anecdotes*, i, 357. Seward speaks of the *Recollections* as printed in the *Poetry of Anna Matilda* (1788). Quoted also in Sanford, *Studies*, p. 617.

47 Waller to Lenthall, Mar. 13. *Tanner MSS;* printed in Sanford, *Studies*, p. 617; *Moderate Intelligencer*, quoted in Gardiner, *Civil War*, ii, 183.

48 Whitelocke, *Memorials* (1732), p. 136. Read in the House on Mar. 20, *C. J.*, iv, 84.

and Crooke and Sir William Waller and there for the time being Waller established his headquarters.[49]

But while the armies had been busy in the field and the negotiators between King and Parliament had made new efforts to come to an agreement, in these early months of 1645 events had moved fast and far in the direction of a new order. On January 4—the day that Laud's attainder was determined—there had been enacted an ordinance forbidding the use of the Prayer Book and setting in its place a Directory for Public Worship, Presbyterian in form and spirit, though adaptable to other Nonconformist communions, and adopted as the official order for all church services. On February 17 the Ordinance for the New Model army had gone into effect and under Fairfax's direction that new engine of warfare was being forged. Finally, on April 3, was enacted the Self-Denying Ordinance by which all members of Parliament in the army laid down their commissions and the Presbyterian leaders, Manchester and Essex, were deprived of their posts by this adroit move which evaded a direct attack upon them. In consequence, with the beginning of the new campaign England entered on another phase of the Civil Wars. And if the Presbyterians seemed to gain ground at the expense of the Anglicans in church affairs and still maintained their ascendancy in Parliament, it was evident that the Independents gained still more in the army. They did not, indeed, replace the Presbyterians there at once, but little by little in the ensuing years the New Model saw more and more of them rising through their military skill and their fierce devotion to the principles and the leader of their party to higher posts until in the end they virtually controlled the veteran force under the command of Fairfax and Cromwell.

MARCH-MAY, 1645

Thus far this spring campaign had been not unlike its predecessors and with no more result. But while Fairfax organized the New Model and Rupert was doing his best at Oxford to reorganize and equip the King's depleted and discouraged forces, Goring, boasting that "for pursuing Waller, if he go as fast as Cromwell I cannot overtake him,"[50] harassed without harming Waller and Cromwell, and the King made another move. On March 6 he sent his son, Prince Charles, with a council of which Hyde was the leading member, to Bristol as general of the four loyal counties. Against Goring's opposition, Hopton was added to that council, and plans were laid to trap Cromwell, who had advanced against Bridgport on March 26 before he could rejoin Waller

[49] *Perfect Diurnall*, Mar. 24–31.
[50] Letters, Mar. 22–30, *Clarendon Mss*, 1841, 1856.

who had written him to return to him at Ringwood.[51] But when the Royalists attempted to surprise Cromwell at "Chiloxford" in the night, he offered battle despite his inferior forces and they withdrew while he rejoined Waller.[52] Thence the Parliamentary commanders separated, Cromwell reaching Sturminster and Waller Shaftesbury on March 31, on their way to their chief objectives, Bath and Bristol, while Goring, harassing Waller by night attacks, hastened to Prince Charles's assistance by way of Wells.[53] On April 9, Waller and Cromwell joined forces at Salisbury, and Cromwell wrote two letters describing the situation of affairs at that moment:

For the Right Honourable Sir Thomas Fairfax, General of the Army: Haste, Haste: These: At Windsor

SIR,

Upon Sunday last we marched towards Bruton in Somersetshire, which was General Goring's headquarter; but he would not stand us, but marched away, upon our approach, to Wells and Glastonbury, whither we held it unsafe to follow him lest we should engage our body of Horse too far into that enclosed country, not having foot enough to stand by them; and partly because we doubted the advance of Prince Rupert with his force to join with Goring, having some notice from Colonel Massey of the Prince his coming this way.

General Goring hath Greenvil[54] in a near posture to join with them. He hath all their garrisons in Devon, Dorset and Somersetshire, to make an addition to him. Whereupon, Sir William Waller having a very poor infantry of about 1,600 men, lest they, being so inconsiderable, should engage our horse, we came from Shaftesbury to Salisbury to secure our foot, to prevent the being necessitated to a too unequal engagement and to be nearer a communication with our friends.

Since our coming hither, we hear Prince Rupert is come to Marshfield, a market town not far from Trowbridge. If the enemy advance altogether how far we may be endangered, that I humbly offer to you, entreating you to take care of us, and to send us with all speed such an assistance to Salisbury as may enable us to keep the field and to repel the enemy if God assist us—at least to secure and countenance us so as that we be not put to the shame and hazard of a retreat, which will lose the Parliament many friends in these parts, who will think themselves abandoned upon our departure from them. Sir, I beseech you send what foot and horse you can spare towards Salisbury, by the way of Kingscleere, with what convenient expedition may be. Truly we look to be attempted upon every day.

[51] Waller to Lenthall, Mar. 27, *Tanner Mss*, printed in Sanford, p. 618.
[52] Probably on Mar. 29. Sanford, p. 621n.
[53] Culpepper to Goring, Apr. 1, *Tanner Mss*, printed in Sanford, p. 621.
[54] Sir Richard Grenvile.

These things being humbly represented to your knowledge and care, I subscribe myself,

Your most humble servant,

Sarum, April 9th
(ten o'clock at night) 1645. OLIVER CROMWELL.[55]

The second letter was to his cousin, Colonel Edward Whalley, who was apparently not far away:

For the Hon. Col. Edward Whalley, at his quarters: haste these

SIR,

I desire you to be with all my troops and Colonel Fiennes his troops also at Wilton at a rendezvous by break of day tomorrow morning, for we hear the enemy has a design upon our quarters to morrow morning.

Sir, I am your cousin and servant,

Sarum, Wednesday night
at 12 o'clock [Apr. 9, 1645.] OLIVER CROMWELL.[56]

But if the Parliamentary commanders had accomplished little and Goring less, the King's position was now difficult, and becoming desperate. He himself was at Oxford which was being threatened more and more by the encircling forces of the Parliament. His son was at Bristol in dire need of men and supplies; Maurice at Chester; Rupert hastening hither and thither endeavoring to bring his army into condition to face the enemy. On March 11 he was at Ludlow, on the 24th at Sheffield, on the 31st at Hereford, seeking recruits and heartening up his despondent subordinates.[57] From blockading Plymouth, Grenvile advanced to Taunton, held by Blake for the Parliament, and by the time that Cromwell wrote, Rupert and Maurice were planning a junction with Charles's forces from Oxford. It was evident that the King was now at bay. Whatever Rupert's high courage, the Royalist army was almost hopelessly overmatched in numbers. East, north, and south, with the exception of outlying posts, the whole country was in the hands of Parliament. The west was going or had gone, save for a few strongholds like Bristol, Hereford, Exeter, and the Marquis of Winchester's Basing House. The King had scarcely more than ten thousand troops, ill supplied and disheartened and Oxford was all but surrounded by his enemies. It was at this moment that the Parliament took fresh steps to bring the matter to a head once for all.

[55] *Harley Mss*, vol. clxvi, p. 189; Carlyle, Letter XXIV. Read in the House of Commons on Apr. 12. Fresh supplies had already been ordered to them.

[56] In Neale, *Seats of Noblemen*, 2nd ser. (1829), vol. iv, from the original then at Melbury, Dorset. Repr. in Sanford, *Studies*, p. 623; and Firth, *Ludlow's Memoirs*, App. II. Abstract in Lomas-Carlyle, Suppl. 11.

[57] Warburton, *Prince Rupert and the Cavaliers*, iii, ch. 1.

While Waller, Cromwell and Goring were maneuvering for the possession and protection of Bath and Bristol, and Rupert was endeavoring to rally the West, at Westminster events were shaping fast toward a new order. Goring's old captor, Fairfax, since his appointment as commander-in-chief on February 21, had struggled with the problem which had brought the Houses into conflict, that of the nomination of his officers. In their choice the Independents were finally successful, though Fairfax's list of Independent officers was approved by the Lords by the narrow margin of one proxy vote. On March 24 a new Self-Denying Ordinance had passed the Commons and on April 3 the Lords. By it, members of Parliament in the army were not to be immediately disqualified but were to resign their commissions within forty days. Significantly nothing was said about their reappointment, and still more significantly, though Essex, Manchester and Denbigh tendered their formal resignations on April 2 and Waller was soon begging to be relieved, Cromwell's position was still undefined.[58] Yet the design was obvious enough. Fairfax had taken no part in the quarrels of the commanders which had led to the Self-Denying Ordinance. His religious position was not clear, and it has been said, doubtless with some truth, that he did not know whether he was a Presbyterian or an Independent. He was a soldier who was but little interested in such theological distinctions, and who had revealed that his first concern was the army and his first instinct was to fight. He was no politician, and was thus eminently fitted for a command in which, as all agreed, the motive force was Cromwell, the idol of the Independents.

In consequence, while the spring campaign went on in the west, Fairfax remained in London and Windsor organizing the New Model. There was need of it, as there was need of assistance for the forces of Waller and Cromwell. As early as March 26, Waller had advised the Commons of his soldiers' discontent and their "extremity of want." With his troops almost two years behind in their pay and in a pitiable and mutinous state, he presently begged to be relieved of his command and return to his place in the House. His forty days' grace stipulated in the Self-Denying Ordinance nearly at an end, on April 17 he was ordered to return from Salisbury and deliver his command to Fairfax,[59] and, accompanying the returning army which reached headquarters on the 20th,[60] Cromwell went at once to Windsor to pay his respects to Fairfax before retiring, with Waller, from the service.[61]

[58] *C. J.*, iv, 75, 100; *L. J.*, vii, 277, 299, 302.

[59] *Cal. S. P. Dom.* (1644–5); *C. J.*, iv, 112.

[60] *C. J.*, iv, 118. The *Encyclopedia Britannica* says Cromwell reached London Apr. 19, which would have been impossible.

[61] Sprigg, *Anglia Rediviva*, p. 11.

OXFORD, APRIL–MAY, 1645

Before Cromwell finished his leave-taking, orders arrived from the Committee of Both Kingdoms to interpose his two regiments and others under his command, with those of Colonel Fiennes, between Oxford and the Royalists in Hereford and Worcester. It was necessary to move rapidly to anticipate Charles and Maurice in their plan to convey their ordnance to Rupert,[62] then awaiting a junction with their forces in Hereford, whence it was proposed to march by way of Chester and Pontefract against the Scots. In consequence Cromwell hastened with all the force he could collect to prevent that junction. The night of Monday, April 21, found him in Caversham Bridge near Reading. Turning north to Watlington which he reached on Wednesday the 23rd, he was joined by a body of Holborne's horse, increasing his force to 1500 men. Learning of the Royalists' dispositions and movements, he continued on to Wheatley Bridge, spending the night at Islip, where, having failed to surprise Northampton's horse, he watched all night to prevent the King from passing.[63] Attacked by the Royalists the next morning, as Dugdale relates:

> "The Rebells under ye command of Ma-generall Cromwell with 1500 Horse and Dragoons did beate up ye Earl of Northampton's Horse at Islip and the townes adjacent and took above 100 Horse, Capt. Wilmot and above 20 more being then slayne." [64]

Thus defeating this force of some thousand Royalists from Alford and endeavoring to hinder the King from leaving Oxford, having secured his prisoners, Cromwell marched against the strongly fortified post of Bletchingdon House. Its commander, young Windebank, urged on, it was reported, by his frightened wife, surrendered almost at once, and shortly thereafter was shot for his cowardice, at Oxford.[65] From there Cromwell wrote his first letter as an independent commander to the Committee of Both Kingdoms, describing his movements and enclosing the articles of surrender:

[*To the Committee of Both Kingdoms*]

My Lords and Gentlemen,

According to your Lordships' appointment, I have attended your service in these parts, and have not had so fit an opportunity to give you an account as now.

[62] *Cal. S. P. Dom.* (1644–5), p. 419; Heath, *Chronicle*, p. 74; Rushworth, vi, 23.

[63] *Perfect Diurnall*, Apr. 22, 25; *Cal. S. P. Dom.* (Add. 1625–1649), p. 681; Vicars, *Burning Bush*, p. 141; Heath, *Chronicle*, p. 74; Rushworth, p. 24; Whitelocke, p. 144.

[64] Dugdale, *Diary*.

[65] Dugdale, *Diary;* Heath, *Chronicle*, pp. 74–5; *Micro-Chronicon* (1647).

So soon as I received your commands, I appointed a rendezvous at Watlington. The body being come up, I marched to Wheatley Bridge, having sent before to Major-General Browne for intelligence, and it being market-day at Oxford, from whence I likewise hoped, by some of the market-people, to gain notice where the enemy was.

Towards night I received certain notice by Major-General Browne, that the carriages were not stirred, that Prince Maurice was not here; and by some Oxford scholars, that there are four carriages and wagons ready in one place, and in another five, all, as I conceived, fit for a march.

I received notice also that the Earl of Northampton's regiment was quartered at Islip; wherefore in the evening I marched that way, hoping to have surprised them, but, by the mistake and failing of the forlorn-hope, they had an alarm there, and to all their quarters, and so escaped me; by means whereof they had time to draw all together.

I kept my body all night at Islip, and, in the morning, a party of the Earl of Northampton's regiment, the Lord Wilmot's and the Queen's, came to make an infall upon me. Sir Thomas Fairfax's regiment was the first that took the field; the rest drew out with all possible speed. That which is the General's troop charged a whole squadron of the enemy, and presently broke it. Our other troops coming seasonably on, the rest of the enemy were presently put into confusion; so that we had the chase of them three or four miles; wherein we killed many, and took near two-hundred prisoners, and about four-hundred horse.

Many of them escaped towards Oxford and Woodstock, divers were drowned, and others got into a strong house in Bletchington, belonging to Sir Thomas Coggin; wherein Colonel Windebank kept a garrison with near two-hundred men, whom I presently summoned; and after a long Treaty, he went out, about twelve at night, with these terms here enclosed; leaving us between two and three-hundred muskets, besides horse arms, and other ammunition, and about threescore-and-eleven horses more.

This was the mercy of God, and nothing more due than a real acknowledgment; and though I have had greater mercies, yet none clearer; because, in the first God brought them to our hands when we looked not for them; and delivered them out of our hands, when we laid a reasonable design to surprise them, and which we carefully endeavoured. His mercy appears in this also, that I did much doubt the storming of the house, it being strong and well manned, and I having few dragoons, and this being not my business; and yet we got it.

I hope you will pardon me if I say, God is not enough owned. We look too much to men and visible helps: this hath much hindered our success. But I hope God will direct all to acknowledge Him alone in all.

Your most humble servant,

Bletchington,
April 25th, 1645.

OLIVER CROMWELL.[66]

[66] Pr. in *L. J.*, vii, 339–40; thence *Old Parl. Hist.*, xiii, 459–60. Carlyle XXV. Abstract in Rushworth. Read in the House of Commons, Apr. 28th and noted in *C. J.*, iv, 124.

Articles of Agreement, upon the Surrender of Bletchington House, between Lieutenant General Cromwell and Colonel Wyndebanke, April the 24th, 1645.

1. First, it is agreed, that all officers of horse of commission of the garrison shall march away, with the horse, sword, and pistol.

2. That the Colonel and the Major are to march, with their horse, swords.

3. That all the soldiers in the garrison are to march away, leaving their arms, colours, and drums, behind them; and for such officers of horse as retreat hither for safety, they are to march away with their swords.

4. That Mr. Hutchinson, Mr. Ernly, Mr. Edes, and Mr. Pitts, being gentlemen that came to visit the colonel, and not engaged, shall march away, with their horses, swords and pistols.

5. That all other arms and ammunition shall be delivered up immediately to Lieutenant General Cromwell, without embezzling, except as abovementioned.

6. That a safe conduct be granted by the Lieutenant General, for all the above-mentioned, to Oxford.

7. That the Colonel's wife, his two servants, and chaplain, march away along with the Colonel, with their horses.

8. That the lady of the House shall enjoy her goods as before, without plunder, and all her family.[67]

The next day, still apparently at Bletchingdon, Cromwell sent his report to Fairfax, enclosing another copy of the Articles.

To Sir Thomas Fairfax

RIGHT HONOURABLE,

I met at my rendezvous at Watlington, on Wednesday last, where I stayed somewhat long for the coming up of the body of horse which your Honour was pleased to give me the command of. After the coming whereof, I marched with all expedition to Wheatley Bridge, having sent before to Major-General Browne for what intelligence he could afford me of the state of affairs in Oxford (I being not so well acquainted in those parts), and the condition, and number of the enemy in Oxford. As himself informed me by letters, that Prince Maurice his forces were not in Oxford, as I supposed; and that, as he was informed by four very honest and faithful gentlemen that came out of Oxford to him a little before the receipt of his letter, that there were twelve pieces of ordnance with their carriages and wagons ready for their march; and in another place five more pieces with their carriages, ready to advance with their convoy; after I received this satisfaction from Major-General Browne, I advanced this morning, being Thursday, the twenty-fourth of April, near Oxford. There I lay before the enemy. Perceiving it at Oxford, and they being in readiness to advance, sent out a party of horse against me—part of the Queen's regiment, part of the Earl of Northampton's regiment, and part of the Lord Wilmot's regiment who made an infall upon me.

[67] Pr. in *L. J.*, vii, 340.

Whereupon your Honour's regiment (lately mine own) I drew forth against the enemy (who had drawn themselves into several squadrons, to be ready for action); and your Honour's own troop therein I commanded to charge a squadron of the enemy; who performed it so gallantly that, after a short firing, they entered the whole squadron and put them to a confusion. And the rest of my horse presently entering after them, they made a total rout of the enemy, and had the chase of three or four miles, and killed two-hundred, took as many prisoners, and about four-hundred horses, and the Queen's colours, richly embroidered, with the Crown in the midst, and eighteen flower-de-luces wrought about all in gold, with a golden cross on the top. Many escaped to Oxford, and divers were drowned. Part of them likewise betook themselves to a strong House in Bletchington where Colonel Windebank kept a garrison, with near two-hundred horse and foot therein; which, after surrounded, I summoned, but they seemed very dilatory in their answer. At last, they sent out Articles to me of surrender, which I have sent your Honour enclosed; and after a large treaty thereupon, the surrender was agreed upon between us. They left behind them between two and three hundred muskets, seventy horses, besides other arms and ammunition.

I humbly rest,

Your Honour's humble servant,

Apr. 26th, 1645. OLIVER CROMWELL.[68]

The loss of Bletchingdon House was a severe blow to the King, upsetting as it did his plans to march to the west.[69] Nor was this all the damage to his cause. Encouraged by this success and by news of Parliamentary victories in Worcestershire, Cromwell harried the country about Oxford, cutting off Charles's communication with Worcester and the west, attacking stray parties of Royalists, taking many prisoners, clearing the countryside of horses, and blocking the despatch of Charles's ordnance and ammunition. These activities he himself described to the Committee of Both Kingdoms at Derby House in a letter of April 28 from Faringdon a few miles southwest of Oxford.[70]

To the Right Honourable Committee of Both Kingdoms, at Derby House

MY LORDS AND GENTLEMEN,

Since my last it has pleased God to bless me with more success in your service. In pursuance of your commands, I marched from Bletchington to Middleton Stonnie, and from thence towards Whitny as privately as I could, believing that to be a good place for interposing between

[68] Carlyle, App. 7, from *An Abstract of a letter from Lieutenant-general Crumwell to Sir Thomas Fairfax, dated 26 April*, etc. Carlyle dates the letter, incorrectly, Apr. 24.

[69] Trevor to Ormond, May 8. Carte, *Original Letters*, i, 84.

[70] Cp. also Heath, *Chronicle*, p. 75; Rushworth, vi, 25; Clarendon; *Perfect Diurnall*, Apr. 30; *Ludlow's Memoirs* (Firth's ed.) i, 119; Whitelocke, p. 144; Vicars, (*Burning Bush*, p. 142) says Cromwell's name was so terrible that Vaughan and his party had little courage and begged quarter.

the King and the West, whether he intended Goring and Greenevill, or the two princes. In my march, I was informed of a body of foot which were marching towards Faringdon (which indeed were a commanded party of 300 which came a day before from Faringdon, under Col. Richard Vaughan, to strengthen Woodstock against me, and were now returning). I understood they were not above three hours march before me. I sent after them, my forlorn overtook them as they had gotten into enclosures not far from Bampton Bush, skirmished with them, they killed some of my horses, mine killed and got some of them, but they recovered the town before my body came up, and my forlorn not being strong enough was not able to do more than they did. The enemy presently barricadoed up the town; got a pretty strong house. My body coming up about eleven in the night, I sent them a summons. They slighted it; I put myself in a posture that they should not escape me, hoping to deal with them in the morning. My men charged them up to their barricadoes in the night, but truly they were of so good resolution that we could not force them from it, and indeed they killed some of my horses, and I was forced to wait until the morning. Besides, they had got a pass over a brook; in the night they strengthened themselves as well as they could in the Store House. In the morning I sent a drum to them, but their answer was, they would not quit except they might march out upon honourable terms. The terms I offered were to submit all to mercy; they refused with anger. I insisted upon them and prepared to storm. I sent them word to desire them to deliver out the gentleman and his family—which they did—for they must expect extremity, if they put me to a storm. After some time spent, all was yielded to mercy. Arms I took: muskets, near 200, besides other arms; about two barrels of powder; soldiers and officers near 200, nine score besides officers, the rest being scattered and killed before. The chief prisoners were Colonel Sir Richard Vaughan, Lieut.-Colonel Middleton and Major Lee; two or three captains and other officers.

As I was upon my march, I heard of some horse of the enemy which crossed me towards Evesham. I sent Colonel Fiennes after them, whom God so blessed that he took about thirty prisoners, one hundred horse and three horse colours. Truly his diligence was great, and this I must testify, that I find no man more ready to all services than himself. I would [not] say so if I did not find it. If his men were at all considered, I should hope you might expect very real service from them. I speak this the rather, because I find him a gentleman of that fidelity to you and so conscientious, that he would all his troops were as religious and civil as any, and make[s] it a great par[t] of his care to get them so. In this march, my men also got one of the Queen's troopers and of them and others, about one hundred horses.

This morning, Col. John Fiennes sent me in the gentleman that waits upon the Lord Digbie in his chambers, who was going to General Goring about exchange of a prisoner. He tells me the King's forces were drawn out the last night to come to relieve Sir Richard Vaughan, and Leg commanded them. They were about 700 horse and 500 foot, but I believe they are gone back. He saith many of the horse were volunteer gentlemen, for I believe I have left him few others here. I looked upon his letters and found them directed to Marl[b]orough. He tells me Goring is about the Devizes. I asked him what further orders he had to him; he tells me he was only to bid him follow former orders. I pressed him to know what they were, and all that I could get was that it was to hasten with all he had, up to the King to Oxford. He saith he has about 3000 horse and 1000 foot; that he is discontented that Prince Rupert commanded away his foot. I am now quartered up to Faringdon. I shall have an eye towards him. I have that which was my regiment and a part of Col. Sydney's five troops [that] were recruited—and a part of Col. Vermuyden's and five troops of Col. Fiennes, three whereof, and Sir John [Norwich's] and Captain Hammond's, I sent with the first prisoners to Aylesbury. It's great pity we want dragoons. I believe most of their petty garrisons might have been taken in and other services done; for the enemy is in high fear. God does terrify them. It's good to take the season; and surely God delights that you have endeavoured to reform your armies; and I beg it may be done more and more. Bad men and discontented say it's faction. I wish to be of the faction that desires to avoid the oppression of the poor people of this miserable nation, upon whom one can look without a bleeding heart. Truly it grieves my soul our men should still be upon free quarters as they are. I beseech you help it what and as soon as you can. My Lords, pardon me this boldness; it is because I find in these things wherein I serve you that He does all. I profess his very hand has led me. I preconsulted none of these things.

My Lords and gentlemen I wait your further pleasure, subscribing myself

Farringdon, April 28, 1645. OLIVER CROMWELL.[71]

In pursuance of his plan to isolate the King in Oxford, the next day Cromwell sent a stern summons to Lieutenant-colonel Burgess, hoping to have the garrison at Faringdon delivered to him as Bletchingdon had been.

To the Governor of the Garrison at Faringdon

SIR,

I summon you to deliver into my hands the House wherein you are, and your ammunition, with all things else there, together with your persons, to be disposed of as the Parliament shall appoint, which if you refuse to do, you are to expect the utmost extremity of war. I rest,

Your servant,

April 29th, 1645.

OLIVER CROMWELL.[72]

His summons ignored, he sent even stronger threats later in the day.

To the Governor of the Garrison in Faringdon

SIR,

I understand by forty or fifty poor men whom you forced into your house, that you have many there whom you cannot arm, and who are not serviceable to you.

[71] Pr. in *Notes and Queries*, ser. 4, vol. ii, p. 121, from a contemporary copy in the House of Lords Mss; thence Carlyle, App. 7. Calendared in *Hist. Mss. Comm. Rept.* 6, App. p. 56 b.

[72] Rushworth, vi, 26; repr. in Carlyle, Letter XXVI.

If these men should perish by your means, it were great inhumanity surely. Honour and honesty require this, that though you be prodigal of your own lives, yet not to be so of theirs. If God give you into my hands, I will not spare a man of you, if you put me to a storm.

OLIVER CROMWELL.[73]

But Burgess was not to be frightened as Windebank had been. Failing to take the garrison, with some of his men killed and others wounded or taken prisoners,[74] the tone of Cromwell's next letter to the governor was very different:

To Lieut.-Col. Burgess

SIR,

There shall be no interruption of your viewing and gathering together the dead bodies, and I do acknowledge it as a favour, your willingness to let me dispose of them. Captain Cannon is but a captain; his major is Smith, so far as I know, but he is a stranger to me. I am confident he is but a captain; Master Elmes but an Ancient.[75] I thank you for your civility to them; you may credit me in this. I rest,

Your servant,

April 30. OLIVER CROMWELL.

[P.S.] If you accept of equal exchange, I shall perform my part.[76]

Charles's last campaign had now begun. Major-General Browne joined Cromwell with reinforcements and orders to command the foot,[77] and on May 1 Fairfax set out from Reading to relieve Taunton. On the evening of May 2 Cromwell rode to Newbury to confer with Fairfax who gave him 4,000 more men to block up Charles in Oxford while the main army went on.[78] That night Goring who had hurried from Taunton to the relief of Charles, surrounded Cromwell's quarters at Faringdon and in a skirmish which took place later in the night, after Cromwell's return, emerged victorious.[79] Cromwell's loss was not great but in Royalist circles it was magnified to a disaster, due no

[73] *Ibid.* xxvii

[74] *Micro-Chronicon* (1647) gives the number of killed as 200. Rushworth, vi, 26–7, places the number at only fourteen with ten prisoners. *Mercurius Aulicus* (Apr. 30) states that Cromwell "lost 200 killed; a captain, an ensign, and eight soldiers prisoners" and had a large number wounded.

[75] *I.e.*, Ensign.

[76] *Mercurius Aulicus*, Apr. 30, 1645. Printed by Firth in *Eng. Hist. Rev.*, ii, 148 (1887); Lomas Carlyle, Suppl. 12.

[77] Committee of Both Kingdoms to Cromwell, Apr. 29, *Cal. S. P. Dom.* (1644–45), p. 445.

[78] Yonge's *Diary*, quoted in Gardiner, *Civil War*, ii, 206; Rushworth, vi, 27; *Moderate Intelligencer*, May 3; *Perfect Diurnall*, May 3; Whitelock, p. 145.

[79] Sprigg, *Anglia Rediviva*, p. 18; Rushworth, vi, 27; *Moderate Intelligencer*, May 3; Clarendon, ix, 28.

doubt to the customary boasting of Goring, who was soon sent back to take supreme command in the west by Rupert after long and bitter quarrels between the Prince and his insubordinate lieutenant.

Cromwell continued to block up Oxford and to help organize the new forces. The day after Goring's attack he was at Blewbury looking over recruits for the foot,[80] and at Abingdon to assist in the incorporation of Manchester's regiment in the New Model. Thence he wrote:

For my noble friend, Major-General Skippon

SIR,

These are to certify you that Captain Griffin's troop was reduced this 2nd of May. Sir, I desire you be pleased to show this bearer his lieutenant, such favour and accommodation as other officers receive who are at this time reduced. Sir, I shall ever remain your assured friend and

Your most humble servant,

Abington,
1645, May 3.

OLIVER CROMWELL.[81]

His recommendation was heeded. Lieutenant Caldwell got his money and Cromwell turned to recommend a certain Major Purbeck Temple to Sir Peter Wentworth with no less success, for on May 20th Temple was recommended to Major-General Browne by the Committee of Both Kingdoms for the governorship of Bletchingdon House.[82]

For my honoured friend Sir Peter Wentworth, Knight of the Bath: These in London

SIR PETER WENTWORTH,

Although I never had the honour to have a word from you, yet I hope you have not cast me out of your favour. I'll try you. Major Temple, it seems, has had some recommendation from Major-General Skippon to the government of Newport Pagnell. If it lie in your way to show him any favour herein or any of my friends, I believe the gentleman is very right, forward and noble. Therefore (except you be preengaged) I beg your assistance to him herein. I shall ever say *ditur digniori.*

Sir, no man is more yours than

Your humble servant,

May 4th, 1645.

OLIVER CROMWELL.[83]

[80] *Moderate Intelligencer*, May 3.

[81] Lomas-Carlyle, Suppl. 10, from *Commonwealth Exchequer Papers.* Underwritten is Skippon's order to the Treasurers for a fortnight's pay to be given to Lieutenant Andrew Caldwell and to two other officers and on the reverse side is Caldwell's receipt. Griffin was one of Manchester's captains who had been with Crawford. *Cal. S. P. Dom.* (1644–5), p. 345.

[82] *Ibid.*, pp. 507–8. Temple was later a chief witness in the trials of the regicides.

[83] *Egerton Mss*, 2042, f. 1, in the British Museum. Mentioned in Henfrey, *Numismata Cromwelliana*, p. 180.

On that same day, probably, Cromwell despatched another report of the situation around Oxford, upon receipt of which the Committee of Both Kingdoms advised Fairfax to return four regiments of foot and two of horse to strengthen the army there.

To the Committee of Both Kingdoms

Goring has joined with the Princes' forces in Oxford. Saddles are needed for the new troops.[84] [May 4, 1645?]

On May 4, it was reported, twelve score of Cromwell's prisoners had arrived in London,[85] and others were still with him according to a letter written to Lord Wharton, which has not survived, but to which a reply was duly sent.

To Philip, Lord Wharton

Asking for directions as to the exchange of prisoners and the disposal of excess prisoners. [May 6, 1645][86]

To that, it seems, the Committee of Both Kingdoms replied two days later to make equal exchanges but to exchange none of his excess prisoners for ransom. Cromwell was in Abingdon on May 5 and advanced the next day, with Browne and 7,000 men, to Dorchester, eight miles south of Oxford.[87] Thence, hanging on the rear of the army of Charles who, with Goring, had left Oxford on May 7 to begin the last of his many marches, Cromwell arrived in Newbridge where he stopped a day or so to build a bridge.[88] Charles was at Stow on May 8, with Rupert and Langdale's horse, and on that day Goring attacked Cromwell, took some forty of his horse and two colonels prisoner near Burford.[89]

The campaign was now on, and though Cromwell and Browne were in constant communication with the Commons and the Committee, but few records of their letters have survived, and those only by knowledge of the replies. On May 9, the day that Charles and Goring left Woodstock, the Committee ordered an extract of one of these

[84] The letter itself has not survived, but a note of it is in the Committee's proceedings. *Cal. S. P. Dom.* (1644–5), pp. 457, 459. On May 5th, saddles were ordered to be sent.

[85] *Perfect Diurnall,* May 5.

[86] The Committee of Both Kingdoms replied, May 8. *Cal. S. P. Dom.* (1644–5), pp. 467–8.

[87] *Perfect Diurnall,* May 6; *Perfect Occurrences,* May 6, which lists among the horse regiments under Cromwell, those of Colonels Whalley, [John] Fiennes, Sir Robert Pye—Cromwell's cousin—Vermuyden and Algernon Sidney; and among the foot regiments those of Colonels Montague, [John] Pickering, Rainsborough and Waller.

[88] *Perfect Passages,* May 9, 10; *Perfect Diurnall,* May 9.

[89] Symonds, Richard, "Diary of Royalist Marches," (*Camden Society*), p. 165.

communications reported to the House with recommendation that it receive attention, and the next morning a letter of May 8—which may have been this one—was read in the House.[90]

To the Committee of Both Kingdoms

Desiring money for encouragement of the soldiers and recruits, artillery ammunition, etc., to pursue the enemy. [May 8, 1645?]

MAY 9–JUNE 13, 1645

The Royalist plan was clear. It was to march north against the Scots, while Prince Charles and Goring held the west against Fairfax, and this was no time for the Committee to hesitate. Money and supplies were voted to support Cromwell, and, since his forty days of grace under the Self-Denying Ordinance were nearly at an end, the House extended his commission for another forty days.[91] Whether or not that was merely a step in the plan to put him in the post of lieutenant-general which was still held vacant, it was earnestly requested by Fairfax, and it gave Cromwell an opportunity to further distinguish himself. Charles reached Evesham on May 9 where he was joined by Astley and his foot regiments,[92] and, still on the King's heels, still demanding money and ammunition, Cromwell wrote from Hinton, southeast of Banbury on that day:

To the Hon. Wm. Lenthall, Esq. Speaker of the House of Commons

SIR,

Upon information that his Majesty was marched out of Oxford, myself and Major-General Browne drew towards Hinton, and are resolved to follow them, for (it's thought) they will advance to Worcester, and so for the relief of Chester. We desire some money for the better encouragement of the soldiers, and a proportionable measure of ammunition for our pursuing after the enemy, (*etc.*)

May the 9th, 1645. OLIVER CROMWELL.[93]

Upon receipt of this letter the Committee of Both Kingdoms ordered Cromwell to march into Warwickshire rather than follow the King north, so that the Eastern Association would be protected and a junction with the Scotch would be possible. Charles was to be left to

[90] *Cal. S. P. Dom.* (1644–45), p. 471; *C. J.*, iv, 138.
[91] *C. J.*, iv, 138. Printed in *L. J.*, vii, 365. Clarendon, ix, 29.
[92] For Charles's movements, see Symonds, "Diary," *loc. cit.*
[93] *Weekly Account*, May 7–14, 1645. Reprinted in Sanford, *Studies*, pp. 623–4. Abstract in Lomas-Carlyle, Suppl. 13. A reply to this letter or another of the same date with the same substance, to the Committee of Both Kingdoms, is in *St. P. Dom.*, calendared in *Cal. S. P. Dom.* (1644–5).

Leven and the Scots. According to the newspapers and a Royalist letter,[94] Cromwell was already in Woodstock on the day the Committee made this decision. Wherever he was, he and Browne wrote another plea to the Committee for supplies, which we know of only from the reply.

To the Committee of Both Kingdoms

A plea for the soldiers who are greatly in need of clothes, money and ammunition. Artillery is also needed. May 11, 1645.[95]

Leaving Woodstock with 5000 horse and foot, Cromwell was reported to have been joined on May 12 by twelve colours of horse and ten of foot out of Hertfordshire and Buckinghamshire, from Islip,[96] and on the 13th as marching toward Warwickshire with 8,000 men with Fairfax advancing to join him.[97] On that day the Committee ordered—or suggested—that Cromwell send 2,500 men under Vermuyden to join the Scots in case Charles marched north, and return with the rest to garrison Bletchingdon and block up Oxford, but, since the King's movements were so uncertain, to use his own judgment.[98]

At this distance, ignorant as we are of many of the hidden reasons of politics and the counsels of each side, there seems in many of these marches and counter-marches, these hard ridings here and there, often apparently without result, if not actually aimless, these petty sieges, capture and recapture of towns and castles, something almost fantastic and unreal. They came in part from the necessity of supplies, in part from divided counsels in both camps, in part from poor intelligence, in part from the disposition and the fortunes of the forces engaged, and more especially from the local interests involved and the disinclination of troops to fight out of their own districts. They came in still larger measure from the fact that the whole country was interpenetrated with the rival elements in each neighborhood. Finally, in no small degree they arose from the King's own irresolution, for Charles did not know himself what he ought to do at any given moment, nor was it easy for any man in his position to decide.

Nothing, indeed, more clearly reveals the situation than the entries in the diary of that worthy antiquarian-soldier, Richard Symonds, who, taking note as he followed the King hither and thither of the architecture, armorial bearings, tombs and windows in castle, church and hall, records for us the wanderings of his master in these days. The third of his volumes of the "Marches, Moovings and Actions of

[94] Nicholas to Digby, *Cal. S. P. Dom.* (1644–5), p. 482. *True Informer*, May 13–17.
[95] The reply, written on May 14, is calendared in *Cal. S. P. Dom.* (1644–5), p. 489.
[96] Nicholas to Digby, *Cal. St. P. Dom.*, Charles I, xx, 482.
[97] *True Informations*, in *Cromwelliana*, p. 15.
[98] *Cal. S. P. Dom.* (1644–5), p. 486.

the Royall Army, his Majesty being personally present, from his coming out of his Winter Quarter at Oxford, May 7, 1645," begins, in fact with Thursday, April 24, 1645 when "Cromwell's horse and dragoons ruined some of our horse that quartered about Islip, of the Lord Northampton's command . . . and this day they demanded the delivery up of Bletchingdon." It continues with an entry of May 3 that "This Satterdy Cromwell's forces removed from before Farringdon, els if they had stayd Prince Rupert and General Goring had falne upon them; they were twice repulsed by Farringdon men, with great losse to them."

Thence it relates the coming of Rupert, Maurice and Goring to Oxford, on Sunday and Monday, May 4 and 5, and the departure of Charles, Rupert, Maurice and their followers from Oxford on Wednesday and their marches thereafter. At Stow they were joined by Rupert's army; thence they marched to Evesham, while Goring went west with 3,000 horse. Thence they went toward Worcester, so to Droitwich, to that "private, sweete village", Bisbury, by Tong, Drayton, Uttoxeter, Burton on Trent, Ashby-de-la-Zouch, and Loughborough, to Leicester, which was stormed and the Scots in it killed. But the record of ancestral monuments and armorial bearings, of epitaphs and inscriptions to the dead worthies of the various neighborhoods where the army rested, is not more depressing than the fact here revealed, that if the King hoped to rouse the country in his favor and terrify his enemies, as undoubtedly he did, he failed in his design. His wanderings only served to confuse his enemies as to his intentions, not to dismay, much less to weaken them.

The result was not only great confusion in the news but in the minds of the Parliamentary Committee and commanders themselves; but from that confusion one fact emerged. For the moment, apparently, Cromwell and Browne were pursuing the King and endeavoring to make his return to Oxford impossible. On the 14th of May, according to report within fifteen miles of Charles's army,[99] uncertain as to their orders, they wrote to the Committee for further instructions:

To the Committee of Both Kingdoms

Giving intelligence of an increase in the King's army and his march northward, and declaring that they did not understand whether by the King's marching northward, the Committee meant the King's marching to Chester, since it was not directly north but northwest. May 14, 1645.[100]

[99] Letter May 19, *Cal. S. P. Dom.* (1644–5), p. 503.

[100] The reply, written May 15, is calendared in *Ibid.*, p. 492. During the deliberation as to what was meant by "north" the King advanced near Chester. Cp. Paper of the Scotch Commissioners, in *L. J.*, vii, 392. On May 19th the Committee wrote saying "north" meant to Chester.

Meanwhile, having marched west toward Taunton after meeting Cromwell on May 2, Fairfax was ordered on May 6 to send 4,500 men to Taunton and return to Cromwell with the rest of his forces, which he did, joining Cromwell at Marston, a mile out of Oxford, on May 22, to make plans for a siege.[101] Cromwell, with his headquarters at Wytham Abbey, waited with his army for ammunition.[102] Charles had reached Bushbury on the 16th, Rupert was at Wolverhampton, and by the 25th the royal army had arrived at Burton-on-Trent.[103] On that day probably, Cromwell, still at Wytham Abbey, wrote another letter:

[*To the Committee of Both Kingdoms*]

Asking for money for his troops which have long been unpaid. [May 25, 1645?][104]

From this it would appear that, so far from Browne and Cromwell having continued their pursuit of Charles, they had turned back to join Fairfax and secure Oxford, and that the new campaign, like the others, was to degenerate into sieges, raids and skirmishes. But the King's march toward the east roused new anxieties. On the 26th the Committee wrote Cromwell a letter which seemed to indicate its fear of a Royalist incursion into the Eastern Counties, for he was ordered to go at once with two troops of horse to fortify the Isle of Ely, of which he was still governor, and remain there until June 22, when his second forty-day period of grace under the Self-Denying Ordinance would expire.[105] Two days later, when it was learned that a Royalist force was at Ashby-de-la-Zouch on its way to Newark, another letter ordered him to take four troops of horse and put the Association in a posture of defence,[106] while Fairfax was to be ready to march north at a moment's notice.[107]

Setting out from Aylesbury on May 29, Cromwell was in Cambridge two days later with orders to send for men from Northamptonshire, and advice that Vermuyden would join him and that £2,000 and twenty barrels of gunpowder were on their way to Ely.[108] Thence he sent a letter to the Committee which received it on June 1:

[101] Rushworth, vi, 28, 34; Heath, *Chronicle*, p. 75; *Weekly Account*, Mar. 26; Sprigg' *Anglia Rediviva*, p. 23; *The Copy of a Letter from an eminent Commander*, etc.

[102] Rushworth, vi, 34, says Cromwell stayed at "Witeham."

[103] Symonds, "Diary."

[104] *Cal. S. P. Dom.* (1644–5), p. 523. The letter was referred to the Committee of the Army.

[105] *C. J.*, iv, 155; Letter, Comm. of B. K. to Cromwell, May 26, *Cal. S. P. Dom.* (1644–5), p. 526.

[106] According to Sprigg, *Anglia Rediviva*, p. 30, Cromwell actually took three troops.

[107] Letter, Comm. of B. K. to Cromwell, *Cal. S. P. Dom.* (1644–5), pp. 533–4.

[108] *Mercurius Civicus; Perfect Diurnall: Perfect Occurrences; Weekly Account; C. J.*, iv, 162; Letter Committee to Cromwell, *Cal. S. P. Dom.* pp. 540, 550.

[*To the Committee of Both Kingdoms*]

Asking that orders be sent him for the disposal of the forces of the Eastern Association. Guns and money were needed. [May 31, 1645?][109]

Apparently he wrote another letter to the Committee on June 2, for on the 3rd they sent him a letter approving what he had done and warning him to guard the passes out of Holland into Ely.[110] In consequence, troops were called in from the Associated counties and from Fairfax. Cromwell had assembled 3,000 horse in the Eastern Counties[111] and on June 4 the London Common Council petitioned the Commons to give him command of the new forces, many of them raw recruits, which were increasing daily.[112] Finally, Fairfax himself was reported to be advancing—a piece of news which was extremely welcome to Cromwell, as his letter to his superior indicates:

To Sir Thomas Fairfax

SIR,

I most humbly beseech you to pardon my long silence. I am conscious of the fault, considering the great obligations lying upon me. But since my coming into these parts, I have been busied to secure that part of the Isle of Ely where I conceived most danger to be.

Truly I found it in a very ill posture, and it is yet but weak, without works, ammunition or men considerable, and of money least; and then, I hope, you will easily conceive of the defence; and God has preserved us all this while to a miracle. The party under Vermuyden waits the King's army and is about Deeping; has a command to join with Sir John Gell, if he commands him. So, the Nottingham horse. I shall be bold to present you with intelligence as it comes to me. We heard you were marching towards us, which was a matter of rejoicing to us.

I am bold to present this as my humble suit: that you would be pleased to make Captain Rawlins, this bearer, a captain of horse. He has been so before, was nominated to the Model, is a most honest man. Colonel Sidney leaving his regiment, if it please you to bestow his troop on him, I am confident he will serve you faithfully. So, by God's assistance, will

Your most humble servant,

Huntingdon,
June 4th, 1645.

OLIVER CROMWELL.[113]

Only two other documents written or signed by Cromwell while he was busy fortifying the Eastern Association have come down to us.

[109] Read in meeting of the Committee, *Ibid.*, p. 553; reply, 2 June, *Ibid.*, p. 558. The question of disposal of forces was left to his own judgment.

[110] *Ibid.*, p. 560.

[111] *Perfect Diurnall*, June 4; *Kingdom's Weekly Intelligencer*, June 3–10.

[112] *C. J.*, iv, 163; Whitelock, p. 149; presented to Lords, June 5, *L. J.*, vii, 411–412; *Perfect Diurnall*, June 5.

[113] Rushworth, vi, p. 37; thence Carlyle, Letter XXVIII.

One seems to be a sample of the recruiting letters sent out by the Committee at Cambridge, of which there were, doubtless, several; the second concerns the fortifications of the Isle of Ely.

To the Deputy-Lieutenants of Suffolk

GENTLEMEN,

The cloud of the enemy's army hanging still upon the borders, and drawing towards Harborough, make some supposals that they aim at the Association. In regard whereof, we having information that the army about Oxford was not yesterday advanced, albeit it was ordered so to do. We thought meet to give you intelligence thereof, and therewith earnestly to propound to your consideration, that you will have in readiness what horse and foot may be had, that so a proportion may be drawn forth for this service, such as may be expedient.

And because we conceive that the exigence may require horse and dragoons, we desire that all your horse and dragoons may hasten to Newmarket, where they will receive orders for farther advance, according as the motion of the enemy and of our army shall require. And to allow both the several troops of dragoons and horse one week's pay, to be laid down by the owner; which shall be repaid out of the public money out of the county, the pay of each trooper being 14 shillings per week, and of a dragoon 10s. 6d. per week.

Your servants,

H. MILDMAY	NATHANIEL BACON
W. HEVINGHAM	FRANCIS RUSSELL
TI. MIDLTON	OLIVER CROMWELL
W. SPRING	HUM. WALCOT
MAURICE BARROW	ISAAK PULLER
	ED —— [*illegible*]

Cambridge,
June 6th, 1645.

[P.S.] The place of rendezvous for the horse and dragoons is to be at Newmarket; and for the foot Bury. Since the writing hereof, we received certain intelligence that the enemy's body, with 60 carriages, was upon his march towards the Association, 3 miles on this side Harborough, last night at 4 of the clock.[114]

The officer to whom his next letter is addressed may have been that Major Underwood who was serving under Major-General Browne the previous autumn when most of his troopers ran away for want of pay.[115] "Stony ground staff" apparently refers to a flag-staff once

[114] Carlyle, (Lomas ed.), i, 199, from the original then the property of one John Wodderspoon, Esq. of the *Mercury* office in Norwich. In the catalogue of the *Collection of Merchants of Old New York*, Pt. I, offered for sale on Dec. 9–10, 1912, is listed an order signed byCromwell, "for massing of troops at Newmarket and Bury St. Edmunds." The document is said to be dated June 2, but it is more than likely that it is the same letter. Only Suffolk men would be ordered to rendezvous at those two places. Carlyle suggests that the last signature is that of Edward Clench. It was probably signed by Cromwell on the day it was written.

[115] *Cal. S. P. Dom.* (1644–5), pp. 45, 84, 132.

mounted on an artificial mound behind a gravel-pit which would command a view of the converging of the Cambridge, St. Ives, and and Ely roads and near which seem to have been two encircling "works." [116]

To Captain Underwood

CAPTAIN UNDERWOOD,

I desire the guards may be very well strengthened and looked unto. Let a new breastwork be made about the gravel, and a new work half-musket-shot behind the old work at stony ground staff. Desire Colonel Fothergill to take care of keeping strong guards. Not having more, I rest,

Yours,

Huntingdon,
June 6, 1645.

OLIVER CROMWELL.[117]

NASEBY, JUNE 14, 1645

The reasons for the movements of May, 1646, lay in large measure in the situation of the north and west. Two days after Charles rode out of Oxford, Montrose had won a victory over Baillie's Scotch Covenanting army on May 9 at Auldearn, and Leven, who had been attending a meeting of the Scottish Parliament in Edinburgh, hastened to rejoin his forces in Westmoreland and throw them between Charles and Montrose. Two days later, on May 11, with Blake's defence of Taunton almost at its last gasp, the Royalist army broke up the siege. Unaware of this, Fairfax plodded on to the relief of Taunton, until ordered to undertake the siege of Oxford, which he began on the 22nd, while Charles pursued his northern march and detached Goring to secure the west. In a sense his course was determined not only by Montrose's success but by the failure to take Taunton and the capture of Evesham by Massey, which interrupted his communication between Oxford and Worcester.

Under such circumstances, though the Parliament neglected the appeals of the Scots commissioners for money for Leven's troops, they had despatched Cromwell to Ely to secure the gateway to the eastern counties. After his success in storming and sacking Leicester, Charles seemed in a position to either attack that great stronghold of the Parliament or to join Montrose. He did neither. On June 2, as Symonds records in his Diary, "Because Oxford was weakened, his Majesty turned his course thither." There were doubtless other reasons which lay behind this move. Despite their openly expressed contempt of the "New Noddle" army and its "brutish commander,"

[116] Lomas-Carlyle, iii, 244.
[117] Carlyle, App. 8, from the original in the Baptist College, Bristol.

the news of disputes between Fairfax and the "woodmonger," Browne, "having been at cudgels and his men and Cromwell's likewise,"[118] Charles and Rupert were conscious of their weakness. They had not received the recruits which they expected on their march; they were outnumbered; and, even more than Fairfax, they were hampered by the lack of intelligence.

Nor was the Parliament less moved by the news which came to them of Massey's success at Evesham, Blake's successful defence of Gloucester, and Montrose's victory at Auldearne. Yet they, like Charles, were irresolute. At Daventry on June 7, the King still was divided between plans to march to the relief of Oxford, or to join Montrose, considering means to supply his capital and summon Goring and Gerard from the west. Meanwhile the Parliament had sent word to Fairfax to raise the siege of Oxford and use his own judgment as to his next move. Much relieved, he had begun to march on June 5, proposing to seek out the King and fight. On June 8 he learned that Charles was at Daventry and set out in pursuit of him, and on June 10, as Symonds notes, sent a proposal to exchange prisoners from Newport Pagnell. He was still hampered by the lack of a competent commander of his cavalry, and on June 8 his council of war, seconding a petition from the City to Parliament some days earlier, urged the appointment of Cromwell to the vacant post of Lieutenant-general to command the horse, declaring that:

> "The general esteem and affection which he hath both with the officers and soldiers of the whole army, his own personal worth and ability for the employment, his great care, diligence and courage, and faithfulness in the service you have already employed him in, with the constant presence and blessing of God that has accompanied him make us look upon it as a duty we owe you and the public to make our suit."[119]

To this the Commons assented on June 10[120] and though the Lords demurred, Fairfax, without waiting for Parliament to act, sent a message to Cromwell at Ely appointing him to that post, with a warning of the coming engagement, and orders to join the main army at once.[121] The General was at Kislingbury, eight miles from Daventry on June 12, and the King, having waited too long for the arrival of his artillery; hearing of the proximity of the Parliamentary army; believing Cromwell nearer than he was; and in wholesome fear of him who, as Whitelocke wrote, "began to increase in the favour of the people

[118] Charles I to Henrietta Maria, June 8. *King's Cabinet Opened.*

[119] *Cromwelliana*, p. 18.

[120] *C. J.*, iv, 169–170; *L. J.*, vii, 421, 433; Sprigg, *Anglia Rediviva*, p. 32. *Mercurius Britannicus*, June 9–10; *Perfect Diurnall*, June 10; *Moderate Intelligencer*, June 5–12. The Lords' concurrence was not until June 16, the day the news arrived from Naseby.

[121] Pr. in Rushworth, vi, 39; and in *Mercurius Britannicus.*

and of the army, and to grow great in the envy of many,"[122] began to retire toward Market Harborough on Friday, June 13, with Fairfax in pursuit.

His plan was to seek refuge under the guns of Belvoir Castle and thence make his way to Newark, and to that end he burned his huts and started on his march. But Fairfax and Cromwell were too quick for him. Cromwell had set out at once on receipt of Fairfax's letter. On June 11 he was at Bedford and at six o'clock on the morning of the 13th as the Royalists began to retire, Cromwell, not waiting for the main body of his 4,000 men but riding forward with 600 horse, was welcomed "with a mighty shout" by Fairfax's army at Kislingbury.[123] With Ireton leading the advance and Cromwell in command of the horse, they advanced to Guilsborough as the King reached Harborough. Outnumbered two to one, the Royalists were compelled to turn and fight, and at Naseby, two miles south of Market Harborough, on the morning of June 14, the armies were drawn up.

Charles's forces formed in line of battle on rising ground with open ground in front of them, and when Fairfax arrived on the field he occupied another ridge opposite, just below the crest, in a position covered by a slight hollow, Broadmoor. On Cromwell's advice, the Parliamentary army had been moved somewhat to the left to gain the advantage of the wind blowing in the faces of the enemy and drew back to a higher ridge in their immediate rear. While they retired, Rupert, dissatisfied with his scoutmaster's report that he could not find Fairfax, rode out to survey the field himself and took the slight withdrawal of his opponents to a more favorable position, for retreat. Perceiving the difficulty of an uphill charge through a wet valley unsuitable for cavalry, he ordered his forces to advance to an eminence, Dust Hill; while Fairfax, to avoid being outflanked, drew up his men almost exactly opposite, lining the hedges on his left with Okey's dragoons to enfilade the troops making a frontal attack.

The battle array on each side was the customary one of a centre of infantry with the cavalry on the flanks and a reserve in the rear. On the side of the Royalists, Astley commanded the foot, with Rupert's horse on his right and Langdale's on his left. For the Parliament, Skippon's foot in the centre had on its right Cromwell, opposing Langdale, and on its left, opposing Rupert, Ireton who, at Cromwell's request, had that morning been made Commissary-general; while beyond them, lining the hedge, were Okey's dragoons which Cromwell had ordered there before the battle began.[124] Though

[122] Whilelocke, *Memorials*, p. 149.

[123] Sprigg, *Anglia Rediviva*, p. 35; *Cal. S. P. Dom.* (1644–5), p. 586; *Moderate Intelligencer;* Vicars, *Burning Bush*, p. 159; S. Luke to Lord Roberts, June 12, Ellis, *Original Letters*, 3rd ser. vol. iv, 246.

[124] *A More Particular and Exact Relation* (1645).

Cromwell's paean of victory which he was presently to write, of an enemy which he saw "draw up and march in gallant order towards us, and we a company of poor ignorant men to seek how to order our battle," somehow gives the impression of Royalist superiority, the fact was otherwise. Charles had at the most 7,500 men, and probably fewer; Fairfax at least 14,000 after the arrival of Cromwell and Rossiter, who came up before the battle; and though there were among them many raw recruits, there were as well the veterans of Edgehill, Marston Moor and Newbury, with commanders as experienced as Rupert, Astley or Langdale.

The Royalists were, as they had usually been, outmatched in numbers, but as usual they attacked. The forces met a little below the summit of the ridge which the Parliamentary troops occupied, some of their regiments advancing to meet the Royalist charge. Harassed by the fire of Okey's dragoons, Rupert's men, none the less, were first to strike; and while the foot of each army fought hand to hand with the advantage on the side of the Royalists, Ireton endeavored to assist Skippon's regiments, with disastrous results. He himself was wounded and for a time made prisoner; and Rupert, perceiving his advantage in the disorganization of Ireton's cavalry, drove his charge home and pursued Ireton's men as far as the baggage-train at Naseby, whose guards held him off. At the same time Skippon was wounded and though his infantry outnumbered that of Astley two to one, they were discouraged and their front line broke, its officers throwing themselves into the squares of the second line. Had Rupert not pushed his pursuit of Ireton too far, he might have crushed the centre by a flank attack and so ensured a victory.

But while he rode off the battlefield in the excitement of the chase, the field was won by Cromwell on the right. Against his 3,600 men, Langdale's 2,000 cavalry toiled up the slope till, with the impetus of their charge slackened, Cromwell hurled his regiments against them, drove them back on their reserves and left Astley's left flank exposed. Against it Cromwell threw the main body of his force, detaching the rest to attack the reserve where Charles was stationed. They fled with Charles among them; Rupert had not yet returned from his pursuit of Ireton's men; and the whole strength of Fairfax, Cromwell and Skippon was thrown against the Royalist foot. One regiment held out and was all but annihilated; the rest—chiefly Welsh recruits—threw down their arms and surrendered at discretion; and when Rupert returned the battle was lost. Fairfax reformed his army and Rupert, perceiving the impossibility of attacking it with his cavalry, joined Charles in a retreat which only ended at Leicester, with Fairfax's cavalry in hot pursuit, "slaughtering as they rode."

For the Royalists the defeat was overwhelming and irreparable. The infantry was gone; five thousand of them, including five hundred officers, were prisoners, the rest killed or wounded. The artillery train, with arms for 8,000 men and forty barrels of powder, and all the royal baggage and papers fell in the hands of Parliament. The last was the most disastrous loss of all; for, sent to London with the news of victory, the triumphant Parliamentary leaders hastened to publish the most damaging documents of the "King's Cabinet"—his negotiations with the Irish and the French, the Queen's correspondence, every particle of evidence which might help to reveal and to discredit his maneuvers in preceding years.[125] It was of no avail to plead that they destroyed such evidence as he had of the intrigues of Parliament; that for each of his negotiations there was a corresponding plot of its leaders. Its case against the King seemed clear. The defeat of his army, if not glorious, was decisive; the publication of his papers was disastrous to his cause.

But if the credit of the King was destroyed by Naseby, that of Cromwell was enormously increased. Twice he had saved the Parliamentary army from defeat when defeat seemed all but inevitable. He had approved himself not only an able lieutenant but an outstanding commander of cavalry, and cavalry was the most important arm of the service at that time. To his experience in recruiting, drilling and equipping men was added his leadership in the field, and his Ironsides with him at their head had become the most formidable body of fighting-men in the British Isles, if not indeed in Europe or the world. With their iron head-, back- and breast-pieces; the excellence of their mounts—for Cromwell was a judge of horseflesh—with their stern discipline and with their religious fervor, they were a force to be feared by any antagonist. To this Cromwell had added new tactics. It is perhaps too much to say with the German military writer that "when he swung his leg over the saddle he began a new era in cavalry history." [127] But as the great Gustavus had revolutionized both cavalry and artillery, Cromwell, though he paid less attention to artillery, followed Gustavus in his cavalry. Instead of using it as mounted infantry, riding forward to fire its clumsy pistols and falling back or at best charging slowly on the enemy, he used the force of horse and man charging at a trot, sometimes at short gallop, in compact mass, as a battering ram against opposing ranks, preceded or accompanied with pistol fire and using the sword hand to hand. In this he followed the Swedish system of three lines of men and horses, rather than the Dutch school of six; and in this he was not alone, for Rupert introduced that system into England, with essentially the same tactics as

[125] *The Kings Cabinet opened; or certain packets of secret letters and papers, written with the Kings own hand and taken in his Cabinet at Naseby Field.* 1645.

[126] For an account of Naseby, see Gardiner, *Civil War*, ch. xxxi; Ross, in *Eng. Hist. Rev.*, ii, 688–79.

[127] Col. F. Hoenig, *Oliver Cromwell.*

Cromwell used, and which he learned, apparently, from his enemies.

Rupert, in fact, was a great cavalry leader, as great as Cromwell save in one particular. The chief difference was not in horses or arms or men or even tactics, for Royalist and Parliamentarian were more or less alike in these. It lay in discipline and speed. Rupert depended more on pace, Cromwell on weight and discipline. He kept his men together; he kept himself in hand; he took into consideration the state of the field at any given moment; and there, as in politics, he took advantage of the situation in which he found himself.[128] As Clarendon says of this battle of Naseby after Rupert's men returned from the pursuit of Ireton:

"They having, as they thought, acted their parts, they could never be brought to rally themselves again in order, or to charge the enemy. And that difference was observed shortly from the beginning of the war, in the discipline of the King's troops and of those which marched under the command of Cromwell (for it was only under him, and had never been notorious under Essex or Waller), that though the King's troops prevailed in the charge, and routed those they charged, they never rallied themselves again in order, nor could be brought to make a second charge again the same day: . . . whereas Cromwell's troops, if they prevailed, or thought they were beaten and presently routed, rallied again and stood in good order till they received new orders."[129]

It was to this that Cromwell owed his eminence and success. Beginning with the skirmishes of Winceby, Grantham and Gainsborough, and culminating in Marston Moor and Naseby, he had developed into the great cavalry leader that he was. As yet he had but little experience in sieges, and less as an independent commander of an army. Those were to come; but meanwhile he had become the main hope of his party and now with the overthrow of Charles, the leading figure on the side of Parliament, the hero of the army and of the Independent cause.

Returned to Harborough from the pursuit of the enemy, Cromwell hastened to inform the House of Commons of the victory, not failing to voice his sentiments about liberty of conscience, for the Scots had no part in Naseby and he no longer felt obliged to hold his tongue to avoid antagonizing them.

For the Honourable William Lenthall, Speaker of the Commons House of Parliament: These

SIR,

Being commanded by you to this service, I think myself bound to acquaint you with the good hand of God towards you and us.

[128] Lt. Col. T. S. Baldock, "Cromwell as a Soldier," in *United Service Mag.*, 1899, and C. H. Firth, *Cromwell's Army*, pp. 130 ff.

[129] *History*, ix, 41.

We marched yesterday after the King, who went before us from Daventry to Harborough; and quartered about six miles from him. This day we marched towards him. He drew out to meet us; both armies engaged. We, after three hours fight very doubtful, at last routed his army; killed and took about 5,000, very many officers, but of what quality we yet know not. We took also about 200 carriages, all he had; and all his guns, being 12 in number, whereof two were demi-cannon, two demiculverins, and (I think) the rest sackers. We pursued the enemy from three miles short of Harbrough to nine beyond, even to sight of Leicester, whither the King fled.

Sir, this is none other but the hand of God; and to Him alone belongs the glory, wherein none are to share with Him. The General served you with all faithfulness and honour; and the best commendations I can give him is, that I dare say he attributes all to God, and would rather perish than assume to himself. Which is an honest and a thriving way, and yet as much for bravery may be given to him, in this action, as to a man. Honest men served you faithfully in this action. Sir, they are trusty; I beseech you in the name of God, not to discourage them. I wish this action may beget thankfulness and humility in all that are concerned in it. He that ventures his life for the liberty of his country, I wish he trust God for the liberty of his conscience, and you for the liberty he fights for. In this he rests, who is

Haverbrowe, Your most humble servant,
14 June 1645. OLIVER CROMWELL.[130]

THE CAMPAIGN IN THE WEST
JUNE 13–SEPT. 13, 1645

The results of Naseby were important even beyond the defeat of Charles and the capture of his papers. It deprived the King of what was left of his financial resources, and one of the first concerns of Fairfax and Cromwell was to get the royal plate and money into safe hands, as Cromwell's next letter indicates:

To Sir Samuel Luke, Governor of Newport Pagnell

SIR,

I doubt not but you hear before this time of the great goodness of God to this poor nation, for which we have all cause to rejoice.

[130] Not agreeing with the last paragraph of Cromwell's dispatch, the House of Commons sent only the first part to the press, but at the same time the Lords exercised no such censorship and permitted the entire letter to be printed. Both forms are in the Thomason Collection in the British Museum with notes on each which show the collector's limited knowledge of Cromwell in these early years. On the first is written; "This is Crumwell's owne trew letter" and on the other, "a false letter in the conclusion." The letter is printed in *L. J.*, vii, 434; Rushworth, vi, 45; Harris, *Life* (1762), p. 132; Ellis, *Original Letters*, 1st ser. iii, 305; Carlyle, *Letter* XXIX. Ms. copies are in *Harl. Mss.* 7502, art. 5, p. 7; *Ayscough Mss.* 4182, f. 5. Ellis observes Cromwell's failure in the first sentence to own obligation to the Lords for his commission, but none was due, for it was not until June 16th that his appointment was approved by them.

ST. G
Cardigan
Newcastle Emlyn
Newport
Fishguard Bay
ST DAVID'S
Rock Cas.
Colby Moor 1645
Haverfordwest
St Brides Bay
CARMARTHEN FOREST
Carmarthen
(Flannel)
Kidwelly
Llanelly
Ferry
COAL
MILFORD
Cas. 1648
1644
Pembroke
Stackpole Ho.
Tenby
1644
Carmarthen Bay
Burry
Swansea
St Gowan's Hd
Worms Hd
BRISTOL
Lundy I.
Ilfracombe
Morte Bay
Barnstaple or Bideford Bay
Barnstaple
CLOTH
(Kerseys & Bays)
Hartland Pt
Hartland
Bideford
Torrington
1643
Chulmleigh
1643
Stratton
Rude Bay
Holsworthy
Hatherleigh
Boscastle
Camelford
Launceston
Lifton
Padstow
BODMIN MOOR
Tavistock
CLOTH
Bodmin
St Columb
Liskeard
Braddock 1644
Lostwithiel
Saltash
PLYMOUTH
Plympton
Modbury
Brent
TIN
St Austell
W. Looe
Fowey
TIN
Truro
Grampound
Tregoney
St. Ives
TIN
St Michael's Mount
1646
Penzance
Marazion
Penryn
Helston
Winstanley's Lighthouse 1698
Eddystone Rocks
The Manacles
Lizard Pt
E N

Leominster
WORCESTER
Alcester
Stratford on Avon
Bromyard
Weobley
Kineton
Edge Hill
1642
Bidford
Evesham
Pershore
MALVERN CHASE
Upton
Shipston
Banbury
HEREFORD
HAWOOD FOREST
Ledbury
Chipping Campden
Tewkesbury
1642
Winchcomb
Stow-on-the-Wold
Chipping Norton
Newent
Ross
CORSE WOOD
Barber's Br.
Cheltenham
GLOUCESTER
1643
Goodrich Cas.
Monmouth
Wonastow
Raglan Cas.
Coleford
FOREST OF DENE
Matson Ho.
Northleach
Burford
Woodstock
WHICHWOOD FOREST
Witney
Stroud
Cirencester
Usk
Berkeley
Minchinhampton
Lechlade
Thames
Dursley
Chepstow
1645-48
WENT WOOD
Aust Passage
Thornbury
Tetbury
Wotton
Cricklade
Faringdon
Highworth
Caerleon
Caerphilly
Newport
Wickwar
BRADON FOR.
Malmesbury
Wootton Bassett
Wantage
Lambourn
East Ilsley
CARDIFF
St Fagan's 1646
1648
BRISTOL
KINGSWOOD FOREST
Chipping Sodbury
Castle Combe
Aldbourne Chase
1643
Ramsbury
Donnington Cas.
Marshfield
Chippenham
Keynsham
Lansdown
1643
PEWSHAM
Calne
Marlborough
SAVERNAKE FOREST
Hungerford
Newbury
Pensford
Bath
BLACKMORE
Roundway Down
1643
Bradford
Devizes
1645
Trowbridge
Norton St Philip
CHUTE FOREST
Axbridge
Westbury
Basingstoke
Overton
Huntspill
WELLS
Frome
Shepton Mallet
SELWOOD FOR.
Warminster
Amesbury
Andover
BRIDGWATER
1645
Glastonbury
Bruton
GROVELY WOOD
Hindon
Mere
Nadder
Wilton
SALISBURY
BUCKHOLT FOREST
WINCHESTER
1645
Alresford
Bishop's Lydeard
Sedgemoor 1685
Somerton
Wincanton
GILLINGHAM FOREST
Taunton
Langport
1645
Queen Camel
Wardour Cas.
Romsey
1644-5
Wellington
Martock
Ilchester
Shaftesbury
CRANBORNE CHASE
Petherton
Yeovil
Sherborne
1642
Sturminster
Cranborne
SOUTHAMPTON
Ilminster
FOREST OF BLACKMORE
Hambledon Hill
NEW FOREST
Chard
Crewkerne
Evershot
Blandford
HOLT FOREST
Ringwood
Honiton
Beaminster
Milton Abbas
Axminster
Cerne Abbas
Wimborne Minster
Lymington
MARSHWOOD VALE
Colyton
Lyme
Frampton
Bere
POOLE
Christchurch
Hurst Cas.
AVINGTON FOREST
Carisbrook Cas.
Bridport
Monmouth landed. 1685
Dorchester
Wareham
Corfe Cas.
Lyme Bay
Weymouth
St Alban's Hd
St Catherine's
Portland Bill
landed.
E N G L I S H C

The General commanded me to desire you to convoy the treasure to Northampton, where Col. Cox will receive it and discharge yours. This is desired may speedily be done. Sir, I am

Your humble servant,

June 15th, 1645. OLIVER CROMWELL.[131]

The second result was no less significant. It was the triumph of Cromwell and the Independents. Though the Commons deleted Cromwell's plea for his Independent followers from their printed version of his despatch, it listened with great pleasure to the letter which the Committee had sent to the army, telling of the "great victory, the most absolute as yet attained" and of "the General, Lieutenant-General Cromwell and Major-General Skippon" who "did beyond expression gallantly." [132] Not only in gratitude to their popular commander of the horse, but with the realization that he was indispensable, they passed a resolution that day to retain him in the army "until the pleasure of both Houses of Parliament," with the pay of a lieutenant-general from the time of the establishment of the New Model.[133] The Lords refused to sanction such a measure, for the old Essex-Manchester animosity remained, but they did agree to extend his commission for three months, with the pay of a lieutenant-general from the expiration of the forty-day period he was then serving.[134]

As that action indicates, few disputed the wisdom of Cromwell's former contention that the war should be prosecuted until the King should be forced to acknowledge defeat. Charles was still at large, and his followers, though much dispersed, held numerous strong places throughout England. Dissuaded from his proposal to die fighting on the field, the King had fled from Naseby with Rupert and a few troopers, first to Ashby-de-la-Zouch, then by way of Lichfield and Bewdley to Hereford, where he was joined by Gerard and two thousand troops, and plans were laid to raise more men in Wales. Rupert hastened to Bristol and the King made his way to Raglan Castle to be entertained by the Marquis of Worcester, while, with the fall of Pontefract and Scarborough, the Scots advanced to besiege Hereford.

THE WESTERN CAMPAIGN, JUNE 16–AUGUST 18, 1645

Meanwhile the Parliamentary army was not slow to improve its victory. Instead of pursuing and capturing the King, they turned their attention to the only royal force left in the field, that of Goring. Reaching Great Glynn on June 16, Leicester was taken two days later

[131] Luke's letter book, *Egerton Mss*, vol. 786, f. 54. Printed in Ellis, *Original letters*, ser. iii, vol. iv, p. 257; and in Lomas-Carlyle, Suppl. 14.

[132] *L. J.*, vii, 434.

[133] *C. J.*, iv, 176.

[134] *L. J.*, vii, 433.

and there, on the 20th, Fairfax—now independent of the Committee of Both Kingdoms—called a council of war to decide on the next move.[135] It was agreed to relieve Taunton, so, marching to Warwick on the 23rd, they turned directly south, quartered at Stratford-on-Avon on the 24th, and on the 26th were at Lechlade in Gloucestershire.[136] Thence, taking a fortified church at Highworth, they went through Wanborough to Marlborough where they spent Sunday, the 29th, and from there, by way of Amesbury, Stonehenge, Salisbury, Burchalk and Blandford, to Dorchester.

There the commanders were soon faced with a problem which was to be of some importance—that of the so-called "Clubmen." Weary of being plundered by both sides, the men of Dorset, Somerset and Wilts, had gathered with such weapons as they could muster—many of them, as their name indicates, armed only with clubs—to resist further seizure of their property. A few of the leaders called upon Fairfax and his officers when they reached Dorchester on July 3, and their chief, Holles, was given a hearing; but before Fairfax was required to take measures to deal with their threats, news of a defeat given them at Lyme Regis settled the matter for the moment, and the army was left to face Goring.[137]

The same day, news came to them that he had withdrawn his troops from before Taunton, and as soon as the report was verified at Beaminster, the next evening, Fairfax, with his foot regiments and some 2,800 horse under Cromwell, decided to engage him immediately. Pushing on the six hot miles to Crewkerne the next day, they rested on Sunday, and a Council of War was called on Monday to consider their next move.

The problem confronting the Parliamentary commanders was a peculiar one. Goring had obviously left Taunton to avoid fighting with the conquerors of Rupert and the King, and it seemed difficult to force an engagement on an enemy which lay on the other side of a river and had possession of all the adjacent garrisons. The two armies were about equal in numbers and Fairfax's only chance of victory lay in outmaneuvering his antagonist. In consequence the next three days were spent in various operations looking to that end, and, in spite of their disadvantageous position at Long Sutton near Langport, Goring's irresolution, lack of resourcefulness and poor generalship finally provided the Parliamentary forces the chance of victory. They could not force Goring to fight, for, under the circumstances,

[135] Wogan's "Proceedings of the New Moulded Army," in Carte, *Original Letters*, i, 130.

[136] Fairfax's letter to Parliament, June 26, in *L. J.*, vii, 463–4; replies to his letters, *Cal. S. P. Dom.* (1644–5), pp. 611, 621; Sir S. Luke to "Aulicus Wounded," June 25, in Ellis, *Original Letters*, 3rd ser. vol. iv, p. 267.

[137] Sprigg, *Anglia Rediviva*, pp. 60–62.

that decision lay with him and for the moment he did not choose to risk an engagement.

Waiting for his decision, Cromwell took advantage of the delay to write a letter in favor of the man in whose behalf he had made one of his first pleas in Parliament and who was to vex him much in later years. John Lilburne, who occupies a place in history as a professional martyr, had entered the army. He had been captured at Edgehill, tried for treason at Oxford and saved only by Parliament's threat of reprisals if he were executed. Made lieutenant-colonel in Manchester's dragoons, he had refused to take the Covenant and was denied a commission in the New Model. He had quarrelled with Colonel King, seized Tickhill Castle against his orders, accused King of treason, and was one of Cromwell's witnesses against Manchester. He had been arrested in May because of a letter in which he had declared against the payment of tithes, had been released, and again arrested a month later after the publication of the same sentiments without first being submitted to the licenser. Held only overnight, he appeared next at Long Sutton, to obtain a good word from Cromwell. He had never received the money voted him because of his punishment by the Star Chamber, and arrears in pay were still due him. On behalf of this firebrand Cromwell interceded as he had once before.

[*To the Members at Westminster*]

GENTLEMEN,

Being at this distance from Lon[don], I am forced to trouble you in a business which I would have done myself, had I been there. It is for Lieut. Col. Lilburne, who hath done both you and the Kingdom good service, otherwise I should not have made use of such friends as you are. He hath a long time attended the House of Com[mons] with a petition that he might have reparation, according to their votes, for his former sufferings and losses and some satisfaction for his arrears for his service of the State, which hath been a long time due unto him.

To this day he cannot get his petition read; his attendance hath proved very expensive, and hath kept him from other employment; and I believe that, his former losses and late services (which have been very chargeable) considered, he doth find it a hard thing, in these times, for himself and his family to subsist. Truly, it is a grief to see men ruin themselves through their affection and faithfulness to the public, and so few lay it to heart. It would be an honour to the Parl[iament] and an encouragement to those that faithfully serve them, if provisions were made for the comfortable subsistence of those who have lost all for them. And, I can assure you, that this neglect of those that sincerely serve you hath made some already quit their commands in this army, who have observed oftentimes their wives and children have begged, who have lost their lives and limbs in the kingdom's service. I wish it were looked to betimes.

138 Sprigg, *Anglia Rediviva*, pp. 62–71.

That which I have to request of you is, that you give him your best assistance to get his petition read in the House, and that you will do him all lawful favour and justice in it. I know he will not be unthankful, but adventure as freely in the service of the kingdom as hitherto he hath done.

Hereby you shall lay a special obligation upon your servant,

[Long Sutton,] OLIVER CROMWELL.[139]
July 10, 1645.

On the day of this letter, which was, apparently, written early in the morning, the officers once more took counsel but even while they discussed ways and means to make Goring fight, God, as Cromwell said, delivered him into their hands. His troops advanced into a pass in the hills between Long Sutton and Langport. Perceiving their opportunity, Fairfax and Cromwell mounted instantly, recalled their horse and foot which had been sent to aid Massey a few miles away, turned their artillery against the main body of the enemy drawn up on the hill, and sent their foot soldiers into the pass. Major Bethel with three hundred horse, seconded by Desborough, charged three times their number of Royalists, while musketeers closed in amongst the hedges and opened fire. After an engagement which lasted only a few minutes, Goring's army turned and fled in terror, dashing through Langport and setting fire to it as they went, to hinder the pursuit. But Cromwell and his horse followed through the burning streets, caught the fugitives at the bridge where many were killed, and captured most of the others.[140]

Early the next morning, apparently,—because he speaks of going at once to a rendezvous which took place the next day at Westonmoor, two miles from Bridgewater—Cromwell wrote a long and enthusiastic account of the battle and pursuit to a friend in London.

[*To "a worthy member of the House of Commons"*]

DEAR SIR,

I have now a double advantage upon you, through the goodness of God, who still appears with us. And as for us, we have seen great things in this last mercy,—it is not inferior to any we have had,—as followeth:

We were advanced to Long-Sutton, near a very strong place of the enemy's, called Lamport; far from our own garrisons, without much ammunition, in a place extremely wanting in provisions, the malignant Club-men interposing, who are ready to take all advantages against our parties, and would undoubtedly take them against our army, if they had opportunity. Goring stood upon the advantage of strong passes, staying until the rest of the recruits came up to his Army, with a resolution not to engage until Greenvill

[139] *Copy of a letter from Lt. Col. John Lilburne to a Friend;* repr. in Sanford, *Studies*, p. 629; Lomas-Carlyle, Suppl. 15.

[140] *Kingdom's Weekly Intelligencer;* Sprigge, *Anglia Rediviva*, pp 71–74.

and Prince Charles his men were come up to him. We could not well have necessitated him to an engagement, nor have stayed one day longer without retreating to our ammunition and to conveniency of victual.

In the morning, word was brought us that the enemy drew out. He did so, with a resolution to send most of his cannon and baggage to Bridgewater, which he effected, but with a resolution not to fight, but, trusting to his ground, thinking he could march away at pleasure.

The pass was strait between him and us; he brought two cannons to secure his, and laid his musketeers strongly in the hedges. We beat off his cannon, fell down upon his musketeers, beat them off from their strength, and, where our horse could scarcely pass two abreast, I commanded Major Bethel to charge them with two troops of about 120 horse, which he performed with the greatest gallantry imaginable; beat back two bodies of the enemy's horse, being Goring's own brigade; brake them at sword's-point. The enemy charged him with near 400 fresh horse. He set them all going, until, oppressed with multitudes, he brake through them, with the loss not of above three or four men. Major Desborow seconded him, with some other of those troops, which were about three. Bethel faced about, and they both routed, at sword's-point, a great body of the enemy's horse, which gave such an unexpected terror to the enemy's army that set them all a-running. Our foot in the mean time coming on bravely, and beating the enemy from their strength, we presently had the chase to Lamport and Bridgewater. We took and killed about 2000, brake all his foot. We have taken very many horses, and considerable prisoners; what were slain we know not. We have the Lieutenant-General of the ordnance; Colonel Preston, Colonel Heveningham, Colonel Slingsby, we know of, besides very many other officers of quality. All Major-General Massie's party was with him, seven or eight miles from us, and about twelve-hundred of our foot, and three regiments of our horse. So that we had but seven regiments with us.

Thus you see what the Lord hath wrought for us. Can any creature ascribe anything to itself? Now can we give all the glory to God, and desire all may do so, for it is all due unto Him! Thus you have Long Sutton mercy added to Naseby mercy. And to see this, is it not to see the face of God! You have heard of Naseby; it was a happy victory. As in this, so in that, God was pleased to use His servants; and if men will be malicious and swell with envy, we know Who hath said, If they will not see, yet they shall see, and be ashamed for their envy at His people. I can say this of Naseby, that when I saw the enemy draw up and march in gallant order towards us, and we a company of poor ignorant men, to seek how to order our battle—the General having commanded me to order all the horse—I could not (riding alone about my business) but smile out to God in praises, in assurance of victory, because God would, by things that are not, bring to naught things that are. Of which I had great assurance; and God did it. O that men would therefore praise the Lord, and declare the wonders that He doth for the children of men!

I cannot write more particulars now. I am going to the rendezvous of all our horse, three miles from Bridgewater; we march that way. It is a seasonable mercy. I cannot better tell you than write, that God will go on. We have taken two guns, three carriages of ammunition in the chase. The enemy quitted Lamport; when they ran out at one end of the town, we entered the other. They fired that at which we should chase, which hindered our pursuit; but we overtook many of them. I believe we got near fifteen hundred horse.

Sir, I beg your prayers. Believe, and you shall be established. I rest,

Your servant,

[July 11? 1645] OLIVER CROMWELL.[141]

Goring's army disposed of, it remained to deal with the Somersetshire Clubmen, who on the day after the battle gathered in great numbers on "Knolhill". There Fairfax and Cromwell went to meet them, and with promises of protection and fair dealing sent them home satisfied.[142] Save for scattered forces here and there, Somerset was now cleared of enemies in the field and Fairfax's next objective was to complete the line of fortresses held by Parliament from the English Channel to Bristol Channel and isolate the Royalists in Cornwall and Devon. In consequence the army advanced against Bridgewater, the commanders making their headquarters in the house of one Walter Raleigh, D. D.[143] at Chedsay, two miles from Bridgewater, to whose capture Fairfax and Cromwell now addressed themselves.

Again the problem presented difficulties and five days were passed in deliberation and reconnoitering. On the first of those days Cromwell went to view the town, and narrowly escaped death from a Royalist volley which killed a cornet who was standing nearby.[144] His observations and those of his fellow-officers ended in a determination on July 16 to storm the place and by the night of the 20th, the army was in position about the town. At two o'clock the next morning the signal for assault was given, the portable bridges previously prepared were thrown across the moat, and the attacking forces were soon in possession of the eastern part of Bridgewater. But the drawbridges which connected it with the town proper were drawn up, resistance continued, a summons was ignored, and it was not until the morning of the 23rd, after a vigorous artillery attack that the garrison surrendered.[145] Two alternatives were now open to Fairfax and Cromwell, the one was to march at once into Devon and Cornwall, where the young Prince Charles had taken refuge, the other was to

[141] *Good Newes out of the West, declared in a letter sent from Lieutenant-General Cromwell to a worthy member of the House of Commons*, etc. (1645); Sanford, *Studies*, pp. 625–6, from a pamphlet in Lincoln College Library, Oxford, vol. x, "Battles and Sieges." Carlyle, App. 9.

[142] Sprigg, *Anglia Rediviva*, p. 74.

[143] Walker, *Sufferings of the Clergy*, ii, 71.

[144] *Mercurius Civicus.*

[145] Sprigg, *Anglia Rediviva*, pp. 74–81.

curb the Clubmen. The scarcity of ammunition determined them to take the second course on July 25, and this involved the capture of Bath and Sherborne, whose defenders were encouraging the Clubmen to resist.[146] Their next move, in consequence, was directed against the unorganized and undisciplined bands which roamed the countryside.

During all these operations, Charles had remained in Wales, at Raglan until July 16, and the next day at Cardiff, where he heard the news of Montrose's victory over the Covenanters in Scotland a fortnight earlier. On July 22 he met Rupert at Creeke and they resolved to put "all the new raysed foot" into garrisons in Wales. Thence Rupert returned to Bristol and Charles to Raglan, where he learned that Fairfax and Cromwell had taken Bridgewater on July 23 and that the Scots had begun the siege of Hereford. At first resolving to throw himself into Bristol with Rupert, he was dissuaded from that move by the Welsh gentlemen who "earnestly persuaded his stay and ymediately raised the hoop, hoop," as his diarist Symonds curiously records, though the men of Glamorganshire virtually declined to fight beyond their own borders. The news of Bridgewater's unexpected loss," Symonds continues, "rather stayed him," and he hung about south Wales, negotiating with the Welsh gentlemen until August 4, when events farther south seemed to make his presence there difficult if not dangerous.[147]

But the Parliamentary commanders paid no attention to the King's movements. Continuing their operations designed to clear the western peninsula of Royalists, they advanced to Martook, ten miles southwest of Bridgewater, where they remained some days, Cromwell, according to Vicars, being indisposed.[148] Meanwhile Fairfax took a small detachment of cavalry to Bath which surrendered without resistance; and on August 2, the siege of Sherborne Castle, the seat of the Earl of Bristol, was begun amid threats from the Dorset Clubmen who had regained their courage since Fairfax and Cromwell had attempted to appease them. More determined than those of Somerset and not so easily overawed, so threatening were their demonstrations that Fleetwood was sent with troops to Shaftesbury to quell the disturbance. He brought forty of their leaders back to Sherborne as prisoners,[149] but the rest were not intimidated, and, faced with their threat to rescue their comrades, Cromwell set out for Shaftesbury with Desborough and two regiments of horse. The first group he met dispersed at his request; the second, on Hambledon Hill, were dis-

146 *Ibid.*, p. 83.
147 Symonds, *Diary of the Marches of the Royal Army*, *passim.*
148 Letter, July 30, in Vicars, *Burning Bush*, p. 204.
149 Sprigg, *op. cit.*, p. 86.

posed to fight; and Cromwell describes what happened in his letter to Fairfax:[150]

To the Right Honourable Sir Thomas Fairfax, Commander-in-Chief of the Parliament's Forces

SIR,

I marched this morning towards Shaftesbury. In my way I found a party of clubmen gathered together, about two miles of this side of the town, towards you; and one Mr. Newman in the head of them, who was one of those who did attend you at Dorchester, with Mr. Hollis. I sent to them to know the cause of their meeting. Mr. Newman came to me and told me that the clubmen in Dorset and Wilts, to the number of ten-thousand, were to meet about their men which were taken away at Shaftesbury, and that their intendment was to secure themselves from plundering. To the first, I told them that although no account was due to them, yet I knew the men were taken by your authority, to be tried judicially for raising a third party in the Kingdom; and if they should be found guilty, they must suffer according to the nature of their offence; if innocent, I assured them you would acquit them. Upon this they said, if they have deserved punishment, they would not have any thing to do with them; and so were quieted as to that point. For the other I assured them that it was your great care not to suffer them in the least to be plundered, and that they should defend themselves from violence, and bring to your army such as did them any wrong, where they should be punished with all severity. Upon this, very quietly and peaceably they marched away to their houses, being very well satisfied and contented.

We marched on to Shaftesbury, where we heard a great body of them was drawn together about Hamilton Hill;—where indeed near two-thousand were gathered. I sent a forlorn of about fifty horse, who coming very civilly to them, they fired upon them; and they desiring some of them to come to me, were refused with disdain. They were drawn into one of the old camps,[151] upon a very high hill. I sent one Mr. Lee[152] to them, to certify the peaceableness of my intentions, and to desire them to peaceableness, and to submit to the Parliament. They refused, and fired at us. I sent him a second time, to let them know that if they would lay down their arms no wrong should be done them. They still (through the animation of their leaders, and especially two vile ministers) refused. I commanded your Captain-Lieutenant to draw up to them, to be in readiness to charge, and if upon his falling on they would lay down arms, to accept them and spare them. When he came near, they refused his offer, and let fly at him; killed about two of his men, and at least four horses, and passage not being for above three abreast, kept them out. Whereupon Major Desburgh wheeled about; got in the rear of them, beat them from the work, and did some small execution upon them; I believe killed not twelve of them, but cut very many, and we have taken

[150] See also, *ibid.*, pp. 86–89; Vicars, *op. cit.*, p. 253; *Two great Victories;* Heath, *Chronicle*, p. 83; and the newspapers.

[151] Roman camps.

[152] A Clubman.

about 300, many of which are poor silly creatures, whom if you please to let me send home, they promise to be very dutiful for time to come, and will be hanged before they come out again.

The ringleaders which we have, I hope to bring to you. They had taken divers of the Parliament soldiers prisoners, besides Colonel Fienes his men; and used them most barbarously, bragging they hoped to see my Lord Hopton, that he is to command them. They expected from Wilts great store; and gave out they meant to raise the siege at Sherborne when they were all met. We have gotten good store of their arms, and they carried few or none home. We quarter about ten miles off, and purpose to draw our quarters near to you tomorrow.

Your most humble servant,

[Shrawton?]
August 4th, 1645. OLIVER CROMWELL.[153]

At Shrawton where the army spent the night after the encounter at Hambledon Hill, the captured Clubmen were kept in a church. There they had an opportunity to take thought before Cromwell had a list of their names made and examined the leaders, one by one. This over, Cromwell lectured the entire group before he dismissed them on promise of good behavior:

Speech to the Clubmen

The Clubmen were to have the liberty to defend themselves against plundering but were to refrain in the future from stopping any soldier who went about his business, and meetings such as had been broken up the day before would not be countenanced. Any man whose name was in the list just made deserved to be hanged if he should be taken again opposing Parliament.[154]

With the news of these successes in the west, on August 12, the Parliament voted to extend Cromwell's period of service four months longer.[155] On the following day a letter from him to the Committee of the Army was read in the Commons, of which there remains only a note of the enclosure:

To the Committee of the Army

Enclosing a list of "necessaries for the army." Sherborne, Aug. 9, 1645.[156]

But the extension of Cromwell's commission was not wholly due to the western campaign. It was inspired in still greater measure by

[153] *Perfect Diurnall*, Aug. 4–11 (*Cromwelliana*, p. 20); *Two letters: the one to Lord Fairfax from Sir Thomas Fairfax . . . the other sent to Sir Thomas Fairfax from Lt. Gen. Cromwell.* Printed in Carlyle (Lomas ed.) Letter XXX, from the holograph original in *Tanner Mss*, lx, f. 236.

[154] Sprigg, *Anglia Rediviva*, pp. 89–90.

[155] *C. J.*, iv, 234, 237; *L. J.*, vii, 535.

[156] *C. J.*, iv, 239, 240.

news from the north, where the successes of the Royalist leader, James Graham, created Marquis of Montrose, alarmed not only the Scotch Covenanters but their English allies. Appointed lieutenant-general for Scotland by Charles in February, 1644, he had entered the country in August, collected a small force and within twelve months had won six pitched battles against the Covenanters. Of these, the victory of Alford had been gained on July 2, and while Fairfax and Cromwell were besieging Sherborne, Montrose advanced against Glasgow. On August 15 he defeated his enemies again and entered that city at the same moment that Sherborne Castle fell. Meanwhile Charles, leaving Cardiff, by this time had reached Doncaster with his little force. With Montrose's victories and the possibility of his junction with the King, this seemed no time to dispense with the most successful of the Parliament's commanders.

BRISTOL, AUGUST 15–SEPTEMBER 11, 1645

With his commission renewed, Cromwell continued his operations in the west. The siege of Sherborne went on with mines and batteries being prepared as rapidly as possible under the supervision of Fairfax and Cromwell, who visited the works once or twice each day until a breach was made. On Friday, August 15, the castle was taken,[157] and after its four hundred prisoners were despatched to London and the soldiers had disposed of their plunder in the market on Saturday, the Council of War resolved to attempt Bristol. There Rupert was stationed with 2,000 men, within recruiting distance of Wales and the supporting Clubmen. The city was infected with the plague with a hundred deaths a week, but Fairfax had faith that God would protect his men from sickness no less than bullets, and on Monday, the 18th, the army began its march by way of Castle Cary, Shepton-Mallet and and Chue toward Bristol. On Thursday night Fairfax and Cromwell lay at Keynsham, and attended a rendezvous on the Somerset side of Bristol the next day. Having spent Saturday settling quarters and guards on the other side of the city, they moved their own quarters to a small farm-house near Stapleton, and on Sunday, with everything in readiness for a siege, they sent a note into the city:[158]

To the Citizens of Bristol

An engagement for the safety of persons and estates of the citizens if the city should surrender. August 25, 1645. Signed by Thomas Fairfax and Oliver Cromwell.[159]

[157] Sprigg, *Anglia Rediviva*, p. 93; Vicars, *Burning Bush*, pp. 255–7.

[158] Sprigg, *op. cit.*, pp. 94–100; Rushworth, vi, 65–72.

[159] According to the *Hist. Mss Comm. Rept.* 5, Appendix, this exists among the papers of the Duke of Sutherland, but efforts to locate it have been unsuccessful.

Oliver Cromwell *aet.* 46. From a Portrait, Attributed to John Sailmaker, in the Possession of the Author. The Background is a View of the Siege of Bristol.

Despite the plague, Bristol was not ready to give way, and Rupert, though he realized that Charles's cause was lost and had advised making terms with Parliament, was the heart and soul of resistance. As greatly disturbed as the Parliamentary generals at the rising of the Clubmen, he had striven to disperse and frighten them; and, taking advantage of the respite granted him by the siege of Sherborne, he had raised men and strengthened the defences of Bristol, laid in provisions and prepared to stand a siege. It was not easy for him to protect its long line of walls and entrenchments with the forces at his command; and, knowing his impetuosity, Fairfax and Cromwell feared a sally from the garrison. The night of August 27 they spent in the field awaiting it, but Rupert did not move. The next day they received the disturbing news that the King had invaded the Eastern Association, plundered Huntingdon, and advanced into Bedford. The Scotch army having been defeated, they feared that Charles would soon appear to relieve Bristol.[160] It was a not too confident but nevertheless optimistic council of war which decided after several days' debate to storm Bristol and to send their sympathy and encouragement to the Earl of Leven who, until the day before, had been besieging Hereford without result:[161]

To the Earl of Leven

MAY IT PLEASE YOUR EXCELLENCY AND THE REST, HONOURED FRIENDS AND BELOVED BRETHREN,

We have, not without much grief, received the sad report of your affairs in Scotland; how far God, for his best and secret ends, hath been pleased to suffer the enemy to prevail there. And are (we speak unfeignedly) not less sensible of your evils, than you have been and are of ours, nor than we are of our own. And the greater cause we have of sympathy with you, the more do our bowels yearn towards you, because whatever you now suffer yourselves in your own Kingdom, are chiefly occasioned by your assisting us in ours, against the power that was risen up against the Lord himself, and his anointed ones.

Wherefore we cannot forget your labour of love, but thought good at this season even amongst our many occasions, to let you know that when the affairs of this kingdom will possibly dispense with us, the Parliament allowing, and you accepting of our assistance, we shall be most willing, if need so require, to help and serve you faithfully in your own kingdom, and to engage ourselves to suppress the enemy there, and to establish you again in peace. In the mean time we shall endeavour to help you by our prayers, and to wrestle with God, for one blessing of God upon both nations; between whom, besides many other strong relations and engagements we hope the unity of spirit shall be the surest bond of peace.

160 Sprigg, *op. cit.*, pp. 101–103; *Cal. S. P. Dom.* (1645), pp. 83, 85.
161 Sprigg, *op. cit.*, p. 104.

And this, whatever suggestions or jealousies may have been to the contrary, we desire you would believe, as you shall ever really find to proceed from integrity of heart, a sense of your sufferings, and a full purpose to answer any call of God to your assistance. As become,

Your Christian friends and servants in the Lord,
THOMAS FAIRFAX, OLIVER CROMWELL, THOMAS HAMMOND, HENRY IRETON, [and 21 other officers of the army.][162]

Before Bristol,
Sept. 2nd, 1645.

On September 4th, 2,000 of the well-affected countrymen around Bristol, who had previously promised Cromwell to join the Parliamentary cause, came into camp and had quarters assigned to them. On the same day Fairfax sent his first summons to Rupert, but with Goring's assistance promised and the King's hoped for, Rupert did his best to delay the threatened storm by negotiations.[163] Meanwhile, anticipating the capture of Bristol and a victorious march into Devon and Cornwall, Fairfax and Cromwell sent a resolution to the sheriff of the latter county suggesting the wisdom of non-resistance, in view of the fact that the Cornishmen were now the only considerable party left to the King.

For the High Sheriff of the County of Cornwall and the well affected Gentry, and Inhabitants of that County.

Whereas, besides the great and frequent supplies of men, money and other aids to the enemy which have been raised out of your County above others, to the sad continuation and often reinforcing of the unnatural war against the Parliament. We are given to understand, that the restless enemies of your and our and the Kingdom's peace, being (through God's late returning mercies to us all, and the blessing of the forces of the Parliament) driven almost out of all other parts of the Kingdom and destitute of all dear supplies from elsewhere save that little angle which you possess) do yet persist by all the ways of art and violence, to draw out from amongst you some fresh supplies and reinforcement of their broken forces, whereby they may once again appear in the field to disturb the peace of the Kingdom, and continue and renew the miseries of it by a further war, we being equally careful to prevent (if possible) your ruin or further sufferings as the kingdom's further troubles, have thought good to admonish you and declare to you, as followeth:

(1) We desire you would be, and we pray God to make you once at last sensible of the interest of Religion, and of the rights and liberties of yourselves and the rest of the people of England, of which the power and authority of Parliaments hath been in former ages and is ever like to be (under God) the best conservatory and support, and which by this unnatural war against the Parliament (and that) in a great degree by the aids your Country hath afforded thereunto, have been so much endangered: And if now at

[162] Pr. in Rushworth, vi, 68; and in Sprigg, *Anglia Rediviva*, pp. 106–107.
[163] Letters in Sprigg, pp. 108–114.

last you shall appear sensible thereof, we shall be willing to believe of you, and be glad we may have occasion so to represent you to the Parliament and Kingdom. That the great aids you have formerly afforded the enemy against them, have been only forced or drawn from you by violence or deceit or those that God has suffered hitherto to be possessed of the power over you.

(2) As we believe you have had by this time sufficient sense and experience of the violence and oppressions (besides all other wickedness) of that party so we advise you timely to consider how unlike you are in humane probability to bear and maintain their war alone against the rest of the Kingdom, that is now by God's blessing almost cleared to the Parliament, how heavy the burden is like to be to you in the prosecution of such a war alone, and how great calamity may befall you in the issue of it.

(3) If God shall see good to set those considerations home upon your hearts and incline you to endeavor the freeing of yourselves from the yoke you have been under, from the burden and danger that may befall you, and from the guilt of so much mischief and trouble to the Kingdom as the prolonging of such a war, when otherwise likely to be happily ended. And if upon these considerations you shall apply yourselves to drive the remainder of the enemy out of your Country, if you shall call home, and (as much as in you lies) withdraw, from the enemy the forces which you have sent them, and forbear for future to afford them any more aids or contribution, but stand upon your guard to defend yourselves and country from any further oppressions, plunderings, or invasions, you shall not only be allowed therein, but countenanced and assisted, as you shall desire, by the Parliament's party; and be secured from any invasion or incursions of the Parliament's forces, unless you shall desire any of them for your assistance. You shall likewise have free trading and commerce by sea and land to all places, and with all persons that are not in hostility against the Parliament, and shall have for money what supplies of arms or ammunition you shall need for your said defence. But if, notwithstanding this offer, you shall persist to aid the enemy any further, you must expect and be assured when God shall give leisure and opportunity (as yourselves thereby will give occasion) for the Parliament's forces to come down amongst you, that you shall be accounted and dealt withal in the severest way of war as the most eminent and obstinate disturbers and retarders of the Kingdom's peace, now by God's mercy in a fair way to be speedily settled. Yet hoping better of you for the future (which we shall be glad to hear of) we remain,

Your assured friends,

From before Bristol, Tho. Fairfax
Sept. 8, 1645. Oliver Cromwell[164]

Reluctant to destroy property and cause unnecessary bloodshed, Fairfax had been patient with Rupert but he could afford to wait no longer. The pre-arranged signal for a storm was given at two o'clock on the morning of September 10th, from the top of Prior's Hill Fort, where Fairfax and Cromwell sat during the siege and where a bullet

[164] Original in the *Clarendon Papers*, 25, f. 127–127v, in the Bodleian Library. Calendared in Coxe, *Calendar of the Clarendon State Papers*, no. 1952.

came "within two hands' breadth of them but did them no hurt at all."[165]

Rupert's force was inadequate to defend the four miles of Bristol's wall in the face of a carefully planned attack. After two hours of vigorous bombardment and fighting the Gloucestershire side gave way. The other side of the fortress with its high works proved impregnable to the three regiments assigned to it, one of which was Cromwell's own, commanded by Major Huntington. When he discovered the city had been fired in several places, Fairfax, unwilling to permit its destruction, once more sent word to Rupert that terms would be given if the fire were immediately extinguished. To this Rupert agreed and by seven that night articles were signed, giving Rupert and a specified number of followers liberty to march wherever he wished.[166]

Of the whole episode Cromwell's account in the longest letter he had yet written gives the best description.

For the Honourable William Lenthall, Speaker of the Commons House of Parliament: These

SIR,

It hath pleased the General to give me in charge to represent unto you a particular account of the taking of Bristol, the which I gladly undertake.

After the finishing of that service at Sherborne, it was disputed at a council of war, whether we should march into the West or to Bristol. Amongst other arguments, the leaving so considerable an enemy at our backs, to march into the heart of the Kingdom; the undoing of the country about Bristol, which was exceedingly harassed by the Prince his being but a fortnight thereabouts; the correspondence he might hold in Wales; the possibility of uniting the enemy's forces where they pleased, and especially the drawing to an head the disaffected clubmen of Somerset, Wilts and Dorset, when once our backs were towards them: these considerations, together with the taking so important a place, so advantageous for the opening of trade to London, did sway the balance, and begat that conclusion.

When we came within four miles of the city, we had a new debate, whether we should endeavour to block it up, or make a regular siege. The latter being overruled, Colonel Welden with his brigade marched to Pile Hill, on the south side of the city, being within musket-shot thereof, where in a few days they made a good quarter, overlooking the city. Upon our advance, the enemy fired Bedminster, Clifton, and some other villages, and would have fired the country thereabouts if our unexpected coming had not hindered. The General caused some horse and dragooners under Commissary-General Ireton to advance over Avon, to keep-in the enemy on the north side of the town, until the foot could come up; and after a day, the General, with Colonel

[165] Sprigg, *Anglia Rediviva*, p. 121.
[166] *Ibid.*, pp. 115–123.

Montague's and Colonel Rainsborowe's brigades, marched over at Keynsham to Stapleton, where he quartered that night. The next day, Colonel Montague, having his post assigned with his brigade, was to secure all between Froom and Avon. He came up to Lawford's Gate, within musket-shot thereof. Colonel Rainsborowe's post was near to Durdham Down, where the dragooners and three regiments of horse made good a post upon the Down, between him and the River Avon, on his right hand, and from Colonel Rainsborowe's quarters to Froom River, on his left. A part of Colonel Birch and Major-General Skippon's regiments were to maintain that post.

These posts being thus settled, our horse were forced to be upon exceeding great duty, to stand by the foot, lest the foot, being so weak in all their posts, might receive an affront; and truly herein we were very happy, that we should receive so little loss by sallies, considering the paucity of our men to make good their posts, and the strength of the enemy within. By sallies (which were three or four) I know not that we lost thirty men, in all the time of our siege. Of officers of quality, only Colonel Okey was taken, by mistake going to the enemy, thinking them to be friends, and Captain Guilliams slain in a charge. We took Sir Bernard Asteley; and killed Sir Richard Crane, men very considerable with the Prince.

We had a council of war concerning the storming of the town, about eight days before we took it; and in that there appeared great unwillingness to the work, through the unseasonableness of the weather, and other apparent difficulties. Some inducement to bring us thither was the report of the good affection of the townsmen to us; but that did not answer expectation. Upon a second consideration, it was overruled for a storm, which no sooner concluded, but difficulties were removed, and all things seemed to favour the design; and indeed there hath been seldom the like cheerfulness in officers and soldiers to any work like to this, after it was once resolved on. The day and hour of our storm was appointed to be Wednesday morning, the tenth, about one of the clock. We chose to act it so early because we hoped thereby to surprise the enemy; with this resolution also (to avoid confusion and falling foul one upon another), that when we had recovered the line, and forts upon it, we would not to (*sic*) advance further until day. The general signal unto the storm was the firing of straw, and discharging four piece of cannon at Prior Hill Fort.

The signal was very well perceived by all, and truly the men went on with great resolution, and very presently recovered the line, making way for the horse to enter. Colonel Montague and Colonel Pickering, who stormed at Lawford's Gate, where was a double work, well filled with men and cannon, presently entered, and with great resolution beat the enemy from their works, and possessed their cannon. Their expedition was such that they forced the enemy from their advantages, without any considerable loss to themselves. They laid down the bridges for the horse to enter; Major Desborowe commanding the horse, who very gallantly seconded the foot. Then our foot advanced to the city walls, where they possessed the gate against the Castle Street whereinto were put an hundred men, who made it good. Sir Hardresse Waller, with his and the General's regiment, with no less resolution, entered on the other side of Lawford's Gate, towards Avon River; and put themselves into an immediate conjunction with the rest of the brigade.

During this, Colonel Rainborowe and Colonel Hammond attempted Prior Hill Fort, and the line downwards towards Froome; Colonel Birch and the Major-General's regiment being to storm towards Froome River. Colonel Hammond possessed the line immediately, and beating the enemy from it, made way for our horse to enter. Colonel Rainborowe, who had the hardest task of all at Prior Hill Fort, attempted it, and fought near three hours for it, and indeed there was great despair of carrying the place, it being exceeding high, a ladder of thirty rounds scarcely reaching the top thereof; but his resolution was such that, notwithstanding the inaccessibleness and difficulty, he would not give it over. The enemy had four piece of cannon upon it; which they played with round and case shot upon our men: his Lieutenant-Colonel Bowen and others were two hours at push of pike, standing upon the palisadoes, but could not enter. Colonel Hammond being entered the line, Captain Ireton,[167] with a forlorn of Colonel Riche's regiment (interposing with his horse between the enemy's horse and Colonel Hammond), received a shot with two pistol-bullets, which broke his arm. By means of his entrance, Colonel Hammond did storm the Fort on that part which was inward; by which means, Colonel Rainborowe and Colonel Hammond's men entered the Fort, and immediately put to the sword almost all in it, and as this was the place of most difficulty, so of most loss to us on that side, and of very great honour to the undertakers. The horse did second them with great resolution: both those Colonels do acknowledge that their interposition between the enemy's horse and their foot was a great means of obtaining this strong Fort, without which all the rest of the line to Froome River would have done us little good: and indeed neither horse nor foot would have stood in all that way, in any manner of security, had not the Fort been taken. Major Bethel's were the first horse entered the line; who did behave himself very gallantly, and was shot in the thigh, had one or two shot more, and his horse shot under him. Colonel Birch with his men, and the Major-General's regiment, entered with very great resolution where their post was; possessing the enemy's guns, and turning them upon them.

By this, all the line from Prior Hill Fort to Avon, which was a full mile, with all the forts, ordnance and bulwarks, were possessed by us but one, wherein there were about 120 men of the enemy which the General summoned, and all the men submitted.

The success on Colonel Welden's side did not answer with this; and although the colonels, and other the officers and soldiers both horse and foot testified very much resolution, as could be expected, Colonel Welden, Colonel Ingoldsby, Colonel Herbert, and the rest of the colonels and officers, both of horse and foot, doing what could be well looked for from men of honour; yet what by reason of the height of the works, which proved higher than report made them, and the shortness of the ladders, they were repulsed, with the loss of about 100 men. Colonel Fortescue's Lieutenant-Colonel was killed, Major Cromwell[168] dangerously shot and two of Colonel Ingoldsby's brothers hurt; with some officers.

Being possessed of thus much as hath been related, the town was fired in three places by the enemy, which we could not put out; and this begat a

[167] The brother of Henry Ireton.

[168] Richard, second son of Sir Philip Cromwell, Oliver's uncle.

great trouble to the General and us all, fearing to see so famous a city burnt to ashes before our faces. Whiles we were viewing so sad a spectacle, and consulting which way to make further advantage of our success, the Prince sent a trumpet to the General to desire a treaty for the surrender of the town, to which the General agreed; and deputed Colonel Montague, Colonel Rainborowe, and Colonel Pickering for that service; authorising them with instructions to treat and conclude the Articles, which are these enclosed;[169] for performance whereof hostages were mutually given.

On Thursday about two of the clock in the afternoon, the Prince marched out; having a convoy of two regiments of horse from us; and making election of Oxford for the place he would go to, which he had liberty to do by his Articles.

The cannon which we have taken are about 140 mounted; about 100 barrels of powder already come to our hands, with a good quantity of shot, ammunition, and arms. We have found already between 2000 and 3000 muskets. The Royal Fort had in it victuals for one-hundred-and-fifty men, for three-hundred-and-twenty days; the Castle victualled for near half so long. The Prince had foot of the garrison (as the Mayor of the City informed me), two-thousand five-hundred, and about one thousand horse, besides the trained bands of the town, and auxiliaries 1200, some say 1500. I hear but one man hath died of the plague[170] in all our army, although we have quartered amongst and in the midst of infected persons and places. We had not killed of ours in this storm, nor all this siege, 200 men.

Thus I have given you a true, but not a full account of this great business; wherein he that runs may read, that all this is none other than the work of God. He must be a very Atheist that doth not acknowledge it.

It may be thought that some praises are due to these gallant men, of whose valour so much mention is made: their humble suit to you and all that have an interest in this blessing, is, that in the remembrance of God's praises they may be forgotten. It's their joy that they are instruments to God's glory, and their country's good; it's their honour that God vouchsafes to use them. Sir, they that have been employed in this service know that faith and prayer obtained this city for you. I do not say ours only, but of the people of God with you and all England over, who have wrestled with God[171] for a blessing in this very thing. Our desires are, that God may be glorified by the same spirit of faith by which we asked all our sufficiency, and having received it, it's meet that He have all the praise. Presbyterians, Independents, all had here the same spirit of faith and prayer; the same pretence and answer; they agree here, know no names of difference: pity it is it should be otherwise anywhere. All that believe, have the real unity, which is most glorious, because inward and spiritual, in the Body, and to the Head. As for being united in forms, commonly called Uniformity, every Christian will for peace-sake study and do, as far as conscience will permit; and from brethren, in things of the mind we look for no compulsion, but that of light and reason. In other things, God hath put the sword into the Parliament's hands, for the terror of evil-doers, and the praise of them that do well. If

[169] Pr. in Sprigg, *Anglia Rediviva*, pp. 119–120, *L. J.*, vii, 586.
[170] Originally "black," but corrected to "plague" by Cromwell.
[171] Originally "waited on God."

any plead exemption from it, he knows not the Gospel: if any would wring it out of your hands, or steal it from you under what pretence soever, I hope they shall do it without effect. That God may maintain it in your hands, and direct you in the use thereof, is the prayer of

Bristol, Your humble servant,
September 14th, 1645. OLIVER CROMWELL.[172]

One thing, among others of more importance, the siege of Bristol did—it vindicated Fiennes for his surrender of the place two years earlier, as the Parliamentary officers all agreed. His seat in the House was restored to him and his fellow-officers presently issued a declaration exonerating him from the charges of incompetence and cowardice.[173] On the other hand, Rupert now suffered the same fate as Fiennes. Deprived of his commission by the King, he made his way to Charles at Newark and demanded a court-martial. Its verdict acquitted him of cowardice and infidelity but censured his lack of discretion; though Charles and Rupert were not reconciled until December and then not until Rupert had appealed to Parliament for a pass to leave England.

DEVIZES—BASING HOUSE, SEPTEMBER 11–OCTOBER 14, 1645

It is not surprising that the royal temper was on edge. Fearing the advance of Fairfax on the south, Charles had left south Wales on August 4 and made his way through Brecknock and Radnor to Bridgnorth and so to Lichfield, where he arrived on August 10. By Monday, August 19—the same day that the Parliamentary army began its march from Sherborne toward Bristol—he reached Doncaster where he reviewed his forces—2,200 horse and 400 foot, a little ammunition "carried upon horses," and "three or four carts full of pikes." By Saturday, August 23, as Fairfax and Cromwell prepared for the storm of Bristol, he had reached Stamford and the next day arrived in

[172] The original, with corrections in Cromwell's hand, is at Welbeck; pr. from that copy, in Lomas Carlyle, Letter XXXI. Omitting the first and the last two paragraphs and altered in places to appear as though Fairfax had written the letter, it is pr. in *L. J.*, vii, 584–6. The last part concerning religion was omitted, either because the House of Commons thought it unwise, or for the sake of brevity, in the official pamphlet, *Lieutenant-General Cromwell's Letter*, but was printed by the Independents, says Thomason, and scattered up and down the streets on Sept. 21st, as *The Conclusion of Lieutenant-General Cromwell's Letter*. Later on the last part was also printed in *Strong motives or loving advice*. With a few minor differences the entire letter is in Rushworth, vi, 85; and in Sprigg, *Anglia Rediviva*, pp. 123–128. The passage "Presbyterians, Independents, . . . but that of light and reason," was quoted in Rutherford Scott, *A Survey of the Spiritual Antichrist*, p. 250, in proof of Cromwell's dangerous influence and his sympathy with Familism, Antinomianism and other errors. The letter was read in Parliament on Sept. 17th and ordered to be read in the churches, Sept. 21st. *C. J.*, iv, 277; *Kingdom's Weekly Intelligencer*. Vane and Pierrepont framed a reply which was signed on Sept. 19. *C. J.*, iv, 279.

[173] *Copie of a Declaration* (1646); Sprigg, *op. cit.*, p. 129.

Huntingdon, which was occupied after a skirmish with a body of Suffolk and Essex horse. It seemed for the moment that he might overrun the eastern counties and from all sides men were summoned to their defence. Against such forces Charles's little army could do nothing and he turned again toward the west, reaching Oxford on August 28, and by September 3 he was at Hereford, whence the Scots had withdrawn toward Gloucester on the news of his coming. By Thursday, September 11, he was back at Raglan Castle and there received the news of the fall of Bristol. His position was now doubly dangerous, and sending "letters of buisiness to Oxford," reproaching Rupert and dismissing him from his command, he set out once more on his travels.

Eluding Poyntz and Rossiter who were set to watch him, he determined to join Montrose, but hearing that Chester was hard pressed, he ordered Lord Byron to that stronghold then besieged by Colonel Michael Jones. Urging its defenders to hold out twenty-four hours, he hastened to relieve it. By the 23rd he had reached Chester, but the next day Poyntz and Jones defeated Charles's little army at Rowton Heath, taking a thousand prisoners, and the next morning the King left Chester for Denbigh, thence to Ruthyn and so to Bridgnorth, where, hearing of the loss of Devizes and Berkeley Castle to Fairfax, he pushed on to Lichfield.[174]

His news of those further losses was correct. Fairfax and Cromwell had continued their reduction of the west while Charles marched here and there, a virtual fugitive. On the night of the evacuation of Bristol by Rupert, who rode out for Oxford on September 11, they had moved their headquarters into the once flourishing but now plague stricken city. Four days later a brigade was sent to take Berkeley Castle, while Cromwell with another brigade of four regiments under Montague, Pickering, Sir Hardress Waller and Hammond, was ordered to take Devizes, in the center of Wiltshire, and commanding the traffic between London and the west. All day Saturday, September 20, the soldiers attacked the Castle with musketry fire and granadoes but with no great effect. The following day, as soon as the cannon and mortars were in place, Cromwell sent a summons to the governor, only to receive an answer like that of Rupert, asking for time to secure the King's permission to give up the place.[175] To that Cromwell replied:

To Sir Charles Lloyd, governor of the Castle of Devizes

Wishing him not to let slip such an opportunity; or, if he were otherwise resolved, giving him leave to send forth his lady and such other gentlewomen that were in the castle. Assuring him that "none were more fitting to keep

[174] Symonds, *Diary, passim;* Warburton, *Rupert, passim.*
[175] Sprigg, *Anglia Rediviva*, pp. 133–4.

strongholds, forts and castles than the Parliament, for the use of the King." September 21, 1645.[176]

The governor's only answer was, "Win it and wear it!" and Cromwell, wasting no more words, attacked "with swords, roaring ordnance, and thundering threats from the cannons mouths," [177] till with some of the granadoes falling into the roofless keep that was the powder magazine, the frightened governor sent forth a request at eight o'clock in the morning for a parley. At eleven Cromwell sent the following propositions:

Articles for the surrender of the Castle of Devizes

(1) That all commanders and gentlemen should march to any garrison the king had within thirty miles, with their horse and arms; and that all private soldiers should march away leaving their arms behind them, but not to go to the same garrisons the commanders marched to.

(2) That all gentlemen in the castle should have liberty to go to their own homes or beyond the seas.

(3) That all soldiers that have been formerly in the Parliament service should be delivered up to the lieutenant-general, and all soldiers that would take up arms in the Parliament service should be entertained.[178]

To these Lloyd at once consented, agreeing to march out towards Worcester with his 400 men the following morning, and a report to Lenthall which has not been preserved was sent on the same day.

To William Lenthall, Speaker of the House of Commons

Relating to the taking of the Castle of Devizes and proceedings against Berkeley Castle. Devizes, September 22, 1645.[179]

Two days later, on September 24, Pickering took Laycock House without resistance. Berkeley House was surrendered to Rainsborough on the 26th; and conceiving that the Royalist position in that quarter was sufficiently weakened, Fairfax decided to divide his forces, he himself to go farther west and Cromwell with four regiments of foot and three of horse to turn east to seize the chief garrisons left between London and the west—Basing House and Winchester.[180] Disarming and dispersing Hampshire and Sussex Clubmen on his way, Cromwell reached Winchester on Sunday, September 28,[181]

[176] *Ibid.*, p. 134.

[177] Vicars, *Burning Bush*, pp. 276–7.

[178] Sprigg, *op. cit.*, pp. 134–5.

[179] *C. J.*, iv, 284. Read in the House of Commons, Sept. 25.

[180] Sprigg, *op. cit.*, pp. 158–9; Rushworth, vi, 91. He had 4000 horse and 3000 foot, according to *Mercurius Civicus*, Sept. 18–25.

[181] *Perfect Diurnall*, Sept. 22–29. Dudgale's *Diary*, (ed. Hamper) p. 82, says Cromwell reached Winchester Sept. 27th.

and demanded its immediate surrender from the mayor, William Longland:

To the Mayor of the City of Winchester

SIR,

I come not to this city but with a full resolution to save it, and the inhabitants thereof, from ruin.

I have commanded the soldiers, upon pain of death, that no wrong be done; which I shall strictly observe; only I expect you give me entrance into the city, without necessitating me to force my way; which if I do, then it will not be in my power to save you or it. I expect your answer within half an hour; and rest,

Your humble servant,

28th September 1645,
5 o'clock at night. OLIVER CROMWELL.[182]

Longland replied that it was not in his power to surrender, inasmuch as the city was under the command of William, Viscount Ogle, governor of the garrison there, who declared to Cromwell his intention to hold out to the last. By firing the city gate, however, the soldiers entered the town without much difficulty. Walter Curl, Bishop of Winchester, refused Cromwell's offer of a convoy to conduct him to safety, taking refuge in the castle[183] which was summoned at once and refused.

Two guns were set to work battering the castle while the other four were being repaired. By Friday, the 3rd, Cromwell, having demonstrated to Lord Ogle what six guns could do, sent another summons and was again refused, partly, perhaps, because Sir Hardress Waller's regiment just then arriving, was mistaken for a relieving force of Royalists.[184] The ordnance playing violently on Saturday soon made a breach wide enough for thirty men abreast, through which the enemy sallied out and for a moment beat Cromwell's artillerymen from their guns. The firing continued until the mansion-house was in ruins. With that the governor asked for a treaty and on Monday Cromwell wrote to the House of Commons enclosing the articles which had been wrangled over all the previous night:[185]

For the Right Honourable William Lenthall, Esq., Speaker of the House of Commons:

SIR,

I came to Winchester on the Lord's day, being the 28th of September, with Colonel Pickering commanding his own, Colonel Moun-

[182] Carlyle, App. 9, from *History and Antiquities of Winchester* (1773), ii, 127.

[183] *Diary or Exact Journal*, Oct. 2–9.

[184] *Perfect Diurnall*, Sept. 29–Oct. 6; *True Informations*, Oct. 4; Vicars, *Burning Bush*, pp. 287–8.

[185] Hugh Peter's account, in Sprigg, *Anglia Rediviva*, pp. 141–4. Cp. an account of the siege of Winchester, calendared in Coxe, *Cal. Clarendon Papers*, i, 292.

tague's, and Sir Hardress Waller's regiments. After some dispute with the Governor, we entered the town. I summoned the Castle; was denied; whereupon we fell to prepare our batteries, which we could not perfect (some of our guns being out of order) until Friday following. Our battery was six guns; which being finished,—after one firing of them round, I sent him a second summons for a treaty, which he refused; whereupon we went on with our work, and made a breach in the wall near the Black Tower which, after about 200 shot, we thought stormable, and purposed on Monday morning to attempt it. On Sunday night, about ten of the clock, the Governor beat a parley, desiring to treat. I agreed unto it, and sent Colonel Hammond and Major Harrison in to him, who agreed upon these enclosed Articles.

Sir, this is the addition of another mercy. You see God is not weary in doing you good: I confess, Sir, His favour to you is as visible, when He comes by His power upon the hearts of your enemies, making them quit places of strength to you, as when He gives courage to your soldiers to attempt hard things; His goodness in this is much to be acknowledged.

For the Castle was well manned with 680 foot and horse, there being near 200 gentlemen, officers, and their servants; well victualled, with very great store of wheat and beer, 15,000 weight of cheese, near 20 barrels of powder, 7 piece of cannon; the works were exceeding good and strong. It's very likely it would have cost much blood to have gained it by storm. We have not lost twelve men; this is repeated to you, that God may have all the praise, for it's all His due.

Sir, I rest,

Winton, Your most humble servant,
October 6th, 1645. OLIVER CROMWELL.

[P.S.] I understand exceptions are taken at my giving a pass to Mr. Chichley to come into Cambridgeshire to see his lady. Truly, Sir, I did it upon the suggestion of his lady's being very ill and much desiring to see him, she being (as I believe you will hear) a virtuous woman and sister to a true servant of yours, Colonel Russells. I thought it to be an act of humanity. I shall not hereafter presume. I can say I have done you service by some civilities, nor have I taken liberty this way, I hope I never shall, but out of judgment to serve you. If it offend the House, I ask their pardon, and had rather be chidden by you than accused by them from whom I have not deserved any jealousy of me, who truly bear an upright heart to the public, and am sorry I need this apology.

Sir, Mr. Peeters is to wait upon you with some considerations concerning the army which it may be are not so fit to be committed to writing, yet very fit you should seasonably be acquainted with them, wherein I beseech you to hear him.[186]

[186] Original at Welbeck Abbey with a copy of the Articles enclosed. Calendared in *Hist. Mss. Comm. Rep.* 13, App. I, 282 (*Portland Mss.*). Pr., without the postscript, in *Cont. of Cert. Spec. & Remark. Pass.*, Oct., 3–10 (*Cromwelliana*, p. 25); Sprigg, p. 140; Rushworth, iv, 91. Sprigg, followed by Rushworth, supposed the letter to be addressed to Fairfax, and Carlyle naturally followed their error. Mrs. Lomas, however (Lomas-Carlyle, Letter XXXII) copied her text from the original. The House of Commons voted to give Peter, Cromwell's chaplain, 50 l. for bringing the news, speaking of him as Cromwell's "secretary." *C. J.*, iv, 299.

Articles agreed upon, the 5th of October, 1645, between the right honourable William viscount Ogle, governor of the garrison of the castle of Winton, of the one part, and colonel Robert Hammond and major Thomas Harrison on the behalf of lieutenant-general Oliver Cromwell, of the other party, for the surrender of the said castle.

(1) That the lord Ogle shall deliver up the castle of Winchester, with all the arms, ordnance, ammunition, provision, and all function of war whatsoever, without any embezzlement, waste, or spoil, unto that officer or officers as shall be thereunto appointed by the said lieutenant-general tomorrow, being Monday the 6th of October, by three of the clock afternoon.

(2) That the said lord Ogle shall have his own colours, and one hundred fixed arms for his guard, and one hundred men to carry them.

(3) That the lord Ogle, and all the officers in commission, shall march out of the said castle with their own horse and arms, and their own proper goods, unto Woodstock, whither they shall be safely conveyed.

(4) That there shall be allowed to the lord Ogle and his officers six carriages for the transporting of their goods aforesaid.

(5) That all officers, gentlemen, clergymen, and inhabitants of the city of Winchester, and all officers within the guards, (desiring it), may be at their own time, free from all violence and injury of the Parliament's forces.

(6) That the lord Ogle shall give sufficient hostages for the performance of the articles here constituted on their part to be performed, also for the safe return of the convoy.[187]

The representatives sent by Lord Ogle to treat with Cromwell were Sir Edward Ford and one of his majors. To Sir Edward's father, Sir William Ford, Cromwell granted a request for a special pass instead of forcing him to go to Oxford with the Royalists from Winchester, and when Sir William compounded a few weeks later for his estate, he used this pass as evidence in his case.[188]

Pass

Permitting Sir William Forde freely to pass into London from Winchester. Oct. 6, 1645.[189]

Meanwhile the Committee of Both Kingdoms, not knowing that Cromwell had already been ordered by Fairfax to help Colonel Dalbier reduce Basing House, wrote him two letters asking such assistance there as would not interfere with his own plans,[190] and the day after the evacuation of Winchester, he set out with his train of artil-

[187] *Cromwelliana*, p. 25; Sprigg, *op. cit.*, pp. 142–43; Rushworth, vi, 91–2; *Perfect Diurnall*, Oct. 7.

[188] *Cal. Comm. for Compounding*, p. 932.

[189] Cal. in *Sussex Archaeological Collections* (1867), xix, 92.

[190] Oct. 2, 6, in *Cal. S. P. Dom.* (1645), pp. 172, 176. The county of Hampshire asked especially for Cromwell's services at Basing House, *Ibid.*, p. 180.

lery for the scene of his last military disagreement with Manchester. Now the commanding officer, experienced in reducing garrisons, and not distracted by the possibility of a relieving force to drive him away, there was little doubt in Cromwell's mind, or in those of the London news writers, that Basing House could hold out long against this joint attack. None the less its first episode was unfortunate; for shortly after the arrival of the army at Basingstoke, Colonel Hammond and Major King, going from the town to view the horse on the other side of Basing House, were captured and carried into the garrison. Immediately Cromwell sent in a demand for the safety of his officers, which, though it has not survived, was evidently brief and stern:

To John Paulet, Marquis of Winchester, governor of Basing House

If any wrong or violence be offered to either Colonel Hammond or Major King during their captivity, the best in the house shall not expect quarter. [c. Oct. 9, 1645.][191]

On the day Cromwell's guns were put in action against the place Cromwell wrote an order of a different character to Colonel Thomas Herbert, for one of his men, possibly that Captain George Jenkins who was to die at Drogheda four years later.

For Mr. Herbert, Commissioner of Parliament in the Army

SIR,

I desire you to deliver unto Capt. Jenkins for the use of his troop two serviceable horses, having lost two lately at the Leaguer before Basing for which this shall be your sufficient warrant. Dated this 10 d. Octob. 1645.

OLIVER CROMWELL.[192]

While, then, the fugitive King, with Bristol and Chester gone, with Fairfax on the south and Poyntz and Jones on the north, having learned of Montrose's defeat at Philiphaugh on September 23, rode out the only way left to him, toward Newark and the east, Cromwell pressed the siege of Basing House. The game was almost over, as Charles realized, and though reinforced by Maurice with a regiment of horse and ordering Goring to join the royal army wherever it might be, he instructed Culpepper to send the Prince of Wales to France, and with a heavy heart set out on his last march.[193]

Meanwhile the siege of Basing House went on. That great fortified mansion of the premier Marquis of England, the Catholic John

[191] Mentioned in *Weekly Account*, Oct. 8–15.

[192] Superscribed "Jo. Chapman in Capt. Jenkins tr. warrt." Holograph original in *S. P. Dom. Charles I*, dxxxix, no. 132. Cal. in *Cal. S. P. Dom.* (1625–49), p. 624.

[193] Symonds, *Diary, ut supra.*

Paulet, a man of "goodness, piety and unselfish loyalty," which "would have become an emperor to dwell in," as Cromwell's chaplain and war correspondent, Hugh Peter, told the Commons, had been regarded as impregnable. A year earlier it had withstood a three months' siege, which had been one of the more dramatic episodes of the war. It was not merely a fortress; it was a storehouse of money, jewels, plate and works of art; and it contained a garrison which numbered many Catholics and some men of letters and artists like the great engraver, Hollar. It was, then, not only an important post, commanding as it did the road to the west, but it was a rich prize for plunder, as was pointed out, and "a nest of idolatrous Papists." There was now no hope of relief from Oxford as there had been a year before, and Cromwell and Dalbier were experienced soldiers. None the less the Marquis refused to surrender, and while Dalbier's guns pounded away on one side of the house, Cromwell's artillery began its cannonade on the other on Friday, with such effect that by Monday night the order was given to storm the place the following morning—October 14—at daybreak.[194]

That night the men snatched a few hours of sleep while Cromwell, according to Peter, spent much of his time in prayer and Scripture reading. Strengthened by the text which was such comfort to iconoclasts, "They that make them are like unto them, so is every one that trusteth in them,"[195] he prepared to attack these idol-worshippers, the twentieth garrison which had fallen to Parliament since the New Model army had taken the field. Spurred on by their hatred of those Catholics who refused to yield and asked no quarter, and perhaps not uninfluenced by the hope of rich plunder, Cromwell's men pushed forward their attack. The assault was brief and bloody. A quarter of the garrison was killed, including the comely but vituperative daughter of a clergyman, many gentlemen of quality and six priests.

The plunder was prodigious and Cromwell allowed his men full play. Though Hammond spared the lives of the Marquis and Sir Robert Peake in return for the civil treatment accorded him during his own captivity, the Marquis was stripped of his fine attire and a great store of food, money, iron, lead, clothing and household goods was seized by the soldiers and sold to the country people who flocked to the spoil of what its owner called "Loyalty House." The place itself was left a mass of smouldering ruins, while Cromwell wrote an account of its capture to Lenthall with a recommendation that it be "utterly slighted." But from the siege arose a controversy which was recalled in later years to blacken his reputation. Like a wise commander, like Fairfax himself, Cromwell did not needlessly expose himself in the attack, and Colonel Dalbier, jealous that Cromwell

[194] *Weekly Account*, Oct. 8–15.

[195] Peter's account in Sprigg, *Anglia Rediviva*, p. 152.

had been given the credit which he felt would have been his had Cromwell not arrived, complained that his superior officer had "stood at a great distance off, out of gun-shot behind a hedge," instead of leading his men in storming the stronghold[196]—a charge of cowardice which, like that at Edgehill, scarcely stands examination.

To the Hon. William Lenthall, Speaker of the House of Commons

SIR,

I thank God, I can give you a good account of Basing. After our batteries placed, we settled the several posts for the storm. Colonel Dalbier was to be on the north side of the House near the Grange, Colonel Pickering on his left hand, and Sir Hardress Waller's and Colonel Montague's regiments next him. We stormed, this morning, after six of the clock. The signal for falling on was the firing four of our cannon, which being done, our men fell on with great resolution and cheerfulness. We took the two houses without any considerable loss to ourselves. Colonel Pickering stormed the New House, passed through, and got the gate of the Old House; whereupon they summoned a parley, which our men would not hear.

In the meantime Colonel Montague's and Sir Hardress Waller's regiments assaulted the strongest work, where the enemy kept his court of guard; which, with great resolution, they recovered; beating the enemy from a whole culverin, and from that work: which having done, they drew their ladders after them, and got over another work, and the house-wall, before they could enter. In this Sir Hardress Waller, performing his duty with honour and diligence, was shot in the arm, but not dangerous.

We have had little loss; many of the Enemy our men put to the sword, and some officers of quality; most of the rest we have prisoners, amongst which the Marquis and Sir Robert Peake, with divers other officers, whom I have ordered to be sent up to you. We have taken about ten pieces of ordnance, with much ammunition, and our soldiers a good encouragement.

I humbly offer to you, to have this place utterly slighted, for these following reasons: It will ask about eight-hundred men to manage it; it is no frontier; the country is poor about it; the place exceedingly ruined by our batteries and mortar-pieces, and by a fire which fell upon the place since our taking it. If you please to take the Garrison at Farnham, some out of Chichester, and a good part of the foot which were here under Dalbier, and to make a strong quarter at Newbury with three or four troops of horse, I dare be confident it would not only be a curb to Dennington, but a security and a frontier to all these parts; inasmuch as Newbury lies upon the river, and will prevent any incursion from Dennington, Wallingford or Farringdon into these parts; and by lying there, will make the trade most secure between Bristol and London for all carriages. And I believe the gentlemen of Sussex and Hampshire will with more cheerfulness contribute to maintain a garrison on a frontier than in their bowels, which will have less safety in it.

196 Holles, *Memoirs*, in *Maseres Tracts*, p. 200; Sprigg, *Anglia Rediviva*, p. 151; *Perfect Diurnall*, Oct. 13–20.

Sir, I hope not to delay, but march towards the West tomorrow; and to be as diligent as I may in my expedition thither. I must speak my judgment to you, that if you intend to have your work carried on, recruits of foot must be had, and a course taken to pay your army; else, believe me, Sir, it may not be able to answer the work you have for it to do.

I entreated Colonel Hammond to wait upon you, who was taken by a mistake whilst we lay before this Garrison, whom God safely delivered to us, to our great joy; but to his loss of almost all he had, which the enemy took from him. The Lord grant that these mercies may be acknowledged with all thankfulness. God exceedingly abounds in His goodness to us, and will not be weary until righteousness and peace meet and that He hath brought forth a glorious work for the happiness of this poor Kingdom. Wherein desires to serve God and you, with a faithful heart,

Basingstoke,
October 14th, 1645.

Your most humble servant,
OLIVER CROMWELL.[197]

Cromwell mentions his intention to march west the following day, to return to the main army as he had been commanded by Fairfax to do as soon as Winchester and Basing House were taken. The House of Commons suggested in their reply, however, that he might take Dennington Castle first,[198] but by the time he received the letter he was a day's march southwest of Basingstoke and Dennington. Not knowing which master to obey, he decided to carry on with his original order; but meanwhile he wrote a letter to each after his second day's march, explaining his dilemma.

To William Lenthall, Esq., Speaker of the House of Commons

Acknowledging the letter from the House of Commons and explaining the condition of affairs in the west which made it necessary to join Fairfax. On his way west he would endeavour to take Langford House. Their orders regarding Dennington Castle would be carried out if they still considered it advisable. Wallop, Oct. 16, 1645.[199]

The letter to Lenthall was enclosed in the following one to Fairfax, who camped near the Royalist city of Exeter:

[197] *Lieutenant-generall Cromwell's Letter; Perfect Diurnall*, Oct. 13–20 (in *Cromwelliana*, p. 27); Sprigg, pp. 149–150; Vicars, *Burning Bush*, pp. 289–90; *Harl. Mss.* 787, f. 73. Carlyle, Letter XXXIII. Read in the House of Commons, Oct. 15. *C. J.*, iv, 309.

[198] Oct. 15. Also thanking him for the success at Basing House and approving of his suggestion to slight it. *C. J.*, iv, 309.

[199] Read in the House Oct. 17. *C. J.*, iv, 312. See the letter to Fairfax of the same date. Sir H. Vane, Jr. was ordered to inform Cromwell of the resolution to leave Fairfax and himself free to dispose of their forces as they saw fit. At the same time it was agreed to keep Cromwell in command four months longer. *Ibid.*

To the Right Honourable Sir Thomas Fairfax, General of the Parliament's Army: Haste: These

SIR,

In two days march I came to Wallop, twenty miles from Basing, towards you. That night I received this enclosed from the Speaker of the House of Commons, which I thought fit to send you; and to which I returned an answer, a copy whereof I have also sent enclosed to you.

I perceive that it's the desire to have the place taken-in. But truly I could not do other than let them know what the condition of affairs in the West are, and submit the business to them and you. I shall be at Langford tomorrow night, if God please. I hope the work will not be long. If it should, I will rather leave a small part of the foot (if Horse will not be sufficient to take it in), than be detained from obeying such commands as I shall receive. I humbly beseech you to be confident that no man hath a more faithful heart to serve you than myself, nor shall be more strict to observe your commands than

Wallop, Your most humble servant,
October 16th, 1645. OLIVER CROMWELL.

[P.S.] I beseech you to let me have your resolution in this business with all the possible speed that may be; because whatsoever I be designed to, I wish I may speedily endeavour it, time being so precious for action in this season.[200]

Meanwhile to encourage his soldiers in the proposed attack on Langford House, Cromwell ordered the payment of a gratuity promised at Winchester:

Warrant to Col. Thos. Herbert, Commissioner of Parliament for the Army

Forasmuch as a gratuity of 5s. was promised each foot soldier of the army as were at the taking of Winchester Castle, and (they) being speedily to engage upon other the enemy's garrisons, I desire you, for their better encouragement (out of such moneys as the Committee of Hampshire shall give for the provisions gained from the enemy and now in Winchester Castle), to pay unto a field or other chief officer commanding the regiments such a sum as may be distributed amongst the private soldiers according to that proportion, for which this, together with their receipts, shall be your warrant.

Sarum, October 17, 1645. O. CROMWELL.[201]

The same day Cromwell's summons was sent to the governor of Langford House, who, considering what had just occurred at Winchester and Basing House, immediately offered to surrender upon

[200] *Sloane Mss.* 1519, fol. 127. The date is difficult to read: Ayscough's Catalogue dates it Oct. 18th while a recent copyist dates it the 15th. The signature only is Cromwell's. Carlyle, Letter XXXIV.

[201] *S. P. Dom.* dxi, 24; pr. in *Cal. S. P. Dom.*, (1645–47), p. 198.

articles. John Hewson, once a cobbler but destined for a seat in Cromwell's Other House, and Thomas Kelsey, who was ten years later to be one of Cromwell's Major-Generals, were the two men selected to draw up the treaty which was enclosed in the following letter:

To the Honourable William Lenthall, Esquire, Speaker to the Honourable House of Commons: These

SIR,

I gave you an account the last night, of my marching to Langford House, whither I came this day, and immediately sent them in a summons. The Governor desired I should send two officers to treat with him, and I accordingly appointed Lieutenant-Colonel Hewson and Major Kelsey thereunto. The treaty produced the Agreement which I have here enclosed to you.

The General, I hear, is advanced as far west as Collumpton, and hath sent some horse and foot to Tiverton. It is earnestly desired, that this force might march up to him, it being convenient that we stay a day for our foot that are behind and coming up.

I wait your answer to my letter from Wallop: I shall desire that your pleasure may be speeded to me, and rest, Sir,

Your humble servant,

Salisbury, 17th October,
(12 at night) 1645. OLIVER CROMWELL.[202]

Articles of agreement made between Sir Bartholomew Bell, Knight, and Major Edmond Uvedale, Commanders-in-Chief of Langford Garrison, and Lieutenant-Colonel Hewson and Major Thomas Kelsey, on the behalf of Oliver Cromwell, Lieutenant-General to Sir Thomas Fairfax's army.

(1) The house and garrison to be delivered up at 12 o'clock to-morrow.

(2) All arms and ammunition to be delivered to the use of the Parliament without any embezzling.

(3) The Commanders-in-Chief, with fifteen gentlemen of the garrison, to march away with horses and arms, and the private soldiers without arms, to Oxford in ten days; to have a troop of horse for their guard the first day, and a trumpet with a pass the rest of the way.

(4) The rest of the gentlemen, not exceeding fourteen, to march with their swords, pistols, and horses, if they can lawfully procure them.

(5) The Commanders-in-Chief to have a cart or waggon to carry their goods to Oxford.

(6) Any of the gentlemen desiring to go to any other garrison or army of the King's to have passes for that purpose.

202 Lomas-Carlyle, Letter, XXXV, from the original in the possession of Captain Lindsay. Pr. in *Weekly Account*, no. 42; and in *Several letters from Col. Gen. Poyntz and Lieut. Gen. Cromwell, etc.* Read in Parliament, Oct. 20. *J. C.*, iv, 315.

(7) The goods remaining in the garrison to be delivered to the owners upon demand within two days.

(8) Lieutenant-Colonel Bowles and Major Fry to be left hostages until these articles be performed.[203]

The surrender of Langford House was marked by an incident which illustrates the discipline kept by Cromwell and the praise he received for it. As the Royalist garrison withdrew, six soldiers who, contrary to the articles of surrender, had plundered Lord Ogle on his departure from Winchester, repeated their offence at the expense of the Langford officers. Four days later a council of war at Blandford found them guilty. Lots were drawn; the loser was hanged; the other five sent to Sir Thomas Glemham, the new governor of Oxford, to deal with as he saw fit; and he, acknowledging the "noble spirit" which had animated Cromwell, set them free.[204] Meanwhile, moving on to Cerne the next day and to Chard on the 23rd,[205] Cromwell there received orders from Fairfax to join him at Crediton. Riding ahead of his brigade, Cromwell arrived at headquarters the next day to find a council of war debating whether to relieve Plymouth or to besiege Exeter[206] from which Goring had retired on news of Cromwell's approach.[207] In this Cromwell joined and after long dispute it was resolved on the day following to ignore Plymouth for the moment, to advance to Topham, east of Exeter, and establish winter quarters in the neighborhood.

For some weeks, owing to sickness which increased with the cold and wet of the early winter, active military operations ceased. At one time, while the headquarters were at Ottery St. Mary, late in November, half of the foot soldiers were incapacitated.[208] Among the victims of this epidemic, which was apparently influenza, was Colonel John Pickering of Cromwell's brigade, a brother of Sir Gilbert Pickering; and from his headquarters at Tiverton, where he had been since December 2, Cromwell wrote to the governor of Lyme Regis in regard to the funeral:[209]

[203] *Hist. Mss. Comm. Rept.* 6, App. p. 81 (House of Lords Mss.); Sprigg, *Anglia Rediviva*, pp. 156–7.

[204] Sprigg, on p. 144, says this was done at Winchester, but he was not with Cromwell at the time and had the story only from hearsay. An item in the *Moderate Intelligencer*, Oct. 23–30, when Glemham had not yet acted in the case, gives the true story. Gardiner, ii, 362, follows Sprigg.

[205] *Moderate Intelligencer*, Oct. 23–30. In one place it says Cromwell was in Chard the 20th but the rest of the news item shows this date to be a mistake.

[206] Sprigg, p. 159; *Perfect Diurnall.*

[207] *Ibid*, Oct. 25; *Moderate Intelligencer.*

[208] Sprigg, p. 167.

[209] *Cal. S. P. Dom.* (1644), p. 497; Roberts, G., *History of Lyme Regis* (1823), p. 69.

To Colonel Ceely at Lyme Regis Castle: These

SIR,

It's the desire of Sir Gilbert Pickering that his deceased brother, Colonel Pickering, should be interred in your garrison; and to the end his funeral may be solemnised with as much honour as his memory calls for, you are desired to give all possible assistance therein. The particulars will be offered to you by his Major, Major Jubbs, with whom I desire you to concur herein, and believe it, Sir, you will not only lay a huge obligation upon myself and all the officers of this army, but I dare assure you the General himself will take it for an especial favour, and will not let it go without a full ackowledgment. But what need I prompt him to so honourable action whose own ingenuity will be argument sufficient herein; whereof rests assured

Your humble servant,

Tiverton,
10th December 1645.

OLIVER CROMWELL.[210]

PARLIAMENT, THE SCOTS AND THE KING, OCTOBER–DECEMBER, 1645

With the fall of Basing House and Langford House and the posting of the army in the neighborhood of Exeter, the campaign of 1645 was virtually ended and interest shifted from the field to the negotiations of Parliament, the King and the Scots for the ending of the war. The first move for settlement had come from the Scots, irritated by the failure to receive their pay, and demanding negotiations with the King and the establishment of Presbyterian government. As early as the second week in October, Parliament had protested the activities of the Scots and insisted on the withdrawal of their garrisons from the northern towns. In turn the Scotch commissioners drew up their terms of peace to be presented to the King, and agreed to support him if he would consent to a church establishment framed by the parliaments and assemblies of the two kingdoms, in effect the Presbyterian system. With this the long threatened break between the Independents and the Presbyterians seemed about to come, and in it the King saw an opportunity to divide and rule. For such a trial of strength the "Dissenters," "sects" or Independents were now prepared. While the Presbyterians had improved their position in the City and in the Assembly of Divines, the Independents under the lead of Vane in the Commons and of Cromwell in the army, had gained still more in numbers and prestige. Cromwell's motion for an order

[210] Original in the Bodleian Library, *Select Clarendon Papers*, vol. ix, 1. Pr. in Polwhele's *Traditions and Recollections* (1826), p. 22, when the original was in the possession of Rev. G. Moore of Grampound. Polwhele misread the word Lyme Regis for Pendennis. Carlyle, App. 8, made the same mistake. Pendennis Castle was in Royalist hands on this date under the governorship of John Arundel. Three days after C wrote this letter, Col. Ceely was elected M.P. for Bridport, (co. Dorset) in the place of Giles Strangways, esq., who was disabled to sit.

of accommodation a year earlier had produced but little result; and though the Assembly had been commanded in the preceding April to produce a plan of church government, on October 13 its members finally refused. In consequence, the Lords ordered the renewal of Cromwell's Accommodation Order on November 6, agreed to by the Commons eight days later; and the first meeting of the committee on November 16 revealed the final breach.

The Independents demanded full liberty of conscience; the City protested; the Houses withdrew their demand for the surrender of the northern posts by the Scots who had meanwhile moved south to Newark and again insisted on the settlement of religion and negotiations with the King. To this last the Commons now agreed and prepared another set of propositions to be sent to Charles. These covered much of the same ground as their predecessors, extending the list of delinquents and adding certain provisions of new import. They now demanded that Essex, Northumberland, Warwick and Pembroke should be given dukedoms; Manchester and Salisbury, marquisates; Robartes, Wharton, Saye and Sele, Willoughby of Parham and the elder Fairfax, earldoms. Holles was to be a viscount; Fairfax, Cromwell, and the elder Vane were to be created barons; and to these were added substantial rewards. Sir Thomas Fairfax was to have £5,000 a year; Cromwell and Waller, £2,500 each; Haselrig and Stapleton, £2,000; Brereton, £1,500; and Skippon, £1,000, a year.[211]

Nor was this all the negotiation of that period. The Scots learned that the Independents were proposing to the King that if he would allow them to withdraw to Ireland, they would give up to him the New Model and the fortresses. At the same time the Queen had refused to support the establishment of Presbyterianism though she agreed to support the Scotch demands on Charles; and the new Pope, Innocent X, sent Cardinal Rinuccini to Ireland to act as his personal representative; while the French minister, Mazarin, in the midst of these various threads of diplomatic complexities, endeavored as best he could to persuade Charles and Henrietta Maria to come to terms of accommodation with their rebellious subjects.

The project of the emigration of the Independents to Ireland seems at this distance sufficiently preposterous; but it was no more extraordinary than the Great Emigration to New England a decade earlier. At this moment Sir Hardress Waller was writing to his friend Sir Philip Percival, sometime Irish official, now member for Newport, of his conversations with Cromwell over the Irish situation and the possibility of conquering Ireland with the Parliamentary army. Cromwell's "spirit," Waller wrote, "leads much that way, especially for the support of Munster and to begin the war there, which, were he

[211] *C. J.*, iv, 360; *Perfect Diurnall*, Dec. 1.

sent over, I would look upon the work as done."[212] If nothing had been done in the matter of selecting a Lord Deputy for Ireland, he suggested, Cromwell might be petitioned to go over in that capacity; but Percival replied that such a petition had already been circulated, but had been "stayed" for some reason and that Lord Lisle, the son of the Earl of Leicester, who had been a commander in Ireland since 1642, had been named for the place.[213]

Meanwhile the peace negotiations had gone on. On the same day that the King, still wandering to and fro, reached Bridgnorth to learn that the Earl of Derby's Lathom House was lost, that Beeston Castle had surrendered and that Sir William Vaughan had been refused admission to Ludlow Castle,[214] he opened negotiations with the Lords. He was the more moved to this in that Dorset, Southampton, Hertford and Lindsey had insisted that he end the war, and, when he rejected the Independent proposals, had even offered to surrender Charles to Parliament if their estates were secured to them. It was apparent that the King's cause was lost, though he continued to hope for French aid and proposed to come to Westminster to negotiate in person.[215] None the less, on December 7, he sent word for the Prince of Wales to leave England and for the Duke of York to go to Ireland; to destroy the fortifications of Exeter, Newark, Chester, Oxford and Worcester and to concentrate the remnants of the army at Worcester in order either to relieve the Prince of Wales's hard-pressed forces in Devon and Cornwall or to make a dash into Kent and Sussex.

It was evident that though Rupert had rejoined the King on December 8, he no longer had Charles's confidence; and while these hollow proposals and wild designs went on, Charles pressed his concurrent negotiations with the Scots and Parliament. On December 26 he renewed his request to return to Westminster for forty days under guarantees of his safety from Parliament, and agreed to put the militia in charge of a committee which was to include Cromwell. That request, like the Parliament's demands for settlement, was denied;[216] and though the Scots had meanwhile invited Charles to their camp, he delayed until he had exhausted the possibilities of negotiations with the Parliament and the Independents. By the first days of 1646, the situation had begun to clarify. Parliament refused Charles's offer to come to Westminster and his proposal to restore the church to its old status with toleration for dissenters; and at this moment the news of his negotiations with Ireland and the Pope destroyed his last hope of accommodation. It was in vain that he dis-

[212] Waller to Percival, Dec. 4, *Hist. Mss Comm. Rept.* 7, App. I, p. 236 (*Egmont Mss*).
[213] Waller to Percival, Dec. 22, *Ibid.*, p. 237.
[214] Symonds, *Diary*.
[215] Gardiner, *Civil War*, iii, 17 ff.
[216] *L. J.*, viii, 71; *C. J.*, iv, 392.

avowed his emissary Glamorgan's purpose to bring an Irish army into England and the Papal offer of aid in return for toleration of the English Catholics. His hope of dividing Presbyterians and Independents disappeared. His supporters in Scotland had been executed despite the promise to spare them after Montrose's defeat at Philiphaugh. His fortresses were falling on every hand; and he was left naked to his enemies. All confidence in him was lost, not only among his opponents but among many, if not most, of his own followers; and unless he could somehow secure the support of the Scotch Covenanters, there seemed nothing left but his complete submission to the Parliament.[217]

That Parliament had gradually assumed the prerogatives of sovereignty. To fill its ranks now so depleted that there were seldom, if ever, a hundred and fifty members in the House, it had ordered new elections. By wholesale confiscations of delinquents' property and that of its own absent members, it had replenished its exchequer, and by a sweeping order it finally decreed that all who had not rendered themselves to its authority by March 25, 1646, were liable to forfeiture of their estates. It had paid Pym's debts and rewarded its own followers. It had forbidden creation of new cities or boroughs save by its own consent. It had seized the books and papers of Chief Justice Banks and of Mr. Vaughan and conferred them upon Mr. Maynard and the new Recorder. It had, in short, assumed to itself the powers of the combined legislative and executive branches of the government and little by little the pretence of attending the wishes of the King had disappeared from its debates and votes. But meanwhile differences of opinion had arisen between its two parties. The Independents were still in a numerical minority and, though bound together in their common animosity toward Charles, the Presbyterians had gradually come to perceive the alliance was not wholly favorable to their cause, the more so in that the New Model army leaned to the other side.

JANUARY-APRIL, 1646

The army, meanwhile, had pursued its conquering course. Quartered about Exeter, it was hampered by illness and lack of supplies, and at Tavistock the Prince of Wales planned to fall upon Fairfax with a force which he had gathered to the number, as he estimated, of 11,000 men. But his men were discontented, ill-equipped, and worse disciplined; and when early in January, Fairfax's army received supplies from Parliament, including shoes and stockings of which it was in dire need, plans were laid to attack the Royalists. The troops assembled at Crediton on January 8, and the next day, despite the bitter

[217] Gardiner, *History*, as above.

cold and snow, Cromwell led a brigade of a regiment of horse and two of foot to Lord Wentworth's headquarters at Bovey Tracy, fourteen miles south of Crediton. Surprising the Royalist camp in the early evening when the Royalist officers were playing cards, Cromwell's soldiers eagerly snatched at the stakes; but the officers threw the money out the window and during the scramble which followed escaped out the back door. Four hundred horses were taken and about fifty prisoners, including a major.[218] The results of this successful raid were out of proportion to its immediate circumstances. On news of it and of the appearance of a Parliamentary detachment before Tavistock, the Royalists, believing Fairfax was at hand, broke up their blockade around Plymouth and retired to the north. Upon this Fairfax and part of his forces, marching by way of Ashburton to Totness near Dartmouth, sent a summons to its garrison on January 12, which was refused and they took it by storm six days later.[219]

While Cromwell was thus engaged in the early spring campaign, the Commons, in pursuance of its policy of rewarding its supporters, took special notice of its lieutenant-general. On January 23, it extended his commission for another six months' period and for his "unwearied and faithful services" it referred to a committee the problem of how he might be put in possession of an estate of £2,500 a year for himself and his heirs. For this purpose the Marquis of Worcester's manors of Abberston and Itchell in Hampshire were voted him, with £500 for the purchase of "horse and furniture," and to this the Lords agreed two weeks later.[220]

The west was now almost entirely in the hands of the Parliamentary forces. With Dartmouth in their possession, and the morale of the Royalist army at such a low ebb that "three red coats could chase one hundred of the enemy," as Fairfax wrote to his father,[221] the General's call for 1,000 recruits brought three times the required number of Devonshire men to the meeting-place at Totness where Cromwell addressed them before selecting a sufficient number to make a regiment.[222]

Speech to Three Thousand Devonshire Recruits, January 24, 1646

'We are come to set you, if possible, at liberty from your taskmasters, and by settling Peace, bring Plenty to you again.'[223]

[218] Sprigg, *op. cit.*, p. 177; *Perfect Diurnall*, Jan. 12; Vicars, *Burning Bush*, p. 34.

[219] Sprigg, *op. cit.*, pp. 178–85.

[220] *C. J.*, iv, 416, 418, 419, 424–26, 430–31; *L. J.*, viii, 134, 144; *Perfect Diurnall*, Jan. 19–26.

[221] Bell, *Memorials*, i, 275.

[222] Sprigg, *op. cit.*, p. 186.

[223] *Moderate Intelligencer*, Jan. 1645/6.

Thus reinforced and with the surrender of the last fort of the chain surrounding Exeter to Colonel Hammond the following night,[224] the siege of that stronghold was renewed on the 26th with more assurance. Its commander, Sir John Berkeley, was encouraged to hold out by promises of aid from Hopton; and on Sunday, February 8, news came that some 4,000 Cornishmen had arrived at Launceston to reinforce the Royalist army. In consequence, a rendezvous of all horse and foot was ordered for the next day at Chudleigh. Leaving a small force under Sir Hardress Waller to blockade Exeter, the rest of the army assembled at Crediton on Tuesday and remained until Saturday when they advanced to Chulmleigh.[225] At four o'clock on Monday morning, the entire army set out from Ring-Ash, and at seven drew up in battle array five miles from Torrington driving part of Hopton's force of 10,000 men before it, and it seemed that a last great battle in the west was about to be fought. That night when Fairfax and Cromwell left "Master Rolls' house" near Torrington to set guards and make dispositions to attack the town at daybreak, they heard noises which seemed to indicate that Hopton was withdrawing from the place. A small reconnoitering party which Cromwell had ordered to steal up to the Royalist quarters, was drawn into an engagement, in which the rest of the dragoons, the forlorn hope, and presently the whole of both armies joined. In it the Parliamentary forces were victorious. Before daybreak many of Hopton's men were killed, six hundred of them were made prisoners and the rest took to flight—mostly to their homes—their arms were abandoned and their ammunition was blown up.[226] Hopton, who was injured in the fight, fled with the remnants of his men toward Truro, and Fairfax and Cromwell remained for the time at Torrington, clearing up the prisoners.

Delayed by wet weather, the council of war decided finally to advance into Cornwall to destroy Hopton's force so that Exeter and Barnstaple could honorably surrender, and on February 23 and 24, the various detachments from Torrington, Bideford and Tavistock reached Holsworthy. Defeating some 500 Royalist foot at Launces-

[224] Sprigg, *op. cit.*, p. 187.

[225] According to the story told in 1652 by Col. Wogan in his *Narrative* this move was inspired by a letter to Ireton from one Robert Long, Secretary to the Prince of Wales, then in Truro, advising Ireton of dissension between Hopton and Grenvile, and Charles's intention to leave England. It suggested a speedy advance of Fairfax's army. Ireton, according to this story, showed the letter to Wogan, then to Fairfax and Cromwell, who called a council of war that night, which resolved on the advance to Torrington. Long later denied vigorously and categorically having ever written such a letter. *Clarendon Mss.*, 614; Hyde to Nicholas, Feb. 16, 1652, *Clarendon State Papers*, iii, 47. Cp. Mary Coate, *Cornwall in the Great Civil War*, etc. (1933), p. 201.

[226] Sprigg, *op. cit.*, pp. 189–204; Wogan's Narrative, in Carte, *Original Letters*, i, 140–1.

ton on February 25,[227] from headquarters there, two days later, they advanced cautiously five or six miles over the moors toward Bodmin, expecting every moment to encounter Hopton's horse.[228]

But the Royalists, as Fairfax and Cromwell knew, were in no mood to fight. They were, in fact, seeking safety in flight. Hopton, wounded and at odds with his men, had tried in vain to make a stand at Bodmin, whence he fled before Fairfax's advance. The King was in and about Oxford in no position to aid Hopton. His son, the Prince of Wales, was at Pendennis Castle near Falmouth in no better case; and with Hopton's forces defeated and disorganized and Fairfax scarcely more than twenty miles away, he was preparing to sail for the Scillies. As the Parliamentary army advanced, on March 1 word came that a party of dragoons were engaged with the enemy. Fearing that the remnants of the Royalist forces were endeavoring to break through and join the King, Cromwell set out with some 1,400 horse and dragoons,[229] only to find that the two captains of the dragoons had already driven back the enemy. He spent that night at St. Tudde and there received orders to secure the pass at Ware Bridge, to prevent Hopton's escape to the east to join the King, and there he placed dragoons before advancing toward Bodmin which Hopton had quitted the night before with the poor drunken and discouraged remnants of his command.[230]

That day, March 2, Prince Charles sailed for the Scilly Isles; and three days later Fairfax, from his headquarters at Bodmin, sent a demand for Hopton's surrender. On the 8th his army advanced to within three miles of Truro which it entered on the 10th, when commissioners from both sides met at Tresillian Bridge to discuss terms of surrender.[231] The articles of capitulation were signed on the 14th and six days later the Royalist army of the west had dispersed, some to their homes, others beyond seas, and still others to take service with the Parliament.[232] Only Pendennis Castle and St. Michael's Mount held out for Charles, and their fall was only a matter of time. Hopton accompanied Prince Charles, first to the Scillies, then to Jersey; and resistance to the Parliament in the west was virtually at an end.

While Cromwell was helping to push Hopton farther and farther into the little corner of Cornwall, he was advised of various matters connected with his own fortunes. A letter from his cousin Oliver St.

[227] *Ibid.*, pp. 206–7; Vicars, *Burning Bush*, p. 374; Wogan's Narrative, *loc. cit.*, i, 142–3.

[228] Sprigg, *op. cit.*, p. 209.

[229] Sprigg, (*Anglia Rediviva*, p. 210) says 2000.

[230] *Ibid.*, pp. 210–11; *Perfect Diurnall*, Mar. 2–9; Wogan's Narrative, *loc. cit.*, i, 142–3; Rushworth's letter, Mar. 2, in Vicars, *Burning Bush*, p. 380.

[231] Summons, Mar. 5, Sprigg, *op. cit.*, pp. 214–220; Vicars, *op. cit.*, pp. 387–95.

[232] Articles in Sprigg, *op. cit.*, pp. 229–36.

John informed him of the £2,500 a year granted him by Parliament;[233] and doubtless others brought him news of his favorite daughter Elizabeth. Then in her seventeenth year, she was married on January 13, in Holy Trinity church, Ely, to John Claypole, the son of an old friend in Northamptonshire.[234] The marriage deed is dated two months later, probably because it was difficult to complete the negotiations while her father was on campaign.

Marriage Deed of Elizabeth Cromwell and John Claypole

Certain lands and manors settled on Elizabeth by John Claypole, senior, for her jointure and for the children of the marriage. Elizabeth's dowry was to be £1,250. The parties to the deed are the Claypoles, father and son, Elizabeth Cromwell, "Oliver Cromwell of Ely in the county of Cambridge, Esq., Benjamin Norton of Ely, aforesaid, Esq., and Walter Wells, of Ely aforesaid, Dr. of Phisick." [235]

On this peaceful note the campaign virtually ended. The army returned from Truro to Bodmin Saturday, March 21, and, on the following Wednesday Fairfax, Cromwell and some of their officers went to Plymouth to view the forts and works there, and to arrange for shipping French soldiers home. There they were greeted by a salute of three hundred guns and a banquet given by the governor and the gentlemen of the city;[236] and thence on Friday morning the party returned through Tavistock to Okehampton to wait for the army which was marching up through Launceston. On Sunday they led their forces to their old quarters at Crediton near Exeter and the next day prepared a summons which was sent to Berkeley on Tuesday after the army had surrounded the city. On Thursday the Royalist commander sent commissioners to treat for the surrender and on April 9 Articles were signed by which the city was to be evacuated four days later.[237] While Fairfax went to force the surrender of Barnstaple, Cromwell and other officers remained to see that the Articles for Exeter were carried out by both sides; and with this last service his career in the west ended.[238]

With it, too, ended the organized resistance of the Royalists there and elsewhere. Two garrisons in Cornwall and one in Devon were all that were left of that high-spirited body of Charles's followers which

[233] In Thurloe, *Collection of State Papers*, i, 75.

[234] R. W. Ramsay, "Elizabeth Claypole," in *English Historical Review*, vii, 37 (1892), from the church Register.

[235] *Ibid.*, p. 38, with no mention of where the deed, dated March 9, 1645/6, is to be found.

[236] Amongst the Mss of the Corp of Plymouth is an item of £200 spent in entertaining Fairfax, Cromwell and others. *Hist. Mss. Comm. Rept.* 10, App. IV, p. 543.

[237] Sprigg, *op. cit.*, pp. 239–50.

[238] *Ibid.*, pp. 250–51; Vicars, *Burning Bush*, pp. 407–8.

a twelve-month earlier had dreamed of overthrowing the Parliament's army. Besides them there remained little more than Oxford and Worcester with a few garrisons like Newark which Charles permitted to surrender in early May, and some scattered bodies of his followers. Of these, the command of Sir Jacob Astley "had the honour to play the last stake for the King." On March 21, at the very moment that the remnants of Hopton's army began to evacuate Truro, Astley's force of some 1,500 horse was defeated by Sir Thomas Brereton and Colonel Morgan at Stow-on-the-Wold, and Astley's famous speech to Brereton's officers marks at once the epitaph of the royal cause and the prologue to the next act of the great drama. "You have now done your work," he said to them, "and may go to play, unless you will fall out among yourselves." "Every day," says Clarendon, "brought the news of the loss of some garrison; and as Oxford was already blocked up at a distance by those horse which Fayrefax had sent out of the west to that purpose, or to wait upon the King, and follow him close . . . What should the King do? There was one thing most formidable to him, and which he was resolved to avoid, that was, to be enclosed in Oxford, and so to be given up, or taken . . . as a prisoner to the Independents' army . . . In this perplexity he chose rather to commit himself to the Scottish army"—and with this resolution there began another chapter of the royal tragedy, and of the Civil Wars.[239]

[239] Clarendon, *History*, x, 31, 32.

CHAPTER VIII

PART I

PARLIAMENT AND THE ARMY

With the surrender of Hopton's army, the loss of Bristol, Hereford, Newark, Exeter and many lesser strongholds which fell almost from day to day, the King's cause in the open field was lost. Not only were the royal armies defeated and destroyed but their commanders were gone. Hyde, Capel, Hopton and Culpepper were in the Scillies with Prince Charles. The Queen had long been in France. Newcastle and his chief officers, Goring and many more of the army of the west, had fled to the Continent. Digby and Langdale were in Ireland. Charles himself with his son James and his daughter Elizabeth, Rupert and Maurice, were cooped up in Oxford toward which Fairfax was advancing, sending before him Ireton with a regiment of cavalry. There remained only surrender or diplomacy, and to this problem Charles now addressed himself.

On its part the victorious Parliament confronted problems of its own. It had begun to recruit its ranks, decimated by Royalist desertion and expulsion, with men from the army like Ireton, Skippon, Fleetwood, Ludlow and Fairfax himself; with country gentlemen like Cromwell's old landlord, Henry Lawrence; with Cromwell's relatives like Sir John Barrington; with City men like Peter Temple; till by the middle of the following year more than two hundred seats were filled with these new men, all followers of the triumphing cause of the Houses. But united as they were against monarchy and episcopacy, they were more and more divided against themselves into Independent and Presbyterian. They faced the problem of the Scots army devoted to the latter cause and that of the New Model leaning more and more toward Independency. They had won the war; they confronted the more difficult problem of the peace.

For the moment the chief effect of the collapse of Royalist resistance in the west was upon the army. While it had been busy on this last campaign, Parliament had concerned itself chiefly with the results of its victory. The Marquis of Winchester, Lord Brudenell and others had been sent to the Tower where the master of Basing House would have starved had it not been for the allowance made him by the

Keeper. The filling of the empty seats in the Commons had gone on and it was reported that the recent disturbances in Somerset had been chiefly due to the "undue proceedings in the elections for knights of that county." The futile negotiations of the Parliament and the Scots commissioners with the King proceeded, and Charles's state of mind is revealed in the fact that he had already written six letters to the Parliament without answer and was presently to write eight more. The censorship was strengthened and every reflection on Parliament suppressed. New acts against Catholicism and "idolatry" were passed; martial law was put in force; and measure after measure extended the powers of the Houses. The Prince of Wales was invited to put himself in the hands of Parliament; the King, after his tenth letter, was advised not to come to London until he had agreed to the Parliamentary conditions; and even a petition of the Assembly of Divines was voted a breach of privilege. In every way it became increasingly evident that the recruited House of Commons felt its new strength and importance in proportion to the successes of its army in the field.[1]

THE SURRENDER OF OXFORD, APRIL–JUNE 24, 1646

That army meanwhile had turned to its last task. With Hopton's surrender, Cromwell left to report the situation of affairs to Parliament and Ireton led his regiment toward Oxford in advance of the main force under Fairfax. There was more in this conjunction of the men than their army connection. On April 22 Cromwell arrived at Westminster, was voted the thanks of the House on the next day;[2] and the day after received a letter from Ireton informing him of a proposal from Charles to give himself up. That letter he read to the House on April 25, denouncing Ireton for sending it to him rather than to Parliament, fearing that the army would be accused of dealing independently with political problems; and it was on his motion that Fairfax was instructed to forward all communications from the King to the Houses and to listen to no overture for peace.[3]

It would seem that Cromwell was overcautious, if not disingenuous. Ireton had committed no very grave offense in transmitting such a document to his superior officers for them to deal with as they saw fit. Cromwell's censure of him was so far from personal, however, that on that very day he signed the marriage settlement of his eldest daughter with Ireton, whose courtship had begun when Ireton was in Ely acting as Cromwell's deputy.

[1] Parry's *Parliaments; C. J., passim.*

[2] Sprigg, *op. cit.*, p. 253; *Perfect Diurnall*, Apr. 20–27; *C. J.*, iv, 520.

[3] Ireton to Cromwell, Apr. 23, in Cary, *Memorials*, i, 1; *C. J.*, iv, 523; Whitacre's *Diary*, quoted in Gardiner, *Civil War*, iii, 96.

Marriage Settlement of Bridget Cromwell and Henry Ireton

Assignment of the lease of a farm in Ely from Oliver Cromwell to Henry Ireton in connection with Bridget Cromwell's marriage settlement. April 26, 1646.[4]

For the moment, it seemed that the lieutenant-general was about to resume his old position and duties as a simple member of the House, for on April 28 he was appointed to serve on a committee to consider that matter with which he had been so closely identified, the draining of the fens. Whether he was present at its meeting on the 30th it is impossible to say, for Fairfax had arrived in the vicinity of London and had called for a general rendezvous of the army at Bullington Green in Hampshire, on May 2. It seems probable that such a call must have been superior even to the question of the draining of the fens; for on May 3 and the days following, a council of war on Headington Hill near Oxford settled the plans for the blockade of the royal capital and the surrounding garrisons. In the language of the hunting-field, the fox had been run to earth and it only remained to dig him out.

In fact Charles had already gone. "Early in the morning upon the 27th day of April," as Clarendon records, "he went out of Oxford, attended only by John Ashburnham and a Divine (one Hudson)," and stopping on his way to get news of Montrose if possible, "very early in the morning" of May 5, arrived at the Scots' camp at Newark. He "went to the general's lodging and discovered himself to him; who either was, or seemed to be, exceedingly surprised and confounded at his Majesty's presence, and knew not what to say; but presently gave notice of it to the committee, who were no less perplexed. An express was presently sent to the Parliament at Westminster, to inform them of the unexpected news, as a thing the Scots had not the least imagination of. And the Parliament were so disordered with the intelligence that at first they resolved to command their general to raise the siege before Oxford, and to march with all expedition to Newark, but the Scottish commissioners diverted them from that. . . . So they made a short despatch to them, in which it was evident that they believed the King had gone there by invitation, and not out of his own free choice."[5]

The Parliament was not, apparently, so dumbfounded as Clarendon believed, for, six days earlier than the letter from Leven announcing the King's arrival, they had been advised of his departure from Oxford and on May 4 had declared any one who concealed him a trai-

[4] *Bulletin of the Institute for Historical Research* (November, 1932), p. 73, where the original with seals and signatures missing is said to be in the Museum, Art Gallery and Public Library at Leicester. The name Bridget was misread as Richard.

[5] Clarendon, *History*, x, 33–34.

tor.[6] At once a quarrel arose in the Commons itself and between the Commons and the Lords as to the disposal of the King's person. Feeling ran high. On May 6 the Commons voted to imprison the King in Warwick Castle; the Lords demanded a conference; and Essex in an impassioned speech declared that "they were bound by their Covenant to defend the King's just rights." They had removed his evil counsellors; "nought remains but to disband the armies and make peace. Rather than consent to make the King a prisoner (he spoke for the Lords) they would all die in their place." His speech was effective. The Commons apologized and rescinded its vote and for the moment the quarrel was composed.[7]

In those quarrels Cromwell, busy with the siege of Oxford, had no part. On May 11, Fairfax summoned Oxford and negotiations for its surrender began.[8] The next day Bulstrode Whitelocke came from Westminster to attend the meetings of the council of war, and was "intimately received" by Cromwell.[9] Meanwhile, foreseeing the strained relations between the Scots and the Parliament, David Leslie showed his good faith by insisting that his English colleague Poyntz receive the surrender of Newark which the King ordered. But he lost no time in breaking camp and with the King a virtual prisoner he made his way farther north toward Newcastle whence Leven had already gone, and where orders were received from the Scotch Parliament to keep the King "out of the way of all papists and delinquents." On May 19, the Commons resolved "that this Kingdom hath no further use of the Scots' Army," and six days later it received the King's eleventh letter, written from Newcastle on May 18, renewing his proposals for a peace.

In these negotiations again Cromwell had no share. Though on June 9 he was appointed to a Commons' committee to prepare a declaration concerning the complicity of the Scots in the King's escape,[10] on that day he was present at a full council of war at Marston where thirty-one officers discussed the advisability of reducing Oxford by force or continuing negotiations for a treaty. Its commander, Glemham, with more than 4,000 men, provisions for six months, entrenchments and artillery, made high demands; and the Parliamentary officers, though they did not "conclude a doubt or suspicion of them," knew, none the less, that the Scots had gone north with the King and that his negotiations with the Irish and

[6] *C. J.*, iv, 532.

[7] Letter of W. Sancroft in *Tanner Mss.* 30, quoted in Warburton, *op. cit.*, iii, 229n.

[8] Sprigg, *Anglia Rediviva*, p. 256 ff.

[9] Whitelocke's *Memorials*, pp. 204–5.

[10] *C. J.*, iv, 570. On June 3 he had been included in another committee, one to judge scandalous offences which would bar the offender from the sacrament. *Ibid.*, iv, 562–3.

foreign powers had not been entirely given up. The decision of the Council was to make terms, and a treaty was concluded on Saturday, June 20, for surrender on the following Wednesday.[11]

Nor did these events lack a romantic touch. Ireton was present at Marston where the resolution was made which would practically put an end to military operations and was a member of the commission which negotiated the treaty for the surrender of Oxford. To celebrate the impending conclusion of that treaty, Bridget Cromwell came to army headquarters and, in a fortified house in Holton, five miles east of Oxford, which was very possibly Cromwell's quarters, she and Ireton were married by Fairfax's chaplain as the church register testifies:

June 15, 1646, Hen. Ireton, Commissary-General to Sir Thomas Fairfax, and Bridget, daughter of Oliver Cromwell, Lieutenant-General of the horse to the said sir Thomas Fairfax, was married by mr. Dell in lady Whorwood her house in Holton.[12]

From this festive occasion Cromwell was recalled by troubles which had arisen in Nottingham, concerning which, on the following day, he wrote a letter to John Holles, second Earl of Clare. That peer who, "a man of honour and of courage and who would have been an excellent person, if his heart had not been too much set upon keeping and improving his estate," had gone to the King from Parliament in 1643 with Bedford and Holland, but was so coldly received that he rejoined his friends in Parliament, and was now in its service in Nottingham.

To the Right Honourable the Earl of Clare: These

My Lord,

No command from your Lordship will find me disobedient to observe you. In that which I last received, I had a double obligation. I do admire your Lordship's character of Major White; it's to the life. I I can with some confidence speak it, being no stranger to him. He is of a right stamp in this, that he would have the honestest men disbanded first, the other being more suitable to his and the common design. The General will instantly order the Nottingham horse to Worcester, wherein I shall be your Lordship's remembrancer to him, and in that and in all things, my Lord,

Your most humble servant,

June 16, 1646. Oliver Cromwell.[13]

[11] Sprigg, *op. cit.*, pp. 283 ff. Articles printed in *ibid.*, pp. 267–76. Baillie, the Scotchman, remarks: "The scurvy, base propositions Cromwell has given to the malignants at Oxford has offended many." *Letters and Journals*, ii, 276.

[12] Parish Register. Quoted in Noble, i, 358, where it is referred to as "Horton" parish and dated January instead of June. On p. 134, Noble refers to the parish as "Norton."

[13] Holograph original, endorsed, "Lieutenant General Cromwell's from Oxford,

Fairfax's ordering of forces to Worcester was in anticipation of a concentration at that Royalist post on the surrender of Oxford. Eight days later, some three thousand Royalists marched out of Oxford, amidst flying colours and martial music, and Fairfax replaced Glemham as commander of the city. After the usual formalities of taking possession, including the granting of hundreds of passes, had been attended to, and after he, in consultation with Ireton, Fleetwood, Lambert and Whitelocke, had determined upon the disposition of six regiments no longer needed at Oxford,[14] of which three detachments were sent respectively to three Royalist garrisons,—Wallingford Castle, Worcester and Raglan,—Cromwell's work was done for the time being. The six months' extension of his command which had been voted in January was apparently not renewed, so that his connection with the army was for the moment at an end. Thanks to the generosity of Parliament he was in a comfortable financial position, once the source of his £2,500 a year had been determined; and thus equipped he moved with his family to London in this summer of 1646 to set up his household in Drury Lane with his wife, his mother and four children. His two eldest sons were dead; his two eldest daughters married; and all of his sisters had found husbands save Elizabeth who lived with a former neighbor in Ely; and there remained at home only Richard, Henry, Mary and Frances.

As to his activities in the parliamentary struggles of that busy summer there remains no evidence; but there can be no doubt that he took deep interest in them. The Parliament had won the war, it remained to win the peace; and those months were filled with discussion of its terms. From his virtual imprisonment at Newcastle the King continued to bombard the Houses, the City and the Scotch Committee of Estates with his proposals, which seemed to look toward peace and toleration; but whatever else he did, he sowed dissension among his enemies. Though the Independents had gained perceptibly in strength in the Commons by the recent recruiting of membership, the Presbyterians were still a majority of that House. They dominated the Lords and the Assembly of Divines. They were strong in the City; and the position of Vane and his party, though supported by the army, was not without its difficulties in Parliament and Cromwell with his strong hand and his ability to sway those members who were neither strongly Presbyterian nor strongly Independent was a welcome addition to their ranks.

16 June 1646. White's regiment for Worcester," is amongst the Portland Papers at Welbeck Abbey. Calendared in *Hist. Mss. Comm. Rept.* 13, App. II, p. 137. Lomas-Carlyle, Suppl. 16, Major Charles White, of Nottingham, has many unfavourable notices in Mrs. Hutchinson's *Memoirs*.

[14] On June 29th. Whitelocke, *Memorials*, p. 213.

THE NEWCASTLE PROPOSITIONS, JULY–AUGUST, 1646

This was the more true in that the Houses now endeavored to come to terms with Charles. As a result of long discussion, on July 4, the Houses sent to the King the so-called Propositions of Newcastle. They were not unlike their previous proposals. As before they demanded indemnity for all past offence; the signature of the Solemn League and Covenant by the King; the abolition of episcopal government; the confirmation of the Assembly of Divines; the reformation of religion in accordance with the decisions of that Assembly and of Parliament; the old penalties against Roman Catholics; with measures for Sabbath observance, the suppression of "innovations" in the worship of God, and of pluralities, and for the "better advancement of preaching" and reforming of the universities and the colleges of Westminster, Eton and Winchester. To these they added demands for the control of the militia for twenty years, and the suppression of all other armed forces at the discretion of Parliament; the confirmation and extension of the liberties of the City and of Scotland; the nullification of all patents of nobility since Lyttleton took away the Seal; the confirmation of all treaties between England and Scotland since the coming of the Scots' army. To these they added a long list of persons to be excepted from indemnity or otherwise punished; and, finally, a demand for Charles's approval of all the measures passed under the Great Seal by the Lords and Commons in his absence.

To these the King replied, on August 1, that no just peace could be arranged unless the power of the crown were recognized. He proposed to come to London under safe conduct from the Houses and the Scots' commissioners, send for his son and there arrange a peace.[15] To this the Commons demurred; especially since his counter-proposal was accompanied by a letter from the Scots' commissioners which proposed to withdraw their forces from England on payment of their expenses and to consult with Parliament on the disposal of the King. Those expenses they reckoned at £1,800,000 but agreed to take less than a third of that amount, and on September 1 the Houses voted £400,000, half to be paid before the Scottish army left, the rest in instalments at fixed intervals.

It had, then, come to bargaining between the Parliament and the Scots for the person of the King, and while Charles hoped against hope for aid from Montrose or from France, while he ordered Ormond to break off negotiations with the Irish, and strove to find some means of dividing or conciliating his enemies, his fate was determined between the Parliament and the Scots. Of Cromwell's part in all this no evidence remains. Apart from his personal concerns—among them,

[15] *L. J.*, viii, 460–461.

doubtless, the payment of his grant from Parliament—he took his old place as a working member of the House.

One of the first matters which arose was the resurrection of an old quarrel in a way which Cromwell could hardly have welcomed. John Lilburne, although incarcerated in Newgate prison, was being his usual obnoxious self and no inconsiderable amount of time was spent in reading his various outbursts in Parliament. Manchester, he declared, whose "head had stood too long on his shoulders" had caused his arrest, and he would not be quiet until Cromwell's charges against Manchester, fully proved in the Commons, he said, were revived.[16] The entire edition of his pamphlet, *The Sum of the Charge given in by Lieutenant General Cromwell against the Earl of Manchester*,[17] which urged the renewal of those charges that had been laid aside by the Commons to induce the Lords to pass the New Model Ordinance, was ordered burned; and Lilburne, brought before the House on July 11, refusing to kneel and stopping his ears with his fingers to shut out the words of the charge against him, was committed to the Tower for seven years.[18]

On the same day that sentence was pronounced, Cromwell was named to a committee to search out the framers of a "Remonstrance" of the City to the King,[19] which, coinciding as it did with the Newcastle Propositions, greatly annoyed the Commons, more especially since there was a growing sentiment in favor of the King, of which this remonstrance was a symptom. So many and so persistent, nevertheless, were the grumblings against Royalists who were permitted to live freely within Parliament quarters, that a large standing committee, of which Cromwell was a member, was appointed to receive all such complaints and to consider the cases of ministers who claimed to be wrongfully sequestered from their livings.[20]

Among these various matters was the situation of a group of poor inhabitants of the hamlet of Hapton, south of Norwich, whose religious views differed from those of one Robert Browne, tenant of Thomas Knyvett whom Cromwell had forced out of Lowestoft some three years earlier when the town had attempted to fortify itself against Parliament forces. It was largely through Cromwell that Knyvett was later discharged by the Sequestration Committee because of his voluntary surrender; and it was thus with some assurance that Cromwell asked him to intercede with Browne:[21]

[16] *L. J.*, viii, 429.
[17] Printed in *L. J.*, viii, 430.
[18] *Ibid.*, 432.
[19] *C. J.*, iv, 615–16. Cp. *A Remonstrance of many thousand citizens and other free born people of England.*
[20] *C. J.*, iv, 625. Appointed July 23.
[21] See Mrs. Lomas's summary of Knyvett's relations with Cromwell, in Lomas-Carlyle, i, 123n–124n.

For my noble Friend Thomas Knyvett, Esquire, at his House at Ashwellthorpe, Norfolk: These

SIR,

I cannot pretend to any interest in you for anything I have done, nor ask any favour for any service I may do you. But because I am conscious to myself of a readiness to serve any gentleman in all possible civilities, I am bold to be beforehand with you to ask your favour on the behalf of your honest poor neighbours of Hapton, who, as I am informed, are in some trouble, and are likely to be put to more, by one Robert Browne, your tenant, who, not well pleased with the way of those men, seeks their disquiet all he may.

Truly nothing moves me to desire this, more than the pity I bear them in respect of their honesties, and the trouble I hear they are like to suffer for their consciences. And however the world interprets it, I am not ashamed to solicit for such as are anywhere under a pressure of this kind; doing herein as I would be done by. Sir, this is a quarrelsome age; and the anger seems to me to be the worse, where the ground is things of difference in opinion; which to cure, to hurt men in their names, persons or estates, will not be found an apt remedy. Sir, it will not repent you to protect those poor men of Hapton from injury and oppression: which that you would is the effect of this letter. Sir, you will not want the grateful acknowledgment, nor utmost endeavours of requital from

Your most humble servant,

London,
July 27th, 1646.

OLIVER CROMWELL.[22]

Five days before Cromwell wrote his letter to Knyvett, Worcester had surrendered to Rainsborough, and on July 29 Wallingford Castle in Berkshire capitulated to Fairfax, leaving only two strongholds in England—Pendennis and Raglan—unsubdued. The siege of the former was being adequately managed, and it was on his way to the latter in Monmouthshire that the General stopped in Bath on the day that Cromwell wrote the following note in behalf of a man who had joined Fairfax's army a year before:[23]

For his Excellency Sir Thomas Fairfax, General of the Parliament's Forces: These

SIR,

I was desired to write a letter to you by Adjutant Fleming. The end of it is, to desire your letter in his recommendation. He will

[22] Printed in *Gentleman's Magazine*, liv, 337 (1784), from the original once in the possession of the Lords Berners, descendants of Knyvett, thence Carlyle, Letter XXXVI. In Carlyle's time only a copy remained in their hands, at Ashwellthorpe. The original was listed for sale in 1931 by Sotheby & Co. in their catalogue. Included in the library of Dr. Roderick Terry sold by the American Art Association on May 2 and 3, 1934. Catalogue, p. 66, with photostat.

[23] *Cal. S. P. Dom.* (1645–47), p. 28. He is in Sprigg's army list, *Anglia Rediviva*, p. 328.

acquaint you with the sum thereof, more particularly what the business is. I most humbly submit to your better judgment, when you hear it from him.

Craving pardon for my boldness in putting you to this trouble, I rest,

Your most humble servant,

July 31st, 1646. OLIVER CROMWELL.[24]

One by one the royal strongholds fell, Pendennis on August 17, Raglan two days later, and the castles of north Wales, beginning with Flint on August 24 and ending with Harlech more than six months later, on March 13, 1647. Meanwhile arose the great problem of what to do with the army which had brought about the downfall of the royal cause. With that was joined the other question which confronted Parliament, that of the Irish war which was still going on, and to that question Parliament had addressed itself.

The situation there was extraordinarily complex. In the beginning Charles had virtually turned the reduction of Ireland over to Parliament and what interest he had was in the hands of the Duke of Ormond. To that he had added a commission to Lord Herbert, son of the Marquis of Worcester, styled Lord Glamorgan, in 1645, in the hope of raising troops for his service in England. It was a disastrous enterprise. Ormonde presently took him prisoner and though Charles repudiated both Glamorgan and his mission, the charge of negotiating with the Irish rebels remained to further weaken the royal cause.

The Irish problem was, as always, difficult and never more difficult than at this moment. There were five parties in Ireland in 1646, each with its own army—those of the English Royalists under Ormonde; the Scots under Monro; the Irish Confederates under Owen Roe O'Neill; the Papal force directed by the legate Rinuccini; and the Parliamentary army under Coote; with other less organized commands. On June 5, Monro was beaten by O'Neill at Benburb; and on September 26, Ormonde, fearing the triumph of the native Irish over the English, and knowing that no help could be expected from the King, sent for aid to Westminster. The Parliament was in a peculiar situation. On the one hand it could not view with equanimity the success of the papal forces or that of the Confederacy of the native Irish; on the other it hesitated to reinforce the Royalist Ormonde. In a sense the end of the English war provided it with an opportunity, and the disbandment of Fairfax's army with an instrument.

The Independents were for sending regiments of the New Model to Ireland; the Presbyterians opposed; and on the last day of July the question came to a vote. With Haselrig, Cromwell appeared as a teller for the Yeas on the proposal of referring the relief of Ireland to a

[24] Original, signed by Cromwell, amongst the *Sloane Mss*, 1519, f. 144, in the British Museum. Carlyle, Letter XXXVII. Mentioned in Henfrey, *Numismata Cromwelliana*, p. 180.

grand committee, with Denzil Holles and Sir Philip Stapleton as tellers for the Noes. As happened more often than not that summer, the Independents were defeated;[25] and, with Cromwell's place as teller taken by Sir John Evelyn, the House decided not to send the six regiments of Fairfax's army to Ireland.[26] In place of them, a new force was to be raised and at the next meeting of the House of Commons, the Irish Committee reported the number of men each county could be called upon to contribute.[27]

Amid these quarrels of Independents and Presbyterians, Cromwell pursued his duties as before in the capacity of a private member of the House. He was named on August 4 to a committee to consider a petition for a new church at Tothill Fields, Westminster, and the maintenance of ministers there and at three churches near by. Six days later he took an interest in a libel charge of Sir Richard Onslow against the poet George Wither, in which he was again a teller with Haselrig against Holles and Stapleton, and again he lost when a fine of £500 was imposed upon Wither.[28] The Presbyterian-Independent difficulty grew. It was proposed to disband Massey's brigade of Presbyterians; the Lords countermanded the Commons' order to that effect; but Fairfax followed the Lower House, and to him Cromwell wrote in some agitation:

For his Excellency Sir Thomas Fairfax, the General: These

SIR,

Hearing you were returned from Ragland to the Bath, I take the boldness to make this address unto you.

Our Commissioners sent to the King came this night to London. I have spoken with two of them, and can only learn these generals, that there appears a good inclination in the Scots to the rendition of our town, and to their march out of the Kingdom. When they bring in their papers, we shall know more. Argile, the Chancellor, and Dunfarlin are come up. Duke of Hamilton is gone from the King into Scotland. I hear that Montrose his men are not disbanded. The King gave a very general answer. Things are not well in Scotland; would they were in England! We are full of faction and worse.

I hear for certain that Ormond hath concluded a peace with the rebels.[29] Sir, I beseech you command the Solicitor to come away to us. His help would be welcome. Sir, I hope you have not cast me off. Truly I may say, no [one]

[25] *C. J.*, iv, 631.

[26] *Ibid.*, p. 632.

[27] *Ibid.*, pp. 633–4.

[28] *C. J.*, iv, 632, 640.

[29] The treaty Ormond had made was signed in March, calling for 10,000 Irish to come to the King's assistance in return for conditions no English Protestant could endure. It was proclaimed on July 30.

more affectionately honours nor loves you. You and yours are in my daily prayers. You have done enough to command the uttermost of,

Your faithfullest and most obedient servant,

London,
Aug. 10th, 1646. OLIVER CROMWELL.

[P.S.] I beseech you, my humble service may be presented to your Lady.

[P.S.] The money for disbanding Massey's men is gotten, and you will speedily have directions about them from the Commons House.[30]

If he was agitated, his confusion was understandable, for the news in his hurried letter revealed the complex situation of the time. The return of the Parliament's commissioners—the Earls of Pembroke and Suffolk, Sir Walter Earle, Sir John Hippesley, Robert Goodwin and Luke Robinson—with the King's answer to the Newcastle Propositions, again divided Independents from Presbyterians. The one regarded the Scots as intriguing enemies; the other as allies; though both agreed that they should be paid and sent home. The King's reply, as Cromwell observes, was "general" and that problem remained. The "faction" was only too evident in every action of the House. The Irish question was extremely difficult, and if, as it appeared, the Royalists and the Irish rebels had come to an agreement, the authority of Parliament in Ireland was seriously threatened. In all, the situation was in the highest degree unsatisfactory if not dangerous, especially if the King could somehow unite Scotland and Ireland against the Parliament.

Through these involved issues Cromwell, like his fellow members, made his way. On August 11 he was on a committee to confer with various persons in regard to borrowing money for Ireland. On the 14th he was on another to consider the third reading of an ordinance for punishing printers or "contrivers" of scandalous pamphlets against the Scots, which the Presbyterians pushed through the House against Independent opposition.[31] And amid these squabbles he found time to write two letters which echo his former lieutenant-generalcy. The date of the first is not certain but since its subject, Mr. Heron of Higney, Hunts, compounded for delinquency on August 18, it probably was about that time.

Certificate

These are to certify whom it may concern that Mr. John Heron laid down his arms in Devonshire the latter end of November, Anno Dom: 1645; and

[30] Holograph original in *Sloane Mss*, 1519, f. 131. Carlyle, Letter XXXVIII. Mentioned in Henfrey *Numismata Cromwelliana*, p. 180. The second postscript has been squeezed in above the first although evidently written after it.

[31] *C. J.*, iv, 641, 644.

willingly submitted himself to the General, Sir Thomas Fairfax, his Dispose, to which I was a witness. And gave him my protection to live unmolested in his own country about that time.

[c. Aug. 18, 1646.] OLIVER CROMWELL.[32]

The second letter is for Major Henry Lilburne, brother to Colonel Robert and Lieutenant-colonel "Freeborn" John Lilburne, and the probable writer of a letter to the King in November 1647 warning Charles of a plot to murder him.[33] Presently appointed governor of Tynemouth Castle, he was slain in 1648 by his own soldiers as a Royalist sympathizer.

To John Rushworth, Esquire, Secretary to his Excellency at Bath: These

MR. RUSHWORTH.

I must needs entreat a favour on the behalf of Major Lilburne, who has a long time wanted employment, and by reason thereof his necessities may grow upon him.

You should do very well to move the General to take him into favourable thoughts. I know a reasonable employment will content him. As for his honesty and courage, I need not speak much of, seeing he is so well known both to the General and yourself.

I desire you answer my expectation herein so far as you may. You shall very much oblige, Sir,

Your real friend and servant,

The House [of Commons],
26th August [1646]. OLIVER CROMWELL.[34]

THE AGREEMENT WITH THE SCOTS, AUGUST–DECEMBER, 1646

Through all of the events of the late summer and early autumn of 1646 there ran the question of the disposal of the Scots' army, and in this, as in other matters, the antagonism of Presbyterian and Independent deepened week by week. In division after division that antagonism grew with Cromwell among the Independent minority. One of the most disputed questions was the amount of money to be paid to the Scots, and when the sum of £400,000 was finally fixed upon and a committee including Cromwell was named to borrow half from the City, on the question of asking the Lords' concurrence, he once more found himself a teller for the minority against that move, with his old colonel, Stapleton, on the other side.[35] With this, with his membership on a committee to consider the issuing of writs for an

[32] Original in *S. P. Dom. Interr.* clxxxvii, 717. *Cal. Comm. for Compounding*, p. 1457.
[33] Cp. S. R. Gardiner, *Civil War*, iv, 15n.
[34] *Sloane MSS.*, 1519, fol. 146, Carlyle XXXIX. Mentioned in Henfrey, *Numismata Cromwelliana*, p. 181.
[35] *C. J.*, iv, 663, 665.

election at Newcastle, and another of very different character concerning the seizure of the estates and employees of the Levant Company by Sir Sackville Crowe, ambassador at Constantinople, and a demand for his recall,[36] he took his part in those affairs which filled in the time between the greater issues of the day.

Among these greater issues the chief was the disposal of the King, which as the Scots prepared to return to their own country, absorbed the attention of all parties. Charles rejected the proposal of the Queen's council in France to give way to the Presbyterians. He entertained, though he did not accept, proposals from the Independents to establish moderate episcopacy, "pass delinquents and waive Ireland" till the Scots were gone and he could negotiate with Parliament. He listened to the advice of the French ambassador and of the Queen's agents to concede everything to the Scots. He even prepared an elaborate if futile plan of his own to first recover his royal authority then settle the church in conjunction with the Parliament. But the number and complexity of these various negotiations revealed the wide divergence of the antagonistic elements—the English Presbyterians and the Scots, the Independents and the Royalists, and behind them all the Queen and her advisers, French and English, and the still unsettled problem of the Irish war.

But if Charles was still King, he was no less a prisoner. Of the goodly company which had set forth with him four years before, he alone was left. Knights, bishops, castles, even the Queen had gone. Only the King and a few pawns remained. Yet though checked on every side, his person was inviolable and he could not yet believe that he was checkmated. He pursued his negotiations with the Independents and the Presbyterians, with the Scots and Parliament, with the Queen and France, still hoping for division among his enemies and his return to power, despite the fact that as September ended the disposal of his person was debated in Parliament and a committee appointed, of which Cromwell was one, to discuss that question with the Scots' commissioners.[37] The death of Essex on September 14 removed a potential supporter of the royal cause and one of the chief opponents of the Independent group. So "wonderfully exalted" did that group appear and so opportune and mysterious was the removal of Essex, that though Ludlow declares that he died from becoming overheated in a stag hunt in Windsor Forest, others did not hesitate to hint at poison.[38]

After the Parliamentary recess during which Essex died, Cromwell

[36] *Ibid.*, p. 666, 671; *Cal. S. P. Dom.* (1645–7), p. 469.

[37] *C. J.*, iv, 675.

[38] Ludlow, *Memoirs*, (Firth ed.), i, 144; Walker, *History of Independency*, p. 43; *Old Parl. Hist.*, xv, 98–9; Clarendon, *History*, v, 42; *Micro-Chronicon*, Sept. 14; *L. J.*, viii, 490. Gardiner (*Civil War*, iii, 148) places Essex's death on Sept. 16.

was again at Westminster taking part in every phase of Parliamentary business. On October 1, he and Edmund Prideaux were commissioned to bring in Sir John Clotworthy's accounts for the army destined for Ireland. On that same day he was a teller with Vane against Waller and Stapleton on the question of the disposal of the Parliamentary Great Seal which had been in the custody of three peers who were thanked for their services as commissioners and paid £1,000 for them.[39] In the existing situation, the problem of the Seal had become an acute issue, for on it hung in some measure the supremacy of King or Commons. Cromwell and Vane believed that the Seal should be in the custody of the Houses. The Commons disagreed with them; but some three weeks later Lords and Commons voted that the Speakers of the two Houses should exercise authority as Commissioners of the Great Seal, so that Vane and Cromwell won their point and Charles and the Presbyterians lost an advantage. To this Cromwell added lesser activities.[40] On October 3, he was a member of a committee to consider the petition of one John Baldwin of Kent;[41] and within a week he was writing to Fairfax in behalf of certain Staffordshire gentlemen who had petitioned for £4,000 of Royalist fines to pay their militia instead of having the money paid into Goldsmiths' Hall as had lately been the case, with the result that the county committees were hard pressed for money to pay their men:

For his Excellency Sir Thomas Fairfax: These

Sir,

I would be loath to trouble you with anything; but indeed the Staffordshire Gentlemen came to me this day, and with more than ordinary importunity did press me to give their desires furtherance to you. Their letter will show what they entreat of you. Truly, Sir, it will not be amiss to give them what ease may well be afforded, and the sooner the better, especially at this time.

I have no more at present, but to let you know the business of your Army is like to come on tomorrow. You shall have account of that business as soon as I am able to give it. I humbly take leave, and rest,

Your Excellency's most humble servant,

London,
October 6th, 1646.

Oliver Cromwell.[42]

It is not clear what Fairfax was expected to do beyond lending his influence to the petition, but as Cromwell points out, "especially at this time" it was well to make friends wherever possible, for Presby-

[39] *C. J.*, iv, 679, 680.
[40] Parry's *Parliaments*, p. 469.
[41] *C. J.*, iv, 681.
[42] *Sloane Mss*, 1519, fol. 148. Cromwell's hand throughout. Carlyle XL.

terians and Independents were coming to close grips. The chief problem was the treatment of the King. Amid its renewed activity in filling vacant seats and ordering the sale of the sequestered estates of great noblemen like the Earl of Worcester and the Marquis of Winchester, and of lesser lords and gentlemen, those of Parliament finally agreed eight days after Essex's death to dispose of the person of the King "as both the Houses shall think fit." On October 9, with only seven earls and five barons present, the Lords finally agreed with the Commons' ordinance abolishing episcopal government;[43] and with the King a prisoner at the disposal of the Houses and the church system gone, it might have seemed that the great purpose of the Puritan revolution was achieved, and that it only remained to construct a new system.

But this was far from true; there still remained great problems to be settled before that system could be framed. There were the Scots' forces to be disposed of; the English army to be reorganized or disbanded; the Irish war to be ended; and some arrangement made with the King. Thus while Charles negotiated and intrigued with Parliament, with Presbyterians and Independents, with the Scots and France, with the City and with his Royalist supporters in England, Scotland and Ireland, the Parliament addressed itself to the various phases of a settlement. They were, in effect, three—the Scots, the army and Ireland—and through the autumn and early winter of 1646 apart from their negotiations with the King the Houses were chiefly absorbed in these.

With them all Cromwell was concerned. In that little group which at this juncture managed the business of governing England—or at least kept it in subjection—by virtue of his military reputation, his proved ability, his place in the House and on the Committee of Both Kingdoms, and his position as an Independent leader, he had risen to new importance; but despite this the record of his activities in these months seems little more than that of an ordinary member of the House. None the less that record, rightly interpreted, reveals much of the spirit and issues of this period which, apparently uneventful in comparison with what had gone on before and what was about to happen, was nevertheless of much significance, and in nothing more than this—that it hints at the rising influence of the party to which he belonged. The Presbyterians had long held the upper hand, but the French agent in London now recorded that "the credit of the Independents increases every day." [44]

That was apparent in many little ways. By October 10, in a thin house, with Cromwell and Haselrig as tellers against Stapleton and Lewes, they mustered 56 votes to 54 on a mtoion to use a ballot-box

[43] *C. J., passim;* see also Parry's *Parliaments.*
[44] Grignon to Brienne, Oct. 22/Nov. 1, 1646. *Record Office Transcripts.*

for selecting persons for offices, preferments and rewards, which seems to indicate their growing confidence in being able to control such prizes for the future.[45] Two other committees on which he served in October—one on the 15th to prepare an ordinance to prevent the arrest of anyone in pursuance of his duties as an agent of the Parliament; and another on the 17th to investigate the seizure by the Marquis of Hereford of the late Earl of Essex's property in his London house[46]—were of no partisan significance, and on the 20th he again acted as a teller for the minority in a division on a no less insignificant ordinance sent down from the Lords.[47]

In the intervals of his duties in Parliament he found time to write on Sunday, October 25, a letter in language appropriate to that day, to his strong family feeling, to his Puritan character, and with a rare touch of humor:

For my beloved Daughter Bridget Ireton, at Cornbury, the General's Quarters

DEAR DAUGHTER,

I write not to thy husband; partly to avoid trouble, for one line of mine begets many of his, which I doubt makes him sit up too late; partly because I am myself indisposed at this time, having some other considerations.

Your friends at Ely are well. Your Sister Claypole is (I trust in mercy) exercised with some perplexed thoughts. She sees her own vanity and carnal mind, bewailing it; she seeks after (as I hope also) that which will satisfy. And thus to be a seeker is to be of the best sect next to a finder; and such an one shall every faithful humble seeker be at the end. Happy seeker, happy finder! Who ever tasted that the Lord is gracious, without some sense of self, vanity, and badness? Who ever tasted that graciousness of His, and could go less in desire, and less in pressing after full enjoyment? Dear Heart, press on; let not husband, let not anything cool thy affections after Christ. I hope he will be an occasion to inflame them. That which is best worthy of love in thy husband is that of the image of Christ he bears. Look on that, and love it best, and all the rest for that. I pray for thee and him; do so for me.

My service and dear affections to the General and Generaless. I hear she is very kind to thee; it adds to all other obligations. My love to all. I am

Thy dear Father,

Octob. 25, 1646,
London.

OLIVER CROMWELL.[48]

[45] *C. J.*, iv, 690; Whitacre's *Diary*, *Add. Mss.*, 31, 116, f. 285, British Museum.

[46] *C. J.*, iv, 695, 696.

[47] *Ibid.*, 700.

[48] Carlyle, XLI, from the original in the *Harleian Mss*, 6988, fol. 224, and from an exact copy which was sent to Carlyle with the notation, 'Memo: The above letter of Oliver Cromwell Jn° Caswell Merch^{t} of London had from his Mother Linnington, who had it from old Mrs. Warner, who liv'd with Oliver Cromwell's daughter.—And was copied from the original letter which is in the hands of John Warner Esqr

Such troubled times as these were full of property disputes, of private quarrels and personal grievances, and in the settlement of these Cromwell took his part. On October 29 he was added to a committee for investigating the business of the suit of the Countess of Peterborough against William Lord Monson, Viscount Castlemaine, for lands held by the latter.[49] The same day he wrote a letter to Mr. Robert Jenner, M.P. for Cricklade, of the Committee for Compounding. "My Lord Cromwell," fourth baron and Earl of Ardglass in Ireland, in whose behalf the letter was written was a descendant of Thomas Cromwell. His career was characteristic of the time-servers of the period. First siding with Parliament, he had "deserted the House," then taken service with the King against the Irish rebels; and finally compounded under the provisions of November, 1645, and taken the Covenant. He differed from many others of like sort only in having a champion of influence; and it is notable that, probably due to this circumstance, his fine of £800 was later abated.

To my very loving Friend Mr. Jenner, at Goldsmith Hall: These

My Lord Cromwell, upon putting in of his particular into Goldsmiths' Hall, knowing what the whole value of his estate amounted unto yearly, gave it in at 470 l. in general, which was the true value of the whole lying in several counties; but not being so perfect in particular values of the several parcels of his estate having trusted it constantly to the managing of others, did give in his lands in Staffordshire, Derbyshire and Cheshire at 350 l. per ann. whereas the true value is but 255 l. And his lands in Wiltshire but 120 l. whereas the true value is 215 l. per ann., both amounting to the said sum of 470 l. for which he compounded. My Lord desires that he may have liberty to set the several values upon his several parcels of land all amounting to the said sum of 470 l., and that he may have his letters to the several counties accordingly. What favour you shall show my Lord Cromwell herein you shall oblige

Your very loving friend,

29 Octob. 1646. OLIVER CROMWELL.[50]

Two days after writing this letter, as a member of the Committee of Both Kingdoms, Cromwell, with five of his colleagues, in response to a resolution of Parliament, signed an order for the secretary, Gualter Frost, to receive the sum involved from the Committee at Goldsmiths' Hall.

of Swanzey, by Chas Norris, 25th Mar: 1749.' Printed also in Thomas Cromwell's *Life of Cromwell* (1821), p. 467. Cornbury House was in Oxfordshire, "now disguised," says Carlyle, as "Blandford Lodge."

[49] *C. J.*, iv, 708, 709.

[50] Original in *S. P. Dom. Interr.* A, lxxviii, 479. Calendared in *Cal. Comm. for Compounding* (1643–60), p. 951; and in Waylen, *House of Cromwell*, p. 274. Summary in Lomas-Carlyle, Suppl. 17.

Resolution

Die Veneris, 30 Octob. 1646.

RESOLVED

That this House doth agree with the Committee, that for the preservation of the Isles of Guernsey, Aldernay and Sarque from present danger, four hundred men to be forthwith sent thither with provision for victual for them. And that for the better carrying on of this work the sum of one thousand pounds be forthwith advanced and paid by the Committee at Goldsmiths' Hall to such person or persons as the Members of both Houses that are of the Committee of Both Kingdoms shall appoint, whose acquittance shall be a good discharge for the same.

H. ELSYNGE, Clerk
Parl: D: Com.

We do appoint Mr. Frost or his Assigns to receive the Thousand pounds in this order mentioned, to be disposed by this Committee for the uses above expressed. Derbyhouse, 31 of Octob. 1646.

NORTHUMBERLAND WARWICK
W. PIERREPONT H. VANE, JR.
OLIVER CROMWELL. JO. CREWE[51]

Of no great importance in itself—save in that it shows the anxiety of the authorities for the safety of the three Channel Islands threatened by the presence of Prince Charles's council in Jersey—it reveals something of the machinery of the revolutionary government at this time. With the decimated Parliament as the supreme authority; the Committee of Both Kingdoms as at once an executive and a creature of the Scottish and English Parliaments; the committees of Sequestration and Compounding as collectors of revenue, with lesser bodies for various administrative purposes; with treasurers of the army and navy; with the Committee at Goldsmiths' Hall as a treasury and exchequer; and with the Great Seal in the hands of the Speakers of the two Houses, it was a disordered and anomalous if effective arrangement of carrying on the business of government under such conditions as had prevailed during four years of war. It was, in effect, an engine of revolution rather than of civil government; for such government as there was rested chiefly in the hands of local authorities. Writs still ran in the King's name and that of the Houses; courts still functioned, however haltingly; such ecclesiastical business as there was, rested not in Convocation but in the Assembly of Divines and in some fashion administration was carried on. But it was only too evident that this awkward machinery was at best a temporary expedient and depended for its functioning not on the system but on the group of able and determined men who managed it.

[51] *S. P. Dom. Interr.* G ccxlv, 73, and G iii, 276. Calendared in *Cal. Comm. for Compounding.*

Of these Cromwell was now one, yet there is little or no evidence of it. Though still designated as lieutenant-general,[52] he was officially only a member of the House of Commons and by virtue of his place there and by its authority, a member of the great Committee. Such record as we have of him is chiefly in that capacity. He was doubtless present at the Earl of Essex's funeral for which Parliament adjourned on October 22, and it is probable that ten days later he attended that of his sister, Anna Sewster, at Wistow, Hunts.,[53] but during November, 1646, he seems to have devoted himself assiduously to his duties as a member of Parliament and of the Committee of Both Kingdoms. On the 3rd he was a teller for the minority in endeavoring to prevent the introduction of an ordinance for continuing the Committee and Treasurers for the Army for ten months more. On the 21st he was successful in a division to refuse a certain Edward Vaughan permission to remain on the Committee for Montgomeryshire. He was a member of two committees of the House, one to consider the losses of several persons whose places had been taken from them by the abolition of the Court of Wards; another to decide on cases resulting from putting into execution the ordinance for the sale of bishops' lands, passed on the 30th.[54]

During the month of December the negotiations between Charles, the Scots and the English Parliament went on. The King who had in November proposed to abdicate for a time, asked again to come to London, and the Scots, whose Parliament had voted to support the King, prepared to evacuate their positions in England. Money was being raised to pay them; and Lords and Commons disputed as to where the King should be confined, whether, as the Lords urged, at Newmarket, or as the Commons insisted successfully, at Holmby House in Northamptonshire. Whatever part he played behind the scenes, there is but little evidence of Cromwell's share in these great events. That his counsels carried weight, there can be little doubt; and though the importance of the Committee of Both Kingdoms had dwindled considerably since the surrender of Oxford, the varied business of Parliament and his prominence in it are revealed by the fact that he was placed on five special committees before the middle of the month. Of these, one to consider ways and means to keep in hand the disaffected in London and Westminster; another to satisfy the arrears of pay for the army were of importance.[55] Others of less

[52] *C. J.*, iv, 634.

[53] Noble, i, 89; ii, 231. Four years her brother's junior, she was the mother of two boys and four girls. Robina, the only one of the four left in 1654, who presumably spent much time in her uncle's household where her grandmother lived, married Sir William Lockhart, the man who became the Protector's ambassador to France.

[54] *C. J.*, iv, 713, 726, 727, 730; *L. J.*, viii, 585.

[55] *C. J.*, v, 4, 9.

significance and widely different character were for the consideration of Sir John Sedley's defeat in a Kent election; the investigation of the printing of a sermon by Mr. Dell, Fairfax's chaplain; and the examination of a book by certain London ministers.[56] He was a teller for the losing Yeas, on December 12, in a vote for discharging from imprisonment one Francis Sympson.[57] On the 17th he was placed on a committee to meet the next day to examine information on words reported to have been spoken by Sir John Evelyn; and on the 18th he was at Derby House discussing Irish affairs with the Committee of Both Kingdoms.[58] These, with such like business as was common to the members of the House absorbed his time during that critical period.

The growing strength of the Independents had become clearly perceptible late in November when they succeeded in sending a Commons' declaration to the Scots, without first submitting it to the Lords for approval, asserting the right of the English Parliament to dispose of the King's person while he was on English soil. Meanwhile the Scottish Parliament had met and showed signs of refusing the King shelter in Scotland. The Scotch army was thus left in a dilemma but the English Parliament tactfully avoided the rupture which seemed inevitable by proceeding with peaceful negotiations. None the less rumors of coercion were afoot, for on December 14, Montrose's friend, Lord Napier, wrote to the Earl of Mar that Cromwell was "advancing northward with a considerable power, and a little money to the Scotts army, which if they will not accept he will fall on as his orders caryes." [59] The story was not true but it revealed the difficulties of the situation. They were soon cleared up. The next day the Articles of Agreement between the Parliament's committee and the Scotch committee were inserted in the *Commons Journals* and the following day in the *Lords Journals*. Two days before they were finally signed, Cromwell wrote to Fairfax giving him the news:

For his Excellency Sir Thomas Fairfax, General of the Parliament's Armies: These

SIR,

Having this opportunity by the Major-General to present a few lines unto you, I take the boldness to let you know how our affairs go since you left the Town.

We have had a very long petition from the City. How it strikes at the army and what other aims it has, you will see by the contents of it; as also what the prevailing temper is at this present, and what is to be expected from men.

[56] *Ibid.*, pp. 6, 10, 11.
[57] *Ibid.*, p. 12.
[58] *Ibid.*, p. 17; *Cal. S. P. Irish* (1647–60), p. 727.
[59] *Hist. Mss, Comm. Rept.* (Earl of Mar & Kellie Mss), p. 204.

But this is our comfort, God is in heaven, and He doth what pleaseth Him; His and only His counsel shall stand, whatever the designs of men, and the fury of the people be.

We have now, I think, almost perfected all our business for Scotland. I believe Commissioners will speedily be sent down to see agreements performed; it's intended that Major-General Skippon have authority and instructions from your Excellency to command the Northern Forces, as occasion shall be, and that he have a Commission of Martial Law. Truly I hope that the having the Major-General to command this Party will appear to be a good thing, every day more and more.

Here has been a design to steal away the Duke of York from my Lord of Northumberland. One of his own servants, whom he preferred to wait on the Duke, is found guilty of it; the Duke himself confessed so. I believe you will suddenly hear more of it.

I have no more to trouble you; but praying for you, rest,

Your Excellency's most humble servant,

London,
December 21st, 1646. OLIVER CROMWELL.[60]

These various developments came to a head on December 23, when the Articles with the Scots were signed by Cromwell and his fellow committee members at Derby House,[61] arranging a time and place for the payment of £400,000 and the departure of the unwanted army:

Articles of Agreement between Committees of Lords and Commons of the Parliament of England and Commissioners of the Parliament of Scotland, authorized thereunto by the Parliaments of each Kingdom respectively.

I. That 400,000 l. be paid to the Kingdom of Scotland, in manner hereafter express'd, for the pay of their army brought into the Kingdom of England for the assistance of this Kingdom, and of their forces that came into the garrison of Berwick, by virtue of the treaties between the two kingdoms of the 29th of November 1643; and for due recompence and full satisfaction for all the pains, hazard, and charges which they have undergone, and for whatsoever other sums of money or recompense the Kingdom of Scotland can claim of the Kingdom of England, by virtue of the said treaties.

II. That the 200,000 l. now ready, part of the said 400,000 l. shall be forthwith sent to the city of York, and shall there forthwith be told by the treasurers in whose custody the money now is, or by such as they, or any two of them, shall appoint; and by such as shall be appointed by the Kingdom of Scotland, or by Sir Adam Hepburne, Treasurer of the Scots army, or his deputies, except 12,000 l. part thereof, which, at the desire of the Scots Com-

[60] *Sloane Mss*, 1519, fol. 150. Holograph. Carlyle, Letter XLII.

[61] Gardiner says it was signed December 16, and gives *L. J.* as the reference, but there is nothing there to confirm the date. *Old Parl. Hist.* gives Dec. 23 as the correct date. An ordinance of Jan. 13, 1646–7 concerning payment mentions articles "dated 23 Dec. 1646." *Cal. S. P. Dom.* (1645–7), p. 514.

missioners, is reserved to be paid here in London, and is accepted for so much of the first 100,000 l. appointed to be paid at Northallerton; the which 12,000 l. the said Scots Commissioners have power to receive here in manner as aforesaid, and to discharge the Kingdom of England thereof.

III. That the first 100,000 l. except the sum of 12,000 l. before excepted shall be told within six days after the arrival of the said money at York, and the second 100,000 l. within six days after that.

IV. That the money, so told as aforesaid, shall be sealed up in the several bags, each to contain 100 l. by the seal of both parties appointed as aforesaid to tell the same; and shall be forthwith put into chests, 1000 l. in each chest, and the said chests also sealed up by the aforesaid persons appointed to tell the said money.

V. That the said persons appointed by the Kingdom of Scotland to tell the said money shall continue with the same, to see, that there shall be no alteration made thereof after the telling and sealing the same as aforesaid.

VI. That within five days after the 200,000 l. is told at York, 100,000 l. thereof shall be paid at Northallerton to Sir Adam Hepburne or his deputies or to such others as by the Kingdom of Scotland shall be appointed to receive the same, except only the 12,000 l. reserved to be paid in London as aforesaid.

VII. That the delivery of 100 chests of money, or of 1000 bags, so as aforesaid sealed up, to the persons mentioned in the foregoing Article, except before excepted, shall be, and be accounted, the payment of the said 100,000 l. and acquittances are thereupon to be given for the same to the said treasurers for their discharge, by Sir Adam Hepburne, or his deputies, or any other authorized by the Kingdom of Scotland.

VIII. That when the said 100,000 l. except before excepted, is come to Topcliffe in the County of York, and before it pass any further towards Northallerton for the payment of the same as aforesaid, the Kingdom of Scotland shall there deliver hostages; Sir Walter Riddell, Knt., George Hume, of Wedderburn, Esq., Sir Patrick Mackegie, Knt., Alexander Strachan, of Thorneton, Esq., Sir James Wood, Knt., Sir James Lumsden, younger, Knt., Sir Arthur Forbes, Knt., Thomas Craig, of Rickerton, Esq., Sir William Ker, Knt., Robert Douglas, of Tilly-Whilley, Esq., Col. John Welden, John Lesley, of Pitcaple, Esq., or any six of them, for assurance that the Scots shall quit all their quarters, passes, and garrisons on the south side Tyne; and shall deliver up to such forces as both Houses of the Parliament of England, or such as shall be by them authorized, shall appoint all the aforesaid places, together with all the ordnance, arms, and ammunition belonging to the Kingdom of England, within ten days after the first 100,000 l. shall be paid as aforesaid, and for assurance that they shall deliver up the town of Newcastle, with the High Castle in the same; the Castle of Tinmouth, with all the works belonging thereunto; the Spanish works, the Shields-Field Fort, and all other forts and works on the north side Tyne, together with all ordnance, arms, and ammunition therein, belonging to the Kingdom of England, unto such forces or persons as shall be appointed by both Houses of the Parliament of England; or by any of them thereunto authorized, to receive the same, when and at such time as notice is given that the second 100,000 l. is come to the north of the River of Tees, as is hereafter expressed in the tenth Article.

IX. That within one day after the performance of all the particulars mentioned in the said former article, the said hostages of the Kingdom of Scotland shall be again redelivered unto them, within half a mile of the works on the north side of Newcastle.

X. That after the garrisons of Hartlepool, Stockton, Durham, and all other garrisons, quarters, and passes on the south side of Tyne, are quitted by the Scots army and forces; and, after that all the said army and forces are removed to the north side of Tyne, which is to be done in ten days after the payment of the first 100,000 l. as aforesaid, that then the other 100,000 l. shall be brought to the north side of the River Tees.

XI. That the second 100,000 l. being come to the north side of the said River of Tees, upon notice thereof given to the General or Commander-in-Chief of the Scots Army, in writing, from him that commands the convoy, they shall deliver up the town of Newcastle, with the High Castle in the same; the Castle of Tinmouth, with all the works belonging thereunto; the Spanish works, the Shields-Field Fort, and all other forts and works on the north side Tyne, other than is provided for in the 15th Article, together with all ordnance, arms, and ammunition therein, belonging to the Kingdom of England, unto such forces or persons as shall be appointed by both Houses of the Parliament of England, or by any by them thereunto authorized to receive the same.

XII. That for the more speedy delivery and receiving the said towns of Newcastle and Castle of Tinmouth, the said forces that are to be put into those garrisons, are to march before the said money and convoy.

XIII. That when the Scots army and forces are marching out of, and the English forces are entering into, Newcastle and Tinmouth Castle; and that there be 500 of the garrison appointed by both Houses of Parliament entered into Newcastle, and not above 500 of the Scots forces remaining therein; that then Sir William Selby, of Berwick in the county of Northumberland, Knt., Ralph Delaval, of Seaton Delaval in the county of Northumberland, Esq., Sir Edward Loftus, of Middleham in the county of York, Viscount Ely, Sir Thomas Trollopp, in the county of Lincoln, Bart., Henry Mildmay, of Graces in the county of Essex, Esq., Sir Richard Erle, of Straglethorpe in the county of Lincoln, Bart., Sir Ralph Hare, of the county of Norfolk, Bart., and Sir Lionel Tolmache, of the county of Suffolk, Bart., or any six of them, shall be given hostages by the Kingdom of England to the Kingdom of Scotland for assurance that the latter 100,000 l. of the 200,000 l. shall be paid unto the Kingdom of Scotland, on the north side of the works within six days after the delivery of Newcastle, Tinmouth Castle, and places aforesaid, in manner aforesaid, to such persons, and in such manner, as is expressed in the sixth and seventh Articles for the payment of the first 100,000 l. and acquittances are thereupon to be given, as in the said seventh Article is expressed.

XIV. That upon the delivery of the said latter 100,000 l. of the 200,000 l. the hostages of the Kingdom of England are forthwith to be redelivered.

XV. That upon the coming of the latter 100,000 l. out of Newcastle, hostages, as in the eighth Article, shall be delivered to the Kingdom of England, by the Kingdom of Scotland, for assurance that all the Scots armies and forces shall march out of the Kingdom of England within ten days after the payment of the latter 100,000 l. That they will permit and suffer that the fortifications of Berwick and Carlisle may be slighted, according to the Large Treaty and Treaty of Berwick, which shall accordingly be slighted within ten days after payment of the last 100,000 l. And that the said towns be quitted; and all ordnance, arms and ammunition therein, belonging to the Kingdom of England be, within the said ten days, delivered unto such persons as shall be appointed by both Houses of the Parliament of England, or such as shall be by them, or any authorized by them for that purpose, appointed to cause and see Berwick and Carlisle slighted in manner as aforesaid; and are hereby authorized to call in the aid of the country for the doing thereof as they shall see cause; and likewise the Parliament of Scotland, or any of them authorized, are to appoint such persons as they shall think fit to see this performed.

XVI. That within four days after the Scots army and forces shall be marched out of the Kingdom of England, and the said garrisons of Berwick and Carlisle quitted as aforesaid, the Hostages of the Kingdom of Scotland shall be re-delivered unto them.

XVII. That the public faith of the Kingdom of England is hereby given for the payment of the latter 200,000 l. as is hereafter expressed; That for the better satisfaction and security of some private persons of the Kingdom of Scotland who have advanced great sums of money, provisions and other necessaries during these troubles, the sum of 50,000 l. shall be paid to the said persons, whose names are expressed in an ordinance of both Houses for that effect, at twelve months after the payment of the last 100,000 l. of the first 200,000 l. out of the receipts of such monies as shall come in and be received by fines and compositions made, and to be made, with papists and delinquents estates. And that other 50,000 l. shall also be paid at the said twelve months after the payment of the last 100,000 l. of the first 200,000 l. That the last 100,000 l. of the 400,000 l. shall be paid within twelve months after that, *viz.*, two years after the payment of the last 100,000 l. of the first 200,000 l. and that out of such ways and means as both Houses of Parliament shall think fit.

Signed at Derby-House in Westminster, the 23d Day of December, 1646.

NORTHUMBERLAND,
WARWICK,
MANCHESTER,
WILLIAM WALLER,
W. PIEREPOINT,
GILBERT GERRARD,
W. ARMYNE,
ARTHUR HESILRIG,
OLIVER CROMWELL,
PH. STAPYLTON,
RO. WALLOPP,
JOHN CREW,
OL. ST. JOHN.[62]

LOUDON,
LAUDERDALE,
CHARLES ERSKINE,
HUGH KENNEDY,
ROBERT BARCLAY,

[62] Printed in *Old Parl. Hist.*, xv, 236–42 with signatures; in *L. J.*, viii, 614–615; and *C. J.*, v, 13, 36–38.

ARMY AND PARLIAMENT, DECEMBER, 1646–MARCH, 1647

Such was the arrangement made with the Scots which Cromwell signed. In it two things are notable. The first is that it does not bear the name of Sir Henry Vane; the second is that there is nothing in the Articles in regard to the surrender of the King to Parliament. That was understood; but even the signers of this elaborate agreement seem to have balked at the statement of its real purpose. None the less that purpose was clear. In the words of Charles's followers, the Scots had "sold their King." Whatever justification there was for that transaction in his own intrigues and "ineffectual wiles," in his adherence to episcopacy, or in the charge that his success would have meant "the restoration of the system which Laud had praised and which Strafford had supported," the emotions roused by this bargain between Parliament and the Scots were not to be calmed by any appeal to reason. It was interpreted by Royalists as an act of treachery and remained to embitter politics for many years.

Of Cromwell's share in it beyond his signature of the Articles there is no evidence. Nor is there any record of his part in the stirring events of the following weeks save as his activities are a part of the doings of Parliament. Even there the record is curiously dull and unrevealing. To all intents and purposes it is that of any other member of the House. On Christmas Day, 1646, a petition from the soldiers of Colonel Massey's regiment, lately disbanded by Fairfax, was referred to a Committee for the Pay of Soldiers, to which Cromwell and others were added.[63] On the next day the Lords voted a reply to the King's fourteenth letter received on the 14th of December requesting permission to come to London under safe-conduct, that they would "have no treaty on the propositions," [64] and thus closed the door to direct negotiations. The following Monday Cromwell and Sir Dudley North were ordered to bring in an ordinance for appointing a successor to John Hobart, dismissed as sheriff of Cambridge and Huntingdon "by reason of sickness and other manifest hindrances;[65] and on the 31st the House framed a resolution "to proceed against all who preach or expound the Scriptures . . . except they be ordained either here or in some reformed church." Against the inclusion of the words "or expound the Scriptures," as tellers, Cromwell and Haselrig protested vainly. The declaration was ordered printed and a committee, of which Cromwell was a member, appointed to receive complaints.[66]

Though it is generally agreed that the Presbyterians were now in

[63] *C. J.*, v, 28.
[64] *L. J.*, viii, 630.
[65] *C. J.*, v, 31.
[66] *C. J.*, v, 34, 35.

the ascendant, a week later another division showed the Independents to be in temporary control. The agreement with the Scotch Commissioners included the transfer of Charles to the hands of Parliament. The issue which arose at once as to who should be delegated to receive the captive was settled by the appointment, on January 7, of Sir James Harrington, Member for Rutland, supported by the Independents with Cromwell and Haselrig as tellers.[67] On that day, too, the Commons resolved to bring in an ordinance to settle on Cromwell lands from the Marquis of Winchester's estates in Hampshire to make up the income of £2,500 a year voted him nearly twelve months earlier.[68] With all the curious inconsistency and the regard for law which even in these times of stress and strain of revolution distinguished the English character, it was discovered twelve days later that the Marquis seemed to have only a life interest in these lands and an ordinance was demanded for replacing them with "lands of like value confiscated from papists and delinquents and not yet disposed of or assigned." [69]

Though there is no evidence of his share in great matters of policy, it appears that Cromwell was more than usually busy that month with affairs of the House. He was appointed to four new committees —one to examine a book on the Navy by an Andrew Burrell who ten months before had brought charges against the Navy Commissioners;[70] one to prepare an ordinance to visit and regulate the University of Oxford;[71] one to draw up instructions for the newly appointed judges on circuit, to bring in an ordinance to regulate differences between landlords and tenants, and to nominate judges for Wales;[72] and one to advise with the Committee of Accompts.[73] With this his name disappears from the *Commons Journals* not to reappear until the middle of April. Yet despite these minor assignments, that his absence, due to a dangerous "impostume in the head," meant much to the Independents is evidenced by the remark of Sir Edward Hyde's London correspondent at this time that thereby his party was "weaker in the House,"[74] and every division during his absence reveals the Presbyterian preponderance.

[67] *Ibid.*, p. 45.

[68] He had already been assigned Abbotston and Itchin, Winchester's only clear-title lands. *C. J.*, iv, 426.

[69] *Ibid.*, v, 44, 57. A year later he was in possession of £1680 per annum out of the Marquis of Worcester's estates. Cp. his letter, Mar. 21, 1647–8. In 1650 Chepstow was given to him. Cp. *Cal. Com. for Compounding*, and Lomas-Carlyle, i, 294n.

[70] Jan. 9. *C. J.*, v, 47. Cp. *Cal. S. P. Dom.* (1645–7), p. 512.

[71] Jan. 13. *C. J.*, v, 51.

[72] Jan. 21. *C. J.*, v, 60.

[73] Jan. 25. *C. J.*, v, 63.

[74] Letter of Intelligence, Feb. 8/18. *Clarendon Mss*, 2, 439. Calendared in Coxe, *Cal. of the Clarendon Mss.*, i, 361.

Yet though his loss was felt, it must not be assumed that it was entirely responsible for the sudden ascendancy of the Presbyterians. So long as the removal of the Scots' army was at stake and the King was in its hands, many neutral members of the House had voted with the Independents as the only safeguard against the restoration of Charles. Once the Scots had gone and the King was in the hands of Parliament, that danger was removed and they swung to the Presbyterians on the great issues which now confronted the government—and it is notable, among the other results of the Articles, that from this time the influence of Vane notably declined. It was replaced for the moment by that of the Presbyterian leaders. What Pym and Hampden had been to an earlier period; what Vane and St. John had just been to the Parliament and what Cromwell and Ireton were now to the army, Holles and Stapleton were to the House at this moment.

The first of the issues which they faced was the disposition of the King. Negotiations with the Scots completed and the money ready to be paid over, on January 26 the Parliament's commissioners with the Scots' army informed Charles of their orders to convey him to Holdenby or Holmby House in Northamptonshire. Four days later, on receipt of their first payment of £100,000, the Scots' commissioners took their leave of him; their garrison marched out of Newcastle, and with no more ceremony than the changing of the guard, the English troops marched in. A week later the second instalment of £100,000 was paid, and by February 11 the Scots' army had gone. Meanwhile Charles had set out from Newcastle on February 3, travelling by easy stages, welcomed everywhere by enthusiastic crowds and met at Nottingham by Fairfax himself. He arrived at Holmby House on the 16th, convinced of his subjects' loyalty and believing that he would yet defeat his enemies.

With Charles in their possession, the Presbyterian majority in Parliament turned to the next great problem which confronted them, the disposition of the army, whose disbandment would leave them in supreme control. Three days after Charles arrived at Holmby, they passed a resolution to disband all the infantry save that in garrisons; the cavalry having already been reduced to some 6,600 men. Their plan was simple. They feared that the army with its Independent leanings might interfere with their programme; they faced the still unsolved problem of the Irish war; and, combining these two elements, they proposed an ingenious solution of using the disbanded Independents to conquer the Irish rebels. To the discharged men they proposed to offer service in Ireland, where Ormonde had agreed to surrender Dublin to the Parliament, with the King's consent.

Having thus, as they conceived, settled the problem of the rank and file, they next struck at the high command, voting that, save Fairfax, there should be no officer above the rank of colonel in the new army which they proposed to keep on foot to defend themselves; and to ensure their own predominance, they added to this a provision that all of its officers must take the Covenant.

The success of this maneuver depended on an element of which they had taken insufficient account. They assumed that, now the King was in their hands, there was no party left to challenge the authority of the Parliament, and that their orders would be unquestioningly obeyed. But they had not reckoned on the possibility that the men thus summarily disposed of would not tamely submit to have their future determined for them, especially since their pay was so long in arrears and the Parliament seemed disposed to treat that obligation lightly or neglect it altogether. In consequence they roused the bitter animosity of the soldiers, inspired at once by their shabby treatment and their Independent leanings, so that the Independent-Presbyterian cleavage which had been so evident in Parliament was presently transferred to a breach between army and Parliament. So strong was the feeling that, unless Cromwell was misinformed, some two hundred men were raised near Covent Garden to prevent the soldiers "from cutting the Presbyterians' throats."[75]

This seemed to Charles another opportunity to pursue his favorite, fatal policy of attempting to divide and rule. With his usual incautious duplicity he proposed publicly to agree to the establishment of Presbyterianism for three years and to Parliamentary control for ten, while his private letters, which promptly found their way to Westminster, outlining his real hopes, at once revealed and defeated his design.[76] Here, then, were the conflicting plans and interests—the King, clinging to the recovery of his royal authority; the Parliamentary Presbyterians determined to retain their dominance over both Charles and the army; and the Independents resolved not to be pushed aside by the politicians in the House nor to submit to Presbyterian authority in matters ecclesiastical. On this basis came a new alignment and a new struggle among these various elements.

Apparently little involved in all of this, Cromwell was recovering from his illness, concerning which he wrote to Fairfax who, having conducted Charles from Nottingham to Holmby House, was about to move his headquarters nearer London:

For his Excellency Sir Thomas Fairfax, General of the Parliament's Armies

SIR,

It hath pleased God to raise me out of a dangerous sickness; and I do most willingly acknowledge that the Lord hath (in this visita-

[75] See Cromwell's letter of March 11.

[76] Bellièvre to Mazarin, Feb. 12/22. *Record Office Transcripts,* quoted in Gardiner, *Civil War*, iii, 215.

tion) exercised the bowels of a Father toward me. I received in myself the sentence of death, that I might learn to trust in him that raiseth from the dead, and have no confidence in the flesh. It's a blessed thing to die daily, for what is there in this world to be accounted of. The best men according to the flesh, and things, are lighter than vanity. I find this only good, to love the Lord and his poor despised people, to do for them, and to be ready to suffer with them: and he that is found worthy of this hath obtained great favour from the Lord; and he that is established in this shall (being conformed to Christ and the rest of the Body) participate in the glory of a Resurrection which will answer all.

Sir, I must thankfully confess your favour in your last letter. I see I am not forgotten; and truly, to be kept in your remembrance is very great satisfaction to me; for I can say in the simplicity of my heart, I put a high and true value upon your love, which when I forget, I shall cease to be a grateful and an honest man.

I most humbly beg my service may be presented to your Lady, to whom I wish all happiness, and establishment in the truth. Sir, my prayers are for you, as becomes

Your Excellency's most humble servant,

March 7th, 1646. OLIVER CROMWELL.

[P.S.] Sir, Mr. Rushworth will write to you about the Quartering, and the letter lately sent you; and therefore I forbear.[77]

The postscript as to the army's quartering was supplemented presently by a protest from the county of Essex against its being stationed at Saffron Walden where the troops were being concentrated as part of the projected reorganization of the forces. The Presbyterians would have been better advised to keep the regiments apart. They would have been even wiser not to have provoked them still further. But on March 8, feeling secure in their authority, they resolved that "no officer that shall command under Sir Thomas Fairfax shall be above a colonel" and that "no member of this House shall have the command . . . of any of the Forces that are now to be kept in the Kingdom of England",[78] which would have compelled the higher officers who desired to stay in the army to take service in the projected expedition to Ireland, and thus at one stroke remove them from possible opposition at home and compel them to serve the purpose of Parliament abroad. Such a provision naturally affected Cromwell most of all, and he was inevitably drawn into the quarrel with the

[77] Holograph original in *Sloane Mss*, 1519, f. 158, dated inside 1647, but outside 1646. Cal. in Ayscough's *Catalogue*, i, 193, with date 1646. Pr. in Ellis, *Original Letters*, 1st ser., iii, 319, with date 1647. Carlyle (Letter LIV) put the letter in 1647–8, but the content is sufficient to place it a year earlier. Cromwell had a serious illness in February, 1646–7, while a year later his name appears every few days in connection with Parliamentary affairs.

[78] *C. J.*, v, 107–8.

Presbyterian majority, as his letter to Fairfax written on—or more probably after—March 11,[79] clearly reveals:

For his Excellency Sir Thomas Fairfax, General of the Parliament's Army: These

SIR,

Your letters about your new quarters, directed to the Houses, came seasonably, and were to very good purpose. There want not in all places men who have so much malice against the army as besots them: the late Petition, which suggested a dangerous design upon the Parliament in coming to those quarters doth sufficient evidence the same: but they got nothing by it, for the House did assoil the army from all suspicion, and have left you to quarter where you please.

Never were the spirits of men more embittered than now. Surely the Devil hath but a short time. Sir, it's good the heart be fixed against all this. The naked simplicity of Christ, with that wisdom He please to give, and patience, will overcome all this. That God would keep your heart as He has done hitherto, is the prayer of

Your Excellency's most humble servant,

[c. March 11th, 1646-7] OLIVER CROMWELL.

[P.S.] I desire my most humble service may be presented to my Lady. Mr. Allen desires Colonel Baxter,[80] sometime Governor of Reading, may be remembered. I humbly desire Colonel Overton may not be out of your remembrance. He is a deserving man, and presents his humble service to you. Upon the Fast [day divers] soldiers were raised (as I hear), both horse and foot, near 200 in Covent Garden, to prevent [the sectaries] from cutting the Presbyterians' throats! These are fine tricks to mock God with.[81]

One thing his letter evidences, as even the Presbyterian majority in Parliament were beginning to realize. The soldiers were getting out of hand; and on March 17 the Commons ordered the Committee of the Army to ask Fairfax that his directions to his regiments to quarter not less than twenty-five miles from London be more strictly observed.[82] To this Cromwell added his own letter to the General:

For his Excellency Sir Thomas Fairfax, General of the Parliament's Army: These

SIR,

This enclosed order I received; but, I suppose, letters from the Committee of the Army to the effect of this are come to your hands before this time. I think it were very good that the distance of twenty-five

[79] Fairfax's letter from Saffron Walden and the Essex petition were both read in the House March 11th. *C. J.*, v, 110.

[80] *I.e.*, Col. John Barkstead.

[81] *Sloane MSS*, 1519, f. 129. Carlyle Letter XLIII. Mentioned in Henfrey, *Numismata Cromwelliana*, p. 181. The words in brackets are supplied where the manuscript is too much damaged to be sure what the actual words are.

[82] *C. J.*, v, 115.

miles be very strictly observed; and they are to blame that have exceeded the distance, contrary to your former appointment. This letter I received this evening from Sir William Massam, a member of the House of Commons; which I thought fit to send you; his house being much within the distance of twenty-five miles of London.[83] I have sent the officers down, as many as I could well light of.

Not having more at present, I rest,

Your Excellency's most humble servant,

London,
March 19th, 1646. OLIVER CROMWELL.[84]

How acute the situation was, appears from a letter of intelligence on March 20 that Cromwell that gone to Bury to quiet the army.[85] Whether he had or not, it would seem from his letter to Fairfax that he had not yet put in an appearance in the House since his illness. Whatever his other activities, he was not too busy to write one of those many letters so common in the lives of men like him, in behalf of one Thomas Edwards, born near Huntingdon and admitted sizar of Sidney Sussex College in 1614, two years before Cromwell entered. To the chairman of the Committee for the Advance of Money he wrote:

For the Right Honourable Edward, Lord Howard: These

MY LORD,

Your favours give me the boldness to present the humble suit of this poor man to your Lordship, whose power (as he tells me) may confer upon him that which he seeks, which is a dividend clerk's place in the Prerogative office. I have had many promises from Mr. Hill of doing the man a favour, but I hear he is now out of town. Sir Nathaniel Brent knows him. And truly that which commends him to the place is partly his merit, he having served there as an under clerk about sixteen or seventeen years, and in all that time his behaviour has been such as I believe the strictest man could not detect him. My Lord, believe me I would not put you to this trouble did I not know the man to be a most religious honest man. I have known him so near this twenty[86] years, we having had much of our education together. I dare profess to your Lordship that I believe his modesty and integrity have kept him from being preferred hitherunto. He having so good a pretence, I hope your Lordship will befriend his just desire, and pardon this trouble and boldness to, my Lord,

Your most humble and most faithful servant,

March 23, 1646. OLIVER CROMWELL.[87]

[83] Married to Cromwell's cousin Elizabeth Barrington, Masham, member for Essex, had a house called Otes.

[84] Holograph original in *Sloane Mss*, 1519, f. 152. Carlyle, Letter XLIV. Mentioned in Henfrey, *Numismata Cromwelliana*, p. 181.

[85] Coxe, (*Cal. Clarendon Mss*, i, 415) puts this in 1647–8, but it should be here.

[86] Should be thirty.

[87] Holograph original in *S. P. Dom. Interr.* A, cvi, 19. Pr. in *Eng. Hist. Rev.*, xiv, 737; and in Lomas-Carlyle, Suppl. 18.

Were it not for the fact that in public business, as in all human affairs, the most important and the most trivial incidents of life jostle each other continually for our attention, it would seem absurd for Cromwell to interest himself at this critical conjuncture with such things as these. Yet his next letters are of the same character. The first, to Sir Dudley North of Catlidge Hall near Newmarket and member for Cambridgeshire, brings to attention once more that John Hobart, sometime committeeman for Cambridgeshire, and now replaced as sheriff by this Tristan Dymond.[88] The other finds Cromwell still pursuing a place for Edwards:

For the Honourable Sir Dudley North: These

SIR,

It being desired to have the Commission of the Peace renewed in the Isle of Ely,—with some addition, as you may perceive; none left out; only Mr. Diamond, now High Sheriff of the County, and my Brother Desborow added, there being great want of one in that part of the Isle where I live,—I desire to join with me in a Certificate; and rest,

Your humble servant,

March 30th, 1646 [sic] OLIVER CROMWELL.[89]

For my Noble Friends, Henry Darlye and John Gurdon Esquires: These

GENTLEMEN,

I wrote a letter to my Lord Howard on the behalf of this bearer, Mr. Edwards, to desire he may be placed in that office to which he has been related near seventeen years. He is (I am persuaded) a godly man. I have known him above thirty years. I believe the reason he has not been preferred is more because of his modesty and honesty than for any other cause. Now you will have opportunity to right him. He is a very able clerk. The place he desires is a dividend clerk's place in the Prerogative, for which he hath so long served, and from which he hath been so long and unduly kept. He hath a family in town to maintain. I would not write thus confidently for him but upon known grounds.

I rest, your humble servant,

Martii ult. 1647. OLIVER CROMWELL.[90]

It is not surprising that Cromwell's name disappears for a time from public affairs. Whatever his position in the House and on the Com-

[88] *C. J.*, v, 36.

[89] Carlyle, App. 8, from the original once in the possession of the Rev. W. S. Spring Casborne, of Pakenham, Suffolk; a descendant of the North family. The letter is dated 1646, but there can be no doubt that Cromwell has made a mistake. The new year began on March 25th and the habit of a year made him write 1646 instead of the new year, 1647.

[90] Holograph original in *S. P. Dom. Interr.*, A, cvi, 20. *Cal. Comm. for Advance of Money*, p. 685. Pr. in *Eng. Hist. Rev.*, xiv, 738. Lomas-Carlyle, Supp. 18.

mittee of Both Kingdoms, the situation in which he found himself was uncomfortable and threatening to become impossible. The Presbyterian majority in the House was doing its best to get rid of the Independents in an army which was in no mood to disband until its arrears of pay were met. No longer lieutenant-general, with his opinions carrying little weight in the decisions at Westminster, Cromwell was at a loss to know which way to turn. His training and his official status as well as his conscience made him unwilling to question Parliamentary authority. His sympathies lay with the soldiers who had enabled Parliament to overthrow the King and though he did what he could to keep the army quiet and away from London, it was not without bitterness that he remarked to Edmund Ludlow whom he met in Sir Robert Cotton's garden about this time:

> "If thy father were alive, he would let some of them hear what they deserved; that it was a miserable thing to serve a Parliament to whom let a man be never so faithful if one pragmatical fellow amongst them rise up and asperse him, he shall never wipe it off. Whereas, when one serves under a general he may do as much service and yet be free from all blame and envy." [91]

So discouraged was he toward the end of March that he even considered taking service in Germany where the Lutherans were endeavvoring to exclude the Calvinists from the peace then being negotiated in Westphalia. The Elector Palatine's plan to request Parliament for its army to recover his estates, occasioned frequent conferences with Cromwell,[92] who saw in this an escape from the impossible situation then developing. None the less, upset and irritated as he was, he believed that if Parliamentary authority should be removed, only confusion could follow; and he protested in the House, "In the presence of Almighty God, before whom he stood, that he knew the army would disband and lay down their arms at their door, whensoever they should command them." [93]

LEVELLERS AND AGITATORS, MARCH, 1647

Many members of that House had not the same confidence, for events in the army had indicated that the soldiers were not disposed to give way without protest. Two movements had begun to combine

[91] Ludlow, *Memoirs* (Firth, ed.), i, 144–5. Ludlow places this conversation in September, 1646, but it was not until this time that there was reason for such dejection.

[92] Bellièvre, July 15/25, *R. O. Transcripts*, (quoted in Gardiner, *Civil War*, iii, 222n,) declares that the Elector had intended to ask Parliament for troops 'et qu'il avait en ce sujet de grandes conferences avec Cromwell . . . qui se croyoit lors necessité de quitter l'Angleterre.'

[93] Walker, *History of Independency*, p. 31, where it is said to be in connection with an ordinance for disbanding, but Gardiner thought the words were probably spoken in the discussion of an ordinance for raising money. Walker goes on to say the assur-

to oppose the Parliament. The first was the rise of a group or party known as "Levellers" beginning to make its way among the more extreme elements of the army and presently to develop into a formidable force. The second was the organization of the regiments themselves and the appointment or election of agents, "Adjutators" or "Agitators," to represent their interests in the conflict with Parliament over disbandment and pay. Encouraged, nevertheless, by Cromwell's pledge of the obedience of the army, the Presbyterian leaders went on with the project of enlisting the disbanded men in the Irish war. To that end commissioners from Parliament met a body of officers presided over by Fairfax at Saffron Walden church on March 21 to present their plan. But, asked the officers, who was to command; what regiments were to go; how were they to be paid; and, above all, what of the arrears and indemnity for their past services? These queries they embodied in a petition signed by many officers, among them the two Hammonds, Pride, Robert Lilburne and Okey. To this the soldiers added a petition of their own requesting payment of arrears, exemption from impressment in future wars, pensions for widows and orphans of those killed, indemnity for their losses in service, and money to meet the expense of their quarters.

To this the Parliament demurred. Cromwell, supported by Ireton, opposed it so frankly that he aroused the wrath of the party of protest, among whose members, as usual, John Lilburne was conspicuous, charging him with double dealing:

"O dear Cromwell, the Lord open thine eyes and make thy heart sensible of those snares that are laid for thee in that vote of the House of Commons of 2,500 l. (per annum) . . . As poor Mordecai . . . said unto Queen Esther, so say I to thee . . . Thou great man, Cromwell! Think not with thyself that thou shalt escape in the Parliament House more than all the rest of the Lamb's poor despised redeemed ones, and therefore, O Cromwell, if thou altogether holdest thy peace, or stoppest and underminest, as thou dost our and the army's petitions at this time, then shall enlargement and deliverance arise to us poor afflicted ones, that have hitherto doted too much on thee, O Cromwell, from another place than you silken Independents; . . . and therefore, if thou wilt pluck up thy resolutions, and go on bravely in the fear and name of God, and say with Esther, 'If I perish, I perish'; but if thou would not, know that here before God, I arraign thee at his dreadful bar, and there accuse thee of delusions and false words deceitfully, for betraying us, our wives and children, into the Haman-like tyrannical clutches of Holles and Stapleton, against whom we are sufficiently able to preserve ourselves if it were not for thee, O Cromwell, that art led by the nose by two unworthy covetous earthworms, Vane and St. John—I mean, young Sir Henry Vane and solicitor St. John, whose baseness I sufficiently anatomatised unto thee in thy bed above a

ance was maliciously given by Cromwell to widen the breach between Presbyterians and army, and that at the same time he was conspiring with the Agitators to refuse to disband.

year ago . . . O Cromwell, I am informed this day by an officer out of the army and by another knowing man yesterday that came a purpose to me out of the army, that you and your agents are likely to dash in pieces the hopes of our outward preservation—their petition to the House, and will not suffer them to petition till they have laid down their arms whensoever they shall command them, although I say no credit can be given to the House's oaths and engagements to make good what they have promised. And if this be true, as I am too much afraid it is, then I say, Accursed be the day that ever the House of Commons bribed you with a vote of 2,500 l. to betray and destroy us. Sir, I am jealous over you with the height of godly jealousy." [94]

It is in the involved and complicated events of these months that there rests in large part the various charges of hypocrisy, double-dealing or treachery levelled against Cromwell. They came from men as widely separated in politics and nature as Lilburne and Clarendon, Walker, Wildman and Wogan; from Royalists and Levellers, Presbyterians and Republicans. Beginning with the differences between the army and Parliament, they proceeded to the question of the disposal of the King, and were finally crowned with the accusation of Cromwell's having designed that end from the first with a view to making himself the master of the state.

To Lilburne's attack Clarendon added when he came to write his *History* a more definite account of Cromwell's actions, which, though it came to him at second hand, represents the current opinion of the time:

"Cromwell hitherto carried himself with that rare dissimulation (in which sure he was a very great master), that he seemed exceedingly incensed against this insolence of the soldiers, was still in the House of Commons when any such addresses were made, and inveighed bitterly against the presumption, and had been the cause of the commitment of some of the officers. He proposed that the general might be sent down to the army, who, he said, would conjure down this mutinous spirit quickly; and he was so easily believed that he himself was sent once or twice to compose the army; where after he had stayed two or three days, he would return again to the House and complain heavily of the great license that was got into the army . . . And in these and the like discourses, when he spake of the nation's being to be involved in new troubles, he would weep bitterly, and appear the most afflicted man in the world . . . [95]

The charge against Cromwell was, in effect, that he first induced Parliament to pass the disbanding ordinance by his assurance that the army would obey it without protest, and that he and Ireton then stirred up the army to resist. To this accusation his absence from the House and from the Committee of Both Kingdoms in this critical

[94] Lilburne to Cromwell, March 25. *Jonah's Cry out of the Whale's Belly*, (1647), p. 4; quoted in Gardiner, *Civil War*, iii, 226n–227n.

[95] *History*, x, 88–9.

period contributed—and though that absence was occasioned in part by his illness, it was continued long after his recovery. "Young Vane and Cromwell," says a news letter, "often forbear coming to the House," and Holles complained that Cromwell and his friends absented themselves from the Committee.[96] The story persisted, and Butler wrote years later in his *Hudibras:*

"So Cromwell with deep oaths and vows,
Swore all the Commons out o' th' house,
Vowed that the redcoats would disband
Ay marry would they, at their command;
And trolled them on, and swore and swore
Till th' Army turned them out of door." [97]

To this view Colonel Wogan lent his testimony:

"Crumwell all this whille, sate in the House, and both Houses ordered that the most parte of the army should disband or goe for Ireland, except those that were to stay in the kingdome as a standing armie, wch was to be all Presbyterians. Crumwell seemed to be as forward for this as any in the House." [98]

Clement Walker in his *History of Independency*, published in the following year, takes this view:

"To the passing of this Ordinance Cromwell's protestation in the House with his hand upon his brest . . . conduced much: this was maliciously done of Cromwell to set the army at a greater distance with the Presbyterian party and bring them and the Independent party neerer together . . . And at the same time when he made these protests in the House he had his Agitators (Spirits of his and his son Ireton's conjuring up in the Army though since conjured down by them without requital) to animate them against the major part of the House . . . to engage them against disbanding and going for Ireland . . . and to insist upon many other high demands, some private, as souldiers, some publique, as statesmen." [99]

Later in that year when the Agitators, as Walker indicates, found themselves at odds with Cromwell and Ireton, they wrote:

"We hope it will be no discouragement unto you, though your Officers, yea, the greatest officers, should apostatise from you; It's well known that the great Officers which now oppose, did as much oppose secretly when wee refused to disband according to the Parliament's Order; and at last they confessed the Providence of God was the more wonderfull, because those resolutions to stand for Freedom and justice began among the Souldiers only." [100]

[96] *Clarendon Mss*, 2,504; Holles, *Memoirs*, in Maseres, *Tracts*.

[97] *Hudibras*, pt. ii, canto ii.

[98] "Colonel Wogan's Narrative" in the *Clarke Papers*, Firth's ed., i, 425.

[99] *History of Independency*, ed. 1648, pt. i, p. 31.

[100] *A Copy of a Letter sent by the Agents of Several Regiments*, (1647), quoted by Firth in his preface to the *Clarke Papers*, i, xix.

To this again Colonel John Wildman, a leader of the Levellers, in his *Putney Projects* written a few months later, adds his evidence—or opinion:

"I shall not prejudge the singleness of Cromwell's or Ireton's hearts as to public good, in their first associating with the Army at Newmarket, but it's worth the knowing that they both in private opposed those gallant endeavours of the Army for their country's freedom. Yea, their arguments against them were only prophesies of sad events; confusion and ruin, said they, will be the portion of the actors in that design, they will never be able to accomplish their desires against such potent enemies. They were as clearly convinced, as if it had been written with a beam of the Sun, that an apostate party in Parliament (viz. Hollis his faction) did subject our laws and liberties to their inordinate wills and lusts, and exercised such tyranny, injustice, arbitrariness, and oppression, as the worst of arbitrary courts could never parallel. But to oppose a party of tyrants so powerful; *hic labor hac opus est*, there was a lion and a bear in the way. And lest mere suspicion of their compliance with the Army in any attempt to affront those insulting tyrants should be turned to their prejudice, they were willing, at least by their creatures, to suppress the soldiers first most innocent and modest petition. C. Rich sent several orders to some of his officers to prevent subscription of that petition. And the constant importunity and solicitation of many friends could not prevail with Cromwell to appear, until the danger of imprisonment forced him to fly to the Army (the day after their first rendezvous) for shelter. And then both he and Ireton joining with the Army, and assuming offices to themselves (acting without commissions and being outed by the self-denying Ordinance of Parliament, and the General having no power to make general officers) they were engaged in respect to their own safety to crush and overturn Hollis his dominneering, tyrannical action. And to that end their invasion of the people's freedom, their injustice and oppression, was painted in the most lively colours to the people's eyes, and petitions to the General against those obstructors of justice in parliament, drawn by Cromwell himself, were sent to some counties to subscribe, and then the most mellifluous enamouring promises were passed to petitioners of clearing and securing their rights and liberties, then the General engaged himself to them that what he wanted in expression of his devotion to their service should be supplied in action: and hereby their names were ingraven in the peoples hearts for gallant patriots, and the most noble heroes of our age." [101]

The matter came to a head in the Commons on March 30 with the passage of Holles's vigorous resolution that "All those who shall continue in their distempered condition . . . shall be proceeded against as enemies of the State."[102] Carried in the absence of several Independents who had left the House thinking that nothing would be done until the next day, it was a challenge to them and to the army which deepened the gulf between the two parties and between the Parliament and the army.

[101] Quoted in Firth, *Clarke Papers*, i, xix–xx.
[102] *L. J.*, ix, 115. Two months later the declaration was recalled.

Meanwhile the disposition of the armed forces became the chief concern of the Houses. The first question was the command of the troops destined for Ireland, and early in April Skippon and Cromwell were nominated by the Independents and Sir William Waller and Sir Edward Massey by the Presbyterians for that post.[103] The result was a compromise. Skippon was selected as Field-Marshal and Massey as Lieutenant-General of horse.[104] Six days later it was decided to keep several regiments in England, among them Cromwell's, under the command of Major Huntington.[105] Cromwell was present that day, on one of his now rare visits to the House, and acted as a teller on a minor issue of paying some gentlemen from Ireland £600 for their traveling expenses; to which he was opposed and forced a compromise of half that sum.[106] On April 14, he was named to a committee to instruct commissioners appointed to obtain the King's answer to the Newcastle Propositions and to consider the sale of bishops' lands;[107] and the next day the "ordinance in the hands of Mr. Lisle concerning Lieutenant-general Cromwell" was put on the calendar for April 20.[108]

That ordinance had to do with the matter of Cromwell's remuneration long since voted to him by the Commons. Nothing was done until May 5, when a commission of survey was ordered to be passed under the Great Seal for determining the value of the "manors, lands and hereditaments" in Gloucester and Monmouth to be granted to Cromwell and his heirs forever, lands which had been the property of the Marquis of Worcester.[109] To this was added other minor business for Cromwell in the House during the month of April. On the 20th he and six others were instructed to prepare an ordinance setting aside the second Tuesday of each month as a day of recreation for "young scholars, apprentices and servants" and for the suppression of the observance of "Holy Days."[110] Another committee on which he sat was ordered to examine papers entitled "A new-found Stratagem framed in the old Forge of Machiavellism and put upon the inhabitants of the County of Essex" and "An Apology of the Soldiery to their Commissioner Officers"; and on the strength of their report various men were ordered brought before the House.[111]

[103] Sir P. Percivalle to Lord Inchiquin, *Hist. Mss. Comm. Rept.* (Egmont Mss), i, 384.

[104] *C. J.*, v, 133.

[105] *Ibid.*, 137; *Perfect Diurnall*, Apr. 5–12.

[106] Letter of Intelligence in *Clarendon Mss*, 2504. *C. J.*, v, 137.

[107] *Ibid.*, 142.

[108] *Ibid.*

[109] *Ibid.*, p. 162. See *Gloucestershire Notes and Queries*, iii, 79 (1887), for details of lands acquired at this time which included the Seignory of Gower valued at £479 per annum.

[110] *C. J.*, v, 148.

[111] Apr. 23. *C. J.*, v, 153, 154; *Clarke Papers*, i, 15.

These pamphlets revealed the growing dissatisfaction of the army with Parliament, which had already taken other forms. Following the votes of April 8 as to which regiments should go to Ireland, six commissioners from the Committee of Derby House went to Saffron Walden on April 15 to confer with Fairfax on the reluctance exhibited by the soldiers to go to Ireland; and while Fairfax was engaged with them, some two hundred officers gathered in the church to prepare a statement of their case. "If the same conduct they have had"—that is to say Fairfax and Cromwell—their spokesmen declared, "might be continued also as to the service of Ireland, it would conduce much to their encouragement and personal engagement".[112] "Fairfax and Cromwell, and we all go!" they cried and the next day most of the cavalry officers and a hundred officers of infantry signed an appeal to Parliament to give them back their old generals.[113]

THE AGITATORS, APRIL–MAY, 1647

As Parliament and the army developed their positions throughout April, the issue between them grew clearer. On April 27 the Commons sought a compromise, passing a resolution by 114 to 7 to pay six weeks' arrears to disbanded men who did not wish to go to Ireland. In despair and disgust at such parsimony, the Independents, apparently, refused to vote.[114] Finally, on the last day of April, three troopers, Edward Sexby, William Allen and Thomas Sheppard[115]—two of them of some note in Cromwell's later life—arrived at Westminster with a letter signed by themselves and thirteen other troopers representing eight regiments.[116] A copy of the letter which expressed much the same sentiments as did the petition denounced just a month before, was presented to Skippon, who had accepted the post of Field Marshal, and another to Cromwell. Both copies were brought to the House which, greatly disturbed by this threatened mutiny, ordered these officers, with Fleetwood and Ireton—all now members of Parliament—to go at once to Saffron Walden to assure the soldiers that an ordinance of indemnity would be drawn up at once, that a con-

[112] *Clarke Papers*, i, 7.

[113] *Perfect Diurnall*, Apr. 17; *Moderate Intelligencer*, Apr. 15–22; Waller, *Vindication*. Holles, in his *Memoirs*, p. 239, says that Cromwell, Ireton, Fleetwood, Rainsborough and Fairfax stayed away from the army to give time for disorders to increase.

[114] *C. J.*, v, 155.

[115] Sexby, agent for Fairfax's regiment, presently in command of a regiment, died in the Tower for plotting against Cromwell's life. Allen, of Cromwell's regiment, went as Adjutant General to Ireland in 1651. (Cp. Firth's discussion of Allen's identity in *Clarke Papers*, i, 432.) Sheppard was a trooper in Ireton's regiment.

[116] *For our faithful and ever honored commanders . . . Sir Thomas Fairfax, Major-General Skippon, Lieutenant-General Cromwell*, etc. Pr. in Cary, *Memorials*, i, 201–205; *L. J.*, ix, 164.

siderable part of their arrears would be paid before disbanding and the rest as soon as possible.[117]

The concession thus extracted by force came too late to prevent united action by the troops. Sexby, Allen and Sheppard represented a new element in the situation, the so-called Agents or Agitators, who, while Parliament had haggled and hesitated over disbandment, had during April developed an organization of their own. The eight regiments of horse which these men represented had each chosen two agents or commissioners, presently called Agitators, to lay their cause before Parliament, with this result. The example set by the cavalry was followed by the whole army and by the end of the first week in May each troop or company had chosen representatives, which in turn, regiment by regiment, chose two Agitators, forming, as Clarendon observed, a House of Commons of the Army, with the Council of Officers as a House of Peers.

This was a new and startling development not only for the Parliament but for the officers, since this new party was committed not only to justice for the soldiers but to doctrines of equality and democracy which, in conjunction with the theories of the Levellers, at once supplementing and infusing the principles of the Agitators, injected a new and dangerous factor into the already too disturbed situation of affairs. In the midst of this movement, on May 2, Cromwell, Skippon and Ireton met at the *Sun* Inn at Saffron Walden to discuss the problem. To it meanwhile was added another complication. As a newsletter from one of the officers relates:

> "About halfe an houre after the afternoone sermon was ended there came Lievtennant Colonell Tubbs[118] to my Quarters, and informed mee that there was Intelligence given to him that morning that there was private orders sent by Collonell Middleton, Collonell of the Auxilliaries to the severall Captaines that commanded under his command for the being in a posture ready to rise against the Army, which he was informed should be that night; whereupon he raised his Regiment for their better securitie, and drew them to a Rendezvous; but after hee had spoke with the Major Generall, Lievtennant Generall, and Commissary Generall and informed them of the bussinesse, they came together to the Major Generall's Quarters, and satt very late about it." [119]

Under such circumstances, with the horse setting guards, with the soldiers in the town "much nettled" "and every man provided powder and bullett and kept guards with their swords drawne at the street corners," the officers debated far into the night. As a result they determined to send a letter the next day to the colonel of each regiment ordering him and one officer of each troop to present themselves for further questioning:

[117] *C. J.*, v, 158; *Perfect Diurnall*, Apr. 30; Rushworth, vi, 474–5.
[118] Should be Jubbs, who was Lieutenant Colonel of Hewson's regiment.
[119] *Clarke Papers*, i, 21–22. Cp. *Essex Archaeological Society Collections*, v, 78 (1870).

To the Colonels or chief officers of the respective regiments

SIR,

We desire you upon receipt hereof forthwith to repair hither yourself, with some commission officer of every troop in your regiment, to give unto us the best account you can concerning the present temper and disposition of the regiment, in relation to some late discontents reported to have been amongst the soldiers; and to receive from us an account of such things as we are appointed by the honourable House of Commons to impart to the army, concerning the care of that House for their indemnity and arrears. You are, with the said officers, to be here with as much speed as possibly you may, but at farthest fail not to be here on Thursday next. We remain,

Your assured friends,

P. SKIPPON.
OLIVER CROMWELL.
H. IRETON.[120]

Walden,
May 3d, 1647.

The same day the three officers sent a joint report to the House:

To William Lenthall, Esq., Speaker of the House of Commons

SIR,

We have sent out orders to summon the officers of the several regiments to appear before us on Thursday next; to the end we may understand from them the true condition and temper of the soldiers in relation to the discontents lately represented; and the better to prepare and enable them,—by speaking with them, and acquainting them with your votes,—to allay any discontents that may be among the soldiers.

We judged this way most likely to be effectual to your service; though it ask some time, by reason of the distance of the quarters. When we shall have anything worthy of your knowledge, we shall represent it; and in the mean time study to approve ourselves,

Your most humble servants,

PH. SKIPPON.
OLIVER CROMWELL.
H. IRETON.[121]

May 3, 1647.

It was at this crisis in the relations between the army and Parliament that a new element was injected into the situation. From his seclusion in Holmby House the King had followed with interest the increasing differences between the Presbyterians and the Independents. He had already presented two unsatisfactory answers to the Newcastle Propositions and amid their quarrel with the army the Houses had been engaged in amending their original proposals. Each side was making concessions and Charles's third answer was conciliatory in the extreme. It was to the effect that on his coming to London

[120] *Clarke Papers*, i, 20–21; Lomas-Carlyle, Suppl. 19.
[121] Cary, *Memorials*, i, 205–206; Carlyle, App. 10.

in conjunction with Parliament he would establish Presbyterianism for three years after which the form of church government should be determined by the Assembly of Divines with twenty additions nominated by the crown; that he would not take the Covenant until he had an opportunity to discuss the matter with his own chaplains; that he would enforce the laws against Papists and for the observation of the Sabbath. As to the militia he agreed to give its control to Parliament for ten years; as to Ireland he would "give satisfaction"; and he suggested a general act of oblivion, agreeing to approve all acts done under the new Great Seal, consent to confirm the privileges and customs of London, new and old, and negotiate with respect to royal officials on his return to Westminster.[122]

Thus as the Parliament and the army drew apart, the Presbyterians in the Parliament and the King approached each other so nearly that it seemed probable some compromise might be reached. That this alarmed the Independents and the army leaders was only natural and it was no less natural that they should also approach the King. Even while Cromwell, Skippon and Ireton waited for the meeting with the officers of the regiments, there arose a rumor that the Cambridgeshire foot planned to fetch the King from Holmby to the army.[123] That story was hotly denied by the *Perfect Diurnall* which repudiated any suggestion that the army had invited the King to join it against Parliament. Yet it would appear from various circumstances that the story was true. It was reported that such a move had come from Ireton's regiment at Ipswich, and unless he had received some such invitation it is difficult to explain Charles's letter to the army that "We will not engage our people in another war. Too much blood has been shed already . . . let the army know that we highly respect their expressions . . . "[124] Nor is there anything extraordinary in such an invitation at such a crisis as this. Each side was well aware of the possibility of a breach; as is revealed, among other things, by the fact that at this moment the Independent officers of the London Militia, a force of 18,000, were replaced by Presbyterians with the sanction of the House.[125]

THE MEETINGS AT SAFFRON WALDEN, MAY 7–20, 1647

By Friday, May 7, 150 officers of foot and 30 officers of horse had gathered at Saffron Walden to listen to an address by Skippon, urging them to follow him to Ireland. His appeal was not convincing. Less distinguished and less influential than Fairfax or Cromwell, he was a

[122] *L. J.*, ix, 193. Quoted in Gardiner, *Select Documents*, 227 ff.

[123] Relation from Walden, May 5, *Clarke Papers*, i, 25.

[124] *Perfect Diurnall*, May 8; *Moderate Intelligencer; Carte MSS.*, xx, f. 630; *Clarke Papers*, i, 27–8.

[125] *C. J.*, v, 160; *L. J.*, ix, 143; H. A. Dillon in *Archaeologia*, lii.

Presbyterian, and confessing his own reluctance to go to Ireland, he succeeded only in persuading the officers to declare that they would go with him as soon as with any one except the General or the Lieutenant-General.[126] After brief debate they separated to confer with their respective regiments, agreeing to meet again a week later. Of this unsatisfactory preliminary conference the Parliamentary commissioners sent a report to the Commons:

To William Lenthall, Esq., Speaker of the House of Commons

SIR,

According to our orders sent out to the officers of the Army, many of them appeared at the time appointed. The greatest failing was of Horse officers; who, by reason of the great distance of their quarters from this place (being some of them above three-score miles off), could not be here: yet there were, accidentally, some of every regiment except Colonel Whalley's present at our meeting;—which was upon Friday morning about ten of the clock.

After some discourse offered unto them, about the occasion of the meeting, together with the deep sense the Parliament had of some discontents which were in the Army, and of our great trouble also that it should be so, we told them, we were sent down to communicate the House of Commons' votes unto them, whereby their care of giving the army satisfaction might appear: desiring them to use their utmost diligence with all good conscience and effect, by improving their interests in the soldiers, for their satisfaction; and that they would communicate to their soldiers the votes, together with such informations as they received then from us, to the end their distemper might be allayed. After this had been said, and a copy of the votes delivered to the chief officer of every respective regiment, to be communicated as aforesaid, we desired them to give us a speedy account of the success of their endeavours; and if in anything they needed our advice or assistance for furthering the work, we should be ready here at Saffron Walden to give it them, upon notice from them.

We cannot give you a full and punctual account of the particular distempers, with the grounds of them: because the officers were desirous to be spared therein by us, until they might make a further inquiry amongst the soldiers, and see what effect your votes and their endeavours might have with them. We desire as speedy an account of this business as might well be; but, upon the desire of the officers, thought it necessary for the service to give them until Saturday next to bring us an account of their business, by reason the regiments were so far distant.

As anything falls out worthy of your knowledge, we shall represent it; and in the mean time study to approve ourselves,

Your most humble servants,
PH. SKIPPON.
OLIVER CROMWELL.
H. IRETON.
CHARLES FLEETWOOD.[127]

Saffron Walden,
May 8, 1647.

[126] *Clarke Papers*, i, 28–30.

[127] Pr. in Cary, *Memorials*, i, 207, from the *Tanner MSS*. Carlyle, App. 10.

The following day Cromwell and Skippon sent a formal request for an investigation of the letters which had occasioned their mission to Walden:

To the Eight Horse Regiments

SIR,

When we were in London there were three letters delivered (the one to the General, the other two to us, all of the same effect) in the name of the 8 Regiments of Horse, whereof yours is one; which importing matter of dangerous consequence were imparted to the House of Commons, we desire you to use your best endeavours to enquire where they had their rise, and to bring with you when you come on Saturday next the best account thereof you can, and so we rest,

Your very assured friends,

PHILLIPP SKIPPON.

Walden, May 9. OLIVER CROMWELL.[128]

Their position was, in fact, extremely delicate. On the one hand they were members of Parliament, commissioned to compose the differences with the army; on the other they were looked up to by that army as their old commanding officers; and there is something humorous in the circumstance that while Cromwell was engaged in these difficult negotiations, he was appointed on May 14 by the House to a committee to regulate the University of Oxford. So far did the Presbyterian majority seem from the realities of the situation.

Those realities were only too apparent to the commissioners. On May 15 some two hundred officers, having conferred with their regiments, assembled again at headquarters, and with Skippon presiding and Cromwell apparently sitting beside him, silent save for his opening assurance that the Field-Marshal expressed the sense of all the commissioners, the conference began. The first day was consumed in speeches by colonels Lambert, Whalley, Okey, Hewson, Sheffield and some lesser officers;[129] and at five the next afternoon when the assembly met again, Whalley presented a Declaration[130] signed by 223 officers, and one by one its supporters aired the grievances of their regiments with such heat that more than once Skippon was compelled to ask that they "hear one another with sobriety." However much they differed among themselves, their complaints were essentially the same. They wanted, first, their pay—more than the miserable six

[128] *Clarke Papers*, i, 32–33. The letter referred to is the one produced in the House April 30 (pr. in Cary, *Memorials*, i, 201) from the regiments under command of Fairfax, Cromwell, Ireton, Fleetwood, Okey, Butler, Sheffield, and Rich.

[129] *Clarke Papers*, i, 33–45.

[130] *Declaration of the Armie under Sir Thomas Fairfax, as it was lately presented at Saffron Walden in Essex unto Major Generall Skippon, Lieutenant Generall Cromwell*, etc. 1646 [sic].

weeks' arrears proposed by Parliament. They complained of the arrest of one of their number by the commissioners without Fairfax's consent; of Parliament's tolerance of the attacks on them; and demanded the right of petition to their general, of consideration by Parliament of their original petition and permission to publish a vindication of their conduct.

It can hardly be doubted that such moderate demands from men who had borne the burden and heat of the fighting for four years must have appealed strongly to their commanders. To further pacify the men, toward the close of the meeting Cromwell rose to announce that Parliament proposed to add a fortnight's pay to the six weeks' arrears already promised; asked three officers from each regiment to remain for further consultation, and appealed to the army to support the Parliament:

Speech in Saffron Walden Church. May 16.

Gentlemen, by the command of the Major-General, I will offer a word or two to you. I shall not need to remind you what the occasion of this meeting was, and what the business we are sent down about: you see by what has passed that it was for us to learn what temper the army was in, and truly to that end were the votes of the Parliament communicated by us to you, that you should communicate them to the army, that so we might have an accompt from you. That accompt is received, but it being in writing and consisting in many particulars, we do not yet know what the contents of those papers are. But this I am to let you know: that we shall deal very faithfully through the grace of God with those that have employed us hither and with you also. The further consideration of these businesses will be a work of time. The Major-General and the rest of the gentlemen think it not fit to necessitate your stay here from your several charges; but because there may be many particulars that may require further consideration in these papers that are here represented, it is desired that you would stay here a field officer at the least of every regiment, and two captains. For the rest, it is desired of you that you would repair to your several charges, and that when you are there, you would renew your care and diligence in pressing [on] the several soldiers under your commands the effect of those votes that you have already read. That likewise you would acquaint them as particularly with those two things that the Major-General did impart to you, which he had in a letter from the Speaker of the House of Peers, to wit the addition of a fortnight's pay, a fortnight to those that are to go for Ireland, and a fortnight to those that do not go, and likewise there is an Act of Indemnity very full already passed the House of Commons. Truly, gentlemen, it will be very fit for you to have a very great care in the making the best use and improvement that you can both of the votes and of this that hath been last told you, and of the interest which all of you or any of you may have in your several respective regiments, namely to work in them a good opinion of that authority that is over both us and them. If that authority falls to nothing, nothing can follow but confusion. You have hitherto fought to maintain that duty, and truly as you have vouchsafed your hands in defending that, so [vouchsafe] now to express your industry and interest to preserve it, and therefore I have nothing more to say to you. I shall desire that you will be pleased to lay this to heart that I have said.[131]

Finally, Lambert was appointed to tabulate the returns from the various regiments and dispatch a summary to Fairfax, and the next day the four Commissioners wrote a preliminary report to the House of Commons:

To William Lenthall, Esq., Speaker of the House of Commons

SIR,

We having made some progress in the business you commanded us upon, we are bold to give you this account, which, although it come not with that expedition you may expect and your other affairs require, yet we hope you will be pleased to excuse us with the weight of the affair: in comparison whereof nothing that ever yet we undertook was, at least to our apprehension, equal; and wherein, whatever the issue prove, our greatest comfort is, that our consciences bear us witness we have, according to our abilities, endeavoured faithfully to serve you and the Kingdom.

The officers repaired to us at Saffron Walden upon Saturday last, according to appointment, to give us a return of what they had in charge from us at our last meeting; which was, to read your votes to the soldiers under their respective commands for their satisfaction, and to improve their interest faithfully and honestly with them to that end; and to give us a perfect account of the effect of their endeavours, and a true representation of the temper of the Army.

At this meeting, we received what they had to offer us, which they delivered to us in writing, by the hands of some chosen by the rest of the officers then present, and in the name of the rest of the officers and of the soldiers under their commands, which was not done till Sunday in the evening. At which time, and likewise before upon Saturday, we acquainted them all with a letter from the Earl of Manchester, expressing that an Act of Indemnity, large and full, had passed the House of Commons;[132] and that two weeks pay more was voted to those that were disbanded, as also to them that undertook the service of Ireland. And, thinking fit to dismiss the officers to their several commands,—all but some that were to stay here about further business,—we gave them in charge to communicate these last votes to their soldiers, and to improve their utmost diligence and interest for their best satisfaction.

We must acknowledge, we found the army under a deep sense of some sufferings, and the common soldiers much unsettled; whereof, that which we have to represent to you will give you a more perfect view. Which, because it consists of many papers, and needs some more method in the representation of them to you than can be done by letter, and forasmuch as we were sent down by you to our several charges to do our best to keep the soldiers in

131 *Clarke Papers*, i, 72; Lomas-Carlyle, Suppl. 21.
132 *C. J.*, v, 174 (14th May 1647).

order,—we are not well satisfied, any of us, to leave the place nor duty you sent us to, until we have the signification of your pleasure to us. To which we shall most readily conform; and rest,

Your most humble servants,
PH. SKIPPON.
OLIVER CROMWELL.
H. IRETON.
CHARLES FLEETWOOD.[133]

Walden,
May 17th, 1647.

It had been suggested at the meeting on May 16th that two of the Commissioners be sent to represent the desires of the army to Parliament. On the receipt of the Commissioners' letter, the House of Commons sent a similar order dated May 18th, which was acknowledged by all four:

To William Lenthall, Esq., Speaker of the House of Commons

SIR,

Upon the order you sent us of the 18th instant we have herewith sent up two of ourselves (Lieutenant-General Cromwell and Colonel Fleetwood) to give an account to the House of the business we are employed in here according to certain heads by a report here agreed upon for that purpose by us all who are

Your most humble servants,
PHIL: SKIPPON.
OL: CROMWELL.
HEN: IRETON.
CHARLES FLEETWOOD.[134]

Walden,
May 20th, 1647.

The next day Cromwell appeared with Fleetwood at Westminster with this authorization and the written report of the proceedings, agreed upon and signed by the Commissioners at Walden May 20th:

The Heads of a Report to be made to the Honourable House of Commons by Lieutenant General Cromwell and Colonel Fleetwood in the name of themselves and the rest of the Officers in the Army and members of that House lately sent down to the Army whose names are subscribed.

1. That according to the appointment (whereof we have formerly given account) the Officers met here again on Saturday last to return an account of their proceedings and successes in communicating the votes and improving the same together with their utmost interest and power for the satisfaction of the soldiers and quieting of all distempers, as also to give a full account of the tempers of the Army in relation to the late discontent appearing therein.

2. That on Sunday evening we received a summary account in writing agreed upon and signed by about 24 of the Officers, and presented to us by

133 Cary, *Memorials*, i, 214–16, from *Tanner MSS*. Carlyle, App. 10.
134 *Clarke Papers*, i, 94. Paraphrased in Lomas-Carlyle, Suppl. 22.

some of the chief in the name and presence of the rest of the subscribers which we have now sent up.

3. That at the same time from the 8 Regiments of Horse and 8 of Foot now lying within the association the several chief Officers present for the respective Regiments gave us account by word of mouth all of them to this effect. That they had communicated the votes and done their endeavors according to order and do find their soldiers very quiet and in no visible distemper at present, but having divers grievances sticking upon them, which (they said) were contained in the respective papers then given in by them, and all of them did also expressly declare, That the effect and substance of those their grievances was contained in the said Summary then given in, except only those Officers whose distinct returns for their several charges given to us in writing are these following, which we have likewise sent up, vizt.

1. One from three Officers of Colonel Lilburne's regiment for the remaining soldiers of these three companies only.
2. One from the Field Officers and 5 captains of the General's regiment of Foot.
3. One from Captain Hall for the Life Guard.
4. One from Colonel Sheffield, his Major and 2 Captains.

To that from the General's Regiment there was exception made by three Captains and some other Officers of that Regiment, as also by 7 soldiers chosen and intrusted by their fellows of 7 Companies, who declared their grievances to be as in the Summary and have given in a paper to that purpose which we have also sent up.

To that from Colonel Sheffield there was exception made by Captain Rainborrow, and Captain Evelyn's Lieutenant for their respective Troops, and by private soldiers for other Troops, of that Regiment chosen and intrusted by their fellows, who brought the hands of all the soldiers of the Regiment to attest their grievances, which because contained for substance within the Summary we do not trouble the House withal. Colonel Sheffield replied, That he knew of no such thing while he stayed with that Regiment, but the other averred it was publicly agreed on upon the rendezvous after he was gone.

[4.] That we received also in writing other distinct accounts from some other Officers of Horse and Dragoons lying out of the Association, vizt.

[1.] One from two Lieutenants, two Cornets, and a Quarter Master of Colonel Grave's Regiment.

[2.] One from the Major and two Captains of Dragoons of the three Troops lying about Holdenby.

[3.] One from two other Captains of Dragoons for their two Troops lying in Shropshire.

But we find that these accounts were made by the respective officers without the immediate privity of all their Soldiers or the other Officers and Troops of the same Regiments, and that they had not since the former meeting here had time to draw out their Troops from the rest of those Regiments to acquaint them fully with the votes, or gain a certain account of them, the great distance of all from those of their Quarters not admitting it to be so done within that time, and therefore we have given order that the votes, together with what is since added of the arrears, be effectually communicated to them all, and a certain account to be returned from each as soon as may be.

5. That from Sir Robert Pye's Regiment of Horse (we suppose for the same reason) we have had no return from any officer yet appearing, nor do we yet hear whether they have received the votes. The copy whereof for them was (in defect of any officer of that Regiment at the first meeting) delivered to an officer of Colonel Grave's Troops for both those Regiments.

6. We have also received some other papers which at present we thought not necessary to trouble the House withal.

7. That on Monday another paper was delivered to us by Lieutenant Colonel Jackson, subscribed by himself and other officers that dissented from the rest to clear themselves from mistake or misapprehensions in their said dissenting, which we have likewise sent.

8. That since the said General meeting the Officers (who by consent of the rest had subscribed it) drew up and perfected the Summary, have showed us, and we have read over.

1. The particular returns in writing from the 8 Regiments of Horse, and 8 of Foot lying in the association out of which the Summary was extracted.

2. A request of them in writing signed by the officers that brought in the same unto them, desiring that they would take the pains to frame and perfect the said Summary.

By all which we find,

1. That those officers had good ground for what they did in the Summary, the said particular returns of grievances being full to the heads of the Summary and many of them exceeding.

2. That whereas many of them for matter or expressions were brought confused and full of tautologies, impertinencies, or weaknesses answerable to Soldiers dialect, they drew the matter of them into some form more fit for view or judgment.

3. That whereas many of them for matter or expressions were such as might have given greater offense, they did, by their persuasions with the inferior Officers and soldiers that came with them (intrusted for the rest), bring them to lay aside many more offensive things, and to be satisfied in the heads of the Summary, and therein endeavored to bring them as low and to as much moderation as they could.

4. That their end and reason for going in that method and undertaking the Summary seems (most probably) to be to gain the precedent effects, and to avoid further offense to the Parliament, so as the Army's tenderness towards the authorities and privileges of the Parliament, and the Parliament's favorable construction and consideration of the Army might seem to remove all discontents and prevent any more inconveniency.

5. That the Officers thus joining with the soldiers again in a regular way to make known and give vent to their grievances hath contributed much to allay precedent distempers, to bring off the soldiers much from their late ways of correspondency and actings amongst themselves, and reduce them again towards a right order and regard to their Officers in what they do.

6. That the said several returns do generally express a passionate sense of the scandal concerning the petition to the King, protesting against the thing and the appearance of it amongst them in a great detestation thereof and importunity for their clearing therein.

1. The same particular returns themselves the said Officers that showed them to us desired they might keep, both for their own justification in what they had done, and especially because the Officers and soldiers that brought them being all satisfied in the Summary.

 1. It was their own request the particular papers might not be produced in public to discover the weaknesses or rashness of those that sent them, which they are very sensible of.

 2. The Officers therefore conceived it might be better (if the Parliament pleased) to take no notice of them.

[7.] That though (in the charge to the Officers at their first meeting) we expressed not, nor did intend to expect to have any such returns of grievances, but only an account of what effect the votes with the Officers' endeavors had for quieting of distempers, and to know what distempers had been or should remain, to the end we might the better understand how to apply ourselves to pay them, and give the better account to the House, yet now upon the whole matter we humbly conceive, that the way it hath fallen into, the course taken by the said Officers and admitted by us (being all upon a kind of necessity as providence hath cast it for preventing worse) hath hitherto proved for the best, and may (through the goodness of God with the wisdom of the Parliament) be turned to a good issue.

[8] Lastly. That what hath been publicly said or done by us in the transacting or prosecution of this great affair hath been with the advice and unanimous consent or with the allowance and approbation of us all.

All which we humbly submit to the Parliament's better judgment and the good pleasure of God.

PHILLIP SKIPPON. H. IRETON.
OLIVER CROMWELL. CHARLES FLEETWOOD.[135]

May 20, 1647.

Upon the reading of the report in the Commons, it was at once resolved to have ordinances prepared which would meet the chief demands of the Agitators.[136] The position of the Presbyterians was now becoming desperate. They disbelieved Cromwell's assurance that though the army would not go to Ireland, it would disband if ordered

[135] *Clarke Papers*, i, 94–9. *C. J.*, v, 181.
[136] *C. J.*, v, 181.

to do so.[137] They were prepared to come to terms with Charles but were faced with the possibility that the army would not follow them. Thus they turned to their old allies, the Scots, proposing to send Charles to Scotland and with the aid of the Scots' army and English Royalists to restore the King and set up a Presbyterian church government in both kingdoms. To accomplish this it was essential to keep the army quiet and Charles's removal to Scotland a profound secret; and to this end Fairfax was sent to the army, two of the commissioners were summoned from Walden to London to report, and the Committee for Ireland was ordered to consider the time and manner of disbandment. Convinced of an army plot to seize the King, the Presbyterians talked publicly of bringing him to Northampton or Windsor,[138] and privately of sending him to Scotland; and on May 25 framed a plan to scatter the army by appointing a different place for the disbandment of each regiment and, in defiance of their promise of satisfaction on May 21, to give the soldiers the alternative of service in Ireland or immediate dismissal.[139]

The Agitators at once protested and everything gained by the meeting at Walden was lost. With growing suspicion on both sides, any hope of an understanding was gone. "I doubt," said a letter written apparently by Ireton to Cromwell, "the disobligeing of soe faithfull an army will be repented of; provocation and exasperation makes men thinke of that they never intended. . . . I assure you that passionate and violent councell which is given thus to provoke the Army will in time be apprehended to be destructive, or my observation fails me." [140]

Whether or not the wish was father to the thought, the warning was more than justified. The army and its Agitators were deeply stirred by the revelations of Parliament's ingratitude and treachery and took steps to organize against the House. The first regiment slated for disbandment was the General's and the date set was the first of June. But before the orders of Parliament could be carried out the soldiers had acted. On May 29 two hundred officers met at Bury St. Edmunds and recommended a general rendezvous at Newmarket, whose purpose was evidently to put the army in a position to resist if necessary;[141] and when the Parliamentary commissioners arrived at Chelmsford, they found Fairfax's regiment had already gone. Their mission thus hopeless, the commissioners were recalled on June 2, and each side prepared to face the fact that Parliament and the army were now definitely at odds.

137 Letter of Intelligence, May 24, *Clarendon Mss*, 2520.
138 Joachimi to States General, May 23/June 7, *Add. Mss.*, 17, 667, f. 456.
139 *C. J.*, v, 183.
140 Dated May 27, *Clarke Papers*, i, 101–102.
141 Letter of Intelligence, May 29, *Clarke Papers*, i, 111.

THE SEIZURE OF THE KING, JUNE 1–4, 1647

In this great crisis of his life, Cromwell seems to have remained in London, [142] where his son Richard, now nearing twenty-one, was admitted to Lincoln's Inn, with Oliver St. John's protegé, later the Protector's secretary, John Thurloe, acting as one of his securities.[143] There at Cromwell's house in Drury Lane near Charing Cross, sectaries and officers "resorted thither as to their headquarters with all their projections and were entertained with small beer and bread and butter," and, as this hostile contemporary notes, "No men of more abstemiousnesse ever effected so vile and flagitious an enterprise upon so just a government," as the projected army mutiny.[144] What share Cromwell himself had in this enterprise it is impossible to prove or to disprove from any written evidence. That he was fully aware of it there can be little doubt; that he was the master-mind of the whole plot it is as difficult to demonstrate as the charge that from the first he strove to sow dissension between the House and the army; but that he finally took the side of the latter and rose to power on its ultimate success is evident enough.

Amid these plots and counter-plots, with Presbyterians and Agitators each seeking possession of the person of the King and the command of the artillery, whatever share he had in the inception of the plan, one thing seems provable. It is that two days after the council of war at Bury St. Edmunds Cromwell was present at another meeting, as the Leveller John Harris testifies:

"The army and council . . . did agree and enter into an engagement . . . to employ all their force to break and prevent . . . raising another army, and to defend . . . the liberties and native birthrights of all the free Commons of England . . . in pursuance whereof it was by some persons at L.-Gen. Cromwell's . . . [house in Drury Lane on May 31] he himself being present . . . resolved that forasmuch as it was probable that . . . Holles and his party had a determination privately to remove the King to someplace of strength, or else to set him at the head of another army, that therefore Cornet Joyce should with as much speed and secrecy as might be, repair to Oxford, to give instructions for the securing the garrison magazine and train . . . and then forthwith to gather . . . a party of horse . . . and either secure the person of the King from being removed by any other, or, if occasion were, to remove him to some place of better security."[145]

[142] Rushworth, vi, 494–500; *Parl. Hist.*, iii, 582–8; Masson, *Milton*, iii, 537–538n.

[143] Sir J. Burrow's *Anecdotes*, quoted in Noble, i, 159.

[144] *Court and Kitchin of Mrs. Joan Cromwell* (pr. in *Secret History of James I*, 1811, p. 404). Mrs. Cromwell, we are further told, found herself several score pounds out of purse by this entertaining, so as soon as Cromwell's ends had been gained, she closed her doors once more and returned to her former privacy, and frugality. Later she used the piece of gold plate Cromwell received for defeating the Levellers for discharging her former expense.

[145] *The Grande Designe; or a discovery of that form of slavery entended . . . by a*

To this another witness adds that about this time there was a meeting at the *Star* Tavern in Coleman Street between Cromwell, Fiennes, Hugh Peter and others to discuss the disposal of the King;[146] and, fearing to be anticipated by the Commons, acting under the officers' instructions, Joyce reached Oxford on June 1. Its garrison, advised of the situation, refused to surrender to the Parliament its artillery and a sum of £3,500 sent down to pay them off; and at the head of 500 troopers collected from various regiments, Joyce arrived at Holmby the next day. Its guard had already been won over by the Agitators; and when the Parliamentary commissioners demanded Joyce's business, he replied that he had come "with authority from the soldiers to seize Colonel Graves . . . to prevent a plot to convey the King to London." As to what happened, the letter which he wrote "with direction that it should be delivered to Lieutenant-General Cromwell, or in his absence to Sir Arthur Haselrig or Colonel Fleetwood," [147] reveals something of his orders, his mission, his state of mind, and of Cornet Joyce himself:

"SIR,

Wee have secured the King, Graves is runne away, hee gott out about one a'clock in the morning and soe went his way. Itt is suspected hee is gone to London; you may imagine what hee will doe there. You must hasten an answere to us, and lett us knowe what wee shall doe. Wee are resolved to obey noe orders but the Generall's; wee shall followe the Commissioners directions while wee are here, if iust in our Eyes. I humbly entreat you to consider what is done and act accordingly with all the hast you can; wee shall not rest night nor day till wee heare from you.

Yours and the Kingdomes
Faithfull Servant till death,

Holdenby this 4th of June
at 8 of the Clock in the Morning.

GEORGE JOYCE."[148]

Misdated by a day, Joyce's letter expresses the situation on the morning of June 3, when, having seized the house, he handed in at the demand of the commissioners, a written statement that the soldiers were "endeavoring to prevent a second war discovered by the design of some men privately to take away the King, to the end he might side with that intended army to be raised, which, if effected, would be to the utter undoing of the kingdom." Alarmed at the possibility that Graves would return with a rescue party, Joyce and his men feared to

powerful party in the Parliament and Lieutenant-General Cromwell, etc. By Sirrahniho [John Harris?] (Dec. 8, 1647).

[146] Testimony of Wybert Gunter, a servant at the *Star*, against Peter, in 1660. *Exact and Impartiall Account of the Trial of the Regicides*, p. 157–58.

[147] Whitacre's Diary, *Add. Mss*, 31,116, f. 312b.

[148] *Clarke Papers*, i, 118–119. The letter is not directed to Cromwell but there seems to be no doubt that it is the one referred to by Whitacre.

await further instructions, and against the protest of the commissioners, he interviewed the King that night, proposing his removal to a safer place. To this Charles consented on promise of safe-conduct, permission to take his servants, and a guarantee that he would not be compelled to do anything against his conscience.

In consequence, at six o'clock the next morning, June 4, Charles appeared before Joyce and his company, who agreed to his provisions. "What commission have you to secure my person?" he asked Joyce, who, first evading the question, replied finally, turning to his men, "Here is my commission. It is behind me." "It is," replied Charles, "as fair a commission and as well written as I have seen a commission written in my life; a company of handsome, proper gentlemen as I have seen in a great while;"[149] and with these jesting words rode out toward Newmarket, stopping the first night, by curious coincidence, at Hinchinbrook, lately inherited by Colonel Montagu from his father, Sir Sidney.[150]

Such was the dramatic episode of the seizure of the King, and with the arrival in Parliament on June 3 of the news of Joyce's march and on its heels a letter announcing the failure of the Parliamentary commissioners for disbandment, Cromwell knew that flight alone could save him from the wrath of Holles and the Presbyterians. This would almost certainly be visited on his head; and Clarendon's account of his actions, however biased, describes the next step in the proceedings:[151]

"But . . . the most active officers and agitators were known to be his own creatures and such who neither did nor would do anything but by his direction. So that it was resolved by the principal persons of the House of Commons, that when he came the next day into the House, which he seldom omitted to do, they would send him to the Tower; presuming that if they had once severed his person from the army they should easily reduce it to its former temper and obedience. For they had not the least jealousy of the General Fayrefax, whom they knew to be a perfect Presbyterian in his judgment, and that Cromwell had the ascendant over him purely by his dissimulation, and pretence of conscience and sincerity. There is no doubt Fayrefax did not then, nor long after, believe that the other had those wicked designs in his heart against the King, or the least imagination of disobeying the Parliament.

"This purpose of seizing upon the person of Cromwell could not be carried so secretly but that he had notice of it; and the very next morning after he had so much lamented his desperate misfortune in having lost all reputation and credit and authority in the army, and that his life would be in danger if he were with it, when the House expected every minute his presence, they

149 *True Impartial Narration*, printed in Rushworth, vi, 513; Narrative of Col. Montague, one of the commissioners, in *L. J.*, ix, 249–50.

150 Fairfax to the Parliament, in *L. J.*, ix, 248; and in Heath, *Chronicle*, p. 131.

151 See also Ludlow's *Memoirs* (Firth's ed.), i, 164.

were informed that he was met out of the town by break of day, with one servant only, on the way to the army; where he had appointed a rendezvous of some regiments of the horse, and from thence he writ a letter to the House of Commons," explaining his conduct.[152]

CROMWELL'S FLIGHT TO THE ARMY, JUNE 4, 1647

At almost the same moment that Charles rode to Huntingdon on his way to Newmarket, Cromwell and his chaplain, war correspondent, "familiar" and "jester" as his enemies called him, Hugh Peter, who had recently been engaged as an election agent to fill up the depleted ranks of the Commons, were riding hard for the army by way of Ware. There they stopped for refreshment, and there, as was testified some fourteen years later by a witness with a remarkable memory, one of them said "They should bring [the King] to justice, try him for his life and cut off his head."[153] About the time that Charles reached Hinchinbrook, Cromwell and Peter arrived at the army rendezvous on Kentford Heath, three miles beyond Newmarket.[154] There Cromwell found Fairfax agitated by the news of Joyce's exploit,[155] and there the commanders were advised the next morning of the King's arrival in Huntingdon. At once Colonel Whalley who had already been despatched to take charge at Holmby, was sent fresh orders to conduct the King thither;[156] Cromwell adding to Fairfax's orders a message to Whalley to "use anything but force to cause His Majesty to return."[157]

Cromwell's major, Huntington, later testified how greatly disturbed Fairfax was on the receipt of Joyce's letter, and what share Cromwell had in the King's seizure:

> "The General being troubled thereat, told Commissary-General Ireton that he did not like it, demanding withal 'who gave those orders.' He replied 'that he gave orders only for securing the King there, and not for taking away from thence.' Lieutenant-Gen. Cromwell, coming then from London, said 'that if this had not been done, the King would have been fetched away by order of Parliament, or else Col. Graves, by the advice of the Commissioners, would have carried him to London, throwing themselves upon the favour of Parliament for that service. The same day Cornet Joyce, being told that the General was displeased with him for bringing the King from Holdenby; he answered 'that Lieutenant-General Cromwell had given him orders at London to do what he had done, both there and at Oxford."[158]

[152] Clarendon, *History*, x, 88–9.
[153] Dr. Wm. Young's testimony in Peter's trial. *Exact and Impartiall Account of the Trial of the Regicides*, p. 156.
[154] Wildman, *Putney Projects*.
[155] Fairfax to Lenthall, June 4, *L. J.*, ix, 243.
[156] Fairfax to Lenthall, June 4, *L. J.*, ix, 243.
[157] Berkeley, *Memoirs*, in Maseres, *Tracts*, p. 359.
[158] *Sundry Reasons inducing Major R. H. to lay down his commission* (Aug. 2, 1648). Repr. in Maseres, *Tracts*, pp. 398–9.

Huntington himself was charged—somewhat improbably—with framing the plan to seize the King and it was charged that the troopers to whom he gave private instructions could "witness how far he was engaged in it before [Cromwell and Ireton] knew of it."[159] But it is not likely that so grave a step would or could have been planned or taken by a subordinate officer without the knowledge and at least the consent of his superior officers.

Writing years later, Clarendon attributes to Cromwell a letter written supposedly on his way to Newmarket:

To the House of Commons. [June 3?]

"He had the night before received a letter from some officers of his own regiment that the jealousy the troops had conceived on him and of his want of kindness towards them was much abated, so that they believed, if he would be quickly present with them they would all in a short time by his advice be reclaimed, upon this he made all the haste he could, and did find that the soldiers had been abused by misinformation, and that he hoped to discover the fountain from whence it sprung; and in the mean time desired that the General, and the other officers in the House, and such as remained about the town might be presently sent to their quarters; and that he believed it would be very necessary in order to the suppression of the late distempers, and for the prevention of the like for some time to come, that there might be a general rendezvous of the army; of which the General would best consider when he came down; which he wished might be hastened."[160]

It seems obvious that this was not precisely what he wrote, if he wrote at all; for he must have known that the general rendezvous was ordered and that Fairfax was there or on his way to it; but, however garbled, it perhaps represents some communication to the House excusing and explaining his sudden departure, though there seems to be no further record of such an explanation.

In any event, the army commanders, like Parliament, faced a new and difficult situation; and while Joyce's letter was read in the House, and Haselrig and Fleetwood were denying all knowledge of it, the General's messenger met the royal party near Cambridge on the afternoon of June 5. Charles, though he refused to return to Holmby, agreed to lodge in Sir John Cutts's house at Childerley, some five or six miles northwest of Cambridge. The next day the army headquarters were moved to Cambridge and on June 7, Fairfax, Cromwell, Ireton, Hammond and some other officers rode to Childerley—Fairfax to kiss the King's hand again, Cromwell and Ireton to "behave themselves

[159] *Back Blow to Major Huntingdon for his treacherous accusation of Lt. Gen. Cromwell and Commissary Gen. Ireton* (Sept. 1, 1648). Repr. in Maseres, *Tracts*.

[160] Clarendon, *History*, x, 89.

with good manner towards him."[161] There was discussed the question of the King's removal, and with Joyce and Charles present to testify, it was agreed that Joyce had acted on his own initiative in bringing the King away.[162] Thereafter, since Charles refused to return to Holmby, it was determined to allow him to proceed to his house at Newmarket, by back lanes so that his Cambridge adherents would have no opportunity to express their enthusiasm or perhaps attempt a rescue.[163] Under such conditions the King went on to Newmarket; the officers returned to their headquarters; and the army Agitators proceeded with the formulation of their grievances to be presented to Parliament.

That body meanwhile, confronted with these problems, had begun to weaken, as was shown in its treatment of that irrepressible pamphleteer John Lilburne who had recently presented three petitions to the House. The first two had been ignored; the third was ordered burned; but now a fourth demanding, like that of the Agitators a week earlier, a reformation of the House and of the officials, the redress of the soldiers' grievances and the restoration of the City Militia Committee, by a majority of 128 to 112 was laid over for future consideration. The changed attitude of the Commons represented the difficulties which gathered in its path. Those difficulties were revealed in the news which reached it from day to day. On June 1 it received a letter from Fairfax containing the opinions and advice of the Council of War of May 29 and on June 3 its commissioners returned from the army to report that "it was in a distemper, and did march away from the place of rendezvous." On that same day the news arrived of Joyce's expedition. Thoroughly alarmed, the Commons voted the next day by 154 to 123 to consider the payment of full arrears and finally by 96 to 79 to expunge from its records the resolution declaring the aggrieved soldiers as enemies of the state. On June 5 the Houses learned that Charles was at Newmarket and had a message from him that he had acted under duress and expected the Parliament to protect him, the laws of the land, and its own honor. In reply, the Presbyterians secretly appealed to the Scots for aid, ordered Massey to rouse the City against the army, and, in conjunction with the Scots' commissioners, sent a message to the Queen and the Prince of Wales for the latter to head another Scotch invasion of England, which the Presbyterians agreed to support.

[161] Clarendon, *History*, x, 95. Cp. also *Perfect Diurnall*, June 10. It was here, says Heath, that Cromwell "plaid his masterpiece of dissimulation, professing himself a devoted servant of H. M.'s interest and that the strangeness of this action of the army proceeded of meer care of his person." *Chronicle*, p. 130.

[162] Newsletter, June 7th, in *Clarke Papers*, i, 124–125.

[163] For the interview at Childerley, see Rushworth, vi, 549–50; Whitelocke, p. 252; *Perfect Declaraton; Perfect Diurnall*, June 10; *Conference at Childersley*, etc.; Montague to Manchester, June 8, *L. J.*, 249–50; and *Clarke Papers*.

Thus were the lines drawn between the two parties, and it seemed that a new civil war was near. Meanwhile the army had prepared its manifestos, and at the second rendezvous at Kentford Heath near Newmarket on June 5, its *Humble Representation* [164] denouncing the Presbyterian leaders, agreed that the soldiers would not disperse until their grievances were redressed and they were guaranteed immunity for their refusal to disband. To that, apparently under Cromwell's influence, was added a request for the creation of a Council of the Army of those general officers who had sided with the soldiers, with two commissioned officers and two privates from each regiment, which should decide the terms of security and satisfaction of the soldiers' claims. In such fashion was erected a new instrument of government to set against the authority of Parliament, and in this body Cromwell took his place with Fairfax, Ireton and their colleagues. Army and Parliament now stood face to face, and when on June 7 the House was threatened by a mob of "Reformadoes" composed of former soldiers of Essex, Waller and Massey, and appealed to by the City to raise cavalry and dispose of the King's person, it voted £10,000 for the pay of the rioters, resolved that the forces destined for Ireland should be quartered at Worcester, and in general made such dispositions as it could to raise a force to oppose the mutinous army. That force was largely Presbyterian while the army, despite the fact that its Independents were a minority, leaned to that party.

THE ADVANCE TOWARD LONDON, JUNE 9–28, 1647

The initiative had now passed to the army which had already begun to move toward London. When on June 9, commissioners from Parliament arrived at Cambridge to negotiate with Fairfax and his officers, they were referred to the *Solemn Engagement*,[165] and asked to read their proposals at the head of each regiment,[166] the next morning on Triploe Heath, seven miles south of Cambridge, to which the army had now advanced. That army, more than twenty thousand strong, there referred the whole matter to the new Council of War,[167] and, under Fairfax's orders, this formidable force moved on toward St. Albans. At Royston, where the officers quartered for the night, an

[164] *Humble Representation of the Dissatisfaction of the Army . . . June 4 and 5.* In Rushworth, vi, 505–510.

[165] *Solemn Engagement of the Army . . . read and assented unto and subscribed by all officers and souldiers . . . at the general rendezvous . . . on June 5.* In Rushworth, vi, 510–512.

[166] Nottingham to Manchester, June 10, in *L. J.*, ix, 253.

[167] *Perfect Diurnall;* Fairfax to Lenthall, June 8, *L. J.*, ix, 248, and Rushworth, vi, 550–551. Cp. also *Ibid.*, p. 556.

answer to Parliament was embodied in a manifesto to the City authorities, in reply to their recent petition in regard to the army.

Though signed by all the officers, it is possible, even probable, that Cromwell, aided perhaps by Ireton, was responsible for the actual composition of the letter, as well as its general inspiration:

To the Right Honourable the Lord Mayor, Aldermen, and Common Council of the City of London: These, Haste

RIGHT HONOURABLE AND WORTHY FRIENDS,

Having, by our letters and other addresses presented by our General to the Honourable House of Commons, endeavoured to give satisfaction of the clearness of our just demands; and also, in papers published by us, remonstrated the ground of our proceedings in prosecution thereof;—all which having been exposed to public view, (we are confident) have come to your hands, and at least received a charitable construction from you;—the sum of all our desires as soldiers is no other than a desire of satisfaction to our demands as soldiers; and reparation upon those who have, to the uttermost, improved all opportunities and advantages, by false suggestions, misrepresentations and otherwise, for the destruction of this army with a perpetual blot of ignominy upon it. Which we should not value if it singly concerned our own particulars, being ready to deny ourselves in this, as we have done in other cases, for the Kingdom's good: but under this pretence, finding no less involved than the overthrow of the privileges both of Parliament and People; wherein rather than they shall fail in their designs, or we receive what in the eyes of all good men is just endeavour to engage the kingdom in a new war, and this singly by those who, when the truth of these things shall be made to appear, will be found the authors of these evils that are feared;—as having no other way to protect themselves from question and punishment but by putting the Kingdom into blood, under pretence of the honour of and their love to the Parliament, as if that were dearer to them than us; or as if they had given greater proof of their faithfulness to it than we.

But we perceive that, under these veils and pretences, they seek to interest in their design the city of London:—as if that city ought to make good their miscarriages, and should prefer a few self-seeking men before the welfare of the public. And indeed we have found these men so active to accomplish their designs, and to have such apt instruments for their turn in that city, that we have cause to suspect they may engage many therein upon mistakes,—which are easily swallowed, in times of such prejudice against men that have given (we may speak it without vanity) the most public testimony of their good affections to the public, and to that city in particular.

For the thing we insist upon as Englishmen,—and surely our being soldiers hath not stripped us of that interest, although our malicious enemies would have it so,—we desire a settlement of the peace of the Kingdom and of the liberties of the subject, according to the votes and declarations of Parliament, which, before we took up arms, were, by the Parliament, used as arguments and inducements to invite us and divers of our dear friends out; some of which have lost their lives in this war, which being, by God's blessing, finished, we think we have as much right to demand, and desire to see, a happy settlement, as we have to our money, or the other common interest of soldiers which we have insisted upon. We find also the ingenuous and honest people, in almost all the parts of the Kingdom where we come, full of the sense of ruin and misery if the Army should be disbanded before the peace of the Kingdom, and those other things before mentioned, have a full and perfect settlement.

We have said before, and profess it now, We desire no alteration of the Civil Government. We desire not to intermeddle with, or in the least to interrupt, the settling of the Presbyterian Government. Nor do we seek to open a way to licentious liberty, under pretence of obtaining ease for tender consciences.

We profess, as ever in these things, when the State have once made a settlement, we have nothing to say but to submit or suffer. Only we could wish that every good citizen, and every man that walks peaceably in a blameless conversation, and is beneficial to the Commonwealth, may have liberty and encouragement; it being according to the just policy of all States, even to justice itself.

These are our desires, and the things for which we stand; beyond which we shall not go. And for the obtaining of these things, we are drawing near your city;—professing sincerely from our hearts, [that] we intend not evil towards you; declaring, with all confidence and assurance, that if you appear not against us in these our just desires, to assist that wicked Party that would embroil us and the Kingdom, nor we nor our Soldiers shall give you the least offence. We come not to do any act to prejudice the being of Parliaments, or to the hurt of this [Parliament] in order to the present settlement of the Kingdom. We seek the good of all. And we shall here wait, or remove to a farther distance there to abide, if once we be assured that a speedy settlement of things be in hand,—until they be accomplished. Which done, we shall be most ready, either all of us, or so many of the Army as the Parliament shall think fit, to disband, or go for Ireland.

And although you may suppose that a rich city may seem an enticing bait to poor hungry soldiers to venture far to gain the wealth thereof,—yet, if not provoked by you, we do profess, rather than any such evil should fall out, the soldiers shall make their way through our blood to effect it. And we can say this for most of them, for your better assurance, that they so little value their pay, in comparison of higher concernments to a public good, that rather than they will be unrighted in the matter of their honesty and integrity (which hath suffered by the Men they aim at and desire justice upon), or want the settlement of the Kingdom's peace, and theirs with their fellow-subjects' Liberties, they will lose all. Which may be a strong assurance to you that it's not your wealth they seek, but the things tending in common to your and their welfare; which that they may attain, you shall do like fellow-subjects and brethren if you solicit the Parliament for them, on their behalf.

If after all this, you, or a considerable part of you, be seduced to take up arms in opposition to, or hindrance of, these our just undertakings, we hope by this brotherly premonition, to the sincerity whereof we call God to witness, we have freed ourselves from all that ruin which may befall that great and populous City; having hereby washed our hands thereof.

We rest,

Your affectionate Friends to serve you,

	TH. FAIRFAX.	H. IRETON.
	OLI. CROMWELL.	ROB. LILBURN.
	RO. HAMMOND.	JOHN DISBOROW.
	THO. HAMMOND.	THO. RAINSBOROW.
	HARDRES WALLER.	J. LAMBERT.
Royston,	NATH. RICH.	T. HARRISON.
June 10th, 1647.	THO. PRIDE.[168]	

Such was the retort of the new authority in the state to Parliament; such the threat to the City if it persisted in supporting that Parliament; such the conception of government which its signers held—and such the means by which in the space of a month Oliver Cromwell turned from Parliament to the army and took another step toward power. No period of his life has roused more controversy than these weeks; none of his actions has been more bitterly attacked; none of his motives has been more violently questioned than those involved in this movement. Was he, as his enemies alleged, a hypocrite and dissembler from the start; did he first lull the Parliament into false security and encourage it to mistreat the soldiery, then rouse the army to resist the injustice and ingratitude of Parliament? Was he the moving spirit of the seizure of the King? Did he encourage the Agitators secretly while denouncing them in public? Did he conspire with every element of discontent and, under pretence of upholding Parliamentary sovereignty, contrive a deep-laid plan to overthrow its power and by means of the army rise to greater heights? Did he foresee and plan the downfall of the King and Parliament alike and with infinite cunning, patient subtlety, fraud, force and persuasion, compel all parties to his will?

It is the crux of Cromwell's character and on the events of the summer of 1647 there hangs in large measure the judgment of the case. The commonest charge against Cromwell is hypocrisy—and the commonest basis for that is defective chronology. Writing immediately after the events of this summer, the Presbyterian, Sir William Waller charges that Cromwell stole away to the army,

> "after he had publicly in the House of Commons disclaimed all intelligence with the army as to their mutinous proceedings, and invoked the curse of God upon himself and his posterity if ever he should join or combine with them in any actings or attempts contrary to the orders of the House."[169]

[168] In *L. J.*, ix, 257; Rushworth, vi, 554; *Old Parl. Hist.*, xv, 431; Carlyle, (Lomas ed.) i, 266–69. The texts differ from each other in minor points.

[169] Waller, *Vindication and Answer of the XI Secluded Members*, p. 139.

In so far Waller seems to confirm Clarendon who wrote much later and, in this case, largely from hearsay; and he seems, in turn, to be confirmed by the Presbyterian leader Holles, who, writing in the year following these events, adds that Cromwell was among the officers who earlier disclaimed connection with the mutiny declaring that:

"As Cromwell did openly in the House, protesting, for his part, he would stick to Parliament, whilst underhand they sent their encouragements and directions" [to the army when the trouble first began, and even when he returned from the army on his earlier visit to Saffron Walden] "he who made these solemn protestations with some great imprecations on himself if he failed in his performance, did notwithstanding privily convey thence his goods (which many of the Independents likewise did) leaving City and Parliament as marked out for destruction, and then without leave of the House (after some members missing him and fearing him gone; and having notice of it came and showed himself a little in the House) did steal away that evening."[170]

Attacking Cromwell on wholly different grounds and from precisely the opposite direction, the Leveller, Major John Wildman, writing in the latter part of 1647, accuses Cromwell of treachery to the army, alleging that Cromwell and Ireton

"were willing, at least by their creatures, to suppress the soldiers' first most innocent and modest petition; and Colonel Rich sent several orders to some of his officers to prevent subscriptions to that petition, and the constant importunity and solicitation of many friends could not prevail with Cromwell to appear until the danger of imprisonment forced him to fly to the army."[171]

Thirty-five years later another of Cromwell's opponents, the Presbyterian Sir Harbottle Grimston, just before his death, told Bishop Burnet that:

"when the House of Commons and the army were a quarrelling, at a meeting of the officers it was proposed to purge the army, that they might better know what to depend on, Cromwell upon that said he was sure of the army; but there was another body that had more need of purging, namely the House of Commons, and he thought the army only could do that"; and further that when two officers who had heard him say it were produced in the House to testify, "when they withdrew Cromwell fell down upon his knees and made a solemn prayer to God, attesting his innocence and his zeal for the House; he submitted himself to the providence of God, who, it seems, thought fit to exercise him with calumny and slander, but he committed his cause to Him; this he did with great vehemence and many tears."[172]

[170] Holles, *Memoirs.*
[171] *Putney Projects.*
[172] Burnet, *History* (1823), i, 25.

Thus with Holles and Wildman, Huntington, Grimston and Clarendon, Royalist, Leveller and Presbyterian joining accusations of hypocrisy and double-dealing, the case might well seem proved. One may admit at once that the event seems to bear them out. Cromwell did attend the House; he did protest allegiance to the Parliament, and very probably in the emotional fashion which was natural to him and his party but gave offence to the more decorous Royalist and Presbyterian. He did maintain relations with the army. He did, at last, leave Parliament, more or less secretly, and take refuge with the army. He did take part in its proceedings and become a member of its Council; he did compose and sign a statement of its position and his own to Parliament, with whatever stronger measures he took presently; and he did, finally, through this welter of intrigue and war, rise to the highest position in the state.

All this may be granted at once; but there are two corollaries to the charges of his enemies. The first is the time element. Conditions changed almost from day to day and, naturally and inevitably, Cromwell changed with them. Had he not done so, not only would the Presbyterians have won and the Independents lost, but Cromwell would have found himself in the Tower—if not worse. The second is the *tu quoque* or "alternative" argument which though apt to produce more heat than light, has its uses. The charges of Royalist, Presbyterian and Leveller each assume that its supporters were possessed of the whole secret of truth and righteousness, that its opponents were invariably wrong and dishonest. That belief was held no less firmly by Cromwell and his friends. Whether or not it be the task of history to adjudicate between "right" and "wrong" in such a case as this, or whether it can ever be possible to so adjudicate, it is its duty to set forth the facts, and the facts are these.

There were at this moment three parties in religious questions and four parties in the state. The Anglicans adhered to episcopal government, the Presbyterians to a presbytery, the Independents to a wider liberty than that afforded by either bishops or presbyters. In some measure this division was followed in politics. There Royalists and Presbyterians joined in support of monarchy, the former unreservedly, the latter on conditions of their own. To this the Independents at this time agreed more nearly with the Presbyterians, though on different terms. Beyond them still lay the extremer schools in general classified as Levellers, anxious to break down distinctions of rank and birth and class, a true social revolutionary element. Each was deeply convinced of the profound and immutable righteousness of its cause; each was prepared to fight and die for it; and each in consequence, was prepared to use all means at its command—argument, negotiation, even conspiracy and force—to gain its blessed ends.

In this great conflict of ideas and ideals, of personal ambitions and political theories, of religious emotions and ecclesiastical dispute, with its appeal to every means of human effort to achieve its aims, high, low, intellectual, spiritual, material, the Independents won, the Royalists, the Presbyterians and the Levellers lost; and in that Independent victory Cromwell was the chief instrument of success. He wielded the same weapons as his enemies but with more vigor and success. He took advantage of his opportunities as they came along, upheld by the conviction that his cause was right and that he was supported in it by his God, of whom he was the human instrument. He was not the first, nor will he be the last, to identify himself with the purposes of the Deity or to believe that what personal ambition he may naturally have had was wholly for his cause and not for himself. For how shall God's purposes be fulfilled or justified save by the elevation and success of His instrument? If that break or fail, the purpose goes with it, and how shall the will of God be manifest to men save by the elevation of his instrument; or be interpreted save by that instrument? If this be hypocrisy, make the most of it. Nor, viewing all the evidence, can one believe Cromwell a far-seeing plotter who foresaw because he had contrived the various steps to his own victory, who perceived the end from the beginning and made his way toward it with deep cunning and profound hypocrisy. Here as elsewhere, he seems rather a creature of circumstance and opportunity, prepared, as in his battles, to know when to strike and when to hold his hand. It is true that, in the words of the motto at the head of one of his earliest biographies, 'he who knows not how to dissimulate knows not how to rule'; and it is also true that many were deceived, but rather by his silence than his speech. But it is also true that in most respects he differed only from his enemies by virtue of superior abilities and success in management of men: that had they succeeded and had he failed, the charges would have been the same but with the parts reversed.

There is, finally, one other consideration. It is that of the necessity to choose, not between good and evil as men like Charles and Holles and the Levellers conceived, but that commonest of all choices in human experience, between two evils; and it is only too apparent that this was Cromwell's situation at this time. Any real and permanent alliance between Charles and the Independents on the basis of general religious toleration was practically inconceivable. An alliance between the King and the Presbyterians, on the other hand, was possible, if not probable, and such an alliance would spell the doom of the Independent cause. The triumph of the Presbyterians would be as fatal to that cause as the triumph of the Anglicans, and no less fatal to Cromwell himself as the very words of his opponents testify. Whatever his original share in bringing civil war, whatever his relations with the army, the fact was that the soldiers had been badly treated by the Presbyterian majority in the Parliament and were on the eve of still worse treatment. Soldiers and officers alike were irritated and alarmed, and even Fairfax joined in the movement to secure their rights. The army had mutinied, the Parliamentary Presbyterians were preparing a new Scotch alliance, royal co-operation and a Presbyterian army, to put it down. They obviously planned to arrest and imprison Cromwell as the first step in the suppression of the army mutiny, and it was evident to all, not least to Cromwell himself, that another civil war was highly probable. What, then, was he to do—stay in London and be sent to the Tower or the scaffold and see his cause go down before the Presbyterian-Royalist onslaught, or join his companions in arms and co-religionists and overpower the Presbyterian-Parliamentarians before they could seize him and crush the Independents? Such was the hard alternative choice offered to him between his allegiance to the forms of Parliamentary government and the facts of practical politics. And there was one thing more. It was the growing strength of the Agitators and the Levellers; it was the possibility of anarchy.

Among these dangers and disturbances he had to pick his way, and it is evident that he found choice difficult. How slow he was to move is indicated by Sir Gilbert Pickering's testimony ten years later of Cromwell's unwillingness to be "drawn to head that violent and rash part of the army at Triploe Heath when they would not disband," and that it was not until the third letter demanding his leadership and vowing to go on without him if he refused, that he decided finally with which side to cast his lot.[173] It is only natural that his defeated enemies should accuse him of hypocrisy and treachery, but if such a hard choice in such hard circumstances be hypocrisy and treachery, what choice should he have made, or what would have been the effect on his party and his cause if he had chosen otherwise? Or, indeed, what would the triumph of his enemies have meant to England—and to him?

As Berkeley wrote of him in later years:

> "After Cromwell quitted the Parliament, his chief dependence was on the army, which he endeavoured by all means to keep in unity, and if he could not bring it to his sense, he, rather than suffer any division in it, went over himself and carried his friends with him into that way which the army did choose."[174]

That was the logic of the situation; it was the course of a practical politician, willing to be a hero but unwilling to be a martyr, especially an ineffective martyr, for his cause.

[173] Walter Gostelow to Cromwell, Dec. 3, 1656. Thurloe, *State Papers*, v, 674.
[174] Berkeley, *Memoirs*, in Maseres, *Tracts*, i, 364.

The situation at this moment was extremely critical. The King was at Newmarket still dreaming of regaining his authority, through Parliament, the Presbyterians and the Scots, with foreign aid, or with the support of the army. Parliament clung stubbornly to its claims of supreme authority. The army leaders, professing their peaceful intentions but demanding justice to their forces, were on the march toward London. The City authorities, on receipt of the letter announcing the intention of the army to occupy the capital, appealed to Parliament to forbid its approach nearer than twenty-five miles of the City. The Lords increased that distance to thirty, the Commons to forty miles;[175] but Fairfax replied from Royston that his headquarters that night would be at St. Albans, within the twenty-five mile limit.[176] The City authorities called out the trained bands and ordered the shops to close; but those orders only revealed their own weakness, for the trained bands refused to move and only the Westminster regiment and a few militia obeyed the summons.[177] City and Parliament were no longer looked up to by the counties as the chief authority and Fairfax's letter noted petitions from Norfolk, Suffolk and Essex supporting the army's cause.[178] To these was drafted a reply, which was apparently never sent, defining once more the position of the army and its officers:

To Several Counties

Honoured Gentlemen and our Christian Friends,

We suppose you have received some information from our printed papers concerning our late proceedings with the Parliament in relation to our affairs as soldiers. We mean the business of Ireland, of our arrears, the Declaration against us as enemies after so many experiences in blood of our fidelity to the Kingdom, and all these managed and carried on by a prevailing party who have abused and misled the Parliament against their faithful friends and the Kingdom's interest in many particulars. As to these things we have named, we desire to refer you to our printed papers, and the declarations we are setting forth; but the truth is, whilst these things were in agitation, that great design of the prevailing party against the Parliament and this kingdom's interest does discover itself in their transactions with us. We are unavoidably involved as subjects both, respectively, to ourselves and the public, to keep our swords in our hands. We hope within three or four days to publish a Declaration which we are confident will give satisfaction to all honest and reasonable men of our proceedings. In the mean time we thought fit to give you this brief account, that we are come near London without the least intent of giving occasion of a new war, but hope fully to prevent it. We seek not ourselves but the accomplishing those

[175] *L. J.*, ix, 256–8; *C. J.*, v, 209.
[176] *L. J.*, ix, 261.
[177] *Clarke Papers*, i, 132–3.
[178] Pr. in *L. J.*, ix, 263. Cp. *C. J.*, v, 237.

ends and obtaining those things which the Parliament held forth as arguments to invite us to undertake this war, vizt., the recovery of the rights and liberties of the subject, the opposing tyranny and oppression, the obtaining a firm and well grounded peace, and those other things which the Parliament held forth in their several Declarations, without which we had not engaged ourselves. And now, having through the good hand of God brought the war to an end, we would be loath the Kingdom should lose so blessed a fruit and harvest of our labor as we perceive some bad men are designing to defeat it of. We meddle not with matters of Religion or Church Government, leaving those to the Parliament. We desire as much as any to maintain the authority of Parliament, and the fundamental government of the Kingdom. We seek justice against those that have wronged us and the Kingdom. To which we desire the concurrence of you and all good men, and rest,

Your very affectionate friends,[179]

St. Alban's,
June 13, 1647.

At this moment a Declaration[180] prepared by Ireton, who had become or was becoming the political philosopher of the Independent group, was signed by the officers on June 14 and delivered to the Parliamentary commissioners with the army the next day. Long and confused, it was, none the less, a remarkable document. It proposed the "purging" of Parliament and some provision for ending the existing Parliament and choosing a new House of Commons. To it was annexed a charge of high treason against those eleven Presbyterian members of the House who were accused of responsibility for the recent disturbances—for the disbanding ordinance, discouragement of the army for further engagement in Parliamentary service, and plotting another war.[181] At the head of the list of the Eleven Members thus proscribed was the name of Denzil Holles, the reputed author of the declaration that the promoters of the army petition were enemies of the state, and accused of holding secret correspondence with the Queen and inviting the Scots to invade England.[182]

"Here"—with the letter of the officers to the City—Holles wrote later "they first take upon them openly to intermeddle with the business of the kingdom." Under his direction the Commons had

[179] Written by the officers of the army, but apparently never sent. Pr. in *Clarke Papers*, i, 130–2. The declaration mentioned in the first part of the letter was signed the next day.

[180] *A Declaration or Representation from his Excellency*, etc., pr. in Rushworth, vi, 564–70.

[181] *Heads of a charge delivered in the name of the Army, . . . unto the Commissioners of Parliament, . . . against Denzil Holles, Sir Philip Stapleton, Sir William Lewis, Sir John Clotworthy, Sir William Waller, Sir John Maynard, Knights, Major General Massey, Mr. Glyn, Recorder of London, Colonel Walter Long, Colonel Harley, and Anthony Nichols, Esq.*, etc. Pr. in Rushworth, vi, 570–571. Cromwell and Lambert are said to have assisted Ireton in drafting the declarations (Whitelocke, p. 254).

[182] *Old Parl. Hist.*, xv, 470; xvi, 70.

passed ordinances to enable the Presbyterian-dominated Committee for Irish affairs to raise horse and foot, the City to raise cavalry, and a new Committee of Safety was named to join with the reformed City Committee of Militia to oppose Fairfax's advance on London. The Declaration of the army which virtually asserted the right of the army to speak for the people, challenged the arbitrary power of Parliament no less than that of the crown, setting in place of both the authority of the "people." It had one unanswerable argument in its favor; it had the force; and despite the efforts of the Presbyterians to encourage desertion from its ranks, it was not only united in itself but its leaders soon won over the City commissioners sent to negotiate.

None the less Parliament delayed so long in acting upon the army's demands that on the 24th another protest was sent by the officers,[183] to which the House on the following morning retorted by a resolution that no judgment could be given to suspend the eleven members before particulars and proofs were presented. Meanwhile Holles and his party endeavored to come to terms with the King and the Scots, but Fairfax and his officers were prepared to forestall them with Charles. While the army rested about St. Albans and the various parties sought to come to some accommodation or to strengthen their own positions, the King's petition to be allowed to have with him the Duke of Richmond, Sir William Fleetwood and two of his chaplains was granted. Finally, requested by Parliament to go to Richmond, south of the Thames and farther away from the army headquarters, he agreed to move and presently began his progress to the south.

As the star of the Presbyterians waned, that of the army and especcially that of Cromwell, rose to the ascendant. Friends and enemies alike observed that he "carry'd his Business with great Subtilty"[184] and it was evident that he was the dominant figure in the army's councils. That was apparent in the business which then was the chief concern of all parties, the custody of the King. On June 24, Charles with his guards and the Parliamentary commissioners left Newmarket, arriving at Royston on the morning of the 25th;[115] and on that day Cromwell, at the new army quarters in Berkhampstead, wrote to Whalley in regard to the treatment of the royal party:

To Colonel Whalley

Sir,

Having received yesterday's vote from the House, which puts the Commissioners into the same capacity that they were at Holdenby,

[183] *Humble Remonstrance from his Excellency Sir Thomas Fairfax*, etc. In Rushworth, vi, 585–91.

[184] Whitelocke, *Memorials*, p. 255.

[185] Montagu to Manchester, June 25, *L. J.*, ix, 296.

we hold you free of all further charge, save to look to your guards that his Majesty make no escape, and therein you must be careful and more now than ever.

Dr. Hammond and the other of his Majesty's Chaplains[186] (so much desired) went through this town this morning, coming towards you; perhaps the Commissioners will put you upon it to keep them from the King, so [see?] you are exact only in faithfulness to your trust and that during that only, for now you can be as civil as some others that pretend to be more. Let such distrustful carriages be provided for by those gentlemen who perhaps will incur some difficulty in the way wherein you have been faulted.

We commend ourselves kindly unto you and rest,

Your affectionate friends and servants,
OLIVER CROMWELL.
June 25, 1647. JOHN HEWSON.

Prithee be very careful of the King's securing, and although you have had some opportunity of putting all upon others that's unacceptable, yet be never a whit more remiss in your diligence.[187]

The day after Cromwell sent orders to Whalley concerning the King, Charles reached Hatfield where he spent Sunday, June 27, and the next day news reached Westminster that he had attended divine service there according to the ritual of the Church of England. Upon this, as Cromwell had foreseen, the Parliamentary commissioners were instructed to remove his chaplains and the Duke of Richmond from his company. The Parliamentary leaders, intent on the enforcement of Presbyterianism in so far as that lay in their power, did not seem to realize the precariousness of their own position; yet the dangers which confronted them were imminent and threatening, as even they began to perceive. On the very day that Charles reached Hatfield a letter had come to Westminster from the army leaders so menacing that the eleven threatened members had requested and received permission to withdraw from the House.[188] The army headquarters had been advanced to Uxbridge, within striking distance of London. On the 28th the officers replied to the Parliament's request for its terms by demanding the abandonment of its warlike preparations, its negotiations with the Scots and the Continent, its encouragement of desertion from the army; the payment of the soldiers till a settlement was reached; and an agreement not to bring the King nearer London than the place of the army headquarters was distant from the capital.

[186] Dr. Henry Hammond, uncle of Colonel Robert, and one of the King's favorite chaplains, was a canon of Christ Church, Oxford. The other chaplain was Dr. Gilbert Sheldon, afterwards Archbishop of Canterbury. Both were ejected in 1648 and imprisoned.

[187] *Clarke Papers*, i, 140; Lomas-Carlyle, Suppl. 23.

[188] *C. J.*, v, 225.

ARMY NEGOTIATIONS WITH THE KING, JULY 1–16, 1647

For the moment the proceedings against the eleven members was postponed, and, agreeing to a request for a conference, on July 1 Fairfax appointed ten of the chief officers, including Cromwell, to meet with Parliamentary commissioners at the *Katherine Wheele* Inn the next morning and from time to time thereafter to discuss the *Humble Remonstrance*.[189] With these negotiations under way, the army removed to Reading, and the King, first going to Windsor, was presently established in Lord Craven's house at Caversham just across the river from the army. The army leaders were the more moved to discuss the situation with the King personally because their own disputes with the Parliament had led them to believe that it might not be the King's fault if he had not succeeded in satisfying the Presbyterians. They were soon undeceived. The King still talked as if he could impose his will on Parliament and army alike; till Ireton, irritated by this, bluntly declared, "Sir, you have an intention to be the arbitrator between the Parliament and us; and we mean to be it between your Majesty and the Parliament."[190] In those few words he summed up the whole issue; and, feeling unequal to negotiating with the King, he and his colleagues sought a Royalist intermediary to assist them in the task.

This they found in the person of Sir John Berkeley, sometime governor of Exeter which he had surrendered to Fairfax and Cromwell some fourteen months before, honored by them and trusted by Charles, and now returning from France commissioned by the Queen to discover the army's intentions toward the King. On July 3, Sir Allen Apsley, last Royalist governor of Barnstaple which had surrendered a few days after Exeter, was given a pass to go to France,[191] and on the way thither he met Berkeley at Tunbridge. "He told me," Berkeley explains in his *Memoirs*, "that he was going to me from Cromwell and some other officers of the Army with letters and a cypher and instructions."[192] To this Berkeley added his version of a letter from Cromwell which Apsley gave him:

To Sir John Berkeley

'That he should desire me to remember that, in some conferences with Colonel Lambert, and other officers of the Army, upon the rendering of Exeter, I had taken notice of the Army's bitter inveighing against the King's

[189] Commission printed in *L. J.*, ix, 312.

[190] Berkeley's *Memoirs*, Maseres' *Tracts*, p. 360.

[191] *L. J.*, ix, 313.

[192] Memoirs of Sir John Berkeley, repr. from 1699 edition, in Maseres, *Tracts*, pp. 355–394. How Apsley, believing Berkeley to be in France, chanced to encounter him at Tunbridge is not pointed out.

person, as if he had been the worst of men, and their excessive extolling the Parliament; both which being without any colour of ground, I had concluded, that those discourses were not out of any persuasion of mind, but affected to prepare men to receive the alteration of Government, which they intended that the Parliament should effect, by the assistance of the Army; which I had said, was not only a most wicked, but a very difficult, if not an impossible, design, for a few men, not of the greatest quality, to introduce a popular Government against the King and his party, against the Presbyterians, against the nobility and gentry, against the laws established, both ecclesiastical and civil, and against the whole genius of the nation, that had been accustomed, for so many ages, to a monarchical government. Whereas, on the other side, if they would but consider, that those of their party had no particular obligations to the crown, (as many of the Presbyterians had) and therefore ought less to despair of his Majesty's grace and favour;—that, under that pretext, they had deceived many well-meaning men, and had brought great things to pass; but that now the mask was taken off, and they were discovered to have sought their own advantages—and, at the same time, that the power to do themselves much good, or much hurt to others, was now almost wrested out of their hands; and that this had been done by the Independent Party, who could establish themselves, no way under Heaven, so justly and prudently, as by making good what the Presbyterians had only pretended to do, that is, the restoring King and People to their just and ancient rights; which would so ingratiate them with both, that they would voluntarily invest them with as much trust and power as subjects are capable of: Whereas, if they grasped at more, it would be with the general hatred, and with their own destruction. To this discourse of mind, they now informed me that, at that time, they had only given a hearing, but no consent, as proceeding from an interest much divided from theirs: but that they had since found, by experience, all, or the most part, of it, to be so reasonable, that they were resolved to put it in practice, as I might perceive by what had already passed. They desired for the present nothing of me, but that I would present them humbly to the Queen and Prince, and be suitor to them in their names, not to condemn them absolutely, but to suspend their opinions of them, and their pretensions towards his Majesty, and judge them rather by their future behavior; of the innocence whereof they had already given some testimonies to the world, and would do more and more, daily. When I should have done this office, they desired I would come over into England, and become an eye-witness of their proceedings."[193]

Under such conditions and in such a mood, one after another, the officers crossed to Caversham to confer with Charles. Taking the lead in these negotiations, with Fairfax's approval, Cromwell interviewed the King on July 4 with such apparent satisfaction to both parties that it was openly predicted by the army leaders that an understanding would be reached in a fortnight.[194] According to Major Hunting-

[193] Berkeley's *Memoirs*, pp. 356–8.

[194] Letter of Intelligence, *Clarendon Mss*, 2544; Coxe, *Cal. of Clar. Papers*, i, 382; *Clarke Papers*, i, 148; Bell, *Memorials*, i, 343–371.

ton, Cromwell and Ireton continually solicited Charles by messengers proffering anything he should desire—access of letters, servants, chaplains, friends, wife, children and revenue. The French ambassador whom they met at Caversham on July 9, reported that Fairfax and Cromwell seemed willing even to tolerate Roman Catholics,[195] and it appeared that if Charles could be persuaded to any "reasonable" constitutional settlement there was no question of his restoration. The reason for this was obvious. To St. John's advice not to do the King's business too fast, Cromwell replied that it could not be helped because the army was so inclined to the King.[196] In him they saw an opportunity denied them by Parliament, and with his authority and their own force a settlement of their grievances and the kingdom's affairs seemed easy of accomplishment.

The officers appear to have urged no personal aggrandizement of any of their numbers, a circumstance so suspicious to Charles that—save for Huntington—he mistrusted them all.[197] Either at Caversham or two days later at army headquarters, Bellièvre questioned Cromwell as to this extraordinary phenomenon, and, as the ambassador reported, Cromwell replied with a cryptic saying, "No one rises so high as he who knows not whither he is going," which, reported later to the French minister de Retz, moved him to say, unwisely, that he "knew he [Cromwell] was a fool."[198]

While these negotiations went on at Caversham, events outside grew more and more disquieting. News came of the efforts of the Presbyterians in Parliament to raise troops in London, of Poyntz's plan to put the Northern Army in Scotch hands.[199] Intercepted letters to Scotland increased their fears; and on July 6 a delegation from the army appeared at the door of the House to demand the impeachment of the eleven members.[200] To this the Commons after some days of debate replied on July 12 by an order to the accused members to bring in their answer after a week's time. Meanwhile England was flooded with pamphlets in a new paper war. Much of it Walker attributed to Cromwell and his party endeavoring to lull the people into a sense of security "till the grandees had wrought their will on City and Houses."[201] The Presbyterians attacked Cromwell personally; but he was disdainful of their charges that he was a hypo-

[195] Newsletter, July 16/26, *Roman Transcripts* R. O., quoted by Gardiner.

[196] Huntington, *Sundry Reasons* (Maseres, *Tracts*, p. 400); Letter of Intell., *Clar. Mss*, Coxe, *Calendar*, i, 383.

[197] Berkeley, *Memoirs*, p. 361.

[198] De Retz, *Memoires* (1859), iii, 242.

[199] *Clarke Papers*, i, 167.

[200] *A Particular Charge of Impeachment.*" In *Old Parl. Hist.* xvi, 70–92.

[201] Walker, *History of Independency*, pp. 36–37.

crite and a loose liver, asking an officer who complained of this,[202] "If . . . we shall quarrel with every dog in the street that barks at us and suffer the kingdom to be lost with such a fantastical thing?"[203] Meanwhile the army grew more and more restive and the Agitators began to demand a march on London as the only way to settle the dispute.

It was at this moment that on July 12, the day that the Commons gave the eleven members a week to prepare their answer to the charge of treason, Sir John Berkeley reached Reading to be met by an officer, some hours after his arrival, with Cromwell's excuses for not seeing him until ten that evening when the Committee of Parliament would adjourn. At that time Cromwell, with Rainsborough and Sir Hardress Waller, made his appearance and, after some generalities, Berkeley explained that the Queen's instructions had been to persuade Charles to accede to the army's demands in so far as his conscience and honor would permit. To that Cromwell replied, according to Berkeley,

> "that whatever this world might judge of them, they would be found no seekers of themselves farther than to have leave to live as subjects ought to do, and to preserve their consciences; and that they thought no men could enjoy their lives and estates quietly without the King had his rights, which they had declared in general terms already to the world, and would more particularly very speedily, wherein they would comprise the several interests of the Royal, Presbyterian and Independent parties, as far as they were consisting with each other."[204]

Convinced of the desire of Cromwell and Ireton to reach an agreement with the King and of the Agitators' error in doubting their sincerity, Berkeley entered upon his hopeless task. The next day, following Cromwell's directions, he called upon Fairfax to obtain permission to see the King. Three days later, at Caversham, Cromwell told Berkeley with tears in his eyes that he had witnessed "the tenderest sight that ever his eyes beheld"—the meeting of Charles and his three youngest children. The King, he said, "was the uprightest and most conscientious man of his three kingdoms" and "the Independents were under infinite obligations to him for having rejected the Scots' propositions at Newcastle, which his Majesty's interest seemed to invite him to"; and, says Berkeley, he "concluded

[202] *Works of Darkness Brought to Light; Remonstrance of the Young Men and Apprentices;* Lilburne, *Jonah's Cry out of the Whale's Belly*, or *Certain Epistiles to Oliver Cromwell and John Goodwin.*

[203] *Clarke Papers*, i, 205.

[204] Berkeley's *Memoirs*, pp. 360–361.

with me by wishing that God would be pleased to look upon him according to the sincerity of his heart towards his Majesty".[205]

None the less the negotiations hung fire. At times Cromwell assured Berkeley that he wished the King would be more frank, at times that he wished Ireton would hasten the completion of the proposals and make the terms easier for Charles to accept;[206] but at no time does it appear that he impressed Berkeley as a hypocrite, though others were not then nor thereafter so convinced as Berkeley of Cromwell's sincerity.

It was no wonder that men were suspicious of him and of each other. Rumors multiplied of forces being collected against the army. Poyntz was arrested by his own men and the news was sent to Reading at this juncture, but Fairfax at once ordered his release. Though the Commons passed an ordinance to expel the "reformadoes" of Essex's, Waller's, and Manchester's armies from London, it was hard to drive them out, especially since the City had begun to sympathize with the Parliament. To conciliate the apprentices, an ordinance giving them, with scholars and servants, a holiday on the second Tuesday of each month passed the House. In return the grateful apprentices on their first holiday, which fell on the 15th, petitioned for the suppression of conventicles, for the restoration of the King, the maintenance of the Covenant and the disbandment of the army. Such circumstances, with the increasing fear of Scotch invasion backed by the Presbyterians, served to further irritate the army, and these, with the delay in the negotiations, strengthened the demand of the Agitators for a march on the City. To quiet the disturbance, there was ordered finally a "Council of War" at Reading on July 16, which, in effect, resolved itself into a general debate on the whole situation at the time and, taking wider range, the whole foundation of English government.

PART II

THE ARMY COUNCILS

THE MEETING AT READING, JULY 16–17, 1647

The "General Council of War" [207] called for the morning of July 16 to consider the demands of the Agitators for a march on London was, as the event was to prove, a turning-point in the affairs of England, of Charles and of Oliver Cromwell. To it were summoned officially

[205] *Ibid.*, p. 365.
[206] *Ibid.*, p. 364.
[207] So called, though it was really a Council of the Army.

under the presidency of Fairfax, Lieutenant-General Cromwell, Commissary-General Ireton, Lieutenant-General Hammond, Adjutant-Generals Deane, Evelyn and Tulidah, Quartermaster-General Grosvenor, thirteen colonels,[208] three lieutenant-colonels, seven majors, nineteen captains and two lieutenants, in all fifty-two officers. It would appear from a newsletter of the day following the meeting that there were more than that number present, for the writer speaks of "above 100 officers besides Agitators, who now in prudence we admitt to debate." The meeting itself and especially the admission of the Agitators reveals the critical situation confronting the officers and the reasons for calling the council. As the writer of the newsletter—probably John Rushworth—says:

"It is not more than necessary they [the Agitators] should be [admitted] considering the influence they have upon the souldiers, . . . and . . . it is the singularest part of wisdom in the General and the officers so to carry themselves considering the present temper of the Army, so as to be unanimous in the Councills, including the new persons into their number. It keeps a good accord, and obtains ready obedience, for to this hour never any troop or company yet mutiny'd, and if a man consider the alterations of officers that are now admitted, and interests of officers that are gone, it is the greatest wonder that there is unanimity still . . . think it not strange if it should be advised to march nearer to London, as an expedient to obtain satisfaction . . . in declaring against forreign forces coming in, the putting reformado's out of the line, and suspending the 11 members . . . to putt the Militia of the Citty of London into the same hands it was before . . . Tho' this was much prest with reasons and earnestness by the Agitators, yet the Generall and the Officers after many houres debate so satisfy'd them . . . that they submitted it to the Generall and Officers . . ."[209]

The Council of War at Reading, July 16, 1647

The debate was, as this reporter says, long and animated and in it Cromwell took a leading part. It began, in fact, according to our account of it from the pen of William Clarke, assistant to Rushworth, the Secretary to the General and Council of War, with a motion by Cromwell for a committee, "many thinges then nott being fitt for debate, and the Councill of Warre to be adjourned till the afternoone." That motion being apparently defeated, the debate began. Throughout the morning, in spite of Cromwell's continued efforts to adjourn in order to consider the matter more at length, it turned on the question of an immediate march to London, to which Cromwell was strongly opposed, and was seconded in this by Rainsborough.

[208] Whalley, Rainsborough, Lambert, Sir H. Waller, Okey, Scroope, Tomlinson, Fleetwood, Harrison, Pride, Barkstead, Horton, Rich.

[209] *Clarke Papers*, i. 214–5.

Against them the Agitators, Allen in particular and others like Major Tulidah, urged immediate and direct action. As Clarke reports the debate, it ran somewhat as follows:[210]

Commissary-General Ireton demurred to any delay, and urged the consideration at once of the point whether the army should march to London or no; on which Major Tulidah declared that all the proposals would be of no effect without a march to London.

Lieut.-Gen. Cromwell: "Marching up to London is a single proposal, yet it does not drop from Jupiter, as that it should be presently received and debated without considering our reasons. For I hope this [temper] will ever be in the Agitators—I would be very sorry to flatter them—I hope they will be willing that nothing should be done but with the best reason and with the best and most unanimous concurrence. Though we have this desire backed with such reasons, certainly it was not intended [to say] we had no reason to weigh those Reasons; for I think we shall be left to weigh these Reasons. All this paper is filled with Reasons; the dissatisfaction in particulars; the disadvantages of removal from London; the advantages of marching towards London. You are ripe for a conclusion and get a conclusion; but let this be offered to the General and Council of War."

Col. Rainborowe prayed for a little time, in order to come prepared with other reasons. Ireton urged that the great point was not to get power into one man's hands more than another, but to settle the liberties of the kingdom, and to show what the army would do with the power when they got it.

Lieut.-Gen. Cromwell: "I desire we may withdraw and consider. Discourses of this nature will, I see, put power into the hands of any[211] that cannot tell how to use it, of those that are like to use it ill. I wish it with all my heart in better hands, and I shall be glad to contribute to get it into better hands. If any man or company of men will say that we do seek ourselves in doing this, much good may it do him with his thoughts. It shall not put me out of my way. The meeting at six o'clock. It is not to put an end to this business of meeting,[212] but I must consult with myself before I consent to such a thing,[213] but really to do such a thing [I must consult] before I do it. And whereas the Commissary[214] does offer that these things were desired before satisfaction be given to the public settlement,[215] there may be a conveniency of bringing in that to the Council of War next sitting, if it be ready and thought fit to be brought in. If these other things be in

[210] Firth prints the entire speeches in his edition of the *Clarke Papers;* Mrs. Lomas printed only Cromwell's with so much of the substance of the others as is needed to link Cromwell's together. In general this account of the speeches follows that of Mrs. Lomas in her edition of Carlyle.

[211] Probably "many," or "some."

[212] "Marching"?

[213] *i.e.*, marching on London.

[214] Ireton.

[215] *i.e.*, that new things are being brought up before the main point (satisfaction to the kingdom) is decided.

preparation we may bring them in that we may not be to seek for a Council of War if we had our business ready."

CAPTAIN CLARKE believed that they all sought the good of the kingdom and had no intention of beginning a fresh war. MR. ALLEN urged that they should not stand idle while they discussed matters, but ought at once to take the power out of the hands of those who might destroy the kingdom. IRETON reiterated his argument that not quarrelling with others but the satisfaction of the kingdom was the main point, and after two or three other speeches, the Council adjourned.

In some measure, at least, Cromwell had his way, for the morning meeting adjourned with the appointment of a committee of eighteen men representing the two parties, on which, among others, he sat with Ireton and their supporters, and on the other side the Agitators including Sexby and Allen, to "looke over the Engagements" before proceeding with the arguments. Again when the Council met in the afternoon, he began the session with a discussion of the "paper" which had occasioned the meeting:

LIEUT.-GEN. CROMWELL: "If you remember, there are in your paper five particulars that you insist upon. Two of them are things new, that is to say, things that yet have not been at all offered to the Parliament or their commissioners, that is the second and the fourth.[216] The second, which concerns the Militia of the city, and the fourth which concerns the release of those prisoners that you have named in your paper, and those that are imprisoned in the several parts of the kingdom, of whom likewise you desire a consideration might be had now the judges are riding their circuits.

To the first [we give you] this account: that upon your former paper delivered[217] and upon the weight and necessity of the thing, there has been a very serious care taken by the General, he having, as I told you to-day, referred the preparing of somewhat for the Parliament concerning that to Col. Lambert and myself; and an account of that has been given to the General at our meeting in the inner room; and if it please you, that which has been in preparation may be read together with the Reasons of it. That paper that now it is desired may be read to you is part of it an answer to a former paper that was sent to the Commissioners concerning the excluding of the Reformadoes out of the lines of communication, and the purging of the House of Commons, and the discharging or sending away into Ireland the men that had deserted the army. The General did order a paper to that purpose to be sent to the Commissioners; and that paper that now is to be read to you of a reply to the Commissioners; and there is an addition of this business concerning the Militia, with the Reasons to enforce the desire of it."

[216] 2nd. That the Militia of the City of London be returned into the hands "of those in whom it lately was," etc.

4th. That all prisoners illegally committed be set at liberty and reparation given them—Lilburne, Musgrave and others named. The *Representation* is printed in the *Clarke Papers*, i, 170.

[217] The paper on the London Militia presented on July 6.

The Papers Read[218]

Lieut.-Gen. Cromwell: "Care taken of all them only two, which are concerning the suspending of the eleven members[219] and the discharging of prisoners.

I am commanded by the General to let you know in what state affairs stand between us and the Parliament and into what way all things are put. Tis very true that you urge in your papers, concerning that effect that an advancing towards London may have, and of some supposed inconveniences that our drawing back thus far may bring upon us; but I shall speak to that presently. Our businesses they are put into this way, and the state of our business is this: We are now endeavouring as the main of our work to make a preparation of somewhat that may tend to a general settlement of the peace of the kingdom and of the rights of the subject, that Justice and Righteousness may peaceably flow out upon us. That's the main of our business. These things are but preparatory things to that that is the main; and you remember very well that this, that is the main work of all, was brought to some ripeness. The way that our business is in is this: for the redressing of all these things it [is] a treaty, a treaty with Commissioners sent from the Parliament down hither, to the end that an happy issue may be put to all these matters that so much concern the good of the kingdom, and therein our good is so that they must be finished in the way of a treaty. The truth of it is, you are all very reasonably sensible, that if those things were not removed that we think may lose us the fruit of a treaty, and the fruit of all our labours, it's in vain to go on with a treaty, and it's dangerous to be deluded by a treaty. And therefore I am confident of it, that lest this inconveniency should come to us, lest there should come a second war, lest we should be deluded by a long treaty, your zeal hath been stirred up to express in your paper that there is a necessity of a speedy marching towards London to accomplish all these things. Truly I think that possibly that may be that that we shall be necessitated to do. Possibly it may be so; but yet I think it will be for our honour and our honesty to do what we can to accomplish this work in the way of a treaty. And if I were able to give you all those reasons that lie in the case I think it would satisfy any rational man here. For certainly that is the most desirable way, and the other a way of necessity, and not to be done but in way of necessity. And truly, instead of all reasons, let this serve; that whatsoever we get by a treaty, whatsoever comes to be settled upon us in that way, it will be firm and durable, it will be conveyed over to posterity, as that that will be the greatest honour to us that ever poor creatures had, that we may obtain such things as these are which we are now about. And it will have this in it too, that whatsoever is granted in that way, it will have firmness in it. We shall avoid that great objection that will lie against us, that we have got things of the Parliament by force, and we know what it is to have that stain lie upon us. Things, though never so good, obtained in that way, it will exceedingly

[218] *Book of Army Declarations*, p. 77, paper entitled *An Answer to the Commissioners of the Army*, etc.

[219] That the eleven members impeached by the army "be forthwith sequestered and disenabled from sitting in the House."

weaken the things, both to ourselves and to all posterity; and therefore I say, upon that consideration, I wish we may be well advised what to do. I speak not this that I should persuade you to go about to cozen one another; it was not in the General's, nor any of our hearts.

[You demand] that we that are Commissioners should be very positive and peremptory to have these things immediately granted, I believe, within the compass of that time which your papers mention, within so many days. And for the other two things that they take no care of, that is the members impeached [and the prisoners] these are two additional[s] which will be likewise taken care of to be considered and answered, not with words and votes, but with content and action. For there needs no more of our representing of them than these papers that have been read. In effect there hath been consideration had of the matters in your papers. And if these be not granted in a convenient time and answer given by the way proposed[220] you are yet put in such a way, in taking such a course of doing things as you have proposed sooner than that we could not have put ourselves into a posture of doing.[221]

I hope in God that if we obtain these things in this way we propose to you, and [in] this convenient time, that we shall think ourselves very happy that we have not gone any other way for the obtaining them. That which we seek [is] to avoid the having of a second war and the defeating of those [things] that are so dear to us, whose interest ought to be above our lives to us. If we find anything tending that way to delay us or disappoint us of those honest things we are to insist upon, I hope it cannot nor shall not be doubted that the General nor any of us will be backward for the accomplishment of those things we have proposed. It remains that you have some short account, as the time will bear, of that that has been so long in preparation, which is that that tends to the General Settlement, and the General hath commanded the Commissary to let you have a brief state of that."

Captain Clarke here objected that the "way of treaty" would be too dilatory; that the great thing was to remove corrupt persons from power and place men of known integrity in their room, and that they [the army] were very desirous that the paper presented to his Excellency might be represented [to Parliament] as immediately from them, and from this honourable Council and by the Agitators, which they conceived would put vigour and strength into the business and effect what was so earnestly desired.

Lieut.-Gen. Cromwell: "I may very easily mistake that which the other officer offered to your Excellency. Two particulars which might receive retardment or obstruction by carrying them on in a way of treaty, I mentioned indeed, particulars which were that of the eleven members and that of the prisoners, and meant that those[222] should go as the sense of the whole army. He conceives it will add more vigour and strength to the desire and make

[220] The two clauses here are inverted.

[221] Cromwell's meaning appears to be that if the Parliament refuse, they will, by their refusal, give the army a better reason for taking another course than any that the army could have found for itself. This seems to be referred to by Allen when he says "The Lieut-Genl hath exprest that if things be not ended in such a way, then there is a ground to go on in some other way."

[222] The MS. has "means by those that."

our desires more easily granted [to] present not only those but all the rest [as the sense of the whole army]. If it be so all the rest will be obstructed if they go by way of treaty. There may be perhaps some mistake or forgetfulness in that which I offered to you. I think truly there is no objection lies in that which is said. For, so far as I know and discern of these things and the way of management of them, if we convey [this paper] to the Commissioners and by them to the Parliament as the sense of the whole [army] represented by the Agitators to the General and assented to by the Council of War, and it so becomes the sense not only of the army that is the offended part but also [of] the commanding part of it; and [if] we represent it to them with that positiveness that hath been spoken of, to be sent up to London, to which we desire an answer, and expect an answer within some few days, that is to say, within so short a time as they can have it consulted, we may call this a treaty, but I think it signifies nothing else but what that gentleman speaks of.[223] Therefore for my part I think they differ in nothing but in words and not in substance.

"I suppose there are resolutions not to enter upon a further treaty till we have an answer to these things, and if you have patience to hear that which is offered you to be acquainted with from the Commissary General, I suppose that business may be so disposed of.[224] Therefore I shall desire that if it please the General that you may[225] have an account of that other business by the Commissary General."

Mr. Allen assured the General that they were satisfied that he and his Council had endeavoured to manage affairs with care and fidelity, but this made it the sadder that the Parliament gave so little care to them. Truly a treaty would have been an honourable way, but they had waited so long that their patience was expended. "The Lieut.-General hath expressed, that if things be not ended in such a way, then there is a ground to go on in some other way." It was in most of their thoughts that those they had been treating with did not intend to conclude things in such a way, and that perhaps God had allowed them to act thus, in order to show to the army the need of using another way to attain them. They believed that the presentation of their proposals and the advance of the army would be the most likely way to obtain the answer to those things which they desired, while delay brought danger every day of running into confusion.

Lieut.-Gen. Cromwell: "If that that I say of the Treaty be applied to one thing, which I mean of another, then there may haply be a very great misunderstanding of me; if[226] that which I speak of [the] Treaty, that relates to those things that are prepared for a general settlement of the kingdom, be applied to the obtaining of these things which are to precede a

[223] Firth's emendation of this passage is adopted as it makes the sense much clearer.

[224] Here follows in the MS., "As that it may be seen to all the world that it is an effectual means to procure these things to be granted as marching to London would do," but Firth believes that this sentence belongs at the end of the preceding paragraph.

[225] MS., "that the Commissioners General may by you."

[226] "but" in MS. The symbols for "the," "that," "but," "if," and "was," are so similar in the system of shorthand used by Clarke that they are very likely to have been mistaken for each other.

treaty, then[227] that that I have said to you hath been mistaken throughout, instead[228] of giving me satisfaction of that point which sticks so with every one, of danger and delay. But that which I say of the Treaty, in answer to that [which] is offered in your paper [is] that we should obtain these by positive demand within a circumscribed time, and going[229] of the Commissioners.[230] Yet using the name will not offend if we do not the things, that is [if] we do not treat of those things.[231]

"Give me leave to offer one thing to your consideration which I see you make to be your ground of marching towards London; because it came in my mind, I am sorry I did it, but this came in my mind, and I would not offer it to you but because I really know it is a truth. We are, as our friends are elsewhere, very swift in our affections and desires; and truly I am very often judged for one that goes too fast that way, and it is the property of men that are as I am, to be full of apprehensions that dangers are not so real as imaginary; to be always making haste, and more sometimes perhaps than good speed; we are apt to misapprehensions that we shall be deluded through delay, and that there are no good intentions in the parliament towards us, and that we gather from the manifold bearing of those words that we have represented to them. Give me leave to say this to you; for my own part, perhaps I have as few extravagant thoughts, overweaning [thoughts] of obtaining great things from the Parliament, as any man; yet it hath been in most of our thoughts that this Parliament might be a reformed and purged parliament, that we might see [there] men looking at public and common interests only. This was the great principle we had gone upon, and certainly this is the principle we did march upon when we were at Uxbridge and when we were at St. Albans, and surely the thing was wise and honourable and just, and we see that providence hath led us into that way. It's thought that the Parliament does not mend—what's the meaning of that? That is to say, that company of men that sits there does not mean well to us. There is a party there that have been faithful from the sitting of the parliament to this very day; and we know their interests, and [they] have ventured their lives through so many hazards, they came not to the House but under the apprehensions of having their throats cut every day. If we well consider what difficulties they have passed, then[232] we may not run into that extreme of thinking too hardly of the Parliament; if we shall consider that their business of holding their heads above water is the common work and every other day['s work] and to-day that which we desire is that which they have struggled for as for life, and sometimes they have been able to carry it, others not, and yet daily they get ground. If we [wish to] see a purged Parliament, I pray let me persuade every man that he would

227 "is" in MS.

228 "and instead" in MS.

229 Departure.

230 *Cf.* what he says above.

231 Firth paraphrases this, "There is no harm in nominally using the Commissioners for this purpose if we do not treat with them, but merely turn them into messengers." This sense however seems a little doubtful. An alternative reading might be, "Using the name of a treaty generally will do no harm if we take care that certain things are settled before we begin to treat." The sense, in any reading, is obscure.

232 "that" in text.

be a little apt to hope the best; and I speak this to you as out of a clear conscience before the Lord, I do think that [that part of] the Parliament is upon the gaining hand, and that this work that we are now upon tends to make them gain more; and I would wish that we might remember this always, that [what] we and they gain in a free way, it is better than twice so much in a forced, and will be more truly ours and our posterities; and therefore I desire not to persuade any man to be of my mind, but I wish that every man would seriously weigh these things."

Mr. Allen said that his Honour (speaking his own hopes) told them that the prevailing part of the Parliament was a gaining part; but although they would gladly think so, they could not. Rather it seemed to them that their friends there were the losing party, and always would be so unless a march to London might conduce to quell those who were acting in such manner as to make them losers.

To this Ireton replied that seeing how many of the other party had left the House, it must be that their friends were on the gaining hand. As to the march upon London and the way of sending up the desires of the army, he could not but believe that the latter would be more effectual if it went as a paper agreed upon by the General, the Council of War and the Agitators, rather than merely given in by the Commissioners. He expected no great matter from the Treaty, and much desired to shorten the work, but saw no reason to blame the Commissioners of Parliament, who had patiently waited. If there had been delay the fault lay with themselves. He and another [probably Lambert] had the proposals for the first of these in hand, and would be glad of suggestions from others.

As to the march upon London, he did not think that should be unless their proposals were offered and rejected, nor that they should seek to gain their object by force if it could be got in any other way. As to the earlier march (in June) the army was then, as it were, proscribed, and the open enemies of the army had the power in Parliament and were in danger of bringing about another war. But these men were now withdrawn from the House and nothing was needed but their actual sequestration, which might justly be demanded; thus the former reasons for a march had now disappeared.

Allen replied that Ireton's justification for the former march was that the army were then unowned, and the House was then unpurged. Truly, he confessed they were now owned in name, but he doubted not in nature, to be the Parliament's army, for if they were, Parliament would not suffer them to be traduced and reviled as they had been in pulpit and in press. And as to the purging of the House, the [eleven] members were at present debarred from sitting, but the ordinance for sequestering them (which was almost everything) was still wanting. His fear was that while they were still laying the foundation of their plan for a settlement, some would step in and take the matter out of their hands.

Lieut.-Gen. Cromwell: "This I wish in the general, that we may all of us so demean ourselves in this business that we speak those things that tend to the uniting of us, and that we do none of us exercise our parts to strain things, and to let in things to a long dispute, or to unnecessary contradictions, or to the stirring up of any such seed of dissatisfaction in one another's minds as may in the least render us unsatisfied one in another. I do not speak this that anybody does do it, but I say this ought to *become* both you and me, that we so speak and act as that the end may be union and a right understanding one with another. Truly if I thought that which was last spoken by Mr. Allen had been satisfactory to that end for which he spake it, I should not have said anything to you. But for that [answer] which he made to the Commissary [General's argument] of the Parliament's owning of us, and what a thing that was to us, and how much tending to the settlement of the peace of the kingdom to say or to think 'it is but a titular thing that, and but in name only that they do own [us],' I think is a very great mistake. For really it did at that time lay the best foundation could be expected for the preventing an absolute confusion in this kingdom, and I think if we had not been satisfied in that, we should not have been satisfied in anything. And [it is a very great mistake] to think that this is any weighty argument, 'it is but titular, because they suffer scandalous books [to] flock up and down'—I would not look they should love us better than they love themselves, and how many scandalous books go out of [*i.e.*, concerning] them.

We have given them, the Parliament,[233] more to do than to attend [to] scandalous books. I hope that will not weigh with any man, and I desire we may put this debate to a conclusion, or else let us answer those things that are really and weightily objected, as truly that was [not]. They have given us so[234] real a testimony that they cannot give more. They cannot disown us without the losing of all rational and honest people in the kingdom, and therefore let us take it as a very great and high owning of us; let not us disown that owning. If any man would [say] by that which was objected we would have peace, a perfect settlement of all we seek and we would march to London to say we forced them.[235] Really, really, have what you will have, that [which] you have by force I look upon it as nothing. I do not know that force is to be used except we cannot get what is for the good of the kingdom without force. All the arguments must tend to this, that it is necessary to use force, to march up with the army, and not to tarry four days. [Was not the argument thus][236] we shall be baffled, denied, and shall never march up, but still be patient and suffer, even to have the ruin of the kingdom as hath been imagined [if we do not march within four days]. [We] expect a speedy answer [to that] which hath been offered, and to make that critical[237] to us whether they own us or intend to perfect the settlement as we expect. The kingdom would be saved, though[238] we do not march within four days, if we had these things granted to us. If these things be

[233] "and the Parliament" in MS.

[234] "as" in MS.

[235] Firth thinks this may be paraphrased thus, "If any man urges, we would have a perfect settlement of all we seek, and would therefore march to London. Say we did force them to grant what we ask."

[236] MS., "if the argument was not thus." This clause is transferred from the line below.

[237] *i.e.*, crucial or decisive.

[238] "if" in text. These two signs seem often to be confused.

granted to us, we may march to York. I wish we may respite our determination till that four or five days be over, till we see how things will be, except you will urge reasons to show it to be of absolute necessity to all those ends to determine just now that we will march up to London tomorrow or next day. I am sorry that we be not satisfied with that which has been proposed as to this very thing, and [hope] that[239] having had assurance these things were put into such a way as hath been offered to you, that you will rest contented with this as at this time, except you will show us some absolute reasons."

Major Tulidah said that the Lieut.-General had put the matter to a good issue, for the weight of the business lay there. They all agreed that the things in their proposals were necessary, but differed as to the way of accomplishing them. He desired a "sweet and honourable way of treating" as much as any one; but did not see that they were any further than when they were at Uxbridge, if as far. If advancing to Uxbridge put their friends in Parliament into such a way that they had liberty to speak, if it put them on their legs, nothing would expedite them to speak boldly for the kingdom like an advance to the city. As to forcing things, it was only desired to force them this once that there might be no more forcing—that by the sword, they might take the sword "out of those hands that are enemies to justice." He did not believe that they would gain anything except by marching to London.

Lieut.-Gen. Cromwell: "Truly the words spoken by Major Tulidah were [spoken] with affection, but we are rational [men]. I would fain know with what reason or colour of reason he did urge any reason, but only with affirmation of earnest words. For that declaration of the Parliament, the Parliament hath owned us, and taken off that that any man can loyally or rationally charge us with. If that upon his apprehensions or any man's else we shall quarrel with every dog in the street that barks at us, and suffer the kingdom to be lost, with such a fantastical thing? I desire that nothing of heat or earnestness may carry us here, nor nothing of affirmation, nor nothing of that kind may lead us, but that which is truly reason, and that which hath life and argument in it.

"To that which was alleged that by our marching[240] to Uxbridge, we opened those honest men's mouths to speak for us, this is not to be answered with reason, but this is matter of fact, and better known to some of us than it is to Major Tulidah or any of you. 'Tis true there was a fear and an awe upon the Parliament by our marching to Uxbridge, there was something of that, for those eleven members were afraid to be in the House. If you will believe that which is not a fancy, they have voted very essential things to their own purging, and I believe this, if we will believe that which is the truth in fact[241] upon that very one vote that was passed concerning the

[239] "if" in MS.

[240] MS., "alleged of our marching."

[241] On July 5 a vote was passed that no person who had been in actual war against the Parliament or accepted pardons from the King, or taken any part in bringing about the cessation or otherwise assisting the Rebellion in Ireland, or were sequestered by Parliament for delinquency, should presume to sit in the House of Commons.

putting a fine or penalty [on those] that knew themselves to be guilty, and that if they did not go out should accuse themselves to be liable to sequestration[242] I believe there will go twenty or thirty men out of the House of Commons. And if this be [not] an effect and demonstrance of their[243] happy progress and that by use of that liberty that they have had by our [not] drawing near, I appeal to any man? And if they shall, as I said before, disown us, and we give them no cause to do it, but pressing only just and honourable and honest things from them, judge ye, what can the world think of them and of us? But [what can the world think if] we shall do that, whilst we are upon the gaining hand that shall really stop their mouths, to open their mouths in a little for us; that whiles they are, as fast as they can, gaining the things we desire, if we shall be so impatient that whiles they are struggling for life, that they are unable to help us, and gained more within these three days than in ten days, for ought I know we may by advancing stop their mouths.[244]

"They will not have wherewithal to answer that middle party in the House, who is answered with this reason, 'you see the army is contented to go backward, you see the army is willing to make fair representations[245] of that they have from us.' I profess, I speak it in my conscience, that if we should move until we had made these proposals to them, and see what answer they will give them, we shall not only disable them, but divide among ourselves, and I as much fear that as anything; and if we should speak to your satisfactions you must speak to our satisfactions, though there be great fears of others I shall very much question the integrity of any man that[246] would not have it spoken."

Cornet Joyce asked whether the Parliament, in owning them to be their army, owned their act in fighting of the King.

Mr. Sexby conceived that what the Parliament had done was from fear, not love; first, because those who had deserted them (the army) were better looked upon and much better paid than they were; and second, because they were treated with, "for truly Parliaments or armies never treat with friends, but enemies."

Major Disbrowe urged them to keep to the business in hand. The re-

(*Commons Journals*, v. 233.) Those who infringed this order were by a second vote of July 9, to be liable to the penalties imposed in the Newcastle propositions on those who had sat in the Oxford Parliament; *i.e.*, to be guilty of high treason and their estates to be sequestered (*ibid.* p. 238.) Gardiner, *Constitutional Documents*, p. 217. (*Note by Firth.*)

242 The report here is very confused. What Cromwell said was probably this: "If we will believe that which is the truth in fact, not that which is a fancy, they have voted very essential things to their own purging." (*Note by Firth.*)

243 "the" in MS.

244 Firth suggests that Cromwell's argument is, "Shall we do that whilst they are upon the gaining hand in order to open their mouths for us, that shall really stop their mouths. If we shall be so impatient—and that whilst they are as fast as they can gaining us the things we desire, and have gained us more in the last three days than in ten days whilst they were struggling for life and could not help us—for aught I know, we may by advancing stop their mouths."

245 MS., "fancy representations."

246 "I" in MS.

port of his speech is rather confused, but he seems to have said that as in any case it would take a few days to prepare to march to London, they might, if they were expeditious in discussing the matter, send off their proposals and get an answer by the time they were ready to start.

LIEUT. SCOTTON said that if they could obtain their desires, they would be willing to waive the march to London; but the great point was that Lieut.-Col. Lilburne should be freed.

CORNET SPENCER said that he had just come from the city, where the militia officers were taking the names of all the apprentices and ordering them to be ready at an hour's warning; and that the King having come to Maidenhead, their friends in London wished the army had come with the King and would march up to London [this last too confusedly expressed for the meaning to be certain].

LIEUT.-GEN. CROMWELL: "Truly Sir, I think neither of these two things that gentleman spoke last are any great news. For the one of them, the listing of apprentices, I doubt they have listed them twice over; I am sure we have heard [it] more than twice over. For the other [that our friends in London] would rejoice to see us come up, what if we [be] better able to consult what is for their good than themselves. It is the general good of them and all the people of the kingdom that's the question;—what's for their good, not what pleases them. I do not know that all these considerations are arguments to have satisfaction in these things that we have in proposition. Though[247] you be in the right and I in the wrong, if we be divided I doubt we shall all be in the wrong. . . . Whether of them will do our work, let them speak without declaring. Let us not think that this is a greater argument, that they love those that deserted, that they have paid them and not us, which was Mr. Sexby's argument, which if it had weight in it, I should have submitted to it. The question is singly this: whether or no we shall not in a positive way desire the answer to these things before we march towards London, when perhaps we may have the same things in the time that we can march. Here is the strictness of the question."

COL. RICH said that the debate resolved itself into two points; first, concerning the paper and the five particulars, whether they should go up as they were or whether the paper should first be insisted upon, and whether this should be presented to the Commissioners of Parliament as from the Council or from the Commissioners of the army; the former being, he thought, the better way. Second, to answer the Lieut.-General's question; whether they should march forthwith to London or wait four days.

LIEUT. CHILLENDEN thought that the paper might go "concluding all things in it."

COM. IRETON said he would have the five particulars to go but not the paper itself, as it proposed the march to London, which he believed would lose them every friend they had either in Parliament or in the city. As to the expression "that they should not only be sequestered but disabled," he saw no justice in it, and prayed the army to avoid it. *Here the Report ends.*[248]

[247] "If" in MS.
[248] *Clarke Papers*, i, 176 *et seq.*

Though the debate lasted until midnight, the business of the Council was unfinished. There remained, in fact, the most important item of all to be considered, no less than a new constitution for England, on which Ireton and Lambert had been engaged for a considerable period. Ireton had by this time become the political thinker—or theorist—of the revolutionary party, the Sieyès of the movement. As Whitelocke wrote in later years, "Colonel Ireton was chiefly employed or took upon him the business of the pen," and ". . . was therein encouraged and assisted by Lieutenant-general Cromwell, his father-in-law, and by Colonel Lambert."[249] The *Engagement of the Army* of June 5 and the *Remonstrance* of June 14 were in form and doubtless in spirit apparently his work. He had taken part in the treaty between the army and the Parliament, and with Lambert he seems to have been commissioned to draw up a plan of accommodation among the various parties to the great dispute. His suggestion he now presented in the form of a paper entitled "The Heads of the Army Proposals," to settle the disturbed affairs of the kingdom.

Its fifteen "heads," to which were added five supplementary articles, formed the most complete and, it seems at this distance, in general the fairest plan yet made for the settlement of affairs. As to Parliament, it proposed biennial sessions of at least 120 days, with no session more than 240 days, and committees to carry on such business as was referred to them during the intermission. Extraordinary sessions were callable by the King with the advice of a Council of State, which was to have a more important constitutional position than the old Privy Council. It proposed further a redistribution of seats "according to some rule of equality or proportion," "proportionable to the respective rates . . . in the common charges and burdens of the kingdom," with free elections under regulations determined by the Commons itself. Members of the House were to be free from the consequences of "dissent" against the peers or the King himself and no official could be protected against judgment by the King "other than by their equals or according to the law of the land."

To secure the safety of Parliament, the militia was to be in its hands for ten years. None in arms against the Parliament were to hold office for five years; and the Council of State was to control the armed forces and foreign affairs, under direction of Parliament, which for ten years should have the disposition of great offices of State. To these main heads there followed provisions voiding peerages created since the beginning of the war, with declarations against Parliament and grants under the Great Seal after its removal. The treaties between England and Scotland were to be confirmed, the "Cessation" in Ireland denounced and the war there left to the

[249] Whitelocke, *Memorials*, 254.

Parliament; and the ordinance for taking away the court of wards and liveries be confirmed "provided His Majesty's revenue be not damnified therein" or its officers left without reparation.

As to the church, there should be an act taking away "all coercive power, authority and jurisdiction of Bishops and all other Ecclesiastical Officers"; the repeal of acts "enjoining the use of the Book of Common Prayer" or making illegal any other religious meetings; provision for discovering and disabling Papists; the repeal of acts enforcing the taking of the Covenant; in brief religious liberty. This done "His Majesty's person, his Queen, and royal issue may be restored to a condition of safety, honour and freedom . . . without diminution to their personal rights or further limitation to the exercise of the royal power." To this were joined terms of composition for "delinquency," in general on the basis of a year's revenue or five per cent of the property. To these again was added a curious and highly varied bill of rights or redress of grievances—the right of petition, the removal of excise, of forest laws and monopolies and inequalities of taxation, tithe reform, cheaper lawsuits, prevention of the defrauding of creditors through abuse of the laws for imprisonment for debt, the presence of two witnesses in capital cases, no compulsion to incriminate one's self or his relations in criminal suits, and no "molestation or ensnaring religious and peaceable people for nonconformity". Finally, it demanded that the large powers of committees and deputy-lieutenants be recalled, finances reorganized and provision made for payment of army arrears, the public debts and damages of the war, especially to those whose "debt or damages are great and their estates small."

Such was the statesmanlike, if somewhat confused, plan which Ireton and Lambert brought forward after long and earnest consideration and consultation with many men, including Charles himself. As against the royal proposals or those of Parliamentary Presbyterians, it reveals a scope and generosity in sharp contrast to the narrower and more selfish ideas of either King or Commons. It involved the granting of religious and political liberty far in advance of its generation, and its very qualities made it the more impossible of acceptance. The debate upon Ireton's proposals, brief and unsatisfactory as our account of it is, reveals the difficulties of the proposals, not least in the obscure and all but incoherent record of Cromwell's remarks on it.

The Council of War at Reading, July 17, 1647.

COMMISSARY IRETON. That these papers doe nott concerne the Army in particular butt the whole Kingdome in generall.

LIEUT. GEN. [CROMWELL]. That all prejudices might bee removed.

COMMISSARY IRETON. There could bee butt 2 wayes: either by Treatie, or else to have such an intire proposall of particulars prepared, as might neede the lesse delay in the way of Treatie. The Commissioners are those that your Excellency was pleased to appoint. Itt was offer'd to us by the Commissioners of the Parliament parte, whether wee would draw out particulars or an intire proposall of all together? Though there was noe publique proposall, yet wee did satisfie our selves how longe and teadious itt would have bin to draw out particulars by way of debate by the Commissioners there; and therefore I was, with the consent of your Excellency and the rest of the Commissioners, sequestred from that imployment of the Treatie to make some preparation of particulars fitt to tender to your Excellency and the Army . . . if any body could thinke of any other particulars that concern'd the Kingdome every man was as free to doe as my selfe or any other, and would have bin as well accepted; and for my owne part I should have bin glad that any other would have sett himselfe on worke as I did.

One thinge, the Parliament have sent propositions to the Kinge; wee have nott had any from them.

The propositions read[250]

LIEUT.-GEN. CROMWELL: But you would not have a Parliament dissolved without the consent of the Houses in 120 days?

COL. LAMBERT: [They may sit] longer than that, that except the Council of State, and the King shall think fit; if you involve themselves in it if they may sit without the consent of both Houses.

LIEUT.-GEN. CROMWELL: They may be adjourned if the King and Council of State think fit; it may be as convenient to have a Parliament continued as to [have it] out itself whether it will or no.

If it does not conclude it public, as that it be here read or no. If there be any thing afterwards that shall be desired to be offered for any addition the Council of War will meet, and the Agitators [may] send so many as they shall select to get any alteration; but it would not be read here but that it be passed by with silence.[251]

To this objection, not to the matter but to the procedure, offered by his father-in-law, Ireton replied in effect that either to pass the articles as they stood or to agree to Cromwell's proposal might be inconvenient and he suggested that the matter be referred to a committee; for, as he said, these proposals were made "not for a present conclusion but consideration; for I cannot say the things have been so considered as to satisfy myself in them." To this the Agitator Allen added his "one word," "that we are most of us but young Statesmen" and these things are of "great weight, having relation

[250] The propositions, or *Heads of Proposals*, are printed in Rushworth, vii, 731; *Old Parl. Hist.*, xvi, 212; Gardiner, *Constitutional Documents*, p. 232. The present discussion is on the second clause of the first head. Parliament might sit 240 days at the outside, and must sit at least 120 days. The spelling of the opening speeches has been retained to show the character of the original; the rest has been modernized.

[251] *Clarke Papers*, i, 212–14.

to the settling of a Kingdome, which is a great work . . . we all expect to have a share in and desire that others may also," and so seconded the idea of referring the matter to a committee and spending more time in debate. Finally Ireton ended the discussion, urging that all men read and consider these proposals, choose a small committee to perfect them and finally offer the revised version as a solution of the national problem.

In consequence on the next day, July 18, Fairfax appointed a committee of twelve officers, six each from the horse and foot, headed by Ireton, and twelve Agitators, to perfect the proposals, adding that "Lieutenant General Cromwell be present with the said Council when he can."[252] To this he added on the same day the appointment of another committee of officers, including neither Cromwell nor Ireton, to attend him daily at his quarters to "advise upon all emergencies of the affairs of the Army."[253] Whether mere details of army management or graver problems, those "emergencies" were pressing, and, as partial concession to the demands of the city and the Parliament to remove further from London, the next week the army took up its quarters at Bedford, establishing the King at Woburn, the seat of the Earl of Bedford, and there began the discussion of Ireton's proposals and new negotiations between the army, the Parliament, the Scots and the King.

THE REBELLION OF THE CITY, JULY 21–AUGUST 6, 1647

Charles, learning of the events in Westminster in the preceding fortnight, consulted daily by Lauderdale on behalf of the Scots,[254] and provided by Berkeley with a copy of the *Army Proposals* before they were officially presented to him,[255] found himself in a position which was always to his liking, that of an arbiter among factions disputing for his favor. He was convinced of two things, in both of which he was wrong. The first was that he was a skilled negotiator, the second that he was the one unchanging, indispensable element in the state; and on the basis of these two misconceptions he entered with new enthusiasm on his favorite occupation of endeavoring to achieve his own ends by playing the various factions against each other. Encouraged by the news from the capital and from Scotland, he advised Fairfax and Cromwell through Major Huntington that he was ready to treat with the army. In response to that message several officers went to Woburn, but the only satisfaction they received was the assurance that the King was not against them.[256]

[252] *Clarke Papers*, i, 216.
[253] *Ibid.*, i, 217.
[254] Berkeley's *Memoirs*, p. 366.
[255] *Ibid.*
[256] Huntington, *Sundry Reasons*, p. 401–402.

It was little wonder that he was encouraged by the news from London, for while the army had been engaged in these discussions and in the move to Bedford, the City mob had once more taken a hand in public affairs, and many members, fearing the trend of events, had quietly left their places. Each day after July 16 the Presbyterian majority sank by the departure of its supporters.[257] On July 19, as the army began to move, the eleven members presented their defence to the Houses, drawn up apparently by Prynne, in answer to the accusations of the army. That answer, however logically convincing, was not acceptable, for the Houses voted command of all the land forces to Fairfax,[258] and the next day gave each of the eleven members leave "to follow his own occasions," which they interpreted by securing leave for six months' absence and passports to leave the country.[259] In view of these events, Cromwell, Waller, Hammond and Rich in the name of Fairfax assured the Parliamentary commissioners that the army was satisfied with Parliament and was prepared to consider a settlement.[260]

Meanwhile the City had rebelled. On July 21, "reformadoes," apprentices and watermen signed an engagement in Skinners' Hall to maintain the Covenant and restore the King on his terms of May 12 giving up episcopacy for three years and the militia for ten. Five days later, on July 26, a petition to repeal the ordinance re-establishing the Parliamentary Committee of Militia in the City was presented to the Houses. The nine peers present in the Upper House were overawed by the mob which accompanied the City delegation, agreed to its terms and hastily adjourned. The Commons, invaded, insulted and even attacked by the mob, consented to repeal the ordinance; then, with the Speaker held in his chair by members of the mob, were forced to pass a resolution to recall the King to London. With the news of this outbreak it was evident to the army leaders that unless they acted quickly they would have to face a new alliance of the King, the Scots, the Presbyterians and the City and they hastened to put their troops in motion toward the capital. By the 29th they were on the march, while the City authorities, aided, it was charged, by Presbyterian leaders like Holles, strove feverishly to put the City in a posture of defence.

Between the City and the Army the Parliament virtually disappeared as a force in politics. When the Houses assembled on July 30, fifty-seven Independent members were missing from their seats and neither House had a Speaker. Whether of his own accord or as a result of strong persuasion by Cromwell and Ireton, Lenthall had

257 *C. J.*, v, 245 ff; Letters of Intell., July 22, *Clarendon Mss*, 2559.

258 *L. J.*, ix, 338.

259 *C. J.*, v, 251.

260 Nottingham to Manchester, *L. J.*, ix, 355.

fled to the army,[261] and Manchester, despite his Presbyterian leanings, had accompanied the Independents to the same refuge. The little handful of Presbyterians that remained were still undaunted. They recalled the eleven members, chose new Speakers, revived the Committee of Safety and ordered Fairfax not to come nearer than thirty miles to London, and if he were nearer, to retire.[262] But Parliamentary Presbyterianism was at its last gasp. The army was already at Colnbrook[263] between Windsor and Twickenham and planning to block up the City by holding both banks of the river.

The prophecy of Sir Jacob Astley had come true; the King's opponents had fallen out among themselves; and Charles found a situation to his liking in this struggle between the parties which had overthrown him in the field. When the *Army Proposals* were presented to him, he disdainfully rejected them. There was not one of his old supporters he would consent to except from pardon, and he would not be content with less than the definite establishment of episcopacy. His position was expressed in his brief statement, "You cannot do without me." "You will fall to ruin if I do not sustain you,"[264] he continued; and in that conviction of being indispensable he went on to the end. It was in vain, as Clarendon relates, that Cromwell expostulated with Charles's devoted but distressed followers, Berkeley and Ashburnham:

"When he [Huntington] observed Cromwell to grow colder in his expressions for the King than he had formerly been, he expostulated with him in very sharp terms, for abusing him and making him the instrument to cozen the King; and though the other endeavoured to persuade him that all should be well, he informed his majesty of all he had observed, and told him that Cromwell was a villain, and would destroy him if he were not prevented; . . . Cromwell himself expostulated with Mr. Ashburnham, and complained that the King could not be trusted, and that he had no affection or confidence in the army, but was jealous of them and of all the officers; that he had intrigues in the Parliament, and treaties with the Presbyterians of the city to raise new troubles; that he had a treaty concluded with the Scotch commissioners to engage the nation again in blood; and therefore he would not be answerable if any thing fell out amiss, and contrary to expectation; and that was the reason, besides the old animosity, that had drawn on the affront which the commissioners had complained of."[265]

It is at this point, as the second great basis of the charge of hypocrisy, treachery and ambition levelled against Cromwell, that his antagonists have found support for their arguments. He had first

[261] See *Clarke Papers*, i, 219, for collected evidence concerning Lenthall's flight.
[262] *Old Parl. Hist.*, xvi, 193.
[263] *Perfect Weekly Account.*
[264] Berkeley's *Memoirs*, p. 368.
[265] Clarendon, *History*, x, 125.

denounced the army for its mutiny and then joined it; he had within a fortnight professed adherence to Charles and he now abandoned him. In each case the charge is true; but in each instance the old adage holds that "circumstances alter cases." Like his fellow-officers he was confronted not by a theory but by a condition; and Clarendon's own words which follow on his account of Cromwell's interview with Huntington give some clue to his attitude and his plans. If the Presbyterians and Royalists distrusted Cromwell, he had, like his companions in arms, come to believe that he could not trust the King. He and they knew of Charles's negotiations with the Scots, the City and the Presbyterians. And, as Clarendon points out, there was another element:

"At this time [there was] a new faction grown up in the army, which were, either by their own denomination or with their own consent, called *Levellers;* who spake insolently and confidently against the King and Parliament and the great officers of the army; professed as great malice against all the lords as against the King, and declared that all degrees of men should be levelled, and an equality should be established, both in titles and estates, throughout the kingdom. Whether the raising this spirit was a piece of Cromwell's ordinary witchcraft, in order to some of his designs, or whether it grew amongst those tares which had been sowed in that confusion, certain it is, it gave him real trouble at last . . . but the present use he made of it [was, that] upon the licentious discourse of that kind which some soldiers upon the guard usually made, the guard upon the King's person was doubled and a restraint put upon the great resort of people who came to see the King . . ."[266]

If Cromwell distrusted Charles, he was no less distrusted by the King, supported by Huntington in his suspicions of Cromwell's designs. Though Cromwell assured Huntington that all would be well, the situation of affairs was far from promising. So far had events moved in the preceding months, that, as often happens in revolutionary periods, the officers even seemed at this moment to occupy a middle ground between the King, the Presbyterians and the Levellers, and as the only substantial element in the confused welter of factions had been sought as a refuge both by Lenthall and Manchester with their fellow-members of both Houses. The leaders still hoped for an accommodation with the King despite his rejection of their proposals; but in the face of the rebellion of the City they could not stand still. From Colnbrook they had advanced with a force of some twenty thousand men to Hounslow Heath by August 3 and there received a message from the Common Council of London on the day following, disclaiming any desire for more bloodshed. To this, as to the votes of Parliament, the Council of War drew up a declaration

[266] Clarendon, *History*, x, 126.

the same day denouncing the illegality of the choice of new Speakers for the Houses "by some Gentlemen at Westminster," declaring no free and legal Parliament sat there and that the votes of July 29 were null and void.[267] To this, on the next day, the nine Lords and fifty-seven commoners who had fled to the army, added their engagement to live and die with Fairfax,[268] and with this the troops began their advance on the City.

THE ARMY IN LONDON, AUGUST 6–26, 1647

On August 6, with the fugitive members of Parliament in their midst, the army marched into the City, the foot-soldiers in the lead and Cromwell with his regiment riding in advance of the main body of horse under Fairfax. Welcomed at Hyde Park by the Lord Mayor and Aldermen and at Charing Cross by the Common Council,[269] they reached Westminster where in the heavily guarded Houses of Parliament Lenthall and Manchester resumed their seats with Fairfax in a chair placed specially for him. The way for this reconciliation had been paved by a series of resolutions before his arrival. On receipt of a formal report and declaration that he and the army "are advanced to Town, in regard of the force and violence offered to the Parliament, in order to the safe and free sitting of the Parliament," the Commons, thoroughly cowed by this display of force, hastened to resolve that,

> "This House doth approve of the coming up of the General and the Army, for the safe sitting of the Parliament, and that Thanks be given to the General and the Army for the same."

To this the Lords added their blessing, resolving that,

> "This House doth approve the Declaration of Sir Thomas Fairfax, and his Proceedings in bringing up the Army."[270]

A "gratuity" of a month's pay to the non-commissioned officers and soldiers was ordered, a thanksgiving appointed "for the safe Return of the Members of *both Houses*." The Speaker acknowledged "God's great Mercies in this action"; Fairfax was given command of the Tower; and the surrender of Parliament was complete. Thence Fairfax, Cromwell and Skippon with the whole army rode to the Tower to turn out the Lieutenant, Colonel West, and replace him with a strong Independent, Colonel Tichborne; and the next day the

[267] *L. J.*, ix, 375–8.

[268] *Ibid.*, p. 385. Rushworth, vi, 755. Percivale, in *Hist. Mss. Comm. Rept.* (Egmont Mss, I, ii, 440) gives a different list, including Cromwell's name.

[269] *Perfect Diurnall*, Aug. 6; Rushworth, vii, 756; *Perfect Summary of Passages*.

[270] *C. J.*, v, 268; *L. J.*, ix, 379.

greater part of their forces marched over London Bridge into Kent and Surrey.[271]

Fairfax, suffering from a recent illness, rode in a carriage with Mrs. Cromwell and Lady Fairfax.[272] Cromwell himself rode at the head of the cavalry; and as the grim veterans of the New Model, the heroes of Marston Moor and Naseby, horse, foot and dragoons, with their renowned commanders at their head, regiment by regiment, fierce and threatening, made their way through London streets, the City, like the Parliament, learned its lesson. Against such forces its trained bands and mobs of apprentices were as helpless as the politicians of the House of Commons. The military demonstration took the heart out of the City authorities and, like the Parliament, they hastened to conciliate their formidable antagonists. They planned a dinner to Fairfax and his officers, which, however, Fairfax declined;[273] and with this last gesture London's futile protest passed into history.

London having been overawed, there remained the Parliament to be dealt with. On the day that Fairfax declined to accept the peace-offering of the City dignitaries, an excited delegation of Independents, including the officer-members from the army, met in the Commons with a subdued group of Presbyterians. From the Lords they received a resolution that the revocation, on July 26, of the ordinance of July 23 declaring all who signed a petition to permit the King to come to Parliament were traitors was obtained by force and that all other acts and ordinances made in the absence of the Speakers since July 26, when "there was a visible, insolent and actual force" upon the Houses, were null and void. The contest on this critical motion was close and bitter. It was carried at first by 95 to 94; then three members, the Presbyterians Rolle, Ashurst and Irby, called from a committee and protesting that their votes had not been counted, it was lost by 97 to 95.[274]

Nor was this a temporary success, for the day following saw the Independents even more clearly outnumbered. The votes taken in the absence of the Speakers were, indeed, repealed, but had they been annulled, the members responsible for them would have been held guilty of unconstitutional proceedings, as the army claimed they should be. With this new triumph of the Presbyterians who seemed about to dominate Parliament again, the Agitators were roused to renew their demand for a "purge" of the Houses and the expulsion of such members of this "pretended" Parliament as were

[271] Holles, *Memoirs*, p. 290; Walker, (*Hist. of Independency*, p. 45) adds, "The consequences of these two actions were, that immediately the City decayed in Trade above 200000 l. a week: and no more bullion came to the Mint."

[272] *Perfect Occurrences*, Aug. 6–13; *Cal. S. P. Dom.* xxi, 598; *Clarendon, Mss*, 2572.

[273] Whitelocke, p. 264.

[274] *C. J.*, v, 270.

opposed to them. More and more impatient with the actions and the speeches of the majority, Cromwell and his fellow Independent officers were inclined to agree with them. "These men," he said to Ludlow of the eleven members, "will never leave till the Army pulls them out by the ears."[275] Confronted with such threats, those members did not wait. Holles fled to St. Malo; Massey and Poyntz to Holland; Waller, Lewis, Clotsworthy, Long and Stapleton to Calais, where Stapleton soon died. Nichols was under arrest; and only Glyn, Harley and Sir John Maynard remained at large in England, as the Presbyterian emigrés like those Girondins, who managed to escape their enemies the Jacobins in the French Revolution, followed the Royalists into exile.

None the less the movement for a purge of Parliament went on. On August 18 the Army Council met at Kingston where it drew up a declaration in support of the Agitators' demand for a purge of Parliament. To this Cromwell lent his voice.[276] Toward Holles and Stapleton he was especially hostile. "I know nothing to the contrary," he declared, "but that I am as well able to govern the kingdom as either of them";[277] and though Fairfax refused to join in the movement, Cromwell acted on his own responsibility. On August 19 the Houses received a remonstrance from Fairfax for the army, insisting that "the Members who sat while the Speakers were absent, shall not sit again till they have cleared themselves."

For two weeks the Houses had wrangled over the Null and Void Ordinance which repealed all the acts since July 26. On August 20 Cromwell took matters in his own hands. Stationing a regiment of horse in Hyde Park, he and his fellow officer-members of the House set a guard outside, took their seats, and after Cromwell and Ireton had stated their case, passed the measure over the opposition of the Presbyterians, thus accomplishing their ends without the grave step of a formal purge.[278] With that the Presbyterian party began to melt away and in Parliament, as in the City and the country, the army was left supreme. The sessions of the Houses went on, but with the average attendance in the House of Lords reduced to seven and with scarcely more than a hundred and fifty members in the House on even the most important questions, Parliament became as impotent as it was thin. In effect, as Clarendon observed, authority had passed to the new "parliament," that of the army, with its

[275] *Ludlow's Memoirs*, (i, 148) places the statement at an earlier date by several months, but Huntington's *Sundry Reasons* (p. 402) indicates this as the correct date; and there seems to be no reason why Cromwell should have considered the use of violence earlier.

[276] Fairfax, *Short Memorials*, in *Somers Tracts*, v, 393.

[277] Walker, *Anarchia Anglicana*, p. 21; Huntington, *Sundry Reasons*, p. 405.

[278] *C. J.*, v, 280; Holles, *Memoirs*, p. 289; Newsletter, *Roman Trans. R. O.* qu. in Gardiner, iii, 351.

"upper house" of the Council of Officers and its "Commons" of Agitators and soldiers' representatives.

THE NEGOTIATIONS WITH THE KING, AUGUST–SEPTEMBER, 1647

This was reflected, among other things, in relations with the King. With the removal of the army headquarters to Kingston, Charles was transferred to Henry VIII's old palace of Oatlands at Walton-on-the-Thames not far away, and on August 24 he was taken to Hampton Court while the army, two days later, removed its headquarters to Putney.[279] There he was permitted to live in royal state with his servants, and many visitors, Fairfax and Cromwell among them, were much at court. So frequent, indeed, were their visits that Presbyterians and Levellers believed that Cromwell and Ireton had some secret agreement with Charles. Cromwell was to be an earl 'with a blue ribbon,' his son to be of the Prince's bedchamber.[280] To Berkeley Cromwell repeated the gossip passed on to him by that Lady Carlisle who was reputed to have been the informant of the Parliamentary leaders of the King's proposed attempt on the five members and who now, apparently, resumed her old rôle. According to her, Berkeley himself had said that Cromwell was to be created Earl of Essex and captain of the King's guards; and it appeared to Berkeley that this trouble-maker was endeavoring to convince the Agitators of Cromwell's ambitious designs.[281]

Though the officers still hoped to come to some accommodation with the King, jealousy, doubts, and fears of treachery were the natural result of the negotiations and intrigues which now centered about Hampton Court. Almost daily Ashburnham brought a message from the King to Putney; and the Agitators were so disturbed at the fraternizing of Cromwell and Ireton with the "malignants," Berkeley and Ashburnham, that Cromwell was compelled to ask the King's representatives to come less often and send their messages privately. He was so suspected, he told them, that he was afraid to lie in his own quarters.[282] Berkeley acquiesced but Ashburnham did not; and the rumor spread that Berkeley was piqued because the two officers showed his colleague more respect than himself.

Concerning this situation, Clarendon, writing from the current gossip of the time, contributes his testimony to the personal relationships among these various characters in the drama. Ashburnham and Berkeley, he says, were both opinionated men, each undervaluing

[279] *L. J.*, ix, 406; *Perfect Diurnall*, Aug. 28; Herbert, *Memoirs* (1839), p. 48–9; Clarendon, x, 115; Berkeley, p. 371–2.

[280] Holles, *Memoirs*, p. 264.

[281] Berkeley, *Memoirs*, p. 371; Wildman, *Truth's Triumphs*, p. 7.

[282] Berkeley, pp. 371–2.

the other's understanding, Ashburnham depending wholly on Cromwell and Ireton. Warned of the suspicions of the Agitators, neither consulted Cromwell much directly thereafter, fearing the jealousy both of the soldiers and of Parliament:

"And so Sir Edward Ford, who had married Ireton's sister, but had been himself an officer in the King's army . . . and a gentleman of good meaning, . . . was trusted to pass between them. . . . Berkeley who had not found that respect from Cromwell and Ireton that he expected . . . had applied himself to others . . . not of so great names, but greater interest, as he thought in the soldiers. His chief confidence was in Dr. Stanes . . . quarter-master-general of the army, and one Watson . . . scout-master-general . . . both of the council of war, both in good credit with Cromwell . . . notable fanatics and professed enemies to the Scots and Presbyterians . . . they seemed very much to blame Ireton's stubbornness towards the King and to fear that he often prevailed upon Cromwell against his own inclinations. . . . They were the first who positively advertised the King . . . that Cromwell would never do him service, and the first who seemed to apprehend that the King's person was in danger, and that there was some secret design upon his life."[283]

It was easy for Clarendon and his informants, wise in the event, to foresee that which was to happen to Charles in the next few months. It was more difficult for those then absorbed in an endeavor to find some means of settlement for the kingdom; nor is there any evidence that at this moment there was any design of making away with the King in the minds of either Cromwell or Ireton. We lack, unfortunately, any records of the debates in the Council of Officers, if any records of those meetings were kept, but it is not inconceivable that the disposal of the King may have been discussed there, as it certainly was among the Agitators and the Levellers.

It may be that Ireton, and even Cromwell, contemplated the removal of the King at this time; it may be that they perceived the end from the beginning and worked toward it; it may be that they foresaw because they planned that tragedy. It was the settled conviction of men like Clarendon and other Royalists that from the first Cromwell designed to make himself supreme, that he plotted, deceived and conspired to that end; that at this moment, in particular, he saw and seized his opportunity to make his way by holding the army in play, seizing the person of the King, overawing Parliament, hoodwinking his fellow officers and the Agitators, and so maneuver among these various elements till he rose to the head of affairs. It is a pleasing theory and it has the advantage of plausible simplicity. It explains so easily and into it may be fitted much of the evidence without much strain. There was motive and opportunity; there was

[283] Clarendon, *History*, x, 135.

the undoubted fact that events moved in that direction to that conclusion; there is the testimony of Holles, Clarendon and Wildman—Presbyterian, Royalist and Leveller—who, divided in all else, united in their charge of Cromwell's ambition and treachery.

It would seem conclusive but for one circumstance. It does not fit the facts we know of Cromwell. It may, indeed, be true; for we know little of what goes on in the minds of even those whom we know best. But, taking all the evidence we have of Cromwell's character as revealed by his speeches, conversations, writings and actions, it is difficult to believe that he was such a finished actor and conspirator, with a mind so tortuous that it deceived all parties in the state. What evidence we have seems to show rather the reverse, that he was a forthright, direct, simple man of action rather than of thought, much less of far-seeing tortuous designs. We have had so far no great amount of evidence on which to base a final judgment of his mental processes and his character, but what we have all goes to show that, so far from being a conspirator, he met each issue and emergency as it came along, not with involved theory and indirection but with blunt practicality. So far as one may judge, he had not seen much further than the immediate problem—one step enough for him. From his first utterance in Parliament on behalf of Beard to his latest comment on Ireton's *Proposals*, he appears the same—a man determined to push his own simple Independent doctrines through. The evidence as to his position on Ireton's plan of settlement is too slight a basis for wide generalizations, but such as it is, it appears to represent a man careless of theory, not much concerned with forms and theories of government, but intent on solving the immediate problem at all costs, keeping in view only one great aim, that of the success of the Independents and their principles.

Against the theory of personal ambition, far-seeing treachery and hypocrisy, this may be set as being somewhat more in accord with all the evidence available. Amid the gusts of passion which swept England in these years, amid the waves of emotion which rose higher and higher with the deepening quarrel, amid the storm and stress of civil war, he rode the whirlwind, but it seems hard to prove that he did much to direct the storm. If he met plan with plan, if he outwitted King and Parliament and Levellers, at worst he turned the weapons of his enemies against them, at best he kept faith with the doctrines of his own party; and his success is no argument for or against his honesty nor that of his opponents, whether King or Presbyterian, Leveller or Republican. But one thing seems certain—whether or not he made the opportunity, in peace and war all his success lay in perceiving and seizing each opportunity as it came along—and by whatever means, he meant to have his way.

It is apparent that he had become a dominant figure in the councils of the army and was reckoned its most influential figure, but as yet rather by his ability and character than by his office, for he was officially Fairfax's subordinate. That perplexed officer found himself in a difficult position. As he explained later in his *Short Memorial* defending his conduct, he was, in effect, from the formation of the army council after the rendezvous at Newmarket little more than a figurehead. "I never gave my free consent to anything they did," he says, "but being yet undischarged of my place, they set my name in a way of course to all their papers whether I consented or not."[284] He seems, none the less in fact, to have agreed with much, if not most, of the policy of the army council and to have approved of its negotiations with the King. A soldier devoted to his military duties, he was no politician, and he believed, as he wrote, "that tender, equitable, and moderate dealing towards his majesty, his royal family, and his late party, so far as may stand with safety to the kingdom, is the most hopeful course to take away the seeds of war or future feuds amongst us for posterity, and to procure a lasting peace and agreement in this now distracted nation."[285]

It was an admirable programme which lacked only the straightforward acquiescence of Charles and Cromwell to succeed. But Fairfax was too simple and too much of a soldier to direct the complex and shifting forces then loose in England. He was unable to do more than keep the army under discipline, and that was difficult enough. For the rest he was willing—or forced—to be content to leave the politics to other hands. On August 30 he issued a commission for "the General's Committee of Officers," to which he named Cromwell, Ireton, General Hammond and nine others, including Berkeley's correspondents, Stane and Watson, "to be a general committee to receive and take into consideration all business which shall by me be referred or shall otherwise be tendered unto you . . . and propose to me what you conceive may be fit to be done upon the same." Of these he appointed four—Cromwell, Ireton, Hammond and Rainsborough —"to be one" especially to consult with the officers and Agitators. On this committee there devolved, in consequence, the conduct of the political activities of the army, and in it Cromwell and his son-in-law Ireton were the dominant influence.[286]

At this moment, by a curious chance, two days after his appointment, Cromwell wrote a letter which reveals the strange vicissitudes of fortune and affairs in the preceding years in an extraordinary way. In reply to "advices" from North Wales he addressed his old neighbor, John Williams, sometime Bishop of Lincoln, later a prisoner in the Tower for opposing Laud, and, after the raising of the royal standard,

[284] *Short Memorial*, p. 9.
[285] *Old Parl. Hist.* xvi, 104.
[286] *Clarke Papers*, i, 223–5.

created Archbishop of York. That prelate had fortified his ancestral estate of Conway Castle for the King; had been dispossessed by a Royalist Colonel, Sir John Owen, had appealed to a Parliamentary commander to oust Owen, and now held Conway Castle for the Parliament. At this moment he appealed to the man whom he had earlier denounced to Charles as the worst enemy the King had, with "all the properties of evil beasts," and to his "advices" Cromwell now replied:

For the Right Honourable my Lord of York: These

My Lord,

Your advices will be seriously considered by us. We shall endeavour our uttermost, so to settle the affairs of North Wales as, to the best of our understandings, to most public good thereof and of the whole. And that without private respect, or to the satisfaction of any humour, which has been too much practised by the occasion of our troubles.

The drover you mention will be secured (as far as we are able) in his affairs, if he come to ask it. Your kinsman shall be very welcome to me; I shall study to serve him for kindred's sake; among whom let not be forgotten, My Lord,

Your cousin and servant,

September 1st, 1647. Oliver Cromwell.

The Governor of Conway will not be forgotten, to prevent his abuse.[287]

While still at Putney, whence he wrote to Williams, a new turn in the negotiations took place. On August 26 the Parliament had decided to submit to Charles the old Newcastle Propositions, with a few changes. Cromwell was reported to agree with Ireton in his assurance that the King was not expected to agree to this proposal, asking "if the King did not wonder at these votes?" Charles was, in fact, entirely at a loss to know what this maneuvre meant. Since the army leaders concurred with the vote of the Parliament, he feared they had decided to recall their own proposals which were more lenient than these new Propositions. It was interpreted by some as a threat to force the *Army Proposals* on the King; and now as then it is extremely difficult to interpret this new move. Nor does the explanation attributed to Cromwell clear the matter up. As Major Huntington testifies, he sent word to Charles that,

"really it was the truth . . . that we (speaking of the Parliament) intended nothing else by it but to satisfy the Scot, who otherwise might be troublesome, . . . that they would not have his Majesty mistrust them . . . that if the Army remained an army, his Majesty should trust the proposals with what was promised, to be the worst of his conditions, which should be made

287 *Gentleman's Magazine* (1789), lix, 877; Sanford, p. 238n; Carlyle, XLV.

for him." Then, Huntington goes on to say, "striking his hand on his breast in his chamber at Putney," Cromwell bade him tell the King "he might rest confident and assured of it."[288]

The situation of affairs was now approaching a point where some settlement seemed imperative. The country was clamoring for peace; the soldiers and their representatives, the Agitators, were no less desirous of arrears and disbandment. Their arguments were simple and direct. The war was over, why should such forces be kept on foot at such expense; why was it not possible for the leaders to come to some agreement among themselves and let nation and army return to their normal lives? Why should the people be made to suffer because the politicians could not come to terms? They were all at hand. King, army and Parliament were all within that little area about London; Charles kept something of his old state at Hampton Court; Parliament was in session; the Army Council was in being; it only remained to come to some agreement among them to settle the kingdom, pay the soldiers and let them all go home.

But the case was not as simple as it seemed. Charles was determined to be restored as nearly as possible without conditions and to do what he could for episcopacy. The Presbyterians were no less determined to establish their own system of church government, and they were a powerful if not a dominant element in Parliament. The Independents were bent on religious toleration free from either episcopal or presbyterial interference and they were in control of the army. In its ranks, as Cromwell pointed out, those groups which revolution always breeds—in this case Levellers—were prepared to take advantage of any breach of authority to press their doctrines of equality and induce anarchy or the rule of the sword. And there remained, besides, the ever present fear of another Scottish invasion in behalf of Presbyterianism; the City mob; and the Irish war.

The army, like the nation, was desirous of peace, and at this moment it held the upper hand. But peace involved a settlement with the King and Parliament and various problems were concerned in it. There was the question of the army's pay; of the control of the militia; of the relations between the King and Parliament; of amnesty for the adherents of each side; of church settlement; and behind them all the constitutional problem raised by the *Army Proposals*. Believing that no settlement which ignored the monarchy could ever be arrived at, Charles felt himself in a position to dictate its terms. The Independents felt that it was necessary to win the King to their side. The Parliamentary Presbyterians stood their ground, firm in their conviction that no settlement was possible without consent of the Houses, and strengthened by the support of their Scotch allies.

[288] Huntington, *Sundry Reasons*, p. 403.

It was to keep that union, apparently, that the Houses had offered Charles the old Newcastle Propositions, as Cromwell assured him they "intended nothing else but to satisfy the Scot." Why, then, asked Charles, had the officer members not opposed them in the House? He was told, disingenuously as it seems now, that "they only concurred with the rest of the House that their unreasonableness might the better appear to the kingdom." "If the army remained an army," Cromwell commissioned Huntington to tell the King, "his Majesty should trust the [army] proposals with what was promised to be the worst of his condition which should be made for him"; and of this, he added "striking his hand on his heart," Charles "might rest confident and assured." Ireton added stronger assurances that the army "would purge and purge and never leave purging the Houses, till they had made them of such a temper as to do his Majesty's business." Meanwhile Lauderdale on behalf of the rising party of the King in Scotland was hinting to Charles of Scottish support and even negotiating with the Parliamentary vice-admiral Batten in a design to bring his command in the fleet to the side of the King and Scots. This was the more dangerous in that, within a fortnight, Batten, summoned before the admiralty committee, threw up his commission, was presently succeeded by Rainsborough, under whom the fleet refused to serve, and, in the following spring, put him ashore while Batten sailed with eleven ships to join the Prince of Wales in Holland.

With such discontent among the forces both on land and sea, if the situation of the Parliament was precarious, that of the army was as the Roman correspondent wrote, with perhaps some exaggeration, 'never nearer its ruin,' and its leaders were using every means in their power to legalize its position. In one respect they had an advantage. King and even Parliament had the law on their side, but the army leaders had the force, so long as they could control it. The Agitators and the Levellers threatened their position even there and they were doubly anxious to join hands with Charles before their position became untenable. They were prepared even to negotiate with the Scots on the basis of granting all reasonable demands on condition the Scots would not send in an army to assist the King. Save as the agents of Parliament, they had no legal standing. Now that the war was over and they were at odds with Parliament, the position of the officers before the country was more than dubious, and none more so than that of those who, like Cromwell, were at once members of the Commons and the Army Council. It was essential, then, to somehow legalize their position and to that end they entered on negotiations with almost every element, but especially with Charles, seeking almost desperately to find a way out of the dilemma, not only for the sake of the kingdom and their cause but for themselves.

It is not easy to explain this sudden approval of the officers to the resubmission of the Newcastle Propositions. It may be that the Independents feared that, once on his throne again, Charles would repudiate his agreement with the army and that a treaty with the Parliament would be held more binding. It may be that it was advanced for trading purposes. It may be, as the Royalists declared, that it was a mere blind, covering deeper designs. In any event, when on September 7 the revised Newcastle Propositions were presented to the King, first sending a draft of his proposed answer to Cromwell and Ireton, Charles informed the Houses that he preferred the *Army Proposals* which he commended to the consideration of the Parliament;[289] and in return Cromwell and Ireton agreed to support Charles's demand for a personal treaty.[290]

The situation was now still more confused. While Cromwell, Ireton and Vane supported Charles in his refusal to accept the Newcastle Propositions, the Agitators were more and more convinced that Cromwell was in private agreement with the King and more and more opposed to acceptance of his decision. The Commons was no less suspicious of Cromwell and he had scarcely a friend left in the House.[291] But if both Parliament and the Agitators were opposed to Cromwell, the Agitators were no less opposed to the Commons which still included many who had sat while the Speakers were with the army. From his imprisonment in the Tower Lilburne had been agitating for a purge; the soldiers were of like mind, especially since if they marched back to London they might be able to secure their pay by force. On September 6 Cromwell granted Lilburne's request for a personal interview and visited him in the Tower but with no more result than Lilburne's promise that if he were released he would leave England and not, as Cromwell feared, stir the army to mutiny.[292]

Among these cross-currents it was hard to steer one's way. The King was endeavoring to gain time by negotiation while the Hamiltons in Scotland were forming a party in his interest. Parliament and the army leaders were each striving to bring him to their terms, and each was suspicious of the other's aims. The Agitators were equally suspicious of them both. The soldiers were anxious for their pay and though Fairfax was reducing them to discipline and reported early in September that he had six thousand foot and two thousand horse ready to go to Ireland when their arrears were paid, he never ceased to urge that they be satisfied. On September 7 he and his council appealed to the City authorities for a loan of £50,000, only

289 *L. J.*, ix, 434; Berkeley, *Memoirs*, p. 372.
290 Huntington to Fairfax, Sept. 9, *Clarke Papers*, i, 225.
291 Berkeley, *Memoirs*, p. 372; Whitelocke, p. 269.
292 *An Additional Plea.*

to be refused two days later.[293] Cromwell was especially opposed to permitting the army to follow the dictates of the Agitators and took a leading part at Putney on September 9 in the expulsion of Major Francis White from the Council of the Army for declaring—injudiciously perhaps, but truthfully enough it seems at this distance—that there was "now no visible authority in the kingdom but the power and force of the sword."[294] It was dangerous doctrine to spread abroad at this moment. There was no place for such a firebrand among such combustibles as were to be found everywhere.

Cromwell had no mind to permit the army to fall into the hands of the Agitators and the country into anarchy, and the Council turned from White's expulsion to discuss the best way to peace on the basis of the restoration of the King. In that discussion Cromwell played his part as the antagonist of religious uniformity, even declaring his disinclination "to cast down the foundation of Presbytery and set up Independency."[295] From this meeting he turned—if the news-sheets are correct, to a journey to the Isle of Wight some time between September 4 and 12,[296] but he was in his place in the House of Commons on September 14, supporting a motion to search for precedents on the jurisdiction of the Lords in Lilburne's case, and so bringing on his head a charge of being a "perfidious hypocrite" from that splenetic firebrand.[297]

On that same day Cromwell wrote to Colonel Michael Jones, commander of the Parliamentary forces in Ireland to congratulate him on his victory of August 8 at Dungan Hill near Trim. To him, on the King's orders, Ormond had surrendered Dublin and though the disturbed condition of English affairs had thus far kept reinforcements from reaching him, his victory over Preston enabled him to maintain himself against the Irish rebel army under Owen Roe O'Neill and hold the country about Dublin for the Parliament.

For the Honourable Colonel Jones, Governor of Dublin and Commander-in-Chief of all the Forces in Leinster: These

SIR,

The mutual interest and engagement[298] we have in the same cause gives me occasion, as to congratulate, so abundantly to rejoice in God's gracious dispensation unto you and by you. We have (both in England and Ireland) found the immediate presence and assistance of God,

[293] Whitelocke, pp. 268–9; *Perfect Diurnall.*
[294] *Humble Proposals of the Adjutators; Copy of a Letter . . . by Francis White.*
[295] *Two declarations from Sir Thomas Fairfax and the General Councell.*
[296] *Mercurius Melancholicus.*
[297] *C. J.*, v, 301; *Two letters writ by . . . John Lilburne.*
[298] Carlyle printed "interest and agreement"; Mrs. Lomas "corrected" it to read "engagement and agreement." The present version follows the manuscript.

in guiding and succeeding our endeavours hitherto; and therefore ought (as I doubt not both you and we desire), to ascribe the glory of all to him and to improve all we receive from him unto him alone.

Though it may be for the present a cloud may lie over our actions, to them who are not acquainted with the grounds of our t[ransactions?]; yet we doubt not but God[299] will clear our integrity and innocency from any other ends we aim at but his glory and the public good. And as you are an instrument herein, so we shall as becometh us upon all occasions, give you your due honour. For mine own particular, wherein I may have your commands to serve you, you shall find none more ready than he that sincerely desires to approve himself.

Your affectionate friend and humble servant,

14 September 1647. OLIVER CROMWELL.[300]

Apart from its religious character, it reveals that Cromwell was fully conscious of the suspicion under which he lay. His position, like that of his fellow officers on the Council was extremely difficult. For a week, since Charles had declared his preference for the *Army Proposals*, frequent meetings between the King and the leading members of the Parliament and the Army Council seemed to indicate that a settlement was close at hand. At Putney, on September 16, the Army Council resolved to proceed by degrees with the various matters involved in such a settlement and to ask Parliament to draw up bills securing its privileges and the settlement of the militia to be presented to Charles for his assent.[301] The decision was by no means unanimous and the debate was so violent that Rainsborough, who headed the party opposed to further negotiation with the King, became so infuriated with Cromwell, who insisted that negotiations should go on, that he told Cromwell that "one of them must not live."[302] Yet, like his fellow-negotiators, denounced by Agitators, Presbyterians and Royalists in the pamphlets which poured from the presses, Cromwell went on with his duties in the council of officers and the Parliament apparently undisturbed by such incidents.[303] And it is not without humor, that after months of relief from committee work, on September 15, he who was concerned most of all with the settlement of the kingdom, was asked to serve on one committee to consider a petition of the aldermen and inhabitants of

299 "God's" in the original. The word has been followed by others subsequently erased and the *s* of "God's" was not erased. Mrs. Lomas pointed out most of Carlyle's mistakes in transcrbing this letter, but she had her footnote on this point refer to the "God" in the first paragraph.

300 Holograph original in Trinity College Library, Dublin, F. 3. 181, Kindly transcribed by Professor E. Curtis. Carlyle, XLVI.

301 *Intentions of the Army;* Whitelocke, p. 270.

302 Ford to Hopton, Sept. 20, *Clarendon Mss*, 2597.

303 Fairfax's request for Parliament to stop the libels and the resulting ordinance had no effect upon the circulation of these attacks. *L. J.*, ix, 441, 457.

Colchester and another on the ordinance for the payment of tithes.[304]

Nothing could seem more removed from the great problem which pressed upon the nation than these petty details, yet they reveal that Cromwell was not merely lieutenant-general of the army but a member of the Commons and as such able to make his influence felt in the next issue which came before that body. On September 21 the King's reply to the Houses expressing his preference for the *Army Proposals* rather than the Newcastle Propositions was laid before Parliament and the next day the Commons was crowded with members to take part in the decision which must then be made. Was Parliament to make a fresh attempt to treat with Charles, or should it declare that he had forever forfeited his right to his title? It was moved that the House go into committee to discuss the great problem. Henry Marten, a leader of that group of Independents soon to be styled Republicans, made a counter-proposal that no further addresses be made to the King. To this Cromwell, with the fear of military anarchy before his eyes, together with Ireton, St. John, Vane and Fiennes, argued for a grand committee and a personal treaty with the King.[305]

Speech in the Commons, September 21, 1647

"Consider," Cromwell urged, "how that there was a party in the army labouring for the King, and that a great one; how the City was endeavouring to get another party in the army; and that there was a third party . . . little dreamt of, that was endeavouring to have no other power rule but the sword."[306]

With Sir John Evelyn, Cromwell acted as teller for the Ayes with Rainsborough on the other side; and though both Lords and Commons resolved that the King "hath denied his consent to the propositions for peace," by 84 to 34 the committee was voted.[307] But once in the grand committee the alignment shifted. The House rejected any consideration of a personal treaty and voted to submit selected portions of the Newcastle Propositions once more to Charles. The next day, when Cromwell and Ireton were compelled to be at Putney, the Presbyterians took advantage of their absence to include in these selections the abolition of episcopacy, and to make only one more application to the King[308]—a virtual vote of "no addresses."

All the evidence goes to show that at this moment, for whatever

[304] *C. J.*, v, 301–2.

[305] Ford to Hopton, Sept. 28, *Clarendon Mss*, 2604; *Clarendon St. P.*, ii, App. xxxix; Berkeley, p 372. Cp. Whitelocke, p. 271.

[306] Ford to Hopton, Sept. 28, *loc. cit.*

[307] *C. J.*, v, 312.

[308] *Ibid.*, 314; *Clarke Papers*, i, 230n.

reason, Cromwell and Ireton were bitterly opposed to breaking off negotiations with Charles. Among the newsletters of the period one relates that:

"The last week his Majesty's answers to the propositions being considered of in the House was voted to be a denial, and that the King's drift therein was to put a difference between the Parliament and the army and between the English and Scottish nation; whereupon a sharp debate grew whether the King should be sent unto any more, or whether they should forthwith proceed to the settlement of the kingdom; to the latter most of the orators inclined, and in likelihood would have led the House that way, but that it was opposed by Cromwell and Ireton, who said it was no fit time to proceed with such vigour, the King having gotten so great a reputation in the army, and therefore advised them to proceed . . . towards the satisfaction of the kingdom and the army. . . . There have been . . . some desperate motions. . . . But all those speeches have been stopped by Cromwell and Ireton, whose civilities are visible, but the reality of their intentions not clearly discerned."[309]

To this Ford adds his testimony. In connection with his report of Cromwell's speech, he wrote to Hopton that "It was moved earnestly in the House that the malignants might be removed from court and also that the King might be removed further off from headquarters because of the confluence of people to him . . . might beget an ill influence and danger in the army, but it was opposed by Cromwell and Ireton."[310] Whatever their object in keeping Charles close at hand, it is evident that, for the moment at least, they were not inclined to give up their negotiations with him, much less to let him fall into the hands of Parliament or be removed from their influence.

During these critical days of late September and early October, 1647, Cromwell's energies were divided between the Army Council and the Commons. On September 30 he was named to a committee to consider a proposition on religion to be submitted to Charles and six days later he was put on a larger committee to prepare a proposition concerning the establishment of Presbyterian government with provisions for tender consciences.[311] On that same day he was directed to communicate the thanks of the House to citizens of London petitioning for the propagation of the preaching of the gospel. On October 9th he was not included in a list of absentees, and on the 12th he was appointed on a committee to investigate the Fellows of certain Cambridge colleges charged with being malignants.[312] On the 13th the committee on Presbyterian government submitted a high-

[309] *Clarendon Mss.* 2602; quoted in Firth, *Clarke Papers*, i, 230n.
[310] Ford to Hopton, as above.
[311] *C. J.*, v, 321, 327.
[312] *Ibid.*, v, 327, 329–30, 331.

ly important report, no less than a proposal to set up that system for three years with provision for permitting other forms of worship.

Whatever share, if any, Cromwell had in framing this plan, there is no doubt that he was deeply interested in it as his presence as a teller on three successive motions proves. On the first—the proposal to establish Presbyterianism for three years—he was a teller for the affirmative, which was beaten by the narrow margin of 38 to 35. On the second—that a time limit be imposed on this experiment—he was successful by 44 to 30; and on the third—that the period be limited to seven years—he was again beaten by 41 to 33. It seems from this that while he was in accord with the Presbyterians up to the point of admitting the policy of establishing that form of church government, he parted with them in his desire to limit the experiment to a shorter period than they were willing to admit. The result was that 'the end of the next session of Parliament'—a curiously vague date—was resolved upon; and, after the adoption of some other clauses, further discussion was postponed.[313]

This question of the establishment of a Presbyterian system was closely related to the general problem which confronted the army leaders. Though present at most of the sessions of Parliament and taking his share in the debates and votes, Cromwell none the less continued in close communication with the King's representatives. This was the more important in that it seemed that an agreement between Charles and the army officers might be reached at any moment, and several new and more important men were admitted as counsellors to the King in the hope that under their influence he could be induced to come to terms. But by October 11 it became evident that the negotiators were as far apart as ever and the King's new advisers were ordered to return to London. It was at this moment, according to report, that Cromwell began to suspect that nothing could ever be settled between the King and the army and inclined to turn to compromise with the Presbyterians; though Ireton, rumor said, was not ready to abandon negotiations with the King and had a serious disagreement with Cromwell, even offering to give up his command in the army.[314]

Whether or not the wish was father to the thought, that compromise between Charles and the army leaders was impossible, and whether that influenced Cromwell in his actions and votes in the Commons on October 13 regarding the establishment of Presbyterianism, it is evident that he kept in close touch with both army and Parliament. From the debate and divisions on the establishment of Presbyterianism, he seems to have hastened back to his headquarters to be con-

[313] *Ibid.*, 332.
[314] Letter of Intelligence, *Clarendon Mss*, 2622.

fronted with a question of a very different character. This was the case of Sir George Middleton, brother-in-law of Whalley, a captain in Cromwell's own regiment, later a spy for Charles II during the Protectorate, and as such arrested and condemned to death but doubtless through the influence of his connections, pardoned and exiled.[315] It would seem that Middleton had fallen out with some of the soldiers, that his trial had been delayed, and that to prevent charges of favoritism, Cromwell wrote Fairfax:

For his Excellency Sir Thomas Fairfax: These

SIR,

The case concerning Captain Middleton hears ill, inasmuch as it is delayed (upon pretences) from coming to a trial. It is not (I humbly conceive) fit that it should stay any longer. The Soldiers complain thereof, and their witnesses have been examined. Captain Middleton, and some others for him, have made stay thereof hitherto. I beseech your Excellency to give order it may be tried on Friday, or Saturday at farthest, if you please; and that so much may be signified to the Advocate.

Sir, I pray excuse my not-attendance upon you. I scarce miss the House a day, where it's very necessary for me to be. I hope your Excellency will be at the headquarter tomorrow, where, if God please, I shall wait upon you. I rest,

Your Excellency's most humble servant,

Putney, October 13th, 1647. OLIVER CROMWELL.[316]

From such diverse affairs, great and small, Cromwell was called to face another crisis. At this moment two new Scottish commissioners, Lanark and Loudon, joined Lauderdale in London on October 11, to inspire Charles with hope and the army leaders with fear. The army was, in fact, on the horns of a dilemma. If the Scots invaded England, could the army march north to meet them leaving the King, the Parliament and the City in its rear, with a nation weary of war and ready to make peace on almost any terms? If the army should be forced to leave to meet a Scotch invasion, it was proposed by some of the officers, Cromwell possibly among them, that the King should be taken with them, and when the Army Council met on October 14, that was a principal topic of discussion. To such a move Charles was naturally opposed. His negotiations with Cromwell and Ireton had obviously broken down and each side naturally accused the other of bad faith.

Cromwell's position and activities at this moment partook of the nature of his dual capacity as soldier and politician. He spent his time between the Council of Officers and the House of Commons, keep-

[315] Noble, ii, 153.

[316] Holograph original in *Sloane MSS*, 1519, f. 160. Carlyle, XLVII.

ing close watch on every move of Parliament, army and the King. Writing from Putney, he had told Fairfax that he would wait on him on the 14th, the day of the meeting of the Army Council. On that day the religious question was debated in the House, but, whether or not he was present, the decision to tolerate neither the Papists nor the Book of Common Prayer bears no evidence of his influence.[317] The day following he seems to have been present in his place, as he was ordered to supply two committees with information as to the "late force" upon the House, and as to relief of certain persons to whom money was owed.[318] On October 16 the propositions to be sent to the King were returned from the Lords with certain additions, and on a division as to whether the manner of address to the King should be considered immediately, Cromwell and Marten acted as tellers for the affirmative, but were beaten.[319]

His anxiety for a speedy settlement was understandable. The soldiers were getting out of hand, the influence of the Agitators was increasing and the Levellers were gaining ground. A week earlier, on October 9, the representatives of five regiments had drawn up a manifesto, *The Case of the Army truly stated*,[320] calling for the immediate purging of the House and for its dissolution within a year. To this they added a demand for a "law paramount" establishing biennial parliaments chosen by manhood suffrage, and endowed with supreme authority in all legislation. Against the system of King, Lords and Commons, as against the old system of county and borough constituencies with their various traditional and anomalous franchise, the Levellers set their new doctrine of equality and popular sovereignty, based on a new instrument of government, a written constitution which should be the supreme law of the land.

However posterity was to justify their principles, this radical revolutionary party, in still greater measure than even Ireton, labored under three great disadvantages—they were far in advance of their generation, they were a minority of a minority, and they were out of touch with the enormous majority of popular opinion. They were none the less dangerous. Aggrieved by the withholding of their arrears of pay, suspicious of long and tortuous negotiations of their leaders, desirous of justice and of peace, the soldiers formed a threatening element. Negotiations on the basis of existing institutions had failed or seemed about to fail, and, impatient of delay, they sought a new and revolutionary basis of settlement. Of all this Cromwell was well aware. He knew that many officers, including his own son-in-law Ireton—and Ireton perhaps most of all—were not unfavorable to

317 *C. J.*, v, 333.
318 *Ibid.*, 334. This probably refers to army arrears.
319 *Ibid.*, 335.
320 Published in October, 1647.

such a settlement, and he was anxious to avert such a crisis as seemed to impend, most of all to prevent the divisions in the army and between the army and Parliament coming to an open breach.

While, then, the Houses and the Levellers prepared their new systems, in Army Council as in Parliament he strove for compromise and agreement. On October 18, the day the Levellers presented their petition to Fairfax, he was in Parliament taking part in its discussions of the propositions to be presented to the King, then making their slow way through the House and was appointed to a committee to consider the so-called "Ninth Paper," relating to the method of selecting officers, ambassadors and foreign agents under the new arrangement for continuing monarchical government.[321] Two days later, when a proposal concerning the exemption from pardon for delinquents came up, he won the point for which he argued—that the number exempted from pardon should not exceed seven—by a notable speech, three hours long, in which he defined his position. Of it only a fragmentary notice has come down to us, yet that fragment is not without interest and significance.

Speech in the Commons, October 20, 1647

"Three days ago," wrote the Roman correspondent, "to this effect Cromwell . . . [spoke] for three hours striving with as much hypocrisy as dissimulation . . . to persuade the Parliament that he and General Fairfax and all the heads of the army had not in any way a part in the designs of those regiments which had [mutinied] but that their purpose and wish from the beginning of the war had been none other than to serve the King and to establish the power of the monarchy. Throughout his whole speech he spoke very favorably of the King, concluding that it was necessary to re-establish him as quickly as possible."[322]

If we accept this as a statement of his convictions, Cromwell's position, like that of the other parties to the dispute, was fairly clear. In general it may be said that the King clung to his purpose of defending his friends, the monarchy and the church. The Parliamentary Presbyterians desired to limit monarchy and episcopacy, or to replace the latter with the Presbyterian system. The Levellers were prepared to abolish both monarchy and the Established church. Independents like Cromwell seem at this moment to be content with curbing the crown and permitting a limited episcopacy with toleration for the other sects. Assuming the premise which his opponents rejected—that of his good faith—it would seem that Cromwell at this time was seeking a middle ground; that he felt that Charles's support of

[321] *C. J.*, v, 336.

[322] Newsletter, Oct. 22/Nov. 1, *Roman Transcripts*, R. O., quoted in Gardiner, *Civil War*, iii, 381.

the Independents was essential to the success of their cause; and that, with all the difficulties they had encountered in coming to an agreement with the King, they believed that such an agreement was still possible. Apart from other considerations, they felt that sooner or later he must appreciate the facts of the situation and yield to their superior force. They could not realize that his convictions were as strong as their own; that he never lost his faith that something would come to his relief; that he felt his person to be inviolable; and that, prisoner as he was, he was still the King.[323]

If we assume with the Royalists that Cromwell was a traitor and a hypocrite, or if we assume with Cromwell's apologists that Charles was a dissembler, all this must perforce fall to the ground. The problem, like all such which rest on the determination of sincerity is difficult, if not impossible. But we cannot assume that all the honesty was on one side, all the dishonesty on the other. There was sincerity and dissimulation on both sides, for each side was deeply convinced of the eternal righteousness of its cause; and—though each side would have denied it bitterly—each side was prone to act on the maxim that the end justified the means.

Meanwhile the business of life went on, in Parliament as in the army, with Cromwell taking his part in it. He was not merely a member of Parliament, he was lieutenant-general of the army, and though he seems to have been regular in his attendance in the House, he apparently returned to his quarters at Putney every night, if we may judge by the circumstance that on October 22 he was put on a committee to consider the satisfaction of the army arrears[324] and that same day wrote from Putney to Fairfax in regard to the replacement of the deputy-governor of Hull, John Mauleverer, by the Fifth Monarchist, Colonel Robert Overton:

To his Excellency Sir Thomas Fairfax: These

SIR,

Hearing the Garrison of Hull is much distracted in the present government, and that the most faithful and honest officers have no disposition to serve there any longer under the present Governor; and that it is their earnest desires, with all the faithful and trusty inhabitants in the Town, to have Colonel Overton sent to them to be your Excellency's deputy over them, I do humbly offer to your Excellency, whether it might not be convenient that Colonel Overtown be speedily sent down; that so that garrison may be settled in safe hands. And that your Excellency would be pleased to send for Colonel Overton, and confer with him about it, that either the regiment in the town may be so regulated as your Excellency may be confident that the garrison may be secured by them; or otherwise it may be drawn

[323] *C. J.*, v, 337.
[324] *C. J.*, v, 344.

out, and his own regiment in the Army be sent down thither with him. But I conceive, if the regiment in Hull can be made serviceable to your Excellency, and included in the Establishment, it will be better to continue it there, than to bury a regiment of your Army in that garrison.

Sir, the expedition will be very necessary, in regard of the present distraction there. This I thought fit to offer to your Excellency's consideration. I shall humbly take leave, and subscribe myself, Your Excellency's

Most humble [and faithful servant,

Putney, October 22d, 1647. OLIVER CROMWELL.][325]

The next glimpse of him is a communication of like character on October 26, to General Thomas Mytton, asking if Carnarvonshire had just cause for its complaint that too many horse were being stationed there at the county's expense. To this Mytton replied on November 2, agreeing that the complaint was just. In itself the correspondence seems of small importance, yet it reveals the great underlying fact which, in a measure obscured by greater events and so more or less neglected by historians, is none the less of fundamental importance in these and later years. It is that England, though possessed of a King and nominally governed by a Parliament, was, in effect, in the hands of an armed force quartered on a population which, however helpless, for the most part bitterly resented this military occupation. The greater part of them were virtually a conquered people at the mercy of their conquerors and among the elements to be considered, not the least was the underlying dissatisfaction of the great majority. More than ever it appeared that the army was, as it were, alone in the midst of its enemies, and its officers, unless they could come to some accommodation with the King and meanwhile keep their own followers under discipline, might well be the victims not the victors of the civil war.

Every day made a solution of their problem more necessary and more difficult. None realized this better than the army leaders themselves, and it is not without importance to consider the preamble of their new proposals, the so-called *Agreement of the People* in connection with this insignificant letter of Cromwell to Mytton. On October 28, some ten days after the *Case of the Army* was presented to Fairfax, a meeting of the Army Council was called in Putney church, and to it were invited, as before, Wildman, Sexby and other leaders of the Levellers, to consider the situation of affairs and to find a solution if possible.

[325] *Sloane MSS*, 1519, f. 164; Carlyle, XLVIII. The letter is not in Cromwell's hand and all after "humble," including the signature, has been torn off.

THE MEETING AT PUTNEY
OCTOBER 28–NOVEMBER 11, 1647

The assembly of the representatives of the army in Putney church was a momentous meeting destined to last through three long session days. In the preceding weeks there had been drawn up the *Agreement of the People* by the Levellers as an answer at once to the position of the Parliament and the King, and Ireton's *Heads of the Army Proposals*. The language of the preamble revealed that the Levellers, no less than the officers, knew the precarious position in which the army stood.

"Having by our late labours and hazards made it appear to the world at how high a rate we value our just freedom, and God having so far owned our cause as to deliver the enemies thereof in our hands, we do now hold ourselves bound . . . to take the best care we can for the future . . . for as it cannot be imagined that so many of our countrymen would have opposed us in this quarrel if they had understood their own good, so we may hopefully promise to ourselves that when our common rights and liberties shall be cleared, their endeavours will be disappointed that seek to make themselves our masters. . . ."[326]

To that end they proposed a new instrument and system of government. Its first provisions rested on the dissoluion of the existing Parliament and the choice of another, of four hundred members, on the basis of population as nearly as they could guess, to be chosen every two years, to meet from mid-June to mid-December every year. Save for persons receiving alms, servants and wage-earners, all "housekeepers" of twenty-one, who had not aided the King and who had not opposed the army's policies, were eligible for the franchise and for election to the House. This body was to appoint a Council of State to which its own members were eligible; erect and abolish courts of law and public offices; refrain from impressing for foreign war; make laws from which no rank or station should be excepted. As to religion it proposed that it be reformed "to the greatest purity in doctrine, worship and discipline, according to the Word of God," and maintained out of the public treasury, with full toleration—save for public profession of Catholicism—to all who "abuse not this liberty to the civil injury of others, or to actual disturbance of the public peace."

Such, with much detail as to the choice of representatives, was the proposal of the Levellers set against that of Ireton. It included many things, but, save for the denunciation of those who had supported

[326] S. R. Gardiner, *Const. Docts.*, p. 232.

Charles, it seems to ignore both King and monarchy, and, directly or indirectly, it was aimed, like the arguments of its authors, against the efforts of Cromwell and Ireton to come to some accommodation with the King. That was apparent from the first. In the absence of Fairfax who was reported "being not well, and at Turnham Green," Cromwell presided and,

The Officers being met, first said,

LIEUTENANT-GENERAL CROMWELL.

That the Meeting was for public business. Those that had anything to say concerning the public business might have liberty to speak.

To that Sexby answered, "Mr. Allen, Mr. Lockyer, and myself are three," with, it appears, two soldiers, one of Cromwell's own regiment and one of Colonel Whalley's, "with two other gentlemen, Mr. Wildman and Mr. Petty"; and with this the argument began by a formal statement from Ireton regarding the reasons for the meeting "in a friendly way, not by command or summons, to invite some of those gentlemen to come in with us."

Sexby was not appeased. He had, he said, been "desired by the Lieutenant General to [let him] know the bottom of their desires," and this he did in no uncertain terms.[327]

On behalf of the agitators Sexby declared that there were two causes of their misery. They sought to satisfy all men, but in going about to do it had dissatisfied all men. They had laboured to please the King, but unless they all cut their throats, they would not please him; and they had all supported a House which would prove rotten studs;[328] *i.e.*, the Parliament. Wherefore he prayed the Lieut.-General and Commissary-General—whose credit and reputation had been much blasted upon these two matters—to consider of those things which should be offered them.

LIEUT.-GEN. CROMWELL: "I think it is good for us to proceed to our business in some order, and that will be if we consider some things that are lately past. There hath been a book printed called *The Case of the Army Stated*, and that hath been taken into consideration, and there hath been somewhat drawn up by way of exception to things contained in that book, and I suppose there was an answer brought to that which was taken by way of exception, and yesterday the gentleman that brought the answer he was dealt honestly and plainly withal, and he was told that there were new designs a driving and nothing would be a clearer discovery of the sincerity of [their] intentions, than[329] their willingness that were active to bring what they had to say to be judged of by the General Officers and by this General

[327] *Clarke Papers*, 226 ff. Here as elsewhere, Mrs. Lomas' admirable brief summaries of the remarks of other speakers than Cromwell are, in general, retained.

[328] *i.e.*, the uprights in a lath and plaster wall.

[329] "as" in MS.

Council, that we might discern what the intentions were. Now it seems there be divers that are come hither to manifest those intentions according to what was offered yesterday, and truly I think, that the best way of our proceeding will be to receive what they have to offer. Only this, Mr. Sexby, you were speaking to us two. [I know not why], except you think that we have done somewhat or acted somewhat different from the sense and resolution of the General Council. Truly, that that you speak to, was the things that related to the King and things that related to the Parliament; and if there be a fault, I may say it and I dare say, it hath been the fault of the General Council, and that which you do speak, both in relation to the one and the other, you speak to the General Council I hope, though you named us two. Therefore truly I think it sufficient for us to say, and 'tis that we say—I can speak for myself, let others speak for themselves—I dare maintain it, and I dare avow I have acted nothing but what I have done with the public consent, and approbation and allowance of the General Council. That I dare say for myself, both in relation to the one and to the other. What I have acted in Parliament in the name of the Council or of the army I have had my warrant for from hence. What I have spoken in another capacity, as a member of the House, that was free for me to do; and I am confident that I have not used the name of the army, or interest of the army, to anything but what I have had allowance from the General Council for, and [what they] thought fit to move the House in. I do the rather give you this account, because I hear there are some slanderous reports going up and down upon somewhat that hath been offered to the House of Commons [by me] as being the sense and opinion of this army and in the name of this army, which, I dare be confident to speak it, hath been as false and slanderous a report as could be raised of a man. And that was this: That I should say to the Parliament and deliver it as the desire of this army, and the sense of this army, that there should be a second address to the King by way of propositions. I dare be confident to speak it, what I delivered there I delivered as my own sense, and what I delivered as my own sense I am not ashamed of. What I delivered as your sense, I never delivered but what I had as your sense."

After a few words from Col. Rainborowe, Commissary Ireton denied all desire or purpose to set up the King, or to set up the Parliament or any other men whatsoever, to be their law-makers, but neither would he concur with any who were not willing to attempt all ways to preserve both Parliament and King. It was thought fit to let the agitators know what the General Council had done, which was now drawn up in writing as follows (*read*), and he thought it fit that the Council should have an answer.

Mr. Allen: We read the paper amongst them and this is the answer (*read*).

Ireton complained that the agitators set themselves up as a "divided party or distinct Council," and set down their resolutions as things in which they demanded the compliance of others, rather than as seeming willing to show compliance themselves. But upon some things that the Lieut.-General and some others of the Committee offered them, they had descended a little from their height and had now sent some "to hear what we have to say to them or to offer something to us." Wherefore he prayed that they might proceed.

Some remarks from Buff Coat (supposed to be Everard) followed, and then the second answer of the agitators—*i.e.*, "the Agreement of the People," was read. This demanded 1. Equal electoral districts. 2. The dissolution of the Long Parliament on Sept. 30, 1648. 3. Biennial Parliaments, to be elected every March and sit for five months. 4. The limitation of the powers of future Parliaments so as to guarantee complete toleration; a full indemnity for acts done during the late public differences, and good and equal laws. It attacked the privileges of the peerage and protested against the proposed treaty with the King.

Lieut.-Gen. Cromwell: "These things that you have now offered, they are new to us; they are things that we have not at all (at least in this method and thus circumstantially) had any opportunity to consider of them, because they come to us but thus, as you see; this is the first time we had a view of them.

Truly this paper does contain in it very great alterations of the very government of the kingdom, alterations from that government that it hath been under, I believe I may almost say, since it hath been a nation; I say I think I may almost say so, and what the consequences of such an alteration as this would be, if there were nothing else to be considered, wise men and godly men ought to consider, I say, if there were nothing else [to be considered] but the very weight and nature of the things contained in this paper. Therefore, although the pretensions in it and the expressions in it are very plausible, and if we could leap out of one condition into another, that had so specious things in it as this hath, I suppose there would not be much dispute, though perhaps some of these things may be very well disputed. How do we know if, whilst we are disputing these things, another company of men shall gather together, and they shall put out a paper as plausible perhaps as this? I do not know why it might not be done, by that time you have agreed upon this, or got hands to it, if that be the way. And not only another and another, but many of this kind. And if so, what do you think the consequence of that would be? Would it not be confusion? Would it not be utter confusion? Would it not make England like the Switzerland country, one canton of the Swiss against another, and one county against another? I ask you whether it be not fit for every honest man seriously to lay that upon his heart? And if so, what would that produce but an absolute desolation—an absolute desolation to the nation—and we in the meantime tell the nation: "It is for your liberty, 'tis for your privilege, 'tis for your good." Pray God it prove so, whatever course we run. But truly I think we are not only to consider what the consequences are (if there were nothing else but this paper) but we are to consider the probability of the ways and means to accomplish: that is to say [to consider] if[330] according to reason and judgment, the spirits and temper of the people of this nation are prepared to receive and to go on along with it, and [if] those great difficulties [that] lie in our way [are] in a likelihood to be either overcome or removed. Truly, to anything that's good, there's no doubt on it, objections may be made and framed; but let every honest man consider whether or no there be not very real objections [to this] in point of difficulty. I know a man may answer all difficulties with faith,

[330] MS., "that."

and faith will answer all difficulties really where it is, but[331] we are very apt all of us to call that faith that perhaps may be but carnal imagination and carnal reasonings. Give me leave to say this, there will be very great mountains in the way of this, if this were the thing in present consideration; and therefore we ought to consider the consequences, and God hath given us our reason that we may do this. And it is not enough to propose things that are good in the end, but it is our duty as Christians and men to consider consequences and to consider the way, even supposing[332] this model were an excellent model, and fit for England and the kingdom to receive.

But really I shall speak to nothing but that that, as before the Lord, I am persuaded in my heart tends to uniting of us in one to that that God will manifest to us to be the thing that He would have us prosecute; and he that meets not here with that heart and dares not say he will stand to that, I think he is a deceiver. I say it to you again, and I profess unto you, I shall offer nothing to you but that I think in my heart and conscience tends to the uniting of us and to the begetting a right understanding among us; and therefore this is that I would insist upon, and have it cleared among us.

It is not enough for us to insist upon good things; that every one would do—there is not forty of us but we could prescribe many things exceeding plausible, and hardly anything worse than our present condition, take it with all the troubles that are upon us. It is not enough for us to propose good things, but it behoves honest men and Christians that really will approve themselves so before God and men, to see whether or no they be in a condition [to attempt], whether, taking all things into consideration they may honestly endeavour and attempt that that is fairly and plausibly proposed. For my own part I know nothing that we are to consider first but that, before we would come to debate the evil or good of this [paper] or to add to it or subtract from it,[333] which I am confident, if your hearts be upright as ours are—and God will be judge between you and us—if we should come to anything, you do not bring this paper with peremptoriness of mind, but to receive amendments, to have anything taken from it that may be made apparent by clear reason to be inconvenient or unhonest. This ought to be our consideration and yours, saving [that] in this you have the advantage of us—you that are the soldiers, you have not—but you that are not [soldiers] you reckon yourselves at a loose and at a liberty, as men that have no obligation upon you. Perhaps we conceive we have; and therefore this is that I may say—both to those that come with you and to my fellow-officers and all others that hear me—that it concerns us, as we would approve ourselves before God, and before men that are able to judge of us, if we do not make good [our] engagements, if we do not make good that that the world expects we should make good. I do not speak to determine what that is, but if I be not much mistaken, we have in the time of our danger issued out Declarations; we have been required by the Parliament, because our Declarations were general, to declare particularly what we meant; and having done that, how far that obliges or not obliges [us], that is by us to be con-

331 MS., "and."

332 "but suppose" in MS.

333 The words "if we should come to anything," seem to belong to the previous clause. (*Note by Firth.*)

sidered, if we mean honestly and sincerely and to approve ourselves to God as honest men. And therefore, having heard this paper read, this remains to us; that we again review what we have engaged in, and what we have that lies upon us. He that departs from that that is a real engagement and a real tie upon him, I think he transgresses without faith, for faith will bear up men in every honest obligation, and God does expect from men the performance of every honest obligation. Therefore I have no more to say but this: We having received your paper shall amongst ourselves consider what to do; and before we take this into consideration, it is fit for us to consider how far we are obliged, and how far we are free; and I hope we shall prove ourselves honest men where we are free to tender anything to the good of the public. And this is that I thought good to offer to you upon this paper."

Mr. Wildman said that having been appointed as a mouth-piece at the meeting of gentlemen, soldiers and agents the day before, he would say something in reply to his Honour, the chief weight of whose speech seemed to be that he and his brother officers would consider their obligations and how far they were engaged, before considering the paper, adding that God would protect men in keeping honest promises. But, so far as he comprehended the meaning of those from whom he came, every past obligation must be considered again, whether it were just or no, for if by a clearer right it appeared not so, they judged (and so does he) that a man might honestly recede from it. Therefore the first thing was to consider the honesty of what was offered.

Commissary Ireton, after objecting to the theory that a man can withdraw from all engagements to another if he alters his mind about their justice, as subversive of law and the Commonwealth, and observing that it comes strangely from one who agrees with this book [*i.e.*, the Case of the Army] in which every punctilio of Engagement is insisted on, declared that there were many things in the paper which he should rejoice to see obtained, and if they were free from all engagements, he should concur further than at present he can. But they were under engagements; the army itself was under engagements, and however much this gentleman might hold himself absolved, he believed those of the army who came with him would hold themselves bound by them. Therefore they must consider how far they were obliged by their former declarations, and unless the Council would meet from day to day and consider the matter themselves, he proposed that a Committee be appointed for the purpose.

Col. Rainborowe said that he had not expected to be there and it would probably be the last time. He came thither not about the paper, but because he had learnt that his regiment was to be taken from him, but rather than lose it, Parliament should exclude him from the House or imprison him, for whilst he was employed abroad he would not be undone at home. As to the paper, whoever had done it had done it with much respect to the good of his country. It had been said that a man, being engaged, must perform his engagements, but he was wholly confident that every honest man was bound to God and his conscience, let him be engaged in what he will, to decline it if convinced that it is his duty. There were two objections made to this thing. 1. Division; but he believed that honest things would keep them together. 2. Difficulties; but if they had thought of difficulties they would never have looked an enemy in the face, and whatever the difficulties might be, even if they had death before them and the sea on either side and behind, yet if they were convinced that the thing was just, they were bound to carry it on. It was said: "it's a huge alteration, it's a bringing in of new laws"; this kingdom has been under this government ever since it was a kingdom. "If writings be true, there hath been many scufflings between the honest men of England and those that have tyrannised over them," and the just laws which English men are born to were intrenchments once. But even if they are what the people have always been under, "if the people find that they are [not] suitable to freemen as they are," there is no reason why anything should not be gained "that might be more advantageous to them than the government under which they live." He prayed that the justness of the thing might be considered, and, that established—that nothing might deter them from doing that which was just to the people.

Lieut.-Gen. Cromwell: "Truly I am very glad that this gentleman that spoke last is here, and not sorry for the occasion that brought him hither; because it argues that we shall enjoy his company longer than I thought we should have done."

Col. Rainborowe: "If I should not be kicked out."

Lieut.-Gen. Cromwell: "And truly then I think it shall not be long enough. But truly I do not know what the meaning of that expression is, nor what the meaning of any hateful word is here. For we are all here with the same integrity to the public; and perhaps we have all of us done our parts not frighted with difficulties, one as well as another; and I hope have all purposes henceforward, through the grace of God, to do so still. And therefore truly I think all the consideration is, that amongst us we are almost all soldiers; all considerations [of not fearing difficulties] or words of that kind do wonderfully please us, all words of courage animate us to carry on our business, to do God's business [and] that which is the will of God. I say it again, I do not think that any man here wants courage to do that which becomes an honest man and an Englishman to do. But we speak as men that desire to have the fear of God before our eyes, and men that may not resolve to do that which we do in the power of a fleshly strength, but to lay this as the foundation of all our actions, to do that which is the will of God. And if any man have a false deceit—on the one hand, deceitfulness, that which he doth not intend, or a persuasion on the other hand, I think he will not prosper.

"But to that which was moved by Col. Rainborow, of the objections of difficulty and danger of the consequences, they are not proposed to any other end, but [as] things fitting consideration, not forged to deter from the consideration of the business. In the consideration of the thing that is new to us, and of everything that shall be new that is of such importance as this is, I think that he that wishes the most serious advice to be taken of such a change as this is—so evident and clear [a change]—whoever offers that there may be most serious consideration, I think he does not speak impertinently. And truly it was offered to no other end than what I speak. I shall say no more to that.

"But to the other, concerning Engagements and breaking of them. I do not think that it was at all offered by anybody that though an Engagement were never so unrighteous, it ought to be kept. No man offered a syllable or tittle [to that purpose]. For certainly it's an act of duty to break an unrighteous Engagement; he that keeps it does a double sin, in that he made an unrighteous Engagement, and [in] that he goes about to keep it. But this was only offered, and I know not what can be more fit;[334] that before we can consider of this [paper] we labour to know where we are and where we stand. Perhaps we are upon Engagements that we cannot with honesty break, but let me tell you this, that he that speaks to you of Engagements here, is as free from Engagements to the King as any man in all the world; and I know that[335] if it were otherwise, I believe my future actions would provoke some to declare it. But I thank God I stand upon the bottom of my own innocence in this particular; through the grace of God I fear not the face of any man; I do not. I say we are to consider what Engagements we have made, and if our Engagements have been unrighteous, why should we not make it our endeavours to break them. Yet if unrighteous Engagements,[336] it is not [good to make] a present breach of them unless there be a consideration of circumstances. Circumstances may be such as I may not now break an unrighteous Engagement, or else I may do that which I do[337] scandalously, though[338] the thing be good. If that be true concerning the breaking of an unrighteous Engagement, it is much more verified concerning Engagements disputable whether they be righteous or unrighteous. If so, I am sure it is fit we should dispute [them], and if, when we have disputed them, we see the goodness of God enlightening us to see our liberties, I think we are to do what we can to give satisfaction to men. But if it were so, as we made an Engagement in judgment and knowledge, so we go off from it in judgment and knowledge. But there may be just engagements upon us, such as perhaps it will be our duty to keep; and if so, it is fit we should consider; and all that I said [was] that we should consider our Engagements, and there is nothing else offered, and therefore what need anybody be angry or offended. Perhaps we have made such Engagements as may in the matter of them not bind us, [yet] in some circumstances they may. Our Engagements are public Engagements. They are to the kingdom, and to every one in the kingdom that could look upon what we did publicly declare; could read or hear it read. They are to the Parliament, and it is a very fitting thing that we do seriously consider of the things. And shortly, this is that I shall offer: that because the kingdom is in the danger it is in, because the kingdom is in that condition it is in, and time may be ill spent in debates, and it is necessary for things to be put to an issue—if ever it was necessary in the world it is now—I should desire this may be done:—

"That this General Council may be appointed [to meet] against a very short time, two days, Thursday if you would, against Saturday, or at furthest against Monday: that there might be a Committee out of this Council appointed to debate and consider with those two gentlemen and with any

334 Transposed from the line below, after "this paper."
335 MS., "it."
336 *i.e.*, if our engagements are unrighteous.
337 "did" in MS.
338 "if" in MS.

others that are not of the army that they shall bring, and with the agitators of those five Regiments; that so there may be a liberal and free debate had amongst us; that we may understand really as before God the bottom of our desires, and that we may seek God together, and see if God will give us an uniting spirit. Give me leave to tell it you again, I am confident there sits not a man in this place that cannot so freely act with you but if he sees that God hath shut up his way that he cannot do any service in that way as may be good for the kingdom, he will be glad to withdraw himself, and wish you all prosperity. And if this heart be in us as is known to God, that searcheth our hearts and trieth the reins, God will discover whether our hearts be not clear in this business. Therefore I shall move that we may have a Committee amongst ourselves [to consider] of the Engagements, and this Committee to dispute things with others, and a short day [to be appointed] for the General Council. I doubt not but if in sincerity we are willing to submit to that light that God shall cast in among us, God will unite us and make us of one heart and one mind. Do the plausiblest things you can do, do that which hath the most appearance of reason in it that tends to change, at this conjuncture of times, you will find difficulties. But if God satisfy our spirits, this will be a ground of confidence to every good man, and he that goes upon other grounds, he shall fall like a beast. I shall desire this, that you or any other of the agitators or gentlemen that can be here will be here, that we may have free discourses amongst ourselves of things, and you will be able to satisfy each other. And really, rather than I would have this kingdom break in pieces before some company of men be united together for a settlement, I will withdraw myself from the army to-morrow and lay down my commission. I will perish before I hinder it."

Bedfordshire Man: Hoped that the engagements of the army had given nothing away that was the people's rights. As to the change of Government, there might be dangers in it, but there might be more dangers without it. Moved that there might be free liberty to act for the people's good and that all who conceived themselves bound up would desist, and not hinder the people in a more perfect way.

Capt. Awdeley urged the immediate appointing of a Committee.

Lieut.-Col, Goffe begged to put his honour in mind of what he moved even now, (viz. that there might be a seeking of God in the things that now lie before them), mourned the withdrawal of God's presence and urged that they should seriously set themselves to seek the Lord; and proposed the morrow as the best day.

Lieut.-Gen. Cromwell: "I know not what [time] Lieut.-Col. Goffe means for tomorrow for the time of seeking God. I think it will be requisite that we do it speedily, and do it the first thing, and that we do it as unitedly as we can, as many of us as well may meet together. For my part I shall lay aside all business for this business, either to convince or be convinced as God shall please. I think it would be good that tomorrow morning be spent in prayer, and the afternoon might be the time of our business. I do not know if[339] these gentlemen do assent to it that tomorrow in the afternoon might be the time."

339 "that" in MS.

LIEUT.-COL. GOFFE agreed to this.

COMMISSARY IRETON acknowledged himself as much moved by what LIEUT.-COL. GOFFE had said; feared they none of them walked as closely with God as they should, urged that the main thing was for each of them individually to wait upon God, and proposed that the next forenoon should be set apart for all to spend in prayer, but either in private or public as each thought best.

Agreed for the meeting for prayer to be at Mr. Chamberlain's.

LIEUT.-GEN. CROMWELL urged that they should not meet as two contrary parties but as some desirous to satisfy or convince each other.

MR. PETTY had only done what was desired by the agents that sent him, but not knowing their sense as to the meeting, he could only give his own consent to it.

BUFF COAT spoke to the same effect.

LIEUT.-GEN. CROMWELL: "I hope we know God better than to make appearances of religious meetings covers for designs as for insinuations amongst you. I desire that God that hath given us some sincerity will own us according to His own goodness and that sincerity that He hath given us. I dare be confident to speak it, that [design] that hath been amongst us hitherto is to seek the guidances of God, and to recover that presence of God that seems to withdraw from us;[340] and our end is to accomplish that work which may be for the good of the kingdom. It seems to us in this as much as anything we are not of a mind,[340] and for our parts we do not desire or offer you to be with us in our seeking of God further than your own satisfactions lead you but only [that] against tomorrow in the afternoon (which will be designed for the consideration of these businesses with you) you will do what you may to have so many as you shall think fit, to see what God will direct you to say to us. That—whiles we are going one way and you another—we be not both destroyed. This requires spirit. It may be too soon to say, it is my present apprehension; I had rather we should devolve our strength to you than that the kingdom for our division should suffer loss.[341] For that's in all our hearts, to profess above anything that's worldly the public good of the people; and if that be in our hearts truly and nakedly, I am confident it is a principle that will stand. Perhaps God may unite us and carry us both one way. And therefore I do desire you, that against tomorrow in the afternoon, if you judge it meet, you will come to us to the Quartermaster-General's quarters, where you will find us [at prayer] if you will come timely to join with us, [or] at your liberty, if afterwards, to speak with us, there[342] you will find us."

MR. WILDMAN wished to return to the earlier business of the meeting. It was said that as the agents insisted on Engagements in the "Case of the Army" it was therefore contrary to their principles that an Engagement which was unjust should lawfully be broken.[343] The principle that a man

[340] "And it seems as much to us in this as anything we are not all of a mind. And to accomplish that work which may be for the good of the kingdom is our end." MS.

[341] See quotation from Berkeley, above.

[342] "and there" in MS.

[343] See Ireton's speech, above.

once engaged, though the engagement appeared to be unjust, must sit down and suffer under it—and that therefore, if they were engaged to submit to the laws made by Parliament, they must swear obedience even to unrighteous laws—seemed to him very dangerous and contrary to the first declaration of the army.[344] The agents desired nothing but the union of the army, but the necessities of the kingdom were such that it might be lost by two or three days' delay, as there might be an agreement by propositions between the King and Parliament. They [the agents] were satisfied that their way was just and meant to go on with it. The main thing was to secure the rights of the people in their Parliaments, as insisted on by the Declaration of June 14. If the thing was just or the people's due, no Engagement could bind them from it, therefore it was only the justice of the thing that needed to be considered.

COM. IRETON declared that he was far from holding that if a man had engaged himself to what it were sin to perform, he was still bound to do it; but what they were talking of was not so much of what was sinful before God as of what was just between man and man; and he conceived that the great foundation of right and justice betwixt man and man was that they should keep covenant one with another. If the principle of covenant, of contract were taken away, what right had a man to his estate or his good. When he heard that the keeping of engagements was to depend only on the "wild or vast notion of what in every man's conception is just or unjust" he trembled at the endless consequences of it. It was argued that if this engagement were just, then all the engagements made before, if they were against it, were unjust; but there was a great deal of equivocation as to what is just and unjust.

WILDMAN and IRETON carried on their contention for some time, interrupted only by a suggestion from CAPT. AWDELEY that if they tarried long, the King would come and say who would be hanged first.

LIEUT.-GEN. CROMWELL: "Let me speak a word to this business. We are now upon that business which we spake of consulting with God about, and therefore for us to dispute the merit of those things, I judge it altogether unreasonable[345] unless you will make it the subject of debate before you consider it among yourselves. The business of the Engagement[s] lies upon us. They[346] are free in a double respect; they made none, and if they did, then the way out is now, and [it is a way] which all the members of the army, except they be sensible of it [may take] and at one jump jump out of all [engagements] and it is a very great jump, I will assure you.[347] As we profess we intend to seek the Lord in the thing, the less we speak in it [now] the better, and the more we cast ourselves upon God the better.

I shall only speak two things to Mr. Wildman in order to our meeting. Methought he said: if there be delay he fears this business will be determined,

[344] *i.e.*, the "Declaration of the Army" of June 14, 1647.

[345] "about it" in MS.

[346] "they," *i.e.*, the representatives of the five regiments and the agents of the Londoners. (*Note by Firth.*)

[347] This seems to be sarcastic: they made no engagements, or if they did, they now say they are free to break them all; and all the army may take the like big jump, unless they happen to be sensible of their obligations. (*Note by Mrs. Lomas.*)

the propositions will be sent from the Parliament, and the Parliament and King agree, and so those gentlemen that were in that mind to go on in their way will be cut off in point of time to their own disadvantage. And the other thing he said was, that these gentlemen who have chosen Mr. Wildman and that other gentleman[348] to be their mouth at this meeting to deliver their minds, they are upon the matter engaged in what they have resolved upon, and they come as engaged men upon their own resolution. If that be so, I think there neither needs consideration of the former, for you will not be anticipated. If that be so, you [can] work accordingly. And though you do meet us, yet having that resolution, you cannot be prevented in your way[349] by any proposition or any such thing; though we should have come hither and we should meet tomorrow as a company of men that really would be guided by God. If any come to us tomorrow only to instruct us and teach us, how far that will consist with the liberty of a free[350] [debate] or an end of satisfaction, I refer to every sober-spirited man to think of and determine.[351] I think it is such a pre-engagement that there is no need of talk of the thing. And I see then, if that be so, things are in such an irrevocable way—I will not call it desperate—as there is no hope of accommodation or union, except we receive the counsels—I will not call it the commands—of them that come to us. I desire that we may rightly understand this thing. If this be so, I do not understand what the end of the meeting will be. If this be not so, we[352] will [not] draw any man from their engagements further than the light of God shall draw them from their engagements; and I think, according to your own principle, if you be upon any Engagement you are liable to be convinced unless you be infallible. If we may come to an honest and single debate, how we may all agree in one common way for public good; if we meet so, we shall meet with a great deal the more comfort and hopes of a good and happy issue and understanding of the business. But if otherwise, I despair of the meeting, or at least I would have the meeting to be of another notion, a meeting that did represent the agitators of five Regiments to give rules to the Council of War. If it signify this, for my own part I shall be glad to submit to it under this notion. If it be a free debate what may be fit for us all to do, with clearness and openness before the Lord, let us understand, that we may come and meet so and in that sincerity.[353] Otherwise I do verily believe we shall meet with prejudice, and we shall meet to prejudice—really to the prejudice of the kingdom and of the whole army. Thus, if we be absolutely resolved upon our way and engaged beforehand, the kingdom will see it is such a real actual division as admits of no reconciliation, and all those that are enemies to us and friends to our enemies, will have the clearer advantage upon us, to put us into inconveniency. And I desire if there be any fear of God among us, I desire that we may declare ourselves freely, that we do meet upon these terms."

[348] Petty.

[349] MS., "in your way you cannot be prevented."

[350] MS., "the liberty of a free liberty."

[351] The last two words transferred from three lines before.

[352] MS., "that they," *i.e.*, Cromwell and the Council. The reporter changes into *oratio obliqua* for a moment. (*Note by Firth.*)

[353] Four words transferred from the previous line.

COL. RAINBOROWE supported Wildman's argument, but believed there was "no such distance betwixt these gentlemen as is imagined," but that they would hear reason and be advised by the Council, and hoped for a happy meeting on the morrow.

BUFF COAT said that he would break an hundred obligations a day "if afterwards God should reveal Himself."

MR. WILDMAN: Provided that which is done tends to either self-destruction or destruction of one's neighbour.

LIEUT.-GEN. CROMWELL: "I think clearly you were understood to put it upon an issue where there is clearly a case of destruction, public destruction and ruin; and I think this will bring it into consideration whether or no our Engagements have really in them that that hath public destruction and ruin necessarily following. Or whether or no we may not give way too much to our own doubts or fears? And whether it be lawful to break a covenant upon our own doubts and fears will be the issue. I think [best] if we agree to defer the debate, to nominate a Committee."

After some remarks from RAINBOROWE, IRETON and WILDMAN, MR. LOCKYER observed that he gathered that destruction was something near, and that the cause thereof was supposed to be "the going of the proposals to the King." Thought that they should be brought hither, that it might be seen what they were.

LIEUT.-GEN. CROMWELL: "The question is whether the propositions will save us, or [whether they will] not destroy us. This discourse concludes nothing."

CAPT. MERRIMAN thought that fundamentally both parties of them desired the same thing, and hoped that their meeting would be for good, not evil.

BUFF COAT: Although the gentleman who has come along with them [Wildman] has declared their resolutions, yet if God gives them further light, they will not deny it. They have not come resolved *nolens volens* and desire there may be better thoughts of them than that.

LIEUT. CHILLENDEN hoped that the hearts of the gentlemen of the five regiments tended to peace and that they would willingly come on the morrow and join "with sweet compliance in communicating counsels."

LIEUT.-GENERAL CROMWELL: "That which this gentleman[354] hath moved I like exceeding well; he hath fully declared himself concerning the freedom of their spirit as to principles. In general they aim at peace and safety, and really I am persuaded in my conscience it is their aim [to act] as may be most for the good of the people, for really if that be not the supreme good to us under God (the good of the people) our principles fall. Now if that be in your spirits and our spirits it remains only that God show us the way, and lead us [in] the way, which I hope He will. And give me leave [to add] that there may be some prejudices upon some of your spirits, and [upon] such men that do affect your way, that they may have some jealousies and apprehensions that we are wedded and glued to forms of government; so that whatsoever we may pretend, it is in vain for [you] to speak to us, or to hope

[354] *i.e.*, Buff Coat.

for any agreement from us to you; and I believe [also] some such apprehensions as [to] some part of the legislative power of the kingdom, where it may rest besides in the Commons of the kingdom. You will find that we are far from being so particularly engaged to anything to the prejudice of this—further than the notorious engagements that the world takes notice of—that we should not concur with you that the foundation and supremacy is in the people, radically in them, and to be set down by them in their representations.[355] And if we do so [concur, we may also concur] how we may run to that end that we all aim at for[356] that that does remain and therefore let us only name the Committee."

LIEUT.-COL. GOFFE was fully persuaded that if God carried them to meet sincerely, and freely open themselves before the Lord, they might be found going on according to His will.

MR. ALLEN questioned whether "these gentlemen" had power to debate, and if not, thought they should have recourse to those that sent them to see what powers might be given them. Unless they could have a full debate, the meeting would be "useless and endless."

LIEUT.-GEN. CROMWELL: "That gentleman says he will do what he can to draw all or the most of them hither to be heard tomorrow; and I desire Mr. Wildman, that if they have any friends that are of a loving spirit, that would contribute to this business of a right understanding [they would come with him]. And I say no more but this, I pray God judge between you and us when we do meet, whether we come with engaged spirits to uphold our own resolutions and opinions or whether we shall lay down ourselves to be ruled by[357] that which he shall communicate."[358]

From this long, animated, and at times acrimonious, debate three things are evident. The first is the animosity of the Levellers against Ireton, and in less degree against Cromwell, whom Ireton was accused in hostile pamphlets of having betrayed. The second is the denunciation of the "Engagement" or the Army *Proposals* by the Levellers. The third is the conciliatory language of Cromwell. Naturally he was named to the committee of eighteen, with generals Ireton, Hammond and Deane, Colonels Rainsborough, Waller, Rich, Scrope, Tomlinson, Overton, Okey and Tichborne from among the officers. On their part the Levellers were represented by Sexby, Allen, Lockyer, Clarke, Stenson and Underwood; and, apart from the prayer-meeting, were to "confer with the Agitators of the five regiments and such gentlemen as shall come with them about the "Agree-

[355] "Some people believe we are engaged to maintain the authority of the House of Lords. Waller asserts that Cromwell and Ireton privately entered into an engagement to maintain the rights of the House of Lords in August 1647, when the nine Lords joined the army." *Vindication*, p. 192. (*Note by Firth.*)

[356] MS., "or."

[357] "and" in MS.

[358] *Clarke Papers*, i, 226–279; Lomas-Carlyle, Suppl. 25.

ment" now brought in, and their own declarations and engagements."[359]

Under such conditions on the next day, October 29, they assembled once more and as the secretary records:

"Att the meeting of the officers for calling uppon God, according to the appointment of the Generall Councill, after some discourses of Commissary Cowling, Major White and others,"

this second meeting began, not with a speech by the presiding officer, but with a religious exhortation by a Captain Clarke, which was followed with a prayer. To that Adjutant General Deane added a motion for a meeting at this place—the Quartermaster General's quarters—on the following Monday, "the council day," from 8 to 11, to seek God, &c."; and with this the debate began again. After some discussion by Lieutenant Colonel Goffe, the Fifth Monarchist, who had been kept awake the night before by "the conjunction that is betweene Antichrist, or that mystery of iniquity . . . the church . . . with kings and great men," and the stuttering "Buff Coat," Everard, of Cromwell's regiment, who had signed the letter accompanying the *Agreement*, Cromwell finally came to the heart of the argument:

"I think it would not be amiss that those gentlemen that are come would draw nigher.

"I must offer this to your consideration, whether or no we, having set apart this morning to seek God, and to get such a preparedness of heart and spirit as might receive that, that God was minded to have imparted to us, and this having taken up all our time, all this day, and it having been so late this last night as indeed it was when we brake up, and we having appointed a committee to meet together to consider of that paper, and this committee having had no time or opportunity that I know of, not so much as a meeting, I make some scruple or doubt whether or no it is not better,—[I know] that danger is imagined [near at hand] and indeed I think it is,—but be the danger what it will, our agreement in the business is much more [pressing] than the pressing of any danger, so by that we do not delay too. That which I have to offer [is] whether or no we are [as] fit to take up such a consideration of these papers now as we might be to-morrow. Perhaps if these gentlemen, which are but few, and that committee should meet together, and spend their time together an hour or two, the remainder of the afternoon, and all this company might meet about nine or ten o'clock at furthest, they[360] [might] understand one another so well as we might be prepared for the general meeting to have a more exact and particular consideration of things than [we can have] by a general loose debate of things,

[359] *Clarke Papers*, i, 279.
[360] MS., "and they."

which our committee, or at least many[361] of us have [not] had any, or at least not many thoughts about."

COL. RAINBOROWE urged that as they were all met there together they might go on, and thought that the more public the debate was, the better. The Committee might still meet for an hour or two afterwards.

MR. EVERARD desired that the Council might at once consider upon some way of easing them. He did not desire to ruinate any wholesome laws, but only such as would not stand with the peace of the kingdom.

CAPT. AWDELEY desired to second this gentleman's motion. While they debated, they did nothing.

LIEUT.-GEN. CROMWELL: "I think it is true. Let us be doing, but let us be united in our doing. If there remain nothing else but present action[362] I think we need not be in Council here. But if we do not rightly and clearly understand one another before we come to act, if we do not lay a foundation of action before we do act, I doubt whether we shall act unanimously or no. And seriously, as before the Lord, I knew no such end of our speech the last night, and appointing another meeting, but in order to a more perfect understanding of one another what we should do, and that we might be agreed upon some principles of action. And truly, if I remember rightly, upon[363] the delivery of the paper that was yesterday, this was offered, that the things [that] are now upon us are things of difficulty, the things are therefore things that do deserve consideration, because there might be great weight in the consequences; and it was then offered, and I hope is still so in all our hearts, that we are not troubled with the consideration of the difficulty, nor with the consideration of anything but this; that if we do difficult things we may see that the things we do have the will of God in them, that they are not only plausible and good things but seasonable and honest things, fit for us to do. And therefore it was desired that we might consider before we could come to these papers, in what condition we stood in respect of former engagements; however[364] some may be satisfied that there lie none upon us, or none but such as it's duty to break, it's sin to keep. Therefore that was yesterday promised [that] there may be a consideration had of them—and I may speak it as in the presence of God that I know nothing of any Engagements, but I would see liberty in any man, as I would be free from bondage to anything that should hinder me from doing my duty—and therefore that was first in consideration. If our obligation be nothing, or if it be weak, I hope it will receive satisfaction why it should be laid aside, that the things that we speak of are not obliged. And therefore if it please you I think it will be good for us to frame our discourse to what we were, where we are, what we are bound to, what we are free to; and then I make no question but that this may conclude what is between these gentlemen in one afternoon. I do not speak this to make obligations more than what they

361 MS., "any."

362 The MS. inserts after "action," "I mean doing in that kind, doing in that sort," and after "here," "such kind of action, action of that nature."

363 MS., "that upon."

364 MS., "which however."

were before, but as before the Lord. You will see what they are[365] and when we look upon them we shall see if[366] we have been in a wrong way, and I hope it will call upon us for the more double diligence."

COL. RAINBOROWE had hoped that the Committee was to decide whether the paper "did hold forth justice and righteousness," but if they were to spend ten days in discussing what engagements they had broken, or whether they had broken any or no, or what they had kept, he believed evil would overtake them before they had set upon the work at all; he therefore prayed that the agreement might be read and debated on, and that they would either accept it or think of some other way.

LIEUT.-GEN. CROMWELL: "I shall but offer this to you. Truly I hope that we may speak our hearts freely here; and I hope there is not such an evil amongst us as that we could or would exercise our wits or our cunning to veil over any doubleness of heart that may possibly be in us. I hope, having been in such a presence as we have been this day, we do not admit of such a thought as this into our hearts. And therefore if the speaking of that we did speak before, and to which I shall speak again, with submission to all that hear me—if the declining to consider this paper may have with any man a working[367] upon his spirit through any jealousy that it aims at delay; truly I can speak it as before the Lord, it is not at all in my heart, but sincerely this is the ground of it. I know this paper doth contain many good things in it, but this is the only thing that doth stick with me, the desiring to know my freedom to this thing. Though this doth suggest that that may be the bottom of all our evils—and I will not say against it because I do not think against it—though this doth suggest the bottom of all our evils, yet for all of us to see ourselves free to this [so] as we may unanimously join upon this, either to agree to this or to add more to it, [or] to alter as we shall agree, this impediment lies in our way [even] if every man be satisfied with it but myself: That this is the first thing that is to be considered, that we should consider in what condition we stand to our former obligations, that if we be clear we may go off clear, if not, we may not go on. If I be not come off [clear] with what obligations are made, if I be not free to act to whatsoever you shall agree upon, I think this is my duty; that I should not in the least study either to retard your work or hinder it, or to act against it, but wish you as much success as if I were free to act with you. I desire we may view over our obligations and engagements, that so we may be free, upon honest and clear grounds, if this be [possible]."

COL. RAINBOROWE: "My desire——"

LIEUT.-GEN. CROMWELL: "I have but one word to prevent you in, and that is for imminent danger. It may be possibly so [imminent] that [it] may not admit of an hour's debate, nor nothing of delay. If that be so, I think that's above all law and rule to us."

365 Cromwell at this point seems to have produced the book of *Army Declarations*, printed by Matthew Simmons in September 1647. (*Note by Firth.*)

366 MS., "that."

367 MS., "work."

COL. RAINBOROWE urged that they should read the paper and not at this time consider the engagements.

COM. COWLING declared the necessity of expedition, especially considering the state of the army, now upon free quarters.

MAJOR WHITE[368] thought that any particular engagements should yield to the public good.

LIEUT.-GEN. CROMWELL: "I desire to know what the gentleman means concerning particular engagements; if he means those that are in this book? If those that are in this book [they are the engagements of the army]. But if he means engagements personal from particular persons, let every man speak for himself. I speak for myself, I disavow all, and I am free to act, free from any such——"

MAJOR WHITE: If they be such as are passed by the Representative [*i.e.*, the General Council] of the army, the army is bound to go on with them.

COL. HEWSON: All the engagements declared for have been by the Representative of the army, and are the cause of the cloud now hanging over their heads.

MR. PETTUS proposed that the agreement might be read, and that "when any of the matter shall come to touch upon any engagement" so as to break it, then the engagement might be shown and debated.

COM.-GEN. IRETON declared that he himself was not personally or privately engaged in any way, and if he was he would not let his engagements stand in any man's way. Nor did he care for the engagements of the army so much for their own sake as for the army's, which had hitherto carried on the interests of God and His people, and must not now incur the scandal of neglecting engagements and of deceiving the world, giving occasion to think that they are the disturbers of the peace of mankind. He agreed to the plan of reading the paper first, taking into consideration its relation to their engagements amongst other things afterwards.

After a few words from COL. RAINBOROWE, the Agreement was read, and a long debate followed upon the first Article, the supporters of which demanded manhood suffrage.

This was opposed by IRETON, whose view was that "no person hath a right to an interest or share in the disposing or determining the affairs of the kingdom, and in choosing those that shall determine what laws we shall be ruled by here . . . that hath not a permanent fixed interest in this kingdom . . . that is the persons in whom all land lies, and those in corporations in whom all trading lies." He desired equal electoral districts and agreed to an extension of the franchise, but believed that manhood suffrage would be subversive of all rights of property and a taking away of the "fundamental Civil Constitution" of the kingdom.

COL. RAINBOROWE argued hotly in favour of the Article, and at length declared that Ireton and his party not only believed that they [the proposers of the agreement] were for anarchy, but wished to make all the world believe it too.

LIEUT.-GEN. CROMWELL: "I know nothing but this, that they that are the most yielding have the greatest wisdom; but really, Sir, this is not right

[368] Firth points out that this can hardly be Major Francis White, as he had been expelled from the Council.

as it should be. No man says that you have a mind to anarchy, but the consequence of this rule tends to anarchy, must end in anarchy; for where is there any bound or limit set if you take away this [limit] that men that have no interest but the interest of breathing [shall have no voice in elections]. Therefore I am confident on't we should not be so hot one with another."

The debate continued, being chiefly a duel between IRETON and RAINBOROWE, the former being supported by COL. RICH, the latter by MR. PETTUS, COM. COWLING, MR. WILDMAN and MR. SEXBY. SEXBY declared that they—the soldiers—had risked their lives to recover their birthrights, and now they were told that "except a man hath a fixed estate in this kingdom, he hath no right in this kingdom." He wondered they were so much deceived. If they had no rights in the kingdom, they were mere mercenary soldiers. But they have as much a birthright as those two [Cromwell and Ireton] who are their lawgivers, and he is resolved to give up his birthright to no man. The poor and the mean of the kingdom have been the means of its preservation; they are as free from anarchy as their opposers, and they will not lose that which they have contended for.

HUGH PETERS apparently desired a compromise, being "clear the point of elections should be amended."

LIEUT.-GEN. CROMWELL: "I confess I was most dissatisfied with that I heard Mr. Sexby speak of any man here, because it did savour so much of will. But I desire that all of us may decline that, and if we meet here really to agree to that which was for the safety of the kingdom, let us not spend so much time in such debates as these are, but let us apply ourselves to such things as are conclusive, and that shall be this: Everybody here would be willing that the Representative might be mended, that is, it might be better than it is. Perhaps it may be offered in that paper[369] too lamely. If the thing be insisted upon [as] too limited, why perhaps there are a very considerable part of copyholders by inheritance that ought to have a voice, and there may be somewhat too, reflects upon the generality of the people. I know our debates are endless. If we think to bring it to an issue this way, and I think if you do [desire to] bring this to a result,[370] it were well if we may resolve upon a committee.[371] If I cannot be satisfied to go so far as these gentlemen that bring this paper (I say it again), I profess I shall freely and willingly withdraw myself, and I hope to do it in such a manner that the army shall see that I shall, by my withdrawing, satisfy the interest of the army, the public interest of the kingdom and those ends these men aim at."

COL. RAINBOROWE had heard nothing yet to satisfy him. He was not against a committee, and would be as ready as any one to draw back if he saw that what he wished would destroy the kingdom; but until he did see that he should refuse to sell his birthright.

MR. SEXBY thought it a miserable thing that they had fought all this time for nothing. If he [Cromwell] had advertised them of it, he would have had

[369] "That paper" is the *Heads of the Proposals*, "this paper," the *Agreement* now presented.

[370] Clause transposed from end of the speech.

[371] "Cromwell, when in difficulties, generally moved for a Committee."—Firth, Preface to 3rd vol. of *Clarke Papers*.

fewer men under his command. And as to putting off this question and going to another, the army would settle upon no other until this was done. Was loath to make divisions, but unless this was put to a question, he despaired of an issue.

CAPT. CLARKE urged moderation, not making reflections upon each other, but with "droppings of love" upon one another's hearts.

CAPT. AWDELEY complained that apparently the dispute was going to last until the 10th [*i.e.*, the Ides] of March. They [the two disputing parties] had brought things into a fair pass, and if their reasons were not satisfied and every one did not fetch water from their wells, they threatened to withdraw. Wished they might all rise and go to their duties.

LIEUT.-GEN. CROMWELL: "Really for my own part I must needs say, whiles we say we would not make reflections we do make reflections; and if I had not come hither with a free heart to do that that I was persuaded in my conscience is my duty I should a thousand times rather have kept myself away. For I do think I had brought upon myself the greatest sin that I was [ever] guilty of if I should have come to have stood before God in that former duty without saying that[372] which I did say and shall persevere to say, that I cannot against my conscience do anything.

"They that have stood so much for liberty of conscience, if they will not grant that liberty to every man, but say it is a deserting I know not what—if that be denied me, I think there is not that equality that [is] professed to be amongst us.[373] I said this and I say no more, but[374] make your businesses as well as you can, we might bring things to an understanding, it was to be brought to a fair composure, and when you have said, if you should put this paper to the question without any qualifications I doubt whether it would pass so freely, if we would have no difference we ought to put it; and let me speak clearly and freely, I have heard other gentlemen do the like, I have not heard the Commissary General answered, not in a part to my knowledge, not in a tittle, if therefore when I see there is an extremity of difference between you, to the end it may be brought nearer to a general satisfaction, and if this be thought a deserting of that interest, if there can be anything more sharply said, I will not give it an ill word. Though we should be satisfied in our consciences in what we do, we are told we purpose to leave the army or to leave our commands as if we took upon us to do it in matter of will. I did hear some gentlemen speak more of will than anything that was spoken this way, for more was spoken by way of will than of satisfaction, and if

[372] MS., "and if that my saying."

[373] Compare with these remarks about freedom of conscience a similar passage in Speech III. (vol. ii. p. 383). "The remainder of this speech is simply a chaos of detached phrases from different sentences. The argument seems to be, 'If you claim liberty to follow your consciences, but will not grant me liberty to follow mine, there is no equality between us. Though we conscientiously believe that under certain circumstances we ought to resign our commands, you taunt us as if we were following our wills instead of our consciences and accuse us of deserting the cause. Can anything be more harshly said.' In answer to Sexby's demand for an immediate vote Cromwell again proposes that the question should be referred to a committee to try to make a fair compromise." (*Note by Firth.*)

[374] "that" in MS.

there be not a more equality in our minds, I can but grieve for it, I must do no more."

After further arguments from IRETON, RAINBOROWE and PETTUS.

LIEUT.-GEN. CROMWELL: "Here's the mistake; [the whole question is] whether that's the better Constitution in that paper or that which is [now]. But if you will go upon such a ground as that although a better Constitution was offered for the removing of the worse, yet some gentlemen are resolved to stick to the worse, there might be a great deal of prejudice upon such an apprehension. I think you are by this time satisfied that it is a clear mistake; but it is a dispute[375] whether or no this be better; nay, whether it be not destructive to the kingdom."

During the further discussion which followed, LIEUT. CHILLENDEN moved that according to the Lieut.-General's motion, a committee might be chosen; CAPT. AWDELEY explained that his complaints against delay were not only against Lieut.-Gen. Cromwell and the Commissary General but against all "that would dispute till we have our throats cut." He would die in asserting that it is the right of every free-born man to elect.

IRETON again protested against altering the Constitution, and declared that if there were any thing that was a foundation of liberty at all, it was "that those who shall chose the law-makers shall be men freed from dependence upon others."

LIEUT.-GEN. CROMWELL: "If we should go about to alter these things, I do not think that we are bound to fight for every particular proposition. Servants while servants are not included. Then you agree that he that receives alms is to be excluded."

MR. EVERARD said he came from the agents of the five regiments in consequence of the Lieut.-General's desire for an understanding, who had prayed them to show their wish for unity by coming. He was marvellously taken up with the plainness of the Lieut.-General's carriage, and although he was warned by some that they would be kept in debate and dispute until all would go to ruin, he said "I will bring them to you. You shall see if their hearts be so; for my part I see nothing but plainness and uprightness of heart made manifest to you." The one thing in which they differed was that the other party conceived that this debating and disputations would do the work, while they believed they must put themselves into the privileges which they wanted.

SIR HARDRESS WALLER agreed with the last speaker that disputings would not do the thing, and thought they should let all the powers, "Parliament or King or whoever they are," know "that these are our rights and if we have them not we must get them the best way we can."

LIEUT.-GEN. CROMWELL: "I think you say very well, and my friend at my back [Everard], he tells me that [there] are great fears abroad, and they talk of some things such as are not only specious to take a great many people with, but real and substantial, and such as are comprehensive of that that hath the good of the kingdom in it. Truly if there be never so much desire of carrying on these things [together] never so much desire of conjunction, yet if there be not liberty of speech to come to a right understanding of

[375] *i.e.*, it is disputable.

things, I think it shall be all one as if there were no desire at all to meet. I may say it with truth that I verily believe there is as much reality and heartiness amongst us [as amongst you] to come to a right understanding, and to accord with that that hath the settlement of the kingdom in it. Though when it comes to particulars we may differ in the way, yet I know nothing but that every honest man will go as far as his conscience will let him, and he that will go further I think he will fall back. And I think when that principle is written in the hearts of us, and when there is not hypocrisy in our dealings, we must all of us resolve upon this, that 'tis God that persuades the heart; if there be a doubt of sincerity, it's the devil that created that effect; and 'tis God that gives uprightness, and I hope with such an heart that we have all met withal; if we have not, God find him out that came without it, for my part I do it."

Despite Cromwell's soothing words, this was by no means the end of the long argument. To them Ireton added a defence of his Army *Proposals* against those of the Levellers; Sir Hardress Waller an appeal for unity in the face of the grave dangers confronting them; Colonel Rainsborough a motion that the army might be called to a rendezvous and "things settled." Upon this there followed a sharp interchange between Ireton and Rainsborough as to the meaning of some phrases in the Army *Proposals*, and the angry denial of an Agitator of the charge that it was his party which had provoked the disturbances. With further defence by Ireton of his Proposals against the arguments of Wildman, speaking, he declared, for the Agents or Agitators, the meeting ended on a note of entire disagreement between them as to the form and powers of the system to be established. It was expressed concisely by Wildman voicing the fear that, were the King restored, as Ireton urged,—as to "indemnity, I do not say it was asking of the King pardon; it is rendering us up, [because the King is under constraint] and therefore is null in law."[376] This issue ran through the whole debate, and was one of the elements in the situation as it developed in succeeding months. It is a motive force in all revolutions. What will happen to the revolutionaries if the old order is restored? What have they to expect, or to hope for, if those they overthrew should come once more to power? It is the motive of fear which drives men farther than they might go were that fear removed, and leads them in many instances to remove the source of that fear.

As a result of this long debate, on the next day, October 30, there was a meeting of the committee of officers at the Quartermaster General's, at which there were eighteen men present, Cromwell and Ireton among them. The list of the other members is not without interest, for there were present, besides the Agitator-Levellers, Sexby and Allen, with four others like them designated merely as "Mr.," a

[376] *Clarke Papers*, i, 280–363; thence Lomas-Carlyle, Suppl. 25.

group of men of some importance in the next few months. There sat the determined enemy of the King, Colonel Rainsborough, with Colonels Lilburne and Rich, Lieutenant Colonel Goffe and two men to whose charge Charles was to be committed at Windsor on another stage of his journey to the scaffold—Captain Merriman and Lieutenant Colonel Cobbett.

Before that committee came the consideration "of the papers of the Armie, and the paper of the People's Agreement, and to collect and prepare somewhat to bee insisted uppon and adheer'd unto for settling the Kingedome, and to cleare our proceedinges hitherto." The committee determined on six general points to be "insisted uppon and adheer'd unto." They were to dissolve the existing Parliament on the first of the next September, and to make provision for biennial Parliaments and the continuance of their sitting—that is that they could not be dissolved by the monarch, save by their own consent. In the intervals between parliamentary sessions there was to be a Council of State appointed by the Houses with other needful committees, and the King could not call an extraordinary Parliament without its advice and warrant. As to the election of members, a redistribution of seats should be made, eliminating the old charters and privileges and spreading representation with "more perfection of equality," together with provisions for the constitution of the new electorate thus created. To it all those who had served Parliament were to be admitted, all against the Parliament excluded from both franchise or membership. Finally, no peers created since May 21, 1642, "or hereafter to be made" should sit or vote in Parliament without the consent of both Houses.[377]

Such was the programme laid down by the committee, to which was added presently another series of constitutional proposals. Throughout the long debate it is clear that the Council of Officers inclined to uphold Cromwell in rejecting the demands of the Agitators that no more applications be made to Charles. It was perhaps no wonder that men like Wildman felt there must be some secret arrangement between Cromwell and Ireton and the King, and that the Agitators and Levellers and perhaps the army generally might be betrayed by those leaders. Nor was that feeling lessened by the fact that Cromwell's wife, his daughter, Mrs. Ireton, and his cousin Whalley's wife had lately been at court, where Ashburnham had taken Mrs. Cromwell by the hand, and the others with their escorts had been led into the court and 'feasted.'[378]

Had they known of the royal plans they would have been more angry than they were, for Charles was listening to the proposals of the Scots to escape to them and wage a new war for his throne. He

[377] *Clarke Papers*, i, 363–7.
[378] *Clarendon St. Papers*, ii, App. xl.

had given his word not to attempt such an escape, and to this Ashburnham had added his parole; but with that curious twisted conscience which so many men possess, and Charles not least among them, he found another way. He sent Ashburnham to suggest to the army that "the court was so much Scottified that he feared there would be workings to get the King away";[379] and in some mysterious fashion incomprehensible to the ordinary mind, he seems to have conceived that this, in effect, relieved him of his parole. Alarmed by this warning, Whalley posted guards within the palace, and on complaint that they disturbed the sleep of the Princess Elizabeth, asked the King to renew his pledge not to endeavor to escape. This Charles refused to do, and Fairfax was notified at once. On the 31st, the guard at Hampton Court was increased and the next day most of the royal attendants, including Berkeley and Ashburnham, were dismissed.[380]

The whole situation was disturbing to the army leaders. It seemed evident to them that there were plots and intrigues centering about Charles of which they knew nothing, and consequently feared. By November 1, when the army council renewed its discussions, this change was evident in Cromwell's attitude. He had not yet come to the Agitators' side, but his speeches lacked the conviction of three days before. With his fellow-officers he had, as it were, moved to the left; and where they had been prepared earlier to accept Ireton's *Army Proposals*, they were now more and more inclined to support the Agitators' *Case of the Army Stated*.

They had, in fact, reached that point which all successful revolutions reach in time. From the creation of a "revolutionary atmosphere" they had proceeded to reform; then to armed resistance; then to the overthrow of the existing government. They now faced the creation of a new system to replace the old. In that Ireton had led the way with his *Army Proposals*, endeavoring, in effect, to combine new and old, to keep King, Lords and Commons, even episcopacy, with altered powers and greater authority in the Parliament, and toleration for the sects. Between the King and the Presbyterians this proved impossible; and if the revolutionary party was to go on to its goal, it seemed imperative to find a new system, if not of compromise with their opponents, one to be imposed on them by force. As Cromwell pointed out in his opening speech, the officers were not wholly free agents. On the one side they had the King, the Parliament, the Presbyterians and the Scots; on the other the party of the Levellers, some already, as Allen said, "declaring against the name and title of King and Lords." How strong this feeling was, Sexby's remarks revealed. "I think," he said, in considering the proposal to

379 Whalley, *More Full Relation*, p. 2.
380 *Ibid.*, pp. 2–4.

retain the old system, however modified, "we are going to set up the power which God will destroy. We are going to set up the power of Kings, some part of it which God will destroy; and which will be but as a burdensome stone, that whosoever shall fall upon it, it will destroy him."

Between him and the "Saints," like Goffe and Cromwell, was a great gulf fixed. The one demanded political, the other religious liberty. To the one the form of government was everything; to Cromwell, as he said, government was 'but dross and dung in comparison with Christ.' The Levellers proposed to recover the popular rights, lost, they conceived, with that curious perversion of history which Ireton denounced, at the Norman Conquest. Each desired the supremacy of law, but the one demanded political, if not economic, equality, the other held to the rights of religious liberty, of property, of class and rank and an ordered state; and into this argument between the champions of liberty and those of equality, Cromwell plunged.[381]

At the Meeting of the General Council of the Army on November 1 [1647]

LIEUT.-GEN. CROMWELL first moved that every one might speak their experiences as the issue of what God had given in answer to their prayers.

CAPT. ALLEN[382] made a speech expressing the experiences of himself and other godly people: that the work that was before them was to take away the negative voice of the King and Lords.

CAPT. JOHN CARTER, COMMISSARY COWLING and LIEUT.-COL. HENRY LILBURNE gave their experiences.

LIEUT.-GEN. CROMWELL: "To that which hath been moved concerning the negative vote, or things which have been delivered in papers and otherwise may present a real pleasing:—I do not say that they have all pleased, for I think that the King is King by contract, and I shall say as Christ said, 'Let him that is without sin cast the first stone'; and mind that word of bearing one with another; it was taught us to-day. If we had carried it on in the Parliament and by our power without any things laid on [us of] that kind, so that we could say that we were without transgression, I should then say it were just to cut off transgressors, but considering that we are in our own actions failing in many particulars, I think there is much necessity of pardoning of transgressors.

"For the actions that are to be done and those that must do them: I think it is their proper place to conform to the Parliament that first gave them their being; and I think it is considerable[383] whether they do contrive

[381] Cp. Gardiner, *Civil War*, iv, 3ff., and Pease, *The Leveller Movement*, pp. 215 ff.

[382] Francis Allen, of Ingoldsby's regiment; Major Allen of Berkshire. Thurloe, iv. 285. (*Note by Firth.*)

[383] "Considerable," *i.e.*, "to be considered of." The sense seems to be: "I think they ought to consider whether they intend to suppress the royalists(?) by the power

to suppress the power of that power or no. If they do continue [? contrive] to suppress them, how they can take the determination of commanding men, conducting men, quartering men, keeping guards, without an authority otherwise than from themselves, I am ignorant of. And therefore I think there is much need in the army to conform to those things that are within their sphere. For those things that have been done in the army,—as this of the *Case of the Army truly Stated*—there is much in it useful and to be condescended to, but I am not satisfied how far we shall press [it]. Either they are a Parliament or no Parliament. If they be no Parliament, they are nothing and we are nothing likewise.[384] If they be a Parliament, we are to offer it to it. If I could see a visible presence of the people, either by subscriptions or number, [I should be satisfied with it]; for in the government of nations that which is to be looked after is the affections of the people, and that I find which satisfies my conscience in the present thing.

[Consider the case of the Jews.] They were first [divided into] families where they lived, and had heads of families [to govern them], and they were [next] under judges, and [then] they were under kings. When they came to desire a king, they had a king; first elective, and secondly by succession. In all these kinds of government they were happy and contented. If you make the best of it, if you should change the government to the best of it, it is but a moral[385] thing. It is but as Paul says 'dross and dung in comparison of Christ';[386] and when[387] we shall so far contest for temporal things that[388] if we cannot have this freedom we will venture life and livelihood for it; when every man shall come to this condition, I think the State shall come to desolation. Therefore the considering of what is fit for the kingdom does belong to the Parliament—well composed in their creation and election—how far, I shall leave it to the Parliament to offer it. There may be care,—That the elections or forms of Parliament are very illegal, as I could name but one, for a corporation to choose two. I shall desire that there may be a form for the electing of Parliaments. And another thing is[389] the perpetuity of the Parliament, that there is no assurance to the people but that it is perpetual, which does satisfy the kingdom[390] and for other things that are

of the Parliament." (*Note by Firth.*) But it would seem that it was the suppression of the power of Parliament against which Cromwell was arguing rather than that of the royalists, in which case the sense probably is: "whether they are contriving to suppress the exercise of power by that (Parliamentary) power or no."

[384] Because the Parliament gave us our being. See p. 539 above.

[385] Possibly should be "small."

[386] Philippians iii. 8.

[387] MS., "why."

[388] MS., "yet."

[389] MS., "as."

[390] Sentence transposed. Cromwell's argument may be thus summed up: "Leave the settlement of government to Parliament, but provide that Parliament be rightly constituted. There may be care taken that future Parliaments be well composed, as to their creation and election. Elections to Parliament are sometimes illegal, as for instance for corporations to choose two. I shall desire that there may be a form for the electing of Parliament. Another thing to be provided against is the perpetuity of the same Parliament; there is no security, at present, that it shall not be perpetual." The policy advocated is that set forth in the Army Declaration of June 14. Compare Cromwell's remarks on pp. 533, 534 above. (*Note by Firth.*)

to the King's negative vote, as may cast you off wholly, it hath been the resolution of the Parliament and of the army. If there be a possibility of the Parliament's offering those things to the King that may secure us, I think there is much may be said for the doing of it.

"As for the present condition of the army, I shall speak somewhat of it. For the conduct of the army, I perceive there are several declarations from the army, and disobligations to the General's order, by calling rendezvous and otherwise. I must confess I have a commission from the General and I understand that [*i.e.* what] I am to do by it. I shall conform to him according to the rules and discipline of war, and according to those rules I ought to be conformable;[391] and therefore I conceive it is not in the power of any particular men or any particular man in the army to call a rendezvous of a troop or regiment or [in the] least[392] to disoblige the army from those commands of the general. This way is destructive to the army and to every particular man in the army. I have been informed by some of the King's party that if they give us rope enough we will hang ourselves. [We shall hang ourselves] if we do not conform to the rules of war, and therefore I shall move what we shall centre upon. If it have but the face of authority, if it be but a hare swimming over the Thames, he will take hold of it, rather than let it go."[393]

After speeches from CHILLENDEN, ALLEN and LIEUT.-COL. JUBBES, RAINBOROWE moved that the papers of the Committee might be read.

LIEUT.-COL. GOFFE: "I think that motion that was made by the Lieut.-General should not die, but that it should have some issue. I think it is a vain thing to seek God if we do not hearken after His answer, and something that was spoken by the Lieut.-General moves me to speak at this time, and that was upon this ground. It was concluded by the Lieut.-General upon what was spoken by one here that that was not the mind of God that was spoken by him. I could wish we might be wary of such expressions." God hath spoken in several ages in sundry ways. A prophet would come and say upon his bare word that he had received such a message from the Lord. Now He speaks not by one man but in all our hearts, and it is a dangerous thing to refuse what comes from God.

It seems to me clear that a voice from heaven has told us that we have sinned against the Lord by tampering with His enemies; I desire that we may wait upon God and see if He hath not spoken to us, and if the Lord hath spoken to us, I pray God keep us from that sin, that we do not hearken to the voice of the Lord.

391 Sir William Waller said of Cromwell: "Although he was blunt, he did not bear himself with pride or disdain. As an officer he was obedient, and did never dispute my orders or argue upon them." *Recollections* by Sir William Waller (p. 125).

392 MS., "at least."

393 Cromwell's general meaning is plain enough, though the illustration he uses is difficult to understand. The army, he urges, must have some civil authority to support it, therefore it ought to own the authority of the Parliament. He would lay hold of any commission from Parliament, any simulacrum of authority, anything that came from Westminster, from the other side of the Thames. Possibly the illustration was suggested by the story of the multitude of rats swimming over the Tweed which is told in a newsletter of Sept. 1647. (*Clarendon State Papers*, ii. App. 39.) (*Note by Firth.*)

LIEUT.-GEN. CROMWELL: "I shall not be unwilling to hear God speaking in any; but I think that God may [as well] be heard speaking in that which is to be read as otherwise.[394] But I shall speak a word to[395] that which Lieut.-Col. Goffe said, because it seems to come as a reproof to me, and I shall be willing to receive a reproof when it shall be in love and shall be [so] given. That which he speaks was, that at such a meeting as this we should wait upon God and [hearken to] the voice of God speaking in any of us. I confess it is an high duty, but when anything is spoken [as from God] I think the rule is, Let the rest judge.[396] It is left to me to judge for my own satisfaction, and the satisfaction of others, whether it be of the Lord or not, and I do no more. I do not judge conclusively, negatively, that it was not of the Lord, but I do desire to submit it to all your judgments whether it was of the Lord or no. I did offer some reasons which did satisfy me, I know not whether I did others. If in those things we do speak and pretend to speak from God, there be mistakes of fact—if there be a mistake in the thing, in the reason of the thing—truly I think it is free for me to show both the one and the other, if I can. Nay, I think it is my duty to do it; for no man receives anything in the name of the Lord further than [to] the light of his conscience appears. I can say in the next place—and I can say it heartily and freely—as to the matter he speaks, I must confess I have no prejudice, not the least thought of prejudice upon that ground—I speak it truly as before the Lord—but this I think; that it is no ill advertisement to wish us in our speeches of righteousness and justice to refer us to any engagements that are upon us, and that which I have learnt in all [our] debates I have still desired, [that] we should consider where we are, and what engagements are upon us, and how we ought to go off as becomes Christians. This is all that I aimed at and I do aim at. I must confess I had a marvellous reverence and awe upon my spirit when we came to speak. [We said] let us speak one to another what God hath spoken to us;[397] and as I said before, I cannot say that I have received anything that I can speak as in the name of the Lord—not that I can say that anybody did speak that which was untrue in the name of the Lord—but upon this ground, that when we say we speak in 'the name of the Lord,' it is of an high nature."

LIEUT.-COL. GOFFE made an apology for what he had said before.

MR. ALLEN thought the great difference between them was in the interest of King and Lords, some declaring against the name and title of King and Lords. As for the King, if the setting of him up be not consistent with, and is prejudicial to the liberties of the kingdom, then down with him; but if he might be so set up (as the speaker thought he might) then set him up; this being not only their judgment, but that of those who set forth the case of the army.

COL. RAINBOROWE objected that what Mr. Allen spoke reflected upon himself and some others, as if they were against the name of King and Lords.

MR. SEXBY: Truly the Lord has put you, or suffered you to run into such

[394] The papers of the Committee, which Rainborowe had just moved to have read.

[395] MS., "in."

[396] Cromwell is perhaps referring to St. Paul's directions concerning those speaking in unknown tongues and prophesying. See 1 Cor. xiv. 29.

[397] See opening Meeting.

a state that you know not where you are. We find in the word of God "I would heal Babylon, but she would not be healed." I think we have gone about to heal Babylon when she would not. We have gone about to wash a Blackamore, to wash him white, which he will not. "I think we are going about to set up the power which God will destroy. We are going about to set up the power of Kings, some part of it, which God will destroy; and which will be but as a burdensome stone, that whosoever shall fall upon it, it will destroy him."

LIEUT.-GEN. CROMWELL:[398] I think we should not let go that motion which Lieut.-Col. Goffe made, and so I cannot but renew that caution that we should take heed what we speak in the name of the Lord. As for what that gentleman spoke last (but it was with too much confidence) I cannot conceive that he altogether meant it. I would we should all take heed of mentioning our own thoughts and conceptions with that which is of God. What this gentleman told us [was] that which [he conceived] was our great fault. He alludes to such a place of Scripture, "We would have healed Babylon but she would not." The gentleman applied it to us, as that we had been men that would have healed Babylon and God would not have had her healed. Truly though that be not the intent of that Scripture, yet I think it is true, that whosoever would have gone about to heal Babylon when God had determined [to destroy her] he does fight against God, because God will not have her healed. Indeed when we are convinced that it is Babylon we are going about to heal, I think it's fit we should then give over our healing; and yet certainly in general it is not evil to desire an healing. But since I hear no man offering nothing to speak to us as a particular dictate from God, I shall desire to speak a word or two.[399] I should desire to draw to some conclusion of that expectation of ours. Truly, as Lieut.-Col. Goffe said, God hath in several ages used several dispensations, and yet some dispensations more eminently in one age than another. I am one of those whose heart God hath drawn out to wait for some extraordinary dispensations, according to those promises that he hath held forth of things to be accomplished in the later time, and I cannot but think that God is beginning of them. Yet certainly [we do well to take heed] upon the same ground that we find in the epistle of Peter, where he speaks of the Scriptures as "a more sure word of prophecy" than their testimonies was, to which, says he, you do well to take heed, as a light shining in a dark place.[400] If, when we want particular and extraordinary impressions, we shall either alto-

[398] When Wildman criticises this speech, Ireton is said to reply to him, as if he had been the speaker. But the whole speech is so extremely like Cromwell and so utterly unlike Ireton; the involved strain of religious argument—of which Cromwell was so fond—is so different from Ireton's clear, sharp, business-like way of speaking, that it is impossible not to believe that Cromwell was the speaker. Besides, his opening words, "I cannot but renew the caution that we should take heed what we speak in the name of the Lord" clearly refer to the beginning of Cromwell's last speech, "I shall not be unwilling to hear God speaking in any." Ireton had never said a word about anything of the sort. As to the two short subsequent answers, it is probable that they are attributed to the Commissary-General by mistake and were really made by Cromwell. (*Note by Mrs. Lomas.*)

[399] Several words transposed.

[400] 2nd Peter i. 19.

gether sit still because we have them not, and not follow that light that we have; or shall go against or short of that light that we have, upon the imaginary apprehension of such divine impressions and divine discoveries in particular things—which are not so divine as to carry their evidence with them, to the conviction of those that have the spirit of God within them—I think we shall be justly under a condemnation. Truly we have heard many speaking to us; and I cannot but think that in many of those things, God hath spoke to us. I cannot but think that in most that have spoke there have been some things of God made forth to us; and yet there hath been several contradictions in what hath been spoken. But certainly God is not the author of contradictions. The contradictions are not so much in the end as in the way. I cannot see but that we all speak to the same end, and the mistakes are only in the way. The end is to deliver this nation from oppression and slavery, to accomplish that work that God hath carried us on in, to establish our hopes of an end of justice and righteousness in it. We agree thus far. I think we may go thus far further, that we all apprehend danger from the power of the King and from the Lords. All that have spoke have agreed in this too, though the gentleman in the window[401] when he spoke [of] set[ting] up, if he should declare it, did not mean all that that word might import. I think that seems to be general among us all, that if it were free before us, whether we should set up one or other, there is not any intention of any in the army, of any of us, to set up the one [or the other]. I do to my best observation find an unanimity amongst us all that we would set up neither.[402] Thus far I find us to be agreed, and thus far as we are agreed, I think it is of God. But there are circumstances in which we differ as in relation to this. I must further tell you, that as we do not make it our business or intention to set up the one or the other, so neither is it [our intention] to preserve the one or the other with a visible danger and destruction to the people and the public interest. So that that part of difference that seems to be among us is whether there can be a preservation [of them with safety to the kingdom]. First of all, on the one part, there is this apprehension: that we cannot with justice and righteousness at the present destroy, or go about to destroy, or take away or [altogether] lay aside both, or all the interest they have in the public affairs of the kingdom; and those that do so apprehend would strain something in point of security, would rather leave some hazard—or at least if they see that they may consist without any considerable hazard to the interest of the kingdom, do so far [wish] to preserve them. On the other hand those that differ from this, I do take it in the most candid apprehension that they seem to run[403] thus: that there is not any safety or security to the liberty of the kingdom and to [the] public interest, if you do retain these at all; and therefore they think this a consideration to them paramount [to] the consideration of particular obligations of justice, or matter of right or due towards King or Lords. Truly I think it hath pleased God to lead me to a true and clear stating our agreement and our difference; and if this be so we are the better prepared to go [on]. If this be not so, I shall desire that any one that hath heard me [will] declare [it] if he do think that

[401] Allen.
[402] *i.e.*, neither King nor Lords.
[403] *i.e.*, argue.

the thing is mis-stated as to our agreement or difference; and I shall go on, only in a word or two, to conclude that we have been about. As to the dispensations of God, it was more particular in the time of the law [of Moses than in the time of the law] written in our hearts, that word within us, the mind of Christ;[404] and truly when we have no other more particular impression of the power of God going forth with it, I think that this law and this [word] speaking within us—which truly is in every man who hath the spirit of God—we are to have a regard to; and this to me seems to be very clear what we are to judge of the apprehensions of men to particular cases, whether it be of God or no. When it doth not carry its evidence of the power of God with it, to convince us clearly, our best way is to judge the conformity or disformity of [it with] the law written within us, which is the law of the spirit of God, the mind of God, the mind of Christ. As was well said by Lieut.-Colonel Jubbs, for my part I do not know any outward evidence of what proceeds from the spirit of God more clear than this, the appearance of meekness and gentleness and mercy and patience and forbearance and love, and a desire to do good to all and to destroy none that can be saved,[405] and as he said of the spirit of malice and envy and things of that nature, I cannot but take that to be contrary to this law. For my part I say, where I do see this, where [? there] I do see men speaking according to that law, which I am sure is the law of the spirit of life, and I think there is this radically in that heart where there is such a law, or leads us against all opposition. On the other hand I think that he that would decline the doing of justice—where there is no place for mercy,—and the exercise of the ways of force for the safety of the kingdom where there is no other way to save it; and would decline these out of the apprehensions of danger and difficulties in it, he that leads that way on the other hand doth truly lead us from that which is the law of the spirit of life, the law written in our hearts. And truly having thus declared what we may apprehend of all that hath been said, I shall wish that we may go on to our business; and I shall only add several cautions on the one hand and the other.

"I could wish that none of those whose apprehensions run on the other hand,—that there can be no safety in a consistency with the person of the King or the Lords, or their having the least interest in the public affairs of the kingdom,—I do wish them that they will take heed of that which some men are apt to be carried away by, [that is], apprehensions that God will destroy these persons or that power; for that they may mistake in. And though [I] myself do concur with them, and perhaps concur with them upon some ground that God will do so, yet let us [not] make those things to be our rule which we cannot so clearly know to be the mind of God. I mean in particular things let us not make those our rules that this is to be done, [this] is the mind of God, we must work to it.[406] At least let those to whom this is not made clear, though they do think it probable that God will destroy them, yet let them make this rule to themselves, though God have a purpose

[404] Hebrews viii. 10; 1 Corinthians ii. 16. So Cromwell elsewhere observes of certain things that they are 'written in better books than those of paper; written, I am persuaded, in the heart of every good man.' See Speech, Sept. 4, 1654. (*Note by Firth.*)

[405] *Cf.* Speech, July 4, 1653.

[406] *Cf.* Cromwell's speech on p. 478 above.

to destroy them, and though I should find a desire to destroy them—though a Christian spirit can hardly find it for itself—yet God can do it without necessitating us to do a thing which is scandalous, or sin, or which would bring a dishonour to His name; and therefore let those that are of that mind wait upon God for such a way when the thing may be done without sin, and without scandal too. Surely what God would have us do, He does not desire we should step out of the way for it. This is the caution, on the one hand that we do no wrong to one or other, and that we abstain from all appearance of wrong, and for that purpose avoid the bringing of a scandal to the name of God and to His people upon whom His name is called. On the other hand, I have but this to say: That those who do apprehend obligations lying upon them—either by a general duty or particularly in relation to the things that we have declared, a duty of justice, or a duty in regard of that engagement—that they would clearly come to this resolution, that if they found in their judgments and consciences that those engagements lead to anything which really cannot consist with the liberty and safety and public interest of this nation, they would account the general [duty] paramount [to] the other, so far as not to oppose any other that would do better for the nation than they will do. If we do act according to that mind and that spirit and that law which I have before spoken of, and in these particular cases do take these two cautions, God will lead us to what shall be His way, as many of us as He shall incline their minds to, and the rest in their way in a due time."

Capt. Bishop declared that the endeavour to preserve the King—"that man of blood"—was the cause that the kingdom was in a dying condition.

Mr. Wildman followed, in answer to the speech of "that gentleman that spoke last but one" (*i.e.* the speech of Cromwell above) and, in answer to his criticisms, there are two short explanations, attributed in the MS. to the "Com.-Gen.," but which must have been made by the Lieut.-General if the speech above is his, *viz.:*—

1. That he did not speak of destroying the King and the Lords—he had not heard any man charge all the Lords as deserving punishment—but of reserving any interest to them in the public affairs of the kingdom: and

2. That he had said that some men did apprehend that an interest might be given to the King and Lords with safety, while others thought that it could not be done without destruction to the kingdom.[407]

It was evident long before the end of the discussions that the principles of the *Agreement of the People* were gaining ground. At the meeting of the Committee on November 2 that was reflected in the

[407] "It is evident that either the attribution of the long speech to Cromwell or of these two short observations to Ireton is a mistake, and the style shows the latter to be far the more likely of the two.

The debate went on for a long time after this, the chief subject of it being the restrictions to be imposed on the House of Lords, but Cromwell did not speak again.

Other debates followed, of which we have only very scanty notices, and on the 5th (when Cromwell appears to have been absent) the party of the agitators carried a vote for a general rendezvous of the army." (Note by Mrs. Lomas.) *Clarke Papers*, I, 363–406; Lomas-Carlyle, Suppl. 25.

new provisions which were added to those laid down on October 30 by the same body. Those new provisions were six in number. First and most significantly it was unanimously agreed that Parliament's power extended "to the enacting, altering and repealing of all lawes, to the conclusive exposition and Declaration of law, and to finall judgment without further appeale," which effectually barred the interposition of the King and weakened, if it did not actually end the power of the crown as it had previously been exercised. The second—which was apparently not unanimous—was to the effect that no law should be repealed nor new law made "to bind the Commons of England," nor any judgment, trial or order be valid against any "Commoner," without consent of the House of Commons. This was followed by three unanimous decisions to the effect that all commoners, ministers of state and officers of justice—save peers—were subject to "the power and judgment of the House of Commons without further appeale," and that no person condemned by Parliament should be capable of pardon or protection from the King or have his fine remitted without consent of the Houses. To this, finally, was added a long provision accepted unanimously that "positive compulsions" in matters of religion "are not intrusted to any human power"; that pressing men for war, save in defence of the kingdom, was "likewise reserved"; that no commoner was to be questioned as to his share in "the late warre or publique contests" without consent of the Commons; and that the articles already adopted as to Parliament and the franchise were "reserved by the people represented as their fundamental rights not to bee given away or abrogated by their Representatives."[408]

The army programme thus followed in general the scheme laid down by Ireton which would have kept the King but deprived the crown of most of its old prerogatives and made the House of Commons the sole ruler of England, with such checks as could be put on it by King and Lords through personal or extraconstitutional means. To this again the Committee of Officers added further limitations on the royal authority the next day, November 3. The meeting began with an extraordinary prologue which revealed something of the suspicion and unrest of the time. Fairfax was apparently charged with "wearing the Kinge's Colours," and it was reported that soldiers were saying "Lett my Collonell bee for the Devill and hee will, I will bee for the Kinge," and that 400 of Colonel Lilburne's regiment had declared for Charles and proposed to the people of Dunstable where they were quartered that "they would take clubs, and bringe the Kinge to Whitehall." That there was some basis for this fear of a rising sentiment of royalism among some of the soldiery, a newsletter of a few days later presently confirmed. Its story ran that Major

[408] *Clarke Papers*, i, 407–10.

White of Fairfax's own regiment told his men "that the kingdom must be under another government (which he said, to see how they would like it)," but to his discomfiture "the whole regiment threw up their hats and cried 'A King, a King.' And thereupon White got to his horse and made some haste out of the field."[409]

The debate in the committee on the militia and the delinquents which followed this informal discussion of the fears of some of the officers turned on a proposal that Parliament should control the militia for ten years. This was followed by a proposition that tithes be abolished and a land tax put in their place, or that church lands should be sold for the use of the state which should provide for the ministers—in effect what was to be done later in the French Revolution with the confiscation and sale of church property and the enactment of the Civil Constitution of the Clergy. In such fashion does history repeat itself—if never precisely in the same words at least to the same effect.[410]

There is but little record of the important meetings of the Army Council between Wednesday, November 3, and Monday, November 8, when these great issues were being debated and the policy of the army thus laid down. On November 4 the Council considered alterations in their propositions to the King, and the discussion on the question of suffrage gave the Levellers a decided victory in extending the franchise to virtually all but servants and beggars.[411] Again on Friday the 5th and Saturday the 6th they went on with their argument, Fairfax, who had been ill, again in his place, and Cromwell apparently absent attending his duties in Parliament. There on November 5 a committee of the two Houses reported its propositions to be sent to Charles, then voted on in their final form.[412]

The tide had now definitely turned in the Army Council against Cromwell and Ireton.[413] There Rainsborough "intimated that the army was not disposed to make any more addresses to the King . . . Ireton opposed the same all he could, and in testimony of dissent left the council, protesting he could come no more there to be partaker of the high neglect and violation of reason and justice which he observed to reign amongst them." His plan to keep in communication with the King and to achieve reform through him and through Parliament was overpowered by the Levellers' design to have the new constitution derive directly from "the people," that is to say, in effect, from the army. To that end Rainsborough had expressed the sentiment of his party in opposition to further communication with

409 Newsletter, Nov. 15. *Clarendon State Papers*, ii, App. xlix.

410 *Clarke Papers*, i, 410–11.

411 *Perfect Occurrences; Copy of a Letter.*

412 *C. J.*, v, 350–351.

413 Newsletter, Nov. 8, *Clarendon St. Papers*, ii, App. xli; *Clarke Papers*, i, 440.

the King, and carried a motion for a general rendezvous of the army. It was no doubt his motion which implied the settlement of the constitutional question in the spirit of the Levellers, that caused Ireton to withdraw. Meanwhile Charles—who had told Ashburnham of his plan to escape to Jersey and had been advised rather to remove to London with the aid of the Scots—further complicated the situation by asking the Houses for permission to come to London to negotiate.

For Cromwell the situation was extremely difficult. He had negotiated with Charles with little or no definite result; he had turned to Parliament with scarcely more effect; he had most recently tended to accept the plans of the Levellers; and he had, in consequence, roused the suspicions of all three. He went so far in the direction of the Levellers that at this moment, on November 6, he permitted a discussion on the question 'whether it were safe either for the army or the people to suffer any power to be given to the King.'[414] On that same day the House, irritated by the King's request to come to London for a personal treaty, voted that the King was 'bound in justice and by the duty of his office' to assent to all laws made in Parliament. Matters had now come to an *impasse*. The King did not propose to yield up his authority; the Parliament insisted on being the dominant power in the state; the Scots were preparing to support the King in return for his concessions to the Presbyterians; the Levellers were proposing to take authority from the hands of King and Lords alike; and meanwhile army discipline declined, the country was threatened with anarchy, and Royalist reaction again raised its head.

Cromwell hoped for some form of constitutional authority to which he could cling, as he said, 'even though it were but as a hare swimming over the Thames.' To this the Levellers retorted by offering a new form of constitution. As the King's declaration described their plan, it was "to have annulled the House of Lords . . . to purge the House of Commons . . . bring in new members . . . and then draw up an impeachment against the King's Majesty to take away his life . . . and in the meantime to have his Majesty kept . . . where they might guard his person." Thus with the rendezvous voted, fearing its result, Cromwell consented to a discussion in the Army Council on November 8 on the general question of the King's authority, though he was not prepared to adopt the Levellers' principle of manhood suffrage, much less to relax the army discipline:

At a Council of Officers, Putney, November 8.

The LIEUT.-GENERAL spoke much to express the danger of their principles who had sought to divide the army; that the first particular of that which they called the Agreement of the People did tend very much to anarchy

[414] *Copy of a letter;* Newsletter, Nov. 8, *loc. cit.*

[i.e.] that all those who are in the kingdom should have a vote in electing representatives.

CAPT. WILLIAM BRAY made a long speech to take off what the Lieut.-Gen. said; but Cromwell moved and carried a resolution praying the Lord General to send the representative officers and agitators back to their regiments until the rendezvous should be over.[415]

By this adroit move Cromwell contrived to eliminate the more aggressive Levellers from the Army Council and divide them from each other. This done, the Council decided on the next day to appoint a committee to examine the *Agreement of the People* to see how far it was consistent with the other engagements of the army;[416] while Fairfax, seeking means to quiet the soldiery, wrote to the Speaker to ask that the lands of the Deans and chapters be sold to pay the army's arrears.[417]

PART III

THE BREAKDOWN OF NEGOTIATION

THE FLIGHT OF THE KING, NOVEMBER 11–15, 1647

While these arrangements were being made to reduce or to destroy the power of monarchy, Charles was laying his own plans for an escape, in conjunction with his devoted followers, Berkeley and Ashburnham. The former counselled the stationing of vessels at three ports, by one of which Charles could escape to the Continent; the latter still believed that with diplomacy Charles could remain in England and retain his throne. When his plan to bring the King to London failed, casting about for a refuge for his royal master, he recalled a conversation he had held a short time before with the nephew of Charles's chaplain, Dr. Henry Hammond. This was Colonel Robert Hammond, Cromwell's cousin through his marriage with John Hampden's daughter, and now newly appointed governor of the Isle of Wight. That transfer from the turmoil at Putney Hammond had welcomed and had told Ashburnham that he was glad to leave because "he found the army resolved to break all promises to the King and he would have nothing to do with such perfidious actions."[418] To him, in consequence, Ashburnham now resolved to escape with the King. Hampton Court was no longer considered safe. The Levellers seemed determined to have not only Charles's abdication but his

[415] *Clarke Papers*, i, 226.

[416] *Ibid.*, i, 415.

[417] Fairfax to Lenthall, Nov. 9. Rushworth, vii, 687. According to the new establishment, Cromwell's salary, beginning Nov. 3, 1647, was £3 a day. *Cal. S. P. Dom.* (1625–49), p. 715.

[418] Berkeley's *Memoirs*, *loc. cit.*, 373–375; Ashburnham's *Narrative*, ii, 106–112.

life, and the King had just been warned by an anonymous letter, written possibly by Henry Lilburne, brother of John Lilburne and lieutenant-colonel in his brother Robert's regiment, the most mutinous in the army, that there was a design to murder him.[419]

That there was some design to put Charles out of the way appeared in the meeting of the council of officers on November 11 when the fanatical Fifth Monarchist Harrison declared that the King was "a man of blood" and should be prosecuted. If one may fairly interpret the ensuing remarks, Cromwell, though opposed to such a solution of the problem, was aware of the possibility of being compelled to consider it in the last resort and it would seem that this was the first public admission on his part of that eventuality:

At a Council of Officers, Putney, November 11

The Lieut.-General answered him by putting several cases in which murder was not to be punished. As in the case if a man that had killed his son should get into a garrison, whether he might raise war, or not give conditions to that place. Stated the case of David upon Joab's killing of Abner, that he spared him upon two prudential grounds: one that he would not hazard the spilling of more blood, in regard the sons of Zeruiah were too hard for him.

IRETON "answered in the same case," and further urged they were not to go in any unlawful way in order to bring a delinquent to justice; and

The LIEUT.-GENERAL said that we [must not?] do the work when it is disputable and the work of others to do it, [but only] if it be an absolute and indisputable duty for us to do it.[420]

On this note, after a few words from Fairfax and Cowling, the debate came to an end. The hints thrown out by Harrison, the sentiments expressed by the Levellers, were not to be ignored. There was evidently a strong feeling among many men in the army that Charles must be not only dethroned but killed. Nothing could be worse for the cause which Cromwell represented than the assassination of the King by the fanatical element in the army. It would certainly be attributed to the connivance, the negligence, or even the instigation of the army leaders and it would prejudice their cause hopelessly before the country. This, in Cromwell's view, must be avoided at all costs and scarcely was the debate at an end than he wrote to warn Colonel Whalley who commanded the King's guards against a possible attempt on Charles's life by the Levellers.

To Colonel Edward Whalley

DEAR COS. WHALLEY,

There are rumours abroad of some intended attempt on

[419] The letter, signed "E.R." is pr. in *Old Parl. Hist.*, xvi, 328. Cp. Gardiner, *Civil War*, iv, 15.

[420] *Clarke Papers*, I, 417–18; Lomas-Carlyle, Suppl. 25.

his Majesty's person. Therefore I pray have a care of your guards, for if any such thing should be done, it would be accounted a most horrid act.
* * * * * *

Yours,
[Nov. 11?, 1647.] [Oliver Cromwell.][421]

The part of the letter not included in the pamphlet which published the King's letters seems to have contained a statement that, in prosecution of the murderous design of the Levellers, a "new guard was the next day to [have been] put upon his Majesty, of that party."[422] If this information was correct, it was of the utmost importance and Whalley showed the letter to the King on November 11, probably as soon as he received it,[423] not, as he said, to frighten Charles, but in case Charles had heard of such a design from another quarter, to assure him that the general officers abhorred such a plot and would take every precaution to prevent its being carried out.[424]

The plans of the Levellers and the warning of the officers that the King's life was in danger fitted in with the plans of Charles so admirably that the coincidence seemed almost too striking to be accidental; and it was later charged that the whole design was framed by the officers themselves. But nothing could have suited the King's plans better. He had long since consented to the pleas of those who urged him to escape and the preparations of his followers were now complete. He had ordered Ashburnham, Berkeley and William Legge, sometime governor of Oxford, to meet him that night outside his windows at Hampton Court; and, having written three letters explaining his flight, one to Whalley, with a postscript, "I assure you that it was not the letter you shewed me today that made me take this resolution . . . but I confess that I am loth to be made a close prisoner under pretence of securing my life,"[425] he stepped out of the window and hastened through the dark and stormy night, with his three followers, toward Southampton.

It was some little time before it was discovered that the King was not in his room writing letters for the foreign post as he customarily did on Thursday night. The possibility of his being in one of the other 1500-odd rooms of the palace was considered, but the officers at Putney were notified of his disappearance.[426] At midnight Cromwell wrote to Lenthall.

421 Fragment pr, in *His Majesties most gracious declaration left by him on his table at Hampton Court, 11 Novemb. 1647*, p. 7. Carlyle, L.

422 Berkeley, *Memoirs*, p. 377.

423 Whalley, *More full relation*, etc. (Nov. 22, 1647), p. 6.

424 *Ibid.*

425 *L. J.*, ix, 520.

426 Whalley, *op. cit.*, p. 5.

To the Honourable William Lenthall, Speaker of the House of Commons

[SIR,]

* * * His Majesty [has] withdrawn himself [from Hampton Court] at nine o'clock.

The manner is variously reported; and we will say little of it at present, but that his Majesty was expected at supper, when the Commissioners and Colonel Whalley missed; upon which they entered the room, and found his Majesty had left his cloak behind him in the Gallery in the private way. He passed, by the backstairs and vault, towards the water-side.

He left some letters upon the table in his withdrawing room, of his own handwriting; whereof one was to the Commissioners of Parliament attending him, to be communicated to both Houses, and followeth in these words: *etc.*

[OLIVER CROMWELL.][427]

[Hampton Court, Twelve at night,
11th November 1647.]

The next day Cromwell's letter was read in the Commons,[428] and another of which only a line remains, which he must have written shortly thereafter to Manchester, was read in the Lords:

For the Right Honourable the Earl of Manchester, Speaker of the House of Lords.

* * * the King, with nine horses, last night went over Kingston Bridge * * *

[November 12, 1647][429]

Meanwhile, with his destination unknown save to himself and his companions, Charles rode southwest till on the following day, near Southampton, Berkeley and Ashburnham left the King and Colonel Legge to make their way to the Earl of Southampton's house at Titchfield, while Berkeley and Ashburnham crossed to the Isle of Wight, to warn Hammond of the King's approach, to prepare for his reception at Carisbrooke Castle, or, failing that, to find a ship to take him to France. Hammond, though friendly to the King, was appalled at the responsibility thus thrust upon him. Divided between his loyalty to Charles and his duty as an officer of the army, he 'turned deathly pale, trembled for an hour or more, and passionately exclaimed that he was undone.' Persuading Berkeley and Ashburnham to take him and the governor of Cowes Castle to Charles, he found the King no less distressed at the sight of the Parliamentary officers and the realization that he was to be taken to Carisbrooke not only

[427] Rushworth, vii, 871; Carlyle, Letter XLIX.
[428] *C. J.*, v, 356.
[429] *L. J.*, ix, 519.

for security but as a prisoner,[430] which presently he was, while Hammond advised his superiors of the King's presence.

Neither at Westminster nor at Putney was there any notion where the King had gone until Hammond's letters arrived on November 15, asking for instructions. They were a great relief, for Parliament, the City and even the army leaders were alarmed. Every conceivable rumor of the escape was afloat, among them the story that Fairfax and Cromwell had concealed Charles to save him from the Agitators;[431] but once Parliament was assured that he was neither in France nor with the Scots, but a prisoner at Carisbrooke, it turned its attention to the question of how and why he had escaped.

Upon the King's escape to Carisbrooke and Cromwell's share in it, controversy has raged from that day to this. Taken in connection with the maneuvers and debates of the preceding months, Cromwell's negotiations with the King, the Parliament, the Agitators and the army officers, a plausible argument may be—and has been—made that he planned the whole design from the first, to secure the supreme power for himself. It would appear from Clarendon's account that Cromwell was satisfied with this outcome, for as the great historian of the Rebellion writes, when the news arrived:

"All these doubts were quickly cleared, and within two days Cromwell informed the House of Commons that he had received letters from colonel Hammond of all the manner of the King's coming to the Isle of Wight, and the company that came with him; that he remained then in the castle at Carisbrooke till the pleasure of the Parliament should be known. He assured them that colonel Hammond was so honest a man, and so much devoted to their service, that they need have no jealousy that he might be corrupted by any body; and all this relation he made with so unusual a gaiety, that all men concluded that the King was where he wished he should be. And from hence all those discourses, which are mentioned before to have fallen out after, took their original too probably."[432]

Yet even Clarendon, despite his hatred of Cromwell, does not intimate that Cromwell was privy to a plot to remove the King to Carisbrooke as the first step to the scaffold. Besides rumor, that charge rests largely on the lines of one of Cromwell's friends, admirers and servants, Andrew Marvell, who in later years suggested that:

"Twining subtle fears with hope
He wove a net of such a scope
That Charles himself might chase
To Carisbrooke's narrow case,
That thence the royal actor borne
The tragic scaffold might adorn!"

[430] Berkeley, *Memoirs*, pp. 375–81; Ashburnham's *Narrative*.
[431] Newsletter, Nov. 12, *Roman Transcripts*, Record Office.
[432] Clarendon, *History*, x, 138.

It is easy to argue in the light of the event, as Clarendon indicates—and there is no argument more often used and more fallacious than that of *post hoc, propter hoc*—that because Charles fled to Carisbrooke and finally was condemned by the High Court of Justice, the one was a step to the other and since Cromwell was a moving spirit in the execution of the King, he was also the moving spirit in his flight. There is no contemporary evidence to that effect. Cromwell could hardly have known of Charles's destination, for even on the road to Southampton there was an argument as to whether the King should seek the Isle of Wight or go still farther west and find a ship for France. The only possible ground for arguing that Cromwell was involved in a complicated plot to seize the King's person is that Berkeley, Ashburnham and Legge, one or all, were equally involved in a piece of treachery—which is wholly inconceivable, whether one regards them as traitors or as dupes.

The argument that Cromwell planned the King's flight and his imprisonment at Carisbrooke rests on the facts that he was a relative of both Whalley and Hammond; that he wrote a letter to Whalley warning him of an attempt on Charles; that an anonymous letter to the same effect reached the King at about the same time; that the flight was welcomed by Cromwell; and that it was the first step to the scaffold for the King. It rests further on the assumptions that it was Cromwell's design to frighten the King off by having Whalley show his letter to Charles; that Cromwell himself inspired, if he did not write, the anonymous note of warning; that Whalley knew of the presence of Berkeley, Ashburnham and Legge with horses at Thames Ditton ready for a flight; that on the night of the escape he set no sentinel over the King's lodgings and left the way open for escape; that it was somehow planned between Whalley, Hammond and Cromwell that the King should be directed to the Isle of Wight; and that Ashburnham was "an unconscious agent" of all this.[433]

This may in part be true; but it involves a superhuman series of intrigues and coincidences—and no less superhuman skill on Cromwell's part. That he may have had some understanding with Whalley is not inconceivable; that he was at least not displeased at Charles's escape is understandable; that he took advantage of the situation as it developed is in accordance with his whole career. But that he could have foreseen that the King would seek refuge in, or be taken to, Carisbrooke or any other Parliamentary garrison seems inconceivable. He may have wished to get rid of Charles as William III was anxious to be quit of James, and, like William, made flight easier. Beyond that, in view of the evidence, it is impossible to go.[434]

433 The latest and most detailed statement of this view of the case is by Mr. Belloc—Mr. Buchan absolutely dissenting. For the contemporary accounts see below.

434 Until Berkeley's *Memoirs* and Ashburnham's *Narrative* were published Crom-

THE ARMY MEETING, NOVEMBER 15–19, 1647

Such was the romantic and disastrous episode of Charles's effort to escape. It was natural that Cromwell should be pleased at the King's flight. It relieved him and his fellow officers of an unpleasant dilemma. The King was now beyond the reach of the Agitators and of assassination, of the Scots and Parliament. As Clarendon relates:

"And now the Parliament maintained no farther contests with the army, but tamely submitted to whatsoever they proposed, the Presbyterians in both Houses and in the city being in a terrible agony that some close correspondences they had held with the King . . . would be discovered. . . . But Cromwell had more cause to fear a fire in his own quarters. . . . The Agitators, who were first formed by him to oppose the Parliament and to resist the destructive doom of their disbanding . . . now the King was . . . in such a place as the army could have no recourse to him and the Parliament was become of so soft a temper . . . he desired to restrain that liberty which they (the Agitators) had so long enjoyed, and to keep them within stricter rules of obedience . . . and to hinder their future meetings and consultations concerning the settling the government of the kingdom; which he thought ought now to be solely left to the Parliament, whose authority for the present he thought best to uphold. . . . And the suppression of this license put Cromwell to the expense of all his cunning, dexterity and courage. . . ."[435]

But the officers escaped one dilemma only to face another. That Cromwell was having trouble with the Levellers there can be no doubt. Colonel Rainsborough and the Republican Henry Marten spoke openly of impeaching him, and according to one report, some of the more violent Levellers planned to murder him in his bed the night before the rendezvous. Appealing to all the regiments for unity of people and soldiers against the army "grandees,"[436] the leaders of the Levellers, it was reported, planned to secure Fairfax and cut the throats of any members who refused to follow them in their design of prosecuting the King.[437] It was at this moment, then, with the King a prisoner in Carisbrooke, with Parliament preparing to make another effort to come to terms with him, and the Scots preparing to support him, if need be by force of arms, that another meeting of the army was called to deliberate on the new situation of affairs and more especially to consolidate its own position.

The revolutionary movement had now arrived at that stage which

well's innocence of the charge of inveigling the King away was open to serious question but since that time there is direct evidence on one side against pure conjecture—including contemporary rumors, it is true—on the other.

[435] Clarendon, *History*, x, 139.

[436] *Letter sent from several Agitators of the Army to their Respective Regiments.*

[437] *Walwyn's Wiles*, p. 18.

all such enterprises reach sooner or later. The wilder and more aggressive enemies of society were loose and it remained to see whether the leaders of the movement could curb the spirits they had raised, or whether it would go on, as Cromwell feared, to anarchy. The rendezvous had been called for Corkbush Field, near Ware, some thirty miles north of London, for November 15, and in preparation for it, on the preceding day, the officers drew up a statement of their position in the form of a manifesto to the soldiers. Accepting in some measure the proposals of the Agitators and Cromwell's views, it proposed a speedy dissolution of the existing Parliament and a new basis of franchise to make the Commons more nearly representative of the people, and declared that unless discipline was restored, Fairfax, in whose name it was issued, would lay down his commission. To this was added an engagement for the soldiers to sign, promising allegiance to the General and the Army Council.[438] Though it is commonly said that Ireton wrote many or most of these various documents, the whole manifesto was so much in accord with the ideas expressed by Cromwell in the Army Council on November 1, that it is not unreasonable to suppose that Cromwell may have inspired, if he did not actually have a hand in writing it.[439]

A Remonstrance from his Excellency Sir Thomas Fairefax, and his Council of War, concerning the late Discontent and Distraction in the Army; with his Excellency's Declaration of himself, and Expectation from the Army thereupon, for the future uniting of the Army.

That, ever since the Engagement of the Army at Newmarkett Heath, his Excellency, with the General Officers and General Council of the Army (to which that Engagement refers) have been doing their Duty and best Endeavour for the Good of the Army and Kingdom, according to the Ends of that Engagement, and the Declarations and other Papers that have since passed from the Army.

And in this (according to their Consciences, and the best of their Understandings) they have done the utmost they could, without present Destruction to the Parliament, which in their Opinions would inevitably have put the Kingdom into Blood and Confusion, and so both the Army and Kingdom into an Incapacity, or past all rational Hopes, of attaining or enjoying that Satisfaction or Security for which the Engagement was entered into; and if they have neglected any Thing wherein they might have done better, they have been ready (as still they are) to be convinced thereof, and to amend the Default, and to hearken to what any Man would soberly offer for that Purpose, or to lead them to any Thing better.

That, while they have been thus doing their Duty (besides many other Interruptions or Diversion by the Designs and Workings of Enemies), they have of late found the greatest Interruption to their Proceedings by a few

[438] *L. J.*, ix, 529.

[439] See Gardiner, *Civil War*, iv, 22.

Men, Members of the Army, who (without any Authority, or just Call thereunto, that we know of, assuming the Name of Agents for several Regiments) have (for what Ends we know not) taken upon them to act as a divided Party from the said Council and Army, and, associating themselves with, or rather (as we have just Cause to believe) give themselves up to be acted or guided by, divers private Persons that are not of the Army, have endeavoured, by various Falsehoods and Scandals, raised and divulged in Print, and otherwise, against the General, the General Officers and Council to possess the Army and Kingdom with jealousies of them, and Prejudices against them [as if they were fallen from their Principles, had broke all their Engagements and Declarations, and thereby all their Engagements and Declarations, and thereby forfeited their Trust, and were in their whole Proceedings false and treacherous both to the Army and Kingdoms.] And, by these and other Practices, the said Agents and their Associates have laboured to make Parties and Factions in the Army, to raise Discontents, Mutinies, and Disorders therein, to divide the Soldiers from the Officers, and both Officers and Soldiers amongst themselves, and to withdraw several Parts of the Army from their Duty and Obedience to the General's Orders, (and that) in Things most necessary for the Safety of the Army and Kingdom.

And thus, while they causelessly cry out against Breach of Engagements and Dividing the Army, they themselves have made, or endeavoured to make, the greatest Breaches of their Engagements, and greatest Dividing of the Army, that can be; a Dividing most truly contrary to the Engagements, a Dividing which is as bad and destructive as Disbanding, even the Dissolution of all that Order, Combination, and Government, which is the Essence of an Army; and, under false and delusive Pretences (that the Engagements have been broken), they have endeavoured really to loosen and draw the Army off from its former Engagements, and to draw it into new Engagements, different from, and (in some Things) destructive to, the former; and have thus endangered the greatest Forfeiture of the Faith, and Honour of the Army, that ever it incurred.

And whilst they cry out there is nothing done, they themselves have made the greatest Obstructions to the doing of any Good for the Army or Kingdom, both in the Hindrance and Delays to our Proceedings, and the Expence of Time which with their Workings have occasioned (either to have satisfied them (if it had been possible), or else to salve and quiet those Discontents and Distractions which they have raised in the Army); and also by the Occasions which the Parliament and Kingdom (yea even our best Friends in both) have thus received, to discourage them from Compliance with, or Confidence in, an Army so uncertain, so unsettled, so divided.

For these Causes, the General hath thought fit to rendezvous the Army, or such Parts of it as are not fixed upon necessary Duty elsewhere; and having (with the Advice of the General Council) sent to the Parliament more importunately than before, for speedy Satisfaction to the Army in their just Desires (especially in Point of Provision for constant Pay to avoid Free Quarter, and of Security for Arrears), thought it best (with the same Advice) to dismiss most of the Officers and Agitators from the Headquarters for a Fortnight, unto their respective Regiments, to satisfy and compose these Discontents and Division, which have thus been raised in them; and, for

Ease to the Country, and Accommodation to the Soldiery (with respect to the Season of the Year), thought fit to contract the Quarters of the Army in Three Brigades, and to draw them to Three several Rendezvous not far from each other, and this in order to One general Rendezvous, if there should be any Occasion; and in this the several Regiments of Horse and Foot have been appointed to contract Quarters, in order to those several Rendezvous, by taking them directly in Order as their several Quarters lay before without any other Respect or Consideration: But even these Things the said pretended Agents and their Associates have laboured to pervert and make Advantage of, to the aforesaid Ends of Discontent and Distraction, and to represent the same treacherous Counsels and Designs which they had before suggested: And what Good they could not deny to be in the Things, they assume to themselves, as gained by their Procurements; and so greedily catch at the sole Credit of it, as if the General and his Council (but for them) had not done it; and, by Letters or Messages contradicting the General's order, they have (under such scandalous Pretences) laboured to draw divers Regiments, from the Quarters and Rendezvous to which they were ordered, unto the First Rendezvous near Ware, in a disorderly and confused Manner, to the Oppression of the Country, and Disaccommodation (if not Quarreling and Distraction) of the Soldiery and Quartering.

That, without Redress of these Abuses and Disorders, his Excellency cannot nor will any longer undergo or undertake further to discharge his present Trust, to the Parliament, and the Army and Kingdom.

That, though he is far above any such low Thoughts as to court or woo the Army to continue him their General; yet, to discharge himself to the utmost, and bring the Business to a clear and certain Issue, his Excellency doth now Declare,

That he is yet willing to adhere to, and to conduct, and live and die with the Army, in the lawful Prosecution of these Things following:

First, for the Soldiery to obtain:

1. Present Provision for constant Pay while continued; to enable them to discharge Quarters.
2. The present Stating of Accompts, and Security for Arrears; with an effectual and speedy Course to raise Monies thereupon.
3. Sufficient Indemnity, and Commissioners in every County for that Purpose.
4. Provision for maimed Soldiers, and the Widows and Orphans of Men slain in the Service (and that in a certain and more honourable Way); with Commissioners in every County for that Purpose.
5. Provisions for Freedom from Pressing, according to the First Petition of the Army.
6. Provision for Freedom of Apprentices that have served in this War, with a Penalty upon Masters refusing to give it.

Secondly, for the Kingdom:

A Period to be set for this present Parliament (to end so soon as may be with Safety), and Provision therewith to be made for future Parliaments; for the Certainty of their Meeting, Sitting and Ending; and for the Freedom and Equality of Elections thereto; to render the House of Commons (as near as may be) an equal Representative of the People that are to elect.

And (according to the Representation of the Army, of June the 14th) to leave other Things to, and acquiesce in the Determinations of, Parliament; but to mind the Parliament of, and mediate with them for, Redress of the common Grievances of the People, and all other Things that the Army have declared their Desires for.

That, upon his Excellency's continued Conjunction in these Things, he expects that, for the particular Circumstances of them, the Army shall (according to their aforesaid First Engagements) acquiesce in what shall be agreed unto by the general Council of the Army to which that Engagement refers; and for the Matter of Ordering, Conduct, and Government of the Army, that every Member of it shall be observant of, and subject to, his Excellency, his Council of War, and every One of his Superior Officers, according to the Discipline of War; for Assurance whereof, he expects that as many as are satisfied herewith, and agree hereunto, do severally subscribe to what is hereunder written for that Purpose.

We, the Officers and Soldiers of Regiment of , whose Names are here subscribed, do hereby Declare That we are satisfied in his Excellency the General's continued Conjunction with the Army, in the lawful Prosecution of the Things here before declared to be prosecuted for the Soldiery and Kingdom respectively; and for the particular Circumstance of them, we shall (according to the general Engagement of the Army above-mentioned) acquiesce in what shall be agreed unto by the General Council of the Army to which that Engagement refers: And for the Matter of Ordering, Conduct, and Government of the Army, we shall be observant of, and subject to, his Excellency, his Council of War, and every One of us to our Superior Officers in this Regiment and the Army, according to the Discipline of War.

Signed, by the Appointment of his Excellency Sir Thomas Fairefax and the Council of War.

Hertford, Nov.
the 14th 1647. Jo. Rushworth, Secretary."[440]

Thus prepared, on November 15 the officers rode to the rendezvous. There they found not only the four regiments of horse and three of foot ordered to meet the General, but two others, those of Robert Lilburne and Harrison, the one having been ordered to the north, the other to another rendezvous. It was an open mutiny, for, apart from having disobeyed their orders, Lilburne's men had driven away most of their officers and had stuck copies of the *Agreement of the People* in their hats, with a motto, "England's freedom! Soldiers' rights!" Despite this the officers held the upper hand. The forces before them were scarcely more than a fourth of the army, and the soldiers of the seven regiments were not disposed to follow their leaders. Rainsborough who approached Fairfax with a copy of the *Agreement* was waved aside; the few other officers who called on their men to support him, save for Major Scott who was a member of

[440] *L. J.*, ix, 529.

Parliament, were arrested and the soldiers readily signed the engagement. Harrison's regiment yielded to Fairfax's persuasion and followed suit; but Lilburne's men refused.

For a moment it seemed that there might happen what all commanders dread, a conflict between units of their own troops, if not a general mutiny, for Lilburne's regiment had long been a source of uneasiness. There was perhaps no real danger, for the loyal soldiery greatly outnumbered the mutineers; but Cromwell gave them no time for further protest. When the men refused to obey his order to tear the offending papers from their hats, he drew his sword and rode among them, seized the leaders, and overawed the men. The ringleaders were brought before a hastily improvised court-martial; three of them were at once condemned, allowed to throw dice for their lives, and the loser was shot down by a firing squad before the regiments.[441]

A second and third rendezvous were held at Windsor and Kingston with no sign of disturbance. On November 19th, Cromwell related to the House how the Leveller spirit which had threatened the very existence of the army had been quelled, and gave Fairfax credit for the good condition and submissiveness of the army. Convinced that Cromwell had acted only to advance his own power, Edmund Ludlow joined others in as loud a "No" as he could in the vote of the House to express its gratitude to Cromwell for his services. None the less Cromwell was ordered to declare to Fairfax that the House of Commons would at all times be ready to receive and answer such addresses as he might see fit to make to them.[442]

Meanwhile, since the King's removal from Hampton Court left no further reason for keeping the army so near London, its headquarters were moved from Putney to Windsor,[443] but, though this relieved the City from its presence, its leaders were not disposed to let the citizens forget their obligations. Demands for money to pay the troops having failed, Colonel Hewson was ordered to march on the city to collect the assessments, without which free quarter could no longer be avoided. This threat of a second occupation of the capital by the troops alarmed the Commons, which on the day following Cromwell's report of the mutiny, ordered him to write Hewson and persuade the general to countermand his orders, while at the same time it urged the City authorities to pay promptly and avoid military occupation at whatever cost.[444] In such fashion and under such circumstances the army, having in its power King, Parliament and City, and provided with a programme for revision of the constitution, set

441 Rushworth, vii, 875; *Clarendon St. Papers*, ii, App. xli; *L. J.*, ix, 527; *Clarke Papers*, i, liv; *Perfect Diurnall*, Nov. 19; Maseres, *Tracts*, Preface.

442 *C. J.*, v, 364; Ludlow, i, 173; Rushworth, vii, 880; *Perfect Diurnall*, Nov. 19.

443 *L. J.*, ix, 536.

444 *C. J.*, v, 364; Rushworth, vii, 884.

forth on another stage of its career, with Cromwell as its dominant spirit. It only remained to impose its will upon the other parties in the state.

THE NEGOTIATION WITH THE KING, THE "SADDLE LETTER" AND THE "ENGAGEMENT"
NOVEMBER 16–DECEMBER 23, 1647

The army mutiny and the threat of an attack upon London were not the only striking events of this period. At this moment Charles offered to make further concessions; and but for lack of confidence in him, Parliament might well have come to an arrangement with the King. On the day after the rendezvous at Corkbush Field, November 16, he sent a message proposing a compromise. He still held out for episcopacy and restoration of the bishops' lands, but he agreed that the bishops might be assisted by presbyters both in ordination and in jurisdiction, with powers "so limited that they be not grievous to the tender consciences of others." He agreed further to the establishment of Presbyterianism for three years, pending a final settlement by King and Parliament; with full liberty of worship meanwhile to himself, to "all others of his judgment" and still others of "too tender consciences" to submit to this system. The final settlement was to give "full liberty to all those who shall differ on conscientious grounds" from it, except Roman Catholics and atheists. To this Charles added an agreement to surrender the militia for his lifetime, if its control should be guaranteed to his successors; and, with a recommendation to the Houses to consider the demands of the army relating to "the succession of Parliaments and their due election," he requested once more a "personal treaty" in London.

It was a fair proposal and it was backed by the all but unanimous desire of the nation for peace and settled government at almost any price. To deny it was a heavy responsibility not only in ethics but in politics; and though in private the Scots commissioners denounced it as tolerating heresy and schism, and the Parliamentary leaders had no confidence in Charles, it seemed difficult, if not impossible, to them to refuse its terms. The army leaders, Ireton in particular, were no less disturbed; nor does it seem incredible that they, like some men in Parliament, apart from their convictions, had some fears for their personal safety if Charles was on the throne supported by a people weary of war and spoliation. They certainly feared a combination of King and Parliament and on November 18 or 19 Huntington reports that Ireton,

"standing by the fireside at his headquarters at Kingston, and some speaking of an agreement likely to be made between King and Parliament now the person of the King was out of the power of the army, replied, with a discontented countenance, that he hoped it would be such a peace as we might with a safe conscience fight against them both."[445]

To this was added the fear of the Scots. On the very day that Huntington says that Ireton made this remark, the Scots' commissioners presented to the Parliament a protest against the way Charles had been treated—his removal to Holmby House, his wanderings and his confinement since, and the lack of respect shown to his wishes and his person. The concurrent presentation of Charles's moderate proposals and the Scots' warning boded ill for the Independents and the army leaders. It was only too apparent that Charles and the Scots' commissioners had come to some agreement, and that, unless something intervened, Parliament would find it difficult or impossible to refuse the terms offered by the King. In that case the position of the army, and especially of its Independent leaders, would be precarious. Hated by the great majority of the English people; anathema to Scotch and English Presbyterians; at odds with the majority in the House; disliked and distrusted by the King; if all these elements should combine, the situation of men like Cromwell and Ireton would be desperate. What, then, were they to do; where did their own safety and the future of their cause reside? Short of a miracle, where could they look for help?

The first consideration was delay, and though the King's proposal for a personal treaty was presented on November 16, it was nine days before the Lords found an answer. That answer, though not precisely in the negative, was provisional. On November 25, the Lords named a committee to select from the Newcastle and Hampton Court proposals various articles to present once more to Charles "for our present security"; and the next day sent these Four Propositions to the Commons to be passed. The last of these gave the existing Parliament the right to adjourn itself to any place the Houses thought desirable, a condition, they well knew, to which Charles could never consent unless he was sincere in agreeing to abandon control of Parliament. In brief, somewhere and somehow in this period, the army leaders and the Lords, if not the Commons, under Independent influence seem to have changed their minds, or at least their policy, concerning the possibility of arriving at an agreement with the King.

What occasioned this change of heart; what was the miracle which saved the army leaders from an accommodation between King and Parliament; what arguments were offered to persuade the members to ignore the popular demand for peace? The usual answer is given in one of the most dramatic stories told of Cromwell's life, that of the so-called "Saddle Letter." It derives primarily from the life of Cromwell's friend, Roger Boyle, Lord Broghill, first Earl of Orrery,

[445] Huntington, *Sundry reasons*, in Maseres, *Tracts*, p. 404.

written by his chaplain, Thomas Morrice. As told by Orrery himself, that nobleman, one of Cromwell's most intimate friends, and a trustworthy witness, asked Cromwell in 1649 why the army had not tried longer to come to terms with Charles, to which Cromwell is said to have replied:

"The reason why we would once have closed with the King was this; we found the Scots and the Presbyterians began to be more powerful than we; and if they made up matters with the King we should have been left in the lurch: therefore we thought it best to prevent them by offering first to come in upon any reasonable conditions; but while we were busied in these thoughts there came a letter from one of our spies who was of the King's bedchamber, which acquainted us that on that day our final doom was decreed; that he could not possibly tell what it was, but we might find out if we could intercept a letter sent from the King to the Queen, wherein he declared what he would do. The letter, he said, was sewed up in the skirt of a saddle, and the bearer of it would come with the saddle upon his head about ten of the clock that night to the Blue Boar Inn in Holborn, for there he was to take horse and go to Dover with it. This messenger knew nothing of the letter in the saddle but some persons in Dover did. We were at Windsor when we received this letter, and immediately upon the receipt of it Ireton and I resolved to take one trusty fellow with us, and with troopers' habits to go to the inn in Holborn; which accordingly we did, and set our man at the gate of the inn, when the wicket only was open, to let people in and out. Our man was to give us notice when any person came there with a saddle, whilst we, in the disguise of common troopers, called for cans of beer, and continued drinking till about ten o'clock. The sentinel at the gate then gave notice that the man with the saddle was come in. Upon this we immediately arose, and, as the man was leading out his horse saddled, came up to him with drawn swords and told him we were to search all that went in and out there, but as he looked like an honest man we would only search his saddle and dismiss him. Upon that we ungirt his saddle, and carried it into the stall where we had been drinking, and left the horseman with our sentinel. Then, ripping up one of the skirts of the saddle, we there found the letter of which we had been informed. As soon as we had the letter we opened it, in which we found the King had acquainted the Queen that he was now counted on by both the factions, the Scotch Presbyterians and the army, and which bid fairest for him should have him, but he thought he should close with the Scots sooner than the others. Upon this we took horse and went to Windsor, and finding we were not likely to have any tolerable terms from the King, we immediately, from that time forward, resolved his ruin."[446]

Such is the story told to account for the change which took place in the attitude of Cromwell and Ireton toward the King at about this time, accepted by eminent authorities and so embalmed in history. It seems to be confirmed by other evidence. Writing to Hammond

[446] Morrice, "Biography of Orrery," in *A Collection of State Letters of . . . Roger Boyle . . . first earl of Orrery* (1743), i, 219–28.

on November 21, Ireton told Charles's jailer of the suspicions at headquarters and urged him to guard the King well, rather with his soldiers than with inhabitants of the Isle of Wight—though that seems an extraordinary suggestion to make to the commander of a garrison. "The Lieutenant-General," he added in a postscript, "is at London or Putney, and on scout, I know not where."[447] Wherever Cromwell was on November 21, he was in a committee of the House on the day following, considering a petition "of many freeborn people of England," urging the acceptance of the *Agreement of the People*, which, upon the committee's report, was voted seditious and he apparently returned to Windsor that afternoon or the next day. The objections to accepting Orrery's story have often been pointed out—that a spy could hardly have known the subject of Charles's letter to his wife; that the shortest and safest way from Carisbrooke to Paris was not by way of London; and that the timing was just short of miraculous.

As to the truth or falsity of this it is difficult to decide. Orrery died almost exactly thirty years after the episode for which his story is the chief authority, though he doubtless told it long before that time. To support it other testimony has been adduced; of which the first item is Dugdale's statement that Cromwell was said to intend the restoration of the King,

> "but that after he was brought to Hampton Court a certain letter from the Queen was intercepted by them and privately opened; the contents whereof were that she did thereby acquaint him that the Scots were raising or preparing to raise an army in order to his restoration, or expressions to that effect, and that Cromwell having seen this letter and made it up artificially that no violation of the seal could appear, conveyed it to the King, and the next morning sent Ireton on purpose to his Majesty, to enquire of him what he knew of any hostile preparations then in hand by the Scots to the purpose aforesaid. Unto which the King briefly saying that he did neither know nor believe anything thereof, Ireton returned with the answer, and that thereupon both of them concluding that his Majesty was not to be further trusted they did thenceforth resolve to proceed against him."[448]

To this is added the story printed in Herbert's *Memoirs*, some twenty years later, apparently from Dugdale, that:

> "It hath been suggested by some . . . that the King by a letter from the Queen was acquainted [with the Scotch preparations] which letter was intercepted, the seal violated, and the letter read by some great officers of the army, members of the Commons House."[449]

These stories are fortified by two others. The first is a rumor voiced by Roger Coke in 1696 that Cromwell and Ireton discovered

[447] *Letters between Hammond and the Derby House Committee*, p. 22.
[448] Dugdale, *Short view of the late troubles* (1681), p. 378.
[449] Sir Thomas Herbert, *Memoirs* (1702), p. 63.

Charles's intention to break with them as soon as he was restored to power.[450] This story is further reinforced by the statement of Wagstaffe in his *Vindication*, published in 1711, that he heard that Charles's Saddle Letter was in the hands of one Millington, an auctioneer, who refused him sight of it;[451] and in 1743 by Spence who, in his *Anecdotes*, declares that Richardson was told by Bolingbroke that Pope told him that Harley had once had in his hands this Saddle Letter—for which he offered £500 unavailingly,[452] and also the Queen's letter to Charles. Those letters, according to this tale, reveal Charles having replied to the Queen's appeal "not to yield too much to the traitors," that "she need not have any concern in her mind on that head, for whatever agreement they might enter into, he could not look upon himself as obliged to keep any promises made so much on compulsion whenever he had power enough to break them." To this Richardson adds that Bolingbroke quoted Charles to the effect that "he should know in due time how to deal with the rogues who, instead of a silken garter, should be fitted with a hempen cord."

Such is the sum of the evidence for this romantic tale; and from it two things appear. The first is that these stories relate to two different communications, the one from the Queen to Charles, the other from Charles to the Queen; the one seized at Hampton Court, the other at the *Blue Boar* Inn. The second is that they have a common element—the King's dissimulation as the cause of the break of Cromwell and Ireton with Charles. Though there seems no evidence that such a letter as the one supposed to have been seized at the *Blue Boar* Inn was ever presented to the Houses, it is apparent that the Lords, said at this time to have been under Independent influence, proved unwilling to accept the King's proposals, and it is generally agreed that something in that week changed Cromwell and Ireton from being at least apparent champions of an agreement with the King and his restoration, to another state of mind. For such a reversal of their position the story of the Saddle Letter provides a romantic explanation. It may be true in part, in part wholly true; yet there are other and less dramatic explanations possible. This was not the first of Charles's letters and those of the Queen to be intercepted; and from them, from their conversations with him, and from his every action, the King's character, views and intrigues were well known. Whatever else there was in the Saddle Letter, if all it contained is told by Orrery, there was, at least no news, but Cromwell and Ireton may well have needed some such concrete evidence to convince their colleagues of the King's lack of good faith.

However much Cromwell's attitude toward the King may have

[450] Coke, *Detection* (1699), i, 166.
[451] Wagstaffe, *Vindication* (1711), p. 13.
[452] Spence, *Anecdotes* (1820), p. 298; Richardson, *Richardsoniana* (1776).

changed, no rumor of a shift in his position had yet circulated, for on the very day of the supposed capture of the Saddle Letter, the Venetian ambassador, usually a most reliable gleaner of gossip, wrote:

"Cromwell, whose advice and co-operation have hitherto directed the action of Fairfax, is believed to favor the King, prudently realizing that neither he nor Fairfax could subsist for long against the secret detestation of Parliament."[453]

The reasons for the change of heart in Cromwell and Ireton, if it occurred at all at this moment, need no dramatic incident to explain them; they can be accounted for by the well known facts of the political situation of the time. Once more matters approached a crisis. The Levellers' mutiny and their demand for the deposition or the death of Charles; the threatening attitude of the Scots' commissioners; the rising tide of Royalism in the country as evidenced by the action of Parliament and the army protests against seditious libels; the evident drawing together of the elements opposed to army and Parliament in support of Charles—all these produced a situation fraught with danger to the Independent leaders and their cause. Had Orrery never told the story of the Saddle Letter, it would not be hard to interpret the attitude of Cromwell and Ireton. They were confronted by a world of enemies, which, save for the Levellers, centered in the King. Even the army could not be wholly trusted, partly because of the late mutiny, partly because it contained no inconsiderable element once in the royal ranks. If the Independents were to win, they must divide their enemies and somehow parry the danger from the King.

The first step was the consideration of the King's message and the *Agreement of the People* which reached the Houses almost simultaneously. The latter they dismissed at once as "seditious and contemptuous." The former they countered with their Four Propositions, which, debated for some weeks, were finally turned into the Four Bills passed by the Lords on December 14. Of these the first conferred the control of the militia upon Parliament for a space of twenty years; the second confirmed and justified all acts and declarations during the late war; the third made null and void all honors conferred since May, 1642; the fourth asserted the right of Parliament to adjourn to any other place. To these they added a list of twelve propositions and twenty-three "qualifications," which, in effect, reiterated and even emphasized their previous demands, including the long list of those excepted from indemnity. Among them only one was notably different from the proposals of Newcastle and Hampton Court. It was to the effect that no one should be questioned or penalized for nonconformity. This was a concession to the Independents, though the preceding article established Presbyterian government.[454]

[453] *Cal. S. P. Venetian* (1647–52), p. 30.

[454] Parry, *Parliaments;* Gardiner, *Select Doc'ts.*

The irresistible force had finally met the immovable object. If it seemed that Parliament could not meet the King's demands, it seemed no less certain that Charles could not meet those of Parliament which had grown more exacting, as it appeared to his supporters, in proportion as he had given way to them. And to that problem was added the Scots' commissioners' refusal to agree to the Propositions.[455]

On November 25, the day that the Lords suddenly sprang into action to pass four of the Newcastle Propositions as an answer to Charles's request for a personal treaty, a meeting of the General Council of the Army took place at Windsor;[456] and on the following Sunday, the King having been advised of the action of the Lords, his follower, Berkeley, appeared at another meeting of the Council, with a letter from Hammond and another from Charles, virtually demanding that the army place him in control of affairs.

This visit to the army was, according to Berkeley, due to the insistence of Colonel Hammond, who, greatly alarmed by the army mutiny, as were Charles and his followers, had refused the demand of Parliament for Ashburnham, Berkeley and Legge, and had sent his chaplain to urge the officers "to make use of their success upon the Adjutators." Writing to Cromwell and Ireton "conjuring them by their engagement, by their interest, by their honour and conscience, to come to a speedy close with the King," he sent Berkeley on his way; and that gentleman's adventure forms one of the most picturesque incidents in this history and is best told in his own words. On his journey he met first the headquarters' chaplain, one Traughton, who told him that the army had not yet come to a resolution about the King. Nearer Windsor, Berkeley was overtaken by Cornet Joyce, who said that "it had been discoursed among the Adjutators, 'whether, for their justification, the King ought not to be brought to trial'; which he held in the affirmative."

"Quickly weary of his discourse," as Berkeley says, the King's messenger sought Fairfax's quarters where he found a general meeting of the officers, to whom he presented his letters and was requested to withdraw. He was recalled in half an hour, and, as his story goes on to say:

"The General looked very severely upon me, and, after his manner, said, 'That they were the Parliament's Army, and therefore could not say anything to his Majesty's motion of peace but must refer those matters to them; to whom they would send his Majesty's Letters.' I then looked about, upon *Cromwell* and *Ireton*, and the rest of my acquaintance; who saluted me very coldly, and had their countenances quite changed towards me, and shewed me *Hammond's* letter, which I had delivered to them, and smiled with much

[455] Clarendon, *History*, x, 142.
[456] *Clarke Papers*, i, 415.

disdain upon it. I saw that *that* was no place for me, and therefore went to my lodging. . . . At last I sent my servant out . . . to see if he could light upon any of my acquaintance. At last he met with one that was a General Officer, who whispered in his ear and bad him tell me, that he would meet me at twelve at night, in a Close behind the *Garter* Inn. I came at the hour, and he not long after. I asked him what news? and, he replied, 'None good;' and then continued this discourse.

'You know, that I and my friend engaged ourselves to you; that we were zealous for an Agreement. And, if the rest were not so, we were abused; that, if there was an intention to cozen us, it would not be long hid from us; that, whatever we should discover, should not be secret to you; that we, since the tumults of the Army, did mistrust *Cromwell;* and, not long after, *Ireton;* whereof I informed you. I come now to tell you, that we mistrust neither; but know them, and all of us, to be the archest villains in the world. For we are resolved, notwithstanding our engagements, to destroy the King and his Posterity; to which Ireton made two Propositions, this afternoon; one, that you should be sent prisoner to *London*, the other, that none should speak with you upon pain of death. . . . The way that is intended to ruin the King, is to send eight hundred, of the most disaffected of the Army, to secure his person, (as believing him not so now,) and then bring him to a trial; and I dare think no farther. This will be done in ten days; and therefore, if the King can escape, let him do it as he loves his life.'

I then inquired what was the reason of this horrid change; what had the King done to deserve it; He said, 'Nothing; and that to our grief; for, we would leap for joy, if we could have any advantage against him. I have pleaded hard against this Resolution this day; but have been laughed at for my pains.'

I then said, 'Well, but still, why is this horrid perfidiousness resolved-on since there appears no occasion for it, the officers being superior at the rendezvous?'

He answered 'that he could not tell certainly; but he conceived this to be the ground of it: That, though one of the Mutineers was shot at the late Rendezvous, and eleven made prisoners, and the rest, in appearance, overquelled, yet they were so far from being so indeed, that there have been with *Cromwell* and *Ireton*, one after another, two third parts of the Army to tell them, that, though they were certainly to perish in the attempt, they would leave nothing unessayed, to bring the Army to their sense; and if all failed, they would make a division in the Army, and join with any that would assist in the destruction of their opposers. *Cromwell* and *Ireton*, therefore, argued thus; If the Army divide, the greatest part will join with the Presbyterians, and will, in all likelihood, prevail to our ruin; and we shall be forced to make applications to the King, wherein we shall rather crave than offer any assistance; and when his Majesty shall give it us, and afterwards have the good fortune to prevail, if he shall then pardon us, it is all we can pretend-to, and more than we can promise ourselves; and, thereupon, concluded, 'That, if we cannot bring the Army to our sense, we must go to theirs; a schism being evidently destructive.' And, therefore, *Cromwell* bent all his thoughts to make his peace with the Party that was most opposite to the King; in which Peters was instrumental. He then acknowledged, (as he had formerly done, upon the like occasion) that the Glories of the World had so dazzled his eyes that he could not discern clearly the great Works the Lord was doing, and said, that he was now resolved to humble himself, and desire the prayers of the Saints, that God would be pleased to forgive him his Self-seeking. These arts, together with comfortable messages to the prisoners (that they should be of good cheer, for no harm should befall them, since it had pleased God to open his eyes)—perfected his Reconciliation; and he was re-instated in the Fellowship of the Faithful.'

I then asked this Gentleman, whether I should not endeavour to deliver my letters from the King to *Cromwell* and *Ireton;* he replied, 'By all means, lest they should mistrust that I had discovered them.' "[457]

Such is the curious story of that honest and disturbed King's messenger as to his encounter with the army authorities at this critical moment. From this interview he returned to his lodgings to send to Hammond a general account of the conditions in the army and to Charles a "passionate supplication" to escape. The next morning, as he goes on to say:

"I sent Colonel *Cook* to *Cromwell*, to let him know that I had letters and instructions from the King. He sent me word by the same messenger, that he durst not see me, it being very dangerous to us both, and bid me be assured, that he would serve his Majesty as long as he could do it without his own ruin; but desired that I would not expect that he should perish for his sake."

Here, as at so many periods of his career, Cromwell was presented with a choice, not, as the Royalists would have contended, between good and evil, but between two evils. From their standpoint Cromwell and his fellow-officers should have made terms with Charles, divided the army, and suppressed the Levellers, restored the King to his throne and trusted to his generosity. According to the Levellers, the officers should have repudiated Charles, sentenced him to death or deposition—and no sentence short of death would have been effective—and set up a new government on the lines of the *Agreement of the People*. Cromwell and his associates were unwilling to embrace either alternative; but more and more, in the face of Charles's known negotiations with the Scots, they leaned or were driven toward the position of the Levellers, for reasons of personal safety as well as of principle.

None the less it would appear from other evidence that it was Cromwell's interference which prevented the issuance of a warrant for the arrest of Berkeley, Ashburnham and Legge.[458] In view of Berkeley's narrative, of Cromwell's earlier warning to Hammond to spy on the King, and of his negotiations with the Levellers, it is

[457] Berkeley, *Memoirs*, *loc. cit.*, pp. 383–86.
[458] Letter of Intelligence, Dec. 2, in *Clarendon St. Papers*, ii, App. xlii.

apparent that he and Ireton were walking slippery paths, where a misstep might well cost them not only their positions but their lives, and it seems no less evident that they were well aware of it.

While Charles endeavored to come to an arrangement with the army and the Scots, and Cromwell endeavored to keep on terms both with the King and the Levellers, the Army Council again approached the Parliament. On Sunday, December 5, a Humble Representation was put in final form to present to the Houses. It requested that pay might be made constant and regular, that the "supernumeraries" be paid and disbanded, and, in consequence, that free quarter might be avoided.[459] This was the more important in that, concurrently with the presentation of this remonstrance, the Houses received petitions from Middlesex and Herts against the "intolerable burden and bondage" of free quarter. Though the Lords contented themselves with reading the Army Council's petition, the Commons thanked the officers and promised relief speedily.

Meanwhile Charles came to terms with the Scots. On December 15 an agreement known as the "Engagement" was sent to them and two days before the King rejected the Four Bills, he signed this momentous document.[460] By it he agreed to confirm the League and Covenant once he was restored, provided "none who is unwilling shall be constrained to take it." He further agreed to establish Presbyterianism for three years, after which the form of church government was to be determined by an Assembly of Divines reinforced by twenty of his own nominees, with proper provisions for suppressing some ten dissenting sects, including the Independents. On their part the Scots agreed that if Charles were not allowed to come to London for a personal treaty and the English forces would not disband, they would send an army to support the royal cause, on receipt of the £200,000 of "Brotherly Assistance" not yet paid to them by the Parliament; possession of certain fortresses and towns as "places of retreat and magazine" in this new invasion; and payment of their expeditionary force and of their army in Ireland.[461]

Whatever other results it had—and they were many and serious—this Scotch Engagement served to compose the quarrels in the army and in Parliament. At once Cromwell came to terms with Rainsborough and the Levellers, and motions were made in the Army

[459] *C. J.*, v, 376; *Old Parl. Hist.* xvi, 370–96. Heath, (*Chronicle*, p. 156–7) notes in this connection that men would be disbanded in one brigade and their arms taken by the officers. Later the same men would be listed in another brigade and the old arms sold to the state to re-arm them. Cromwell, he says, had amassed a magazine of these arms in the City. When they were rumored to belong to the Reformadoes, investigation showed they were Cromwell's and the affair was hushed up.

[460] King to Parliament, Dec. 28, in Heath *Chronicle*, p. 160–161. The Engagement is printed in Gardiner, *Const. Doc'ts.*, p. 259–264.

[461] *Clar. Mss.*, vii, 2685, 2686. Quoted in Gardiner, *Sel. Docts.*, 259ff.

Council at Windsor on Tuesday, December 21, to forgive the mutineers and set them at liberty.[462] On the following day a great prayer-meeting was held there from nine in the morning until seven that night, and Ireton with many other officers prayed fervently making "such sweet musick as the heavens never before knew."[463] So complete was the reconciliation that the meeting ended with a resolution to recommend Rainsborough for the post of vice-admiral—a move which at once conciliated the Levellers' leader and removed him from the army. Two days later the appointment was confirmed by the House. Thus was the army once more united, one of the chief instigators of disturbance removed to a post where he was no longer any danger to this unity, and Cromwell and Ireton were confirmed in their direction of affairs.

It was a shrewd maneuver, and Cromwell, asked how he could ever trust a man like Rainsborough, replied:

> "That he had now received particular assurance from Colonel Rainsborough as great as could be given by any man, that he would be conformable to the judgment and directions of himself and Commissary-General Ireton, for the management of the business at sea."[464]

It was probably at this point that Sir Arthur Haselrig remarked to Cromwell, "If you prove not an honest man, I will never trust a fellow with a great nose for your sake";[465] and on that note of humorous, if grudging, admiration—and a little doubt—the episode ended.

Even in such crises as these the ordinary business of life must go on; and the day after the prayer-meeting and the settlement of the difficulties with the Agitators, Cromwell found time to recommend to the head of Trinity College, Cambridge, a certain Dudley Wyatt. Matriculated at that college in 1628, taking his degree in course, becoming a Fellow in 1633, he disappeared from the college in 1645 to go to the Queen's court in France and be embalmed in Clarendon's *History* as a messenger hastening here and there between the King, the royal army and the Queen. From that narrative he disappears on a journey of various gentlemen to the Prince in Jersey in June, 1646, to reappear again in history and in his former college post by virtue of Cromwell's letter:

462 Rushworth, vii, 943.
463 *Clar. State Papers*, ii, App. xliv; *Perfect Diurnall*, Dec. 27.
464 Huntington, "Sundry Reasons," in Maseres, *Select Tracts*, p. 406.
465 *A Word to General Cromwell*, (1647), p. 19.

[*To Dr. Thomas Hill, Master of Trinity College, Cambridge*]

SIR,

As I am informed, this Gentleman the Bearer hereof, in the year 1641, had leave of his College to travel into Ireland for seven years; and in his absence he (being then actually employed against the Rebels in that Kingdom) was ejected out of his fellowship by mistake, the College Registry being not looked into, to inquire the cause of his non-residence.

I cannot therefore but think it a just and reasonable request, that he be readmitted to all the benefits, rights and privileges which he enjoyed before that ejection; and therefore desire you would please to effect it accordingly. Wherein you shall do a favour will be owned by

Your affectionate friend and servant,

Windsor, 23rd Decemb. O. CROMWELL.[466]
1647.

THE VOTE OF NO ADDRESSES,
DECEMBER 23, 1647–3 JANUARY, 1648.

On the day that he wrote the letter for Wyatt, a meeting of the Council of Officers, which Cromwell doubtless attended, considered the Commons' ordinance against officers quartering in private houses;[467] and apparently the next day, December 24, took place another great prayer-meeting opened by Cromwell, Ireton, Tichborne and others, with prayers and Scripture reading. There, as Clarendon, confirmed by Whitelocke, declares, the great decision was finally made, and "it was resolved that the King should be prosecuted for his life, as a criminal person; of which his majesty was advertised speedily by Watson, quartermaster-general of the army, who was present, and had pretended from the first coming of the King to the army to have a desire to serve him, and desired to be now thought to retain it; but the resolution was a great secret, of which the Parliament had not the least intimation or jealousy, but was, as it had been, to be cozened by degrees to do what they never intended."[468]

Finally, during the last week of December, 1647, the council was occupied with disbanding the supernumerary forces according to the votes of Parliament—with which, as the officers assured its commis-

[466] *Papers relating to Trin. Coll.* vol. 3, in the Muniment Room of Trinity College, Cambridge, "docketed in the hand of one Porter, Clerk to Thomas Parne, about 1724, 'L. P. Cromwell's Letter concerning Sir Dudley Wyatt.' " Pr. in Hartshorne's *Book Rarities in the University of Cambridge* (1829), p. 277, from a copy in *Harl. Mss*, no. 7053, f. 153 b. which bears a note: "Upon this letter, Sir Dudley Wyatt was readmitted." A contemporary copy was offered for sale by Walter V. Daniell in 1912 (Cat. item no. 3312.) Carlyle, LI.

[467] Rushworth, vii, 943.

[468] Clarendon, *History*, x, 147; Whitelocke, pp. 284–5.

sioners, the army would live and die.[469] A declaration in regard to disbanding was signed on the 30th and the next day the chief officers dined with the commissioners, took a loving farewell of them and gave them a parting salute of twenty-five guns.[470] Meanwhile events outside the army circles had moved rapidly. On December 26, the Scots, feeling that their bargain with the King was not good enough, secured from him additional articles to the Engagement, providing that Scotchmen should have equal employment with the English in public offices and that the King or the Prince of Wales should reside in Scotland. Thus fortified, on December 28, the King replied to the Four Bills and their accompanying propositions. Pointing out that the Scots' commissioners were strongly opposed to the proposals of the Parliament, and that those proposals would divest the crown of all authority and place supreme power in the Parliament, he declined to entertain them. He appealed to the judgment of posterity; he begged once more for a personal treaty; but left the way open for further negotiation. At the same time he pushed forward his plans for flight and the Scots began to set their forces in order. The day of his proposed escape to Jersey was set to coincide with his refusal of the Four Bills; and, possibly suspicious of such an attempt, on that same day Hammond dismissed Berkeley, Ashburnham and Legge from attendance on the King and ordered them to leave the castle. These precautions were evidently taken on the authority of a letter from Cromwell written, if that assumption is correct, about December 25 or 26, warning Hammond of the danger of escape:

For Col. Robin Hammond, Governor of the Isle of Wight, these, at Carisbrooke Castle, haste, post haste

DEAR ROBIN, am I forgotten?

Thou art not, I wish thee much comfort in thy great business, and the blessing of the Almighty upon thee.

This intelligence was delivered this day, *viz.*, that Sir George Cartwright[471] hath sent three boats from Jersey and a barque from Sharbrowe[472] under the name of Frenchmen, but are absolutely sent to bring the King (if their plot can take effect) from the Isle of Wight to Jersey, one of which boats is returned back to Jersey with news, but it is kept very private.

I wish great care be taken. Truly I would have the castle well manned; you know how much lieth upon it. If you would have any thing more done let your friends know your mind they are ready to assist and secure you.

You have warrant now to turn out such servants as you suspect; do it suddenly for fear of danger. You see how God hath honoured and blessed

[469] Rushworth, vii, 946.
[470] *Ibid.*, 953–4; *Perfect Diurnall*, Dec. 31, Jan. 1.
[471] Carteret.
[472] Cherbourg.

every resolute action of these [?] for Him; doubt not but He will do so still.

Let the Parliament ships have notice of Cartwright's design that so they may look out for him.

I have no more but rest,

Your true servant,

[?December 1647] O. CROMWELL.[473]

With this the matter finally came before the House on January 3, when the King's letter rejecting the Four Bills was read. Here, finally, Cromwell took his stand. Of his speech there are various accounts; and of them two—differing in detail but supplementing each other—have come down to us. The first is that of Clarendon:

Speech in the House of Commons Jan. 3, 1647–8

"Cromwell declared that the King was a man of great parts and a great understanding, but that he was so great a dissembler, and so false a man, that he was not to be trusted; and thereupon repeated many particulars, whilst he was in the army, when his majesty wished that such and such things might be done, which being done to gratify him, he was displeased, and complained of it: that whilst he professed with all solemnity that he referred himself wholly to the Parliament, and depended wholly upon their wisdom and counsel for the settlement and composing the distractions of the kingdom, he had at the same time secret treaties with the Scots' commissioners how he might embroil the nation in a new war and destroy the Parliament. He concluded, that they might no farther trouble themselves with sending messages to him, or farther propositions, but that they might enter upon those counsels which were necessary towards the settlement of the kingdom without having further recourse to the King."[474]

The second is that of a contemporary pamphlet, often reprinted, which makes Cromwell say:

"That it was now expected the Parliament should govern and defend the kingdom by their own power and resolutions, and not teach the people any longer to expect safety and government from an obstinate man, whose heart God had hardened; that those men who had defended the Parliament from so many dangers with the expense of their blood, would defend them herein with fidelity and courage against all opposition. Teach them not, by neglecting your own and the kingdom's safety, in which their own is involved, to think themselves betrayed and left hereafter to the rage and malice of an irreconcileable enemy,—whom they have subdued for your sake, and therefore are likely to find his future government of them insupportable and fuller of revenge than justice,—lest despair teach them to seek their safety by some other means than adhering to you, who will not stick to yourselves. How

[473] Holograph original amongst the Mss of the Marquis of Lothian at Newbattle. Pr. in *Clarke Papers*, ii, xxv; Lomas-Carlyle, Suppl. 26.

[474] Clarendon, *History*, x, 146.

destructive such a resolution in them will be to you all, I tremble to think, and leave you judge."[475]

The question of breaking off relations with the King was one of the most momentous problems which had confronted Parliament since the passage of the Grand Remonstrance; and as the one had begun, so, in a sense, the other ended the long contest with the monarchy. And as the one had been the occasion of violent debate, so the other, despite the purging and reconstitution of the Commons, despite the absence of the Eleven Members on the side of the Presbyterians, and all of the Royalists, found no inconsiderable opposition. In that debate Cromwell took his share, and in what spirit a Royalist account indicates:

"Of his power and greatness we have a very pregnant instance by his lordly carriage in the House, upon debate of that vote which denies all addresses to or returns from his Majesty; for when Mr. Maynard stood up and gave reasons against the passing of such a vote . . . then Mr. Cromwell (to show that this was no time to speak sense and reason) stood up, and the glow-worm glistening in his beak, he began to spit fire; and as the devil quoted Scripture against our Saviour, so did he against his sovereign, and told the House: It is written, Thou shalt not suffer an hypocrite to reign; and what then (I pray you) will become of himself? But to show that it was so decreed, I am told he laid his hand upon the hilt of his sword, as the only graceful conclusion of so gallant a piece of oratory."[476]

That gesture made a great impression on all who heard his speech, as the speech evidently profoundly moved his audience. As Walker says:

"He laid his hand upon his Sword at the latter end of his speech, that sword which being by his side could not keep him from trembling when S[ir] Philip Stapleton baffled him in the House of Commons. This concluding Speech, having something of menace in it, was thought very prevalent with the House."[477]

Whether his argument or his threat prevailed, the House voted in an extraordinarily large division, by 141 to 92, not to address the King further, and followed this with a vote not to receive messages from him.[478] On this the doors were unlocked, candles brought in and, most of the Presbyterians having left, the Committee of Both

[475] *Treason Arraigned, in answer to Plain English* (1660); thence Stainer, *Speeches of Cromwell*, no. 9. Printed also in Walker, *History of Independency*, pp. 71–72; repr. in Heath, *Chronicle*, pp. 161–162; and in *Old Parl. Hist.*, xiv, 492–3.

[476] *Mercurius Pragmaticus*, Jan. 4–11, and quoted in Carlyle, (Lomas ed.), i, 290n.

[477] Walker, *History of Independency*, p. 72.

[478] *C. J.*, v, 415.

Kingdoms was revived as a Committee of Safety at Derby House and declared independent of Parliament.[479] This done, Cromwell went to Lord Wharton's house and wrote to Hammond of the transactions of the eventful day:

For Colonel Robert Hammond, Governor of the Isle of Wight: These. For the Service of the Kingdom. Haste, post haste.

DEAREST ROBIN,

Now (blessed be God) I can write and thou receive freely. I never in my life saw more deep sense, and less will to show it unchristianly, than in that which thou didst write to us when we were at Windsor, and thou in the midst of thy temptation, which indeed, by what we understand of it, was a great one, and occasioned the greater by the letter the General sent thee; of which thou wast not mistaken when thou didst challenge me to be the penner.

How good has God been to dispose all to mercy! And although it was trouble for the present, yet glory has come out of it; for which we praise the Lord with thee and for thee. And truly thy carriage has been such as occasions much honour to the name of God and to religion. Go on in the strength of the Lord; and the Lord be still with thee.

But, dear Robin, this business hath been (I trust) a mighty providence to this poor Kingdom and to us all. The House of Commons is very sensible of the King's dealings, and of our brethren's, in this late transaction. You should do well, if you have anything that may discover juggling, to search it out, and let us know it. I may be of admirable use at this time; because we shall (I hope) instantly go upon business in relation to them, tending to prevent danger.

The House of Commons has this day voted as follows: 1st, They will make no more Addresses to the King; 2nd, None shall apply to him without leave of the two Houses, upon pain of being guilty of high treason; 3rd, They will receive nothing from the King, nor shall any other bring anything to them from him, nor receive anything from the King; lastly, the Members of both Houses who were of the Committee of Both Kingdoms are established in all that power in themselves, for England and Ireland, which they had to act with Both Kingdoms; and Sir John Evelyn of Wilts is added in the room of Mr. Recorder and Nathaniel Fiennes in the room of Sir Philip Stapleton, and my Lord of Kent in the room of the Earl of Essex. I think it good you take notice of this, the sooner the better.

Let us know how it's with you in point of strength, and what you need from us. Some of us think the King well with you, and that it concerns us to keep that Island in great security, because of the French, &c., and if so,

[479] Walker, *op. cit.*, p. 72; *Moderate Intelligencer*, Dec. 30–Jan. 6; *C. J.*, v, 417; *Cal. S. P. Dom.* (1648–9), p. 1 (with a list of members including those added on Jan. 22. These are practically the same as the former committee except that the Scottish members were removed as well as three English Presbyterians—Essex and Stapleton, who were dead, and Glyn, who was in the Tower.

where can the King be better? If you have more force you will be sure of full provision for them.

3d January 1647
(My Lord Wharton's,
near ten at night.)

The Lord bless thee. Pray for
Thy dear friend and servant,
O. CROMWELL.[480]

THE ATTEMPT AT COMPROMISE
JANUARY, 1648

With this the die was cast and England moved toward the dictatorship of the revolutionary element. Bitterly as many Englishmen have resented the comparison, different as were the Jacobins and the Independents, especially on the religious side, there is a certain similarity between this new Committee of Safety and the French revolutionary Committee of Public Safety a century and a half later. Each was dominated by the leaders of the revolutionary party; each faced the problem of a hostile majority at home and foreign invasion, of the formation of a new system of government, and of a prisoner King, still clinging to a disestablished church. From this new Committee of Safety the Scottish members of the old Committee of Both Kingdoms were naturally removed. Of the Presbyterian members of the old committee, Essex and Stapleton were dead and Glyn was in the Tower. With those exceptions the new committee was merely a revival of the old. Like the Girondins, the Presbyterians were crushed or cowed, and there remained only the Independents with their rivals and allies, the Levellers, in control of this supreme executive committee, of which Cromwell was the dominant figure.

In this new arrangement, Parliament, like the French Convention, was little more than a registering authority. Even the Army Council disappeared. On Saturday, January 8, the General Council of the Army met for the last time, and voted to agree with Parliament in all questions relating to the King, surrendering its authority to the Committee at Derby House. All of its members were invited to dine with Fairfax at Windsor Castle the next day, to take leave of each other before dispersing to their various commands, and there issued a Declaration of adherence to Parliament.[481] As to the Lords, that slender group had divided 10 to 10 on the Vote of No Addresses but its opposition was soon crushed. On January 14, according to Walker, the Independents had 'by strategy' cleared the House of Presbyterians and carried an invitation to the army to come to Whitehall. Before the vote had passed, the troops were on the move. By eight

[480] Pr. in Birch, *Hammond Letters*, p. 23; Harris, *Life of Cromwell*, p. 509; Forster, iv, 234–6; Carlyle, LII. The letter with Cromwell's signature was in the collection of Lady Beryl Gilbert until it was sold by Sotheby to Ramsay in 1918 (*Autograph Prices Current*, III, where it is dated 2 Jan.).

[481] Rushworth, vii, 958–962; *Perfect Diurnall*, Jan. 8.

o'clock on the morning of January 15, the foot was at Whitehall, the horse at the Mews, "to guard the Parliament," and the Lords promptly concurred with the Vote of No Addresses.[482] Thus swiftly, efficiently and bloodlessly, the Independents seized supreme authority.

That circumstance was marked by a new burst of activity on the part of the irrepressible John Lilburne, who, with the Leveller-Army Agent, Wildman, occupied the attention of the House for a few days and served, among other things, to relieve the tension of the greater issues. Lilburne, brought before the House, defended himself as usual by an attack on others; in this case a charge that Cromwell and Ireton were dealing with the King for their own advantage.[483] It was an old story based on gossip of Charles's having offered Cromwell the title of his ancestor's patron, Thomas Cromwell, Earl of Essex and Knight of the Garter;[484] strengthened by a report that Cromwell had private correspondence with Hammond at Farnham[485] to put the Prince of Wales on the throne. The charge failed to be sustained and Lilburne and Wildman were committed to Newgate.[486]

It was improbable that Cromwell would exchange his real authority for an empty title, however eminent. He was busy with the conduct of the government; yet here, as at various other times, though his influence was doubtless dominant, there is small record of his activities. He was not present at the first meeting of the Committee at Derby House on January 20, but he attended four of the other six in that month and five of the eight in February.[487] Neither there nor in Parliament is there any notice of his actions, save two. On January 24 he informed the Committee of the desire of Major General Laugharne, previously banished, to come to London;[488] and in Parliament, some mysterious Scotch agent, "V51," casually mentioned that he had moved that £1,000 be given a Mr. Ashurst in consideration of his losses.[489]

These trifling notices bear little relation to his real activities in these days. He was busy with the problem of the new government which must replace Charles I's authority. In view of his refusal to yield supremacy to Parliament, that monarch's return to power now seemed impossible. What was to take its place? Still convinced, ap-

482 Rushworth, vii, 962.

483 Walker, *op. cit.*, pp. 72–73; *C. J.*, v, 432; *L. J.*, ix, 662; Rushworth, vii, 965–7; Grignon to Brienne, 17/27 Jan. *Record Office Transcripts.*

484 *Moderate Intelligencer*, Jan. 19; *C. J.*, v, 436–7.

485 Walker, *op. cit.*, pp. 77–78.

486 Rushworth, vii, 969.

487 *Cal. S. P. Dom.* (1648–9), pp. 6 ff.

488 Comm. of Both Houses to Fairfax, *Cal. S. P. Dom.* (1648–9), p. 8.

489 "V51" to Hamilton, in Hamilton Collection at the Register House in Edinburgh, Chest 53, no. 91. £1000 was voted to William Ashurst in January. *C. J.*, v, 450.

parently, that some form of monarchy was not only advisable but necessary to escape anarchy, it seems that, with Oliver St. John, he strove to conciliate all remaining members of House and army, and it has been suggested that the two men discussed the old plan of negotiation with the Queen and Prince of Wales with a view of putting the Prince on the throne, under the authority of the Houses. Whatever his plans and motives, he singled out the chief republicans,[490] inviting to dinner at his house in King Street their leaders and the "grandees" of army and Parliament, to discuss the possibilities of settling the government.[491]

On the discussions, of which the debate at the dinner in King Street was only one of a series, hinged the next step in the revolution. The old system was destroyed; it remained to find a new; and, in the situation of affairs that was not easy; nor is it easy to determine Cromwell's position at this time. Long before, in the army councils, Waller had observed Cromwell's disposition to draw men out and reserve his own opinions and actions to the last;[492] and now he used the same technique. As the Republican Ludlow testifies of the debate in Cromwell's house, some argued for monarchy, some for aristocracy, some for democracy, while Cromwell, neither theorist nor controversialist, listened to them all. Finally, after the fashion of his earlier days, he ended the discussion by throwing a cushion at Ludlow's head, and running downstairs pursued by Ludlow carrying another. The long discussion had at least one effect on him; for the next day, passing Ludlow in the House, Cromwell observed that he was now convinced of the desirability but not of the feasibility of an equal commonwealth.[493]

The task of bringing together the various elements in some agreement as to the form of government was, in fact, Cromwell's chief business in these days. He approached them all. He tried to come to terms with the Republican Henry Marten only to part with him, according to rumor, 'much more an enemy than before.'[494] He "bestowed two nights' oratory on Sir Henry Vane Jr." with no more effect; and when he told Ludlow of his entertainment of various members of the Commonwealth party in his chamber and Ludlow replied acidly that he knew of Cromwell's ability to cajole them and give them good words when he had occasion to make use of them, Cromwell burst forth in a rage, that 'they were a proud people only considerable in their own conceits.'[495]

[490] Newsletter, Jan. 7/17, *Record Office Transcripts;*—to Lanark, Feb. 1, *Hamilton Papers*, p. 148.

[491] Ludlow, *Memoirs* (ed. Firth), i, 185–6.

[492] See p. 334.

[493] Ludlow, *op. cit.*, i, 185–186.

[494] Letter, Feb. 22, *Hamilton Papers*, p. 154.

[495] Ludlow, p. 186.

It was not the first time, nor the last, that the man of action has had to contend with theorists, and with small result. Nor did he have much more success with the other groups. He arranged a meeting of the leading Independents and Presbyterians, ministers as well as members of Parliament, at a dinner at Westminster designed to reconcile the two parties, but the task proved too difficult.[496] He even tried to bring the City, the Army and the Parliament together, and was probably one of the "chief officers" who on February 4 accompanied Fairfax to dinner with the Lord Mayor and some aldermen.[497]

The very record of Cromwell's activities at this time is the best indication of the disturbed condition of affairs. The test of the success of a revolution lies less in the overthrow of an existing government than in the creation of a new system to take its place, and though the Independents held the country and the Parliament down by control of the army, it was evident to them, and not least to Cromwell, that the situation could not last. There must be found some more permanent basis of authority.

To the great majority of the English people this still resided in the King and at this moment, despite, or on account of, his imprisonment, his position had improved. From every direction came evidence that the country was weary of what was, in effect, the dictatorship of the revolutionary leaders. Every post brought news of discontent and rumors of conspiracies and disturbances. For this there seemed good reason. The war had now been over for a year and more; yet the army was still in being and settlement of the kingdom apparently as far off as ever. Whatever might be urged of the distrust of Charles on the part of the leaders of Parliament and the army, his proposals for a settlement seemed to most men more reasonable than those of his opponents; and to most men it began to seem that his enemies were not desirous of a settlement save on the basis of his elimination, or even that of monarchy, from the government. The City was uneasy; the country much disturbed; Wales on the eve of a rebellion; Scotland committed to the royal cause. A new burst of pamphleteering, in the main now as favorable to the royal cause as it had earlier been opposed to it, revived monarchical spirit and alarmed the leaders of the army and of Parliament. For the moment, at least, the revolutionary spirit seemed to have spent its force, and there ensued that period common to all revolutions, a loss of momentum on the part of its forces and a reaction in favor of its opponents. At best it had come to a dead center; at worst it might easily begin to turn in the other direction. "The revolutionary leader," as one of Cromwell's

[496] *Ibid.*, pp. 183–184.

[497] Rushworth, vii, 986; Walker, *History of Independency*, (1661), i, 83.

biographers has said, "treads a path of fire," and he cannot, in consequence, like a legitimate ruler, stand still.

It was apparently about this time that there was written the famous ballad *O Brave Oliver*, copied later in the year by Thomason. It revealed, among other things, not only that hate and fear of Cromwell which marked him in the minds of his opponents as their most dangerous antagonist and the chief foe of monarchy, but the possibility of his rising to supreme power on the ruins of that monarchy. Thus early the shadow of the man on horseback fell across the path which England trod.

O Brave Oliver

The army is come up, hay hoe,
The army is come up, hay hoe!
   to London it is brought,
   and who would have thought
It ever would have proved soe?
   for the indipendants
   ar superindendants
Over kingdome and Cyty also.
Then O fine Oliver, O brave, O rare Olliver, O,
Dainty Olliver, O gallant Olliver, O!

* * * *

For Olliver is all in all,
For Olliver is all in all,
   and Olliver is here,
   and Olliver is there,
And Olliver is at whitehall.
   And Olliver notes all,
   And Olliver voats all,
And claps his hand upon his bilboe.
Then O fine Olliver, O brave Olliver, &c.

You shall have a Kinge, but whome?
You shall have a Kinge, but whome?
   That you cannot tell,
   nor never shall well
Perhaps to the day of doome;
   for good Sir Thomas
   great matters did promise.
Was ever Kinge served soe?—
To make roome for Olliver, O fine Olliver, &c.

Now Olliver must be he,
Now Olliver must be he,
   for Olliver's nose
   is the Lancaster rose,

And thence comes his soverainety.
For Olliver teaches,
And Olliver preaches,
And prayeth upon his tip-toe.
Then O fine Olliver, O rare Olliver, &c.

But doe you not heare? what news?
But doe you not heare? what news?
The Prince they say
will come thys way,
And the Scots will him not refuse.
I wish he may enter
this Land to the Center,
And winne it, and give a right blow.
Then O base Olliver, O s—— Olliver, O,
Stinking Olliver, O Trayter Olliver, O,
Damned Olliver, O![498]

Despite the vote of No Addresses, Charles remained King; and at this moment there was introduced into the Commons an extraordinary Declaration. It contained, among other things, what seemed to his supporters the basis for a direct attack upon his person, in the form of the revival of an earlier charge that, with the Duke of Buckingham, he had conspired against his father's life. To most men this seemed monstrous and incredible, and against it the leading lawyers of the House, Maynard and Selden in particular, protested violently. Maynard declared that by their vote of No Addresses the Houses had, in effect, ended their own existence. Selden objected no less vigorously to the insinuation that Charles had conspired with Buckingham to poison James, declaring that he had served on the committee appointed to investigate that charge and had found nothing which reflected upon Charles. But, as Clarendon observed bitterly, "the other side meant not to maintain their resolution by discussion." They had the votes, and the Declaration was carried on February 11 by a vote of 80 to 50.[499] In the course of the debate on it Cromwell was reported to have "made a sever invective against monarchical government."[500] In consequence, Maynard left the House for many months and Cromwell, who supported the Declaration vigorously, went so far as to move to expel Selden. As Nicholas's London correspondent wrote:

"Mr. Selden told the House that he was one of the Committee to examine the business of poisoning King James in the Duke of Buckingham's time, but could find nothing at all reflecting upon this King, and therefore moved the

[498] Printed in Hyder E. Rollins, *Cavalier and Puritan* (1923), pp. 221–223.

[499] *C. J.*, v, 462; *Old Parl. Hist.* xvi, 1–24; Clarendon, *History*, x, 149.

[500] *Mercurius Elencticus;* Fraser to Lanark, Feb. 15, *Hamilton Papers*, Add. *Camden Miscellany*, ix, 9.

House that that article might be deserted. Whereupon the Lieutenant General moved, that that Gentleman who made that motion might be expelled the House; which Sir Simon D'Ewes (who troubles himself much in relicks and records) took much in snuff, and told the House that he had a premeditated speech upon that particular; but finding Mr. Selden like to speed so ill for declaring his mind, he desired that he might have liberty to sit down, and say nothing."[501]

Few things in his career at this period reveal more clearly how deeply Cromwell was committed to the party bent on disposing of the King than his attack on monarchy and his motion against Selden. Little by little, and now more and more rapidly, Cromwell and Charles had begun to come to open antagonism. If the one had grown from a mere country gentleman to be member of Parliament, a captain of horse, colonel, lieutenant-general, and now the recognized leader of the party opposed to the monarchy, the other had declined from his high estate, from king to fugitive to prisoner, now on his way to trial, then to the scaffold. If the one had risen to be a hero and a dictator, the other was about to become a martyr, then a saint. Already there was some dim consciousness of this in the minds of many men; and from this month of March there is apparent an effort on the part of various elements to evade this conclusion of the revolutionary movement, and on the other hand to maintain it in the face of rising opposition in the country at large, as Cromwell and his fellows strove desperately to rally the opposition elements into a coherent group.

From these momentous events, the notices of Cromwell's activities turn to minor matters in connection with his official duties and his family. On February 16th, he was named on the committee for Cambridge and Huntingdon counties and the Isle of Ely, in the ordinance for raising £20,000 for the relief of Ireland.[502] A week later he, with Ireton and fifteen other officers, was appointed by Fairfax to sit at Whitehall every day at nine and at two to consider petitions and other business of the army. His attendance on this Committee of officers,[503] with that on the Committee of Both Houses, left him little time for attendance at the House of Commons. On Thursday, the 24th, and on Friday, Cromwell met with the Officers to examine members of Fairfax's life guard, recently ordered disbanded, about the carrying away of their colours.[504]

While Cromwell was thus occupied with public business, his eldest

[501] Letter of Intelligence, Feb. 17, Coxe, *Clarendon Mss*, 2724, 2725; *Clarendon State Papers*, ii, App. xlv.

[502] *L. J.*, x, 53–54.

[503] *Perfect Diurnall*, Feb. 24; Rushworth, vii, 1008.

[504] Rushworth, vii, 1009.

son who, according to a news sheet of the preceding October, was captain of the General's life guard,[505] was apparently following his own youthful footsteps in one respect at least. Cromwell had been married at the age of twenty-one years and four months; and when Richard was precisely that age the first indication of his having fallen in love appears in a letter from his father to Colonel Richard Norton—member of Parliament for Hampshire and Cromwell's friend since their service in Manchester's army—who was to act as go-between in the marriage settlement.

For my noble Friend Colonel Richard Norton: These

DEAR NORTON,

I have sent my son over to thee, being willing to answer Providence; and although I confess I have had an offer of a very great proposition, from a father, of his daughter, yet truly I rather incline to this in my thoughts; because, though the other be very far greater, yet I see difficulties, and not that assurance of godliness; yet indeed fairness. I confess that which is told me concerning [the] estate of Mr. M. is more than I look for, as things now stand.

If God please to bring it about, the consideration of piety in the parents, and such hopes of the gentlewoman in that respect, make the business to me a great mercy; concerning which I desire to wait upon God.

I am confident of thy love; and desire things may be carried with privacy. The Lord do His will: that's best; to which submitting, I rest,

Your humble servant,

25th February 1647. O. CROMWELL.[506]

The efforts to find some basis of accord among the opponents of the King left little time for other matters and the business of the Derby House Committee, like that of Parliament, was very light in the first three months of 1647; so light, in fact, that during March it held only nine short meetings of which Cromwell attended six.[507]

505 *Mercurius Pragmaticus*, Oct. 5–12. "And truly, if you knew what a large family Mr. Lieut.-Gen. hath in the army, you could not much blame him for being so craving daily for money, whereof honest John Lilburne hath given me a perfect muster. 1. Himself, Lieut.-Gen. and Col. of horse. 2. One of his sons, Capt. of the General's life-guard. 3. His other son, Capt. of a troop in Col. Harrison's regiment. 4. His brother-in-law Desborough, Col. of the General's regiment of horse. 5. His son-in-law Ireton, Commissary Gen. of the horse, and Col. of horse. 6. His brother Ireton, Quarter-master-general of the horse, and Capt. of horse. 7. His cousin Whaley, Col. of horse. 8. And his brother Whaley lately made Judge-Advocate." There is, of course, some slight possibility that the reference is not to Richard but to Cromwell's son-in-law, John Claypole, later captain of the Protector's life-guard.

506 Pr. in Harris, p. 514–15, from the original in the hands of R. Symmer. Pr. also in Noble, i, 319, and Forster, *Lives of eminent British statesmen*, iv, 247. Lomas-Carlyle, Letter LIII, from the holograph original, then in the Morrison Collection but sold in 1918. Calendared in *Hist. Mss. Comm. Rept.* 2 App. (Prescott Mss.), p. 98.

507 *Cal. S. P. Dom.* (1648–9), pp. 23–35 *passim*.

That was not due to the lack of importance of the issues before it. The plans for a campaign in Ireland; the discontent and disturbances in Wales; the disbanding of the "supernumerary" troops; the Scotch threat, and the situation at Carisbrooke were enough to absorb its energies. But they were most of them matters which called rather for political maneuvering outside of administrative or legislative bodies, and in consequence the part which Cromwell played in Parliament and the Committee was in sharp contrast to his more important activities outside those bodies.

On March 1, he and Sir Anthony Irby were ordered by the Commons to look into the question of the dissolution of the Eastern Association and to bring in a report on it, and the matter of an army auditor, one Henry Beard, on the following Saturday.[508] Apparently they were also appointed to nominate Commissioners for the Great Seal, for, according to Whitelocke, Cromwell and his party agreed on the Earl of Kent, Sir Thomas Widdrington, Speaker of the House, and Whitelocke himself; and on March 2 Irby carried an ordinance to that effect to the Upper House.[509] In the Committee at Derby House on March 7, Cromwell presented a letter from Colonel Jubbs, enclosing a printed paper, and was instructed to send both to Fairfax. A week later he was ordered to inform the General of Colonel Hammond's situation and ask Fairfax to do what he thought fit about it.[510]

But his chief business and that of the Committee was to rally strength from every quarter to its cause, and Walker testifies that Cromwell pleaded with the House for such support. In that he was only partially successful. He was answered that its members were chosen to pursue only one interest—the common good, safety and liberty of the people—and whoever had any "peculiar" interest was not fit to sit there.[511] In particular the Republicans were unimpressed by Cromwell's appeal. Men like Ludlow and Marten, with Marten's supporter and client, Lilburne, were no less opposed to Cromwell's ascendancy than they were to monarchy. They were even more afraid of a dictator than they were of a king. Marten in particular was reported to be so convinced of Cromwell's treachery that "he provided and charged a pistol, and took a dagger in his pocket, that if the one did not, the other should despatch"[512] Cromwell if he deserted the party opposed to Charles. It was said that this threat frightened him into supporting the vote of No Addresses; but it is more probable that he was influenced by the possibility of impeach-

[508] *C. J.*, v, 475.
[509] Whitelocke, p. 294; *C. J.*, v, 477.
[510] *Cal. S. P. Dom.* (1648–9), pp. 25, 29.
[511] Walker, *History of Independency*, pp. 82–3.
[512] *Declaration of some of the Proceedings of Lieut. Col. John Lilburne.* (1648)

ment by Marten and Rainsborough and still more probable that the general situation forced him to make terms with them. Despite his efforts, Walker observes that Marten was unreconciled; that he favored bringing in Scotch aid rather than permit Cromwell's dominance, declaring that "there was nothing he would not do to destroy Cromwell and his party, who was the falsest of mankind."[513] Already the dread of a military dictatorship was disturbing the minds of the revolutionary party; and amid the various evidences that Cromwell was rising to the first place in affairs none is more convincing than the antagonism of the more advanced republicans.

FAMILY AND PERSONAL AFFAIRS FEBRUARY–APRIL, 1648

That antagonism was heightened by the introduction of a bill to grant him the lands necessary to make up the £2,500 a year voted him two years before in recompense for his services. Casting about to find lands suitable to supplement those confiscated from the Earl of Worcester's estates in Hampshire, Parliament had ordered various county committees to investigate the remainder of Worcester's properties. Only one report, that from Monmouth, seems to have survived.[514] There various estates, ranging in value from Chepstow Castle valued at £18/3/8 a year to the Lordship of Magor at more than £266, were assigned to him, and an ordinance granting him properties in Southampton, Gloucester, Monmouth and Glamorgan passed the Commons on March 7 and the Lords two days later.[515] What their value really was it is hard to judge. The estimates ranged from Cromwell's own figure of £1,680 submitted to Parliament on March 21,[516] to that of Clement Walker who reckoned them worth between five and six thousand pounds.[517] "It is farther said," con-

[513] — to Lanark, Mar. 14, *Hamilton Papers*, Add.; *Camden Miscellany* X; *Westminster Projects*, Mar. 23.

[514] *Day Book of Orders*, Interr. G 118, p. 969–974. *Cal. S. P. Dom.* (1648–9), p. 40–41. Drawn up Feb. 10, 1647/8. Lands designated for Cromwell were Chepstow Castle, worth £18/3/8; Domum de Chepstow Codllvos, £53/4/8; Magor, £266/18/1; Redwick Miles Court, £60/16/4½; Barton and Hardwick, £45/14/3; Tithe of Magor and Hardwick, £20.

[515] Pr. in *L. J.*, x, 104–5. Lands there specified are: the Manors of Charleton, Clanfield and Blendworth and all of Worcester's lands in Catherton, co. Southampton (already in Cromwell's possession); the Manors of Tyddenham and Wolleston with the patronage to the churches there, in co. Gloucester; the Manors and Lordships of Chepstow and Magor with their rights in Chepstow, Magor, St. Bride's, Gouldcliff, Wash, Whilston, Redwicke, Christ Church, Lanston, Penhouse, Shernewton, Pewterry, Mounton, and Carwent, in co. Monmouth; the Manors and Lordships of Gower, Swansey, Kythall, Longher, Oistermouth, Liniccon, Pennard, Trisday, and Kilvey, in co. Glamorgan.

[516] See next letter.

[517] Walker, *op. cit.*, p. 81.

tinues Walker, "those lands are bravely wooded"; and that much, at least, seems true for, anticipating the passage of the ordinance, Cromwell had already asked the Navy Commissioners to consider the purchase of 2,000 timber trees on his land—once the Earl of Worcester's, but assigned to him some months previously—within six miles of Portsmouth.[518]

Whether or not Walker's estimate of the value of Cromwell's land grants is more nearly correct than Cromwell's own, his is only one side of the story. In the first place, the new schedule of army salaries lately approved by Parliament[519] reduced Cromwell's salary from £4 to £3 a day. In addition to this reduction of income, two weeks after the ordinance was passed Cromwell voluntarily offered £1,000 a year for five years out of the Earl of Worcester's estate for the war in Ireland. This leaves according to his calculation of its value, only £680 a year for his own use. His further offer to remit £1,500 back pay as Lieutenant-General and two years arrears as Governor of the Isle of Ely left him little income apart from his private means and his reduced army salary. His written offer was presented to the Derby House Committee, reported to Parliament by Sir John Evelyn on March 24th, and accepted immediately with due thanks.

To the Committee of Lords and Commons sitting at Derby House

The two Houses of Parliament having lately bestowed one thousand six hundred eighty pounds *per annum* upon me and my heirs, out of the Earl of Worcester's estate; the necessity of affairs requiring assistance, I do hereby offer one thousand pounds annually to be paid out of the rents of the said land; that is to say, five hundred pounds out of the next Michaelmas rent, and so on, by the half years, for the space of five years, if the war in Ireland shall so long continue, or that I live so long; to be employed for the service of Ireland, as the Parliament shall please to appoint; provided the said yearly rent of one thousand six hundred eighty pounds become not to be suspended by war or other accident.

And whereas there is an arrear of pay due unto me whilst I was Lieutenant-General unto the Earl of Manchester, of about Fifteen hundred pounds audited and stated; as also a great arrear due for about two years being Governor of the Isle of Ely; I do hereby discharge the State from all or any claim to be made by me thereunto, 21° Martii 1647.

O. Cromwell.[520]

The rewards voted to its successful generals by Parliament raised one of the great issues which always accompany such movements as this. "Revolutions," Napoleon is said to have observed, "are only the

518 Committee of the Navy to Commissioners of the Navy, Feb. 22, *St. P. Dom.* dxvii; *Calendar* (1648–9), p. 357. Pat. 21 Charles I, pt. I, no. 74.

519 Feb. 9th, *C. J.*, v, 460; *Perfect Diurnall*, Feb. 13.

520 *C. J.*, v, 513; Carlyle (Lomas ed.) i, 296–297.

transfer of property from one hand to another." They are, of course, much more than this; but *vae victis* is never truer than in a civil war, and whatever the high motives and noble aspirations of the leaders of the Puritan Revolution, they profited greatly in a material way from their success. The sums voted to the commanders by Parliament were, like the estates bestowed on Cromwell, taken from the property of the Royalists; nor were these rewards confined to the higher command nor to the votes of Parliament. Apart from such confiscation as that which handed over the Marquis of Worcester's estates directly to Cromwell, and apart from the public acknowledgment of military services, there were many ways in which the triumphant party acquired the property of its conquered opponents. From highest to lowest, the shrewder and more energetic of the Parliamentarians made their fortunes in English and Irish lands, by direct grant or by purchasing confiscated estates at a fraction of their value. It is a matter of more than merely curious interest that such a strong Republican as Ludlow emerged from the civil wars with a comfortable fortune and that such a leading Leveller as Wildman was reported to have bought land in twenty counties, and lived on an estate which he had bought from his Republican friend Marten, who had acquired it by like means from the government. He was perhaps the worst and most successful of the speculators in confiscated lands, but between him and those granted estates for eminent services there were a multitude of others; so that to the political and spiritual opposition between the parties there was added the material grievance of the dispossessed Royalists which was to endure for generations.

This settlement of the rewards for his services accomplished, on March 25 Cromwell was in the House to be thanked for his generous offer and to bring two messages from Fairfax: the one concerned with paying off discharged soldiers of which he submitted lists; the other concerning the pay of Dutch soldiers petitioning for arrears.[521] Then, although the Independent leaders were meeting frequently to discuss the form of government to be set up,[522] and it was reported by a Scotch agent in London that they had voted for monarchy to prevent it being forced on them by the Scotch army, Cromwell chose the anniversary of the King's accession, then being enthusiastically celebrated in London, to go into the country. His visit was on personal business. In the Great Lodge of Merdon Manor near Winchester lived a certain Richard Mayor, whom Cromwell describes as "wise and honest," but one of his tenants characterized as "witty but thrifty even to miserliness, and an unscrupulous oppressor of his tenant-

[521] *C. J.*, v, 514.

[522] Letter to Lanark, *Hamilton Papers*, i, 170, says it was reported that they had voted for monarchy to avoid having it forced on them by the Scots.

ry."[523] To arrange a marriage between Richard Cromwell and Dorothy Mayor, Cromwell journeyed to Farnham where he expected to meet his friend Colonel Norton who was assisting in the marriage negotiations, and who, like "Brother" Francis Russell, and Cromwell himself, was a colonel in the Eastern Association and a member of Parliament, from which, again like Russell, he had been absenting himself, as Cromwell takes pains to point out:

For my noble Friend Col. Richard Norton: These

DEAR DICK,

It had been a favour indeed to have met you here at Farnham, but I hear you are a man of great business; therefore I say no more: if it be a favour to the House of Commons to enjoy you, what is it to me. But, in good earnest, when will you and your Brother Russell be a little honest, and attend your charge. Surely some expect it, especially the good fellows who chose you.

I met with Mr. Mayor; we spent two or three hours together last night. I perceive the gentleman is very wise and honest, and indeed much to be valued. Some things of common fame did a little stick: I gladly heard his doubts, and gave such answer as was next at hand, I believe, to some satisfaction. Nevertheless I exceedingly liked the gentleman's plainness and free dealing with me. I know God has been above all ill reports, and will in His own time vindicate me; I have no cause to complain. I see nothing but that this particular business between him and me may go on. The Lord's will be done.

For news out of the North there is little, only the mal [ignant] party is prevailing in the Parliament of S[cotland]. They are earnest for a war; the ministers oppose as yet. Mr. Marshall is returned, who says so, and so do many of our letters. Their great Committee of Dangers have two malignants for one right. It's said they have voted an army of 40,000 in Parliament; so some of yesterday's letters. But I account my news ill bestowed, because upon an idle person.

I shall take speedy course in the business concerning my Tenants; for which, thanks. My service to your Lady. I am really,

March 28, 1648, Your affectionate servant,

Farnham, O. CROMWELL.[524]

Apart from its personal significance, the letter is important in its revelation of the situation of affairs and Cromwell's state of mind.

[523] *Victoria County History of Southampton*, iii, 419, from a manuscript account of the customs of the manor, written by a tenant, Richard Morley.

[524] Harris, p. 515, from the original then in the possession of R. Symmer. Also in Noble, i, 320. Lomas-Carlyle, Letter LV, from the original in the Morrison Collection until it was sold in 1918. Ms. copy by Birch in *Ayscough Mss*, 4162, f. 56, also from the original. In *Hist. Mss. Comm. Rept.* 2, App. (Prescott Mss), p. 98, is mention of a letter of the same date from Cromwell to his son Richard. The letter may be this one but described as being addressed to Richard Cromwell because of the salutation "Dear Dick."

He was acutely conscious of the doubts of his own rectitude which even Mr. Mayor seems to have expressed to him. He is no less concerned with the prospect of war with the Scots; nor is the Royalist reaction wholly absent from his thoughts, nor the indifference of men like Norton and Russell to the cause.

It was doubtless this visit to Farnham which gave rise to the rumor that Cromwell had gone to consult with Hammond in regard to the King;[525] but it is evident that this was not the case. The marriage negotiations were resumed, but for the moment no agreement was reached; and once more in London Cromwell wrote again to Norton in regard to them:

[*For Colonel Richard Norton*]

DEAR NORTON,

I could not in my last give you a perfect account of what passed between me and Mr. M., because we were to have a conclusion of our speech that morning after I wrote my letter to you. Which we had; and having had a full interview of one another's minds, we parted with this: That both would consider with our relations, and according to satisfactions given there, acquaint each other with our minds.

I cannot tell how better to do it, to receive or give satisfaction, than by you who (as I remember), in your last, said that, if things did stick between us, you would use your endeavour towards a close.

The things insisted upon were these (as I take it). Mr. Mayor desired 400*l. per annum* of Inheritance lying in Cambridgeshire and Norfolk, to be presently settled, and to be for maintenance, wherein I desired to be advised by my Wife. I offered the land in Hampshire for present maintenance, which I dare say, with copses and ordinary fells, will be, *communibus annis*, 500*l. per annum:* besides 500*l. per annum* in Tenants' hands holding but for one life, and about 300*l. per annum*, some for two lives, some for three lives. But as to this, if the latter be not liked of, I shall be willing a further conference be had in [regard to] the first.

In point of jointure I shall give satisfaction, and as to the settlements of lands given me by the Parliament, satisfaction to be given in like manner, according as we discoursed. In what else was demanded of me, I am willing (so far as I remember any demand was) to give satisfaction. Only, I having been informed by Mr. Robinson that Mr. Mayor did, upon a former match, offer to settle the Manor wherein he lived, and to give 2,000*l.* in money, I did insist upon that; and do desire it may not be with difficulty. The money I shall need for my two little wenches, and thereby I shall free my Son from being charged with them. Mr. Mayor parts with nothing in present but that money, saving their board, which I should not be unwilling to give them, to enjoy the comfort of their society; which it's reason he smart for, if he will rob me altogether of them.

Truly the land to be settled,—both what the Parliament gives me, and my own,—is very little less than 3,000*l. per annum*, all things considered,

[525] Walker, *History of Independency*, pp. 77–78.

if I be rightly informed. And a lawyer of Lincoln's Inn, having searched all the Marquis of Worcester's writings, which were taken at Ragland and sent for by the Parliament, and this gentleman appointed by the Committee to search the said writings, assures me there is no scruple concerning the title. And it so fell out that this gentleman who searched was my own lawyer, a very godly able man, and my dear friend, which I reckon no small mercy. He is also possessed of the writings for me.

I thought fit to give you this account, desiring you to make such use of it as God shall direct you, and I doubt not but you will do the part of a friend between two friends. I account myself one, and I have heard you say Mr. Mayor was entirely so to you. What the good pleasure of God is, I shall wait; there is only rest. Present my service to your Lady, to Mr. Mayor, &c. I rest,

Your affectionate servant,

April the 3d 1648 O. CROMWELL.

[P.S.] I desire you to carry this business with all privacy. I beseech you to do so, as you love me. Let me entreat you not to lose a day herein, that I may know Mr. Mayor's mind, for I think I may be at leisure for a week to attend this business, to give and take satisfaction; from which perhaps I may be shut up afterwards by employment. I know thou art an idle fellow, but prithee neglect me not now; delay may be very inconvenient to me; I much rely upon you. Let me hear from you in two or three days. I confess the principal consideration as to me, is the absolute settlement of the Manor wherein he lives; which he would do but conditionally, in case he prove to have no son, and but 3,000*l.* in case have a son. But as to this, I hope farther reason may work him to more.[526]

THE ROYALIST REACTION, APRIL–MAY, 1648

Cromwell's suggestion that he might soon find further "employment" was more than justified, though not, perhaps, precisely in the form in which it was intended. A Royalist reaction had begun. Not only were the Scots raising forces in pursuance of the Engagement and the King engaged in a plot to escape, but there were being woven the threads of a widespread conspiracy looking toward the overthrow of the military government and Charles's restoration. Ireland was not only not unpacified but various of its factions were looking toward union against the common enemy—the Parliamentary army under Colonel Jones. Wales was on the edge of insurrection; and everywhere in England there were efforts being made to rouse the people against the government and in favor of the King.

In the face of these dangers, the Derby House Committee met on April 1st and 3rd to discuss plans for a new campaign in Ireland and

[526] Harris, p. 516–17; Noble, i, 321. Lomas-Carlyle, Letter LVI, from the original in the Morrison Collection until 1918. Listed in sale catalogue of J. Herbert Foster Library to be sold by Anderson Galleries, Mar. 14, 1922, item no. 46 (with facs. of portion.) Copy in *Ayscough Mss.* 4162, fol. 56.

the curbing of the imminent Welsh rising; and with this may be said to begin another chapter in the revolutionary movement. The first business was that of Ireland, and, present at both sessions, Cromwell and his colleagues began with signing a warrant for money to be sent into Munster:

To Sr. Adam Loftus, knt. Treasurer at Warres for ye Kingdome of Ireland

Whereas you have received the sum of Five thousand pounds from Alderman Andrewes and Mr. Maurice Thompson appointed to be the Treasurers for the Ordinance of 20000 l. per mensem for the relief of Ireland. These are therefore to will and require you to cause the said money to be transmitted to Bristol to be there in a readiness to be transported into Munster with Col. Wm. Jephson, Major Richard Salwey and John Swinsen, Esquires, who are appointed by both Houses of Parliament to go Commissioners into that Province. The above said money you are there to issue according to such warrants and directions as you shall from time to time receive from the said Commissioners or any two of them, hereof you are not to fail and for sodoing this shall be your sufficient warrant. Dated at Derby House this 3d of April 1648.

(Signed) WARWICK
ARTHUR ANNESLEY
W. PIERREPONT
O. CROMWELL
J. TEMPLE
GILBERT GERARD [527]

Meeting three times a week in the first three weeks of April, Cromwell and his fellow members of the committee found themselves confronted again with new and perplexing problems. The first of these was that of the King himself. Had he succeeded in escaping, it might well have meant the end of the predominance of the army and the downfall of the Independents. Already he had made one unsuccessful attempt on March 20, of which the committee learned a fortnight later. It had failed but it might well be renewed with more success, especially in the hands of that determined and energetic Presbyterian Royalist Colonel Titus against whom Cromwell now warned Hammond. On the strength of that warning the Colonel was expelled from the Castle but he remained on the island in correspondence with the King, and with him and Charles's other devoted followers at hand, especially Henry Firebrace who had engineered the first plot, the emergency was imminent and acute.[528]

[527] Original in *State Papers Domestic*, *Charles I*, dxxxix, no. 505; cal. in *Cal. S. P. Dom.* (1625–1649), p. 715.

[528] *Firebrace's Narrative*, in Herbert's *Memoirs*, (1702).

For Colonel Robert Hammond

Dear Robin,

Your business is done in the House: your 10 l. by the week is made 20 l.; 1000 l. is given you; and Order to Mr. Lisle to draw up an Ordinance for 500 l. per annum to be settled upon you and your heirs. This was done with smoothness; your friends were not wanting to you. I know thy burden; this is an addition to it: the Lord direct and sustain thee.

Intelligence came to the hands of a very considerable person, that the King attempted to get out of his window; and that he had a cord of silk with him whereby to slip down, but his breast was so big the bar would not give him passage. This was done in one of the dark nights about a fortnight ago. A gentleman with you led him the way, and slipped down. The Guard, that night, had some quantity of wine with them. The same party assures that there is aquafortis gone down from London, to remove that obstacle which hindered; and that the same design is to be put in execution in the next dark nights. He saith that Captain Titus and some others about the King are not to be trusted. He is a very considerable person of the Parliament who gave this intelligence, and desired it should be speeded to you.

The gentleman that came out of the window was Master Firebrace; the gentlemen doubted are Cresset, Burrowes and Titus; the time when this attempt of escape was, the 20th of March.

Your servant,

April 6th, 1648. Oliver Cromwell.[529]

The danger at which Cromwell hints in his letters was imminent. The celebration of the King's accession in London had been greater than any public demonstration since his return from Spain two decades earlier. The City was lighted with innumerable bonfires; all coaches were stopped to make their occupants drink the King's health; the streets were full of crowds shouting for the King and cursing his jailer in whose behalf Cromwell had just pushed an appropriation through the Parliament. It was reported that the Independents began to look with favor once more on the King, and it seems evident that Cromwell's efforts to bring about an understanding between the City, the Army and the Parliament had failed. At this moment, on April 8, Walker reports that Cromwell approached the London Council with a proposition for an alliance of some sort. The story goes that Cromwell's agent, Solicitor Glover, offered the restitution of the Tower and control of the militia, with release of the imprisoned aldermen in return for the support of the City. When the offer was rejected, Walker says, Cromwell was so nettled that he demanded of Glover by what authority he had made it; to which Glover retorted by exhibiting a warrant signed by "Fairfax, Crom-

[529] Birch, p. 40. Carlyle, LVII. Original in cipher.

well, Mr. Recorder, and Sir Henry Vane, Jr., which Cromwell had the impudence to put in his pocket."[530]

The crisis did not pass without the use of force. On April 9 some thousands of London apprentices met in Moorfields in defiance of a City ordinance, pelted with bricks and stones the trained band which the Lord Mayor sent to disperse them, and disarmed its members, and thence triumphantly marched through Fleet Street and the Strand, shouting for the King and encouraged by the spectators as they advanced toward Westminster. Not until they were almost at the Mews, at about eight in the evening, did news of the disorder come to Fairfax. As it happened, Cromwell and Ireton were there, and Cromwell ordered out the cavalry, fell upon the mob, killed its leader and one or two others, and drove the rest before him back into the City. That night the crowd rallied, secured Ludgate and Newgate, seized arms at the Armory, and took possession of the City, which they held until, on the next day, part of a regiment of foot and some troops of horse burst through Moorgate, drove the mob into Leadenhall and took its leaders prisoner.[531]

Nor was this all the disturbing news which alarmed the Parliament. Hardly had it voted a day of thanksgiving for the City's deliverance, when a delegation of "renegado" officers from Lord Inchiquin's regiment in Munster presented itself before the House of Commons. Warning its members that Inchiquin intended to declare against Parliament and the Independents, they informed the House of his "good correspondence" with the Presbyterians in Parliament, and of a treaty between the Independents and the native Irish under Owen Roe O'Neill. As usual the cry of treachery was raised and Alderman Allen, the goldsmith, moved that every member should be offered an Engagement or Covenant, that it might be discovered what members were enemies.

The debate was short and sharp. According to Walker, who was apparently present, Cromwell suggested

"That being to debate this business to-morrow, whosoever with crosse Arguments shall spin out the debate and so retard our proceedings (by my consent) shall be noted with a Black Coal."[532]

To this piece of characteristic impatience with Parliamentary proceedings it was answered that "this tended to take away freedom of debate, which was the life of Parliament and of all Councils," and the debate was held. It only served to deepen the breach between

[530] Walker, *History of Independency*, p. 83.

[531] Newsletter, Apr. 10, *Clarke Papers*, ii, 3–4. Cp. Walker, pp. 83–5, who credits the Independents with having induced the boys to gather. Cp. also Rushworth, vii, 1051; and *L. J.*, x, 188, 190.

[532] Walker, *op. cit.*, pp. 86–87.

the two parties. On the Presbyterians' insistence that this was only another "purging" of the House and that the Independents should clear themselves of the charge of treating with O'Neill before they gave a purgation to others, the matter was dropped, as evidently too dangerous to all parties save the Royalists in the existing situation of affairs.[533] The government had all it could do to maintain itself in the face of the dangers which now threatened it on every hand and this was no time to investigate the devious negotiations and intrigues of its various elements; for, as the Royalists were saying, "If the rogues fell out among themselves, the honest party would come into its own," and it seemed that this might happen almost any day in the disturbed condition of whole country.

From these disputes and distractions Cromwell was called upon to consider various pieces of business more personal to himself. The first of these was his own salary. Among the papers at the Record Office is a certificate by Captain John Blackwell, one of the Treasurers at War, that Cromwell's pay for twenty-eight days amounted to £84, and annexed to it is Cromwell's receipt for that amount:

Receipt for Pay

Received then of Sir John Wollaston, kt. and the rest of the Treasurers at War, By virtue of a warrant from the right Honorable the Committee of Lords and Commons for the Army, Bearing date the xii of April instant in full of xxviii days pay for myself as Lieutenant General of the Army under Command of his Excy Thomas Lord Fairfax according to the establishment of the 3d of November last: the sum of eighty four pounds, the said pay to commence the viiith of April instant 1648.	lxxxiiii l.

OLIVER CROMWELL [534]

The second item relates to a characteristic incident of the sequestration policy. Like many others of their kind, in 1645 Sir Oliver Cromwell, with an estate of some £1,200 a year, and his son Henry, had petitioned to compound, and fines had been imposed on them which the debt-ridden estate could not afford to pay. On April 8, 1648, in consequence, Sir Oliver appealed to the Sequestration Committee, pleading that he had been declared delinquent at the beginning of the war "for some opposition he should make against the Parliament's forces under the command of Lieutenant-General Cromwell at Ramsey," possibly on that visit already noted, and that he had been well-nigh ruined by his long sequestration. He therefore

[533] *Ibid.*
[534] Original in *S. P. Dom.* Charles I, dxxxix, 508; *Cal. S. P. Dom.* (1625–49), p. 715.

appealed for the remittance of his fine, and, more fortunate than many of his fellow-sufferers, he had the support of his nephew, in opposing whom he had incurred the fine. That intercession was so successful that the sequestration, with the fine of £841, was discharged by the House of Commons, and the old man, now eighty-four, was saved from ruin.[535]

The third item of such incidental business is a letter to the lieutenant to Governor Boys of Dover Castle, Colonel Kenrick, later a militia commissioner for Kent, relating to the application of the unknown bearer for a post:

To Colonel Kenrick, Lieutenant of Dover Castle

SIR,

This is the gentleman I mentioned to you. I am persuaded you may be confident of his fidelity to you in the things you will employ him in.

I conceive he is fit for any civil employment, as having been bred towards the law, and having beside very good parts. He hath been a captain-lieutenant: and therefore I hope you put such value upon him, in civil way, as one that hath borne such a place shall be thought by you worthy of. Whereby you will much oblige.

[London] Yours affectionate servant,
April 18th, 1648. O. CROMWELL.

[P.S.] I expect to hear from you about your defects in the Castle, that so you may be timely supplied.[536]

To such minutiae of daily business which press on public men even in such times of crises may be added an order by the House on the day he wrote the letter to Kenrick, that Cromwell should prepare an ordinance to satisfy the arrears of Colonel Richard Fortescue, Governor of Pendennis Castle, and find new employment for him in the army.[537] Two days later he was ordered by the Committee at Derby House to suggest to the House of Commons that a reward be given to those who apprehended a certain Browne Bushell, suspected conspirator who had escaped from a messenger of the Admiralty Committee while on his way to be questioned at Derby House.[538]

These were only incidental to the main business which then absorbed the energies of Cromwell and his fellow-Independents. London was now frankly hostile to them and in favor of the monarchy. Wales was in all but open rebellion. The Scots were arming; and

[535] *Cal. Com. for Comp.*, p. 978–9; *C. J.*, v, 533; *Perfect Diurnall*, 17 Apr.; Whitelocke, *Memorials*, p. 300.

[536] *Gentleman's Magazine*, lxi, 520 (1791); Carlyle, LVIII.

[537] *C. J.*, v, 536.

[538] *Cal. S. P. Dom.* (1648–9), p. 50.

England was favorable to restoration of the monarchy. The Independents were prepared to support a restoration; and by the date of Cromwell's letter to Kenrick, it was said to be admitted by the Independents themselves that "nobody would trust them and they would trust nobody,"[539] and there is no reason to doubt that they would have welcomed an understanding with the King. There is, in fact, a story that they made another effort to come to terms with Parliament and the King by means of a lady who was despatched from Lime Street with a letter to Charles. On her return Berkeley and Colonel Legge were sent to him to seek some such understanding.[540]

Save for the army, the Independent leaders had few supporters, and it was even questionable how long they could control the troops. They sought allies on every hand. Seconded by Vane, on April 27, Cromwell urged the House to come to an agreement with the City, remove the army and leave the trained bands in charge of Skippon who was trusted by army and City alike.[541] The motion met with no opposition and the next day the House, voting on the settlement of the kingdom, decided by a great majority of 165 to 99 not to alter "the fundamental government by King, Lords and Commons."[542]

Despite the large majority, it is evident that the Republicans and Levellers were strong. There can be but little doubt that Cromwell voted with the majority as his next movements indicate. From this division he repaired at once to Windsor to a council of war summoned to deal with the Agitators who had met a few days earlier at St. Albans to deplore the ambition of "the grandees" and adopt the *Agreement of the People* as their solution of the constitutional problem. Again the Independent officers were between the upper and nether millstones. With the country and Parliament in favor of the King, the Agitators pressing for a virtual republic, what were they to do?

As usual the Council of Officers opened its proceedings with a prayer-meeting; and as usual Cromwell urged officers and Agitators alike to examine into the causes of England's misfortunes. As one of those present testifies:

Speech at the Council of War at Windsor, April 29, 1648

"He did press very earnestly on all those present to a thorough consideration of our actions as an army, as well as our ways particularly as private Christians, to see if any iniquity could be found in them, and what it was,

539 Murray to Lanark, Apr. 18, *Hamilton Papers*, p. 185, and *Hist. Mss. Comm. Rept.* 11 App., vi, 121; Ford to Hopton, *Clarendon Mss*, 2763.

540 *Tricks of the State* (Apr. 29, 1648), quoted in Gardiner, *Civil War*, iv, 99n.

541 *Mercurius Pragmaticus; L. J.*, x, 234.

542 *C. J.*, v, 547.

that if possible we might find it out, and so remove the cause of such sad rebukes which were upon us by reason of our iniquities."[543]

However inspiring, this was far from definite. What else he said we may only judge from the reports of his enemies. According to a contemporary story recorded by Walker, he urged that there were but three possibilities open to the army. The first was to join the Levellers and 'new model' church and state. The second was to restore Charles with more limited powers. The third was to depose him, disinherit the Prince of Wales and crown the little Duke of Gloucester, appointing a Protector for the time being. Whether or not he made such a proposal, this was the common-sense of the situation as it presented itself to men in the position of the army officers; and it is possible that he said something which hinted at these alternatives. But it is difficult to believe that he advanced the arguments attributed to him by a group of Royalists in favor of the third plan. That solution was the best, he is alleged to have said,

"for that would necessitate the continuance of our Army, which secures our persons, will enforce our reasons, make just our demands, and facilitate their grant; for the Blood that will flow from the cheap veins of the Common souldiers, whereof England hath plenty, and we will not want; For the money, London is our bank, and from their purses it shall drain into our coffers."[544]

Such words are wholly unlike Cromwell and it is not probable that he uttered them; yet, apart from the gratuitous sneer at the common soldiers, which seems to have been inserted by a writer striving to discredit Cromwell, there were sentiments here which must have been present in the minds of more than one of the officers. For were peace to come and were the army disbanded, what would become of them? With no force at their back, what could they hope from King or Parliament? The army in being was at once their argument, their hope of accommodation, their guarantee of life and liberty. Without it, they were naked to their enemies.

For two days they wrestled with this great problem with no definite results save for a reprimand to the Agitators; but the third morning brought an end to their arguments and prayers, for there arrived the startling news that Adjutant-General Fleming had been killed in a Welsh uprising and that the population of south Wales was in arms or hiding in the hills. With tears in their eyes, the officers answered this challenge with a resolution to subdue the kingdom once more and, that accomplished, to bring the King to account for the blood that he had caused to be shed.[545]

543 Allen's "Narrative," Somers' *Tracts*, vi, 500.
544 *Remonstrance of the Colchester Knights*. Pr. in Walker, pp. 162–166.
545 Allen's "Narrative," Somers' *Tracts*, vi, 499–501.

The Puritan Revolution had now reached the point to which all such movements come sooner or later. Its leaders had succeeded in overthrowing the old system but as yet they had not been able to set another in its place nor to reconcile the people in general, much less their opponents, to a provisional government which was, in effect, a rule of force. Their opponents, though defeated, were not crushed; the nation was restless under military rule. The great majority was anxious for the return of peace and settled government, regular and not too burdensome taxes in place of confiscation, sequestration and assessments, the resumption of orderly trade and business, and some sense of security. There was, as always in such cases, a reaction in favor of the older system, which, with all its faults, had provided these conditions. Such was the situation which encouraged Royalists to make an effort to throw off the heavy yoke of an army and a rump Parliament. And such, in turn, as always in such cases, was the ground for the charge of the army that the responsibility for the bloodshed was not theirs nor that of the Parliament, but was on the shoulders of those who opposed them, the King in particular, "that man of blood," as he now came to be called, who must be brought to account for all the deaths and destruction of the civil war.

But first their enemies must be crushed and this was no small task. The British Isles seethed with discontent. There were great bodies of soldiery now disbanded or about to be disbanded, ready to revolt. The Scots were preparing an expedition to restore the King. The City favored him. The Royalists from Northumberland to Kent were planning to rise against those whom they regarded not only as their enemies but as the enemies of England, and almost every county was the seat of a conspiracy. Of these disaffected areas three were the most dangerous. The first was the north with the activities of Langdale and the threat of Scotch invasion. The second was Wales, already in revolt. The third was that of the southeastern counties and the capital. In consequence the army leaders hastened to secure the threatened areas, and to each the man who seemed best fitted was despatched with all speed.

To the north Fairfax ordered Lambert, who, besides being himself a Yorkshireman, had seen most of his service in that region and in the preceding August had pacified the mutinous soldiers of the northern army who had arrested their commander, Poyntz. Lambert had little difficulty in disposing of Langdale, driving him into Carlisle and retaking the strongholds seized by the Royalists; but the Scotch advance, coupled with the Royalist surprise and capture of Pontefract and the defection of Scarborough, left him in a difficult situation and he had all that he could do to maintain himself until relief came from other quarters.

That relief could not be sent at once. Fairfax who had remained to take charge of the situation in the capital and the adjacent counties and to be at or near the army headquarters, found his hands full in keeping rebellion down. To Cornwall he sent Sir Hardress Waller, and to south Wales he ordered Cromwell to hasten with two regiments of horse, which, with the troops already there under Colonel Horton, raised the forces under Cromwell's command to some 8,000 men. This, the largest body of Parliamentary troops under any of the commanders, indicated that the army leaders considered the Welsh situation most serious and it was perhaps for that reason, among others, that Cromwell was entrusted with the task of suppressing the rebellion in that quarter. Under such conditions there began the Second Civil War; and under such conditions Cromwell advanced to his next great triumph.[546]

[546] *Perfect Diurnall*, May 1, 2; Fairfax to Lenthall, May 1, in Cary, *Memorials*, i 393; *Moderate Intelligencer*, May 5.

CHAPTER IX

THE SECOND CIVIL WAR AND THE EXECUTION OF THE KING

MAY, 1648–JANUARY, 1649

With the outbreak of hostilities in Wales and the preparations in Scotland for an invasion of England in the early months of 1648, there began a new phase of the Puritan Revolution and a new epoch in the life of Oliver Cromwell. Save for occasional and sporadic outbreaks, England had now been at peace for nearly two years. That interval had been largely consumed in vain efforts to arrive at a solution of the constitutional and ecclesiastical problems raised by the war; in quarrels in Parliament and in the army and between Parliament and the army; in negotiations with the King; in an infinity of intrigues, proposals and counter-proposals among the various elements in the state. Despite these activities, in large part on account of them, England seemed as far from the determination of her political problem as she had been two years earlier; and despite the long drawn out discussions in the Assembly of Divines, as far from the solution of the ecclesiastical dispute as she had been at the Hampton Court conference more than forty years before. From all of these arguments there had emerged only one definite result—the irreconcilable opposition among the three elements in church and state, the Anglicans, the Presbyterians, and the Independents.

Of these the supporters of Charles and the Establishment were numerically far superior to their opponents; but despite the divergences between the Presbyterians and the sects, those opponents had the advantage of greater unity and superior leadership both in peace and war. They controlled both Parliament and the army, and though a free election would have swept them from power in a month, there was no possibility of such a contingency. The only hope of the majority lay in the division of its enemies, and at this moment it seemed that there was a possibility of this. The Agitators were more or less at odds with the officers and with Parliament, but Parliament was sharply divided against itself; and the Independent minority of the revolutionary minority maintained its position only by the ability of its leaders and their ascendancy over the army. The City had now more or less definitely swung to the side of the monarchy, as had the country in general. It was strongly felt that the time had come to

N O
REFER
Principal Commercial Centres
Head ports
Customs ports
Cathedral cities
Other towns and villages
Castles
The figures against the roa
of Ogilby's
BERWICK UPON TWEED
English Camp 1639
Holy I.
Duns
Lauder
Greenlaw
Galashiels
Coldstream (Monck's H.Q.)
Kelso
Selkirk
Jedburgh
Wooler
Hawick
Alnwick
Rothbury
Morpeth
Langholm
Lockerbie
Longtown
Annan
Brampton
Hexham
Newburn 1640
NEWCASTLE (Glass)
Sunderland
CARLISLE
1645
INGLEWOOD FOREST
WESTWARD FOREST
Penrith
WHINFELL FOREST
DURHAM
Hartlepool
Bishop Auckland
Staindrop
Darlington
Guisborough
COAL
86
9
8
62

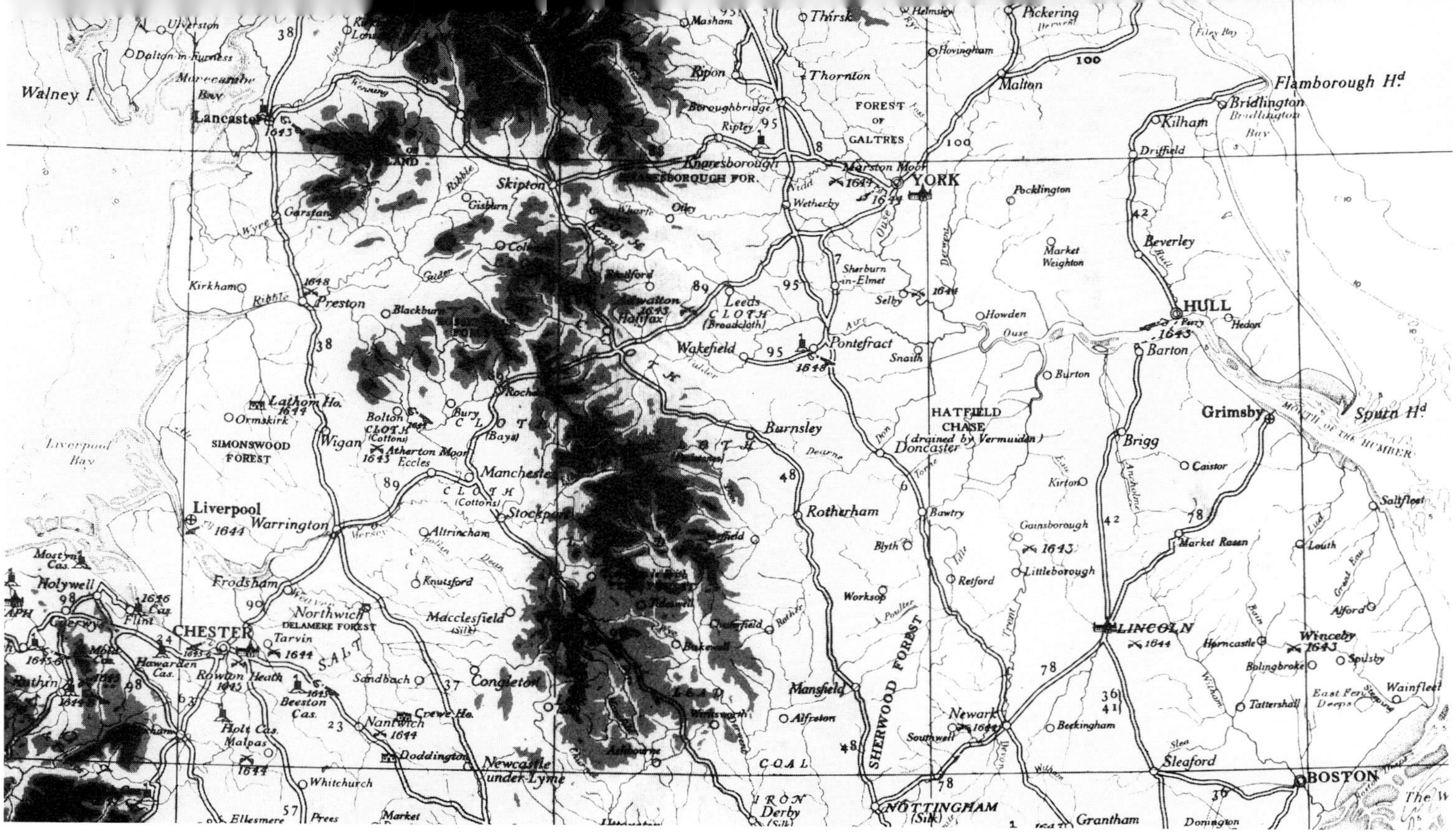

Flamborough Hd
Spurn Hd
Walney I.
Morecambe Bay
Liverpool Bay
Ulverston
Dalton-in-Furness
Lancaster
Garstang
Kirkham
Preston
Wigan
Ormskirk
Lathom Ho.
SIMONSWOOD FOREST
Liverpool
Warrington
Frodsham
CHESTER
Holywell
Flint
Hawarden Cas.
Rowton Heath
Tarvin
Northwich
DELAMERE FOREST
Beeston Cas.
Holt Cas.
Malpas
Nantwich
Crewe Ho.
Doddington
Whitchurch
Ellesmere
Prees
Sandbach
Congleton
Newcastle under-Lyme
Macclesfield
Knutsford
Altrincham
Stockport
Manchester
Atherton Moor
Eccles
Bolton
Bury
Blackburn
Gisburn
Skipton
Otley
Knaresborough
Ripley
Ripon
Masham
Boroughbridge
Thirsk
Thornton
FOREST OF GALTRES
Helmsley
Hovingham
Pickering
Malton
Marston Moor
YORK
Wetherby
Pocklington
Market Weighton
Leeds
CLOTH (Broadcloth)
Halifax
Wakefield
Pontefract
Sherburn in-Elmet
Selby
Snaith
Howden
Barnsley
Rotherham
Doncaster
HATFIELD CHASE (drained by Vermuiden)
Bawtry
Blyth
Worksop
Retford
Gainsborough
Littleborough
Mansfield
Alfreton
SHERWOOD FOREST
Southwell
Newark
NOTTINGHAM
Derby
Grantham
Beckingham
LINCOLN
Sleaford
BOSTON
Donington
Tattershall
Bolingbroke
Horncastle
Winceby
Spilsby
Wainfleet
Alford
Louth
Saltfleet
Market Rasen
Caistor
Grimsby
Brigg
Kirton
Burton
Barton
HULL
Hedon
Beverley
Driffield
Kilham
Bridlington
Bridlington Bay
Filey Bay
MOUTH OF THE HUMBER
Ouse
Trent
Witham
Ancholme

give the nation peace and settled government and most men saw that possibility only in the King. To this the Scots agreed, provided that their form of religious faith were imposed on England, while Wales, which had furnished a considerable part of the royal armies in the last stages of the civil war, was whole-heartedly for Charles.

In the face of this it might have seemed that the position of the Independent leaders was all but desperate, especially in view of the late Leveller mutiny and the activities of the Agitators, that their hand was against every one and every one's hand against them and they were bound to fall before their enemies. But they had the advantage which an organized, disciplined and experienced force has over an unorganized opposition. So long as they could control the army, they were the masters of England, and their hold on the army, especially Cromwell's ascendancy among the soldiers, was unshaken. The rank and file would, and did, grumble, but they obeyed; and there was no force in England, nor, as it proved, in Great Britain or the British Isles, which could stand against it under his command.

To accomplish its overthrow and the restoration of the King—for without its overthrow his restoration was inconceivable—it was necessary for its opponents to combine, but combination was difficult if not impossible for them. None the less there had been serious attempts to combine these diverse elements. In the early months of 1648, efforts were made to unite the various Irish factions—the Royalists under Ormond, the forces of Lord Inchiquin, who in April deserted the Parliament for the King, and the Supreme Council of the confederated Catholics. At the same time the Welsh were approached and a design for a Welsh rising framed. The Scots had already been won over to throw in their lot with Charles, and during April, 1648, while the Parliamentary army was being reorganized, it seemed that there might be formed a combination powerful enough to rescue Charles from his prison and restore him to the throne. To this was added the discontent of the soldiers about to be disbanded, and it was from this direction that the first blow came. In connection with the disbandment plans, the troops raised in Wales by Colonel Laugharne had mutinied and marched to join Colonel Poyer at Pembroke Castle. Declaring for the King, Poyer had driven the Parliamentary commander, Fleming, out of Pembroke town, seized Tenby Castle, issued a proclamation for the King and the Prayer Book and overrun all Pembrokeshire.

To suppress him and Laugharne's deserters, Fairfax had sent Colonel Horton to superintend the disbandment of the other troops; but meanwhile Colonel Fleming had been defeated and killed, and when Horton arrived he had found all south Wales in revolt, and Colonel Laugharne on the side of the rebels. None the less he acted with courage and resolution and on May 8 he met the mutineers at

St. Fagan's and defeated them after a brief engagement. For the moment the peril from the west seemed at an end; but even while Cromwell hastened to the support of Horton, new and graver dangers threatened the Parliamentary supremacy, which the Houses had sought to bolster up on May 2 by an ordinance against blasphemy and heresy which went far beyond any pronouncements of Star Chamber or High Commission. On that very day there arrived the news that, five days before, Sir Marmaduke Langdale at the head of a force of Scotch Royalists had seized Berwick, and another party had surprised Carlisle. On May 1 Sir Philip Musgrave returned to his old post as governor of Carlisle and, with Langdale, agreed to surrender to the Scots such places as they held whenever called upon. The next day a letter from the Scottish Parliament demanded the imposition of the Covenant, the establishment of Presbyterian government, the readmission of the excluded members, and the disbandment of the army of "sectaries." To this the Houses had replied with their resolution not to alter the government by King, Lords and Commons; agreeing to maintain the Covenant and join the Scots in presenting once more to Charles their old proposals. When to this was added on the next day, May 4, a petition from the county of Essex supported by two thousand men on foot, asking that the army be disbanded and the King restored, and when the City expressed its resentment of military rule so strongly that Parliament felt compelled to withdraw Fairfax's men from garrison and permit the City authorities to name the lieutenant of the Tower and its own committee of militia, it seemed that the Royalist reaction might well succeed. Thus while Cromwell marched toward Wales, the country at large, profoundly irritated by the supremacy of the army, seemed prepared to join the Scots in the restoration of the King.

Against this the army was determined to fight; and it was reported that the Council of Officers resolved on May 5, while Cromwell was on his way to Wales, "That neither this king nor any of his posterity should ever reign kings of England."[1] In the face of what seemed a universal desire for his restoration, officers and soldiers alike seemed bent on the exclusion of Charles from the throne; and the Royalists who had all along contended that this was the fundamental cause of the failure of negotiations with the King seemed justified. In any event, whatever had gone before, it seems apparent that from the outbreak of this second civil war, the issue lay between the King and the army, between monarchy and military supremacy.

However much they may have regretted the shedding of more blood, the outbreak of the second civil war relieved the army leaders of many of their difficulties. It ended the long and fruitless negotiations with the King; it offered not merely a clear-cut issue but a relief

[1] *Mercurius Politicus.*

from long inaction which had brought with it the rise of discontent among the soldiery. Welsh rebellion and Scotch invasion were things all men could understand. It was essential to put down the one and repel the other. The Royalists had hoped that the soldiers would refuse to follow their leaders; but this was too much to expect from seasoned veterans, and though many of the men were unwilling to go, they were prevailed upon by their officers to obey.[2] At the same time the removal of the troops from Whitehall, the Mews, and finally the Tower—a move which Cromwell had previously recommended—relieved the irritation of the City and conciliated its authorities.[3] It was a shrewd maneuver; for it secured the army from a revolt of the capital during its absence against the Welsh and Scots, and, if successful there, London would be again at its mercy as it had been before.

The leaders of the army and the Parliament had another advantage over the followers of Charles. However they differed among themselves, they were united in opposition to the King; but however united his supporters were in their desire to restore the monarchy, Irish Catholics, Welsh Episcopalians and Scotch Presbyterians disliked each other, if possible, more than they hated their mutual enemies. The English Royalists distrusted the Scotch; and each feared the results of a restoration by the aid of Irish Catholics. Moreover, Charles's supporters were as divided in geography as they were in theology. As earlier, the leaders of Parliament and the army held the inner lines and if it was difficult for the Welsh and the Scots to act in unison, it was impossible for the Irish to lend them any aid. With all the friendly feeling toward him among his English subjects, it was no less difficult to transmute that feeling into acts. England was in the grip of a veteran army which controlled the machinery of administration. The Royalists were largely disarmed, impoverished by the sequestration and compounding policy, and watched carefully not only by officials but by many unofficial agents of intelligence, chiefly ministers and congregations of the nonconformist sects. Their ranks were decimated by the war; their leaders dead or in exile; their King a prisoner; their strongholds dismantled or destroyed; and with all of the devotion of his followers, it seemed impossible at this moment to make head against the commanders of the army and the leaders of the Parliament.

THE CAMPAIGN IN WALES, MAY 3–24, 1648

It was under these circumstances that Cromwell set out on his march to crush or overawe the Welsh rebels. Leaving London on

[2] *Moderate Intelligencer*, May 5.
[3] Cary, *Memorials*, i, 393.

May 3, he and his command were in Gloucester on the morning of the 8th; and there, two miles from the city, he reviewed his troops, making a short speech at the head of each regiment; of which the substance and the circumstances are reported by one who was present, and who curiously enough, bore a name made famous by a later revolutionary leader—John Hancock:

Speech to Each Regiment at Gloucester, May 8, 1648

"Lieut. Gen. Cromwel rode to the head of each [regiment] making a short speech touching their present design and engagement, which done, he further declared that he had often times ventured his life with them and they with him, against the common enemy of this kingdom, and a far more potent power and strength than now they are to engage withal; and therefore desired them to arm themselves with the same resolution as formerly and to go on with the same courage, faithfulness and fidelity, as sundry times they had done, and upon several desperate attempts and engagements and that for his part, he protested to live and die with them: the Lieut. Gen. had no sooner declared himself but they all threw up their caps giving a great shout and hallow, crying out with one unanimous consent that they would venture their lives and fortunes under his conduct and command against any enemy either domestic or foreign. After the Lieut. Gen. had taken a view of each regiment he gave orders to march and accordingly about 3 of the clock they advanced: their number doth consist of about 6500 horse and foot, exceeding well armed, and brave resolute men."[4]

Thus assured of the spirit and temper of his troops, either at Gloucester or not far distant, the next day Cromwell wrote two letters; the one to Fairfax urging that troops be sent to garrison Bristol, the other to warn a captain of Gloucestershire militia to be on his guard and use his best endeavors to suppress Royalist gatherings and secure men dangerous to the cause of Parliament:

[*For his Excellency the Lord Fairfax, General: These*]

My Lord,

You hear in what a flame these western parts are. I cannot but mind your Excellency that the enemy are designing to surprise many places and we shall still play the after-game. I think it of absolute necessity that some men be put into Bristol, especially since Chepstow is taken, with which (as I heard) they hold correspondency. Sir, Bristol must have a fixed garrison of foot. I beseech you recommend it to the Parliament, that it may be done, there cannot be less than 600 men for it. Lieut.-Col. Rolphe would be a fit man; he is able to give help in the business by his father Skippon his interest, and it would be well taken if your Lordship would recommend him;

[4] John Hancock to —? 8 May, pr. in *The Declaration of Lieutenant-Generall Cromwell concerning his present design and engagement against Col. Poyer.*

there is necessity of speed in my opinion, the city desire it. I take leave and rest,

Your Excellency's most humble servant,

May 9th, 1648. O. CROMWELL.

[P.S.] My Lord, Lieut.-Col. Blackmore is with me; he is a godly man and a good soldier. I beg a commission to make him an adjutant-general to the army. He is very able, as most ever were in this army.[5]

[*To Captain Thomas Roberts*]

MR. ROBERTS,

Being informed that divers Papists and delinquents do gather themselves together upon pretence of hunting meetings, giving out dangerous speeches, riding up and down armed to the hazard of the peace of this kingdom, I do desire and authorise you to gather to you such of your friends and persons well affected to the Parliament's cause, and attach them, causing them to be brought to Gloucester, that there they may be secured until the pleasure of the Parliament be further known. I rest,

Your friend and servant,

May 9th, 1648. O. CROMWELL.

Underneath—Writ of Assistance

I desire you from time to time to give such assistance to Captain Thomas Roberts in suppressing insurrections and tumults, and apprehending suspected persons, as he shall desire from you.

Given under my hand this ninth day of May, 1648.

OLIVER CROMWELL.

To all officers, horse and foot, under the General the Lord Fairfax.[6]

From Gloucester Cromwell advanced to Monmouth, which he reached on May 10,[7] and there learned of Horton's victory at St. Fagan's, near Cardiff. With it the insurrection in south Wales virtually collapsed, but there remained various scattered strongholds in the hands of the rebels, among them, sixteen miles away, Chepstow Castle which had been betrayed to Sir Nicholas Kemeys a few days before in the absence of its governor, Colonel Hughes. Here Cromwell had a personal interest, for the lordship of Chepstow[8] and much

[5] Holograph original in *Egerton MSS.*, 2620, f. 1. Pr. in *Eng. Hist. Rev.* (1887), ii, 148–9; Lomas-Carlyle, Suppl. 27. Cromwell's request concerning Blackmore was granted, but Rolph was retained in the Isle of Wight where two or three weeks later he was accused of a design to assassinate the king while ostensibly helping him to escape. He was placed in charge after Hammond's departure somewhat later.

[6] Enclosed in a petition to the Protector by Roberts, May 25, 1655. Holograph original in *S. P. Dom.* Interr. c, 117, i. *Cal. S. P. Dom.* (1655), p. 331.

[7] Rushworth, vii, 1118; *Perfect Diurnall*, 17 May.

[8] It was not actually put in his possession until 1650 and even in 1651 he was not able to collect his rents. *Cal. Com. for Comp.* p. 603. Cp. *Ibid.*, pp. 1705–1715. The Manors of Tidenham and Wollaston in Gloucestershire but a few miles east of Chepstow were also among Cromwell's grants.

of the lands through which he marched had but recently been granted to him by Parliament. He reached Chepstow on May 11, but it was only after a sharp encounter with the Royalists that he secured the town and for three days he attempted in vain to force an entrance to the Castle. Leaving Colonel Ewer to continue the siege, he ordered the stronghold to be stormed, and ten days later, on May 25, it surrendered after a breach had been made in its walls.[9]

From Chepstow, with Colonels Pride, Deane and Thornhaugh, Cromwell marched through various villages to which he had recently acquired title, to Cardiff, twenty-eight miles away. There he wrote two letters—one to the Derby House Committee, which has survived only through a note in the *Commons Journals*, and one to Vice-admiral John Crowther, then, apparently, on station at or near Cardiff, each asking for aid in his enterprise:

To the Committee at Derby House

Desiring powder, ammunition, arms, guns, and shot for carrying on the work of reducing Wales; with some intercepted letters enclosed, and a "Declaration in the Name of the Gentlemen and Inhabitants of Wales." Cardiff, May 15, 1648.[11]

To Captain Crowther

SIR,

I received both yours this morning, and cannot but acknowledge your great forwardness to serve the public. I have here enclosed sent you an order for the taking up of vessels for the transporting of soldiers and the oats of the horses. My men shall be at the water-side tomorrow. If they can provide victuals, they shall. If not I shall give you notice that we may bring it out of your vessels.

Sir, I remain,

Your very humble servant,

Cardiff,
May 16, 1648. OLIVER CROMWELL.[12]

Relieved by Horton's victory of the necessity of fighting an enemy whom he had expected to meet beyond Chepstow, he sent five troops of horse and some dragoons into Shropshire, Cheshire and north Wales to suppress or overawe the disaffected there; but Fairfax

[9] *A Great Fight at Chepstow Castle;* Rushworth, vii, 1118.

[10] *Perfect Diurnall*, 17 May; Rushworth, vii, 1118.

[11] Read and acted upon in the House of Commons, May 20. *C. J.*, v, 566. Item in *Moderate Intelligencer*, May; repr. in *Cromwelliana*, p. 39.

[12] Pr., from the original at Wincham in Cheshire, in *A Discourse of the Warr in Lancashire* ed. by W. Beaumont (Chetham Society), p. 98. Lomas-Carlyle, Supp. 29.

promptly ordered them to join Colonel Harrison in Lancashire[13] to meet the menace of the Scots which had increased while Wales was being pacified. There remained to Cromwell, therefore, only the capture of three castles in south Wales—Chepstow, Tenby and Pembroke—and the disposal of his prisoners. This latter problem he settled by shooting two at Cardiff, and sending "240 of the Welsh Batchelors . . . to Barbadoes,"[14] selling them "for 12d. a head to be transported into barbarous plantations, whereby to expell the Canaanites and make new plantations in old England for the Godly."[15]

While Cromwell was thus engaged in suppressing insurrection in south Wales, he was advised by the Committee in London of the situation in the rest of the country. That situation was of the gravest danger to the army and to Parliament. London had been full of Royalist demonstrations, which had the effect of throwing its Council into the arms of a Parliament at that moment dominated by the Presbyterians. Unwilling to drive their opponents into an agreement with the Scots, then about to invade England, the Independents had offered little opposition to the virtual restoration of the London militia and even the Tower to the City committee in return for the Council's declaration to live and die with the Parliament. They knew that this meant a renewal of negotiations with the King, but they knew also that those negotiations had been, and probably would be, fruitless; and, what was most important of all, they knew that the situation of the country at large left them no alternative but to come to terms with the English Presbyterians.

The nation was thoroughly aroused. The Royalist spirit in London only echoed that in Kent and Essex, which were on the verge of insurrection. Fairfax's intended march to the north to oppose the Scots was hastily abandoned and he and Ireton turned south to meet the danger nearer home. To increase that danger, six ships in the Downs mutinied against the unpopular vice-admiral, Rainsborough, declared for the King and blocked up Dover. Hoping to satisfy the sailors, Parliament hastened to appoint the Earl of Warwick as Lord High Admiral, but the mutiny had encouraged the gentry of Kent to plan a rendezvous at Blackheath of twenty thousand men of that county with an equal number from Essex. The Kentishmen were reported reluctant to fight, but the threat was serious, and to Blackheath, accordingly, Fairfax and Ireton advanced in time to prevent

[13] Fairfax to Derby House Com., *Old Parl. Hist.*, xvii, 151. Eight hundred of his horse arrived in Lancashire. A. M. to Strickland, 2 June, *Hist. Mss. Comm. Rept.* 11, App. vi; *Hamilton Papers*, p. 124.

[14] Rushworth, vii, 1130.

[15] Walker, p. 95.

this Royalist demonstration. Thence to Gravesend and so by way of Rochester, Fairfax marched to Maidstone where he defeated the Royalist forces under the Earl of Norwich, and occupied the place while Dover surrendered to Colonel Rich and Canterbury to Ireton.

The commander of the Cavaliers, George Goring, Earl of Norwich and father of that George, Lord Goring, who had played such a part in the first civil war, after his defeat at Maidstone on June 1 marched to Chelmsford in Essex, where he was joined by Sir Charles Lucas, brother of Lord Lucas of Colchester, and by Lord Capel who held a commission as commander-in-chief of the eastern counties. Disappointed in their hope that London would rise, the Royalist commanders, despite the efforts of Whalley and Honeywood, were able to occupy Colchester on June 12, where, with the arrival of Fairfax and Barkstead on the next day, they were blockaded and besieged. Meanwhile Parliament, alarmed by the Royalist insurrection, voted indemnity to any one who would withdraw from the rising, and on June 8, in an effort to conciliate the Presbyterians, revoked its old order disabling the impeached members from sitting.

While Lambert maintained himself in the north in the face of the betrayal of Pontefract Castle to the Royalists by one of his own officers and the loss of Scarborough, and while Fairfax and his lieutenants besieged Colchester, the "war of movement" centered in the west. Thanks to the policy of Parliament which had dismantled the fortresses at the end of the first civil war, the Royalists had but few opportunities to establish centers of resistance in central England which remained quiet. Sir Hardress Waller subdued the Cornwall Royalists; but in North Wales Sir John Owen was still in control; and between them Cromwell went on to complete the pacification of South Wales.

PEMBROKE, MAY 24–JULY 11

Having disposed of his prisoners, from Cardiff Cromwell made his way to Swansea where he established his headquarters on May 19.[16] There he found himself again on his own recently acquired property, the lordship of Swansea, which included that castle and borough, and, just around the bay, Oystermouth Castle. In the other direction lay his immediate objectives, Tenby and Pembroke. Colonel Horton was already besieging the first, and Cromwell pushed on to Pembroke, where he arrived on May 24; and there, having received the news of Chepstow's submission, he made his report on May 30:

[16] "Minute Book of the Common Hall," *Gloucestershire Notes and Queries*, iii, 79–80.

To the Committee at Derby House

"Saying that he had given order to Colonel Ewer to march with his regiment to Coventry and had sent thither also two troops of Colonel Thornhaugh's horse."

Pembroke, May 30, 1648.[17]

Tenby Castle surrendered to Horton on May 31, with five or six hundred prisoners and Horton soon joined Cromwell before Pembroke, whence Cromwell reported the fall of Tenby:

To the Committee at Derby House

"Relating the taking of Tenby Castle in the County of Pembroke, and asking for orders on the disposal of prisoners taken in the castle. Supplies are needed." Pembroke, June 2, 1648.[18]

The Derby House Committee had kept Cromwell advised of the situation in the rest of the country in May and early June, giving him notice that part of his forces would be sent to Lambert's aid in the north and warning him of possible danger from the six mutinous ships.[19] Among the vessels which had remained loyal to the Parliament, the *Lion* at Milford Haven had, through the activities of Hugh Peter, furnished Cromwell with two drakes, two demi-culverins and two culverins for the siege of Pembroke Castle. To provide them with shot and shell, Cromwell wrote:

To my noble Friends the Committee of Carmarthen: These

GENTLEMEN,

I have sent this bearer to you to desire we may have your furtherance and assistance in procuring some necessaries to be cast in the iron-furnaces in your county of Carmarthen, which will the better enable us to reduce the Town and Castle of Pembroke.

The principal things are: shells for our [mo]rtarpiece;[20] the depth of them we desire may be fourteen inches and three-quarters of an inch. That which I desire at your hands is, to cause the service to be performed, and that with all possible expedition; that so (if it be the will of God), the service being done, these poor wasted countries may be freed from the burden of the Army.

In the next place, we desire some demi cannon-shot, and some culverin-shot, may with all possible speed be cast for us, and hasted to us also.

[17] Mentioned in a letter to Fairfax from the Committee, in *S. P. Dom. Interr.* 24 E, 97; *Cal. S. P. Dom.* (1648–9), p. 101.

[18] Read and referred to the Committee of the Army. *C. J.*, v, 588.

[19] *Cal. S. P. Dom.* (1648–9), pp. 84–5, 92, 105, 110, 112.

[20] Paper torn.

We give you thanks for your care in helping us with bread and water &c. You do herein a very special service to the State; and I do most earnestly desire you to continue herein, according to our desires in the late letters. I desire that copies of this paper[21] may be published throughout your country, and the effects thereof observed for the ease of the county, and to avoid the wronging of the country men.

Not doubting of your care to give assistance to the public in the services we have in hand, I rest,

Your affectionate servant,

The Leaguer before Pembroke,
9th June 1648.

O. CROMWELL.[22]

The ancient and massive castle of Pembroke was defended by some three hundred former soldiers of Parliament, many of whom had long been under Colonel Poyer, Parliamentary governor of the Castle, who had turned Royalist and had refused to turn the Castle over to Colonel Fleming whom Fairfax, suspecting Poyer's fidelity, had sent to relieve him some months before. With him was Major-General Laugharne, "very sick of mind and body,"[23] with some of his men who had refused to disband at the order of Parliament as supernumeraries. The garrison was already on restricted rations but, knowing their position as "renegadoes," they were prepared for a desperate resistance.

To take this strong position so resolutely defended, Cromwell had some 3,000 men, no great supply of food, and insufficient artillery. According to tradition he was laid up with gout at Lamphey House;[23] but whatever his own health—and there is no other record of his suffering from gout—he showed great sympathy for Laugharne, restoring the cattle which his men had taken from Laugharne's wife and permitting her and Laugharne's doctor admission to the Castle.[24] To make his task still more difficult, while Fairfax was still in Kent he ordered Cromwell, through the Committee at Derby House, to send Colonel Ewer's regiment, released from Chepstow, to Whalley in Essex; at the same time urging Cromwell to send all available forces to the north under a competent commander, or even to go himself.[25] Before those orders reached Cromwell he had written to the Commit-

[21] Some Proclamation, seemingly.

[22] The original was in the hands of Richard Williams, Esq., Stapleton Hall, Hornsey when it was pr. in Brayley's *Graphic and Historical Illustrator* (London, 1834), p. 355; and repr. in *Notes and Queries*, 2nd ser. iii, 261 (1857). It later formed part of the Morrison Collection until it was dispersed. Pr. in Carlyle, App. 11.

[23] Recovered, at least in body, by June 19. Cp. Phillips, *Memorials of Civil Wars in Wales*, ii, 392.

[23] Phillips, *History of Pembrokeshire*, p. 506.

[24] *Moderate Intelligencer*, June 1–8; *Perfect Occurrences*, June 9–15.

[25] Com. of Derby House to Cromwell, 9 June, *Cal. S. P. Dom.* (1648–9), pp. 115–116. See also June 12, *Ibid.*, p. 120.

tee to advise them of the situation of the Pembroke garrison, where a mutiny of the starving soldiers was expected to put the place in his hands within a fortnight:

[*To a member of the Committee of Derby House*]

SIR,

All that you can expect from hence is a relation of the state of this Garrison of Pembroke, which is briefly thus:

They begin to be in extreme want of provision, so as in all probability they cannot live a fortnight without being starved. But we hear that they mutinied about three days since; cried out, "Shall we be ruined for two or three men's pleasure? Better it were we should throw them over the walls." It's certainly reported to us that within four or six days they'll cut Poyer's throat, and come all away to us. Poyer told them, Saturday last, that if relief did not come by Monday night, they should hang him.

We have not got our guns and ammunition from Wallingford as yet, but, however, we have scraped up a few, which stand us in very good stead. Last night we got two little guns planted, which in twenty-four hours will take away their Mills, and then, as Poyer himself confesses, they are all undone. We made an attempt to storm it about ten days since; but our ladders were too short, and the breach so as men could not get over. We lost a few men, but I am confident the enemy lost more. Captain Flower, of Colonel Dean's regiment, was wounded; and Major Grigg's Lieutenant and Ensign slain; Captain Burges[26] lies wounded, and very sick. I question not, but within a fortnight we shall have the town; Poyer hath engaged himself to the officers of the town not to keep the castle longer than the town can hold out. Neither indeed can it; for we can take away his water in two days, by beating down a staircase, which goes into a cellar where he hath a well. They allow the men half-a-pound of beef, and so much bread a day, but it is almost spent.

We must rejoice at what the Lord hath done for you in Kent. Upon our thanksgiving for that victory, which was both from sea and leaguer, Poyer told his men, that it was the Prince was coming with relief. The other night they mutinied in the town. Last night we fired divers houses;[27] which runs up the town still; it much frights them. Confident I am, we shall have it in fourteen days by starving. I am, Sir,

Your servant,

Leager before Pembroke,
June 14th 1648.

OLIVER CROMWELL.[28]

[26] Benjamin Burges.

[27] By cannon-volleys.

[28] *Perfect Diurnall*, 20 June; *Perfect Weekly Account*, 21 June; Rushworth, vii, 1159. Carlyle dated this letter June 14th and Mrs. Lomas, stating that he did it "probably only by inadvertence," changed it to June 16th. The newspapers both give it the latter date and Rushworth undoubtedly copied from one of them. But a letter from Cromwell was read in the Derby House Committee on June 19th, and ordered reported in Parliament (*Cal. S. P. Dom.* 1648–9, p. 135), hardly giving time enough for a letter written on the 16th to reach London. Moreover, the *Commons Journals* (v, 608), as

In that, at least, Cromwell was mistaken for the castle held out for nearly a month after this letter was written, and much happened in that interval at Pembroke and elsewhere. According to local tradition, it was only taken by the treachery of a Mr. Edmonds who showed Cromwell the staircase of which he speaks, leading into a cellar in which was the castle well, and was presently hanged by Cromwell for his pains.[29] However that may be, it was reported on July 4 that the town had only "a little rainwater and biscuit left," and a week later the place surrendered.[30]

But Cromwell's activities were not confined to the siege of Pembroke. While it went on, with Fairfax's siege of Colchester and Lambert's efforts to make head against the Royalists and the Scots in the north, Cromwell, like his fellow commanders everywhere, was endeavoring to stamp out disaffection and seize its promoters. In pursuit of that enterprise he wrote from before Pembroke a series of letters, orders, instructions and warnings to a number of persons of which the first was a letter on June 17 to a certain Major Saunders, sometime of Derbyshire, now commanding for the Parliament in Brecknockshire, presently to sit on the High Court of Justice, and later to be arrested for joining Major Wildman in a protest against the Protectorate. The individuals mentioned were characteristic figures of the time and place. Sir Trevor Williams had earlier commanded for the Parliament in Monmouthshire, but had apparently deserted that cause and, with Sheriff William Morgan,[31] was wanted for conspiring with the late Sir Nicholas Kemeys in the betrayal of Chepstow Castle to the Royalist insurgents. And it is not without some interest to note that among Cromwell's more remote ancestors was a certain Margaret Kemeys, from whose brother, Ievan, Sir Nicholas was directly descended.[32] Of the others, Colonel William

Carlyle says, reports on June 20th the reading of a letter from Cromwell dated June 14th. Either this letter must have been dated June 14th, therefore, or Cromwell wrote another letter on June 14th to the Derby House Committee. The only evidence of the latter possibility is an order in the House of Commons, also on June 20th, empowering the Committee to appoint Colonel Wogan Governor of the Castle of Aberystwith "according to Cromwell's wishes." This letter makes no such request, but it is possible that the letter was not printed in its entirety in the newspapers. In the absence of better evidence that a second letter was written and because this letter was printed in *Perfect Diurnall* on June 20th, Carlyle's dating rather than Mrs. Lomas's has been followed.

[29] *Notes and Queries*, 2nd ser., iv, 16.

[30] Phillips, *Civil War in Wales*.

[31] Of Pencoad Castle. His father, Sir Edward Morgan was sheriff in 1643. (Charles I's notes, in Phillips, *op. cit.*, ii, 258.)

[32] The family trees of the Welsh families of the names of Morgan, Williams, and Kemeys are curiously intertwined. Cromwell's great-great-grandfather, Morgan Williams, had a grandmother, Margaret Kemeys. Sir Nicholas married Jane, a sister of Sir Trevor Williams's father, whose first wife was a daughter of a Thomas Morgan. By Langevie, Cromwell probably meant Llangibby, for it was at that place Sir Trevor

Herbert had commanded Montgomery Castle for the King from 1645 to 1647; Captain John Nicholas, presently made governor of Chepstow, rose to high rank in the Protectorate; and "Rumsey" is probably Edward Rumsey, Parliamentary commissioner for south Wales.

[*To Major Thomas Saunders*]

SIR,

I send you this enclosed by itself, because it's of greater moment. The other you may communicate to Mr. Rumsey as far as you think fit and I have written. I would not have him or other honest men be discouraged that I think it not fit, at present, to enter into contests; it will be good to yield a little, for public advantage, and truly that is my end, wherein I desire you to satisfy them.

I have sent, as my letter mentions, to have you remove out of Brecknockshire; indeed, into that part of Glamorganshire which lieth next Monmouthshire, for this end: we have plain discoveries that Sir Trevor Williams, of Langevie, about two miles from Usk in the county of Monmouth, was very deep in the plot of betraying Chepstow Castle; so that we are out of doubt of his guiltiness thereof. I do hereby authorise you to seize him; as also the High Sheriff of Monmouth, Mr. Morgan, who was in the same plot.

But, because Sir Trevor Williams is the more dangerous man by far, I would have you seize him first, and the other will easily be had. To the end you may not be frustrated and that you be not deceived, I think fit to give you some characters of the man, and some intimations how things stand. He is a man, as I am informed, full of craft and subtlety, very bold and resolute; hath a house at Langevie well stored with arms, and very strong; his neighbours about him very malignant, and much for him; who are apt to rescue him if apprehended, much more to discover anything which may prevent it. He is full of jealousy, partly out of guilt, but much more because he doubts some that were in the business have discovered him, which indeed they have, and also because he knows that his servant is brought hither, and a minister to be examined here, who are able to discover the whole plot.

If you should march directly into that country and near him it's odds he either fortifies his house, or gives you the slip; so also, if you should go to his house, and not find him there, or if you attempt to take him, and miss to effect it, or if you make any known inquiry after him, it will be discovered.

Wherefore, to the first, you have a fair pretence of going out of Brecknockshire to quarter about Newport and Carleon, which is not above four or five miles from his house. You may send to Colonel Herbert, whose house lieth

had his castle, although even nearer to Usk is a tiny place called Llangefiew which corresponds more nearly of Cromwell's spelling. Colonel William Herbert, from 1645 to 1647 governor of Montgomery Castle, the seat of Lord Herbert of Cherbury, was no near relative of its owner, and disappears during the Protectorate after petitioning to be made a ship's captain. John Claypole, Cromwell's son-in-law, had a sister Elizabeth who married "William Herbert of Colebrook," Monmouth, cousin of Sir Trevor Williams' wife. This was in all probability Colonel Herbert. (Cp. Le Neve's, *Knights*, p. 340.) See Cromwell's letter to him of June 26, 1648.

in Monmouthshire; who will certainly acquaint you where he is. You are also to send to Captain Nicholas, who is at Chepstow, to require him to assist you, if he should get into his house and stand upon his guard. Sam. Jones, who is Quartermaster to Colonel Herbert's troop, will be very assisting to you, if you send to him to meet you at your quarters, both by letting you know where he is, and also in all matters of intelligence. If there shall be need, Captain Burges his troop, now quartered in Glamorganshire, shall be directed to receive orders from you.

You perceive by all this that we are (it may be) a little too much solicitous in this business; it's our fault, and indeed such a temper causeth us often to overact business. Wherefore, without more ado, we leave it to you, and you to the guidance of God herein, and rest,

Yours,

June 17th, 1648. O. Cromwell.

P.S. If you seize him, bring, (and let him be brought with a strong guard), to me. If Captain Nicholas should light on him at Chepstow, do you strengthen him with a good guard to bring him. If you seize his person, disarm his house; but let not his arms be embezzled. If you need Captain Burges his troop, it quarters between Newport and Cardiff.[33]

The more public letter which Cromwell enclosed with this to Saunders and which Mr. Rumsey was to be permitted to see, has disappeared; but on the same subject is a note from Cromwell found years ago in the attic of St. Jillians, the old manor-house belonging to the wife of Edward, Lord Herbert of Cherbury. It is devoid of address but from its content it was undoubtedly intended for Lord Herbert's son Richard, a Royalist sympathizer who soon afterward inherited his father's title.

["*To the Honourable Richard Herbert, at St. Jillian's*"]

Sir,

I would have you to be informed that I have good report of your secret practices against the public advantage; by means whereof that arch-traitor, Sir Nicholas Kemys, with his horse, did surprise the Castle of Chepstow: but we have notable discovery from the papers taken by Col. Hewer on recovering the Castle that Sir Trevor Williams of Llangibby was the malignant who set on foot the plot.

Now I give you this plain warning by Capt. Nicholas and Capt. Burgess that if you harbour or conceal either of the parties, or abet their misdoings, I will cause your treasonable nest to be burnt about your ears.

Leager before Pembroke,
June 18th, 1648. Oliver Cromwell.[34]

[33] Superscribed "For your selfe." Printed, from the original then in the hands of one Hans Wintrop Mortimer, Esq., in Harris, *Life of Cromwell* (1762), p. 508. Repr. in Forster, iv, 238–9; Williams, *Monmouthshire*, p. 184; Willett, *Stranger in Monmouthshire*, p. 299; Carlyle, Letter LX.

[34] Carlyle, App. 11. The letter is just as Carlyle copied it from an old Welsh news-

Both Williams and Morgan seem to have been captured, but their only penalty was the sequestration of their estates, which was discharged soon afterward, on appeal, by the Barons of the Exchequer.[35]

The next letter concerns some conspiracy or misdemeanor which has since disappeared without a trace except for this one allusion. The persons involved are equally shrowded in mystery except possibly "Edwards" who may be that Captain William Edwards who was discharged upon parole by the Derby House Committee in November, 1648. Colonel Hughes was governor of Chepstow until, in his absence, it was betrayed to the Royalists.

To Colonel Hughes

SIR,

It's of absolute necessity that Collington and Ashe do attend the Council of War, to make good what they say of Edwards. Let it be your special care to get them into Monmouthshire thereunto. What Mr. Herbert and Mrs. Cradock hath promised to them in point of indemnity, I will endeavour to have it performed; and I desire you to certify as much to them for their encouragement. I pray do this speedily after receipt hereof, and I shall remain,

Your servant,

June 26th, 1648. O. CROMWELL.[36]

The same day Cromwell wrote to another Parliamentary colonel a letter:

To Col. William Herbert

Desiring him to quarter his troop in any part of Monmouthshire that he judges most advantageous for the public service. June 26, 1648. *Signed*.[37]

To these may be added the summary given by a London news-sheet of a letter received July 5th which was written by Cromwell on June 27th to the Derby House Committee:

"That they within the Town and Castle cannot hold out above 10 days at farthest; that Poyer sent out a message to the Lieut.-Gen. admiring that a David should be so persecuted by a Saul, having been always faithful to the Parliament of England ever since the beginning of these wars; but the

paper, the *Monmouthshire Merlin*, for Sept. 1845, probably with the address and place added and "Llangibby" modernized.

[35] *Cal. Comm. for Compounding*, p. 2947.

[36] Found in Moyne's Court, Monmouthshire, the seat of Colonel Hughes, and pr. in 1791 in *The Topographer*, iv, 125–9; thence Carlyle, App. 11. Repr. in Willett, *Stranger in Monmouthshire*, p. 260.

[37] Lomas-Carlyle, Suppl. 30, with no hint as to where the letter or even a printed copy of it can be found.

honour of Parliament, and their General lying so deep at stake, the Lieut.-Gen. would not admit of any response, or capitulation, though the Governor inclined thereunto. An insurrection was made near the siege, 500 countrymen, horse and foot, joined under pretence of stopping some passes, that the Lo. Inchequin (whom they gave out were near the shore) might not land. A party of the Leaguer horse was commanded out, to the number of 250, who fell upon this pretended well meaning, though royal, party (as seemed afterwards by their commanders), gave no quarter to them, killed 10, wounded many, the rest fled upon the mountains by the sea side; Pembroke much discontented hereat."[38]

In the same packet was a letter to Fairfax which reveals the difficulties which confronted Cromwell. Not only was he lacking in arms and ammunition, but a recent storm had resulted in the dumping of his siege train in the mud at the mouth of the Severn from which it was dug with great expenditure of time and energy. None the less he had despatched six troops to Lambert, with instructions to give him what aid they could in the suppression of disaffection in Cheshire where he was then endeavoring to raise forces for Parliament:

To his Excellency the Lord Fairfax, General of the Parliament's Army: These

My Lord,

I have some few days since despatched horse and dragoons for the north. I sent them by the way of West Chester, thinking it fit so to do in regard of this enclosed letter which I received from Colonel Duckenfield, requiring them to give him assistance in the way. And if it should prove that a present help would not serve the turn, then I ordered Captain Pennyfeather's troop[39] to remain with the Governor [Duckenfield]: and the rest immediately to march towards Leeds, and to send to the Committee of York, or to him that commands the forces in chief there, for directions whither they should come, and how they shall be disposed of.

The Number I sent are six troops, four of horse, and two of dragoons; whereof three are Colonel Scrope's, and Captain Pennyfeather's troop, and the other two dragoons. I could not, by the judgment of the Colonels here, spare more, nor send them sooner, without manifest hazard to these parts. Here is (as I have formerly acquainted your Excellency) a very desperate enemy, who, being put out of all hope of mercy, are resolved to endure to the uttermost extremity; being very many gentlemen of quality, and men thoroughly resolved. They have made some notable sallies upon Lieutenant-Colonel Reade's quarter,[40] to his loss. We are forced to keep divers posts, or

[38] *Moderate Intelligencer*, June 29 to July 6. Repr. in *Cromwelliana*, p. 41.

[39] Of Colonel Horton's regiment of horse.

[40] After the surrender of Tenby Castle, Reade had joined Cromwell before Pembroke. Formerly a captain of foot in Colonel Holborne's regiment in Essex's army, he was now in command of Colonel Overton's regiment of foot, Overton being governor of Hull at this time.

else they would have relief, or their horse break away. Our foot are about three or four-and-twenty hundred, we being necessitated to leave some in garrisons.

The Country, since we sat down before this place, have made two or three insurrections, and are ready to do it every day; so that, what with looking to them, and disposing our horse to that end, and to get us in provisions, (without which we should starve) this country being so miserably exhausted and so poor, and we no money to buy victuals, that indeed, whatever may be thought, it's a mercy we have been able to keep our men together in the midst of such necessities, the sustenance of the foot (for the most part) being but bread and water. Our guns, through the unhappy accident at Berkley, not yet come to us; (and indeed it was a very unhappy thing they were brought thither), the winds having been also so cross, that since they were recovered from sinking, they could not 'come to us,' and this place not being to be had without fit instruments for battery, except by starving. And truly I believe the enemy's straits does increase upon them very fast, and that within a few days an end will be put to this business; which surely might have been before, if we had received things wherewith to have done it. But it will be done in the best time.

I rejoice much to hear of the blessing of God upon your Excellency's endeavours. I pray God teach this nation, and those that are over us, and your Excellency and all us that are under you, what the mind of God may be in all this, and what our duty is. Surely it is not that the poor godly people of this Kingdom should still be made the object of wrath and anger, nor that our God would have our necks under a yoke of bondage; for these things that have lately come to pass have been the wonderful works of God; breaking the rod of the oppressor, as in the day of Midian, not with garments much rolled in blood, but by the terror of the Lord; who will yet save His people and confound His enemies, as in that day. The Lord multiply His spirit upon you, and bless you, and keep your heart upright; and then, though you be not conformable to the men of this world, nor to their wisdom, yet you shall be precious in the eyes of God, and He will be to you a sun and a shield.

My Lord, I do not know that I have had a letter from any of your Army, of the glorious successes God has vouchsafed you. I pray pardon the complaint because I long to rejoice with you. I take leave; and rest,

My Lord,
Your most humble and faithful servant,
OLIVER CROMWELL.

Before Pembroke,
June 28th, 1648.

[P.S.] Sir, I desire you that Colonel Lehunt may have a commission to command a troop of Horse, the greatest part whereof came from the enemy to us; and that you would be pleased to send blank commissions for his inferior officers,—with what speed may be.[41]

[41] *Sloane Mss*, 1519, f. 180; Carlyle, LXI. Col. Lehunt, formerly a captain in Fleetwood's regiment of horse in Manchester's army, was one of the officers of the revolted army who did not desert the Parliament. In 1651 he had command of a regiment of foot in Ireland.

The siege of Pembroke, like that of Colchester, was a test of endurance for both sides. If the defenders fought on to the bitter end despite the scarcity of food and water, the besiegers showed a dogged resolution in the face of adverse circumstances; but as at Colchester the result could never have been doubted, for there was nowhere that the garrison of either place could look for relief. Yet not until July 4, after the arrival of the heavy guns so long delayed, first by accident, then by lack of wind to enable the ship which carried them to make its way to Pembroke, could Cromwell get his batteries into action. After that there was no hope for the defenders of Pembroke. From time to time, apparently, Cromwell and Poyer exchanged messages until finally, on July 10, Cromwell considered the situation of the garrison desperate enough to send an ultimatum and a revised list of articles of surrender:

To Colonel John Poyer

SIR,

I have (together with my Council of War) renewed my propositions. I thought fit to send them to you with these alterations, which if submitted unto I shall make good. I have considered your condition and my own duty; and (without threatening) must tell you that if (for the sake of some) this offer be refused, and thereby misery and ruin befall the poor soldiers and people with you, I know where to charge the blood you spill. In case this offer be refused, send no more to me about this subject.

I rest your servant,

July 10, at 4 o'clock
this afternoon, 1648

O. CROMWELL.[42]

Articles for the Surrender of Pembroke

1. That Major-General Laugharne, Col. Poyer, Col. Humphrey Mathews, Capt. William Bower, and David Poyer, do surrender themselves to the mercy of the Parliament.

2. That Sir Charles Kemeys, Sir Henry Stradling, Mr. Miles Button, Major Prichard, Lieut.-Col. Stradling, Lieut.-Col. Laugharne, Lieut.-Col. Brabazon, Mr. Gamage, Major Butler, Major Francis Lewis, Major Mathews, Major Harnish, Capt. Roach, Capt. Jones, Capt. Hugh Bowen, Capt. Thomas Watts, and Lieut. Young, do within six weeks next following depart the Kingdom, and not to return within two years from the time of their departure.

3. That all officers and gentlemen not before-named, shall have free liberty to go to their several habitations, and then live quietly, submitting to the authority of Parliament.

4. That all private soldiers shall have passes to go to the several houses

[42] *Perfect Occurrences*, No. 81; Repr. in Phillips' *Civil War in Wales*, i, 396; and Lomas-Carlyle, Suppl. 30.

without being stripped, or having any violence done to them—all the sick and wounded men to be carefully provided for, till able to go home, &c.

5. That the townsmen shall be free from plunder and violence, and enjoy their liberties as heretofore they have done, having freedom to remove themselves and families whither they shall think fit, &c.

6. That the Town and Castle of Pembroke, with all the arms, ammunition, and ordnance, together with the victuals and provisions for the garrison, be forthwith delivered unto Lieut. General Cromwell, or such as he shall appoint, for the use of the Parliament.

Oliver Cromwell.
David Poyer.[43]

The following day Poyer surrendered Pembroke "at the mercy of Parliament," but that mercy did not extend to him. He, with Laugharne and Colonel Powell were first carried to Nottingham by Cromwell and later sent to London and forced to draw lots to determine which should suffer death. The lot fell on Poyer, who was shot nine months later in the Piazza in Covent Garden. Meanwhile before he set out on his march to the north, Cromwell sent his report of Pembroke to Parliament, with a copy of the articles of surrender and an explanation of the exceptions he had made:

For the Honourable William Lenthall, Esquire, Speaker to the House of Commons: These

Sir,

The town and Castle of Pembroke were surrendered to me this day, being the eleventh of July, upon the propositions which I send you here enclosed. What arms, ammunition, victual, ordnance and other necessaries of war are in town, I have not to certify you, the Commissioners I sent in to receive the same not being yet returned, nor likely suddenly to be; and I am unwilling to defer the giving you an account of this mercy for a day.

The persons excepted are such as have formerly served you in a very good cause, but, being not apostatised I did rather make election of them than of those who had always been for the King, judging their iniquity double, because they have sinned against so much light, and against so many evidences of Divine Presence going along with and prospering a righteous cause, in the management of which they themselves had a share.

I rest,

July 11, 1648 Your most humble servant,
O. Cromwell.[44]

[43] In *Welbeck Abbey Mss*: cal. in *Hist. Mss. Comm. Rept.* 13 (Welbeck) i, 480. Pr. in *Perfect Diurnall*, July 10–16; *Perfect Occurrences*, No. 81; Phillips, *op. cit.*, ii, 397. Substance in Rushworth, vii, 1190. *Perfect Diurnall* mentions a letter from Cromwell to Fairfax and the Committee of Derby House.

[44] Original at Welbeck Abbey: cal. in *Hist. Mss. Comm. Rept.* 13, (Welbeck) i, 480. Copy in *Tanner Mss*, lxii, 159. Pr. in Grey's *Examination of Neale's History of the Puritans*, ii, App. p. 129; Carlyle, Letter LXII; thence Phillips, *Civil War in Wales*, ii, 397.

PRESTON, JULY 12–AUGUST 20, 1648

Such was the end of the insurrection in south Wales, and while the finishing touches were being put on the suppression of the insurgents, Cromwell prepared to go to the assistance of his companions in arms. Those commanders were in need of all the aid he could bring. Fairfax was still engaged in the siege of Colchester, whose defence was even longer and more stubborn than that of Pembroke. Lambert was falling back before the advance of the Scots under Hamilton, who had crossed the border on July 8 with 10,500 men. Meanwhile Henry Rich, Earl of Holland, who had earlier deserted the King, returned to his old allegiance, and, commissioned general by the Prince of Wales and financed by the sale of Lady Carlisle's pearls, left London on July 4 for Kingston hoping to raise a force to relieve Colchester. But he was defeated on July 7 by Sir Michael Livesey and three days later his forces were surprised and captured by Colonel Scrope at St. Neots and Holland was sent to Warwick Castle as a prisoner. The young Prince Charles was no more successful. As part of the Royalist design in connection with the Scotch invasion, he sailed from Holland with nineteen ships and a force estimated, no doubt with great exaggeration, at twenty thousand men, reached the Thames, took some prizes, issued a proclamation, and sailed back to Holland.

All these abortive efforts of the Royalists had no effect on the military arrangements of either Fairfax or Cromwell, but they had one important result on Cromwell's personal fortunes. The young Duke of Buckingham had involved himself in the Royalist adventure, and though, unlike Holland who was presently executed, he escaped to the continent, he was stripped of his estates. Among them was the lordship of Newhall, with six hundred acres and a great manor house at Boreham near Chelmsford, which his father had bought from the crown for £30,000, and whose income was reckoned at £1,309 three years later, in 1651, when it was sold to Cromwell for five shillings.[45]

Of the events in the south and east Cromwell knew little. Pembroke taken, he hurried to join Lambert; but before he left, he took measures to prevent the Royalists securing another stronghold as a center for revolt, as his notation on the following letter testifies:

"To the Mayor and Aldermen of Haverfordwest

"We being authorised by Parliament to view and consider what Garrisons and places of strength are fit to be demolished; and we finding that the Castle of Haverford is not tenable for the services of the State, and yet that

[45] See *Essex Arch. Soc. Trans.* N. S. xi, 75 (1909); Wright, *History of Essex*, i, 104, where Cromwell is said to have exchanged it for Hampton Court and that in 1653 Newhall was sold for £18,000. Parliament resolved to propose this exchange in 1652, but in 1659 Richard Cromwell mentioned it as "a portion for my sister Frances." *C. J.*

it may be possessed by ill-affected persons, to the prejudice of the peace of these parts: These are to authorise and require you to summon-in the Hundred of Roose and the inhabitants of the Town and County of Haverfordwest; and that they forthwith demolish the several walls and towers of the said Castle; so as that the said Castle may not be possessed by the Enemy, to the endangering of the peace of these parts.

"Given under our hands, this 12th of July 1648.

"Roger Lort. John Lort.
"Sam Lort. Tho. Barlowe.

"We expect an account of your proceedings, with effect, in this business, by Saturday being the 15th of July instant."

To which the Lieutenant General appends:

If a speedy course be not taken to fulfil the commands of this Warrant, I shall be necessitated to consider of settling a Garrison.

OLIVER CROMWELL.[46]

To this the Mayor and Aldermen promptly replied with a request for powder to blow up the castle;[47] but Cromwell had no powder to spare and retorted with another suggestion for its disposal:

To the Mayor and Aldermen of Haverfordwest

Whereas upon view and consideration with Mr. Rogert Lort, Mr. Samson Lort, and the Mayor and Aldermen of Haverfordwest, it is thought fit, for the preserving of the peace of this County, that the Castle of Haverfordwest should be speedily demolished:

These are to authorise you to call unto your assistance, in the performance of this exercise [?], the inhabitants of the Hundreds of Dungleddy, Dewisland, Kemis, Roose and Kilgerran; who are hereby required to give you assistance.

Given under our hands this 14th of July 1648.

OLIVER CROMWELL.[48]

With this last precaution, Cromwell hastened north to the aid of Lambert in his opposition to Hamilton whose raw recruits, with little money and less artillery, were advancing slowly southward, plundering as they went and thereby alienating the people they had come to help. Under Hamilton's ineffective leadership only their superior numbers enabled them to drive back Lambert, who contented himself with holding them in play till he was reinforced, fighting some rear-guard skirmishes as he retired, in one of which Cromwell's son Henry, a captain in Colonel Harrison's regiment, took a part.[49] Leaving a

[46] In the town archives of Haverfordwest; pr. in the *Welshman* (Carmarthen, Dec. 29, 1848); thence *Notes and Queries*, 2nd ser. iii, 44; John Timbs, *Abbey, Castles and Ancient Halls*, ii, 494–5; Carlyle, App. 11.

[47] *Ibid.*

[48] *Ibid.*

[49] Rushworth, vii, 1200–01. Henry Cromwell's lieutenant was killed in the skirmish.

garrison in Appleby Castle, Lambert withdrew to Bowes and Barnard Castle, hoping to hold the Stainmore pass against Hamilton and expecting aid from Yorkshire and Cromwell, of whose advent he had been advised.[50]

For two reasons the Scotch army made no effort to follow Lambert beyond Appleby. The first was Hamilton's incapacity as a general; the second was the situation of his army and of Scotch politics. He had scarcely more than a third of the force which he had expected to lead into England and he was ill supported from home. If Scotland was not, like England, in the throes of civil war, its political condition fell just short of that; and Hamilton himself had played a part which forfeited the confidence of all parties. He had been an enemy of Strafford and had, according to report, contributed to the Earl's condemnation. He had fallen out with Montrose; made friends with the Parliamentary leaders; deserted the King and allied himself with Argyll and the Covenanters. He had in turn fallen out with them and refused to sign the Solemn League and Covenant; and though he turned again to the King, he had so antagonized Charles's advisers that Charles abandoned him and he was imprisoned by the Royalists. Liberated by Fairfax's troops, he had again sought the King, persuaded him to accept Presbyterianism, and finally triumphing over Argyll, gained the virtual mastery of the government and projected this invasion.

But he was hated by the ministers; the General Assembly branded him as a traitor to the Covenant; while the ablest of Scotch generals, Leslie, like Argyll, refused to join in the new enterprise, and Hamilton was left with only the support of the Estates. Fortunately the Prince of Wales's declaration that he would accept the invitation to come to Scotland only on condition that he could use his Prayer Book was not generally known, and though he did not reach Scotland, the influence of the Royalists and the Scotch Estates sufficed to provide Hamilton with such men and supplies as he had for his expedition.

It would seem that in so far as the Royalists had a unified plan, it lay in the seizure of such strongholds as those of Pembroke and the great fortress of Pontefract, in raising such rebellions here and there as would distract and divide the forces of the Parliamentary army, and pave the way for Hamilton. In some measure that had succeeded, and had Hamilton been a capable general with an experienced army, he might have carried all before him while Fairfax was engaged before Colchester, and Cromwell before Pembroke. But various difficulties made this impossible. While Hamilton, like Lambert, awaited reinforcements, Cromwell hastened north, leaving his quarters in south Wales on July 14 or 15 with his ill-equipped regiments. Thirty troops

[50] *Perfect Diurnall*, July 10–16. Rushworth, vii, 1191.

of horse sent on ahead joined Lambert at Bowes on July 27, but the rest moved more slowly.[51] Whether or not they were 'in a bog' at Monmouth with a threat of mutiny to protest the lack of pay and equipment, as a Royalist news-sheet announced,[52] the foot were in a pitiable state when they reached Gloucester,[53] as Cromwell's report to the Committee at Derby House revealed:

To the Committee at Derby House

His "poor wearied soldiers" have advanced as far as Gloucester and shoes and stockings are urgently needed for the long march into the North. Two Welsh troops are with him.[54] [Gloucester, July 24?]

On receipt of the letter at Derby House on July 27, the Committee replied urging him to hasten his march and take with him a Hertfordshire troop, assuring him that the Committee of the Army would be earnestly solicited to have shoes ready for him at Northampton and stockings at Coventry;[55] and the next day the House voted to send him 3,000 pairs of each.[56] Advancing as far as Warwick Castle, Cromwell there awaited money and supplies for three or four days, until he received a letter from Lambert and instructions from the Committee at Derby House to hasten northward.[57] On Saturday the last day of July, he left Warwick with three regiments of foot, one of horse, and a small party of dragoons, reaching Leicester the next day to find the first consignment of shoes and stockings from Northampton and Coventry awaiting him,[58] and to receive a visit from the

[51] *Perfect Diurnall*, July 31–Aug. 7; Rushworth, vii, 1211. Cp. *Ibid.*, 1205.

[52] *Mercurius Pragmaticus*, July 25–Aug. 1. "Noll Cromwell is fallen into a bog at Monmouth, where his men mutiny for want of pay, and will not budge one foot northward, notwithstanding all the exhortations of his best-gifted commanders; which caused a messenger to post away with all speed from Derby House, with a large promise of shoes, stockings, and money, to meet them (if they would march) in their way northward, at Northampton; but the devil a foot will these saints stir; for, as the state is hide-bound in matter of money, so the new Christians are wind-bound; and though the states gazettes bespoke Oliver's advance as far as Gloucester, yet the last intelligence thence says that his soldiers are no men of metal without money, as well as their commanders; and that they have as little mind to look northward, as Nol's nose hath to turn eastward towards Westminster."

[53] Colonel Henry Herbert parted from him not far from Gloucester on July 25th. Herbert to Lenthall, July 28 (*Hist. Mss. Comm. Rept.* 13 (Welbeck) i, 492.

[54] *Cal. S. P. Dom.* (1648–9), p. 217; *C. J.*, v, 650; *Perfect Diurnall*, July 28; Rushworth, vii, 1206.

[55] *Cal. S. P. Dom.* (1648–9), pp. 217, 219.

[56] *C. J.*, v, 650; *Perfect Diurnall*, July 28. Cromwell had 1200 horse and 3000 foot.

[57] Rushworth, vii, 1208; *Moderate Intelligencer*, July 27–Aug. 3; *Perfect Diurnall*, July 29; *C. J.*, v, 650.

[58] *Moderate Intelligencer*, July 27–Aug. 3. On Aug. 2 the Derby House Committee ordered payment for 2500 pairs of shoes provided at Northampton.

mayor and aldermen with gifts of "wyne, biskets, sugar, beare and tobacko" for himself and his officers.[59]

Meanwhile his status changed. There was naturally some question as to the post of commander-in-chief of the forces now about to be joined, and to prevent dispute between Lambert and Cromwell the Derby House Committee took the matter in hand. The day that Cromwell reached Leicester the Committee wrote him:

"In regard of the place and quality you bear in the army, there will be none in the North who will pretend to a command-in-chief while you are there, yet to take away all colour to any such pretence, we have written to all the commanders of forces there to obey your orders."[60]

In the light of this commission, Cromwell wrote at once to Lambert:

To Major-General Lambert

"Desiring him to forbear engaging before he came up." [c. August 4, 1648][61]

It was no wonder that Cromwell was anxious for Lambert not to risk an engagement before he was reinforced, and that he desired to have the full control of the situation in his hands as his was the full responsibility. That responsibility was great. Though the risings in England had been put down, the danger was far from over, and a defeat, even a doubtful victory over the Scots, would be disastrous to his cause and to himself. Not only was the Royalist reaction still strong and the resentment against the rule of the army still stronger, but the various revolutionary elements were far from united even among themselves. Few, even in Parliament, were convinced that this second civil war was in the best interest of the country, and many feared that the success of the army would plunge the nation into still deeper distress. No one knew better than Cromwell that he must win and win decisively if his cause and his party were to maintain themselves; and in that hope he hastened to the assistance of Lambert.

For the antagonism of the nation toward the army, and Cromwell in particular, there was accumulating evidence. Apart from the continued resistance of Colchester and the Royalist sentiment throughout the country, at this moment Parliament voted the 'enlargement' of John Lilburne, who was recognized as the heart and soul and mind and especially the pen of the revolutionary element and was expected

[59] *Cal. S. P. Dom.* p. 230. *Hist. Mss. Comm. Rept.* 8 App. pt. I (Leicester Corp. Mss.) p. 429.

[60] *Cal. S. P. Dom.* (1648–9), p. 227.

[61] *Perfect Diurnall*, Aug. 7–14.

to make trouble for Cromwell. "It will not be long," exulted the Royalist *Mercurius Pragmaticus*, "ere Mr. Speaker and Noll Cromwell be both brought to the stake."[62] Nor was this sentiment confined to Royalists. On August 1 the Lords voted down a resolution 'that those who invited the Scots are traitors'; and on that same day Major Robert Huntington gave an account of the King's being carried from Holmby "by orders of Lieutenant-General Cromwell." In explanation of why he left the army, he carried his narrative, which was embodied in the *Lords' Journals*,[63] back to the time when Parliament had ordered the disbandment of the army, including in it charges against Cromwell and Ireton, especially in regard to Cromwell's connection with the King, and of Cromwell's determination to seize supreme power for himself. In it Huntington set down the main points of what he declared was Cromwell's frequently reiterated philosophy of government.

"First, That every single Man is Judge of Just and Right, as to the Good and Ill of a Kingdom.

"2. That the Interest of honest Men is the Interest of the Kingdom. And that those only are deemed honest Men by him, that are conformable to his Judgement and Practice, may appear in many Particulars: To instance but One; in the Choice of Colonel Rainsborough to be Vice Admiral. Lieutenant General Cromwell being asked, 'How he could trust a Man whose Interest was so directly opposite to what he had professed, and one whom he had lately aimed to remove from all Places of Trust.' He answered 'That he had now received particular Assurance from Colonel Rainsborough, as great as could be given by Man, that he would be conformable to the Judgement and Direction of himself and Commissary General Ireton, for the managing of the whole Business at Sea.'

"3. That it is lawful to pass through any Forms of Government, for the accomplishing his Ends: And therefore, either to purge the Houses, and support the remaining Party by Force everlastingly, or to put a Period to them by Force, is very lawful, and suitable to the Interest of honest Men.

"4. That it is lawful to play the Knave with a Knave."[64]

In spite of this the House of Commons refused to admit an accusation against Cromwell palpably designed to bring about his removal from the army and so crippling it that the triumph of the Royalist cause would be a certainty.[65] It was generally believed that Lilburne was released just at that time because the Presbyterians hoped he would join Huntington in impeaching Cromwell,—as he might have done if he had not looked upon Cromwell as a lesser evil than the

[62] August 2nd.

[63] *Sundry Reasons inducing Major Huntington to lay down his commission.* Printed in *L. J.*, x, 408–12; Thurloe, i, 94–8; *Old Parl. Hist.*, xvii, 360.

[64] *L. J.*, x, 411.

[65] Ludlow's *Memoirs*, (ed. Firth), i, 196.

Scotch. But in this his liberators were disappointed, for he did not hesitate to inform Cromwell of his support in spite of the hardships he had suffered. "I am no staggerer from my first principles that I engaged my life upon," wrote Lilburne in a letter sent on August 3, by Edward Sexby, "nor from you, if you are what you ought to be, and what you are now strongly reported to; although, if I persecuted or desired revenge for an hard and almost starving imprisonment, I could have had of late the choice of twenty opportunities to have paid you to the purpose; but I scorn it, especially when you are low, and this assure yourself, that if ever my hand be upon you, it shall be when you are in your full glory, if then you shall decline from the righteous ways of truth and justice: which if you will fixedly and im-impartially prosecute I am yours, to the last drop of my heart bloud. . . ."[66]

The day Lilburne wrote to him, Cromwell reached Nottingham, with his army increased by the Leicestershire, Nottinghamshire and Derbyshire forces. There he must have written the letter to Derby House which that Committee enclosed in a letter to Lord Grey of Groby on August 8th.[67]

To the Committee at Derby House

There are five or six hundred horse in Leicestershire ready to go north with the army. [c. August 5, 1648.]

Cromwell advanced to Mansfield on Sunday, August 6, and so to Rotherham by Tuesday.[68] He had expected to be in Doncaster by Monday, but probably did not reach there until Wednesday, having learned, no doubt, that the ammunition which was being sent from Hull was delayed.[69] It had not arrived when he reached Doncaster, but rather than waste time waiting for it, he advanced with part of his forces a few miles north on the main road to Pontefract, making contact with its besiegers. The castle was evidently not to be taken save by starving out the garrison, but he drove the Royalist horse from the town into the castle and took prisoner many of the foot. Exchanging some of his raw recruits for more experienced men who had been occupied in the siege and who would be more useful to him in the coming conflict with Hamilton, he left some 2,000 troops to block up Pontefract and Scarborough and went on to meet the Scots.[70]

[66] Quoted in *Legal Fundamental Liberties* (1649), p. 32; pr. in Ludlow, i, 200; *Clarke Papers*, ii, 254.

[67] *Cal. S. P. Dom.* (1648–9), p. 236.

[68] *Perfect Diurnall*, Aug. 7–14.

[69] Derby House Comm. to Fairfax, 2 Aug. *Cal. S. P. Dom.* (1648–9), p. 230; Same to Cromwell, 2 Aug., *Ibid.*

[70] *Moderate Intelligencer*, Aug. 10–17.

It was about this time that there was published a pamphlet entitled *The Declaration of Lieutenant-General Cromwell concerning the Citizens of London.* In commending the people of Bristol for their assistance, it contains a warning, if not a threat, to the turbulent and discontented Londoners. It compares the generosity of the men of Bristol toward the army during the siege of Pembroke with the attitude of the Londoners toward the army, to the disadvantage of the latter, and whether addressed to the governor of Bristol[71] or to the mayor of that city, Gabriel Sherman, it might be interpreted as having been intended to keep the mutinous capital in awe of the army while Cromwell was engaged in his campaign against the Scots.

To the City of Bristol

Whereas I should long since have acquainted you of the many favours we received from the City of Bristol, by the mediation of Mr. Peters, when we lay before Pembrook, they affording us not only a great supply of Beer, but linen for our wounded and sick soldiers, a mercy seasonable and necessary, and at this present sensibly felt; yet in this very poor condition, we can do no more but acknowledge it with thankful hearts to God, and by promising to hazard our lives in a farther adventure for them, and the Kingdom in this our Northern expedition, much enabled and encouraged by the benefit and remembrance of those former favours, together with the supply of 2500 pair of shoes from Northampton and the like quantity of stockings from the city of Coventry, and our joy is that God hath cleared up our way by the appearance of his providence in his former assistances, and believe it, Sir, as long as we have life, we shall keep to first principles, though a poor naked despised party, and die by the sides of our faithful officers, in the owning of that only, which God and reason allows, as for those against whom we now march, it's our opinion they, if victors, will put no difference between Cavaliers, Presbyterians, and Independents, but we trust He that hath hitherto gone along with us, will assist us in this enterprise to blunt somewhat the edge of their delights and that they shall reap as those before them, of that stamp, both old and new, will not Englishmen consider of whom it is said they are the best servants but the worst masters in the world we grieve for that famous city of London, over whom we never desired to insult, nor marched we through with any such intent, but to let them and the world see and understand how false their reports were concerning our endeavours to come up and plunder them, but let them know their destruction (if they perish) will be of themselves, not us.

And not withstanding all their high and strange expressions against us, who have been instrumental of more good to them, then to all the Kingdom, and received the least from them, yet we profess ourselves their servants in the work in hand: and for you noble Citizens of Bristol you have had wonderful experiences and deliverances, do not lose them; we appoint no Government to you nor this Kingdom, we shall stoop, we hope as low as the lowest

[71] Col. Charles Doyley was appointed Governor in March 1647. Whether he served until Col. John Haggett who was appointed in July 1649, is uncertain.

and look no other way upon ourselves, and take no other notice of the workings of providence, then as instruments used by the eternal, since our new modelling for subduing those who have and would inslave both soul and body to their wills, not God's, and reasons: and so many of us as shall outlive these troubles, you shall see will be willing to resign all kind of power and trust, when such an agreement or settlement is made, as may put us in capacity to live under the worst of shades, free from tyranny and persecution.[72]

While Cromwell thus prepared to fall upon the Scots, neither his friends nor his enemies were idle. Hamilton, having received reinforcements, took Appleby Castle and moved south to Kendal, and Lambert whose position at Bowes was thus outflanked, advanced to Richmond to guard Yorkshire or throw himself across the Scotch lines of communication. There he was advised that Hamilton planned to relieve Pontefract and so advanced to a point between Knaresborough and Leeds, while Cromwell's forces waited for supplies at Doncaster. Hamilton's difficulties meanwhile increased. Continual rain and torrential streams hampered the advance and the lack of horses delayed his movements. Still more he faced a problem of command. Sir George Monro had been recalled from Ireland by the Estates to aid Hamilton, and though the invasion had already begun before he arrived, he set out with some two hundred foot and a thousand horse, but was held back to bring up the artillery. Meanwhile the Scottish commanders fell out among themselves. Hamilton's second in command, the Earl of Callander, treated his superior officer with contempt and refused to recognize Monro as an equal. Monro in turn refused to take orders from Callander and, in fact, never joined Hamilton at all, but was left behind with a mixed Scotch and English force some miles in the rear.[73]

Thus divided, Hamilton's command advanced to Hornby, northeast of Lancaster, to argue over their next move. Only when Langdale arrived with news of Parliamentary forces gathering in Yorkshire, did they agree to join forces with him at Preston. Meanwhile Cromwell and Lambert met at Leeds to plan their joint attack. On August 11 the artillery and ammunition arrived and the next day the two Parliamentary armies joined forces between Knaresborough and Wetherby. Cromwell estimated that he had 9,000 men to meet a Scotch force of 24,000;[74] but as not seldom happened, he overestimated the difference in numbers. The difference in quality was still more marked. Hamilton's men were for the most part raw levies;

[72] [Early Aug., 1648] *The Declaration of Lieutenant Generall Cromwel concerning the Citizens of London, and their high and strange expressions against the Army* . . . (14 Aug.).

[73] *A Letter from Holland.*

[74] Cromwell's letter, Aug. 20, 1648.

many of his foot were said to be unable to handle a pike and many of his cavalry unable to keep their seats. In leadership and experience the Scots were even more hopelessly overmatched; and as Napoleon said, "In war it is not men but a man that counts."

Cromwell's plan was to surprise Hamilton if possible. Sending the artillery to Knaresborough to take the main road west, he hastened along the shortest road toward Preston, picking up Ashton's command on his way. The first night of his march, August 13, he stopped at the little town of Otley and the next day reached Skipton. There, or somewhere on the way, he signed an order

Order

Whereas I am informed that Lieut. Swayne, Lieut. to Capt. Cook's troop of horse hath taken two horses of great value from Captain William Harrison, for the restoring whereof he hath had letters, or orders from his superior officers. Notwithstanding the said horses are not restored. It is therefore ordered that they be instantly delivered to the bearer for Capt. Harrison's use, and that the said Capt. Cooke see this order duly observed.
Aug. 14, 1648. O. CROMWELL.[75]

From Skipton the army marched the next day to Gisburn on the banks of the Ribble and so to Hodder Bridge on the Ribble's tributary, the Hodder. There a council of war was held on the 16th, which determined to keep to the north bank of the Ribble and attack Hamilton at Preston. Thence they advanced to Stonyhurst to make camp. Thus far the surprise seems to have been complete. Though Langdale was informed that Cromwell was but three miles away, he seems to have given the report little credence,[76] and the Scotch army was widely scattered for forage on the very eve of the attack. Callander and Middleton on their way to Wigan, were sixteen miles to the south with the cavalry; Monro's forces were to the north; and Langdale's 3,600 English troops were six miles to the east. Informed of Cromwell's approach, Callander dashed back—without his command—to consult Hamilton who arrived in Preston on the morning of the 17th, unaware of the fact that Langdale was already being furiously attacked by the whole Parliamentary army.

That officer's command, though outnumbered more than two to one by Cromwell's veterans, had taken up its position in fields enclosed by hedges and resisted desperately for some four hours until

[75] Written on the bottom of the order is the notation, dated Aug. 15 at Leeds, "This is a true copy of the original Capt. Cooke read and besides it was read to him in presence of us whose names are subscribed. Abraham Burton: Tho. Staveley: Timothy Hurst." In the Tangye Collection in the London Museum. Calendared in Lomas-Carlyle, Suppl. 31.

[76] Clarendon, xi, 73–4; Burnet, vi, 58; Turner, *Memoirs*, p. 63; *Civil War Tracts of Lancashire*, p. 268.

Ashton's reinforcements enabled Cromwell to drive them from their position. On it fell, in fact, the brunt of the whole engagement and Hamilton had just ordered Baillie to lead the foot across the Ribble when news came that Langdale was defeated and being driven toward Preston with the Parliamentary army in pursuit. Hamilton, in consequence, countermanded his orders to Baillie, but Callander intervened, persuading Hamilton to abandon Langdale to his fate, join Baillie's infantry to Middleton's cavalry on its way back from Wigan and fight with the Ribble in front of them, instead of in their rear.

It was a plausible if selfish and disastrous suggestion, which Hamilton adopted, though he himself rode out with some horse to Langdale's assistance. His slender reinforcement did no good. Driven from their hedge strongholds, what was left of Langdale's horse joined Monro, the remnants of the foot surrendered. Langdale and Hamilton made good their escape and joined Baillie as Cromwell's forces occupied the north bank of the Ribble, drove Hamilton's men from the bridge and put themselves between the Scots and their line of retreat to the north.

Thus cut off from Monro and from Scotland, Baillie and Turner were for fighting it out; but, as earlier, Callander had his way and the invaders began their retreat to the south. It was at this point that Cromwell wrote his first report of the battle to solicit help in following up his victory.

For the Honourable Committee of Lancashire sitting at Manchester (*I desire the Commander of the Forces there to open this Letter if it come not to their hands*)

GENTLEMEN,

It hath pleased God, this day, to show His great power by making the Army successful against the common Enemy.

We lay the last night at Mr. Sherburn's of Stonihurst, nine miles from Preston, which was within three miles of the Scots quarters. We advanced betimes next morning towards Preston, with a desire to engage the enemy; and by that time our forlorn had engaged the Enemy, we were about four miles from Preston, and thereupon we advanced with the whole Army: and the enemy[77] being drawn out upon a moor betwixt us and the town, the Armies on both sides engaged; and after a very sharp dispute, continuing for three or four hours, it pleased God to enable us to give them a defeat; which I hope we shall improve, by God's assistance, to their utter ruin: and in this service your countrymen have not the least share.

We cannot be particular, having not time to take account of the slain and prisoners; but we can assure you we have many prisoners, and many of those of quality; and many slain; and the Army so dissipated. The principal part whereof, with Duke Hambleton, is on south side Ribble and Darwain Bridge,

[77] Langdale's command.

and we lying with the greatest part of the Army close to them; nothing hindering the ruin of that part of the enemy's Army but the night. It shall be our care that they shall not pass over any ford beneath the Bridge, to go northward, or to come betwixt us and Whalley.

We understand Colonel-General Ashton's are at Whalley; we have seven troops of horse and dragoons that we believe lie at or near Clitheroe. This night I have sent order to them expressly to march to Whalley, to join to those companies; that so we may endeavour the ruin of this enemy. You perceive by this letter how things stand. By this means the enemy is broken; and most of their horse being gone northwards, and we having sent a considerable party at the very heel of them, and the enemy having lost almost all his ammunition, and near four-thousand arms, so that the greatest part of the foot are naked: and therefore, in order to perfecting this work, we desire you to raise your county; and to improve your forces to the total ruin of that enemy, which way soever they go; and that you shall accordingly do your part, doubt not of their total ruin.

We thought fit to speed this to you; to the end you may not be troubled if they shall march towards you, but improve your interest aforesaid, that you may give glory to God for this unspeakable mercy. This is all at present from,

Your very humble servant,

17 Aug. 1648. OLIVER CROMWELL.[78]

Callander's advice was as disastrous as ever. Leaving Ashton with 4,000 men to hold Preston, Cromwell with some 5,500 troops hastened after Hamilton, whose retreat was covered by Middleton's horse which had finally come up, and the Scotch army made its weary and dispirited way through the rain and mud to Wigan. Thence, the weather having cleared somewhat, Hamilton ordered a night march, hoping to cross the Mersey at Warrington and join Byron in north Wales. At Winwick, on the morning of the 19th, Cromwell caught up with them and in a desperate engagement the Scots were driven back with a loss of some 3,000 men. At Warrington he caught them again, and again on Callander's advice, bitterly against his will, Baillie surrendered the remainder of his infantry, some 4,000 men in all. The next day Cromwell wrote to Lenthall the details of the first great victory in which he held supreme command:[79]

[78] Pr. in many old pamphlets. Repr., with a letter to Sir Ralph Ashton with which Cromwell's letter was enclosed, in Ormerod, *Tracts relating to Lancashire during the Civil War* (Chetham Society, 1844), p. 256; Carlyle, Letter LXIII.

[79] Authorities for Preston are: *Memoirs of Henry Guthrie* (1702), p. 234–5; *Letter from Holland;* Langdale's "Impartiall relation of the fight at Preston," in *Civil War Tracts of Lancashire* (Chetham Society), p. 267; Turner's *Memoirs*, 1632–70 (Bannatyne Club, 1829); Clarendon, xi, 75; Hodgson, *Memoirs*, Edinb. 1808; Carte, *Original Letters*, i, 160–62; Musgrave's relation (*Clarendon Mss*, 2867); Burnet, *Memoirs of James and William, dukes of Hamilton* (1677), p. 358 ff; Baillie, iii, 456; Hoenig, Capt. F. "Battle of Preston" in *Royal United Service Inst. Journal*, xlii, 830; *Bloudy Battle at Preston.*

To the Honourable William Lenthall, Esquire, Speaker of the House of Commons: These

SIR,

I have sent up this gentleman to give you an account of the great and good hand of God towards you, in the late victory obtained against the enemy in these parts.

After the conjunction of that party which I brought with me out of Wales with the northern forces about Knaresborough and Weatherby, hearing that the enemy was advanced with their army into Lancashire, we marched the next day, being the 13th of this instant August, to Oatley (having cast off our train, and sent it to Knaresborough, because of the difficulty of the marching therewith through Craven, and to th' end we might with more expedition attend the enemy's motion): and on the 14th to Skipton, the 15th to Gisborn, the 16th to Hodder Bridge over Ribble;[80] where we held a council of war. At which we had in consideration, whether we should march to Whalley that night, and so on, to interpose between the enemy and his further progress into Lancashire and so southward, which we had some advertisement the enemy intended, and since confirmed that they intended for London itself; or whether to march immediately over the said Bridge, there being no other betwixt that and Preston, and engage the enemy there, who we did believe would stand his ground, because we had information that the Irish forces under Monro lately come out of Ireland, which consisted of twelve-hundred horse and fifteen-hundred foot, were on their march towards Lancashire to join with them.

It was thought that to engage the enemy to fight was our business, and the reason aforesaid giving us hopes that our marching on the north side of Ribble would effect it, it was resolved we should march over the Bridge; which accordingly we did; and that night quartered the whole Army in the field by Stonihurst Hall, being Mr. Sherburn's house, a place nine miles distant from Preston. Very early the next morning we marched towards Preston; having intelligence that the enemy was drawing together thereabouts from all his out-quarters, we drew out a forlorn of about two-hundred horse and four-hundred foot, the horse commanded by Major Smithson, the foot by Major Pounel. Our forlorn of horse marched within a mile where the enemy was drawn up, in the enclosed grounds by Preston, on that side next us, and there, upon a moor, about half a mile distant from the enemy's Army, met with their scouts and outguard, and did behave themselves with that valour and courage as made their guards (which consisted both of horse and foot) to quit their ground, and took divers prisoners; holding this dispute with them until our forlorn of foot came up for their justification, and by those we had opportunity to bring up our whole Army.

So soon as our foot and horse were come up, we resolved that night to engage them if we could, and therefore, advancing with our forlorn, and

[80] Over Hodder rather, which is the chief tributary of the Ribble and little inferior to the main stream in size. Ribble from the Northeast, Hodder from the North, then a few miles farther, Calder from the South; after which the Ribble pursues its old direction, till, far down, the Darwen from the East and South falls in near Preston, and the united waters, drain into the Irish sea.

putting the rest of our Army into as good a posture as the ground would bear (which was totally inconvenient for our horse, being all enclosure and miry ground), we pressed upon them. The regiments of foot were ordered as followeth. There being a lane, very deep and ill, up to the enemy's Army, and leading to the town, we commanded two regiments of horse, the first whereof was Colonel Harrison's and next was my own, to charge up that lane; and on either side of them advanced the battle,—which were Lieutenant-Colonel Read's, Colonel Dean's and Colonel Pride's on the right, Colonel Bright's and my Lord General's on the left, and Colonel Ashton with the Lancashire regiments in reserve. We ordered Colonel Thornhaugh's and Colonel Twisleton's regiments of horse on the right, and one regiment in reserve for the lane; and the remaining horse on the left: so that, at last, we came to a hedge-dispute, the greatest of the impression from the enemy being upon our left wing, and upon the battle on both sides the lane, and upon our horse in the lane: in all which places the enemy were forced from their ground, after four hours dispute, until we came to the town; into which four troops of my regiment first entered, and, being well seconded by Colonel Harrison's regiment, charged the enemy in the town and cleared the streets.

There came no bands[81] of your foot to fight that day but did it with incredible valour and resolution; among which Colonel Bright's, my Lord General's, Lieutenant-Colonel Read's and Colonel Ashton's had the greatest work, they often coming to push of pike and to close firing, and always making the enemy to recoil. And indeed I must needs say, God was as much seen in the valour of the officers and soldiers of these before-mentioned as in any action that hath been performed; the enemy making, though he was still worsted, very stiff and sturdy resistance. Colonel Dean's and Colonel Pride's, outwinging the enemy, could not come to so much share of the action; the enemy shogging[82] down towards the Bridge, and keeping almost all in reserve, that so he might bring fresh hands[83] often to fight, which we not knowing, but lest we should be outwinged, placed those two regiments to enlarge our right wing, which was the cause they had not at that time so great a share in that action.

At the last the enemy was put into disorder, many men slain, many prisoners taken; the Duke, with most of the Scots horse and foot, retreated over the bridge, where, after a very hot dispute betwixt the Lancashire regiments, part of my Lord General's, and them, being at push of pike, they were beaten from the bridge, and our horse and foot, following them, killed many and took divers prisoners, and we possessed the bridge over Darwent and a few houses there; the enemy being driven up within musket-shot of us where we lay that night,[84] we not being able to attempt farther upon the enemy, the night preventing us. In this posture did the enemy and we lie

[81] "hands" in the *Chetham* Book.

[82] "*Shog* is from the same root as *shock;* 'shogging,' a word of Oliver's in such cases, signifies moving by pulses, intermittently. Ribble Bridge lay on the Scotch right; Dean and Pride, therefore, who fought on the English right, got gradually less and less to do. Cromwell uses the term 'shogging down' also in his account of the battle of Dunbar." Lomas-Carlyle.

[83] Perhaps this also should be "bands."

[84] The Darwen between us and them.

the most part of that night. Upon entering the town, many of the enemy's horse fled towards Lancaster, in the chase of whom went divers of our horse, who pursued them near ten miles, and had execution of them, and took about five-hundred horse and many prisoners. We possessed in this fight very much of the enemy's ammunition, I believe they lost four or five thousand arms. The number of slain we judge to be about a thousand; the prisoners we took were about four-thousand.

In the night the Duke was drawing off his Army towards Wiggon; we were so wearied with the dispute that we did not so well attend the enemy's going off as might have been, by means whereof the enemy was gotten at least three miles with his rear, before ours got to them. I ordered Colonel Thornhaugh to command two or three regiments of horse to follow the enemy, if it were possible to make him stand till we could bring up the Army. The enemy marched away seven or eight thousand foot and about four-thousand horse; we followed him with about three-thousand foot and two-thousand five-hundred horse and dragoons, and, in this prosecution, that worthy gentleman, Colonel Thornhaugh, pressing too boldly, was slain, being run into the body and thigh and head by the enemy's lancers.[85] And give me leave to say, he was a man as faithful and gallant in your service as any, and one who often heretofore lost blood in your quarrel, and now his last. He hath left some behind him to inherit a father's honour, and a sad widow; both now the interest of the Commonwealth.

Our horse still prosecuted the enemy, killing and taking divers all the way. At last the enemy drew up within three miles of Wiggon, and by that time our Army was come up, they drew off again, and recovered Wiggon before we could attempt any thing upon them. We lay that night in the field close by the enemy, being very dirty and weary, and having marched twelve miles of such ground as I never rode in all my life, the day being very wet. We had some skirmishing, that night, with the enemy, near the town, where we took General Van Druske and a colonel, and killed some principal officers, and took about a hundred prisoners; where I also received a letter from Duke Hamilton, for civil usage towards his kinsman Colonel Hamilton,[86] whom he left wounded there. We took also Colonel Hurrey and Lieutenant-Colonel Ennis [Innes], sometimes in your service. The next morning the enemy marched towards Warrington, and we at the heels of them. The town of Wiggon, a great and poor town, and very malignant, were plundered almost to their skins by them.

We could not engage the enemy until we came within three miles of Warrington, and there the enemy made a stand, at a pass near Winwicke.

[85] " 'Run through with a lancier in Chorley, he wanting his arms,' says Hodgson. This is the Colonel Thornhaugh so often mentioned, praised and mourned for, by Mrs. Hutchinson."

[86] Claud Hamilton; see Turner *supra*. " 'Colonel Hurry' is the ever-changing Sir John Hurry, sometimes called Urry and Hurrey, who whisks like a most rapid actor of all work, ever on a new side, ever charging in the van, through this Civil-War Drama. The notablest feat he ever did was leading Prince Rupert on that marauding party, from Oxford to High Wycombe, on the return from which Hampden met his death (Clarendon, ii. 351). Hurry had been on the Parliament-side before. He was taken, at last, when Montrose was taken; and hanged out of the way." Carlyle.

We held them in some dispute till our Army came up, they maintaining the pass with great resolution for many hours; ours and theirs coming to push of pike and very close charges, and forced us to give ground; but our men, by the blessing of God, quickly recovered it, and charging very home upon them, beat them from their standing, where we killed about a thousand of them, and took (as we believe) about two-thousand prisoners, and prosecuted them home to Warrington Town, where they possessed the bridge, which had a strong barricado and a work upon it, formerly made very defensive. As soon as we came thither, I received a message from Lieut.-General Bailly, desiring some capitulation; to which I yielded. Considering the strength of the pass, and that I could not go over the River within ten miles of Warrington with the Army, I gave him these terms: That he should surrender himself and all his officers and soldiers prisoners of war, with all his arms and ammunition and horses, to me, I giving quarter for life, and promising civil usage. Which accordingly is done: and the Commissioners deputed by me have received, and are receiving, all the arms and ammunition, which will be, as they tell me, about four-thousand complete arms, and as many prisoners: and thus you have their infantry totally ruined. What colonels and officers are with Lieut.-General Bailly, I have not yet received the list.

The Duke is marching with his remaining Horse, which are about three-thousand, towards Namptwich, where the gentlemen of the county have taken about five-hundred of them, of which they sent me word this day. The country will scarce suffer any of my men to pass, except they have my hand-[writing;] telling them, They are Scots. They bring in and kill divers of them, as they light upon them. Most of the nobility of Scotland are with the Duke. If I had a thousand horse that could but trot thirty miles, I should not doubt but to give a very good account of them, but truly we are so harassed and haggled out in this business, that we are not able to do more than walk an easy pace after them. I have sent post to my Lord Grey, to Sir Henry Cholmely and Sir Edward Roads [Rodes] to gather all together, with speed, for their prosecution; as likewise to acquaint the Governor of Stafford therewith.

I hear Munroe is about Cumberland with the horse that ran away,[87] and his Irish horse and foot, which are a considerable body. I have left Colonel Ashton's three regiments of foot, with seven troops of horse (six of Lancashire and one of Cumberland), at Preston; and ordered Colonel Scroop with five troops of horse and two troops of dragoons, with two regiments of foot (Colonel Lassalls' and Colonel Wastal's), to embody with them, by which I hope he will be able to make a resistance till we can come up to them, and have ordered them to put their prisoners to the sword if the Scots shall presume to advance upon them, because they cannot bring them off with security.

Thus you have a narrative of the particulars of the success which God hath given you: which I could hardly at this time have done, considering the multiplicity of business, but truly, when I was once engaged in it, I could hardly tell how to say less, there being so much of God [in it]; and I am not willing to say more, lest there should seem to be any of man. Only give me leave to add one word, showing the disparity of forces on both sides; that so

[87] Northward from Preston on the evening of the 17th.

you may see, and all the world acknowledge, the great hand of God in this business. The Scots Army could not be less than twelve-thousand effective foot, well armed, and five-thousand horse; Langdale not less than two-thousand five-hundred foot, and fifteen-hundred horse: in all twenty-one-thousand; and truly very few of their foot but were as well armed if not better than yours, and at divers disputes did fight two or three hours before they would quit their ground. Yours were about two-thousand five-hundred horse and dragoons of your old Army; about four-thousand foot of your old Army; also about sixteen-hundred Lancashire foot, and about five-hundred Lancashire horse: in all, about eight-thousand six-hundred. You see by computation about two-thousand of the enemy slain; betwixt eight and nine thousand prisoners, besides what are lurking in hedges and private places, which the country daily bring in or destroy. Where Langdale and his broken forces are, I know not, but they are exceedingly shattered.

Surely, Sir, this is nothing but the hand of God, and wherever anything in this world is exalted, or exalts itself, God will pull it down, for this is the day wherein He alone will be exalted. It is not fit for me to give advice, nor to say a word what use should be made of this, more than to pray you, and all that acknowledge God, that they would exalt Him, and not hate His people, who are as the apple of His eye, and for whom even Kings shall be reproved; and that you would take courage to do the work of the Lord, in fulfilling the end of your magistracy, in seeking the peace and welfare of the people of this Land, that all that will live quietly and peaceably may have countenance from you, and they that are implacable and will not leave troubling the Land may speedily be destroyed out of the land. And if you take courage in this, God will bless you, and good men will stand by you, and God will have glory, and the Land will have happiness by you in despite of all your enemies. Which shall be the prayer of,

Your most humble and faithful servant,

Warrington, O. CROMWELL.
20 August, 1648.

Postscript. We have not, in all this, lost a considerable officer but Colonel Thornhaugh, and not many soldiers, considering the service; but many are wounded, and our horse much wearied. I humbly crave that some course may be taken to dispose of the prisoners. The trouble, and extreme charge of the country where they lie, is more than the danger of their escape. I think they would not go home if they might, without a convoy, they are so fearful of the country, from whom they have deserved so ill. Ten men will keep a thousand from running away.[88]

From the surrender at Warrington, Hamilton escaped with the horse and many of the Scotch nobles, and from there Cromwell wrote three letters. The first was to Sir Henry Cholmley, commander of part of the Yorkshire militia, and to Sir Edward Rodes, a county

[88] *Chetham-Society* Book, *ut supra*, pp. 259–267, from a Pamphlet pr. by Husbands, Aug. 23, 1648. Carlyle, Letter LXIV. See Walker's sarcastic remarks about the last paragraph of this "laureate" letter. *Hist.* of *Indep.* p. 136.

commissioner, later high sheriff of Yorkshire, who with Colonel Charles White, in command of some Nottinghamshire horse and Colonel Francis Hacker with troops of Leicester, Nottingham and Derby horse, were summoned to help hunt down the Scotch fugitives:

For the Honourable Sir Henry Cholmley and Sir Edward Rodes: near Pontefract Haste, haste.

[GENTLEMEN,]

We have quite tired our horse in pursuit of the enemy. We have killed, taken and dissipated all his foot, and left him only some horse, with whom the Duke is fled into Delamere Forest, having neither foot nor dragoons. They have taken five-hundred of them there, I mean the country forces, as they send me word this day.

They are so tired, and in such confusion, that if my horse could but trot after them, I could take them all, but we are so weary, we shall scarce be able to do more than walk after them. I beseech you therefore, let Sir Henry Cholmley, Sir Edward Rodes, Colonel Hacker, and Colonel White and all the countries about you, be sent to, to rise with you and follow them. For they are the miserablest party that ever was. I durst engage myself with five-hundred fresh horse, and five-hundred nimble foot, to destroy them all. My horse are miserably beaten out, and I have ten-thousand of them prisoners.

We have killed we know not what, but a very great number, having done execution upon them at the least thirty miles together, besides what we killed in the two great fights, the one at Preston and the other at Warrington. The enemy was four and twenty thousand horse and foot in the day of the fight, whereof eighteen-thousand foot and six thousand horse, and our number about six-thousand foot and three-thousand horse at the utmost.

This is a glorious day. God help England to answer His minds! I have no more, but beseech you in all your parts to gather into bodies, and pursue them. I rest,

Your most humble servant,

Warrington,
August 20th, 1648. OLIVER CROMWELL.

[P. S.] The greatest part, by far, of the nobility of Scotland are with Duke Hamilton.[89]

His estimate of the number of nobles with Hamilton, like many of his estimates of his opponents, was much exaggerated; but he was none the less, perhaps the more, energetic on that account, and he pursued his success unrelentingly. In his letter to the Derby House Committee of August 23, he mentions having written to Lord Grey,

[89] Underwritten is an order that it be shown to the Committee of York, Col. Bethel and Capt. Crackinthorp, again signed by Cromwell. Original in the Tangye Collection in the London Museum. Carlyle, Letter LXV.

whose deposition at Hamilton's[90] trial notes the receipt of the letter, doubtless similar to the orders sent to Cholmley and Rodes:

To the Lord Grey of Groby

'Enjoining him to pursue the Scottish forces with all vigour. The greatest part of the nobility of Scotland are with Duke Hamilton.' Warrington, August 20, 1648.[90]

The third letter written at this time of which we have knowledge "to acquaint the Governor of Stafford [Captain Henry Stone] therewith," has not come to light, but it was doubtless of the same character, closing the net about the fugitive Scots. Their situation was now hopeless and Cromwell left them to Lambert and the other commanders while he turned back to Preston. While Hamilton vainly sought refuge and Monro led his army toward Scotland, Cromwell wrote from Wigan an order for further pursuit to the committee at York and an explanation of the situation to the Committee at Derby House:

For the Committee at York

GENTLEMEN,

I have intelligence even now to my hands that Duke Hamilton with a wearied body of horse is drawing towards Pomfret; where probably he may lodge himself, and rest his horse, as not daring to continue in these countries where we have driven him, the country-people rising in such numbers, and stop his passage at every bridge.

Major-General Lambert with a considerable force pursues him at the heels. I desire you that you would get together what force you can, to put a stop to any further designs he may have and to be ready to join with Major-General Lambert, if there shall be need. I am marching northward with the greatest part of the Army, where I shall be glad to hear from you. I rest, gentlemen,

Your very affectionate friend and servant,

Wigan,
August 23rd 1648.

OLIVER CROMWELL.

[P.S.] I could wish you would draw out whatever force you have; either to be in his rear or to impede his march. For I am persuaded if he, or the greatest part of those that be with him be taken, it would make an end of the business of Scotland.

O. CROMWELL.[91]

[90] *Clarke Trials*, fol. 124: quoted partly in Gardiner, *Civil War*, iv, 192, and partly in Burnet, *Memoirs of the Dukes of Hamilton*, p. 387. Hamilton had refused two summons to yield upon mercy.

[91] MS. copy in the Tangye Collection in the London Museum. Pr. in *Packets of Letters from Scotland and the North*, no. 24 (Aug. 29, 1648). Carlyle, LXVI.

For the Right Honourable the Committee of Lords and Commons at Derby House: These. Haste, haste

MY LORDS AND GENTLEMEN,

I did not (being straitened with time) send you an account of the great blessing of God upon your Army. I trust it is satisfactory to your Lordships that the House had it so fully presented to them.

My Lords, it cannot be imagined that so great a business as this could be without some loss; although I confess very little compared with the weightiness of the Engagement; there being on our part not one hundred slain, yet many wounded. And to our little it is a real weakening, for indeed we are but a handful, and I submit to your Lordships, whether you will think fit or no to recruit our loss; we having but five poor regiments of foot, and our horse so exceedingly battered as I never saw them in all my life. It is not to be doubted but your enemy's designs are deep. This blow will make them very angry. The principles they went on were such as should a little awaken Englishmen; for I have it from very good hands of their own party that the Duke made this the argument to his army: That the lands of the country and . . .[92] which accordingly is done in part, there being a transplantation of many women and children and of whole families in Westmoreland and Cumberland, as I am credibly informed. Much more might be said, but I forbear. I offer it to your Lordships that money may be to pay the foot and horse to some equality. Some of those that are here since fourteen days before I marched from Windsor into Wales have not had any pay; and amongst the horse my own regiment and some others are much behind. As long as this cost of war must continue I wish your Lordships may manage it for the best advantage, and not be wanting to yourselves in what is necessary, which is the end of my offering these things to you. My Lords, money is not for contingencies so as were to be wished; we have very many things to do which might be better done if we had wherewithal. Our foot want clothes, shoes and stockings. These ways and weather have shattered them all to pieces. That which was the great blow to our horse was (besides the weather and incessant marches) our march ten miles to fight with the enemy, and a fight continuing four hours in as dirty a place as ever I saw horses stand in; and, upon the matter, the continuance of this fight two days more together in our following of the enemy, and lying close by him in the mire . . . until at length we broke him at a near . . . a great party of our horse having . . . miles towards Lancaster; who came up . . . to us, and were with us in all the action. These things I thought fit to intimate, not knowing what is fit to ask, because I know not how your affairs stand, nor what you can supply.

I have sent Major-General Lambert, upon the day I received this enclosed, with above two thousand horse and dragoons and about fourteen hundred foot in prosecution of the Duke and the nobility of Scotland with him; who will, I doubt not, having the blessing of God with him in the business. But

[92] A line or two is illegible but Carlyle suggested the missing part meant that the Scots were to share the English lands among them and go to inhabit the conquered country.

indeed his horse are exceedingly weak and weary. I have sent to Yorkshire and to my Lord Gray to alarm all parts to a prosecution, and if they be not wanting to the work, I see not how many can escape. I am marching myself back towards Preston; and so on towards Monro or otherwise, as God shall direct.

As things fall out, I shall represent them to you; and remain, My Lords and Gentlemen,

Your most humble,

Wigan,
August 23rd, 1648.

OLIVER CROMWELL.[93]

THE EXPEDITION TO SCOTLAND.

The day before Cromwell reached Wigan, while Monro with his forces made his way toward the Scotch border, Hamilton, separated from Callander and Langdale, managed to get as far as Uttoxeter, beyond which his soldiers refused to go. Captain Stone, governor of Stafford, who had received Cromwell's letter of August 20, had already taken Major-General Middleton prisoner, and was soon negotiating with the Duke in Uttoxeter. Hamilton offered to return quietly with a few companions to Scotland, but Stone purposely delayed until Lambert arrived to make Hamilton and all his subordinates prisoners of war. Langdale was captured soon afterward in an ale-house near Nottingham, but Callander escaped to Holland.[94] With the leaders secured, Parliament lost no time in deciding the fate of its prisoners. Of the common soldiers the majority, who had served under compulsion, were permitted to return to Scotland while of the volunteers as many as would be needed were to be shipped to Virginia or Barbadoes, and the rest to service in Venice.

Hamilton's defeat virtually ended the Royalist insurrection in England. A few days after news of Preston was brought to the defenders of Colchester they yielded themselves "to the mercy of the Parliament and General," of which, the agreement went on to suggest, "there hath been large experience." The Earl of Norwich, father of Colonel Goring, with Lord Capel was accordingly left to the mercy of Parliament; but to the discredit of Fairfax, or perhaps even more to that of Ireton who influenced the General,[95] that mercy was not extended to the commanders. On the grounds that officers who con-

[93] *Tanner Mss.* lvii, (1) 229. Original signed inside and out by Cromwell and sealed with the Cromwell arms. Carlyle, App. 12. Mentioned in Henfrey, *Numismata Cromwelliana*, p. 182. This was probably the letter in which Cromwell enclosed a long list of prisoners. It was brought to the House on Aug. 25th. *Perfect Diurnall*, Aug. 25.

[94] *Parliament Scout; Moderate Intelligencer;* Burnet, vi, 64.

[95] Heath believed that Ireton persuaded Fairfax, to make him odious, because Fairfax was the only impediment to Cromwell's greatness. *Chronicle*, p. 179.

tinued to hold an untenable position and so caused unnecessary bloodshed forfeited their right to quarter, and that they had broken their parole given earlier at the time of their composition at Goldsmiths' Hall, the Council of War condemned to death Sir Charles Lucas, Sir George Lisle, and Sir Bernard Gascoigne. The first two were promptly shot but Sir Bernard, who was a Florentine by birth, was reprieved at the last moment because his captors feared reprisals if they or their friends or children "for many generations" should visit Italy.

The Royalists' bitter condemnation of Fairfax and his Council upon the treatment meted out to the soldiers and townspeople at Colchester was in sharp contrast to the tribute paid to Cromwell by Hamilton at his trial: "Indeed he was so very courteous and so very civil as he performed more than he promised," the Duke said, "and I must acknowledge his favour to those poor wounded gentlemen that I left behind, that were by him taken care of, and truly he performed more than he did capitulate for."[96]

THE PURSUIT OF MONRO, AUGUST 28–SEPTEMBER 8, 1648

The day Fairfax marched into Colchester, Cromwell was with his army in Skipton again, hoping to place himself between Monro and Scotland. The Derby House Committee had given him orders[97] which corresponded with his own decision, to pursue his advantage and regain Berwick and Carlisle. In consequence, on his return across the hills into Yorkshire he sent a report of his movements in fulfillment of those orders, to William Pierrepont:

To Mr. Pierpont

Telling of his movements since Preston and asking that letters be sent to the Committees of Lancashire and York and to Colonels Ashton, Lassell, Wastall and Bright, ordering them to follow him on his march to assist him. The army is in need of supplies. Skipton, August 28, 1648.[98]

Cromwell travelled at too slow a pace to interpose his army between Monro and the border; nor did that remnant of the Scotch army, quartered for a few days near Appleby, wait for an encounter with the victorious Lieutenant-General. It was no lack of courage which hurried Monro northward, only a knowledge that from a military point of view the Royalist cause in England was, for the moment at least, completely lost. The disaster at Preston seemed to be a

[96] *Clarke Trials*, fol. 116b.

[97] Committee to Cromwell, in *Cal. S. P. Dom.* (1648–9), pp. 255–6, and in *L. J.*, x, 520.

[98] Letters were accordingly sent by the Committee at Derby House and a reply, dated Sept. 1, was written to Cromwell. *Cal. S. P. Dom.* (1648–9), pp. 263–6.

signal for a general collapse. Not only had Colchester surrendered by the end of August but the capitulation of Deal Castle in the Downs had left Sandown the only spot in southern England not in the hands of the so-called Parliamentary army. Moreover, Prince Charles, who had sailed up the Thames as far as the Medway to do battle with Warwick, was prevented by a gale from attacking and forced by lack of drinking-water to retreat to the shores of Holland. The leaders of the Royalist insurrection who had been unable to agree as to what, exactly, would have followed success, never had to settle the question. By the time Cromwell reached Knaresborough in his pursuit of Monro, nothing remained but to take a few scattered strongholds. In Cromwell's view, God had once more upheld the right and the transgressors were overthrown, as he wrote to his old friend and relative, Mr. Solicitor:

For my worthy Friend Oliver St. John, Esquire, Solicitor-General: These, at Lincoln's Inn

DEAR SIR,

I can say nothing but surely the Lord our God is a great and glorious God. He only is worthy to be feared and trusted, and His appearances patiently to be waited for. He will not fail His people. Let every thing that hath breath praise the Lord.

Remember my love to my dear brother H. V[ane]. I pray he make not too little, nor I too much, of outward dispensations.[99] God preserve us all, that we, in simplicity of our spirits, may patiently attend upon them. Let us all not be careful what use men will make of these actings. They shall, will they, nill they, fulfil the good pleasure of God, and so shall serve our generations. Our rest we expect elsewhere: that will be durable. Care we not for tomorrow, nor for anything. This Scripture has been of great stay to me; read it: *Isaiah* eighth, 10, 11, 14;—read all the chapter.[100]

[99] Alluding to this message in 1656 when, as a result of the publication of his *Healing Question*, he was placed in confinement by the Protector, Vane reminded Cromwell: "The message which in former times you sent me is in my memory still. It was immediately after the Lord had appeared with you against Duke Hamilton's army, when you bid a friend of mine tell your brother Vane (for so you then thought fit to call me), that you were as much unsatisfied with his passive and suffering principles as he was with your active. And indeed I must crave leave to make you this reply at this time; that I am as little satisfied with your active and self-establishing principles, in the lively colours wherein daily they show themselves, as you are or can be with my passive ones, and am willing in this to join issue with you and to beg of the Lord to judge between us and to give the decision according to truth and righteousness." Letter in *The Proceeds of the Protector . . . against Sir Henry Vane* (1656).

[100] The chapter referred to is all about the vain desires of the wicked. The three verses: "Take council together and it shall come to naught; speak the word, and it shall not stand. For God is with us. Sanctify the Lord of Hosts, and let Him be your fear, and let Him be your dread. And He shall be for a sanctuary:—but for a stone of stumbling and for a rock of offence to both the Houses of Israel; for a gin and for

I am informed from good hands, that a poor godly man died in Preston the day before the fight and, being sick, near the hour of his death, he desired the woman that looked to him to fetch him a handful of grass. She did so, and when he received it, he asked whether it would wither or not, now it was cut? The woman said, Yea. He replied, so should this army of the Scots do, and come to nothing, so soon as ours did but appear, or words to this effect; and so immediately died.

My service to Mr. W. P., Sir J. E., and the rest of our good friends. I hope I do often remember you.

Yours,

Knaresborough,
1st Sept. OLIVER CROMWELL.

My service to Frank Russell and honest Pickering.[101]

"Mr. W. P." and "Sir J. E." to whom Cromwell sent his greetings, were, presumably, William Pierrepoint, the son of the Earl of Kingston, to whom Cromwell had written from Skipton, and Sir John Evelyn of Wilts, both members of the Derby House Committee and both friends of Cromwell and St. John. This letter and the next, to still another member of that committee, were probably enclosed in the same packet, possibly with an official report.

The news of the battles of Preston and Warrington reached Parliament on August 23 and a day of thanksgiving was set for the "wonderful great mercy and success." There the matter dropped; for, with Holles and others of the excluded members, whose disenabling had been recalled, in their seats since August 14, the Parliamentary Presbyterians were not likely to rejoice much over an Independent victory. The dream of a king restored by a Royalist-Presbyterian combination was to be postponed for a dozen years. None the less the Presbyterians persisted. The next day the Houses repealed the Vote of No Addresses and it seemed that they were about to open negotiations with Charles once more.

If Cromwell was not surprised when this news reached him a week later, he was none the less disturbed as his letter to his friend Philip, Lord Wharton, indicates. That letter to congratulate Wharton on the birth of his son Thomas, later to be known as the greatest rake and the greatest Whig in England, reached Wharton at about the time he received news that his estate in Westmoreland had been plundered by a party of Monro's horse, which soon afterward, hearing of Cromwell's approach, took refuge in Appleby.[102]

a snare to the inhabitants of Jerusalem! And many among them shall stumble and fall, and be broken, and be snared, and be taken."

[101] Copy by Birch in *Ayscough Mss*, 4107, f. 13. Carlyle, Letter LXVII.

[102] *Perfect Occurrences*, Sept. 1–8; *Cromwelliana*, p. 45.

For the Right Honourable the Lord Wharton: These

My Lord,

You know how untoward I am at this business of writing, yet a word. I beseech the Lord make us sensible of this great mercy here, which surely was much more than * * * the House expresseth. I trust * * * the goodness of our God, time and opportunity to speak of it to you face to face. When we think of our God, what are we. Oh, His mercy to the whole society of saints, despised, jeered saints! Let them mock on. Would we were all saints. The best of us are (God knows) poor weak saints, yet saints; if not sheep, yet lambs, and must be fed. We have daily bread, and shall have it, in despite of all enemies. There's enough in our Father's house, and He dispenseth it as our eyes * * * behind, then we can * * * we for him. I think, through these outward mercies (as we call them), faith, patience, love, hope, all are exercised and perfected, yea, Christ formed, and grows to a perfect man within us. I know not how well to distinguish, the difference is only in the subject. To a worldly man they are outward, to a saint Christian, but I dispute not.

My Lord, I rejoice in your particular mercy. I hope that is so to you. If so, it shall not hurt you; not make you plot or shift for the young Baron to make him great. You will say, he is God's to dispose of, and guide for; and there you will leave him.

My love to the dear little Lady,[103] better than the child. The Lord bless you both. My love and service to all friends high and low; if you will, my Lord and Lady Mulgrave and Will Hill. I am truly,

Your faithful friend and humblest servant,

Sept. 2, 1648. O. Cromwell.[104]

As Cromwell hurried north in a vain effort to cut Monro off from Scotland, Lambert, who had been ordered to his assistance, was on his way with four regiments of horse, not following Cromwell up the great North Road through Boroughbridge, Northallerton and Darlington, but marching toward Carlisle.[105] Wherever Cromwell was on September 6—probably near Durham—he wrote to "Mr. Pierrepoint and others" of the Derby House Committee, a letter known to us only by reference to it in conjunction with the reply to a latter communication,[106] but which probably contained an account of his movements and his plans. The next day he was certainly in Durham, as

[103] Wharton's second wife, daughter of Arthur Goodwyn of Upper Winchenden, who, with John Hampden, sat for Buckinghamshire in the Long Parliament until his death.

[104] Thurloe, *State Papers*, i, 99. Lord Mulgrave was presently to sit in the first Council of State. Will Hill, Carlyle thought, was the Puritan merchant of London who was ruined by his loans to public service. Morely likely, as Mrs. Lomas suggests, he was the William Hill who was a Justice of the Peace for Bucks. Lomas-Carlyle, i, 354 &n.

[105] *Perfect Diurnall*, Sept. 2, 4.

[106] See Letter, Sept. 11, to Derby House Committee.

is evidenced by a note which he dictated, whose address is missing, in regard to some petition which had come into his hands, all further knowledge of which is lost, and which is of no importance save as indicating his movements and his whereabouts:

[*No address*]

SIR,

The enclosed petition coming to my hands, I could not but recommend it to you, as being the fittest instrument to do them right, being near to information which will lead you to what will be most fit to be done. I desire therefore you would please to give them their desires in the petition, as being in my opinion very just.

I remain,

Your very humble servant,

Duresme,
September 7, 1648.

O. CROMWELL.[107]

What is of far more importance is his proclamation before he left Durham[108] ordering the arrest of the stragglers from Hamilton's army, or their destruction if they resisted:

DECLARATION

WHEREAS the Scottish Army, under the command of James Duke of Hamilton, which lately invaded this nation of England, is, by the blessing of God upon the Parliament forces, defeated and overthrown, and some thousands of their soldiers and officers are now prisoners in our hands, so that, by reason of their great number, and want of sufficient guards and watches to keep them so carefully as need requires (the Army being employed upon other duty and service of the Kingdom), divers may escape away, and many, both since and upon the pursuit, lie in private places in the country:

I thought it very just and necessary to give notice to all, and accordingly do declare, That if any Scottishmen (officers or soldiers) lately members of the said Scottish Army, and taken or escaped in or since the late fight and pursuit, shall be found straggling in the countries, or running away from the places assigned them to remain in till the pleasure of the Parliament, or his Excellency the Lord General be known,—It will be accounted a very good and acceptable service to the country and Kingdom of England, for any person or persons to take and apprehend all such Scottishmen, and to carry them to any officer having the charge of such prisoners; or, for want of such officer, to the Committee or Governor of the next Garrison for the Parliament within the county where they shall be so taken; to be secured and kept in prison, as they shall find most convenient.

[107] Original, signed by Cromwell, in the Tangye Collection in the London Museum. Lomas-Carlyle, Suppl. 32.

[108] He reached Newcastle Sept. 9th (Rushworth, vii, 1260), although a letter from York said he expected to be there a day earlier (*Ibid.*, 1259).

And the said Committee, Officer, or Governor respectively, are desired to secure such of the said prisoners as shall be so apprehended and brought unto them, accordingly. And if any of the said Scottish officers or soldiers shall make any resistance, and refuse to be taken or render themselves, all such persons well-affected to the service of the Parliament and Kingdom of England, may and are desired to fall upon, fight with, and slay such refusers: but if the said prisoners shall continue and remain within the places and guards assigned for the keeping of them, that then no violence, wrong, nor injury be offered to them by any means.

Provided also, and special care is to be taken, That no Scottishman residing within this kingdom, and not having been a member of the said Army, or such of the said Scottish prisoners as shall have liberty given them, and sufficient passes to go to any place appointed, may not be interrupted or troubled hereby.

O. CROMWELL.[109]

[Durham,] September 8th 1648.

BERWICK AND CARLISLE, SEPTEMBER 8–OCTOBER 2, 1648

The day that Cromwell issued his declaration, he and his army celebrated a Day of Thanksgiving. They had good reason, for though on that day Monro crossed the Tweed and escaped them, England was free of her invaders. The same day Lambert was believed to be but two days' march south of Durham and on Saturday, September 9, Cromwell advanced to Newcastle[110] where he and his army remained over Sunday, reaching Morpeth on Monday. There that evening he wrote two letters. Of one of them only a record remains. It was read, with his letter of the 6th in the House of Commons and both were sent to the Committee of the Army, from whose reply we gather that they were the usual request for supplies:

"To Mr. Pierrepont and others"

Asking for ships and a supply of clothes for the foot and money for paying his regiment and £1400 with which to buy a supply of bread. He has just marched from Newcastle to Morpeth. Sept. 11, 1648.[111]

The other letter calls the Lord General's attention to the sad plight of the family of Lieutenant-Colonel Cowell, who had but lately died:

For his Excellency the Lord Fairfax, General of all the Parliament's Armies: These

MY LORD,

Since we lost Lieutenant-Colonel Cowell, his wife came to me near Northallerton, much lamenting her loss, and the sad condition she and her children were left in.

[109] *Packets of Letters*, Sept. 11; *Cromwelliana*, p. 46.
[110] Rushworth, vii, 1260.
[111] *Cal. S. P. Dom.* (1648–9), pp. 282–6; *L. J.*, x, 520.

He was an honest worthy man. He spent himself in your and the kingdom's service. He being a great trader in London, deserted it to serve the kingdom. He lent much moneys to the State; and I believe few outdid him. He hath a great arrear due to him. He left a wife and three small children but meanly provided for. Upon his deathbed he commended this desire to me, that I should befriend his to the Parliament or to your Excellency. His wife will attend you for letters to the Parliament, which I beseech you to take into a tender consideration.

I beseech you to pardon this boldness to,

Your Excellency's most humble servant,

Sept. 11th, 1648.[112] OLIVER CROMWELL.[113]

On the evening of Tuesday, September 12, Cromwell reached Alnwick to get his first reports of the situation in Scotland which he was about to invade. That news was of the most comforting character. Unwilling to have war waged on Scottish soil, the Committee of Estates, seconded by Hamilton's brother, the Earl of Lanark, in response to Cromwell's request forbade any Englishman who had fought against the English Parliament to enter Scotland. In consequence Musgrave, who on being thus left behind, had thrown himself into Appleby, on October 9 fell an easy prey to the Parliamentary forces.

But if the Estates had thought to prevent Cromwell's expedition into Scotland, by this unchivalrous maneuver they were soon undeceived. They were in no position to oppose such an invasion and Scotland, if not as turbulent as Ireland, was deeply divided into factions. The overthrow of Hamilton had restored to power his rival, Argyll, and with him the Scotch ministers who had earlier opposed Hamilton and his "Engagers" in the plan of invading England. To the side of Argyll rallied Chancellor Loudon who broke with the Estates, General Leslie, the Highlanders under the Campbell influence and their old enemies, and the Lowland peasantry, known as "Whiggamores" or "Whigs." The latter, under Leven, seized Edinburgh with the Castle; and the Committee of Estates took refuge with Monro at Stirling, where Argyll's followers, quartered at Falkirk, attempting to treat with the Committee, were surprised by Monro's army which killed some and took others prisoner. With Scotland thus divided against itself, its invasion seemed comparatively easy for the veteran army of the Parliament flushed with a recent and overwhelming victory over the Scottish invaders.

With a partial knowledge of the situation in Scotland, Cromwell

[112] Carlyle inserted "Alnwick," but if anything is to be inserted it should be "Morpeth."

[113] *Landsdowne Mss*, 1236, f. 89. Carlyle, Letter LXIX.

wrote to someone, probably at Derby House, what he knew of his position:

[*To Sir William Armyn?*]

Monday we marched from Newcastle to Morpeth, Tuesday to Alnwick; we left our guns behind us there,[114] as knowing we can send for them at pleasure. We have sent a strong party of horse with Major General Lambert's, towards Belford, and with him a summons to Berwick. The English Cavaliers under Sir Tho. Tildesly, being about 1500, lie on this side of Berwick, as not being suffered to come; it's believed they will come in if summoned. Monroe marched through with 3000, and is joined with Lanerick, having 5000 more. Argyle lies at Hedington, 12 miles be-hither Edinburgh, with an army of 10000 men. They lie within 4 miles one of another, and must fight or agree. Old Leven is possessed of Edinburgh Castle. David Leslie is Lieut. General to Argyle. We find no bread in this country, but shall have bisquit from Newcastle till new corn come, which is upon the ground in abundant measure. Lieut.-Col. Ashfield is with us, with six companies of Major-Gen. Skippon's regiment. Col. Ashton is marched towards Carlisle, with Lancashire foot. Alnwick, Sept. 14, 1648.[115]

The next day he sent a summons to Lodovic Leslie, who held Berwick for the Committee of Estates:

For the Governor of Berwick: These

SIR,

Being come thus near, I thought fit to demand the town of Berwick to be delivered into my hands, to the use of the Parliament and kingdom of England, to whom of right it belongeth.

I need not use any arguments to convince you of the justice hereof. The witness that God hath borne against your army in their invasion of this kingdom which desired to sit in peace by you, doth at once manifest His dislike of the injury done to a nation that meant you no harm, but hath been all along desirous to keep amity and brotherly affection and agreement with you.

If you deny me in this, we must make a second appeal to God, putting ourselves upon Him, in endeavouring to obtain our rights, and let Him be judge between us. And if your aims be anything beyond what we profess,

[114] Meaning at Newcastle or Morpeth.

[115] Rushworth, vii, 1264. In Cromwell's letter of the Sept. 20, q.v., he mentions having written to Armyn from Alnwick. If this is the letter, which is probable, some of the original was omitted when it was published in whatever source Rushworth found it. In a letter from Derby House to Fairfax of Sept. 22, a letter from Cromwell is mentioned with a summary of what is contained in this letter. *Cal. S. P. Dom.* (1648–9), p. 289. Armyn was member for Grantham, and one of the commissioners for the North.

He will requite it. If further trouble ensue upon your denial, we trust He will make our innocency to appear.

I expect your answer to this summons, this day, and rest,

Your servant,

Alnwick,
Sept. 15th, 1648. O. C.[116]

Leslie replied at once that he held the town in trust for the Committee of Estates and would await their orders. On that same day Loudon at Falkirk wrote to Cromwell a protestation of his friendship, expressing his disapproval of the late warfare and enclosing a statement of the attempt and failure to treat with Monro.[117] The letter was delivered to Cromwell two days later by Sir Andrew Carr and Major Straughan and, among other things, revealed to him the deep division in Scotch opinion, for Argyll and Loudon were both determined to restore Berwick and Carlisle to England, and the Estates no less determined to hold them as long as possible.

Two days and nights of the stay in Alnwick were spent in the Castle.[118] The next day, after advancing probably to within three or four miles of the Scotch border, Cromwell wrote to the Committee of Estates warning them of the consequence of a refusal to restore the two towns:

For the Right Honourable the Committee of Estates for the Kingdom of Scotland: These

RIGHT HONOURABLE,

Being upon my approach to the borders of the kingdom of Scotland, I thought fit to acquaint you of the reason thereof.

It's well known how injuriously the kingdom of England was lately invaded by the Army under Duke Hamilton, contrary to the Covenant and our leagues of amity, and against all the engagements of love and brotherhood between the two nations. And notwithstanding the pretence, of your late Declaration, published to take with the people of this kingdom, the Commons of England in Parliament assembled declared the said Army so

[116] *L. J.*, x, 517; *Parliamentary History*, xvii, 485. The two texts being slightly different, the former has been followed. The signature in the latter is "Oliver Cromwell." The summons was read, with other papers sent by Cromwell to Parliament, on Sept. 26. Carlyle, Letter LXX.

[117] Loudon to Cromwell, 15 Sept. *L. J.*, x, 518.

[118] Robert Watson wrote from the Castle 20 Sept.; "I was tould by the now commaunder in chiefe, Leiwtenant Generall Cromwell that his lordship [the earl of Northumberland] would take it as an acceptable service from any of his servants . . . Theire was quartered upon me 140 and upwardes, who remaind upon my sold charge two dayes and nights which to supply was noe small coast to me." *History of Northumberland* (1895), ii, 135.

entering as enemies to the kingdom; and those of England who should adhere to them, as traitors. And having received command to march with a considerable part of their Army, to oppose so great a violation of faith and justice; what a witness God, being appealed to,[119] hath borne, upon the engagement of the two Armies, against the unrighteousness of man, not only yourselves, but this kingdom, yea and a great part of the known world will, I trust, acknowledge, how dangerous a thing is it to wage an unjust war; much more, to appeal to God the Righteous Judge therein. We trust He will persuade you better by this manifest token of His displeasure, lest His hand be stretched out yet more against you, and your poor people also, if they will be deceived.

That which I am to demand of you is the restitution of the garrisons of Berwick and Carlisle into my hands, for the use of the Parliament and kingdom of England. If you deny me herein, I must make our appeal to God, and call upon Him for assistance, in what way He shall direct us; wherein we are, and shall be, so far from seeking the harm of the well-affected people of the kingdom of Scotland, that we profess as before the Lord, that (what difference an Army, necessitated in a hostile way to recover the ancient rights and inheritance of the kingdom under which they serve, can make) we shall use our endeavours to the utmost that the trouble may fall upon the contrivers and authors of this breach, and not upon the poor innocent people, who have been led and compelled into this action, as many poor souls now prisoners to us confess.

We thought ourselves bound in duty thus to expostulate with you, and thus to profess, to the end we may bear our integrity out before the world, and may have comfort in God, whatever the event be. Desiring your answer, I rest,

[Near Berwick] Your Lordships' humble servant,

September the 16th, 1648. O. Cromwell.[120]

Cromwell did not know at that time what he afterward learned, that his letter could not be delivered, since the Committee of Estates had been forced by the triumph of the Whiggamores to take refuge in Stirling. Keeping in touch with the various Scotch factions, he sent his letter to the Estates by three of his own men, who carried with them as well a letter of credence to the Marquis of Argyll, whom he addressed as an ally against the Estates:

For the Right Honourable the Lord Marquis of Argyle, and the rest of the well-affected Lords, Gentlemen, Ministers, and People now in arms in the Kingdom of Scotland: Present

My Lords and Gentlemen,

Being (in prosecution of the common enemy) advanced, with the army under my command, to the borders of Scotland, I thought

[119] On Preston Moor.

[120] Original in the Register House in Edinburgh, *State Papers*, no. 207; thence,

fit, to prevent any misapprehension or prejudice that might be raised thereupon, to send your Lordships these Gentlemen, Colonel Bright, Scoutmaster-General Rowe, and Mr. Stapylton, to acquaint you with the reasons thereof: concerning which I desire your Lordships to give them credence.

I remain, My Lords,

Your very humble servant,

Sept. 16, 1648. O. CROMWELL.[121]

Two days later, from his headquarters at a manor-house three or four miles south of Berwick, he sent a letter in reply to Loudon by that nobleman's own messengers to explain his position, both military and political, and his plans against "the common enemy":

To the Right Honourable the Earl of Loudon, Chancellor of the Kingdom of Scotland:

To be communicated to the Noblemen, Gentlemen, and Burgesses now in arms, who dissented in Parliament from the late Engagement against the King of England.

RIGHT HONOURABLE,

We received yours from Falkirk of the 15th September instant. We have had also a sight of your Instructions given to the Laird of Greenhead and Major Strahan, as also other two papers concerning the treaty between your Lordships and the enemy, wherein your care of the interest of the kingdom of England, for the delivery of their towns[122] unjustly taken from them, and desire to preserve the unity of both nations, appears. By which also we understand the posture you are in to oppose the enemies of the welfare and the peace of both the kingdoms, for which we bless God for His goodness to you, and rejoice to see the power of the kingdom of Scotland in a hopeful way to be invested in the hands of those who, we trust, are taught of God to seek His honour, and the comfort of His people.

And give us leave to say, as before the Lord, who knows the secret of all hearts, that, as we think one especial end of Providence in permitting the enemies of God and goodness in both kingdoms to rise to that height, and exercise such tyranny over His people, was to show the necessity of unity amongst those of both nations, so we hope and pray that the late glorious dispensation, in giving so happy success against your and our enemies in our victories, may be the foundation of union of the people of God in love and amity; and to that end we shall, God assisting, to the utmost of our power endeavour to perform what may be behind on our part, and when we shall, through any wilfulness, fail therein, let this profession rise up in judgment against us, as having been made in hypocrisy, a severe avenger of which God hath lately appeared, in His most righteous witnessing against the Army

Thurloe, i, 100. Pr. in *L. J.*, x, 517–18, somewhat altered, and in *Old Parl. Hist.* xvii, 486–7. Carlyle, Letter LXXII. Loudon's reply, Sept. 30, expressing willingness to help Cromwell is in *Old Parl. Hist.*, xviii, 28–9.

[121] Thurloe, *State Papers*, i, 100. Carlyle, Letter LXXI.

[122] Berwick and Carlisle, which by agreement in 1646–7 were not to be garrisoned except by consent of *both* Kingdoms.

under Duke Hamilton, invading us under specious pretences of piety and justice. We may humbly say, we rejoice with more trembling[123] than to dare to do so wicked a thing.

Upon our advance to Alnwick, we thought fit to send a good body of our horse to the borders of Scotland, and thereby a summons to the Garrison of Berwick; to which having received a dilatory answer, I desired a safe-convoy for Colonel Bright and the Scoutmaster[124]-General of this Army to go to the Committee of Estates in Scotland, who, I hope, will have the opportunity to be with your Lordships before this come to your hands, and, according as they are instructed, will let your Lordships in some measure (as well as we could in so much ignorance of your condition) know our affections to you. And understanding things more fully by yours, we now thought fit to make [you] this return.

The command we received, upon the defeat of Duke Hamilton, was, to prosecute this business until the enemy were put out of a condition or hope of growing into a new Army, and the garrisons of Berwick and Carlisle were reduced. Four regiments of our horse and some dragoons, who had followed the enemy into the south parts, being now come up; and this country not able to bear us, the cattle and old corn thereof having been wasted by Monro and the forces with him; the Governor of Berwick also victualling his garrison from Scotland side; and the enemy yet in so considerable a posture as by these gentlemen and your papers we understand, still prosecuting their former design, having gotten the advantage of Stirling Bridge, and so much of Scotland at their backs to enable them thereunto, and your Lordships' condition not being such, at present, as may compel them to submit to the honest and necessary things you have proposed to them for the good of both the kingdoms: we have thought fit, out of the sense of our duty to the commands laid upon us by those who have sent us, and to the end we might be in a posture more ready to give you assistance (and not be wanting to what we have made so large professions of), to advance into Scotland with the Army. And we trust, by the blessing of God, the common enemy will thereby the sooner be brought to a submission to you: and we thereby shall do what becomes us in order to the obtaining of our garrisons, engaging ourselves that, so soon as we shall know from you that the enemy shall yield to the things you have proposed to them, and we have our garrisons delivered to us, we shall forthwith depart out of your kingdom, and in the meantime be more tender towards the Kingdom of Scotland, in the point of charge, than if we were in our own native kingdom.

If we shall receive from you any desire of a more speedy advance, we shall readily yield compliance therewith, desiring also to hear from you how affairs stand. This being the result of a Council of War, I present it to you as the expression of their affections and of my own, who am,

My Lords,

Your most humble servant,
O. CROMWELL.[125]

Cheswick,
this 18th of September, 1648.

[123] "Rejoice with trembling," (Second Psalm).

[124] Thurloe had "Lieutenant-General."

[125] Thurloe, *State Papers*, i, 101; *L. J.*, x, 519–20; *Old Parl. Hist.* xvii, 492–95. Carlyle Letter LXXIII. Read in the House of Lords Sept. 26. *L. J.*, x, 512.

While he was thus engaged in preparing for his advance into Scotland, the Committee at Derby House repeated its order to Cromwell to take Berwick and Carlisle without fail. It added that Lindisfarne, or Holy Island, near by, must be watched with the greatest care to thwart a design of which it had notice, that the squadron which had rebelled against the Parliament and was now in the service of the Prince of Wales in Holland might attempt to seize it and aid the Scots, or at least hamper the movements of the Parliamentary army.[126] Parliament, which had watched the proceedings in the north with the greatest interest, adjourned on September 13 for a brief recess, having previously agreed to a new negotiation with the King and appointed fifteen commissioners to confer with him.[127] The Levellers and the Republicans like Ludlow had done their best to prevent the re-opening of communication with Charles and after the negotiations began they did their best to put an end to them. But Independents joined with Presbyterians to renew their efforts for a settlement, and with Holles and Vane at their head, the commissioners once more embarked upon their hopeless task.

Parliament had set a limit of forty days from September 18 for the new conversations; and Charles, liberated from his confinement in Carisbrooke, went to Newport to meet the commissioners, who presented to him the old Hampton Court proposals. The negotiation began inauspiciously, with Charles's refusal to accept the first of the proposals—that he should withdraw all of his declarations against the Parliament—though he presently consented to that proviso. That concession was, however, qualified by his stipulation that nothing agreed upon should be valid unless agreement was reached on every point. To that, as merely a device to delay a settlement, the Independents were opposed, but when debate on the issue took place in the Commons on September 26, they were outnumbered by the Presbyterians and did not venture to divide. The King's position made a most unfortunate impression on the army, and the regiments at Newcastle and before Berwick appealed to Fairfax in support of the petition of the London Levellers against further negotiations. To Fairfax at his new headquarters in St. Albans, Ireton, irritated by the situation at Newport, wrote to urge the purging of the House and even offered to throw up his commission.

To Cromwell these were minor matters. He doubtless felt that there was nothing to be hoped from an endeavor to come to terms with Charles, and he had, besides, the difficulties and responsibilities of his campaign to face. They were enough to absorb all his energies;

[126] Committee to Cromwell, Sept. 19, *Cal. S. P. Dom.* (1648–9), pp. 283–4. Extract in *Old Parl. Hist.*, xvii, 481.

[127] Full list in *Cal. S. P. Dom.* (1648–9), p. 277.

for, in addition to his negotiations with the Scots and his preparation to retake Berwick and Carlisle, he found that some of his own men had been guilty of the plundering for which he had so strongly denounced the Scots. Accordingly, on September 20, he issued a vigorous proclamation against such practices:[128]

PROCLAMATION

WHEREAS we are marching with the Parliament's Army into the kingdom of Scotland, in pursuance of the remaining part of the enemy who lately invaded the kingdom of England, and for the recovery of the garrisons of Berwick and Carlisle:

These are to declare that if any officer or soldier under my command shall take or demand any money, or shall violently take any horses, goods or victual, without order, or shall abuse the people in any sort, he shall be tried by a Council of War; and the said person so offending shall be punished according to the Articles of War made for the government of the army in the kingdom of England, which is death.

Each colonel, or other chief officer in every regiment is to transcribe a copy of this, and to cause the same to be delivered to each captain of his regiment; and every said captain of each respective troop and company is to publish the same to his troop or company, and to take a strict course that nothing be done contrary hereunto.

Given under my hand, this 20th September 1648,

CROMWELL.[129]

As for his other actions and his plans, they are best expressed in a long report to the Committee at Derby House written on that same day at Norham on the southern bank of the Tweed, and read in the Lords six days later:

To the Right Honourable the Committee of Lords and Commons at Derby House

MY LORDS AND GENTLEMEN,

I did, from Alnwick, write to Sir William Armyn[130] an account of our condition; and recommended to him divers particular considerations about your affairs here in the North, with desire of particular things to be done by your Lordships' appointment in order to the carrying-on of your affairs. I send you here enclosed a copy of the summons that was sent to Barwick when I was come as far as Alnwick; as also of a letter written to

[128] In a regiment raised by Colonel Wren in the bishoprick of Durham which had only recently joined the main army many men were guilty of plundering. They were cashiered and the horses stolen were returned. The whole regiment was ordered back to Northumberland. *Perfect Diurnall*, Oct. 2–9.

[129] In *Moderate Intelligencer*, Sept. 21–28; *Perfect Diurnall*, Sept. 25. Repr. in Rushworth, vii, 1274; *Cromwelliana*, p. 46; Carlyle (Lomas ed.), i, 366.

[130] *L. J.*, x, 512.

the Committee of Estates of Scotland: I mean those who we did presume were convened as Estates, and were the men that managed the business of the war. But there being, as I hear since, none such; the Earl of Roxburgh and some others having deserted, so that they are not able to make a Committee; I believe the said letter is suppressed,[131] and retained in the hands of Colonel Bright and Mr. William Rowe, for whom we obtained a safe convoy to go to the Estates of that Kingdom with our said letter; the Governor of Barwick's answer to our summons leading us thereunto. By advantage whereof, we did instruct them to give all assurance to the Marquis of Argyle and the honest party in Scotland (who we heard were gathered together in a considerable Body about Edinburgh, to make opposition to the Earl of Lanerick, Monroe, and their Armies), of our good affection to them. Wherewith they went the 16th of this month.

Upon the 17th of this month Sir Andrew Car and Major Straughan, with divers other Scottish Gentlemen, brought me this enclosed letter, signed by the Lord Chancellor of Scotland, as your Lordships will see. They likewise showed me their Instructions, and a paper containing the matter of their Treaty with Lanerick and Monroe; as also an Expostulation upon Lanerick's breach with them, in falling upon Argyle and his men, contrary to agreement, wherein the Marquis of Argyle hardly escaped, they having hold of him, but seven-hundred of his men were killed and taken.[132] These papers also I send here enclosed to your Lordships.

So soon as those Gentlemen came to me, I called a Council of War; the result whereof was the letter directed to the Lord Chancellor; a copy whereof your Lordships have also here enclosed, which I delivered to Sir Andrew Car and Major Straughan; with which they returned upon the 18th, being the next day.

Upon private discourse with the gentlemen, I do find the condition of their affairs and their Army to be thus: The Earl of Lanerick, the Earl of Crawford-Lindsay, Monroe, and their Army, hearing of our advance, and understanding the condition and endeavours of their adversaries, marched with all speed to get the possession of Sterling-Bridge; that so they might have three parts of four of Scotland at their backs, to raise men, and to enable themselves to carry on their designs, and are about 5,000 foot and 2,500 horse. The Earl of Leven, who is chosen General; the Marquis of Argyle, with the honest lords and gentlemen, David Lesley being the Lieutenant-General: having about 7,000 foot, but very weak in horse, lie about six miles on this side the Enemy. I do hear that their infantry consists of men who come to them out of conscience, and generally are of the godly people of that nation, which they express by their piety and devotion in their quarters; and indeed I hear they are a very godly and honest body of men.

I think it is not unknown to your Lordships what directions I have received from you for the prosecution of our late victory, whereof I shall be bold to remember a clause of your letter; which was, "That I should "prosecute the remaining party in the North, and not leave any of "them (wherever they shall go) to be a beginning of a new Army; "nor cease to pursue the

[131] Not 'suppressed,' though it could not be received except unofficially.
[132] Bishop Guthry's *Memoirs*.

victory till I finish and fully complete it, with "their rendition of those Towns of Barwick and Carlisle, which most "unjustly, and against all obligations, and the treaties (then) in force, "they surprised and garrisoned against us."

In order whereunto, I marched to the Borders of Scotland, where I found the country so exceedingly harassed and impoverished by Monroe and the Forces with him, that the country was in no sort able to bear us on the English side, but we must have necessarily ruined both your Army and the subjects of this Kingdom, who had not bread for a day, if we had continued among them. In prosecution of your orders, and in answer to the necessity of your friends in Scotland, and their desires, and considering the necessity of marching into Scotland, to prevent the Governor of Barwick from putting provisions into his Garrison on Scotland side (whereof he is at present in some want, as we are informed), I marched a good part of the Army over Tweed yesterday about noon, the residue being to come after as conveniently as we may.

Thus have I given to your Lordships an account of our present condition and engagement, and having done so, I must discharge my duty in remembering to your Lordships the desires formerly expressed in my letters to Sir William Armyn and Sir John Evelyn, for supplies; and in particular for that of shipping to lie upon these coasts, who may furnish us with ammunition or other necessaries wheresoever God shall lead us; there being extreme difficulty to supply us by land, without great and strong convoys, which will weary-out and destroy our horses and cannot well come to us if the Tweed be up, without going very far about.

Having laid these things before you, I rest, my Lords,

Norham, Your most humble servant,

September 20th, 1648. O. CROMWELL.

P.S. Whilst we are here, I wish there be no neglect of the business in Cumberland and Westmorland. I have sent orders both into Lancashire and the Horse before Pontefract. I should be glad your Lordships would second them, and those other considerations expressed in my desires to Sir William Armyn thereabouts.[133]

This with the enclosures[134] were presented to Parliament on September 28th and ordered printed. Cromwell's actions were approved and it was voted that he was to be ordered to join the party which had been opposed to Hamilton.[135]

The next day Cromwell wrote to the new Committee of Estates an apology for the recent plundering:

133 *Transactions of several matters between Lt. Gen. Cromwell and the Scots . . .*; Repr. in *Old Parl. Hist.*, xvii, 481; *L. J.*, x, 516–17. Pub. by order of the House of Commons of Sept. 28. Carlyle, App. 13.

134 See above.

135 *L. J.*, x, 516–20; *Cal. S. P. Dom.* (1648–9), p. 290.

For the Right Honourable the Committee of Estates of the Kingdom of Scotland, at Edinburgh: These:

RIGHT HONOURABLE,

We perceive that there was, upon our advance to the Borders, the last Lord's Day,[136] a very disorderly carriage by some horse, who, without order, did steal over the Tweed, and plundered some places in the kingdom of Scotland, and since that, some stragglers have been alike faulty, to the wrong of the inhabitants, and to our very great grief of heart.

I have been as diligent as I can to find out the men who have done the wrong, and I am still in the discovery thereof, and I trust it shall appear to you that there shall be nothing wanting on my part that may testify how much we abhor such things, and to the best of my information I cannot find the least guilt of the fact to lie upon the regiments of this army, but upon some of the Northern horse, who have not been under our discipline and government, until just that we came into these parts.

I have commanded those forces away back again into England, and I hope the exemplarity of justice will testify for us our great detestation of the fact. For the remaining forces, which are of our old regiments, we may engage for them their officers will keep them from doing any such things, and we are confident that, saving victual, they shall not take anything from the inhabitants, and in that also they shall be so far from being their own carvers, as that they shall submit to have provisions ordered and proportioned by the consent, and with the direction, of the committees and gentlemen of the country, and not otherwise, if they please to be assisting to us therein.

I thought fit, for the preventing of misunderstanding, to give your Lordships this account; and rest, My Lords,

Your most humble servant,

Norham, the 21st of September 1648.

O. CROMWELL.[137]

The critical moment of Cromwell's visit to Scotland had now arrived. By September 21, in spite of the refusal of Berwick to surrender, the entire Parliamentary army, including Lambert's command, had crossed the Tweed. That night Cromwell made his headquarters at Lord Mordington's house, two miles north of Berwick, within the Scotch borders, and the next day—Friday the 21st—hearing that Argyll, Lord Elcho, Sir Charles Erskine and Sir John Scot were coming to pay their respects, he rode out to meet them.

[136] Sept. 17th.

[137] Original, dated and signed by Cromwell, is in the Register House in Edinburgh (*State Papers*, no. 209); Pr. in Thurloe, i, 103; Facsimile in W. B. Sanders, *Facs. of National MSS of Scotland*, ii, xcix. Summary in *34th Rept. Deputy Keeper of Public Records*, App. p. 305–6 (1873). Carlyle, Letter LXXIV. A reply from Loudon, sent with Cromwell's next letter, to Lenthall, was pr. in *Moderate Intelligencer*, Oct. 5–12, and repr. in *Cromwelliana*, p. 47.

The two parties soon came to terms. Argyll promised to send orders from the Committee of Estates the next day to Lodovic Leslie to surrender Berwick. Elcho and Scot were accordingly despatched with this message, but Leslie insisted on first sending for orders to his superior officer, the Earl of Lanark[138] who had joined Monro and the remnants of Hamilton's army at Haddington. It was with the greatest reluctance that Lanark brought himself to treat with Argyll to lay down his arms and to order Leslie to give up Berwick, but he had virtually no alternative and by September 26 he consented to what he considered a humiliating surrender.

While Lanark was bringing himself to this conclusion, Cromwell, awaiting his answer to Leslie, sent Lambert with most of the horse toward Edinburgh to encourage the Whiggamore leaders and remained with three or four regiments to block up Berwick.[139] When Lanark finally gave way, and, under his orders, Leslie marched out of Berwick on September 30, Cromwell immediately took possession of the place, sent Colonel Bright to receive the surrender of Carlisle, and prepared to march to Edinburgh. But before he left Berwick he wrote another long report of his proceedings and plans to Parliament:

[*To the Honourable William Lenthall, Speaker of the House of Commons: These*]

SIR,

I have formerly represented to the Committee at Derby House,[140] how far I have prosecuted your business in relation to the commands I did receive from them, to wit: that I having sent a party of horse with a summons to Berwick, and a letter to the Committee of Estates, which I supposed did consist of the Earl of Lanerick and his participates, and a letter of kindness and affection to the Marquis of Argyle and the well-affected party in arms at Edinburgh, with credence to Colonel Bright and Mr. William Rowe, Scoutmaster of the Army, To let them know upon what grounds and with what intentions we came into their kingdom, and how that, in the mean time, the Marquis of Argyle and the rest at Edinburgh had sent Sir Andrew Carr, Laird of Greenhead, and Major Straughan to me, with a letter, and papers of instructions, expressing their good affection to the kingdom of England, and disclaiming the late Engagement; together with my answer to the said letters and papers, duplicates of all which I sent to the Committee at Derby House, and therefore forebear to trouble you with the things themselves. I think now fit to give you an account, what further progress has been made in your business.

The two Armies being drawn up, the one under Lanerick and Munro at

138 A letter in the Braye MSS (*Hist. MSS. Comm. Rept.* 10, App. VI) says Cromwell and Argyll went to the walls of Berwick and the latter had private conversation with Leslie.

139 *Perfect Diurnall*, Oct. 2–9.

140 Letter, September, 20.

Stirling, and the other under the Earl of Leven and Lieutenant-General Lesley betwixt that and Edinburgh; the heads of the two Armies being upon treaties concerning their own affairs, and I having given (as I hoped) sufficient satisfaction concerning the justice of your cause, and the clearness fo my intentions in entering that kingdom,—did (upon Thursday being the one and twentieth of September, and two days before the Tweed being fordable), march over Tweed at Norham into Scotland, with four regiments of horse, and some dragoons, and six regiments of foot, and there quartered; my head-quarters being at the Lord Mordington's House.

Where, hearing of the Marquis of Argyle, the Lord Elcho, and some others, were coming to me from the Committee of Estates assembled at Edinburgh, I went, on Friday the two and twentieth of September, some part of the way to wait upon his Lordship. Who, when he was come to his quarters, delivered me a letter, of which this enclosed is a copy, signed by the Lord Chancellor, by warrant of the Committee of Estates. And after some time spent in giving and receiving mutual satisfaction concerning each other's integrity and clearness (wherein I must be bold to testify for that noble Lord the Marquis, the Lord Elcho, and the other gentlemen with him, that I have found nothing in them but what becomes Christians and men of honour), the next day it was resolved, that the command of the Committee of Estates to the Governor of Berwick, for rendering the town, should be sent to him, by the Lord Elcho and Colonel Scott, which accordingly was done. But he, pretending that he had not received the command of that place from those that now demanded it of him, desired liberty to send to the Earl of Lanerick, engaging himself then to give his positive answer, and intimating it should be satisfactory.

Whilst these things were transacting, I ordered Major-General Lambert to march towards Edinburgh, with six regiments of horse and a regiment of dragoons, who accordingly did so, and quartered in East Louthian, within six miles of Edinburgh; the foot lying in his rear at Coperspeth and thereabout.[141]

Upon Friday, the 29th of September, came an order from the Earl of Lanerick, and divers other Lords of his party, requiring the Governor of Berwick to march out of the town; which accordingly he did, on Saturday the last of September, at which time I entered; having placed a garrison there for your use. The Governor would fain have capitulated for the English but we, having this advantage upon him, would not hear of it: so that they are submitted to your mercy, and are under the consideration of Sir Arthur Heselrige, who (I believe) will give you a good account of them; and who has already turned out the malignant Mayor, and put an honest man in his room.

I have also received an order for Carlisle, and have sent Colonel Bright, with horse and foot to receive it, Sir Andrew Carr and Colonel Scott being gone with him to require an observance of the order; there having been a treaty and an agreement betwixt the two parties in arms in Scotland, to disband all forces, except fifteen-hundred horse and foot under the Earl of Leven, which are to be kept up to see all remaining forces disbanded.

And having some other things to desire from the Committee of Estates at

[141] What follows is published as a fragment in the Newspapers.

Edinburgh for your service, I am myself going thitherward this day; and so soon as I shall be able to give you a further account thereof, I shall do it. In the mean time, I make it my desire that the garrison of Berwick (into which I have placed a regiment of foot, and shall be attended also by a regiment of horse) may be provided for, and that Sir Arthur Heselrige may receive commands to supply it with guns and ammunition from Newcastle, and be otherwise enabled by you to furnish this garrison with all other necessaries, according as a place of that importance will require. Desiring that these mercies may beget trust and thankfulness to God the only author of them, and an improvement of them to His glory and the good of this poor kingdom, I rest,

Your most humble servant,

Berwick,
October 2, 1648. O. CROMWELL.[142]

To Fairfax, at army headquarters, he sent a duplicate of this report and a short note concerning some military details:

For his Excellency the Lord General Fairfax, at St. Albans: These

MAY IT PLEASE YOUR EXCELLENCY,

I received your late directions with your commissions, how they shall be disposed, which I hope I shall pursue to your satisfaction.

I having sent an account to the House of Commons, concerning affairs here, am bold (being straitened in time) to present you with a duplicate thereof, which I trust will give you satisfaction. I hope there is a very good understanding between the honest party of Scotland and us here, and better than some would have. Sir, I beg of your Excellency to write to Sir A. Haselrige to take care of Berwick; he having all things necessary for the garrison, at Newcastle; which is left destitute of all, and may be lost if this be not [done]. I beg of your Lordship a commission to be speeded to him. I have no more at present; but rest, My Lord,

Your most humble servant,

Berwick,
October 2d, 1648. O. CROMWELL.[143]

THE ADVANCE INTO SCOTLAND, OCTOBER 2–9, 1648

Leaving Berwick on Monday, October 2nd, Cromwell arrived the next day at Seaton, the home of the Earl of Winton, where Lambert had established headquarters, while Argyll continued his journey to Edinburgh six miles away.[144] The new Committee of Estates which,

[142] *Tanner MS.* lvii. 330, Signed. (in Cary's *Memorials* ii. 18); Newspapers (*Cromwelliana*, p. 48). *Old Parl. Hist.* xviii, 25–28 from orig. ed. pr. by Husbands, by order of the House, Oct. 10. Carlyle, Letter LXXV.

[143] Holograph original is in the *Sloane MSS*, 1519, f. 183; thence Carlyle, Letter LXXVI.

[144] Margetts to Browne, Oct. 3, *Hist. MSS. Comm. Rept.* 10, App. IV, (Braye MSS), p. 171.

encouraged by Lambert's proximity, Argyll and the Whiggamores had constituted, sent two representatives on Wednesday to invite Cromwell to enter the city. He accepted the invitation at once and was welcomed by the Earl of Leven, Argyll, the Earl of Cassell, Lord Burghley, David Leslie, Lord Warriston and many others, "with great demonstrations of joy" and "all the solemnity due the deliverer of their country."[145]

Established at the house of the Countess of Moray in the Canongate, he supped that evening with Argyll and Johnston of Warriston.[146] The next day, October 5, feeling that the provisions of the treaty with Hamilton's party were not sufficiently rigorous, he presented to the Committee of Estates a formal demand for the exclusion in the future of all "Engagers" from offices of trust in Scotland:

For the Right Honourable the Committee of Estates for the Kingdom of Scotland: These

RIGHT HONOURABLE,

I shall ever be ready to bear witness of your Lordships' forwardness to do right to the kingdom of England, in restoring the garrisons of Berwick and Carlisle; and having received so good a pledge of your resolutions to maintain amity and a good understanding between the Kingdoms of England and Scotland, it makes me not to doubt but that your Lordships will further grant what in justice and reason may be demanded.

I can assure your Lordships, that the kingdom of England did foresee that wicked design of the malignants in Scotland to break all engagements of faith and honesty between the nations, and to take from the kingdom of England the towns of Berwick and Carlisle. And although they could have prevented the loss of those considerable towns, without breach of the treaty, by laying forces near unto them, yet such was the tenderness of the Parliament of England not to give the least suspicion of a breach with the kingdom of Scotland, that they did forbear to do anything therein. And it is not unknown to your Lordships, when the malignants had gotten the power of your kingdom, how they protected and employed our English malignants, though demanded by our Parliament, and possessed themselves of those towns, and with what violence and unheard-of cruelties they raised an Army, and began a war, and invaded the kingdom of England, and endeavoured, to the uttermost of their power, to engage both kingdoms in a perpetual quarrel, and what blood they have spilt in our kingdom, and what great loss and prejudice was brought upon our nation, even to the endangering the total ruin thereof.

And although God did, by a most mighty and strong hand, and that in a wonderful manner, destroy their designs, yet it is apparent that the same ill-affected spirit still remains; and that divers persons of great quality and power, who were either the contrivers, actors, or abettors of the late unjust

[145] *Perfect Diurnall*, Oct. 16; Ludlow, i, 203; Clarendon, xi, 99.
[146] Guthry, *Memoirs*, p. 297; *True Account.*

war made upon the kingdom of England, are now in Scotland, who undoubtedly do watch for all advantages and opportunities to raise dissensions and divisions between the Nations.

Now forasmuch as I am commanded to prosecute the remaining part of the Army that invaded the kingdom of England, wheresoever it should go, to prevent the like miseries: And considering that divers of that Army are retired into Scotland, and that some of the heads of those malignants were raising new forces in Scotland to carry on the same design, and that they will certainly be ready to do the like upon all occasions of advantage: And forasmuch as the kingdom of England hath lately received so great damage by the failing of the kingdom of Scotland in not suppressing malignants and incendiaries as they ought to have done, and by suffering such persons to be put in places of great trust in the kingdom, who by their interest in the Parliament and the countries, brought the kingdom of Scotland so far as they could, by unjust Engagement, to invade and make war upon their brethren of England:

My Lords, I hold myself obliged, in prosecution of my duty and instructions, to demand, that your Lordships will give assurance in the name of the kingdom of Scotland, that you will not admit or suffer any that have been active in, or consenting to, the said Engagement against England, or have lately been in Arms at Stirling or elsewhere in the maintenance of that Engagement, to be employed in any public place or trust whatsoever. And this is the least security I can demand. I have received an order from both Houses of the Parliament of England,[147] which I hold fit to communicate to your Lordships, whereby you will understand the readiness of the kingdom of England to assist you who were dissenters from the Invasion, and I doubt not but your Lordships will be as ready to give such further satisfaction as they in their wisdoms shall find cause to desire.

Your Lordships' most humble servant,

Edinburgh,
October 5th, 1648. O. CROMWELL.[148]

While Cromwell was thus achieving a bloodless triumph in Scotland, the Houses had reassembled and the negotiations with Charles had dragged on. Parliament was, indeed, all but in abeyance for the time being. The average number of peers present in August had been eleven, in September that number sank to nine, and during that month the highest division in the Commons revealed scarcely more than a hundred members in their seats. Interest centered wholly in the northern operations and in the negotiations with the King. The latter had followed their usual course, but with certain new and disturbing elements. Though in the last days of August the Presbyterians had

[147] Votes of September 28th; *C. J.*, vi. 37; 'received the day we entered Edinburgh' (Rushworth, *ubi supra*).

[148] Printed by Order of Parliament in *Lieut. General Cromwels letter to the Speaker of the House of Commons concerning his proceedings in Scotland. With a letter . . . to the Committee of Estates. . . .* Repr. in *Old Parl. Hist.* xliii, 70–72; Carlyle, Letter LXXVII.

pushed through an ordinance in Parliament establishing an unlimited Presbyterian system for England, their representatives at Newport were so fearful of the danger of military intervention, it is said, that Holles and Grimston threw themselves on their knees before Charles begging him to come to terms before the army could intervene. On the other hand, Vane pleaded for the tolerant *Heads of the Proposals*; and Charles retorted with a plan for granting the purchasers of bishops' lands leases for ninety-nine years and a three-year Presbyterian experiment with limited toleration for the sects. Again he agreed to give up the militia to Parliament for ten years, leave Ireland to the Houses and give the City control of its armed forces and the Tower.

Those proposals were not acceptable to the Commons, which, on October 2, the day that Cromwell left Berwick on his advance into Scotland, rejected them without a division. Failing to meet the demands of Parliament and despairing of accommodation, the King planned an escape, despite his parole, and meanwhile enlarged his concessions. He agreed to bishops limited by presbyters, to give up the militia for twenty years and to settle Ireland in accordance with the decision of Parliament. With such proposals and counter-proposals the fruitless discussions went on, and though they were extended for more than the forty days originally voted, there appeared less and less chance of an agreement, if either side had ever hoped for one.[149]

Nor were these all of the negotiations of the time. In these very days there was being signed at Munster the great Treaty of Westphalia which, after seven years of negotiation, brought to an end the Thirty Years' War and produced a new alignment of European forces from which the English Royalists, the Queen in particular, hoped to find some help for English monarchy. At the same time there were carried on in Edinburgh a series of conversations between the English leaders, Cromwell, Lambert and Haselrig, and the Scotch Presbyterians headed by Argyll and Johnston of Warriston,[150] from which each side hoped to derive some advantage for its cause. At these meetings three Presbyterian ministers, Robert Blair, but lately made moderator of the Scotch General Assembly, David Dickson and James Guthry, were present,[151] and Blair recorded his opinion of Cromwell at this time. Whatever impression Cromwell made upon his English fellow-countrymen, he did not win the entire confidence of the Scots. As the *Life* of Blair relates:

"When they came to Cromwell he had a long discourse to them with a fair flourish of words, and sometimes tears, taking God to be a witness of

149 *C. J.; L. J.*
150 Rushworth, vii, 1295.
151 *Memoirs of Henry Guthry* (1702), p. 248–9.

their sincerity and good intentions, etc. . . . Blair put three questions to Cromwell: 1. What was his opinion of monarchical government? To which Cromwell answered that he was for monarchical government, and that in the person of this King and his posterity. 2. What was his opinion anent the toleration? Answered that he was altogether against toleration. 3. What was his opinion anent the government of the Kirk? To this Cromwell answered: 'O now, Mr. Blair, you article me too severely, you must pardon me that I give you not a present answer to this; I must have some time to deliberate.' Thus he shifted to answer that query, because he had often professed to Mr. Blair that he was for Independency. After they came out from Cromwell, Mr. Dickson, rubbing his elbow, said 'I am very glad to hear this man speak as he does.' Mr. Blair replied, 'And do you believe him?' 'If you knew him as well as I do, you would not believe one word he says. He is an egregious dissembler and a great liar. Away with him, he is a greeting [weeping] devil.' "[152]

That opinion was not confined to Blair. Montrose believed that at this moment Cromwell entered into agreement with Argyll to destroy the monarchy. "Of this," Montrose went on to say, "Cromwell on his return to England was wont to brag among his party far more than of his victory at Preston."[153] To that Clarendon added his testimony:

"Whoever considers the wariness in the wording and timing this protestation [of the Scotch Parliament just before the King's execution], the best end whereof could be no other than the keeping the King always in prison, and so governing without him in both kingdoms, (which was thought to have been the purpose and agreement of Cromwell and Arguyle when they parted), must conclude that both the commissioners and they who sent them laboured and considered more what they were to say in the future, than what they were to do to prevent the present mischieve they seemed to apprehend."[154]

Whatever took place in those unrecorded conversations, Loudon assured Cromwell in writing on Friday, October 6, that the Estates had accepted the terms set out in his letter to them.[155] Realizing that further resistance was useless and that Cromwell was in command of the situation, Monro agreed to disband his troops, but the Scots not under Argyll's influence were angry. Leslie, who had greeted Cromwell formally on his arrival and who gave the English officers an equally formal dinner the evening they left Edinburgh, otherwise stayed conspicuously away from him.[156] Monro's soldiers were even less restrained in their hostility. As a contemporary observer records,

[152] William Row (Blair's son-in-law), *Life of Robert Blair*, (edited by Thomas McCrie for the Wodrow Society, 1848), p. 210.

[153] Wishart, *Memoirs of Montrose* (1893), p. 223.

[154] Clarendon, *History*, xii, 10.

[155] In *Old Parl. Hist.*, xviii, 72–4.

[156] Margetts to Brown, Oct. 10. *Hist. Mss. Comm. Rept.* 10, App. VI, p. 172.

"Gnashing their teeth" and threatening to kill Cromwell and Lambert, they stole horses from the visiting officers and soldiers and so abused the English that they were afraid to walk the streets or even to lie in their beds. Despite his agreement with Argyll and the Estates, it was apparent that Cromwell and his men were in a hostile country.

In this unfriendly atmosphere Cromwell departed from Edinburgh on the evening of Saturday, October 7, after Argyll had taken him and his officers to view the Castle and Leslie had given them a banquet there. The new Committee of Estates, now dominated by the Argyll faction, persuaded him to leave two regiments of horse and two troops of dragoons at Seaton, under command of Lambert, whose "discreet, humble, ingenious, sweet and civil deportment" had gained him "more huge and ingenious respect and interest from the general parties" than Cromwell "to whom went the honour of the occasion."[157]

From Edinburgh Cromwell went to Dalhousie where, on the next day, he wrote a letter of recommendation for Colonel Montgomery whose proposal to sell two thousand of the "common prisoners" to the King of Spain had Cromwell's approval:

For the Honourable William Lenthall, Esquire, Speaker of the Honourable House of Commons: These

SIR,

Upon the desire of divers noblemen and others of the kingdom of Scotland, I am bold to become a suitor to you on the behalf of this gentleman, the bearer, Colonel Robert Montgomery, son of the Earl of Eglinton, whose faithfulness to you in the late troubles may render him worthy of a far greater favour than I shall, at this time, desire for him: for I can assure you, that there is not a gentleman of that kingdom that appeared more active against the late invaders of England than himself.

Sir, it's desired that you would please to grant him an order for two-thousand of the common prisoners that were of Duke Hamilton's Army. You will have very good security that they shall not for the future trouble you: he will ease you of the charge of keeping them, as speedily as any other way you can dispose of them; besides their being in a friend's hands, so as there need be no fear of their being ever employed against you.

Sir, what favour you shall please to afford the gentleman will very much oblige many of your friends of the Scottish nation; and particularly

Your most humble servant,

Dalhousie, near Edinburgh,
Oct. 8, 1648.

O. CROMWELL.[158]

[157] Margetts to Brown, Oct. 3, *Ibid.*, pp. 171–72.

[158] Original in *Tanner MSS*, lvii, 346. Pr. in Cary, *Memorials*, vi, 57; Carlyle, Letter LXXVIII. Mentioned in Henfrey, *Numismata Cromwelliana*, p. 182. Read in Parliament, Oct. 21, *C. J.*, vi, 57.

It was a characteristic transaction on Cromwell's part. Such a policy had been carried out with the Welsh prisoners; it was to be adopted in Ireland; and among the curious anomalies of history is the fact that a leader and a party so devoted to liberty of the individual could be so ruthless in their disposal of their prisoners. In this case it proved difficult to fill Montgomery's quota. Many of the prisoners had been "engaged to go to foreign plantations"; others had been released to go to their homes in Scotland to save their keep. Montgomery finally managed to get his 2,000 together, but, failing to receive the promised remittance from Spain, offered the men to France; but that negotiation was broken off by the recall of the French ambassador after the execution of the King; and what became of the unfortunate men we do not know.

The day following his letter recommending Montgomery to Lenthall, still at Dalhousie, Cromwell wrote again to the Speaker, this time a formal report, enclosing a copy of his letter of October 5 to the Committee of Estates and Loudon's reply, so bringing his account of events up to the date of his letter:

To the Honourable William Lenthall, Esquire, Speaker of the Honourable House of Commons: These

SIR,

In my last, wherein I gave you an account of my despatch of Colonel Bright to Carlisle, after the rendition of Berwick, I acquainted you with my intentions to go to the headquarters of my horse at the Earl of Wynton's, within six miles of Edinburgh; that from thence I might represent to the Committee of Estates what I had further to desire in your behalf.

The next day after I came thither, I received an invitation from the Committee of Estates to come to Edinburgh, they sending to me the Lord Kirkcudbright and Major-General Holborn[159] for that purpose; with whom I went the same day, being Wednesday 4th of this instant October. We fell into consideration, what was fit further to insist upon. And being sensible that the late agreement between the Committee of Estates and the Earls of Crawford, Glencarn, and Lanerick, did not sufficiently answer my instructions, which was, to disenable them from being in power to raise new troubles to England: therefore I held it my duty, not to be satisfied only with the disbanding of them, but considering their power and interest, I thought it necessary to demand concerning them and all their abettors, according to the contents of the paper here enclosed.

Wherein (having received that very day your votes for giving them further assistance) I did in the close thereof acquaint them there with it; reserving such further satisfaction to be given by the kingdom of Scotland, as the Parliament of England should in their wisdom see cause to desire. The Committee of Estates sent the Earl of Cassilis, Lord Warriston, and two gentlemen more to me, to receive what I had to offer unto them, which upon

[159] James Holborne. He had had command of a regiment of foot in Essex's army.

Thursday I delivered. Upon Friday I received by the said persons this enclosed answer, which is the original itself.

Having proceeded thus far as a soldier, and I trust, by the blessing of God, not to your disservice; and having laid the business before you, I pray God direct you to do further as may be for His glory, the good of the nation wherewith you are intrusted, and the comfort and encouragement of the saints of God in both kingdoms and all the world over. I do think the affairs of Scotland are in a thriving posture, as to the interest of honest men: and [Scotland is] like to be a better neighbour to you now than when the great pretenders to Covenant, religion and treaties (I mean Duke Hamilton, the Earls of Lauderdale, Traquair, Carnegy, and their confederates), had the power in their hands. I dare say that that party, with their pretences, had not only, through the treachery of some in England (who have cause to blush), endangered the whole State and kingdom of England; but also brought Scotland into such a condition, as that no honest man who had the fear of God, or a conscience of religion, the just ends of the covenant and treaties, could have a being in that kingdom. But God, who is not to be mocked or deceived, and is very jealous when His Name and religion are made use of to carry on impious designs, hath taken vengeance of such profanity, even to astonishment and admiration. And I wish from the bottom of my heart, it may cause all to tremble and repent, who have practised the like, to the blaspheming of His Name, and the destruction of His people; so as they may never presume to do the like again! And I think it is not unseasonable for me to take the humble boldness to say thus much at this time.

All the enemy's forces in Scotland are now disbanded. The Committee of Estates have declared against all of that party's sitting in Parliament.[160] Good elections are made in divers places, of such as dissented from and opposed the late wicked Engagement; and they are now raising a force of about 4000 horse and foot, which until they can complete, they have desired me to leave them two regiments of horse and two troops of dragoons. Which accordingly I have resolved, conceiving I had warrant by your late votes so to do, and have left Major-General Lambert to command them.

I have received, and so have the officers with me, many honours and civilities from the Committee of Estates, the City of Edinburgh, and ministers; with a noble entertainment, which we may not own as done to us, but as your servants. I am now marching towards Carlisle, and I shall give you such further accounts of your affairs as there shall be occasion.

I am, Sir,

Your humble servant,

Dalhousie, Oct. 9th, 1648. OLIVER CROMWELL.[161]

PONTEFRACT, OCTOBER 9–NOVEMBER 16, 1648

From Dalhousie Cromwell marched southwest into England and the next news of him came from Carlisle where he wrote again to Parliament:

[160] Of Scotland.

[161] *Lieut. General Cromwells letter to the Speaker . . . concerning his proceedings in Scotland. With a letter . . . to the Committee of Estates and the answer thereto.* Carlyle, Letter LXXIX.

[*To William Lenthall, Speaker of the House of Commons?*]

Relating the delivery of the city and citadel of Carlisle. Carlisle, October 14, 1648.[162]

Cromwell had now performed his task. He had beaten the Scots' army at Preston, driven them from England; compelled the surrender or disbandment of their remaining forces; and come to an arrangement with Argyll and Johnston of Warriston, which, whatever its nature, was regarded as enough to cost them their lives a dozen years later when Charles II was restored, as being one of the principal steps in the events which brought his father to the scaffold. There remained to him only to compel the surrender of the few remaining strongholds which were not yet in the hands of Parliament, and to this task he now addressed himself.

From Carlisle the army turned eastward toward Newcastle. On the way, Cromwell, Haselrig and the Cumberland Committee ordered the defences of Cockermouth Castle and Appleby to be "slighted";[163] and on October 17, he and his officers were welcomed at Newcastle where, two days later, they were given a banquet by the mayor.[164] This was not the only honor offered him. On that same day Sir Henry Mildmay moved in the Commons that for his unparalleled services a jewel worth £800 be given Cromwell, but the motion was laid aside on the ground that the soldiers' necessities were too great to spend such a sum in such fashion.[165]

Late in the evening of the 20th he reached Durham[166] where he spent the next day in trying cases of misdemeanor among the soldiers. There that night he received a request from the York Committee to reduce Pontefract which still held out for Charles. Replying that two regiments of foot and two of horse were on their way, he sent for three troops of Derbyshire dragoons to meet him there and promised that he would come as soon as possible. The next day being Sunday, there was a Day of Thanksgiving held for the success in Scotland and Monday was spent in a council of war, where, among other things, a soldier was condemned to be shot for plundering during the Scotch expedition. On Tuesday he left with Haselrig for Sir Henry Vane's seat, Barnard Castle, where the northern counties had arranged to have a meeting to consider the formation of an Association.[167] There he signed a commission for a man who was to become,

[162] Read in the House Oct. 20. *C. J.*, vi, 57; *Perfect Diurnall*, Oct. 20; Whitelock, *Memorials*, p. 343; *Old Parl. Hist.*, xviii, 84.

[163] Rushworth, vii, 1306.

[164] *Perfect Diurnall*, 30 Oct., 1648.

[165] *Old Parl. Hist.*, xviii, 82.

[166] *Perfect Diurnall*, 30 Oct., 1648.

[167] *Ibid.*

in 1675, the founder of the town of Salem in the province of New Jersey:

To John Fenwick, Major: These

You are hereby ordered and required to command as Major under Colonel Thomas Barwis in his regiment of horse which was lately raised in the county of Westmoreland and is to assist the garrison of Carlisle. You are to exercise the officers and soldiers under your command according to the discipline of war. And they are hereby required to yield obedience unto you a major of the said regiment. And all this you are authorized unto, until the pleasure of the Parliament or the Lord General be known. Given under my hand and seal at Bernard Castle this 24th of Oct. 1648.

O. CROMWELL.[168]

He was, apparently, engaged in the formation of a garrison for Carlisle, for on the next day he signed an order for the colonel under whom Fenwick was to serve to proceed there and take up his duties:

To Colonel Thomas Barwis

Ordering him to repair to Carlisle and take command of the regiment of horse lately raised in Westmorland, employing the said regiment for the service of the garrison of Carlisle, and the security of those parts, and for the quelling of all insurrections in Westmorland and Cumberland; and acting under the orders of Sir Arthur Hasilrige. Bernard Castle, Oct. 25, 1648.[169]

On that same day the representatives of the four northern counties sent a report to advise Parliament of the results of the Barnard Castle conference and what they considered necessary for the garrisons of Berwick and Carlisle.[170] The safety of that district thus secured, Cromwell probably began his journey southward again on October 26, for on the 28th he had reached Boroughbridge, whence he wrote to Lenthall in behalf of Lieutenant-Colonel Cholmley:

For the Honourable William Lenthall, Esquire, Speaker to the House of Commons: These

SIR,

I do not often trouble you in particular businesses; but I shall be bold now, upon the desire of a worthy Gentleman, Lieutenant-Colonel Cholmley, to entreat your favour on his behalf.

[168] Original in the possession of the New Jersey Historical Society, Transcript, with a facsimile of the signature, in the *Proceedings* of the Society, N. S. xiv, 512–13. Cp. *Newark* (N. J.) *Sunday Call*, July 14, 1929.

[169] Summary in Lomas-Carlyle, Suppl. 33, from the original then in the possession of Captain Charles Lindsay. Mentioned in Waylen's *House of Cromwell* (1st ed. p. 274), and in Henfrey (p. 181), as of Oct. 24th.

[170] Oct. 25th. Read in House, Nov. 6. *Perfect Diurnall*, 6 Nov.

The case stands thus. His son Major Cholmley, who was killed in the Fight against the Scots at Winnick,[171] was Custom-master at Carlile; the Gentleman merited well from you. Since his death, his aged Father, having lost this his eldest Son in your service, did resolve to use his endeavour to procure the place for a younger Son, who had likewise been in your service; and resolving to obtain my letter to some friends about it, did acquaint an undertenant of the place to his Son with this his purpose to come to me to the borders of Scotland to obtain the said letter;—which the said tenant[172] did say, was very well.

And when the said Lieutenant-Colonel was come for my letter, this tenant immediately hastens away to London; where he, in a very circumventing and deceitful way, prefers a petition to the House of Commons; gets a reference to the Committee of the Navy; who approve of the said man, by the mediation of some gentlemen:—but I hear there is a stop of it in the House.

My humble suit to you is, that if Colonel Morgan do wait upon you about this business (I having given you this true information of the state of it, as I have received it), you would be pleased to further his desire concerning Lieutenant-Colonel Cholmley's younger Son, that he may have the place conferred upon him; and that you would acquaint some of my friends herewith.

By which you will very much oblige,

Your most humble servant,

Burroughbriggs,
October 28th, 1648.

O. CROMWELL.[173]

The siege of Pontefract to which Cromwell was advancing had lost all semblance of a serious military operation. Sir Henry Cholmley, appointed by the Yorkshire Committee as the colonel in charge, though conducting the siege in a most dilatory manner, had refused to give way to Colonel Rainsborough whom Fairfax had sent up to take command. Thinking, no doubt, that Cromwell would soon arrive to straighten out the situation, Rainsborough waited at Doncaster. Meanwhile the 500 foot and 150 horse who held the castle roamed the countryside unchallenged, stealing all the cattle and corn they could lay their hands upon against the time when Cromwell should arrive to renew the blockade. From desperate men who, with the example of Colchester before them, hoped for no quarter, desperate deeds could be expected, and among them, at this moment a dramatic event startled the army and the country.

More than once small parties of the garrison had successfully attacked the Parliamentary besiegers. Finally, determined to seize

[171] Carlyle, following Cary, printed "Berwick"; but Winwick was a skirmish between Chester and Warrington.

[172] Cary printed "servant," Carlyle added "or under-tenant," needlessly.

[173] *Tanner Mss.*, vol. lvii, 393. Pr. in Cary, *Memorials*, ii, 46; Carlyle, App. 14. Sealed with "Private Seal V," Henfrey, p. 185.

Rainsborough with the idea of exchanging him for Langdale who was imprisoned at Nottingham,[174] a small party of Cavaliers entered Doncaster on October 29th, overpowered the guards, and four of their number gained admittance to Rainsborough's lodging by pretending to have a letter from Cromwell and made him prisoner. Once in the street, observing the small number of his captors, he struggled fiercely to escape and in the confusion was killed.[175] His death was construed by Parliament and by Cromwell as the deliberate murder of a man who had been one of the first to advocate the trial of the King. Greatly distressed at the loss of such a valued officer, Cromwell did what he could upon his arrival, to discover the murderers[176] and to prevent further raids.

In pursuance of that vigorous policy, from his quarters in Byron House, not far from Pontefract, he sent orders to one of Sir Henry Cholmley's subordinates, a Yorkshire colonel and the Lord General's brother:

To Col. Charles Fairfax

SIR,

Being informed by Sir Edward Rodes this evening that there is a party of the enemy's horse gone out of Pontefract Castle, and having some apprehension that they will attempt somewhat upon the horse-guard in the park by coming upon their rear, I desire you that you would send to their assistance five files of musketeers, who will give them time to mount their horses if the enemy shall attempt upon them with horse and foot. I desire you to send the commander of the guard there this enclosed note. Not having more, I rest

Byron,
Nov. 2, at 8 at night.

Your affectionate servant,
CROMWELL.[177]

Establishing himself at Knottingley for the serious and lengthy business of taking Pontefract, Cromwell proceeded to settle several posts to prevent further plundering,[178] and called upon the Derby House Committee to send supplies. The only remaining trace of that letter is in the minutes of the Committee, who referred it to the Commons who, in turn, sent it to the Committee of the Army.[179]

[174] Langdale escaped, however, on Oct. 28th.

[175] Rushworth, vi, 1315; Carte, *Papers*, i, 193; *Perfect Diurnall*, Nov. 1; *Full and exact relation; Packets of Letters;* Clarendon, xi, 123.

[176] On Nov. 3, the House ordered him to make an official inquiry. *Perfect Diurnall*, Nov. 3.

[177] From the signed original in the Tangye Collection, London Museum. Lomas-Carlyle, Suppl. 34.

[178] *Perfect Diurnall*, Nov. 6.

[179] *Cal. S. P. Dom.* (1648–9), p. 321; *C. J.*, vi, 77.

To the Committee at Derby House

Concerning the condition of the forces at Pontefract. Requesting supplies and ammunition without which the work there and at Scarborough could not be carried on. November 5, 1648.[180]

Though deeply engaged in his military operations, Cromwell, like all his party, was not unmindful of the negotiations with the King dragging their slow and inconclusive length along at Newport. Meanwhile matters had taken another turn. Released from the long siege of Colchester, Ireton retired from the headquarters at St. Albans and took up his quarters at Windsor where, it is said, he busied himself with drawing up the remonstrance of the army against the effort to come to some accommodation with the King. Already his regiment had petitioned that Charles should be brought to trial and already a party in Parliament was desirous that the army should endeavor to stop the Newport negotiations. But though Ludlow who was foremost in urging this drastic course found Ireton opposed to premature action, and though Cromwell had thus far remained aloof, both men had come to thoroughly distrust Charles, and Ireton had gone so far as to demand bluntly that Fairfax see "impartial justice done upon all criminal persons, and that the same justice be meted out to King or nobleman as to the poorest commoner.[181] The death of Rainsborough deepened the hatred of the army toward the King; and while Cromwell was busy with the siege of Pontefract, that idea spread from the Levellers, who had long advocated it to more moderate men.

Alarmed over the situation, no less at the idea of bringing Charles to trial than at the wild projects of reform proposed by the more radical of the army representatives, not only Presbyterians like Holles and Grimston but Independents like Hammond, Pierrepont and even Vane were prepared to moderate the terms proposed by Parliament. If Charles could be brought to countenance moderate episcopacy and toleration, they were in a mood to conclude a treaty on that basis for the sake of peace and to prevent more violent counsels being adopted by the army. Nor is it easy at this distance to see why this could not be done, for Charles had more than once agreed to more drastic terms than these. The commonest explanation is that the Parliamentary commissioners, like the army representatives, had no confidence in the King, believing that, no matter what he promised, he would repudiate his agreement once he was in power. If that is true, there seems but little reason for such protracted negotiations, nor, indeed, negotiations of any kind. Though his letters

[180] Referred by the Committee to the House, Nov. 10, and to the Committee of the Army, Nov. 15. *S. P. Dom. Interregnum*, 10 E, 189; *Cal. S. P. Dom.* (1648–9), p. 321.

[181] *The true copy of a Petition . . . by . . . the Regiment under . . . Commissary General Ireton*. Oct. 19.

reveal that Charles was even then ordering Ormond to disregard his orders given to satisfy Parliament, to many Royalists it seemed that the whole thing was a blind, that the negotiators had no intention of coming to an agreement and that their continual protests that they could not get the King to accept the most reasonable of their proposals was merely a maneuver by which they hoped to discredit him with the people and pave the way to his removal. In the words of Clarendon, "it was easily discerned that it was moved and prosecuted only by them who did not intend that the treaty itself should have any good effect, and which they were not yet ready and prepared enough to prevent, the army not having finished what they were to do in all parts. . . . And it quickly appeared . . . that delay was their only business."[182]

To this he adds that "it is almost evident that the major part of both Houses of Parliament was at that time so far from desiring the execution of all those concessions, that, if they had been able to have resisted the wild fury of the army, they would have been themselves suitors to have declined the greatest part of them."[183] He was right at least in this—that the impulse to do away with Charles came from the army and its Independent supporters in Parliament. The position of Vane is, as usual, equivocal. According to Burnet, he strove to prolong the treaty with the object of delaying matters till the army could be brought up to London.[184] He thus apparently confirms the Royalist suspicions, though it has been pointed out that there is no corroborative evidence for this charge—and Burnet may have got his story from Clarendon.

This much at least is certain—the Stuart followers continued in this belief and though Vane refused to sit on the High Court of Justice or sign the death-warrant of Charles I, he, with Argyll and Johnston of Warriston, was condemned to death after the Restoration. Of the others, Cromwell and Ireton were already dead, but the vengeance of the Royalists pursued them beyond the grave. Ireton seems to have been determined on the removal of the King. His remark in September that he thought it best "to permit the King and Parliament to make an agreement, and to wait till they had made a full discovery of their intentions, whereby the people, becoming sensible of their danger, would willingly join to oppose them,"[185] indicates two things. The first is that he identified the "people" with the army; the second is that, as its spokesman and representative, he foreshadowed what actually happened within the next two months—

[182] Clarendon, *History*, xi, 180.

[183] *Ibid.*, 189.

[184] Burnet, *History of my own Time*, (ed. Airy,) 1, 74. Cp. Firth, art. "Vane" in *D. N. B.*

[185] Ludlow, *Memoirs*, i, 204.

first the elimination of the Presbyterians from Parliament, then the execution of the King.

Despite these indications of sentiment against Charles among the Republicans like Ludlow and Marten, the growing strength of the Levellers, and the tendency of men like Ireton to support that cause, there is little evidence of Cromwell's position at this time. He was opposed to Vane's plan for limited episcopacy and toleration. He was no less opposed to Charles; but as yet there is no proof that he contemplated the execution of the King. Such evidence as we have is contained in a letter considered from internal evidence to have been written to Colonel Robert Hammond by Cromwell from his headquarters at Knottingley, whence he directed the siege of Pontefract.

It is evident from it that he had heard that a party among the Independents, including Vane, Hammond and Pierrepont, was prepared to come to an accommodation with the King on the basis of episcopacy and toleration; and in half serious, half playful fashion he set himself to oppose that solution. The language reveals, among other things, the close relationship among these men. Hammond was known to all his friends as "Robin"; "Brother Heron" was the term Cromwell used sometimes in addressing or speaking of the younger Vane; and hence "Heron's brother" was Cromwell himself. "Brother Fountayne" is another name by which he referred to himself here as on several other occasions.[186] Some complaint was evidently being made amongst the Independents that Cromwell had not treated the Scots with sufficient harshness, and he felt called upon to defend himself and his companions against the charge of having turned Presbyterian. "Sir Roger" then would be one of the two who accompanied him to Edinburgh—probably Lambert, since a letter from the headquarters in Scotland signed "J. L." expresses the same views in justification of the alliance with Argyll.[187] Cromwell's "wise friend," it has been suggested,[188] is Pierrepont who, with Vane, was at Newport.

[*To Col. Hammond*]

Knottingley, November 6, 1648.

Dear Robin,

I trust the same spirit that guided thee heretofore is still with thee; look to thy heart, thou art where temptations multiply. I fear lest our friends should burn their fingers, as some others did not long since, whose hearts have ached since for it. How easy is it to find arguments for what we would have; how easy to take offence at things called Levellers, and

[186] Nickoll, *Original letters and papers addressed to Oliver Cromwell* (1743), pp. 78, 84.
[187] *Clarke Papers*, ii, preface, p. xxiv.
[188] By Gardiner.

run into an extremity on the other hand, meddling with an accursed thing. Peace is only good when we receive it out of our Father's hand, it's dangerous to snatch it, most dangerous to go against the will of God to attain it. War is good when led to by our Father, most evil when it comes from the lusts that are in our members. We wait upon the Lord, who will teach us and lead us whether to doing or suffering.

Tell my brother Herne I smiled at his expression concerning my wise friend's opinion, who thinks that the enthroning the King with presbytery brings spiritual slavery, but with a moderate episcopacy works a good peace. Both are a hard choice. I trust there's no necessity of either, except our base unbelief and fleshly wisdom make it so; but if I have any logic it will be easier to tyrannise having that he[189] likes and serves his turn, than what you know and all believe he so much dislikes.

But as to my brother himself, tell him indeed I think some of my friends have advanced too far, and need make an honourable retreat, Scots treaties having wrought some perplexities; and hindering matters from going so glib as otherwise was hoped, especially taking in some doubts that Sir Roger and brother Fountayne are also turned Presbyterians. Dear Robin, tell brother Herne that we have the witness of our consciences that we have walked in this thing (whatsoever surmises are to the contrary) in plainness and godly simplicity, according to our weak measure, and we trust our daily business is to approve our consciences to Godward, and not to shift and shark,[190] which were exceeding baseness in us to do, having had such favour from the Lord, and such manifestations of His presence, and I hope the same experience will keep their hearts and hands from him, against whom God hath so witnessed,[191] though reason should suggest things never so plausible.

I pray thee tell my brother Herne thus much from me; and if a mistake concerning our compliance with presbytery perplex an evil business (for so I account it), and make the wheels of such a chariot go heavy, I can be passive and let it go, knowing that innocency and integrity loses nothing by a patient waiting upon the Lord. Our papers are public; let us be judged by them. Answers do not involve us.[192] I profess to thee I desire from my heart, I have prayed for it, I have waited for the day to see union and right understanding between the godly people (Scots, English, Jews, Gentiles, Presbyterians, Independents, Anabaptists, and all). Our brothers of Scotland (really Presbyterians) were our greatest enemies. God hath justified us in their sight, caused us to requite good for evil, caused them to acknowledge it publicly by acts of state, and privately, and the thing is true in the sight of the sun. It is an high conviction upon them. Was it not fit to be civil, to profess love, to deal with clearness with them for removing of prejudice, to ask them what they had against us, and to give them an honest answer? This we have done,

189 *i.e.*, the King.

190 Firth, followed by Mrs. Lomas, suggests "shirk" as an emendation adding that the spelling of the seventeenth century points to the conclusion that "e" (and the "i" here is equivalent to "e") before "r" was almost universally pronounced like "a," as it still is in "Derby," &c.

191 The King.

192 *i.e.*, We are bound by our own words, not by the answers made by the Scots. Gardiner suggests that Cromwell perhaps refers to the answer made by the Committee of Estates on October 6, in which they speak of "these covenanted kingdoms."

and not more. And herein is a more glorious work in our eyes than if we had gotten the sacking and plunder of Edinburgh, the strong castles into our hands, and made conquest from Tweed to the Orcades; and we can say, through God we have left by the grace of God such a witness amongst them, as if it work not yet[193] there is that conviction upon them that will undoubtedly bear its fruit in due time.

Tell my brother Herne, I believe my wise friend would have had a conquest, or if not, things put in a balance;[194] the first was not very unfeasible, but I think not Christian, and I was commanded the contrary by the two Houses; as for the latter, by the providence of God it is perfectly come to pass, not by our wisdom, for I durst not design it, I durst not admit of so mixed, so low a consideration; we were led out (to the praise of our God be it spoken) to more sincere, more spiritual considerations; but I said before the Lord hath brought it to a balance; if there be any dangerous disproportion it is that the honest party (if I may without offence so call them) in my apprehension are the weaker, and have manifold difficulties to conflict withal. I wish our unworthiness here cast not the scale both there and here the wrong way. I have but one word more to say. Thy friends, dear Robin, are in heart and in profession what they were, have not dissembled their principles at all. Are they not a little justified in this, that a lesser party of a Parliament hath made it lawful to declare the greater part a faction, and made the Parliament null, and call a new one, and to do this by force, and this by the same mouths that condemned it in others.

Think of the example and of the consequence, and let others think of it too, if they be not drenched too deep in their one [own] reason and opinions. Robin, be honest still. God keep thee in the midst of snares. Thou hast naturally a valiant spirit. Listen to God, and He shall increase it upon thee, and make thee valiant for the truth. I am a poor creature that write to thee, the poorest in the work,[195] but I have hope in God, and desire from my heart to love His people, and if thou hast opportunity and a free heart, let me hear from thee how it is with thee. This bearer is faithful, you may be very free to communicate with him; my service to all my friends, and to my dear brother Herne whom I love in the Lord, I rest,

Thy true and faithful friend

Knottingley,
November 6, 1648. HERON[s] BROTHER.[196]

Whatever the reason for the curious use of nicknames, whether it was merely playfulness or whether there was a certain element of caution in it—for, if things went wrong, this letter contained much dangerous matter—and whatever the tortuous religious phraseology

[193] "By reason the poor souls are so wedded to their government." In the copy amongst the *Clarke Mss.*

[194] "*i.e.*, A mixed government established in which the Argyle and Hamilton parties would counterbalance each other." (*Note by Firth.*)

[195] "world," *Clarke Mss.*

[196] From the Mss. of the Marquis of Lothian at Newbattle. Copy. Ms. copy also in *Clarke Mss.* xvi, at Worcester College and printed in the *Clarke Papers*, ii, 49. Lomas-Carlyle, Suppl. 35.

so characteristic of Cromwell involved, one thing seems certain. It is that Cromwell was opposed to an agreement with the King; he was scarcely less opposed to Presbyterianism; and he inclined to the position of the Levellers. Had the letter been published, it must have brought grim smiles to the faces of the Scottish Presbyterians who had been confronted with the choice of opposing a powerful and victorious English army or submitting to the "high conviction" that peace and alliance was the safer part, by "spiritual considerations." In any event it makes Cromwell's position on religion clear. He desired universal and complete toleration—save perhaps to Roman Catholics and Episcopalians, whom, whether purposely or inadvertently, he omits from his categories of the "godly." It is too much to say, from what evidence we have, that at this time Cromwell was bent on the death of Charles; but it is not too much to say—as his own words testify—that he sympathized more deeply with those who proposed that solution of the political problem than with their opponents; that he encouraged those who were unwilling to come to an accommodation with the crown, and that he warned those who were willing to make such accommodation. Taking into account the fact that he was the most powerful figure in the army, which in effect was the dominant influence in the state, his position certainly lent weight to the opinion that the King must be put out of the way.

Charles felt the net closing around him. He had already planned two efforts to escape; his followers were even more alarmed than he, and, with the signature of the Peace of Westphalia, his wife bestirred herself to seek the aid of foreign powers, this time not to restore her husband to the throne but to save his life. How dangerous the situation appeared to Charles is revealed in his long letter written during the negotiations to his son, which contains this significant passage:

> "We know not but this may be the last time we may speak to you or the world publicly; we are sensible into what hands we are fallen. . . . These men which have forced laws which they were bound to observe, will find their triumphs full of troubles."[197]

In such fashion and such mood the great antagonists approached the climax of their long rivalry. Like Cromwell, though from a very different position, Charles did not doubt "but God's providence will restrain our enemies' power, and turn their fierceness to his praise"; but unlike the imprisoned King, Cromwell could not 'busy himself in retiring into himself.' With all of his concern over the Newport negotiations, he had before him the immediate task of reducing Pontefract, and for the moment his chief concern and his chief correspondence was in connection with that operation.

[197] Clarendon, xi, 191.

On the same day that he wrote his letter to Hammond in regard to the larger question of the settlement of the kingdom, he addressed an order for the placing of guards about Pontefract Castle:

For the Honourable Col. Fairfax in Pontefract: These

SIR,

I did order a company of my Lord General's regiment to be with the guard of horse in the park this night, but finding it fit to dispose of that company to another place, I thought fit to desire of you that you would send six files of musketeers to the guard in the park this night in the room of the other. I shall have occasion also to remove one of the troops from the guard in the park to another place, wherefore I desire you that you would only retain twenty horse of the troop that is to do duty in the town, and send the rest to strengthen the guard of horse in the park. I hope within a night or two, now tools are come, we shall not put you to so much trouble. I rest, Sir,

Your affectionate servant,

Nottingley, O. CROMWELL.[198]
Nov. 6, 1648.

This was the beginning of a series of communications relating in one way or another to the siege, the next of which is of a somewhat different character.

For the Honourable Col. Fairfax at Pontefract: These

SIR,

I understand that one Richard Gagge and two boys of John Ward's (whose father is now in the Castle) were, upon their coming to Knottingley, apprehended and carried prisoners to Pontefract, upon suspicion that they were going into the Castle. The business being cleared up to me to the contrary, I desire you would set them at liberty and to cause such things as were taken from them to be restored; which will very much oblige, Sir,

Your very humble servant,

Knottingley,
Nov. 7th, 1648. O. CROMWELL.[199]

Two days later Cromwell felt that it was time to send a formal demand for the surrender of the garrison, which he did in a fashion quite different from some of his more peremptory messages to other commanders.

[198] From the signed original in the Tangye Collection in the London Museum. Printed in Lomas-Carlyle, Suppl. 36.

[199] From the signed original in the Tangye Collection in the London Museum, pr. in Lomas-Carlyle, Supple. 36. If the John Ward whose sons he had before him was the Puritan poet, it is hard to see why he was in the Castle.

For the Governor of Pontefract Castle

SIR,

Being come hither for the reduction of this place, I thought fit to summon you to deliver your garrison to me, for the use of the Parliament. Those gentlemen and soldiers with you may have better terms than if you should hold it to extremity. I expect your answer this day, and rest,

Your servant,

November, 9th, 1648. O. CROMWELL.[200]

The summons was, naturally, of no avail, and he settled down to a military operation which for length, leisureliness and final dramatic incident had no parallel in either of the civil wars. It is, indeed, difficult at this distance and in the absence of detailed information to understand the reasons for the whole incident of Pontefract, and not least the position of Cromwell, despite the long and apologetic letter which he wrote presently to explain why the siege presented such difficulties. Among these was the problem of keeping his men in hand. Whatever the zeal of their leaders, the soldiers must be paid, and in consequence he wrote to Colonel Fairfax who was in immediate command of the operation in regard to that and other matters connected with the siege.

For the Honourable Col. Charles Fairfax at Pontefract: These

SIR,

I have perused your letter. I am very sorry that your condition should be so strait. I pray you, strive with difficulties as far as you can, and for my part I will do what lies in me to get you supplied. I shall upon this occasion send expressly to the Committee for a fortnight's pay for you, and if I be denied I shall think I am not fairly dealt withal. I shall let them know that I think present money and nothing else will keep the men together. And truly, if that my lending of you a hundred pounds for the present will do you any service you shall have it in the morning if you please to send for it. I have written to Lincoln and Leicester to keep in Captain Jackson's and the other company of foot for a fortnight; their officers promised me they should perform duty as before until they had an answer. I desire you to send them this enclosed order. I take it not ill at all that you

[200] Pr. in the *Moderate Intelligencer*, Nov. 9–16, 1648; Rushworth, vii, 1352; Carlyle, Letter LXXX. The *Mod. Intell.* adds that Governor Morris kept his men in ignorance of the summons; but as the writer could hardly have known that; as this was the usual statement about almost every incident of the kind; and as the garrison made such an extraordinarily long and desperate resistance, there seems no reason to believe the statement.

give only word, nor can I take anything ill at your hands, I pray you still account me

Your true and faithful friend and servant,

Knottingley,
Nov. 10th, 1648.

O. CROMWELL.[201]

For the Honourable Col. Charles Fairfax, at Pontefract: These

SIR,

The bearer has been with me, complains exceedingly of her poverty, as not able to get victuals for her family, and yet is forced to maintain soldiers much beyond her ability. I desire that what favour can be afforded her, you would do it, at the desire of

Your humble servant,

Knottingley,
November 11th, 1648.

O. CROMWELL.[202]

For the Honourable Colonel Fairfax, in Pontefract: These

SIR,

The bearer, Mrs. Gray, is desirous to go into the Castle to see a brother of her who lies sick in the Castle. I desire you would let her have a drum and give her your pass to return within a limited time. I rest, Sir,

Your very humble servant,

Knottingley,
November 11th, 1648.

O. CROMWELL.[202]

With these letters from Cromwell to Fairfax, there has been preserved one from Colonel Fairfax to Cromwell concerning a Mr. Dawson whose 267 "fatt oxen" were taken from him, with a suggestion as to how he might be repaid. On the upper right hand corner is a note or endorsement:

"Sir, I allwaies approve of what comes from you and I thinke this to bee the most equall.

O. CROMWELL."[203]

The letter thus endorsed was apparently returned to Fairfax, and meanwhile Cromwell bestirred himself to secure the needed supplies from the Committee at Derby House. His letter of requisition, besides an account of his troops' necessities, gives a vivid picture of

[201] From the signed original in the Tangye Collection, London Museum. Pr. in Lomas-Carlyle, Suppl. 36. A postscript, "Sir, I shall desire you to speed this letter by an express to York," has been crossed out in the original.

[202] Signed original in the handwriting of William Clarke, in the Tangye Collection. Photographic reproduction in Tangye, *Two Protectors*, opp. pp. 133 & 137. Printed in Lomas-Carlyle, Suppl. 36.

[203] Original in the Tangye Collection.

such an operation as this siege and the methods of supporting an army under such conditions as that of the men apparently being reduced to sleeping out of doors and living off of the country, which in a cold and wet November made operations doubly difficult. It reveals, as well, the fact that in this siege, unlike others in which he had been engaged, he had been greatly hampered by the absence of adequate artillery, and that this, among other reasons, had caused it to be so long drawn out, though why he had not been able to get guns enough is not easy to understand.

For the Right Honourable the Committee of Lords and Commons sitting at Derby House: These present

My Lords and Gentlemen,

So soon as I came into these parts, I met with an earnest desire from the Committee of this county to take upon me the charge here, for the reducing of the garrison of Pomfret. I received also commands from my Lord General to the same effect. I have had the sight of a letter to the House of Commons, wherein things are so represented, as if this siege were at such a pass that the prize were already gained. In consideration whereof, I thought fit to let you know what the true state of this garrison is, as also the condition of the country, that so you may not think my desire for such things as would be necessary to carry on this work unreasonable.

My Lords, the Castle hath been victualled with two-hundred and twenty or forty fat cattle, within these three weeks, and they have also gotten in (as I am credibly informed) salt enough for them and more, so that I apprehend they are victualled for a twelvemonth. The men within are resolved to endure to the utmost extremity, expecting no mercy, as indeed they deserve none. The place is very well known to be one of the strongest inland garrisons in the kingdom, well watered, situated upon a rock in every part of it, and therefore difficult to mine. The walls very thick and high, with strong towers, and if battered, very difficult of access, by reason of the depth and steepness of the graft. The country is exceedingly impoverished, not able to bear free-quarter, nor well able to furnish provisions, if we had moneys. The work is like to be long, if materials be not furnished answerable. I therefore think it my duty to represent unto you as followeth: viz.—

1. That moneys be provided for three complete regiments of foot, and two of horse; 2. That money be provided for all contingencies which are in view, too many to enumerate. 3. That five-hundred barrels of powder, six good battering-guns, with three-hundred shot to each gun, be speedily sent down to Hull: 4. We desire none may be sent less than demi-cannon. 5. We desire also some match and bullet. And if it may be, we should be glad that two or three of the biggest mortar-pieces with shells may likewise be sent.

And although the desires of such proportions may seem costly, yet I hope you will judge it good thrift; especially if you consider that this place hath cost the kingdom some hundred-thousands of pounds already. And for aught I know, it may cost you one more, if it be trifled withal, besides the dishonour of it, and what other danger may be emergent, by its being in such hands.

It's true, here are some two or three great guns in Hull, and hereabouts, but they are unserviceable, and your garrisons in Yorkshire are very much unsupplied at this time.

I have not as yet drawn any of our foot to this place[204] only I make use of Colonel Fairfax's and Colonel Maleverie's foot regiments and keep the rest of the guards with the horse, purposing to bring-on some of our foot to-morrow, the rest being a little dispersed in Lincoln and Nottingham Shires (these parts being not well able to bear them) for some refreshment; which after so much duty they need, and a little expect.

And indeed I would not satisfy myself nor my duty to you and them, to put the poor men, at this season of the year, to lie in the field, before we be furnished with shoes, stockings and clothes, for them to cover their nakedness (which we hear are in preparation, and would be speeded) and until we have deal-boards to make them courts-of-guard, and tools to cast up works to secure them.[205]

These things I have humbly represented to you; and waiting for your resolution and command, I rest,

Your most humble servant,

Knottingley, near Pontefract, OLIVER CROMWELL.[206]
15th November, 1648.

Informed of his request for supplies by the Committee, the Commons voted on November 17 to provide him with all the material necessary to reduce this last stronghold of Royalism in England.[207] It was the last stronghold in more senses than one; for while Cromwell had been engaged in his attempt to reduce it, affairs outside had moved fast and far toward the elimination of the King himself. Throughout the month of October the Houses, the commissioners and the King had wrestled with the problem of a settlement. Reduced as Parliament was—with an average of ten peers present, and with 167 as the largest division on the most important question which came before it in that month—it found itself divided between Lords and Commons on the question of meeting the royal proposals for a settlement. The Lords accepted the King's plans for the church, the Commons rejected them. The Lords proposed "an expedient" to

[204] *i.e.*, not any of the regular foot of the army; Fairfax's and Mauleverer's being Yorkshire militia regiments. [Note by Mrs. Lomas.]

[205] Concerning the want of necessaries, compare the letter from Col. Rainborowe to Fairfax, written on October 15, preserved amongst the *Clarke MSS.* at Littlecote. Also, a letter from Robert Spavin, Cromwell's secretary, dated November 2. Both speak of the cordiality of the Yorkshire colonels, Charles Fairfax and Mauleverer, and both complain of Sir Henry Cholmley's animosity. "Cholmley," writes Spavin, "a very knave, hates us to the death; leapt at the news of Col. Rainborowe being killed." (See *Hist. MSS. Commissioners' Report on Mr. Leyborne-Popham's MSS.*, pp. 7, 8.). [Note by Mrs. Lomas.]

[206] Pr. in *Propositions sent in a letter from Lieutenant-General Cromwell and his Officers to the Committee of Derbyhouse. Packets of Letters;* Carlyle, Letter LXXXI.

[207] *C. J.*, vi, 81.

harmonize their views, but presently abandoned it, as King and Parliament broke on the question of the religious settlement, and the Commons proceeded on its course of proscribing his supporters. November saw the same progress in the punishment of Royalists, the same lack of progress in accommodation with the King, until on November 24 Charles's final answer came. He would not consent to the destruction of the English church. "What is a man profited," the last words of his refusal ran, "if he shall gain the whole World and lose his own Soul?"

THE ARMY REMONSTRANCE, NOVEMBER 16–20, 1648

With those words, if he did not seal his own death-warrant, he at least turned from Charles the King to Charles the Martyr in the minds of the Anglicans. The means for his destruction were already being forged. Four days before his answer arrived, there had come to the Commons a "Remonstrance of his Excellency, Thomas, Lord Fairfax, and of the Generall Counsell of Officers, held at St. Albans, the 16th of November," which embodied the position of the army leaders, and in a sense sealed the fate of Charles.

That *Remonstrance* was largely if not wholly the work of Ireton,[208] who, encouraged by the success of his earlier petition[209] to the General, had busied himself at Windsor in drawing up this longer and more specific document which set forth the reasons for meting out justice to a King who was a traitor to the "people" and could only be treated with as a person outside and independent of the nation. Any scruples which might have been entertained by the officers were removed by the King's rejection of the Parliamentary proposals; and that rejection was welcomed by Ireton as removing the last obstacle to an attack upon Charles. As he wrote to Hammond, "It hath pleased God . . . to dispose the hearts of your friends in the army as one man . . . to interpose in this treaty, yet in such wise both for matter and manner as, we believe, will not only refresh the bowels of the saints, . . . but be of satisfaction to every honest member of parliament."[210]

He was, in fact, bent on the destruction of the King; and he summed up his manifesto with a demand for the punishment of

"That capitall and grand Author of our troubles, the person of the King, by whose commissions, commands, or procurement, and in whose behalfe and for whose interest only (of will and power) all our warres and troubles

[208] *A Remonstrance of his Excellency*, etc. (1648) Adopted on Nov. 18; reached Parliament on Nov. 20. Cp. Gardiner, *Civil War*, iv, 233.

[209] *The True Copy of a Petition . . . by . . . the Regiment under the Command of Comm.-Gen. Ireton*, Oct. 19, 1648.

[210] *Letters between Hammond and the Committee at Derby House*, p. 87.

have been (with all the miseries attending them), may be speedily brought to justice for the treason, blood, and mischiefe he is therein guilty of."

Nor was he content with the death of Charles. He demanded besides,

"That for further satisfactions of publique justice, Capitall punishment may be speedily executed upon a competent number of his chiefe instruments also, both in the former and latter warre, and (for that purpose) that some such, of both sorts, may be pitcht upon to be made examples of justice in that kind, as are really in your hands or reach, so as their exception from pardon may not be a mockery of justice in the face of God and man."[211]

The reasons for this stern demand were set forth at some length. They were that Charles had stirred up civil war, invited in the Scots, that he was, in general, responsible for the bloodshed of the preceding years, and in particular that he would not be bound by any concessions that he should make or be compelled to make, that no form of words would be held binding by him; for, as the *Remonstrance* said:

"We know besides, what Court maxims there are among the King's party concerning some fundamental rights of the Crown which the King cannot give away . . . but if all other pretexts fail, their non-obligation to what is wrested from them by force . . . will serve such a King's conscience for a shift to make a breach where he finds his advantage."

Against the King was revived the old grievance of his imprisonment of men in 1628 and his attempt on the five members in 1642. It is obvious that the army leaders felt that were the King restored their own position would be precarious. He was reckoned by them not only an untrustworthy but a revengeful man, and it was inconceivable that were he once more on the throne, he would not punish them. Every argument of personal safety as well as principle, therefore, led them to demand the execution of the King. It was of no avail for his supporters to argue that it was Parliament which had taken the first steps toward civil war, that it was Parliament which had first invited in the Scots, and that if Charles had rejected the proposals of Parliament to destroy the church, Parliament had in turn rejected his promise to modify the Establishment. It was of no avail for the matter had been determined, and Ireton's argument was, in effect, only the rationalization of the conclusion that Charles must die.

On the necessity of removing "the chief delinquent" the most advanced party in the army was agreed, but as to what was to happen after that was by no means clear. Charles had been guilty, according to Ireton's argument, of endeavoring to turn a limited into an absolute monarchy. That constitutional question was not of such great

[211] Ireton's *Remonstrance of his Excellency.*

importance to the more radical element in the army, nor even to Cromwell, as the fact that the King had encouraged the second civil war. That was the deadly and unpardonable sin. He and his followers had ventured to challenge the decree of the Almighty as evidenced in the result of the first civil war. They had defied the judgment of the trial by battle; they had caused the shedding of more blood, and at least since August, 1647, in the words of his enemies, Charles was "the man of blood" in all their talk of him.

He was now to be called to account for that, and in the view of the more extreme party this was the principal matter. That, in fact, is always the first instinct of revolutionary parties—to destroy its enemies and overthrow the old system. It is no doubt a sound instinct, for without the destruction of the old, obviously no new order can be established. Yet even to many men in the front rank of the revolutionary element that was not enough. If he were removed; if, as the *Remonstrance* demanded, not only should a number of his supporters in the second civil war perish with him and the army become supreme; even if the Prince of Wales and the Duke of York, refusing to surrender, should be declared incapable of governing and sentenced to die if found in English territory—if all these things happened, what then? What form of government should England have?

To the Republicans the answer was obvious. As Burnet said of Ireton, they "stuck at nothing that might have turned England into a Commonwealth." To the men of lesser intelligence and even more fervid feelings, to Fifth Monarchists like Harrison, there was some dim notion of a millennium and a rule of the Saints. To others, mere soldiers like Ewer, there was only the question of killing an enemy who had sought their lives. But to many more, like Lilburne, that was only the beginning, not the end of the matter. It was necessary to provide for the future before breaking entirely with the past. On this point the *Remonstrance* was far from clear. Even accepting its doctrine of the sovereignty of the people, how was that to be translated into efficient and popular administration? Ireton seems to have envisaged a Parliament elected by property-holders and empowered to make laws and exercise judicial authority over public offenders, "either according to the law where it has provided, or their own judgment where it has not." As to the executive—whether it was to be a separate function vested in an individual or exercised by a Supreme Council—the document was vague.

That vagueness was natural. The circle had come round from the supremacy of the crown to that of Parliament; but the substitution of a Parliament, or a Parliament and a Council, for the old system of King, Lords and Commons, Privy Council and royal courts, left many and apparently insuperable difficulties. It is always easier to tear down than to build, and it is hard to build an arch without a keystone. To Ireton and those of his way of thinking as to all such men at such times, the first and imperative step to a new order was the disposition of the King, and though they talked of deposition or disinheritance, it was obvious that there was but one answer, though they shrank from mentioning it.[212]

To many others the case was not so clear, as was apparent when, on November 16, the *Remonstrance* was presented formally to the Council of Officers which had been meeting for a week or more in the old abbey church of St. Albans debating this great problem of the settlement of the kingdom. Those meetings had developed widely differing views. On the one hand the advanced party was prepared to accept the principles of Ireton's draft which had apparently been laid before them on November 10; on the other many were opposed to such action, fearing that the country would turn upon the army as the chief cause of the nation's difficulties. To this party Fairfax himself inclined, refusing utterly to consider a petition against Charles from the regiments of Fleetwood, Whalley and Barkstead, and vowing that he would support King and Parliament as soon as they had come to an agreement.

Meanwhile another element had been injected into this disturbed situation. While the officers at St. Albans and the Parliament at Westminster discussed the situation, on November 15 there was held at the *Nag's Head* Tavern in London, a meeting of representatives of Levellers and advanced Independents, attended, among others, by John Lilburne and John Wildman, lately released from prison.[213] It was called, according to Lilburne, by "some Independents," and, it has been said, at the suggestion of Cromwell;[214] and there the problem was discussed again. At that meeting, as Lilburne says, "the just ends of the War were exactly laid open by Mr. Wildman as ever I heard in my life"; but after long debate, he goes on to say, the Independents "plainly told us, the chief things first to be done by the Army was first to cut off the King's Head, &c., and force and thoroughly purge, if not dissolve, the Parliament." To that proposal Lilburne was opposed, and with his usual insistence "pressed to know the bottom of their center, and in what they would absolutely rest for a Future Settlement." It was, as he pointed out, to the advantage of the people to keep both King and Parliament, however bad they

[212] As Clarendon wrote, "it was generally concluded they should never be able to settle their new form of government whilst he lived . . . some were for actual deposing of him . . . others for . . . poison . . . or . . . assassination [and] . . . a third sort . . . who pressed to have him brought to a public trial . . . all the Levellers and Agitators of the army, in the head of which Ireton and Harryson were." *History*, xi, 224–7.

[213] Lilburne, *The Legal Fundamental Liberties of the People of England*, (June, 1649).

[214] Gardiner, *Civil War*, iv, 238 (1905 ed.).

were, as "one Tyrant to balance another . . . and not suffer the Army (so much as in us lay) to devolve all the government of the Kingdom into their wills and swords. . . . And if we should do this, our slavery for the future . . . might probably be greater than it ever was . . . and so our last error would be greater then our first." "At which," he goes on to say, "the Gentlemen Independents were some of them most desperately cholerick," but finally they agreed to choose "four and four of a side to debate and conclude of some heads towards the accomplishment of an Agreement of the People," which accordingly they did, and so presently drew up still another scheme of government.

With all of his cantankerousness, Lilburne had put his finger on the real difficulty of the situation. What would happen if the King were gone; would England not descend into military rule? That, as he pointed out, was the real danger of the situation; and to avoid that, he and the dissenting officers at St. Albans, together with the Parliament, insisted on either an arrangement with the King, or some more definite plan for future government. Save for the advanced Independents, most men, even many Levellers like Lilburne, inclined to a government of King and Parliament. At St. Albans after two days of debate Ireton's proposals finally prevailed, though greatly modified and with many reservations, especially that of a new effort to come to terms with Charles, and the addition of various constitutional provisions.

Those new provisions were still vague. They conceived a Parliament—or rather a House of Commons—elected by those who had not supported Charles and who would agree to these proposals. It should have supreme power. There was no mention of a Council of State nor a House of Lords, and any future King was to be chosen or elected "as upon trust from the people" and was to have no veto power. Having referred this scheme to Parliament, the Council of Officers sent another message to Charles, desiring a permanent constitutional settlement. That was to be reached by bringing the existing Parliament to an end and choosing a new House of Commons by a more equal franchise; establishing a Council of State which should control the militia; and appointing great officers of state by Parliament for ten years, thereafter by the King from names submitted to him by Parliament. The army was to be kept in being and presently given a fixed establishment; and five men were to be excepted from pardon, the rest of the Royalists moderately fined.

Nothing could better illustrate the complexity of the situation which confronted the English people at this time than the fact that, apart from the position of the King, there were now four proposals for a settlement—those of the *Remonstrance*, of the Army Council, of Parliament, and of the Independent-Leveller group. It was perhaps small wonder that, being what he was, Charles hesitated, dissembled, and, buoyed up by the hope of escape and the disagreements among his enemies, dreamed of setting the parties against each other so that he could divide and rule. His dreams bore little relation to the realities of the situation. On November 20 the *Remonstrance*[215] was laid before the Commons, and though that House postponed consideration of the army's proposals and refused to break absolutely with the King, its commissioners took leave of him a week later, and the last of the many negotiations was at an end. Thenceforth the issue lay between Charles and the army; and with this the position of Cromwell became of greater, if not of supreme, importance. What that position was, it is not easy to discover from direct evidence, yet there is much that goes to show that he was inclining to the extreme position of Ireton and his followers, if he had, indeed, not already embraced it.

PONTEFRACT, NOVEMBER 20–DECEMBER 6, 1648

On the day that the *Army Remonstrance* was presented to Parliament, Cromwell wrote to Fairfax to advise him of the views held by those officers in his command who had lately requested him to present to Fairfax their petitions, which were not unlike those of the regiments of Whalley, Barkstead and Fleetwood.[216] The letter enclosing these petitions was considered of enough importance to warrant publishing it with extracts from the *Remonstrance*.[217] It is evident that, in a measure, it supported the plan of bringing Charles to "justice," though Cromwell, according to his habit, was careful to express his views in generalities:

For his Excellency the Lord General Fairfax

My Lord,

I find a very great sense in the officers of the regiments of the sufferings and the ruin of this poor kingdom, and in them all a very great zeal to have impartial justice done upon Offenders; and I must confess, I do in all, from my heart, concur with them; and I verily think and am persuaded they are things which God puts into our hearts.

I shall not need to offer anything to your Excellency: I know God teaches you, and that He hath manifested His presence so to you as that you will give glory to Him in the eyes of all the world. I held it my duty, having

[215] *C. J.*, vi, 81. *The Remonstrance*, besides being printed in various contemporary pamphlets is in *Old Parl. Hist.*, xviii, 161–238.

[216] Officers to Cromwell, Nov. c. 18, signed by J. Blackmore, Edw. Scotten, Jos. Wallington and 14 others, endorsed "From his own regiment of horse to be printed before their petition to the general." *Hist. Mss, Comm. Rept. Leyborne-Popham* Mss, p. 9.

[217] *The Demands of Lord Fairfax and the General Council*, etc.

received these petitions and letters, and being desired by the framers thereof, to present them to you. The good Lord work His will upon your heart, enabling you to it; and the presence of Almighty God go along with you. Thus prays, My Lord,

Knottingley, Nov. 20, 1648.

Your most humble and faithful servant,
O. CROMWELL.[218]

To this Cromwell added, on the same day, a letter to the Committee for Compounding, which further defines his position in regard to those who had committed the unpardonable sin—the effort to overthrow the domination of the army by the second civil war. Against them he was extraordinarily bitter, for, he pointed out—and this is some measure of the dangerous situation in which the army felt itself—"how near you were brought to ruin." Sir John Owen had headed the north Welsh in that rising, had been defeated and captured and was then a prisoner at Windsor under charge of high treason. He had, however, with the Earl of Cambridge and Lords Holland, Capel and Goring, been merely condemned to banishment some ten days before Cromwell's letter, and Cromwell now wrote in violent protest against such lenient treatment of those who had ventured to appeal "against all the witnesses God had borne" to the righteousness of the Independent cause as evidenced by its success in the first civil war.

For my honoured Friends Robert Jenner and John Ashe, Esquires: These

GENTLEMEN,

I received an order from the Governor of Nottingham, directed to him from you, To bring up Colonel Owen, or take bail for his coming up to make his composition, he having made an humble petition to you for the same. I must profess to you, I was not a little astonished at the thing.

If I be not mistaken, the House of Commons did vote all those traitors that did adhere to, or bring in, the Scots in their late invading of this kingdom under Duke Hamilton, and not without very clear justice, this being a more prodigious Treason than any that had been perpetrated before; because the former quarrel on their part was that Englishmen might rule over one another; this to vassalise us to a foreign nation.[219] And their fault who have appeared in this summer's business is certainly double to theirs who were in the first, because it is the repetition of the same offence against all the witnesses that God has borne, by making and abetting to a second war.

[218] *The Demands of Lord Fairfax and the Generall Council*, etc.; Rushworth, vii, 1339; Carlyle, Letter LXXXIII.

[219] "Here was the sting, for we have never to forget that Oliver, like Milton, was ever English of the English." Morley, *Cromwell*, p. 266.

And if this was their justice,[220] and upon so good grounds, I wonder how it comes to pass that so eminent actors should so easily be received to compound. You will pardon me if I tell you that, if it were contrary to some of your judgments that at the rendition of Oxford, though we had the town in consideration, and blood saved to boot, yet two years purchase was thought too little to expiate their offence;[221] but now, when you have such men in your hands, and it will cost you nothing to do justice; now after all this trouble and the hazard of a second war, for a little more money all offences shall be pardoned!

This gentleman was taken with Sir Marmaduke Langdale, in their flight together: I presume you have heard what is become of him. Let me remember you that out of this garrison was fetched not long since (I believe whilst we were in heat of action) Colonel Humphrey Mathews, than whom this cause we have fought for has not had a more dangerous enemy; and he not guilty only of being an enemy, but he apostatised from your cause and quarrel; having been a colonel, if not more, under you, and the desperatest promoter of the Welsh rebellion amongst them all. And how near you were brought to ruin thereby, all men that know anything can tell; and this man was taken away to composition, by what order I know not.[222]

Gentlemen, though my sense does appear more severe than perhaps you would have it, yet give me leave to tell you I find a sense amongst the officers concerning such things as these, even to amazement; which truly is not so much to see their blood made so cheap, as to see such manifest witnessings of God (so terrible and so just) no more reverenced.

I have directed the Governor to acquaint the Lord General herewith, and rest,

Gentlemen,

Your most obedient servant,

Knottingley, near Pontefract, OLIVER CROMWELL.[223]
November 20th, 1648.

In sharp contrast to this, two days later, still at Knottingley, Cromwell signed a pass for the man who had held Newark for the King at the outset of the first civil war:

[220] House of Commons.

[221] When Oxford was surrendered the malignants there were to have a composition not exceeding two years revenue for estates of inheritance (Rushworth, vi, 280) which the Presbyterians like Jenner and Ashe had exclaimed against as being too lenient. "Very different now," says Carlyle, "when the new Malignants, though a doubly criminal set, are bone of their own bone."

[222] The order, as Cromwell probably knew, was made by the Committee for Compounding on Sept. 26, that Matthews might prosecute his composition. His fine of £1,397/6/8 was paid the following spring, of which £500 was to be paid "to Mr. Thomason, for the library of mss bought from him." *Cal. Comm. for Comp.*, p. 1855.

[223] Endorsed, "Lieutenant-General Cromwell about prisoners." Original in *Sloane Mss*, 1519, f. 186, with signature only. Carlyle, Letter LXXXII. Mentioned in Henfrey, *Numismata Cromwelliana*, p. 181.

To all the officers and soldiers under my command

I do hereby engage myself that Sir John Digby, gnl., and his servant shall have free liberty to come to Pontefract and to return back again into the Castle. And likewise I do hereby require all officers and soldiers to permit the said Sir John Digby and his servant to pass to Pontefract as above said without trouble or molestation. Given under my hand this 22nd day of Novemb. 1648.

O. CROMWELL.[224]

But Cromwell was not merely the besieger of Pontefract, he was in command of the whole northern area, and in this capacity he wrote in regard to the payment of the Hull garrison and the maintenance of the garrison of Wressel Castle, the property of the Dukes of Northumberland and "one of the most propre" and luxurious castles north of the Trent.[225] Garrisoned by its owner for Parliament, it had been under the command of Major Fenwick until Cromwell had ordered him to Carlisle, and with Pontefract, Scarborough, Berwick, Carlisle and Hull it was part of that chain of fortresses which controlled northern England.

Warrant

Requiring all who shall demand any money in relation to the monthly tax upon any of the towns, formerly assigned to the maintenance of the garrison of Wressell Castle, that they forbear the levying of the same till further order. But that the money be employed for the said garrison according to order.

Knottingley, November 23, 1648 O. CROMWELL.[226]

Again in his capacity of commander of the northern area two days later Cromwell wrote to the Treasurer of the County Committee of West Riding,[227] to solicit funds for Hull:

For my noble Friend Thomas St. Nicholas, Esquire

SIR,

I suppose it's not unknown to you how much the country is in arrear to the garrison of Hull; as likewise how probable it is that the garrison will break, unless some speedy course be taken to get them money;

[224] From the original in the possession of Mr. C. D. Blake, Boston, Mass.

[225] Parliament ordered it demolished in 1650. Its ruins still stand on the east bank of the Derwent in Yorkshire.

[226] Summary from *Hist. Mss. Comm. Rept.* 3, App., p. 87 (Duke of Northumberland Mss.), where it is taken from a contemporary copy in vol. xvi of the Duke of Northumberland Mss.

[227] Ten years later Recorder for Canterbury.

the soldiers at the present being ready to mutiny, as not having money to buy them bread, and without money the stubborn townspeople will not trust them for the worth of a penny.

Sir, I must beg of you that, as you tender the good of the country, so far as the security of that garrison is mentioned,[228] you would give your assistance to the helping of them to their money which the country owes them. The Governor[229] will apply himself to you, either in person or by letter. I pray you do for him herein as in a business of very high consequence. I am the more earnest with you, as having a very deep sense how dangerous the event may be, of their being neglected in the matter of their pay. I rest upon your favour herein, and subscribe myself,

Sir,
Your very humble servant,

Knottingley,
November 25th, 1648. O. CROMWELL.[230]

Such was the business which engaged Cromwell's attention at the time when the fate of the King and, in a sense, of the nation hung in the balance, and it is no unfair question why he stayed on at the siege of Pontefract when such tremendous issues were being debated at St. Albans and at Westminster. His presence at the siege seems to have served no good purpose for it was not until long after he left that the place surrendered, nor is there any indication in his correspondence that he anticipated its speedy reduction nor, indeed, that the siege was pressed with great severity, had that been possible. He was in close touch with the movements in the world of politics, but it is surprising that he who had been the chief figure in the debates of the army hitherto, alone of all the general officers, save Lambert, absented himself from these important consultations. Whatever the reason, it was, at least, good policy. He held aloof from the clash of opinions and arguments and thus avoided making enemies; yet that again is unlike the man who hitherto had been in the forefront of debate and negotiations as of battle.

No reasonable explanation has been given or attempted, nor has his absence been considered especially remarkable by his biographers —though the siege of Pontefract was no such great nor vital operation as to absorb the energies of the greatest of the Parliamentary commanders in this greatest of crises.[231] There is little record of him at this important period. When John Lilburne wrote his *Legal Fundamental Liberties*, which was published in June of the year fol-

[228] Altered to "motioned" by Carlyle.

[229] Col. Robert Overton.

[230] Oldmixon, *History of England* (1730), ii, 352; Kimber's (anonymous) *Life of Cromwell* (3rd ed., London, 1731), p. 96; Carlyle, Letter LXXXIV.

[231] Mr. Buchan speaks of his being "strangely absent in the north"; Gardiner offers no explanation.

lowing, he told something of his own impressions of Cromwell as he saw him at this moment:

> "Having been in the North about my own business, I saw Crumwel, and made as diligent scrutinies into things about him, as I could, which I then to myself judged, savoured more of intended self-exalting, than anything really and heartily (of what before I had strongly heard of him) to the through-advancement of those things that were worthy to be accounted indeed the Liberties and Freedoms of the Nation."

This, it appears from Lilburne's narrative, was just before the meeting at the *Nag's Head* Tavern, for, as he goes on to say, "being come to London, my self and some other of my friends, by two messengers . . . sent a message down to him at Pomfret . . . his express answer to which . . . was principally directed by the Independents," who appointed the meeting at the *Nag's Head.* Thereafter various conferences between Lilburne and his friends, "nick-named Levellers" as he says, and representatives of the "Gentlemen Independents"—"Mr. Ireton, the Stear-man himself . . . Mr. Peters, the grand Journey or Hackney-man of the Army . . . and Colonel Harrison, . . . then extremely fair and gilded." First at Windsor, where they were welcomed by Ireton and his party, then at Whitehall, where they were joined by some members of Parliament, Independents and Levellers conferred, and, presently, "when the army came to town . . . there came the General, Cromwell, and the whole gang of Creature-Colonels, and other officers . . . and there Ireton shewed himself an absolute king, if not an Emperor."[232]

Whether or not Ireton was Cromwell's counsellor or his mouthpiece or merely his colleague or ally in this enterprise of eliminating Charles, it is impossible to say. If they wrote to each other, as doubtless they did, the letters have never come to light,[233] but there can be but little doubt that they were in accord. For this there is an extraordinary letter to Colonel Robert Hammond as evidence. On Hammond, as governor of Carisbrooke and Charles's jailer, had fallen the heaviest burden of them all. Torn between his allegiance to Parliament and his duty as an officer, not unfriendly to the King, and fearful of the situation in which he found himself, he wrote at this moment to Cromwell to propose retiring from his post and to ask for some assurance and advice, and to him Cromwell addressed one of the most remarkable letters which he ever wrote:

[232] Lilburne, *Legal Fundamental Liberties.*

[233] Gardiner seems to believe that they did but that the letters were too dangerous to be kept and so were destroyed. If so, it is hardly necessary to say that they would be, on the whole, the most important of all of Cromwell's correspondence.

To Colonel Robert Hammond: These

Dear Robin,

No man rejoiceth more to see a line from thee than myself. I know thou hast long been under trial. Thou shalt be no loser by it. All must work for the best.

Thou desirest to hear of my experiences. I can tell thee: I am such a one as thou didst formerly know, having a body of sin and death, but I thank God, through Jesus Christ our Lord there is no condemnation, though much infirmity, and I wait for the redemption. And in this poor condition I obtain mercy, and sweet consolation through the Spirit, and find abundant cause every day to exalt the Lord, and abase flesh, and herein I have some exercise.

As to outward dispensations, if we may so call them, we have not been without our share of beholding some remarkable providences, and appearances of the Lord. His presence hath been amongst us, and by the light of His countenance we have prevailed. We are sure, the good-will of Him who dwelt in the bush has shined upon us, and we can humbly say, We know in whom we have believed, who is able and will perfect what remaineth, and us also in doing what is well-pleasing in His eyesight.

I find some trouble in your spirit; occasioned first, not only by the continuance of your sad and heavy burden, as you call it, upon you, but by the dissatisfaction you take at the ways of some good men whom you love with your heart, who through this principle, That it is lawful for a lesser part, if in the right, to force [a numerical majority] &c.

To the first: call not your burden sad or heavy. If your Father laid it upon you, He intended neither. He is the Father of lights, from whom comes every good and perfect gift, who of His own will begot us, and bade us count it all joy when such things befall us; they being for the exercise of faith and patience, whereby in the end we shall be made perfect (James i.).

Dear Robin, our fleshly reasonings ensnare us. These make us say, heavy, sad, pleasant, easy. Was there not a little of this when Robert Hammond, through dissatisfaction too, desired retirement from the Army, and thought of quiet in the Isle of Wight?[234] Did not God find him out there? I believe he will never forget this. And now I perceive he is to seek again; partly through his sad and heavy burden, and partly through his dissatisfaction with friends' actings.

Dear Robin, thou and I were never worthy to be door-keepers in this service. If thou wilt seek, seek to know the mind of God in all that chain of Providence, whereby God brought thee thither, and that person to thee; how, before and since, God has ordered him, and affairs concerning him: and then tell me, whether there be not some glorious and high meaning in all this, above what thou hast yet attained? And, laying aside thy fleshly reason, seek of the Lord to teach thee what that is; and He will do it. I dare be positive to say, it is not that the wicked should be exalted, that God should so appear as indeed He hath done. For there is no peace to them. No, it is set upon the hearts of such as fear the Lord, and we have witness upon witness, That it shall go ill with them and their partakers. I say again, seek

[234] 6th September of the foregoing Year.

that spirit to teach thee; which is the spirit of knowledge and understanding, the spirit of counsel and might, of wisdom and of the fear of the Lord. That spirit will close thine eyes and stop thine ears, so that thou shalt not judge by them, but thou shalt judge for the meek of the earth, and thou shalt be made able to do accordingly. The Lord direct thee to that which is well-pleasing in His eyesight.

As to thy dissatisfaction with friends' actings upon that supposed principle, I wonder not at that. If a man take not his own burden well, he shall hardly others', especially if involved by so near a relation of love and Christian brotherhood as thou art. I shall not take upon me to satisfy, but I hold myself bound to lay my thoughts before so dear a friend. The Lord do His own will.

You say: "God hath appointed authorities among the nations, "to which active or passive obedience is to be yielded. This "resides in England in the Parliament. Therefore active or "passive" &c.[235]

Authorities and powers are the ordinance of God. This or that species is of human institution, and limited, some with larger, others with stricter bands, each one according to its constitution. I do not therefore think the authorities may do anything, and yet such obedience [be] due, but all agree there are cases in which it is lawful to resist. If so, your ground fails, and so likewise the interference. Indeed, dear Robin, not to multiply words, the query is, Whether ours be such a case? This ingenuously is the true question.

To this I shall say nothing, though I could say very much; but only desire thee to see what thou findest in thy own heart as to two or three plain considerations. First, whether *Salus Populi* be a sound position?[236] Secondly, whether in the way in hand,[237] really and before the Lord, before whom conscience must stand, this be provided for, or the whole fruit of the war like to be frustrated, and all most like to turn to what it was, and worse? And this, contrary to engagements, declarations, implicit covenants with those who ventured their lives upon those covenants and engagements, without whom perhaps, in equity, relaxation ought not to be? Thirdly, Whether this Army be not a lawful power, called by God to oppose and fight against the King upon some stated grounds; and being in power to such ends, may not oppose one name of authority, for those ends, as well as another, the outward authority that called them, not by their power making the quarrel lawful, but it being so in itself? If so it may be acting will be justified *in foro humano*.—But truly these kinds of reasonings may be but fleshly, either with or against: only it is good to try what truth may be in them. And the Lord teach us.

My dear friend, let us look into providences; surely they mean somewhat. They hang so together; have been so constant, so clear and unclouded. Malice, swoln malice against God's people, now called Saints, to root out their name; and yet they, by providence, having arms, and therein blessed with defence and more. I desire, he that is for a principle of suffering would not too much slight this. I slight not him who is so minded: but let us beware lest fleshly reasoning see more safety in making use of this principle than

[235] "Obedience."

[236] The safety of the people the supreme law.

[237] By this Parliamentary Treaty with the King.

in acting. Who acts, and resolves not through God to be willing to part with all? Our hearts are very deceitful, on the right and on the left.

What think you of Providence disposing the hearts of so many of God's people this way, especially in this poor Army, wherein the great God has vouchsafed to appear. I know not one officer among us but is on the increasing hand. And let me say it is here in the North, after much patience, we trust the same Lord who hath framed our minds in our actings, is with us in this also. And this contrary to a natural tendency, and to those comforts our hearts could wish to enjoy with others. And the difficulties probably to be encountered with, and the enemies, not few, even all that is glorious in this world, with appearance of united names, titles and authorities, and yet not terrified,[238] only desiring to fear our great God, that we do nothing against His will. Truly this is our condition.[239]

And to conclude. We in this Northern Army were in a waiting posture, desiring to see what the Lord would lead us to. And a Declaration[240] is put out, at which many are shaken: although we could perhaps have wished the stay of it till after the treaty, yet seeing it is come out, we trust to rejoice in the will of the Lord, waiting His further pleasure. Dear Robin, beware of men, look up to the Lord. Let Him be free to speak and command in thy heart. Take heed of the things I fear thou hast reasoned thyself into, and thou shalt be able through Him, without consulting flesh and blood, to do valiantly for Him and for His people.

Thou mentionest somewhat as if, by acting against such opposition as is like to be, there will be a tempting of God. Dear Robin, tempting of God ordinarily is either by acting presumptuously in carnal confidence, or in unbelief through diffidence: both these ways Israel tempted God in the wilderness, and He was grieved by them. The encountering difficulties, therefore, makes us not to tempt God; but acting before and without faith. If the Lord have in any measure persuaded His people, as generally He hath, of the lawfulness, nay of the duty, this persuasion prevailing upon the heart is faith, and acting thereupon is acting in faith, and the more the difficulties are, the more faith. And it is most sweet that he that is not persuaded have patience towards them that are, and judge not: and this will free thee from the trouble of others' actings, which, thou sayest, adds to thy grief. Only let me offer two or three things, and I have done.

Dost thou not think this fear of the Levellers (of whom there is no fear) that they would destroy nobility, had caused some to rake up corruption;

[238] Come or coming over to this opinion.

[239] "Briefly stated, Cromwell's argument was that the victories of the army, and the convictions of the godly, were external and internal evidence of God's will, to be obeyed as a duty. It was dangerous reasoning, and not less dangerous that secular and political motives coincided with the dictates of religious enthusiasm. Similar arguments might be held to justify not merely the temporary intervention of the army, but its permanent assumption of the government of England. Practical good sense and conservative instincts prevented Cromwell from adopting the extreme consequences of his theory; with most of his comrades the logic of fanaticism was qualified by no such considerations." Firth's *Cromwell*, p. 213.

[240] Remonstrance of the Army, presented by Ewer on Monday. [Note by Mrs. Lomas.]

to find it lawful to make this ruining hypocritical agreement, on one part?[241] Hath not this biased even some good men? I will not say, their fear will come upon them; but if it do, they will themselves bring it upon themselves. Have not some of our friends, by their passive principle (which I judge not, only I think it liable to temptation as well as the active, and neither good but as we are led into them by God,—neither to be reasoned into, because the heart is deceitful), been occasioned to overlook what is just and honest, and [to] think the people of God may have as much or more good the one way than the other? Good by this Man, against whom the Lord hath witnessed; and whom thou knowest. Is this so in their hearts; or is it reasoned, forced in?

Robin, I have done. Ask we our hearts, whether we think that, after all, these dispensations, the like to which many generations cannot afford, should end in so corrupt reasonings of good men, and should so hit the designings of bad? Thinkest thou, in thy heart, that the glorious dispensations of God point out to this? Or to teach His people to trust in Him, and to wait for better things, when, it may be, better are sealed to many of their spirits? And as a poor looker-on, I had rather live in the hope of that spirit, and take my share with them, expecting a good issue, than be led away with the other.

This trouble I have been at, because my soul loves thee, and I would not have thee swerve, nor lose any glorious opportunity the Lord puts into thy hand. The Lord be thy counsellor. Dear Robin, I rest thine,

November 25, 1648.

OLIVER CROMWELL.[242]

Of this extraordinary letter various interpretations have been made and it reveals, at least, Cromwell's elusive character which has troubled even his admirers. Cromwell's latest biographer has seen in it "the whole history of his inner life while he was sweeping over northern England like a flame—fragments of Ireton's old philosophy, some of the Levellers' speculations which had been creeping into his mind, his own perplexed musings over Scripture texts."[243] Carlyle has been both lyric and dithyrambic over it. On the other hand it has been declared that Cromwell's earlier letter to Hammond on November 6, "bears evidence of Cromwell's inability as yet definitely to make up his mind on the great question of the trial of the King"; and that in his letter regarding Sir John Owen[244] "lay the root of Cromwell's cry for justice on delinquents, in which, after long hesita-

[241] "Surely we have here laid bare before us Cromwellian opinion in the making. As in other men, the wish was father to the thought. The desire, whether for private or for public ends, shapes the thoughts, and, in Cromwell's case, as the desires swept a wider compass than with most men, the thoughts took a larger scope, and, to some extent, jostled with one another. The cloudy mixture would clear itself soon enough." Gardiner's *Cromwell*, p. 101.]

[242] Birch, p. 101. Carlyle, Letter LXXXV.

[243] Buchan, *Cromwell*, p. 234.

[244] See pp. 691.

tion, he had at last included a cry for justice on the King." In this letter to Hammond, Gardiner believes that "Cromwell strove to justify his change of ground in the spirit of one who argues because he has made up his mind, not in that of one who has resolved to follow the argument whithersoever it may lead him," in effect the rationalization of a position already taken.[245]

What, then, was that position and why did Cromwell take his stand on it? There was—there must be—Hammond had argued, an authority in each state to which obedience was owed, to which resistance, active or passive, is forbidden, and this in England resided in the Parliament. To this Cromwell replied, with the proviso that "there are cases in which it is lawful to resist" and asks is "ours such a case?" All "outward dispensations," he replies to his own question, indicate that it is, "We are sure the good-will of Him who dwelt in the bush has shined on us"—in brief, success has demonstrated the righteousness of the cause. Next, he inquires, is *Salus Populi* a "sound position?"; and thirdly, "Whether this Army be not a lawful power?" There was no need to fear the Levellers he insisted; and, however cryptic and however to be interpreted, he adds a curious sentence—"Good by this Man, against whom the Lord hath witnessed; and whom thou knowest."[246] Finally, with that proud depreciation of himself and his cause which marks much of his writing, he concludes: "As a poor looker-on, I had rather live in the hope of that spirit and take my share with them, expecting a good issue, than be led away with the other."

It is no wonder that controversy has raged over such a letter as this; that a hostile critic has remarked that Cromwell with "cautious obscurity, shadowy significance, . . . suavity, tenderness, subtlety, alludes to more than he mentions; suggests more than pronounces his own . . . intention, and opens an indefinite view, all the hard features of which he softly puts aside."[247] It is no wonder that even such a champion as John Morley observes that "from the point of a modern's carnal reasoning all this has a thoroughly sophistic flavour, and leaves a doubt of its actual weight in Oliver's own mind." "What, he inquires, "if this be the real Cromwell, and represents the literal working of his own habit and temper?"[248] And what, one may inquire practically, lay behind the language of his letters to Hammond?

It meant, if it meant anything, that he approved of bringing Charles to account or "justice" for all the evils which had befallen

[245] Gardiner, *Civil War*, iv, 248, 251, 252.

[246] Or as Gardiner punctuates it: "Good, by this man against whom the Lord hath witnessed, and whom thou knowest!" However punctuated, its meaning is clear enough.

[247] Mozley, *Essays*.

[248] Morley, *Cromwell*, p. 268.

England since the beginning of the civil war. It meant more than that, for, having brought the King to trial, was it conceivable that Charles should be acquitted and turned back a free man—and a King! It meant that Cromwell concurred with Ireton that the King must be put out of the way, and, however wrapped in the mysteries of religious phraseology, it meant that Cromwell was prepared to push the matter through to that conclusion.

There remain two more questions to which this letter gives no answer. One is the reason for Cromwell's long stay at Knottingley, which may be variously interpreted; the other is his view of the future. Assuming that the King was to be removed, what then? That question was not confined to the Presbyterians or the Levellers. It was felt by men as different as Fairfax and Lilburne; it must have been in the minds of nearly every one. Had Cromwell, then, considered it? For that there is no evidence, save Lilburne's feeling that Cromwell entertained ambitions for the headship of the state—and the eventual solution of the great problem.

Yet were Charles gone, who would succeed him? Not the young princes then in exile, for it was inconceivable that they could be brought back to be, like their father, at the mercy of the army; certainly not Vane nor Fairfax, nor any man in the army or in Parliament—save perhaps one. Despite the charges of his enemies, despite the language of Royalists and Levellers at the time and thereafter, it is impossible to prove that such a worldly idea ever entered Cromwell's head, much less that he conceived himself in such a post. Yet had he not, he would have been, one must imagine, much more or less than human. With all of the talk of Parliament and a Supreme Council, he had little faith in deliberative bodies, little patience with deliberative processes save as they served his own purposes. "Far into the future," Gardiner truly says of him, "he could not look"; but had he looked but a little way, could he have seen another man then in England so fit to rule as he? With all his commendation of the army *Remonstrance*—which, in fact, left the question of an individual executive in the air—it is difficult to see Cromwell believing in such a committee as it suggested, either of a Council or of a Parliament, as the head of a state; for more than once, before this and thereafter, both in word and deed, he expressed his opinion of such government. And more—had God not shown him favor, had he not been chosen to bear the cause to victory, and was not that, in his own words an "outward dispensation" of God's purpose? Was he not a "chosen vessel" and a Saint; and who but the leader of the Saints should rule? If not he, who then?

It is not necessary to assume with the Royalists that Cromwell planned and plotted the King's death and his own ascendancy from the beginning. He met the problems as they came along; yet somewhere along the way the idea that he might be called to the highest post must have occurred to him. It occurred to many others who expressed it publicly, and, if in no other way, he could hardly have been unaware of it, for it was scarcely less than common talk, and for this there was a good reason. It was the constitution and personnel of the army in which he was the dominant figure. This was not the army which had begun the Civil War. It bore as little relation to that volunteer organization as the existing Parliament bore to the body elected eight years before. It had been twice formally reorganized; once at the formation of the New Model and once in the last months of 1647; and both times under the influence of Cromwell, and measurably in his image.

Lilburne's taunt of the "Creature-Colonels" had within it a certain grain of truth, since in no small measure the new leaders of the regiments were Cromwell's creation as well as his followers. Though it differed in many respects from the Grande Armée which Napoleon created out of the revolutionary forces in France a century and a half later, there were also many points of resemblance between that force and this. The old colonels were largely gone, with the old generals. Essex, Manchester, Sir William Waller, Holles, Stapleton, and the Presbyterians in general, had disappeared, and those who remained were, like Fairfax and Monk, soldiers rather than politicians. In place of the old colonels there had risen men like Harrison, Okey, Ewer, Barkstead, Corbet, Berry, men of lower social status and more radical opinions than those who had begun the civil war, prepared to proceed to extremes from which the older officers would have shrunk, from which, in fact, many had shrunk, and many more, with Fairfax at their head, were drawing back with horror and dismay. And if the Cromwellian colonels were in many ways like the Napoleonic marshals the men were no less changed. They bore the same relation to the volunteers and drafted troops which had begun the civil wars six years earlier that the soldiers of Napoleon's Grande Armée bore to the first French revolutionary levies.

Though a large proportion of the officers were no doubt moved by spiritual considerations, there were among them professional soldiers like Monk who had once been in the royal service, as well as thousands of the rank and file who had once followed Charles and Rupert. Each side had, in fact, enlisted where it could. If the King had French in his service, the Parliament had Dutch, and in the lists of the officers under Cromwell one finds Scotch, Irish and Welsh names, with some like Tulidah, Dalbier and Vermuyden, which suggest more distant origins. This was a natural result of a period of civil war when peaceful occupations were interrupted and men were driven to the pursuit of arms for a livelihood, but it reveals the Cromwellian army in a somewhat different light than that of a force wholly devoted to a cause which inspired each of its members with deep religious fervor. There were, indeed, some regiments largely composed of such men, but even in them, and still more in the army generally, the professional element was notable; nor can one doubt but that, with all respect to its religious quality, it was its stern discipline and its experience as much as its spiritual element which made it so formidable.

But its directing spirits were more than mere soldiers; they were consciously endeavoring to found a new order. As long ago as when Cromwell formed his troop in Cambridge, Baxter says:

"When he lay at Cambridge long before with that famous Troop which he began his Army with, his Officers purposed to make their Troop a gathered Church, and they all subscribed an Invitation to me to be their Pastor, and sent it me to Coventry: I sent them a Denial, . . . And afterwards meeting Cromwell at Leicester he expostulated with me for denying them. These very men that then invited me to be their Pastor, were the Men that afterwards headed much of the Army, and some of them were the forwardest in all our Changes; which made me wish that I had gone among them, however it had been interpreted; for then all the Fire was in one Spark."

But to this was added another element which he noted on his visit to the army after Naseby:

"But when I came to the Army among Cromwell's Soldiers, I found a new face of things which I never dreamt of: I heard the plotting Heads very hot upon that which intimated their Intention to subvert both Church and State. . . . Abundance of the common Troopers, and many of the Officers, I found to be honest, sober, Orthodox Men, and others tractable ready to hear the Truth, and of upright Intentions: But a few proud, self-conceited, hot-headed Sectaries had got into the highest places, and were Cromwell's chief favourites, and by their very heat and activity bore down the rest, or carried them along with them, and were the Soul of the Army, though much fewer in number than the rest (being indeed not one to twenty throughout the Army; their strength being in the Generals and Whalleys and Rich's Regiments of Horse, and in the new placed Officers in many of the rest).

"I perceived that they took the King for a Tyrant and an Enemy, and really intended absolutely to master him, or to ruine him; and that they thought if they might fight against him, they might kill or conquer him; and if they might conquer, they were never more to trust him further than he was in their power; . . . They said, What were the Lords of England but William the Conquerour's Colonels? or the Barons but his Majors? or the Knights but his Captains?"[249]

The army had become not merely veteran and professional but had developed a character of its own, a separate interest, a sort of political unity, and a feeling of solidarity as an element in the state, a real *imperium in imperio*. What Lilburne and many others feared had,

[249] *Reliquiae Baxterianae*, (1696), i, 50–51.

in fact, already come to pass. The army was the dominating influence in affairs and Cromwell the dominant figure in the army. With all of his ability and character, Fairfax was scarcely more than the nominal commander-in-chief of the forces under him. He was no match for a man like Cromwell, who, as Clarendon truly said, "overwitted" him, especially in the situation now developing.

That situation came rapidly to a crisis. Before Hammond received Cromwell's letter, that letter no longer mattered. Charles still cherished hope of an escape and, closely watched by the army representatives, plans were laid to transfer him to a safer place. To that Hammond refused to lend himself, save by direct order from Parliament, and it became necessary, therefore, to remove him from his post. On November 21 Fairfax replied to Hammond's remonstrances by summoning him to headquarters and replaced him with Colonel Ewer, a former "serving man" risen to command during the civil wars, distinguishing himself at the siege of Chepstow where he acted with "needless violence and cruelty." He had sat on the court which condemned Lucas and Lisle to death after the surrender of Colchester and most recently he had been entrusted with the presentation of the *Army Remonstrance* to the House. If violence were intended, Ewer was a man fit for it and prepared to use it. As Herbert records of him, he "received the King with small observance," "his look was stern, his hair and large beard were black and bushy . . . hardly could one see a man of more grim aspect, and no less robust and rude was his behaviour,"[250] for his manners were, if possible, even worse than his appearance.

The replacement of Hammond by Ewer foreshadowed the nature of the next act in the drama. Before Ewer arrived, Hammond had notified the Speaker of the House of Lords of his orders and had given charge of the King to three officers with instructions to prevent the removal of Charles except by the command of Parliament, even if they were compelled to call on the trained bands of the Isle of Wight to protect him. When Ewer arrived with orders from headquarters to secure the King until Parliament had acted on the Remonstrance, among whose provisions was one for his trial, Hammond at first resisted, then accompanied Ewer to headquarters at Windsor, but was arrested, while the Council of Officers sent instruction to remove the King to the harsh and unhealthy prison of Hurst Castle. Refusing to make an effort to escape, Charles was carried thither, and there, on December 1, began the last stage of his imprisonment before he was brought to trial.

[250] Herbert, *Two last years of Charles I*, pp. 85–6 (1702).

The Religious successfull and truly Valliant
Lieutenant Generall Cromwell

The First Published Portrait of Cromwell. From Ricraft, *Survey of England's Champions and Truth's Faithfull Patriots*, 1647.

PART II

THE EXECUTION OF THE KING

PRIDE'S PURGE, DECEMBER 6, 1647

Meanwhile events moved fast elsewhere. The King was now secure; there remained the Parliament; and against it, following the suggestion so often thrown out by the advanced Independents like Ireton, the army proceeded without delay. It was necessary first to come to an agreement with the Levellers and on November 28, the day that Hammond was arrested at Farnham, the group of officers headed by Ireton and the delegation of Levellers headed by Lilburne, conferring at Windsor had agreed that there should be a meeting of the various parties—four civilians, four army and four Parliamentary Independents, and four Levellers—to which Lilburne added that he would even invite four Presbyterians, if they would come. For the moment the Levellers were quieted, and though Lilburne presently denounced the "dissembling, juggling knaves . . . especially the cunningest of Machiavilians, Commissary Henry Ireton" as having grossly deceived him and his colleagues, this move served its purpose of eliminating a dangerous element for the time being. With this the army was ready to move and, issuing a declaration for impartial justice, regular payment of the soldiers and speedy enactment of salutary laws, Fairfax advised the Lord Mayor of London that the army was about to advance again upon the capital and expected an immediate payment of £40,000 out of the City assessments.

The Commons, once more confronted with the threat of naked force, had even less to offer in the way of resistance than when, sixteen months earlier, it had the City, the "reformadoes" and the Presbyterian officers on its side. It refused to follow Prynne in his violent demand that the soldiers be declared "rebels." It did, indeed, "direct the Speaker to request the General to keep at a distance," but that was a feeble and futile gesture, and it urged the Lord Mayor to meet Fairfax's demands. There was, in fact, nothing else to do. On December 1 Holles informed the House of Charles's final answer to the commissioners and debate on his report was set for the next day; but on that day the army entered the City and Westminster; Fairfax took up his quarters in Whitehall; and the debate was postponed indefinitely.

Before it began, news arrived on December 4 of the transfer of the King to Hurst Castle; and, after long and acrimonious discussion, the Presbyterians, who had plucked up a little courage in the face of this pressing danger, carried an innocuous resolution that the King had been removed 'without the knowledge or consent of Parliament.' A motion to accept the King's answer to the proposals of Parliament, which was urged by Fiennes, was supported by the Independents who hoped to find in it the excuse for intervention which they sought. That hope was denied them, for the Presbyterians carried a motion to delay, but meanwhile various circumstances precipitated the catastrophe which the Presbyterians had been seeking desperately to avoid.

While the Commons struggled to escape the clutches of the army, the committee of Independents and Levellers at Westminster had completed and adopted a new *Agreement of the People*, despite the opposition of Ireton. The City began to show signs of increasing restlessness. The Presbyterians were looking for allies and were prepared to treat with Charles. With the possibility of a combination of Royalists, Presbyterians and the City to bring back the King, the army hastened to forestall that possibility. When on December 5 there was held a meeting of the officers at Whitehall to consider their next step, the doom of the Parliamentary Presbyterians was sealed.

There were but three courses left to the officers, now that they had finally broken with the King. They could dissolve Parliament and call a general election—which would have been suicide. They could, as Cromwell did later, drive the whole House of Commons out; or they could do what had been so often suggested and what they finally determined on—"purge" the House of those opposed to them. In consequence on the morning of December 6, without orders from Fairfax it was said, all the approaches to the House of Commons were occupied by soldiery. Colonel Pride, who was in command of the House of Commons' guard in the Commons' lobby, holding a list of the proscribed members which had been previously drawn up, had them pointed out to him by Lord Grey of Groby as they sought to enter. They were stopped and those who resisted were carried off as prisoners to a room known as the Queen's Court. Those who managed to enter the House indulged in another futile gesture, sending their serjeant-at-arms to demand the release of the prisoners from the commander of their guard, who replied that he took no orders save from his General.

Thus was the House of Commons "purged" of some forty men. To the remnant the Council of Officers promptly sent a demand for renewal of the charges against the survivors of the eleven members formerly excluded, and for the trial of Major-General Browne accused of inviting the Scots. To this they added presently another demand that all who had voted to readmit the eleven members or had opposed the vote declaring that those who called in the Scots were traitors, or had opposed the army in any way, should be excluded from the House.

In such fashion were the Presbyterians eliminated from politics; and in such fashion did the army become the sole arbiter of English fortunes.

In all of this, so far as external appearances were concerned, Cromwell took no part. The siege of Pontefract Castle was now in its sixth month, and despite his presence, it showed no signs of coming to an end. Nor was he destined to receive its surrender, though Clarendon declares that he was bent on its capture because he desired to "take full vengeance" on its garrison "for the loss of Rainsborough to whose ghost he designed an ample sacrifice." It did not, indeed, surrender for four months more, and then under dramatic circumstances which enabled the leaders of the defence to make good their escape in romantic fashion. Meanwhile Cromwell was summoned to the center of affairs. On November 28, the day on which Hammond was arrested and Ireton and the Levellers began to confer at Windsor, Fairfax ordered him to repair immediately to headquarters,[251] and he replied, apparently at once, approving the *Remonstrance* and assuring Fairfax that the General's own regiment, with those of Cromwell, Okey, Harrison and "some others," would come up to London, leaving Lambert in charge of affairs in the north:

For his Excellency the Lord-General Fairfax

SIR,

We have read your declaration here, and see in it nothing but what is honest and becoming Christians and honest men to say and offer. It's good to look up to God, who alone is able to sway hearts to agree to the good and just things contained therein. I verily believe the honest party in Scotland will be satisfied in the justness thereof; however, it will be good that Will Rowe be hastened with instructions thither.

I beseech you command him (if it seems good to your Excellency's judgment) to go away with all speed; what is timely done herein may prevent misunderstandings in them. I hope to wait speedily upon you, at least to begin my journey upon Tuesday.[252] Your own regiment will be coming up. So will Okey's, mine, Harrison's and some others. The two garrisons have men enow (if provided for) to do that work. Lambert will look to them.

I rest, my Lord,

Your Excellency's most humble and faithful servant,

November [29?] 1648. O. CROMWELL.[253]

[251] Fairfax to Cromwell, in *Clarke Papers*, ii, 62–3.

[252] This must mean Tuesday, December 5, as Cromwell reached London on the evening of Wednesday the 6th, and it is not likely that when so urgently summoned, he would take more than a week to make the journey. On the other hand, two days would indeed mean travelling "post haste." Perhaps he got away a little sooner.

[253] *Egerton Mss.* 2620, f. 3. Endorsed by Wm. Clarke. Printed in the *English Historical Review*, 1887, p. 149. Lomas-Carlyle, Suppl. 27.

It seems evident that, besides approving the *Remonstrance*, he favored the seizure, close imprisonment and trial of the King, and though, as usual, there are few or no writings of his extant for this period of his life, it is not difficult to judge of his position. There is still no clue to his long stay at Pontefract. The military situation in the north was evidently well within the powers of Lambert to control; and what we know of the siege seems to indicate that it was far from being prosecuted vigorously—though the winter made it all but impossible to take the place, and there was no hurry.

It has been suggested that, as at other times, he remained in the background until the stage was set, then, like the actor which the Royalists said he was, he entered at the great moment to take the leading part. One thing is certain. William Rowe had succeeded Watson as scoutmaster-general and it was essential that at this crisis the continued support of Argyll and his party should be assured before the next act of the drama was unfolded at Whitehall. Apparently in advance of the regiments now ordered to London, hastening to Westminster, Cromwell arrived at Whitehall on the evening of the day of Pride's Purge. It is inconceivable that he had not been informed of the intention of the army to put pressure upon Parliament, though of the plan as it was carried out he could not well have known, for it was decided on with haste and secrecy. He none the less approved of it. As Ludlow said, "He declared that he had not been acquainted with this design; yet since it was done, he was glad of it, and would endeavour to maintain it.[254]

With this he resumed his seat in the Council of Officers and in the remnant of the House of Commons and amid the great events of the ensuing days, took up the old externals of his daily life. On the day of his first appearance, December 7, the morning after Pride's Purge, there appeared also one of his particular detestations, that "evil liver" Henry Marten, now returned from his adventure in Berkshire and the north, and either by him or by Cromwell's chief object of dislike in later years, Sir Henry Vane the younger, there was proposed and carried a vote of thanks for his recent achievements in the field.[255] To this was added, the next day, another of those minutiae of which his life was full, a recommendation in behalf of an obscure Devonshire man who had been declared delinquent for "going into the King's quarters to gather in his debts," and who compounded on December 14:

[254] Ludlow, *Memoirs*, (Firth ed.), i, 211–212.

[255] Wood, (*Athenae Oxoniensis*, ii, 661) says Henry Marten, who made his appearance also on the 7th after a long absence, interrupted a discussion on the secured members to ask consideration of Cromwell's deserts. Walker (*Anarchia Anglicana*, p. 34) says Sir Henry Vane proposed the thanks. See also *C. J.*, vi, 94, and newspapers

Certificate

These are to certify all those whom it may concern that John Kellond of Totnes in the County of Devon, Esq., was in Cornwall at the time of the disbanding of the horse at Truro, and is comprised within those Articles, and ought to enjoy the full benefit of them. Witness my hand and seal this 8th of December, 1648.

O. CROMWELL.[256]

Insignificant as it is, it is in one way a notable document; for it is, like his letter in behalf of the old Royalist governor of Newark, in such sharp contrast to his attitude toward those who in one way or another had fallen into the power of the army and Parliament for their efforts to restore the King in the second civil war. On them he had small mercy or none, as his letter in regard to Sir John Owen testifies. Nor was Owen alone. As Lilburne said, "Oliver had his hands full with Poyer, Goring, Holland, Hamilton and Langdale," for he still had them in custody, together with Owen and many others taken prisoner in the recent war. Above all the King; and on this the irrepressible Marten who could never resist the opportunity to jest even, as it proved later, in the face of death, coined his epigram. The Commons prisoners had been taken to an inn called "Hell"; and, as he said, "Since Tophet is prepared for kings, it is fitting their friends should go to Hell."[257]

Before that final conclusion was reached, however, the army had another problem to determine. Its first requirement was money and, though he failed to get his £40,000 from the City, Fairfax secured some £28,000 from a subcommittee of the Committee for Advance of Money at Weavers' Hall. Thereafter, under threat of quartering his soldiers on the City, he demanded more from the harassed citizens. The next concern was Parliament, now reduced to half a hundred men or less, many of them officers like Cromwell, deeply devoted to the army's cause. This body promptly complied with the army's demands. It voted to expel those of the eleven members still alive; revoked the repeal of the Vote of No Addresses; annulled the votes which had authorized the Treaty of Newport, but let off Hamilton, Goring and other leaders of the second civil war with fines and banishment. It soon became apparent, however, that Cromwell's view that the punishment of these men was not sufficient was supported by the army against whose dominance they had rebelled.

On December 14, in consequence, Major-General Browne, Sir John

[256] *S. P. Dom.*, G ccvii, 651; *Cal. Comm. for Comp.*, p. 1878. Kellond's fine was set at £544/11.

[257] Gardiner, *Civil War*, iv, 272, from *Mercurius Pragmaticus*.

Clotworthy, Sir William Waller, Sir Edward Massey and Lionel Copley, all former members of the army and all Presbyterians, were arrested on the charge of having joined in the invitation to the Scots, and with this Cromwell once more entered on the scene. If these men were convicted, under any pretense of a trial, some evidence against them must be found and whether because of a letter to Cromwell from Hamilton, then a prisoner at Windsor, or to secure testimony against this new batch of prisoners, or both, on December 14, as *Mercurius Pragmaticus* records:

"This day Duke Oliver set forth in state towards Windsor, upon an entreaty by letter from Duke Hamilton to come and conferre with him, now that design is ripe for execution. It's thought that cunning coward (for as yet we must not call him traytor) hath told tales."[258]

The malice of the writer was unjustified, for he adds, four days later:

"Munday, Decem. 18, came information, that much discourse had passed between Hamilton and Cromwell at Windsor, but in conclusion he protested he was not invited in by his Majesty, nor by any member of Parliament."[259]

The rumor that the Duke had "discovered all he can to save himself and ruin others"[260] was totally unjustified. As Burnet wrote years later in his *Memoirs of the Dukes of Hamilton*:

"Cromwel came several times to him to draw from him some Discoveries of his Correspondents in England, and gave him great assurances of Life, Rewards and Secrecy; but he rejected the Proposition with horrour and disdain, though often repeated; and apprehending they might get his Brother into their hands, sent him" a note "written with the Juyce of a Lemon," to beware of the same trial.[261]

From this and other evidence it appears that Cromwell visited Hamilton more than once, but his visits were unsuccessful in every sense; for Hamilton's refusal to betray his allies and associates was presently to cost him his own life without being of any advantage to his fellow-adventurers or to the King.[262]

[258] *Mercurius Pragmaticus*, Dec. 14.

[259] *Ibid.*, Dec. 18.

[260] *Mercurius Elencticus*, Dec. 12–19; cp. *Perfect Diurnall*, Dec. 14.

[261] Burnet, *Memoirs of the Dukes of Hamilton*, p. 379 (1677).

[262] A dozen years later, when Cromwell's "familiar," Hugh Peters, was tried and convicted, one of the witnesses testified that Cromwell lived at "Master Baker's house in Windsor in December, and met frequently with Peters, Colonel Rich and Ireton in rooms occupied by Ireton and his wife in the house of the witness, one Starkey. But it is probable that his memory was at fault as to the time. There is no evidence that Ireton was at Windsor at this time, and Cromwell's other movements are traceable and leave no time for him to have spent any considerable period there. *Exact Account of the Trial of the Regicides*, pp. 158–160.

However Cromwell spent his time, one thing is notable. Though Ireton was present at every meeting of the Council of Officers from November 7 to February 22,[263] Cromwell, though he came to London early in December, attended but two of the thirteen meetings in that period, once on the day after he went to Windsor, December 15, and once on December 29.[264] Each session was, in its way, of the greatest importance, and in view of the prominent part which Cromwell had played in the meetings at Saffron Walden, it is remarkable that there is no record of his having taken part in the long debate upon the new *Agreement of the People*, which began on December 14 with the question as to "whether the Magistrate have or ought to have any compulsive and restrictive power in matters of religion." Adjourned first to discuss "the other part of the Agreement," then that part "in relation to justice," there were present for the debate on religion not merely members of the Council but various clergymen.

In it Ireton took the leading part, and, like many such debates, it dragged its slow length along through an infinity of theological subtleties without arriving at any conclusion. At that meeting Cromwell was not present, being on his visit to Windsor; but on the day following, December 15, he was there to discuss the all-important question of the hour.[265] It was expressed in the resolution that "the Kinge bee forthwith sent for to bee brought under safe guards to Windsor Castle, and there to be secur'd in order to the bringing of him speedily to justice." To that end a committee of seven was appointed—of whom it is noteworthy that none was above the rank of lieutenant-colonel—to meet from day to day "to consider of the best ways and grounds for the speedy bringing of the King to Justice," and "the like concerning Duke Hamilton, Lord Goreing, Lord Capell, Lord Loughborow" and presently the Earl of Holland, Sir Lewis Dives, Sir John Owen and Sir Henry Lingen; and to these were added the names of five other lesser men, accused of being spies, to be proceeded against by the Judge Advocate.

The programme laid down in the *Remonstrance* was carried out with such haste that on this very day, probably at the close of this meeting, as one of its results a letter was sent to Lieutenant-Colonel Cobbett and others at Hurst Castle announcing that Colonel Harrison with a convoy of horse and dragoons had been sent to bring the King to Windsor; and with this the Council went on in its next session to discuss the *Agreement*.[266] While that discussion was still going on,

263 *Clarke Papers*, ii, App.

264 No record of attendance was taken—or at least preserved—for the meeting on Dec. 23, and he may, of course, have been present then.

265 *Clarke Papers*, ii, App. (Table of Attendance).

266 *Clarke Papers*, ii, 131–2. Another *Agreement* by certain Londoners had been handed to Ireton on Dec. 11 which seems to have modified his opinions.

Cromwell went, on December 18, to welcome the Lord High Admiral, the Earl of Warwick, to confer about the danger from the new fleet then being prepared by Prince Charles,[267] and on the same day he wrote another letter of recommendation. This was in behalf of a certain Dr. Isaac Dorislaus, sometime Judge Advocate of the army, Judge of the Admiralty Court, and most recently an emissary to his native land, Holland, in regard to the revolted ships concerning which Cromwell had just been consulting Warwick. He was presently to help prepare the charge of high treason against Charles and within six months, despatched as a special envoy to the States General, was to be assassinated by the infuriated Royalist refugees.

To the Right Worshipful the Master and Fellows of Trinity Hall in Cambridge: These

GENTLEMEN,

I am given to understand that by the late decease of Dr. Duck, his chamber is become vacant in the Doctors Commons, to which Dr. Dorislaus now desireth to be your tenant: who hath done service unto the Parliament from the beginning of these wars, and hath been constantly employed by the Parliament in many weighty affairs, and especially of late, beyond the seas, with the States General of the United Provinces.

If you please to prefer him before any other, paying rent and fine to your College, I shall take it as a courtesy at your hands whereby you will oblige,

Your assured friend and servant,

18th December, 1648. OLIVER CROMWELL.[268]

"THE CHIEF DELINQUENT"

Parliament now disposed of, arrangements were made to deal with the King, and as matters were being put in train at Westminster, Harrison arrived at Hurst Castle on the evening of December 17, to announce that Charles was to be taken to Windsor, but left the next day without an interview with the King. On the morning of the 19th, Charles was taken to the mainland by Cobbett. Guarded by a troop of horse, he went on by way of Winchester, where he was welcomed by the authorities, and so to Farnham, to be met four miles beyond by another party of horse headed by Harrison, with "a velvet montero on his head, a new buff coat . . . and a crimson scarf about his waist"—which confirms Lilburne's description of him as "fair and gilded." Under his new guard, the unsuspecting King went on past Bagshot, where he had been told that the fastest horse in England was ready for his escape, to learn that the animal had fallen lame and

[267] *Perfect Diurnall*, Dec. 18; Rushworth, vii, 1366; Whitelocke, 362.

[268] *Trinity Hall Mss.;* pr. in *Cambridge Portfolio* (1849), ii, 390; Carlyle, Letter LXXXVI.

his last chance of liberty was gone. Still unconscious of the fate that awaited him, still believing that he had been brought for further discussions, he arrived at Windsor on December 23 and there put under double guard.

While Charles travelled the first stage of his journey to his death Cromwell was busy taking the measure of the situation and preparing his own plans. Having failed in his purpose of getting information from Hamilton against the King and those who had invited in the Scots, he had attended the meeting of the Council on December 15 which appointed the committee to formulate the means of bringing Charles to trial. On December 18, besides his meeting with Warwick, he had, according to the testimony of that capable lawyer and later Cromwellian official, Bulstrode Whitelocke, a conference with Lenthall, Sir Thomas Widdrington, Colonel Deane and Whitelocke himself. The next day, the 19th, the others visited Cromwell "who lay in one of the King's rich beds at Whitehall." Two days later, as Charles was making his journey to Windsor, Cromwell again met Whitelocke and Widdrington and "discoursed freely together about the present affairs and actions of the army and the settlement of the kingdom," though Whitelocke does not record what we should most like to know—that is what they said. On the next day, December 22, Whitelocke and Widdrington proposed that the Council of Officers should reply to the messages of the Commons and take steps to restore the excluded members, and that "heads for a declaration" should be drawn up, if the approval of the Council of Officers and of Parliament could be first secured.[269]

On that day Cromwell and Ireton wrote two letters, one to Harrison, whom they knew to be on the road from Farnham to Windsor with his royal prisoner, and one to Colonel Whichcott, the governor of Windsor, in regard to the details of guarding Charles and the preparations which had been determined on to that end:

To Col. Harrison at Windsor or by the way to Farnham thitherward

SIR,

Col. Tomlinson is to be speeded away to Windsor with instructions to himself, Lt.-Col. Cobbett, and Captain Merriman,[270] for securing of the King, answerable to the several heads you desire resolution in. So soon as he comes you may come away, and your presence here is both desired and needed. But before you come away, we desire you to appoint three or four troops out of your convoy (of the surest men and best officered) to remain about Windsor, to whom you may assign quarters in the next parts of Middlesex and Surrey, advising with the Governor therein, and to

[269] Whitelocke, pp. 362, 363.

[270] Cobbett and Merriman were the two officers who had been sent by Fairfax to the Isle of Wight to demand the removal of the King.

keep guard by a troop at a time within the Castle, and for that purpose to receive orders from Col. Thomlinson; and we desire you also out of the chief of the King's servants last allowed (upon advice with Lt.-Col. Cobbett and Captain Merriman) to appoint about the number of six (such as are most to be confided in, and who may best supply all offices) to stay with and attend the King for such necessary uses, and the rest we desire you to send away, not as discharged from the benefit of their places, but only as spared from extraordinary attendance. This is thought fit to avoid any numerous concourse which many servants, with their followers and their relations or acquaintance, would draw into the Castle; and for the said reason it is wished that such of the servants retained as are least sure, and not of necessity to be constantly in the King's lodgings, may be lodged in the town, or the lower part of the Castle, wherein the Governor is to be advised with.

Capt. Mildmay[271] (we presume) will be one of those you'll find to retain. The dragoons of your convoy send away to the quarters formerly intended, which (as we remember) were in Bedfordshire. We bless God by whose providence you are come on so well with your charge.

We remain,

Your true friends to serve you,

Westminster, OLIVER CROMWELL [272]

Dec. 22nd, 1648. HENRY IRETON, etc.

For Colonel Whitchcott, Governor of Windsor Castle, haste: These[273]

SIR,

Captain Brayfield of Col. Hewson's regiment with his own and two other companies of foot are ordered to come to you, and to receive orders from you for the better securing of the Castle and the person of the King therein. You may quarter them in the town and in Eyton[274] (if not in the Castle). Col. Harrison is also writ unto to appoint three or four troops of horse out of his convoy to remain near Windsor, and to quarter in the next parts of Middlesex and Surrey, as you shall advise, and keep guard by a troop at a time within the Castle. It is thought fittest, that the Horse guard or part of it, be kept within the Upper Castle, and that at least one company of foot at a time be upon guard there, and that the bridge betwixt the Castles (if you think fit) be drawn up in the night, and kept drawn ordinarily in the day. Also, that no other prisoners be lodged in that part of the Castle besides the King, unless Duke Hamilton in some close rooms where he may not have intercourse with the King, and he rather to

[271] Anthony Mildmay (brother of Sir Henry), in the Parliament's service, attendant on the King.

[272] Printed in the *Clarke Papers*, ii, 140, Lomas-Carlyle, Suppl. 38.

[273] (*Note by Firth.*) "In October, 1642, Col. John Venn occupied Windsor Castle for the Parliament. In April, 1645, the House of Commons recommended Col. Christopher Whichcote (to use his own spelling of his name) as Venn's successor. Whichcote, who had commanded a brigade under Essex in Cornwall, and had signed the capitulation of Sept. 1, 1644, seems to have been removed from his governorship in 1651. He died about 1655." *Clarke Papers*, ii, 144.

[274] Eton.

be in Winchester Castle[275] (where Sir Thomas Payton was), if you can safely dispose of the other prisoners elsewhere; but the King (by all means) must be lodged in the Upper Castle, in some of the safest rooms, and Col. Thomlinson, Lt.-Col. Cobbett and Capt. Merriman to have lodgings there, and those Gentlemen of the Army (being about six or seven) who are appointed to attend and assist them in the immediate watching about the King to be also lodged (if it may be) in the Upper Castle, or at least within the Tower; some of his allowed servants also (that were of immediate attendance about his person) must necessarily be lodged in the Upper Castle, about which Col. Harrison and Lt.-Col. Cobbett will advise with you. Col. Thomlinson and with him Lt.-Col. Cobbett and Capt. Merriman are appointed to the charge of the immediate securing of the King's person (as you will see by their instructions, which they will show you), and for their assistance and furtherance therein you are desired to appoint such guards of foot for the immediate securing of him, and to guard the rooms where he and they shall lodge, as they shall desire, and that you order those guards from time to time to observe the orders of Col. Thomlinson, Lt.-Col. Cobbett, and Capt. Merriman therein.

The horse also (as to the immediate guarding of the King) are appointed to receive orders from Col. Thomlinson, but as to the safe-guarding of the garrison, all (both horse and foot) are to be at your command. We thought this distribution better for your ease, and for the leaving you more free to look to the security of the whole garrison than to burden you both with it, and with the immediate charge of the King's person, where you have also so many prisoners to look to.

It is thought convenient that (during the King's stay with you) you turn out of the Castle all malignant or Cavalierish inhabitants (except the prisoners), and as many others of loose and idle persons as you can well rid out, and to stint the number of prisoners' servants to the lowest proportion you well can.

You are desired also to restrain any numerous or ordinary concourse of unnecessary people into that part of the Castle, of whose affection and faithfulness to the public there is not good assurance, or who have not necessary occasions there, and to suffer no public preaching in the Chapel, or any like occasion for concourse of people. 'Tis good the prisoners this while be strictly kept in, and withheld from intercourse or communication one with another, and that the guards of the gates at the upper Castle have a list of the King's allowed servants now retained and their followers, as also of the Officers and Gentlemen of the Army that are to watch the King with their servants, that those guards may know whom they are ordinarily to let in, and the guards at the outer gate of the lower Castle to have knowledge of the same list, and of all other dwellers and lodgers within the lowest part. The Lord be with you and bless you in this great charge. To His good pleasure I commit you and it.

Your faithful friend and servant,

Westminster, OLIVER CROMWELL.
Dec. 22nd, 1648. HENRY IRETON.[276]

[275] Winchester Tower?

[276] Printed in the *Clarke Papers*, ii, 142. Lomas-Carlyle, Suppl. 39.

Those letters only anticipated the action of the Council of Officers which met on the next day, December 23, just as Charles arrived at Windsor. That meeting, at which no record of attendance or debate was taken—or at least preserved—instructed Colonel Thomlinson and three other officers as to their duties "in and for the securing of the King's escape." Drawn up in the form of eight articles, setting forth in minute detail the precautions to be taken, the instructions were adopted unanimously by the Council with the exception of Article Five, forbidding the King conversation with any one save in the presence of one of the officers. To that safeguard Cromwell alone objected, as being unnecessarily harsh, or, as has also been suggested, possibly because he thought it would be an obstacle to a treaty with Charles.[277]

On that day, as well, the handful of Lords remaining in the Upper House, consisting of "The Earl of Denbigh, Speaker, and 4 Earls," ordered that "All Lords within . . . 20 miles . . . do peremptorily make their appearance in the House of Peers on Thursday morning next [the 28th] to attend the great Affairs of this Kingdom, *relating in an extraordinary manner to all the Peerage* of England;"[278] and the House of Commons resolved "That it be referred to a Committee to consider how to proceed *in a way of Justice against the King and other Capital Offenders*,"[279] a resolution curiously like that passed in the Council of Officers eight days earlier. The whole business now in train, it only remained to carry out the plans thus laid; and it is notable that, according to Whitelocke, on this same fateful December 23, discussion of the great problem was resumed at Speaker Lenthall's house, 'some being favourable to crowning the Duke of Gloucester.'[280]

In the face of these various circumstances it might seem that Cromwell and Ireton had not merely determined the destruction of the King but had planned the whole programme down to the last moment of his life; yet this view has been challenged and evidence adduced to weaken or destroy such a conclusion. It has been strongly urged that Ireton's plan, now that the King's trial had been determined on, was to convict him "then leave him in prison till he consented 'to abandon his negative voice, to part from Church lands' and 'to abjure the Scots' " and that "Cromwell even went further than this. In opposition to Ireton, he now asked that the King's trial might be deferred until the subjects, such as Norwich and Capell, who had stirred up the last war, had been brought to trial." To support this view, three pieces of evidence are adduced. The first is the letter of

277 *Clarke Papers*, ii, 144–6, and 146n, quoting *Clarke Mss.*, xvi, 61.
278 *L. J.*, x, 636.
279 *C. J.*, vi, 102.
280 Whitelocke, p. 364.

the French ambassador, Brienne, to the French minister, Grignon, on December 21, to the effect that "The difference between Cromwell and Ireton is only whether to begin with him [the King] as the latter wishes, or to proceed first against the Lords and other principal persons whom they hold prisoners, which is the advice of Cromwell." The second is a letter of the same date written by a person described as a Royalist agent who signs himself "John Lawrans" to Secretary Nicholas, then at Caen in Normandy.

"The petty ones of the levelling conspiracy," he wrote, were most eager for the death of the King, but "now—which is strange to tell—I have been assured that Cromwell is retreating from them, his designs and theirs being incompatible as fire and water, they driving at a pure democracy and himself at an oligarchy; and it will appear that the wild remonstrance and the present design of taking away the King's life is forwarded by him only to make the Levellers vent all their wicked principles and intentions; that having declared themselves, they may become the more odious and abominable, and so be the more easily suppressed, when he see the occasion to take them off and fall openly from them."[281]

To this he adds that "when the Council of War was discussing the question of the King's trial, Pride, as he believed at Cromwell's instigation, brought in 'a strange, ranting letter' to the effect that it was irrational to kill Charles I when Charles II would be at large—to 'exchange a King in their power for a King out of their power, potent in foreign alliances and strong in the affections of the people.' "

The third piece of evidence is a private letter of January 8, 1648—the day of the first meeting of the High Court of Justice for the trial of the King—which says that "Our Councils will not endure any mediations, no, not hear again of Ireton's proposals 'that it were perhaps safer to have the King live prisoner for to dispose him a while to abandon his negative voice.' "[282]

From this evidence the conclusion has been drawn that "Cromwell and his allies among the officers desired at this time to save the King's life if it was possible to do so without injury to the cause for which they had fought." That may be true—though there is in it a large proviso—yet the fact remains that all the evidence so far adduced seems to indicate, not that Cromwell desired either to kill or save the King, but that he preferred to bring the lesser men to trial first. As to the votes of Parliament on December 23, Lawrans wrote that this was a threat intended only for bargaining purposes. As he says:

"This is evident by what the Speaker said to a friend of mine in discourse on Saturday night [December 23]—that if the King came not off roundly now in point of concession, he would be utterly lost; which saying implies

[281] Quoted in Gardiner, *Civil War*, iv, 281–2 and notes from *Clarendon MSS*, 2,968.
[282] *Ibid.*, from *Carte MSS*, xxiii, f. 425.

thus much—they have applied themselves, and are now bartering with his Majesty."[283]

Even assuming the trial was held, the charges brought against him would be such that he could easily acquit himself as he had been assured by a friend who had it from Nicholas Love, one of its members. As for the appointment of the Commons' committee—for Lawrans naturally did not know of the committee of the Council of Officers—there was nothing much to fear.

"Truly sir," he went on to tell the Secretary, "I have it from good hands—some of them Independents—that what I have here represented is a true draft of their intentions; but whether his Majesty will comply with them so far as to part with his negative voice and be no more—as I have often said—than a Duke of Venice, which I hear is the hard condition they intend to impose on him, is not known, and it is very hard to believe."[284]

Matters had now reached a crisis more acute than any which had hitherto confronted the men in charge of affairs, and all groups bestirred themselves to find a way out of a situation which seemed to point inexorably to the deposition or even to the death of Charles. On December 19, four of the little group of peers had visited Fairfax, as Lawrans said, "to cast down their honours at his Excellency's feet, and protested their desire is not to maintain peerage, or any other privilege whatsoever that might be conceived prejudicial to the public interest."[285]

This humiliation availed little beyond a mission of one of their number, Hamilton's distant relative, the Earl of Denbigh, in a last appeal to Charles. That mission had as little result as the appeal to Fairfax, for Charles refused to see the man who, it was reported, had held Fairfax's stirrup for him two days before. On Christmas Day there was, apparently, a meeting, not of the Council of Officers, but, according to Whitelocke, of a "Committee to consider how to proceed against the King," at which, according to a report in *Mercurius Melancholicus*, Cromwell spoke, urging that if the King would accept the conditions now offered, his life should be spared, purely as a matter of policy.[286] To that, it would appear from the same authority, the committee agreed, but a determined minority of six still insisted on a trial.

Though even at a time when every day, almost every hour, is of importance to an understanding of what and how things happened in this supreme crisis of the English monarchy, it is difficult to follow the precise sequence of events which led to the downfall of Charles,

[283] Lawrans to Nicholas, Dec. 25, *Clarendon MSS*, 2,972.
[284] *Ibid.*
[285] Same to same, Dec. 21, *Ibid.*, 2,968.
[286] Paraphrased in Gardiner, *Civil War*, iv, 285.

and still more difficult to disengage the part which Cromwell played in it, yet something may be learned. The same day that the Army Council took measures to reduce Charles's royal state,[287] December 26, the question of proceeding capitally against the King came up in the House of Commons, and from two sources it is possible to determine what Cromwell said on that occasion. The first is the record of his speech by Walker:

Speech in the House of Commons (Dec. 26?) 1648

"When it was first moved in the House of Commons to proceed capitally against the King, Cromwel stood up and told them, That if any man moved this upon design, he should think him the greatest Traytor in the world, but since providence and necessity had cast them upon it, he should pray God to bless their Councels, though he were not provided on the sudden to give them counsel."[288]

In almost the same words and in the same sense, Lawrans reported the speech to Nicholas, though he dated it—with far less probability—January 2:

"Mr. Speaker, if any man whatsoever had carried on this design of deposing the King and disinheriting his posterity, or if any man had yet such a design, he should be the greatest traitor and rebel in the world. But since the Providence of God hath cast this upon us, I cannot but submit to Providence, though I am not yet provided to give you my advice."[289]

The speech, like his letter to Hammond, is characteristic of a man who in such crises always turned, as his followers would have said, for counsel to the Almighty, and who, as his enemies declared, disguised his own suggestions, actions, plans and ambitions under a cloak of such hypocrisy. This is the root of the quarrel between his champions and his adversaries—in how far was he "sincere"? Did he honestly believe that he was literally guided by divine authority; did he deceive himself; or did he use this device to deceive others and avoid responsibility? To that there are two answers, diametrically opposed and wholly incompatible. Whichever one accepts, he must, at least admit one thing. It is that, in distinction from his early frank, rude, injudicious, even dangerous, habits of speech which brought him into continual conflict with authority, even in compari-

[287] They resolved that all ceremonies of state with the King be left off and to reduce the number of his attendants. Walker, *Anarchia Anglicana*, p. 54, dated Dec. 27, quoted in Whitelocke, p. 365. No meeting was held on Dec. 27, but one was held on the 26th.

[288] Walker, *op. cit.*, p. 54, dated Dec. 27.

[289] Lawrans to Nicholas, Jan. 8. *Clarendon State Papers*, ii, App. L. Calendared, with this quotation omitted, in Coxe, *Cal. of Clarendon Papers*, no. 2,995.

son with his first utterances in the Commons, Cromwell had developed a style which was a model of circumspection. When he emerged from the position of a subordinate to that of a leading personality, he retained, indeed, that Puritanical phraseology which had marked his writings and his speeches since his conversion. It may have been what is called "genuine" or "sincere," or it may not; but one thing is certain. It was of enormous use to him. If, in Talleyrand's famous saying, language was invented to conceal thought, no one ever excelled some of Cromwell's utterances in that respect.

It may have been, or have become, a second nature to him. It may have been, as his supporters believed, merely the outward expression of profound religious conviction, or, as his enemies claimed, of profound dissimulation. Whatever it was, nothing could have suited the situation in which he found himself as well as this semi-mystical, religious almost apocalyptic language. To make no other test, it is difficult, if not impossible, to find in any of these later utterances any which, had matters gone wrong, could have been used against him in a court of law. His deeds were known and spoke for themselves; his orders and appeals for assistance in his military enterprises were no less obvious; but as for the rest—unlike so many utterances of so many of his associates—on his words he could never have been convicted, save of extreme religious emotion. Yet, viewing his words in the light of the situation and of the event, it seems obvious that he had been "led" to agree to Charles's death.

There is one other question which arises here. It is the age-long, perennial problem as to how far a political leader directs and in how far he is driven on his course by the current of events. To that no answer has been found save that at times he seems to be the motive power, at others only in the grip of forces beyond his own control or that of any man. In such cases it is his part to gauge those forces and ride the crest of the tide with them. For this, Cromwell, like all such successful men, had two great qualifications. He had extraordinary military capacity—and the man who can lead his followers to the destruction of their fellow-men with the greatest skill and good fortune has always been the great hero of his generation. Not all of them have had political ability commensurate with their military talents; but among those who have possessed both qualities in a high degree, Napoleon and Cromwell have been the most conspicuous in modern times. That leadership each owed in no small degree to the ascendancy of an individual over his fellows which arises from the intangible quality known as personality. That, again, though a question of will power, is in no small measure a question of words. In each of these Cromwell, like Napoleon, excelled—in what he said, in how he said it, and in what he refrained from saying.

In Cromwell's case, his armor of humility, of meek submission to the will of God, whether real or assumed, was impregnable. It was difficult, if not impossible, for any one to pierce that humble reliance on outward dispensations of divine grace in which he wrapped himself. It was impossible to refute his continual challenge to his opponents to produce like manifestations of God's approval on their side. Assuming that God's favor was determined by such means, the argument was triumphant and unanswerable. As he would have said, "If God be with me, who can be against me?"; nor was this almost ostentatious humility less infuriating to his opponents because—if one accepted his premise—his argument was unanswerable.

In all he did he was exceedingly fortunate, or adroit. It is not necessary to stress the point that at various critical periods he had not been at the center of the disturbance, and, though obviously in touch with the various elements in the political maelstrom by which he was surrounded, and part of which he was, he had been able to preserve himself from being sucked down in it as so many of his earlier colleagues were. Apart from the direct favor of the Deity, what, then, were the sources of Cromwell's strength?

With all the good intentions of his admirers who have attributed his worldly success entirely to his high moral and spiritual qualities and the righteousness of his cause, they have unconsciously done him something less than justice. There were men in his own time who equalled, if they did not much surpass him in moral and spiritual qualities, yet rose to no such worldly eminence. There have been men notably deficient in the higher qualities who have risen to great place; and even had Cromwell been the unprincipled scoundrel which his enemies painted him, had he been, as Clarendon described him a "great, bad man," "against whom damnation was pronounced and for which hell was prepared," he might have achieved a great place in the world merely by his qualities of worldly leadership.

Whatever strength he derived from the sense of the greatness of his cause, of the perpetual approval of the Almighty, of the conviction of righteousness, of the consciousness of the certain victory of the eternal and immutable principles for which he fought, these obscure, even while they reinforce and dignify the more practical qualities and means by which he met and overcame his enemies. His military genius owed something perhaps to the inspiration of his cause, as did his political ability; but each rested chiefly on his judgment of men and of situations and his capacity to seize his opportunities in council and in field and to make the most of them. He was, in brief, more than his most ardent admirers painted him. He was not merely the hero of Puritanism; he was a master of war and politics; and so, rather than by his spiritual qualities, he achieved the place he held and led his cause and party to success.

THE HIGH COURT OF JUSTICE

At this moment he had need of all his qualities, worldly as well as unworldly, for the Puritan Revolution which owed its triumph chiefly to his talents had reached its climax in the votes of the Army Council and the Commons to bring the King to "justice." It had been decided that Charles was to be tried and the committee of the officers had been wrestling for some time with the problems which that decision had entailed. Before what body could a King be brought, what charges could be laid against him, and, if adjudged guilty, what should be his punishment and by what authority could it be inflicted? In a sense the questions were academic. The army had the power and was, like the Commons, controlled by men who had determined on the punishment of the King. Yet even at such times men seek to justify themselves by some appearance of legality, and it was not easy to formulate charges, much less to find a body of sufficient authority, to try a man who was not merely the chief executive of the nation but a crowned and anointed King, who in the minds of most of his subjects had a character apart and above that of a mere officer of state. Thus if a court should be erected to try Charles, it would, in a sense, be on trial itself before the whole nation. Every sentiment of prudence, therefore, required that this last solemn function must have as much semblance of legality and as much authority as could be summoned to its aid.

The last act of the great tragedy began with the first day of January, 1649, when the Commons resolved "That the —— and Commons in Parliament assembled do declare and adjudge, that, by the fundamental laws of this Kingdom, it is Treason in the King of England . . . to levy War against the Parliament and Kingdom of England."[290] This, then, was the indictment which was to be brought against Charles, that he was a rebel and a traitor to his Kingdom and recreant to his trust. It came back, in fact, to Calvin and Buchanan—"Let us not believe there is given no other commandment but to obey and suffer . . . I affirm that if they wink at Kings wilfully raging over and treading down the poor community . . . they dreadfully betray the people's liberty," in the former's words. Resistance to royal oppression, even to the point of tyrannicide, and an extreme limitation of monarchy in the latter's teaching—these were the principles which dominated Charles's opponents.

The charge of high treason thus formulated, the next step was the procedure. For such a trial there was, naturally, no existing court, but that had been provided for by the men who pressed the trial forward, and who introduced and passed an ordinance through the Commons establishing a "High Court of Justice" for this special pur-

[290] *C. J.*, vi, 107.

pose. To that end, moreover, a list of its members already drawn and presented and approved with the ordinance. Chief Justices St. John and Rolle and Chief Baron Wilde were appointed as judges and a hundred and fifty "commissioners," or jurymen were named at the same time. It was evident even to the framers of this plan that it would be difficult or impossible to find and keep together such a number, much less to secure quick action from them, and there was inserted a proviso that of these men but twenty were needed to form a quorum. Of these, six were named from the House of Peers; and third on the list of the commoners was the name of Lieutenant-General Cromwell, following those of Lord Monson and Lord Grey of Groby and followed in turn by a phalanx of officers, Skippon, Ireton, Harrison, Whalley, Rich, Pride, Hewson, Okey, Barkstead, Desborough and many lesser men, with six aldermen of London—and General Fairfax who at once refused to serve.

Resolution and ordinance were sent at once to the Upper House for its approval, but the blank space left in the resolution for "the Lords" was never filled. That House had now sunk to the lowest level in its history. On December 29 there had been present only the Speaker, the Earls of Pembroke and Kent and Lord Grey.[291] On January 2, when the Commons' ordinance and resolution came up to them there were, as the *Perfect Diurnall* chronicled, "many more Lords . . . than usual of late" that is, as it declared, sixteen, though the *Lords Journals* reckoned only eleven, besides the Speaker, the Earl of Denbigh. That little body revealed courage beyond its numbers. Manchester asserted that declaring the King a traitor was against every fundamental principle of law. Northumberland agreed and added that "Not one in twenty of the people in England are yet satisfied whether the King did levy war against the Houses first, or the Houses first against him"; and though Pembroke remained neutral, Denbigh is reported to have vowed that he would rather "be torn in pieces" than take the place as a commissioner to which he had been named. The Lords defeated a motion to postpone consideration of the Commons' ordinance and resolution, resolved unanimously not to concur with the resolution but to 'cast it out,' and adjourned for a week to make it more difficult for the Commons' remnant to proceed.[292]

Thus rebuffed, the little group which now made up the House, did not hesitate. On January 3, refusing a request from Henrietta Maria to visit her husband, they passed again the resolution rejected by the Lords and hurried through the first and second reading of a new ordinance for a High Court of Justice. This, omitting the three judges first named, who refused to serve, reduced the number of "commis-

291 *L. J.*, x, 641.

292 *Mercurius Pragmaticus; L. J.*, x, 641–2.

sioners" to 135, made them judges as well as jury, and appointed a committee—of which Cromwell was one—to put the ordinance or "act" into its final form.[293]

This was not Cromwell's only business in the House. In the strange mingling of great and small which distinguishes his career—or that of any man in Parliament—on January 1 besides being named as a commissioner to try the King, he was appointed to a committee to 'consider excise and other treasuries and to prevent obstructions in revenue collections' and on January 4 he was on a committee to 'withdraw and present to the House in the form of two questions upon the debate on amendments to the ordinance for the High Court of Justice.'[294] The passage of that ordinance, or "act" as it was called, was accompanied by a series of resolutions which justified the change of name. They were to the effect that "the people are, under God, the original of all just power; that the Commons of England . . . being chosen by the people, have the supreme power . . . and that whatsoever is enacted or declared for law by the Commons . . . hath the force of law . . . although the consent and concurrence of King or House of Peers be not had."

It might be supposed that such critical periods would produce important documents, but here, as at so many like periods of his career, the only writing that seems to have survived from Cromwell's pen is, perhaps significantly, only one of those inconsequential ephemeridae of which his life was full—a protection for a certain Sir Henry Jerneghan from depredations by the soldiery in Norfolk:

To all officers and soldiers whom this may concern

These are to command and require you, and every of you, that you henceforth forbear to molest the person, seize, take plunder, or carry away any of the horses, oxen, sheep, corn, household stuff, or any other goods whatsoever of, or belonging to, Sir Henry Jerneghan, of Cossey, in the county of Norfolk, as you and every of you will answer the contrary at your utmost perils. Given under my hand and seal at Whitehall the 4th day of Jan. 1648.

O. CROMWELL.[295]

Two days later, on January 6, was passed the "Act of the Commons of England assembled in Parliament for the erecting of a High Court of Justice, for trying Charles Stuart, King of England," with a list annexed of 135 men besides clerks, counsellors and officials, and second on the list is the name of Cromwell.[296] And it is not without

[293] *C. J.*, vi, 110.

[294] *Ibid.*, 107, 111.

[295] Original in the Mss of Lord Stafford, of Cossey Hall, Norfolk. Pr. in *Hist. Mss. Comm. Rept.* no. 10, App. III, p. 166. Calendared in Lomas-Carlyle, Suppl. 40.

[296] Firth & Rait, *Acts & Ordinances*, i, 1,253.

interest to note that Cromwell was first on the list after Fairfax, that his name was followed by those of Ireton, Waller and Skippon and that the last name on the list was that of Cromwell's Cambridge colleague, John Lowry.

It would appear that in these critical days he was present in the House, though, as the Army Council was meeting concurrently at Whitehall, it is possible, if not probable, that he and other officer-members of Parliament were able to fulfil both their functions with no great trouble. There is no record of his attendance at the Council meetings of January 4th and 5th, but on January 6th he was not only present but took part in the debate. That debate was on the first article of the *Agreement of the People*, which was still under discussion and the particular point involved was the setting a period for the ending of the existing Parliament. This Ireton urged should be no later than the last day of April, adducing the old argument of fear, or, as he said, "Itt will bee a greater securitie in case the Army should bee forced to remove, when the ill-affected partie may come in againe." To this Cromwell demurred, arguing, "That itt will bee more honourable and convenient to put a period to themselves." But, retorted Ireton, if Parliament should decide the date for its own dissolution, "all the indeavours will bee used for Parliaments to come in the old way, butt if men finde there is noe avoidance of this Parliament butt by this Agreement, there is nothing so much likely to keepe men's hands off from opposing this Agreement. The people may think if they oppose this Agreement they oppose the ending of this Parliament."

"Then," said Cromwell, with much penetration, "you are afraid they will doe [so]?" "If the generality of people could see the end of this Parliament, [they] would bee for the opposing of any thinge of this kinde; or would waite for the expiring of that to looke for a succession of new Parliaments in the old way and old forme of a King agen."[297]

It was a brief but significant exchange. It revealed that Ireton was fully conscious that the majority of people in England were against his plan and the army, that they only waited an opportunity to restore something of the old order. That, if the Agreement went into effect and a new electorate were created, would end his hopes once and for all, he seems not to have doubted; but Cromwell put his finger on the important question. Given a free vote would the people not oppose the whole business? And what conclusion did he draw from that, and what position did he take? He took great credit to himself in later years for his efforts to get, or to allow, Parliament to dissolve itself, instead of, as it happened, being dissolved by force—and, again as it happened, by himself:

[297] *Clarke Papers*, ii, 170–171.

"So willing were we, even very tender and desirous, if possible that these men might quit their places with honour"[298]

and again:

"I pressed the Parliament, as a member, to period themselves,—once and again, and again, and ten nay twenty times over."[299]

None the less Ireton won his point and the clause in the *Agreement* stood as he had written it.

THE TRIAL OF THE KING

As a result of long and earnest conferences and planning, at two o'clock on Monday, January 8, 1648–9, in accordance with the vote of the House of Commons, that body known as the High Court of Justice assembled in the Painted Chamber at Westminster for its first meeting. By the refusal of any peers to serve and by the known or expressed disinclination of others to take part in its proceedings, of the original list of 150 names reduced to 135, only some fifty-three now appeared.[300] The composition of this body was no less extraordinary than the means by which it had been called into being or the purpose for which it was created, and to understand what it was and did it is necessary to have some knowledge of the men who composed it.

The most famous body which goes under the name of "court" in English history, its membership reveals much of the situation of affairs which gave it birth and the position of the more advanced revolutionary party whose creature it was. It is easy to guess who prepared the list of "commissioners" or "judges" presented to the Commons to be approved as members of the Court. It is impossible to prove who drew it up or when; but it is not difficult to understand the principles which underlay the selection. It was necessary first to have a majority of "safe" men who could be depended on; but it was also desirable to find names which would carry weight in any judgment finally pronounced. That last was not easy. From the beginning, the lawyers, even those who had thus far been identified with the revolutionary movement, hastened to dissociate themselves from the proceedings. The three first selected to preside—Wilde, Rolle, even Oliver St. John—refused to serve. Robert Nicholas who had prosecuted Laud and was noted for his violence, though he had been proclaimed a rebel by the King, declined to lend his services. Whitelocke went into the country to escape pressure being brought on him to take part in the proceedings and with him went Sir Thomas Widdrington, while the Attorney General, Steele, was overtaken by

[298] Speech, July 4, 1653.
[299] Speech, Sept. 12, 1654.
[300] *State Trials*, iv, 1,053.

a providential illness. With one voice the legal profession, irrespective of party, denounced what they regarded as a judicial farce.

For obvious reasons the army and Parliament were more amenable, yet something of the same difficulty presented itself even there. None of the House of Lords was now available and in the handful of the Commons there were few men of distinction left. Of the pronounced Republicans it was found possible to secure the services of Ludlow, Marten, Scot and Jones, of whom the first and last were army officers; but Algernon Sidney repudiated the whole proceeding both publicly and privately, and Sir Henry Vane, despite his intimacy with Cromwell, refused to take any part whatever in the trial and retired to his country-seat. None the less, the whole, or almost the whole, of the remaining members of the Commons were drawn into the body of commissioners.

The army was in a different situation; yet of its general officers only Cromwell and Ireton remained, with Thomas Hammond, who refused to sign the death-warrant. Fairfax, Skippon, Lambert and others declined, as did such notable leaders as Haselrig, Fleetwood and Desborough. The body or hard core of the Court was composed chiefly of the "Cromwellian colonels"—Waller, Whalley, Barkstead, Okey, Pride, Harrison, Hewson, Ewer, Rowe, Goffe and Horton, and it was pointed out by their contemptuous though defeated enemies that most of these were men who had risen from the lower ranks of society under Cromwell's patronage. Okey and Pride had been draymen or brewer's employees; Hewson, a cobbler; Barkstead, the "thimble-seller," a goldsmith; Ewer, a serving-man; Harrison, the son of a butcher; Goffe, a salter; Horton, Haselrig's servant. To these may be added a group described with more or less accuracy as Cromwell's "creatures" or "tools," like Lilburne, Danvers, Downes, Fleetwood and Lisle, again most of them "Cromwellian colonels." There were three London aldermen, Andrews, Pennington, and Tichborne, who was also Lieutenant of the Tower. There were, besides, men like Smith and Waite who pleaded at their trial that they had been intimidated by Cromwell into serving, and that "weak and shifty" creature, Millington.

Finally there were some who were, or claimed to be, present in an effort to help Charles. This Sir Hardress Waller pleaded later in his defence, though his plea was weakened by the fact that he was present at most sessions and signed the death-warrant. To his name may be added that of the renegade courtiers, Sir Henry Mildmay, sometime keeper of the King's jewel house, and the bankrupt Sir John Danvers, with that of William, Lord Monson, son of the old master of the armoury at the Tower, though Mildmay and Monson refused to sign the warrant. Far more probably, the presence of Charles's jailer, Colonel Matthew Thomlinson, whose name appeared three times on January 27—though he declared later that it was a clerk's error—may be thus explained. It is easy to understand the presence—and absence—of men like Fairfax and Sidney. It is scarcely less difficult to see that aldermen Pennington and Andrews were drawn in to lend the weight of the City to the Court.

Though we know nothing of the inner workings of the Court, save in its public appearances, something may be judged from the attendance lists. Since in most cases the names in those lists seem to be roughly in the order that they appear in the ordinance constituting the Court, except for late-comers who were added as they entered, it is impossible to trace any grouping or even any association of individuals. The general status and rank of the men who were active on the High Court of Justice, however, is of considerable significance. Of the 135 men chosen to judge Charles, forty-seven refused to appear at the first meeting of the commissioners or at any subsequent session. Included in that number were thirty-five members of Parliament, at least ten army officers and several members of the legal profession. Of the ninety-one names which are on the attendance lists as having appeared at least once, three are almost certainly errors. They are not named in the ordinance among the 135, and can not be identified. Two—Wm. Tomlinson and Thomas Heath—appear only once, and the third name, John Deane, occurs in four attendance lists, none of which include the name of Richard Deane who attended most of the other meetings. It appears then that eighty-eight men attended the sessions of the High Court of Justice at least once.[301] Of these, sixty-

[301] The Commissioners who took part in the proceedings of the High Court of Justice with the number of times they attended are as follows:

Smith, Blackistone	23	meetings
Scrope, Pride	22	"
Whalley, Barkstead, Cromwell, Waller, Hewson, Pelham, Venn, Danvers	21	"
Carew, Mauleverer, Okey, Tichborne, Norton, Scot, Purefoy, Holland, P. Temple	20	"
Hutchinson, Jones, Millington, Bradshaw, Edwards, Ewers, Goffe, Marten	19	"
Blagrave, Cawley, Constable, Ludlow, Moor, Rowe	18	"
Bourchier, Garland, Harrison, Fry, Lisle, Potter, Horton, Downes	17	"
Grey, Love, Walton, Dixwell, Ireton	16	"
T. Challoner, Say, R. Deane*	15	"
Hammond, Livesey, Allen, J. Temple	14	"
Harvey, Heveningham, Mayne, Stapley, Alured	13	"
Brown, Lassells, Mounson, Lilburne	11	"
Clement, Pennington	10	"
Mildmay, Wogan	9	"

M. Corbet, 8 meetings; Andrews, J. Challoner, 7 meetings; Waite, 6 meetings; Fleetwood, 5 meetings; Lister, Morley, Pickering, Dove, J. Deane,** 4

nine were members of Parliament, of whom sixteen were also army officers. The nineteen who were not members of Parliament include fifteen army officers, an alderman of London, and two men—Edmund Wild and Vincent Potter—whose place in public life is unknown.

Such was the constitution of this extraordinary "Court," composed of just such men as make up such bodies at such times. In it one thing is notable; it is that it contained sixty-nine members of Parliament; and when it is recalled that the number on divisions was seldom over fifty, it seems evident that the High Court of Justice and the remnant of the House—to say nothing of the Army Council, for thirty-one of the commissioners were officers—were rather closely allied in membership. This, then, was the body named to try Charles I, nor was it all made up at once, nor was it wholly unanimous. Of the eighty-eight men involved, of whom not more than seventy-one were ever present at one time, scarcely more than half were active participants. Some like Fairfax and Sidney drew out at once, with Fagg, Dove, Lister, Morley, John Corbet and that Sir Thomas Wroth who had first moved that Charles should be impeached. Of the men who were presently to sign the death-warrant, two—Sir Richard Ingoldsby and Miles Corbet—claimed at their trials that they had sat only on the last fatal day, though the records show that Miles Corbet was marked as present at eight sessions but not on January 29. Though the clerks were not infallible nor their records beyond question, it seems probable that their lists of members present are, on the whole, at least relatively accurate and that they represent in general the attendance and that in turn the character of the Court.

Thus constituted, the Court chose its assistants and officers. The president, Bradshaw, was not present at this first meeting, nor did he appear until January 12, but there were minor officers to be appointed. As serjeant-at-arms, was chosen one Edward Dendy, sometime holder of that office in the House of Commons, whose son in later years petitioned to succeed his father when the Restoration came. For counsel they chose the Attorney General, William Steele of Gray's Inn, who declined on account of illness and was excused on the report of a committee which the suspicious Court sent to investigate; with that Dr. Dorislaus in whose behalf Cromwell had lately written; and a certain John Aske, otherwise unknown to fame. In default of the Solicitor General, Prideaux, who, like Steele, refused to serve, was named John Cook of Gray's Inn, a man of dubious

meetings; Fagg, Sidney, M. Thomlinson, Wallop, 3 meetings; Harrington, Wild, 2 meetings; Anlaby, J. Corbet, Fairfax, Ingoldsby, Wroth, W. Tomlinson,** Heath,** 1 meeting.

* Including the times J. Deane was marked present, this number would be 19.

** Probably should be included with some other name.

reputation then, and still more dubious career thereafter. On him fell the chief burden of the prosecution in the absence of Steele.

The sequence of events in the proceedings of the Court seems to evidence a more or less carefully prepared plan of action. On the morning of the 9th, the serjeant-at-arms read the proclamation of the trial, first in Westminster Hall, where the Chancery Court was in session, then at Cheapside and the Old Exchange, inviting men to come forward with evidence against the King.[302] On the next day, January 10, forty-five of the commissioners met again in the Painted Chamber to choose some ushers and messengers and elect a President. For that post they chose John Bradshaw, a man of moderate talents and position, sometime judge of the sheriff's court in London, more recently chief justice of Chester and a judge in Wales who had lately been created a serjeant-at-law and had distinguished himself by a harangue in Chester against the King. Under the circumstances, Bradshaw was probably the best that the managers of the trial could do and every effort was made to dignify his post. He was given the deanery of Westminster as a residence, provided with a strong guard and adorned with a splendid scarlet robe to which he added a "high-crowned beaver hat lined with plate to ward off blows." He was at that moment in the country so that William Say was ordered to take his place till his return. For clerks the commissioners chose a Mr. Greaves who was excused on account of "great and important employment" and John Phelps the new clerk of the Commons, and Andrew Broughton were named. With this and the appointment of one John King as a crier, the Court was now complete; the doors were thrown open to the public, the crier read the proclamations and summonses were issued for the absentees.

So formed, the real proceedings of the Court began. On Friday, January 12, it met again in the Painted Chamber to appoint sub-committees and plan the conduct of the trial. It ordered Waller and Harrison to request Fairfax to provide "sufficient guards" for the Court during its sessions and instructed the committee for planning the trial, together with Cromwell, Whalley, Waller, Scot, Harrison and Deane, to meet in the Court of Wards for that purpose. It determined that the Lord President and counsel conduct the trial "according to instructions to be given them by the Court"—and with this extraordinary provision it revealed that the "commissioners" were to be judges, jury and prosecutors combined. And it is notable that neither then nor at any other time was it suggested that Charles be allowed or assigned legal assistance for his defence.

Of these early meetings there is one small piece of evidence which was given by a certain Thomas Walkeley, who, among many others, was attracted by this great spectacle, and ten years later at the trial

[302] Walker, *Anarchia Anglicana*, p. 68.

of Hugh Peter told of his experience and of his sight of Cromwell at this time. "I came," he said, "out of Essex in at Aldgate," and,

"just as I came in a Proclamation was read for trial of his majesty; I went down the next day to the Painted Chamber at Westminster, where I saw Oliver Cromwell, John Goodwin and Peters, and others; John Goodwin sat in the middle of the table, and he made a long speech or prayer, I know not whether, but Mr. Peters stood there: After John Goodwin had done his prayer, it was desired that strangers might avoid the room; then came up Cook, and Dorislaus, and Humphreys, and Ask, and Dendy, and several others, and stood by Bradshaw at the upper end of the table; but Cromwell stood up and told them it was not necessary that the people should go out; but that was over-ruled."[303]

This is almost if not quite the only intimate glimpse of Oliver Cromwell at the beginning of this great enterprise. Its first week's work was ended by a meeting of thirty-eight commissioners on the next day, Saturday, January 13, which did little more than order the serjeant-at-arms to secure the vaults under the Painted Chamber to prevent another Gunpowder Plot, and to determine that the trial should be held in Westminster Hall, where the courts of King's Bench and Chancery sat, and that the Hall was to be fitted up for that purpose. Such were the preparations for the trial within the Court itself, and such the matters with which Oliver Cromwell busied himself chiefly in that period. Outside that Court, meanwhile, was much activity. It was not to be supposed that such a proceeding as the trial of the King could go unchallenged even by many who had supported the revolution to this point and before the High Court was constituted protest had begun. On January 4—the day that the Commons had voted itself the supreme authority in the state—it had appointed a committee to go to Mr. Prynne to "know if he would own and avow a scandalous Book or Pamphlet, 'A brief Memento to the present Unparliamentary Juncto, touching their present Intentions and Proceedings to depose and execute Charles Steward, their lawful King.' " To which Mr. Prynne, who had lost his ears under that lawful king, replied that he would give no answer until commanded by a lawful authority.

Parliament had naturally sunk into obscurity in the face of the developments in the Painted Chamber. The Lords were virtually all gone. On January 9 there were seven men present, including the Speaker; on the next day there were only three; and the usual attendance during the month was four. Since the Commons, on January 3, had voted itself power to legislate without the concurrence of the Lords, the Upper House no longer carried any weight in public af-

[303] Testimony at Peter's trial. *Exact and impartial account*, pp. 160–1. *State Trials*, v, 1124.

fairs, and when it sent down some ordinances the Commons only admitted its messengers by a vote of 31 to 18 and replied contemptuously by a vote of 33 to 19 that it would send its answer by messengers of its own. While the Lords went through the motions of a legislative body, to celebrate and confirm its sole direction of affairs the Commons ordered a new Great Seal with a view of itself on one side and on the other an inscription, "In the first year of freedom, by God's blessing restored, 1648."

All this gives point to a letter of January 12 which declared that a motion had been lately made in the Commons to suppress the House of Lords entirely. Against this, according to the author, Cromwell seemed to be very violent and asked them if they were all mad to take these courses to incense the Peers at this time when they needed to study a near union. In this appeal he was successful, for when the House divided, he and thirty-two others went out and only eighteen remained.[304] He had throughout been extremely active in the preparations for the trial of the King as a member of successive committees relating to the organization of the High Court of Justice. Retaining his place in the diminished House of Commons and in the Army Council, now a member of the High Court of Justice, as usual he mingled great things with small in his various capacities as soldier, legislator and now judge. On the first day of the meeting of the Court, he received a bond of £500 from one John Fussell of Dorset to guarantee that Fussell should not raise any forces or arms against the Parliament but should live peaceably,[305] and the very fact that it was given to Cromwell seems of some significance. On January 12 he was put on a Commons' committee to "consider how £300,000 can be raised from Deans' and Chapters' Lands," of which £200,000 was for the Navy, the rest for public services in general;[306] and though he may not have been in the House at that time, and there was no meeting of the Army Council, it is apparent from these little items how fully his time was occupied between the three bodies of which he was a member.

To this he and the managers of the trial added another activity—the recruiting of the Court and the meeting or suppressing of the rising opposition to their plans. Prynne was not alone in his censures. The London ministers in particular were holding meetings with a view to a public protest—a thing which had to be avoided at all costs—and efforts were made to silence them. As *Mercurius Pragmaticus* records under date of January 9, "Cromwell, Ireton and Peters made it their business this weeke again to compass the city and visit the ministers with threats" and Peters carried a file of

[304] Letter Jan. 12. *Clarendon State Papers,* ii, l–li.
[305] *Cal. St. Pap. Dom., Charles I,* (1648), p. 345.
[306] *C. J.,* vi, 116.

musketeers to overawe a Mr. Cawley, who slipped away and appealed to Fairfax, who said that "Peters was a knave and had no command from him. And when Hugh returned he was check'd but defended by Cromwell and Ireton that sent him on work to abuse his Excellency, whom they make but a meer stalking horse for their designs, and in effect but Deputy-General, upon courtesie, to carry on their present proceedings."[307]

Those proceedings meanwhile had gone on. On Monday January 15, the Court met again, this time "openly," with fifty-eight members present, but at once went into secret session; and, with various proclamations, appointed two committees, one headed by Ireton to advise the counsel as to the charge against the King, the other headed by Ludlow to make preparations for the trial. Two days later, on Wednesday, January 17, it met again with fifty-six men present for further preliminary business, in particular that of making the charge against the King 'more brief.' Sir Robert Cotton's house was appointed as Charles's residence during the trial; a guard of thirty officers was appointed for his immediate custody, two always to be outside his bedchamber. A court of guard for two hundred men was ordered to be built in the garden, and ten companies of foot placed constantly on guard; a dais to be raised in Westminster Hall for the judges; two rails to be erected between the Court and the people; guards set along the leads and at windows that looked into the Hall; two hundred halberts provided to arm the guards; and "all back doors from the house called *Hell* . . . stopped up during the King's trial." The Lord President was to be lodged at Sir Abraham Williams's house, and the judges were to meet in the Exchequer chamber and so come into the court. Every precaution was thus taken to prevent escape, rescue or public tumult, and to secure the safety of the Court, as trustworthy troops were ordered up and stationed at strategic points to overawe the City and Westminster.

The stage was now set for the last act of the Tragedy of King Charles the First. The cast was all assembled. The judges sat in the Painted Chamber; the Lords, still going through the motions of meeting, the Commons still doing routine business, in their respective chambers; the Army Council, which was the real power, meeting from day to day to put the last touches on the *Agreement of the People.* That Agreement was completed apparently on January 15,—the same day as the charge against the King—and presented for the approval of the House of Commons five days later—the date set for the opening of the trial. Were there any question as to how that trial would

[307] The same story is told by Walker, *Anarchia Anglicana*, p. 67,—but with more detail and with "Cawley" changed to "Calamy"—from the letter of the London Ministers to Fairfax. Cf. p. 735.

end, it must have been dispelled by the terms of the *Agreement*, since in its provisions there was no place for a King.

That omission is no less significant than the fact that between January 13 and February 22 there are no minutes nor table of attendance of the Army Council surviving. They were, apparently, too dangerous to be preserved, and if they ever existed, it seems they must have been destroyed, probably at the Restoration. It is, therefore, impossible to prove from direct evidence precisely what Cromwell did and said in those eventful days; yet there is little question as to what he did. As a member of Parliament, of the High Court of Justice and of the Army Council, he was at the very heart of things, and from various notices it is possible to determine something of his activities. On January 17 when the High Court of Justice ordered the charge against the King made 'still more brief' and set the beginning of the trial for January 20, Cromwell was named to two Commons' committees, one to consider a petition from the Portsmouth garrison, the other "to select persons to meet with the Parliament of Scotland." Far more important, on that same day he was added by the High Court of Justice to the committee for the conduct of Charles's trial.[308] There can be but little doubt that he, like his colleagues, was busier with the Army Council and the High Court than with the parliamentary business, for Parliament was now a negligible quantity. In these tragic days a handful of three or four peers met and adjourned; the largest number on divisions in the Commons was fifty-two; and in its *Journals* the only mention of the King during the month was to authorize Dr. Juxon "to continue with the King in private, under the same restraint the King is."

That entry foreshadowed the result of the trial. On January 18 the High Court sat to listen to the final draft of the charges against the King. On the next day Charles who had been brought from Windsor to St. James and thence carried to Whitehall, on January 19, in a closely guarded sedan chair, was removed by water to Sir Robert Cotton's house near the west end of Westminster Hall. That journey provides us with another glimpse of Cromwell. A dozen years later when Henry Marten was being tried for his life for his part in the death of the King, one of the witnesses against him, Sir Purbeck Temple, testified that

"Cromwell heard the King was landed at Sir Robert Cotton's stairs. Went to the window looking at the King as he came up the garden, he turned white as the wall, spoke to Bradshaw and Sir Henry Mildmay, drew them and Sir William Brereton, who had concluded some business, aside, and said 'My Masters, he is come, he is come, and now we are doing that great work that the whole nation will be full of: Therefore I desire you to let us

[308] *State Trials*, iv, 1063.

resolve here what answer we shall give the King when he comes before us, for the first question that he will ask us will be by what authority and commission do we try him?' None answered, but presently Marten said 'In the name of the Commons and Parliament assembled and all the good people of England.' "[309]

Besides this there is another story of as great, or little, probability among the legends which grew up about this last stage of Charles's earthly pilgrimage. It is to the effect that, about this time, Cromwell's kinsman, Colonel John Cromwell, Sir Oliver's son, was sent from Holland by Prince Charles with a blank paper with the King's signet and that of the Prince, both confirmed by the States General, for Cromwell to write his own conditions on which he would save Charles's life. Colonel Cromwell saw his cousin Oliver 'shut up in his own house' and after discussing the matter went away to wait for an answer. After some hours he was told that Cromwell and the other officers had been "seeking God" and were resolved that the King must die.[310] Whatever truth there may be in the details of such narratives, one thing emerges clearly. The decision hung largely on Cromwell; and, among the incidental evidences of his dominant position at this time is the curious fact that at this moment a letter from the States General recommending ambassadors was sent to him, with a duplicate to Fairfax.[311]

This was not the only effort made to prevent the trial and to save the King's life—for it was felt on every hand that the verdict was a foregone conclusion. On January 17, some forty-seven London ministers presented their protest to Fairfax against the exclusion and imprisonment of the majority of the Commons, the seizure of the King and the proceedings of the army. "We shall not need to fear the threatenings which some few of us have received," they added, "not from yourselves, yet from messengers directed immediately from yourselves" to the effect that "if the soldiers do us a mischief we may thank ourselves. That if there follow another war, you will give quarter to none that stands against you. That you will spare neither man, woman nor child, English nor stranger."

Those were strong words, which point more or less obliquely in the direction of Cromwell's "familiar," Hugh Peter, who in all contemporary accounts played a conspicuous part at this moment, for which he later paid with his life. But they are no stronger than the words recorded by Sidney as coming from Cromwell at this time. Writing eleven years later he repeated the fateful words which, in this session of the 19th, indicated the stern resolution of the leading man among the commissioners:

309 *Exact and impartial account*, p. 248.
310 Heath, *Flagellum* (1663), p. 53; Echard, ii, 638; Fellowes, *Hist. Sketches*, p. 241.
311 *Hist. Mss Comm. Rept.* 13, App. I (Welbeck Abbey), i, 509.

"I was at Penshurst when the act for the trial passed," Sidney wrote, "and, coming up to town, I heard my name was put in, and that those that were nominated for judges were then in the Painted Chamber. I presently went thither, heard the act read, and found my own name with the others. A debate was raised how they should proceed upon it, and, after having been some time silent to hear what those should say who had had the directing of the business, I did positively oppose Cromwell, Bradshaw and others, who would have the trial to go on, and drew my reasons from these two points: first, the king could be tried by no court; secondly, that no man could be tried by that court. This being alleged in vain, and Cromwell using these formal words, 'I tell you we will cut off his head, with the crown on it,' I replied, 'You may take your own course, I cannot stop you, but I will keep myself clean from having any hand in this business,' immediately went out of the room and never returned."[312]

The great moment had now arrived. On January 20 the *Agreement of the People* was presented to the House of Commons for its approval, but the House, though it returned its "hearty thanks" to the General and the Council of Officers, laid the matter aside, voting that the *Agreement* should be considered as soon as "the necessity of the present weighty and urgent affairs would permit." Those weighty and urgent affairs now centered in the adjoining Westminster Hall where at that moment the trial of the King began. There on a dais at the southern end had been placed seats for the judges, in front of them a barrier or bar and in front of it and facing the judges a chair covered with crimson velvet had been set for the royal prisoner-defendant, behind it a space reserved for the King's guards and attendants and a body of troops under Colonel Axtell. In the corners above the Court were galleries for ladies and distinguished visitors and the body of the Hall was reserved for the public which crowded to the spectacle.

Into the great Hall thus arranged there marched the judges with the officers of the Court, guarded by twenty men with partizans, to take their places on the seats or benches hung with scarlet, Bradshaw in his crimson velvet chair in the middle of the first row, an assistant on each side. In the center of the last row of judges according to a print of the time, which may have been only the artist's fancy, sat Oliver Cromwell.[313] The judges seated, the act establishing the Court was read and the roll called, each man standing to answer to his name, and with this came the first of those interruptions which the managers had feared. After the name of Bradshaw, was called that of Fairfax, whereupon from her place in the gallery, according to Clarendon, Lady Fairfax cried, "he had more wit than to be there," which "put the court into some disorder."[314]

[312] Blencowe, *Sidney Papers*, p. 237.
[313] But see Downes' testimony below.
[314] *History*, xi, 235.

The Court thus constituted and the interruption over, the King was brought in by Colonel Thomlinson, attended by Colonel Hacker, thirty-two officers with partizans and the King's servants. "After a stern looking upon the court," Charles sat down, then rose again and looked over the guards and the crowd and, paying no respect to the Court and keeping on his hat, he sat down again and proceedings were resumed. They began by the reading of the charge by Cook. That charge, now reduced to the shortest form which the counsel and officers could agree upon, was, of necessity perhaps, a statement of a theory of government as well as an indictment, for under existing law no such indictment could be laid against the crown.

It began, therefore, with the assertion that "Charles Stuart, being admitted King of England" was "therein trusted with a limited power to govern by, and according to the laws of the land, and not otherwise; and by his trust, oath, and office" was "obliged to use the power committed to him for the good and benefit of the people, and for the preservation of their rights and liberties." Then came the charge, that "out of a wicked design to erect and uphold in himself an unlimited and tyrannical power, to rule according to his will, and to overthrow the rights and liberties of the people," he had "traitorously and maliciously levied war against the present Parliament, and the people therein represented" by various acts enumerated in the charge. In particular he had "renewed or caused to be renewed" the war in 1648 and commissioned his son, Prince Charles, and others, and still continued the issuance of such commissions to "rebels and revolters, both English and foreigners, and to the Earl of Ormond and the Irish." All these, the charge concluded, "have been, and are carried on for the advancement and upholding of a personal interest of will, power, and pretended prerogative to himself and his family, against the public interest, common right, liberty, justice and peace of the people of this nation."[315]

Such was the charge against Charles Stuart, which Bradshaw called on the King to answer, in words which echoed Marten, "in the behalf of the Commons assembled in Parliament and the good people of England." Before he could reply, Lady Fairfax answered for him from the gallery. "It's a lie," she cried, "not half, nor a quarter of the people of England! Oliver Cromwell is a rogue and a traitor."[316] Infuriated by the new interruption, Axtell ordered his men to fire into the gallery, but they disobeyed, and Lady Fairfax was persuaded to leave the Court. But she had had her say, and in it she had not merely voiced the opinion of most of the spectators as to the legality of the proceedings and the truth of the charge against the King but she had pointed out the man whom most of them, and people gen-

[315] *State Trials*, vol. iv.
[316] *Ibid.*, v, 1146

erally, credited with pressing the case against Charles to this fatal conclusion.

Charles had endeavored to stop Cook in his address to the Court; he had touched the solicitor with his cane, whose head fell off, "at which he wondered," and it was regarded as an ill omen. At his description of himself as a traitor and murderer, he had laughed aloud; and when Bradshaw had asked him, in effect, what he had to say for himself, he demanded to know by what authority he had been called before this body, refusing to proceed until that question had been answered. Bradshaw replied in the words put into his mouth by Marten, "by the authority of the Commons of England, assembled in Parliament, in the behalf of the People of England"; but to that he incautiously added a few words of his own: "by which people you are elected King." These raised at once a highly debatable, if not wholly false, theory of government, and thus palpably gave the case into Charles's hands. Like his father, James I, he was fond of argument; he was never so happy or so much at ease as in a disputation; and he was very good at it. He was, he said, a king not by election for "England was never an elective kingdom; it was a hereditary kingdom for near this thousand years." He was, he said, a king by inheritance and with this obvious retort he carried off the honors of the day.

The trial had begun badly for the prosecution in more ways than these. The crowds were sympathetic to the King; and though he was led away by the soldiers who under Axtell's orders shouted "Justice! Justice!" the crowds retorted, "God save the King!" The second day of the trial, Monday, January 22, Charles replied to the charge in an able argument which he later committed to paper. "Having already made my protestations," he argued in his memorandum, "not only against the illegality of this pretended Court, but also, that no earthly power can justly call me (who am your King) in question as a delinquent," he would not deign to reply to the charges against him, but for one thing "the duty I owe to God in the preservation of the true liberty of my people."[317]

"How," he inquired, "can any free-born subject of England call life, or anything he possesseth his own, if power without right daily make new, and abrogate the old fundamental laws of the land?" The proceedings against him, he declared were warranted neither by the law of God or of the land. How could the House of Commons, without the King or Lords, pretend to make laws or to erect a court? Admitting, but not granting, that the people could delegate such power, "you have never asked the question of the tenth man in this kingdom" and without a majority of the people, where, he inquired, is your authority? With this he struck a still higher note. "I speak,"

[317] *State Trials*, iv, 1085–87.

he said, "not for my own right alone . . . but also for the true liberty of all my subjects, which consists not in the power of government, but in living under such laws, such a government, as may give themselves the best assurance of their lives, and property of their goods."[318]

To that argument there was but one answer which such a body as the High Court of Justice could make, and after some altercation Bradshaw made it. He ordered the King removed from the court. The situation had now reached its last great crisis. It was evident from the beginning that Charles would be pronounced guilty. That verdict, indeed, virtually had already been given in the Army Council. But there were two difficulties which still confronted his accusers. The first was the danger that he might be saved at the last moment. On this very day there arrived a third protest from the Scots against his execution and it was reported that Cromwell had put a guard on Fairfax, suspecting or accusing him of an intention to deliver Charles.[319] From every direction there poured in appeals and threats in an endeavor to save his life. Even to Republicans like Sidney his execution seemed an abhorrent thing. It was, in that view, proper enough to depose or disinherit him, but there was, as Charles said, no law by which he could legally be put to death, save only the law of force. "I doubt not," wrote Major White to Fairfax, "but the sword may do it; but how righteous judgment that may be, that God and future generations will judge."

But if nothing availed against the will and power of those who had determined on Charles's death, nothing availed against the King's determination not to plead or to recognize the Court, and when he was brought before it for the third time on January 23 with no more result than before, Bradshaw ordered the clerk to "record his default" and the Court adjourned to the Painted Chamber to deliberate what should be done next. That deliberation lasted long, but its result was a foregone conclusion. On the very day that Charles was adjudged guilty "by default," the Commons remnant resolved "That the Style to be used in all writs, *etc.* shall be *Authoritate* [*sic*] *Parliamenti Angliae*,"[320] and it is evident that on that day the doom of Charles was sealed. There was no public session of the Court on the 24th or on the 25th, while the examination of the witnesses to Charles's share in the war went on in the Painted Chamber. At the end of that formal and fantastic proceeding the first vote was taken on a resolution that "this court will proceed to sentence of condemnation against Charles Stuart, King of England . . . for tyrant, traitor and murtherer . . . for being a public enemy to the Commonwealth

318 *Ibid.*, 1087–91.

319 News brought to Rouen by a servant of Lady Sidley's, Carte, *Original Letters*, i, 212.

320 *C. J.*, vi, 123.

of England . . . that this vote shall extend to death." It further recorded that the commissioners present, of whom there were forty-six,[321] "were present at these votes." That number was evidently unsatisfactory, and it was declared that this was merely a "preliminary" expression of opinion. A committee was appointed to draw up the sentence, significantly leaving a blank for the manner of Charles's punishment and renewed efforts were made to bring more members into the Court. By the morning of January 26 those efforts resulted in the appearance of sixty-two men in the Painted Chamber. The charge of high treason was omitted as being not only legally absurd but repugnant to the good sense of various members, and with this concession to the objectors it was voted that Charles should be put to death on the charges in the sentence "by the severing of his head from his body." Of the numbers voting for or against this resolution there is no record, but it is all but inconceivable that it was unanimous, for it is certain that a considerable number of those present did not sign the death-warrant, and it is no unreasonable supposition that they voted against the death-sentence, if not against the whole proceeding. At any rate there were enough. The death-warrant had already been prepared and apparently by the morning of the 26th some of the more determined members of the Court, including Cromwell, had already signed it. One further question remained. The proceedings of the Court after the opening sessions had been secret, and it was first proposed that sentence should be pronounced on him in Westminster Hall, but without bringing him into court.

Somehow and some time between the 24th and the 26th that idea was abandoned, and on Saturday the 27th the Court reassembled in Westminster Hall and Charles was brought before it to be welcomed by shouts of "Justice! and execution!" Prevented from speaking, the King was compelled to listen to a harangue from Bradshaw who stressed the "past forbearance" of the Court, before which he said Charles had been called to answer 'in the name of the people of England.' Again he was interrupted by a lady who cried from the gallery, "Not half of the people!" When order was restored, Bradshaw went on to say that the Court had agreed upon a sentence but would listen to the King, if he did not question its jurisdiction. To this Charles answered that he had taken his course not for his own advantage but in behalf of his subjects' liberties, and asked to be heard before the Lords and Commons.[322]

This touched a delicate problem which had evidently appealed to some of the Court, and one of them, Downes, according to later re-

[321] *State Trials*, iv, 1111; Muddiman, *Trial of Charles I*, says 47 and lists 45.

[322] As Gardiner says with unconscious ingenuousness, "In other words he wished to appeal from the Court to a political assembly," *Civil War*, iv, 312.

ports and to his own testimony, was only prevented from rising in his place to support Charles's plea by Cromwell's angry interference. In any event it seems that he secured a recess of the Court and, incidentally, gave another glimpse of Cromwell at this time.

"I remember," Downes said at his trial, "the persons between whom I sat, as it fell out, were one Mr. Cawly, and col. Walton . . . these were the words I spake to them, 'Have we hearts of stone? Are we men?' They laboured to appease me; they told me I would ruin both myself and them; said I, 'if I die for it I must do it.' Cromwell sat just the seat below me, the hearing of me make some stir, whispering, he looked up to me, and asked me if I were myself? What I meant to do, that I could not be quiet? 'Sir,' said I, 'no, I cannot be quiet,' upon that I started up in the very nick; when the President commanded the Clerk to read the Sentence, I stepping up, and as loud as I could speak, spoke to this effect . . . 'I am not satisfied to give my consent to this sentence, but have reasons to offer you against it, and I desire the Court may adjourn to hear me' . . . So accordingly they did adjourn into the Inner Court of Wards; when they came there I was called upon by Cromwell to give an account why I had put this trouble and disturbance upon the Court?"

Whereupon Downes, according to his own story, delivered himself of a long speech against the actions of the Court; and to him, in turn, as he says,

"Cromwell did answer with a great deal of storm; he told the president, that now he saw what good reason the gentleman had to put such a trouble and disturbance upon them; saith he, 'sure he doth not know that he hath to do with the hardest-hearted man that lives upon the earth; however it is not fit that the Court should be hindered from their duty by one peevish man,' he said, 'the bottom was known, that he would fain save his old master'; and desired the Court, without any more ado, would go and do their duty."[323]

Which, reassembling after a half an hour, they did by denying the King's demand and preventing him from speaking. With that Bradshaw made a long harangue, quoting precedents of past depositions, notably those of Edward II, Richard II and Mary, Queen of Scots, and called on the clerk to read the formal sentence. The King's efforts to reply and to protest were stopped by the declaration that they came too late, and the members of the Court were requested to express their approval of the sentence which they did by rising. Charles, still protesting brokenly, was dragged from the Court by his guards, among renewed cries of "Justice! Justice!" from the soldiery, instigated by their officers, especially Axtell, and the murmurs of the crowd.

Such was the grim spectacle of the condemnation of Charles I;

[323] *Trial of the Regicides; State Trials*, v, 1212–13.

such the part that Cromwell played in it; and such the document to which he had set his signature three days earlier:

Death Warrant of Charles I.

At the high Court of Justice for the tryinge and iudginge of Charles Steuart Kinge of England January xxixth Anno Dni 1648.

Whereas Charles Steuart Kinge of England is and standeth convicted attaynted and condemned of High Treason and other high Crymes, And sentence uppon Saturday last was pronounced against him by this Court to be putt to death by the severinge of his head from his body Of wch sentence execucion yet remayneth to be done, These are therefore to will and require you to see the said sentence executed In the open Streete before Whitehall uppon the morrowe being the Thirtieth day of this instante moneth of January betweene the houres of Tenn in the morninge and Five in the afternoone of the same day wth full effect And for soe doing this shall be yor sufficient warrant And these are to require All Officers and Souldiers and other the good people of this Nation of England to be assistinge unto you in this Service Given under our hands and Seales

To Colonell Ffrancis Hacker, Colonell Huncks and Lieutenant Colonell Phayre and to every of them.

				Valentine Wanton	L.S.
				Symon Mayne	L.S.
				Tho. Horton	L.S.
				John Jones	L.S.
Jo. Bradshawe	L.S.	Per. Pelham	L.S.	John Moore	L.S.
Tho. Grey	L.S.	Ri. Deane	L.S.	Gilbt. Millington	L.S.
O. Cromwell	L.S.	Robert Tichborne	L.S.	G. Fleetwood	L.S.
Edw. Whalley	L.S.	H. Edwardes	L.S.	J. Alured	L.S.
M. Livesey	L.S.	Daniel Blagrave	L.S.	Robt. Lilburne	L.S.
John Okey	L.S.	Owen Rowe	L.S.	Will. Say	L.S.
J. Davers	L.S.	William Purefoy	L.S.	Anth. Stapley	L.S.
Jo. Bourchier	L.S.	Ad. Scrope	L.S.	Greg. Norton	L.S.
H. Ireton	L.S.	James Temple	L.S.	Tho. Challoner	L.S.
Tho. Mauleverer	L.S.	A. Garland	L.S.	Tho. Wogan	L.S.
Har. Waller	L.S.	Edm. Ludlowe	L.S.	John Venn	L.S.
John Blakiston	L.S.	Henry Marten	L.S.	Gregory Clement	L.S.
J. Hutchinson	L.S.	Vinct. Potter	L.S.	Jo. Downes	L.S.
Willi. Goff	L.S.	Wm. Constable	L.S.	Tho. Wayte	L.S.
Tho. Pride	L.S.	Rich. Ingoldesby	L.S.	Tho. Scot	L.S.
Pe. Temple	L.S.	Willi. Cawley	L.S.	Jo. Carew	L.S.
T. Harrison	L.S.	Jo. Barkestead	L.S.	Miles Corbet	L.S.
J. Hewson	L.S.	Isaa. Ewer	L.S.		
Hen. Smyth	L.S.	John Dixwell	L.S.[324]		

As to the framing of that fatal document some controversy has arisen in regard to when it was drawn up and when and how the signatures were obtained. It has been argued that it was originally

[324] Thoms, *Death Warrant of Charles I*, from the original in the House of Lords.

drawn on January 23rd, on January 25th or on January 26th, and that it was signed at various times between January 24th and 29th. In a sense these questions are insignificant. The main issue was never much in doubt in the minds of those who planned the trial and execution of the King; yet the means by which they persuaded or compelled enough of their fellows to share in that course can never lack a certain interest or importance, for, obviously, had not enough men joined with them, their purpose could never have been carried out.

It is apparent from the document itself, still more from its signatures, and most of all from the testimony given in the trials of the regicides, that it was difficult to secure enough votes among the judges to condemn Charles to death, and still more difficult to get men to sign the death-warrant for the King which might well be, and in no few cases was, their own. Whoever signed it first, it seems apparent that not more than twenty-eight had signed before the 27th, so that the rest of the signatures must have been obtained after the death sentence was pronounced. There are many stories of that last hectic day before Charles's execution which throw some light on its events and on the doings of Cromwell in particular.

Among them are two which have found currency in history. The one is that Cromwell called on members of the Court who were also members of the Commons to sign the death-warrant when they took their places in the House, and compelled them to sign. Later in the day, when the warrant lay in the Painted Chamber for signatures, as Colonel Ewer testified, "My Lord, I did see a pen in Mr. Cromwell's hand, and he marked Mr. Marten in the face with it, and Mr. Marten did the like to him." It is no less apparent that the death-warrant, partly signed, was set aside for a time, perhaps in the hope that Charles might be frightened into submission. Meanwhile it was changed. There was inserted in place of whatever the original may have been, the words "upon Saturday last" as the time when sentence was pronounced against Charles, and in place of perhaps "twenty-sixth" or "twenty-seventh," the word "Thirtieth" was spread out to cover the erased date. The name of Colonel Huncks remained as one of the three officers entrusted with the execution of the warrant, but in place of the other two—who evidently declined to serve—there were inserted the names of Colonel Francis Hacker and Lieutenant Colonel Phayre; and the name of Garland was evidently written over another which had been erased.

From these incidents and from other evidence it is apparent that even at the last moment, and even more as the last moment approached, there were deep searchings of the heart among many of the men engaged, and that many drew back, so that only the determination of Cromwell and his immediate circle drove the matter on. It so happened that at this moment the ambassador from the States General, Adrian Pauw, appeared with his colleague Joachim to plead with the English authorities, Parliament in particular, for Charles's life. They saw Fairfax in his chamber with a number of officers, and asked to speak with him alone. Soon after Fairfax had withdrawn with the ambassadors, Cromwell entered with some officers without asking permission or performing any act of civility. Fairfax and Cromwell dared not open the letters of credence, Pauw told the States General, except in the presence of the officers, and neither went about without a guard of at least three hundred horse. Pauw praised Fairfax for his civility, Cromwell for his ability and eloquence.[325]

That was only the last of a series of protests. Apart from the three appeals from the Scots, and the blank sheet with the signatures of Charles and his son for the managers of Charles's trial to fill up as the price of the King's life, besides countless private protests, there had arrived letters from Louis XIV to Cromwell and Fairfax pleading for mercy for King Charles.[326] The Royalists were naturally bitterly opposed to the trial and still more to the execution of the King; the Presbyterians were only second in their objection; the people in general were against it; and had this great and growing sentiment in the nation found a leader, Charles's life might have been saved. Many besides Louis XIV looked to Fairfax to take that part. But whether or not Fairfax had the courage, the talents or the initiative to oppose Cromwell, he realized that any effort to save Charles would have meant a prompt and bloody civil war and he shrank from that responsibility; and save for him there was no one able and willing to head a movement to save the King.

We shall probably never know exactly what went on in the closely guarded sessions of the High Court in the Painted Chamber, neither arguments nor votes, but it seems at least possible, if not indeed probable, that the commissioners disagreed among themselves to the last and that the final vote, so far from being unanimous was sharply divided. So far as we may judge from what little evidence we have, it was very possibly the votes of the Cromwellian colonels and "creatures" which turned the scale against the King. For that there are two kinds of testimony. The one is the list of the signers of the death-warrant; the other, which is less dependable, is the testimony adduced at the trials of the regicides ten years later; and to these may be added other evidence which seems to bear them out.

The first is indisputable and is what one expects. The second bears

[325] Pauw's relation to the States General, Mar. 1/11, sent to the Doge of Venice, *Cal. St. P. Venetian, 1647–52*, p. 90. For Ewer's testimony, see *State Trials*, v.

[326] *Mss de Brienne*, Bibliotheque Nacionale, Paris. Printed in Guizot, *History of Oliver Cromwell*, (1854), i, 327–28.

on the great question as to who drove the trial through. Of that there seems but little doubt. The popular verdict was correct. It was Cromwell, or Cromwell and Ireton, who pushed the matter on, pleading, arguing, even threatening, in their efforts to compel men to attend the meetings of the commissioners, vote for conviction and sign the death-warrant. For this, apart from the testimony of the regicides, there is that of Thomas Waite:

"I came to London the day before the sentence was given; I went to the house, (thought nothing) . . . I was sent for to the house, and my name was in the act unknown to me; but one sent a note in my lord Gray's name, that he would speak with me. I went to him and I said, my lord, what would you do with me? Saith he, I did not send for you; whereupon Cromwell and Ireton laid hold on me; said they, we sent for you, you are one of the High Court; no, said I, Not I, my judgment is against it. They carried me to the Court. When the king desired to speak with his parliament, I rising up, one told me I must not be heard . . . Mr. Downes did move, and they did adjourn the Court, and I was glad to get out; Cromwell laughed and smiled and jeered in the Court of Wards."

To this he added presently another piece of testimony as to how his signature was obtained. Grey, he said, had assured him that the King would not die.

"The next day, on Monday, I went to the house, they were labouring to get hands for his execution at the door; I refused and went into the house; saith Cromwell, 'those that are gone in shall set their hands, I will have their hands now.' . . .[327]

Clarendon tells the well-known story of how Sir Richard Ingoldsby happened to sign the death-warrant:

"He was named amongst those who were appointed to be judges of the King . . . he was never once present with them . . . and having no other passion in any part of the quarrel but his personal kindness to Cromwell. The next day after the horrid sentence was pronounced, he had occasion to speak with an officer, who, he was told, was in the Painted Chamber; where, when he came thither, he saw Cromwell, and the rest of those who had sat upon the King, and were then, as he found afterwards, assembled to sign the warrant for his majesty's death. As soon as Cromwell's eyes were upon him, he ran to him, and taking him by the hand, drew him by force to the table; and said, 'though he had escaped him all the while, he should now sign that paper as well as they'; which he, seeing what it was, refused with great passion, saying he knew nothing of the business, and offered to go away. But Cromwell and others held him by violence; and Cromwell, with a loud laughter, taking his hand in his, and putting the pen between his fingers, with his own hand writ 'Richard Ingolsby,' he making all the resist-

[327] *State Trials*, v, 1215–16.

ance he could; and he said, if his name there were compared with what he had ever writ himself, it could never be looked upon as his own hand."[328]

To this Colonel Axtell contributed his testimony as to his share in the trial. "I was there," he said, "at the command of my General," and being pressed by the court as to whether it was the express command of Fairfax, he testified that Fairfax "gave his orders every morning to his adjutant-general or to his major-general." Pressed still further as to what major-general gave him his orders, he answered somewhat obscurely, "There was Cromwell and Ireton," who, as he swore, told him they had had the orders from Fairfax.[329]

These stories were told, it has been said, by men eager to save their lives and throw the blame on others who were dead, and that they are not to be considered evidence. To that summary dismissal of this evidence there are several objections. The first is that not all of the men who testified were on trial for their lives; the second is that their tales are extraordinarily similar though they had no opportunity of collusion in their evidence; the third is that they bear the mark of truth, they are not the work of cowards trying to lie their way to liberty; the fourth is that they are confirmed by outside evidence. Of this there is one striking instance. In later years Lieutenant General Drummond told Bishop Burnet of Cromwell's appeal to the Scots to support him in pressing for Charles's death. As Drummond said,

"Upon this Cromwell entered into a long discourse of the nature of regal power according to the principles of Mariana and Buchanan. He thought a breach of trust in a King ought to be punished more than any crime whatsoever; he said, as to their covenant, they swore to the preservation of the King's person in defence of the true religion; if, then, it appeared that the settlement of the true religion was obstructed by the King, so that they could not come at it but by putting him out of the way, then their oath could not bind them to the preserving him any longer. He said, also, their covenant did bind them to bring all malignants, incendiaries, and enemies to the cause to condign punishment, and was not this to be exercised impartially? What were all those on whom publick justice had been done, especially those who suffered for joining with Montrose, but small offenders acting by commission from the King, who was therefore the principal, and so the most guilty?"[330]

It was a moving plea, but it did not move the Scots. There must have seemed, indeed, something grimly amusing in such an argument from such a man, especially based on the preservation of a "true religion" by one to whom presbyterianism was only less objectionable than episcopacy. Over the Scots he had no power, but, apart from

328 Clarendon, *History*, xvi, 235.
329 *State Trials*, v, 1167.
330 Burnet, *History of My Own Time*, rev. ed. (1753), I, 56–7

those on the High Court of Justice who, like himself, were determined to put the King to death, there were unquestionably some officers to whom his arguments must have seemed like threats. Despite the tendency of men to throw the blame on those who are beyond the reach of punishment, it seems apparent that it was Cromwell who approached them, and his line of reasoning may be deduced from his argument to the Scots. Against this may be set the words of Mrs. Hutchinson whose literary skill produced a portrait of her husband which remains the classic description of a Puritan gentleman, without fear and without reproach. In it she takes occasion to deny the charge of compulsion by Cromwell:

"The gentlemen that were appoynted his [the King's] iudges, and divers others, saw in him a disposition so bent on the ruine of all that oppos'd him, and of all the righteous and iust things they had contended for, that it was upon the consciences of many of them that if they did not execute iustice upon him, God would require at their hands all the blood and desolation which should ensue by their suffering him to escape, when God had brought him into their hands. Although the mallice of the mallignant party and their apostate brethren seem'd to threaten them, yett they thought they ought to cast themselves upon God, while they acted with a good conscience for him and their country. Some of them after, to excuse, belied themselves, and sayd they were under the awe of the armie, and overperswaded by Cromwell, and the like; but it is certeine that all men herein were left to their free liberty of acting, neither perswaded nor compelled; and as there were some nominated in the commission who never sate, and others who sate at first, but durst not hold on, so all the rest might have declin'd it if they would, when it is apparent they should have suffer'd nothing by so doing. For those who then declin'd were afterwards, when they offer'd themselves, recei'd in againe, and had places of more trust and benefitt then those who run the utmost hazard; which they deserv'd not, for I know upon certeine knowledge that many, yea the most of them retreated not for conscience, but for feare and worldly prudence, foreseeing that the insolency of the armie might grow to that height as to ruine the cause, and reduce the kingdome into the hands of the enemie; and then those who had bene most courageous in their country's cause should be given up as victims. These poore men did privately animate those who appear'd most publiquely, and I knew severall of them in whom I liv'd to see that saying of Christ fulfill'd, "He that will save his life shall loose it, and he that for my sake will loose his life shall save it. . . ."[331]

As Mrs. Hutchinson saw the matter at distance of some fifteen or twenty years this doubtless all was true so far as she and her husband were concerned; yet if a question has been raised as to the evidence of the regicides, it is no more than fair to evaluate hers. She was fortunate in being the daughter of a devoted Royalist, Sir Allen Apsley, through whom and others of like sort, acting under her persistent and devoted pleas, her husband was not even brought to trial

[331] Lucy Hutchinson, *Memoirs of the Life of Colonel Hutchinson*, ii, 157.

for his life, though on the basis of his record he was certainly as guilty of Charles's death as any who were executed at the Restoration. Nor is it probable that it was necessary for Cromwell and Ireton to deal with a man whose principles were well known and whose vote could be depended on.

Yet again that leaves the old question open as before—in how far did Cromwell lead and in how far was he pushed to the trial and execution of the King? Here, as elsewhere, he seems the man of action, not of far-sighted statesmanship, unless one credits him, as the Royalists did, with a mere effort to clear his way to the headship of the state. It seems more probable that he was urged on his course by two motives—one the pressure from the army which he found irresistible, the other the desire to remove the immediate obstacle. As to what came next in his mind, it seems impossible to say. The *Agreement of the People* left the question of the executive open, nor is it probable that even its framers, not even Ireton, had thought that problem through—unless, again, the Royalists were right. Yet that must involve far-sighted ambition, long preparation, deep conspiracy of which no hint remains, and a capacity for secrecy and combination of almost superhuman quality.

However this may be, the die was cast and the great tragedy proceeded to its final act. It was not long delayed. If, in the words of the notebook of his ancestor's great patron, Cromwell and his colleagues had acted on the principle embodied in its entry, "The Abbott of Redyng to be tryed & excecutyd at Reding";[332] they now adopted another even better known: "If it were done when 'tis done then 'twere well it were done quickly."[333] Hardly had the warrant been read and Charles dragged from the Court when preparations for his execution were begun. Failing in his last appeal from the decision of the Court, Charles was taken first to Cotton's house, then to Whitehall where he spent the night. On Sunday, the 28th, he was attended by Bishop Juxon, who read prayers to him, and at five o'clock was carried to St. James's, as there began the building of a scaffold outside Whitehall. Meanwhile the members of the Assembly of Divines had petitioned that the King's life be spared. Fairfax later wrote that "My afflicted and troubled mind for it and my earnest endeavors to prevent it will sufficiently testify my dislike and abhorrence of the fact,"[334] and Fairfax's son Brian, and Charles's devoted follower, Herbert, confirmed that testimony. Brian Fairfax declared that "on the night of January 29, some of the general's friends proposed to him to attempt the next day to rescue the king,

[332] Merriman, *Thomas Cromwell*, i, 87, from *Letters and Papers*, *Henry VIII*, xiv (ii), 399.

[333] Shakespeare, *Macbeth*.

[334] Sir Thomas Fairfax, *Short Memorials*, p. 9.

telling him that twenty thousand men were ready to join with him; he said he was ready to venture his own life, but not the lives of others against the army united against them."[335] Herbert added his testimony to the effect that on January 30, Fairfax "being all that morning, as indeed at other times, using all his power and interest to have the execution deferred for some days, forbearing his coming among the officers, and fully resolved with his own regiment to prevent the execution or have it deferred till he could make a party in the army to second his design."[336] His reluctance to engage in a third civil war, especially in an enterprise which, in the excited state of the army, would have been a desperate, if not a hopeless venture is understandable. He was not a clever man and he was perhaps "overwitted" by Cromwell, but Clarendon's further description of him and his attitude scarcely does him justice, however flattering it is to Cromwell. "Out of the stupidity of his soul," says Clarendon, "he was throughout overwitted by Cromwell and made a property to bring that to pass which could very hardly have been otherwise effected." In any event, it was too late now, and he, like others, resigned himself to the inevitable.

Not least Charles, who, now that death approached, rose to meet it like a King. The story of his last hours is one of the most affecting in English history. He was visited on Monday by his daughter, the Princess Elizabeth, then thirteen, who, it was said, never recovered from the shock of her father's death, and by his son, the little Duke of Gloucester, then aged ten, between whom he divided his jewels. To his daughter he declared that she should not sorrow for he was about to "die gloriously for the laws and liberties of this land and for maintaining the true Protestant religion." His son he begged never to accept the crown from his father's murderers. He sent tender messages to his wife; he commanded his children to forgive his judges and executioners, and so dismissed them to prepare for the scaffold.

That grim platform had been erected just in front of the west side of the Banqueting House of Whitehall Palace. On the morning of Tuesday, January 30, after three days of soliciting the remaining signatures to the death-warrant, the commissioners met in the Painted Chamber, directed five ministers, including Nye, to minister to the King, ordered the scaffold to be covered with black and tried desperately to find some one who would behead the King. That was not easy, but it proved easier than to discover the name of the actual executioner in later years. That done, it was necessary to draw up an order to him—or them—to be signed by Hacker, Huncks or Phayre, to whom the conduct of the execution had been entrusted. And again at this moment, we get a glimpse of Cromwell; for ten years later

[335] B. Fairfax, *Life of Buckingham*, p. 7.
[336] Herbert, *Memoirs* (1702), p. 135.

when Hacker was tried, Huncks gave his evidence as to what happened at that last crucial moment.

"That day the king died, a little before the hour he died, I was in Ireton's chamber, where Ireton and Harrison were in bed together, there was Cromwell, col. Hacker, lieut. col. Phayre, Axtell and myself; standing at the door; this warrant for the execution was there produced and you [Hacker] were reading of it, but Cromwell addressed himself to me, commanding me by virtue of that warrant, to draw up an order for the Executioner; I refused it, and upon refusing of it there happened some cross passages. Cromwell would have no delay. There was a little table that stood by the door, and pen, ink, and paper being there, Cromwell stepped and writ. (I conceive he wrote that which he would have had me to write). As soon as he had done writing, he gives the pen over to Hacker; Hacker he stoops and did write (I cannot say what he writ) away goes Cromwell, and then Axtell; we all went out; afterwards they went into another room."[337]

Questioned further, Huncks repeated his story, and, asked what Cromwell said to him and whether he had not called him a coward, replied, "He said I was a froward, peevish fellow."

This done there was one last curious touch which gives another glimpse of Cromwell. At the trial of Hugh Peter, a certain Richard Nunnelly testified on that Tuesday:

"I came with a warrant of 40 or £50,000 to Oliver Cromwell, being doorkeeper to the Committee of the Army. 'Nunnelly,' says Oliver Cromwell, 'will you go to Whitehall? Surely you will see the beheading of the king;' and he let me into Whitehall."[338]

The King walked with no appearance of hesitation out on to the scaffold, holding in his hand a little piece of paper with notes of the address which he made to the fifteen persons on the scaffold, chiefly to Thomlinson, in which according to report, he declared that nothing lay so heavily on his conscience as the death of the Earl of Strafford.[339] Then handing some personal pieces of jewelry to his companions, his "George," his watch, his cane and other things, he put off his cap and doublet, laid his head on the block and with one stroke it was severed from his body. The executioner held it up in silence to the crowd which groaned and wept in horror—and the scene was over. Yet again we have a bit of evidence as to Cromwell, though of doubtful authenticity. As Heath relates:

"The very same day appointed for this Murther Cromwell and the Officers assembled together, to consider of some means if possible (with security still to the Nation) of saving the Kings life, and many tedious expedients were

[337] *State Trials*, v. 1180–1.

[338] *Ibid.*, 1127.

[339] Charles's speech on the scaffold, in Muddiman, *Trial of Charles I*, p. 260–264, the latest and best account. Cp. also Payne-Gallwey, *Scaffold George of Charles I.*

offered by some not so bloody as the rest, & speedy Remonstrance to the Parliament proposed, and in the mean while the King should be Respited. Cromwell likewise seemed very forward, expressing how glad he should be if such a thing might be effected, for he was not ignorant, he said, what calumny that action would draw upon the Army and themselves in particular, though they did nothing therein but in obedience to the Parliament. But before we (said he) proceed in so weighty a matter, let us seek God to know his mind in it; hereto they agreed and Oliver began a long-winded prayer and continued in it till a Messenger whom he had appointed for that purpose, came rapping at the dore and hastily told them that they need not trouble themselves about the King for the work was done, which being unexpected to many of them, did at present astonish them while Cromwell holding up his hands, declared to them, that it was not the pleasure of God he should live, and therefore he feared they had done ill to tempt Him against his wil or words to that effect."[340]

This seems a fantastic tale, yet Sir Thomas Herbert, who was present in these last hours, records in his *Memoirs* that, accompanying the corpse of Charles after the execution he and Bishop Juxon stepped aside into the long gallery where they met Fairfax, who asked Herbert

"how the King did? Which he thought strange (it seems thereby that the General knew not what had passed,) . . . but being with the Officers of the Army then at Prayer, or Discourse in Colonel Harrison's Apartment (being a Room at the hither end of that Gallery looking towards the Privy-Garden) His Question being answer'd, the General seem'd much surpriz'd; and walking further in the Gallery, they were met by another great Commander, Cromwell, who knew what had so lately passed; for he told them, They should have Orders for the King's Burial speedily."[341]

To this finally may be joined the story told apparently by the Earl of Southampton to some one who told it to Pope, whence it found its way into that treasury of Spence's *Anecdotes* and thence into an infinity of history, fiction and art. It was to the effect that:

"The night after King Charles was beheaded my Lord Southampton and a friend of his got leave to sit up by the body in the Banqueting House at Whitehall. As they were sitting very melancholy there, about two o'clock in the morning they heard the tread of somebody coming very slowly upstairs. By-and-by the door opened, and a man entered very much muffled up in his cloak, and his face quite hid in it. He approached the body, considered it very attentively for some time, and then shook his head, sighed out the words, 'Cruel necessity!' He then departed in the same slow and concealed manner as he had come. Lord Southampton used to say that he could not distinguish anything of his face; but that by his voice and gait he took him to be Oliver Cromwell."[342]

340 *Flagellum*, p. 56. Copied in *Arbitrary Government Displayed to the Life* (1682), p. 42–43.

341 Herbert, *Memoirs* (1839), p. 194.

342 Spence, *Anecdotes*, p. 286.

Such, if the tale is true, is the last meeting of the little boys who forty-seven years before had first seen each other at Hinchinbrook, and to whom in those intervening years had come such great and tragic experiences, each driven on by circumstance and character to this great conclusion.

No impartial person at this distance from the scene but must realize that, whatever the righteousness of the revolutionary cause, whatever sympathy he may have with it, whatever political necessity there seemed to be for the death of Charles, his "trial" was judicial murder. It was pushed forward by a small group of men determined to kill the King. It was essentially what is called a "face-saving" gesture to avoid the charge of murdering him. The solemn parody of judicial process could not conceal the purpose of its managers. It deceived no one. Many, if not most, of the judges themselves realized its character; and even with such a packed jury it was not easy to secure a conviction on charges which most men knew were legally absurd. The fact that no lawyer of any standing in England, not even the prosecutors of Laud and Strafford would take part in this tragic farce reveals its character. One may have the lowest opinion of Charles; one may be bitterly opposed to the cause for which he stood; one may believe that his death was a blessing to mankind; but he cannot think that he was justly tried or justly convicted on the charges brought against him by these men.

There are, however, two points of view which have been important in the judgment of this event and of the men who played a part in it. The first is the profound belief in religious and political liberty, which seeks excuses for the excesses of its champions. The second is the conviction that the principles and practices of Puritanism were more in accord with the designs of the Almighty than those of either the Episcopalians or the Presbyterians, that they were more pleasing to God, who approved of and supported them. Accepting these premises, with the doctrine that almost anything may be forgiven men who are deeply "sincere," a strong case has been made out for the men who put Charles I to death. With that—accepting these premises—no argument is possible, whatever the character of the court and its proceedings.

To that another element has lent some strength. It is the natural human pleasure in the fall of the highly placed and powerful. In much of the literature which Charles's execution has produced there is an underlying sense of satisfaction that it was precisely the kind of men who pushed it forward, which lends to it not merely a dramatic quality but a righteous dignity. It was the triumph of what Cromwell called "this poor people" over the great and mighty of the land; it was the circumstance that half a hundred men, many of whom had come from the lower ranks of society, had challenged monarchy and aristocracy and made their challenge good. It is the spirit loosely known as "democracy" which rejoices at the fall of monarchy and glorifies the men who bring it to the ground. In that view the trial and execution of the King somehow strengthened the cause of "popular" government. It somehow dignified the "common people" to kill a king. This, again, is a natural human trait to which it is futile to object for since the middle of the nineteenth century it has been the dominant note of modern politics.

With neither of these is history much concerned. What is of more importance is the question of the result of Charles's trial and execution. That question takes two forms. The first is the immediate effect on the fortunes of the English people; the second is what may be called the verdict of history. So far as the immediate effect is concerned, if one regards the orderly processes of administration, law, justice, peace and prosperity and consequent content as the chief ends of government, Charles's execution was disastrous. With all of its promoters' devotion to ideal forms of government, whether the system proposed by Ireton, or the more advanced republicanism of men like Ludlow, the King's execution ensured a military dictatorship for England. There was no other alternative. A general election, whether according to the old system, or even according to the one proposed by Ireton, would have overthrown the domination of the army within a twelvemonth—as it did ten years later. It is as inconceivable that the Royalists could have been prevented from voting for any considerable period as it was that the Nonconformists could have been excluded from the franchise after the accession of Charles the Second.

The only alternative, then, was the rule of the Saints, that is of the army, and under whatever guise or disguise, that is what England experienced. It may be that this was a small price to pay for the advance in self-government, that it was but an incident in the progress to a new and better life. It may be that the position of England in foreign politics during the next decade more than counterbalanced the defects of her government at home, which it did so much to extenuate and conceal. But the fact remains that for the next ten years England was in the grip of a military despotism such as she had never known. It not merely failed to convert her people to the ideas and ideals of those who now took charge of government, which no appeal to those ideals or to glory managed to conceal, but to the vast majority of the English people even the old abuses of the monarchy began to seem almost beneficent in comparison with what they experienced at the hands of the champions of liberty.

This, in some measure at least, the more far-sighted even of the army leaders must have anticipated; yet it is understandable that the little group at the heart of the revolutionary movement should have killed the King. In a sense they had arrived at a point where they had but little choice. The more radical elements in the army were bent on his destruction. To them, as to all such men of such mentality at such times, it seemed that once the man whom they conceived to be the author of all their troubles were eliminated, those troubles would be over. The future would somehow settle itself. Even to more thoughtful army leaders the death of Charles seemed necessary. While he was alive, even though kept close prisoner, it was said, there would be, as there had been already, plots and conspiracies, intrigues and perhaps rebellion to restore him to the throne. "Stone dead," as Essex said of Strafford, "hath no fellow." Short of this they had but two alternatives. The one was to accept the settlement made by the constitutional revolution of 1640–1 and the more recent proposals of the King, and restore Charles on those terms. The other was to depose him and induce or compel one of his sons to to take the throne under some sort of a regency. For obvious reasons neither of these solutions seemed practicable. The army leaders distrusted Charles; and, even had they desired, they would have found it difficult to persuade their followers to restore him; and they could not have induced any of his sons to accept the crown, if for no other reason than because those sons distrusted the army leaders as much as the officers distrusted Charles.

In such a situation, confronted by such hard alternatives and offered a plausible, if fallacious, system to take the place of monarchy it is not surprising that a few determined men were able to force the trial and execution of the King. If, as Cromwell said later, it was not, "done in a corner," that was true only of the appearance of the King in the public sessions of the court and on the scaffold. The real business was done in the Painted Chamber, in the Court of Wards and in the House of Commons; and it was done in haste. Haste was, indeed, essential to the plan; for with time to organize protest outside the Court, and for more mature deliberation within the Court itself, it may be doubted whether it could have been put through. That very haste was indicative of the fact that Charles's execution was a political mistake from almost any standpoint but one—that of the continued domination of the army clique or "junto." The millennial dreams of Fifth Monarchists like Harrison whose followers believed that he would rise from the dead to lead them to victory were scarcely more visionary than the plans of Ireton, Ludlow and Marten, for England was not ready for a republican form of government.

To this feeling the conduct of Charles in his last days contributed, and the sentiments which that conduct evoked became the platitudes of literature. "Nothing in his life so became him as the leaving of it," has been the commonest reflection on his character; yet if Montaigne be right, if, as he says, a man's life is to be judged in great measure by the way he departs from it, there is much to be said for Charles. The well-known lines of Marvell, who was of the triumphant party, evidence the impression which the King had made.

> "*He* nothing common did or mean
> Upon that memorable Scene;
> But with his keener Eye
> The Axes edge did try:
> Nor call'd the *Gods* with vulgar spight
> To vindicate his helpless Right,
> But bow'd his comely Head,
> Down as upon a Bed."[343]

And he adds lines less well known, yet of far more significance as coming from one who was presently to be a servant of the new masters of England:

> "This was that memorable Hour,
> Which first assur'd the forced Pow'r."

Once again, ending his praise of Cromwell, he strikes the same note in his paean of victory over the conquest of Ireland:

> "But thou the Wars and Fortunes Son
> March indefatigably on;
> . . . .
> The same *Arts* that did *gain*
> A *Pow'r* must it *maintain*."

Charles did much more than die for his principles. The heroism of his last hours did much to efface the memory of his earlier mistakes. If his people did not wholly forget what he had done, they forgave him for it. If, as Clarendon said honestly, "he was not the best King, if he was without some parts and qualities which have made some kings great and happy," "in that very hour when he was thus wickedly murdered . . . he had as great a share in the hearts and affections of his subjects in general, was as much beloved, esteemed, and longed for by the people in general of the three nations, as any of his predecessors had ever been."

The verdict of history has in general borne out Clarendon. It has been expressed in three schools of thought. To the extreme monarchists, what Clarendon called the "unparalleled murder and parricide" of Charles has raised him to the rank of saint and martyr. To the extreme republicans his execution was, in the words of Mrs. Macaulay, an "eminent act of justice." To the Catholic Lingard it was the work not of the nation but of "a small faction of bold and ambitious spirits"; to the judicious constitutional historian Hallam, who con-

[343] *Horatian Ode on Cromwell's return from Ireland.*

demned Charles's early acts and had no sympathy with his policy, his execution seemed unnecessary and unjustifiable. Carlyle naturally approved of it as striking "a damp through the heart of Flunkeyism universally in the world," while Mr. Trevelyan has grown dithyrambic over it.

But this is not the sober judgment of true Liberals. Men like Goldwin Smith and John Morley have deprecated such unseemly rejoicings over the death of even an enemy; and though Frederic Harrison declared that "to bring the King to judgment was no mere act of earthly justice"—which is unquestionably true, though not in the sense he meant—the better judgment is that of men like Gardiner and Morley. The one declared that the result of the Puritan Revolution up to that point had been purely negative and that the death of Charles did not clear the way to peace. The other, expressing the same idea in different form concludes that "The death of the king made nothing easier and changed nothing for the better; it removed no old difficulties, and it added new."

Such, in brief, is the verdict of history. What, then, did Cromwell think of Charles's trial and execution, and what part did he play in it? As to the first question, the answer is simple. As a leading actor in the tragedy he was bound to defend it. In the next year he spoke of "the great fruit of the war, to wit, the execution of exemplary justice upon the prime leader of all this quarrel," and later still of "turning the tyrant out in a way which Christians in after times will mention with honour and tyrants look at with fear . . . an eminent witness of the Lord for blood-guiltiness." There is no evidence that he regretted the part he played, save broken sentences here and there which may or may not reveal some sense of repentance.

As to his share in the movement which culminated in the trial and death of Charles it is evident that he was deeply implicated in the whole matter from beginning to end. The problem remains—was he the chief mover in that enterprise; was he opposed to it and driven by events beyond his own control; was he, as he had once described himself, a "looker-on," who became its chief beneficiary in a worldly sense; or was he a mere passive instrument in the hands of circumstance? To that question many and varying answers have been given. Clarendon and Marvell, differing in all else, seem to have joined in believing that he was a moving force in the great tragedy.

To the author of the *Flagellum* there is, of course, no problem. Like all the advanced Royalists he believed that Cromwell planned the end from the beginning; that his was the iron will and ambition which pushed the matter to its fatal conclusion; and that, even at the last moment, his was the adroit device which prevented reconsideration and possible revocation of a policy which to many, if not most, of those who had thus far consented to it, was in the nature of a threat to bring the King to terms, not serious regicide.[344]

Beside this may be set the testimony of Bishop Burnet, who, having lived through these days; having known and talked to many of the principal actors; and being in many ways the best informed and most trustworthy reporter of his time, set down his judgment of the situation.

"Ireton," he wrote, "was the person that drove it on, for Cromwell was all the while in some suspense about it. Ireton had the principles and the temper of a Cassius in him; he stuck at nothing that might have turned England to a Commonwealth. . . . Fairfax was much distracted in his mind, and changed purposes often every day. The Presbyterians and the body of the City were much against it, and were everywhere fasting and praying for the King's preservation. There was not above 3,000 of the army about the town; but these were selected out of the whole army as the most engaged in enthusiasm; and they were kept at prayer in their way almost day and night, except when they were upon duty; so that they were wrought up to a pitch of fury, that struck a terror into all people. On the other hand the King's party was without spirit; and as many of themselves have said to me, they could never believe his death was really intended until it was too late. They thought all was a pageantry to strike a terror, and to force the King to such concessions as they had a mind to extort from him."[345]

Whether or not that is the natural excuse given both by men who lent themselves to the trial and by men who should have rallied to Charles's defence, it is common to both parties. As Clarendon observes, "they who wished the King best, and stood nearest to the stage where these parts were acted, did not believe that there were those horrid intentions that shortly after appeared."[346] Yet those intentions were evident enough, however incredible they appeared to many men.

The problem still remains—was Cromwell among those who hesitated, or did he, with Ireton, push the matter to its grim conclusion? The worst charge that has been brought against him—that from the beginning to the end he plotted, planned and conspired for the death of Charles that he might seize power for himself—is incapable of proof, save by that process of arriving at a moral certainty by the presumption that an effect is the result of a predetermined cause. There is more real evidence that he was driven on in part by circumstance, to which he lent himself, or in which he saw and seized his

[344] Heath, *Flagellum*, (1663), p. 56. Cp. *supra*, p. 750.
[345] Burnet, *History of My Own Times*, i, 63.
[346] Clarendon, *History*, xi, 228.

opportunities, along a course which was not wholly distasteful to him, and which he found it easier to follow than to forsake. There is a certain amount of testimony to the effect that, once having taken the road which led to the death of Charles, he hurried the journey in all ways possible and encouraged his more reluctant colleagues to accompany him; and in that sense was responsible for the King's execution.

Yet in this as in his whole career, what he really thought and planned it is impossible to say with any certainty; partly because it is always difficult to read the human heart and partly because we have so little evidence. His share in the death of Charles is typical of the whole and we must end this stage of his career as we began. If there is scarcely a man who rose to such eminence of whose early years so little is really known, there is scarcely one whose rise to power is so difficult to trace. In this respect, as in others, Charles had the worst of it, then and thereafter. His mind was an open book where all who chose might read, and he committed to paper more indiscretions than any ruler in history. On the other hand, Cromwell is the opportunity and despair of biographer and historian. He not merely kept his own counsel but he wrote little from which his thoughts and motives can be guessed, and of that little only part has been preserved.

In consequence, with little straining of the evidence, it has been possible to paint him as a hypocritical and ambitious Machiavellian plotter after the manner of an Italian tyrant, and as a noble, single-minded hero of liberty with no thought of personal advancement. It is possible largely because the testimony is not only so scanty but is so susceptible of such widely differing interpretations. It is frequently not so much what he said as what he refrained from saying that is most important, and the silent spaces in his life seem often more significant than the records he has left. It is not merely difficult, it is often impossible to reconstruct from his written words or from such of his conversations as have come down to us, any wholly satisfactory account of his real inner thoughts, his plans, his ambitions or his maneuvres. Save to the penetrating insight of his ardent admirers or detractors, his letters give only the barest suggestion of what we want to know, his speeches little more. As one of his earliest biographers declares, "Questionless his . . . Privacy and Silence in his Managements were to him Assistance beyond all Arts and Sciences."[347] To his contemporaries as to us he was an elusive and enigmatic figure in politics in this period of his life. It is easy to read into that life the characteristics he developed in his later years; it is still easier to personify in him the cause which he fought for; it

[347] Anon. *Life of Oliver Cromwell* (Midwinter), p. 125.

was not easy then, nor is it now, to penetrate his thoughts and ambitions and secret purposes as he advanced to the next stage of his career.

It is not without significance that so many of his portraits are adorned with masks of a fox and a lion as symbols of his nature, or that the oft-quoted motto of one of his earlier biographers is "*Qui nescit dissimulare, nescit regnare*"—"he who knows not how to dissimulate, knows not how to rule." To many of the charges brought against him by his enemies the best that can be said is the Scotch verdict of "Not Proven"; and his best defence rests not so much in his own words or deeds as in the cause which he personified and his success with that of his cause. Like Cromwell himself, his champions have rested their case rather on the ends than the means; and whether one accepts the result of his strivings as the will of God or as the poet's dictum that "Whatever is, is right," the conclusion is the same. For the historian the eternal rights and wrongs of such a debatable issue must yield to the problem of how Cromwell accomplished his purposes and ambitions and what we know of it. Such as it is, here is the evidence, scanty, disjointed, often inconsequential, from which one must of necessity draw such conclusions as are possible. Whatever the righteousness of his cause, whatever its inspiration, this is the only record which remains of the human means by which he achieved his human ends.

THE END OF VOLUME ONE